# REED'S
## NAUTICAL COMPANION

# REED'S
## NAUTICAL COMPANION

### THE COMPREHENSIVE
### SHIPBOARD REFERENCE

**Editor**

Ben Ellison

**Editorial Team**

Nancy Hauswald
Elbert Maloney
Jon Cheston
Dr. Paul Gill
Michael Carr

**Second Edition**

**THOMAS REED**
PUBLICATIONS INC

VK
555
.R44
1998

© 1998 Thomas Reed Publications, Inc.
13A Lewis Street
Boston MA 02113
U.S.A.
Tel.: 617-248-0700 Fax: 617-248-5855
Web Site: www.treed.com
E-mail publisher: jdk@treed.com
E-mail editor: editor@treed.com


ISBN 1-884666-24-8


Printed in the U.S.A. by:

Banta Press

**LEGAL NOTES**

# Contents

# PREFACE

We are proud to present the second edition of *Reed's Nautical Companion*.

The *Companion* is the comprehensive shipboard reference for the navigators of commercial and recreational vessels plying the waters of North America and the Caribbean. It is equally at home in the wheelhouse of a tugboat as it is in the navigation station of a sailing yacht. The common characteristic of our readers is an appreciation of the complexities and value of safe navigation.

We call this book the *Companion* because it nicely complements our annual *Nautical Almanacs*. For example, each of *Reed's* three *Almanacs* — *East Coast*, *West Coast*, and *Caribbean* — provides the most complete tide and current predictions available in one volume for its respective area, while the *Companion* provides a thorough explanation of the physics of tides and currents, and contains secondary reference material that does not change annually. Where the *Almanacs* are loaded with specific data like aids to navigation, chartlets, and lists of radio resources; the *Companion* discusses the techniques of piloting, different types of charts, and the mechanics of radio waves.

The *Companion* also stands alone as a reference and learning tool. Almost every subject of importance to navigators and captains is covered here. Although not directed primarily at novices, the basics of every subject are generally outlined. We often provide more advanced material, as well as useful tables and illustrations. Please note the new Table of Useful Tables on page 547.

The *Companion* contains a complete USCG-accepted copy of the *International and Inland Navigation Rules,* which are not only important but *required* aboard all vessels over 12 meters in U.S. waters. The USCG also accepts *Reed's Almanacs* as replacements for *Light Lists, Tide and Current Tables,* and *Coast Pilots* that are required on board commercial fishing and towing vessels. In short, Reed's provides all the essential navigational data you need except a current set of charts.

We are proud of the editorial team who helped to update this edition. They are all experts in their fields and are dedicated to understanding and explaining their subjects thoroughly. Often, they have written volumes of material on subjects that we have condensed to a chapter or two here. There is an amazing amount of material in this book. Let us suggest that you first scan the contents page of each chapter. We are confident that you will find numerous topics that you would like to explore, or reference tables and techniques that you would like to have within reach of your chart table.

As you come to know and use *Reed's Companion*, please bear in mind that this is more than a simple reference book; REED'S is a system! The *Companion* supplements much of the material in the annually published *Almanacs;* together they provide as much reference material as any mariner needs. Each spring we publish a free supplement that includes an update to all of our books. To receive a supplement, please return the postage-paid reply card found in any edition of *Reed's Almanacs*. And, check our Web site from time to time for the up-to-minute information pertinent to *Reed's* books, as well as a link list to all the Web sites mentioned in this book. *Reed's* is an ongoing information system for navigators… join us.

Sincerely,

Ben Ellison, Editor
Jerald Knopf, Publisher

# Acknowledgements

We are very grateful to all the organizations and persons that contributed to this new edition of *Reed's Nautical Companion*.

The principal writers are profiled on the inside back cover. Here is what they did:

Elbert Maloney was responsible for updating the Rules and writing pithy commentary on them. "Mack" also rewrote large portions of the chapters on communications, seamanship, and safety.

Jon Cheston wrote or rewrote all three of the navigation chapters and also finished the chapter on weather. Michael Carr wrote the first draft of that chapter, just before he headed off across the Atlantic on a Whitbread racing boat.

Dr. Paul Gill wrote the chapter on emergency medicine.

Ben Ellison wrote or rewrote many bits and pieces. He also reorganized the chapters and created many of the illustrations.

Many other persons and organizations contributed to this book; chief among them is Nancy Hauswald. Nancy is the new Research Editor for *Reed's Almanacs*, as well as our copy editor. She worked hard to make all the above writers look good in print.

We are especially indebted to Geoff Kuenning who voluntarily copy edited the original edition.

Carl Sederquist wrote the section on satellites in the communications chapter.

Meteorologist Ken McKinley was the source of much information in the weather chapter.

The section on theory in the chapter on tides and currents was originally published as *Restless Tides* and is republished with permission from the User Services Branch, Oceanographic Products and Services Division, National Ocean Service.

Illustrations in Chapter 9, "Medical Emergencies," are copyright by William P. Hamilton and all rights are reserved.

The illustrations in Chapter 5, "Emergency Navigation," were done by Chris McLarty and modeled with permission on those of David Burch in his book *Emergency Navigation*.

Several illustrations in this book are reprinted from *Bowditch, The American Practical Navigator*, with permission from Marine Navigation Dept. of the National Imagery and Mapping Agency.

The international code flags illustration is reproduced with permission of the Controller, H. M. Stationary Office.

Color buoyage illustrations are reproduced with the permission of the United States Coast Guard.

The Beaufort sea state and cloud photographs are reproduced from the *Guide to Sea State, Wind, and Clouds*, with permission of the National Weather Service, National Oceanic and Atmospheric Administration.

Numerous writers contributed to the first edition of this book, and many of their words are still in it. They are: John J. Kettlewell, Leslie Kettlewell, Kim Hollamby, Jean Fowler, Thomas B. Stableford, Lt. Cdr. Harry J. Baker, Robin Ekblom, Arthur Somers, Roger Taylor, Kathleen Karny, and Catherine Degnon.

# THE STORY OF REED'S

From its depression-era roots to its continued success in the age of electronic navigation, *Reed's Nautical Almanac* has served countless thousands of ships, yachts, and small craft in peace and war. It has saved lives, helped deliver babies, and taught sound navigation skills to generations of sailors. Although hundreds of people have assisted its publication over the years, *Reed's Almanac* owes its existence to the inspired dedication of one man: Oswald M. Watts.

One of the youngest British Merchant Navy officers ever to hold a Master's certificate, Capt. Watts left the sea in 1927. For a time he eked out a precarious living delivering yachts, teaching navigation, and editing *Pearson's Nautical Almanac*. While working on *Pearson's* – and using it on his deliveries all around Britain – Watts became convinced that he could create a better almanac, designed specifically for the yachts, fishing boats, and small commercial vessels operating in the treacherous waters around the British Isles. In June 1931, Watts came to the Sunderland office of Thomas Reed & Co with a proposal.

Founded in 1782, Reed's was one of the oldest nautical publishers in the world. In 1859, the company produced its first textbook for officers taking the new Masters' and Mates' certificates. Their *Reed's Seamanship,* first published in the 1830s, sold more than 100,000 copies. How, Watts asked, would they like a chance to publish something even more successful?

Watts' idea was that he should compile, and Reed's should publish, a standard reference so comprehensive that it would have a place on every yacht and merchant ship's chart table. In one volume it would assemble all the knowledge a navigator would need to pilot a vessel in the Home Trade Waters around the British Isles.

Reed's editors were enthusiastic. With an agreement sealed by a handshake, Watts returned to London to compile the first issue of the new almanac for publication by January 1, 1932.

The reams of data that today are assembled and processed with the help of sophisticated computer programs, Watts then produced by hand, often working alone through the night. To provide comprehensive coverage of Home Trade Waters, he had to draw up a complete list of lights and buoys for British and Continental ports from Brest to the Elbe, including Denmark, the Faeroes, and Iceland. He had to prepare the tidal data for countless ports, calculate course and distances from port to port, and write whole sections on maritime law, signalling, and pilotage.

Published in January 1932, the first edition of *Reed's Home Trade Nautical Almanac and Tide Tables* was 990 pages long and an instant success. Watts immediately began work on the second edition, bolstered by scores of appreciative letters from professional seamen and yachtsmen alike. Many offered helpful suggestions that Watts was able to incorporate into subsequent editions, a tradition of reader feedback that continues today.

During the 1930s Watts opened a chandlery off London's Piccadilly where he continued to compile and edit successive editions of *Reed's*. When the war clouds began to gather over Europe, Watts started a sea school where yachtsmen could learn what they would need to know to serve in the Royal Naval Volunteer Reserve in the coming conflict. When war finally broke out, the *Reed's Nautical Almanac* that had been a convenience for sailors became a lifeline for professional mariners.

As the bombs fell on London during the Blitz, Watts continued to work on the next year's *Almanac*. In the preface to the 10th edition, he wrote: "No new features have been introduced into *Reed's Almanac* for 1941 for the main reason that the majority of the pages have been prepared in London during night after night of incessant bombing and gunfire, which has made it a physical impossibility. We in London are glad to bear many of the horrors of modern warfare so that some at least may be lifted from the shoulders of our seafarers – Royal and Merchant Navy men both." Reed's finest hour came in 1944, when the government ordered 3,000 extra copies of the *Almanac* for use on vessels involved in the Normandy D-Day landings.

After the war, yachtsmen who had served in the Royal and Merchant Navies continued to use *Reed's Almanac*, which had seen them through the hostilities. The *Almanac* had become what Watts had promised: as essential as a compass and, aboard many boats, the only reference apart from charts that any navigator ever used. Watts continued to edit Reed's until his retirement in 1981; he died only a few years afterward.

*Reed's Nautical Almanac* has continued to maintain the standard for complete and accurate information set by Capt. Watts. Every edition since World War II has incorporated new features and improvements. Many have been culled from readers' suggestions or have reflected new technologies being used on board, while others were simply dreamt up by Watts and the editors who followed him. Signal flags were joined by satellite navigation. Sections on first aid, customs regulations, and lifeboat navigation were added. A doctor friend of Watts even wrote a section on childbirth at sea, which was later used by yachtsman Colin Swale to deliver his wife Rosie's 12-lb. baby on board the couple's 30-foot catamaran off the coast of Italy. "We never thought it would be used," Watts said of the section, which has since been expanded and updated.

The first North American edition was published in 1974, and today our Boston, Massachusetts-based publishing company continues to uphold Capt. Watts' high standards, while meeting the ever-growing needs of coastal and offshore navigators.

By 1993, the amount of essential reference information that did not require annual updates had grown so much that, at the suggestion of many readers, it was published in a separate reference volume – and the first edition of *Reed's Nautical Companion* was born.

In 1994, we published our first Caribbean edition. Cuba, Hispanola, and the Bahamas had been previously included in the North American East Coast edition, but mariners were clamoring for more. Today the Caribbean almanac covers all the islands and the coastline from Mexico to Venezuela.

In 1996, federal budget cuts forced the National Oceanic and Atmospheric Administration to stop publishing the tide and current tables, leaving *Reed's Almanacs* as one of the few sources of official tide and current data. To fill the need left by NOAA's decision, we began publishing a North American West Coast edition that covers Alaska to the Baja peninsula. All of *Reed's Nautical Almanacs* are recognized by NOAA and accepted by the USCG as official tide and current data.

NOAA's decision to stop publishing tide tables also left hundreds of newspapers without a source of accurate local tide information. Again, Reed's stepped in to fill the need; our Newstide Service provides customized local tide tables to newspapers throughout America's coastal communities.

Creating those tables would have been a long and dreadfully laborious project for Captain Watts, but since the late 1980s, high-speed computers have been dramatically changing the way *Reed's Almanacs* are published. Today, sophisticated programs process raw tide and current data through a series of algorithms and result in the tide predictions that appear in *Reed's*. In 1997, Reed's opened its doors on the World Wide Web at **www.treed.com,** now home to the midyear supplement that updates notices to mariners and daily tide predictions for locations throughout the U.S.

Reader feedback continues to drive improvements to *Reed's Almanacs*, but suggestions today are more likely to come via e-mail – often directly from computers on board readers' boats. In an era when laptop computers threaten to eclipse the paper chart, *Reed's Almanacs* continue to find a home in the nav stations and wheelhouses of serious mariners.

*Reed's Almanacs* have also become a common site on commercial fishing vessels and tugboats, which are required to carry a variety of navigational publications on board. In the mid-1990s, the Coast Guard accepted *Reed's* as a replacement for many of the texts required on board.

With this second edition of *Reed's Nautical Companion,* we have even further extended our commitment to navigation and seamanship education. Growing numbers of sailing and navigation schools now teach from the *Companion;* the Coast Guard accepts it as fulfilling several federal vessel safety program requirements; and it still covers childbirth!

Capt. Watts would be proud.

# NAVIGATION RULES

1

# INTRODUCTION

*"Study of the rules is a rewarding pastime, practical and captivating. They constitute a remarkable document with an immense assigned task — the prevention of collisions between a vast array of vessels in a vast array of circumstances: vessels barely visible at 100 yards to vessels the size of horizontal skyscrapers; drifting without power or traveling at 30 knots or more; following unmarked lanes or crisscrossing open waters offering nothing more than an educated guess as to their intended course; in all conditions of weather, clear or fog, calm or storm; and often with no common language between their drivers.*

*But despite this enormous assignment, they do the job. Collisions can always be traced to at least one violation of the Rules. The key to avoiding further proof of this is a thorough understanding of the Rules and how to apply them, including the rules on what to do if an approaching vessel does not obey the rules."*

*— David Burch*

*"A collision at sea will ruin your whole day."*        *— Anonymous*

Just as there are "Rules of the Road" for vehicles on the streets, there are "Nautical Rules of the Road" for vessels on the water. The proper name for these are "Navigation Rules," and for most of the users of this book there are two sets of rules, much alike, but not identical.

For the high seas — the open oceans — there are the International Rules, the full name of which is the International Regulations for Prevention of Collisions at Sea, 1972. The Coast Guard often abbreviates these as the "COLREGS" — sometimes "72 COLREGS" — to distinguish them from earlier versions. With the ratification of the treaty including these regulations, they became U.S. laws. There are 38 numbered Rules, organized in five Parts: A — General,

B — Steering and Sailing Rules, C — Lights and Shapes, D — Sound and Light Signals, and E — Exemptions. There are also four Annexes (I through IV) with technical specifications and requirements.

For inland waters, most nations use the International Rules, perhaps supplemented by a few local regulations to cover domestic situations. (Canada's modifications are printed at the end of this chapter). The United States, however, takes advantage of the authorization in International Rule 1(b) to establish the Inland Navigation Rules. These are applicable on most, but not all, "inland waters." The U.S. Inland Rules are numbered 1 through 38 with wording that closely, in some cases exactly, matches the International Rules (there is no Inland Rule 28, but the number is included as a blank so that the following Rules will match the International Rules numbers). There are the corresponding four Annexes, slightly different from the International Rules in requirements, plus a U.S. only Annex V, the U.S. Pilot Rules.

Both sets of Rules are written in terms of "vessels," and this means all watercraft regardless of size, from personal watercraft (jet-skis and the like) to supertankers. Of course, common sense and good judgement must be applied in situations such as right of way, but no small boat is excused in any manner from compliance with the Rules.

The International and Inland Rules both use metric measurements for size, dimensions, and short distances (such as the spacing of lights); longer distances (such as for the visibility of lights) remain measured in nautical miles. A conversion table for metric values used in the Rules can be found on page 100.

For all skippers, thorough knowledge of the Navigation Rules is absolutely essential. This knowledge should be in their heads — when a dangerous situation develops, it's too late to look "in the book" for the applicable Rule and the appropriate action.

**Rules**

## Chapter Organization

This chapter is organized so that you can easily compare the International and Inland versions. They are printed in parallel — International on the left, Inland on the right. Usually it is quite obvious where they differ; the most important differences are noted in the commentary text.

The comments printed in shaded boxes alongside the rules were written for *Reed's* by Elbert "Mack" Maloney. He manages to point out essential aspects of the rules in a way that is useful for both beginning and experienced mariners.

In addition to the complete rules with Annexes, this chapter contains the U.S. COLREGS demarcation lines, which define the border between U.S. Inland Rules and the International Rules.

At the end of the chapter we have published the Canadian Rules, which are modifications or additions to the International Rules.

**Note: This publication fulfills the requirement that a vessel over 12 M (39.4 ft.) in length in U.S. Inland waters must carry a copy of the Rules on board.**

## Notice

In October, 1996, President Clinton signed Public Law 104-324. Section 701 of that Act made seven changes to the Inland Navigation Rules. As this book goes to press in February of 1998, the U.S. Coast Guard has not yet "promulgated" these changes; that is, they have not yet printed or started to enforce them. *Reed's* has printed the up-to-date text of the rules with the new changes, which, according to our sources, are legally in effect and actually have been since Oct., 1996. The changes are each noted in the remarks.

On February 4, 1998, the USCG issued a number of changes (effective March 6, 1998) to Annex I, the Pilot Rules, and the Interpretive Rules; we managed to get all of them into this chapter just before publication.

Aside from the above, the text of these Rules is exactly the same as the most recent USCG publication, COMDTINST M16672.2C. We expect that the next printing of USCG Rules will reflect all these changes. Any further changes to the Rules will be published in our annual supplement and on our web site, *www.treed.com*.

# PART A — GENERAL RULES

**International**                                    **Inland**

## Rule 1    Application

(a) These Rules shall apply to all vessels upon the high seas and in all waters connected therewith navigable by seagoing vessels.

(b) Nothing in these Rules shall interfere with the operation of special rules made by an appropriate authority for roadsteads, harbours, rivers, lakes, or inland waterways connected with the high seas and navigable by seagoing vessels. Such special rules shall conform as closely as possible to these rules.

(c) Nothing in these Rules shall interfere with the operation of special rules made by the Government of any State with respect to additional station or signal lights, shapes or whistle signals for ships of war and vessels proceeding under convoy, or with respect to additional station or signal lights, or shapes for fishing vessels engaged in fishing as a fleet. These additional station or signal lights, shapes or whistle signals shall, so far as possible, be such that

## Rule 1    Application

(a) These Rules apply to all vessels upon the inland waters of the United States and to vessels of the United States on the Canadian waters of the Great Lakes to the extent that there is no conflict with Canadian law.

(b) (i) These Rules constitute special rules made by an appropriate authority within the meaning of Rule 1(b) of the International Regulations.

(ii) All vessels complying with the construction and equipment requirements of the International Regulations are considered to be in compliance with these Rules.

(c) Nothing in these Rules shall interfere with the operation of any special rules made by the Secretary of the Navy with respect to additional station or signal lights and shapes or whistle signals for ships of war and vessels proceeding under convoy, or by the Secretary with respect to additional station or signal lights and shapes for fishing vessels engaged in fishing as a fleet. These additional station or signal lights and shapes or whistle signals shall, so far as possible, be such that they can-

---

### *Rule 1*

The U.S. Inland Rules and the International Rules are mutually exclusive; waters are subject to one or the other, but not both, although in many cases the Rules are the same. The boundary between them is termed a "COLREGS Demarcation Line." These lines are described in Federal Regulations (published later in this chapter), and are shown on all applicable charts. The Demarcation Lines must be studied carefully and clearly understood; there are areas of U.S. waters that would logically be thought of as "inland" — along the northeast Maine coast, in the lower Florida Keys, all of Puget Sound, and others — but which are subject to the International Rules.

Both the International and Inland Rules provide for exceptions and special provisions for naval vessels. This covers the unusual shape of some vessels such as aircraft carriers. The Inland Rules also prescribe a special light for submarines due to their large bulk that is underwater and out of sight; this is an amber (yellow) all-round light flashing three times at one-second intervals, followed by a dark interval of three seconds.

| International | Inland |
|---|---|
| they cannot be mistaken for any light, shape or signal authorized elsewhere under these Rules. | not be mistaken for any light, shape, or signal authorized elsewhere under these Rules. Notice of such special rules shall be published in the Federal Register and, after the effective date specified in such notice, they shall have effect as if they were a part of these Rules. |
| (d) Traffic separation schemes may be adopted by the Organization for the purpose of these Rules. | (d) Vessel traffic service regulations may be in effect in certain areas. |
| (e) Whenever the Government concerned shall have determined that a vessel of special construction or purpose cannot comply fully with the provisions of any of these Rules with respect to the number, position, range or arc of visibility of lights or shapes, as well as to the disposition and characteristics of sound-signalling appliances, such vessel shall comply with such other provisions in regard to the number, position, range or arc of visibility of lights or shapes, as well as to the disposition and characteristics of sound-signalling appliances, as her Government shall have determined to be the closest possible compliance with these Rules in respect of that vessel. | (e) Whenever the Secretary determines that a vessel or class of vessels of special construction or purpose cannot comply fully with the provisions of any of these Rules with respect to the number, position, range, or arc of visibility of lights or shapes, as well as to the disposition and characteristics of sound-signaling appliances, the vessel shall comply with such other provisions in regard to the number, position, range, or arc of visibility of lights or shapes, as well as to the disposition and characteristics of sound-signaling appliances, as the Secretary shall have determined to be the closest possible compliance with these Rules. The Secretary may issue a certificate of alternative compliance for a vessel or class of vessels specifying the closest possible compliance with these Rules The Secretary of the Navy shall make these determinations and issue certificates of alternative compliance for vessels of the Navy. |
|  | (f) The Secretary may accept a certificate of alternative compliance issued by a contracting party to the International Regulations if he determines that the alternative compliance standards of the contracting party are substantially same as those of the United States. |

## Rule 2

This is often referred to unofficially as the "Rule of Good Seamanship" or the "General Prudential Rule." This Rule first states that all the Rules must be complied with, and the customary practices of good seamanship must be followed. But it then goes on to recognize that there may be "special circumstances." Its intention is to apply common sense to the interpretation and application of the Rules, and to prevent any perversion of the Rules to avoid the consequences of their misconstruction or misapplication. It recognizes that a departure from the strict language of the Rules may be required to avoid immediate danger — no vessel has the right of way *through* another vessel! There may be special situations where a departure from the Rules is not only desirable, but is required. Should a collision result, strict literal compliance with the Rules may not be a defense.

| International | Inland |
| --- | --- |

## Rule 2    Responsibility

(a) Nothing in these Rules shall exonerate any vessel, or the owner, master or crew thereof, from the consequences of any neglect to comply with these Rules or of the neglect of any precaution which may be required by the ordinary practice of sea-men, or by the special circumstances of the case.

(b) In construing and complying with these Rules due regard shall be had to all dangers of navigation and collision and to any special circumstances, including the limitations of the vessels involved, which may make a departure from these Rules necessary to avoid immediate danger.

## Rule 3    General Definitions

For the purpose of these Rules, except where the context otherwise requires:

(a) The word "vessel" includes every description of watercraft including nondisplacement craft and seaplanes, used or capable of being used as a means of transportation on water.

(b) The term "power-driven vessel" means any vessel propelled by machinery.

(c) The term "sailing vessel" means any vessel under sail provided that propelling machinery, if fitted, is not being used.

(d) The term "vessel engaged in fishing" means any vessel fishing with nets, lines, trawls or other fishing apparatus which restrict maneuverability, but does not include a vessel fishing with trolling lines or other fishing apparatus which do not restrict maneuverability.

(e) The word "seaplane" includes any aircraft designed to maneuver on the water.

(f) The term "vessel not under command" means a vessel which, through some exceptional circumstance, is unable to maneuver

## Rule 2    Responsibility

(a) Nothing in these Rules shall exonerate any vessel, or the owner, master, or crew thereof, from the consequences of any neglect to comply with these Rules or of the neglect of any precaution which may be required by the ordinary practice of sea-men, or by the special circumstances of the case.

(b) In construing and complying with these Rules due regard shall be had to all dangers of navigation and collision and to any special circumstances, including the limitations of the vessels involved, which may make a departure from these Rules necessary to avoid immediate danger.

## Rule 3    General Definitions

For the purpose of these Rules and this Act, except where the context otherwise it requires:

(a) The word "vessel" includes every description of watercraft, including nondisplacement craft and seaplanes, used or capable of being used as a means of transportation on water;

(b) The term "power-driven vessel" means any vessel propelled by machinery;

(c) The term "sailing vessel" means any vessel under sail provided that propelling machinery, if fitted, is not being used;

(d) The term "vessel engaged in fishing" means any vessel fishing with nets, lines, trawls, or other fishing apparatus which restricts maneuverability, but does not include a vessel fishing with trolling lines or other fishing apparatus which does not restrict maneuverability;

(e) The word "seaplane" includes any aircraft designed to maneuver on the water;

(f) The term "vessel not under command" means a vessel which, through some exceptional circumstance, is unable to maneuver

Rules

| International | Inland |
|---|---|

as required by these Rules, and is therefore unable to keep out of the way of another vessel.

(g) The term "vessel restricted in her ability to maneuver" means a vessel which, from the nature of her work, is restricted in her ability to maneuver as required by these Rules and is therefore unable to keep out of the way of another vessel. The term "vessels restricted in their ability to maneuver" shall include but not be limited to:

(i) a vessel engaged in laying, servicing or picking up a navigation mark, submarine cable or pipeline;

(ii) a vessel engaged in dredging, surveying or underwater operations;

(iii) a vessel engaged in replenishment or transferring persons, provisions or cargo while underway;

(iv) a vessel engaged in the launching or recovery of aircraft;

(v) a vessel engaged in mine clearance operations;

(vi) a vessel engaged in a towing operation such as severely restricts the towing vessel and her tow in their ability to deviate from their course.

(h) The term "vessel constrained by her draft" means a power-driven vessel which, because of her draft in relation to the available depth and width of navigable water, is severely restricted in her ability to deviate from the course she is following.

(i) The word "underway" means that a vessel is not at anchor, or made fast to the shore, or aground.

(j) The words "length" and "breadth" of a vessel mean her length overall and greatest breadth.

(k) Vessels shall be deemed to be in sight of one another only when one can be observed visually from the other.

---

as required by these Rules, and is therefore unable to keep out of the way of another vessel;

(g) The term "vessel restricted in her ability to maneuver" means a vessel which, from the nature of her work, is restricted in her ability to maneuver as required by these Rules and is therefore unable to keep out of the way of another vessel; vessels restricted in their ability to maneuver include, but are not limited to:

(i) a vessel engaged in laying, servicing, or picking up a navigation mark, submarine cable, or pipeline;

(ii) a vessel engaged in dredging, surveying, or underwater operations;

(iii) a vessel engaged in replenishment or transferring persons, provisions, or cargo while underway;

(iv) a vessel engaged in the launching or recovery of aircraft;

(v) a vessel engaged in mine clearance operations; and

(vi) a vessel engaged in a towing operation such as severely restricts the towing vessel and her tow in their ability to deviate from their course.

(h) The word "underway" means that a vessel is not at anchor, or made fast to the shore, or aground;

(i) The words "length" and "breadth" of a vessel mean her length overall and greatest breadth;

(j) vessels shall be deemed to be in sight of one another only when one can be observed visually from the other;

## International

(l)  The term "restricted visibility" means any condition in which visibility is restricted by fog, mist, falling snow, heavy rainstorms, sandstorms or any other similar causes.

### Rule 3

There are four of these definitions of particular importance to skippers of small craft. The Rules are written in terms of "vessels," and this means *all watercraft regardless of size or description* — a rowboat or dinghy, a personal watercraft (PWC), a recreational craft or fishing boat, a cruise ship, freighter, or tanker — these are all "vessels" as far as the Navigation Rules are concerned. Of course, common sense and good judgement must be applied in situations such as right of way, but no small boat is excused in any manner from compliance with the Rules.

A "sailing vessel" has that status *only* if it is not using mechanical propulsion. Even if the sails are up and being used, if the engines are running it is a "power-driven" vessel and does *not* have the special privileged status of a sailboat.

A sport-fishing boat with trolling lines out is *not* considered a "vessel engaged in fishing" with a special status and privileges. Such lines are not considered a restriction in her ability to maneuver.

Note carefully the definition of "underway." Remember that even when you are "just drifting" you are still underway as regards the Navigation Rules; a vessel that is drifting is sometimes informally described as "underway with no way on." This is particularly relevant in foggy situations or other conditions of restricted visibility.

Note also that the Inland Rules contain definitions not in the International Rules, such as "Western Rivers."

## Inland

(k) The term restricted visibility" means any condition in which visibility is restricted by fog, mist, falling snow, heavy rainstorms, sandstorms, or any other similar causes;

(l) "Western Rivers" means the Mississippi River, its tributaries, South Pass, and Southwest Pass, to the navigational demarcation lines dividing the high seas from harbors, rivers, and other inland waters of the United States, and the Port Allen-Morgan City  Alternate Route, and that part of the Atchafalaya River above its junction with the Port Allen-Morgan City Alternate Route including the Old River and the Red River;

(m) "Great Lakes" means the Great Lakes and their connecting and tributary waters including the Calumet River as far as the Thomas J. O'Brien Lock and Controlling Works (between mile 326 and 327), the Chicago River as far as the east side of the Ashland Avenue Bridge (between mile 321 and 322), and the Saint Lawrence River as far east as the lower exit of Saint Lambert Lock;

(n) "Secretary" means the Secretary of the department in which the Coast Guard is operating;

(o) "Inland Waters" means the navigable waters of the United States shoreward of the navigational demarcation lines dividing the high seas from harbors, rivers and other inland waters of the United States and the waters of the Great Lakes on the United States side of the International Boundary;

(p) "Inland Rules," or "Rules," mean the Inland Navigational Rules and the annexes thereto, which govern the conduct of vessels and specify the lights, shapes, and sound signals that apply on inland waters; and

(q) "International Regulations" means the International Regulations for Preventing Collisions at Sea, 1972, including annexes currently in force for the United States.

**Rules**

# PART B — STEERING AND SAILING RULES

| International | Inland |
|---|---|
| SECTION I<br>CONDUCT OF VESSELS IN<br>ANY CONDITION OF VISIBILITY | SUBPART I<br>CONDUCT OF VESSELS IN<br>ANY CONDITION OF VISIBILITY. |

## Rule 4    Application

Rules in this Section apply in any condition of visibility.

## Rule 5    Lookout

Every vessel shall at all times maintain a proper lookout by sight and hearing as well as by all available means appropriate in the prevailing circumstances and conditions so as to make a full appraisal of the situation and of the risk of collision.

## Rule 4    Application

Rules in this subpart apply in any condition of visibility.

## Rule 5    Lookout

Every vessel shall at all times maintain a proper lookout by sight and hearing as well as by all available means appropriate in the prevailing circumstances and conditions so as to make a full appraisal of the situation and of the risk of collision.

---

### *Rule 4*

The International Rules divide Part B — Rules 4 through 19 — into three "Sections"; the Inland Rules uses the term "Subparts" for these subdivisions. There is no practical effect in the use of these different titles.

The Rules of Section/Subpart I — Rules 5 through 10 — are applicable in conditions of both normal and restricted visibility.

### *Rule 5*

This is a basic Rule, the violation of which is so often the cause of small-craft accidents — collisions with other boats or stationary objects. On smaller vessels, the "lookout" is nominally the helmsman, and this is acceptable if he is aware of his responsibility and performs his duties. He must be able to hear as well as see potential dangers. If in doubt, a skipper should post an additional person with the *sole* duties of lookout; this is particularly necessary in situations of reduced visibility. It is even possible that two lookouts will be necessary — one forward and one aft. Should a collision occur, failure to have a proper lookout would be strongly held against you in court.

This is also the Rule that is obviously violated by all single-handing skippers on long voyages, or even on voyages of more than a few hours.

Note that the Rule states that a lookout is required "at all times" — this includes when a vessel is at anchor.

## Rule 6    Safe Speed

Every vessel shall at all times proceed at a safe speed so that she can take proper and effective action to avoid collision and be stopped within a distance appropriate to the prevailing circumstances and conditions.

In determining a safe speed the following factors shall be among those taken into account:

(a)  By all vessels:

(i) the state of visibility;

(ii) the traffic density, including concentrations of fishing vessels or any other vessels;

(iii) the maneuverability of the vessel with special reference to stopping distance and turning ability in the prevailing conditions;

(iv) at night, the presence of background light such as from shore lights or from back scatter of her own lights;

(v) the state of wind, sea, and current, and the proximity of navigational hazards;

## Rule 6    Safe Speed

Every vessel shall at all times proceed at a safe speed so that she can take proper and effective action to avoid collision and be stopped within a distance appropriate to the prevailing circumstances and conditions.

In determining a safe speed the following factors shall be among those taken into account:

(a) By all vessels:

(i) the state of visibility

(ii) the traffic density, including concentrations of fishing vessels or any other vessels;

(iii) the maneuverability of the vessel with special reference to stopping distance and turning ability in the prevailing conditions;

(iv) at night, the presence of background light such as from shore lights or from back scatter of her own lights;

(v) the state of wind, sea, and current, and the proximity of navigational hazards;

**Rules**

---

### Rule 6

This is another basic Rule — so obvious that it shouldn't need comment. But note that no specific speed is stated in terms of knots or miles per hour. The sole focus is on preventing collisions, and a "safe speed" will be determined by the prevailing conditions, with six common sense factors specifically listed. (Numerical speed limits found in some harbors and waterways are not part of the Navigation Rules; they must not be exceeded, and under some conditions may actually be greater than a "safe speed.")

Note that this Rule is applicable in *all* conditions of visibility — normal and restricted.

If you have radar on your boat, and you are using it, you are responsible for using it properly — too many small-craft skippers do not know how to plot radar targets. Learn the capabilities and limitations of your radar set and how to meet the legally required determination of risk of collision.

The commonly used phrase of "stopping in half of the distance of visibility" does not appear in the Rules and is not applicable in many cases, such as when radar is being used.

| International | Inland |
|---|---|
| (vi) the draft in relation to the available depth of water. | (vi) the draft in relation to the available depth of water. |
| (b) Additionally, by vessels with operational radar: | (b) Additionally, by vessels with operational radar; |
| (i) the characteristics, efficiency and limitations of the radar equipment; | (i) the characteristics, efficiency and limitations of the radar equipment; |
| (ii) any constraints imposed by the radar range scale in use; | (ii) any constraints imposed by the radar range scale in use; |
| (iii) the effect on radar detection of the sea state, weather and other sources of interference; | (iii) the effect on radar detection of the sea state, weather, and other sources of interference; |
| (iv) the possibility that small vessels, ice and other floating objects may not be detected by radar at an adequate range. | (iv) the possibility that small vessels, ice and other floating objects may not be detected by radar at an adequate range; |
| (v) the number, location and movement of vessels detected by radar. | (v) the number, location, and movement of vessels detected by radar; and |
| (vi) the more exact assessment of the visibility that may be possible when radar is used to determine the range of vessels or other objects in the vicinity. | (vi) the more exact assessment of the visibility that may be possible when radar is used to determine the range of vessels or other objects in the vicinity. |

## Rule 7    Risk of Collision

(a) Every vessel shall use all available means appropriate to the prevailing circumstances and conditions to determine if risk of collision exists. If there is any doubt such risk shall be deemed to exist.

(b) Proper use shall be made of radar equipment if fitted and operational, including long-range scanning, to obtain early warning of risk of collision and radar plotting or equivalent systematic observation of detected objects.

(c) Assumptions shall not be made on the basis of scanty information, especially scanty radar information.

## Rule 7    Risk of Collision

(a) Every vessel shall use all available means appropriate to the prevailing circumstances and conditions to determine if risk of collision exists. If there is any doubt such risk shall be deemed to exist.

(b) Proper use shall be made of radar equipment if fitted and operational, including long-range scanning, to obtain early warning of risk of collision and radar plotting or equivalent systematic observation of detected objects.

(c) Assumptions shall not be made on the basis of scanty information, especially scanty radar information.

### Rule 7

Radar is fine if you have it and use it correctly, but it is not essential to the determination of "risk of collision." The very basic means is by visual observation — a "seaman's eye." Early on, establish a compass bearing to the other vessel, and re-measure it at frequent intervals — if it doesn't change, with neither vessel maneuvering, there is real risk of collision. Even if it does change, there is still a possible risk, especially if the other vessel is a tug towing a barge astern — *never* try to pass between a tug and its tow!

| International | Inland |
|---|---|
| (d) In determining if risk of collision exists, the following considerations shall be among those taken into account: | (d) In determining if risk of collision exists, the following considerations shall be among those taken into account: |
| (i) such risk shall be deemed to exist if the compass bearing of an approaching vessel does not appreciably change; | (i) such risk shall be deemed to exist if the compass bearing of an approaching vessel does not appreciably change; and |
| (ii) such risk may sometimes exist even when an appreciable bearing change is evident, particularly when approaching a very large vessel or a tow or when approaching a vessel at close range. | (ii) such risk may sometimes exist even when an appreciable bearing change is evident, particularly when approaching a very large vessel or a tow or when approaching a vessel at close range. |

**Rules**

## Rule 8    Action to avoid a Collision

(a) Any action taken to avoid collision shall, if the circumstances of the case admit, be positive, made in ample time and with due regard to the observance of good seamanship.

(b) Any alteration of course and/or speed to avoid collision shall, if the circumstances of the case admit, be large enough to be readily apparent to another vessel observing visually or by radar; a succession of small alterations of course and/or speed should be avoided.

(c) If there is sufficient sea room, alteration of course alone may be the most effective action to avoid a close-quarters situation, provided that it is made in good time, is substantial, and does not result in another close-quarters situation.

(d) Action taken to avoid collision with another vessel shall be such as to result in passing at a safe distance. The effectiveness of the action shall be carefully checked until the other vessel is finally past and clear.

## Rule 8    Action To Avoid Collision

(a) Any action taken to avoid collision shall, if the circumstances of the case admit, be positive, made in ample time and with due regard to the observation of good seamanship.

(b) Any alteration of course or speed to avoid collision shall, if the circumstances of the case admit, be large enough to be readily apparent to another vessel observing visually or by radar; a succession of small alterations of course or speed should be avoided.

(c) If there is sufficient sea room, alteration of course alone may be the most effective action to avoid a close-quarters situation, provided that it is made in good time, is substantial, and does not result in another close-quarters situation.

(d) Action taken to avoid collision with another vessel shall be such as to result in passing at a safe distance. The effectiveness of the action shall be carefully checked until the other vessel is finally past and clear.

---

### Rule 8

Another very logical Rule, but one that is often slighted. If you are approaching another vessel and some action is required of you, such as a change of course or speed, make it soon enough to be effective, *and make it of sufficient size to be apparent to the other skipper.* From a distance, a change of course is usually more apparent than a change of speed, but don't hesitate to slow down or stop if this is required for safety. Slowing down has the added advantage of giving you more time to assess the situation. The phrase "all way off" means dead in the water without forward movement — no "coasting."

| International | Inland |

## RELATIVE BEARINGS VERSUS COMPASS BEARINGS

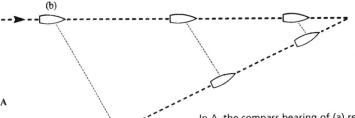

A

In A, the compass bearing of (a) relative to (b) is constant, and therefore risk of collision exists. In this particular case the relative bearing of (a) to (b) is also constant.

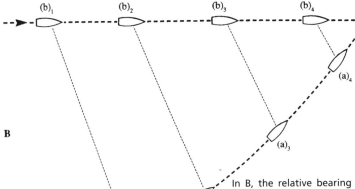

B

In B, the relative bearing of (b)$_1$ from (a)$_1$ is abaft the beam. At (a)$_2$ the bearing is approximately abeam and at (a)$_3$ and (a)$_4$ is moving ahead of the beam. The compass bearing, however, remains constant and therefore risk of collision exists.

(e) If necessary to avoid collision or allow more time to assess the situation, a vessel shall slacken her speed to take all way off by stopping or reversing her means of propulsion.

(f) (i) A vessel which, by any of these rules, is required not to impede the passage or safe passage of another vessel shall, when required by the circumstances of the case, take early action to allow sufficient sea room for the safe passage of the other vessel.

(ii) A vessel required not to impede the passage or safe passage of another vessel is not relieved of this obligation if approach-

(e) If necessary to avoid collision or allow more time to assess the situation, a vessel shall slacken her speed or take all way off by stopping or reversing her means of propulsion.

(f) (i) A vessel which, by any of these rules, is required not to impede the passage or safe passage of another vessel shall, when required by the circumstances of the case, take early action to allow sufficient sea room for the safe passage of the other vessel.

(ii) A vessel required not to impede the passage or safe passage of another vessel is not relieved of this obligation if approach-

| **International** | **Inland** |
|---|---|

ing the other vessel so as to involve risk of collision and shall, when taking action, have full regard to the action which may be required by the rules of this part.

(iii) A vessel, the passage of which is not to be impeded, remains fully obliged to comply with the rules of this part when the two vessels are approaching one another so as to involve risk of collision.

## Rule 9    Narrow Channels

(a) A vessel proceeding along the course of a narrow channel or fairway shall keep as near to the outer limit of the channel or fairway which lies on her starboard side as is safe and practicable.

(b) A vessel of less than 20 meters in length or a sailing vessel shall not impede the passage of a vessel which can safely navigate only within a narrow channel or fairway.

(c) A vessel engaged in fishing shall not impede the passage of any other vessel navigating within a narrow channel or fairway.

(d) A vessel shall not cross a narrow channel or fairway if such crossing impedes the passage of a vessel which can safely navigate only within such channel or fairway. The latter vessel may use the sound signal prescribed in Rule 34(d) if in doubt as to the intention of the crossing vessel.

(e)  (i) In a narrow channel or fairway when overtaking can take place only if the vessel to be overtaken has to take action to permit safe passing, the vessel intending to overtake shall indicate her intention by sounding the appropriate signal prescribed in Rule 34(c)(i). The vessel to be overtaken

---

ing the other vessel so as to involve risk of collision and shall, when taking action, have full regard to the action which may be required by the rules of this part.

(iii) A vessel, the passage of which is not to be impeded, remains fully obliged to comply with the rules of this part when the two vessels are approaching one another so as to involve risk of collision.

## Rule 9    Narrow Channels

(a)  (i) A vessel proceeding along the course of a narrow channel or fairway shall keep as near to the outer limit of the channel or fairway which lies on her starboard side as is safe and practicable.

(ii) Notwithstanding paragraph (a)(i) and Rule 14(a), a power-driven vessel operating in narrow channels or fairways on the Great Lakes, Western Rivers, or waters specified by the Secretary, and proceeding downbound with a following current shall have the right-of-way over an up-bound vessel, shall propose the manner and place of passage, and shall initiate the maneuvering signals prescribed by Rule 34(a)(i), as appropriate. The vessel proceeding upbound against the current shall hold as necessary to permit safe passing.

(b) A vessel of less than 20 meters in length or a sailing vessel shall not impede the passage of a vessel that can safely navigate only within a narrow channel or fairway.

(c) A vessel engaged in fishing shall not impede the passage of any other vessel navigating within a narrow channel or fairway.

(d) A vessel shall not cross a narrow channel or fairway if such crossing impedes the passage of a vessel which can safely navigate only within that channel or fairway. The latter vessel shall use the danger signal prescribed in Rule 34(d) if in doubt as to the intention of the crossing vessel.

(e)  (i) In a narrow channel or fairway when overtaking, the vessel intending to overtake shall indicate her intention by sounding the appropriate signal prescribed by Rule 34(c) and take steps to permit safe passing. The overtaken vessel, if in agreement, shall sound the same signal. If in

**Rules**

| International | Inland |
|---|---|
| shall, if in agreement, sound the appropriate signal prescribed in Rule 34(c)(ii) and take steps to permit safe passing. If in doubt she may sound the signals prescribed in Rule 34(d). | doubt she shall sound the danger signal prescribed in Rule 34(d). |
| (ii) This Rule does not relieve the overtaking vessel of her obligation under Rule 13. | (ii) This Rule does not relieve the overtaking vessel of her obligation under Rule 13. |
| (f) A vessel nearing a bend or an area of a narrow channel or fairway where other vessels may be obscured by an intervening obstruction shall navigate with particular alertness and caution and shall sound the appropriate signal prescribed in Rule 34(e). | (f) A vessel nearing a bend or an area of a narrow channel or fairway where other vessels may be obscured by an intervening obstruction shall navigate with particular alertness and caution and shall sound the appropriate signal prescribed in Rule 34(e). |
| (g) Any vessel shall, if the circumstances of the case admit, avoid anchoring in a narrow channel. | (g) Every vessel shall, if the circumstances of the case admit, avoid anchoring in a narrow channel. |

## Rule 9

This is basically the waterborne equivalent of driving on the right-hand side of the road. The needs of a vessel that must have the available deeper water are protected.

The term "narrow" should be construed with respect to the size of the vessels using the waterway.

A vessel required to "not impede" should take *early* action to keep clear of the other vessel by a *wide* margin. This might be a vessel that otherwise would be the "stand-on" vessel, but whose status is changed by the practical considerations of Rule 9.

Sound signals are required, but under different circumstances in the International and Inland Rules.

On the Great Lakes, Western Rivers — essentially the Mississippi River and its tributaries — and other specified waters, the Inland Rules specifically provide privileged status to a vessel proceeding with the current. In other areas that may have tidal currents or normal river flows, this Rule does not apply, but common courtesy should lead to giving a vessel going with the current, and thus being less maneuverable, the right-of-way over a vessel opposing the current flow.

In Rule 9(d), the Inland Rules require the whistle signal of doubt or danger — five short blasts sounded rapidly. Under the International Rules, this signal is optional. The "bend" signal of one prolonged blast is also used by vessels entering a waterway from a side channel or coming out of a berth or slip; see Rule 34(g). Note that the Rules do not provide for a "long" blast, only short blasts (approximately one second) or prolonged blasts (four to six seconds duration).

In October, 1996, Inland Rule (e)(i) was changed to limit its provisions to power-driven vessels. Its wording does not parallel that of the corresponding International Rule. *See note on page 4.*

## Rule 10　Traffic Separation Schemes

(a) This Rule applies to traffic separation schemes adopted by the Organization and does not relieve any vessel of her obligation under any other rule.

(b) A vessel using a traffic separation scheme shall:

(i) proceed in the appropriate traffic lane in the general direction of traffic flow for that lane;

(ii) so far as practicable keep clear of a traffic separation line or separation zone;

(iii) normally join or leave a traffic lane at the termination of the lane, but when joining or leaving from either side shall do so at as small an angle to the general direction of traffic flow as practicable.

(c) A vessel shall so far as practicable avoid crossing traffic lanes, but if obliged to do so shall cross on a heading as nearly as practicable at right angles to the general direction of traffic flow.

(d) (i) A vessel shall not use an inshore traffic zone when she can safely use the appropriate traffic lane within the adjacent traffic separation scheme. However, vessels of less than 20 meters in length, sailing vessels and vessels engaged in fishing may use the inshore traffic zone.

(ii) Notwithstanding subparagraph (d)(i), a vessel may use an inshore traffic zone when en route to or from a port, offshore installation or structure, pilot station, or any other place situated within the inshore traffic zone, or to avoid immediate danger.

(e) A vessel other than a crossing vessel or a vessel joining or leaving a lane, shall not normally enter a separation zone or cross a separation line except:

(i) in cases of emergency to avoid immediate danger;

(ii) to engage in fishing within a separation zone.

(f) A vessel navigating in areas near the

## Rule 10　Traffic Separation Schemes

(a) This Rule applies to traffic separation schemes and does not relieve any vessel of her obligation under any other Rule.

(b) A vessel using a traffic separation scheme shall:

(i) proceed in the appropriate traffic lane in the general direction of traffic flow for that lane;

(ii) so far as practicable keep clear of a traffic separation line or separation zone;

(iii) normally join or leave a traffic lane at the termination of the lane, but when joining or leaving from either side shall do so at as small an angle to the general direction of traffic flow as practicable.

(c) A vessel shall so far as practicable avoid crossing traffic lanes, but if obliged to do so shall cross on a heading as nearly as practicable at right angles to the general direction of traffic flow.

(d) (i) A vessel shall not use an inshore traffic zone when she can safely use the appropriate traffic lane within the adjacent traffic separation scheme. However, vessels of less than 20 meters in length, sailing vessels and vessels engaged in fishing may use the inshore traffic zone.

(ii) Notwithstanding subparagraph (d)(i), a vessel may use an inshore traffic zone when en route to or from a port, offshore installation or structure, pilot station, or any other place situated within the inshore traffic zone, or to avoid immediate danger.

(e) A vessel other than a crossing vessel or a vessel joining or leaving a lane, shall not normally enter a separation zone or cross a separation line except:

(i) in cases of emergency to avoid immediate danger;

(ii) to engage in fishing within a separation zone.

(f) A vessel navigating in areas near the

**Rules**

## International

terminations of traffic separation schemes shall do so with particular caution.

(g) A vessel shall, so far as practicable, avoid anchoring in a traffic separation scheme or in areas near its terminations.

(h) A vessel not using a traffic separation scheme shall avoid it by as wide a margin as is practicable.

(i) A vessel engaged in fishing shall not impede the passage of any vessel following a traffic lane.

(j) A vessel of less than 20 meters in length or a sailing vessel shall not impede the safe passage of a power-driven vessel following a traffic lane.

(k) A vessel restricted in her ability to maneuver when engaged in an operation for the maintenance of safety of navigation in a traffic separation scheme is exempted from complying with this Rule to the extent necessary to carry out the operation.

(l) A vessel restricted in her ability to maneuver when engaged in an operation for the laying, servicing or picking up of a submarine cable, within a traffic separation scheme, is exempted from complying with this Rule to the extent necessary to carry out the operation.

terminations of traffic separation schemes shall do so with particular caution.

(g) A vessel shall, so far as practicable, avoid anchoring in a traffic separation scheme or in areas near its terminations.

(h) A vessel not using a traffic separation scheme shall avoid it by as wide a margin as is practicable.

(i) A vessel engaged in fishing shall not impede the passage of any vessel following a traffic lane.

(j) A vessel of less than 20 meters in length or a sailing vessel shall not impede the safe passage of a power-driven vessel following a traffic lane.

(k) A vessel restricted in her ability to maneuver when engaged in an operation for the maintenance of safety of navigation in a traffic separation scheme is exempted from complying with this Rule to the extent necessary to carry out the operation.

(l) A vessel restricted in her ability to maneuver when engaged in an operation for the laying, servicing or picking up of a submarine cable, within a traffic separation scheme, is exempted from complying with this Rule to the extent necessary to carry out the operation.

### Rule 10

Obviously, the International Rule is much more specific about proper behavior regarding Traffic Separation Schemes than the Inland Rule.

This is an important rule and there are two aspects of it that are particularly critical to smaller vessels. First, all crossing vessels must cross on a heading as nearly as practicable at right angles to the lane, thereby presenting a full profile to vessels using the lane.

Second, a vessel — even if under sail — is required "not to impede the safe passage of a power-driven vessel following a traffic lane." The aim should be to cross as quickly as possible, which means using the engine when necessary and not trying to counteract any sideways effect of the tidal stream.

In the illustration at upper right, Yacht A is counteracting the effect of the tidal stream to make her track at 90° to the lane, but her profile to vessels in the lane is considerably reduced. This has two results. First, her time in crossing the lane is much increased; second, her reduced profile means that she is less visible, both visually and on radar screens, than if she presented a full profile. The action taken by Yacht A is incorrect. Yacht B is correctly presenting her full profile in the lane and is not attempting to counteract the tidal stream. Although her track is longer than that of Yacht A, she will cross in less

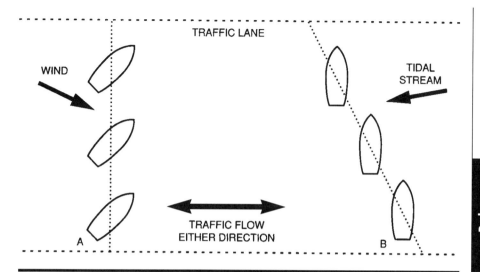

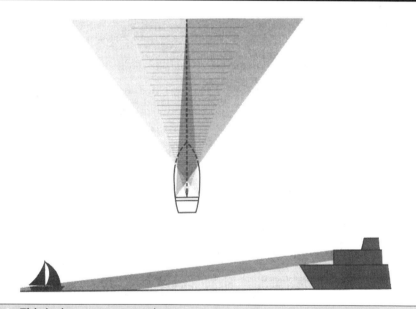

time. This is the correct procedure.

Also illustrated is the fact that there is a blind area ahead of and on each bow of any vessel — the larger the vessel the larger the blind area. As a general guideline, if you are within a mile of a medium-to-large vessel, i.e. 10,000 to 15,000 tons, then you are in the blind arc. A simple test: If you cannot see the captain's bridge, then the chances are the captain cannot see you.

Avoid either remaining in, or crossing the bow within, the blind arc. The actual area of the arc is a function of the size of the vessel, the size of the yacht, the height of eye of the vessel, and its beam. It is the yacht hull that has to be seen, not the mast.

| International | Inland |
|---|---|

## SECTION II
## CONDUCT OF VESSELS IN SIGHT OF ONE ANOTHER

### Rule 11  Application

Rules in this section apply to vessels in sight of one another.

### Rule 12  Sailing Vessels

(a) When two sailing vessels are approaching one another, so as to avoid risk of collision, one of them shall keep out of the way of the other as follows:

(i) when each has the wind on a different side, the vessel which has the wind on the port side shall keep out of the way of the other;

(ii) when both have the wind on the same side, the vessel which is to windward shall keep out of the way of the vessel which is to leeward;

(iii) if a vessel with the wind on the port side sees a vessel to windward and cannot determine with certainty whether the other vessel has the wind on the port or on the starboard side, she shall keep out of the way of the other.

## SUBPART II
## CONDUCT OF VESSELS IN SIGHT OF ONE ANOTHER

### Rule 11  Application

Rules in this subpart apply to vessels in sight of one another.

### Rule 12  Sailing Vessels

(a) When two sailing vessels are approaching one another, so as to involve risk of collision, one of them shall keep out of the way of the other as follows:

(i) when each has the wind on a different side, the vessel which has the wind on the port side shall keep out of the way of the other;

(ii) when both have the wind on the same side, the vessel which is to windward shall keep out of the way of the vessel which is to leeward; and

(iii) if a vessel with the wind on the port side sees a vessel to windward and cannot determine with certainty whether the other vessel has the wind on the port or on the starboard side, she shall keep out of the way of the other.

### Rule 11

The Rules of Section/Subpart II — Rules 11 through 18 — are applicable *only* when each vessel can see the other. They do *not* apply under conditions of "restricted visibility" — fog, mist, heavy rain or snow, etc., when the vessels cannot see each other. The mere darkness of night is not a status of restricted visibility, unless one or more of the conditions listed above prevail.

### Rule 12

In considering the relative status of two vessels coming into a situation where danger of collision might exist, the Navigation Rules now use the terms of "stand-on" and "give-way." The long-used and well-known terms of "privileged" and "burdened" are no longer in the Rules, but continue in everyday speech. Note also that the term "right-of-way" for one vessel over another does not appear anywhere in either set of Rules.

This Rule requires that a sailing vessel that cannot determine whether or not she should keep out of the way of the other must assume that she should and act accordingly. *This is an excellent consideration for any situation of two vessels of any type or size encountering each other.*

| International | Inland |
|---|---|
| (b) For the purposes of this Rule the windward side shall be deemed to be the side opposite to that on which the mainsail is carried or, in the case of a square-rigged vessel, the side opposite to that on which the largest fore-and-aft sail is carried. | (b) For the purpose of this Rule the windward side shall be deemed to be the side opposite to that on which the mainsail is carried or, in the case of a square-rigged vessel, the side opposite to that on which the largest fore-and-aft sail is carried. |

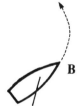

When B is in doubt about A's tack, it is the responsibility of B to keep clear.

## Rule 13   Overtaking

(a) Notwithstanding anything contained in the Rules of Part B, Sections I and II, any vessel overtaking any other shall keep out of the way of the vessel being overtaken.

(b) A vessel shall be deemed to be overtaking when coming up with another vessel from a direction more than 22.5 degrees abaft her beam; that is, in such a position with reference to the vessel she is overtaking, that at night she would be able to see only the sternlight of that vessel but neither of her sidelights.

(c) When a vessel is in any doubt as to whether she is overtaking another, she shall assume that this is the case and act accordingly.

## Rule 13   Overtaking

(a) Notwithstanding anything contained in Rules 4 through 18, any vessel overtaking any other shall keep out of the way of the vessel being overtaken.

(b) A vessel shall be deemed to be overtaking when coming up with another vessel from a direction more than 22.5 degrees abaft her beam; that is, in such a position with reference to the vessel she is overtaking, that at night she would be able to see only the sternlight of that vessel but neither of her sidelights.

(c) When a vessel is in any doubt as to whether she is overtaking another, she shall assume that this is the case and act accordingly.

**International**

**Inland**

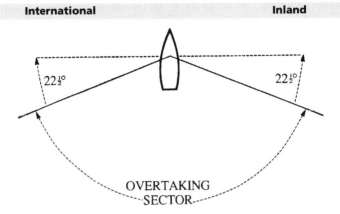

OVERTAKING
SECTOR

(d) Any subsequent alteration of the bearing between the two vessels shall not make the overtaking vessel a crossing vessel within the meaning of these Rules or relieve her of the duty of keeping clear of the overtaken vessel until she is finally past and clear.

(d) Any subsequent alteration of the bearing between the two vessels shall not make the overtaking vessel a crossing vessel within the meaning of these Rules or relieve her of the duty of keeping clear of the overtaken vessel until she is finally past and clear.

### Rule 13

The zone in which a vessel is deemed to be "overtaking" is the same as that defined for the arc of visibility of the overtaken vessel's sternlight. A vessel coming up astern of a slower vessel is considered to have greater maneuverability and, as such, is the "give-way" vessel. She must take appropriate action until she is finally past and well clear of the overtaken vessel — once a vessel's status is "overtaking," it does not change as she moves out of the sector that created that status.

Although not a part of this Rule, it is required that an overtaking vessel indicate its desire to pass with a whistle signal and get the consent of the overtaken vessel to be passed; see Rule 34(c). This is required by the Inland Rules for all waters, but by the International Rules only in a narrow channel or fairway. In actual practice, VHF radio contact, usually on Channel 13, is often substituted for the whistle signals — "I will pass you on one whistle (or two whistles) if that is OK with you." (See Rule 34(h).)

### Rule 14   Head-on Situation

(a) When two power-driven vessels are meeting on reciprocal or nearly reciprocal courses so as to involve risk of collision, each shall alter her course to starboard so that each shall pass on the port side of the other.

(b) Such a situation shall be deemed to exist when a vessel sees the other ahead or nearly ahead and by night she could see

### Rule 14   Head-on Situation

(a) Unless otherwise agreed, when two power-driven vessels are meeting on reciprocal or nearly reciprocal courses so as to involve risk of collision, each shall alter her course to starboard so that each shall pass on the port side of the other.

(b) Such a situation shall be deemed to exist when a vessel sees the other ahead or nearly ahead and by night she could see

| **International** | **Inland** |
|---|---|
| the masthead lights of the other in a line or nearly in a line and/or both sidelights and by day she observes the corresponding aspect of the other vessel. | the masthead lights of the other in a line or nearly in a line or both sidelights and by day she observes the corresponding aspect of the other vessel. |
| (c) When a vessel is in any doubt as to whether such a situation exists, she shall assume that it does exist and act accordingly. | (c) When a vessel is in any doubt as to whether such a situation exists, she shall assume that it does exist and act accordingly. |

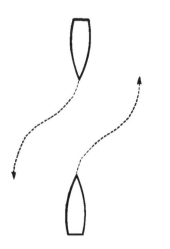

(d) Notwithstanding paragraph (a) of this Rule, a power-driven vessel operating on the Great Lakes, Western Rivers, or waters specified by the Secretary, and proceeding downbound with a following current shall have the right-of-way over an upbound vessel, shall propose the manner of passage, and shall initiate the maneuvering signals prescribed by Rule 34(a)(i), as appropriate.

---

### Rule 14

Other than overtaking, the encounter of two vessels is either "meeting" or "crossing." Meeting is defined as "head-on or nearly head-on," with no numeric definition of "nearly"; courts have, however, accepted as meeting situations where each vessel was in a forward arc of not greater than one point (11¼°).

Meeting is a more serious and urgent matter than overtaking because the rate of closure is the *sum* of the speed of each vessel rather than the difference. If a vessel is in any doubt that the encounter is a meeting situation, she should assume that it is and act accordingly, steering to the right. Neither vessel is "stand-on" or "give-way"; both have responsibilities. Note that this Rule applies only to *power-driven* vessels meeting other *power-driven* vessels; a meeting of a power-driven vessel with, for example, a sailing vessel, is not covered.

Meetings are normally "port-to-port," but the Inland Rules do allow for deviation if agreed to by both vessels; this is most likely to occur in winding rivers and channels.

Whistle signals are required, and may be supplemented by flashing light signals, but are different between the International and Inland Rules; see Rule 34(a) and (b). In the Inland Rules, VHF radio communications may be substituted for the whistle signals; see Rule 34(h). In the International Rules, radio communications are not an acceptable substitute for whistle signals, but are often used as a supplement.

| International | Inland |
|---|---|

## Rule 15   Crossing Situation

When two power-driven vessels are crossing so as to involve risk of collision, the vessel which has the other on her own starboard side shall keep out of the way and shall, if the circumstances of the case admit, avoid crossing ahead of the other vessel.

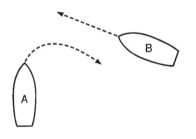

## Rule 15   Crossing Situation

(a) When two power-driven vessels are crossing so as to involve risk of collision, the vessel which has the other on her starboard side shall keep out of the way and shall, if the circumstances of the case admit, avoid crossing ahead of the other vessel.

(b) Notwithstanding paragraph (a), on the Great Lakes, Western Rivers, or waters specified by the Secretary, a power-driven vessel crossing a river shall keep out of the way of a power-driven vessel ascending or descending the river.

---

### Rule 15

If the situation between two vessels encountering each other does not fit the definitions of overtaking or meeting, then it must be "crossing." Note that for the Rule to be applicable, there must be a "risk of collision" — no risk, no need to apply the Rule, but it is better to be safe than sorry!

This is the Rule that has led to the principle of a "danger zone," from dead ahead to two points (22½°) abaft the beam on the starboard side (the same arc as covered by the green sidelight). If you see another vessel in your danger zone, with risk of collision, you must yield to her and take evasive action. But note that this applies only for visual contacts — if you "see" another vessel only by radar, then Rule 19 governs.

Note that Inland Rule 15(b), applicable in specified, but not all, inland waters, requires that a power-driven vessel crossing a river keep out of the way of another power-driven vessel going either up or downstream. There is no consideration of the relative maneuverability of the vessels, nor of which has the other on its starboard side. There is no corresponding International Rule.

In October, 1996, Inland Rule 15(b) was changed. It now applies only to a power-driven vessel crossing a river. There is no corresponding International Rule. See note on page 4.

### Rule 16

Having stated in Rules 12 through 15 which sailing or power-driven vessel must give way to another vessel in various situations, this Rule now specifies just how the give-way vessel must act. Early and meaningful action will not only serve to lessen the danger of collision, but will also be more apparent to the skipper of the stand-on vessel.

|          International          |          Inland          |

## Rule 16   Action by Give-way Vessel

Every vessel which is directed to keep out of the way of another vessel shall, so far as possible, take early and substantial action to keep well clear.

## Rule 17   Action by Stand-on Vessel

(a) (i) Where one of two vessels is to keep out of the way the other shall keep her course and speed.

(ii) The latter vessel may, however, take action to avoid collision by her maneuver alone, as soon as it becomes apparent to her that the vessel required to keep out of the way is not taking appropriate action in compliance with these Rules.

(b) When, from any cause, the vessel required to keep her course and speed finds herself so close that collision cannot be avoided by the action of the give-way vessel alone, she shall take such action as will best aid to avoid collision.

(c) A power-driven vessel which takes action in a crossing situation in accordance with sub-paragraph (a)(ii) of this Rule to avoid collision with another power-driven vessel shall, if the circumstances of the case admit, not alter course to port for a vessel on her own port side.

(d) This rule does not relieve the give-way vessel of her obligation to keep out of the way.

## Rule 16   Action by Give-way Vessel

Every vessel which is directed to keep out of the way of another vessel shall, so far as possible, take early and substantial action to keep well clear.

## Rule 17   Action by Stand-on Vessel

(a) (I) Where one of two vessels is to keep out of the way, the other shall keep her course and speed.

(ii) The latter vessel may, however, take action to avoid collision by her maneuver alone, as soon as it becomes apparent to her that the vessel required to keep out of the way is not taking appropriate action in compliance with these Rules.

(b) When, from any cause, the vessel required to keep her course and speed finds herself so close that collision cannot be avoided by the action of the give-way vessel alone, she shall take such action as will best aid to avoid collision.

(c) A power-driven vessel which takes action in a crossing situation in accordance with subparagraph (a)(ii) of this Rule to avoid collision with another power-driven vessel shall, if the circumstances of the case admit, not alter course to port for a vessel on her own port side.

(d) This rule does not relieve the give-way vessel of her obligation to keep out of the way.

---

### Rule 17

The stand-on vessel may be said to have the "right-of-way," but with this status comes specific responsibilities and required actions. It is unacceptable and contrary to the Rules to hold one's course and speed right on into a collision — you could be said to be "right, dead right!" The stand-on vessel *may* take action just as soon as it becomes clear that the give-way vessel is not taking the actions required by the Rules; she is *required* to take action when the situation develops that collision cannot be avoided by action of the give-way vessel alone. The actions to be taken are not specified in the Rules, and may be whatever is required by the circumstances. Rule 17(c), however, does prohibit, under normal conditions, a turn by a stand-on vessel toward a vessel on her port side. The distinction between permissive and mandatory actions should be fully understood.

| International | Inland |
|---|---|

## Rule 18 Responsibilities Between Vessels

Except where Rules 9, 10, and 13 otherwise require:

(a) A power-driven vessel underway shall keep out of the way of:

   (i) a vessel not under command;

   (ii) a vessel restricted in her ability to maneuver;

   (iii) a vessel engaged in fishing;

   (iv) a sailing vessel.

(b) A sailing vessel underway shall keep out of the way of:

## Rule 18 Responsibilities Between Vessels

Except where Rules 9, 10, and 13 otherwise require:

(a) A power-driven vessel underway shall keep out of the way of:

   (i) a vessel not under command;

   (ii) a vessel restricted in her ability to maneuver;

   (iii) a vessel engaged in fishing; and

   (iv) a sailing vessel.

(b) A sailing vessel underway shall keep out of the way of:

---

### Rule 18

Note that Rule 18 applies *only* if Rules 9, 10, and 13 do not require other specific action. For example, a sailing vessel that is overtaking a power-driven vessel is the give-way vessel, regardless of Rule 18(a)(iv), because Rule 13 takes precedence.

These lists are often thought of as a "pecking order" between various types of vessels for situations not involving narrow channels, Traffic Separation Schemes, and the overtaking encounter, but this is *not* correct! The sequence of the listing of various types of vessels in each paragraph is *not* an indication of relative status of these categories; the subparagraphs are a total list of applicable types of vessels, not a priority listing within any list. Each paragraph should be read independently of the others for the category of vessel concerned.

A vessel "not under command" is usually one that has suffered a loss of propulsion or steering control. A vessel "restricted in her ability to maneuver" would typically be a dredge, one laying an underwater cable, a Coast Guard vessel servicing an aid to navigation, etc.

Remember: (1) A vessel under sail does not have the privileges of that category if she is also being propelled by machinery; and, (2) a sport-fishing boat with trolling lines out is not a "vessel engaged in fishing."

International Rule 18(e) and Inland Rule 18(d), in practical terms, apply to a seaplane taxiing on the water. Such aircraft, when taking off and landing, are unable to maneuver to keep clear of vessels.

| International | Inland |
|---|---|
| (i) a vessel not under command; | (i) a vessel not under command; |
| (ii) a vessel restricted in her ability to maneuver; | (ii) a vessel restricted in her ability to maneuver; and |
| (iii) a vessel engaged in fishing; | (iii) a vessel engaged in fishing. |
| (c) A vessel engaged in fishing when underway shall, so far as possible, keep out of the way of: | (c) A vessel engaged in fishing when underway shall, so far as possible, keep out of the way of; |
| (i) a vessel not under command; | (i) a vessel not under command, and |
| (ii) a vessel restricted in her ability to maneuver. | (ii) a vessel restricted in her ability to maneuver. |
| (d) (i) any vessel other than a vessel not under command or a vessel restricted in her ability to maneuver shall, if the circumstances of the case admit, avoid impeding the safe passage of a vessel constrained by her draft, exhibiting the signals in Rule 28. | |
| (ii) A vessel constrained by her draft shall navigate with particular caution, having full regard to her special condition. | |
| (e) A seaplane on the water shall, in general, keep well clear of all vessels and avoid impeding their navigation. In circumstances, however, where risk of collision exists, she shall comply with the Rules of this Part. | (d) A seaplane on the water shall, in general, keep well clear of all vessels and avoid impeding their navigation. In circumstances, however, where risk collision exists, she shall comply with the Rules of this Part. |

SECTION III
CONDUCT OF VESSELS IN
RESTRICTED VISIBILITY

SUBPART III
CONDUCT OF VESSELS IN
RESTRICTED VISIBILITY

## Rule 19   Conduct of Vessels in Restricted Visibility

(a) This Rule applies to vessels not in sight of one another when navigating in or near an area of restricted visibility.

(b) Every vessel shall proceed at a safe speed adapted to the prevailing circumstances and conditions of restricted visibility. A power-driven vessel shall have her engines ready for immediate maneuver.

## Rule 19   Conduct of Vessels in Restricted Visibility

(a) This Rule applies to vessels not in sight of one another when navigating in or near an area of restricted visibility.

(b) Every vessel shall proceed at a safe speed adapted to the prevailing circumstances and conditions of restricted visibility. A power-driven vessel shall have her engines ready for immediate maneuver,

Rules

| International | Inland |
|---|---|
| (c) Every vessel shall have due regard to the prevailing circumstances and conditions of restricted visibility when complying with the Rules of Section I of this Part. | (c) Every vessel shall have due regard to the prevailing circumstances and conditions of restricted visibility when complying with Rules 4 through 10. |
| (d) A vessel which detects by radar alone the presence of another vessel shall determine if a close-quarters situation is developing and/or risk of collision exists. If so, she shall take avoiding action in ample time, provided that when such action consists of an alteration of course, so far as possible the following shall be avoided: | (d) A vessel which detects by radar alone the presence of another vessel shall determine if a close-quarters situation is developing or risk of collision exists. If so, she shall take avoiding action in ample time, provided that when such action consists of an alteration of course, so far as possible the following shall be avoided: |
| (i) an alteration of course to port for a vessel forward of the beam, other than for a vessel being overtaken; | (i) an alteration of course to port for a vessel forward of the beam, other than for a vessel being overtaken; and |
| (ii) an alteration of course toward a vessel abeam or abaft the beam. | (ii) an alteration of course toward a vessel abeam or abaft the beam. |
| (e) Except where it has been determined that a risk of collision does not exist, every vessel which hears apparently forward of her beam the fog signal of another vessel, or which cannot avoid a close-quarters situation with another vessel forward of her beam, shall reduce her speed to the minimum at which she can be kept on her course. She shall, if necessary, take all her way off and in any event navigate with extreme caution until danger of collision is over. | (e) Except where it has been determined that a risk of collision does not exist, every vessel which hears apparently forward of her beam the fog signal of another vessel, or which cannot avoid a close-quarters situation with another vessel forward of her beam, shall reduce her speed to the minimum at which she can be kept on course. She shall, if necessary, take all her way off and, in any event, navigate with extreme caution until danger of collision is over. |

## Rule 19

Section/Subpart III of Part B consists of the single Rule 19.

For this Rule to be applicable, *both* of two conditions must be met — vessels must be in or near an area of restricted visibility, and they must *not* be in sight of each other. A vessel might be in quite clear weather, but adjacent to a fog bank, rainsquall, etc., that did, *or might*, conceal another vessel — this Rule would then be applicable. The range of visibility is not specified; common sense must be applied — the distance would be less in confined waters than on the high seas.

The requirement of Rules 19(b) and (e) for a safe speed ties back to Rule 6(a) with its very specific conditions and requirement for stopping distance. The requirements of Rule 19(c) tie in with the provisions of Rule 5, Lookouts; Rule 7, Risk of Collision; and Rule 8, Action to Avoid Collision. If you have radar, Rule 19(d) should be read in conjunction with Rule 6(b).

Sound signals are required; see Rule 35.

## PART C  LIGHTS AND SHAPES

**International**                                    **Inland**

### Rule 20  Application

(a) Rules in this Part shall be complied with in all weathers.

(b) The Rules concerning lights shall be complied with from sunset to sunrise, and during such times no other lights shall be exhibited, except such lights as cannot be mistaken for the lights specified in these Rules or do not impair their visibility or distinctive character, or interfere with the keeping of a proper lookout.

(c) The lights prescribed by these Rules shall, if carried, also be exhibited from sunrise to sunset in restricted visibility and may be exhibited in all other circumstances when it is deemed necessary.

(d) The Rules concerning shapes shall be complied with by day.

(e) The lights and shapes specified in these Rules shall comply with the provisions of Annex I to these regulations.

### Rule 20  Application

(a) Rules in this Part shall be complied with in all weathers.

(b) The Rules concerning lights shall be complied with from sunset to sunrise, and during such times no other lights shall be exhibited, except such lights as cannot be mistaken for the lights specified in these Rules or do not impair their visibility or distinctive character, or interfere with the keeping of a proper lookout.

(c) The lights prescribed by these Rules shall, if carried, also be exhibited from sunrise to sunset in restricted visibility and may be exhibited in all other circumstances when it is deemed necessary.

(d) The Rules concerning shapes shall be complied with by day.

(e) The lights and shapes specified in these Rules shall comply with the provisions of Annex I of these Rules.

---

#### *Rule 20*

For this Rule, "in all weathers" means regardless of the state of visibility, good or bad. Navigation lights may be shown at any time during the day, and most towing vessels do so. They must be shown in daytime if visibility is restricted and, of course, must be shown at night. Shapes — commonly called "dayshapes" — are for daytime use only; they should be ignored if seen at night.

The requirement of Rule 20(b) that no other lights be shown that would impair the visibility of navigation lights is most important — but have you ever seen a cruise ship all lit up?!

In order not to overly complicate the basic Navigation Rules, specifications for lights and shapes, and requirements for the placement of these on vessels, are given in Annex I. There are differences between this Annex in the International and in the Inland Rules.

Note that there are color illustrations of various vessels' light configurations starting on page 176.

| International | Inland |
|---|---|

## Rule 21   Definitions

(a) "Masthead light" means a white light placed over the fore and aft centerline of the vessel showing an unbroken light over an arc of the horizon of 225 degrees and so fixed as to show the light from right ahead to 22.5 degrees abaft the beam on either side of the vessel.

(b) "Sidelights" mean a green light on the starboard side and a red light on the port side, each showing an unbroken light over an arc of the horizon of 112.5 degrees and so fixed as to show the light from right ahead to 22.5 degrees abaft the beam on its respective side. In a vessel of less than 20 meters in length, the sidelights may be combined in one lantern carried on the fore and aft centerline of the vessel.

## Rule 21   Definitions

(a) "Masthead light" means a white light placed over the fore and aft centerline of the vessel showing an unbroken light over an arc of the horizon of 225 degrees and so fixed as to show the light from right ahead to 22. 5 degrees abaft the beam on either side of the vessel, except that on a vessel of less than 12 meters in length the masthead light shall be placed as nearly as practicable to the fore and aft centerline of the vessel.

(b) "Sidelights" mean a green light on the starboard side and a red light on the port side, each showing an unbroken light over an arc of the horizon of 112.5 degrees and so fixed as to show the light from right ahead to 22.5 degrees abaft the beam on its respective side. On a vessel of less than 20 meters in length, the sidelights may be combined in one lantern carried on the fore and aft centerline of the vessel, except that on a vessel of less than 12 meters in length the sidelights, when combined in one lantern, shall be placed as nearly as practicable to the fore and aft centerline of the vessel.

---

### Rule 21

The term "masthead" light is somewhat a misnomer — this light is seldom, if ever, actually at the head (top) of the mast; that position is usually reserved for an anchor light. The masthead light may be below, well below, the head of the mast, provided that the location meets the requirements of Annex I as to its height "above the hull (gunwale)"; these heights vary according to the size of the vessel.

Note that the Inland Rules have less restrictive provisions for the masthead light and sidelights on vessels less than 12 meters (39.4 ft.) in length that do not appear in the International Rules.

The high rate of "flashing lights," 120 or more flashes per minute, is specified to prevent confusion with Quick-Flashing lights on aids to navigation, which flash at a nominal rate of 60 per minute.

The "special flashing light" is a feature of the Inland Rules only; it is used to mark the forward end of a barge pushed ahead. Note that its arc of visibility can be slightly different from a masthead light, but is always not less than 180°.

| International | Inland |
|---|---|
| (c) "Sternlight" means a white light placed as nearly as practicable at the stern showing an unbroken light over an arc of the horizon of 135 degrees and so fixed as to show the light 67.5 degrees from right aft on each side of the vessel. | (c) "Sternlight" means a white light placed as nearly as practicable at the stern showing an unbroken light over an arc of the horizon of 135 degrees and so fixed as to show the light 67.5 degrees from right aft on each side of the vessel. |
| (d) "Towing light" means a yellow light having the same characteristics as the "sternlight" defined in paragraph (c) of this Rule. | (d) "Towing light" means a yellow light having the same characteristics as the "sternlight" defined in paragraph (c) of this Rule. |
| (e) "All-round light" means a light showing an unbroken light over an arc of the horizon of 360 degrees. | (e) "All-round light" means a light showing an unbroken light over an arc of this horizon of 360 degrees. |
| (f) "Flashing light" means a light flashing at regular intervals at a frequency of 120 flashes or more per minute. | (f) "Flashing light" means a light flashing at regular intervals at a frequency of 120 flashes or more per minute. |
| | (g) "Special flashing light" means a yellow light flashing at regular intervals at a frequency of 50 to 70 flashes per minute, placed as far forward and as nearly as practicable on the fore and aft centerline of the tow and showing an unbroken light over an arc of the horizon of not less than 180 degrees nor more than 225 degree and so fixed as to show the light from right ahead to abeam and no more than 22·5 degrees abaft the beam on either side of the vessel. |

## Rule 22   Visibility of Lights

The lights prescribed in these Rules shall have an intensity as specified in Section 8 of Annex I to these Regulations so as to be visible at the following minimum ranges:

(a) In vessels of 50 meters or more in length:
  a masthead light, 6 miles;
  a sidelight, 3 miles;
  a sternlight, 3 miles;
  a towing light, 3 miles;
  a white, red, green or yellow all-round light, 3 miles.

## Rule 22   Visibility of Lights

The lights prescribed in these Rules shall have an intensity as specified in Annex 1 to these Rules, so as to be visible at the following minimum ranges:

(a) In a vessel of 50 meters or more in length:
  a masthead light, 6 miles;
  a sidelight, 3 miles;
  a sternlight, 3 miles;
  a towing light, 3 miles;
  a white, red, green or yellow all-round light, 3 miles; and
  a special flashing light, 2 miles.

Rules

31

| International | Inland |
|---|---|
| (b) In vessels of 12 meters or more in length but less than 50 meters in length:<br>    a masthead light, 5 miles; except that where the length of the vessel is less than 20 meters, 3 miles;<br>    a sidelight, 2 miles;<br>    a sternlight, 2 miles;<br>    a towing light, 2 miles;<br>    a white, red, green or yellow all-round light, 2 miles. | (b) In a vessel of 12 meters or more in length but less than 50 meters in length:<br>    a masthead light, 5 miles, except that where the length of the vessel is less than 20 meters, 3 miles;<br>    a sidelight, 2 miles;<br>    a sternlight, 2 miles;<br>    a towing light, 2 miles;<br>    a white, red, green or yellow all-round light, 2 miles; and,<br>    a special flashing light, 2 miles. |
| (c) In vessels of less than 12 meters in length:<br>    a masthead light, 2 miles;<br>    a sidelight, 1 mile;<br>    a sternlight, 2 miles;<br>    a towing light, 2 miles;<br>    a white, red, green or yellow all-round light, 2 miles. | (c) In a vessel of less than 12 meters in length:<br>    a masthead light, 2 miles;<br>    a sidelight, 1 mile;<br>    a sternlight, 2 miles;<br>    a towing light, 2 miles;<br>    a white, red, green or yellow all-round light, 2 miles; and a special flashing light, 2 miles. |
| (d) In inconspicuous, partly submerged vessels or objects being towed:<br>    a white all-round light, 3 miles. | (d ) In an inconspicuous, partly submerged vessel or object being towed:<br>    a white all-round light, 3 miles. |

## Rule 22

The basic requirement of Rule 22 is the intensity of each navigation light; this is for the guidance of the designers and manufacturers of the hardware. The stated ranges provide a necessary input into the formula used in Annex I to calculate the intensity. A light is "legal" if it meets the intensity requirement of Annex I, even though under some conditions of visibility it cannot be seen at the ranges stated in this Rule for that type of light.

The stated ranges also provide guidelines for vessel operators and enforcement agencies in the field.

Both sets of Rules state the visibility requirement in terms of "miles"; this is a nautical mile even on inland waters normally using statute miles for distances. Annex I translates these visibility distances to technical measurements of luminous intensity for use in the design and manufacture of navigation lights.

The Inland Rules state a visibility requirement of two miles for a "special flashing light"; this light does not appear in the International Rules. This light is yellow, as is the light for air-cushion vessels when operating in the non-displacement mode, but the frequency of the flashes is different allowing an observer to differentiate between them.

| **International** | **Inland** |
|---|---|

## Rule 23  Power-driven Vessels Underway

(a)  A power-driven vessel underway shall exhibit:

(i) a masthead light forward;

(ii) a second masthead light abaft of and higher than the forward one, except that a vessel of less than 50 meters in length shall not be obliged to exhibit such light but may do so;

(iii) sidelights;

(iv) a sternlight.

(b) An air-cushion vessel when operating in the non-displacement mode shall, in addition to the lights prescribed in paragraph (a) of this Rule, exhibit an all-round flashing yellow light.

## Rule 23  Power-driven Vessels Underway

(a) A power-driven vessel underway shall exhibit:

(i) a masthead light forward;

(ii) a second masthead light abaft of and higher than the forward one, except that a vessel of less than 50 meters in length shall not be obliged to exhibit such light but may do so:

(iii) sidelights; and

(iv) a sternlight;

(b) An air-cushion vessel when operating in the non-displacement mode shall, in addition to the lights prescribed in paragraph (a) of this Rule, exhibit an all-round flashing yellow light where it can best be seen.

*Rules*

---

### *Rule 23*

This Rule establishes what might be termed the basic requirements for navigation lights, sometimes called "running lights," for vessels underway. Subsequent Rules will cover vessels towing and being towed, vessels under sail or being rowed, fishing vessels, pilot vessels, and other categories and situations.

There are differences between the International and Inland Rules. In general, the Inland Rules provide more options and are less rigorous regarding placement.

Note that the International Rules contain a provision for craft less than 7 meters long operating at speeds not greater than 7 knots (the vessel can be capable of greater speeds, but must not be operated at more than 7 knots while using this Rule). This provision does not appear in the Inland Rules. In turn, the Inland Rules contain a special provision for vessels on the Great Lakes that does not appear in the International Rules.

Nowhere in either set of Rules does the term "range lights" appear, but the two masthead lights, where fitted on larger vessels, do form a range similar to that established by two aids to navigation. This "range" is very helpful in determining the orientation of a ship seen at a distance at night — the white masthead lights can be seen at a considerably greater distance than the red and green sidelights.

In October, 1996, Inland Rule 23(a)(i) was changed. The revised Rule eliminates the exception for vessels less than 20 meters in length; these craft must now have their masthead light located in the forward half of the vessel. The Rule is now directly comparable with the corresponding International Rule. *See note on page 4.*

| International | Inland |
|---|---|
| (c) (i) A power-driven vessel of less than 12 meters in length may, in lieu of the lights prescribed in paragraph (a) of this Rule, exhibit an all-round white light and side-lights; | (c) A power-driven vessel of less than 12 meters in length may, in lieu of the lights prescribed in paragraph (a) of this Rule, exhibit an all-round white light and side-lights. |
| (ii) a power-driven vessel of less than 7 meters in length whose maximum speed does not exceed 7 knots may, in lieu of the lights prescribed in paragraph (a) of this Rule, exhibit an all-round white light and shall, if practicable, also exhibit sidelights; | (d) A power-driven vessel, when operating on the Great Lakes, may carry an all-round white light in lieu of the second masthead light and sternlight prescribed in para-graph (a) of this Rule. The light shall be carried in the position of the second mast-head light and be visible at the same mini-mum range. |
| (iii) the masthead light or all-round white light on a power-driven vessel of less than 12 meters in length may be displaced from the fore and aft centerline of the ves-sel if centerline fitting is not practicable, provided that the sidelights are combined in one lantern which shall be carried on the fore and aft centerline of the vessel or located as nearly as practicable in the same fore and aft line as the masthead light or the all-round white light. | |

## Rule 24   Towing and Pushing

(a)  A power-driven vessel when towing shall exhibit:

(i) instead of the light prescribed in Rule 23 (a)(i) or (a)(ii), two masthead lights in a vertical line. When the length of the tow, measuring from the stern of the towing vessel to the after end of the tow exceeds 200 meters, three such lights in a vertical line;

(ii) sidelights;

(iii) a sternlight;

(iv) a towing light in a vertical line above the sternlight;

(v) when the length of the tow exceeds 200 meters, a diamond shape where it can best be seen.

(b) when a pushing vessel and a vessel being pushed ahead are rigidly connected in a composite unit they shall be regarded as a power-driven vessel and exhibit the lights prescribed in Rule 23.

## Rule 24   Towing and Pushing

(a) A power-driven vessel when towing astern shall exhibit:

(i) instead of the light prescribed either in Rule 23 (a)(i) or 23(a)(ii), two masthead lights in a vertical line. When the length of the tow, measuring from the stern of the towing vessel to the after end of the tow exceeds 200 meters, three such lights in a vertical line;

(ii) sidelights;

(iii) a sternlight;

(iv) a towing light in a vertical line above the sternlight; and

(v) when the length of the tow exceeds 200 meters, a diamond shape where it can best be seen.

(b) When a pushing vessel and a vessel being pushed ahead are rigidly connected in a composite unit they shall be regarded as a power-driven vessel and exhibit the lights prescribed in Rule 23.

| International | Inland |
|---|---|
| (c) A power-driven vessel, when pushing ahead or towing alongside, except in the case of a composite unit, shall exhibit: | (c) A power-driven vessel, when pushing ahead or towing alongside, except as required by paragraphs (b) and (i) of this Rule, shall exhibit: |
| (i) instead of the light prescribed in Rule 23(a)(i) or (a)(ii), two masthead lights in a vertical line; | (i) instead of the light prescribed either in Rule 23(a)(i) or 23(a)(ii), two masthead lights in a vertical line; |
| (ii) sidelights; | (ii) sidelights; and |
| (iii) a sternlight. | (iii) two towing lights in a vertical line. |
| (d) A power-driven vessel to which paragraphs (a) or (c) of this Rule apply shall also comply with Rule 23(a)(ii). | (d) A power-driven vessel to which paragraphs (a) or (c) of this Rule apply shall also comply with Rule 23(a)(i) and 23(a)(ii). |
| (e) A vessel or object being towed, other than those mentioned in paragraph (g) of this Rule, shall exhibit: | (e) A vessel or object other than those referred to in paragraph (g) of this Rule being towed shall exhibit: |
| (i) sidelights; | (i) sidelights; |
| (ii) a sternlight; | (ii) a sternlight; and |
| (iii) when the length of the tow exceeds 200 meters, a diamond shape where it can best be seen. | (iii) when the length of the tow exceeds 200 meters, a diamond shape where it can best be seen. |

*Rules*

### Rule 24

This Rule covers both "towing," which means towing astern on a hawser or cable or with the towed vessel alongside, and "pushing," which means only pushing the "towed" vessel ahead of the towing vessel.

For determining the need for different lights and dayshapes for longer tows, the distance is measured from the stern of the towing vessel to the stern of the towed vessel; thus, it is the sum of the length of the towline and the towed vessel.

Note carefully that the lights seen from astern of vessels pushing ahead or towing alongside are quite different in waters governed by the Inland and by the International Rules.

Note that the two masthead lights for towing vessels with tows of 200 meters or less, and the three masthead lights used with longer tows, may be shown either forward or aft on towing vessels 50 meters or more in length. If the multiple lights are shown forward, there will be a single, higher masthead light aft; if the two or three lights are shown aft, there will be a single, lower masthead light forward. The single masthead light is not required of shorter towing vessels, but may be shown.

Note that the diamond dayshape required on the towed vessel or object for tows over 200 meters in length has no corresponding light for nighttime. Note also that the diamond shape is shown only on the towed vessel or object, and not on the towing vessel even though the triple masthead lights may not be noticeable during the day (these lights will normally be shown in the daytime, although not required by the Rules).                                        *(cont.)*

35

REED'S NAUTICAL COMPANION

| International | Inland |
|---|---|
| (f) Provided that any number of vessels being towed alongside or pushed in a group shall be lighted as one vessel: | (f) Provided that any number of vessels being towed alongside or pushed in a group shall be lighted as one vessel, except as provided in paragraph (iii): |
| (i) a vessel being pushed ahead, not being part of a composite unit, shall exhibit at the forward end, sidelights; | (i) a vessel being pushed ahead, not being part of a composite unit, shall exhibit at the forward end, sidelights and a special flashing light; |
| (ii) a vessel being towed alongside shall exhibit a sternlight and, at the forward end, sidelights. | (ii) a vessel being towed alongside shall exhibit a sternlight and, at the forward end, sidelights and a special flashing light; and |
|  | (iii) when vessels are towed alongside on both sides of the towing vessel, a stern-light shall be exhibited on the stern of the outside vessel on each side of the towing vessel, and a single set of side-lights as far forward and as far outboard as is practicable, and a single special flashing light. |
| (g) An inconspicuous, partly submerged vessel or object, or combination of such vessels or objects being towed, shall exhibit: | (g) An inconspicuous, partly submerged vessel or object being towed shall exhibit: |
| (i) if it is less than 25 meters in breadth, one all-round white light at or near the forward end and one at or near the after end except that dracones need not exhibit a light at or near the forward end; | (i) if it is less than 25 meters in breadth, one all-round white light at or near each end; |

## Rule 24 (cont.)

The Inland Rule 24(a) is quite explicit, stating "a vessel when towing astern." The corresponding International Rule merely states "a vessel when towing," but this has been interpreted as meaning only towing astern.

Neither the International nor the Inland Rules clearly cover the situation of more than one vessel or object being towed in line astern. A reasonable inter-pretation of the Rules, however, can focus on the language "a vessel or object towed astern" — nothing is said about confining the requirement to the *last* vessel in a string. This would seem to require *each* vessel or object to be simi-larly lighted with sidelights and a sternlight.

In October, 1996, Inland Rule 24(f) was changed. The requirement for the lighting of barges pushed ahead and alongside was revised. The revision reflects the situation on the Western Rivers where often multiple barges are pushed by a single power-driven vessel. The Rule is still not directly compara-ble with the corresponding International Rule. *See note on page 4.*

Note that at Rule 24(i) the International and Inland Rules "get out of step." International (i) corresponds to Inland (j), and Inland (i) has no International counterpart.

| International | Inland |
|---|---|
| (ii) if it is 25 meters or more in breadth, two additional all-round white lights at or near the extremities of its breadth; | (ii) if it is 25 meters or more in breadth, four all-round white lights to mark its length and breadth; |
| (iii) if it exceeds 100 meters in length, additional all-round white lights between the lights prescribed in sub-paragraphs (i) and (ii) so that the distance between the lights shall not exceed 100 meters; | (iii) if it exceeds 100 meters in length, additional all-round white lights between the lights prescribed in sub-paragraphs (i) and (ii), so that the distance between the lights shall not exceed 100 meters: *Provided,* that any vessels or objects being towed alongside each other shall be lighted as one vessel or object; |
| (iv) a diamond shape near the aftermost extremity of the last vessel or object being towed and, if the length of the tow exceeds 200 meters, an additional diamond shape where it can best be seen and located as far forward as is practicable. | (iv) a diamond shape at or near the after most extremity of the last vessel or object being towed; and<br><br>(v) the towing vessel may direct a searchlight in the direction of the tow to indicate its presence to an approaching vessel. |
| (h) Where from any sufficient cause it is impracticable for a vessel or object being towed to exhibit the lights or shapes prescribed in paragraph (e) or (g) of this Rule, all possible measures shall be taken to light the vessel or object towed, or at least to indicate the presence of such vessel or object. | (h) Where from any sufficient cause it is impracticable for a vessel or object being towed to exhibit the lights prescribed in paragraph (e) or (g) of this Rule, all possible measures shall be taken to light the vessel or object towed, or at least to indicate the presence of the unlighted vessel or object. |
| (i) Where from any sufficient cause it is impracticable for a vessel not normally engaged in towing operations to display the lights prescribed in paragraph (a) or (c) of this Rule, such vessel shall not be required to exhibit those lights when engaged in towing another vessel in distress or otherwise in need of assistance. All possible measures shall be taken to indicate the nature of the relationship between the towing vessel and the vessel being towed as authorized by Rule 36, in particular by illuminating the towline. | (i) Notwithstanding paragraph (c), on the Western Rivers (except below the Huey P. Long Bridge on the Mississippi River) and on waters specified by the Secretary, a power-driven vessel when pushing ahead or towing alongside, except as paragraph (b) applies, shall exhibit:<br><br>(ii) sidelights; and<br><br>(iii) two towing lights in a vertical line.<br><br>(j) Where from any sufficient cause it is impracticable for a vessel not normally engaged in towing operations to display the lights prescribed by paragraph (a), (c), or (i) of this Rule, such vessel shall not be required to exhibit those lights when engaged in towing another vessel in distress or otherwise in need of assistance. All possible measures shall be taken to indicate the nature of the relationship between the towing vessel and the vessel being assisted. The searchlight authorized by Rule 36 may be used to illuminate the tow. |

**Rules**

37

# REED'S NAUTICAL COMPANION

## SHAPES

### VESSEL SAILING AND USING POWER

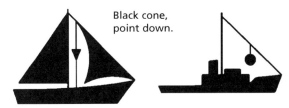

Black cone, point down.

**VESSEL AT ANCHOR**

Black ball.

Vessel of less than 7 m. in length, when at anchor, not in or near a narrow channel, fairway or anchorage, shall not be required to exhibit the ball.

### VESSEL TOWING

If length of tow exceeds 200 m., a black diamond shape to be exhibited on each vessel.

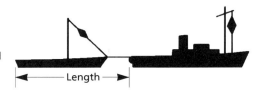

Length

**VESSEL RESTRICTED IN ABILITY TO MANEUVER**

Black ball over black diamond over black ball.

### VESSEL ENGAGED IN UNDERWATER OPERATIONS

Two black balls on the side of the obstruction.

Two black diamonds on the side on which vessels may pass.

PASS THIS SIDE

OBSTRUCTION THIS SIDE

If vessel is too small to exhibit above shapes, a rigid replica of code flag A (white and blue) shall be flown.

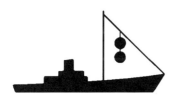

**VESSEL NOT UNDER COMMAND**

Two black balls

**VESSEL ENGAGED IN MINESWEEPING**

Three black balls

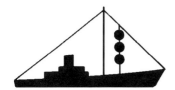

**VESSEL AGROUND**

Three black balls to be exhibited.
Not required for vessel under 12m.

**VESSEL ENGAGED IN FISHING**

Two black cones, points together.
May be replaced by basket if under 20m.

If outlying gear extends more than
150m. horizontally, a black cone point up
is shown in direction of gear.

**VESSEL CONSTRAINED BY HER DRAUGHT**

A black cylinder

| International | Inland |
|---|---|
| **Rule 25 Sailing Vessels Underway and Vessels Under Oars** | **Rule 25 Sailing Vessels Underway and Vessels Under Oars** |

(a) A sailing vessel underway shall exhibit:

(i) sidelights;

(ii) a sternlight.

(b) In a sailing vessel of less than 20 meters in length, the lights prescribed in paragraph (a) of this Rule may be combined in one lantern carried at or near the top of the mast where it can best be seen.

(c) A sailing vessel underway may, in addition to the lights prescribed in paragraph (a) of this rule, exhibit at or near the top of the mast, where they can best be seen, two all-round lights in a vertical line, the upper being red and the lower green, but these

(a) A sailing vessel underway shall exhibit:

(i) sidelights; and

(ii) a sternlight.

(b) In a sailing vessel of less than 20 meters in length, the lights prescribed in paragraph (a) of this Rule may be combined in one lantern carried at or near the top of the mast where it can best be seen.

(c) A sailing vessel underway may, in addition to the lights prescribed in paragraph (a) of this Rule, exhibit at or near the top of the mast, where they can best be seen, two all-round lights in a vertical line, the upper being red and the lower green, but these

---

### Rule 25

A sailboat that is underway shows the same sidelights and sternlight as a powerboat, but does not show a masthead light. From ahead of a sailboat you see only her sidelights; from astern, only her sternlight (which gives her the same appearance as a powerboat from astern). There are, however, variations and additional lights permitted but not required.

Note that the red-over-green all-round lights at or near the masthead are in addition to the normal sidelights and sternlight, which must be shown. However, the optional "tricolor" light at or near the masthead is in lieu of the normal sidelights and sternlight, which must not be shown if the tricolor light is lit.

**Remember:** A vessel with sails up, but also being propelled by machinery, even a small outboard motor, must show the lights of a power-driven vessel — not those of a sailing vessel. The tricolor light cannot be used in this circumstance. A white forward "masthead" light must be shown.

The Inland Rules exempt a sailboat less than 12 meters from the requirement to show a cone, point downward, when under sail and power during daylight; there is no such exemption in the International Rules.

It is desirable that a sailboat less than 7 meters in length show normal running lights, but she *may* alternatively show a white light, typically a flashlight or electric lantern shown on the sails; this is quite effective in making known the small craft's presence.

A rowboat will normally just show a white light in the direction of another vessel; it could show the same lights as a sailboat, but will rarely have the capability.

| **International** | **Inland** |
|---|---|

lights shall not be exhibited in conjunction with the combined lantern permitted by paragraph (b) of this Rule.

(d) (i) A sailing vessel of less than 7 meters in length shall, if practicable, exhibit the lights prescribed in paragraph (a) or (b) of this Rule, but if she does not, she shall have ready at hand an electric torch or lighted lantern showing a white light which shall be exhibited in sufficient time to prevent collision.

(ii) A vessel under oars may exhibit the lights prescribed in this Rule for sailing vessels, but if she does not, she shall have ready at hand an flashlight or lighted lantern showing a white light which shall be exhibited in sufficient time to prevent collision.

(e) A vessel proceeding under sail when also being propelled by machinery shall exhibit forward where it can best be seen a conical shape, apex downwards.

## Rule 26   Fishing Vessels

(a) A vessel engaged in fishing, whether underway or at anchor, shall exhibit only the lights and shapes prescribed in this Rule.

(b) A vessel when engaged in trawling, by which is meant the dragging through the water of a dredge net or other apparatus used as a fishing appliance, shall exhibit:

(i) two all-round lights in a vertical line, the upper being green and the lower white, or a shape consisting of two cones with their apexes together in a vertical line one above the other.

(ii) a masthead light abaft of and higher than the all-round green light; a vessel of less than 50 meters in length shall not be obliged to exhibit such a light but may do so;

(iii) when making way through the water, in addition to the lights prescribed in this paragraph, sidelights and a stern-light.

---

lights shall not be exhibited in conjunction with the combined lantern permitted by paragraph (b) of this Rule.

(d) (i) A sailing vessel of less than 7 meters in length shall, if practicable, exhibit the lights prescribed in paragraph (a) or (b) of this Rule, but if she does not, she shall have ready at hand an electric torch or lighted lantern showing a white light which shall be exhibited in sufficient time to prevent collision.

(ii) A vessel under oars may exhibit the lights prescribed in this Rule for sailing vessels, but if she does not, she shall have ready at hand an electric torch or lighted lantern showing a white light which shall be exhibited in sufficient time to prevent collision.

(e) A vessel proceeding under sail when also being propelled by machinery shall exhibit forward where it can best be seen a conical shape, apex downward. A vessel of less than 12 meters in length is not required to exhibit this shape, but it may do so.

## Rule 26   Fishing Vessels

(a) A vessel engaged in fishing, whether underway or at anchor, shall exhibit only . the lights and shapes prescribed in this Rule.

(b) A vessel engaged in trawling, by which is meant the dragging through the water of a dredge net or other apparatus used as a fishing appliance, shall exhibit:

(i) two all-round lights in a vertical line, the upper being green and the lower white, or a shape consisting of two cones with their apexes together in a vertical line one above the other.

(ii) a masthead light abaft of and higher than the all-round green light; a vessel of less than 50 meters in length shall not be obliged to exhibit such a light but may do so; and

(iii) when making way through the water, in addition to the lights prescribed in this paragraph, sidelights and a stern-light.

**Rules**

| International | Inland |
|---|---|
| (c) A vessel engaged in fishing, other than trawling, shall exhibit: | (c) A vessel engaged in fishing, other than trawling, shall exhibit: |
| (i) two all-round lights in a vertical line, the upper being red and the lower white, or a shape consisting of two cones with their apexes together in a vertical line one above the other; | (i) two all-round lights in a vertical line, the upper being red and the lower white, or a shape consisting of two cones with their apexes together in a vertical line one above the other; |
| (ii) when there is outlying gear extending more than 150 meters horizontally from the vessel, an all-round white light or a cone apex upwards in the direction of the gear; | (ii) when there is outlying gear extending more than 150 meters horizontally from the vessel, an all-round white light or a cone apex upward in the direction of the gear; and |
| (iii) when making way through the water, in addition to the lights prescribed in this paragraph, side lights and a stern-light. | (iii) when making way through the water, in addition to the lights prescribed in this paragraph, sidelights and a stern-light. |
| (d) The additional signals described in Annex II to these Rules apply to a vessel engaged in fishing in close proximity to other vessels engaged in fishing. | (d) The additional signals described in Annex II to these Rules apply to a vessel engaged in fishing in close proximity to other vessels engaged in fishing. |
| (e) A vessel, when not engaged in fishing, shall not exhibit the lights or shapes prescribed in this Rule, but only those pre-scribed for a vessel of her length. | (e) A vessel, when not engaged in fishing, shall not exhibit the lights or shapes prescribed in this Rule, but only those pre-scribed for a vessel of her length. |

### Rule 26

A fishing vessel is defined as one engaged in fishing with nets, lines, trawls, or other gear that restricts her ability to maneuver. It does not include sport-fishing boats with trolling lines, which are not considered to pose any such restriction.

Note that a distinction is made between trawling and other kinds of fishing, with different special lights but the same dayshape. Underway but not making way through the water, or at anchor, *only* these special lights are shown. If making way, these lights *plus* sidelights and a sternlight must be shown (if 50 meters or longer, a second higher masthead light is required aft). Note also that a basket is no longer authorized in the International Rules as a dayshape for smaller fishing vessels.

A "fishing vessel" when *not* engaged in fishing must show the normal lights for a vessel of her size; she must not display the special fishing lights.

In October, 1996, Inland Rules 26(b)(i), (c)(i), and (d) were changed. The first two changes deleted the alternative basket dayshape. The third change brought the Inland Rules into parallel wording with the International Rules. Now all of Inland Rule 26 is essentially in conformity with the International Rule. *See note on page 4.*

| International | Inland |
|---|---|

## Rule 27 Vessels Not Under Command or Restricted in Their Ability To Maneuver

| | |
|---|---|
| **Rule 27 Vessels Not Under Command or Restricted in Their Ability To Maneuver** | **Rule 27 Vessels Not Under Command or Restricted in Their Ability To Maneuver** |
| (a) A vessel not under command shall exhibit: | (a) A vessel not under command shall exhibit: |
| (i) two all-round red lights in a vertical line where they can best be seen: | (i) two all-round red lights in a vertical line where they can best be seen-; |
| (ii) two balls or similar shapes in a vertical line where they can best be seen; | (ii) two balls or similar shapes in a vertical line where they can best be seen; and |
| (iii) when making way through the water, in addition to the lights prescribed in this paragraph, sidelights and a stern-light. | (iii) when making way through the water, in addition to the lights prescribed in this paragraph, sidelights and a stern-light. |

**Rules**

### *Rule 27*

Definitions for "vessel not under command" and "vessel restricted in her ability to maneuver" are given in Rule 3(f) and (g) respectively. These vessels cannot physically comply with the requirements of the Navigation Rules, thus they are granted special privileges, and their status is indicated by special lights.

Typically, a vessel not under command is one that has suffered a steering failure or a loss of propulsion power. The term "vessel restricted in her ability to maneuver" is applicable to one attached to the bottom for work, such as a dredge, or one engaged in work in a limited area, such as a Coast Guard buoy tender servicing an aid to navigation, or a ship laying underwater cables. A tug towing a barge is *not* normally considered to be restricted in her ability to maneuver, but there may be exceptional situations where this status is warranted and the additional lights and shapes may be displayed.

A vessel engaged in diving operations may or may not be restricted in her ability to maneuver. A salvage vessel with "hard hat" divers down — supplied with air from pumps on the surface — is definitely restricted in her ability to maneuver and should show the lights of Rule 27(d) or (e). On the other hand, a dive boat with free-swimming SCUBA divers in the water is definitely not restricted and should not show the signals of Rule 27(e). Such a craft should fly the "diver's flag" (red with one white diagonal stripe) that signifies "Divers in the water — keep clear." This flag is not a part of the Navigation Rules, but is widely used and is legally required by many state and local authorities.

Note that Rule 27(e) specifically requires "a rigid replica" of the International Code flag "A"; preferably, this would be two or more in a cruciform configuration so that it could be seen from any direction. All too often, vessels are seen flying the cloth flag — this does not meet the requirement of the Rules.

| International | Inland |
|---|---|
| (b) A vessel restricted in her ability to maneuver, except a vessel engaged in mine clearance operations, shall exhibit: | (b) A vessel restricted in her ability to maneuver, except a vessel engaged in mine clearance operations, shall exhibit: |
| (i) three all-round lights in a vertical line where they can best be seen. The highest and lowest of these lights shall be red and the middle light shall be white; | (i) three all-round lights in a vertical line where they can best be seen. The highest and lowest of these lights shall be red and the middle light shall be white; |
| (ii) three shapes in a vertical line where they can best be seen . The highest and lowest of these shapes shall be balls and the middle one a diamond; | (ii) three shapes in a vertical line where they can best be seen. The highest and lowest of these shapes shall be balls and the middle one a diamond; |
| (iii) when making way through the water, a masthead light or lights, sidelights and a sternlight, in addition to the lights prescribed in sub-paragraph (i); | (iii) when making way through the water, masthead lights, sidelights and a sternlight, in addition to the lights prescribed in subparagraphs (b)(i); and |
| (iv) when at anchor, in addition to the lights or shapes prescribed in sub-paragraphs (i) and (ii), the light, lights or shape prescribed in Rule 30. | (iv) when at anchor, in addition to the lights or shapes prescribed in subparagraphs (b) (i) and (ii), the light, lights or shapes prescribed in Rule 30. |
| (c) A power-driven vessel engaged in a towing operation such as severely restricts the towing vessel and her tow in their ability to deviate from their course shall, in addition to the lights or shapes prescribed in Rule 24(a), exhibit the lights or shapes prescribed in sub-paragraphs (b)(i) and (ii) of this Rule. | (c) A vessel engaged in a towing operation which severely restricts the towing vessel and her tow in their ability to deviate from their course shall, in addition to the lights or shapes prescribed in subparagraphs (b)(i) and (ii) of this Rule, exhibit the lights or shape prescribed in Rule 24. |
| (d) A vessel engaged in dredging or underwater operations, when restricted in her ability to maneuver, shall exhibit the lights and shapes prescribed in sub-paragraphs (b)(i), (ii) and (iii) of this Rule and shall in addition, when an obstruction exists, exhibit: | (d) A vessel engaged in dredging or underwater operations, when restricted in her ability to maneuver, shall exhibit the lights and shapes prescribed in subparagraphs (b)(i), (ii) and (iii) of this Rule and shall, in addition, when an obstruction exists, exhibit: |
| (i) two all-round red lights or two balls in a vertical line to indicate the side on which the obstruction exists; | (i) two all-round red lights or two balls in a vertical line to indicate the side on which the obstruction exists; |
| (ii) two all-round green lights or two diamonds in a vertical line to indicate the side on which another vessel may pass; | (ii) two all-round green lights or two diamonds in a vertical line to indicate the side on which another vessel may pass; |
| (iii) when at anchor, the lights or shapes prescribed in this paragraph instead of the lights or shape prescribed in Rule 30. | (iii) when at anchor, the lights or shape prescribed by this paragraph instead of the lights or shapes prescribed in Rule 30 for anchored vessels. |
| (e) Whenever the size of a vessel engaged in diving operations makes it impracticable to exhibit all lights and shapes prescribed in paragraph (d) of this Rule, the following shall be exhibited: | (e) Whenever the size of a vessel engaged in diving operations makes it impracticable to exhibit all lights and shapes prescribed in paragraph (d) of this Rule the following shall instead be exhibited: |

| **International** | **Inland** |
|---|---|
| (i) three all-round lights in a vertical line where they can best be seen. The highest and lowest of these lights shall be red and the middle light shall be white; | (i) Three all-round lights in a vertical line where they can best be seen. The highest and lowest of these lights shall be red and the middle light shall be white. |
| (ii) a rigid replica of the International Code flag "A" not less than 1 meter in height. Measures shall be taken to ensure its all-round visibility. | (ii) A rigid replica of the International Code flag "A" not less than 1 meter in height. Measures shall be taken to insure its all-round visibility. |
| (f) A vessel engaged in mine clearance operations shall, in addition to the lights prescribed for a power-driven vessel in Rule 23, or to the lights or shape prescribed for a vessel at anchor in Rule 30 as appropriate, exhibit three all-round green lights or three balls. One of these lights or shapes shall be exhibited near the foremast head and one at each end of the fore yard. These lights or shapes indicate that it is dangerous for another vessel to approach within 1,000 meters of the mine clearance vessel. | (f) A vessel engaged in mine clearance operations shall, in addition to the lights prescribed for a power-driven vessel in Rule 23, or to the lights or shape prescribed for a vessel at anchor in Rule 30, as appropriate, exhibit three all-round green lights or three balls. One of these lights or shapes shall be exhibited near the foremast head and one at each end of the fore yard. These lights or shapes indicate that it is dangerous for another vessel to approach within 1,000 meters of the mine clearance vessel. |
| (g) Vessels of less than 12 meters in length, except those engaged in diving operations, shall not be required to exhibit the lights and shapes prescribed in this Rule. | (g) A vessel of less than 12 meters in length, except when engaged in diving operations, is not required to exhibit the lights or shapes prescribed in this Rule. |
| (h) The signals prescribed in this Rule are not signals of vessels in distress and requiring assistance. Such signals are contained in Annex IV to these Regulations. | (h) The signals prescribed in this Rule are not signals of vessels in distress and requiring assistance. Such signals are contained in Annex IV to these Rules. |

## Rule 28   Vessels Constrained by Their Draft

A vessel constrained by her draft may, in addition to the lights prescribed for power-driven vessels in Rule 23, exhibit where they can best be seen three all-round red lights in a vertical line, or a cylinder.

## Rule 28 (Reserved)

---

### *Rule 28*

Under the International Rules, a vessel "constrained by her draft" remains obligated to conform to the Rules covering a meeting or crossing situation. She has no additional right-of-way over another vessel and is required to navigate with "particular caution," but the other vessel is, in turn, required not to impede her safe passage; see Rule 18(d).

There is no Rule 28 in the Inland Rules.

| International | Inland |
|---|---|

## Rule 29   Pilot Vessels

(a)  A vessel engaged on pilotage duty shall exhibit:

(i) at or near the masthead, two all-round lights in a vertical line, the upper being white and the lower red;

(ii) when underway, in addition, sidelights and a sternlight;

(iii) when at anchor, in addition to the lights prescribed in sub-paragraph (i), the light, lights or shape prescribed in Rule 30 for vessels at anchor.

(b)  A pilot vessel when not engaged on pilotage duty shall exhibit the lights or shapes prescribed for a similar vessel of her length.

## Rule 29   Pilot Vessels

(a) A vessel engaged on pilotage duty shall exhibit:

(i) at or near the masthead, two all-round lights in a vertical line, the upper being white and the lower red;

(ii) when underway, in addition, sidelights and a sternlight; and

(iii) when at anchor, in addition to the lights prescribed in subparagraph (i), the anchor light, lights, or shape prescribed in Rule 30 for anchored vessels.

(b)  A pilot vessel when not engaged on pilotage duty shall exhibit the lights or shapes prescribed for a similar vessel of her length.

### Rule 29

The lights of pilot vessels are easily remembered by the rhyme "White over red — pilot ahead." (As contrasted with "Red or green over white — they're fishing tonight.")

White-over-red lights are also used by fishing vessels when hauling in their nets if fishing in close proximity to other fishing vessels (Annex II). However, these lights are used in conjunction with white-over-green lights so there is little likelihood of confusion with a pilot vessel.

## Rule 30   Anchored Vessels and Vessels Aground

(a)  A vessel at anchor shall exhibit where it can best be seen:

(i) in the fore part, an all-round white light or one ball;

(ii) at or near the stern and at a lower level than the light prescribed in sub-paragraph (i), an all-round white light.

(b) A vessel of less than 50 meters in length may exhibit an all-round white light where it can best be seen instead of the lights prescribed in paragraph (a) of this Rule.

(c) A vessel at anchor may, and a vessel of 100 meters and more in length shall, also use the available working or equivalent lights to illuminate her decks.

## Rule 30   Anchored Vessels and Vessels Aground

(a) A vessel at anchor shall exhibit where it can best be seen:

(i) in the fore part, an all-round white light or one ball; and

(ii) at or near the stern and at a lower level than the light prescribed in sub-paragraph (i), an all-round white light.

(b) A vessel of less than 50 meters in length may exhibit an all-round white light where it can best be seen instead of the lights prescribed in paragraph (a) of this Rule.

(c) A vessel at anchor may, and a vessel of 100 meters or more in length shall, also use the available working or equivalent lights to illuminate her decks.

| International | Inland |
|---|---|
| (d) A vessel aground shall exhibit the lights prescribed in paragraph (a) or (b) of this Rule and, in addition, where they can best be seen: | (d) A vessel aground shall exhibit the lights prescribed in paragraph (a) or (b) of this Rule and, in addition, if practicable, where they can best be seen: |
| (i) two all-round red lights in a vertical line; | (i) two all-round red lights in a vertical line; and |
| (ii) three balls in a vertical line. | (ii) three balls in a vertical line. |
| (e) A vessel of less than 7 meters in length, when at anchor, not in or near a narrow channel, fairway, or anchorage, or where other vessels normally navigate, shall not be required to exhibit the lights or shape prescribed in paragraphs (a) and (b) of this Rule. | (e) A vessel of less than 7 meters in length, when at anchor, not in or near a narrow channel, fairway, anchorage, or where other vessels normally navigate, shall not be required to exhibit the lights or shapes prescribed in paragraphs (a) and (b) of this Rule. |
| (f) A vessel of less than 12 meters in length, when aground, shall not be required to | (f) A vessel of less than 12 meters in length, when aground, shall not be required to |

Rules

## Rule 30

Small craft less than 7 meters in length are not required to show an anchor light or shape if anchored out of the way of all other water traffic. Larger craft and vessels must comply with Rule 30 wherever anchored (see Inland exception below) — this includes the showing of an "anchor ball" dayshape, a requirement that is all too frequently ignored by small craft.

Any vessel at anchor may, and vessels of 100 or more meters in length must, show deck or working lights to increase her visibility to other vessels. A vessel made fast to a mooring is "at anchor." A vessel dragging its anchor is not "made fast to the bottom" and, therefore, is not a vessel at anchor, but rather a vessel underway.

The Inland Rules only provide for "special anchorage areas" in which anchor lights and shapes are not required for craft less than 20 meters in length. These are generally established off marinas and yacht clubs where boats are left unmanned on moorings for days at a time and electric power is not available for showing anchor lights. There are only a limited number of these; they are described in *Coast Pilots* and are outlined on applicable large-scale charts. There is no provision in the International Rules for areas where anchor lights and shapes are not required.

International Rule 30(d) requires vessels of 12 meters or more length when aground to show the three "anchor balls" day signal or two all-round red lights at night; few small craft are equipped to meet this requirement, and thus, nearly all fail to comply. The Inland Rules have the same requirement, but add "if practicable" without defining the limits of practicability.

A vessel is not considered "aground" for the purposes of this Rule if she is intentionally placed in contact with the bottom or against the bank to hold her position; in this case, the vessel is underway with no way on.

| International | Inland |
|---|---|
| exhibit the lights or shapes prescribed in sub-paragraphs (d)(i) and (ii) of this Rule. | exhibit the lights or shapes prescribed in subparagraphs (d)(i) and (ii) of this Rule. |
| | (g) A vessel of less than 20 meters in length, when at anchor in a special anchorage area designated by the Secretary, shall not be required to exhibit the anchor lights and shapes required by this Rule. |

## Rule 31   Seaplanes

Where it is impracticable for a seaplane to exhibit lights and shapes of the characteristics or in the positions prescribed in the Rules of this Part, she shall exhibit lights and shapes as closely similar in characteristics and position as is possible.

## Rule 31   Seaplanes

Where it is impracticable for a seaplane to exhibit lights and shapes of the characteristics or in the positions prescribed in the Rules of this Part, she shall exhibit lights and shapes as closely similar in characteristics and position as possible.

---

### Rule 31

When on the water, a seaplane (or amphibian) is a "vessel" in terms of the Navigation Rules. "In this part" refers to Rules 20 through 30.

---

# PART D — SOUND AND LIGHT SIGNALS

## Rule 32   Definitions

(a) The word "whistle" means any sound-signalling appliance capable of producing the prescribed blasts and which complies with the specifications in Annex III to these Regulations.

(b) The term "short blast" means a blast of about one second's duration.

(c) The term "prolonged blast" means a blast of from four to six seconds' duration.

## Rule 32   Definitions

(a) The word "whistle" means any sound-signaling appliance capable of producing the prescribed blasts and which complies with specifications in Annex III to these Rules.

(b) The term "short blast" means a blast of about 1 second duration.

(c) The term "prolonged blast" means a blast of from 4 to 6 seconds' duration.

---

### Rule 32

This Rule broadens the term "whistle" to include sound-producing devices that are more likely to be found on smaller vessels — if it can make a sound that meets the requirements of the Rules and Annex III, it's a whistle. Note that there are only two kinds of whistle blasts — short and prolonged; the term "long blast" does not appear in either set of the Navigation Rules.

| **International** | **Inland** |

## Rule 33  Equipment for Sound Signals

(a) A vessel of 12 meters or more in length shall be provided with a whistle and a bell, and a vessel of 100 meters or more in length shall, in addition, be provided with a gong, the tone and sound of which cannot be confused with that of the bell. The whistle, bell and gong shall comply with the specifications in Annex III to these Regulations. The bell or gong or both may be replaced by other equipment having the same respective sound characteristics, provided that manual sounding of the prescribed signals shall always be possible.

(b)  a vessel of less than 12 meters in length shall not be obliged to carry the sound signalling appliances prescribed in paragraph (a) of this Rule, but if she does not, she shall be provided with some other means of making an efficient sound signal.

## Rule 33  Equipment for Sound Signals

(a) A vessel of 12 meters or more in length shall be provided with a whistle and a bell, and a vessel of 100 meters or more in length shall, in addition, be provided with a gong, the tone and sound of which cannot be confused with that of the bell. The whistle, bell and gong shall comply with the specifications in Annex III to these Rules. The bell or gong or both may be replaced by other equipment having the same respective sound characteristics, provided that manual sounding of the prescribed signals shall always be possible.

(b) A vessel of less than 12 meters in length shall not be obliged to carry the sound signaling appliances prescribed in paragraph (a) of this Rule, but if she does not, she shall be provided with some other means of making an efficient sound signal.

*Rules*

---

### *Rule 33*

There are only three types of sound-signal equipment mentioned in the Rules — whistle, bell, and gong, with the latter only required on vessels 100 meters or more in length. Even if the sound of a bell or gong can be created by other means (electronic), manual sounding must always be possible. There is no use of the term "fog horn" in the Rules; "fog" signals are sounded on the same whistle as used for other purposes.

Automatically timed fog signals are widely used, but caution is advised lest your signals get in synchronization with those of another vessel and you don't hear that vessel.

---

## Rule 34  Maneuvering and Warning Signals

(a)  When vessels are in sight of one another, a power-driven vessel underway, when maneuvering as authorized or required by these Rules, shall indicate that maneuver by the following signals on her whistle:

one short blast to mean "I am altering my course to starboard"

two short blasts to mean "I am altering my course to port";

three short blasts to mean "I am operating astern propulsion".

## Rule 34  Maneuvering and Warning Signals

(a) When power-driven vessels are in sight of one another and meeting or crossing at a distance within half a mile of each other, each vessel underway when maneuvering as authorized or required by these Rules:

(i) shall indicate that maneuver by the following signals on her whistle: one short blast to mean "I intend to leave you on my port side"; two short blasts to mean "I intend to leave you on my starboard side"; and three short blasts to mean "I am operating astern propulsion".

## Rule 34

This Rule contains the most significant variations between the International and Inland Rules — and these differences must be clearly understood.

The International Rules whistle signals for power-driven vessels underway in sight of each other are signals of actions being taken — they are required between two such vessels in sight of one another, and do not require a reply.

The Inland Rules whistle signals for power-driven vessels are signals of intent — they are required in sight of one another and are meeting or crossing at a distance within half a mile of each other. These signals require a reply.

The meanings of the one and two short-blast signals are *different* in the two sets of Rules. Be sure of which set governs the waters you are on at all times so that you may properly sound your signals and interpret the signals of other vessels. These signals are not to be used in conditions of restricted visibility. Fortunately, the very important signal of doubt or danger — five or more short and rapid blasts — is the same on all waters.

The three-blast sound signal in both sets of Rules has the same meaning. "Operating astern propulsion" means only that; it does not necessarily mean that the vessel has stopped or is making sternway. The deciding factor is the operation of the propulsion machinery, not the movement of the vessel.

In both sets of Rules, the one, two, three, and five or more short blast signals may be supplemented by light signals with the corresponding number of one-second flashes at one-second intervals. Note that the light signals may not be substituted for the sound signals.

The International Rules require that this light be white; the light signals need not be synchronized with the whistle blasts, and may be repeated after an interval of ten seconds. The Inland Rules allow either white or yellow; the light flashes must be synchronized with the whistle blasts and cannot be repeated separately. The required visibility ranges are different for the two sets of Rules.

Note that Rule 34 is applicable only to power-driven vessels — vessels under sail are not required to sound maneuvering signals (unless, of course, they are also using mechanical propulsion, in which case they are not sailing vessels).

In waters governed by the International Rules, a power-driven vessel may sound a whistle signal to a sailing vessel to indicate action being taken. However, in Inland Rules waters, a power-driven vessel should not sound whistle signals of intent to a sailing vessel, as that vessel cannot reply.

In overtaking situations, the signals of the International Rule are applicable only if the encounter occurs in a narrow channel and the overtaken vessel must maneuver to allow safe passage of the other. In the Inland Rules, the signals are required in all circumstances if the vessels will come within a half-mile of each other.

The signals of the two sets of Rules are quite different, with the International being more complex.

| **International** | **Inland** |
|---|---|

**International**

(b)  Any vessel may supplement the whistle signals prescribed in paragraph (a) of this Rule by light signals, repeated as appropriate, while the maneuver is being carried out:

(i) these light signals shall have the following significance:

one flash to mean "I am altering my course to starboard"

two flashes to mean "I am altering my course to port"

three flashes to mean "I am operating astern propulsion";

(ii) the duration of each flash shall be about one second, the interval between flashes shall be about one second, and the interval between successive signals shall be no less than ten seconds;

(iii) the light used for this signal shall, if fitted, be an all-round white light, visible at a minimum range of 5 miles and shall comply with the provisions of Annex I to these regulations.

(c) When in sight of one another in a narrow channel or fairway:

(i) a vessel intending to overtake another shall, in compliance with Rule 9(e)(i), indicate her intention by the following signals on her whistle:

two prolonged blasts followed by one short blast to mean "I intend to overtake you on your starboard side";

two prolonged blasts followed by two short blasts to mean "I intend to overtake you on your port side";

**Inland**

(ii) upon hearing the one– or two–blast signal of the other shall, if in agreement, sound the same whistle signal and take the steps necessary to effect a safe passing. If, however, from any cause the vessel doubts the safety of the proposed maneuver, she shall sound the danger signal specified in paragraph (d) of this Rule and each vessel shall take appropriate precautionary action until a safe passing agreement is made.

(b) A vessel may supplement the whistle signals prescribed in paragraph (a) of this Rule by light signals:

(i) These signals shall have the following significance: One flash to mean "I intend to leave you on my port side"; two flashes to mean "I intend to leave you on my starboard side"; three flashes to mean "I am operating astern propulsion";

(ii) The duration of each flash shall be about 1 second; and

(iii) The light used for this signal shall, if fitted, be one all-round white or yellow light, visible at a minimum range of 2 miles, synchronized with the whistle and shall comply with the provisions of Annex I to these Rules.

(c) When in sight of one another:

(i) a power-driven vessel intending to overtake another power-driven vessel shall indicate her intention by the following signals on her whistle: One short blast to mean "I intend to overtake you on your starboard side"; two short blasts to mean "I intend to overtake you on your port side"; and

Rules

| International | Inland |
|---|---|
| (ii)the vessel about to be overtaken when acting in accordance with Rule 9(e)(i) shall indicate her agreement by the following signal on her whistle: One prolonged, one short, one prolonged and one short blast, in that order. | (ii) the power-driven vessel about to be overtaken shall, if in agreement, sound a similar sound signal. If in doubt she shall sound the danger signal prescribed in paragraph (d). |

(d) When vessels in sight of one another are approaching each other and, from any cause, either vessel fails to understand the intentions or actions of the other, or is in doubt whether sufficient action is being taken by the other to avoid collision, the vessel in doubt shall immediately indicate such doubt by giving at least five short and rapid blasts on the whistle. Such signal may be supplemented by a light signal of at least five short and rapid flashes.

(e) A vessel nearing a bend or an area of a channel or fairway where other vessels may be obscured by an intervening obstruction shall sound one prolonged blast. Such signal shall be answered with a prolonged blast by any approaching vessel that may be within hearing around the bend or behind the intervening obstruction.

(f) If whistles are fitted on a vessel at a distance apart of more than 100 meters, one whistle only shall be used for giving maneuvering and warning signals.

(d) When vessels in sight of one another are approaching each other and, from any cause, either vessel fails to understand the intentions or actions of the other, or is in doubt whether sufficient action is being taken by the other to avoid collision, the vessel in doubt shall immediately indicate such doubt by giving at least five short and rapid blasts on the whistle. This signal may be supplemented by a light signal of at least five short and rapid flashes.

(e) A vessel nearing a bend or an area of a channel or fairway where other vessels may be obscured by an intervening obstruction shall sound one prolonged blast. This signal shall be answered with a prolonged blast by any approaching vessel that may be within hearing around the bend or behind the intervening obstruction.

(f) If whistles are fitted on a vessel at a distance apart of more than 100 meters, one whistle only shall be used for giving maneuvering and warning signals.

(g) When a power-driven vessel is leaving a dock or berth, she shall sound one prolonged blast.

(h) A vessel that reaches agreement with another vessel in a meeting, crossing, or overtaking situation by using the radiotelephone as prescribed by the Bridge-to-Bridge Radiotelephone Act (85 Stat. 165; 33 U.S.C. 1207), is not obliged to sound the whistle signals prescribed by this Rule, but may do so. If agreement is not reached, then whistle signals shall be exchanged in a timely manner and shall prevail.

| International | Inland |
|---|---|

## Rule 35   Sound Signals in Restricted Visibility

In or near an area of restricted visibility, whether by day or night, the signals prescribed in this Rule shall be used as follows.

(a) A power-driven vessel making way through the water shall sound at intervals of not more than 2 minutes one prolonged blast.

(b) A power-driven vessel underway, but stopped and making no way through the water, shall sound at intervals of not more than 2 minutes two prolonged blasts in succession with an interval of about 2 seconds between them.

(c) A vessel not under command, a vessel restricted in her ability to maneuver, a vessel constrained by her draft, a sailing vessel, a vessel engaged in fishing and a vessel engaged in towing or pushing another vessel shall, instead of the signals prescribed in paragraphs (a) or (b) of this Rule, sound at intervals of not more than 2 minutes three blasts in succession, namely one prolonged followed by two short blasts.

(d) A vessel engaged in fishing, when at anchor, and a vessel restricted in her ability to maneuver when carrying out her work at anchor, shall instead of the signals prescribed in paragraph (g) of this Rule sound the signal prescribed in paragraph (c) of this Rule.

(e) A vessel towed or, if more than one vessel is towed, the last vessel of the tow, if manned, shall at intervals of not more than 2 minutes sound four blasts in succession, namely one prolonged followed by three short blasts. When practicable, this signal shall be made immediately after the signal made by the towing vessel.

## Rule 35   Sound Signals in Restricted Visibility

In or near an area of restricted visibility, whether by day or night, the signals prescribed in this Rule shall be used as follows:

(a) A power-driven vessel making way through the water shall sound at intervals of not more than 2 minutes one prolonged blast.

(b) A power-driven vessel underway, but stopped and making no way through the water, shall sound at intervals of not more than 2 minutes two prolonged blasts in succession with an interval of about 2 seconds between them.

(c) A vessel not under command; a vessel restricted in her ability to maneuver, whether underway or at anchor; a sailing vessel; a vessel engaged in fishing, whether underway or at anchor; and a vessel engaged in towing or pushing another vessel shall, instead of the signals prescribed in paragraphs (a) or (b) of this Rule, sound at intervals of not more than 2 minutes, three blasts in succession; namely, one prolonged followed by two short blasts.

(d) A vessel towed or, if more than one vessel is towed, the last vessel of the tow if manned, shall at intervals of not more than 2 minutes sound four blasts in succession; namely, one prolonged followed by three short blasts. When practicable, this signal shall be made immediately after the signal made by the towing vessel.

(e) When a pushing vessel and a vessel being pushed ahead are rigidly connected in a composite unit they shall be regarded as a power-driven vessel and shall give the signals prescribed in paragraphs (a) or (b) of this Rule.

### Rule 35

International Rule 35(f) and Inland Rule 35(e) refer to a "composite unit" of a rigidly connected pushing vessel and vessel being pushed. This is a rare situation, as the normal means of connection of wires and winches does not meet this definition. See also Rule 24(b).

| International | Inland |
|---|---|
| (f) When a pushing vessel and a vessel being pushed ahead are rigidly connected in a composite unit they shall be regarded as a power-driven vessel and shall give the signals prescribed in paragraphs (a) or (b) of this Rule. | (f) A vessel at anchor shall, at intervals of not more than 1 minute, ring the bell rapidly for about 5 seconds. In a vessel of 100 meters or more in length the bell shall be sounded in the forepart of the vessel and immediately after the ringing of the bell the gong shall be sounded rapidly for about 5 seconds in the after part of the vessel. A vessel at anchor may, in addition, sound three blasts in succession; namely, one short, one prolonged and one short blast, to give warning of her position and of the possibility of collision to an approaching vessel. |
| (g) A vessel at anchor shall, at intervals of not more than one minute, ring the bell rapidly for about five seconds. In a vessel of 100 meters or more in length the bell shall be sounded in the forepart of the vessel and immediately after the ringing of the bell the gong shall be sounded rapidly for about five seconds in the after part of the vessel. A vessel at anchor may, in addition, sound three blasts in succession, namely one short, one prolonged and one short blast to give warning of her position and of the possibility of collision to an approaching vessel. | (g) A vessel aground shall give the bell signal and, if required, the gong signal prescribed in paragraph (f) of this Rule, and shall, in addition, give three separate and distinct strokes on the bell immediately before and after the rapid ringing of the bell. A vessel aground may, in addition, sound an appropriate whistle signal. |
| (h) A vessel aground shall give the bell signal and, if required, the gong signal prescribed in paragraph (g) of this Rule, and shall, in addition, give three separate and distinct strokes on the bell immediately before and after the rapid ringing of the bell. A vessel aground may, in addition, sound an appropriate whistle signal. | (h) A vessel of less than 12 meters in length shall not be obliged to give the above-mentioned signals but, if she does not, shall make some other efficient sound signal at intervals of not more than 2 minutes. |
| (i) A vessel of less than 12 meters in length shall not be obliged to give the above-mentioned signals but, if she does not, shall make some other efficient sound signal at intervals of not more than 2 minutes. | (i) A pilot vessel when engaged on pilotage duty may, in addition, to the signals prescribed in paragraphs (a), (b) or (f) of this Rule, sound an identity signal consisting of four short blasts. |
| (j) A pilot vessel when engaged on pilotage duty may, in addition to the signals prescribed in paragraphs (a), (b) or (g) of this Rule, sound an identity signal consisting of four short blasts. | (j) The following vessels shall not be required to sound signals as prescribed in paragraph (f) of this Rule when anchored in a special anchorage area designated by the Secretary: <br> (i) a vessel of less than 20 meters in length; and <br> (ii) a barge, canal boat, scow, or other nondescript craft. |

| International | Inland |
|---|---|

## Rule 36  Signals to Attract Attention

If necessary to attract the attention of another vessel, any vessel may make light or sound signals that cannot be mistaken for any signal authorized elsewhere in these Rules, or may direct the beam of her searchlight in the direction of the danger, in such a way as not to embarrass any vessel. Any light to attract the attention of another vessel shall be such that it cannot be mistaken for any aid to navigation For the purpose of this Rule,the use of high-intensity intermittent or revolving lights, such as strobe lights, shall be avoided.

## Rule 36  Signals To Attract Attention

If necessary to attract the attention of another vessel, any vessel may make light or sound signals that cannot be mistaken for any signal authorized elsewhere in these Rules, or may direct the beam of her searchlight in the direction of the danger, in such a way as not to embarrass any vessel.

## Rule 37  Distress Signals

When a vessel is in distress and requires assistance she shall use or exhibit the signals described in annex IV to these Regulations.

## Rule 37  Distress Signals

When a vessel is in distress and requires assistance she shall use or exhibit the signals described in Annex IV to these Rules.

---

### *Rule 36*

Note carefully that a signal "to attract the attention of another vessel" is not a distress signal. It is often used by fishing vessels with nets out. A searchlight should be shown only in the direction of the danger; it should never be directed toward the other vessel, lest it blind the helmsman.

The International Rule specifically eliminates the use of strobe lights for the purpose of attracting attention. The Inland Rule does not have this prohibition, but it should be noted that such a light is listed as a distress signal in waters subject to these Rules.

### *Rule 37*

Because the primary intent of the Navigation Rules is to prevent collisions, the details of distress signals are not included in the basic Rules — only a reference to Annex IV, where they may be found.

# PART E - EXEMPTIONS

| International | Inland |
|---|---|

## Rule 38 Exemptions.

Any vessel (or class of vessels) provided that she complies with the requirements of the International Regulations for Preventing Collisions at Sea, 1960, the keel of which is laid or which is at a corresponding stage of construction before the entry into force of these Regulations may be exempted from compliance therewith as follows:

(a) The installation of lights with ranges prescribed in Rule 22, until four years after the date of entry into force of these Regulations.

(b) The installation of lights with color specifications as prescribed in Section 7 of Annex I to these Regulations, until four years after the date of entry into force of these Regulations.

(c) The repositioning of lights as a result of conversion from Imperial to metric units and rounding off measurement figures, permanent exemption.

(d) (i) The repositioning of masthead lights on vessels of less than 150 meters in length, resulting from the prescriptions of Section 3(a) of Annex I to these Regulations, permanent exemption.

(ii) The repositioning of masthead lights on vessels of 150 meters or more in length, resulting from the prescriptions of Section 3(a) of Annex to these Regulations, until nine years after the date of entry into force of these Regulations.

(e) The repositioning of masthead lights resulting from the prescriptions of section 2(b) of annex I to these Regulations, until nine years after the date of entry into force of these Regulations.

(f) The repositioning of sidelights resulting from the prescriptions of Sections 2(g) and 3(b) of Annex I to these Regulations, until nine years after the date of entry into force of these Regulations.

(g) The requirements for sound signal appliances prescribed in Annex III to these Regulations, until nine years after the date of entry into force of these Regulations.

## Rule 38 Exemptions

Any vessel or class of vessels, the keel of which is laid or which is at a corresponding stage of construction before the date of enactment of this Act provided that she complies with the requirements of:

(a) The Act of June 7, 1897 (30 Stat. 96), as amended (33 U.S.C. 154-232) for vessels navigating the waters subject to that statute;

(b) Section 4233 of the Revised Statutes (33 U.S.C. 301-356) for vessels navigating the waters subject to that statute;

(c) The Act of February 8, 1895 (28 Stat. 645), as amended (33 U.S.C. 241-295) for vessels navigating the waters subject to that statute, or

(d) Sections 3, 4, and 5 of the Act of April 25, 1940 (54 Stat. 163) as amended (46 U.S.C. 526 b, c, and d) for motorboats navigating the waters subject to that statute; shall be exempted from compliance with the technical Annexes to these rules as follows:

(i) the installation of lights with ranges prescribed in Rule 22, until 4 years after the effective date of these Rules, except that vessels of less than 20 meters in length are permanently exempt;

(ii) the installation of lights with color specifications as prescribed in Annex to these Rules, until 4 years after the effective date of these Rules except that vessels of less than 20 meters in length are permanently exempt;

(iii) the repositioning of lights as a result of conversion to metric units and rounding off measurement figures, are permanently exempt; and

(iv) the horizontal repositioning of masthead lights prescribed by Annex I to these rules:

(1) on vessels of less than 150 meters in length, permanent exemption.

(2) on vessels of 150 meters or more in length, until 9 years after the effective date of these Rules.

| International | Inland |
|---|---|

(h) The repositioning of all-round lights resulting from the prescription of Section 9(b) of Annex I to these Regulations, permanent exemption.

### Rule 38

Most of the exemptions are in the nature of "phase-in" requirements; those stated with a specific number of years have now all expired. There are a few permanent exemptions; the Inland Rules are more lenient with respect to smaller vessels.

(v) the restructuring or repositioning of all lights to meet the prescriptions of Annex I to these Rules, until 9 years after the effective date of these Rules;

(vi) power-driven vessels of 12 meters or more but less than 20 meters in length are permanently exempt from the provisions of Rule 23(a)(i) and 23 (a)(iv) provided that, in place of these lights, the vessel exhibits a white light aft visible all round the horizon; and

(vii) the requirements for sound-signal appliances prescribed in Annex III to these Rules, until 9 years after the effective date of these Rules.

**Rules**

## ANNEX I — POSITIONING AND TECHNICAL DETAILS OF LIGHTS AND SHAPES

### 1. Definition

The term "height above the hull" means height above the uppermost continuous deck. This height shall be measured from the position vertically beneath the location of the light.

*Added to Inland Annex (2/4/1998):*
(b) High-speed craft means a craft capable of maximum speed in meters per second (m/s) equal to or exceeding:
$3.7 \, \nabla^{0.1667}$; where $\nabla$ = displacement corresponding to the design waterline (meters$_3$). Note: The same formula in pounds and knots is: 1.98 (lbs) $\nabla^{0.1667}$; where $\nabla$ = displacement corresponding to design waterline in pounds.

### § 84.01 Definitions.

(a) The term "height above the hull" means height above the uppermost continuous deck. This height shall be measured from the position vertically beneath the location of the light.

(c) The term "practical cutoff" means, for vessels 20 meters or more in length, 12.5 percent of the minimum luminous intensity (Table 84.15(b)) corresponding to the greatest range of visibility for which the requirements of Annex I are met.

(d) The term "Rule" or "Rules" means the Inland Navigation Rules contained in Sec. 2 of the Inland Navigational Rules Act of 1980 (Pub. L. 96-591, 94 Stat 3415, 33 U.S.C. 2001, December 24, 1980) as amended.

### 2. Vertical positioning and spacing of lights

(a) On a power-driven vessel of 20 meters or more in length the masthead lights shall be placed as follows:

(i) the forward masthead light, or if only one masthead light is carried, then that light, at a height above the hull of not less than 6 meters and, if the breadth of the vessel exceeds 6 meters, then at a height above the hull not less than such breadth, so however that the light need not be placed at a greater height above the hull than 12 meters;

### § 84.03 Vertical positioning and spacing of lights.

(a) On a power-driven vessel of 20 meters or more in length the masthead lights shall be placed as follows:

(1) The forward masthead light, or if only one masthead light is carried, then that light, at a height above the hull of not less than 5 meters and, and, if the breadth of the vessel exceeds 5 meters, then at a height above the hull not less than such breadth, so however that the light need not be placed at a greater height above the hull than 8 meters;

57

| International | Inland |
|---|---|
| (ii) when two masthead lights are carried the after one shall be at least 4.5 meters vertically higher than the forward one. | (2) When two masthead lights are carried the after one shall be at least 2 meters vertically higher than the forward one. |
| (b) The vertical separation of masthead lights of power-driven vessels shall be such that in all normal conditions of trim the after light will be seen over and separate from the forward light at a distance of 1,000 meters from the stem when viewed from sea level. | (b) The vertical separation of the masthead lights of power-driven vessels shall be such that in all normal conditions of trim the after light will be seen over and separate from the forward light at a distance of 1,000 meters from the stem when viewed from water level. |
| (c) The masthead light of a power-driven vessel of 12 meters but less than 20 meters in length shall be placed at a height above the gunwale of not less than 2.5 meters. | (c) The masthead light of a power-driven vessel of 12 meters but less than 20 meters in length shall be placed at a height above the gunwale of not less than 2.5 meters. |
| (d) A power-driven vessel of less than 12 meters in length may carry the uppermost light at a height of less than 2.5 meters above the gunwale. When, however, a masthead light is carried in addition to sidelights and a sternlight or the all-round light prescribed in Rule 23(c)(i) is carried in addition to sidelights, then such masthead light or all-round light shall be carried at least one meter higher than the sidelights. | (d) The masthead light, or the all-round light described in Rule 23(c), of a power-driven vessel of less than 12 meters in length shall be carried at least one meter higher than the sidelights. |
| (e) One of the two or three masthead lights prescribed for a power-driven vessel when engaged in towing or pushing another vessel shall be placed in the same position as either the forward masthead light or the after masthead light provided that, if carried on the aftermast, the lowest after masthead light shall be at least 4.5 meters vertically higher than the forward masthead light. | (e) One of the two or three masthead lights prescribed for a power-driven vessel when engaged in towing or pushing another vessel shall be placed in the same position as either the forward masthead light or the after masthead light, provided that the lowest after masthead light shall be at least 2 meters vertically higher than the highest forward masthead light. |

## Annex I

The placement of navigation lights and their technical specifications are primarily concerns of the builder of the vessel, but the owner/operator is the person who will have to answer to the Coast Guard if her vessel is found to have lights that are not properly located or spaced, or which do not cover the specified arcs of visibility, or do not have the required intensity (visibility range) set forth in the Rules.

Annex I includes specific dimensions for dayshapes, but includes a provision for vessels less than 20 meters in length to use shapes that are smaller and more in proportion to the size of the craft, with reduced separation distances. All shapes are black.

There are minor differences between the International and Inland Rules. In general, the Inland Rules have lesser requirements, reflecting the smaller sizes of vessels and the closer distances in operations. Note that the USCG made a number of changes to the Inland Annex on 2/4/1998.

| International | Inland |
|---|---|

**International**

(f) (i) The masthead light or lights prescribed in Rule 23(a) shall be so placed as to be above and clear of all other lights and obstructions except as described in sub-paragraph (ii).

(ii) When it is impracticable to carry the all-round lights prescribed by Rule 27(b)(i) or Rule 28 below the masthead lights, they may be carried above the after masthead light(s) or vertically in between the forward masthead light(s) and after masthead light(s), provided that, in the latter case, the requirement of Section 3(c) of this Annex shall be complied with.

(g) The sidelights of a power-driven vessel shall be placed at a height above the hull not greater than three quarters of that of the forward masthead light. They shall not be so low as to be interfered with by decklights.

(h) The sidelights, if in a combined lantern and carried on a power-driven vessel of less than 20 meters in length, shall be placed not less than one meter below the masthead light.

(i) When the Rules prescribe two or three lights to be carried in a vertical line, they shall be spaced as follows:

(i) on a vessel of 20 meters in length or more such lights shall be spaced not less than 2 meters apart, and the lowest of these lights shall, except where a towing light is required, be placed at a height of not less than 4 meters above the hull;

(ii) on a vessel of less than 20 meters in length such lights shall be spaced not less than 1 meter apart and the lowest of these lights shall, except where a towing light is required, be placed at a height of not less than 2 meters above the gunwale;

(iii) when three lights are carried they shall be equally spaced.

(j) The lower of the two all-round lights prescribed for a vessel when engaged in fishing shall be at a height above the sidelights not less than twice the distance between the two vertical lights.

(k) The forward anchor light prescribed in Rule 30(a)(i), when two are carried, shall not be less than 4.5 meters above the after one. On a vessel of 50 meters or more in length this forward anchor light shall be placed at a height of not less than 6 meters above the hull.

**Inland**

(f) (1) The masthead light or lights prescribed in Rule 23(a) shall be so placed as to be above and clear of all other lights and obstructions except as described in paragraph (f)(2) of this section.

(2) When it is impracticable to carry the all-round lights prescribed in Rule 27(b)(i) below the masthead lights, they may be carried above the after masthead light(s) or vertically in between the forward masthead light(s) and after masthead light(s), provided that, in the latter case, the requirement of § 84.05(d) shall be complied with.

(g) The sidelights of a power-driven vessel shall be placed at least one meter lower than the forward masthead light. They shall not be so low as to be interfered with by decklights.

(h) (Reserved)

(i) When the Rules prescribe two or three lights to be carried in a vertical line, they shall be spaced as follows:

(1) On a vessel of 20 meters in length or more such lights shall be spaced not less than 1 meter apart, and the lowest of these lights shall, except where a towing light is required, be placed at a height of not less than 4 meters above the hull;

(2) On a vessel of less than 20 meters in length such lights shall be spaced not less than 1 meter apart and the lowest of these lights shall, except where a towing light is required, be placed at a height of not less than 2 meters above the gunwale;

(3) When three lights are carried they shall be equally spaced.

(j) The lower of the two all-round lights prescribed for a vessel when engaged in fishing shall be at a height above the sidelights not less than twice the distance between the two vertical lights.

(k) The forward anchor light prescribed in Rule 30(a)(i), when two are carried, shall not be less than 4.5 meters above the after one. On a vessel of 50 meters or more in length this forward anchor light shall be placed at a height of not less than 6 meters above the hull;

Rules

59

| International | Inland |
|---|---|

## 3. Horizontal position and spacing of lights

(a) When two masthead lights are prescribed for a power-driven vessel, the horizontal distance between them shall not be less than one half of the length of the vessel, but need not be more than 100 meters. The forward light shall be placed not more than one quarter of the length of the vessel from the stem.

(b) On a power-driven vessel of 20 meters or more in length the sidelights shall not be placed in front of the forward masthead lights. They shall be placed at or near the side of the vessel.

(c) When the lights prescribed in Rule 27(b)(i) or Rule 28 are placed vertically between the forward masthead light(s) and the after masthead light(s) these all-round lights shall be placed at a horizontal distance of not less than 2 meters from the fore and aft centerline of the vessel in the athwartship direction.

*Added to Inland Annex 2/4/1998:*
(d) When only one masthead light is prescribed for a power-driven vessel, this light must be exhibited forward of amidships. For a vessel of less than 20 meters in length, the vessel shall exhibit one masthead light as far forward as is practicable.

## § 84.05 Horizontal positioning and spacing of lights.

(a) Except as specified in paragraph (e) of this section, when two masthead lights are prescribed for a power-driven vessel, the horizontal distance between them must not be less than one quarter of the length of the vessel but need not be more than 50 meters. The forward light must be placed not more than one half of the length of the vessel from the stem.

(b) On a power-driven vessel of 20 meters or more in length the sidelights shall not be placed in front of the forward masthead lights. They shall be placed at or near the side of the vessel.

(c) When the lights prescribed in Rule 27(b)(i) are placed vertically between the forward masthead light(s) and the after masthead light(s) these all-round lights shall be placed at a horizontal distance of not less than 2 meters from the fore and aft centerline of the vessel in the athwartship direction.

(e) On power-driven vessels 50 meters but less than 60 meters in length operated on the Western Rivers and those waters specified in § 89.25, the horizontal distance between masthead lights shall not be less than 10 meters.

## 4. Details of location of direction–indicating lights for fishing vessels, dredgers, and vessels engaged in underwater operations

(a) The light indicating the direction of the outlying gear from a vessel engaged in fishing as prescribed in Rule 26(c)(ii) shall be placed at a horizontal distance of not less than 2 meters and not more than 6 meters away from the two all-round red and white lights. This light shall be placed not higher than the all-round white light prescribed in Rule 26(c)(i) and not lower than the sidelights.

(b) The lights and shapes on a vessel engaged in dredging or underwater operations to indicate the obstructed side and/or the side on which it is safe to pass, as prescribed in Rule 27(d)(i) and (ii), shall be placed at the maximum practical horizontal distance, but in no case less than 2 meters, from the lights or shapes prescribed in Rule 27(b)(i) and (ii). In no case shall the upper of these lights or shapes be at a greater

## § 84.07 Details of location of direction-indicating lights for fishing vessels, dredgers, and vessels engaged in underwater operations.

(a) The light indicating the direction of the outlying gear from a vessel engaged in fishing as prescribed in Rule 26(c)(ii) shall be placed at a horizontal distance of not less than 2 meters and not more than 6 meters away from the two all-round red and white lights. This light shall be placed not higher than the all-round white light prescribed in Rule 26(c)(i) and not lower than the sidelights.

(b) The lights and shapes on a vessel engaged in dredging or underwater operations to indicate the obstructed side and/or the side on which it is safe to pass, as prescribed in Rule 27(d)(i) and (ii), shall be placed at the maximum practical horizontal distance, but in no case less than 2 meters, from the lights or shapes prescribed in Rule 27(b)(i) and (ii). In no case shall the upper of these lights or shapes be at a greater

| International | Inland |
|---|---|

height than the lower of the three lights or shapes prescribed in Rule 27(b)(i) and (ii).

**5. Screens for sidelights**

The sidelights of vessels of 20 meters or more in length shall be fitted with inboard screens painted matt black, and meeting the requirements of Section 9 of this Annex. On vessels of less than 20 meters in length the sidelights, if necessary to meet the requirements of Section 9 of this Annex, shall be fitted with inboard matte black screens. With a combined lantern, using a single vertical filament and a very narrow division between the green and red sections, external screens need not be fitted.

**6. Shapes**

(a) Shapes shall be black and of the following sizes:

(i) a ball shall have a diameter of not less than 0.6 meter;

(ii) a cone shall have a base diameter of not less than 0.6 meter and a height equal to its diameter;

(iii) a cylinder shall have a diameter of at least 0.6 meter and a height of twice its diameter;

(iv) a diamond shape shall consist of two cones as defined in (ii) above having a common base.

(b) The vertical distance between shapes shall be at least 1.5 meters.

(c) In a vessel of less than 20 meters in length shapes of lesser dimensions but commensurate with the size of the vessel may be used and the distance apart may be correspondingly reduced.

**7. Color specification of lights**

The chromaticity of all navigation lights

---

height than the lower of the three lights or shapes prescribed in Rule 27(b)(i) and (ii).

**§ 84.09 Screens.**

(a) The sidelights of vessels of 20 meters or more in length shall be fitted with matte black inboard screens and meet the requirements of § 84.17. On vessels of less than 20 meters in length, the sidelights, if necessary to meet the requirement of § 84.17, shall be fitted with matte black inboard screens. With a combined lantern, using a single vertical filament and a very narrow division between the green and red sections, external screens need not be fitted.

(b) On power-driven vessels less than 12 meters in length constructed after July 31, 1983, the masthead light, or the all-round light described in Rule 23(c), shall be screened to prevent direct illumination of the vessel forward of the operator's position.

**§ 84.11 Shapes.**

(a) Shapes shall be black and of the following sizes:

(1) A ball shall have a diameter of not less than 0.6 meter;

(2) A cone shall have a base diameter of not less than 0.6 meter and a height equal to its diameter;

(3) A diamond shape shall consist of two cones (as defined in paragraph (a)(2) of this section) having a common base.

(b) The vertical distance between shapes shall be at least 1.5 meters.

(c) In a vessel of less than 20 meters in length shapes of lesser dimensions but commensurate with the size of the vessel may be used and the distance apart may be correspondingly reduced.

**§ 84.13 Color specification of lights.**

(a) The chromaticity of all navigation lights shall conform to the following standards, which lie within the boundaries of the area of the diagram specified for each color by the International Commission on Illumination (CIE), in the "Colors of Light Signals," which is incorporated by reference. It is Publication CIE No. 2.2. (TC-1.6), 1975, and is available from the Illumination Engineering Society, 345 East 47th Street, New York, NY, 10017. It is also available for inspection at the Office

| International | Inland |
|---|---|
| shall conform to the following standards, which lie within the boundaries of the area of the diagram specified for each color by the International Commission on Illumination. The boundaries of the area for each color are given by indicating the corner co-ordinates, which are shown below. | of the Federal Register, Room 8401, 1100 L Street N.W., Washington, D.C., 20408. This incorporation by reference was approved by the Director of the Federal Register. (b) The boundaries of the area for each color are given by indicating the coordinates, which are shown below: |

| (i) | White | | | | | | |
|---|---|---|---|---|---|---|---|
| | $x$ | 0.525 | 0.525 | 0.452 | 0.310 | 0.310 | 0.443 |
| | $y$ | 0.382 | 0.440 | 0.440 | 0.348 | 0.283 | 0.382 |
| (ii) | Green | | | | | | |
| | $x$ | 0.028 | 0.009 | 0.300 | 0.203 | | |
| | $y$ | 0.385 | 0.723 | 0.511 | 0.356 | | |
| (iii) | Red | | | | | | |
| | $x$ | 0.680 | 0.660 | 0.735 | 0.721 | | |
| | $y$ | 0.320 | 0.320 | 0.265 | 0.259 | | |
| (iv) | Yellow | | | | | | |
| | $x$ | 0.612 | 0.618 | 0.575 | 0.575 | | |
| | $y$ | 0.382 | 0.382 | 0.425 | 0.406 | | |

## 8. Intensity of lights

(a) The minimum luminous intensity of lights shall be calculated by using the formula:

$$L = 3.43 \times 10^6 \times T \times D^2 \times K^{-D}$$

where L is luminous intensity in candelas under service conditions,

T is threshold factor $2 \times 10^{-7}$ lux,

D is range of visibility (luminous range) of the light in nautical miles,

K is atmospheric transmissivity. For prescribed lights the value of K shall be 0.8, corresponding to a meteorological visibility of approximately 13 nautical miles.

(b) A selection of figures derived from the formula is given in the luminosity table.

## § 84.15 Intensity of lights.

(a) The minimum luminous intensity of lights shall be calculated by using the formula:

$$L = 3.43 \times 10^6 \times T \times D^2 \times K^{-D}$$

where L is luminous intensity in candelas under service conditions,

T is threshold factor $2 \times 10^{-7}$ lux,

D is range of visibility (luminous range) of the light in nautical miles,

K is atmospheric transmissivity. For prescribed lights the value of K shall be 0.8, corresponding to a meteorological visibility of approximately 13 nautical miles.

(b) A selection of figures derived from the formula is given in Table 84.15(b).

| Range of Visibility (luminous range) of light in nautical Miles D | Minimum luminous Intensity of light in candelas for K = 0.8 L |
|---|---|
| 1 | 0.9 |
| 2     Luminosity Table/ | 4.3 |
| 3     Table 84.15(b) | 12 |
| 4 | 27 |
| 5 | 52 |
| 6 | 94 |

**Note to International Rule:** The maximum luminous intensity of navigation lights should be limited to avoid undue glare. This shall not be achieved by a variable control of the luminous intensity.

| International | Inland |
|---|---|

## 9. Horizontal sectors

(a) (i) in the forward direction, sidelights as fitted on the vessel shall show the minimum required intensities. The intensities shall decrease to reach practical cut-off between 1 degree and 3 degrees outside the prescribed sectors.

(ii) for sternlights and masthead lights and at 22.5 degrees abaft the beam for sidelights, the minimum required intensities shall be maintained over the arc of the horizon up to 5 degrees within the limits of the sectors prescribed in Rule 21. From 5 degrees within the prescribed sectors the intensity may decrease by 50 per cent up to the prescribed limits; it shall decrease steadily to reach practical cut-off at not more than 5 degrees outside the prescribed sectors.

(b) All-round lights shall be so located as not to be obscured by masts, topmasts or structures within angular sectors of more than 6 degrees, except anchor lights prescribed in Rule 30, which need not be placed at an impracticable height above the hull.

---

*Also added to Inland Annex 2/4/1998:*
Note to paragraph (c): Two unscreened all-round lights that are 1.28 meters apart or less will appear as one light to the naked eye at a distance of one nautical mile.

---

## 10. Vertical sectors

(a) The vertical sectors of electric lights as fitted, with the exception of lights on sailing vessels underway shall ensure that:

(i) at least the required minimum intensity is maintained at all angles from 5 degrees above to 5 degrees below the horizontal;

(ii) at least 60 per cent of the required minimum intensity is maintained from 7.5 degrees above to 7.5 degrees below the horizontal.

(b) In the case of sailing vessels underway the vertical sectors of electric lights as fitted shall ensure that:

(i) at least the required minimum intensity is maintained at all angles from 5 degrees above to 5 degrees below the horizontal;

---

## § 84.17 Horizontal sectors.

(a) (1) In the forward direction, sidelights as fitted on the vessel shall show the minimum required intensities. The intensities shall decrease to reach practical cut-off between 1 and 3 degrees outside the prescribed sectors.

(2) For sternlights and masthead lights and at 22.5 degrees abaft the beam for sidelights, the minimum required intensities shall be maintained over the arc of the horizon up to 5 degrees within the limits of the sectors prescribed in Rule 21. From 5 degrees within the prescribed sectors the intensity may decrease by 50 percent up to the prescribed limits; it shall decrease steadily to reach practical cut-off at not more than 5 degrees outside the prescribed sectors.

(b) All-round lights shall be so located as not to be obscured by masts, topmasts or structures within angular sectors of more than 6 degrees, except anchor lights prescribed in Rule 30, which need not be placed at an impracticable height above the hull, and the all-round white light described in Rule 23(d), which may not be obscured at all.

---

*Added to Inland Annex 2/4/1998:*
(c) If it is impracticable to comply with paragraph (b) of this section by exhibiting only one all-round light, two all-round lights shall be used suitably positioned or screened to appear, as far as practicable, as one light at a minimum distance of one nautical mile.

---

## § 84.19 Vertical sectors.

(a) The vertical sectors of electric lights as fitted, with the exception of lights on sailing vessels underway and on unmanned barges, shall ensure that:

(1) At least the required minimum intensity is maintained at all angles from 5 degrees above to 5 degrees below the horizontal;

(2) At least 60 percent of the required minimum intensity is maintained from 7.5 degrees above to 7.5 degrees below the horizontal.

(b) In the case of sailing vessels underway the vertical sectors of electric lights as fitted shall ensure that:

(1) At least the required minimum intensity is maintained at all angles from 5 degrees above to 5 degrees below the horizontal;

| International | Inland |
|---|---|

**International**

(ii) at least 50 percent of the required minimum intensity is maintained from 25 degrees above to 25 degrees below the horizontal.

(c) In the case of lights other than electric, these specifications shall be met as closely as possible.

## 11. Intensity of nonelectric lights

Nonelectric lights shall, so far as practicable, comply with the minimum intensities, as specified in the Table given in Section 8 of this Annex.

## 12. Maneuvering light

Notwithstanding the provisions of paragraph 2(f) of this Annex the maneuvering light described in Rule 34(b) shall be placed in the same fore and aft vertical plane as the masthead light or lights and, where practicable, at a minimum height of 2 meters vertically above the forward masthead light, provided that it shall be carried not less than 2 meters vertically above or below the after masthead light. On a vessel where only one masthead light is carried the maneuvering light, if fitted, shall be carried where it can best be seen, not less than 2 meters vertically apart from the masthead light.

## 13. Approval

The construction of lights and shapes and the installation of lights on board the vessel shall be to the satisfaction of the appropriate authority of the State whose flag the vessel is entitled to fly.

**Inland**

(2) At least 50 percent of the required minimum intensity is maintained from 25 degrees above to 25 degrees below the horizontal.

(c) In the case of unmanned barges, the minimum required intensity of electric lights as fitted shall be maintained on the horizontal.

(d) In the case of lights other than electric lights these specifications shall be met as closely as possible.

## § 84.21 Intensity of nonelectric lights.

Nonelectric lights shall, so far as practicable, comply with the minimum intensities, as specified in the Table given in § 84.15.

## § 84.23 Maneuvering light.

Notwithstanding the provisions of § 84.03(f), the maneuvering light described in Rule 34(b) shall be placed approximately in the same fore and aft vertical plane as the masthead light or lights and, where practicable, at a minimum height of one-half meter vertically above the forward masthead light, provided that it shall be carried not less than one-half meter vertically above or below the after masthead light. On a vessel where only one masthead light is carried the maneuvering light, if fitted, shall be carried where it can best be seen, not less than one-half meter vertically apart from the masthead light.

## § 84.25 Approval. (Reserved)

*Added to Inland Annex 2/4/1998:*

## § Sec. 84.27 High-speed craft.

(a) The masthead light of high-speed craft with a length to breadth ratio of less than 3.0 may be placed at a height related to the breadth lower than that prescribed in Sec. 84.03(a)(1), provided that the base angle of the isosceles triangle formed by the side lights and masthead light when seen in end elevation is not less than 27 degrees as determined by the formula in paragraph (b) of this section.

(b) The minimum height of masthead light above sidelights is to be determined by the following formula: $\tan 27° = {}^X/_Y$; where Y is the horizontal distance between the sidelights and X is the height of the forward masthead light.

## ANNEX II — ADDITIONAL SIGNALS FOR FISHING VESSELS FISHING IN CLOSE PROXIMITY

| International | Inland |
| --- | --- |

### 1. General

The lights mentioned herein shall, if exhibited in pursuance of Rule 26(d), be placed where they can best be seen. They shall be at least 0.9 meter apart but at a lower level than lights prescribed in Rule 26(b)(i) and (c)(i). The lights shall be visible all round the horizon at a distance of at least 1 mile but at a lesser distance than the lights prescribed by these Rules for fishing vessels.

### § 85.1 General.

The lights mentioned herein shall, if exhibited in pursuance of Rule 26(d), be placed where they can best be seen. They shall be at least 0.9 meter apart but at a lower level than lights prescribed in Rule 26(b)(i) and (c)(i) contained in the Inland Navigational Rules Act of 1980. The lights shall be visible all around the horizon at a distance of at least 1 mile but at a lesser distance than the lights prescribed by these Rules for fishing vessels.

### 2. Signals for trawlers

(a) Vessels, when engaged in trawling, whether using demersal or pelagic gear, may exhibit:

(i) when shooting their nets: two white lights in a vertical line;

(ii) when hauling their nets: one white light over one red light in a vertical line;

(iii) when the net has come fast upon an obstruction: two red lights in a vertical line.

(b) Each vessel engaged in pair trawling may exhibit:

(i) by night, a searchlight directed forward and in the direction of the other l vessel of the pair;

(ii) when shooting or hauling their nets or when their nets have come fast upon an obstruction, the lights prescribed in 2(a) above.

### § 85.3 Signals for trawlers.

(a) Vessels, when engaged in trawling, whether using demersal or pelagic gear may exhibit:

(1) When shooting their nets: two white lights in a vertical line;

(2) When hauling their nets: one white light over one red light in a vertical line;

(3) When the net has come fast upon an obstruction: two red lights in a vertical line.

(b) Each vessel engaged in pair trawling may exhibit:

(1 ) By night, a searchlight directed forward and in the direction of the other vessel of the pair;

(2) When shooting or hauling their nets or when their nets have come fast upon an obstruction, the lights prescribed in paragraph (a) above.

### 3. Signals for purse seiners

Vessels engaged in fishing with purse seine gear may exhibit two yellow lights in a vertical line. These lights shall flash alternatively every second and with equal light and occultation duration. These lights may be exhibited only when the vessel is hampered by its fishing gear.

### § 85.5 Signals for purse seiners.

Vessels engaged in fishing with purse seine gear may exhibit two yellow lights in a vertical line. These lights shall flash alternately every second and with equal light and occultation duration. These lights may be exhibited only when the vessel is hampered by its fishing gear.

---

### *Annex II*

This annex provides the necessary details for the additional lights authorized by Rule 26.

## ANNEX III — TECHNICAL DETAILS OF SOUND SIGNAL APPLIANCES

| International | Inland |
|---|---|

### 1. Whistles

**(a) Frequencies and range of audibility**

The fundamental frequency of the signal shall lie within the range 70-700 Hz. The range of audibility of the signal from a whistle shall be determined by those frequencies, which may include the fundamental and/or one or more higher frequencies, which lie within the range 180-700 Hz (±1 per cent) and which provide the sound pressure levels specified in paragraph 1(c) below.

**(b) Limits of fundamental frequencies**

To ensure a wide variety of whistle characteristics, the fundamental frequency of a whistle shall be between the following limits:

(i) 70-200 Hz, for a vessel 200 meters or more in length;

(ii) 130-350Hz, for a vessel 75 meters but less than 200 meters in length;

(iii) 250-700 Hz, for a vessel less than 75 meters in length.

**(c) Sound signal intensity and range of audibility**

A whistle fitted in a vessel shall provide, in the direction of maximum intensity of the whistle and at a distance of 1 meter from it, a sound pressure level in at least one 1/3 octave band within the range of frequencies 180-700 Hz (±1 per cent) of not less than the appropriate figure given in the table right.

The range of audibility in the table is for information and is approximately the range at which a whistle may be heard on its forward axis with 90 per cent probability in conditions of still air on board a vessel having average back-ground noise level at the listening posts (taken to be 68 dB in the octave band centered on 250 Hz and 63 dB in the octave band centered on 500 Hz).

In practice, the range at which a whistle may be heard is extremely variable and depends critically on weather conditions; the values given can be regarded as typical, but under conditions of strong wind or

### Subpart A—Whistles

**§ 86.01 Frequencies and range of audibility.**

The fundamental frequency of the signal shall lie within the range 70-525 Hz. The range of audibility of the signal from a whistle shall be determined by those frequencies, which may include the fundamental and/or one or more higher frequencies, which lie within the frequency ranges and provide the sound pressure levels specified in § 86.05.

**§ 86.03 Limits of fundamental frequencies.**

To ensure a wide variety of whistle characteristics, the fundamental frequency of a whistle shall be between the following limits:

(a) 70-200 Hz, for a vessel 200 meters or more in length;

(b) 130-350 Hz, for a vessel 75 meters but less than 200 meters in length;

(c) 250-525 Hz, for a vessel less than 75 meters in length.

**§ 86.05 Sound signal intensity and range of audibility.**

A whistle on a vessel shall provide, in the direction of the forward axis of the whistle and at a distance of 1 meter from it, a sound pressure level in at least one-third octave band of not less than the appropriate figure given in Table 86.05 within the following frequency ranges (± 1 per cent):

(a) 130-1200 Hz, for a vessel 75 meters or more in length;

b) 250-1600 Hz, for a vessel 20 meters but less than 75 meters in length

(c) 250-2100 Hz, for a vessel 12 meters but less than 20 meters in length.

NOTE: The range of audibility in the table is for information and is approximately the range at which a whistle may usually be heard on its forward axis in conditions of still air on board a vessel having average background noise level at the listening posts (taken to be 68 dB in the octave band centered on 250 Hz and 63 dB in the octave band centered on 500 Hz).

| International | Inland |
|---|---|
| high ambient noise level at the listening post the range may be reduced. | In practice, the range at which a whistle may be heard is extremely variable and depends critically on weather conditions; the values given can be regarded as typical, but under conditions of strong wind or high ambient noise level at the listening post the range may be much reduced. |

**Sound Signal Intensity Table — *International Only***

| Length of vessel in meters | $1/3$ octave band level at 1 meter in dB referred to $2 \times 10^{-5}$ N/m$^2$ | Audibility range in nautical miles |
|---|---|---|
| 200 or more | 143 | 2 |
| 75 but less than 200 | 138 | 1.5 |
| 20 but less than 75 | 130 | 1 |
| Less than 20 | 120 | 0.5 |

**Table 86.05 — *Inland Only***

| Length of vessel in meters | Fundamental frequency range (Hz) | For measured frequencies (Hz) | $1/3$ - octave band level at 1 meter in dB referred to $2 \times 10^{-5}$N/m$^2$ | Audibility range in nautical miles |
|---|---|---|---|---|
| 200 or more | 70-200 | 130-180<br>180-250<br>250-1200 | 145<br>143<br>140 | 2 |
| 75 but less than 200 | 130-350 | 130-180<br>180-250<br>250-1200 | 140<br>138<br>134 | 1.5 |
| 20 but less than 75 | 250-525 | 250-450<br>450-800<br>800-1600 | 130<br>125<br>121 | 1.0 |
| 12 but less than 20 | 250-525 | 250-450<br>450-800<br>800-2100 | 120<br>115<br>111 | 0.5 |

## (d) Directional properties

The sound pressure level of a directional whistle shall be not more than 4 dB below the prescribed sound pressure level on the axis at any direction in the horizontal plane within ±45 degrees of the axis. The sound pressure level at any other direction in the horizontal plane shall be not more than 10 dB below the prescribed sound pressure level on the axis, so that the range in any direction will be at least half the range on the forward axis. The sound pressure level shall be measured in that one-third octave band which determines the audibility range.

## § 86.07 Directional properties.

The sound pressure level of a directional whistle shall be not more than 4 dB below the sound pressure level specified in § 86.05 in any direction in the horizontal plane within ±45 degrees of the forward axis. The sound pressure level of the whistle at any other direction in the horizontal plane shall not be more than 10 dB less than the sound pressure level specified for the forward axis, so that the range of audibility in any direction will be at least half the range required on the forward axis. The sound pressure level shall be measured in that one-third octave band which determines the audibility range.

| International | Inland |
|---|---|

## (e) Positioning of whistles

When a directional whistle is to be used as the only whistle on a vessel, it shall be installed with its maximum intensity directed straight ahead. A whistle shall be placed as high as practicable on a vessel, in order to reduce interception of the emitted sound by obstructions and also to minimize hearing damage risk to personnel. The sound pressure level of the vessel's own signal at listening posts shall not exceed 110 dB (A) and so far as practicable should not exceed 100 dB(A).

## (f) Fitting of more than one whistle

If whistles are fitted at a distance apart of more than 100 meters, it shall be so arranged that they are not sounded simultaneously.

## (g) Combined whistle systems

If, due to the presence of obstructions, the sound field of a single whistle or of one of the whistles referred to in paragraph 1(f) above is likely to have a zone of greatly reduced signal level, it is recommended that a combined whistle system be fitted so as to overcome this reduction. For the purposes of the Rules a combined whistle system is to be regarded as a single whistle. The whistles of a combined system shall be located at a distance apart of not more than 100 meters and arranged to be sounded simultaneously. The frequency of any one whistle shall differ from those of the others by at least 10 Hz.

---

### § 86.09 Positioning of whistles.

(a) When a directional whistle is to be used as the only whistle on the vessel and is permanently installed, it shall be installed with its forward axis directed forward.

(b) A whistle shall be placed as high as practicable on a vessel, in order to reduce interception of the emitted sound by obstructions and also to minimize hearing damage risk to personnel. The sound pressure level of the vessel's own signal at listening posts shall not exceed 110 dB (A) and so far as practicable should not exceed 100 dB (A).

### § 86.11 Fitting of more than one whistle.

If whistles are fitted at a distance apart of more than 100 meters, they shall not be sounded simultaneously.

### § 86 13 Combined whistle systems.

(a) A combined whistle system is a number of whistles (sound emitting sources) operated together. For the purposes of the Rules a combined whistle system is to be regarded as a single whistle.

(b) The whistles of a combined system shall:

(1) Be located at a distance apart of not more than 100 meters;

(2) Be sounded simultaneously;

(3) Each have a fundamental frequency different from those of the others by at least 10 Hz, and;

(4) Have a tonal characteristic appropriate for the length of vessel which shall be evidenced by at least two-thirds of the whistles in the combined system having fundamental frequencies falling within the limits prescribed in § 86.03, or if there are only two whistles in the combined system, by the higher fundamental frequency falling within the limits prescribed in § 86.03.

NOTE: If due to the presence of obstructions the sound field of a single whistle or of one of the whistles referred to in § 86.11 is likely to have a zone of greatly reduced signal level, a combined whistle system should be fitted so as to overcome this reduction.

---

## Annex III

There are technical differences between the International and Inland Rules regarding the frequency of whistle sounds for various sizes of vessels and other specifications.

---

### § 86.15 Towing vessel whistles.

A power-driven vessel normally engaged in pushing ahead or towing alongside may, at all times, use a whistle whose characteristic

| International | Inland |
|---|---|

**Inland**

falls within the limits prescribed by § 86.03 for the longest customary composite length of the vessel and its tow.

**International**

## 2. Bell or gong

### (a) Intensity of signal

A bell or gong, or other device having similar sound characteristics, shall produce a sound pressure level of not less than 110 dB at a distance of 1 meter from it.

### (b) Construction

Bells and gongs shall be made of corrosion-resistant material and designed to give a clear tone. The diameter of the mouth of the bell shall be not less than 300 mm for vessels of 20 meters or more in length, and shall be not less than 200 mm for vessels of 12 meters or more but of less than 20 meters in length. Where practicable, a power-driven bell striker is recommended to ensure constant force ,but manual operation shall be possible. The mass of the striker shall be not less than 3 per cent of the mass of the bell.

## 3. Approval

The construction of sound signal appliances, their performance and their installation on board the vessel shall be to the satisfaction of the appropriate authority of the state whose flag the vessel is entitled to fly.

**Inland**

## Subpart B – Bell or gong.

### § 86.21 Intensity of signal.

A bell or gong, or other device having similar sound characteristics, shall produce a sound pressure level of not less than 110 dB at 1 meter.

### § 86.23 Construction.

Bells and gongs shall be made of corrosion-resistant material and designed to give a clear tone. The diameter of the mouth of the bell shall be not less than 300 mm for vessels of more than 20 meters in length, and shall be not less than 200 mm for vessels of 12 to 20 meters in length. The mass of the striker shall be not less than 3 per cent of the mass of the bell. The striker shall be capable of manual operation .

NOTE: When practicable, a power-driven bell striker is recommended to ensure constant force.

## Subpart C—Approval.

### § 86.31 Approval. (Reserved)

# ANNEX IV — DISTRESS SIGNALS

## 1. Need of Assistance

The following signals, used or exhibited either together or separately, indicate distress and need of assistance:

(a) a gun or other explosive signal fired at intervals of about a minute;

(b) continuous sounding with any fog-signalling apparatus;

(c) rockets or shells, throwing red stars fired one at a time at short intervals;

(d) a signal made by radiotelegraphy or by other signalling method consisting of the group • • • − − − • • • (SOS) in the Morse Code;

(e) a signal sent by radiotelephony consisting of the spoken word "Mayday";

## § 87.1 Need of assistance.

The following signals, used or exhibited either together or separately, indicate distress and need of assistance:

(a) A gun or other explosive signal fired at intervals of about a minute;

(b) A continuous sounding with any fog-signaling apparatus;

(c) Rockets or shells, throwing red stars fired one at a time at short intervals;

(d) A signal made by radiotelegraphy or by any other signaling method consisting of the group • • • − − − • • • (SOS) in the Morse Code.

(e) A signal sent by radiotelephony consisting of the spoken word "Mayday";

## International

(f) the International Code Signal of distress indicated by N.C.;

(g) a signal consisting of a square flag having above or below it a ball or anything resembling a ball;

(h) flames on the vessel (as from a burning tar barrel, oil barrel, etc.);

(i) a rocket parachute flare or a hand flare showing a red light;

(j) a smoke signal giving off orange-colored smoke;

(k) slowly and repeatedly raising and lowering arms outstretched to each side;

(l) the radiotelegraph alarm signal;

(m) the radiotelephone alarm signal;

(n) signals transmitted by emergency position-indicating radio beacons;

(o) approved signals transmitted by radio communication systems.

2. The use or exhibition of any of the foregoing signals except for the purpose of indicating distress and need of assistance and the use of other signals which may be confused with any of the above signals is prohibited.

3. Attention is drawn to the relevant sections of the International Code of Signals, the Merchant Ship Search and Rescue Manual and the following signals:

(a) a piece of orange colored canvas with either a black square and circle or other appropriate symbol (for identification from the air);

(b) a dye marker.

## Inland

(f) The International Code Signal of distress indicated by N.C.;

(g) A signal consisting of a square flag having above or below it a ball or anything resembling a ball;

(h) Flames on the vessel (as from a burning tar barrel, oil barrel, etc.);

(i) A rocket parachute flare or a hand flare showing a red light;

(j) A smoke signal giving off orange-colored smoke;

(k) Slowly and repeatedly raising and lowering arms outstretched to each side;

(l) The radiotelegraph alarm signal;

(m) The radiotelephone alarm signal;

(n) Signals transmitted by emergency position-indicating radio beacons;

(o) Signals transmitted by radiocommunication systems, including survival craft radar transponders meeting the requirements of 47 CFR 80.1095.

(p) A high intensity white light flashing at regular intervals from 50 to 70 times per minute.

### § 87.3 Exclusive use.

The use or exhibition of any of the foregoing signals except for the purpose of indicating distress and need of assistance and the use of other signals which may be confused with any of the above signals is prohibited.

### § 87.5 Supplemental signals.

Attention is drawn to the relevant sections of the International Code of Signals, the Merchant Ship Search and Rescue Manual, the International Telecommunication Union Regulations and the following signals:

(a) A piece of orange-colored canvas with either a black square and circle or other appropriate symbol (for identification from the air);

(b) A dye marker.

---

### *Annex IV*

These distress signals can be used individually or in combination.

The International and Inland Rules are identical, except that the Inland Rules additionally list a high-intensity white light flashing at regular intervals from 50 to 70 times per minute; this is commonly called a "strobe" light.

Note that these signals are both an indication of a state of distress and a request for assistance, a request that must be responded to.

## DISTRESS SIGNALS
## 72 COLREGS

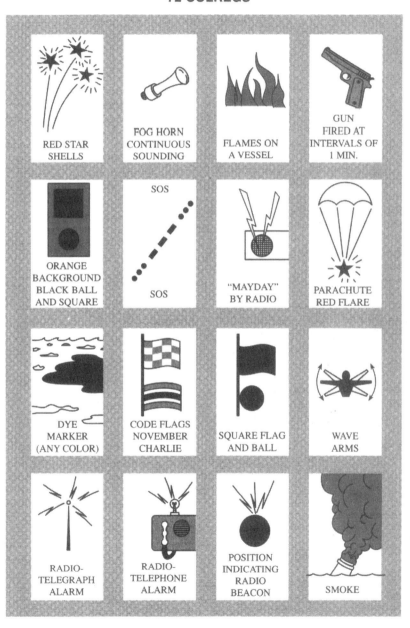

# ANNEX V — PILOT RULES

## Annex V

This Annex — the U.S. Pilot Rules — is found only in the Inland Rules. It is a collection of miscellaneous, unrelated regulations.

Note that from this point forward the Rules chapter is no longer divided into International and Inland columns. The applicability of each section will be noted at the beginning of that section.

### § 88.01 Purpose and applicability.

This Part applies to all vessels operating on United States inland waters and to United States vessels operating on the Canadian waters of the Great Lakes to the extent there is no conflict with Canadian law.

### § 88.03 Definitions;

The terms used in this part have the same meaning as defined in the Inland Navigational Rules Act of 1980.

### § 88.05 Copy of Rules.

After January 1, 1983, the operator of each self-propelled vessel 12 meters or more in length shall carry on board and maintain for ready reference a copy of the Inland Navigation Rules.

### § 88.09 Temporary exemption from light and shape requirements when operating under bridges.

A vessel's navigation lights and shapes may be lowered if necessary to pass under a bridge.

### § 88.11 Law enforcement vessels.

(a) Law enforcement vessels may display a flashing blue light when engaged in direct law enforcement or public safety activities. This light must be located so that it does not interfere with the visibility of the vessel's navigation lights.

(b) The blue light described in this section may be displayed by law enforcement vessels of the United States and the States and their political subdivisions.

### § 88.12 Public Safety Activities.

(a) Vessels engaged in government sanctioned public safety activities, and commercial vessels performing similar functions, may display an alternately flashing red and yellow light signal. This identification light signal must be located so that it does not interfere with the visibility of the vessel's navigation lights. The identification light signal may be used only as an identification signal and conveys no special privilege. Vessels using the identification light signal during public safety activities must abide by the Inland Navigation Rules, and must not presume that the light or the exigency gives them precedence or right of way.

(b) Public safety activities include but are not limited to patrolling marine parades, regattas, or special water celebrations; traffic control; salvage; firefighting; medical assistance; assisting disabled vessels; and search and rescue.

### § 88.13 Lights on barges at bank or dock.

(a) The following barges shall display at night and, if practicable, in periods of restricted visibility the lights described in paragraph (b) of this section:

(1) Every barge projecting into a buoyed or restricted channel.

(2) Every barge so moored that it reduces the available navigable width of any channel to less than 80 meters.

(3) Barges moored in groups more than two barges wide or to a maximum width of over 25 meters.

(4) Every barge not moored parallel to the bank or dock.

((b) Barges described in paragraph (a) of this section shall carry two unobstructed all-round white lights of an intensity to be visible for at least 1 nautical mile and meeting the technical requirements as prescribed in Sec. 84.15 of this chapter.

(c) A barge or group of barges at anchor or made fast to one or more mooring buoys or other similar device, in lieu of the provisions of Inland Navigation Rule 30, may carry unobstructed all-round white lights of an intensity to be visible for at least 1 nautical mile that meet the requirements of Sec. 84.15 of this chapter and shall be arranged as follows:

(1) Any barge that projects from a group formation, shall be lighted on its outboard corners.

(2) On a single barge moored in water where other vessels normally navigate on both sides of the barge, lights shall be placed to mark the corner extremities of the barge.

(3) On barges moored in group formation, moored in water where other vessels normally navigate on both sides of the group, lights shall be placed to mark the corner extremities of the group.

(d) The following are exempt from the requirements of this section:

(1) A barge or group of barges moored in a slip or slough used primarily for mooring purposes.

(2) A barge or group of barges moored behind a pierhead.

(3) A barge less than 20 meters in length when moored in a special anchorage area designated in accordance with Sec. 109.10 of this chapter.

(e) Barges moored in well-illuminated areas are exempt from the light requirements of this section. These areas are as follows:

**Chicago Sanitary Ship Canal;** (1) Mile 293.2 to 293.9; (3) Mile 295.2 to 296.1; (5) Mile 297.5 to 297.8; (7) Mile 298 to 298.2; (9) Mile 298.6 to 298.8; (11) Mile 299.3 to 299.4; (13) Mile 299.8 to 300.5; (15) Mile 303 to 303.2; (17) Mile 303.7 to 303.9; (19) Mile 305.7 to 305.8; (21) Mile 310.7 to 310.9; (23) Mile 311 to 311.2; (25) Mile 312.5 to 312.6; (27) Mile 313.8 to 314.2; (29) Mile 314.6; (31) Mile 314.8 to 315.3; (33) Mile 315.7 to 316; (35) Mile 316.8; (37) Mile 316.85 to 317.05; (39) Mile 317.5; (41) Mile 318.4 to 318.9; (43) Mile 318.7 to 318.8; (45) Mile 320 to 320.3; (47) Mile 320.6; (49) Mile 322.3 to 322.4; (51) Mile 322.8; (53) Mile 322.9 to 327.2. **Calumet Sag Channel;** (61) Mile 316.5. **Little Calumet River;** (71) Mile 321.2; (73) Mile 322.3. **Calumet River;** (81) Mile 328.5 to 328.7; (83) Mile 329.2 to 329.4; (85) Mile 330, west bank to 330.2; (87) Mile 331.4 to 331.6; (89) Mile 332.2 to 332.4; (91) Mile 332.6 to 332.8. **Cumberland River;** (101) Mile 126.8; (103) Mile 191

### § 88.15 Lights on dredge pipelines.

Dredge pipelines that are floating or supported on trestles shall display the following lights at night and in periods of restricted visibility.

(a) One row of yellow lights. The lights must be:

(1 ) Flashing 50 to 70 times per minute;

(2) Visible all around the horizon;

(3) Visible for at least 2 miles on a clear dark night;

(4) Not less than 1 and not more than 3.5 meters above the water;

(5) Approximately equally spaced; and

(6) Not more than 10 meters apart where the pipeline crosses a navigable channel. Where the pipeline does not cross a navigable channel the lights must be sufficient in number to clearly show the pipeline's length and course.

(b) Two red lights at each end of the pipeline, including the ends in a channel where the pipeline is separated to allow vessels to pass (whether open or closed). The lights must be:

(1) Visible all around the horizon; and

(2) Visible for at least 2 miles on a clear dark night; and

(3) One meter apart in a vertical line with the lower light at the same height above the water as the flashing yellow light.

## INTERPRETIVE RULES

**82.1 Purpose.** (a) This part contains the interpretative rules concerning the 72 COLREGS that are adopted by the Coast Guard for the guidance of the public.

**82.3 Pushing vessel and vessel being pushed: Composite unit.** Rule 24(b) of the 72 COLREGS states that when a pushing vessel and a vessel being pushed ahead are rigidly connected in a composite unit, they are regarded as a power-driven vessel and must exhibit the lights under Rule 23. A "composite unit" is interpreted to be a pushing vessel that is rigidly connected by mechanical means to a vessel being pushed so they react to sea and swell as one vessel. "Mechanical means" does not include the following: (a) Lines, (b) Hawsers, (c) Wires, (d) Chains.

**82.5 Lights for moored vessels.** For the purposes of Rule 30 of the 72 COLREGS, a vessel at anchor includes a barge made fast to one or more mooring buoys or other similar device attached to the sea or river floor. Such a barge may be lighted as a vessel at anchor in accordance with Rule 30, or may be lighted on the corners in accordance with 33 CFR 88.13.

**82.7 Sidelights for unmanned barges.** An unmanned barge being towed may use the exception of COLREGS Rule 24(h). However, this exception only applies to the vertical sector requirements.

---

**90.1 Purpose.**(a) This part contains the interpretative rules for the Inland Rules. These interpretative rules are intended as a guide to assist the public and promote compliance with the Inland Rules.

**90.3 Pushing vessel and vessel being pushed: Composite unit.** Rule 24(b) of the Inland Rules states that when a pushing vessel and a vessel being pushed ahead are rigidly connected in a composite unit, they are regarded as a power-driven vessel and must exhibit the lights prescribed in Rule 23. A "composite unit" in interpreted to be the combination of a pushing vessel and a vessel being pushed ahead that are rigidly connected by mechanical means so they react to sea and swell as one vessel. Mechanical means does not include lines, wires, hawsers or chains.

**90.5 Lights for moored vessels.** A vessel at anchor includes a vessel made fast to one or more mooring buoys or other similar device attached to the ocean floor. Such vessels may be lighted as a vessel at anchor in accordance with Rule 30, or may be lighted on the corners in accordance with 33 CFR 88.13.

**90.7 Sidelights for unmanned barges.** An unmanned barge being towed may use the exception of COLREGS Rule 24(h). However, this exception only applies to the vertical sector requirements for sidelights.

## COLREGS DEMARCATION LINES

### DEMARCATION LINES: PURPOSE, AUTHORITY, AND SOURCE

**80.01 General basis and purpose of demarcation lines**

(a) The regulations in this part establish the lines of demarcation delineating those waters upon which mariners shall comply with the International Regulations for Preventing Collisions at Sea, 1972 (72 COLREGS) and those waters upon which mariners shall comply with the Inland Navigation Rules.

(b) The waters inside of the lines are Inland Rules Waters. The waters outside the lines are COLREGS Waters. [CGD 82-029,47 FR 19518, May 6, 1982; CGD 83-003, 48 FR 7442, Feb.22, 1983]

**AUTHORITY**: Rule 1, International Regulations for Preventing Collisions at Sea, 1972 (as rectified); E.O. 11964; Pub. L. 95-75, 91 Stat. 308; 14U.S.C. 2;49CFR 1.46(b),unless otherwise noted. **SOURCE**: CGD 77-118a, 42 FR 35784, July 11, 1977, unless otherwise noted.

## ATLANTIC COAST — First District

**80.105 Calais, ME to Cape Small, ME.** The 72 COLREGS shall apply on the harbors, bays and inlets on the east coast of Maine from International Bridge at Calais, ME, to the southwesternmost extremity of Bald Head at Cape Small.

**80.110 Casco Bay, ME.** (a) A line drawn from the southwesternmost extremity of Bald Head at Cape Small to the southeasternmost extremity of Ragged Island; thence to the southern tangent of Jaquish Island thence to Little Mark Island Monument Light; thence to the northernmost extremity of Jewell Island.

(b) A line drawn from the tower on Jewell Island charted in approximate position latitude 43° 40.6' N, longitude 70° 05.9' W, to the northeasternmost extremity of Outer Green Island.

(c) A line drawn from the southwesternmost extremity of Outer Green Island to Ram Island Ledge Light; thence to Portland Head Light.

**80.115 Portland Head, ME to Cape Ann, MA.** (a) Except inside lines specifically described in this section, the 72 COLREGS shall apply on the harbors, bays, and inlets on the east coast of Maine, New Hampshire, and Massachusetts from Portland Head to Halibut Point at Cape Ann.

(b) A line drawn from the southernmost tower on Gerrish Island charted in approximate position latitude 43° 04.0' N longitude 70° 41.2' W to Whaleback Light; thence to Jeffrey Point Light 2A; thence to the northeasternmost extremity of Frost Point.

(c) A line drawn from the northernmost extremity of Farm Point to Annisquam Harbor Light.

**80.120 Cape Ann, MA to Marblehead Neck, MA.** (a) Except inside lines specifically described in this section, the 72 COLREGS shall apply on the harbors, bays and inlets on the east coast of Massachusetts from Halibut Point at Cape Ann to Marblehead Neck.

(b) A line drawn from Gloucester Harbor Breakwater Light to the twin towers charted in approximate position latitude 42° 35.1' N longitude 70° 41.6' W.

(c) A line drawn from the westernmost extremity of Gales Point to the easternmost extremity of House Island; thence to Bakers Island Light; thence to Marblehead Light. [CGD 81-017, 46 FR 28154, May 26, 1981]

**80.125 Marblehead Neck, MA to Nahant, MA.** The 72 COLREGS apply on the harbors, bays, and inlets on the east coast of Massachusetts from Marblehead Neck to the easternmost tower at Nahant, charted in approximate position latitude 42° 25.4' N, longitude 70° 54.6' W. [CGD 81-017, 46 FR 28154, May 26, 1981]

**80.130 Boston Harbor entrance.** A line drawn from easternmost tower at Nahant, charted in approximate position latitude 42° 25.4' N, longitude 70° 54.6' W, to Boston Lighted Horn Buoy "B"; thence to the easternmost radio tower at Hull, charted in approximate position latitude 42° 16.7' N, longitude 70° 52.6'W. [CGD 81-017, 46 FR 28154, May 26, 1981]

**80.135 Hull, MA to Race Point, MA.**

(a) Except inside lines described in this section, the 72 COLREGS apply on the harbors, bays, and inlets on the east coast of Massachusetts from the easternmost radio tower at Hull, charted in approximate position latitude 42° 16.7'N, longitude 70° 52.6' W, to Race Point on Cape Cod.

(b) A line drawn from Canal Breakwater Light 4 south to the shoreline. [CGD 81-017, 46 FR 28154, May 26, 1981]

**80.145 Race Point, MA to Watch Hill, RI.** (a) Except inside lines specifically described in this section, the 72 COLREGS shall apply on the sounds, bays, harbors and inlets along the coast of Cape Cod and the southern coasts of Massachusetts and Rhode Island from Race Point to Watch Hill.

(b) A line drawn from Nobska Point Light to Tarpaulin Cove Light on the southeastern side of Naushon Island; thence from the southernmost tangent of Naushon Island to the easternmost extremity of Nashawena Island; thence from the southwestern most extremity of Nashawena Island to the easternmost extremity of Cuttyhunk Island; thence from the southwestern tangent of Cuttyhunk Island to the tower on Gooseberry Neck charted in approximate position latitude 41° 29.1' N, longitude 71° 02.3' W.

(c) A line drawn from Sakonnet Breakwater Light 2 tangent to the southernmost part of Sacnuest Point charted in approximate position latitude 41° 28.5'N, longitude 71° 14.8'W.

(d) An east-west line drawn through Beavertail Light between Brenton Point and the Boston Neck shoreline. [CGD 81-017, 46 FR 28154, May 26, 1981]

**80.150 Block Island, RI.** The 72 COLREGS shall apply on the harbors of Block Island.

**80.155 Watch Hill, RI to Montauk Point, NY.** (a) A line drawn from Watch Hill Light to East Point on Fishers Island.

(b) A line drawn from Race Point to Race Rock Light; thence to Little Gull Island Light thence to East Point on Plum Island.

(c) A line drawn from Plum Island Harbor East Dolphin Light to Plum Island Harbor West Dolphin Light.

(d) A line drawn from Plum Island Light to Orient Point Light; thence to Orient Point.

(e) A line drawn from the lighthouse ruins at the southwestern end of Long Beach Point to Cornelius Point.

(f) A line drawn from Coecles Harbor Entrance Light to Sungic Point.

(g) A line drawn from Nichols Point to Cedar Island Light.

(h) A line drawn from Three Mile Harbor West Breakwater Light to Three Mile Harbor East Breakwater Light.

(i) A line drawn from Montauk West Jetty Light 1 to Montauk East Jetty Light 2. [Redisignated by CGD 87-0086, 52 FR 25218, July 6, 1987]

**80.160 Montauk Point, NY to Atlantic Beach, NY.** (a) A line drawn from Shinnecock Inlet East Breakwater Light to Shinnecock Inlet West Breakwater Light 1.

(b) A line drawn from Moriches Inlet East Breakwater Light to Moriches Inlet West Breakwater Light.

(c) A line drawn from Fire Island Inlet Breakwater Light 348° true to the southernmost extremity of the spit of land at the western end of Oak Beach.

(d) A line drawn from Jones Inlet Light 322° true across the southwest tangent of the island on the north side of Jones Inlet to the shoreline. [Redesignated CGD 87-0086, 52 FR 25218, July 6, 1987]

**80.165 New York Harbor.** A line drawn from East Rockaway Inlet Breakwater Light to Sandy Hook Light.

**80.170 Sandy Hook, NJ to Tom's River, NJ** (a) A line drawn from Shark River Inlet North Breakwater Light 2 to Shark River Inlet South Breakwater Light 1.

(b) A line drawn from Manasquan Inlet North Breakwater Light 4 to Manasquan Inlet South Breakwater Light 3.

(c) A line drawn from Barnegat Inlet North Breakwater Light 4A to the seaward extremity of the submerged Barnegat Inlet South Breakwater; thence along the submerged break-water to the shoreline.

## ATLANTIC COAST — Fifth District

**80.501 Tom's River, NJ to Cape May, NJ.** (d) A line drawn from the southernmost point of Longport at latitude 39° 18.2' N. longitude 74° 33.1' W. to the northeasternmost point of Ocean City at latitude 39° 17.6' N. longitude 74° 33.1' W. across Great Egg Harbor Inlet.

(b) A line drawn from the seaward tangent of Pullen Island to the seaward tangent of Brigantine Island across Brigantine Inlet.

(c) A line drawn from the seaward extremity of Absecon Inlet North Jetty to Atlantic City light.

(d) A line drawn from the southernmost point of Longport at latitude 30° 18.2' N, longitude 75° 32.2' W to the northeasternmost point of Ocean City at latitude 39° 17.6' N, longitude 74° 33.1' W across the Great Egg Harbor Inlet.

(e) A line drawn parallel with the general trend of highwater shoreline across Corson Inlet.

(f) A line formed by the centerline of the Townsend Inlet Highway Bridge.

(g) A line formed by the shoreline of Seven Mile Beach and Hereford Inlet Light.

(h) A line drawn from Cape May Inlet West Jetty Light. [CGD 87-0086, 52 FR 25218, July 6, 1987]

**80.503 Delaware Bay.** A line drawn from Cape May Light to Harbor of Refuge Light;

thence to the northernmost extremity of Cape Henlopen.

**80.505 Cape Henlopen, DE to Cape Charles, VA.** (a) A line drawn from the seaward extremity of Indian River Inlet North Jetty to Indian River Inlet South Jetty Light.

(b) A line drawn from Ocean City Inlet Light 6 225° true across Ocean City Inlet to the submerged south breakwater.

(c) A line drawn from Assateague Beach Tower Light to the tower charted at latitude 37° 52.6' N, longitude 75° 26.7' W.

(d) A line formed by the range of Wachapreague Inlet Light 3 and Parramore Beach lookout Tower drawn across Wachapreague Inlet.

(e) A line drawn from the lookout tower charted on the northern end of Hog Island to the seaward tangent of Parramore Beach.

(f) A line drawn 207° true from the lookout tower charted on the southern end of Hog Island across Great Machipongo Inlet.

(g) A line formed by the range of the two cupolas charted on the southern end of Cobb Island drawn across the Sand Shoal Inlet.

(h) Except as provided elsewhere in this section from Cape Henlopen to Cape Charles, lines drawn parallel with the general trend of the highwater shoreline across the entrances to small bays and inlets.

**80.510 Chesapeake Bay Entrance, VA.** A line drawn from Cape Charles Light to Cape Henry Light.

**80.515 Cape Henry, VA to Cape Hatteras, NC.** (a) A line drawn from Rudee Inlet Jetty Light 2 to Rudee Inlet Jetty Light 1.

(b) A line formed by the centerline of the highway bridge across Oregon Inlet.

**80.520 Cape Hatteras, NC to Cape Lookout, NC.** (a) A line drawn from Hatteras Inlet Lookout Tower at latitude 35° 11.8' N. longitude 75° 44.9' W. 255°  true to the eastern end of Ocracoke Island.

(b) A line drawn from the westernmost extremity of Ocracoke Island at latitude 35° 04.0' N, longitude 76° 00.8' W to the northeastern extremity of Portsmouth Island at latitude 35° 03.7' N, longitude 76° 02.3' W.

(c) A line drawn across Drum Inlet parallel with the general trend of the highwater shoreline.

**80.525 Cape Lookout, NC to Cape Fear, NC.** (a) A line drawn from Cape Lookout Light to the seaward tangent of the southeastern end of Shackleford Banks.

(b) A line drawn from Morehead City Channel Range Front Light to the seaward extremity of the Beaufort Inlet west jetty.

(c) A line drawn from the southernmost extremity of Bogue Banks at latitude 34° 38.7' N, longitude 77° 06.0' W across Bogue Inlet to the northernmost extremity of Bear Beach at latitude 34° 38.5' N, longitude 77° 07.1' W.

(d) A line drawn from the tower charted in approximate position latitude 34° 31.5' N, longitude 77° 20.8' W to the seaward tangent of the shoreline on the northeast side of New River Inlet.

(e) A line drawn across New Topsail Inlet between the closest extremities of the shore on either side of the inlet from latitude 34° 20.8' N, longitude 77° 39.2' W to latitude 34° 20.6' N, longitude 77° 39.6' W.

(f) A line drawn from the seaward extremity of the jetty on the northeast side of Masonboro Inlet to the seaward extremity of the jetty on the southeast side of the Inlet.

(g) Except as provided elsewhere in this section from Cape Lookout to Cape Fear, lines drawn parallel with the general trend of the highwater shoreline across the entrance of small bays and inlets.

**80.530 Cape Fear, NC to Little River Inlet, NC.** (a) A line drawn from the abandoned lighthouse charted in approximate position latitude 33° 52.4' N longitude 78° 00.1 W across the Cape Fear River Entrance to Oak Island Light.

(b) Except as provided elsewhere in this section from Cape Fear to Little River Inlet, lines drawn parallel with the general trend of the highwater shoreline across the entrance to small inlets.

## ATLANTIC COAST — Seventh District

**80.703 Little River Inlet, SC to Cape Romain, SC.** (a) A line drawn from the western-most extremity of the sand spit on Bird Island to the easternmost extremity of Waties Island across Little River Inlet.

(b) From Little River Inlet, a line drawn parallel with the general trend of the highwater shoreline across Hog Inlet; thence a line drawn from Murrels Inlet Light 2 to Murrels Inlet Light 1; thence a line drawn parallel with the general trend of the highwater shoreline across Midway Inlet, Pawleys Inlet and North Inlet.

(c) A line drawn from the charted position of Winyah Bay North Jetty End Buoy 2N south to the Winyah Bay South Jetty.

(d) A line drawn from Santee Point to the seaward tangent of Cedar Island.

(e) A line drawn from Cedar Island Point west to Murphy Island.

(f) A north-south line (longitude 79° 20.3' W) drawn from Murphy Island to the northern-most extremity of Cape Island Point.

**80.707 Cape Romain, SC to Sullivans Island, SC.** (a) A line drawn from the western extremity of Cape Romain 292° true to Racoon Key on the west side of Racoon Creek.

(b) A line drawn from the westernmost extremity of Sandy Point across Bull Bay to the northernmost extremity of Northeast Point.

(c) A line drawn from the southernmost extremity of Bull Island to the easternmost extremity of Capers Island.

(d) A line formed by the overhead power cable from Capers Island to Dewees Island.

(e) A line formed by the overhead power cable from Dewees Island to Isle of Palms.

(f) A line formed by the centerline of the highway bridge between Isle of Palms and Sullivans Island over Breach Inlet.

**80.710 Charleston Harbor, SC.**

(a) A line formed by the submerged north jetty from the shore to the west end of the north jetty.

(b) A line drawn from across the seaward extremity of the Charleston Harbor Jetties.

(c) A line drawn from the west end of the South Jetty across the South entrance to Charleston Harbor to shore on a line formed by the submerged south jetty.

**80.712 Morris Island, SC to Hilton Head Island, SC.** (a) A line drawn from the eastern-most tip of Folley Island to the abandoned lighthouse tower on the northside of Lighthouse Inlet; thence west to the shoreline of Morris Island.

(b) A straight line drawn from the seaward tangent of Folly Island through Folly River Daybeacon 10 across Stono River to the shoreline of Sandy Point.

(c) A line drawn from the southernmost extremity of Seabrook Island 257° true across the North Edisto River Entrance to the shore of Botany Bay Island.

(d) A line drawn from the microwave antenna tower on Edisto Beach charted in approxi-mate position latitude 32° 29.3' N, longitude 80° 19.2' W across St. Helena Sound to the abandoned lighthouse tower on Hunting Island.

(e) A line formed by the centerline of the highway bridge between Hunting Island and Fripp Island.

(f) A line following the general trend of the seaward highwater shoreline across Cabretta Inlet.

**80.715 Savannah River.** A line drawn from the southernmost tank on Hilton Head Island charted in approximate position latitude 32° 06.7'N, longitude 80° 49.3' W to Bloody Point Range Rear Light; thence to Tybee (Range Rear) Light.

**80.717 Tybee Island, GA to St. Simons Island, GA.** (a) A line drawn from the south-ernmost extremity of Savannah Beach on Tybee Island 255° true across Tybee Inlet to the shore of Little Tybee Island south of the entrance to Buck Hammock Creek.

(b) A straight line drawn from the northernmost extremity of Wassaw Island 031° true through Tybee River Daybeacon 1 to the shore of Little Tybee Island.

(c) A line drawn approximately parallel with the general trend of the highwater shore-lines from the seaward tangent of Wassau Island to the seaward tangent of Bradley Point on Ossabaw Island.

(d) A north-south line (longitude 81° 08.4'W) drawn from the southernmost extremity of Ossabaw Island to St. Catherines Island .

(e) A north-south line (longitude 81°10.6' W) drawn from the southernmost extremity of St. Catherines Island to Northeast Point on Blackbeard Island.

(f) A line following the general trend of the seaward highwater shoreline across Cabretta Inlet.

(g) A north-south line (longitude 81° 16.9' W) drawn from the southwesternmost point on Sapelo Island to Wolf Island.

(h) A north-south line (longitude 81°17.1' W) drawn from the southeasternmost point of Wolf Island to the northeasternmost point on Little St. Simons Island.

(i) A line drawn from the northeasternmost extremity of Sea Island 045° true to Little St. Simons Island.

(j) An east-west line from the southernmost extremity of Sea Island across Goulds Inlet to St. Simons Island.

**80.720 St. Simons Island, GA to Amelia Island, FL.** (a) A line drawn from St. Simons Light to the northernmost tank on Jekyll Island charted in approximate position latitude 31°05.9' N longitude 81° 24.5' W.

(b) A line drawn from the southernmost tank on Jekyll Island charted in approximate position latitude 31° 01.6' N longitude 81° 25.2' W to coordinate latitude 30° 59.4' N, longitude 81° 23.7' W (0.5 nautical mile east of the charted position of St. Andrew Sound Lighted Buoy 32); thence to the abandoned lighthouse tower on the north end of Little Cumberland Island charted in approximate position lat. 30° 58.5' N, lon. 81° 24.8' W.

(c) A line drawn across the seaward extremity of the St. Marys Entrance Jetties.

**80.723 Amelia Island, FL to Cape Canaveral, FL.** (a) A line drawn from the southernmost extremity of Amelia Island to the northeasternmost extremity of Little Talbot Island.

(b) A line formed by the centerline of the highway bridge from Little Talbot Island to Fort George Island.

(c) A line drawn across the seaward extremity of the St. Johns River Entrance Jetties.

(d) A line drawn across the seaward extremity of the St. Augustine Inlet Jetties.

(e) A line formed by the centerline of the highway bridge over Matanzas Inlet.

(f) A line drawn across the seaward extremity of the Ponce de Leon Inlet Jetties.

**80.727 Cape Canaveral, FL to Miami Beach, FL.** (a) A line drawn across the seaward extremity of the Port Canaveral Entrance Channel Jetties.

(b) A line drawn across the seaward extremity of the Sebastian Inlet Jetties.

(c) A line drawn across the seaward extremity of the Fort Pierce Inlet Jetties.

(d) A north-south line (longitude 80° 09.7' W) drawn across St. Lucie Inlet.

(e) A line drawn from the seaward extremity of Jupiter Inlet North Jetty to the northeast extremity of the concrete apron on the south side of Jupiter Inlet.

(f) A line drawn across the seaward extremity of the Lake Worth Inlet Jetties.

(g) A line drawn across the seaward extremity of the Boynton Inlet Jetties.

(h) A line drawn from Boca Raton Inlet North Jetty Light 2 to Boca Raton Inlet South Jetty Light 1.

(i) A line drawn from Hillsboro Inlet Light to Hillsboro Inlet Entrance Light 2; thence to Hillsboro Inlet Entrance Light 1; thence west to the shoreline.

(j) A line drawn across the seaward extremity of the Port Everglades Entrance Jetties.

(k) A line formed by the centerline of the highway bridge over Bakers Haulover Inlet.

**80.730 Miami Harbor, FL.** A line drawn across the seaward extremity of the Miami Harbor Government Cut Jetties.

**80.735 Miami, FL to Long Key, FL.** (a) A line drawn from the southernmost extremity of Fisher Island 212° true to the point latitude 25° 45.0' N longitude 80° 08.6' W on Virginia Key.

(b) A line formed by the centerline of the highway bridge between Virginia Key and Key Biscayne.

(c) A line drawn from Cape Florida Light to the northernmost extremity on Soldier Key.

(d) A line drawn from the southernmost extremity on Soldier Key to the northernmost extremity of the Ragged Keys.

(e) A line drawn from the Ragged Keys to the southernmost extremity of Angelfish Key following the general trend of the seaward shoreline.

(f) A line drawn on the centerline of the Overseas Highway (U.S. 1) and bridges from latitude 25° 19.3' N longitude 80° 16.0' W at Little Angelfish Creek to the radar dome charted on Long Key at approximate position latitude 24° 49.3' N longitude 80° 49.2' W [CGD 81-017, 46 FR 28154, May 26, 1981]

## PUERTO RICO AND VIRGIN ISLANDS — Seventh District

**80.738 Puerto Rico and Virgin Islands.** (a) Except inside lines specifically described in this section, the 72 COLREGS shall apply on all other bays, harbors and lagoons of Puerto Rico and the U.S. Virgin Islands.

(b) A line drawn from Puerto San Juan Light to Cabras Light across the entrance of San Juan Harbor.

## GULF COAST — Seventh District

**80.740 Long Key, FL to Cape Sable, FL.** A line drawn from the microwave tower charted on Long Key at approximate position latitude 24° 48.8' N longitude 80° 49.6' W to Long Key Light 1; thence to Arsenic Bank Light 2; thence to Sprigger Bank Light 5; thence to Schooner Bank Light 6; thence to Oxfoot Bank Light 10; thence to East Cape Light 2; thence through East Cape Daybeacon 1A to the shoreline at East Cape.

**80.745 Cape Sable, FL to Cape Romano, FL.** (a) A line drawn following the general trend of the mainland, highwater shoreline from Cape Sable at East Cape to Little Shark River Light 1; thence to westernmost extremity of Shark Point; thence following the general trend of the mainland, highwater shoreline crossing the entrances of Harney River, Broad Creek, Broad River, Rodgers River First Bay, Chatham River, Huston River, to the shoreline at coordinate latitude 25° 41.8' N longitude 81° 17.9' W.

(b) The 72 COLREGS shall apply to the waters surrounding the Ten Thousand Islands and the bays, creeks, inlets and rivers between Chatham Bend and Marco Island except inside lines specifically described in this part.

(c) A north-south line drawn at longitude 81° 20.2' W across the entrance to Lopez River.

(d) A line drawn across the entrance to Turner River parallel to the general trend of the shoreline.

(e) A line formed by the centerline of Highway 92 Bridge at Goodland.

**80.748 Cape Romano, FL to Sanibel Island, FL.** (a) A line drawn across Big Marco Pass parallel to the general trend of the seaward, highwater shoreline.

(b) A line drawn from the northwesternmost extremity of Coconut Island 000° T across Capri Pass.

(c) Lines drawn across Hurricane and Little Marco Passes parallel to the general trend of the seaward, highwater shoreline.

(d) A line from the seaward extremity of Gordon Pass South Jetty 014° true to the shoreline at approximate coordinate latitude 26° 05.7' N longitude 81° 48.1' W.

(e) A line drawn across the seaward extremity of Doctors Pass Jetties.

(f) Lines drawn across Wiggins, Big Hickory, New, and Big Carlos Passes parallel to the general trend of the seaward highwater shoreline.

(g) A straight line drawn from Sanibel Island Light through Matanzas Pass Channel Light 2 to the shore of Estero Island. [CGD 81-017, 46 FR 28154, May 26, 1981]

**80.750 Sanibel Island, FL to St. Petersburg, FL.** (a) A line formed by the centerline of the highway bridge over Blind Pass, between Captiva Island and Sanibel Island, and lines drawn across Redfish and Captiva Passes parallel to the general trend of the seaward, highwater shorelines.

(b) A line drawn from La Costa Test Pile North Light to Port Boca Grande Light.

(c) Lines drawn across Gasparilla and Stump Passes parallel to the general trend of the seaward, highwater shorelines.

(d) A line across the seaward extremity of Venice Inlet Jetties.

(e) A line drawn across Midnight Pass parallel to the general trend of the seaward, highwater shoreline.

(f) A line drawn from Big Sarasota Pass Light 14 to the southernmost extremity of Lido Key.

(g) A line drawn across New Pass tangent to the seaward, highwater shoreline of Longboat Key.

(h) A line drawn across Longboat Pass parallel to the seaward, highwater shoreline.

(i) A line drawn from the northwesternmost extremity of Bean Point to the southeasternmost extremity of Egmont Key.

(j) A straight line drawn from Egmont Key Light through Egmont Channel Range Rear Light to the shoreline on Mullet Key.

(k) A line drawn from the northernmost extremity of Mullet Key across Bunces Pass and South Channel to Pass-a-Grille Channel Light 8; thence to Pass-a-Grille Channel Daybeacon 9; thence to the southwesternmost extremity of Long Key. [CGD 81-017, 46 FR 28154, May 26, 1981]

**80.753 St. Petersburg, FL to the Anclote, FL.**

(a) A line drawn across Blind Pass, between Treasure Island and Long Key, parallel with the general trend of the seaward, highwater shoreline.

(b) Lines formed by the centerline of the highway bridges over Johns and Clearwater Passes.

(c) A line drawn across Dunedin and Hurricane Passes parallel with the general trend of the seaward, highwater shoreline.

(d) A line drawn from the northernmost extremity of Honeymoon Island to Anclote Anchorage South Entrance Light 7; thence to Anclote Key 28° 10.0' N, 82° 50.6' W; thence a straight line through Anclote River Cut B Range Rear Light to the shoreline.

**80.755 Anclote, FL to the Suncoast Keys, FL.** (a) Except inside lines specifically described in this section, the 72 COLREGS shall apply on the bays, bayous, creeks, marinas, and rivers from Anclote to the Suncoast Keys.

(b) A north-south line drawn at longitude 82° 38.3'W across the Chassahowitzka River Entrance.

**80.757 Suncoast Keys, FL to Horseshoe Point, FL.** (a) Except inside lines specifically described in this section, the 72 COLREGS shall apply on the bays, bayous, creeks, and marinas from the Suncoast Keys to Horseshoe Point.

(b) A line formed by the centerline of Highway 44 Bridge over the Salt River.

(c) A north-south line drawn through Crystal River Entrance Daybeacon 25 across the river entrance.

(d) A north-south line drawn through the Cross Florida Barge Canal Daybeacon 48 across the canal.

(e) A north-south line drawn through Withlacoochee River Daybeacon 40 across the river.

(f) A line drawn from the westernmost extremity of South Point north to the shoreline across the Waccasassa River Entrance.

(g) A line drawn from position latitude 29° 16.6'N longitude 83° 06.7' W 300° true to the shoreline of Hog Island.

(h) A north-south line drawn through Suwannee River Wadley Pass Channel Daybeacons 30 and 31 across the Suwanee River.

**80.760 Horseshoe Point, FL to Rock Islands, FL.** (a) Except inside lines specifically described provided in this section, the 72 COLREGS shall apply on the bays, bayous, creeks, marinas, and rivers from Horseshoe Point to the Rock Islands.

(b) A north-south line drawn through Steinhatchee River Light 21.

(c) A line drawn from Fenholloway River Approach Light FR east across the entrance to Fenholloway River.

## GULF COAST — Eighth District

**80.805 Rock Island, FL to Cape San Blas, FL.** (a) A north-south line drawn from the Econfina River Light to the opposite shore.

(b) A line drawn from Gamble Point Light to the southernmost extremity of Cabell Point.

(c) A line drawn from St. Marks (Range Rear) Light to St. Marks Channel Light 11; thence to the southernmost extremity of Live Oak Point; thence in a straight line through Shell Point Light to the southernmost extremity of Ochlockonee Point; thence to Bald Point along longitude 84° 20.5' W.

(d) A line drawn from the south shore of Southwest Cape at longitude 84° 22.7' W to Dog Island Reef East Light 1; thence to Turkey Point Light 2; thence to the easternmost extremity of Dog Island.

(e) A line drawn from the westernmost extremity of Dog Island to the easternmost extremity of St. George Island.

(f) A line drawn across the seaward extremity of the St. George Island Channel Jetties.

(g) A line drawn from the northwesternmost extremity of Sand Island to West Pass Light 7.

(h) A line drawn from the westernmost extremity of St. Vincent Island to the southeast, highwater shoreline of Indian Peninsula at longitude 85° 13.5'W.

**80.810 Cape San Blas, FL to Perdido Bay, FL.** (a) A line drawn from St. Joseph Bay Entrance Range A Rear Light through St. Joseph Bay Entrance Range B Front Light to St. Joseph Point.

(b) A line drawn across the mouth of Salt Creek as an extension of the general trend of the shoreline to continue across the inlet to St. Andrews sound in the middle of Crooked Island.

(c) A line drawn from the northernmost extremity of Crooked Island 000° T to the mainland.

(d) A line drawn from the easternmost extremity of Shell Island 120° true to the shoreline across the east entrance to St. Andrews Bay.

(e) A line drawn between the seaward end of the St. Andrews Bay Entrance Jetties.

(f) A line drawn between the seaward end of the Choctawatchee Bay Entrance Jetties.

(g) An east-west line drawn from Fort McRee Leading Light across the Pensacola Bay Entrance along latitude 30° 19.5' N.

(h) A line drawn between the seaward end of the Perdido Pass Jetties.

**80.815 Mobile Bay, AL to the Chandeleur Islands, LA.** (a) A line drawn across the inlets to Little Lagoon as an extension of the general trend of the shoreline.

(b) A line drawn from Mobile Point Light to Dauphin Island Channel Light No.1 to the eastern corner of Fort Gaines at Pelican Point.

(c) A line drawn from the westernmost extremity of Dauphin Island to the easternmost extremity of Petit Bois Island.

(d) A line drawn from Horn Island Pass Entrance Range Front Light on Petit Bois Island to the easternmost extremity of Horn Island.

(e) An east-west line (latitude 30° 14.7' N) drawn between the westernmost extremity of Horn Island to the easternmost extremity of Ship Island.

(f) A curved line drawn following the general trend of the seaward, highwater shoreline of Ship Island.

(g) A line drawn from Ship Island Light; to Chandeleur Light; thence in a curved line following the general trend of the seaward, highwater shorelines of the Chandeleur Islands to the island at latitude 29° 44.1' N, longitude 88° 53.0' W; thence to lat. 29° 26.5' N, lon. 88° 55.6' W.

**80.825 Mississippi Passes, LA.** (a) A line drawn from latitude 29° 26.5' N, longitude 88° 55.6' W to latitude 29° 10.6' N, longtitude 88° 59.8' W; thence to latitude 29° 03.5' N, longitude 89° 03.7' W; thence to lat. 28° 58.8'N, lon. 89° 04.3' W.

(b) A line drawn from latitude 28° 58.8' N, longitude 89° 04.3' W; to latitude 28° 57.3' N, longitude 89° 05.3' W; thence to latitude 28° 56.95' N, longitude 89° 05.6' W; thence to latitude 29° 00.4' N, longitude 89° 09.8' W; thence following the general trend of the seaward highwater shoreline in a northwesterly direction to latitude 29° 03.4' N, longitude 89° 13.0' W; thence west to latitude 29° 03.5'N, longitude 89° 15.5'W; thence following the general trend of the seaward highward shoreline in a southwesterly direction to latitude 28° 57.7' N, longitude 89° 22.3'W.

(c) A line drawn from latitude 28° 57.7' N, longitude 89° 22.3' W; to latitude 28° 51.4' N, longitude 89° 24.5' W; thence to latitude 28° 51.5' N, longitude 89° 27.1' W; thence to latitude 28° 52.65' N, longitude 89° 27.1' W; thence to the seaward extremity of the Southwest Pass West Jetty located at latitude 28° 54.5' N, longitude 89° 26.1' W.

(d) A line drawn from Mississippi River South Pass East Jetty Light 4 to Mississippi River South Pass West Jetty Light; thence following the general trend of the seaward highwater shoreline in a northwesterly direction to coordinate latitude 29° 03.4' N, longitude 89° 13.0' W; thence west to coordinate latitude 29° 03.5' N, longitude 89° 15.5' W; thence following the general trend of the seaward highwater shoreline in a southwesterly direction to Mississippi River Southwest Pass Entrance Light.

(e) A line drawn from Mississippi River Southwest Pass Entrance Light; thence to the seaward extremity of the Southwest Pass West Jetty located at coordinate latitude 28° 54.5' N, longitude 89° 26.1' W.

**80.830 Mississippi Passes, LA to Point Au Fer, LA.** (a) A line drawn from the seaward extremity of the Southwest Pass West Jetty located at coordinate latitude 28° 54.5' N longitude 89° 26.1' W; thence following the general trend of the seaward, highwater jetty and shoreline in a north, northeasterly direction to Old Tower latitude 28° 58.8' N longitude 89° 23.3' W; thence to West Bay Light; thence to coordinate latitude 29° 05.2' N longitude 89° 24.3' W; thence a curved line following the general trend of the highwater shoreline to Point Au Fer Island except as otherwise described in this section.

(b) A line drawn across the seaward extremity of the Empire Waterway (Bayou Fontanelle) entrance jetties.

(c) An east-west line drawn from the westernmost extremity of Grand Terre Islands in the direction of 194° true to the Grand Isle Fishing Jetty Light.

(d) A line drawn between the seaward extremity of the Belle Pass Jetties.

(e) A line drawn from the westernmost extremity of the Timbalier Island to the easternmost extremity of Isles Dernieres.

(f) A north-south line drawn from Caillou Bay Light 13 across Caillou Boca.

(g) A line drawn 107° true from Caillou Bay Boat Landing Light across the entrances to Grand Bayou du Large and Bayou Grand Caillou.

(h) A line drawn on an axis of 103° true through Taylors Bayou Entrance Light 2 across the entrances to Jack Stout Bayou, Taylors Bayou, Pelican Pass and Bayou de West.

**80.835 Point Au Fer, LA to Calcasieu Pass, LA.** (a) A line drawn from Point Au Fer to Atchafalaya Channel Light 34; thence Point Au Fer Reef Light 33; Atchafalaya Bay Pipeline Light D latitude 29° 25.0' N, longitude 91° 31.7' W; thence Atchafalaya Bay Light 1 latitude 29° 25.3' N, longitude 91° 35.8' W; thence South Point.

(b) Lines following the general trend of the high-water shoreline drawn across the bayou canal inlets from the Gulf of Mexico between South Point and Calcasieu Pass except as otherwise described in this section.

(c) A line drawn on an axis of 140° true through Southwest Pass-Vermillion Bay Light 4 across Southwest Pass.

(d) A line drawn across the seaward extremity of the Freshwater Bayou Canal Entrance Jetties.

(e) A line drawn from Mermentau Channel East Jetty Light 6 to Mermentau Channel West Jetty Light 7.

(f) A line drawn from the radio tower charted in approximate position latitude 29° 45.7' N, longitude 93.06.3' W 115° true across Mermentau Pass.

(g) A line drawn across the seaward extremity of the Calcasieu Pass Jetties.

**80.840 Sabine Pass, TX to Galveston, TX.** (a) A line drawn from the Sabine Pass East Jetty Light to the seaward end of the Sabine Pass West Jetty.

(b) A line drawn across the small boat passes through the Sabine Pass East and West Jetties.

(c) A line formed by the centerline of the highway bridge over Rollover Pass at Gilchrist.

**80.845 Galveston, TX to Freeport, TX.** (a) A line drawn from Galveston North Jetty Light 6A to Galveston South Jetty Light 5A.

(b) A line formed by the centerline of the highway bridge over San Luis Pass.

(c) Lines formed by the centerlines of the highway bridges over the inlets to Christmas Bay (Cedar Cut) and Drum Bay.

(d) A line drawn from the seaward extremity of the Freeport North Jetty to Freeport Entrance Light 6; thence Freeport Entrance Light 7; thence the seaward extremity of Freeport South Jetty.

**80.850 Brazos River, TX to the Rio Grande, TX.** (a) Except as otherwise described in this section lines drawn continuing the general trend of the seaward, high-water shore-lines across the inlets to Brazos River Diversion Channel, San Bernard River, Cedar Lakes, Brown Cedar Cut, Colorado River, Matagorda Bay, Cedar Bayou, Corpus Christi Bay, and Laguna Madre.

(b) A line drawn across the seaward extremity of Matagorda Ship Channel North Jetties.

(c) A line drawn from the seaward tangent of Matagorda Peninsula at Decros Point to Matagorda Light.

(d) A line drawn across the seaward extremity of the Aransas Pass Jetties.

(e) A line drawn across the seaward extremity of the Port Mansfield Entrance Jetties.

(f) A line drawn across the seaward extremity of the Brazos Santiago Pass Jetties.

## PACIFIC COAST — Eleventh District

**80.1105 Santa Catalina Island, CA.** The 72 COLREGS shall apply to the harbors on Santa Catalina Island.

**80.1110 San Diego Harbor, CA.** A line drawn from Zuniga Jetty Light "V" to Zuniga Jetty Light "Z"; thence to Point Loma Light.

**80.1115 Mission Bay, CA.** A line drawn from Mission Bay South Jetty Light 2 to Mission Bay North Jetty Light 1.

**80.1120 Oceanside Harbor, CA.** A line drawn from Oceanside South Jetty Light 4 to Oceanside Breakwater Light 3.

**80.1125 Dana Point Harbor, CA.** A line drawn from Dana Point Jetty Light 6 to Dana Point Breakwater Light 5.

**80.1130 Newport Bay, CA.** A line drawn from Newport Bay East Jetty Light 4 to Newport Bay West Jetty Light 3.

**80.1135 San Pedro Bay - Anaheim Bay, CA.** (a) A line drawn across the seaward extremities of the Anaheim Bay Entrance East Jetties; thence to Long Beach Breakwater East End Light 1.

(b) A line drawn from Long Beach Channel Entrance Light 2 to Long Beach Light.

(c) A line drawn from Los Angeles Main Entrance Channel Light 2 to Los Angeles Light.

**80.1140 Redondo Harbor, CA.** A line drawn from Redondo Beach East Jetty Light 2 to Redondo Beach West Jetty Light 3.

**80.1145 Marina Del Rey, CA.** (a) A line drawn from Marina Del Rey Breakwater South Light 1 to Marina Del Rey Light 4.

(b) A line drawn from Marina Del Rey Breakwater North Light 2 to Marina Del Rey Light 3.

(c) A line drawn from Marina Del Rey Light 4 to the seaward extremity of the Ballona Creek South Jetty.

**80.1150 Port Hueneme, CA.** A line drawn from Port Hueneme East Jetty Light 4 to Port Hueneme West Jetty Light 3.

**80.1155 Channel Islands Harbor, CA.** (a) A line drawn from Channel Islands Harbor South Jetty Light 2 to Channel Islands Harbor Breakwater South Light 1.

(b) A line drawn from Channel Islands Harbor Breakwater North Light to Channel Islands Harbor North Jetty Light 5.

**80.1160 Ventura Marina, CA.** A line drawn from Ventura Marina South Jetty Light 6 to Ventura Marina Breakwater South Light 3; thence to Ventura Marina North Jetty Light 7.

**80.1165 Santa Barbara Harbor, CA.** A line drawn from Santa Barbara Harbor Light 4 to Santa Barbara Harbor Breakwater Light.

## PACIFIC COAST — Twelfth District

**80.1205 San Luis Obispo Bay, CA.** A line drawn from the southernmost extremity of Fossil Point to the seaward extremity of Whaler Is. Breakwater.

**80.1210 Estero-Morro Bay, CA.** A line drawn from the seaward extremity of the Morro Bay East Breakwater to the Morro Bay West Breakwater Light.

**80.1215 Monterey Harbor, CA.** A line drawn from Monterey Harbor Light 6 to the northern extremity of Monterey Municipal Wharf 2.

**80.1220 Moss Landing Harbor, CA.** A line drawn from the seaward extremity of the pier located 0.3 mile south of Moss Landing Harbor Entrance to the seaward extremity of the Moss Landing Harbor North Breakwater.

**80.1225 Santa Cruz Harbor, CA.** A line drawn from the seaward extremity of the Santa Cruz Harbor East Breakwater to Santa Cruz Harbor West Breakwater Light; thence to Santa Cruz Light.

**80.1230 Pillar Point Harbor, CA.** A line drawn from Pillar Point Harbor Light 6 to Pillar Point Harbor Entrance Light.

**80.1250 San Francisco Harbor, CA.** A straight line drawn from Point Bonita Light through Mile Rocks Light to the shore.

**80.1255 Bodega and Tomales Bay, CA.** (a) An east-west line drawn from Sand Point to Avalis Beach.

(b) A line drawn from the seaward extremity of Bodega Harbor North Breakwater to Bodega Harbor Entrance Light 1. [CGD 81-017, 46 FR 28154, May 26, 1981]

**80.1260 Albion River, CA.** A line drawn on an axis of 030° true through Albion River Light 1 across Albion Cove.

**80.1265 Noyo River, CA.** A line drawn from Noyo River Entrance Daybeacon 4 to Noyo River Entrance Light 5.

**80.1270 Arcata-Humboldt Bay, CA.** A line drawn from Humboldt Bay Entrance Light 4 to Humboldt Bay Entrance Light 3.

**80.1275 Crescent City Harbor, CA.** A line drawn from Crescent City Entrance Light to the southeasternmost extremity of Whaler Island.

## PACIFIC COAST — Thirteenth District

**80.1305 Chetco River, OR.** A line drawn across the seaward extremities of the Chetco River Entrance Jetties. [CGD 81-017, 46 FR 28154, May 26, 1981]

**80.1310 Rogue River, OR.** A line drawn across the seaward extremities of the Rogue River Entrance Jetties.

**80.1315 Coquille River, OR.** A line drawn across the seaward extremities of the Coquille River Entrance Jetties.

**80.1320 Coos Bay, OR.** A line drawn across the seaward extremities of the Coos Bay Entrance Jetties.

**80.1325 Umpqua River, OR.** A line drawn across the seaward extremities of the Umpqua Entrance Jetties.

**80.1330 Siuslaw River, OR.** A line drawn across the seaward extremities of the Siuslaw River Entrance Jetties.

**80.1335 Alsea Bay, OR.** A line drawn from the seaward shoreline on the north of the Alsea Bay Entrance 165° true across the channel entrance.

**80.1340 Yaquina Bay, OR.** A line drawn across the seaward extremities of Yaquina Bay Entrance Jetties.

**80.1345 Depoe Bay, OR.** A line drawn across the Depoe Bay Channel entrance parallel with the general trend of the highwater shoreline.

**80.1350 Netarts Bay, OR.** A line drawn from the northernmost extremity of the shore on the south side of Netarts Bay north to the opposite shoreline.

**80.1355 Tillamook Bay, OR.** A line drawn across the seaward extremities of the Tillamook Bay Entrance Jetties.

**80.1360 Nehalem River, OR.** A line drawn approximately parallel with the general trend of the highwater shoreline across the Nehalem River Entrance.

**80.1365 Columbia River Entrance, OR/WA.** A line drawn from the seaward extremity of the Columbia River North Jetty (above water) 155° true to the seaward extremity of the Columbia River South Jetty (above water).

**80.1370 Willapa Bay, WA.** A line drawn from Willapa Bay Light 169.8° true to the westernmost tripod charted 1.6 miles south of Leadbetter Point.

**80.1375 Grays Harbor, WA.** A line drawn across the seaward extremities (above water) of the Grays Harbor Entrance Jetties.

**80.1380 Quillayute River, WA.** A line drawn from the seaward extremity of the Quillayute River Entrance East Jetty to the overhead power cable tower charted on James Island; thence a straight line through Quillayute River Entrance Light 3 to the shoreline.

**80.1385 Strait of Juan de Fuca.** The 72 COLREGS shall apply on all waters of the Strait of Juan de Fuca.

**80.1390 Haro Strait and Strait of Georgia.** The 72 COLREGS shall apply on all waters of the Haro Strait and the Strait of Georgia.

**80.1395 Puget Sound and Adjacent Waters.** The 72 COLREGS shall apply on all waters of Puget Sound and adjacent waters, including Lake Union, Lake Washington, Hood Canal, and all tributaries. [CGD 81-087, 46 FR 61456, Dec. 17, 1981]

## PACIFIC ISLANDS — Fourteenth District

**80.1410 Hawaiian Island Exemption from General Rule.** Except as provided elsewhere in this part for Mamala Bay and Kaneohe Bay on Oahu; Port Allen and Nawiliwili Bay on Kauai; Kahului Harbor on Maui; and Kawailae and Hilo Harbors on Hawaii, the 72 COLREGS shall apply on all other bays, harbors, and lagoons of the Hawaiian Islands (including Midway).

**80.1420 Mamala Bay, Oahu, HI.** A line drawn from Barbers Point Light to Diamond Head Light.

**80.1430 Kaneohe Bay, Oahu, HI.** A straight line drawn from Pyramid Rock Light across Kaneohe Bay through the center of Mokolii Island to the shoreline.

**80.1440 Port Allen, Kauai, HI.** A line drawn from Hanapepe Light to Hanapepe Bay Breakwater Light. [CGD 81-017, 46 FR 28154, May 26, 1981]

**80.1450 Nawiliwili Harbor, Kauai, HI.** A line drawn from Nawiliwili Harbor Breakwater Light to Kukii Point Light.

**80.1460 Kahului Harbor, Maui, HI.** A line drawn from Kahului Harbor Entrance East Breakwater Light to Kahului Harbor Entrance West Breakwater Light.

**80.1470 Kawaihae Harbor, Hawaii, HI.** A line drawn from Kawaihae Light to the seaward extremity of the Kawaihae South Breakwater.

**80.1480 Hilo Harbor, Hawaii, HI.** A line drawn from the seaward extremity of the Hilo Breakwater 265° true (as an extension of the seaward side of the breakwater) to the shoreline 0.2 nautical mile north of Alealea Point.

**80.1490 Apra Harbor, U.S. Territory of Guam.** A line drawn from the westernmost extremity of Orote Island to the westernmost extremity of Glass Breakwater.

**80.1495 U.S. Pacific Island Possessions.** The 72 COLREGS shall apply on the bays, harbors, lagoons, and waters surrounding the U.S. Pacific Island Possessions of American Samoa, Baker, Howland, Jarvis, Johnson, Palmyra, Swains and Wakelslands.

## ALASKA — Seventeenth District

**80.1705 Alaska.** The 72 COLREGS shall apply on all the sounds, bays, harbors, and inlets of Alaska. [CGD 81-017, 46 FR 28154, May 26, 1981]

## CANADIAN RULES

Canada has a set of Rules that modify or supplement the International COLREGS.

The Canadian Rules apply to all vessels within "Canadian waters or fishing zones" and to Canadian vessels in all waters.The first section comprises the Canadian Modifications to the International Rules and must be read along with the appropriate International Rule. The second section comprises all additional rules, and may be read on their own. In both cases, the Canadian Rules usually add to, rather than change, an International Rule.

### CANADIAN RULES THAT DIFFER FROM COLREGS

**Rule 6. Safe Speed — *Canadian Modification***

(c) In the Canadian waters of a roadstead, harbor, river, lake or inland waterway, every vessel passing another vessel or work that includes a dredge, tow, grounded vessel or wreck shall proceed with caution at a speed that will not adversely affect the vessel or work being passed, and shall comply with any relevant instruction or direction contained in any Notice to Mariners or Notice to Shipping.

(d) For the purpose of paragraph (c), where it cannot be determined with certainty that a passing vessel will not adversely affect another vessel or work described in that paragraph, the passing vessel shall proceed with caution at the minimum speed at which she can be kept on her course.

(e) In the Canadian waters of a roadstead, harbor, river, lake or inland waterway, every vessel shall navigate with caution and shall comply with any relevant instruction or direction contained in any Notice to Mariners or Notice to Shipping where abnormal water levels, ice conditions or a casualty to a vessel or aid to navigation may

> (i) make navigation difficult or hazardous,

> (ii) cause damage to property, or

> (iii) block the navigational channel.

**Rule 9. Narrow Channels — *Canadian Modification***

(h) Notwithstanding paragraph (d), in the waters of the Great Lakes Basin, a vessel that can safely navigate only within a narrow channel or fairway shall, if a crossing vessel impedes her passage, use the sound signal prescribed in Rule 34(d) if in doubt as to the intention of the crossing vessel.

(i) Notwithstanding paragraph (e), in a narrow channel or fairway in the waters of the Great Lakes Basin, a vessel shall indicate its intention to overtake, or its agreement to being overtaken, as the case may be, by sounding the whistle signals prescribed in Rule 34(j).

(j) In the Canadian waters of a narrow channel or fairway a barge or an inconspicuous, partly submerged vessel or object shall not be navigated, moored or anchored so as to impede the safe passage of any other vessel or object using those waters.

(k) Notwithstanding paragraph (a) and Rule 14(a), in the Canadian waters of a narrow channel or fairway where there is a current or tidal stream and two power-driven vessels are meeting each other from opposite directions so as to involve risk of collision:

> (i) the vessel proceeding with the current or tidal stream shall be the stand-on vessel

and shall propose the place of passage and shall indicate the side on which she intends to pass by sounding the appropriate signal prescribed in Rule 34(a) or (g),

(ii) the vessel proceeding against the current or tidal stream shall keep out of the way of the vessel proceeding with the current or tidal stream and shall hold as necessary to permit safe passing, and

(iii) the vessel proceeding against the current or tidal stream shall promptly reply to the signal referred to in subparagraph (I) with the same signal, if she is in agreement, and with the sound signal prescribed in Rule 34(d), if she is in doubt.

## Rule 10. Traffic Separation Schemes — *Canadian Modification*

(m) Traffic separation schemes adopted by the Organization shall be described in Notices to Mariners or Notices to Shipping.

(m.1) Subject to paragraphs (o) and (p), paragraphs (a) to (l) apply to any routing system described in Notices to Mariners or Notices to Shipping.

(n) Every power-driven vessel of more than 20 meters in length shall use the route within a traffic separation scheme or a routing system by which it can safely proceed to its destination.

(o) Paragraphs (b), (c) and (h) do not apply to a vessel engaged in fishing with nets, lines, trawls, trolling lines or other fishing apparatus in or near a routing system located in Canadian waters or fishing zones.

(p) Paragraphs (b), (c), (e) and (h) do not apply to a vessel engaged in laying, servicing or picking up a navigation mark, submarine cable or pipeline, dredging, surveying, underwater operations or launching or recovering aircraft in or near a routing system located in Canadian waters or fishing zones, where that vessel

(i) does not prevent other vessels that use the route from navigating safely,

(ii) identifies herself to approaching vessels and informs them of the location and nature of the operation and of her intentions, and

(iii) informs the Department, as soon as possible before the commencement of the operation of

(A) the nature, location and duration of the operation, and

(B) any cautionary advice necessary concerning the operation.

(q) A vessel making a transatlantic voyage shall, as far as practicable, avoid crossing the Grand Banks of Newfoundland north of latitude 43° North.

## Rule 13. Overtaking — *Canadian Modification*

(e) Notwithstanding paragraph (b), in the waters of the Great Lakes Basin, a vessel shall be deemed to be overtaking another vessel when at night she would be able to see

(i) the sternlight of the other vessel, or

(ii) in the case of a power-driven vessel lighted in accordance with Rule 23(c) or (e), the all-round white light or lights of the other vessel but not her sidelights.

## Rule 15. Crossing Situation — *Canadian Modification*

(b) Notwithstanding paragraph (a), in Canadian waters, a vessel crossing a river shall keep out of the way of a power-driven vessel ascending or descending the river, except on the St. Lawrence River northeast of "Île Rouge."

## Rule 21. Definitions — *Canadian Modification*

(g) "Special flashing light" means a yellow light flashing at regular intervals at a frequency of 50 to 70 flashes per minute, placed as far forward and as nearly as practicable on the fore and aft centerline of a vessel and showing an unbroken light over an arc of the horizon of not less than 180 degrees nor more than 225 degrees and so fixed as to show the light from right ahead to abeam and not more than 22.5 degrees abaft the beam on either side of the vessel.

(h) "Blue flashing light" means a blue all-round light flashing at regular intervals at a frequency of 50 to 70 flashes per minute.

### Rule 22. Visibility of Lights — *Canadian Modification*

(e) In vessels being pushed ahead, irrespective of length:

—a special flashing light, 2 miles.

(f) In any government or police vessel:

—a blue flashing light, 2 miles.

### Rule 23. Power-driven Vessels Underway — *Canadian Modification*

(d) Rule 23(c)(ii) does not apply to a Canadian power-driven vessel in any waters or to a non-Canadian power-driven vessel in the Canadian waters of a roadstead, harbor, river, lake or inland waterway.

(e) In the waters of the Great Lakes Basin, a power-driven vessel when underway may, instead of the second masthead light and sternlight prescribed in paragraph (a), carry, in the position of the second masthead light, a single all-round white light or two such lights placed not over 800 millimeters apart horizontally, one on either side of the keel and so arranged that one or the other or both shall be visible from any angle of approach and for the same minimum range as the masthead lights.

### Rule 24. Towing and Pushing — *Canadian Modification*

(j) Notwithstanding paragraphs (e) and (h), within Canadian waters or fishing zones, where it is impracticable for a barge being towed to comply with paragraph (e) the barge shall exhibit the lights prescribed in paragraph (k) to (m).

(k) Subject to paragraphs (l) to (n), every barge shall carry one all-round white light at each end of the barge.

(l) Where two or more barges are grouped together, the group may be lighted as a single barge.

(m) Subject to paragraph (n), where two or more barges are grouped together, the total length of the group exceeds 100 meters and the group is lighted as a single barge, the group shall carry an all-round white light located as closely as possible at the middle point of the group, in addition to the lights prescribed in paragraph (k).

(n) A barge being pushed ahead shall carry, instead of the all-round white lights prescribed in paragraphs (k) and (m), white lights that show an unbroken light over an arc of the horizon of 225 degrees and are fixed so as to show the light from right ahead to 22.5 degrees abaft the beam on either side of the barge.

(o) Notwithstanding paragraph (c), in the waters of the Great Lakes Basin, a power-driven vessel when pushing ahead or towing alongside shall exhibit two towing lights in a vertical line instead of the sternlight prescribed in paragraph (c).

(p) In the waters of the Great Lakes Basin, a special flashing light shall be exhibited at the forward end of a vessel or vessels being pushed ahead, in addition to the lights prescribed in paragraphs (f) and (n).

### Rule 25. Sailing Vessels Underway and Vessels Under Oars — *Canadian Modification*

(f) Notwithstanding paragraph (e), in the Canadian waters of a roadstead, harbor, river, lake or inland waterway, a vessel of less than 12 meters in length proceeding under sail when also being propelled by machinery is not required to exhibit a conical shape, apex downwards, but may do so.

**Rules**

## Rule 26. Fishing Vessels — *Canadian Modification*

(f) Notwithstanding paragraph (d), a vessel engaged in fishing in Canadian waters and fishing zones in close proximity to another vessel or vessels engaged in fishing

(i) may, if it is less than 20 meters in length or fishing with purse seine gear, and

(ii) shall, if it is 20 meters or more in length and fishing other than with purse seine gear,

exhibit and sound the appropriate signals prescribed in Annex II.

## Rule 28. Vessels Constrained by their Draught — *Canadian Modification*

(b) Notwithstanding paragraph (a), in the Canadian waters of a roadstead, harbor, river, lake or inland waterway, no vessel shall exhibit three all-round red lights in a vertical line or a cylinder.

## Rule 30. Anchored Vessels and Vessels Aground — *Canadian Modification*

(g) In the Canadian waters of a roadstead, harbor, river, lake or inland waterway, a barge or an inconspicuous, partly submerged vessel or object may, when at anchor, exhibit the appropriate all-round white lights prescribed by paragraphs 24(g) and (k) to (m) instead of the lights prescribed by paragraphs (a) to (c) of this Rule.

(h) Notwithstanding this Rule, in the Canadian waters of a roadstead, harbor, river, lake or inland waterway, a barge or an inconspicuous, partly submerged vessel or object, when at anchor, is not required to exhibit any light while located within a recognized mooring, storage or booming area that is not an area in or near a narrow channel or fairway or where other vessels normally navigate.

## Rule 33. Equipment for Sound Signals — *Canadian Modification*

(c) Notwithstanding paragraph (b), in the Canadian waters of a roadstead, harbor, river, lake or inland waterway, a vessel that is

(i) less than 12 meters in length,

(ii) built or converted for the purpose of pushing or pulling any floating object, and

(iii) not solely employed in yarding or warping operations,

shall carry the sound signal appliances prescribed in paragraph (a) for a vessel of 12 meters or more in length.

## Rule 34. Maneuvering and Warning Signals — *Canadian Modification*

(g) Notwithstanding paragraph (a), in the waters of the Great Lakes Basin, when power-driven vessels are in sight of one another and meeting or crossing at a distance within half a mile of each other, each vessel underway, when maneuvering as authorized or required by these Rules

(i) shall indicate that maneuver by the following signals on her whistle:

—one short blast to mean "I intend to leave you on my port side",

—two short blasts to mean "I intend to leave you on my starboard side", and

—three short blasts to mean "I am operating astern propulsion", and

(ii) shall, upon hearing the one or two blast signal, referred to in subparagraph (i), of the other vessel indicate her agreement by sounding the same whistle signal and taking the steps necessary to effect a safe passing. If, however, for any cause, a vessel on hearing a one or two blast signal referred to in subparagraph (i) doubts the safety of the proposed maneuver, she shall sound the signal specified in paragraph (d) and each vessel shall take appropriate precautionary action until a safe passing agreement is made.

(h) Notwithstanding paragraph (b), in the waters of the Great Lakes Basin, a vessel may supplement the whistle signals prescribed in paragraph (g) by light signals

    (i) that have the following significance:

        —one flash to mean "I intend to leave you on my port side",

        —two flashes to mean "I intend to leave you on my starboard side",

        —three flashes to mean "I am operating astern propulsion", and

    (ii) the duration of which shall be about one second for each flash.

(i) The light used for a signal referred to in paragraph (h), shall, if fitted, be one all-round white or yellow light, visible at a minimum range of 2 miles, synchronized with the whistle signal referred to in paragraph (g), and shall comply with section 12 of Annex I.

(j) Notwithstanding paragraph (c), in the waters of the Great Lakes Basin, when power-driven vessels are in sight of one another in a narrow channel or fairway,

    (i) the vessel intending to overtake another shall, in compliance with Rule 9(i), indicate her intention by the following signals on her whistle:

        —one short blast to mean "I intend to overtake you on your starboard side",

        —two short blasts to mean "I intend to overtake you on your port side",

    (ii) the vessel about to be overtaken when acting in accordance with Rule 9(i) shall, if in agreement, sound the same signal as given by the other vessel. If in doubt, she shall sound the signal prescribed in paragraph (d).

(k) In the Canadian waters of a roadstead, harbor, river, lake or inland waterway, a power-driven vessel that is leaving a dock or berth shall give a signal of one prolonged blast.

(l) Notwithstanding this Rule and Rule 9, in the Canadian waters of a roadstead, harbor, river, lake or inland waterway, a vessel may use a bridge-to-bridge radiotelephone instead of the prescribed whistle signals to reach agreement in a meeting, crossing or overtaking situation. If agreement is not reached, then whistle signals shall be exchanged in a timely manner and shall prevail.

## Rule 35. Sound Signals in Restricted Visibility — *Canadian Modification*

(k) Notwithstanding paragraph (i), in the Canadian waters of a roadstead, harbor, river, lake or inland waterway, a vessel that is

    (i) less than 12 meters in length,

    (ii) built or converted for the purpose of pushing or pulling any floating object, and

    (iii) not located within a recognized mooring, storage or booming area

shall sound the signals prescribed for a vessel of 12 meters or more in length.

## Rule 38. Exemptions — *Canadian Modification*

(i) For the purposes of paragraphs (d), (e), (f) and (g), the nine years referred to therein shall be considered to commence on July 15, 1977.

(j) Notwithstanding paragraph (i), the nine years referred to in paragraphs (d), (e), (f) and (g) shall be considered to commence on March 1, 1983 for vessels exclusively engaged in inland voyages.

(k) In the case of a vessel not required to be inspected under the Canada Shipping Act, the lights are exempted from compliance with these Regulations if they were,

    (i) before July 15, 1981, where the vessel is 20 meters or more in length, or

    (ii) before June 1, 1984, where the vessel is less than 20 meters in length,

constructed and installed in accordance with the Collision Regulations, as those Regulations read on July 31, 1974, or the Small Vessel Regulations, as those Regulations read on May 31, 1984.

# PART F  ADDITIONAL CANADIAN PROVISIONS

## Rule 39.  Special Signals for Dangerous Goods

In the Canadian waters of a roadstead, harbor, river, lake or inland waterway, a vessel that is taking in, discharging or carrying dangerous goods shall,

(a) when not underway, exhibit where it can best be seen, an all-round red light or the International Code flag "B"; and

(b) when underway, exhibit where it can best be seen, the International Code flag "B," but not an all-round red light.

## Rule 40.  Radar Reflectors

(a) Subject to paragraph (b), a vessel that is less than 20 meters in length or is constructed primarily of non-metallic materials shall be equipped with a passive radar reflector.

(b) Paragraph (a) does not apply where

(i) a vessel operates in limited traffic conditions, daylight, and favorable environmental conditions and where compliance is not essential for the safety of the vessel, or

(ii) the small size of the vessel or its operation away from radar navigation makes compliance impracticable.

(c) The radar reflector prescribed in paragraph (a) shall,

(i) be capable of performance through 360 degrees of azimuth and responsive to a radar frequency of 9.3 GHz (corresponding wave length 3.2 centimeters),

(ii) have an equivalent echoing area of 10 square meters measured perpendicularly to the main radar lobes,

(iii) be mounted or suspended higher than the superstructures and, if practicable, at a height of not less than 4 meters above the water,

(iv) be positioned and painted so as not to be visually prominent,

(v) be capable of maintaining its performance under the conditions of sea states, vibration, humidity and change of temperature likely to be experienced in the marine environment, and

(vi) be clearly marked so as to indicate any preferred orientation of mounting.

(d) The azimuthal polar diagram of the radar reflector prescribed in paragraph (a) shall have a response not less than minus 6 dB with reference to the maxima of the main radar lobes

(i) over a total angle of 240 degrees, and

(ii) within any arc of more than 10 degrees.

## Rule 41.  Transponders

(a) No vessel shall be fitted with a transponder that can transmit radar responder signals or radar beacon signals in the 3 or 10 centimeters marine radar bands unless the use of the transponder is authorized in writing by the Chairman.

(b) The Chairman may authorize the use of a transponder referred to in paragraph (a) if he is satisfied that the transponder will be used in a manner that will not interfere with or degrade the use of radar in navigation.

(c) An authorization referred to in paragraph (a) may contain such conditions as the Chairman considers necessary to ensure that the transponder will be used as described in paragraph (b).

(d) No person shall operate a transponder on a vessel except in accordance with the conditions, if any, contained in the authorization prescribed in paragraph (a).

## Rule 42. Additional Requirements for Exploration or Exploitation Vessels

(a) An exploration or exploitation vessel shall display identification panels bearing the name, identification letters or numerals of the vessel so that at least one panel is visible in any direction.

(b) The name, identification letters or numerals referred to in paragraph (a) shall be

(i) black,

(ii) not less than 1 meter in height,

(iii) displayed on a yellow background, and

(iv) easily visible in daylight and at night by the use of illumination or retro-reflecting material.

(c) Subject to paragraph (h), an exploration or exploitation vessel, when stationary and engaged in drilling or production operations, shall, in lieu of the lights or shapes required by these Rules, exhibit where it can best be seen from any direction a white light or a series of white lights located at an equal height above the water and operating in unison, which light or lights shall

(i) flash the morse letter "U" at intervals of not more than 15 seconds,

(ii) be installed at a height above the water of not less than 6 meters and not more than 30 meters so that at least one light shall remain visible to within 15 meters of the vessel,

(iii) be visible all round the horizon at a nominal range of 15 miles,

(iv) be powered by a reliable power source,

(v) be equipped with an auxiliary power source, and

(vi) be exhibited from 15 minutes before sunset until sunrise and at all times when the visibility in any direction is 2 miles or less.

(d) The horizontal and vertical extremities of an exploration or exploitation vessel that is stationary and engaged in drilling or production operations shall be adequately marked in compliance with the requirements set out in Transport Canada Standards Obstruction Markings (2nd ed.), 1987, TP 382, as amended from time to time.

(e) An exploration or exploitation vessel, when stationary and engaged in drilling or production operations, shall be equipped with a sound-signalling appliance that

(i) is powered by a reliable power source,

(ii) is provided with an auxiliary power source,

(iii) when operating, emits a rhythmic blast corresponding to the Morse letter "U" every 30 seconds,

(iv) has its maximum intensity at a frequency between 100 and 1 000 Hertz,

(v) has a usual range of at least 2 miles,

(vi) is installed at a height above the water of not less than 6 meters and not more than 30 meters, and

(vii) is so placed that the sound emitted is audible, when there is no wind, throughout the required range in all directions in a horizontal plane from the vessel.

(f) An exploration or exploitation vessel, when stationary and engaged in drilling or production operations, shall, whenever the visibility in any direction is 2 miles or less, operate the sound-signalling appliance described in paragraph (e) in lieu of the sound signal described in Rule 35.

(g) Every exploration or exploitation vessel shall comply with the relevant technical requirements contained in the Recommendations for the marking of offshore structures, November 1984, published by the International Association of Lighthouse Authorities

(IALA), as amended from time to time, and the nominal range of lights shall be computed in accordance with Appendix II of Recommendation for the Notation of Luminous Intensity and Range of Lights, 1967, published by the International Association of Lighthouse Authorities (IALA), as amended from time to time.

(h) In the Canadian waters of the Great Lakes Basin, the white light or series of white lights exhibited by an exploration or exploitation vessel when stationary and engaged in drilling or production operations shall have a range of visibility of between 8 and 15 miles.

## Rule 43. Safety Zones Around Exploration or Exploitation Vessels

(a) For the purpose of this Rule, with respect to an exploration or exploitation vessel that is in position for the purpose of exploring or exploiting the non-living natural resources of the sea bed, a safety zone is the area that extends from the outer extremities of the exploration or exploitation vessel to the greater of

(i) 500 meters in all directions, and

(ii) 50 meters beyond the boundaries of the anchor pattern of the vessel.

(b) The Chairman may establish a safety zone greater or smaller than the safety zone referred to in paragraph (a), where such a zone is reasonably related to the nature and function of the exploration or exploitation vessel.

(c) No vessel shall navigate within a safety zone.

(d) Paragraph (c) does not apply to a vessel that

(i) is in distress,

(ii) is attempting to save life or provide assistance to a vessel in distress,

(iii) is operated by or on behalf of the state having jurisdiction over the exploration or exploitation operations, or

(iv) has received permission from the person in charge of the exploration or exploitation vessel to enter the safety zone around that vessel.

(e) All vessels shall comply with any relevant instruction or direction with respect to a safety zone contained in a Notice to Mariners or Notice to Shipping.

## Rule 44. Ocean Data Acquisition Systems (ODAS)

(a) Every Canadian ODAS shall clearly display its identification number on an exterior surface where it can be clearly seen and, if practicable, shall display the name and address of the owner of the ODAS.

(b) Subject to paragraph (f), every ODAS shall be constructed or fitted with a passive radar reflector that has a radar response at least equivalent to a radar reflector required by Rule 40.

(c) Every ODAS that is designed to operate while floating with part of its structure extending above the water shall

(i) be colored yellow,

(ii) have a shape that cannot be confused with the shape of a navigational mark, and

(iii) where technically practicable,

(A) have a topmark consisting of a yellow "X" shape,

(B) exhibit a yellow light visible at a minimum range of five miles that gives a group of five flashes every 20 seconds, and

(C) be equipped with an appliance that emits a sound signal at intervals of not more than two minutes, which sound signal cannot be confused with any other signal prescribed by these Rules or with the sound signal of any aid to navigation in the vicinity of the ODAS.

(d) Subject to paragraph (f), every ODAS designed to operate under water, other than an ODAS referred to in paragraph (e), shall

(i) be escorted by a surface vessel that gives warning of the presence of the ODAS in accordance with Rule 27, or

(ii) have tethered to it a surface float that is marked, provides the radar response, is lighted and sounds the signals specified in paragraph (a) to (c).

(e) Every ODAS designed to operate when resting on the bottom of sea, lake or river with part of its structure extending above the water shall be marked, exhibit lights and shapes, and sound signals in the same manner as an exploration or exploitation vessel.

(f) Paragraphs (b) and (d) do not apply to an ODAS where

(i) the Chairman has determined that the ODAS does not constitute a potential danger to navigation by reason of

(A) it size, material, construction, area or method of operations,

(B) the nature and condition of the waters in the area of operation of the ODAS, and

(C) the use that is or might reasonably be expected to be made of those waters, and

(ii) the Chairman has given the owner of the ODAS notice in writing of that determination.

## Rule 45. Blue Flashing Light

(a) For the purposes of this Rule, "government ship" means a ship or vessel that is owned by and in the service of Her Majesty in right of Canada or of a province and any ship that is owned or operated by a federal, provincial, harbor, river, county or municipal police force (navire d'État).

(b) Any government ship may exhibit as an identification signal a blue flashing light where it

(i) is providing assistance in any waters to any vessel or other craft, aircraft or person that is threatened by grave and imminent danger and requires immediate assistance, or

(ii) is engaged in law enforcement duties in Canadian waters.

## Rule 46. Alternate System of Navigation Lights

(a) For the purposes of this Rule, "alternate system of navigation lights" means a system that includes masthead lights, sidelights, a sternlight and anchor lights (système de feux de navigation de relais).

(b) Subject to paragraph (d), every ship built on or after January 1, 1991 that is required to be inspected under the Act shall be fitted with an alternate system of navigation lights.

(c) Subject to paragraph (d), every ship built before January 1, 1991 that is required to be inspected under the Act shall, before January 1, 1996,

(i) if it is of 500 tons gross tonnage or more, be fitted with an alternate system of navigation lights, or

(ii) if it is of less than 500 tons gross tonnage, be fitted with or carry on board an alternate system of navigation lights.

(d) Paragraph (b) and subparagraph (c)(ii) do not apply to a vessel of less than 15 meters in length.

(d.1) For a ship referred to in paragraph (b) or subparagraph (c)(i), the alternate system of navigation lights shall be supplied by the main source of electric power of the ship and one other source of electric power with which the ship is required to be supplied by section 15 of Annex I.

(e) For a ship referred to in subparagraph (c)(ii), the alternate system of navigation lights shall

(i) be supplied by a source of electrical power with which the ship is required to be supplied by section 15 of Annex I, other than the main source of power of the ship, or

(ii) subject to paragraph (f), consist of nonelectric lights.

(f) Nonelectric lights shall not be used as alternate lights on

(i) a ship or barge whose cargo has volatile or explosive properties that could endanger the ship or barge and its crew, or

(ii) a ship engaged in towing or pushing a ship or barge whose cargo has volatile or explosive properties that could endanger the ships or barge and their respective crews.

## ANNEX I. Positioning and Technical Details of Lights and Shapes

### Annex I, Part 1. Definition — *Canadian Modification*

(b) The term "practical cut-off" means the point on an arc around a source of light at which the intensity of the light is reduced as follows:

(i) for vessels of less than 20 meters in length, where the intensity is reduced to 67 per cent of the minimum required intensity within 3 or 5 degrees as appropriate, outside the horizontal sectors referred to in section 9 of this Annex and described in Rule 21, practical cut-off occurs at the point at which the intensity is reduced to 10 per cent of the minimum required intensity within 20 degrees outside the horizontal sectors referred to in section 9 of this Annex and described in Rule 21,

(ii) for vessels of 20 meters or more in length, practical cut-off occurs at the point at which the intensity is reduced to 12.5 per cent of the minimum required intensity within 3 or 5 degrees, as appropriate, outside the horizontal sectors referred to in section 9 of this Annex and described in Rule 21.

### Annex I, Part 2. Vertical Positioning and Spacing of Lights — *Canadian Modification*

(l) Notwithstanding paragraph (a), in the waters of the Great Lakes Basin, on a power-driven vessel of 20 meters or more in length the masthead lights may be placed as follows:

(i) the forward masthead light, or if only one masthead light is carried, then that light, at a height above the hull of not less than 5 meters, and, if the breadth of the vessel exceeds 5 meters, then at a height above the hull of not less than such breadth, but the light need not be placed at a greater height above the hull than 8 meters,

(ii) where two masthead lights are carried, the after one shall be at least 2 meters vertically higher than the forward one.

(m) Notwithstanding paragraph (d), in the Canadian waters of a roadstead, harbor, river, lake or inland waterway, the masthead light or the all-round white light referred to in Rule 23(c), for a power-driven vessel of less than 12 meters in length shall be carried at least 1 meter higher than the sidelights.

(n) Notwithstanding paragraph (e), in the waters of the Great Lakes Basin, one of the two or three masthead lights prescribed for a power-driven vessel when engaged in towing or pushing another vessel shall be placed in the same position as the forward masthead light or the after masthead light, but where the light is carried on the aftermast the lowest after masthead light shall be at least 2 meters vertically higher than the forward masthead light.

(o) Notwithstanding paragraph (g), in the waters of the Great Lakes Basin, the sidelights of a power-driven vessel may be placed at least 1 meter lower than the forward masthead light but shall not be so low as to be interfered with by deck lights.

(p) Notwithstanding subparagraph (i)(i), in the waters of the Great Lakes Basin, where a vessel of 20 meters in length or more is required to carry two or three lights in a vertical line, these lights may be spaced not less than 1 meter apart, and the lowest of these lights shall, except where a towing light is required, be placed at a height of not less than 4 meters above the hull.

(q) The all-round white lights prescribed for an inconspicuous, partly submerged vessel or object or a barge in Rules 24(g) and (k), respectively, shall be carried at the same height and shall be placed at a height of not less than 2 meters above the water.

### Annex I, Part 3. Horizontal Positioning and Spacing of Lights — *Canadian Modification*

(e) Notwithstanding paragraph (a), in the waters of the Great Lakes Basin, where two masthead lights are prescribed for a power-driven vessel,

> (i) the horizontal distance between them shall be not less than one-quarter the length of the vessel but need not be more than 50 m, and

> (ii) the forward light shall be placed not more than one-half the length of the vessel away from the stem.

### Annex I, Part 4. Details of location of direction-indicating lights for fishing vessels, dredgers and vessels engaged in underwater operations — *Canadian Modification*

(a) The light indicating the direction of the outlying gear from a vessel engaged in fishing as prescribed in Rule 26(c)(ii) shall be placed at a horizontal distance of not less than 2 meters and not more than 6 meters away from the two all-round red and white lights. This light shall be placed not higher than the all-round white light prescribed in Rule 26(c)(i) and not lower than the sidelights.

(b) The lights and shapes on a vessel engaged in dredging or underwater operations to indicate the obstructed side and/or the side on which it is safe to pass, as prescribed in Rule 27(d)(i) and (ii), shall be placed at the maximum practical horizontal distance, but in no case less than 2 meters, from the lights or shapes prescribed in Rule 27(b)(i) and (ii). In no case shall the upper of these lights or shapes be at a greater height than the lower of the three lights or shapes prescribed in Rule 27(b)(i) and (ii).

### Annex I, Part 5. Screens for Lights Other than Sidelights — *Canadian Modification*

5.1 On power-driven vessels of less than 12 meters in length, constructed after July 31, 1983, the masthead light or the all-round light referred to in Rule 23(c), shall be screened to prevent direct illumination of the vessel forward of the operator's position.

### Annex I, Part 7. Color Specification of Lights — *Canadian Modification*

(v) Restricted Blue

> x 0.136 0.218 0.185 0.102

> y 0.040 0.142 0.175 0.105

### Annex I, Part 9. Horizontal Sectors — *Canadian Modification*

(c) Notwithstanding paragraph (b), in the waters of the Great Lakes Basin, the all-round white light or lights referred to in Rule 23(e) shall not be obscured.

### Annex I, Part 10. Vertical Sectors — *Canadian Modification*

(d) Notwithstanding paragraph (a), in the Canadian waters of a roadstead, harbor, river, lake or inland waterway, electric lights on unmanned barges need not comply with the vertical sector requirements but shall maintain the required minimum intensity on the horizontal.

### Annex I, Part 12. Maneuvering Light — *Canadian Modification*

(b) Notwithstanding paragraph (a), in the waters of the Great Lakes Basin, the maneuvering light referred to in Rule 34(h) shall be placed in the same fore and aft vertical plane as the masthead light or lights at not less than 1 meter vertically above or below the after masthead light and, where practicable, shall be placed at the minimum height of 1 meter vertically above the forward masthead light. On a vessel where only one masthead light is carried, the maneuver light, if fitted, shall be carried where it can best be seen and shall be located not less than 1 meter vertically apart from the masthead light.

### Annex I, Part 15. Approval — *Canadian Modification*

(b) For the purpose of paragraph (a), the appropriate Canadian authority is the Chairman.

15. Electric Power Supply

Electric power supplied to any navigation lights shall be in compliance with the provisions of the Transport Canada Ship Safety Electrical Standards, 1987, TP 127, as amended from time to time.

## ANNEX II  Additional Signals For Fishing Vessels Fishing In Close Proximity

### Annex II, Part 4. Special visual signals — *Canadian Modification*

In Canadian waters and fishing zones, a vessel engaged in pair-trawling shall exhibit at the foremast the International Code flag "T" during the daylight hours.

### Annex II, Part 5. Special sound signals — *Canadian Modification*

(a) In Canadian waters and fishing zones, a vessel engaged in fishing as described in Rule 26(f) shall, in any condition of visibility, sound the following signals on her whistle:

(i) 4 blasts in succession, namely, 2 prolonged blasts followed by 2 short blasts when shooting a net or gear,

(ii) 3 blasts in succession, namely, 2 prolonged blasts followed by 1 short blast when hauling a net or gear, and

(iii) 4 blasts in succession, namely, 1 short blast followed by 2 prolonged blasts, followed by 1 short blast when a net or gear is fast to an obstruction.

(b) When in or near an area of restricted visibility, the signals described in paragraph (a) shall be sounded 4 to 6 seconds after the sound signal prescribed in Rule 35(c).

## ANNEX III  Technical Details Of Sound Signal Appliances

### Annex III, Part 1. Whistles — *Canadian Modification*

(h) Notwithstanding paragraph (a), in the Canadian waters of a roadstead, harbor, river, lake or inland waterway, the upper limit of the frequency range referred to in that paragraph may be expanded to be within the range of 180-2 100 Hz (±1 per cent).

(i) Notwithstanding paragraph (c), in the Canadian waters of a roadstead, harbor, river, lake or inland waterway, the whistle on a vessel of 12 meters or more in length but less than 20 meters in length may provide, in the direction of the forward axis of the whistle and at a distance of 1 meter from it, a sound pressure level in at least one 1/3rd-octave band of not less than the appropriate figure shown below within the frequency range of 250-2 100 Hz (±1 per cent):

(i) 250-450 Hz—120 dB

(ii) 450-800 Hz—115 dB

(iii) 800-2 100 Hz—111 dB

(j) In the Canadian waters of a roadstead, harbor, river, lake or inland waterway, a power-driven vessel that is normally engaged in pushing ahead or towing alongside may, at any time, use a whistle whose characteristic falls within the limits prescribed in paragraph (b) for the longest normal length of the vessel and its tow.

### Annex III,  Part 3.  Approval — *Canadian Modification*

(b) For the purpose of paragraph (a), the appropriate Canadian authority is the Chairman.

## ANNEX IV  Distress Signals

**ANNEX IV** — *Canadian Modification* (add two parts)

4. In Canadian waters or fishing zones, in addition to the signals described in section 1, the following signals may be used or exhibited either together or separately to indicate distress and need of assistance:

(a) a square shape or anything resembling a square shape; and

(b) a high intensity white light flashing at regular intervals of 50 to 70 times per minute.

5. Notwithstanding section 2 and paragraph 4(b), a North Cardinal Buoy may use a quick flashing white light flashing at regular intervals of 60 times per minute.

# METRIC CONVERSION TABLE

Conversion of metric measurements used in the Rules to U.S. Customary Units

Metric Measure . . . . . . . . . . . . . . . .U.S. Customary

| | |
|---|---|
| 1000 Meters (M) . . . . . . . . . . . . . . . . . . . . .3280.8 ft. |
| 500 M . . . . . . . . . . . . . . . . . . . . .1640.4 ft. |
| 200 M . . . . . . . . . . . . . . . . . . . . .656.2 ft. |
| 150 M . . . . . . . . . . . . . . . . . . . . .492.1 ft. |
| 100 M . . . . . . . . . . . . . . . . . . . . .328.1 ft. |
| 75 M . . . . . . . . . . . . . . . . . . . . .246.1 ft. |
| 60 M . . . . . . . . . . . . . . . . . . . . .196.8 ft. |
| 50 M . . . . . . . . . . . . . . . . . . . . .164.0 ft. |
| 25 M . . . . . . . . . . . . . . . . . . . . .82.0 ft. |
| 20 M . . . . . . . . . . . . . . . . . . . . .65.6 ft. |
| 12 M . . . . . . . . . . . . . . . . . . . . .39.4 ft. |
| 10 M . . . . . . . . . . . . . . . . . . . . .32.8 ft. |
| 8 M . . . . . . . . . . . . . . . . . . . . .26.2 ft. |
| 7 M . . . . . . . . . . . . . . . . . . . . .23.0 ft. |
| 6 M . . . . . . . . . . . . . . . . . . . . .19.7 ft. |
| 5 M . . . . . . . . . . . . . . . . . . . . .16.4 ft. |
| 4.5 M . . . . . . . . . . . . . . . . . . . . .14.8 ft. |
| 4.0 M . . . . . . . . . . . . . . . . . . . . .13.1 ft. |
| 3.5 M . . . . . . . . . . . . . . . . . . . . .11.5 ft. |
| 2.5 M . . . . . . . . . . . . . . . . . . . . .8.2 ft. |
| 2.0 M . . . . . . . . . . . . . . . . . . . . .6.6 ft. |
| 1.5 M . . . . . . . . . . . . . . . . . . . . .4.9 ft. |
| 1 M . . . . . . . . . . . . . . . . . . . . .3.3 ft. |
| 0.9 M . . . . . . . . . . . . . . . . . . . . .35.4 in. |
| 0.6 M . . . . . . . . . . . . . . . . . . . . .23.6 in. |
| 0.5 M . . . . . . . . . . . . . . . . . . . . .19.7 in. |
| 300 Millimeters (mm) . . . . . . . . . . . . . . . . . . . . .11.8 in. |
| 200 mm . . . . . . . . . . . . . . . . . . . . .7.9 in. |

*Most vessels plying the coastal waters of North America are subject to international, federal, and state regulations. In this chapter we present some of the more important regulations for our readership. Most are laws of the United States, and you should consider them so unless otherwise noted. Some are referred to and elaborated upon in subsequent chapters; they are specifically noted.*

## U.S. COAST GUARD SAFETY EQUIPMENT

This section covers the minimum requirements needed to satisfy United States Coast Guard regulations. Many boaters, especially those venturing offshore, will want to carry additional items. At the very least, most boats should carry backup supplies of flares in case any of them must be used (or in case any fail to work properly).

To meet U.S. Coast Guard standards, all equipment must be Coast Guard approved; approved equipment will be labeled as such. There is no prohibition against carrying *additional* non-approved equipment.

In addition to the equipment listed below, all vessels must comply with the Navigation Rules regarding navigation lights and sound signals. Refer to Chapter 1, *Navigation Rules,* for this information.

## PERSONAL FLOTATION DEVICES (PFDs)

PFDs must be Coast Guard approved and in "good and serviceable" condition. They should be the appropriate size for each person wearing them, must be readily accessible, and must be removed from any plastic or other wrapping. Obviously, they should not be stored in locked or remote lockers. Other gear should not be stored on top of PFDs. All throwable devices must be instantly available.

When applicable, it is important to buy PFDs that are specifically designed for small children. Most adult-sized flotation devices do not fit a smaller person properly and, in fact, may cause the person wearing one to float in a dangerous position. Some states require that PFDs be worn by children of specific ages under certain conditions. Check with your state boating safety officials.

Remember, PFDs will keep you from sink-ing, but not necessarily from drowning. Take the time to select a properly sized PFD to ensure a safe fit. Testing your PFD in shallow water or a guarded swimming pool is a good and reassuring practice.

Though not required by law, it is advisable to wear a PFD at all times when underway. A point often overlooked is the great danger present in using small dinghies away from the large boat. Small boats are inherently less stable and seaworthy than larger ones. PFDs are required on board all vessels large and small, except that there are some federal and state exemptions for racing kayaks, wind surfers, and the like.

### Types Of PFDs

**Type I PFDs** are designed as offshore lifejackets. They provide more buoyancy than other types and are designed to turn an unconscious wearer in the water to a face-up position. Type I jackets come in sizes for adults and children. The smaller jackets provide a minimum of 11 pounds of buoyancy; the larger jackets provide at least 22 pounds of buoyancy.

**Type II PFDs** are designed as near-shore lifejackets and, although they will turn some unconscious wearers to a face-up position in the water, the turning action is not as pronounced as with Type I PFDs. Adult sizes provide at least 15.5 pounds of buoyancy; medium children's sizes provide about 11 pounds. Small children's sizes provide at least 7 pounds of buoyancy.

**Type III PFDs** are to be used in near-shore waters when there is a good chance of a quick rescue. Wearers will usually have to turn themselves face-up in the water and may have to lean back to avoid turning face-down. Type IIIs have the same minimum buoyancy as Type IIs and come in many types and styles. They are often designed with fashion in mind, as well as safety. Float coats and vest styles can often be worn to provide extra warmth in addition to safety.

**Type IV PFDs** are throwable devices intended for use in near-shore waters. They are not designed to be worn in the water. The most common type is the popular flotation cushion, which is often used in dinghies and small craft. Horseshoe buoys, another Type IV PFD, are often found on the stern pulpits of offshore boats. These devices often remain in the sun for long periods and should be inspected frequently for wear. **Note that Type IV PFDs no longer fulfill the PFD requirement for small boats.**

**Type V PFDs** are special-use devices designed for particular water activities. They may be carried instead of another PFD only if used according to the approval condition on that label. These devices include deck suits, work vests, board sailing vests, and HYBRID PFDs. A typical use is aboard offshore oil platforms where a normal PFD would be too bulky or too fragile.

**HYBRID PFDs** are the least bulky of all. They incorporate both inherent buoyancy and inflatable chambers to provide additional buoyancy. Their performance is equal to a Type I, II, or III PFD (as noted on the PFD label) when inflated. Hybrid PFDs must be worn when underway to be acceptable.

### PFD Requirements

**Boats less than 16 feet in length** (including canoes and kayaks of any length) must carry at least one Type I, II, III, or V PFD for each person on board.

**Boats longer than 16 feet** must carry at least one Type I, II, III, or V PFD for each person on board. In addition, at least one Type IV (throwable device) must be carried.

**Note:** If a Type V device is used to count toward requirements, it must be worn.

Federal regulations require PFDs on canoes and kayaks of any size; they are not required on racing shells, rowing skulls, or racing kayaks. State laws may vary.

**Water-skiers** are considered to be aboard the vessel and PFDs are required for them. It is advisable for skiers to wear PFDs that are designed to withstand the potential impact of a fall at high speed.

State laws may differ and be more strict. Some states require skiers to wear a PFD; others may require all children under a specified age to wear a PFD.

### Visual Distress Signals

See Chapter 8, *Safety,* for more information on "Distress and Rescue."

**Coast Guard Requirements**. All vessels used on coastal waters, the Great Lakes, territorial seas, and those waters connected directly to them, up to a point where a body of water is less than two miles wide, must be equipped with U.S.C.G. approved visual distress signals. Vessels owned in the United States operating on the high seas must be equipped with U.S.C.G. approved visual distress signals. The following vessels are not required to carry day signals, but must carry night signals when operating from sunset to sunrise:

(a) Recreational boats less than 16 feet in length;

(b) Boats participating in events such as races, regattas, or parades;

(c) Open sailboats, with no engines and under 26 feet long; and

(d) Manually propelled boats.

**Non-pyrotechnic Devices.** These include a three-foot square orange distress flag with a black square above a black ball (day use only), and an electric distress light that automatically flashes the international SOS signal (night use only). The international SOS signal is three short flashes, followed by three long flashes, followed by three more short flashes (• • • – – – • • •). When flashed four to six times a minutes, this is an unmistakable distress signal, well known to many boaters. These non-pyrotechnic devices must be Coast Guard approved.

**Pyrotechnic Devices.** Again, all of these devices must be Coast Guard approved and be within their marked service life. The four basic types of pyrotechnic devices are:

(a) Handheld red flares;

(b) Orange smoke, handheld or floating (day use only);

(c) Aerial red meteors, fired from a flare gun or a self-contained launcher; and

(d) Parachute flares, fired from a flare gun or a self-contained launcher.

Boats must carry a minimum of three day and night flares or their equivalents to meet requirements; for greater safety, carry a larger number.

**Warning:** Some states, and several countries, consider flare guns as firearms. Check with state authorities or customs officials before carrying these launchers.

**Regulations**

### Notes on flares:

Many types of flares meet the minimum requirements for distress signals, but recent tests indicate a great difference in performance among the various types. As with most things, the more you spend, the better the results. The common 12-gauge flare pistol will launch meteors up to about 250 feet. A 25mm gun can launch either meteors or parachute flares up to 375 feet. Several types of handheld parachute flare launchers can achieve altitudes near 1,000 feet. The higher the launch, the greater the range of visibility. Parachute flares may be visible for up to a minute after launch; meteors last only briefly. The farther from land you travel, the better your distress signals should be. Always carry more than the minimum required.

SOLAS (Safety of Life at Sea) approved flares meet stringent requirements and are preferred for offshore use. There are SOLAS approved devices on the market that may not carry Coast Guard approval. They cannot be used to meet the legal requirements, even though they are excellent distress signals.

Each type of distress signal may come in to play during a rescue. Meteors, or parachute flares, could be used to attract attention, either day or night. Do not waste your limited supply of flares; do not launch one unless you are sure that there is someone to see it — a vessel or low-flying aircraft. Handheld flares or orange smoke could be useful in directing rescue vessels to your location. Orange smoke is particularly useful in attracting aircraft during daylight hours.

Great care should always be taken with any pyrotechnic signal. These devices produce a very hot flame, and the ash and slag can cause injury or ignite flammable material. Handheld flares are particularly notorious for dropping red-hot slag. If possible, put on leather gloves before igniting handheld flares. Always point the devices away from the vessel and downwind. The Coast Guard recommends firing flares at an angle of about 60 degrees above the horizon in calm winds. As the wind increases you may fire the flare closer to the vertical. Never fire the device straight up — watch out for masts and rigging above your head! Look away from the device before firing.

When pyrotechnic devices reach their expiration date they may no longer be used to meet the Coast Guard requirements. Most boaters keep these expired devices as backups to their fresh supply. If expired flares are removed from the boat, make sure that they are disposed of properly. Turn them over to the fire department, police, boating officials, or the Coast Guard Auxiliary. Never "test" fire flares from a boat without the express permission of the Coast Guard; regulations expressly forbid the display of flares except when assistance is needed.

### Fire Extinguishers

Coast Guard approved fire extinguishers are required on boats where the following conditions exist:

(a) Inboard engines are used;

(b) Fuel is stored in closed compartments;

(c) Portable fuel tanks are stored in closed compartments;

(d) Boats with double bottoms not sealed or filled with flotation material;

(e) Closed living spaces;

(f) Flammable materials stowed in closed compartments;

(g) Permanent fuel tanks, or portable tanks that can't be lifted by those aboard.

In practice, most boats with any type of fuel aboard need to carry at least one fire extinguisher. Most boaters will want to carry several.

Extinguishers are classified by a letter and number symbol. The letter indicates the type of fire the unit is designed to extinguish. (Type B, for example, is designed to extinguish flammable liquids such as gasoline, oil, and grease.) The number indicates the relative size of the extinguisher (minimum extinguishing agent weight).

Coast Guard approved extinguishers are handportable, either B-I or B-II classification, and have a specific marine mounting bracket. It is recommended that the extinguishers be mounted in a readily accessible position.

| Class | Foam | Dry $CO_2$ | Chemical | Halon |
|-------|------|------------|----------|-------|
|       | gals | lbs        | lbs      | lbs   |
| B-I   | 1.25 | 4          | 2        | 2.5   |
| B-II  | 2.5  | 15         | 10       | 10    |

All extinguishers must be periodically inspected to make sure they are fully charged and all seals are secure. Pressure gauges should be in the operable range. Weigh extinguishers annually to be sure that the minimum weight is as stated on the extinguisher label. Generally, any use of an extinguisher means it should be replaced or recharged.

Halon units must be inspected and tagged frequently. Their pressure gauges are not accurate indicators of the state of charge.

**Boats less than 26 feet long** must have one type of B-I extinguisher.

**Boats 26 feet to less than 40 feet long** must have at least two B-I extinguishers or one B-II. With an approved fixed system (nonportable, automatic extinguishers), only one additional B-I type need be carried.

**Boats 40 feet to 65 feet long** must carry at least three B-I extinguishers or one B-II and one B-I. If an approved fixed system is installed, two B-I types, or one B-II, will meet the portable extinguisher requirement.

## Ventilation

All boats that use gasoline for electrical generation, mechanical power, or propulsion are required to be equipped with a ventilation system.

**A natural ventilation system** is required for each compartment in a boat that:

1. contains a permanently installed gasoline engine;
2. has openings between it and a compartment that requires ventilation;
3. contains a permanently installed fuel tank and an electrical component that is not ignition-protected;
4. contains a fuel tank that vents into that compartment (including a portable tank); and
5. contains a nonmetallic fuel tank.

A natural ventilation system consists of a supply opening or duct from the atmosphere (located on the exterior surface of the boat) or from a ventilated compartment or from a compartment that is open to the atmosphere, and an exhaust opening into another ventilated compartment or an exhaust duct to the atmosphere.

Each exhaust opening or exhaust duct must originate in the lower one-third of the compartment. Each supply opening or

supply duct and each exhaust opening or duct in a compartment must be above the normal accumulation of bilge water.

**A powered ventilation system** is required for each compartment in a boat that has a permanently installed gasoline engine with a cranking motor for remote starting.

A powered ventilation system consists of one or more exhaust blowers. Each intake duct for an exhaust blower must be in the lower one-third of the compartment and above the normal accumulation of bilge water.

For boats built prior to 1980, there was no requirement for a powered ventilation system; however, some boats were equipped with a blower.

The Coast Guard Ventilation Standard, a manufacturer requirement, applies to all boats built on or after August 1, 1980. Some builders began manufacturing boats in compliance with the Ventilation Standard as early as August 1978. If your boat was built on or after August 1, 1978, it might have been equipped with either (1) a natural ventilation system or, (2) both a natural ventilation system and a powered ventilation system. If your boat bears a label with the words "This boat complies with U.S. Coast Guard safety standards," etc., it is probable that the design of your boat's ventilation system meets applicable regulations.

Manufacturers of boats built after 1980 with remote starters are required to display a label that contains the following information:

| WARNING |
|---|
| Gasoline vapors can explode. Before starting engine, operate blower at least 4 minutes and check engine compartment bilge for gasoline vapors. |

All owners of boats equipped with exhaust blowers are strongly encouraged to take the same precautions before starting a gasoline engine.

All owners are responsible for keeping their boats' ventilation systems in operating condition. This means making sure that openings are free of obstructions, ducts are not blocked or torn, blowers operate properly, and worn components are replaced with equivalent marine type equipment.

**Regulations**

## Backfire Flame Control

Gasoline engines installed in vessels after April 25, 1940, except outboard motors, must be equipped with an acceptable means of backfire flame control. The device must be suitably attached to the air intake with a flame-tight connection and is required to be Coast Guard approved or comply with SAE J-1928 or UL 1111 standards and marked accordingly.

## Sound Producing Devices

Regulations do not specifically require vessels less than 12 meters in length to carry a whistle, horn or bell; however, the Navigation Rules require sound signals to be produced under certain circumstances. Also, many boats will want to have a horn aboard for negotiating locks and opening bridges. When travelling in fog, proper signals must be used.

Vessels 12 meters or more in length are required to carry on board a power whistle or power horn and a bell. For the Courtesy Marine Examination, the Auxiliary requires some type of horn or whistle capable of a four-second blast audible for a half-mile for all boats.

## Navigation Lights

Chapter 1, *Navigation Rules,* covers this subject in detail for all types and sizes of vessels. Here we present a short discussion specifically for sail and power boats less then 20 meters (65.6 feet).

*Power-driven Vessels*
Vessels of less than 20 meters in length should show red/green sidelights (or a combined bow light), a white sternlight, and a white masthead light located in the forward half of the craft. Vessels of less than 12 meters in length may show red and green sidelights (or a combined bow light) and an all-round white light in lieu of separate masthead and sternlights.

Vessels of less than 7 meters with a top speed of less than 7 knots may, in lieu of normal running lights, show an all-round white light and, if practicable, red and green sidelights (International Rules only).

There are distinguishing lights for towing vessels, fishing vessels, pilot boats, air-cushion vessels, and other special types of vessels and vessels in special situations.

Be sure to check the Navigation Rules for proper light locations and ranges of visibility.

*Sailing Vessels*
Vessels under sail less than 20 meters in length have several options. They may show separate red and green sidelights with a white sternlight; the red and green lights may be combined in a single bow fixture. Another option is to show a masthead all-round red light above an all-round green light in addition to the normal sidelights and sternlight. The combined red-green-white masthead light is very popular — it has the advantage of consuming less power while being highly visible offshore. When this tri-color light is shown, normal sidelights and sternlight are not shown, nor are the red-over-green lights.

Vessels less than 7 meters may, instead of running lights, carry a flashlight or lantern to be shown in time to prevent collision.

Sailing vessels under power must show the same lights as a power vessel (the tri-color masthead light may not be used). Some state regulations require sidelights and sternlight on a sailboat of any size.

*Anchor Lights*
Vessels at anchor must show an anchor light unless located in a special anchorage area designated by the Secretary of Transportation.

For vessels less than 50 meters in length, the light should be an all-round white light visible for two miles. It should be located where it may best be seen.

Many sailboats have masthead anchor lights. It must be kept in mind that these are located well above the line of sight of many small coastal vessels likely to be encountered at night. A safer alternative is a light hung at the lowest height from which it can be seen in all directions.

Vessels less than 7 meters in length are not required to display anchor lights when anchored in an area clear of vessel traffic.

*Shapes*
Anchored boats should hang a black ball in the forward part of the vessel.

Sailing vessels under power with sails hoisted must hang an inverted cone (point down) in the forward part of the vessel. (Inland Rules only exempt vessels under 12 meters in length.)

## COURTESY MARINE EXAMINATIONS

Your local Coast Guard Auxiliary is a volunteer organization dedicated to assisting the Coast Guard in promoting boating safety. They offer a free boat inspection called a Courtesy Marine Examination (CME). The CME requirements are at least as stringent as the Coast Guard's guidelines, and in many cases stricter. The examination doesn't enforce the law — it's to promote safety. If your boat passes the test you will receive a Seal of Safety decal to display on your boat.

Following is a list of CME requirements. The list serves as a good overview of the USCG legal equipment minimum, along with some intelligent additions.

Numbering — proper spacing, contrasting color, minimum 3" block letters;

Registration/Documentation — must be on board;

Navigation lights — must operate and show proper configuration;

Sound producing device — horn, whistle, or other (a bell on boats over 12m — 39.4 ft);

Personal flotation device (PFD) — one wearable for each passenger, 2 minimum (Type IV on boats 16 ft or longer);

Fire extinguishers — mounted, minimum for size of boat, HALON, FE241/CO2- current tag;

Visual distress signals (VDS) — INLAND, a VDS, flag, signal light, etc.; INT'L., minimum flares, aerial rockets, or approved signals, not expired;

Backfire flame arrester — approved, tight, clean;

Ventilation — for closed compartments with potential for explosive vapors and an ignition source. Blower must work and warning posted. Fuel tanks secure, over seven gallons considered permanent, and must be grounded/vented. Hoses in good condition, no leaks;

Anchor & tackle — Suitable to boat and the area;

Alternate propulsion — under 16 ft, paddle or oar; if mechanical, separate fuel tank and starting source;

Dewatering device — pumps must work, extra manual bailer;

Overall vessel condition — bilge and equipment area clean, well maintained. Not overloaded, overpowered, or no automotive parts;

Electrical system — batteries secure, terminals covered, well-organized wiring, proper fuses/circuit breakers;

Galley/Heating systems — secure system, proper tank installation; no flammable material nearby;

State requirements — complies with state safety requirements. Contact state boating regulators for current state boating regulations;

Marine sanitation device — approved device, overboard discharge sealed;

MARPOL trash placard — boats 26 ft and longer, written plan over 40 ft;

Pollution placard — boats 26 ft and longer with machinery compartment;

Navigation rules — boats 12m (39.4 ft) and longer;

FCC marine radio license — all radios, radar, EPIRB, etc.

## U.S. DOCUMENTATION

Larger recreational vessels may be documented by the U.S. Coast Guard. A variety of measurements determine the "tonnage" of the vessel for documentation purposes. For documentation, "tonnage" is a measure of volume, not weight; 30 cubic feet equals one measurement ton; not all space is included — there is "gross tonnage" and "net tonnage." The vessel must measure a minimum of five net tons to be documented. This generally means a minimum length of about 30 feet.

The major advantage of documentation for most owners is the establishment of clear title to your boat. Some banks and lenders will require documentation before a loan will be issued. The document is also internationally recognized proof of ownership and origin, which can smooth customs clearance in many foreign countries.

To obtain documentation, write to the National Vessel Documentation Center at the address below, requesting the necessary forms. The center can also be reached at 1-800-799-8362, and the personnel there are very helpful. The application must be on Coast Guard forms filled out precisely as instructed. Forms include declaration of citizenship (for the owners), vessel measurements, builder's certification, certificate of marking, and a special bill of sale. It is highly advisable to fill out an official Coast Guard bill of sale whenever buying or selling a boat. Do this even if you are planning on obtaining state registration. If you later decide to obtain documentation, the official bill of sale will prevent you from having to contact previous owners, who may be hard to reach.

Your official number will have to be carved into a beam or otherwise attached permanently to some interior part of your vessel. The number must be at least three inches high, in block letters, and preceded by the abbreviation "No."

The name of the vessel and its hailing port must be marked together with letters more than four inches high. Recreation vessels may have the name and port at any location. Commercially documented vessels must have the name and port on the stern, plus the name only on each bow.

Bills of sale must be error-free, notarized, and submitted in duplicate. The Coast Guard is notoriously finicky about perfection on these forms. Many private agencies provide documentation services for those desiring assistance in this exacting process.

*National Vessel Documentation Center*
*U.S. Coast Guard*
*2039 Stonewall Jackson Drive*
*Falling Waters, WV 25419-9502*
*Tele: 800-799-8362*

## U.S. STATE REGULATIONS & REGISTRATION

In addition to U.S. federal requirements, the owner/operator may be required to comply with additional regulations specific to the state in which the vessel is registered or operated. State laws vary. A vessel in compliance with the laws of the state of registration may not meet the requirements of another state where operated. To ensure compliance with state boating laws, understand the jurisdiction limits and contact the appropriate boating agency.

*Jurisdiction Limits*
The term "Navigable Waters of the United States" includes all waters navigable continuously from the high seas, including where access is by canals and locks. Also included are bodies of water that cover two or more states which, although not accessible from the ocean, are capable of "interstate commerce." The final inclusion is any waters used for travel to and from a foreign country. These waters are under the jurisdiction of the U.S. Coast Guard. States and local governments, though, can enforce their laws and regulations on these waters, provided that such do not conflict with federal laws and regulations.

Waters other than as defined above are not subject to federal jurisdiction and are regulated only by the states and their political subdivisions.

*Registration*
To obtain information on state boat registrations and rules, contact the appropriate office from the following list. Federal law requires all vessels propelled by machinery (with the exception of racing vessels and tenders under 10 hp) to be registered with the state of principal use if that state has an approved numbering system, or with the Coast Guard. A certificate of number is issued upon registering the

vessel. Federal law requires the registration certificate to be on board whenever the boat is in use. When the boat is moved to a new state of principal use, the certificate is valid for at least 60 days. State laws vary.

State numbers must be painted or permanently attached to each side of the forward half of the vessel. Numbers must be of plain block style, contrasting color, and at least three inches high. The validation stickers must be affixed within six inches of the registration number. Check your state's instructions about the exact position for the validation sticker. No other letters or numbers may be displayed nearby.

The owner of a vessel must notify — within 15 days — the agency that issued the certificate of number, if:

• The vessel is transferred, destroyed, abandoned, lost, stolen or recovered;
• The certificate of number is lost, destroyed, or the owner's address changes; or
• The certificate of number becomes invalid for any reason.

**Note:** Some states require state registration in addition to Coast Guard documentation, and some states have registration requirements that differ from or exceed the Coast Guard rules. Check with the state agency for any differences in your area.

Alabama
*Dept. of Cons. and Natural Resources*
*Marine Police Division*
*64 N. Union St., Room 438*
*Montgomery, AL 36130-1451*
*(334) 242-3673*

Alaska
*Department of Public Safety*
*1979 Peger Rd.*
*Fairbanks, AK 99709-5257*
*(907) 451-5351*

Arizona
*Arizona Game and Fish Dept.*
*2221 W. Greenway Rd.*
*Phoenix, AZ 85023*
*(602) 789-3383*

Arkansas
*Arkansas Game & Fish Commission*
*Boating Safety Division*
*2 Natural Resources Dr.*
*Little Rock, AR 72205*
*(501) 223-6399*

California
*Dept. of Boating and Waterways*
*1629 "S" Street*
*Sacramento, CA 95814*
*(916) 445-6281*

Colorado
*Division of Parks & Outdoor Recreation*
*13787 S. Hwy. 85*
*Littleton, CO 80125*
*(303) 791-1954*

Connecticut
*Dept. Marine Headquarters*
*P.O. Box 280*
*Old Lyme, CT 06371*
*(860) 424-3124*

Delaware
*Division of Fish and Wildlife*
*Richardson and Robbins Building*
*P.O. Box 1401*
*Dover, DE 19903*
*(302) 739-3440*

District of Columbia
*Metropolitan Police Dept.*
*Harbor Patrol Branch*
*550 Water St. SW*
*Washington, DC 20024*
*(202) 727-4582*

Florida
*Dept. of Environmental Protection*
*Division of Law Enforcement*
*3900 Commonwealth Blvd. MS 630*
*Tallahassee, FL 32399-3000*
*(904) 488-5600*

Georgia
*Dept. of Natural Resources*
*Wildlife Resources Division*
*Law Enforcement Section*
*2070 US Hwy., 278, SE*
*Social Circle, GA 30025*
*(770) 918-6408*

Hawaii
*Dept. of Land and Natural Resources*
*Division of Boating and Ocean Recreation*
*333 Queen St., Suite 300*
*Honolulu, HI 96813*
*(808) 587-1975*

Idaho
*Dept. of Parks and Recreation*
*PO Box 83720*
*Boise, ID 83720-0655*
*(208) 334-4180*

Illinois
*Dept. of Conservation*
*Division of Law Enforcement*
*524 S. Second St.*
*Springfield, IL 62701-1787*
*(217) 782-6431*

**Regulations**

Indiana
*Dept. of Natural Resources*
*Law Enforcement Division*
*IGCS, Room W255-D*
*402 W. Washington*
*Indianapolis, IN 46204*
*(317) 232-4010*

Iowa
*Dept. of Conservation*
*Fish and Wildlife Division*
*Wallace State Office Bldg.*
*E. Ninth and Grand Ave.*
*Des Moines, IA 50319-0034*
*(515) 281-8652*

Kansas
*Kansas Wildlife and Parks*
*900 SW Jackson*
*Topeka, KS 66612-1233*
*(913) 296-2281*

Kentucky
*Kentucky Water Patrol*
*Dept. of Fish and Wildlife Resources*
*#1 Game Farm Rd.*
*Frankfort, KY 40601*
*(502) 564-3074*

Louisiana
*Dept. of Wildlife and Fisheries*
*P.O. Box 98000*
*2000 Quail Dr.*
*Baton Rogue, LA 70898-9000*
*(504) 765-2983*

Maine
*Inland Fisheries and Wildlife*
*284 State St. Section #41*
*Augusta, ME 04333*
*(207) 287-2766*

Maryland
*Dept. of Natural Resources*
*Tawes State Office Bldg., B-1*
*580 Taylor Ave.*
*Annapolis, MD 21401*
*(410) 260-8881*

Massachusetts
*Division of Environmental Law*
*Enforcement*
*175 Portland St.*
*Boston, MA 02214-1701*
*(617) 727-3190*

Michigan
*Dept. of Natural Resources*
*Law Enforcement Division*
*P.O. Box 30028*
*Lansing, MI 48909*
*(517) 335-3416*

Minnesota
*Dept. of Natural Resources*
*Attn: Boating Safety*
*500 Lafayette Rd.*
*St. Paul, MN 55155*
*(612) 296-3336*

Mississippi
*Dept. of Wildlife, Fisheries and Parks*
*P.O. Box 451*
*Jackson, MS 39205*
*(601) 364-2185*

Missouri
*Missouri State Water Patrol*
*Dept. of Public Safety*
*P.O. Box 1368*
*Jefferson City, MO 65102-1368*
*(573) 751-3333*

Montana
*Montana Fish, Wildlife and Parks*
*Enforcement Division*
*1420 E. 6th Ave.*
*P.O. Box 200701*
*Helena, MT 59620*
*(406) 444-2452*

Nebraska
*Nebraska Game and Parks Commission*
*Law Enforcement Division*
*2200 N. 33rd St.*
*Lincoln, NE 68503-0370*
*(402) 471-5579*

Nevada
*Department of Conservation and Natural*
*Resources*
*Division of Wildlife*
*1100 Valley Road*
*PO Box 10678*
*Reno, NV 89520-0022*
*(702) 688-1542*

New Hampshire
*Division of Safety Services*
*31 Dock Rd.*
*Gilford, NH 03246*
*(603)293-2037*

New Jersey
*New Jersey State Police Troop F*
*P.O. Box 7068*
*West Trenton, NJ*
*08628-0068*
*(602) 882-2000 ext. 6164*

New Mexico
*Energy, Minerals, & Natural*
*Resources Dept.*
*Parks and Recreation Division*
*P.O. Box 1147*
*Santa Fe, NM 87504-1147*
*(505) 827-7173*

New York
*Bureau of Marine & Recreation Vehicles*
*Agency Bldg. #1, 13th Fl.*
*Empire State Plaza*
*Albany, NY 12238*
*(518) 473-0179*

North Carolina
*Wildlife Resources Commission*
*512 N. Salisbury St.*
*Archdale Building*
*Raleigh, NC 27604-1188*
*(919) 733-7191*

North Dakota
*Game & Fish Dept.*
*Information & Education Division*
*100 N. Bismarck Expressway*
*Bismarck, ND 58501-5095*
*(701) 328-6327*

Ohio
*Dept. of Natural Resources*
*Division of Watercraft*
*4435 Fountain Square Dr.*
*Columbus, OH 43224-1300*
*(614) 265-6485*

Oklahoma
*Lake Patrol Division; Dept. of Public Safety*
*P.O. Box 11415*
*Oklahoma City, OK 73136-0415*
*(405) 425-2143*

Oregon
*State Marine Board*
*435 Commercial St., NE*
*Salem, OR 97310*
*(503) 373-1405 Ext. 244*

Pennsylvania
*PA Fish & Boat Commission*
*Bureau of Boating*
*P.O. Box 67000*
*Harrisburg, PA 17106-7000*
*(717) 657-4538*

Rhode Island
*Dept. of Environmental Management*
*235 Providence Street*
*Providence, RI 02908*
*(401) 277-3071*

South Carolina
*Wildlife and Marine Resources Dept.*
*Division of Law Enforcement & Boating*
*P.O. Box 12559*
*Charleston, SC 29412*
*(803) 762-5034*

South Dakota
*Dept. of Game, Fish, and Parks*
*Division of Wildlife*
*523 E. Capitol*
*Pierre, SD 57501-3182*
*(605) 773-4506*

Tennessee
*TN Wildlife Resources Agency*
*Boating Division*
*P.O. Box 40747*
*Nashville, TN 37204-9979*
*(615) 781-6682*

Texas
*Texas Parks and Wildlife Dept.*
*Law Enforcement Division*
*4200 Smith School Rd.*
*Austin, TX 78744*
*(512) 389-4624*

Utah
*Division of Parks & Recreation*
*1594 W. North Temple Street*
*PO Box 146001*
*Salt Lake City, UT 84114-6001*
*(801) 538-7341*

Vermont
*Vermont State Police HQ*
*103 S. Main Street*
*Waterbury, VT 05671*
*(802) 244-8778*

Virginia
*Dept. of Game and Inland Fisheries*
*P.O. Box 11104*
*Richmond, VA 23230-1104*
*(804)-367-1189*

Washington
*WA State Parks & Recreation Commission*
*P.O. Box 42654*
*Olympia, WA 98504-2654*
*(360) 902-8525*

West Virginia
*Division of Natural Resources*
*Law Enforcement Section*
*Capital Complex, Bldg 3*
*Charleston, WV 25305-0668*
*(304) 558-2783*

Wisconson
*Dept. of Natural Resources*
*Division of Law Enforcement*
*P.O. Box 7921*
*Madison, WI 53707*
*(608) 266-2141*

Wyoming
*Wildlife Law Enforcement*
*Game and Fish Dept.*
*5400 Bishop Blvd.*
*Cheyenne, WY 82006*
*(307) 777-4579*

American Samoa
*Department of Special Operations*
*PO Box 1086*
*Pago Pago, AS 96799*
*011-684 633-2004*

Regulations

111

Guam
*Guam Police Department*
*Special Program Section*
*PO Box 23909*
*GMF Barrigada, Guam 96921*

Northern Marinas [CNMI]
*Boating and Safety Section*
*Department of Public Safety*
*PO Box 791*
*Saipan, CNMI, 96950*
*011-670 233-7233*

Puerto Rico
*Office of the Commissioner of Navigation*
*Dept. of Natural Resources*
*P.O. Box 5887*
*Puerta de Teierra, PR 00906*
*(787) 724-2340*

Virgin Islands
*Department of Planning and Natural*
*Resources*
*396-1 Foster Plaza*
*Annas Retreat*
*St. Thomas, VI 00802*
*(809) 776-8600*

## CANADIAN VESSEL & OPERATOR LICENSING

As *Reed's Companion* goes to press in early 1998, the Canadian Coast Guard and the Minister of Fisheries and Oceans are about to announce a requirement for all boaters, in all types of boats, to meet a minimum basic knowledge requirement. Officially, the target date to begin is January 1, 1999. It is likely that this new regulation will be phased in over a number of years. It is expected that people born after December 31, 1983, will be required to meet the standard. Along with knowledge requirements will be age restrictions that will restrict unaccompanied qualified children less than 12 years of age to boats with engines less than 10 horsepower, and unaccompanied qualified children between 12 and 16 years of age to vessels with less than 40 horsepower.

Vessel licensing or registration in Canada is somewhat similar to the U.S. dual system of state registration or federal documentation. Every vessel principally maintained or operated in Canada that has a motor exceeding 7.5 kW (about 10 hp) or a combination of motors exceeding 7.5 kW total, must be licensed. Vessels larger than 20 "register tons" (an average 36-foot cruiser) may elect to register instead. There are advantages to registering — primarily clear title for securing mortgages and official confirmation of ownership and nationality of captain and vessel when clearing into foreign ports.

Vessel licensing is handled by Canadian customs and is free of charge. The vessel will be issued a license number that must be displayed in block characters not less than 7.5 cm high, and in a color that contrasts with the background. The numbers should be displayed on each side of the bow or on a board attached to each side of the bow. This number is a permanent number for the vessel and remains with it through any subsequent transfers of ownership.

For complete information on Canadian regulations, order the publication "*Small Vessel Regulations*" (P218) from:

*Hydrographic Chart Distribution Office*
*Department of Fisheries and Oceans*
*1675 Russell Road*
*P.O. Box 8080*
*Ottawa, Ontario, Canada K1G 3H6*
*(613) 998-4931; Fax: (613) 998-1217*

## CANADIAN EQUIPMENT REQUIREMENTS

Canada has stricter equipment requirements than the United States. For complete information on these regulations, order the publication *"Small Vessel Regulations"* as mentioned above. We give here a short description of the basic requirements:

### Vessels not over 5.5m (18') in length
1) One approved small-vessel lifejacket or approved flotation device for each person aboard.
2) Two oars and oarlocks, or two paddles.
3) One bailer or one manual pump.
4) If equipped with an inboard motor, permanent fuel tanks or a stove using liquid or gaseous fuel, and one B-I fire extinguisher.
5) Sound signalling device.
6) Lights must comply with Collision Regulations if permanently fitted.

### Vessels 5.5m - 8m (18.0' - 26.2')
All items listed above plus:
7) One approved throwable device — either a cushion, a buoyant heaving line, or an approved lifebuoy.
8) Six approved distress flares: three A, B, or C type flares AND three A, B, C, or D type flares — EXCEPT if vessel is engaged in racing and has no beds/bunks OR operating in a river, canal, or lake in which the boat can never be more than one nautical mile from shore OR boat is propelled by oars or paddles.

### Vessels 8m – 12m in length (26.2' - 39.4')
1) One approved small-vessel lifejacket for each person aboard.
2) One lifebuoy 610 or 762 mm. in diameter.
3) One approved buoyant heaving line not less than 15m in length.
4) One bailer AND one manual or power-driven bilge pump.
5) Twelve pyrotechnic distress signals in a waterproof container; not more than six may be daytime smoke signals.
6) One anchor with not less than 15m of cable, rope, or chain.
7) If equipped with an inboard motor, permanent fuel tanks or a stove using liquid or gaseous fuel, one B-II fire extinguisher.
8) Proper lights and sound signaling apparatus to comply with the International Rules of the Road (see Chapter 1).

### Vessels 12m – 20m in length (39.4' - 65.6')
Items 1–8 above except:
2) One approved 762 mm. lifebuoy or two 610 mm. lifebuoys.
7) Two B-II fire extinguishers, one by entrance to sleeping cabin and one next to the engine space entrance.

Plus:
9) Two fire buckets and one fire axe.

### Vessels over 20m (65.6') in length
Items 1–8 above except:
2) Two approved 762mm lifebuoys, one with an automatic light.
3) One buoyant heaving line not less than 27.5m in length.
7) Two B-II fire extinguishers, one by entrance to sleeping cabin and one next to the engine space entrance. In each accommodation space, one A-II fire extinguisher (maximum of three need be carried). Power fire pump able to reach any part of vessel.

Plus:
9) Four fire buckets and two fire axes.
10) One VHF radio telephone installation.

### Regulation Notes
In Canada, the horseshoe type lifebuoy does NOT fulfill Coast Guard safety requirements.

Note that an approved lifejacket or personal floatation device (PFD) is required for each person on a sailboard.

In Canada, porta-pottie type heads must be permanently installed in the boat and equipped for proper pumpout.

An official copy of the boat's up-to-date license (i.e., in the owner's name) should be on board. A reasonable length of time is allowed to produce it.

Ontario, Manitoba, and Saskatchewan (and possibly additional provinces) have adopted the regulation limiting boats to a top speed of 10 km/h when within 30 meters of shore (approx. 100 feet).

The Small Vessel Regulations will be changed in 1998 to give boaters more options on required safety equipment. Some additional equipment will be required — waterproof flashlights, buoyant heaving lines, and PFDs that actually fit everyone on board.

Regulations

113

## U.S. COAST GUARD BOARDING POLICY

The U.S. Coast Guard is the primary maritime law enforcement agency in the United States.

Authority  Section 89 of Title 14 of the United States Code authorizes the Coast Guard to board vessels subject to the jurisdiction of the U.S. anytime upon the high seas and upon waters over which the United States has jurisdiction, to make inquiries, examinations, inspections, searches, seizures, and arrests.

**What to expect:** A uniformed CG boarding team will notify you that they are coming aboard to conduct a CG boarding. Like other law enforcement officers, they will be armed. Once on board they will conduct an initial safety inspection to identify any obvious safety hazards and to ensure the seaworthiness of your vessel. The boarding officer will then ask to see the vessel registration or documentation and proceed to inspect your vessel. The scope of the vessel inspection, during most boardings, is limited to determining the vessel's regulatory status (e.g., commercial, recreational, passenger, cargo, and/or fishing vessel) and checking for compliance with U.S. civil law applicable to vessels of that status. The CG may also enforce U.S. criminal law. The boarding officer will complete a Coast Guard boarding form and note any discrepancies. You will get a signed copy before they depart.

**Report of Boarding:** When a CG boarding officer issues you a boarding report, they will either issue a yellow copy, if no discrepancies were noted, or a white copy if there were. A white copy will indicate a warning or a notice of violation. The CG boarding officer should explain the procedures to follow in each case. In any event, those procedures are written on the reverse of the form. If you have any questions, ask the CG boarding officer or call the Coast Guard Customer Information Line at 800-368-5647.

## U.S. LAW ENFORCEMENT

The U.S. Coast Guard may impose a civil penalty up to $1,000 for failure to comply with equipment requirements, for failure to report a boating accident, or for failure to comply with other federal regulations. Failure to comply with the Inland Navigation Rules Act of 1980 can result in a civil penalty of up to $5,000.

Improper use of a radiotelephone is a criminal offense. The use of obscene, indecent, or profane language during radio communications is punishable by a $10,000 fine, imprisonment for two years, or both. Other penalties exist for misuse of a radio, such as improper use of Channel 16 on a VHF radio.

### Boating Under the Influence (BUI)

Operating a boat while intoxicated became a federal offense on January 13, 1988. If the blood alcohol level is .10% (.08% in some states) or higher, violators are subject to a civil penalty of up to $1,000, or a criminal penalty of up to $5,000, one year of imprisonment, or both.

### Negligent Operation

The Coast Guard may impose a civil penalty for Negligent or Grossly Negligent Operation of a vessel that endangers lives and/or property. Grossly Negligent Operation is a criminal offense with fines up to $5,000, imprisonment for one year, or both. Examples of Grossly Negligent Operation include:

• Operating a boat in a swimming area;

• Operating a boat under the influence of alcohol or drugs;

• Speeding near other boats or in dangerous waters;

• Hazardous waterskiing practices; and

• Bowriding, riding on seatback, riding on gunwale, riding on transom.

### Termination of Use

The Coast Guard can terminate a voyage if they feel a boat is being operated in an unsafe condition or if an especially hazardous condition exists. You may be directed to port or told to immediately correct the hazardous situation. Your voyage may be terminated if it is declared a "Manifestly

Unsafe Voyage" — the catchall that can be used whenever the Coast Guard feels you are operating in an unsafe manner.

An operator who refuses to terminate the unsafe use of a vessel can be cited for failure to comply with the directions of a Coast Guard officer. Violators may be fined up to $1,000, imprisoned for one year, or both.

## Reporting Accidents

A formal report must be filed with the law enforcement authorities in the state where an accident occurred if more than $500 of damage is done, or a vessel is lost. You have 10 days to file a report.

In the case of fatal accidents, you must notify the authorities immediately. If a person has died or disappeared, you must provide officials with the following information:

• Date, time, and exact of the accident;
• Name of the person (or persons) involved;
• Number and name of the vessel; and
• Name and address of the owner and operator.

In an accident with injuries requiring more than first aid, a formal report must be filed within 48 hours.

## Rendering Assistance

The master of a vessel is obligated by law to provide assistance to any person in danger at sea. The master is subject to a fine and/or imprisonment for failure to do so. Many boaters refer to this great tradition as "The Law of the Sea."

In U.S. waters, the Federal Boating Safety Act of 1971 contains a "Good Samaritan" provision that states:

"Any person...who gratuitously and in good faith renders assistance at the scene of a vessel collision, accident, or other casualty without objection of any person assisted, shall not be held liable for any act or omission in providing or arranging salvage, towage, medical treatment, or other assistance where the assisting person acts as a ordinary, reasonable prudent man would have acted under the same or similar circumstances."

## OPERATOR LICENSES

The U.S. Coast Guard does not require the operator of a recreational boat to have an operator license or permit. If, however, you are carrying passengers for hire, a license is required. There are licenses for various numbers of passengers, size of vessel, and waters used. Contact your local Coast Guard District for further information.

Some states require that children under a specified age — it varies from state to state — must have taken a boating course and received a operator's permit. Several states are contemplating licensing for all vessel operators.

## CUSTOMS CLEARANCE

U.S. recreational craft are not required to "clear"; that is, obtain permission to depart, when leaving a U.S. port for a foreign destination. Clearance may be required when leaving a foreign port — be sure to ask on arrival.

All vessels, U.S. and foreign flag, must "enter" when arriving in the United States from a foreign port. The procedures are simple for U.S. recreational craft, but vary with the arrival port. A single telephone call or visit by an officer will usually take care of the requirements of customs, immigration, public health, and animal and plant quarantine. The surest way to know what is required is to ask before departing on an overseas cruise.

The requirements and procedures for U.S. commercial and all foreign-flag vessels is more complicated, but not onerous. A radio call to the local Coast Guard station will usually provide all necessary guidance.

## POLLUTION REGULATIONS

The Refuse Act of 1899 prohibits throwing, discharging, or depositing any refuse matter of any kind (including trash, garbage, oil, and other liquid pollutants) into the waters of the United States.

The Federal Water Pollution Control Act prohibits the discharge of oil or hazardous substances that may be harmful into U.S. navigable waters. Vessels 26 feet in length and over must display a placard at least five by eight inches, made of durable material, fixed in a conspicuous place in the machinery spaces, or at the bilge pump control station, stating the following:

---

### Discharge of Oil Prohibited

The Federal Water Pollution Control Act prohibits the discharge of oil or oily waste upon or into any navigable waters of the U.S. The prohibition includes any discharge which causes a film or discoloration of the surface of the water or causes a sludge or emulsion beneath the surface of the water. Violators are subject to substantial civil and/or criminal sanctions including fines and imprisonment.

---

Regulations issued under the Federal Water Pollution Control Act require all vessels with propulsion machinery to have a capacity to retain oil mixtures on board. A fixed or portable means to discharge oily waste to a reception facility is required. A bucket or bailer is suitable as a portable means of discharging oily waste on recreational vessels. No person may intentionally drain oil or oily waste from any source into the bilge of any vessel. You must immediately notify the U.S. Coast Guard if your vessel discharges oil or hazardous substances in the water. Call toll-free 800-424-8802 (in Washington, D.C., (202) 267-3675).

Report the following information:

• location
• substances
• color
• size
• source
• time observed

The Act to Prevent Pollution from Ships (MARPOL ANNEX V) places limitations on the discharge of garbage from vessels. It is illegal to dump plastic trash anywhere in the ocean or in navigable waters of the United States. It is also illegal to discharge garbage in the navigable waters of the United States, including the Great Lakes. The discharge of other types of garbage is permitted outside of specific distances offshore as determined by the nature of that garbage.

United States vessels of 26 feet or longer must display in a prominent location, a durable placard at least 4"x 9" that notifies the crew and passengers of the discharge restrictions (as shown).

United States oceangoing vessels of 40 feet or longer that are engaged in commerce or are equipped with a galley and berthing, must have a written Waste Management Plan describing the procedures for collecting, processing, storing, and discharging garbage, and designate the person who is in charge of carrying out the plan.

---

### MARPOL ANNEX V

1) Plastics, including synthetic ropes, fishing nets, and plastic bags may not be discharged in any area.

2) Floating dunnage, lining, and packing materials may not be discharged less than 25 miles from the nearest land.

3) Food waste, paper, rags, glass, metal, bottles, crockery, and similar refuse may not be discharged less than 12 miles from the nearest land.

4) Comminuted or ground food waste, paper, rags, glass, etc. may not be discharged less than 3 miles from the nearest land.

---

## MARINE SANITATION DEVICES

All recreational boats with installed toilet facilities must have an operable marine sanitation device (MSD) on board. Vessels 65 feet and under may use a Type I, II, or III MSD. Vessels over 65 feet must install a Type II or III MSD. All MSDs must be Coast Guard certified.

Type I and II MSDs are flow-through treatment systems that treat the sewage using chemical, electrical, and/or incineration methods before discharging the waste overboard. A Type II MSD treats the sewage more completely than a Type I. If you have this type of treatment system, avoid discharging when in shallow water, near shellfish beds, in confined harbors or near bathing areas.

Type III MSDs are holding tanks for storing the sewage aboard the boat. The tank may be discharged outside the three-mile U.S. territorial limit. Within the limit, or in no-discharge zones, the tank must be emptied at a shoreside pumpout station. When within the limit, the handle of the discharge valve should be removed or padlocked in the closed position to prevent unauthorized use.

## VESSEL BRIDGE-TO-BRIDGE RADIOTELEPHONE REGULATIONS

(Refer to Chapter 6, *Communications,* for a detailed discussion of these regulations.)

The Vessel Bridge-to-Bridge Radiotelephone Act is applicable on navigable waters of the United States inside the boundary lines established in 46 CFR 7. In all cases, the Act applies on waters subject to the Inland Rules. In some instances, the Act may apply all the way out to the three-mile limit, depending on where the boundary lines are located. In no instance does the Act apply beyond the three-mile limit.

26.01    Purpose.
26.02    Definitions.
26.03    Radiotelephone required.
26.04    Use of the designated frequency.
26.05    Use of radiotelephone.
26.06    Maintenance of radiotelephone; failure of radiotelephone.
26.07    Communications.
26.08    Exemption procedures.
26.09    List of exemptions.
26.10    Penalties.

### 26.01 Purpose.

(a) The purpose of this part is to implement the provisions of the Vessel Bridge-to-Bridge Radiotelephone Act. This part:

(1) Requires the use of the vessel bridge-to-bridge radiotelephone;

(2) Provides the Coast Guard's interpretation of the meaning of important terms in the Act; and

(3) Prescribes the procedures for applying for an exemption from the Act and the regulations issued under the Act and a listing of exemptions.

(b) Nothing in this part relieves any person from the obligation of complying with the rules of the road and the applicable pilot rules.

### 26.02 Definitions.

For the purpose of this part and interpreting the Act:

"Secretary" means the Secretary of the Department in which the Coast Guard is operating;

"Act" means the "Vessel Bridge-to-Bridge Radiotelephone Act," 33 U.S.C. Sections 1201-1208;

"Length" is measured from end to end over the deck, excluding sheer;

"Power-driven vessel" means any vessel propelled by machinery; and

"Towing vessel" means any commercial vessel engaged in towing another vessel astern, alongside, or by pushing ahead.

"Vessel Traffic Services" (VTS) means a service implemented under part 161 of this chapter by the U.S. Coast Guard, designed to improve the safety and efficiency of vessel traffic and to protect the environment. The VTS has the capability to interact with marine traffic and respond to traffic situations developing in the VTS area.

"Vessel Traffic Service Area or VTS Area" means the geographical area encompassing a specific VTS area of service as described in Part 161 of this chapter. This area of service may be subdivided into sectors for the purpose of allocating responsibility to individual Vessel Traffic Centers or to identify different operating requirements.

**Note:** Although regulatory jurisdiction is limited to the navigable waters of the United States, certain vessels will be encouraged or may be required, as a condition of port entry, to report beyond this area to facilitate traffic management within the VTS area.

### 26.03 Radiotelephone required.

(a) Unless an exemption is granted under 26.09 and except as provided in paragraph (a)(4) of this section, this part applies to:

(1) Every power-driven vessel of 20 meters or over in length while navigating;

(2) Every vessel of 100 gross tons and upward carrying one or more passengers for hire while navigating;

(3) Every towing vessel of 26 feet or over in length while navigating; and

(4) Every dredge and floating plant engaged in or near a channel or fairway in operations likely to restrict or affect navigation of other vessels except for an unmanned or intermittently manned floating plant under the control of a dredge.

(b) Every vessel, dredge, or floating plant

117

described in paragraph (a) of this section must have a radiotelephone on board capable of operation from its navigational bridge, or in the case of a dredge, from its main control station, and capable of transmitting and receiving on the frequency or frequencies within the 156-162 MHz band using the classes of emissions designated by the Federal Communications Commission for the exchange of navigational information.

(c) The radiotelephone required by paragraph (b) of this section must be carried on board the described vessels, dredges, and floating plants upon the navigable waters of the United States.

(d) The radiotelephone required by paragraph (b) of this section must be capable of transmitting and receiving on VHF FM Channel 22A (157.1 MHz).

(e) While transiting any of the following waters, each vessel described in paragraph (a) of this section also must have on board a radiotelephone capable of transmitting and receiving on VHF FM Channel 67 (156.375 MHz):

(1) The lower Mississippi River from the territorial sea boundary, and within either the Southwest Pass safety fairway or the South Pass safety fairway specified in 33 CFR 166.200, to mile 242.4 AHP (Above Head of Passes) near Baton Rouge;

(2) The Mississippi River-Gulf Outlet from the territorial sea boundary, and within the Mississippi River-Gulf Outlet safety fairway specified in 33 CFR 166.200, to that channel's junction with the Inner Harbor Navigation Canal; and

(3) The full length of the Inner Harbor Navigation Canal from its junction with the Mississippi River to that canal's entry to Lake Pontchartrain at the New Seabrook vehicular bridge.

(f) In addition to the radiotelephone required by paragraph (b) of this section, each vessel described in paragraph (a) of this section while transiting any waters within a Vessel Traffic Service Area, must have on board a radiotelephone capable of transmitting and receiving on the VTS designated frequency in Table 26.03(f) (VTS Call Signs, Designated Frequencies, and Monitoring Areas), located just following this section.

**Note:** A single VHF-FM radio capable of scanning or sequential monitoring (often referred to as "dual watch" capability) will not meet the requirements for two radios.

## 26.04 Use of the designated frequency.

(a) No person may use the frequency designated by the Federal Communications Commission under section 8 of the Act, 33 U.S.C. 1207(a), to transmit any information other than information necessary for the safe navigation of vessels or necessary tests.

(b) Each person who is required to maintain a listening watch under section 5 of the Act shall, when necessary, transmit and confirm, on the designated frequency, the intentions of his vessel and any other information necessary for the safe navigation of vessels.

(c) Nothing in these regulations may be construed as prohibiting the use of the designated frequency to communicate with shore stations to obtain or furnish information necessary for the safe navigation of vessels.

(d) On the navigable waters of the United States, Channel 13 (156.65 MHz) is the designated frequency required to be monitored in accordance with section 26.05(a), except that in the area prescribed in section 26.03(e), Channel 67 (156.375 MHz) is the designated frequency.

(e) On those navigable waters of the United States within a VTS area, the designated VTS frequency is the designated frequency required to be monitored in accordance with §26.05.

**Note:** As stated in 47 CFR 80.148(b), a VHF watch on Channel 16 (156.800MHz) is not required on vessels subject to the Vessel Bridge-to-Bridge Radiotelephone Act and participating in a Vessel Traffic Service (VTS) system when the watch is maintained on both the vessel bridge-to-bridge frequency and a designated VTS frequency.

## 26.05 Use of radiotelephone.

Section 5 of the Act states: (a) The radiotelephone required by this Act is for the exclusive use of the master or person in charge of the vessel, or the person designated by the master or person in charge to pilot or direct the movement of the vessel, who shall maintain a listening watch on the designated frequency. Nothing contained herein shall be interpreted as precluding the use of portable radiotelephone equipment to satisfy the requirements of this Act.

## 26.06 Maintenance of radiotelephone, failure of radiotelephone.

Section 6 of the Act states: (a) Whenever radiotelephone capability is required by this Act, a vessel's radiotelephone equipment shall be maintained in effective operating condition. If the radiotelephone equipment carried aboard a vessel ceases to operate, the master shall exercise due diligence to restore it or cause it to be restored to effective operating condition at the earliest practicable time. The failure of a vessel's radiotelephone equipment shall not, in itself, constitute a violation of this Act, nor shall it obligate the master of any vessel to moor or anchor his vessel; however, the loss of radiotelephone capability shall be given consideration in the navigation of the vessel.

## 26.07 Communications.

No person may use the services of, and no person may serve as, a person required to maintain a listening watch under section 5 of the Act, 33 U.S.C. 1204, unless the person can communicate in the English language.

## 26.08 Exemption procedures.

(a) Any person may petition for an exemption from any provision of the Act or this part;

(b) Each petition must be submitted in writing to U.S. Coast Guard (G-NSR), 2100 Second Street, SW, Washington, D.C. 20593, and must state:

(1) The provisions of the Act or this part from which an exemption is requested; and

(2) The reasons why marine navigation will not be adversely affected if the exemption is granted and if the exemption relates to a local communication system how that system would fully comply with the intent of the concept of the Act but would not conform in detail if the exemption is granted.

## 26.09 List of exemptions.

(a) All vessels navigating on those waters governed by the navigation rules for the Great Lakes and their connecting and tributary waters (33 U.S.C. 241 et seq.) are exempt from the requirements of the Vessel Bridge-to-Bridge Radiotelephone Act and this part until May 6, 1975.

(b) Each vessel navigating on the Great Lakes as defined in the Inland Navigational Rules Act of 1980 (33 U.S.C. 2001 et seq.) and to which the Vessel Bridge-to-Bridge Radiotelephone Act (33 U.S.C. 1201-1208) applies is exempt from the requirements in 33 U.S.C. 1203, 1204, and 1205 and the regulations under sections 26.03, 26.04, 26.05, 26.06, and 26.07. Each of these vessels and each person to whom 33 U.S.C. 1208(a) applies must comply with Articles VII, X, XI, XII, XIII, XV, and XVI and Technical Regulations 1-9 of "The Agreement Between the United States of America and Canada for Promotion of Safety on the Great Lakes by means of Radio, 1973."

## 26.10 Penalties.

Section 9 of the Act states:

(a) Whoever, being the master or person in charge of a vessel subject to the Act, fails to enforce or comply with the Act or the regulations hereunder; or whoever, being designated by the master or person in charge of a vessel subject to the Act to pilot or direct the movement of a vessel fails to enforce or comply with the Act or the regulations hereunder is liable to a civil penalty of not more than $500 to be assessed by the secretary.

(b) Every vessel navigated in violation of the Act or the regulations hereunder is liable to a civil penalty of not more than $500 to be assessed by the secretary, for which the vessel may be proceeded against in any District Court of the United States having jurisdiction.

(c) Any penalty assessed under this section may be remitted or mitigated by the secretary, upon such terms as he may deem proper.

**Regulations**

## VESSEL TRAFFIC SERVICES

"Vessel Traffic Services" are defined in the Radiotelephone Regulations. Following are the specific VTS stations with their call signs, designated frequencies, and monitoring areas.

**Note:** In the event of a communication failure either by the vessel traffic center or the vessel or radio congestion on a designated VTS frequency, communication may be established on an alternate VTS frequency. The bridge-to-bridge navigation frequency, 156.650 MHz (Channel 13), is monitored in each VTS area. It may be used as an alternate frequency, however, only to the extent that doing so provides a level of safety beyond that provided by other means.

## NEW YORK

**Note:** Designated frequency monitoring is required within U.S. navigable waters. In areas which are outside the U.S. navigable waters, designated frequency monitoring is voluntary. However, prospective VTS users are encouraged to monitor the designated frequency.

*New York Traffic   156.700 MHz (Ch. 14)*
The waters of the Lower New York Bay west of a line drawn from Norton Point to Breezy Point and north of a line drawn from Ambrose Entrance Lighted Gong Buoy #1 to Ambrose Channel Lighted Gong Buoy #9 thence to West Bank Light and thence to Great Kills Light. The waters of the Upper New York Bay, south of 40°42.40'N (Brooklyn Bridge) and 40°43.70'N (Holland Tunnel Ventilator Shaft); and in Newark Bay, south of 40°38.25'N (Arthur Kill Railroad Bridge), and south of 40°41.95'N (Lehigh Valley Draw Bridge); and the Kill Van Kull.

*New York Traffic   156.550 MHz (Ch. 11)*
The waters of Raritan Bay east of a line drawn from Great Kills Light to Point Comfort in New Jersey and south of a line drawn from Great Kills Light to West Bank Light to Ambrose Channel Lighted Gong Buoy #9 thence to Ambrose Channel Lighted Gong Buoy #1 and west of a line drawn from Ambrose Channel Lighted Gong Buoy #9, thence to Ambrose Channel Lighted Gong Buoy #1 and west of a line drawn from Ambrose Channel Lighted Gong Buoy #1 to the Sandy Hook Channel

Entrance Buoys (Lighted Gong Buoys #1 and #2).

*New York Traffic   156.600 MHz (Ch. 12)*
Each vessel at anchor within the above areas.

## HOUSTON

*See note under New York.*
The navigable waters north of 29°N, west of 94°20'W, south of 29°49'N, and east of 95°20'W.

*Houston Traffic   156.550 MHz (Ch. 11)*
The navigable waters north of a line extending due west from the southern most end of Exxon Dock #1 (29°43.37'N, 95°01.27'W).

*Houston Traffic   156.600 MHz (Ch. 12)*
The navigable waters south of a line extending due west from the southern most end of E on Dock #1 (29°43.37'N, 95°01.27'W).

## BERWICK BAY

*Berwick Traffic   156.550 MHz (Ch. 11)*
The navigable waters south of 29°45'N, west of 91°10'W, north of 29°37'N, and east of 91°18'W.

## ST. MARYS RIVER

*Soo Control   156.600 MHz (Ch. 12)*
The navigable waters of the St. Mary's River between 45°57'N (De Tour Reef Light) and 46°38.7'N (Ile Parisienne Light), except the St. Mary Falls Canal and those navigable waters east of a line from 46°04.16'N and 46°01.57'N (La Pointe to Sims Point in Potagannissing Bay and Worsley Bay).

## SAN FRANCISCO

*See note under New York.*

*San Francisco Traffic   156.600 MHz (Ch. 12)*
The waters within a 38 nautical mile radius of Mount Tamalpais (37°55.8'N, 122°34.6'W) excluding the San Francisco Offshore Precautionary Area.

*San Francisco Traffic   156.700 MHz (Ch. 14)*
The waters of the San Francisco Offshore Precautionary Area eastward to San Francisco Bay including its tributaries extending to the ports of Stockton, Sacramento and Redwood City.

## PUGET SOUND

**Note:** A Cooperative Vessel Traffic Service was established by the United States and Canada within adjoining waters. The appropriate vessel traffic center administers the rules issued by both nations; however, it will enforce only its own set of rules within its jurisdiction.

*Seattle Traffic       156.700 MHz (Ch. 14)*
The navigable waters of Puget Sound, Hood Canal, and adjacent waters south of a line connecting Marrowstone Point and Lagoon Point in Admiralty Inlet and south of a line drawn due east from the southernmost tip of Possession Point on Whidbey Island to the shoreline.

**Note:** Seattle Traffic may direct a vessel to monitor the other primary VTS frequency 156.250 MHz or 156.700 MHz (Channel 5A or 14) depending on traffic density, weather conditions, or other safety factors, rather than strictly adhering to the designated frequency required for each monitoring area as defined above. This does not require a vessel to monitor both primary frequencies.

*Seattle Traffic       156.250 MHz (Ch. 5A)*
The navigable waters of the Strait of Juan de Fuca east of 124°40'W. Excluding the waters in the central portion of the Strait of Juan de Fuca north and east of Race Rocks; the navigable waters of the Strait of Georgia east of 122°52'W; the San Juan Island Archipelago, Rosario Strait, Bellingham Bay; Admiralty Inlet north of a line connecting Marrowstone Point and Lagoon Point, and all waters east of Whidbey Island north of a line drawn due east from the southernmost tip of Possession Point on Whidbey Island to the shoreline.

*Tofino Traffic       156.725 MHz (Ch. 74)*
The waters west of 124°40'W. Within 50 nautical miles of the coast of Vancouver Island including the waters north of 48°N and east of 127°W.

**Note:** A portion of Tofino Sector's monitoring area extends beyond the defined CVTS area. Designated frequency monitoring is voluntary in these portions outside of VTS Jurisdiction, however, prospective VTS Users are encouraged to monitor the designated frequency.

*Vancouver Traffic   156.550 MHz (Ch. 11)*
The navigable waters of the Strait of Georgia west of 122°52'W, the navigable waters of the central Strait of Juan de Fuca north and east of Race Rocks, including the Gulf Island Archipelago, Boundary Pass and Haro Strait.

## PRINCE WILLIAM SOUND

**Note:** The bridge-to-bridge navigational frequency, 156.650 MHz (Channel 13), is used in these VTSs because the level of radiotelephone transmissions does not warrant a designated VTS frequency. The listening watch required by §26.05 of this chapter is not limited to the monitoring area.

*Valdez Traffic       156.650 MHz (Ch. 13)*
The navigable waters south of 61°05'N, east of 147°20'W, north of 60°N, and west of 146°30'W; and all navigable waters in Port Valdez.

## LOUISVILLE

*See note under Prince William Sound.*

Louisville Traffic                156.650 MHz (Ch. 13)
The navigable waters of the Ohio River between McAlpine Locks (Mile 606) and Twelve-Mile Island (Mile 593), only when the McAlpine upper pool gauge is at approximately 13.0 feet or above.

## RESOURCES

*U.S. Coast Guard's Boating Safety Hotline: (800) 368-5647. You can obtain information on boating safety recalls, report defects in boats, receive answers to boating safety questions, and obtain boating safety literature.*

*See page 160 for addresses of USCG District offices.*

*Canadian Coast Guard
Office of Boating Safety
344 Slater Street, 9th Floor
Ottawa, Ontario  K1A0N7
613-990-3116*

*Canadian Marine Rescue Auxillary safety line: 800-267-6687*

*United Safe Boating Institute
1504 Blue Ridge Road
Raleigh, NC 27607
919-821-0281*

*BOAT U.S. Foundation
880 South Pickett Street
Alexandria, VA 22304-4606
703-823-9550*

*The American Boat & Yacht Council (ABYC)
3069 Solomon's Island Road
Edgewater, MD 21037-1416
410-956-1050*

*The American Bureau of Shipping (ABS)
2 World Trade Center, 106th Floor
New York, NY 10048-0203
212-839-5000*

# ESSENTIAL NAVIGATION

3

# NAVIGATION BASICS

This section is designed for new navigators. It provides information that experienced navigators already know. For them, this chapter can serve as a reminder of essentials.

## CHARTS

You should no sooner head out in your boat without up-to-date charts than you should set out across the Atlantic in a canoe. Don't be lulled into thinking that updated charts aren't important because the positions of hazardous rocks and ledges don't change. The positions of sandbars and other features do change in storms, and the Coast Guard often makes changes in navigational aids.

How do you keep charts up-to-date? Buy the latest editions and correct them continually with information about recent changes and special warnings promulgated by the Coast Guard in weekly Notices to Mariners. See the list on page 160 for the Coast Guard district addresses where you can obtain Local Notices to Mariners for your area. An excerpt from Notices to Mariners is included on page 159.

## Projections

Most of the charts you'll use are Mercator projections in which features on the curved surface of the earth are projected onto a cylinder tangent to the earth's surface at the equator. This type of projection serves navigators well because all directions are represented by straight lines. So, for example, if your intended course is 045°, you can plot it as a straight line in that direction.

Mercator projections have a major drawback, however: Those straight-line courses don't usually take you along the path that is the shortest distance between two points. For short trips, the distances along these so-called "rhumb line" courses are not so much longer than the shortest (great circle) routes that you need to make adjustments to the straight course line on your regular Mercator-type chart.

When you set off on a long ocean passage, though, you'll want to take the shortest route. To figure out the changing

**Mercator Projection**

This projection turns a spherical surface into a flat map by "projecting" the earth's surface onto a cylinder that is tangential to the equator. Lines of longitude become parallel. Longitude is carefully scaled to latitude so that accurate compass courses can be drawn on Mercator charts. Large-area Mercator projections distort reality by showing areas away from the equator as relatively larger than areas closer to the equator.

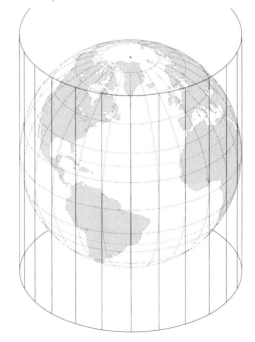

courses to steer along that great circle route, you can use a different type of chart—a gnomonic projection, on which the features on the earth's surface are projected onto a plane surface tangent to the earth at a single point.

A gnomonic chart has limited use because a single course or direction is not drawn in a straight line. But the shortest distance between points on a gnomonic-type chart is a straight line, so you can use it to set long distance routes that are as short as possible. (Other methods of calculating courses over long distances are covered in Chapter 4.)

## Coordinates

The grids on Mercator-type charts are formed by two types of lines: meridians of longitude, where planes through the center of the earth and the poles intersect the earth's surface; and parallels of latitude, where slices of the earth cut parallel to the equator intersect the surface. Meridians are great circles on which units of distance are constant throughout their length. All parallels of latitude except the equator are small circles—the planes that form them do not pass through the earth's center.

## Universal Plotting Sheets

You can make your own Mercator projection chart using a universal plotting sheet. The key is to get the right spacing between the meridians of longitude. Only then will a single direction be in a straight line. On the earth's surface, meridians of longitude are most widely spaced at the equator and gradually converge as latitude increases until the distance between them at the poles is zero. On a Mercator projection—to keep the direction aspect straight—the meridians are parallel rather than converging. The spacing between them changes with changes in latitude.

You use a universal plotting sheet to plot positions obtained in celestial navigation (Chapter 4) in mid-ocean areas lacking coastal features (or to keep a DR reckoning when you don't have a large-scale chart). Its description here can help you understand the Mercator projections you use in everyday navigation.

A universal plotting sheet contains a circle divided into 360° and three parallels of latitude—one drawn horizontally through the center of the circle, and the other two tangent to the circle's top and bottom. (See illustration.) Label the middle latitude

**Essential Nav.**

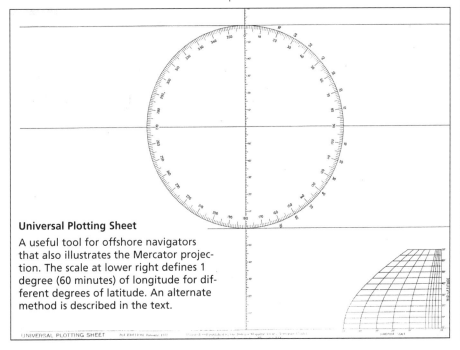

**Universal Plotting Sheet**

A useful tool for offshore navigators that also illustrates the Mercator projection. The scale at lower right defines 1 degree (60 minutes) of longitude for different degrees of latitude. An alternate method is described in the text.

UNIVERSAL PLOTTING SHEET     2nd EDITION January 1977

125

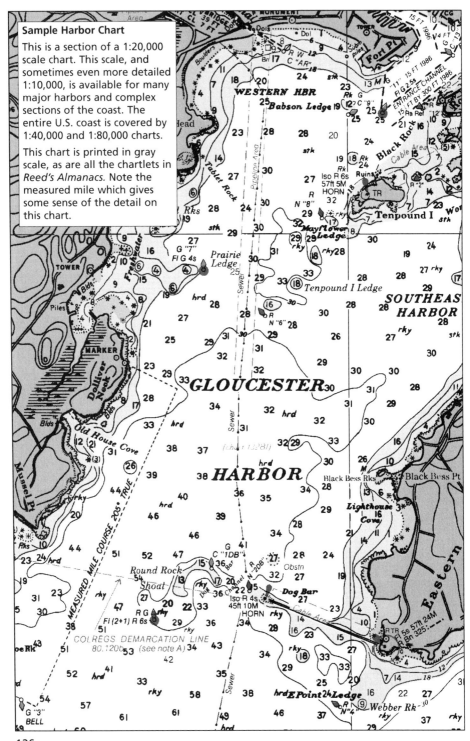

**Sample Harbor Chart**

This is a section of a 1:20,000 scale chart. This scale, and sometimes even more detailed 1:10,000, is available for many major harbors and complex sections of the coast. The entire U.S. coast is covered by 1:40,000 and 1:80,000 charts.

This chart is printed in gray scale, as are all the chartlets in *Reed's Almanacs*. Note the measured mile which gives some sense of the detail on this chart.

with a whole degree nearest your position, say 40° north. Then label the other parallels of latitude accordingly.

To draw the meridians of longitude with the spacing that corresponds to this mid-latitude, find the complement of 40° (90 minus 40 equals 50) and locate 50° on the circle; draw a vertical meridian through it. The distance between this meridian and the north-south line drawn through the center of the circle is one degree of longitude.

By visualizing the placement of meridians corresponding to different latitudes, you can see that the distance between meridians decreases as latitude increases. Because the relationship between distance and latitude is constant (one degree equals 60 nautical miles), you can use the latitude scale on the sides of charts to measure distance. You'll make a big mistake if you use the longitude scale at the top and bottom of charts because the distances between meridians are not constant.

## Compass Rose

The circle drawn on a universal plotting sheet is, in effect, a compass rose. Most Mercator charts have one or more compass roses printed on them to show directions. They usually show both true and magnetic directions, with the outer circle oriented to true north and the inner circle oriented to the magnetic pole.

When setting courses or measuring bearings with a magnetic compass, be sure to use the inner (magnetic) ring to draw directions on the chart.

## Chart Features

### Depths
All charted depths are given with reference to a low water level—often mean low water, for example. The units are feet, fathoms, or meters, as stated under the chart title. In places with no appreciable tide, sea level is the reference point. On metric charts, depths are given in whole meters; shallow depths are given in meters and decimeters—$5_3$ means 5.3 meters. In shallow areas on charts using fathoms, the same practice is followed to subdivide fathoms into feet.

### Heights
Heights are given in feet above a high

water level, such as mean high water. The reference point—called the datum—is chosen so that you can safely assume that clearance under bridges or obstructions will normally be at least as great as indicated on the chart. Depths are based on a similarly conservative assumption.

### Contours
Depth contours delineate areas inside of which the depth does not exceed a certain value. For example, inside the six-fathom curve, the depth everywhere is less than six fathoms. Height contours are also shown on land alongshore.

### Soundings
Because depths can't be printed at every point on the bottom, the least depths are given priority and others are shown in a pattern that avoids cluttering the chart.

### Bottom Surface
To inform your anchoring decisions, as well as for other purposes, charts include information about bottom composition. The possibilities range from the familiar mud, sand, and rocks, to the uncommon marl, shingle, and ooze.

### Navigation Aids
Symbols are used to designate and locate buoys, lights, and other aids. So that you'll be able to recognize them, these symbols are drawn larger than scale, but their positions are given with precision.

### Chart Symbols and Abbreviations
The Coast Guard's Chart No. 1—not a chart but a small paperback book—gives full details of every symbol and abbreviation used and should be included in every navigator's kit. Some useful excerpts from Chart No. 1 start on page 168.

## Pilot Charts

One of several types of special-purpose charts, pilot charts provide important hydrographic, navigational, and meteorological information for planning voyages. Charts covering major ocean basins are issued for each month. A pilot chart of the North Atlantic for June tells you, for example, how far south the icebergs migrate, the frequency of storms, and the likely strengths and directions of winds.

You can't use pilot charts to navigate, but they're an essential tool in voyage plan-

Essential Nav.

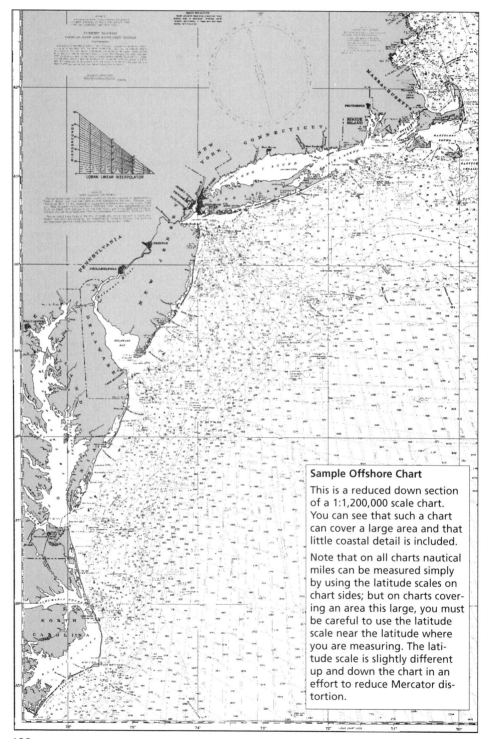

**Sample Offshore Chart**

This is a reduced down section of a 1:1,200,000 scale chart. You can see that such a chart can cover a large area and that little coastal detail is included.

Note that on all charts nautical miles can be measured simply by using the latitude scales on chart sides; but on charts covering an area this large, you must be careful to use the latitude scale near the latitude where you are measuring. The latitude scale is slightly different up and down the chart in an effort to reduce Mercator distortion.

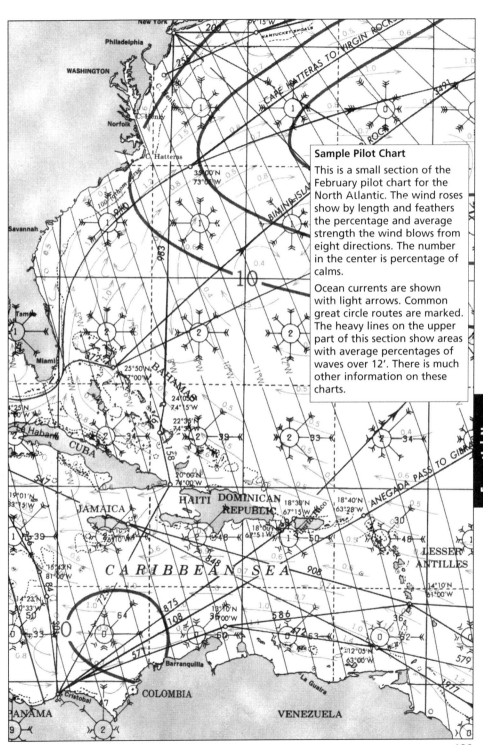

**Sample Pilot Chart**

This is a small section of the February pilot chart for the North Atlantic. The wind roses show by length and feathers the percentage and average strength the wind blows from eight directions. The number in the center is percentage of calms.

Ocean currents are shown with light arrows. Common great circle routes are marked. The heavy lines on the upper part of this section show areas with average percentages of waves over 12'. There is much other information on these charts.

Essential Nav.

ning. Take a moment to look over the wide array of data on the portion of a pilot chart shown on the previous page. You might want to get one for your part of the world even though you're not planning a voyage soon.

## PLOTTING

### Notes

Common mistake number one: Using the directions on the outer (true) ring of the compass rose when using magnetic compasses. When the compasses you use to steer or take bearings are magnetic, you usually don't need to convert the directions to true before plotting them because, on the vast majority of charts, the compass roses include an inner circle with magnetic directions. You simply use the inner circle.

When equipped with magnetic compasses, your need to plot true directions is limited. You should be prepared to plot true directions, for example, on long passages in which variation—the difference between true and magnetic directions—changes.

(Some charts covering very large areas omit the inner ring on their compass roses.) The procedure for converting between true and magnetic directions is covered later.

Common mistake number two: Using the longitude scale (printed at the tops and bottoms of charts) to measure distance. The author pledges to haunt any reader who makes this mistake.

You should, of course, use the latitude scale, for reasons already explained.

In addition, when you're using small-scale charts (covering large areas) you should use that part of the latitude scale that is alongside your track, because the scale is expanded with increasing latitude on Mercator-type charts. Of course, if your large-scale (small area) chart has a separate distance scale printed in a margin, you can use that, but it's not a very salty thing to do.

Common mistake number three: Messing up the transfer of directions from one part of the chart to another. It's not easy to "walk" a line to or from a compass rose without changing its direction, especially when you're bobbing around on a boat

and you're not able to spread out and tape down your chart. Be patient when using a parallel ruler to move the lines; you may need to make several attempts before you succeed. Avoid the temptation to settle for "getting close." That's not good enough. You don't need to add sloppy plotting to navigation errors.

If you lose patience with parallel rulers, try using a protractor with a built-in compass rose. You plot true, not magnetic, directions with a protractor, so be prepared to convert between true and magnetic when you use one.

## Plotting Tools

In addition to a parallel ruler or protractor, you'll need good dividers to measure distance. Adjust the dividers so that they're not so loose as to be floppy nor so tight they aren't easily spread. When adjusted properly, you can measure distances with one hand and hold your parallel ruler (or yourself) in place with the other.

You'll also need a close relative of dividers, a drawing compass, to draw arcs. A drawing compass is a divider with a lead pencil at one point.

A quartz watch tells all the time you'll need for piloting. It should be genuinely water resistant. (More on time in Chapter 4.)

Pencils, sharpeners, and soft-gum erasers are added to this list of plotting tools without apology for insulting your intelligence. With a good eraser you can not only clean up your mistakes, but you'll be able to reuse the same parts of a chart.

### THE COMPASS

Very few smaller craft used mainly on coastal routes are fitted with gyrocompasses, which are precisely oriented to true north by their continuously spinning motion and their sensitivity to the earth's rotation around its north-south axis. Gyrocompasses are expensive and dependent on an uninterrupted supply of electricity.

## Magnetic Compasses

Most recreational and small-craft navigators rely on magnetic compasses, which can be quite accurate and don't need electrical power. They are, however, perturbed by metal objects on the boat, thereby requiring you to convert compass readings to magnetic directions.

Modern magnetic compasses consist of a circular card floating in a fluid-filled enclosed bowl. Magnets attached to the card's underside align it to the magnetic axis. To offset the unwanted influence of magnetic material near the compass, you can adjust the positions of the compensating magnets under the card to reduce the amount of deviation between the card's orientation and the magnetic axis. Normally, it's best to hire a professional compass adjuster to perform the adjustment. The procedure is complicated because the deviation changes as your boat's heading changes. (With changes in heading come changes in the directional relationships between your compass, metal objects on your boat, and the north-south axis.)

Even after careful adjustment, some deviation will likely remain when your compensating magnets can't completely offset the influences of surrounding objects. Therefore, you need to determine the residual deviation on various headings so you can apply corrections to your magnetic compass readings. These values of deviation are normally determined as part of a professional compass adjustment and are recorded on a deviation card—a simple table with compass headings, say, every 30° in one column and the corresponding deviation in the other.

For deviation on headings between those contained on your card, you can interpolate. Or, you can construct a deviation curve showing deviation on all headings. (A deviation card showing this type of curve is illustrated on page 134.)

You can check these values from time to time by taking bearings on ranges; that is, on any object that lines up behind another. You don't have to confine yourself to formal ranges established by the Coast Guard. Ranges abound in most coastal areas. You can use any pair of objects—one nearer, the other farther away—whose locations are precisely given on your chart. If there are plenty of ranges in a variety of directions in your area, you can use them by steering courses along a selected group of ranges—that is, by keeping the objects in line ahead or astern as you move toward or away from them. You then compare the compass directions you're steering with the charted magnetic directions of the ranges. The differences are the deviations on these headings.

If your selection of ranges is limited, you can still determine deviation on various headings by swinging your boat around to various headings while located on a line extending from a single range. As you swing, the direction you measure to the range shouldn't change. The extent to which it does as you change headings equals your deviation on those headings.

It's awkward and imprecise, with your steering compass, to measure bearings that aren't directly ahead or astern. To improve accuracy in this swinging procedure, you can construct and use a pelorus—a device that enables you to accurately measure relative bearings; that is, directions relative to your vessel's bow or, more precisely, its centerline.

With reasonable care you can construct a pelorus with materials readily at hand. Mark a sheet of plywood approximately 12 to 18 inches square with a lubber line along the center. On the center of this square, glue a compass rose from an old chart with the magnetic north and south lines carefully lined up on the lubber line. Then mark a circle of, say, 12 inches diameter on the plywood square, using the center of the compass rose for the purpose. Now, draw lines through each 5° point on the rose to the outer circle mentioned above. You can then further subdivide the degree marks on the outer ring, but you'll probably find you can quite accurately estimate the readings by eye. A small wooden point about nine inches long mounted in the center of the rose completes the pelorus, which you mount so that the lubber line is on the fore and aft line of your vessel.

With a pelorus, you can also measure relative bearings to a single distant object, even a heavenly body, as you swing your vessel and convert them to compass bearings to get deviation. If the object is far away (five miles or more) and you swing in a tight circle so that you stay nearly in the same position, then the bearing to the object should not change appreciably as you swing.

Because you're using a single object and not a range, you don't know the correct magnetic bearing to the object. But you can find that bearing (and deviation on various headings) as you swing: it's the average of all the bearings you observe in your swing.

Here's the procedure. Swing your vessel until her head is on due north (compass) and note the bearing of the object on the pelorus. Repeat this procedure for each quadrant of the compass until you get eight bearings of the object. Then convert these relative pelorus bearings to compass bearings.

For example, with the ship's head on compass north, the pelorus reading will be the actual bearing of the object as you would read it from your compass. Let's assume that this reading is 250°. Then, if you swing the ship's head to 045°, the pelorus bearing would become, say, 200°. The compass bearing of the object would thus be 200° + 45°—or 245°. Carrying on this way you'd obtain a series of roughly similar pelorus bearings; their average would give the correct magnetic bearing of the object. When you compare this average bearing to the bearings measured at each quadrant, you get the deviation at each of these points.

Chapter 4 explains how to determine deviation when you can't see a range or single distant object.

## Digital Compasses

Installing an advanced digital magnetic compass that compensates continuously and automatically to within an accuracy of half a degree is one way to avoid dealing with the deviation problem. If you locate the unit at a dry place on your boat farthest away from large metal parts, you'll get stable readouts at your steering station in the roughest weather. A digital compass interfaces readily with electronic navigation systems, charts, and autopilots.

However, there are drawbacks to weigh against the considerable advantage that digital compasses provide. Like gyrocompasses, digital compasses rely on steady electrical power. Also, their physical make-up can limit their use in taking bearings.

## Compass Correction

You've got to take account of both deviation and variation when you need to convert back and forth between compass and true directions. Deviation and variation are values having both magnitude and direction—east or west. In making these conversions, you can logically determine where to add or subtract east or west values by noting whether magnetic north is left or right of true north on your chart's compass rose; by changing the plus or minus signs associated with east or west deviation when you translate the values from errors to corrections; and by reversing the steps you use to convert from true to compass when you convert from compass to true. Confusing, isn't it?

Or, you can swallow your pride in your capacity to apply logic and simply use the memory device that old salts and beginners alike have used for ages: Can Dead Men Vote Twice At Elections? When you line up this catchy question with its compass-correcting counterpart, the pairing looks like this:

| | | |
|---|---|---|
| **C**an | **C**ompass | |
| **D**ead | **D**eviation | |
| **M**en | **M**agnetic | Add in this |
| **V**ote | **V**ariation | direction |
| **T**wice | **T**rue | |
| **A**t | **A**dd | |
| **E**lections | **E**ast | |

Suppose you want to know the true course that corresponds to your compass course of 060°. You look at your deviation card to find that the deviation on that heading is 6° east. The compass rose on the chart shows a variation of 8° west.

Keeping this pneumonic in mind, you'll remember that you add the 6° easterly deviation to the compass course to get a magnetic course of 066° and then subtract the 8° westerly variation to get a true course of 058°.

Going the other way, from true to compass, you reverse the order and the signs. When you know any three values, you can find the other two. The single memory aid prompts you to correctly handle all the variables going in either direction.

Even so, some mariners like to use a second pneumonic when correcting from true to compass. At the risk of overtaxing your memory of pneumonics, it's included here: True Virgins Make Dull Companions At Weddings.

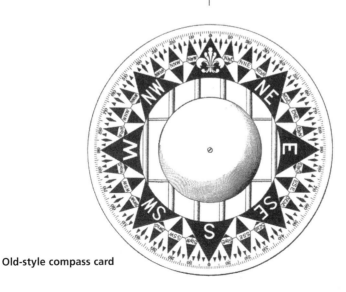

**Old-style compass card**

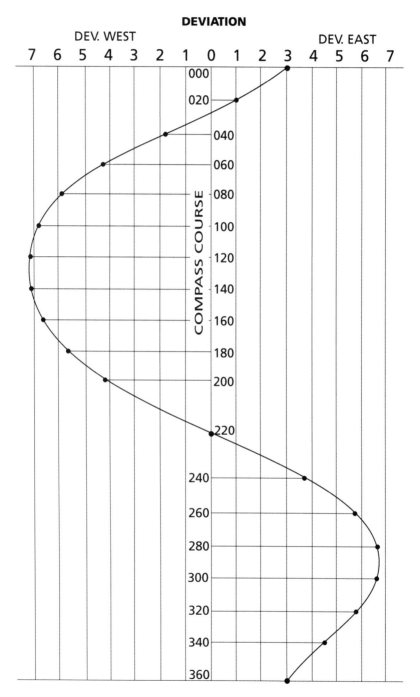

**DEVIATION**

DEV. WEST           DEV. EAST

7   6   5   4   3   2   1   0   1   2   3   4   5   6   7

COMPASS COURSE

**An example of a graphic deviation card,
which shows the method of construction**

# PILOTING

## TRACKS

It's important to attach clear and consistent meanings to your own use of the words "heading," "course," and "track." Although these terms are often used interchangeably and differently by authors and mariners, that shouldn't cause you a problem if you remember several essential distinctions when defining these words in your own mind.

The direction that your boat is headed at any instant is usually somewhat different from the course you're steering. "Not when I'm steering!" you say? Even the best skippers must admit that their boat oscillates around their course. If the oscillation is evenly distributed on both sides of your course, your average heading equals your course. Under some conditions, though, the helmsman tends to head more to one side of course than the other. Steep seas on your starboard quarter, for example, tend to move you to the right of your course as the waves lift your stern and your boat yaws to starboard. If you don't deliberately compensate for this tendency, the difference between your average heading and your intended course can be significant.

Such tendencies usually produce a difference between your intended course and the course you actually make good through the **water**. Your intended course usually differs from your course, or track, made good over the **ground**, as well, for other reasons. One factor is current that moves the whole body of water you're in—and your boat with it—in directions (set) and at speeds (drift) that you can't control. Another factor is leeway, the sideways slippage especially noticeable in sailboats beating to weather. To gauge leeway, look astern and observe your wake. If it's tracking directly astern in line with your boat's centerline, then you have no leeway. If it angles off to windward of that line, the angle it forms with the extension of your centerline is the amount of your leeway. To measure this angle accurately, you can tie a light line to a point on your boat's centerline and trail it astern. If you're making leeway, the line will trail off slightly to windward and you can measure the extent that it does—your leeway.

## DEAD RECKONING, ESTIMATED POSITIONS, AND FIXES

Among the three types of positions you can plot, the one based on dead reckoning—your DR position—is likely to be the least accurate because it's based only on a projection of the course you're steering and your speed through the water. When you take account of known current, leeway and, yes, error at the helm, in advancing your position you're establishing an estimated position (EP). When you establish your position with reference to directions and distances to surrounding or far-off objects, you get a fix. Because the distinctions among these types of positions is very important, they are conventionally plotted with different symbols: a semicircle for a DR position; a square for an EP; and a full circle for a fix—each with a dot in the center to mark its exact location.

When you know what current is acting on you with reasonable confidence, you can project an EP based on it. You do this by drawing a vector diagram on your chart using your course and speed through the water as one entering vector, the set and drift of the current as another, and get the estimated course and speed over the ground as the resulting vector.

### Compensating for Current and Leeway

You can also modify this process to determine an unknown current by comparing the location of a fix (based on a course and speed over the ground) with a corresponding DR position (based on a course and speed through the water). The direction and distance of the resulting vector, from the DR position to the fix, is the set and drift of the current.

Figure 1 illustrates the different kinds of positions defined above. Assuming point A to be the last reliable fix (obtained at, say, 1300 hours), and AB the course steered and the log distance for one hour; then B is the DR position for 1400 hours—i.e., the position the vessel would be in if there were no leeway, no current, the course had been accurately steered, and the distance run through the water accurately indicated.

Essential Nav.

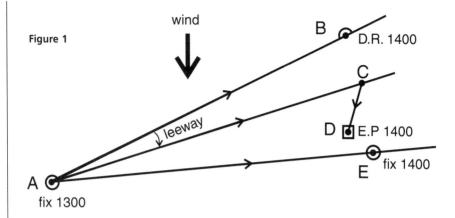

Figure 1

wind

B D.R. 1400

C

leeway

D E.P 1400

E fix 1400

A fix 1300

If the vessel had been making leeway (angle BAC) due to a northerly wind, but was not affected by current, then C would be the EP at 1400 hours. Note that the distance AB and AC are the same.

If, however, a current setting, say, 200° T at 3 knots were encountered, then you'd lay off the set and drift for one hour (200° - 3 miles) on the chart from point C—i.e., CD, and point D is now the EP for 1400 hours. Should a reliable fix, E, be obtained at 1400 hours, you could determine the current actually experienced during the last hour by measuring the direction and distance from C to E (not drawn in figure). The track made good over the ground would be the straight line AE.

You can offset the effects of current by adjusting your course (and speed) so that you're more likely to proceed along your intended track (and arrive on time). To do this, draw a vector diagram starting with the above elements, but apply the current vector to your starting point and reverse its direction. A line with a length equal to your speed through the water, drawn from the end of this reversed current vector to the course and speed through the water vector, completes the triangle and indicates the course to steer to stay on your intended track. (See figure 2.)

For example, say you want to make good a track of 75°. The current is setting 190° at 3 knots of drift. A northerly wind is creating a 5° leeway angle. Your speed through the water is 9 knots. What course should you steer to offset the effects of current and leeway, and what will be your speed over the ground?

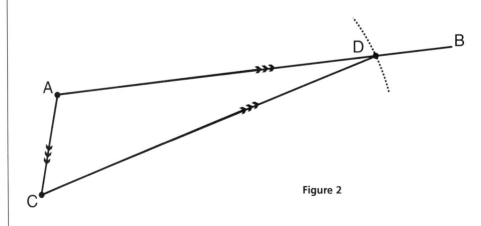

D B

A

C

Figure 2

In the diagram, AB represents the intended track.

1. From your starting point A, lay off the current vector AC representing 3 knots at 190° T (using units from any convenient scale).

2. With center C and radius equal to your speed through the water of 9 knots, strike an arc cutting AB at D.

3. CD represents course required 061° T to compensate for the current.

4. Apply leeway angle of 5° in a windward direction; course will be 056° T.

5. The length of AD, measured in the same units as A, indicates that 8 knots is the speed over the ground.

Illustrated on page 200 is a type of plotting sheet that can make short work of this sort of problem.

## USING THE COURSE CORRECTION TABLE

*Reed's* offers you another way to make allowance for current. By using the table on page 162, you don't have to work out the problem on your chart. This table is based on two facts: 1) The slower your vessel's speed, the more effect current will have on her; and, 2) the more this current is abeam, the more it will push your vessel sideways and, therefore, require a greater course compensation. Should the stream be directly ahead or astern, no course allowance is needed, but the speed will need to be advanced or retarded.

The table—in addition to giving a compensating course adjustment—gives also the speed made good over the ground. You'll likely find that in practical navigation the course correction is more important than the speed correction.

### Correcting Your Course for Current

This section might more accurately be called "How to Find the Course to Steer to Counteract the Effect of Current."

1. Find the speed of the current at the top of the page and the relative angle of the current from the desired track in the left-hand column, C. Read the value from the table.

2. Find at the top of the table the speed of the vessel (through the water) and look down this column until you find the value in #1 above (or its close approximation). Then read off in the left-hand column C the number of degrees of allowance to be made to the course.

3. Make this course correction to the same side, port or starboard, as the current. That is, to counteract a current setting toward the vessel's starboard side, you alter course to starboard.

*Example 1:*
Vessel steering 060° T at 10 knots estimates a current will set 290° T at 3 1/2 knots. What course should be made to compensate?

1. Find speed of current—3 1/2 knots—in column at top of page and 50° (relative angle of the current to the vessel's course) on the left-hand side of the page. The value is 2.681.

2. Find the speed of vessel—10 knots—at the top of the table and value 2.681 in this column—2,760 is the nearest. The course allowance in column C on this line is 16°.

3. Because the current is on the starboard bow you must alter course 16° to the right to counteract its effect. Therefore, the course to steer is 076° T.

*Example 2:*
Vessel steering 200° T, speed 8 knots, current estimated to set 230° T at 1 1/2 knots (i.e., 30° from dead astern). With 1 1/2 knots on top and 30° in column C, value is 0.750. With 8 knots on top and value 0.750 in same column, 5° is found in column C. Current is on port quarter, so alter course 5° to port and steer 195° T.

*Example 3:*
Vessel steering 337° at 14 1/2 knots, current setting 247° at 2 1/2 knots. With 2 1/2 knots on top and 90° in column C, the value is 2.500. With 14 1/2 knots on top and value 2.500 in the same column, 10° is found in column C. Current is abeam to starboard so alter course 10° to starboard. Therefore, course to steer is 347°.

### How to Find the Speed Made Good Over the Ground

1. Enter the table from the top with the speed of the current and from the right-hand column S with relative angle of the current. Read from the table the factor

and name it "C.C." (Current Contribution to vessel's speed over the ground.)

2. Enter table from the top with your vessel's speed (through the water) and from the right-hand column S with the course correction found as above. Read from the table the factor and name it "S.C." (Ship's Contribution to vessel's speed over the ground.)

3. If current is on the bow (that is, ahead of the beam), the vessel's speed over the ground is the difference between S.C. and C.C. If current is abaft the beam, the vessel's speed over the ground is the sum of S.C. and C.C.

*Example 1:*
Vessel's speed through the water is 10 knots; the current is 3 1/2 knots, 50° on the bow; course correction is 16°. What is the vessel's speed over the ground?
1. With 3 1/2 knots at top and 50° on the right in column S, the value of C.C. (by interpolation) is 2.249.

2. With 10 knots at the top and a 16° course correction on the right in column S (by interpolation), the S.C. value is 9.608.

3. Because the current is ahead of the vessel (that is, 50° on the starboard bow) and pushing her back, the difference between S.C. and C.C.—9.608 and 2.249—gives 7.359 knots*, the vessel's speed over the ground. If the current had been on the starboard quarter (that is, helping the vessel along), you'd use the sum of the C.C. and S.C.—11.857 knots—to calculate the speed over the ground.

*If you hadn't interpolated but had used the nearest tabulated figures—C.C. 2.203 and S.C. 9.660—the result would have been 7.457, which is accurate enough for ordinary purposes.

*Example 2:*
Vessel's speed, 8 knots, current speed 1 1/2 knots, 30° on the quarter. Course allowance 5°. What is the vessel's speed over the ground?
1. With 1 1/2 knots and 30°, C.C. is 1.300.

2. With 8 knots and 5°, S.C. is 7.970.

3. Because current is behind vessel, the sum of 9.27 is the speed over the ground.

*Example 3:*
Vessel's speed, 14 1/2 knots, current 2 1/2 knots abeam. Course allowance 10°. What is the vessel's speed over the ground?
1. With 2 1/2 knots and 90°, C.C. is 0.

2. With 14 1/2 knots and 10°, S.C. is 14 1/4.

3. Because the current is abeam, the sum, or difference, is 14 1/4, so the vessel's speed over the ground is 14 1/4 knots— the same as her speed through the water.

## Measuring Speed

To get an accurate measure of your speed through the water, perhaps as a check of the accuracy of your knotmeter, you can time your run on a straight line between any two charted objects. To cancel the effects of current on your answer, you need to make the run twice, in reciprocal directions, and average the results.

### TIME-DISTANCE-SPEED CALCULATIONS

The calculations you do in dead reckoning, compensating for current, and determining current often require you to convert back and forth between speed and distance. You can do this by using a simple algebraic formula, a nautical slide rule or calculator, or the table that starts on page 186. Many electronic navigation instruments have components that do the problems for you; you simply select the speed or distance button.

To do time-distance-speed problems unaided, you can use the formula
$$60D = S \times T \text{ or } D = \frac{S \times T}{60}$$
when dealing with time in minutes, distance in nautical miles, and speed in knots. To remember this formula, think of the address 60 **D** Street. If, for example, your speed is seven knots and you run for 40 minutes, then your distance run, **D**, = **S** x **T**/60 or 7 x 40/60 or **280/60** or 4 2/3 knots.

On a pitching boat, at a cramped navigation station, or in the cockpit, it's a lot easier and quicker to use a nautical (circular) slide rule (commonly available at chandleries). This or the *Reed's* table relieves you of the need to think it through—a welcome relief, especially when you're under stress or discomfort from, say, thick fog or boisterous seas.

## POSITION FIXING

The intersection of two or more lines of position (LOPs) marks a fix. You should use more than two LOPs whenever possible because you can't gauge the accuracy of the lines when you use only two. Try to obtain the LOPs as nearly simultaneously as possible. If there's a significant time interval between the observations you can get a so-called "running fix" by advancing your plots of earlier LOPs up to the time of the last one. A simultaneous fix is usually more reliable than a running fix because accurate advancing of earlier LOPs depends on accurate estimates of current and leeway.

### Some Notes on Bearings

• LOPs based on directions to fixed objects ashore or to beacons fixed to the sea bottom are more reliable than those taken from floating buoys.

• Bearings to objects on the beam and nearby a moving vessel change more rapidly than objects ahead or astern or more distant. Your choice of objects and the sequence of your observing them can benefit from this knowledge.

• A single bearing to an object near your beam can give you an accurate reference point when making a turn (a turning bearing) and when determining if your hook has set or is dragging in the anchoring process (an anchor bearing).

There are other occasions when a single position line may prove useful. For example, you can use: a) an LOP parallel or nearly parallel to your intended track to determine whether or not your vessel is on track; b) a position line that crosses your track at or near 90° to check on speed over the ground; or, c) a single line tangent to a hazardous area (a danger bearing) to keep on the safe side.

• Bearings to ranges (objects in line) can be very accurate and, as pointed out earlier, require no compass correction. You can use any two objects, however dissimilar, whose locations are clearly shown on your chart—a point of land in line with a conspicuous chimney, for example.

• It's essential to relate precisely the object in view to its position on the chart. For example, your observation of the direction to the water's edge of a gradually sloping point of land can vary with the height of tide.

• Radar bearings suffer in accuracy because of the width of the signal, as explained in Chapter 4.

• It's difficult to measure bearings to celestial bodies accurately because of their height and difficult to plot their directions accurately because of their distance, so celestial LOPs are not primarily based on bearings.

• Radio directions can be measured only crudely because receivers are relatively insensitive directionally.

### Some Notes on Distance (or Range) of Objects

• Radar ranges can be quite accurate because they use the navigational strengths of electronic emissions.

• Loran LOPs can be even more accurate than radar ranges by providing precise measurement of the difference in distance between two transmitters.

• Measuring vertical or horizontal angles with a sextant is a seldom used but effective way to find your distance from objects—it's made easier by material presented later in this chapter.

• Even without a sextant, you can relate the known height of objects to distance off when making a landfall by getting a "dipping range" (more later).

### Soundings

LOPs are commonly thought of as straight lines based on bearings, or as arcs based on ranges. It doesn't stretch the concept of an LOP too far, though, to treat lines based on soundings in the same way. Especially where bottom contours form a regular pattern, as off the east coast of Florida, or where depths change abruptly, soundings can provide a reliable indication of position. So, for example, you're able to proceed safely on long stretches of the east coast of Florida by staying on, say, the six-fathom curve, steering more toward shore when the depth exceeds six fathoms, and away when it rises above that depth. Or, when crossing the Gulf Stream toward the Bahamas, you'll know precisely when you've entered the shallow banks by noting when you abruptly come "on soundings."

**Essential Nav.**

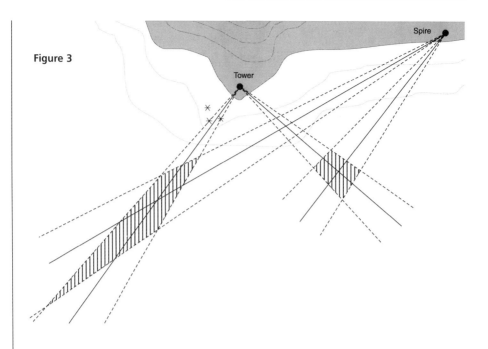

Figure 3

Cruisers in the Bahamas, as in other places, don't even need depthsounders to use "soundings." They learn to estimate depths quite accurately by observing changes in water color, just like the ancient Polynesians did. (Chapter 5 is filled with ways to navigate without instruments.)

Soundings should be used routinely to confirm the plausibility of positions based on other LOPs. And in dense fog, they may provide the primary basis for knowing your position.

### Fix Accuracy

Only in the unlikely event that you're located simultaneously on two ranges can you have complete confidence in a fix based on only two LOPs. You need at least a third LOP, or preferably more, to determine whether you're really at the intersection of the first two. If additional LOPs intersect at the same point, then you're in good shape; if not, and the three or more LOPs form a sizable triangle—a so-called "cocked hat"—then you'd better check for errors in the LOPs.

Common sources of errors in LOPs include failure to take compass deviation fully into account, failure to precisely locate the object observed on the chart, and the inherent difficulty of using a steering compass to take bearings. Even accurate LOPs will intersect in a triangle when a significant time interval separates the observations. In fact, on a fast-moving vessel you should be suspicious if three or more LOPs do intersect at a point. Normally you'd expect them to form a small triangle.

It's sometimes prudent to think of LOPs as giving you an area of possible positions rather than a definitive fix. You can visualize or plot that area by treating each LOP as a cone or band bordered by lines that represent the extent of potential error. If, for example, you judge that a bearing could be off by no more than 3° on either side, then you could safely assume that you're somewhere within an arc of 6° centered on the observed bearing, as illustrated by the shaded area in figure 3.

Where two or more such shaded areas overlap is your area of possible positions.

Note that the shape of the area depends on the angular relationship among the objects observed. The shape for two objects 90° apart is more compact than for two that are close together, or nearly reciprocal, in bearing. So, too, the shape is more compact, and useful, when three LOPs are 120° apart. You should be guided by these results in choosing objects to observe. By doing so, you can minimize the effects of errors in LOPs.

## THE RUNNING FIX

When only one known object is visible and you can't get both a range and bearing to it, you can take bearings to it at different times to obtain a running fix. This is the procedure:

1. Take the first bearing and note the time and log reading, if available; plot the position line on the chart and mark it with its direction and the time.

2. When the bearing has altered enough to make a good crossing angle with the first position line, repeat the procedure.

3. Advance the first line by moving any convenient point on the first line by the "run"—the course and distance made good over the ground during the time interval between observations.

4. Through the end of the run draw a line parallel to the first position line. This line is the first position line advanced and it should be marked by its direction, the time of its observation, and the time (of the second bearing) to which it's advanced.

5. The point where the advanced line crosses the second LOP is the running fix.

The accuracy of these fixes depends not only on the accuracy of the bearings and their angle of crossing, but also on your accuracy in estimating the leeway and current that affect the "run" between bearings. As with a simultaneous fix, you can better asses the reliability of a running fix when you transfer two bearings up to the time of a third. You can generally treat a small "cocked hat" thus formed with greater confidence than a running fix from only two bearings. Also, the principle of the running fix applies when you obtain the position lines from different objects. A bearing of one object may be advanced to cross with a bearing of another object that was not sighted until after the first one was lost to view.

***Example of a running fix, with no current or leeway (fig. 4):***

Vessel steering 270° T and making no leeway. At 2300 a lighthouse, P, bore 315° T, log read 86.2. At 2330 the same light bore 040° T, log read 90.7. If the current was estimated to be nil during the interval between the bearings, what was the ship's position at 2330 hours?

1. Plot the two position lines as described.

2. From any convenient point A on the first LOP lay off the run (AB) 270°, 4 1/2 miles.

3. Through B draw the advanced LOP parallel to PA; the point where it cuts the second bearing is the running fix.

**Figure 4**

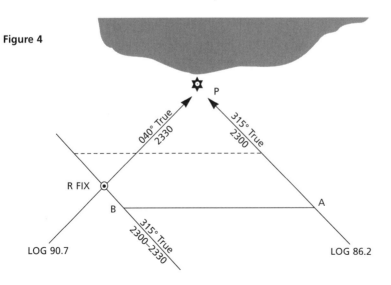

**Figure 5**

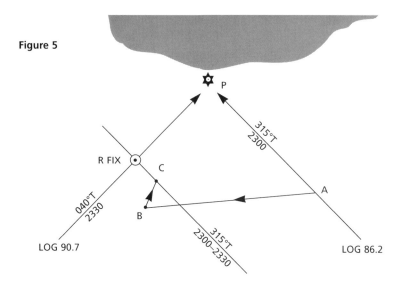

R FIX

C

A

315°T 2300

040°T 2330

B

315°T 2300-2330

LOG 90.7

LOG 86.2

P

**Example of a running fix, in a current and with leeway (fig. 5):**
Vessel steering 270° T and making 5° leeway due to a northerly wind. At 2300 hours a lighthouse, P, bore 315° T, log reading 86.2. At 2330 hours the same light bore 040° T, log reading 90.7. The current was estimated to be setting 010° at 2 knots. Find the vessel's position at 2330.

1. Plot the two position lines as described above.

2. From any convenient point A on the first position line, lay off AB (4 1/2 miles along the wake course adjusted for leeway—265°).

3. From point B lay off BC, the current effect for 30 minutes (1 mile in the direction of 010°). The estimated run, then, is AC.

4. Through point C draw the transferred LOP parallel to PA. The point where it cuts the second bearing is the fix.

### Some Useful Variations in the Running Fix Method
Using the running fix table (page 179) will enable you to approximate distance off an object before it comes abeam. If necessary, then, you can alter course to avoid danger. You can estimate the "distance off" even when you can't locate the observed object on the chart. By using the table you need not plot the bearings on the chart.

### Angles on the Bow
By choosing pairs of bearings in advance, you can determine distance off when the object comes abeam without using the table. When you know the course and the distance run over the ground during the interval between the two bearings, you can determine the "distance off" when the object is abeam by observing any of the following pairs of angles on the bow, because the distance off when abeam equals the distance run over the ground between the observations.

Pairs of angles: (a) 22° and 34°; (b) 25° and 41°; (c) 26 1/2° and 45°; (d) 32° and 59°; (e) 35° and 67°; (f) 37° and 72°; and (g) 45° and 90°.

**Caution:** As with other forms of running fixes, these methods (including the special cases described below), are accurate only when: (a) current and leeway are correctly taken into account; (b) the bearings are accurate; and, (c) the course is accurately steered. When you're affected by current and/or making leeway, you should use the angle between the bearing of the object and the track because in these circumstances the heading is likely to be very different than the track. The "abeam" bearing should always be 90° from the track. When the course and speed over the ground is uncertain, you should treat running fixes with utmost caution.

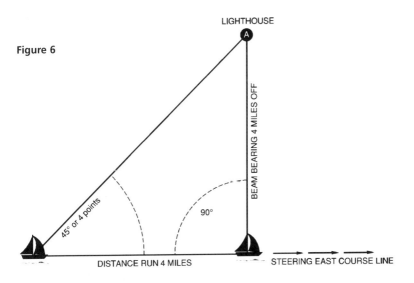

**Figure 6**

LIGHTHOUSE

A

BEAM BEARING 4 MILES OFF

45° or 4 points

90°

DISTANCE RUN 4 MILES                    STEERING EAST COURSE LINE

## Other Special Cases of Running Fixes

The two special cases that follow are especially easy to remember without referring to tables or this book, and so hold great value for those who are operating small vessels.

### Bow and Beam Bearing

When there is no leeway or current, take a bearing of an object when it bears 45° on the bow (if leeway or current are present, take the bearing when they make an angle of 45° with the track). Note the time and log. Note the time and log again when the object is abeam (or 90° to the track).

The distance made good over the ground in the interval between the two bearings equals the distance off when abeam. See figure 6.

*Example:*
Steering 022°, a lighthouse bears 067° at 1638, log 36. At 1704, it comes abeam bearing 112°, log 39 1/2. What is the distance off when abeam? The log shows 3 1/2 miles has been run. Therefore, the vessel is 3 1/2 miles off if there has been no current or leeway.

### Doubling the Angle on the Bow

Using the bow and beam rule, you can't estimate the object's distance off when abeam before you have it on your beam.

By "doubling the angle on the bow" you can find this distance in advance.

To do so, take a bearing of an object on the bow and note the time and log. Carefully watch the change in bearing until it is exactly doubled. Then note the log and time again. The distance made good over the ground between the bearings is the distance off at the time of taking the second bearing. This holds true no matter which pairs of bearings you use, so long as the second bearing doubles the first. For example, 22 1/2° and 45°, or 30° and 60° would be good choices.

*Example:*
Steering 231° at five knots, a lighthouse bears 259°. One hour and 13 minutes later, it bears 287°. What is the position at the second bearing?

The angle on the bow was doubled, from 28° to 56°. In one hour and 13 minutes at five knots the vessel steamed 6.1 miles. Therefore, the vessel's position is 6.1 miles off when the lighthouse bears 287°.

Essential Nav.

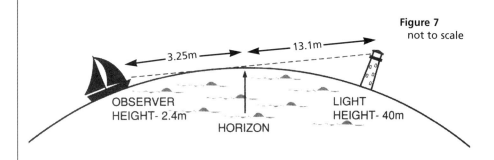

**Figure 7**
not to scale

3.25m

13.1m

OBSERVER
HEIGHT- 2.4m

LIGHT
HEIGHT- 40m

HORIZON

## FINDING THE DISTANCE OF OBJECTS AT SEA

Because of the earth's curvature, the distance you can see a far-off object at sea depends on your height of eye and the height of the object. Figure 7 illustrates this.

In this example, using the top table on page 161, the distance of the horizon from the observer is 3.25 miles; the distance of the light from the horizon is 13.1 miles. The light will first appear when you are 16.35 miles away, provided that visibility is sufficiently clear to allow you to see that far. This is useful information when making a landfall. You can use it not only to determine how far off you are when you first sight the light, but also to predict when you'll first see it.

To check whether or not a newly sighted light is actually on the horizon, lower your eye immediately to see if the light dips below the horizon again. In clear visibility and a heavy swell, the light should alternately rise above and dip below the horizon with your vessel's movement. The distance off from the light at this moment if often referred to as the "dipping range" or "dipping distance."

The lower table on page 161 combines the observer's and object's horizon distances to allow you to find the dipping range of a light in one step. By coupling the dipping range with a bearing to the light, you can fix your position.

### Range of Lights

How far away you can see a light depends not only on your height, the object's height, and atmospheric clarity,

but also on the strength of the beam of light. Different terms are used to sort these factors.

**Luminous range** is the maximum distance at which a light can be seen as determined by the intensity of the light and the meteorological visibility prevailing at the time; it takes no account of height.

**Nominal range** is the luminous range when visibility is unlimited.

**Geographic range** is the maximum distance at which a beam of light can theoretically reach an observer, as limited only by the height of the light and the refraction of the atmosphere. Geographic ranges assume a height of eye of 15 feet (about 5 meters).

The Lights Rising and Dipping Table on page 162 is based on normal atmospheric refraction and should not be used when conditions are abnormal.

The range shown on charts of U.S. waters is the nominal range. All heights of lights are given above high water. Allowance for the state of the tides should be made with lights of small elevation.

Glare from background lighting reduces considerably the range at which lights are sighted. A light of 100,000 candle power has a nominal range of about 20 miles; with minor background lighting, as from a populated coastline, this range is reduced to about 14 miles; and with major background lighting, as from a city or from harbor installations, to about nine miles.

Navigators with a near horizon and using the powerful lights around the U.S. coastline will probably be more concerned with the geographic range of lights.

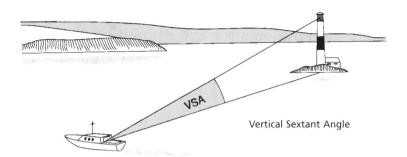

Vertical Sextant Angle

## LOPS BY SEXTANT

### Position by Vertical Sextant Angle

When you know the height of any object you can find your distance off by measuring a vertical sextant angle. If you take a bearing of the object at the same time, you get a fix. Because the heights of lighthouses are given on charts, you'll often use them for this technique. Remember that the stated height is to the center of the light, not to the top of the lighthouse structure. So, measure the light's center. Also, keep in mind that the given height refers to a chart datum related to some water level. In practice, you need not make an allowance for the height of tide or observer's eye unless the object is very low.

A table starting on page 180 enables you to translate a vertical sextant angle into the "distance off." When the height of the object is small, the distances can't be found beyond six miles, so the first page (containing heights only to 150 feet) extends only to six miles. The distance column is graduated for every cable up to three miles and two cables from three to six miles. A cable, or cable's length, is 100 fathoms, or 600 feet, or about 0.1 nautical mile.

*Example 1:*
The sextant angle of a lighthouse 40 meters above high water is measured at 0°24'. To find the distance off, enter the column for 40 meters. Glance down this column until you sight the vertical angle; that is, 24'. Move your eye along this line to the left where you find the distance off in miles and cables—in this case, three miles exactly.

If you want to keep three miles off this lighthouse, you must not let the sextant angle get larger than 0°24'.

### Measuring Vertical Sextant Angles

The sextant measures angles with great precision. It does this with two mirrors that enable you to bring the reflected image of one object into line with the direct image of another object. You move the sextant's arm to bring the two objects in line, and the extent of that movement is indicated on an arc that is graduated in degrees. A micrometer drum and vernier scale on

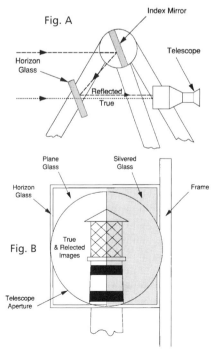

Fig. A

Fig. B

**Essential Nav.**

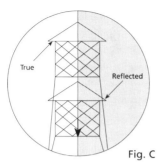

Fig. C

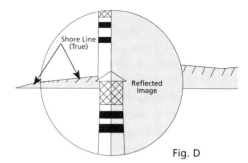

Fig. D

modern sextants enable you to subdivide the degrees into minutes and tenths of minutes of arc. The reading you get is the angular distance between the objects.

To measure vertical angles, set the index to zero. Hold the sextant vertically and view the center of the light (or other object) through the telescope. The light will be seen direct through the plane (or unsilvered) part of the horizon glass, i.e., the true image. It will also be seen as a reflected image in the silvered part. (Figs. A and B.) Both true and reflected images should coincide.

The micrometer head is now turned with the left hand so that the index moves along the arc, away from the telescope end. As soon as the micrometer is turned, the true and reflected images will separate, the reflected image moving downward. (Fig. C). As the reflected image of the light "falls," the sextant is tilted downward to follow its movement. When the center of the light reaches the shoreline the reading is noted. (Fig. D.)

Using the sextant should first be practised on dry land and then on a boat. Try bringing a chimney top down to the base of a wall to begin with.

## Horizontal Sextant Angle Fix

You can obtain a fix by measuring the angles between three objects marked on the chart and using the table on page 184. You get the best results when the objects are roughly equidistant from you and the angles separating them are at least 30°.

### Explanation and Examples of How to Use This Table

Figure 8 illustrates a vessel (S) whose navigator takes simultaneous (or nearly so) horizontal sextant angles. The first angle is between the center object, a church (C), and the right-hand object, a high rock (R). The second angle is between the church (C) and the left-hand object, a lighthouse (L), all marked conspicuously on the chart and clearly visible to the navigator.

The angle between the rock (R) and the church (C) (right-hand angle) is 30°. The distance between R and C is 3.2 miles. The angle between the lighthouse (L) and church (C) (left-hand angle) is 45°. The distance between L and C is 7.1 miles.

With the angle RSC (30°) subtended by the right-hand and center objects, enter the table on page 184 from the side and find the radius of one of the position circles in the column headed by the distance

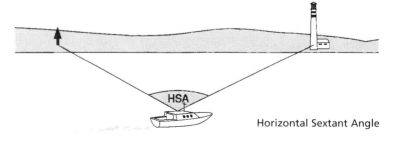

Horizontal Sextant Angle

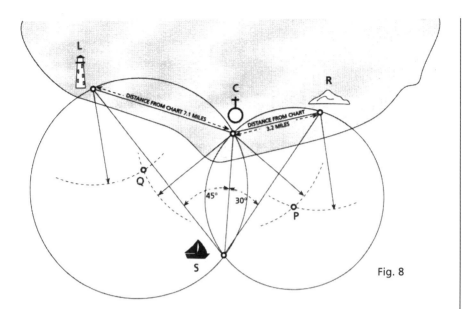

Fig. 8

between the objects. In this case, with 30° at the side and 3.2 miles at the top, the radius (by interpolation), is 3.2. Therefore, draw a short arc with a 3.2 mile radius from both R and C and mark P—their point of intersection. With the same radius, draw around P the circle RCS.

Proceeding in the same way, draw arcs LQ and CQ and circle LCS. The intersection of the two circles (S in the figure) gives the fix.

### Measuring Horizontal Sextant Angles

The horizontal sextant angle between, say, a lighthouse and a beacon, is measured by holding the sextant horizontally with the handle downward. As with the vertical sextant angle, the index is set to zero. The telescope is now pointed at the right-hand object, in figure E, the lighthouse.

Since the angle to be measured will be relatively large, the index is now moved along the arc by means of the release clamp. Actually, the body of the sextant must be swung toward the LEFT while the index arm is held steady in order to keep the reflected lighthouse in view. The reflected image of the lighthouse will appear to move toward the LEFT, so that by letting it follow the true coastline in the unsilvered part of the horizon glass it will eventually approach the beacon.

As soon as the beacon is seen in the horizon glass, the clamp is released. The micrometer head is now turned until the reflected image of the lighthouse is superimposed on the true image of the beacon. The angle may then be read.

Some navigators prefer to point the sextant initially at the left-hand object and move the index bar forward so the right-hand object eventually comes into view.

**Essential Nav.**

Fig. E

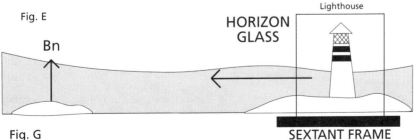

Fig. G

# AIDS TO NAVIGATION

## AIDS TO NAVIGATION SYSTEM

The waters of the United States and its territories are marked by the U.S. Aids to Navigation System. This system encompasses buoys and beacons that conform to the International Association of Lighthouse Authorities (IALA) buoyage guidelines, as well as other short-range aids to navigation.

The U.S. Aids to Navigation System is intended for use with nautical charts. You can't know the exact meaning of a particular aid to navigation unless you consult the appropriate nautical chart. Additional, important information supplementing that shown on charts is contained in the *Light List*, *Coast Pilots*, *Sailing Directions*, and *Reed's*.

### Types Of Marks

The IALA maritime buoyage guidelines apply to buoys and beacons that indicate the lateral limits of navigable channels, obstructions, dangers (such as wrecks), and other important areas or features. This system provides five types of marks: lateral marks, safe-water marks, special marks, isolated danger marks, and cardinal marks. (Cardinal marks are not now used in the United States.) Each type of mark is differentiated from other types by distinctive colors, shapes, and light rhythms. Examples are shown on pages 166 and 167.

**Lateral marks** are buoys or beacons that indicate the port and starboard sides of a route to be followed; they are used in conjunction with a "conventional direction of buoyage."

Generally, lateral aids to navigation indicate on which side of the aid a vessel should pass when navigable channels are entered from seaward and a vessel proceeds in the conventional direction of buoyage. Since all channels do not lead from seaward, certain assumptions must be made so the system can be consistently applied. In the absence of a route leading from seaward, the conventional direction of buoyage generally follows a clockwise direction around land masses.

Virtually all U.S. lateral marks are located in IALA Region B and follow the traditional 3R rule of "red, right, returning." In U.S.

waters, returning from seaward and proceeding toward the head of navigation is generally considered as moving southerly along the Atlantic coast, westerly along the Gulf coast, and northerly along the Pacific coast. In the Great Lakes, the conventional direction of buoyage is generally considered westerly and northerly, except on Lake Michigan where southerly movement is considered as returning from sea. When the direction of "returning" is ambiguous, check your chart carefully to determine the bouyage plan.

A summary of the port- and starboard-hand lateral mark characteristics is contained in the upper portion of the table on page 166.

**Preferred channel marks** are aids that mark channel junctions or bifurcations and often mark wrecks or obstructions. You may normally pass preferred channel marks on either side, but their red-and-green bands indicate the preferred channel.

At a point where a channel divides, when proceeding in the conventional direction of buoyage, a preferred channel in IALA Region B may be indicated by a modified port or starboard lateral mark as also shown in the upper portion of page 166.

CAUTION: It may not always be possible to pass on either side of preferred channel aids. Always consult the appropriate chart.

NOTE: U.S. lateral aids to navigation at certain Pacific islands are located within Region A and thus exhibit opposite color significance. Port-hand marks are red with square or cylindrical shapes; starboard-hand marks are green with triangular or conical shapes.

**Non-lateral marks** have no lateral significance but may be used to supplement the lateral aids to navigation specified above. Occasionally, daybeacons or minor lights outside of a normal channel do not have lateral significance because they do not define limits to navigable waters. These aids use diamond-shaped dayboards and are divided into four diamond-shaped sectors. The side sectors of these dayboards are colored white; the top and bottom sectors are colored black, red, or green as the situation dictates.

**Safe-water marks** indicate fairways, mid-channels, and offshore approach points that have unobstructed water on all sides. You can use the latter when making a landfall. Safe-water marks are red-and-white striped and, if not a spherical buoy, have a red spherical topmark to further aid in identification. If lighted, they display a white light with the characteristic Morse code "A."

**Isolated danger marks** are erected on, or moored above or near, an isolated danger that has navigable water all around it. Don't approach these marks closely without special caution. Isolated danger marks are colored with black-and-red bands and, if lighted, display a group flashing (2) white light. A topmark consisting of two black spheres, one above the other, is fitted for both lighted and unlighted marks.

**Special marks** don't assist in navigation, but rather alert you to a special feature or area. The feature should be described in a nautical document such as a chart, *Light List*, *Coast Pilot*, or *Notice to Mariners*. Some types of areas marked by these aids are spoil areas, pipelines, traffic separation schemes, jetties, anchorages. or military exercise areas. Special marks are yellow and, if lighted, display a yellow light.

**Information and regulatory marks** alert the mariner to various warnings or regulatory matters. These marks have orange geometric shapes against a white background. The preferred channel meanings associated with the orange shapes follow:

1. An open-faced diamond signifies danger.

2. A diamond shape with a cross centered within indicates that vessels are excluded from the marked area.

3. A circular shape indicates that certain operating restrictions are in effect within the marked area.

4. A square or rectangular shape contains directions or instructions lettered within the shape.

**Buoys** are floating aids. They are moored to the seabed by concrete sinkers with various lengths of chain or synthetic rope connecting them to the buoy body.

Buoy positions represented on nautical charts are in approximate positions only because of the practical limitations of positioning and maintaining buoys and their sinkers in precise geographical locations. The Coast Guard normally verifies buoy positions during periodic maintenance visits. Between visits, atmospheric and sea conditions, seabed slope and composition,

Essential Nav.

| Characteristic | Port-Hand Marks | Starboard-Hand Marks |
|---|---|---|
| Color | Green | Red |
| Shape (buoys) | Cylindrical (can) or pillar | Conical (nun) or pillar |
| Dayboard or Topmark when fitted) | Green square or cylinder | Red triangle or cone, point upward |
| Light Color (when fitted) | Green | Red |
| Reflector Color | Green | Red |
| Numbers | Odd | Even |

| Characteristic | Preferred channel to starboard | Preferred channel to port |
|---|---|---|
| Color | Green with one broad red band | Red with one broad green band |
| Shape (buoys) | Cylindrical (can) or pillar | Conical (nun) or pillar |
| Dayboard | Green square, lower half red | Red triangle, lower half green |
| Topmark (when fitted) | Green square or cylinder | Red triangular cone |
| Light (when fitted) | | |
| Color | Green | Red |
| Rhythm | Composite group flashing (2+1) | Composite group flashing (2+1) |
| Reflector Color | Green | Red |

and collisions or other accidents may cause buoys to sink, capsize, or shift from their charted locations.

Buoy moorings vary in length. The length defines a "watch circle," within which buoys can move. Watch circles are not indicated by the symbols representing buoys on charts.

CAUTION: Attempting to pass a buoy close aboard risks collision with a yawing buoy or with an obstruction that the buoy marks. Don't rely on buoys alone to determine your position because buoy reliability is limited. Prudent mariners use bearings from fixed aids to navigation and shore objects, soundings, and various methods of electronic navigation to positively fix their position.

**Beacons** are permanently fixed to the earth's surface. They range from lighthouses to small unlighted daybeacons that exhibit a daymark to make them readily visible and easily identifiable against background features. The daymark conveys, during daylight hours, the same significance as a light at night.

CAUTION: Don't pass fixed aids to navigation close aboard; doing so may put you in danger of collision with riprap or structure foundations, or with the obstruction or danger being marked.

## Reporting Defects In Aids To Navigation

The Coast Guard can't keep the thousands of aids to navigation comprising the U.S. Aids to Navigation System under simultaneous and continuous observation and can't keep every aid to navigation operating properly and on its assigned position at all times. Therefore, for the safety of all mariners, promptly report to the nearest Coast Guard unit any aid to navigation that is either off station or exhibiting characteristics other than those listed in the *Light List*. Prefix radio messages "COAST GUARD" and transmit them directly to one of the U.S. government radio stations listed in *Reed's Nautical Almanac*.

Recommendations and requests pertaining to aids to navigation and reports of navigation aids that are no longer needed should be mailed to the appropriate Coast Guard district.

## LIGHTED AIDS

Most lighted aids have controls that automatically light the aid during darkness and extinguish the light during daylight. These devices don't have equal sensitivity; therefore, all lights do not come on or go off at the same time—a feature that can help you identify aids during twilight periods when some lighted aids are lit while others are not.

Although lights are serviced at periodic intervals to assure reliable operation, there is always the possibility of a light being extinguished or operating improperly.

The condition of the atmosphere has a considerable effect on the distance at which you can see lights. Sometimes, lights are obscured by fog, haze, dust, smoke, or precipitation that is present at the light, or between the light and the observer, but not at the observer, and so may not be recognized by the observer. Atmospheric refraction may cause a light to be seen farther away than it would otherwise appear. A light of low intensity can easily be obscured by unfavorable atmospheric conditions. For this reason, you should consider the intensity of a light when estimating when you'll see it in thick weather. Haze and distance may reduce the apparent duration of the flash of a light. Also, in some atmospheric conditions white lights may have a reddish hue.

Lights placed at high elevations are more frequently obscured by clouds, mist, and fog than lights located at or near sea level.

In cold regions, the lantern panes of unattended lights may become covered in winter with ice or snow, which will greatly reduce the visibility of the lights and may also cause colored lights to appear white.

The increasing use of brilliant shore lights for advertising, illuminating bridges, and other purposes, may cause navigational lights, particularly those in densely inhabited areas, to be outshone and difficult to distinguish from background lighting. You should report such cases so steps can be taken to improve the conditions.

You often see the "loom," or glow, of a powerful light beyond the limit of visibility of the actual rays. The loom sometimes appears sufficiently sharp to obtain a bearing.

At short distances, some flashing lights may show a faint continuous light between flashes.

You can't estimate your distance from a light by its apparent intensity. Always check the characteristics of lights so that you don't mistake distant powerful lights for lower intensity nearby lights.

If you don't sight a light within a reasonable time after prediction, you may need to take steps to resolve the discrepancy to ensure your safety.

The apparent characteristic of a complex light may change with your distance from it. For example, a fixed white light with additional flashes of alternating white and red may, when first sighted in clear weather, show as a simple flashing white light because you can see the flashing white light at a greater distance than the flashing red and fixed white. As you draw nearer, the red flash will become visible and you'll see alternating flashing white and red. When you get still closer, you'll see the fixed white light between the flashes and you'll finally recognize the true characteristics of the light—fixed white, alternating flashing white and red (F W Al WR).

If your vessel is heaving up and down in heavy seas, a light sighted on the horizon may alternately appear and disappear. This may lead the unwary to attribute a false characteristic and, hence, to err in identification. The true characteristic may only be evident after you've closed the distance or increased your height of eye.

Similarly, the effects of wave motion on lighted buoys may lead you to misapprehend a light's characteristics when you can't see flashes that occur when the buoy is in the trough. In addition, buoy motion can reduce the distance at which lights are detected.

Sectors of colored glass are placed in the lanterns of some lights to indicate, in directions from the light, the presence of important navigational features. In general, red sectors mark shoals or warn of other obstructions or of nearby land. Such lights provide approximate bearing information by changing color as you cross the boundary between sectors. These boundaries are indicated in *Reed's* and by dotted lines on charts. All bearings referring to lights are given in true degrees as observed from your vessel toward the light. The accuracy of bearings at the boundaries between light sectors is not good enough to use them as turning bearings or other types of LOPs because the edges of a colored sector cannot be cut off sharply. On either side of the line of demarcation between white, red, or green sectors, there is always a small arc of uncertain color. Moreover, when haze or smoke are present in the intervening atmosphere, a white sector might have a reddish hue. For these reasons, be guided instead by the compass bearing to the light.

The area in which you can observe a light is normally described on a chart by an arc with the light as the center. However, on some bearings obstructions may reduce a light's range In such cases, the extent of the obstructed area might differ with height of eye and distance. When a light is cut off by adjoining land, its bearing when the light disappears may vary with your distance from it and with your height of eye. When the light is cut off by a sloping hill or point of land, the light may be seen over a wider arc by a vessel farther away than by one closer to the light.

The arc drawn on charts around a light is not intended to give information about the distance at which it can be seen, but solely to indicate sectors where its visibility varies or is obstructed.

## Oil Well Structures

Oil well structures in navigable waters are not listed in the *Light List*. However, the structures are shown on nautical charts. Information concerning the location and characteristics of those structures that display lights and sound signals, but that aren't located in obstruction areas, are published in *USCG Local Notices to Mariners*.

In general, at night during drilling operations, a series of white lights is displayed extending from the platform to the top of the derrick. At other times, structures are usually marked with one or more fixed or quick-flashing white or red light, visible for at least one nautical mile during clear weather. Appurtenances to the main structure, such as mooring piles and anchor and mooring buoys, normally are not lighted. In addition, some of the structures are equipped with a sound signal (bell, siren, whistle, or horn). Such bells sound one stroke every 15 seconds; sirens, whistles, or horns sound a single two-second blast every 20 seconds.

Essential Nav.

## LIGHT CHARACTERISTICS

| Abbrev | Example | Explanation | Graphic representation = 30 seconds |
|--------|---------|-------------|-------------------------------------|
| F | F W | FIXED: a continuous steady light | |
| **OCCULTING: total light greater than dark; eclipses equal and repeated regularly** | | | |
| Oc | Oc W 10s | SINGLE OCCULTING: steady light with eclipse regularly repeated | —10s— |
| Oc(n) | Oc(2) W 15s | GROUP OCCULTING: a group of eclipses, number specified, regularly repeated | —15s— |
| Oc(n+n) | Oc(2+1) 15s | COMPOSITE GROUP OCCULTING: successive groups in a period have different numbers of eclipses | —15s— |
| Iso | Iso W 15s | ISOPHASE: a light where the duration of light and darkness are clearly equal | —15s— |
| **FLASHING: single light at regular intervals; duration of light less than dark** | | | |
| Fl | Fl W 4s | SINGLE FLASHING: flash is regularly repeated at less than 50 flashes per minute | —4s— |
| LFl | LFl W 10s | LONG FLASHING: a flash of 2 or more seconds, regularly repeated | —10s— |
| Fl(n) | Fl(2) W 10s | GROUP FLASHING: successive groups of flashes, specified in number, regularly repeated | —10s— |
| Fl(n+n) | Fl(2+1) W 10s | COMPOSITE GROUP FLASHING: successive groups in a period have a different number of flashes | —10s— |
| **QUICK: rapid regularly repeated flashes, between 50 and 80 per minute (usually 60)** | | | |
| Q | Q W | CONTINUOUS QUICK: light in which a flash is regularly repeated | |
| Q(n) | Q(3) W 10s | GROUP QUICK: quick light in which a specified group of flashes is regularly repeated | —10s— |
| VQ + LFl | VQ(6)+LFl 10s | QUICK plus LONG FLASH: quick light in which a sequence of flashes is interrupted by regular eclipses of constant and long duration | —10s— |
| **VERY QUICK: regularly repeated flashes, between 80 and 160 per minute (usually 120)** | | | |
| VQ | VQ W | CONTINUOUS VERY QUICK: very quick light in which flash is regularly repeated | |
| VQ(n) | VQ(3) W 5s | GROUP VERY QUICK: specified group of flashes regularly repeated | —5s— |
| IVQ | IVQ W 10s | INTERRUPTED VERY QUICK: sequence of very quick flashes interrupted by regularly repeated eclipses of constant and long duration | —10s— |
| **ULTRA QUICK: flashes repeated at rate of not less than 160 per minute (usually 180)** | | | |
| UQ | UQ W | CONTINUOUS ULTRA QUICK: ultra quick light in which flash is regularly repeated | |
| IUQ | IUQ W 10s | INTERRUPTED ULTRA QUICK: flashes interrupted by eclipses of long duration | —10s— |
| Mo(a) | Mo(a) W 6s | MORSE CODE: in which appearances of light of two clearly different durations are grouped to represent a character(s) in the Morse code | —6s— |
| F Fl | F W & Fl W P 5s | FIXED AND FLASHING: steady light combined with one brilliant flash at regular intervals | |
| Alt | Alt RW 5s | ALTERNATING: a light that alters in color in successive flashing | —5s— |

## CHARACTERISTICS OF AIDS

### Light Colors
Only green or red lights have lateral significance. When proceeding in the conventional direction of buoyage in Region B:

**Green lights** mark port sides of channels and locations of wrecks or obstructions that you must leave on your port hand. Green lights are also placed on preferred channel marks where the preferred channel is to starboard (that is, aid left to port when proceeding in the conventional direction of buoyage).

**Red lights** mark starboard sides of channels and locations of wrecks or obstructions which must be passed by keeping these lighted aids to navigation on the starboard hand of a vessel. Red lights are also used on preferred channel marks where the preferred channel is to port (i.e., aid to navigation left to starboard when proceeding in the conventional direction of buoyage).

**White** and **yellow** lights have no lateral significance. You can determine the purpose of aids with white or yellow lights by their shapes, colors, letters, and light rhythms.

Most aids to navigation are fitted with retroreflective material to increase their visibility in darkness. Red or green retroreflective material is used on lateral aids.

### Light Rhythms
Light rhythms have no lateral significance. Aids to navigation with lateral significance exhibit flashing, quick, occulting, or isophase light rhythms. Ordinarily, flashing lights (frequency not exceeding 30 flashes per minute) are used. In U.S. waters, lights on lateral aids will normally flash every 2 1/2, 4, or 6 seconds. In situations where lights require a distinct cautionary significance, as at sharp turns, sudden channel constrictions, wrecks or obstructions, a quick-flashing light rhythm is used.

Preferred channel marks exhibit a composite group-flashing light rhythm of two flashes followed by a single flash.

Safe-water marks show a white Morse code "A" rhythm (a short flash followed by a long flash).

Isolated danger marks show a white flashing (2) rhythm (two flashes repeated regularly).

Special marks show yellow lights and normally exhibit a flashing rhythm; however, a fixed rhythm is sometimes used.

Information and regulatory marks, when lighted, display a white light with any light rhythm, except quick flashing, flashing (2), and Morse code "A."

### Daymarks
The first letter of the daymark listing indicates its basic purpose or shape as follows:

**S=Square.** Used to mark the port (left) side of channels when entering from seaward.

**T=Triangle.** Used to mark the starboard (right) side of channels when entering from seaward.

**J=Junction.** May be a square or a triangle. Used to mark channel junctions or bifurcations in the channel. May be used to mark wrecks or other obstructions that may be passed on either side. The color of the top band has lateral significance for the preferred channel.

**M=Safe water.** Octagonal. Used to mark the fairway or middle of the channel.

**K=Range.** Rectangular. When the front and rear daymarks are aligned on the same bearing, the vessel is on the azimuth of the range, which usually marks the center of the channel.

**N=No lateral significance.** Diamond or rectangular shaped. Used for special purposes as a warning, distance, or location marker.

The second letter in a daymark abbreviation indicates its color (G=green, etc.). When there is a third letter with no intervening hyphen, it refers to the color of the center stripe. This designation is used for range daymarks only.

Finally, a hyphen (-) indicates a mark on an intracoastal waterway, as follows:

**-I= Intracoastal Waterway.** Daymark with a yellow horizontal reflective strip.

**-SY=Intracoastal Waterway.** Daymark with a yellow reflective square. Indicates a port-hand mark for vessels crossing the waterway. May appear on a triangular daymark when the intracoastal coincides with a waterway having opposite conventional direction of buoyage.

**Essential Nav.**

**-TY=Intracoastal Waterway.** Daymark with a yellow reflective triangle. Indicates a starboard-hand mark for vessels crossing the waterway. May appear on a square daymark where the intracoastal coincides with a waterway having opposite conventional direction of buoyage.

The following abbreviations cover many of the major designations:

**SG**=Square green daymark with a green reflective border.

**SG-I**=Square green daymark with a green reflective border and a yellow reflective horizontal strip.

**SG-SY**=Square green daymark with a green reflective border and a yellow reflective square.

**SG-TY**=Square green daymark with a green reflective border and a yellow reflective triangle.

**TR**=Triangular red daymark with a red reflective border.

**TR-I**=Triangular red daymark with a red reflective border and a yellow reflective horizontal strip.

**TR-SY**=Triangular red daymark with a red reflective border and a yellow reflective square.

**TR-TY**=Triangular red daymark with a red reflective border and a yellow reflective triangle.

**JG**=Daymark with horizontal bands of green and red, green band topmost, with a green reflective border.

**JG-I**=Daymark with horizontal bands of green and red, green band topmost, with a green reflective border and a yellow reflective horizontal strip.

**JG-SY**=Daymark with horizontal bands of green and red, green band topmost, with a green reflective border and a yellow reflective square.

**JG-TY**=Daymark with horizontal bands of green and red, green band topmost, a green reflective border, and a yellow reflective triangle.

**JR**=Daymark with horizontal bands of green and red, red band topmost, with a red reflective border.

**JR-I**=Daymark with horizontal bands of green and red, red band topmost, a red reflective border and a yellow horizontal strip.

**JR-SY**=Triangular daymark with horizontal bands of green and red, red band topmost, with a red reflective border and a yellow reflective square.

**JR-TY**=Triangular daymark with horizontal bands of green and red, red band topmost, with a red reflective border and a yellow reflective triangle.

**MR**=Octagonal daymark with stripes of white and red with a white reflective border.

**MR-I**=Octagonal daymark with stripes of white and red, with a white reflective border and a yellow reflective horizontal strip.

**CG**=Diamond-shaped green daymark bearing small green diamond-shaped reflectors at each corner.

**CR**=Diamond-shaped red daymark bearing small red diamond-shaped reflectors at each corner.

**KBG**=Rectangular black daymark bearing a central green stripe.

**KBG-I**=Rectangular black daymark bearing a central green stripe and a yellow reflective horizontal strip.

**KBR**=Rectangular black daymark bearing a central red stripe.

**KBR-I**=Rectangular black daymark bearing a central red stripe and a yellow reflective horizontal strip.

**KBW**=Rectangular black daymark bearing a central white stripe.

**KBW-I**=Rectangular black daymark bearing a central white stripe and a yellow reflective horizontal strip.

**KGB**=Rectangular green daymark bearing a central black stripe.

**KGB-I**=Rectangular green daymark bearing a central black stripe and a yellow reflective horizontal strip.

**KGR**=Rectangular green daymark bearing a central red stripe.

**KGR-I**=Rectangular green daymark bearing a central red stripe and a yellow reflective horizontal strip.

**KGW**=Rectangular green daymark bearing a central white stripe.

**KGW-I**=Rectangular green daymark bearing a central white stripe and a yellow reflective horizontal strip.

**KRB**=Rectangular red daymark bearing a central black stripe.

**KRB-I**=Rectangular red daymark bearing a central black stripe and a yellow reflective horizontal strip.

**KRG**=Rectangular red daymark bearing a central green stripe.

**KRG-I**=Rectangular red daymark bearing a central green stripe and a yellow reflective horizontal strip.

**KRW**=Rectangular red daymark bearing a central white stripe.

**KRW-I**=Rectangular red daymark bearing a central white stripe and a yellow reflective horizontal strip.

**KWB**=Rectangular white daymark bearing a central black stripe.

**KWB-I**=Rectangular white daymark bearing a central black stripe and a yellow reflective horizontal strip.

**KWG**=Rectangular white daymark bearing a central green stripe.

**KWG-I**=Rectangular white daymark bearing a central green stripe and a yellow reflective horizontal strip.

**KWR**=Rectangular white daymark bearing a central red stripe.

**KWR-I**=Rectangular white daymark bearing a central red stripe and a yellow reflective horizontal strip.

**NB**=Diamond-shaped daymark divided into four diamond-shaped colored sectors with the sectors at the side corners white and the sectors at the top and bottom corners black, with a white reflective border.

**NG**=Diamond-shaped daymark divided into four diamond-shaped colored sectors with the sectors at the side corners white and the sectors at the top and bottom corners green, with a white reflective border.

**NR**=Diamond-shaped daymark divided into four diamond-shaped colored sectors with the sectors at the side corners white and the sectors at the top and bottom corners red, with a white reflective border.

**NW**=Diamond-shaped white daymark with an orange reflective border and black letters describing the information, or regulatory nature, of the mark.

**NL**=Rectangular white location marker with an orange reflective border and black letters indicating the location.

**NY**=Diamond-shaped yellow daymark with a yellow reflective border

## OTHER SHORT-RANGE AIDS

**Lighthouses** most often have no lateral significance and show no lateral markings. They usually exhibit a white light.

Occasionally, lighthouses use sectored lights to mark shoals or warn of other dangers. Lights so equipped show one color from most directions and a different color or colors over defined arcs as indicated on the chart.

**Large navigational buoys** (LNBs) were developed to replace lightships and were placed at points where it's impractical to build lighthouses. The unmanned LNBs were 40 feet in diameter with light towers approximately 40 feet above the water. These have largely been replaced either with ordinary buoys or Exposed Location Buoys (ELBs), which are somewhat larger than ordinary buoys but have the same markings.

**Seasonal aids to navigation** are placed into service or changed at specified times of the year. The dates shown in the *Light List* are approximate and may vary due to adverse weather or other conditions.

**Ranges** are nonlateral aids that comprise pairs of aids that you can line up to assist you in maintaining a safe course. You must consult the chart when using ranges to determine if the range marks the centerline of the navigable channel and also what section of the range may be safely traversed. Ranges display rectangular dayboards of various colors and are generally lighted. When lighted, ranges may display lights of any color; in most cases, the front light is quick flashing and the rear light is isophase.

**Sound signal** is a generic term used to describe devices that produce an audible signal designed to assist you in fog or

155

other periods of reduced visibility. These devices can be activated manually, remotely, or by a fog detector. Where a fog detector is used, there may be a delay in the automatic activation of the signal. Also, fog detectors may not detect patchy fog.

Sound signals are distinguished by their tone and phase characteristics. Tones vary with the devices producing the sound; for example, diaphones, diaphragm horns, sirens, whistles, bells, and gongs.

Phase characteristics are defined by the signal's sound pattern—the number of blasts and silent periods per minute. Signals sounded from fixed structures generally produce a specific number of blasts and silent periods each minute. Buoy sound signals are generally activated by the motion of the sea and therefore do not emit a regular signal characteristic. It is common, in fact, for a buoy to produce no sound signal when seas are calm.

The *Light List* gives the characteristic of a sound signal. Assume that the signal only operates during times of fog, reduced visibility, or adverse weather unless it is specifically stated that it operates continuously, or the signal is a bell, gong, or whistle on a buoy.

An emergency sound signal is sounded at some locations when the main and standby signals are inoperative.

CAUTION: Don't rely on sound signals to determine your position. You can't accurately determine distance by sound level. Occasionally, even nearby sound signals may not be heard, especially when they're downwind of you. Signals may not be activated when fog is nearby but not right at the location of the signal.

## Variations To The U.S. System

**Intracoastal Waterway aids to navigation:** The Intracoastal Waterway runs parallel to the Atlantic and Gulf coasts from Manasquan Inlet, New Jersey, to the Mexican border. Aids in these waters have some yellow marking on them. Otherwise, their coloring and numbering follow the same system as other U.S. waters. The special Waterway markings consist of a yellow square or yellow triangle and indicate which side the aid should be passed when following the conventional direction of buoyage. The yellow square indicates that

the aid to navigation should be kept on the left side; the yellow triangle indicates that the aid should be kept on the right side.

NOTE: The conventional direction of buoyage in the Intracoastal Waterway is generally southerly along the Atlantic coast and westerly along the Gulf coast.

**The Western Rivers System** — a variation of the standard U.S. Aids to Navigation System described in the preceding sections — is employed on the Mississippi River and its tributaries above Baton Rouge, LA , and on certain other rivers that flow toward the Gulf of Mexico. The Western Rivers System varies from the standard U.S. system as follows:

1. Aids to navigation are not always numbered.

2. Any numbers on aids don't have lateral significance, but rather indicate mileage from a fixed point (normally the river mouth).

3. Diamond-shaped crossing dayboards, red or green as appropriate, are used to indicate where the river channel crosses from one bank to the other.

4. Lights on green aids to navigation show a single-flash characteristic, which may be green or white.

5. Lights on red aids show a group-flash characteristic, which may be red or white.

6. Isolated danger marks are not used.

**Uniform State Waterway Marking System (USWMS):** This system was developed in 1966 to provide an easily understood system for operators of small boats. Although designed for lakes and other inland waterways that are not portrayed on nautical charts, the USWMS is used on other waters as well. It supplements the existing federal marking system and is generally compatible with it.

The conventional direction of buoyage is upstream, or toward the head of navigation.

The USWMS varies from the standard U.S. system as follows:

1. The color black is used instead of green.

2. Three aids to navigation reflect cardinal significance:

a) A white buoy with a red top represents an obstruction and should be passed to the south or west.

b) A white buoy with a black top represents an obstruction and should be passed to the north or east.

c) A red-and-white vertically striped buoy indicates that an obstruction exists between that buoy and the nearest shore.

3. Mooring buoys are white buoys with a horizontal blue band midway between the waterline and the top of the buoy. When lighted, this buoy generally shows a slow-flashing white light.

## Bridge Markings

Bridges across navigable waters are generally marked with red, green, and/or white lights. Red lights mark piers and other bridge parts. Red lights on drawbridges show when they are in the closed position. Green lights on drawbridges show when they are in the open position. The location of these lights varies according to bridge structure.

Green lights are also used to mark the centerline of navigable channels through fixed bridges. If there are two or more channels through the bridge, the preferred channel is also marked by three white lights in a vertical line above the green light.

Red and green retro-reflective panels mark bridge piers and may be placed on bridges not required to display lights.

Main channels through bridges may be marked by lateral red and green lights and dayboards. Adjacent piers are marked with fixed yellow lights when the main channel is marked with lateral aids to navigation.

Centerlines of channels through fixed bridges may be marked with a safe-water mark and an occulting white light when lateral marks are used to mark main channels. The centerline of the navigable channel through the draw span of floating bridges may be marked with a special mark—a yellow diamond with yellow retro-reflective panels—and may exhibit a yellow light that displays a Morse code "B" ( $- \cdots$ ).

Clearance gauges may be installed that indicate vertical clearance. The gauges are located on the right channel pier or pier

protective structure facing approaching vessels.

Drawbridges equipped with radiotelephones display a blue-and-white sign that indicates what VHF channels the bridgetender monitors.

## Electronic Aids To Navigation

### Racons

Some aids to navigation are enhanced by the use of RAdar beaCONS (racons). Racons, when triggered by pulses from your vessel's radar, transmit a coded reply to your radar. This identifies the racon station with a series of dots and dashes that emanate from the racon and appear on your radar screen. This display indicates the approximate range and bearing to the racon. Although racons may be used on both laterally significant and nonlaterally significant aids, the racon signal itself serves for identification purposes only and carries no lateral significance. Racons are also placed on bridges to mark the point of best passage.

All racons operate in the marine radar X-band from 9,300 to 9,500 MHz. Some frequency-agile racons also operate in the 2,900 to 3,000 MHz marine radar S-band.

Racons have a typical output of 100 to 300 milliwatts and so are short-range aids. Reception varies from a nominal range of six to eight nautical miles when mounted on a buoy, to as much as 17 nautical miles for a racon with a directional antenna mounted at a height of 50 feet on a fixed structure. These nominal ranges are a guide; actual ranges vary with many factors.

The beginning of the racon presentation appears on your radar screen about 50 yards beyond the racon position and persists for a number of revolutions of the radar antenna that depends on its rotation rate.

Distance to the racon can be measured to the point at which the racon flash begins, but the figure obtained is greater than your ship's distance from the racon. This is due to the slight response delay in the racon apparatus.

Radar operators may notice some broadening or spoking of the racon presentation when their vessel approaches close to the source of the racon. You can minimize this effect by adjusting the IF gain or sweep

Essential Nav.

gain of your radar. If desired, you can virtually eliminate the racon presentation by operating the FTC (fast time constant) controls of your radar.

**Radar Reflectors**

Many aids to navigation incorporate special fixtures that enhance the reflection of radar energy. These radar reflectors help radar-equipped vessels to detect buoys and beacons. They do not, however, positively identify a radar target as an aid to navigation.

For more information on electronic aids to navigation, see Chapter 4.

## THE CANADIAN
## AIDS TO NAVIGATION SYSTEM

To augment this brief discussion of the Canadian system, consult the Canadian coast pilots and small-craft guides. The Canadian Coast Guard publishes a book titled *The Canadian Aids to Navigation System*.

Canada uses the same IALA Region B system used in the United States in a combined lateral and cardinal system. The shape, color, and light characteristics all indicate the function of the aid to navigation.

In general, the "red right returning" rule applies. In addition, the system of cardinal marks indicates the relative position of obstructions. The cardinal buoys have double cone topmarks. The diagram on page 166 illustrates the significance of the various topmarks.

Canada also has special-purpose buoys that are usually similar to U.S. buoys designed for the same purpose. Daymarks include red triangles and green squares somewhat similar to marks used in the U.S. Intracoastal Waterway.

Canada uses the metric system, and lighthouse heights are given in meters rather than feet. Ranges of lights are still listed in nautical miles.

## NOTICES TO MARINERS

**11370**
19 ed., 08/03/96 LAST LNM 32/97 NAD 83　(CGD8) 33/97
LA – MISSISSIPPI RIVER – NEW ORLEANS TO BATON ROUGE
Add

| | | |
|---|---|---|
| Zito Lighted Mooring Buoy "A", Q W, White with blue band, (Priv maint) | 29°56'46.0"N | 90°10'08.0"W |
| Zito Lighted Mooring Buoy "E", Q W, White with blue band, (Priv maint) | 29°56'55.0"N | 90°09'57.0"W |
| Zito Lighted Mooring Buoy "F", Q W, White with blue band, (Priv maint) | 29°56'56.0"N | 90°09'56.0"W |
| Zito Lighted Mooring Buoy "I", Q W, White with blue band, (Priv maint) | 29°57'05.0"N | 90°09'45.0"W |
| Zito Mooring Buoys (3), "D", "G", "H", White with blue band, (Priv Maint) | 29°56'58.0"N | 90°09'59.0"W |
| Zito Mooring Buoys (2), "B", "C", White with blue band, (Priv maint) | 29°56'47.0"N | 90°10'09.0"W |
| Zito Mooring Buoy "J", White with blue band, (Priv maint) | 29°57'08.0"N | 90°09'47.0"W |

**11371**
34 ed., 04/06/96 LAST LNM 27/97 NAD 83　(CGD8) 33/97
LAKE BORGNE AND APPROACHES – CAT I TO POINT AUX HERBES
Change　Pass Christian West Light "2" to Pass Christian West Light "2A", Fl R 2.5s, 17ft, 3M　30°18'27.4"N 89°14'59.4"W

**11372**
27 ed., 10/12/96 LAST LNM 32/97 NAD 83　(CGD8) 33/97
MS – INTRACOASTAL WATERWAY – DOG KEYS PASS TO WAVELAND
Change　Pass Christian West Light "2" to Pass Christian West Light "2A", Fl R 2.5s, 17ft, 3M　30°18'27.4"N 89°14'59.4"W

**11374**
28 ed., 03/01/97 LAST LNM 26/97 NAD 83　(CGD8) 33/97
AL – MS – INTRACOASTAL WATERWAY – DAUPHIN ISLAND TO DOG KEYS PASS
Add　Bayou Casotte Channel Light "11A", Fl G 6s, 17ft, 3M　30°19'58.7"N 88°30'54.1"W
Bayou Casotte Channel Light "11B", Fl G 6s, 17ft, 3M　30°20'04.7"N 88°30'52.4"W

| (1) No. | (2) Name and Location | N/W (3) Position | (4) Characteristic | (5) Ht | (6) Rng | (7) Structure | (8) Remarks |
|---|---|---|---|---|---|---|---|
| 7432 | – LIGHT 11A | 30 20.0 88 30.9 | Fl G 6s | 17 | 3 | SG on pile. | Ra ref. |
| * | * | * | * | * | * | * | * (33/97) |
| 7433 | – LIGHT 11B | 30 20.1 88 30.9 | Fl G 6s | 17 | 3 | SG on pile. | Ra ref. |
| * | * | * | * | * | * | * | * (33/97) |
| | **\* Delete Heading:**<br>**\* Mississippi Sound**<br>MISSISSIPPI SOUND | | | | | | |
| 8270 | | | | | | | Remove from list.<br>* (33/97) |
| 8565 | – UPPER REACH OUTBOUND RANGE FRONT LIGHT | 30 13.8 88 58.9 | Q W Fl R 6s | 35 36 | 4 | KRW on concrete pile. | Visible 2° each side of rangeline. Passing light visible around horizon. (33/97) |

**Notice to Mariners samples** — Shown are samples of chart (left) and light list changes. Other information includes warnings and proposed changes.

159

## U.S. Coast Guard Districts

17th

Pacific Area    Atlantic Area

9th

13th

14th

11th

1st

5th

7th

8th

**Local Notice to Mariners** are published weekly by each Coast Guard District and contain the latest information about special warnings, changes to aids to navigation, and more. If you would like to receive the LNM for your district, contact the appropriate office listed below. LNMs are also available on the internet at www.navcen.uscg.mil

First District
408 Atlantic Avenue
Boston, MA 02110-3350
Day: 617-223-8338
Night: 617-223-8558

Fifth District
Federal Building
431 Crawford Street
Portsmouth, VA 23704-5004
Day: 804-398-6489
Night: 804-398-6231

Seventh District
Brickell Plaza Federal Building
909 SE 1st Avenue, Rm. 406
Miami, FL 33131-3050
Day: 305-536-5621
Night: 305-536-5611

Eighth District
Hale Boggs Federal Building
501 Magazine Street
New Orleans, LA 70130-3396
Day: 504-589-6234
Night: 504-589-6225

Ninth District
1240 East 9th Street
Cleveland, OH 44199-2060
Day: 216-522-3991
Night: 216-522-3984

Eleventh District
Building 50-6
Coast Guard Island
Alameda, CA 94501-5100
Day: 510-437-2940
Night: 510-437-3700

Thirteenth District
915 Second Avenue
Seattle, WA 98174-1067
Day: 206-220-7280
Night: 206-220-7004

Fourteenth District
Prince Kalanianaole Fed. Bldg.
9th Floor, Room 9139
300 Ala Moana Blvd.
Honolulu, HI 96850-4982
Day: 808-541-2317
Night: 808-541-2500

Seventeenth District
P.O. Box 25517
Juneau, AK 99802-5517
Day: 907-463-2262
Night: 907-463-2000

**NIMA Notice to Mariners.** The National Imagery and Mapping Agency also publishes a weekly Notice to Mariners which includes most coastal aids and chart changes as well as international notices. Contact NIMA, Marine Navigation Department, 4600 Sangamore Road, Bethesda, MD 20816-5003 (301-227-3370); Fax: 301-227-4211; e-mail: NavNotices@nima.mil

**Canadian Notice to Mariners** are now published monthly, one editon for the West Coast and another for the East Coast. You may obtain either edition by contacting the Director General, Marine Navigation Services Directorate, Canadian Coast Guard, Department of Fisheries and Oceans, Ottawa, Ontario, K1A 0N7 (613-990-3037); Fax: 613-998-8428; or on the Web at www.notmar.com

## DISTANCE OF SEA HORIZON IN NAUTICAL MILES

| Height in Meters | Height in Feet | Distance in Miles | Height in Meters | Height in Feet | Distance in Miles | Height in Meters | Height in Feet | Distance in Miles | Height in Meters | Height in Feet | Distance in Miles |
|---|---|---|---|---|---|---|---|---|---|---|---|
| 0.3 | 1 | 1.15 | 4.3 | 14 | 4.30 | 12.2 | 40 | 7.27 | 55 | 180 | 15.4 |
| 0.6 | 2 | 1.62 | 4.9 | 16 | 4.60 | 12.8 | 42 | 7.44 | 61 | 200 | 16.2 |
| 0.9 | 3 | 1.99 | 5.5 | 18 | 4.87 | 13.4 | 44 | 7.62 | 73 | 240 | 17.8 |
| 1.2 | 4 | 2.30 | 6.1 | 20 | 5.14 | 14.0 | 46 | 7.79 | 85 | 280 | 19.2 |
| 1.5 | 5 | 2.57 | 6.7 | 22 | 5.39 | 14.6 | 48 | 7.96 | 98 | 320 | 20.5 |
| 1.8 | 6 | 2.81 | 7.3 | 24 | 5.62 | 15.2 | 50 | 8.1 | 110 | 360 | 21.8 |
| 2.1 | 7 | 3.04 | 7.9 | 26 | 5.86 | 18 | 60 | 8.9 | 122 | 400 | 23.0 |
| 2.4 | 8 | 3.25 | 8.5 | 28 | 6.08 | 20 | 70 | 9.6 | 137 | 450 | 24.3 |
| 2.7 | 9 | 3.45 | 9.1 | 30 | 6.30 | 24 | 80 | 10.3 | 152 | 500 | 25.7 |
| 3.0 | 10 | 3.63 | 9.8 | 32 | 6.50 | 27 | 90 | 10.9 | 183 | 600 | 28.1 |
| 3.4 | 11 | 3.81 | 10.4 | 34 | 6.70 | 30 | 100 | 11.5 | 213 | 700 | 30.4 |
| 3.7 | 12 | 3.98 | 11.0 | 36 | 6.90 | 40 | 130 | 13.1 | 244 | 800 | 32.5 |
| 4.0 | 13 | 4.14 | 11.6 | 38 | 7.09 | 46 | 150 | 14.1 | | | |

## DISTANCE OF LIGHTS RISING OR DIPPING

| Height of Light | | HEIGHT OF EYE | | | | | | | | | | | | |
|---|---|---|---|---|---|---|---|---|---|---|---|---|---|---|
| | | Meters | | | | | | | | | | | | |
| | | 1.5 | 3 | 4.6 | 6.1 | 7.6 | 9.1 | 10.7 | 12.2 | 13.7 | 15.2 | 16.8 | 18.3 | 19.8 |
| | | Feet | | | | | | | | | | | | |
| | | 5 | 10 | 15 | 20 | 25 | 30 | 35 | 40 | 45 | 50 | 55 | 60 | 65 |
| m | ft | | | | | | | | | | | | | |
| 12 | 40 | 9¾ | 11 | 11¾ | 12½ | 13 | 13½ | 14 | 14½ | 15 | 15½ | 15¾ | 16¼ | 16½ |
| 15 | 50 | 10¾ | 11¾ | 12½ | 13¼ | 14 | 14½ | 15 | 15½ | 15¾ | 16¼ | 16¾ | 17 | 17½ |
| 18 | 60 | 11½ | 12½ | 13½ | 14 | 14¾ | 15¼ | 15¾ | 16¼ | 16½ | 17 | 17½ | 17¾ | 18¼ |
| 21 | 70 | 12¼ | 13¼ | 14 | 14¾ | 15½ | 16 | 16½ | 17 | 17¼ | 17¾ | 18 | 18½ | 19 |
| 24 | 80 | 13 | 14 | 14¾ | 15½ | 16 | 16½ | 17 | 17½ | 18 | 18½ | 18¾ | 19¼ | 19½ |
| 27 | 90 | 13½ | 14½ | 15½ | 16 | 16¾ | 17¼ | 17¾ | 18¼ | 18½ | 19 | 19½ | 19¾ | 20¼ |
| 30 | 100 | 14 | 15 | 16 | 16½ | 17¼ | 17¾ | 18¼ | 18¾ | 19¼ | 19½ | 20 | 20½ | 20¾ |
| 34 | 110 | 14½ | 15¾ | 16½ | 17¼ | 17¾ | 18¼ | 19 | 19¼ | 19¾ | 20¼ | 20½ | 21 | 21¼ |
| 37 | 120 | 15¼ | 16¼ | 17 | 17¾ | 18¼ | 19 | 19½ | 20 | 20¼ | 20¾ | 21 | 21½ | 22 |
| 40 | 130 | 15¾ | 16¾ | 17½ | 18¼ | 19 | 19½ | 20 | 20½ | 20¾ | 21¼ | 21½ | 22 | 22½ |
| 43 | 140 | 16¼ | 17¼ | 18 | 18¾ | 19½ | 20 | 20½ | 21 | 21¼ | 21¾ | 22 | 22½ | 23 |
| 46 | 150 | 16¾ | 17¾ | 18½ | 19¼ | 19¾ | 20½ | 21 | 21¼ | 21¾ | 22¼ | 22½ | 23 | 23¼ |
| 49 | 160 | 17 | 18¼ | 19 | 19¾ | 20¼ | 20¾ | 21½ | 21¾ | 22¼ | 22¾ | 23 | 23½ | 23¾ |
| 52 | 170 | 17½ | 18½ | 19½ | 20 | 20¾ | 21¼ | 21¾ | 22¼ | 22¾ | 23 | 23½ | 24 | 24¼ |
| 55 | 180 | 18 | 19 | 20 | 20½ | 21¼ | 21¾ | 22¼ | 22¾ | 23 | 23½ | 24 | 24¼ | 24¾ |
| 58 | 190 | 18½ | 19½ | 20¼ | 21 | 21½ | 22 | 22¾ | 23 | 23½ | 24 | 24½ | 24¾ | 25 |
| 61 | 200 | 18¾ | 20 | 20¾ | 21½ | 22 | 22½ | 23 | 23½ | 24 | 24½ | 24¾ | 25¼ | 25½ |
| 64 | 210 | 19¼ | 20¼ | 21 | 21¾ | 22½ | 23 | 23½ | 24 | 24½ | 24¾ | 25¼ | 25½ | 26 |
| 67 | 220 | 19½ | 20¾ | 21½ | 22¼ | 22¾ | 23¼ | 24 | 24¼ | 24¾ | 25¼ | 25½ | 26 | 26¼ |
| 70 | 230 | 20 | 21 | 22 | 22½ | 23¼ | 23¾ | 24¼ | 24¾ | 25 | 25½ | 26 | 26¼ | 26¾ |
| 73 | 240 | 20½ | 21½ | 22¼ | 23 | 23½ | 24 | 24½ | 25 | 25½ | 26 | 26¼ | 26¾ | 27 |
| 76 | 250 | 20¾ | 21¾ | 22½ | 23¼ | 24 | 24½ | 25 | 25½ | 26 | 26¼ | 26¾ | 27 | 27½ |
| 79 | 260 | 21 | 22¼ | 23 | 23¾ | 24¼ | 24¾ | 25¼ | 25¾ | 26¼ | 26¾ | 27 | 27½ | 27¾ |
| 82 | 270 | 21½ | 22½ | 23¼ | 24 | 24½ | 25¼ | 25¾ | 26¼ | 26½ | 27 | 27½ | 27¾ | 28¼ |
| 85 | 280 | 21¾ | 23 | 23¾ | 24½ | 25 | 25½ | 26 | 26½ | 27 | 27½ | 27¾ | 28 | 28½ |
| 88 | 290 | 22 | 23¼ | 24 | 24¾ | 25¼ | 26 | 26½ | 26¾ | 27¼ | 27¾ | 28 | 28½ | 28¾ |
| 91 | 300 | 22½ | 23½ | 24½ | 25 | 25¾ | 26¼ | 26¾ | 27¼ | 27½ | 28 | 28½ | 28¾ | 29¼ |
| 95 | 310 | 22¾ | 24 | 24¾ | 25½ | 26 | 26½ | 27 | 27½ | 28 | 28½ | 28¾ | 29 | 29½ |
| 98 | 320 | 23 | 24¼ | 25 | 25¾ | 26¼ | 27 | 27½ | 27¾ | 28¼ | 28¾ | 29 | 29½ | 29¾ |
| 100 | 330 | 23½ | 24½ | 25¼ | 26 | 26½ | 27¼ | 27¾ | 28 | 28½ | 29 | 29½ | 29¾ | 30 |
| 104 | 340 | 23¾ | 24¾ | 25¾ | 26¼ | 27 | 27½ | 28 | 28½ | 29 | 29¼ | 29¾ | 30 | 30½ |
| 107 | 350 | 24 | 25 | 26 | 26¾ | 27¼ | 27¾ | 28¼ | 28¾ | 29¼ | 29½ | 30 | 30½ | 30¾ |
| 122 | 400 | 25½ | 26½ | 27½ | 28 | 28¾ | 29¼ | 29¾ | 30¼ | 30¾ | 31 | 31½ | 32 | 32¼ |
| 137 | 450 | 27 | 28 | 28¾ | 29½ | 30 | 30¾ | 31¼ | 31¾ | 32 | 32½ | 33 | 33¼ | 33¾ |

Essential Nav.

## COURSE CORRECTION FOR CURRENT OR LEEWAY
### (Designed by R. C. Fisher)
SPEED OF TIDAL STREAM (OR CURRENT) OVER THE GROUND AND SHIP'S SPEED THROUGH THE WATER

| C | Knots 0.5 | 1.0 | 1.5 | 2.0 | Knots 2.5 | 3.0 | 3.5 | 4.0 | 4.5 | Knots 5.0 | S |
|---|---|---|---|---|---|---|---|---|---|---|---|
| 0 | 0 | 0 | 0 | 0 | 0 | 0 | 0 | 0 | 0 | 0 | 90 |
| 1 | 0.009 | 0.019 | 0.026 | 0.035 | 0.044 | 0.052 | 0.061 | 0.070 | 0.079 | 0.087 | 89 |
| 2 | 0.017 | 0.035 | 0.052 | 0.070 | 0.087 | 0.105 | 0.122 | 0.139 | 0.157 | 0.174 | 88 |
| 3 | 0.026 | 0.052 | 0.079 | 0.105 | 0.131 | 0.157 | 0.183 | 0.209 | 0.236 | 0.262 | 87 |
| 4 | 0.035 | 0.070 | 0.105 | 0.140 | 0.174 | 0.209 | 0.244 | 0.279 | 0.314 | 0.349 | 86 |
| 5 | 0.044 | 0.087 | 0.131 | 0.174 | 0.218 | 0.261 | 0.305 | 0.349 | 0.392 | 0.436 | 85 |
| 6 | 0.052 | 0.105 | 0.157 | 0.209 | 0.261 | 0.314 | 0.366 | 0.418 | 0.470 | 0.523 | 84 |
| 8 | 0.070 | 0.139 | 0.209 | 0.278 | 0.348 | 0.418 | 0.487 | 0.557 | 0.626 | 0.696 | 82 |
| 10 | 0.087 | 0.174 | 0.260 | 0.347 | 0.434 | 0.521 | 0.608 | 0.695 | 0.781 | 0.868 | 80 |
| 12 | 0.104 | 0.208 | 0.312 | 0.416 | 0.520 | 0.624 | 0.728 | 0.832 | 0.936 | 1.040 | 78 |
| 14 | 0.121 | 0.242 | 0.363 | 0.484 | 0.605 | 0.726 | 0.847 | 0.968 | 1.089 | 1.210 | 76 |
| 16 | 0.138 | 0.276 | 0.413 | 0.551 | 0.689 | 0.827 | 0.965 | 1.103 | 1.240 | 1.378 | 74 |
| 18 | 0.155 | 0.309 | 0.464 | 0.618 | 0.773 | 0.927 | 1.082 | 1.236 | 1.391 | 1.545 | 72 |
| 21 | 0.179 | 0.358 | 0.538 | 0.717 | 0.896 | 1.075 | 1.254 | 1.433 | 1.613 | 1.792 | 69 |
| 24 | 0.203 | 0.407 | 0.610 | 0.813 | 1.017 | 1.220 | 1.424 | 1.627 | 1.830 | 2.034 | 66 |
| 27 | 0.227 | 0.454 | 0.681 | 0.908 | 1.135 | 1.362 | 1.589 | 1.816 | 2.043 | 2.270 | 63 |
| 30 | 0.250 | 0.500 | 0.750 | 1.000 | 1.250 | 1.500 | 1.750 | 2.000 | 2.250 | 2.500 | 60 |
| 33 | 0.272 | 0.545 | 0.817 | 1.089 | 1.362 | 1.634 | 1.906 | 2.179 | 2.451 | 2.723 | 57 |
| 36 | 0.294 | 0.588 | 0.882 | 1.176 | 1.469 | 1.763 | 2.057 | 2.351 | 2.645 | 2.939 | 54 |
| 39 | 0.315 | 0.629 | 0.944 | 1.259 | 1.573 | 1.888 | 2.203 | 2.517 | 2.832 | 3.147 | 51 |
| 42 | 0.335 | 0.669 | 1.004 | 1.338 | 1.673 | 2.007 | 2.342 | 2.667 | 3.011 | 3.346 | 48 |
| 46 | 0.360 | 0.719 | 1.079 | 1.439 | 1.798 | 2.158 | 2.518 | 2.877 | 3.237 | 3.597 | 44 |
| 50 | 0.383 | 0.766 | 1.149 | 1.532 | 1.915 | 2.298 | 2.681 | 3.064 | 3.447 | 3.830 | 40 |
| 54 | 0.405 | 0.809 | 1.214 | 1.618 | 2.023 | 2.427 | 2.832 | 3.236 | 3.641 | 4.045 | 36 |
| 58 | 0.424 | 0.848 | 1.272 | 1.696 | 2.120 | 2.540 | 2.986 | 3.392 | 3.816 | 4.240 | 32 |
| 62 | 0.442 | 0.883 | 1.324 | 1.766 | 2.207 | 2.649 | 3.090 | 3.532 | 3.973 | 4.415 | 28 |
| 66 | 0.457 | 0.914 | 1.370 | 1.827 | 2.284 | 2.741 | 3.197 | 3.754 | 4.111 | 4.568 | 24 |
| 70 | 0.470 | 0.940 | 1.410 | 1.879 | 2.349 | 2.819 | 3.289 | 3.759 | 4.229 | 4.698 | 20 |
| 75 | 0.483 | 0.966 | 1.449 | 1.932 | 2.415 | 2.898 | 3.381 | 3.864 | 4.347 | 4.830 | 15 |
| 80 | 0.492 | 0.985 | 1.477 | 1.970 | 2.462 | 2.954 | 3.447 | 3.939 | 4.432 | 4.924 | 10 |
| 85 | 0.498 | 0.996 | 1.494 | 1.992 | 2.490 | 2.989 | 3.487 | 3.985 | 4.483 | 4.981 | 5 |
| 90 | 0.500 | 1.000 | 1.500 | 2.000 | 2.500 | 3.000 | 3.500 | 4.000 | 4.500 | 5.000 | 0 |
| C | 0.5 | 1.0 | 1.5 | 2.0 | 2.5 Knots | 3.0 | 3.5 | 4.0 | 4.5 | 5.0 | S |

| C | Knots 6 | 7 | 8 | 9 | Knots 10 | 12 | 14 | 16 | 18 | Knots 20 | S |
|---|---|---|---|---|---|---|---|---|---|---|---|
| 0 | 0 | 0 | 0 | 0 | 0 | 0 | 0 | 0 | 0 | 0 | 90 |
| 1 | 0.105 | 0.120 | 0.140 | 0.160 | 0.170 | 0.210 | 0.240 | 0.280 | 0.310 | 0.350 | 89 |
| 2 | 0.209 | 0.240 | 0.280 | 0.310 | 0.350 | 0.420 | 0.490 | 0.560 | 0.503 | 0.700 | 88 |
| 3 | 0.314 | 0.370 | 0.420 | 0.470 | 0.520 | 0.630 | 0.730 | 0.840 | 0.940 | 1.050 | 87 |
| 4 | 0.419 | 0.490 | 0.560 | 0.630 | 0.700 | 0.840 | 0.980 | 1.120 | 1.260 | 1.400 | 86 |
| 5 | 0.523 | 0.610 | 0.700 | 0.780 | 0.870 | 1.050 | 1.220 | 1.390 | 1.570 | 1.740 | 85 |
| 6 | 0.627 | 0.730 | 0.840 | 0.940 | 1.050 | 1.250 | 1.460 | 1.670 | 1.880 | 2.080 | 84 |
| 8 | 0.835 | 0.970 | 1.110 | 1.250 | 1.390 | 1.670 | 1.950 | 2.230 | 2.510 | 2.780 | 82 |
| 10 | 1.040 | 1.220 | 1.390 | 1.560 | 1.740 | 2.080 | 2.430 | 2.780 | 3.130 | 3.470 | 80 |
| 12 | 1.247 | 1.460 | 1.660 | 1.870 | 2.080 | 2.490 | 2.910 | 3.330 | 3.740 | 4.160 | 78 |
| 14 | 1.452 | 1.690 | 1.940 | 2.180 | 2.420 | 2.900 | 3.390 | 3.870 | 4.350 | 4.840 | 76 |
| 16 | 1.654 | 1.930 | 2.210 | 2.480 | 2.760 | 3.310 | 3.860 | 4.410 | 4.960 | 5.510 | 74 |
| 18 | 1.854 | 2.160 | 2.470 | 2.780 | 3.090 | 3.710 | 4.330 | 4.940 | 5.560 | 6.180 | 72 |
| 21 | 2.150 | 2.510 | 2.870 | 3.230 | 3.580 | 4.300 | 5.020 | 5.730 | 6.450 | 7.170 | 69 |
| 24 | 2.440 | 2.850 | 3.250 | 3.660 | 4.070 | 4.880 | 5.690 | 6.510 | 7.320 | 8.130 | 66 |
| 27 | 2.724 | 3.180 | 3.630 | 4.090 | 4.540 | 5.450 | 6.360 | 7.260 | 8.170 | 9.080 | 63 |
| 30 | 3.000 | 3.500 | 4.000 | 4.500 | 5.000 | 6.000 | 7.000 | 8.300 | 9.000 | 10.00 | 60 |
| 33 | 3.268 | 3.810 | 4.360 | 4.900 | 5.450 | 6.540 | 7.620 | 8.710 | 9.800 | 10.89 | 57 |
| 36 | 3.527 | 4.110 | 4.700 | 5.290 | 5.880 | 7.050 | 8.230 | 9.400 | 10.58 | 11.76 | 54 |
| 39 | 3.776 | 4.410 | 5.030 | 5.660 | 6.290 | 7.550 | 8.810 | 10.07 | 11.33 | 12.59 | 51 |
| 42 | 4.015 | 4.680 | 5.350 | 6.020 | 6.690 | 8.030 | 9.370 | 10.71 | 12.04 | 13.38 | 48 |
| 46 | 4.316 | 5.040 | 5.750 | 6.470 | 7.190 | 8.630 | 10.07 | 11.51 | 12.95 | 14.39 | 44 |
| 50 | 4.596 | 5.360 | 6.130 | 6.890 | 7.660 | 9.190 | 10.72 | 12.26 | 13.79 | 15.32 | 40 |
| 54 | 4.854 | 5.660 | 6.470 | 7.280 | 8.090 | 9.710 | 11.33 | 12.94 | 14.56 | 16.18 | 36 |
| 58 | 5.088 | 5.940 | 6.780 | 7.630 | 8.480 | 10.18 | 11.87 | 13.57 | 15.26 | 16.96 | 32 |
| 62 | 5.298 | 6.180 | 7.060 | 7.950 | 8.830 | 10.60 | 12.36 | 14.13 | 15.89 | 17.66 | 28 |
| 66 | 5.481 | 6.390 | 7.310 | 8.220 | 9.140 | 10.96 | 12.79 | 14.62 | 16.44 | 18.27 | 24 |
| 70 | 5.638 | 6.580 | 7.520 | 8.460 | 9.400 | 11.28 | 13.16 | 15.04 | 16.91 | 18.79 | 20 |
| 75 | 5.796 | 6.760 | 7.730 | 8.690 | 9.660 | 11.59 | 13.52 | 15.45 | 17.39 | 19.32 | 15 |
| 80 | 5.909 | 6.890 | 7.880 | 8.860 | 9.850 | 11.82 | 13.79 | 15.76 | 17.73 | 19.70 | 10 |
| 85 | 5.977 | 6.970 | 7.970 | 8.970 | 9.960 | 11.95 | 13.95 | 15.94 | 17.93 | 19.92 | 5 |
| 90 | 6.000 | 7.000 | 8.000 | 9.000 | 10.00 | 12.00 | 14.00 | 16.00 | 18.00 | 20.00 | 0 |
| C | 6 | 7 | 8 | 9 | 10 Knots | 12 | 14 | 16 | 18 | 20 | S |

## U.S. COAST GUARD CHART & AIDS DIAGRAMS

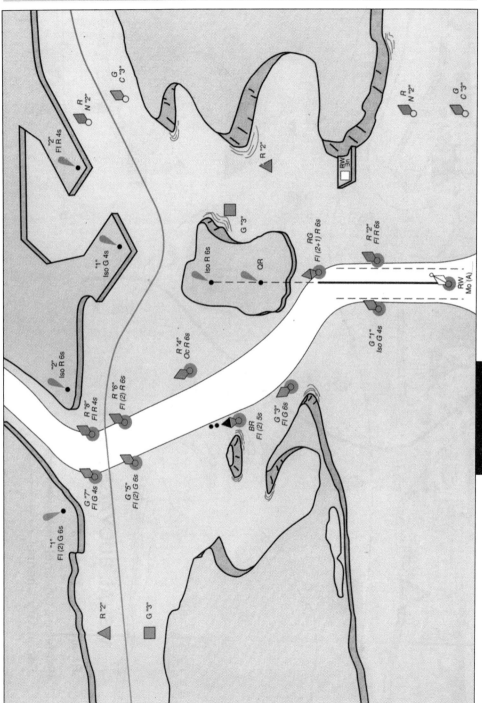

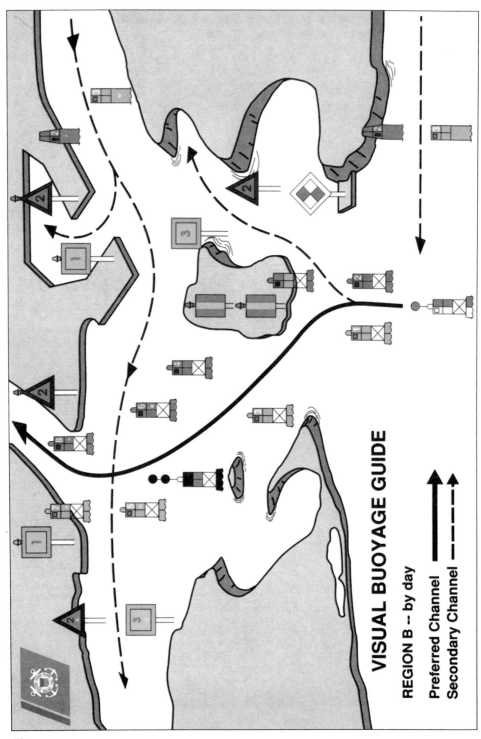

VISUAL BUOYAGE GUIDE

REGION B -- by day

Preferred Channel

Secondary Channel

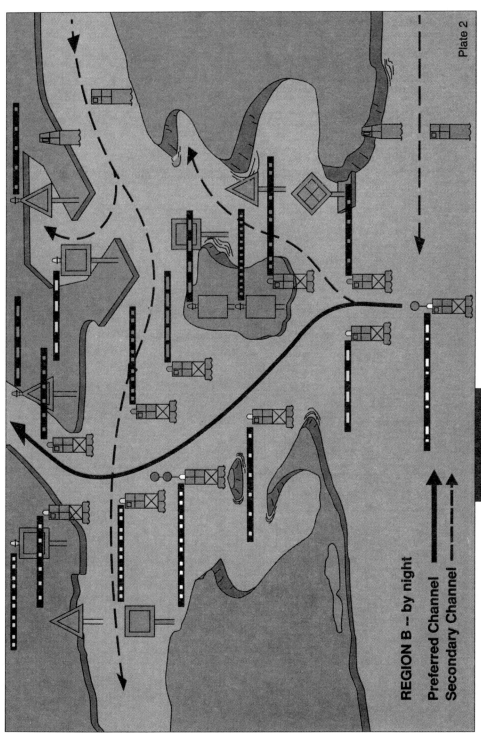

Plate 2

REGION B – by night

Preferred Channel

Secondary Channel

Essential Nav.

## AIDS TO NAVIGATION WITH LATERAL SIGNIFICANCE

### LATERAL SYSTEM AS SEEN ENTERING FROM SEAWARD

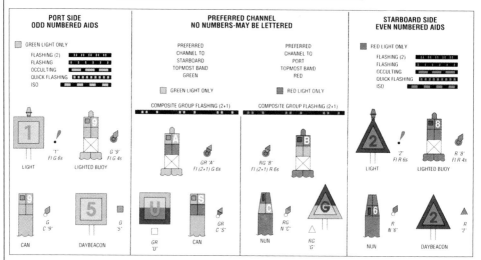

### CARDINAL MARKS (Used commonly in Canada)

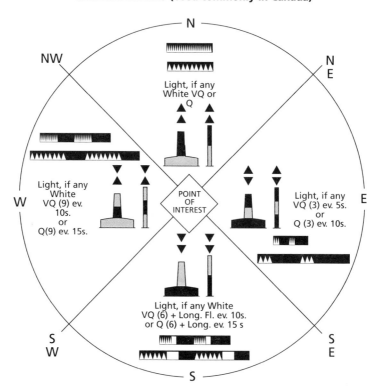

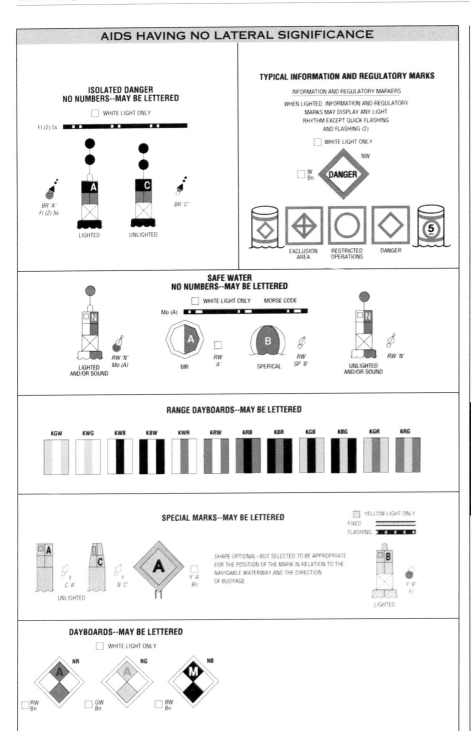

## AIDS HAVING NO LATERAL SIGNIFICANCE

**ISOLATED DANGER**
**NO NUMBERS--MAY BE LETTERED**

☐ WHITE LIGHT ONLY

Fl (2) 5s

BR 'A'
Fl (2) 5s

BR 'C'

LIGHTED          UNLIGHTED

**TYPICAL INFORMATION AND REGULATORY MARKS**

INFORMATION AND REGULATORY MARKERS

WHEN LIGHTED, INFORMATION AND REGULATORY
MARKS MAY DISPLAY ANY LIGHT
RHYTHM EXCEPT QUICK FLASHING
AND FLASHING (2)

☐ WHITE LIGHT ONLY

NW

☐ W
Bn        DANGER

EXCLUSION      RESTRICTED       DANGER
AREA          OPERATIONS

**SAFE WATER**
**NO NUMBERS--MAY BE LETTERED**

☐ WHITE LIGHT ONLY    MORSE CODE

Mo (A)

RW 'N'
Mo (A)

RW
MR     'A'

RW
SPERICAL     SP 'B'

RW 'N'

LIGHTED
AND/OR SOUND

UNLIGHTED
AND/OR SOUND

**RANGE DAYBOARDS--MAY BE LETTERED**

KGW   KWG   KWB   KBW   KWR   KRW   KRB   KBR   KGB   KBG   KGR   KRG

**SPECIAL MARKS--MAY BE LETTERED**

☐ YELLOW LIGHT ONLY
FIXED
FLASHING

Y
C 'A'

Y
N 'C'

A

Y 'A'
Bn

SHAPE OPTIONAL--BUT SELECTED TO BE APPROPRIATE
FOR THE POSITION OF THE MARK IN RELATION TO THE
NAVIGABLE WATERWAY AND THE DIRECTION
OF BUOYAGE

B

Y 'B'
Fl

UNLIGHTED

LIGHTED

**DAYBOARDS--MAY BE LETTERED**

☐ WHITE LIGHT ONLY

NR

A

☐ RW
Bn

NG

A

☐ GW
Bn

NB

M

☐ BW
Bn

## SELECTIONS FROM CHART #1 – CHART SYMBOLS

### LIGHTS/BUOYS BEACONS

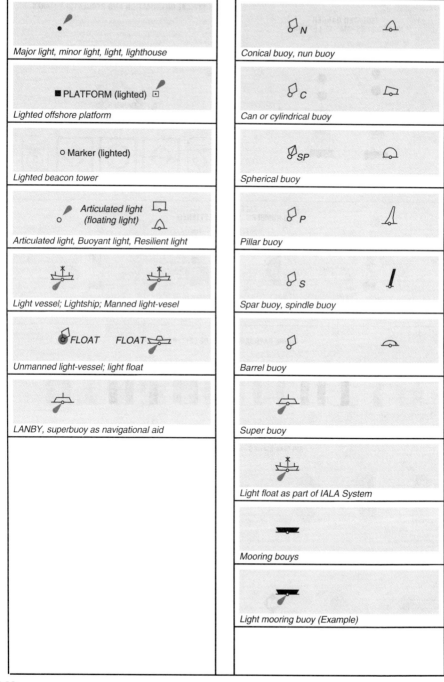

| | |
|---|---|
| Major light, minor light, light, lighthouse | Conical buoy, nun buoy |
| Lighted offshore platform | Can or cylindrical buoy |
| Lighted beacon tower | Spherical buoy |
| Articulated light, Buoyant light, Resilient light | Pillar buoy |
| Light vessel; Lightship; Manned light-vesel | Spar buoy, spindle buoy |
| Unmanned light-vessel; light float | Barrel buoy |
| LANBY, superbuoy as navigational aid | Super buoy |
| | Light float as part of IALA System |
| | Mooring bouys |
| | Light mooring buoy (Example) |

## DEPTHS/NATURE OF SEABED

| Feet | Fm/Mtrs |
|------|---------|
| 0 | 0 |
| 6 | 1 |
| 12 | 2 |
| 18 | 3 |
| 24 | 4 |
| 30 | 5 |
| 36 | 6 |
| 60 | 10 |
| 120 | 20 |
| 180 | 30 |
| 240 | 40 |
| 300 | 50 |
| 600 | 100 |
| 1,200 | 200 |
| 1,800 | 300 |
| 2,400 | 400 |
| 3,000 | 500 |
| 6,000 | 1,000 |

Approximate depth contour

— 5 — (blue or
black) — 100 —

Continuous lines, with values

NOTE
The extent of the blue tint varies with the scale
and purpose of the chart, or its sources.
On some charts, contours and figures are printed
in blue.

| | |
|------|----------------------------|
| S | Sand |
| M | Mud |
| Cy;Cl | Clay |
| Si | Silt |
| St | Stones |
| G | Gravel |
| P | Pebbles |
| Cb | Cobbles |
| Rk; Rky | Rock; Rocky |
| Co | Coral and Coralline algae |
| Sh | Shells |
| S/M | Two layers, eg. Sand over mud |
| Wd | Weed (including Kelp) |
| Kelp | Kelp, Seaweed |
| Sandwaves | Mobile bottom (sand waves) |
| Spring | Freshwater springs in seabed |

Gravel
Area with stones, gravel or shingle

Rock
Rocky area, which covers and uncovers

Coral
Coral reef, which covers and uncovers

Essential Nav.

169

## DEPTHS

| | |
|---|---|
| **ED**<br><br>Existance doubtful | 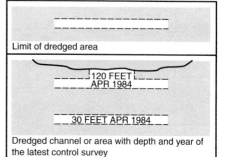<br>Limit of dredged area |
| **SD**<br><br>Sounding doubtful | ```120 FEET```<br>```APR 1984```<br><br>```30 FEET APR 1984```<br>Dredged channel or area with depth and year of the latest control survey |
| **Rep**<br><br>Reported, but not surveyed | |
| ⟨3⟩ Rep (1983)<br><br>Reported with year of report, but not surveyed | 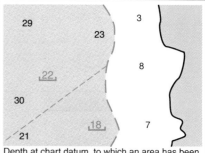 |
| ⟨3⟩ Rep<br><br>Reported but not confirmed sounding or danger | |
| 19  $8_2$  $7\frac{3}{4}$  $8_2$  19<br><br>Sounding in true position (Upright soundings are used on English unit charts and Sloping soundings are used on Metric charts) | Depth at chart datum, to which an area has been swept by wire drag. The latest date of sweeping may be shown in parentheses |
| (23)  •⎯1036<br><br>Sounding out of position | 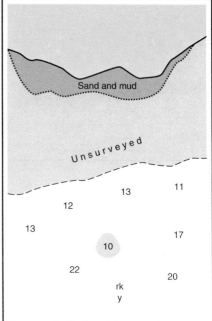 |
| (5)<br><br>Least depth in narrow channel | |
| $\overline{65}$<br><br>No bottom found at depth shown | |
| $8_2$  19  $8_2$  19<br><br>Soundings which are unreliable or taken from a smaller-scale source (Upright soundings are used on English unit charts and Sloping soundings are used on Metric charts) | |
| 6<br><br>Drying heights above chart datum | Unsurveyed or inadequately surveyed area; area with inadequate depth information |

## ROCKS, WRECKS AND OBSTRUCTIONS

| Symbol | Symbol | Description | Symbol | Symbol | Description |
|---|---|---|---|---|---|
| + 35 Rk | 35 Rk | Non-dangerous rock, depth known | Foul | Foul | Remains of a wreck or other foul area, non-dangerous to navigation but to be avoided by vessels anchoring, trawling etc. |
| +Co+ 3₁ Reef Line | | Coral reef which covers | Wks | Wks | |
| Breakers Br | | Breakers | # | Wreckage | |
| | | | Obstn | Obstn | Obstruction, depth unknown |
| Hk | Hk | Wreck, hull always dry, on large-scale charts | 5½ Obstn | 5½ Obstn | Obstruction, least depth known |
| | Hk | Wreck, covers and uncovers, on large-scale charts | 21 Obstn / 5 Obstn | 21 Obstn / 5 Obstn | Obstruction, least depth known, swept by wire drag or diver |
| | Hk | Submerged wreck, depth unknown, on large-scale charts | ⊥ oo Subm piles / Stakes, o------o / Perches Subm piling | | Stumps of posts or piles, wholly submerged |
| | PA | Wreck showing any portion of hull or superstructure at level of chart datum | oo Snags / oo Stumps | | Submerged pile, stake, snag, well or stump (with exact position) |
| Masts / Mast (10 ft) / Funnel | | Wreck showing mast or masts above chart datum only | \|\|\|\|\|\|\|\|\|\|\|\|\| Fsh stks | | Fishing stakes |
| 5½ Wk | | Wreck, least depth known by sounding only | | | Fish trap, fish weirs, tunny nets |
| 21 Wk / 5 Wk | 21 Wk / 5½ Wk / 5½ Wk | Wreck, least depth known, swept by wire drag or diver | | | Fish trap area, tunny nets area |
| | | Dangerous wreck, depth unknown | Obstruction (Fish haven) / (actual shape) | | Fish haven (artificial fishing reef) |
| +++ | | Sunken wreck, not dangerous to surface navigation | Obstn / Fish haven (auth min 42ft) | | Fish haven with minimum depth |
| 8 Wk | | Wreck, least depth unknown, but considered to have safe clearance to the depth shown | Oys | | Shellfish cultivation (stakes visible) |

Essential Nav.

## TIDES AND CURRENTS

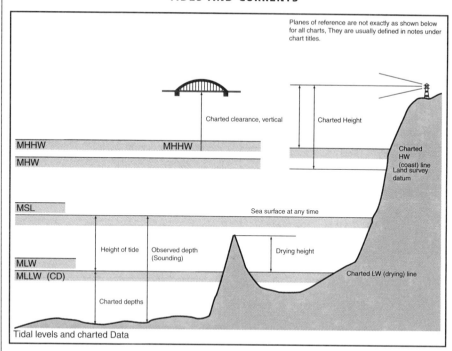

Planes of reference are not exactly as shown below for all charts, They are usually defined in notes under chart titles.

Charted clearance, vertical

Charted Height

MHHW     MHHW

MHW

Charted HW (coast) line Land survey datum

MSL

Sea surface at any time

Height of tide    Observed depth (Sounding)

Drying height

MLW

MLLW (CD)

Charted LW (drying) line

Charted depths

Tidal levels and charted Data

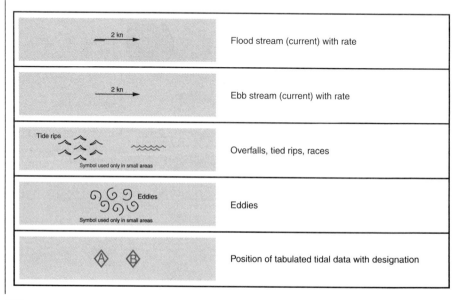

| | |
|---|---|
| 2 kn → | Flood stream (current) with rate |
| 2 kn → | Ebb stream (current) with rate |
| Tide rips   Symbol used only in small areas | Overfalls, tied rips, races |
| Eddies   Symbol used only in small areas | Eddies |
| Ⓐ Ⓑ | Position of tabulated tidal data with designation |

## CULTURAL FEATURES AND LANDMARKS`

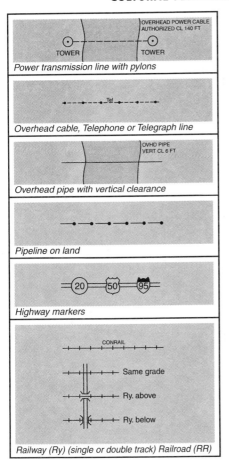

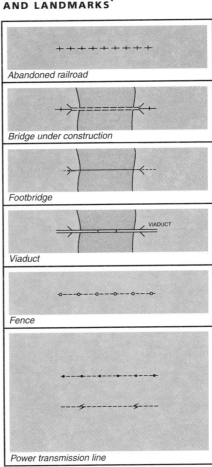

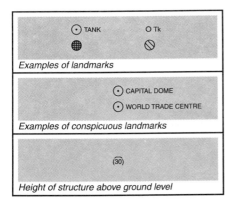

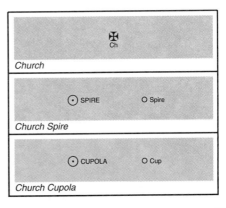

Essential Nav.

## CULTURAL FEATURES

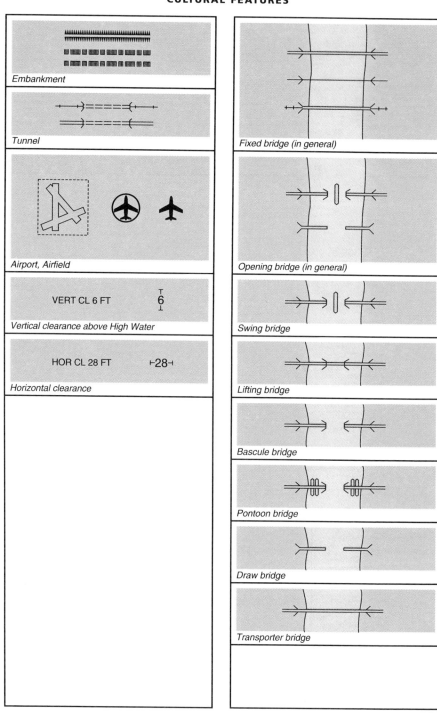

Embankment

Tunnel

Airport, Airfield

VERT CL 6 FT

Vertical clearance above High Water

HOR CL 28 FT

Horizontal clearance

Fixed bridge (in general)

Opening bridge (in general)

Swing bridge

Lifting bridge

Bascule bridge

Pontoon bridge

Draw bridge

Transporter bridge

## RADAR, RADIO, ELECTRONIC POSITION-FIXING SYSTEMS

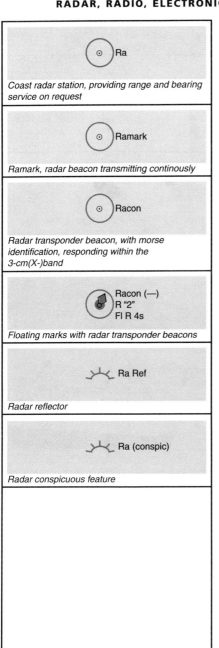

Coast radar station, providing range and bearing service on request

Ramark, radar beacon transmitting continously

Radar transponder beacon, with morse identification, responding within the 3-cm(X-)band

Floating marks with radar transponder beacons

Radar reflector

Radar conspicuous feature

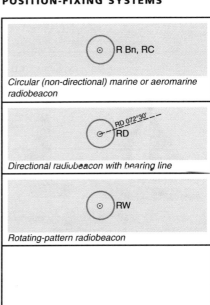

Circular (non-directional) marine or aeromarine radiobeacon

Directional radiobeacon with bearing line

Rotating-pattern radiobeacon

## RECOGNITION OF LIGHTS AND SHAPES
(Complete details in Collision Regulations)
### LIGHTS

SAILING VESSEL UNDERWAY - NOT USING POWER

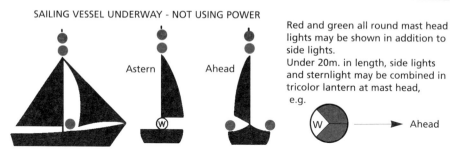

Astern    Ahead

Red and green all round mast head lights may be shown in addition to side lights.
Under 20m. in length, side lights and sternlight may be combined in tricolor lantern at mast head, e.g.

Ahead

Under 7m. in length, if not practicable to exhibit these lights, vessel shall have a white light ready to display to avoid collision.

VESSEL SAILING -
AND USING POWER

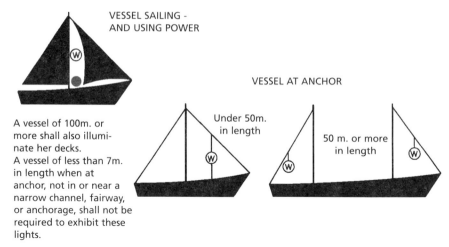

A vessel of 100m. or more shall also illuminate her decks.
A vessel of less than 7m. in length when at anchor, not in or near a narrow channel, fairway, or anchorage, shall not be required to exhibit these lights.

VESSEL AT ANCHOR

Under 50m. in length

50 m. or more in length

POWER DRIVEN VESSEL UNDERWAY

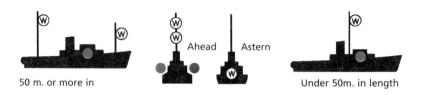

50 m. or more in

Ahead    Astern

Under 50m. in length

Under 12m. may exhibit all round white light and side lights.

Less than 7m. and maximum speed not exceeding 7 knots an all round white light may be shown, and if practicable side lights.

## HOVERCRAFT

Normal lights as for power driven vessels
and when in non-displacement mode an
all round flashing yellow light.

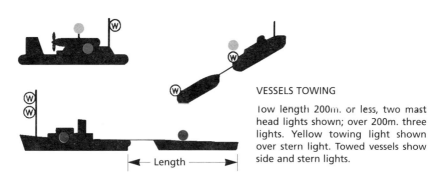

## VESSELS TOWING

low length 200m. or less, two mast
head lights shown; over 200m. three
lights. Yellow towing light shown
over stern light. Towed vessels show
side and stern lights.

## VESSEL ENGAGED IN UNDERWATER OPERATIONS

When making
way also shows
mast head, stern
and side lights.
When at anchor
does NOT show
anchor light.

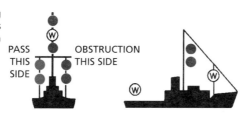

PASS          OBSTRUCTION
THIS          THIS SIDE
SIDE

## VESSEL AGROUND

Two all round red lights
and anchor light(s).

A vessel of less than 12m.
in length shall not be
required to exhibit these
lights.

## VESSELS RESTRICTED IN ABILITY TO MANEUVER

Shows 3 all round lights, red over white over red.
When making way shows mast head,
stern and side lights.
When at anchor shows an
anchor light.

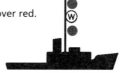

## PILOT VESSEL ON DUTY

2 all round lights, white
over red.
When underway shows
stern and side lights
instead of anchor light.

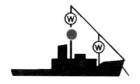

Anchored

Underway,
from astern

Underway,
from ahead

Essential Nav.

### VESSEL CONSTRAINED BY HER DRAFT

Three all round red lights,
with normal navigation lights.

### VESSEL ENGAGED IN MINESWEEPING

Three all round green lights,
with normal navigation lights.

### VESSEL FISHING, OTHER THAN TRAWLING

Two all round lights red over white with one
all round white light in direction of gear if it
extends more than 150m. horizontally.

Each vessel engaged in "pair trawling" may
direct a searchlight forward and in direction
of other vessel.

### VESSEL TRAWLING

Two all round lights green over white,
with normal navigation lights.
Mast head light optional under 50m.

### VESSEL NOT UNDER COMMAND

Two all round red lights and when making way
stern and side lights.

### REMEMBER

A sailing vessel when using its engine - with or without sails - is a power driven vessel within the meaning of the Rules and must act accordingly, showing the appropiate shapes and lights.
Therefore a tricolor lantern may not be used when under power

## RUNNING FIX TABLE

### DISTANCE OFF (at Second Bearing) By TWO BEARINGS AND RUN BETWEEN THEM

EXAMPLE OF USING TABLES. At 0600 steering East (Magnetic) a vessel takes a bearing of a lighthouse 160° (M). Patent Log 56. half an hour later the Patent Log reads 60 and the bearing is found to be 210° (M). Find the distance off at the second bearing. Angle between Course Line and First bearing equals 70°. Angle between First and Second bearing equals 50°. Using Table, with above angles 70° at top and 50° at side, gives 1.2.

Distance run between bearings (PL 60 − 56) = 4 miles. Therefore, 1.2′ × 4 = 4.8 miles.

Vessel's bearing and distance from the lighthouse is therefore 210°, distance 4.8 miles.

Speed must be estimated as accurately as possible if Patent Log is not available.

| Angle between 1st and 2nd Bearings | Angle between Course Line (i.e. Ship's Head) and First Bearing | | | | | | | | | | | | | | | Angle between 1st and 2nd Bearings |
|---|---|---|---|---|---|---|---|---|---|---|---|---|---|---|---|---|
|  | 20° | 25° | 30° | 35° | 40° | 45° | 50° | 55° | 60° | 65° | 70° | 75° | 80° | 85° | 90° |  |
| 10° | 2·0 | 2·4 | 2·9 | 3·3 | 3·7 | 4·1 | 4·4 | 4·7 | 5·0 | 5·2 | 5·4 | 5·6 | 5·7 | 5·7 | 5·8 |  |
| 15° | 1·3 | 1·6 | 1·9 | 2·2 | 2·5 | 2·7 | 3·0 | 3·2 | 3·3 | 3·5 | 3·6 | 3·7 | 3·8 | 3·8 | 3·9 |  |
| 20° | 1·0 | 1·2 | 1·5 | 1·7 | 1·9 | 2·1 | 2·2 | 2·4 | 2·5 | 2·6 | 2·7 | 2·8 | 2·9 | 2·9 | 2·9 | 160° |
| 25° | 0·8 | 1·0 | 1·2 | 1·4 | 1·5 | 1·7 | 1·8 | 1·9 | 2·0 | 2·1 | 2·2 | 2·3 | 2·3 | 2·4 | 2·4 | 155° |
| 30° | 0·7 | 0·8 | 1·0 | 1·1 | 1·3 | 1·4 | 1·5 | 1·6 | 1·7 | 1·8 | 1·9 | 1·9 | 2·0 | 2·0 | 2·0 | 150° |
| 35° | 0·6 | 0·7 | 0·9 | 1·0 | 1·1 | 1·2 | 1·3 | 1·4 | 1·5 | 1·6 | 1·6 | 1·7 | 1·7 | 1·7 | 1·7 | 145° |
| 40° | 0·5 | 0·7 | 0·8 | 0·9 | 1·0 | 1·1 | 1·2 | 1·3 | 1·3 | 1·4 | 1·5 | 1·5 | 1·5 | 1·5 | 1·6 | 140° |
| 45° | 0·5 | 0·6 | 0·7 | 0·8 | 0·9 | 1·0 | 1·1 | 1·2 | 1·2 | 1·3 | 1·3 | 1·4 | 1·4 | 1·4 | 1·4 | 135° |
| 50° | 0·4 | 0·6 | 0·7 | 0·7 | 0·8 | 0·9 | 1·0 | 1·1 | 1·1 | 1·2 | 1·2 | 1·3 | 1·3 | 1·3 | 1·3 | 130° |
| 55° | 0·4 | 0·5 | 0·6 | 0·7 | 0·8 | 0·9 | 0·9 | 1·0 | 1·1 | 1·1 | 1·1 | 1·2 | 1·2 | 1·2 | 1·2 | 125° |
| 60° | 0·4 | 0·5 | 0·6 | 0·7 | 0·7 | 0·8 | 0·9 | 0·9 | 1·0 | 1·0 | 1·1 | 1·1 | 1·1 | 1·2 | 1·2 | 120° |
| 65° | 0·4 | 0·5 | 0·6 | 0·6 | 0·7 | 0·8 | 0·8 | 0·9 | 1·0 | 1·0 | 1·0 | 1·1 | 1·1 | 1·1 | 1·1 | 115° |
| 70° | 0·4 | 0·4 | 0·5 | 0·6 | 0·7 | 0·8 | 0·8 | 0·9 | 0·9 | 1·0 | 1·0 | 1·0 | 1·0 | 1·1 | 1·1 | 110° |
| 75° | 0·4 | 0·4 | 0·5 | 0·6 | 0·7 | 0·7 | 0·8 | 0·8 | 0·9 | 0·9 | 1·0 | 1·0 | 1·0 | 1·0 | 1·0 | 105° |
| 80° | 0·3 | 0·4 | 0·5 | 0·6 | 0·7 | 0·7 | 0·8 | 0·8 | 0·9 | 0·9 | 1·0 | 1·0 | 1·0 | 1·0 | 1·0 | 100° |
| 85° | 0·3 | 0·4 | 0·5 | 0·6 | 0·6 | 0·7 | 0·8 | 0·8 | 0·9 | 0·9 | 0·9 | 1·0 | 1·0 | 1·0 | 1·0 | 95° |
| 90° | 0·3 | 0·4 | 0·5 | 0·6 | 0·6 | 0·7 | 0·8 | 0·8 | 0·9 | 0·9 | 0·9 | 1·0 | 1·0 | 1·0 | 1·0 | 90° |
|  | 160° | 155° | 150° | 145° | 140° | 135° | 130° | 125° | 120° | 115° | 110° | 105° | 100° | 95° | 90° |  |
|  | Angle between Course Line (i.e. Ship's Head) and First Bearing | | | | | | | | | | | | | | |  |

**Note:** When the angles exceed 90° use the right vertical column for the difference between bearings and the bottom horizontal row for the angle between Course Line and First Bearing. Interpolate for accuracy.

Essential Nav.

179

## FINDING DISTANCE OFF WITH SEXTANT

HEIGHT OF OBJECT, TOP LINE METERS — LOWER LINE FEET

| Distance in Miles & Cables (m c) | 12 / 40 | 15 / 50 | 18 / 60 | 21 / 70 | 24 / 80 | 27 / 90 | 30 / 100 | 33 / 110 | 37 / 120 | 40 / 130 | 43 / 140 | 46 / 150 | Distance in Miles & Cables (m c) |
|---|---|---|---|---|---|---|---|---|---|---|---|---|---|
|  | ° ' | ° ' | ° ' | ° ' | ° ' | ° ' | ° ' | ° ' | ° ' | ° ' | ° ' | ° ' |  |
| 0 1 | 3 46 | 4 42 | 5 38 | 6 34 | 7 30 | 8 25 | 9 20 | 10 15 | 11 10 | 12 04 | 12 58 | 13 52 | 0 1 |
| 0 2 | 1 53 | 2 21 | 2 49 | 3 18 | 3 46 | 4 14 | 4 42 | 5 10 | 5 38 | 6 06 | 6 34 | 7 02 | 0 2 |
| 0 3 | 1 15 | 1 34 | 1 53 | 2 12 | 2 31 | 2 49 | 3 08 | 3 27 | 3 46 | 4 05 | 4 23 | 4 42 | 0 3 |
| 0 4 | 0 57 | 1 11 | 1 25 | 1 39 | 1 53 | 2 07 | 2 21 | 2 35 | 2 49 | 3 04 | 3 18 | 3 32 | 0 4 |
| 0 5 | 0 45 | 0 57 | 1 08 | 1 19 | 1 30 | 1 42 | 1 53 | 2 04 | 2 16 | 2 27 | 2 38 | 2 49 | 0 5 |
| 0 6 | 0 38 | 0 47 | 0 57 | 1 06 | 1 15 | 1 25 | 1 34 | 1 44 | 1 53 | 2 02 | 2 12 | 2 21 | 0 6 |
| 0 7 | 0 32 | 0 40 | 0 48 | 0 57 | 1 05 | 1 13 | 1 21 | 1 29 | 1 37 | 1 45 | 1 53 | 2 01 | 0 7 |
| 0 8 | 0 28 | 0 35 | 0 42 | 0 49 | 0 57 | 1 04 | 1 11 | 1 18 | 1 25 | 1 32 | 1 39 | 1 46 | 0 8 |
| 0 9 | 0 25 | 0 31 | 0 38 | 0 44 | 0 50 | 0 57 | 1 03 | 1 09 | 1 15 | 1 22 | 1 28 | 1 34 | 0 9 |
| 1 0 | 0 23 | 0 28 | 0 34 | 0 40 | 0 45 | 0 51 | 0 57 | 1 02 | 1 08 | 1 14 | 1 19 | 1 25 | 1 0 |
| 1 1 | 0 21 | 0 26 | 0 31 | 0 36 | 0 41 | 0 46 | 0 51 | 0 57 | 1 02 | 1 07 | 1 12 | 1 17 | 1 1 |
| 1 2 | 0 19 | 0 24 | 0 28 | 0 33 | 0 38 | 0 42 | 0 47 | 0 52 | 0 57 | 1 01 | 1 06 | 1 11 | 1 2 |
| 1 3 | 0 17 | 0 22 | 0 26 | 0 30 | 0 35 | 0 39 | 0 44 | 0 48 | 0 52 | 0 57 | 1 01 | 1 05 | 1 3 |
| 1 4 | 0 16 | 0 20 | 0 24 | 0 28 | 0 32 | 0 36 | 0 40 | 0 44 | 0 48 | 0 53 | 0 57 | 1 01 | 1 4 |
| 1 5 | 0 15 | 0 19 | 0 23 | 0 26 | 0 30 | 0 34 | 0 38 | 0 41 | 0 45 | 0 49 | 0 53 | 0 57 | 1 5 |
| 1 6 | 0 14 | 0 18 | 0 21 | 0 25 | 0 28 | 0 32 | 0 35 | 0 39 | 0 42 | 0 46 | 0 49 | 0 53 | 1 6 |
| 1 7 | 0 13 | 0 17 | 0 20 | 0 23 | 0 27 | 0 30 | 0 33 | 0 37 | 0 40 | 0 43 | 0 47 | 0 50 | 1 7 |
| 1 8 | 0 13 | 0 16 | 0 19 | 0 22 | 0 25 | 0 28 | 0 31 | 0 35 | 0 38 | 0 41 | 0 44 | 0 47 | 1 8 |
| 1 9 | 0 12 | 0 15 | 0 18 | 0 21 | 0 24 | 0 27 | 0 30 | 0 33 | 0 36 | 0 39 | 0 42 | 0 45 | 1 9 |
| 2 0 | 0 11 | 0 14 | 0 17 | 0 20 | 0 23 | 0 25 | 0 28 | 0 31 | 0 34 | 0 37 | 0 40 | 0 42 | 2 0 |
| 2 1 | 0 10 | 0 14 | 0 16 | 0 19 | 0 22 | 0 24 | 0 27 | 0 30 | 0 32 | 0 35 | 0 38 | 0 40 | 2 1 |
| 2 2 | 0 10 | 0 13 | 0 15 | 0 18 | 0 21 | 0 23 | 0 26 | 0 28 | 0 31 | 0 33 | 0 36 | 0 39 | 2 2 |
| 2 3 | 0 10 | 0 12 | 0 14 | 0 17 | 0 20 | 0 22 | 0 25 | 0 27 | 0 30 | 0 32 | 0 34 | 0 37 | 2 3 |
| 2 4 | 0 10 | 0 12 | 0 14 | 0 17 | 0 19 | 0 21 | 0 24 | 0 26 | 0 28 | 0 31 | 0 33 | 0 35 | 2 4 |
| 2 5 | 0 9 | 0 11 | 0 13 | 0 16 | 0 18 | 0 20 | 0 23 | 0 25 | 0 27 | 0 29 | 0 32 | 0 34 | 2 5 |
| 2 6 | 0 9 | 0 11 | 0 13 | 0 15 | 0 17 | 0 20 | 0 22 | 0 24 | 0 26 | 0 28 | 0 30 | 0 33 | 2 6 |
| 2 7 | 0 9 | 0 10 | 0 12 | 0 15 | 0 17 | 0 19 | 0 21 | 0 23 | 0 25 | 0 27 | 0 29 | 0 31 | 2 7 |
| 2 8 | 0 8 | 0 10 | 0 12 | 0 14 | 0 16 | 0 18 | 0 20 | 0 22 | 0 24 | 0 26 | 0 28 | 0 30 | 2 8 |
| 2 9 | 0 8 | 0 10 | 0 11 | 0 14 | 0 16 | 0 18 | 0 20 | 0 21 | 0 23 | 0 25 | 0 27 | 0 29 | 2 9 |
| 3 0 | 0 8 | 0 9 | 0 10 | 0 13 | 0 15 | 0 17 | 0 19 | 0 21 | 0 23 | 0 24 | 0 26 | 0 28 | 3 0 |
| 3 2 |  |  |  | 0 12 | 0 14 | 0 16 | 0 18 | 0 19 | 0 21 | 0 23 | 0 25 | 0 27 | 3 2 |
| 3 4 |  |  |  | 0 12 | 0 13 | 0 15 | 0 17 | 0 18 | 0 20 | 0 22 | 0 23 | 0 25 | 3 4 |
| 3 6 |  |  |  | 0 11 | 0 13 | 0 14 | 0 16 | 0 17 | 0 19 | 0 20 | 0 22 | 0 24 | 3 6 |
| 3 8 |  |  |  | 0 10 | 0 12 | 0 13 | 0 15 | 0 16 | 0 18 | 0 19 | 0 21 | 0 22 | 3 8 |
| 4 0 |  |  |  | 0 10 | 0 11 | 0 13 | 0 14 | 0 16 | 0 17 | 0 18 | 0 20 | 0 21 | 4 0 |
| 4 2 |  |  |  |  |  | 0 12 | 0 14 | 0 15 | 0 16 | 0 17 | 0 19 | 0 20 | 4 2 |
| 4 4 |  |  |  |  |  | 0 12 | 0 13 | 0 14 | 0 15 | 0 17 | 0 18 | 0 19 | 4 4 |
| 4 6 |  |  |  |  |  | 0 11 | 0 13 | 0 14 | 0 15 | 0 16 | 0 17 | 0 18 | 4 6 |
| 4 8 |  |  |  |  |  | 0 11 | 0 12 | 0 13 | 0 14 | 0 15 | 0 16 | 0 18 | 4 8 |
| 5 0 |  |  |  |  |  | 0 10 | 0 11 | 0 12 | 0 14 | 0 15 | 0 16 | 0 17 | 5 0 |
| 5 2 |  |  |  |  |  |  |  | 0 12 | 0 13 | 0 14 | 0 15 | 0 16 | 5 2 |
| 5 4 |  |  |  |  |  |  |  | 0 12 | 0 13 | 0 14 | 0 15 | 0 16 | 5 4 |
| 5 6 |  |  |  |  |  |  |  | 0 11 | 0 12 | 0 13 | 0 14 | 0 15 | 5 6 |
| 5 8 |  |  |  |  |  |  |  | 0 11 | 0 12 | 0 13 | 0 14 | 0 15 | 5 8 |
| 6 0 |  |  |  |  |  |  |  | 0 10 | 0 11 | 0 12 | 0 13 | 0 14 | 6 0 |

## FINDING DISTANCE OFF WITH SEXTANT

| Distance in Miles & Cables | HEIGHT OF OBJECT, TOP LINE METERS — LOWER LINE FEET | | | | | | | | | | | | Distance in Miles & Cables |
|---|---|---|---|---|---|---|---|---|---|---|---|---|---|
| | 49 / 160 | 52 / 170 | 55 / 180 | 58 / 190 | 61 / 200 | 64 / 210 | 67 / 220 | 70 / 230 | 73 / 240 | 76 / 250 | 79 / 260 | 82 / 270 | |
| m c | ° ′ | ° ′ | ° ′ | ° ′ | ° ′ | ° ′ | ° ′ | ° ′ | ° ′ | ° ′ | ° ′ | ° ′ | m c |
| 0 1 | 14 45 | 15 37 | 16 29 | 17 21 | 18 13 | 19 03 | 19 54 | 20 43 | 21 32 | 22 21 | 23 09 | 23 57 | 0 1 |
| 0 2 | 7 30 | 7 58 | 8 25 | 8 53 | 9 20 | 9 48 | 10 15 | 10 43 | 11 10 | 11 37 | 12 04 | 12 31 | 0 2 |
| 0 3 | 5 01 | 5 19 | 5 38 | 5 57 | 6 15 | 6 34 | 6 53 | 7 11 | 7 30 | 7 48 | 8 07 | 8 25 | 0 3 |
| 0 4 | 3 46 | 4 00 | 4 14 | 4 28 | 4 42 | 4 56 | 5 10 | 5 24 | 5 38 | 5 52 | 6 06 | 6 20 | 0 4 |
| 0 5 | 3 01 | 3 12 | 3 23 | 3 35 | 3 46 | 3 57 | 4 08 | 4 20 | 4 31 | 4 42 | 4 53 | 5 05 | 0 5 |
| 0 6 | 2 31 | 2 40 | 2 49 | 2 59 | 3 08 | 3 18 | 3 27 | 3 36 | 3 46 | 3 55 | 4 05 | 4 14 | 0 6 |
| 0 7 | 2 09 | 2 17 | 2 25 | 2 33 | 2 41 | 2 49 | 2 58 | 3 06 | 3 14 | 3 22 | 3 30 | 3 38 | 0 7 |
| 0 8 | 1 53 | 2 00 | 2 07 | 2 14 | 2 21 | 2 28 | 2 35 | 2 42 | 2 49 | 2 57 | 3 04 | 3 11 | 0 8 |
| 0 9 | 1 40 | 1 47 | 1 53 | 1 59 | 2 06 | 2 12 | 2 18 | 2 24 | 2 31 | 2 37 | 2 43 | 2 49 | 0 9 |
| 1 0 | 1 30 | 1 36 | 1 42 | 1 47 | 1 53 | 1 59 | 2 04 | 2 10 | 2 16 | 2 21 | 2 27 | 2 33 | 1 0 |
| 1 1 | 1 22 | 1 27 | 1 33 | 1 38 | 1 43 | 1 48 | 1 53 | 1 58 | 2 03 | 2 08 | 2 14 | 2 19 | 1 1 |
| 1 2 | 1 15 | 1 20 | 1 25 | 1 30 | 1 34 | 1 39 | 1 44 | 1 48 | 1 53 | 1 58 | 2 02 | 2 07 | 1 2 |
| 1 3 | 1 10 | 1 14 | 1 18 | 1 23 | 1 27 | 1 31 | 1 36 | 1 40 | 1 44 | 1 49 | 1 53 | 1 57 | 1 3 |
| 1 4 | 1 05 | 1 09 | 1 13 | 1 17 | 1 21 | 1 25 | 1 29 | 1 33 | 1 37 | 1 41 | 1 45 | 1 49 | 1 4 |
| 1 5 | 1 00 | 1 04 | 1 8 | 1 12 | 1 15 | 1 19 | 1 23 | 1 27 | 1 30 | 1 34 | 1 38 | 1 42 | 1 5 |
| 1 6 | 0 57 | 1 00 | 1 04 | 1 07 | 1 11 | 1 14 | 1 18 | 1 21 | 1 25 | 1 28 | 1 32 | 1 35 | 1 6 |
| 1 7 | 0 53 | 0 57 | 1 00 | 1 03 | 1 07 | 1 10 | 1 13 | 1 16 | 1 20 | 1 23 | 1 26 | 1 30 | 1 7 |
| 1 8 | 0 50 | 0 53 | 0 57 | 1 00 | 1 03 | 1 06 | 1 09 | 1 12 | 1 15 | 1 19 | 1 22 | 1 25 | 1 8 |
| 1 9 | 0 48 | 0 51 | 0 54 | 0 57 | 1 00 | 1 02 | 1 05 | 1 08 | 1 11 | 1 14 | 1 17 | 1 20 | 1 9 |
| 2 0 | 0 45 | 0 48 | 0 51 | 0 54 | 0 57 | 0 59 | 1 02 | 1 05 | 1 08 | 1 11 | 1 14 | 1 16 | 2 0 |
| 2 1 | 0 43 | 0 46 | 0 48 | 0 51 | 0 54 | 0 57 | 0 59 | 1 02 | 1 05 | 1 07 | 1 10 | 1 13 | 2 1 |
| 2 2 | 0 41 | 0 44 | 0 46 | 0 49 | 0 51 | 0 54 | 0 57 | 0 59 | 1 02 | 1 04 | 1 07 | 1 09 | 2 2 |
| 2 3 | 0 39 | 0 42 | 0 44 | 0 47 | 0 49 | 0 52 | 0 54 | 0 57 | 0 59 | 1 01 | 1 04 | 1 06 | 2 3 |
| 2 4 | 0 38 | 0 40 | 0 42 | 0 45 | 0 47 | 0 49 | 0 52 | 0 54 | 0 57 | 0 59 | 1 01 | 1 04 | 2 4 |
| 2 5 | 0 36 | 0 38 | 0 41 | 0 43 | 0 45 | 0 48 | 0 50 | 0 52 | 0 54 | 0 57 | 0 59 | 1 01 | 2 5 |
| 2 6 | 0 35 | 0 37 | 0 39 | 0 41 | 0 44 | 0 46 | 0 48 | 0 50 | 0 52 | 0 54 | 0 57 | 0 59 | 2 6 |
| 2 7 | 0 34 | 0 36 | 0 38 | 0 40 | 0 42 | 0 44 | 0 46 | 0 48 | 0 50 | 0 52 | 0 54 | 0 57 | 2 7 |
| 2 8 | 0 32 | 0 34 | 0 36 | 0 38 | 0 40 | 0 42 | 0 44 | 0 46 | 0 48 | 0 50 | 0 53 | 0 55 | 2 8 |
| 2 9 | 0 31 | 0 33 | 0 35 | 0 37 | 0 39 | 0 41 | 0 43 | 0 45 | 0 47 | 0 49 | 0 51 | 0 53 | 2 9 |
| 3 0 | 0 30 | 0 32 | 0 34 | 0 36 | 0 38 | 0 40 | 0 41 | 0 43 | 0 45 | 0 47 | 0 49 | 0 51 | 3 0 |
| 3 2 | 0 28 | 0 30 | 0 32 | 0 34 | 0 35 | 0 37 | 0 39 | 0 41 | 0 42 | 0 44 | 0 46 | 0 48 | 3 2 |
| 3 4 | 0 27 | 0 28 | 0 30 | 0 32 | 0 33 | 0 35 | 0 37 | 0 38 | 0 40 | 0 42 | 0 43 | 0 45 | 3 4 |
| 3 6 | 0 25 | 0 27 | 0 28 | 0 30 | 0 31 | 0 33 | 0 35 | 0 36 | 0 38 | 0 39 | 0 41 | 0 42 | 3 6 |
| 3 8 | 0 24 | 0 25 | 0 27 | 0 28 | 0 30 | 0 31 | 0 33 | 0 34 | 0 36 | 0 37 | 0 39 | 0 40 | 3 8 |
| 4 0 | 0 23 | 0 24 | 0 25 | 0 27 | 0 28 | 0 30 | 0 31 | 0 33 | 0 34 | 0 35 | 0 37 | 0 38 | 4 0 |
| 4 2 | 0 22 | 0 23 | 0 24 | 0 26 | 0 27 | 0 28 | 0 30 | 0 31 | 0 32 | 0 34 | 0 35 | 0 36 | 4 2 |
| 4 4 | 0 21 | 0 22 | 0 23 | 0 24 | 0 26 | 0 27 | 0 28 | 0 30 | 0 31 | 0 32 | 0 33 | 0 35 | 4 4 |
| 4 6 | 0 20 | 0 21 | 0 22 | 0 23 | 0 25 | 0 26 | 0 27 | 0 28 | 0 30 | 0 31 | 0 32 | 0 33 | 4 6 |
| 4 8 | 0 19 | 0 20 | 0 21 | 0 22 | 0 24 | 0 25 | 0 26 | 0 27 | 0 28 | 0 30 | 0 31 | 0 32 | 4 8 |
| 5 0 | 0 18 | 0 19 | 0 20 | 0 21 | 0 23 | 0 24 | 0 25 | 0 26 | 0 27 | 0 28 | 0 29 | 0 31 | 5 0 |
| 5 2 | 0 17 | 0 18 | 0 20 | 0 21 | 0 22 | 0 23 | 0 24 | 0 25 | 0 26 | 0 27 | 0 28 | 0 29 | 5 2 |
| 5 4 | 0 17 | 0 18 | 0 19 | 0 20 | 0 21 | 0 22 | 0 23 | 0 24 | 0 25 | 0 26 | 0 27 | 0 28 | 5 4 |
| 5 6 | 0 16 | 0 17 | 0 18 | 0 19 | 0 20 | 0 21 | 0 22 | 0 23 | 0 24 | 0 25 | 0 26 | 0 27 | 5 6 |
| 5 8 | 0 16 | 0 17 | 0 18 | 0 19 | 0 19 | 0 20 | 0 21 | 0 22 | 0 23 | 0 24 | 0 25 | 0 26 | 5 8 |
| 6 0 | 0 15 | 0 16 | 0 17 | 0 18 | 0 19 | 0 20 | 0 21 | 0 22 | 0 23 | 0 24 | 0 25 | 0 25 | 6 0 |
| 6 2 | | | | | 0 18 | 0 19 | 0 20 | 0 21 | 0 22 | 0 23 | 0 24 | 0 25 | 6 2 |
| 6 4 | | | | | 0 18 | 0 19 | 0 20 | 0 21 | 0 21 | 0 22 | 0 23 | 0 24 | 6 4 |
| 6 6 | | | | | 0 17 | 0 18 | 0 19 | 0 20 | 0 21 | 0 21 | 0 22 | 0 23 | 6 6 |
| 6 8 | | | | | 0 17 | 0 18 | 0 18 | 0 19 | 0 20 | 0 21 | 0 22 | 0 22 | 6 8 |
| 7 0 | | | | | 0 16 | 0 17 | 0 18 | 0 19 | 0 19 | 0 20 | 0 21 | 0 22 | 7 0 |

Essential Nav.

## FINDING DISTANCE OFF WITH SEXTANT

| Distance in Miles & Cables | HEIGHT OF OBJECT, TOP LINE METERS – LOWER LINE FEET | | | | | | | | | | | | Distance in Miles & Cables |
|---|---|---|---|---|---|---|---|---|---|---|---|---|---|
| m c | 85 / 280 | 88 / 290 | 91 / 300 | 94 / 310 | 97 / 320 | 101 / 330 | 104 / 340 | 107 / 350 | 110 / 360 | 113 / 370 | 116 / 380 | 119 / 390 | m c |
| | ° ' | ° ' | ° ' | ° ' | ° ' | ° ' | ° ' | ° ' | ° ' | ° ' | ° ' | ° ' | |
| 0 1 | 24 44 | 25 30 | 26 16 | 26 01 | 27 46 | 28 29 | 29 13 | 29 56 | 30 38 | 31 19 | 32 00 | 32 41 | 0 1 |
| 0 2 | 12 58 | 13 25 | 13 52 | 14 08 | 14 45 | 15 11 | 15 37 | 16 03 | 16 29 | 16 55 | 17 21 | 17 47 | 0 2 |
| 0 3 | 8 44 | 9 02 | 9 20 | 9 39 | 9 57 | 10 15 | 10 34 | 10 52 | 11 10 | 11 28 | 11 46 | 12 04 | 0 3 |
| 0 4 | 6 34 | 6 48 | 7 02 | 7 16 | 7 30 | 7 44 | 7 58 | 8 11 | 8 25 | 8 39 | 8 53 | 9 07 | 0 4 |
| 0 5 | 5 16 | 5 27 | 5 38 | 5 49 | 6 01 | 6 12 | 6 23 | 6 34 | 6 45 | 6 56 | 7 08 | 7 19 | 0 5 |
| 0 6 | 4 23 | 4 33 | 4 42 | 4 51 | 5 01 | 5 10 | 5 19 | 5 29 | 5 38 | 5 47 | 5 47 | 6 06 | 0 6 |
| 0 7 | 3 46 | 3 54 | 4 02 | 5 10 | 4 18 | 4 26 | 4 43 | 4 42 | 4 50 | 4 58 | 5 06 | 5 14 | 0 7 |
| 0 8 | 3 18 | 3 25 | 3 32 | 3 39 | 3 46 | 3 53 | 4 00 | 4 07 | 4 14 | 4 21 | 4 28 | 4 35 | 0 8 |
| 0 9 | 2 56 | 3 02 | 3 08 | 3 15 | 3 21 | 3 27 | 3 33 | 3 40 | 3 46 | 3 52 | 3 58 | 4 05 | 0 9 |
| 1 0 | 2 38 | 2 44 | 2 49 | 2 55 | 3 01 | 3 06 | 3 12 | 3 18 | 3 23 | 3 29 | 3 35 | 3 40 | 1 0 |
| 1 1 | 2 24 | 2 29 | 2 34 | 2 39 | 2 44 | 2 49 | 2 55 | 3 00 | 3 05 | 3 10 | 3 15 | 3 20 | 1 1 |
| 1 2 | 2 12 | 2 17 | 2 21 | 2 26 | 2 31 | 2 35 | 2 40 | 2 45 | 2 49 | 2 54 | 2 59 | 3 04 | 1 2 |
| 1 3 | 2 02 | 2 06 | 2 10 | 2 15 | 2 19 | 2 23 | 2 28 | 2 32 | 2 36 | 2 41 | 2 45 | 2 49 | 1 3 |
| 1 4 | 1 53 | 1 57 | 2 01 | 2 05 | 2 09 | 2 13 | 2 17 | 2 21 | 2 25 | 2 29 | 2 37 | 2 37 | 1 4 |
| 1 5 | 1 46 | 1 49 | 1 53 | 1 57 | 2 01 | 2 04 | 2 08 | 2 12 | 2 16 | 2 19 | 2 23 | 2 27 | 1 5 |
| 1 6 | 1 39 | 1 42 | 1 46 | 1 50 | 1 53 | 1 57 | 2 00 | 2 04 | 2 07 | 2 11 | 2 14 | 2 18 | 1 6 |
| 1 7 | 1 33 | 1 36 | 1 40 | 1 43 | 1 46 | 1 50 | 1 53 | 1 56 | 2 00 | 2 03 | 2 06 | 2 10 | 1 7 |
| 1 8 | 1 28 | 1 31 | 1 34 | 1 37 | 1 40 | 1 44 | 1 47 | 1 50 | 1 53 | 1 56 | 1 59 | 2 02 | 1 8 |
| 1 9 | 1 23 | 1 26 | 1 29 | 1 32 | 1 35 | 1 38 | 1 41 | 1 44 | 1 47 | 1 50 | 1 53 | 1 56 | 1 9 |
| 2 0 | 1 19 | 1 22 | 1 25 | 1 28 | 1 30 | 1 33 | 1 36 | 1 39 | 1 42 | 1 45 | 1 47 | 1 50 | 2 0 |
| 2 1 | 1 15 | 1 18 | 1 21 | 1 23 | 1 26 | 1 29 | 1 32 | 1 34 | 1 37 | 1 40 | 1 42 | 1 45 | 2 1 |
| 2 2 | 1 12 | 1 15 | 1 17 | 1 20 | 1 22 | 1 25 | 1 27 | 1 30 | 1 33 | 1 35 | 1 38 | 1 40 | 2 2 |
| 2 3 | 1 09 | 1 11 | 1 14 | 1 16 | 1 19 | 1 21 | 1 24 | 1 26 | 1 29 | 1 31 | 1 33 | 1 36 | 2 3 |
| 2 4 | 1 06 | 1 08 | 1 11 | 1 13 | 1 15 | 1 18 | 1 20 | 1 22 | 1 25 | 1 27 | 1 30 | 1 32 | 2 4 |
| 2 5 | 1 03 | 1 06 | 1 08 | 1 10 | 1 12 | 1 15 | 1 17 | 1 19 | 1 21 | 1 24 | 1 26 | 1 28 | 2 5 |
| 2 6 | 1 01 | 1 03 | 1 05 | 1 07 | 1 10 | 1 12 | 1 14 | 1 16 | 1 18 | 1 20 | 1 23 | 1 25 | 2 6 |
| 2 7 | 0 59 | 1 01 | 1 03 | 1 05 | 1 07 | 1 09 | 1 11 | 1 13 | 1 15 | 1 17 | 1 20 | 1 23 | 2 7 |
| 2 8 | 0 57 | 0 59 | 1 01 | 1 03 | 1 05 | 1 07 | 1 09 | 1 11 | 1 13 | 1 15 | 1 17 | 1 19 | 2 8 |
| 2 9 | 0 55 | 0 57 | 0 58 | 1 00 | 1 02 | 1 04 | 1 06 | 1 08 | 1 10 | 1 12 | 1 14 | 1 16 | 2 9 |
| 3 0 | 0 53 | 0 55 | 0 57 | 0 58 | 1 00 | 1 02 | 1 04 | 1 06 | 1 08 | 1 10 | 1 12 | 1 14 | 3 0 |
| 3 2 | 0 49 | 0 51 | 0 53 | 0 55 | 0 57 | 0 58 | 1 00 | 1 02 | 1 04 | 1 05 | 1 07 | 1 09 | 3 2 |
| 3 4 | 0 47 | 0 48 | 0 50 | 0 52 | 0 53 | 0 55 | 0 57 | 0 58 | 1 00 | 1 02 | 1 03 | 1 05 | 3 4 |
| 3 6 | 0 44 | 0 46 | 0 47 | 0 49 | 0 50 | 0 52 | 0 53 | 0 55 | 0 57 | 0 58 | 1 00 | 1 01 | 3 6 |
| 3 8 | 0 42 | 0 43 | 0 45 | 0 46 | 0 48 | 0 49 | 0 51 | 0 52 | 0 54 | 0 55 | 0 57 | 0 58 | 3 8 |
| 4 0 | 0 40 | 0 41 | 0 42 | 0 44 | 0 45 | 0 47 | 0 48 | 0 49 | 0 51 | 0 52 | 0 54 | 0 55 | 4 0 |
| 4 2 | 0 38 | 0 39 | 0 40 | 0 42 | 0 43 | 0 44 | 0 46 | 0 47 | 0 48 | 0 50 | 0 51 | 0 53 | 4 2 |
| 4 4 | 0 36 | 0 37 | 0 39 | 0 40 | 0 41 | 0 42 | 0 44 | 0 45 | 0 46 | 0 48 | 0 49 | 0 50 | 4 4 |
| 4 6 | 0 34 | 0 36 | 0 37 | 0 38 | 0 39 | 0 41 | 0 42 | 0 43 | 0 44 | 0 45 | 0 47 | 0 48 | 4 6 |
| 4 8 | 0 33 | 0 34 | 0 35 | 0 37 | 0 38 | 0 39 | 0 40 | 0 41 | 0 42 | 0 44 | 0 45 | 0 46 | 4 8 |
| 5 0 | 0 32 | 0 33 | 0 34 | 0 35 | 0 36 | 0 37 | 0 38 | 0 40 | 0 41 | 0 42 | 0 43 | 0 44 | 5 0 |
| 5 2 | 0 30 | 0 32 | 0 33 | 0 34 | 0 35 | 0 36 | 0 37 | 0 38 | 0 39 | 0 40 | 0 41 | 0 42 | 5 2 |
| 5 4 | 0 29 | 0 30 | 0 31 | 0 32 | 0 34 | 0 34 | 0 36 | 0 37 | 0 38 | 0 39 | 0 40 | 0 41 | 5 4 |
| 5 6 | 0 28 | 0 29 | 0 30 | 0 31 | 0 32 | 0 33 | 0 34 | 0 35 | 0 36 | 0 37 | 0 38 | 0 39 | 5 6 |
| 5 8 | 0 27 | 0 28 | 0 29 | 0 30 | 0 31 | 0 32 | 0 33 | 0 34 | 0 35 | 0 36 | 0 37 | 0 38 | 5 8 |
| 6 0 | 0 26 | 0 27 | 0 28 | 0 29 | 0 30 | 0 31 | 0 32 | 0 33 | 0 34 | 0 35 | 0 36 | 0 37 | 6 0 |
| 6 2 | 0 26 | 0 26 | 0 27 | 0 28 | 0 29 | 0 30 | 0 31 | 0 32 | 0 33 | 0 34 | 0 35 | 3 06 | 6 2 |
| 6 4 | 0 25 | 0 26 | 0 27 | 0 27 | 0 28 | 0 29 | 0 30 | 0 31 | 0 32 | 0 33 | 0 34 | 0 34 | 6 4 |
| 6 6 | 0 24 | 0 25 | 0 26 | 0 27 | 0 27 | 0 28 | 0 29 | 0 30 | 0 31 | 0 32 | 0 33 | 0 33 | 6 6 |
| 6 8 | 0 23 | 0 24 | 0 25 | 0 26 | 0 27 | 0 27 | 0 28 | 0 29 | 0 30 | 0 31 | 0 32 | 0 32 | 6 8 |
| 7 0 | 0 23 | 0 23 | 0 24 | 0 25 | 0 26 | 0 27 | 0 37 | 0 38 | 0 29 | 0 30 | 0 31 | 0 31 | 7 0 |

## FINDING DISTANCE OFF WITH SEXTANT

| Distance in Miles & Cables | HEIGHT OF OBJECT, TOP LINE METERS – LOWER LINE FEET | | | | | | | | | | | | Distance in Miles & Cables |
|---|---|---|---|---|---|---|---|---|---|---|---|---|---|
| m c | 122 / 400 | 137 / 450 | 152 / 500 | 168 / 550 | 183 / 600 | 198 / 650 | 213 / 700 | 244 / 800 | 274 / 900 | 305 / 1000 | 457 / 1500 | 610 / 2000 | m c |
| 0 1 | 33 20 | 36 30 | 39 26 | 42 08 | 44 37 | | | | | | | | 0 1 |
| 0 2 | 18 13 | 20 18 | 22 21 | 24 20 | 26 16 | 28 08 | 29 56 | 33 20 | 36 30 | 39 26 | | | 0 2 |
| 0 3 | 12 22 | 13 52 | 15 20 | 16 47 | 18 13 | 19 37 | 21 00 | 23 41 | 26 16 | 28 44 | | | 0 3 |
| 0 4 | 9 20 | 10 29 | 11 37 | 12 45 | 13 52 | 14 58 | 16 03 | 18 13 | 20 18 | 22 21 | | | 0 4 |
| 0 5 | 7 30 | 8 25 | 9 20 | 10 15 | 11 10 | 12 04 | 12 58 | 14 45 | 16 30 | 18 13 | 26 15 | | 0 5 |
| 0 6 | 6 15 | 7 02 | 7 48 | 8 34 | 9 20 | 10 06 | 10 52 | 12 22 | 13 52 | 15 20 | 22 20 | 28 44 | 0 6 |
| 0 7 | 5 22 | 6 02 | 6 42 | 7 22 | 8 01 | 8 41 | 9 20 | 10 39 | 11 56 | 13 13 | 19 25 | 25 10 | 0 7 |
| 0 8 | 4 42 | 5 17 | 5 52 | 6 27 | 7 02 | 7 37 | 8 11 | 9 20 | 10 29 | 11 37 | 17 08 | 22 21 | 0 8 |
| 0 9 | 4 11 | 4 42 | 5 13 | 5 44 | 6 15 | 6 46 | 7 17 | 8 19 | 9 20 | 10 21 | 15 19 | 20 05 | 0 9 |
| 1 0 | 3 46 | 4 14 | 4 42 | 5 10 | 5 38 | 6 06 | 6 34 | 7 30 | 8 25 | 9 20 | 13 51 | 18 13 | 1 0 |
| 1 1 | 3 25 | 3 51 | 4 17 | 4 42 | 5 08 | 5 33 | 5 59 | 6 49 | 7 40 | 8 30 | 12 38 | 16 39 | 1 1 |
| 1 2 | 3 08 | 3 32 | 3 55 | 4 19 | 4 42 | 5 05 | 5 29 | 6 15 | 7 02 | 7 48 | 11 37 | 15 20 | 1 2 |
| 1 3 | 2 54 | 3 16 | 3 37 | 3 59 | 4 20 | 4 42 | 5 04 | 5 47 | 6 30 | 7 13 | 10 45 | 14 12 | 1 3 |
| 1 4 | 2 41 | 3 02 | 3 22 | 3 42 | 4 02 | 4 22 | 4 42 | 5 22 | 6 02 | 6 42 | 10 00 | 13 13 | 1 4 |
| 1 5 | 2 31 | 2 49 | 3 08 | 3 27 | 3 46 | 4 05 | 4 23 | 5 01 | 5 38 | 6 15 | 9 20 | 12 22 | 1 5 |
| 1 6 | 2 21 | 2 39 | 2 57 | 3 14 | 3 32 | 3 49 | 4 07 | 4 42 | 5 17 | 5 52 | 8 46 | 11 37 | 1 6 |
| 1 7 | 2 13 | 2 30 | 2 46 | 3 03 | 3 19 | 3 36 | 3 52 | 4 26 | 4 59 | 5 32 | 8 15 | 10 57 | 1 7 |
| 1 8 | 2 06 | 2 21 | 2 37 | 2 53 | 3 08 | 3 24 | 3 40 | 4 11 | 4 42 | 5 13 | 7 48 | 10 21 | 1 8 |
| 1 9 | 1 59 | 2 14 | 2 29 | 2 44 | 2 58 | 3 13 | 3 28 | 3 58 | 4 27 | 4 57 | 7 25 | 9 50 | 1 9 |
| 2 0 | 1 53 | 2 07 | 2 21 | 2 35 | 2 49 | 3 04 | 3 18 | 3 46 | 4 14 | 4 42 | 7 02 | 9 20 | 2 0 |
| 2 1 | 1 48 | 2 01 | 2 15 | 2 28 | 2 41 | 2 55 | 3 08 | 3 35 | 4 02 | 4 29 | 6 41 | 8 53 | 2 1 |
| 2 2 | 1 43 | 1 56 | 2 08 | 2 21 | 2 34 | 2 47 | 3 00 | 3 25 | 3 51 | 4 17 | 6 23 | 8 30 | 2 2 |
| 2 3 | 1 38 | 1 51 | 2 03 | 2 15 | 2 27 | 2 40 | 2 52 | 3 16 | 3 41 | 4 05 | 6 07 | 8 09 | 2 3 |
| 2 4 | 1 34 | 1 46 | 1 58 | 2 10 | 2 21 | 2 33 | 2 45 | 3 08 | 3 32 | 3 55 | 5 52 | 7 48 | 2 4 |
| 2 5 | 1 30 | 1 42 | 1 53 | 2 04 | 2 16 | 2 27 | 2 38 | 3 01 | 3 23 | 3 46 | 5 38 | 7 30 | 2 5 |
| 2 6 | 1 27 | 1 38 | 1 49 | 2 00 | 2 10 | 2 21 | 2 32 | 2 54 | 3 16 | 3 37 | 5 25 | 7 13 | 2 6 |
| 2 7 | 1 24 | 1 34 | 1 45 | 1 55 | 2 06 | 2 16 | 2 27 | 2 47 | 3 08 | 3 29 | 5 13 | 6 57 | 2 7 |
| 2 8 | 1 21 | 1 31 | 1 41 | 1 51 | 2 01 | 2 11 | 2 21 | 2 41 | 3 02 | 3 22 | 5 02 | 6 42 | 2 8 |
| 2 9 | 1 18 | 1 28 | 1 37 | 1 47 | 1 57 | 2 07 | 2 16 | 2 36 | 2 55 | 3 15 | 4 52 | 6 28 | 2 9 |
| 3 0 | 1 15 | 1 25 | 1 34 | 1 44 | 1 53 | 2 02 | 2 12 | 2 31 | 2 49 | 3 08 | 4 42 | 6 15 | 3 0 |
| 3 2 | 1 11 | 1 20 | 1 28 | 1 37 | 1 46 | 1 55 | 2 04 | 2 21 | 2 39 | 2 57 | 4 24 | 5 52 | 3 2 |
| 3 4 | 1 07 | 1 15 | 1 23 | 1 31 | 1 40 | 1 48 | 1 56 | 2 13 | 2 30 | 2 46 | 4 09 | 5 32 | 3 4 |
| 3 6 | 1 03 | 1 11 | 1 19 | 1 26 | 1 34 | 1 42 | 1 50 | 2 06 | 2 21 | 2 37 | 3 55 | 5 13 | 3 6 |
| 3 8 | 1 00 | 1 07 | 1 14 | 1 22 | 1 29 | 1 37 | 1 44 | 1 59 | 2 14 | 2 29 | 3 43 | 4 57 | 3 8 |
| 4 0 | 0 57 | 1 04 | 1 11 | 1 18 | 1 25 | 1 32 | 1 39 | 1 53 | 2 07 | 2 21 | 3 31 | 4 42 | 4 0 |
| 4 2 | 0 54 | 1 01 | 1 07 | 1 14 | 1 21 | 1 28 | 1 34 | 1 48 | 2 01 | 2 15 | 3 21 | 4 29 | 4 2 |
| 4 4 | 0 51 | 0 58 | 1 04 | 1 11 | 1 17 | 1 24 | 1 30 | 1 43 | 1 56 | 2 08 | 3 12 | 4 17 | 4 4 |
| 4 6 | 0 49 | 0 55 | 1 01 | 1 08 | 1 14 | 1 20 | 1 26 | 1 38 | 1 51 | 2 03 | 3 04 | 4 05 | 4 6 |
| 4 8 | 0 47 | 0 53 | 0 59 | 1 05 | 1 11 | 1 17 | 1 22 | 1 34 | 1 46 | 1 58 | 2 57 | 3 55 | 4 8 |
| 5 0 | 0 45 | 0 51 | 0 57 | 1 02 | 1 08 | 1 14 | 1 19 | 1 30 | 1 42 | 1 53 | 2 50 | 3 46 | 5 0 |
| 5 2 | 0 43 | 0 49 | 0 54 | 1 00 | 1 05 | 1 11 | 1 16 | 1 27 | 1 38 | 1 49 | 2 44 | 3 38 | 5 2 |
| 5 4 | 0 42 | 0 47 | 0 52 | 0 58 | 1 03 | 1 08 | 1 13 | 1 24 | 1 34 | 1 45 | 2 28 | 3 30 | 5 4 |
| 5 6 | 0 40 | 0 45 | 0 50 | 0 56 | 1 01 | 1 06 | 1 11 | 1 21 | 1 31 | 1 41 | 2 32 | 3 22 | 5 6 |
| 5 8 | 0 39 | 0 44 | 0 49 | 0 54 | 0 58 | 1 03 | 1 08 | 1 18 | 1 28 | 1 37 | 2 26 | 3 15 | 5 8 |
| 6 0 | 0 38 | 0 42 | 0 47 | 0 52 | 0 57 | 1 01 | 1 06 | 1 15 | 1 25 | 1 34 | 2 21 | 3 09 | 6 0 |
| 6 2 | 0 36 | 0 41 | 0 46 | 0 50 | 0 55 | 0 59 | 1 04 | 1 13 | 1 22 | 1 31 | 2 16 | 3 02 | 6 2 |
| 6 4 | 0 35 | 0 40 | 0 44 | 0 49 | 0 53 | 0 57 | 1 02 | 1 11 | 1 20 | 1 28 | 2 12 | 2 57 | 6 4 |
| 6 6 | 0 34 | 0 38 | 0 43 | 0 47 | 0 51 | 0 56 | 1 00 | 1 09 | 1 17 | 1 26 | 2 08 | 2 51 | 6 6 |
| 6 8 | 0 33 | 0 37 | 0 42 | 0 46 | 0 50 | 0 54 | 0 58 | 1 07 | 1 15 | 1 23 | 2 04 | 2 46 | 6 8 |
| 7 0 | 0 32 | 0 36 | 0 40 | 0 44 | 0 48 | 0 53 | 0 57 | 1 05 | 1 13 | 1 21 | 2 01 | 2 42 | 7 0 |

Essential Nav.

## HORIZONTAL SEXTANT ANGLE FIX

| Angle Subtended by Objects (°) | 1 | 2 | 3 | 4 | 5 | 6 | 7 | 8 | 9 | Angle Subtended by Objects (°) |
|---|---|---|---|---|---|---|---|---|---|---|
| 30 | 1.00 | 2.00 | 3.00 | 4.00 | 5.00 | 6.00 | 7.00 | 8.00 | 9.00 | 150 |
| 10 | 1.00 | 1.99 | 2.99 | 3.98 | 4.98 | 5.97 | 6.97 | 7.96 | 8.96 | 50 |
| 20 | 0.99 | 1.98 | 2.97 | 3.96 | 4.95 | 5.94 | 6.93 | 7.92 | 8.91 | 40 |
| 30 | 0.99 | 1.97 | 2.96 | 3.94 | 4.93 | 5.91 | 6.90 | 7.88 | 8.87 | 30 |
| 40 | 0.98 | 1.96 | 2.94 | 3.92 | 4.90 | 5.88 | 6.86 | 7.84 | 8.83 | 20 |
| 50 | 0.98 | 1.95 | 2.93 | 3.90 | 4.88 | 5.85 | 6.83 | 7.80 | 8.78 | 10 |
| 31 | 0.97 | 1.94 | 2.91 | 3.88 | 4.86 | 5.83 | 6.80 | 7.77 | 8.74 | 149 |
| 10 | 0.97 | 1.93 | 2.90 | 3.86 | 4.83 | 5.80 | 6.76 | 7.73 | 8.70 | 50 |
| 20 | 0.96 | 1.92 | 2.89 | 3.85 | 4.81 | 5.77 | 6.73 | 7.70 | 8.65 | 40 |
| 30 | 0.96 | 1.91 | 2.87 | 3.83 | 4.79 | 5.74 | 6.70 | 7.66 | 8.61 | 30 |
| 40 | 0.95 | 1.91 | 2.86 | 3.81 | 4.76 | 5.72 | 6.67 | 7.62 | 8.57 | 20 |
| 50 | 0.95 | 1.90 | 2.84 | 3.79 | 4.74 | 5.69 | 6.64 | 7.58 | 8.53 | 10 |
| 32 | 0.94 | 1.89 | 2.83 | 3.77 | 4.72 | 5.66 | 6.61 | 7.55 | 8.49 | 148 |
| 10 | 0.94 | 1.88 | 2.82 | 3.76 | 4.70 | 5.63 | 6.57 | 7.51 | 8.45 | 50 |
| 20 | 0.94 | 1.87 | 2.81 | 3.74 | 4.68 | 5.61 | 6.55 | 7.48 | 8.42 | 40 |
| 30 | 0.93 | 1.86 | 2.79 | 3.72 | 4.65 | 5.58 | 6.51 | 7.44 | 8.38 | 30 |
| 40 | 0.93 | 1.85 | 2.78 | 3.71 | 4.63 | 5.56 | 6.49 | 7.41 | 8.34 | 20 |
| 50 | 0.92 | 1.84 | 2.77 | 3.69 | 4.61 | 5.53 | 6.45 | 7.38 | 8.30 | 10 |
| 33 | 0.92 | 1.84 | 2.75 | 3.67 | 4.59 | 5.51 | 6.43 | 7.34 | 8.26 | 147 |
| 10 | 0.92 | 1.83 | 2.75 | 3.66 | 4.58 | 5.49 | 6.41 | 7.32 | 8.24 | 50 |
| 20 | 0.91 | 1.82 | 2.73 | 3.64 | 4.55 | 5.46 | 6.37 | 7.28 | 8.19 | 40 |
| 30 | 0.91 | 1.81 | 2.72 | 3.62 | 4.53 | 5.44 | 6.34 | 7.25 | 8.15 | 30 |
| 40 | 0.90 | 1.80 | 2.71 | 3.61 | 4.51 | 5.41 | 6.31 | 7.22 | 8.12 | 20 |
| 50 | 0.90 | 1.80 | 2.69 | 3.59 | 4.49 | 5.39 | 6.29 | 7.18 | 8.08 | 10 |
| 34 | 0.89 | 1.79 | 2.68 | 3.58 | 4.47 | 5.36 | 6.26 | 7.15 | 8.05 | 146 |
| 10 | 0.89 | 1.78 | 2.67 | 3.56 | 4.45 | 5.34 | 6.23 | 7.12 | 8.02 | 50 |
| 20 | 0.89 | 1.77 | 2.66 | 3.55 | 4.43 | 5.32 | 6.21 | 7.09 | 7.98 | 40 |
| 30 | 0.88 | 1.77 | 2.65 | 3.53 | 4.42 | 5.30 | 6.18 | 7.06 | 7.95 | 30 |
| 40 | 0.88 | 1.76 | 2.64 | 3.52 | 4.40 | 5.27 | 6.15 | 7.03 | 7.91 | 20 |
| 50 | 0.88 | 1.75 | 2.63 | 3.50 | 4.38 | 5.25 | 6.13 | 7.00 | 7.88 | 10 |
| 35 | 0.87 | 1.74 | 2.62 | 3.49 | 4.36 | 5.23 | 6.10 | 6.97 | 7.84 | 145 |
| 12 | 0.87 | 1.74 | 2.60 | 3.47 | 4.34 | 5.21 | 6.07 | 6.94 | 7.81 | 48 |
| 24 | 0.86 | 1.73 | 2.59 | 3.45 | 4.32 | 5.18 | 6.04 | 6.90 | 7.77 | 36 |
| 36 | 0.86 | 1.72 | 2.58 | 3.44 | 4.30 | 5.15 | 6.01 | 6.87 | 7.73 | 24 |
| 48 | 0.86 | 1.71 | 2.57 | 3.42 | 4.28 | 5.13 | 5.99 | 6.84 | 7.70 | 12 |
| 36 | 0.85 | 1.70 | 2.55 | 3.40 | 4.25 | 5.10 | 5.95 | 6.80 | 7.66 | 144 |
| 12 | 0.85 | 1.69 | 2.54 | 3.39 | 4.23 | 5.08 | 5.93 | 6.77 | 7.62 | 48 |
| 24 | 0.84 | 1.69 | 2.53 | 3.37 | 4.21 | 5.06 | 5.90 | 6.74 | 7.58 | 36 |
| 36 | 0.84 | 1.68 | 2.52 | 3.35 | 4.19 | 5.03 | 5.87 | 6.71 | 7.55 | 24 |
| 48 | 0.83 | 1.67 | 2.50 | 3.34 | 4.17 | 5.01 | 5.84 | 6.68 | 7.51 | 12 |
| 37 | 0.83 | 1.66 | 2.49 | 3.32 | 4.16 | 4.99 | 5.82 | 6.65 | 7.48 | 143 |
| 12 | 0.83 | 1.65 | 2.48 | 3.31 | 4.14 | 4.96 | 5.79 | 6.62 | 7.44 | 48 |
| 24 | 0.82 | 1.65 | 2.47 | 3.29 | 4.12 | 4.94 | 5.76 | 6.58 | 7.41 | 36 |
| 36 | 0.82 | 1.64 | 2.46 | 3.28 | 4.10 | 4.92 | 5.74 | 6.56 | 7.38 | 24 |
| 48 | 0.82 | 1.63 | 2.45 | 3.26 | 4.08 | 4.90 | 5.71 | 6.53 | 7.34 | 12 |
| 38 | 0.81 | 1.62 | 2.44 | 3.25 | 4.06 | 4.87 | 5.68 | 6.50 | 7.31 | 142 |
| 12 | 0.81 | 1.62 | 2.43 | 3.23 | 4.04 | 4.85 | 5.66 | 6.47 | 7.28 | 48 |
| 24 | 0.81 | 1.61 | 2.42 | 3.22 | 4.03 | 4.83 | 5.64 | 6.44 | 7.25 | 36 |
| 36 | 0.80 | 1.60 | 2.41 | 3.21 | 4.01 | 4.81 | 5.61 | 6.41 | 7.21 | 24 |
| 48 | 0.80 | 1.60 | 2.39 | 3.19 | 3.99 | 4.79 | 5.59 | 6.38 | 7.18 | 12 |
| 39 | 0.79 | 1.59 | 2.38 | 3.18 | 3.97 | 4.77 | 5.56 | 6.36 | 7.15 | 141 |
| 12 | 0.79 | 1.58 | 2.37 | 3.16 | 3.96 | 4.75 | 5.54 | 6.33 | 7.12 | 48 |
| 24 | 0.79 | 1.58 | 2.36 | 3.15 | 3.94 | 4.73 | 5.52 | 6.30 | 7.09 | 36 |
| 36 | 0.79 | 1.57 | 2.35 | 3.14 | 3.92 | 4.71 | 5.49 | 6.28 | 7.06 | 24 |
| 48 | 0.78 | 1.56 | 2.34 | 3.12 | 3.91 | 4.69 | 5.47 | 6.25 | 7.03 | 12 |
| 40 | 0.78 | 1.56 | 2.33 | 3.11 | 3.89 | 4.67 | 5.45 | 6.22 | 7.00 | 140 |
| 20 | 0.77 | 1.55 | 2.32 | 3.09 | 3.86 | 4.64 | 5.41 | 6.18 | 6.95 | 40 |
| 40 | 0.77 | 1.54 | 2.30 | 3.07 | 3.84 | 4.61 | 5.37 | 6.14 | 6.91 | 20 |
| 41 | 0.76 | 1.52 | 2.29 | 3.05 | 3.81 | 4.57 | 5.33 | 6.10 | 6.86 | 139 |
| 20 | 0.76 | 1.51 | 2.27 | 3.03 | 3.79 | 4.54 | 5.30 | 6.06 | 6.81 | 40 |
| 40 | 0.75 | 1.50 | 2.26 | 3.01 | 3.76 | 4.51 | 5.26 | 6.02 | 6.77 | 20 |
| 42 | 0.75 | 1.50 | 2.24 | 2.99 | 3.74 | 4.49 | 5.23 | 5.98 | 6.73 | 138 |
| 20 | 0.74 | 1.49 | 2.23 | 2.97 | 3.71 | 4.46 | 5.20 | 5.94 | 6.68 | 40 |
| 40 | 0.74 | 1.48 | 2.21 | 2.95 | 3.69 | 4.43 | 5.17 | 5.90 | 6.64 | 20 |
| 43° | 0.73 | 1.47 | 2.20 | 2.93 | 3.67 | 4.40 | 5.13 | 5.86 | 6.60 | 137° |

## HORIZONTAL SEXTANT ANGLE FIX

| Angle Subtended by Objects | | Distance between Objects | | | | | | | | | Angle Subtended by Objects | |
|---|---|---|---|---|---|---|---|---|---|---|---|---|
| ° | | 1 | 2 | 3 | 4 | 5 | 6 | 7 | 8 | 9 | ° | |
| 43 | | 0.73 | 1.47 | 2.20 | 2.93 | 3.67 | 4.40 | 5.13 | 5.86 | 6.60 | 137 | |
| | 20 | 0.73 | 1.46 | 2.19 | 2.91 | 3.64 | 4.37 | 5.10 | 5.83 | 6.56 | | 40 |
| | 40 | 0.72 | 1.45 | 2.17 | 2.90 | 3.62 | 4.34 | 5.07 | 5.79 | 6.52 | | 20 |
| 44 | | 0.72 | 1.44 | 2.16 | 2.88 | 3.60 | 4.32 | 5.04 | 5.76 | 6.48 | 136 | |
| | 20 | 0.72 | 1.43 | 2.15 | 2.86 | 3.58 | 4.29 | 5.01 | 5.72 | 6.44 | | 40 |
| | 40 | 0.71 | 1.42 | 2.14 | 2.85 | 3.56 | 4.27 | 4.98 | 5.69 | 6.40 | | 20 |
| 45 | | 0.71 | 1.41 | 2.12 | 2.83 | 3.54 | 4.24 | 4.95 | 5.66 | 6.36 | 135 | |
| | 20 | 0.70 | 1.41 | 2.11 | 2.81 | 3.52 | 4.22 | 4.92 | 5.62 | 6.33 | | 40 |
| | 40 | 0.70 | 1.40 | 2.10 | 2.80 | 3.50 | 4.19 | 4.89 | 5.59 | 6.29 | | 20 |
| 46 | | 0.70 | 1.39 | 2.09 | 2.78 | 3.48 | 4.17 | 4.87 | 5.56 | 6.26 | 134 | |
| | 20 | 0.69 | 1.38 | 2.07 | 2.76 | 3.46 | 4.15 | 4.84 | 5.53 | 6.22 | | 40 |
| | 40 | 0.69 | 1.38 | 2.06 | 2.75 | 3.44 | 4.13 | 4.81 | 5.50 | 6.19 | | 20 |
| 47 | | 0.68 | 1.37 | 2.05 | 2.73 | 3.42 | 4.10 | 4.79 | 5.47 | 6.15 | 133 | |
| | 20 | 0.68 | 1.36 | 2.04 | 2.72 | 3.40 | 4.08 | 4.76 | 5.44 | 6.12 | | 40 |
| | 40 | 0.68 | 1.35 | 2.03 | 2.71 | 3.38 | 4.06 | 4.74 | 5.41 | 6.09 | | 20 |
| 48 | | 0.67 | 1.35 | 2.02 | 2.69 | 3.37 | 4.04 | 4.71 | 5.38 | 6.06 | 132 | |
| | 20 | 0.67 | 1.34 | 2.01 | 2.68 | 3.35 | 4.02 | 4.69 | 5.36 | 6.03 | | 40 |
| | 40 | 0.67 | 1.33 | 2.00 | 2.66 | 3.33 | 4.00 | 4.66 | 5.33 | 5.99 | | 20 |
| 49 | | 0.66 | 1.33 | 2.00 | 2.65 | 3.31 | 3.98 | 4.64 | 5.30 | 5.96 | 131 | |
| | 20 | 0.66 | 1.32 | 1.98 | 2.64 | 3.30 | 3.95 | 4.61 | 5.27 | 5.93 | | 40 |
| | 40 | 0.66 | 1.31 | 1.97 | 2.62 | 3.28 | 3.94 | 4.59 | 5.25 | 5.90 | | 20 |
| 50 | | 0.65 | 1.31 | 1.96 | 2.61 | 3.26 | 3.92 | 4.57 | 5.22 | 5.87 | 130 | |
| | 30 | 0.65 | 1.30 | 1.94 | 2.59 | 3.24 | 3.89 | 4.54 | 5.18 | 5.83 | | 30 |
| 51 | | 0.64 | 1.29 | 1.93 | 2.57 | 3.22 | 3.86 | 4.51 | 5.15 | 5.79 | 129 | |
| | 30 | 0.64 | 1.28 | 1.92 | 2.56 | 3.20 | 3.83 | 4.47 | 5.11 | 5.75 | | 30 |
| 52 | | 0.63 | 1.27 | 1.90 | 2.54 | 3.17 | 3.81 | 4.44 | 5.08 | 5.71 | 128 | |
| | 30 | 0.63 | 1.26 | 1.89 | 2.52 | 3.15 | 3.78 | 4.41 | 5.04 | 5.68 | | 30 |
| 53 | | 0.63 | 1.25 | 1.88 | 2.50 | 3.13 | 3.76 | 4.38 | 5.01 | 5.63 | 127 | |
| | 30 | 0.62 | 1.24 | 1.87 | 2.49 | 3.11 | 3.73 | 4.35 | 4.98 | 5.60 | | 30 |
| 54 | | 0.62 | 1.24 | 1.85 | 2.47 | 3.09 | 3.71 | 4.33 | 4.94 | 5.56 | 126 | |
| | 30 | 0.61 | 1.23 | 1.84 | 2.46 | 3.07 | 3.68 | 4.30 | 4.91 | 5.53 | | 30 |
| 55 | | 0.61 | 1.22 | 1.83 | 2.44 | 3.05 | 3.66 | 4.27 | 4.88 | 5.50 | 125 | |
| | 30 | 0.61 | 1.21 | 1.82 | 2.43 | 3.03 | 3.64 | 4.25 | 4.85 | 5.46 | | 30 |
| 56 | | 0.60 | 1.21 | 1.81 | 2.41 | 3.02 | 3.62 | 4.22 | 4.82 | 5.43 | 124 | |
| | 30 | 0.60 | 1.20 | 1.80 | 2.40 | 3.00 | 3.60 | 4.20 | 4.80 | 5.40 | | 30 |
| 57 | | 0.60 | 1.19 | 1.79 | 2.38 | 2.98 | 3.58 | 4.17 | 4.77 | 5.36 | 123 | |
| | 30 | 0.59 | 1.19 | 1.78 | 2.37 | 2.97 | 3.56 | 4.15 | 4.74 | 5.34 | | 30 |
| 58 | | 0.59 | 1.18 | 1.77 | 2.36 | 2.95 | 3.54 | 4.13 | 4.72 | 5.31 | 122 | |
| | 30 | 0.59 | 1.17 | 1.76 | 2.35 | 2.93 | 3.52 | 4.11 | 4.69 | 5.28 | | 30 |
| 59 | | 0.58 | 1.17 | 1.75 | 2.33 | 2.92 | 3.50 | 4.09 | 4.67 | 5.25 | 121 | |
| | 30 | 0.58 | 1.16 | 1.74 | 3.32 | 2.90 | 3.48 | 4.06 | 4.64 | 5.23 | | 30 |
| 60 | | 0.58 | 1.16 | 1.73 | 2.31 | 2.89 | 3.47 | 4.04 | 4.62 | 5.20 | 120 | |
| 61 | | 0.57 | 1.14 | 1.72 | 2.29 | 2.86 | 3.43 | 4.00 | 4.57 | 5.14 | 119 | |
| 62 | | 0.57 | 1.13 | 1.70 | 2.27 | 2.83 | 3.40 | 3.97 | 4.53 | 5.10 | 118 | |
| 63 | | 0.56 | 1.12 | 1.68 | 2.24 | 2.81 | 3.37 | 3.93 | 4.49 | 5.05 | 117 | |
| 64 | | 0.56 | 1.11 | 1.67 | 2.23 | 2.78 | 3.34 | 3.90 | 4.45 | 5.01 | 116 | |
| 65 | | 0.55 | 1.10 | 1.66 | 2.21 | 2.76 | 3.31 | 3.86 | 4.41 | 4.96 | 115 | |
| 66 | | 0.55 | 1.10 | 1.64 | 2.19 | 2.74 | 3.29 | 3.83 | 4.38 | 4.93 | 114 | |
| 67 | | 0.54 | 1.09 | 1.63 | 2.17 | 2.72 | 3.26 | 3.80 | 4.34 | 4.89 | 113 | |
| 68 | | 0.54 | 1.08 | 1.62 | 2.16 | 2.70 | 3.24 | 3.78 | 4.32 | 4.86 | 112 | |
| 69 | | 0.54 | 1.07 | 1.61 | 2.14 | 2.68 | 3.21 | 3.75 | 4.28 | 4.82 | 111 | |
| 70 | | 0.53 | 1.06 | 1.60 | 2.13 | 2.66 | 3.19 | 3.72 | 4.26 | 4.79 | 110 | |
| 71 | | 0.53 | 1.06 | 1.59 | 2.12 | 2.65 | 3.17 | 3.70 | 4.23 | 4.76 | 109 | |
| 72 | | 0.53 | 1.05 | 1.58 | 2.10 | 2.63 | 3.16 | 3.68 | 4.21 | 4.73 | 108 | |
| 73 | | 0.52 | 1.05 | 1.57 | 2.09 | 2.62 | 3.14 | 3.66 | 4.18 | 4.71 | 107 | |
| 74 | | 0.52 | 1.04 | 1.56 | 2.08 | 2.60 | 3.12 | 3.64 | 4.16 | 4.68 | 106 | |
| 76 | | 0.52 | 1.03 | 1.55 | 2.06 | 2.58 | 3.09 | 3.61 | 4.12 | 4.64 | 104 | |
| 78 | | 0.51 | 1.02 | 1.53 | 2.04 | 2.56 | 3.07 | 3.58 | 4.09 | 4.60 | 102 | |
| 80 | | 0.51 | 1.02 | 1.52 | 2.03 | 2.54 | 3.05 | 3.55 | 4.06 | 4.57 | 100 | |
| 82 | | 0.51 | 1.01 | 1.52 | 2.02 | 2.53 | 3.03 | 3.54 | 4.04 | 4.55 | 98 | |
| 84 | | 0.50 | 1.01 | 1.51 | 2.01 | 2.52 | 3.02 | 3.52 | 4.02 | 4.53 | 96 | |
| 86 | | 0.50 | 1.00 | 1.50 | 2.00 | 2.51 | 3.01 | 3.51 | 4.01 | 4.51 | 94 | |
| 90 | | 0.50 | 1.00 | 1.50 | 2.00 | 2.50 | 3.00 | 3.50 | 4.00 | 4.50 | 90 | |
| ° | | | | | | | | | | | ° | |

Essential Nav.

## TIME, SPEED, AND DISTANCE TABLE

for finding distance run in a given time at various Speeds, 2½ to 22 knots

| Min | $2\frac{1}{2}$ | 3 | $3\frac{1}{2}$ | 4 | $4\frac{1}{2}$ | 5 | $5\frac{1}{2}$ | 6 | $6\frac{1}{2}$ | 7 | $7\frac{1}{2}$ | 8 | $8\frac{1}{2}$ | Min |
|---|---|---|---|---|---|---|---|---|---|---|---|---|---|---|
| | | | | | | KNOTS | | | | | | | | |
| 1 | 0.1 | 0.1 | 0.1 | 0.1 | 0.1 | 0.1 | 0.1 | 0.1 | 0.1 | 0.1 | 0.1 | 0.1 | 0.2 | 1 |
| 2 | 0.1 | 0.1 | 0.1 | 0.2 | 0.2 | 0.2 | 0.2 | 0.2 | 0.2 | 0.2 | 0.3 | 0.3 | 0.3 | 2 |
| 3 | 0.1 | 0.2 | 0.2 | 0.2 | 0.3 | 0.3 | 0.3 | 0.3 | 0.3 | 0.3 | 0.4 | 0.4 | 0.4 | 3 |
| 4 | 0.1 | 0.2 | 0.3 | 0.3 | 0.3 | 0.3 | 0.4 | 0.4 | 0.4 | 0.5 | 0.5 | 0.5 | 0.6 | 4 |
| 5 | 0.2 | 0.3 | 0.3 | 0.4 | 0.4 | 0.4 | 0.5 | 0.5 | 0.6 | 0.6 | 0.6 | 0.7 | 0.7 | 5 |
| 6 | 0.3 | 0.3 | 0.4 | 0.4 | 0.5 | 0.5 | 0.6 | 0.6 | 0.7 | 0.7 | 0.8 | 0.8 | 0.9 | 6 |
| 7 | 0.3 | 0.4 | 0.4 | 0.5 | 0.6 | 0.6 | 0.6 | 0.7 | 0.8 | 0.8 | 0.9 | 0.9 | 1.0 | 7 |
| 8 | 0.4 | 0.4 | 0.5 | 0.6 | 0.6 | 0.7 | 0.7 | 0.8 | 0.9 | 0.9 | 1.0 | 1.0 | 1.1 | 8 |
| 9 | 0.4 | 0.5 | 0.6 | 0.6 | 0.7 | 0.8 | 0.8 | 0.9 | 1.0 | 1.1 | 1.1 | 1.2 | 1.3 | 9 |
| 10 | 0.4 | 0.5 | 0.6 | 0.7 | 0.8 | 0.8 | 0.9 | 1.0 | 1.1 | 1.2 | 1.3 | 1.3 | 1.4 | 10 |
| 11 | 0.5 | 0.6 | 0.7 | 0.8 | 0.9 | 0.9 | 1.0 | 1.1 | 1.2 | 1.3 | 1.4 | 1.5 | 1.6 | 11 |
| 12 | 0.5 | 0.6 | 0.7 | 0.8 | 0.9 | 1.0 | 1.1 | 1.2 | 1.3 | 1.4 | 1.5 | 1.6 | 1.7 | 12 |
| 13 | 0.6 | 0.7 | 0.8 | 0.9 | 1.0 | 1.1 | 1.2 | 1.3 | 1.4 | 1.5 | 1.6 | 1.7 | 1.8 | 13 |
| 14 | 0.6 | 0.7 | 0.8 | 1.0 | 1.1 | 1.2 | 1.3 | 1.4 | 1.5 | 1.6 | 1.8 | 1.9 | 2.0 | 14 |
| 15 | 0.7 | 0.8 | 0.9 | 1.0 | 1.2 | 1.3 | 1.4 | 1.5 | 1.6 | 1.8 | 1.9 | 2.0 | 2.1 | 15 |
| 16 | 0.7 | 0.8 | 1.0 | 1.1 | 1.2 | 1.3 | 1.5 | 1.6 | 1.7 | 1.9 | 2.0 | 2.1 | 2.3 | 16 |
| 17 | 0.7 | 0.9 | 1.0 | 1.2 | 1.3 | 1.4 | 1.6 | 1.7 | 1.8 | 2.0 | 2.1 | 2.3 | 2.4 | 17 |
| 18 | 0.8 | 0.9 | 1.1 | 1.2 | 1.4 | 1.5 | 1.7 | 1.8 | 2.0 | 2.1 | 2.3 | 2.4 | 2.6 | 18 |
| 19 | 0.8 | 1.0 | 1.1 | 1.3 | 1.5 | 1.6 | 1.7 | 1.9 | 2.1 | 2.2 | 2.4 | 2.5 | 2.7 | 19 |
| 20 | 0.9 | 1.0 | 1.2 | 1.4 | 1.5 | 1.7 | 1.8 | 2.0 | 2.2 | 2.3 | 2.5 | 2.7 | 2.8 | 20 |
| 21 | 0.9 | 1.1 | 1.3 | 1.4 | 1.6 | 1.8 | 1.9 | 2.1 | 2.3 | 2.5 | 2.6 | 2.8 | 3.0 | 21 |
| 22 | 0.9 | 1.1 | 1.3 | 1.5 | 1.7 | 1.8 | 2.0 | 2.2 | 2.4 | 2.6 | 2.8 | 2.9 | 3.1 | 22 |
| 23 | 1.0 | 1.2 | 1.4 | 1.6 | 1.8 | 1.9 | 2.1 | 2.3 | 2.5 | 2.7 | 2.9 | 3.0 | 3.3 | 23 |
| 24 | 1.0 | 1.2 | 1.4 | 1.6 | 1.8 | 2.0 | 2.2 | 2.4 | 2.6 | 2.8 | 3.0 | 3.2 | 3.4 | 24 |
| 25 | 1.1 | 1.3 | 1.5 | 1.7 | 1.9 | 2.1 | 2.3 | 2.5 | 2.7 | 2.9 | 3.1 | 3.3 | 3.5 | 25 |
| 26 | 1.1 | 1.3 | 1.5 | 1.8 | 2.0 | 2.2 | 2.4 | 2.6 | 2.8 | 3.0 | 3.3 | 3.5 | 3.7 | 26 |
| 27 | 1.2 | 1.4 | 1.6 | 1.8 | 2.1 | 2.3 | 2.5 | 2.7 | 2.9 | 3.2 | 3.4 | 3.6 | 3.9 | 27 |
| 28 | 1.2 | 1.4 | 1.7 | 1.9 | 2.1 | 2.3 | 2.6 | 2.8 | 3.0 | 3.3 | 3.5 | 3.7 | 4.0 | 28 |
| 29 | 1.2 | 1.5 | 1.7 | 2.0 | 2.2 | 2.4 | 2.7 | 2.9 | 3.1 | 3.4 | 3.6 | 3.9 | 4.1 | 29 |
| 30 | 1.3 | 1.5 | 1.8 | 2.0 | 2.3 | 2.5 | 2.8 | 3.0 | 3.3 | 3.5 | 3.8 | 4.0 | 4.3 | 30 |
| 31 | 1.3 | 1.6 | 1.8 | 2.1 | 2.4 | 2.6 | 2.8 | 3.1 | 3.4 | 3.6 | 3.9 | 4.1 | 4.4 | 31 |
| 32 | 1.4 | 1.6 | 1.9 | 2.2 | 2.4 | 2.7 | 2.9 | 3.2 | 3.5 | 3.7 | 4.0 | 4.3 | 4.5 | 32 |
| 33 | 1.4 | 1.7 | 2.0 | 2.3 | 2.5 | 2.8 | 3.0 | 3.3 | 3.6 | 3.9 | 4.1 | 4.4 | 4.7 | 33 |
| 34 | 1.4 | 1.7 | 2.0 | 2.3 | 2.6 | 2.9 | 3.1 | 3.4 | 3.7 | 4.0 | 4.3 | 4.5 | 4.8 | 34 |
| 35 | 1.5 | 1.8 | 2.1 | 2.4 | 2.7 | 2.9 | 3.2 | 3.5 | 3.8 | 4.1 | 4.4 | 4.7 | 5.0 | 35 |
| 36 | 1.5 | 1.8 | 2.1 | 2.4 | 2.7 | 3.0 | 3.3 | 3.6 | 3.9 | 4.2 | 4.5 | 4.8 | 5.1 | 36 |
| 37 | 1.6 | 1.9 | 2.2 | 2.5 | 2.8 | 3.1 | 3.4 | 3.7 | 4.0 | 4.3 | 4.6 | 4.9 | 5.2 | 37 |
| 38 | 1.6 | 1.9 | 2.2 | 2.6 | 2.9 | 3.2 | 3.5 | 3.8 | 4.1 | 4.4 | 4.8 | 5.0 | 5.4 | 38 |
| 39 | 1.7 | 2.0 | 2.3 | 2.6 | 2.9 | 3.3 | 3.6 | 3.9 | 4.2 | 4.6 | 4.9 | 5.2 | 5.5 | 39 |
| 40 | 1.7 | 2.0 | 2.4 | 2.7 | 3.0 | 3.3 | 3.7 | 4.0 | 4.3 | 4.7 | 5.0 | 5.3 | 5.7 | 40 |
| 41 | 1.7 | 2.1 | 2.4 | 2.8 | 3.1 | 3.4 | 3.8 | 4.1 | 4.4 | 4.8 | 5.1 | 5.5 | 5.8 | 41 |
| 42 | 1.8 | 2.1 | 2.5 | 2.8 | 3.2 | 3.5 | 3.9 | 4.2 | 4.6 | 4.9 | 5.3 | 5.6 | 6.0 | 42 |
| 43 | 1.8 | 2.2 | 2.5 | 2.9 | 3.3 | 3.6 | 3.9 | 4.3 | 4.7 | 5.0 | 5.4 | 5.7 | 6.1 | 43 |
| 44 | 1.9 | 2.2 | 2.6 | 3.0 | 3.3 | 3.7 | 4.0 | 4.4 | 4.8 | 5.1 | 5.5 | 5.9 | 6.2 | 44 |
| 45 | 1.9 | 2.3 | 2.7 | 3.0 | 3.4 | 3.8 | 4.1 | 4.5 | 4.9 | 5.3 | 5.6 | 6.0 | 6.4 | 45 |
| 46 | 1.9 | 2.3 | 2.7 | 3.1 | 3.5 | 3.8 | 4.2 | 4.6 | 5.0 | 5.4 | 5.8 | 6.1 | 6.5 | 46 |
| 47 | 2.0 | 2.4 | 2.8 | 3.2 | 3.6 | 3.9 | 4.3 | 4.7 | 5.1 | 5.5 | 5.9 | 6.3 | 6.7 | 47 |
| 48 | 2.0 | 2.4 | 2.8 | 3.2 | 3.6 | 4.0 | 4.4 | 4.8 | 5.2 | 5.6 | 6.0 | 6.4 | 6.8 | 48 |
| 49 | 2.1 | 2.5 | 2.9 | 3.3 | 3.7 | 4.1 | 4.5 | 4.9 | 5.3 | 5.7 | 6.1 | 6.5 | 6.9 | 49 |
| 50 | 2.1 | 2.5 | 2.9 | 3.4 | 3.8 | 4.2 | 4.6 | 5.0 | 5.4 | 5.8 | 6.3 | 6.7 | 7.1 | 50 |
| 51 | 2.2 | 2.6 | 3.0 | 3.4 | 3.9 | 4.3 | 4.7 | 5.1 | 5.5 | 6.0 | 6.4 | 6.8 | 7.2 | 51 |
| 52 | 2.2 | 2.6 | 3.1 | 3.5 | 3.9 | 4.3 | 4.8 | 5.2 | 5.6 | 6.1 | 6.5 | 6.9 | 7.4 | 52 |
| 53 | 2.2 | 2.7 | 3.1 | 3.6 | 4.0 | 4.4 | 4.9 | 5.3 | 5.7 | 6.2 | 6.6 | 7.0 | 7.5 | 53 |
| 54 | 2.3 | 2.7 | 3.2 | 3.6 | 4.1 | 4.5 | 5.0 | 5.4 | 5.9 | 6.3 | 6.8 | 7.1 | 7.6 | 54 |
| 55 | 2.3 | 2.8 | 3.2 | 3.7 | 4.2 | 4.6 | 5.0 | 5.5 | 6.0 | 6.4 | 6.9 | 7.3 | 7.8 | 55 |
| 56 | 2.4 | 2.8 | 3.3 | 3.8 | 4.2 | 4.7 | 5.1 | 5.6 | 6.1 | 6.5 | 7.0 | 7.5 | 7.9 | 56 |
| 57 | 2.4 | 2.9 | 3.4 | 3.8 | 4.3 | 4.8 | 5.2 | 5.7 | 6.2 | 6.7 | 7.1 | 7.6 | 8.1 | 57 |
| 58 | 2.4 | 2.9 | 3.4 | 3.9 | 4.4 | 4.8 | 5.3 | 5.8 | 6.3 | 6.8 | 7.3 | 7.7 | 8.2 | 58 |
| 59 | 2.5 | 3.0 | 3.5 | 3.9 | 4.5 | 4.9 | 5.4 | 5.9 | 6.4 | 6.9 | 7.4 | 7.9 | 8.4 | 59 |
| 60 | 2.5 | 3.0 | 3.5 | 4.0 | 4.5 | 5.0 | 5.5 | 6.0 | 6.5 | 7.0 | 7.5 | 8.0 | 8.5 | 60 |
| Min | $2\frac{1}{2}$ | 3 | $3\frac{1}{2}$ | 4 | $4\frac{1}{2}$ | 5 | $5\frac{1}{2}$ | 6 | $6\frac{1}{2}$ | 7 | $7\frac{1}{2}$ | 8 | $8\frac{1}{2}$ | Min |

**Example 1.** if steaming 7½ knots, what distance has been covered in 41 minutes? Answer = 5.1 miles

## TIME, SPEED, AND DISTANCE TABLE

**for finding distance run in a given time at various Speeds, 2½ to 22 knots**

| | | | | | | | KNOTS | | | | | | | |
|---|---|---|---|---|---|---|---|---|---|---|---|---|---|---|
| Min | 9 | 9½ | 10 | 10½ | 11 | 11½ | 12 | 12½ | 13 | 13½ | 14 | 14½ | 15 | Min |
| 1 | 0.2 | 0.2 | 0.2 | 0.2 | 0.2 | 0.2 | 0.2 | 0.2 | 0.2 | 0.2 | 0.2 | 0.2 | 0.3 | 1 |
| 2 | 0.3 | 0.3 | 0.3 | 0.4 | 0.4 | 0.4 | 0.4 | 0.4 | 0.5 | 0.5 | 0.5 | 0.5 | 0.5 | 2 |
| 3 | 0.5 | 0.5 | 0.5 | 0.5 | 0.6 | 0.6 | 0.6 | 0.6 | 0.7 | 0.7 | 0.7 | 0.7 | 0.8 | 3 |
| 4 | 0.6 | 0.6 | 0.7 | 0.7 | 0.7 | 0.8 | 0.8 | 0.8 | 0.9 | 0.9 | 0.9 | 1.0 | 1.0 | 4 |
| 5 | 0.8 | 0.8 | 0.8 | 0.9 | 0.9 | 1.0 | 1.0 | 1.1 | 1.1 | 1.2 | 1.2 | 1.2 | 1.3 | 5 |
| 6 | 0.9 | 1.0 | 1.0 | 1.1 | 1.1 | 1.2 | 1.2 | 1.3 | 1.3 | 1.4 | 1.4 | 1.5 | 1.5 | 6 |
| 7 | 1.1 | 1.1 | 1.2 | 1.2 | 1.3 | 1.3 | 1.4 | 1.5 | 1.5 | 1.6 | 1.6 | 1.7 | 1.8 | 7 |
| 8 | 1.2 | 1.3 | 1.3 | 1.4 | 1.5 | 1.5 | 1.6 | 1.7 | 1.7 | 1.8 | 1.9 | 1.9 | 2.0 | 8 |
| 9 | 1.4 | 1.4 | 1.5 | 1.6 | 1.7 | 1.7 | 1.8 | 1.9 | 2.0 | 2.0 | 2.1 | 2.2 | 2.3 | 9 |
| 10 | 1.5 | 1.6 | 1.7 | 1.8 | 1.8 | 1.9 | 2.0 | 2.1 | 2.2 | 2.3 | 2.3 | 2.4 | 2.5 | 10 |
| 11 | 1.7 | 1.7 | 1.8 | 1.9 | 2.0 | 2.1 | 2.2 | 2.3 | 2.4 | 2.5 | 2.6 | 2.7 | 2.8 | 11 |
| 12 | 1.8 | 1.9 | 2.0 | 2.1 | 2.2 | 2.3 | 2.4 | 2.5 | 2.6 | 2.7 | 2.8 | 2.9 | 3.0 | 12 |
| 13 | 2.0 | 2.1 | 2.2 | 2.3 | 2.4 | 2.5 | 2.6 | 2.7 | 2.8 | 2.9 | 3.0 | 3.1 | 3.2 | 13 |
| 14 | 2.1 | 2.2 | 2.3 | 2.5 | 2.6 | 2.7 | 2.8 | 2.9 | 3.0 | 3.2 | 3.3 | 3.4 | 3.5 | 14 |
| 15 | 2.3 | 2.4 | 2.5 | 2.6 | 2.8 | 2.9 | 3.0 | 3.1 | 3.3 | 3.4 | 3.5 | 3.6 | 3.8 | 15 |
| 16 | 2.4 | 2.5 | 2.7 | 2.8 | 2.9 | 3.1 | 3.2 | 3.3 | 3.5 | 3.6 | 3.7 | 3.9 | 4.0 | 16 |
| 17 | 2.6 | 2.7 | 2.8 | 3.0 | 3.1 | 3.3 | 3.4 | 3.5 | 3.7 | 3.8 | 4.0 | 4.1 | 4.3 | 17 |
| 18 | 2.7 | 2.9 | 3.0 | 3.2 | 3.3 | 3.5 | 3.6 | 3.8 | 3.9 | 4.1 | 4.2 | 4.4 | 4.5 | 18 |
| 19 | 2.9 | 3.1 | 3.2 | 3.3 | 3.5 | 3.6 | 3.8 | 4.0 | 4.2 | 4.3 | 4.4 | 4.6 | 4.8 | 19 |
| 20 | 3.0 | 3.2 | 3.3 | 3.5 | 3.7 | 3.8 | 4.0 | 4.2 | 4.4 | 4.5 | 4.7 | 4.8 | 5.0 | 20 |
| 21 | 3.2 | 3.3 | 3.5 | 3.7 | 3.9 | 4.0 | 4.2 | 4.4 | 4.6 | 4.7 | 4.9 | 5.1 | 5.3 | 21 |
| 22 | 3.3 | 3.5 | 3.7 | 3.9 | 4.0 | 4.2 | 4.4 | 4.6 | 4.8 | 5.0 | 5.1 | 5.3 | 5.5 | 22 |
| 23 | 3.5 | 3.6 | 3.8 | 4.0 | 4.2 | 4.4 | 4.6 | 4.8 | 5.0 | 5.2 | 5.4 | 5.6 | 5.7 | 23 |
| 24 | 3.6 | 3.8 | 4.0 | 4.2 | 4.4 | 4.6 | 4.8 | 5.0 | 5.2 | 5.4 | 5.6 | 5.8 | 6.0 | 24 |
| 25 | 3.8 | 4.0 | 4.2 | 4.4 | 4.6 | 4.8 | 5.0 | 5.2 | 5.4 | 5.6 | 5.8 | 6.1 | 6.3 | 25 |
| 26 | 3.9 | 4.1 | 4.3 | 4.6 | 4.8 | 5.0 | 5.2 | 5.4 | 5.6 | 5.9 | 6.1 | 6.3 | 6.5 | 26 |
| 27 | 4.1 | 4.3 | 4.5 | 4.7 | 5.0 | 5.2 | 5.4 | 5.6 | 5.9 | 6.1 | 6.3 | 6.5 | 6.8 | 27 |
| 28 | 4.2 | 4.4 | 4.7 | 4.9 | 5.1 | 5.4 | 5.6 | 5.8 | 6.1 | 6.3 | 6.5 | 6.8 | 7.0 | 28 |
| 29 | 4.4 | 4.6 | 4.8 | 5.1 | 5.3 | 5.6 | 5.8 | 6.0 | 6.3 | 6.5 | 6.8 | 7.0 | 7.3 | 29 |
| 30 | 4.5 | 4.8 | 5.0 | 5.3 | 5.5 | 5.8 | 6.0 | 6.3 | 6.5 | 6.8 | 7.0 | 7.3 | 7.5 | 30 |
| 31 | 4.7 | 4.9 | 5.2 | 5.4 | 5.7 | 5.9 | 6.2 | 6.5 | 6.7 | 7.0 | 7.2 | 7.5 | 7.8 | 31 |
| 32 | 4.8 | 5.0 | 5.3 | 5.6 | 5.9 | 6.1 | 6.4 | 6.7 | 6.9 | 7.2 | 7.5 | 7.7 | 8.0 | 32 |
| 33 | 5.0 | 5.2 | 5.5 | 5.8 | 6.1 | 6.3 | 6.6 | 6.9 | 7.2 | 7.4 | 7.7 | 8.0 | 8.3 | 33 |
| 34 | 5.1 | 5.4 | 5.7 | 6.0 | 6.2 | 6.5 | 6.8 | 7.1 | 7.4 | 7.7 | 8.0 | 8.2 | 8.5 | 34 |
| 35 | 5.3 | 5.5 | 5.8 | 6.1 | 6.4 | 6.7 | 7.0 | 7.3 | 7.6 | 7.9 | 8.2 | 8.5 | 8.8 | 35 |
| 36 | 5.4 | 5.7 | 6.0 | 6.3 | 6.6 | 6.9 | 7.2 | 7.5 | 7.8 | 8.1 | 8.4 | 8.7 | 9.0 | 36 |
| 37 | 5.6 | 5.9 | 6.2 | 6.5 | 6.8 | 7.1 | 7.4 | 7.7 | 8.0 | 8.3 | 8.6 | 8.9 | 9.3 | 37 |
| 38 | 5.7 | 6.0 | 6.3 | 6.7 | 7.0 | 7.3 | 7.6 | 7.9 | 8.2 | 8.6 | 8.9 | 9.2 | 9.5 | 38 |
| 39 | 5.9 | 6.2 | 6.5 | 6.8 | 7.1 | 7.5 | 7.8 | 8.1 | 8.5 | 8.8 | 9.1 | 9.4 | 9.8 | 39 |
| 40 | 6.0 | 6.3 | 6.7 | 7.0 | 7.3 | 7.7 | 8.0 | 8.3 | 8.7 | 9.0 | 9.3 | 9.7 | 10.0 | 40 |
| 41 | 6.2 | 6.5 | 6.8 | 7.3 | 7.5 | 7.9 | 8.2 | 8.5 | 8.9 | 9.2 | 9.6 | 9.9 | 10.3 | 41 |
| 42 | 6.3 | 6.7 | 7.0 | 7.4 | 7.7 | 8.1 | 8.4 | 8.8 | 9.1 | 9.5 | 9.8 | 10.2 | 10.5 | 42 |
| 43 | 6.5 | 6.8 | 7.2 | 7.5 | 7.9 | 8.2 | 8.6 | 9.0 | 9.3 | 9.7 | 10.0 | 10.4 | 10.8 | 43 |
| 44 | 6.6 | 7.0 | 7.3 | 7.7 | 8.0 | 8.4 | 8.8 | 9.2 | 9.5 | 9.9 | 10.3 | 10.6 | 11.0 | 44 |
| 45 | 6.8 | 7.1 | 7.5 | 7.9 | 8.2 | 8.6 | 9.0 | 9.4 | 9.8 | 10.1 | 10.5 | 10.9 | 11.3 | 45 |
| 46 | 6.9 | 7.3 | 7.7 | 8.1 | 8.4 | 8.8 | 9.2 | 9.6 | 10.0 | 10.4 | 10.7 | 11.1 | 11.5 | 46 |
| 47 | 7.1 | 7.4 | 7.8 | 8.2 | 8.6 | 9.0 | 9.4 | 9.8 | 10.2 | 10.6 | 11.0 | 11.4 | 11.8 | 47 |
| 48 | 7.2 | 7.6 | 8.0 | 8.4 | 8.8 | 9.2 | 9.6 | 10.0 | 10.4 | 10.8 | 11.2 | 11.6 | 12.0 | 48 |
| 49 | 7.4 | 7.8 | 8.2 | 8.6 | 9.0 | 9.4 | 9.8 | 10.2 | 10.6 | 11.0 | 11.4 | 11.8 | 12.3 | 49 |
| 50 | 7.5 | 7.9 | 8.3 | 8.7 | 9.1 | 9.6 | 10.0 | 10.4 | 10.8 | 11.3 | 11.7 | 12.1 | 12.5 | 50 |
| 51 | 7.7 | 8.1 | 8.5 | 8.9 | 9.4 | 9.8 | 10.2 | 10.6 | 11.1 | 11.5 | 11.9 | 12.3 | 12.8 | 51 |
| 52 | 7.8 | 8.2 | 8.7 | 9.1 | 9.5 | 10.0 | 10.4 | 10.8 | 11.3 | 11.7 | 12.1 | 12.6 | 13.0 | 52 |
| 53 | 8.0 | 8.4 | 8.8 | 9.3 | 9.7 | 10.2 | 10.6 | 11.0 | 11.5 | 11.9 | 12.4 | 12.8 | 13.3 | 53 |
| 54 | 8.1 | 8.6 | 9.0 | 9.5 | 9.9 | 10.4 | 10.8 | 11.3 | 11.7 | 12.2 | 12.6 | 13.1 | 13.5 | 54 |
| 55 | 8.3 | 8.7 | 9.2 | 9.6 | 10.0 | 10.5 | 11.0 | 11.5 | 11.9 | 12.4 | 12.8 | 13.3 | 13.8 | 55 |
| 56 | 8.4 | 8.9 | 9.3 | 9.8 | 10.2 | 10.7 | 11.2 | 11.7 | 12.1 | 12.6 | 13.1 | 13.5 | 14.0 | 56 |
| 57 | 8.6 | 9.0 | 9.5 | 10.0 | 10.5 | 10.9 | 11.4 | 11.9 | 12.4 | 12.8 | 13.3 | 13.8 | 14.3 | 57 |
| 58 | 8.7 | 9.2 | 9.7 | 10.2 | 10.6 | 11.1 | 11.6 | 12.1 | 12.6 | 13.1 | 13.5 | 14.0 | 14.5 | 58 |
| 59 | 8.9 | 9.3 | 9.8 | 10.3 | 10.8 | 11.3 | 11.8 | 12.3 | 12.8 | 13.3 | 13.8 | 14.3 | 14.8 | 59 |
| 60 | 9.0 | 9.5 | 10.0 | 10.5 | 11.0 | 11.5 | 12.0 | 12.5 | 13.0 | 13.5 | 14.0 | 14.5 | 15.0 | 60 |
| Min | 9 | 9½ | 10 | 10½ | 11 | 11½ | 12 | 12½ | 13 | 13½ | 14 | 14½ | 15 | Min |

**Example 2.** How long will it take to steam 6.8 miles (when the course is to be altered)? Vessel's speed is 10½ knots. Answer = 39 minutes.

**Essential Nav.**

## TIME, SPEED, AND DISTANCE TABLE

for finding distance run in a given time at various Speeds, 2½ to 22 knots

| Min | 15½ | 16 | 16½ | 17 | 17½ | 18 | 18½ | 19 | 19½ | 20 | 20½ | 21 | 21½ | 22 | Min |
|-----|------|------|------|------|------|------|------|------|------|------|------|------|------|------|-----|
| | | | | | | KNOTS | | | | | | | | | |
| 1 | 0.3 | 0.3 | 0.3 | 0.3 | 0.3 | 0.3 | 0.3 | 0.3 | 0.3 | 0.3 | 0.3 | 0.4 | 0.4 | 0.4 | 1 |
| 2 | 0.5 | 0.5 | 0.5 | 0.6 | 0.6 | 0.6 | 0.6 | 0.6 | 0.6 | 0.7 | 0.7 | 0.7 | 0.7 | 0.7 | 2 |
| 3 | 0.8 | 0.8 | 0.8 | 0.9 | 0.9 | 0.9 | 0.9 | 1.0 | 1.0 | 1.0 | 1.0 | 1.1 | 1.1 | 1.1 | 3 |
| 4 | 1.0 | 1.1 | 1.1 | 1.1 | 1.1 | 1.2 | 1.2 | 1.3 | 1.3 | 1.3 | 1.3 | 1.4 | 1.4 | 1.5 | 4 |
| 5 | 1.3 | 1.3 | 1.3 | 1.4 | 1.4 | 1.5 | 1.5 | 1.6 | 1.6 | 1.7 | 1.7 | 1.8 | 1.8 | 1.8 | 5 |
| 6 | 1.5 | 1.6 | 1.6 | 1.7 | 1.7 | 1.8 | 1.8 | 1.9 | 1.9 | 2.0 | 2.0 | 2.1 | 2.1 | 2.2 | 6 |
| 7 | 1.8 | 1.9 | 1.9 | 2.0 | 2.0 | 2.1 | 2.1 | 2.2 | 2.2 | 2.3 | 2.4 | 2.5 | 2.5 | 2.6 | 7 |
| 8 | 2.0 | 2.1 | 2.2 | 2.3 | 2.3 | 2.4 | 2.4 | 2.5 | 2.6 | 2.7 | 2.7 | 2.8 | 2.8 | 2.9 | 8 |
| 9 | 2.3 | 2.4 | 2.5 | 2.6 | 2.6 | 2.7 | 2.8 | 2.9 | 2.9 | 3.0 | 3.1 | 3.2 | 3.2 | 3.3 | 9 |
| 10 | 2.6 | 2.7 | 2.7 | 2.8 | 2.9 | 3.0 | 3.1 | 3.2 | 3.2 | 3.3 | 3.4 | 3.5 | 3.6 | 3.7 | 10 |
| 11 | 2.8 | 2.9 | 3.0 | 3.1 | 3.2 | 3.3 | 3.4 | 3.5 | 3.6 | 3.7 | 3.8 | 3.9 | 3.9 | 4.0 | 11 |
| 12 | 3.1 | 3.2 | 3.3 | 3.4 | 3.5 | 3.6 | 3.7 | 3.8 | 3.9 | 4.0 | 4.1 | 4.2 | 4.3 | 4.4 | 12 |
| 13 | 3.4 | 3.5 | 3.6 | 3.7 | 3.8 | 3.9 | 4.0 | 4.1 | 4.2 | 4.3 | 4.4 | 4.6 | 4.7 | 4.8 | 13 |
| 14 | 3.6 | 3.7 | 3.8 | 4.0 | 4.1 | 4.2 | 4.3 | 4.4 | 4.5 | 4.7 | 4.8 | 4.9 | 5.0 | 5.1 | 14 |
| 15 | 3.9 | 4.0 | 4.1 | 4.3 | 4.4 | 4.5 | 4.6 | 4.8 | 4.9 | 5.0 | 5.1 | 5.3 | 5.4 | 5.5 | 15 |
| 16 | 4.2 | 4.3 | 4.4 | 4.5 | 4.6 | 4.8 | 4.9 | 5.1 | 5.2 | 5.3 | 5.4 | 5.6 | 5.7 | 5.9 | 16 |
| 17 | 4.4 | 4.5 | 4.6 | 4.8 | 4.9 | 5.1 | 5.2 | 5.4 | 5.5 | 5.7 | 5.8 | 6.0 | 6.1 | 6.2 | 17 |
| 18 | 4.7 | 4.8 | 4.9 | 5.1 | 5.2 | 5.4 | 5.5 | 5.7 | 5.8 | 6.0 | 6.1 | 6.3 | 6.4 | 6.6 | 18 |
| 19 | 4.9 | 5.1 | 5.2 | 5.4 | 5.5 | 5.7 | 5.8 | 6.0 | 6.1 | 6.3 | 6.5 | 6.7 | 6.8 | 7.0 | 19 |
| 20 | 5.1 | 5.3 | 5.5 | 5.7 | 5.8 | 6.0 | 6.1 | 6.3 | 6.5 | 6.7 | 6.8 | 7.0 | 7.1 | 7.3 | 20 |
| 21 | 5.4 | 5.6 | 5.8 | 6.0 | 6.1 | 6.3 | 6.5 | 6.7 | 6.8 | 7.0 | 7.2 | 7.4 | 7.5 | 7.7 | 21 |
| 22 | 5.7 | 5.9 | 6.0 | 6.2 | 6.4 | 6.6 | 6.8 | 7.0 | 7.1 | 7.3 | 7.5 | 7.7 | 7.9 | 8.1 | 22 |
| 23 | 5.9 | 6.1 | 6.3 | 6.5 | 6.7 | 6.9 | 7.1 | 7.3 | 7.5 | 7.7 | 7.9 | 8.1 | 8.2 | 8.4 | 23 |
| 24 | 6.2 | 6.4 | 6.6 | 6.8 | 7.0 | 7.2 | 7.4 | 7.6 | 7.8 | 8.0 | 8.2 | 8.4 | 8.6 | 8.8 | 24 |
| 25 | 6.5 | 6.7 | 6.9 | 7.1 | 7.3 | 7.5 | 7.7 | 7.9 | 8.1 | 8.3 | 8.5 | 8.8 | 9.0 | 9.2 | 25 |
| 26 | 6.7 | 6.9 | 7.1 | 7.4 | 7.6 | 7.8 | 8.0 | 8.2 | 8.4 | 8.7 | 8.9 | 9.1 | 9.3 | 9.5 | 26 |
| 27 | 7.0 | 7.2 | 7.4 | 7.7 | 7.9 | 8.1 | 8.3 | 8.6 | 8.8 | 9.0 | 9.2 | 9.5 | 9.7 | 9.9 | 27 |
| 28 | 7.2 | 7.5 | 7.7 | 7.9 | 8.1 | 8.4 | 8.6 | 8.9 | 9.1 | 9.3 | 9.5 | 9.8 | 10.0 | 10.3 | 28 |
| 29 | 7.5 | 7.7 | 7.9 | 8.2 | 8.4 | 8.7 | 8.9 | 9.2 | 9.4 | 9.7 | 9.9 | 10.2 | 10.4 | 10.6 | 29 |
| 30 | 7.8 | 8.0 | 8.2 | 8.5 | 8.7 | 9.0 | 9.2 | 9.5 | 9.7 | 10.0 | 10.2 | 10.5 | 10.7 | 11.0 | 30 |
| 31 | 8.0 | 8.3 | 8.5 | 8.8 | 9.0 | 9.3 | 9.5 | 9.8 | 10.0 | 10.3 | 10.6 | 10.9 | 11.1 | 11.4 | 31 |
| 32 | 8.2 | 8.5 | 8.8 | 9.1 | 9.3 | 9.6 | 9.9 | 10.2 | 10.4 | 10.7 | 10.9 | 11.2 | 11.4 | 11.7 | 32 |
| 33 | 8.5 | 8.8 | 9.1 | 9.4 | 9.6 | 9.9 | 10.2 | 10.5 | 10.7 | 11.0 | 11.3 | 11.6 | 11.8 | 12.1 | 33 |
| 34 | 8.8 | 9.1 | 9.3 | 9.6 | 9.9 | 10.2 | 10.5 | 10.8 | 11.0 | 11.3 | 11.6 | 11.9 | 12.2 | 12.5 | 34 |
| 35 | 9.0 | 9.3 | 9.6 | 9.9 | 10.2 | 10.5 | 10.8 | 11.1 | 11.4 | 11.7 | 12.0 | 12.3 | 12.5 | 12.8 | 35 |
| 36 | 9.3 | 9.6 | 9.9 | 10.2 | 10.5 | 10.8 | 11.1 | 11.4 | 11.7 | 12.0 | 12.3 | 12.6 | 12.9 | 13.2 | 36 |
| 37 | 9.6 | 9.9 | 10.2 | 10.5 | 10.8 | 11.1 | 11.4 | 11.7 | 12.0 | 12.3 | 12.6 | 13.0 | 13.3 | 13.6 | 37 |
| 38 | 9.8 | 10.1 | 10.4 | 10.8 | 11.1 | 11.4 | 11.7 | 12.0 | 12.3 | 12.7 | 13.0 | 13.3 | 13.6 | 13.9 | 38 |
| 39 | 10.1 | 10.4 | 10.7 | 11.1 | 11.4 | 11.7 | 12.0 | 12.4 | 12.7 | 13.0 | 13.3 | 13.7 | 14.0 | 14.3 | 39 |
| 40 | 10.4 | 10.7 | 11.0 | 11.3 | 11.7 | 12.0 | 12.3 | 12.7 | 13.0 | 13.3 | 13.6 | 14.0 | 14.3 | 14.7 | 40 |
| 41 | 10.6 | 10.9 | 11.2 | 11.6 | 12.0 | 12.3 | 12.6 | 13.0 | 13.3 | 13.7 | 14.0 | 14.4 | 14.7 | 15.0 | 41 |
| 42 | 10.8 | 11.2 | 11.5 | 11.9 | 12.3 | 12.6 | 12.9 | 13.3 | 13.6 | 14.0 | 14.3 | 14.7 | 15.0 | 15.4 | 42 |
| 43 | 11.1 | 11.5 | 11.8 | 12.2 | 12.5 | 12.9 | 13.2 | 13.6 | 13.9 | 14.3 | 14.7 | 15.1 | 15.4 | 15.8 | 43 |
| 44 | 11.3 | 11.7 | 12.1 | 12.5 | 12.8 | 13.2 | 13.5 | 13.9 | 14.3 | 14.7 | 15.0 | 15.4 | 15.7 | 16.1 | 44 |
| 45 | 11.6 | 12.0 | 12.4 | 12.8 | 13.1 | 13.5 | 13.8 | 14.3 | 14.6 | 15.0 | 15.4 | 15.8 | 16.1 | 16.5 | 45 |
| 46 | 11.9 | 12.3 | 12.6 | 13.0 | 13.4 | 13.8 | 14.2 | 14.6 | 14.9 | 15.3 | 15.7 | 16.1 | 16.5 | 16.9 | 46 |
| 47 | 12.2 | 12.5 | 12.9 | 13.3 | 13.7 | 14.1 | 14.5 | 14.9 | 15.3 | 15.7 | 16.1 | 16.5 | 16.8 | 17.2 | 47 |
| 48 | 12.4 | 12.8 | 13.2 | 13.6 | 14.0 | 14.4 | 14.8 | 15.2 | 15.6 | 16.0 | 16.4 | 16.8 | 17.2 | 17.6 | 48 |
| 49 | 12.7 | 13.1 | 13.5 | 13.9 | 14.3 | 14.7 | 15.1 | 15.5 | 15.9 | 16.3 | 16.7 | 17.2 | 17.6 | 18.0 | 49 |
| 50 | 12.9 | 13.3 | 13.7 | 14.2 | 14.6 | 15.0 | 15.4 | 15.8 | 16.2 | 16.7 | 17.1 | 17.5 | 17.9 | 18.3 | 50 |
| 51 | 13.2 | 13.6 | 14.0 | 14.5 | 14.9 | 15.3 | 15.7 | 16.2 | 16.6 | 17.0 | 17.5 | 17.9 | 18.3 | 18.7 | 51 |
| 52 | 13.5 | 13.9 | 14.3 | 14.7 | 15.1 | 15.6 | 16.0 | 16.5 | 16.9 | 17.3 | 17.7 | 18.2 | 18.6 | 19.1 | 52 |
| 53 | 13.7 | 14.1 | 14.5 | 15.0 | 15.4 | 15.9 | 16.3 | 16.8 | 17.2 | 17.7 | 18.1 | 18.6 | 19.0 | 19.4 | 53 |
| 54 | 14.0 | 14.4 | 14.8 | 15.3 | 15.7 | 16.2 | 16.6 | 17.1 | 17.5 | 18.0 | 18.4 | 18.9 | 19.3 | 19.8 | 54 |
| 55 | 14.2 | 14.7 | 15.1 | 15.6 | 16.0 | 16.5 | 16.9 | 17.4 | 17.8 | 18.3 | 18.8 | 19.3 | 19.7 | 20.2 | 55 |
| 56 | 14.4 | 14.9 | 15.4 | 15.9 | 16.3 | 16.8 | 17.2 | 17.7 | 18.1 | 18.7 | 19.1 | 19.6 | 20.0 | 20.5 | 56 |
| 57 | 14.7 | 15.2 | 15.7 | 16.2 | 16.6 | 17.1 | 17.6 | 18.1 | 18.5 | 19.0 | 19.5 | 20.0 | 20.4 | 20.9 | 57 |
| 58 | 15.0 | 15.5 | 16.0 | 16.4 | 16.9 | 17.4 | 17.9 | 18.4 | 18.8 | 19.3 | 19.8 | 20.3 | 20.8 | 21.3 | 58 |
| 59 | 15.2 | 15.7 | 16.2 | 16.7 | 17.2 | 17.7 | 18.2 | 18.7 | 19.2 | 19.7 | 20.2 | 20.7 | 21.1 | 21.6 | 59 |
| 60 | 15.5 | 16.0 | 16.5 | 17.0 | 17.5 | 18.0 | 18.5 | 19.0 | 19.5 | 20.0 | 20.5 | 21.0 | 21.5 | 22.0 | 60 |
| Min | 15½ | 16 | 16½ | 17 | 17½ | 18 | 18½ | 19 | 19½ | 20 | 20½ | 21 | 21½ | 22 | Min |

**Example 3.** How far will a vessel steam at 17.5 knots in 25 minutes? Answer 7.3 miles

# ADVANCED NAVIGATION

**4**

# ELECTRONIC NAVIGATION SYSTEMS

Radio waves have been used in navigation for more than 100 years, but it's just been in the last several decades that the use of electronic systems has dominated the practice of navigation. In fact, this dominance has reached the point of frightening many mariners who believe that a lot of navigators would be lost, literally, without electronic devices. The only way to relieve yourself of this concern is to know how, from practice, to navigate without electronic systems. And, if you know the basics, you'll understand better how the systems work and when to doubt their intelligence.

## RADIOBEACONS

Radiobeacons were first introduced in U.S. waters in the 1930s as an aid to coastal navigation. Onboard receivers with direction-finding capabilities could indicate the bearing to a transmitting beacon.

When the electrical coil in a directional receiver is oriented 90° from the direction of the beacon, the signal is strongest; when the coil faces the transmitter, the signal is weakest — it's at the null. Although radiobeacons have theoretical ranges up to 200 miles (substantially lower ranges at night when power is deliberately reduced), they are reliable only to about 25 miles.

As other types of electronic aids have gained in use, the number of radiobeacons has been reduced. Also, their mode of operation has changed in recognition that they're now used mostly as single homing devices rather than in groups yielding simultaneous bearing fixes. So now they transmit continuously rather than in time-sharing arrangements with others in their group.

Radiobeacon waves are subject to several kinds of error. Waves crossing a coastline at angles other than 90° are refracted (bent in) toward land. At night, waves reflected off the ionosphere can blur the signal. And, incoming waves can ricochet off rigging and reach the receiver as a second (erroneous) signal. Finally, waves follow a great circle path to the receiver, but you plot directions as rhumb lines on a Mercator chart. To plot the direction to a distant transmitter, you can convert great circle to rhumb line bearings using the Radiobeacon Half-Convergency Correction Table on page 237.

In an emergency, you can use a commercial radio station as a homing device in conjunction with a regular portable radio receiver. Ironically, cheaper sets often serve this purpose better than expensive ones because their antennae are more directionally sensitive — an undesirable feature for most (non-navigation) purposes that higher quality designs often eliminate. Don't be tempted, however, to rely heavily on commercial stations, because all the errors mentioned above come into play. In addition, because the locations of commercial transmitters are seldom given on charts, the results are usually bound to be crude.

Note that Canada, Mexico, and the U.S. are rapidly decommissioning marine radiobeacons. Many relatively recent charts show radiobeacons that are no longer operational. Check *Reed's Almanac* or other up-to-date sources. There are numerous aero beacons in operation that work with RDF receivers and provide similar lines of position.

## DEPTHSOUNDERS

This system is noted here because it's of general interest to navigators and also because it serves as a reminder to use soundings in everyday navigation — an element too often overlooked.

Ocean bottom features are similar to topographical features on land except that they are usually more worn down and gentle. Bathymetric charts based on systematic surveys shows these features as bottom contours alongside continents and along heavily traveled routes between continents. Using a good depthsounder, you can detect when you're passing over a prominent feature like a seamount or canyon. In the absence of such features, you can overlay a trace of soundings taken over time on top of charted contour lines and match them up. This technique works best when you're crossing contour lines at sizable angles.

## HYPERBOLIC ELECTRONIC NAVIGATION SYSTEMS

### The Concept

When you know the difference in your distance from two objects, you know you're on a curved line defined by that difference. By definition, a hyperbolic curve is formed by joining all points that are the same difference in distance between two points. In hyperbolic navigation systems, your receiver measures the difference in time of receipt of radio waves, and you or the set translate the time difference into a distance difference using the known speed of the waves.

It's easy to grasp the concept intuitively by placing yourself on an imaginary football field. If the sound of bells rung simultaneously under each goalpost reached you at the same time, you'd know that you were equidistant from each goalpost, or somewhere on the 50-yard line. If the sound from the bell at the north goalpost reached you sooner than the other one, you'd know that you were closer to that bell. The amount of time difference would determine how much closer you were. Just as the receipt of the sounds at the same time places you on a line, the straight 50-yard line, so, too, the receipt at a specific difference in time places you on the field somewhere on a different line — a hyperbolic curve.

If your recall of high school geometry is a bit murky when it comes to the shape of hyperbolic curves, it should all come back to you when you look at the pattern in the diagram below left. In it, a pair of transmitters takes the place of the goalposts, and the line between them is called the baseline, which is bisected by a line perpendicular to it (centerline) — the 50-yard line in our analogy. All the other lines are hyperbolic curves. Unless you received the signals from each transmitter simultaneously, you'd be on one of these curves. If you received the signal from transmitter X, say, 50 microseconds before the one from M, then you'd be on line CD; if 150 seconds before, then on line EF.

Note that the distance between the lines in this pattern increases with increasing distance from the baseline. Because it does, the potential accuracy of the system is greater when you're nearer the baseline — where the lines converge. In fact, when you're located in the vicinity of the baseline extension (shown as dashed lines) where the divergence of the lines is most pronounced, accuracy may be reduced to unacceptably low levels.

The reading you get from one pair of transmitters gives you a single LOP — the curve you're on. To get a fix, you need to measure the time difference from a second pair that places you on another curve. Your fix is at the intersection of the two curves, as shown below.

**Hyperbolic basics and a sample hyperbolic fix**

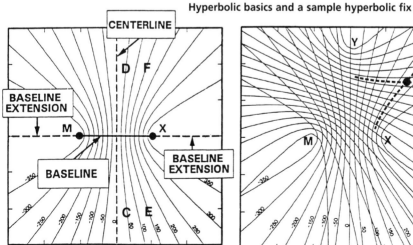
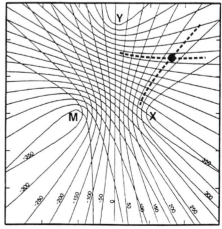

## Decca, Consol, Omega

Decca was the first of several hyperbolic electronic navigation systems developed during and after World War II. (Among these systems, Loran-C remains the most widely used and will be described in some detail later.) Decca was first employed in the 1944 Normandy invasion. Its coverage was later extended beyond the English Channel to the waters off Newfoundland, the North Sea, and the Sea of Japan.

The Consol system, based on an approach developed in Germany during the war, was established in the eastern North Atlantic. Because of the short baseline distance between transmitting towers in this system, the close grouping of towers serves much like a single radiobeacon — but one having a very long range.

The Omega system was devised to overcome the major drawback of other hyperbolic systems — their limited geographic coverage. With eight transmitters located some 5,000 to 6,000 miles apart (see the list of stations on page 237), Omega's coverage is worldwide — a spread made possible by the use of atomic time standards to regulate the very low-frequency, long-range signals.

A very long baseline between transmitters results in less divergence of hyperbolic lines (and less deterioration of accuracy) in locations far away from the baseline than the shorter baseline systems can achieve. This characteristic makes worldwide coverage possible, but the widely spaced geographic locations of stations limits accuracy to about one mile during the day and two miles at night — values that are acceptable in mid-ocean but normally not for inshore work.

The significance of Omega's worldwide coverage has been reduced greatly by the development of satellite navigation systems with universal coverage. By the time the Omega system was fully in place — the eighth station was added in 1981 — the Transit satellite system was fully operational and work on the GPS system had begun.

## SATELLITE SYSTEMS

### Transit

When the Soviets launched Sputnik in 1957, scientists at the Johns Hopkins Applied Physics Lab took careful note of the pronounced Doppler shift in the signal from the passing satellite. As the fast-moving Sputnik approached, the scientists noted that signal frequency was higher than the transmitted frequency. They also observed that the frequency lowered until the satellite reached its closet point of approach (CPA), when the observed frequency equaled the transmitted frequency. Its decrease continued as Sputnik raced away, although the rate of decrease slowed with increasing distance from the observers. This Doppler shift phenomenon that the scientists observed was the same one you experience when an express train rushes by you at a local station and you hear its roaring sound drop sharply in pitch.

The scientists reasoned that they could accurately locate their position on earth by carefully measuring the satellite's Doppler shift and knowing with precision the satellite's position in orbit at the exact instant of each measurement.

By 1964, the military's NAVSAT system was in place with the computers, timing devices, tracking stations, and satellites needed to provide accurate fixes. In 1967, with added Transit satellites, the capability was offered to private and commercial users as the Transit system. Ten Transit satellites were in polar orbits that circled the earth once every 106 minutes at an altitude of 600 miles.

The Transit system provided fixes with 0.1 mile accuracy based on a single satellite pass, provided that the satellite was between 10° and 70° in elevation for a prolonged period. With 10 satellites in use, there were periods normally lasting up to an hour — even more in lower latitudes where the polar orbits were spread farther apart — when no fix was available.

The Transit system went offline at the end of 1996. As *Reed's* goes to press in early 1998, Omega is still operating but will probably be shut down soon. GPS, DGPS, and Loran-C have become the widely accepted and used electronic navigation systems.

## GPS

The Global Positioning System (GPS), with 24 satellites, has overtaken the Transit system and fulfills the dream of all navigators — a system that fixes their position accurately worldwide, in all weather and, unlike Transit, continuously. And, it does all this in three dimensions: giving latitude, longitude, and altitude.

The components of GPS are similar to those of Transit: tracking stations, high-speed computers, and atomic clocks with an error of plus or minus one second in 300,000 years. The tracking systems continuously update orbital information for each satellite, which is transmitted to the satellite along with super-accuracte time. The satellite, in turn, relays this information to your GPS receiver. Your set measures the time it takes to receive a signal and translates time into distance to the satellite. (Your set knows, with precision, the orbital position of the satellite at the instant of measurement.)

In two-dimensional terrestrial systems, a range to an object places you on an LOP consisting of an arc that's part of a circle of position. In contrast, the three-dimensional GPS system places you on a sphere of position, with the satellite at the center of the sphere. In the terrestrial systems, you need observations of two objects, with intersect-

ing LOPs, to get a fix. With GPS, you need measurements from three satellites to locate yourself at a single point in space — because the intersection of only two spheres defines a circle, not a point. (If you're skeptical, blow some bubbles and look at the shape that forms when you get a double bubble.) Actually, the intersection of three spheres defines two points, but your receiver easily dismisses the point that's not at or near the earth's surface. In two-dimensional systems, you need a third observation to determine the accuracy of the other two. For the same reason, GPS uses a fourth satellite in each fix. Continuous fixes are possible in GPS because at least four satellites are within line of sight of a receiver at sea level at any one time.

GPS can provide an accuracy of 16 meters. That is, 95 percent of fixes should fall within this distance of the true position. The impetus for the system came from the military, which uses that accuracy in its advanced weapons systems. Because the military wants to deny that accuracy to potential enemies, the accuracy available to other than authorized military users is deliberately degraded by altering the timing part of the satellites' signals. The degraded signals yield an accuracy of about 100 meters.

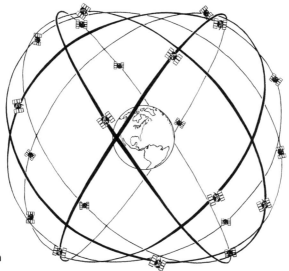

**The GPS Constellation**

There is talk that the U.S. government may end this signal degradation, called Selective Availability, but no time table has been announced. You can easily measure the effects of Selective Availability by leaving your GPS on at a dock and either recording the positions over time or observing a small-scale plot of the positions.

## Differential GPS

One-hundred meter accuracy is adequate for most purposes, but not for navigation in tight quarters. To achieve greater accuracy for civilian users without compromising military objectives, the Differential GPS (DGPS) was developed. Local DGPS stations — often located at radiobeacon sites — receive the satellites' signals. Because these stations know their own locations with precision, they can calculate the exact time it should take to receive the signals and compare that with the actual time of receipt, thereby determining the error. The DGPS stations relay this error information to GPS sets nearby on short-range frequencies.

DGPS is being phased in all along the U.S. and Canadian Coasts. Check *Reed's Nautical Almanac* for up-to-date coverage.

## GPS Receivers

GPS receivers come in the form of permanent installations or portable handheld units. Some receivers display no information directly to the user but relay data to other systems integrating radar and chart information. Even the least expensive handheld units display information on direction and distance to waypoints, speed, and crosstrack error. Many are "differential-ready" and can provide DGPS accuracy when coupled with a separate DGPS receiver.

## GPS Information

For more information about GPS, contact the Coast Guard's Global Positioning Information Center. You can hear a 24-hour-a-day recording by calling 703-866-3826.

If you have questions about GPS, call 703-866-3806 or fax 703-866-3825 and a watchstander will answer them for you (on duty daily from 0600 to 2200 EST).

The Coast Guard broadcasts warnings and information on GPS in their regular Marine Information Broadcasts on VHF Channel 16 (switching 22A) and on medium frequency

2182 (switching 2670). Messages are also broadcast on NAVTEX.

Radio station WWV also broadcasts GPS status reports at 14 and 15 minutes past the hour on 2.5, 5, 10, 15, and 20MHz. WWVH broadcasts these reports at 43 and 44 minutes past the hour on 2.5, 5, 10, and 15MHz. For more information on WWV and WWCH broadcasts, see the "Resources" chapter in *Reed's Nautical Almanacs*.

GPS and Omega publications are available from:

*Commanding Officer*
*Omega NAVSYSCEN/GPSIC*
*Telegraph Road*
*Alexandria, VA 22310-3998.*

## OTHER ADVANCED NAVIGATION SYSTEMS

### Inertial Navigation

Except for dead reckoning, most navigation relies on visual, audio, or radio wave information generated on or off a vessel. The inertial navigation system does not; it's entirely independent of any form of external measurement. If you could afford an installation, you'd be able to advance your position based on a sophisticated sensing of the direction and speed of your movement over the ground.

Inertial navigation uses gyros, accelerometers, and computers to give you DR-type projections "to die for." Three gyros keep the sensing unit in a plane tangent to the earth's surface so that only horizontal movement is detected. Two accelerometers — one oriented east/west, the other north/south — use one of your favorite laws from high school physics, Newton's second (F=MA), to monitor, with exquisite precision, movement in any horizontal direction. And, a computer keeps track by cumulating all movement.

But in that cumulative process lies the only drawback in the system, other than high cost. Just as in a DR track, any errors in an inertial system are cumulative. Gyro friction, variations in the earth's daily rotation, and false interpretation of vertical components of gravity can raise minuscule daily errors to significant levels over time. So even the missile-bearing submarines that carry the most exacting inertial components need to fix their positions by other means after long stretches underway.

## Doppler Sonar

In another advanced system, sonar gear tracks movement over the bottom to determine speed over the ground. Sonar signals are beamed fore and aft and changes in signal frequency induced by the Doppler shift are measured and translated into speed and distance run. The use of both fore and aft beams allows the system to eliminate potential vertical motion errors and to compensate for irregular bottom features. By adding gyros, the system provides both distance and direction traveled over the ground. Here, too, errors are cumulative and can reach up to .85 mile after a 500-mile run. When water depth exceeds 1,000 feet, some systems can use signals reflected off the water mass itself, rather than the bottom.

## LORAN-C

GPS has not yet replaced the most widely used hyperbolic system: Loran-C. Although Loran-C's coverage is not universal, it extends over the continental United States, across the North Atlantic, through the Mediterranean Sea, and in the central Pacific and Japan. It's useful out to about 1,000 miles from land.

The pair of transmitting stations that yield a hyperbolic LOP are designated as master and secondary (slave) stations. A Loran-C chain consists of a master and two to four slaves, designated with the letters W, X, Y, and Z. The stations transmit the signals in sequence. A chain is identified by the time it takes to complete a sequence — its group repetition interval (GRI). The northeastern U.S. chain, whose coverage is shown here, repeats the cycle in 99,600 microseconds and is known as the 9960 chain. (See the "Loran-C Rate Table" on page 238 for a list of U.S. chains.)

The measured time difference (TD) defines the curve you're on. TD curves are overprinted on charts intended for use with Loran-C. With them, you can plot a Loran-C fix at the intersection of two TD lines, interpolating between the charted lines for TD values other than those charted.

Loran-C receivers convert TDs to latitude and longitude coordinates that you can plot in the normal way instead of plotting the intersection of TD curves. Because of potential errors in the TD to lat/long conversion in your receiver, the TD readings, themselves, may be more accurate. For this reason, you should consider plotting the TDs rather than the lat/long coordinates when you need utmost accuracy.

Finally, the repeatability of Loran-C is extremely accurate. That is, the reading you get at an oft-used waypoint, say a ledge marked by a beacon, will be precisely the same the next time you're at that point. In that case, if you note the reading the first time you arrive at the waypoint and navigate to produce the same reading at subsequent arrivals, you can be confident in finding the precise point, because Loran-C is perfectly consistent. Even errors are repeated consistently, so if you know them, you can take account of them in advance. You can realize the full potential of Loran-C, then, by using TD readings observed previously at a location.

**The 9960 Loran Chain**

Typical loran array of master and four slave stations showing coverage area.

**Advanced Nav.**

195

## RADAR

Radar is probably the most versatile electronic navigation aid when coasting. It not only gives position information but also indicates the dangers of collision by tracking other vessels.

Radar consists of four basic units: transmitter, antenna, receiver, and display.

A very short pulse of powerful electromagnetic energy is transmitted from the antenna in a narrow, horizontal beam at the speed of light (300 million meters/second) at the same time a stream of electrons (the trace) is deflected from the center of the cathode-ray tube display out toward the circumference of the tube face at a controlled rate that varies with the range scale in use.

Any object on the bearing of the transmitted pulse re-radiates the energy in many directions and only a very small portion returns to the antenna.

The receiver greatly amplifies and changes this returned signal to positive DC voltage. The DC pulse allows an increase in the flow of electrons to make a bright mark on the screen to record the "echo." This sequence takes place many times each second at a given pulse repetition frequency (PRF). The space between allows a

returned echo to be detected and displayed before the next transmission. PRFs vary with range and/or make of set, between 500 to 2,000 per second. The antenna rotates at about 20 revolutions per minute and is synchronized with the trace rotation so the direction of every echo from the observer is shown on the display.

Even the smallest object returns several echoes before the beam moves on. The energy from the several returned echoes are cumulated to help display the weaker echoes.

A heading marker on the display provides an important reference to direction. When the antenna is pointing ahead, it sends a pulse to the radar display that causes a line to show on the screen that represents the vessel's head. You can refer echoes displayed on the screen to your vessel's head and get the relative bearing of the echo. If the heading marker is not pointing exactly ahead, relative bearings will be wrong. You can quickly check for any such mistake by heading toward a small prominent visible object and see if the radar echo appears under the heading marker.

The horizontal width of the beam is determined by the size of the antenna. Larger antennae produce smaller horizon-

**Good and Bad Radar Returns**
(land masses exaggerated)

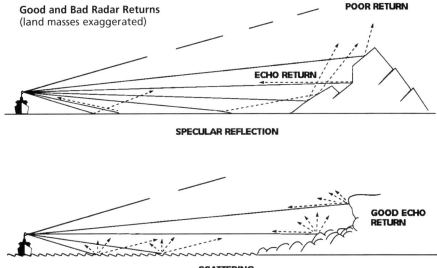

POOR RETURN

ECHO RETURN

SPECULAR REFLECTION

GOOD ECHO RETURN

SCATTERING

**Buoys and small vessels can be lost
in the "clutter" of a rough sea.**

tal beams. Slx-meter antennae produce 0.5°
beams. Antennae on merchant ships produce beams less than 2° wide. Because
small craft can't carry large antennae, their
average antenna size is about 0.5 meter
and produces a 6° wide beam. To allow for
the motion at sea, the vertical span of the
beam is about 20°.

The transmitted pulse has to contain sufficient energy to travel many miles and
produce a detectable echo return. If a peak
power of 1.5 kW is transmitted for 0.5 mil-
lionths of a second (1/2 microsecond), this
produces a pulse 150 meters long. The
pulse is shorter on lower ranges (0.1 mil-
lionths of a second = 30 meters).

The combined effect of pulse length and
horizontal beam width determines picture
resolution and your ability to discriminate
between objects close to each other. The
beam distortion of echoes is evident in the
fact that echoes appear larger at longer
ranges and get smaller as they near the
center of your display. You may not detect
small river or harbor entrances, and
buoyed channels may close. Multiple
objects within the beam at the same range
will show on the screen at that bearing as
a single echo.

The pulse length gives apparent length to
an echo. Any two objects within the pulse
appear as one, which is why the shortest
pulse possible for detection is used on
lower ranges.

The detectability of objects is also determined by their shape, size, aspect, and
material. Metal is a perfect reflector; fiberglass is almost transparent to radar. (This is
why small fiberglass vessels should carry a
radar reflector.) Objects that present a sizable vertical surface return stronger
echoes. (See illustration left.)

Seawater is a very good re-radiator.
Although most of the energy from surrounding seawater is reflected away, the
scattered return from nearby waves may
give stronger echoes than close-by objects
within the waves. Sea clutter normally is
more noticeable to windward because the
backs of the waves give less return to the
antenna.

To remove this clutter around the center
of the display, a special variable suppres-
sion is provided that works outward from
the center, decreasing to nil at about three
miles. Use this sea clutter control with caution — it's easy to remove real echoes
without realizing the extent of the "hole"
in your picture. This is one reason that
small craft are sometimes not detected on
a larger ship's radar display. (See figure
above.)

### Navigating Using Radar

Even with all of the above limitations,
radar is a most useful navigational aid. It
presents a view of the locality that you can
relate to the chart. However, the radar picture will not look quite the same as the
chart. Small insignificant objects may be
enhanced, while small prominent objects
may not give a detectable return. Lower
parts of a distant coast may be below the
radar horizon, in which case the coast will
appear on the radar to be inland from the
charted coast. Or, the slope of the shore
may be so gradual that much of the energy
is reflected away.

Bearings are quite difficult to take with
small-craft radar. You must note your vessel's heading at the instant you take the
bearing and convert the relative bearing to
a true bearing. Care must be taken to rec-
oncile features on the screen with those on

**Advanced Nav.**

197

the chart. And the apparent directions to objects will be displaced by half the radar's beam width. The best radar LOPs are arcs based on radar ranges.

To aid radar navigation, important objects such as lightships or fairway buoys are fitted with responder beacons called racons. These produce an identifying flash on the radar screen along with an enhanced blip.

Some radar presentations are now oriented to compass directions rather than to vessel heading — north is at the top of the screen — although these presentations are not yet widely available on small-craft radars. As the vessel yaws, the heading marker moves while the picture is stable. Another new feature is true motion, where the center spot moves across the screen at your vessel's course and speed.

## The Radar Plot

The majority of small-craft radars are still only able to provide a "ship's head-up" display. The heading marker is always at the top of the screen and any change in the craft's heading shows as rotating move-

ment of the radar picture. When plotting in this mode you need to convert the relative bearings into compass bearings. The relationship between the two changes, of course, with each change of course. Failure to make this adjustment is a frequent cause of mistakes.

You should take bearings of objects with the cursor through the center of the echo and, when taking ranges, use the inner edge of the range marker through the inner edge of the echo. At the moment of bearing, note the heading along with the time. The accuracy of the plot is only as good as the accuracy with which the ship's head was noted.

When your vessel is stopped, all ranges and bearings produce a "true motion picture." All moving objects show the real direction of their movement; stationary objects do not move. When your vessel is moving, all stationary objects appear to move in a direction opposite to your movement and at your speed. A harbor entrance, for example, will appear to come toward you on the screen. All echoes from moving vessels move across the screen in a

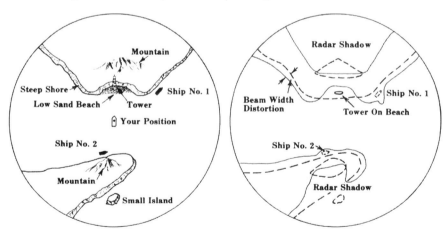

**Distortion effects of radar shadow, beam width, and pulse length.** The left view shows the actual shoreline. The solid lines in the right view represent the radar picture. Note:

- The sand beach is not detected by the radar and the tower looks like a ship in a cove.
- There is a radar shadow behind both mountains, obscuring the small island.
- Beam width distortion causes the land masses to "spread," particularly where the beam is less square to the shore.
- Ship No. 1 appears as a small peninsula because of beam width distortion.
- Ship No. 2 also merges with the land because of both beam width and pulse length distortion. Reducing receiver gain might separate the ship from land.

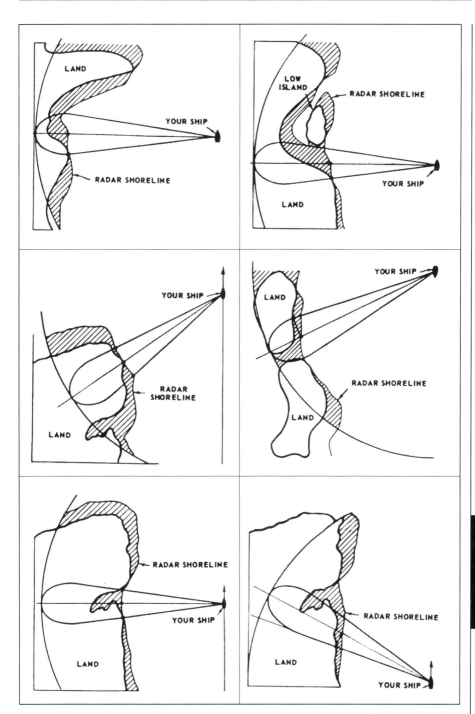

**Effects of ship's position, beam width, and pulse length on radar shoreline.** Note that this distortion will increase with greater beam width and/or more acute beam angles.

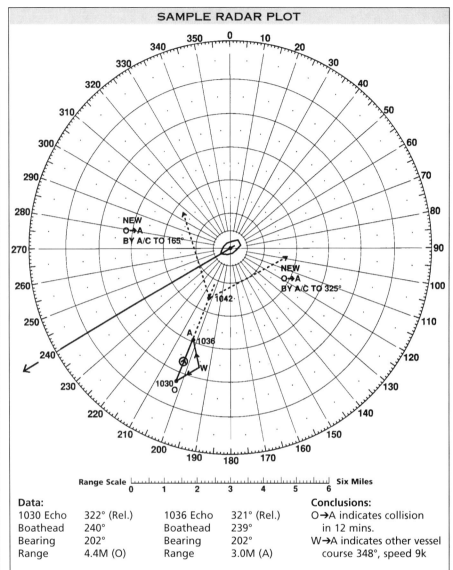

## SAMPLE RADAR PLOT

Range Scale 0 1 2 3 4 5 6 Six Miles

**Data:**

| | | | |
|---|---|---|---|
| 1030 Echo | 322° (Rel.) | 1036 Echo | 321° (Rel.) |
| Boathead | 240° | Boathead | 239° |
| Bearing | 202° | Bearing | 202° |
| Range | 4.4M (O) | Range | 3.0M (A) |

**Conclusions:**
O→A indicates collision
in 12 mins.
W→A indicates other vessel
course 348°, speed 9k

In this example, the navigator has plotted an approaching target at 10:30 and 6 minutes later. By extending the track, he or she can immediately see that a collision is probable. By plotting his own six-minute track, W→O, the navigator can deduce the other vessel's course and speed vector, W→A. The navigator has then predicted the target's position at 10:42. The two dotted lines extending from the 10:42 mark represent relative motion tracks that would keep the target vessel at a one mile Closest Point of Contact. The navigator determines the new course required by vector analysis — the easiest way is to take a parallel of the dotted line back so it runs through the original A, then swing the W→O vector around W until it touches the new line. The course change to 325° is definately preferable, in case the target decides to change course (probably to starboard). This type of plotting sheet, known as a manuevering board, is also useful for other relative motion problems like current drift and set, determining true wind speed and direction, and hurricane avoidance.

direction and rate determined by your own course and speed and the other's course and speed through the water

You can use this difference in movement on your screen to distinguish between stationary objects useful in navigating and moving objects that can pose risks of collision. In order to decide upon a safe action, it is essential to know the other vessel's heading and speed. To do this we divide the movement into its known components to produce a triangle.

To allow time to plot and assess which action to take, the plot should start when the echo is some distance from the center (you).

The triangle of motions is often named by the points 'W', 'O', and 'A'. A series of ranges and bearings are taken in a time interval of six minutes (1/10th hour).

The first position is named O and the time noted. After the six minutes, the range and bearing is taken and marked A. This O → A line is projected past the center to show the closest point of approach (CPA). A CPA of less than one mile should be considered potentially dangerous due to the small scale of the radar picture and the inaccuracy of radar bearings.

In the plotting interval of six minutes, your own vessel will have moved over a known course and distance (1/10th of the speed). This direction and distance is laid back from O and named W. W→O is "Way of Own Ship." Join W to A. This represents the course and speed of the vessel. W→A represents "Way of Another." Use arrows on each line to indicate direction.

With this information, avoiding action can now be planned. Whatever action is decided may be applied to the plot to see the possible effect before the alteration is made. Alternatively, a safe distance can be decided on and taken back to the plot (a new O/A line) to find the alteration needed to achieve this.

To aid visual appreciation of the situation, sketch in a boat shape at the center of the plot in the direction of your own heading and another shape at A in the direction W→A (the other's heading).

With practice and reasonable accuracy, the radar plot gives a good general idea of the situation, assuming the other vessel has maintained course and speed. It is important to continue plotting an approaching echo until it is past and clear, especially after you have made an alteration, to see what effect has been made to the CPA.

The need for radar plotting became apparent soon after radar was introduced for use at sea in the 1940s. Many collisions in the early days were caused by misunderstanding of what was "seen" on the screen. Since then, technology and regulations have come a long way toward improving the situation.

Very few of the modern developments extend to the small-ship's radar, and most are only able to present the original "ship's head up" display. The information may be filtered to the "Rasterscan" type (television) display. Guard rings are available, but the plotting and forecasting of subsequent movements are left to the observer.

## ELECTRONIC CHARTING SYSTEMS

Electronic charts display on a screen the kinds of information contained on paper nautical charts by translating the data into a digitized format that computers can read. When translated into this format, the chart data can be plotted upon with great precision. It can also be integrated with inputs from position systems like GPS and radars, digital compasses, and autopilots to form an electronic system that can guide a vessel safely at any time in all weather throughout the world. That's the good news.

The bad news is that blind reliance on the system without a navigator's monitoring — an attractive temptation — can lead to disaster, and has. Further bad news for the small-vessel operator is that these systems are expensive and not yet reliable enough to substitute for paper charts.

### Data Types

Some electronic charts use raster data; other use vector data. Each has advantages and limitations.

In the raster data type, a scanner moving across a paper chart picks up all the information on the chart for later display on a screen. In this process, information is not sorted into different categories; the chart is simply a dot picture of the paper chart. As a result, the displays can't be selective about what is shown. They can't clean up the picture by filtering out some of the detailed information that would clutter a chart viewed at small scale, or scale information as the user zooms in an out of the chart.

Charts based on vector data, however, can exclude categories of information because the data sets are defined mathematically and can be manipulated individually. Therefore, the display can be tailored to the navigator's needs. Vector data also takes up less storage space, so more charts can be put on a single disk.The problem with vector charts is that it takes a tremendous amount of work to include all the detail of a paper chart and they tend to look a bit chunky and crude. Ideally, electronic charting would blend the two techniques; we are starting to see such systems come to market.

### Screen Types

Data in either form can be shown on a liquid crystal display (LCD) screen or a cathode-ray tube (CRT). LCD units are compact and draw little power, but CRT types — used also in television sets and computer monitors — provide better resolution and a broader range of colors.

### The System's Display

Electronic charting systems offer almost unlimited ways to display and manipulate data from all other electronic sources. With GPS and/or Loran-C input, your vessel's position is shown on the electronic chart. You can watch your vessel's movement in relation to charted features; and, when you enter waypoints, you can monitor your progress toward them and adjust your course when necessary to offset the effects of current. With radar input, you can monitor not only the navigational picture, but also your position in relation to other traffic. The latest systems can even put tide vectors, light list, and pilot book information right on your screen.

The highly scaled down screen image below shows a section of San Francisco harbor with simple route and turning bearing plotted, both of which were done with the flick of a mouse. Two developers of charting software are:

*Nautical Software (ChartView)*
*800-946-2877; www.tides.com*

*Nautical Technologies (The Cap'n)*
*800-637-4020; www.thecapn.com*

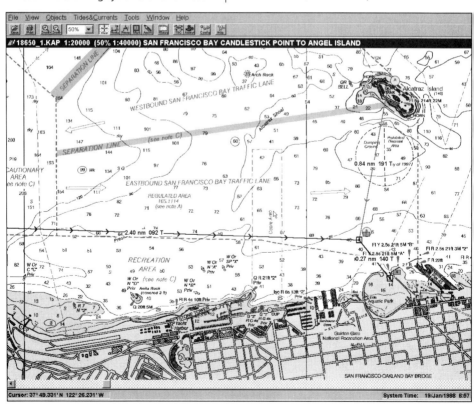

# NAVIGATING WITH A CALCULATOR

The following pages show you how to solve a variety of navigational problems with an electronic calculator.

Calculators can be divided into three main groups: the inexpensive arithmetical type with a decimal base, the scientific or slide rule calculator with algebraic, trigonometrical, and logarithmic functions and a number of memories, and the most expensive calculators that can be programmed for repetition work either manually or by inserting magnetic cards and sometimes having printout facilities.

The middle range of scientific calculators with trigonometrical and logarithmic functions, square root, exponents and reciprocals, with two to three memories, will fulfil the needs of the average navigator. The better the calculator the fewer the key sequences required. Key sequences and functions vary with different calculators, and the manufacturer's handbook should always be studied first.

The examples in this section have all been worked using sin, cos, tan, and inverse (sometimes shown as ARC) keys together with the normal arithmetical functions, all of which are included on most scientific calculators.

## Basic Trigonometrical Functions

Before using these functions consider the method by which they are derived as this will assist you in solving triangular problems. Given any right-angle triangle ABC

(fig. 1) trigonometrical functions are:

$$\sin \text{ angle ABC} = \frac{\text{opposite}}{\text{hypotenuse}} = \frac{AC}{AB}$$

$$\cos \text{ angle ABC} = \frac{\text{adjacent}}{\text{hypotenuse}} = \frac{BC}{AB}$$

$$\tan \text{ angle} = \frac{\text{opposite}}{\text{adjacent}} = \frac{AC}{BC}$$

For example:

$$\sin \text{ angle BAC} = \frac{\text{opposite}}{\text{hypotenuse}} = \frac{BC}{AB}$$

These functions are the same for angle BAC except that adjacent and opposite sides are different.

Triangular problems can usually be easily solved if they can be reduced to right-angle triangles.

### COASTAL NAVIGATION TECHNIQUES

Consider now the solution to one of the simplest navigational problems, finding the distance off from a fixed point. If using the "four points" rule or "doubling the angle" on the bow, one has to wait for specific bearings to appear, i.e., 45° or 30° and 60°.

Using trigonometrical functions, however, the navigator can take the initial bearing at any suitable time. Consider the example in figure 2 where the vessel is on a course of 105° T and needs to know the distance off the headland when abeam.

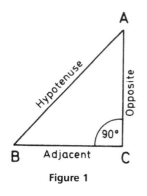

Figure 1

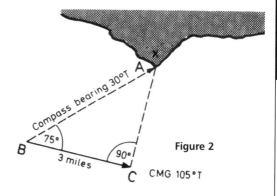

Figure 2

In this example, tidal set and leeway angle are ignored for the sake of simplicity.

Vessel's course = 105° T.

Compass bearing of A = 030° T.

∴ Relative Bearing (RB) = 75° (Angle ABC).

When the vessel is abeam of the fixed point A the relative bearing will be 90° and the log reads 3 miles.

From figure 1 it will be seen that:

$$\frac{AC}{BC} = \tan \text{ angle } ABC$$

$$\therefore AC = BC \times \tan 75$$

$$AC = 3 \times 3.732$$

$$= \underline{11.19 \text{ miles}}$$

Using the calculator to solve the problem the following steps are necessary:

| Quantity | Entry | Reading |
|---|---|---|
| Clear calculator | C | 0 |
| Enter Relative Bearing (RB) | 75 | 75 |
| | tan | 3.732 |
| | × | 3.732 |
| Distance Run | 3 | 3 |
| Answer | = | 11.19 |

Distance off = 11.19 miles

Remember that the distance run must be the distance over the ground and the log reading must therefore be adjusted for tidal set and leeway angle (read on for the method of calculating this).

In many cases, the navigator will wish to know his or her distance off before reaching the abeam position if, for example, there are outlying dangers as in the following example (fig. 3).

The vessel is somewhere in vicinity of A on a course of 080° T and wishes to know if this will clear outlying danger.

At A, first compass bearing is 050° T.

∴ first RB = 30°

Second compass bearing after 3 miles run is 035° T.

∴ second RB = 45°

Now consider the solution to obtain both a "fix" and a probable distance off using trigonometrical functions. (This working will be used to derive a formula which will considerably simplify later calculations.)

In figure 4, the triangle ABD is completed by drawing BD at right angles to AX.

To find XC it is first necessary to evaluate DB and then BX

(1) To find DB referring again to figure 1 it will be seen that:

$$\sin 30° = \frac{DB}{AB} = \frac{DB}{3}$$

Since sin 30° = ½, DB= 1.5 m

(2) To find XB angle DXB is first required. This is (45-30) = 15°

$$\sin 15° = \frac{DB}{XB} = 0.258$$

$$\therefore XB = \frac{DB}{0.258} = \frac{1.5}{0.258} = 5.8 \text{ m.}$$

(3) To find XC

$$\sin 45° = \frac{XC}{5.8}$$

$$\therefore XC = \sin 45° \times 5.8 = 4.1 \text{ m.}$$

**Figure 3**

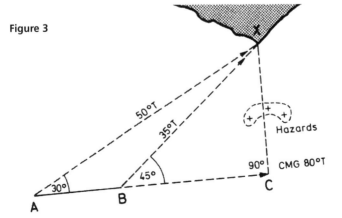

**Figure 4**

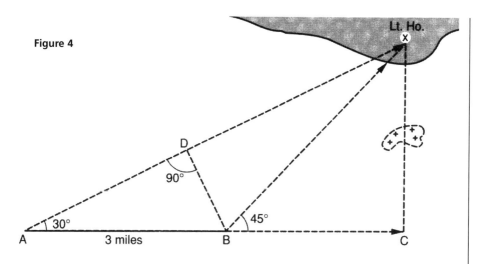

Referring to figure 4, the position at B can be established by describing a circle of radius 5.8 miles with center at X and then drawing XB, the True bearing (not the relative bearing) and the point of intersection is the fix. Similarly with XC, giving the probable position when abeam.

Consider now the key sequences necessary on the calculator, first using the somewhat lengthy calculation shown earlier.

| Quantity | Entry | Reading |
|---|---|---|
| Clear calculator | C | 0 |
| Enter first RB | 30° | 30° |
|  | sin | 0.5 |
|  | × | 0.5 |
| Enter Distance Run | 3 | 3 |
|  | = | 1.5 |
| Store – Memory 1 | M1+ | 1.5 |
| Clear display | C | 0 |
| Enter angle DXB | 15° | 15° |
|  | sin | 0.2588 |
| Store – Memory 2 | M2+ | 0.2588 |
| Clear display | C | 0 |
| Recall Memory 1 | MR1 | 1.5 |
|  | ÷ | 1.5 |
| Recall Memory 2 | MR2 | 0.2588 |
| Answer | = | 5.8 |

Distance off first bearing = 5.8 miles

The key sequences for distance off when abeam will be:

| Quantity | Entry | Reading |
|---|---|---|
| Clear calculator | C | 0 |
| Enter second RB | 45° | 45° |
|  | sin | 0.7071 |
|  | × | 0.7071 |

Enter distance off
at second RB     5.8         5.8
                =         4.1

Distance off when abeam = 4 miles

These somewhat lengthy calculations can be reduced to the following two formulas:

**Formula for Distance Off at 2nd Bearing**

$D2$ = Distance off at 2nd Bearing.

$R$ = Distance between 1st and 2nd Bearings.

$RB1$ = First Relative Bearing

$RB2$ = Second Relative Bearing

$$D2 = \frac{R \sin RB1}{\sin (RB2 - RB1)}$$

In the case above the calculations will therefore be:

$$\frac{3 \sin 30°}{\sin (45-30)} = \frac{3 \times 0.5}{0.258}$$

$$= 5.8 \text{ miles}$$

**Formula for Distance Off when Abeam**

$D2$ = Distance off at Second Bearing

$RB2$ = 2nd Relative Bearing

$DA$ = Distance off when abeam

$DA$ = $D2 \sin RB2$

     = $5.8 \times \sin 45°$

     = 4.1 miles.

These formulas reduce the work to a short key sequence requiring no plotting until you wish to plot your position.

**Advanced Nav.**

**Figure 5**

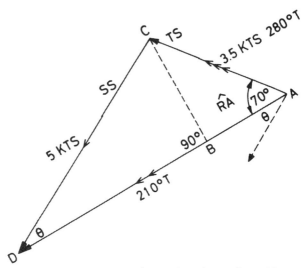

## Tide Correction Angle and Speed Made Good (fig. 5)

As in the previous techniques, a formula can be derived for calculating the tidal correction angle. Omitting the step-by-step calculation, this formula is:

$$\text{Sin } \theta = \frac{\text{TS} \times \text{sin RA}}{\text{SS}}$$

where $\theta$ = Tidal Correction Angle

TS = Tide Speed

RA = Relative angle between tide and course to be made good

SS = Ship's Speed

**Example:**

Current 3.5 kts. 280° T
Ship's speed 5 kts.
Course to be made good 210° T
∴ RA = 70°

$$\text{CB} = \text{CA} \times \text{sin } 70°$$

$$\therefore \text{ sin } \theta = \frac{\text{CA} \times \text{sin } 70°}{\text{CD}}$$

$$= \frac{3.5 \text{ sin } 70°}{5} = \frac{3.5 \times 0.94}{5} =$$

0.658

$$\theta = 41°$$

NOTE: To convert 0.658, use invert and sine keys. Method may vary with different types of calculators.

Speed made good = AD

= CD cos $\theta$ + AC cos 70°

in standard terms

= (Ship's speed × cos $\theta$) + (Tide speed × cos RA)

= (5 × 0.754) + (3.5 × 0.342)

= 4.97 kts.

When R̂A is greater than 90°, the complementary angle is used (e.g., ^RA = 150°, complementary angle = 180 – 150 = 30°) in both correction angle and speed calculations. The latter formula becomes SS cos $\theta$ – TS cos R̂A where R̂A is the complementary angle.

## HORIZONTAL ANGLE FIX

A quick method of calculating the radius of the circle required in the horizontal angle fix omitting the step by step calculation is:

$$\text{Radius} = \frac{\frac{1}{2}\text{AB}}{\text{SIN } \theta}$$

Where AB is the horizontal distance between the two points and $\theta$ is the angle subtended at the vessel.

In figure 6, if the distance AB = 7 miles and angle $\theta$ is 55°

$$\text{Radius} = \frac{\text{AB}}{2 \text{ SIN } \theta} = \frac{7}{2 \times .819} = 4.27 \text{ m}$$

A position line cutting the circle will give a fix.

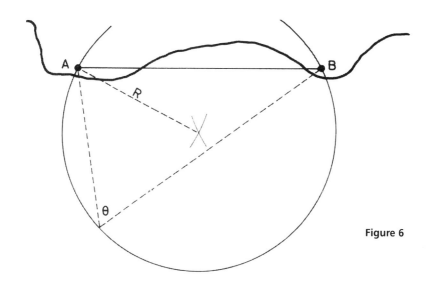

**Figure 6**

## FINDING DR POSITION, COURSE, AND DISTANCE

These formulas produce the same results as old-fashioned traverse tables. The examples may look somewhat lengthy but, with practice, the calculation can be done very quickly and accurately.

### Example A — To find vessel's D. R. position

A vessel in Lat. 17°20′N, Long. 38°41′W steers 320° (N40°W) for 54 miles. What position has she arrived at?

To find D. Lat.               D. Lat. = Distance x cos Co.

| Quantity | | Entry | Reading |
|---|---|---|---|
| Course | → | 40 | 40 |
| | | cos | 0.76604 |
| | | STO 1 | 0.76604 |
| Dist. | → | 54 | 54 |
| | | x | 54 |
| | | RCL 1 | 0.76604 |
| D. Lat. | ← | = | 41.4 |

To find Dep.               Dep = Distance x sin Co.
(intermediate value)

| Quantity | | Entry | Reading |
|---|---|---|---|
| Course | → | 40 | 40 |
| | | sin | 0.64279 |
| | | STO 1 | 0.64279 |
| Dist. | → | 54 | 54 |
| | | x | 54 |
| | | RCL 1 | 0.64279 |
| Dep. | ← | = | 37.7 |

To find D. Long.               D. Long. = $\dfrac{\text{Dep.}}{\text{cos Mean Lat.}}$

Mean Lat. = Initial Lat. + ½ D. Lat. = 17°20′N + 20′.7 - 17°40′.7N (Note: A mental approximation for Mean Lat. will do.)

| Quantity | | Entry | Reading |
|---|---|---|---|
| Mean Lat. | → | 17.68 | 17.68 |
| | | cos | 0.95277 |
| | | STO 1 | 0.95277 |
| Dep. | → | 34.7 | 34.7 |
| | | ÷ | 34.7 |
| | | RCL 1 | 0.95277 |
| D. Long. | ← | = | 36.4 |

| Lat. from | 17°20'N. | | Long. from | 38°41'W. |
|---|---|---|---|---|
| D. Lat. | 4 1'.4N | | D. Long. | 36'.4W |
| **D.R. Position** | **18°01'.4N** | | | **39°17'.4W** |

### Example B — To find the course and distance

What is the true course and distance to steer from Lat. 49°57'N, Long. 6°00'W to Lat. 43°04'N, Long. 9°38'W?

| Lat. from | 49°57'N | | Long. from | 6°00'W |
|---|---|---|---|---|
| Lat. to | 43°04'N | | Long to. | 9°38'W |
| D. Lat. | 6°53'S = 413'S | | D. Long. | 3°38'W = 218'W |

Mean Lat. = 43°04' + 3°26'.5 = 46°30'.5N (Note: A mental approximation for Mean Lat. will do.)

To find Dep.  Departure = D. Long. x cos. mean Lat.

| Quantity | | Entry | Reading |
|---|---|---|---|
| Mean Lat. | → | 46.5 | 46.5 |
| | | cos | 0.68835 |
| | | STO 1 | 0.68835 |
| D. Long. | → | 218 | 218 |
| | | x | 218 |
| | | RCL 1 | 0.68835 |
| Dep | ← | = | 150 |

To find the Course.  tan Co. = $\dfrac{\text{Dep.}}{\text{D. Lat.}}$

| Quantity | | Entry | Reading |
|---|---|---|---|
| Dep | → | 150 | 150 |
| | | ÷ | 150 |
| D. Lat. | → | 413 | 413 |
| | | = | 0.3632 |
| | | arc | 0.3632 |
| Course | ← | tan | 20 |

Therefore, the course is S.20°W.

To find the distance:  Distance = $\dfrac{\text{D. Lat.}}{\text{cos Co.}}$

| Quantity | | Entry | Reading |
|---|---|---|---|
| Course | → | 20 | 20 |
| | | cos | 0.93969 |
| | | STO 1 | 0.93969 |
| D. Lat. | → | 413 | 413 |
| | | ÷ | 413 |
| | | RCL 1 | 0.93969 |
| Distance | ← | = | 439.5 |

So, the course is S.20°W and the distance 439.5 miles.

Note: These formulas assume that the earth is flat, which is why this routine is often referred to as "plane sailing." This assumption is reasonable for distances up to 500 or 600 miles; therefore, do not use for greater distances.

## MIDDLE-LATITUDE SAILING

For distances greater than 500 to 600 miles, the same procedures as in the previous section can be followed, except that a correction has to be applied to the mean latitude.

This corrected MEAN latitude is called the MIDDLE latitude.

### Correction in minutes to apply to MEAN LAT. to obtain MIDDLE LAT.

| MEAN LAT. | DIFFERENCE OF LATITUDE | | | | | | | | | | | | | | | | MEAN LAT. |
|---|---|---|---|---|---|---|---|---|---|---|---|---|---|---|---|---|---|
| ° | 2° | 4° | 6° | 8° | 10° | 11° | 12° | 13° | 14° | 15° | 16° | 17° | 18° | 19° | 20° | 21° | ° |
| 11 | -129 | -125 | -118 | -110 | -100 | -93 | -87 | -80 | -72 | -64 | -57 | -48 | -38 | -29 | -18 | -8 | 11 |
| 12 | -114 | -111 | -105 | -98 | -89 | -83 | -77 | -71 | -64 | -57 | -49 | -42 | -33 | -23 | -15 | -5 | 12 |
| 13 | -102 | -100 | -95 | -88 | -79 | -75 | -69 | -63 | -57 | -51 | -43 | -36 | -27 | -20 | -12 | -3 | 13 |
| 14 | -93 | -90 | -86 | -80 | -72 | -67 | -62 | -57 | -51 | -45 | -38 | -31 | -24 | -16 | -9 | 0 | 14 |
| 15 | -85 | -83 | -79 | -73 | -65 | -61 | -56 | -51 | -46 | -40 | -34 | -27 | -21 | -13 | -6 | +1 | 15 |
| 16 | -79 | -76 | -72 | -66 | -60 | -56 | -51 | -46 | -41 | -36 | -30 | -24 | -17 | -10 | -4 | +4 | 16 |
| 17 | -72 | -70 | -66 | -61 | -55 | -51 | -47 | -42 | -37 | -32 | -27 | -21 | -15 | -8 | -2 | +6 | 17 |
| 18 | -67 | -65 | -61 | -56 | -50 | -46 | -43 | -38 | -34 | -29 | -24 | -18 | -12 | -6 | +1 | +8 | 18 |
| 19 | -62 | -60 | -57 | -52 | -46 | -43 | -39 | -35 | -30 | -25 | -21 | -15 | -9 | -3 | +3 | +10 | 19 |
| 20 | -58 | -56 | -53 | -48 | -42 | -39 | -35 | -31 | -27 | -22 | -18 | -13 | -7 | -1 | +5 | +13 | 20 |
| 22 | -50 | -48 | -45 | -41 | -36 | -33 | -29 | -25 | -22 | -17 | -13 | -8 | -3 | +3 | +9 | +15 | 22 |
| 24 | -44 | -42 | -40 | -36 | -31 | -28 | -24 | -21 | -17 | -13 | -8 | -4 | +1 | +6 | +12 | +17 | 24 |
| 26 | -39 | -37 | -35 | -31 | -26 | -23 | -20 | -16 | -13 | -9 | -5 | 0 | +5 | +10 | +15 | +21 | 26 |
| 28 | -34 | -32 | -30 | -26 | -22 | -19 | -16 | -12 | -9 | -5 | -1 | +3 | +8 | +13 | +18 | +23 | 28 |
| 30 | -30 | -29 | -26 | -22 | -18 | -15 | -12 | -9 | -6 | -2 | +2 | +6 | +11 | +16 | +21 | +26 | 30 |
| 35 | -22 | -21 | -18 | -15 | -10 | -7 | -5 | -1 | +2 | +6 | +10 | +14 | +18 | +23 | +28 | +33 | 35 |
| 40 | -16 | -14 | -12 | -8 | -4 | -1 | +2 | +5 | +8 | +12 | +16 | +20 | +25 | +29 | +34 | +40 | 40 |
| 45 | -11 | -10 | -7 | -3 | +1 | +4 | +7 | +11 | +14 | +18 | +22 | +27 | +31 | +36 | +41 | +47 | 45 |
| 50 | -8 | -6 | -3 | +1 | +6 | +9 | +12 | +16 | +20 | +24 | +28 | +33 | +38 | +44 | +49 | +55 | 50 |
| 55 | -5 | -3 | 0 | +5 | +10 | +14 | +17 | +21 | +25 | +30 | +35 | +40 | +46 | +52 | +58 | 65 | 55 |
| 60 | -3 | -1 | +3 | +8 | +14 | +18 | +22 | +27 | +32 | +37 | +43 | +49 | +55 | +62 | +69 | +77 | 60 |

### Examples:

To find course and distance from 42°03′N 70°04′W to 36°59′N 25°10′W.

| | | |
|---|---|---|
| Departure position | 42°03′N | 70°04′W |
| Destination position | 36°59′N | 25°10′W |

$$\begin{array}{ll} \text{D. Lat.} \quad 5°04′S & \text{D. Long } 44°54′E \\ ″ = 304′ & ″ = 2694′ \end{array}$$

Mean Lat. = 39°31′N
(from table) corr. = - 13′

Middle Lat. 39°18′ = 39.3°

To find Departure
Dep = d.long Cos middle Lat.

| Quantity | | Entry | Reading |
|---|---|---|---|
| Middle Lat. | → | 39.3 | 39.3 |
| | | cos | 0.77384 |
| | | STO 1 | 0.77384 |
| D. Long. | → | 2694 | 2694 |
| | | x | 2694 |
| | | RCL 1 | 0.77384 |
| Departure | ← | = | 2084.73 |

To find the Course.

$$\tan \text{Co.} = \frac{\text{Departure}}{\text{D. Lat.}}$$

| Quantity | | Entry | Reading |
|---|---|---|---|
| Dep | → | 2084.73 | 2084.73 |
| | | ÷ | 2084.73 |
| D. Lat. | → | 304 | 304 |
| | | = | 6.85765 |
| | | arc Tan | 81.7035 |

Course = S 81°42'.17E
To find the Distance.

$$\text{Distance} = \frac{\text{D. Lat.}}{\cos \text{course}}$$

| Quantity | | Entry | Reading |
|---|---|---|---|
| Course | → | 81.7035 | 81.7035 |
| | | cos | 0.14430 |
| | | STO 1 | 0.14430 |
| D. Lat. | → | 304 | 304 |
| | | ÷ | 304 |
| | | RCL 1 | 0.14430 |
| Distance | ← | = | 2106.78 |

Distance = 2106.8

Conversely, suppose the vessel starts from a position 42°03'N 70°04'W and steers S81°42'E for a distance of 2106.8 miles. What would be her D.R.?
To find D. Lat. D. Lat. = distance x cos Co.

| Quantity | | Entry | Reading |
|---|---|---|---|
| Course | → | 81.7 | 81.7 |
| | | cos | 0.14436 |
| | | STO 1 | 0.14436 |
| Distance | → | 2106.8 | 2106.8 |
| | | x | |
| | | RCL 1 | 0.14436 |
| D. Lat. | ← | = | 304.13 |

| Latitude departure | = 42°03'N | Mean Lat. | = 39°31' |
| D. Lat. (304) | = 5°04'S | Corr. | = - 13' |
| Arrival D.R. Lat. | = 36°59'N | Middle Lat. | = 39°18' |

To find Departure Dep. = Dist x Sin Co

| Quantity | | Entry | Reading |
|---|---|---|---|
| Course | → | 81.7 | 81.7 |
| | | sin | 0.98953 |
| | | STO 1 | 0.98953 |
| Distance | → | 2106.8 | 2106.8 |
| | | x | 2106.8 |
| | | RCL 1 | 0.98953 |
| Departure | ← | = | 2084.73 |

To find D. Long

$$\text{D. Long.} = \frac{\text{Dep.}}{\cos \text{mid. lat.}}$$

| Quantity | | Entry | Reading |
|---|---|---|---|
| Mid. Lat. | → | 39.3 | 39.3 |
| | | cos | 0.77384 |
| | | STO 1 | 0.77384 |
| Departure | → | 2084.73 | 2084.73 |
| | | ÷ | 2084.73 |
| | | RCL 1 | 0.77384 |
| D. Long. | ← | = | 2694 |

| Longitude departure | = 70°04'W |
| D. Long. 2694 | = 44°54'E |
| Arrival D.R. Long. | = 25°10'W |

# CELESTIAL NAVIGATION

To find your position without electronic systems when far offshore and off soundings, you need to be able to measure the height (altitude) of the stars, moon, planets, and sun above the horizon; determine the heavenly bodies' locations at the precise time you measure their altitudes; and calculate your distance from the points on earth directly underneath the bodies. (You'll get an explanation below of these steps.)

To measure altitude with sufficient accuracy, you need a decent sextant and practice in its use — including practice at sea on a heaving deck, if possible. You get the locations of the stars, planets, moon, and sun from an almanac. Because you enter the almanac with the precise time of your observations, you need an accurate watch. Finally, to make the necessary calculations, you need either trigonometric tables, a calculator, a computer, or — perish the thought — the ability to solve problems in spherical trigonometry from scratch.

Because *Reed's Publications* recognizes that it's important for you to have the capacity to do celestial navigation when you're offshore, we continue to provide in our *Nautical Almanac* both the tables and the almanac (ephemeris) information you need. Both *Reed's Almanac* and this *Companion* explain the celestial navigation process. (In fact, the clear and elegant explanation of celestial navigation in the *Almanac* has largely been retained as originally written by this publication's founder, Captain O. M. Watts.)

Many calculators and computers carry all or part of the ephemeris in their memories. *Reed's*, nevertheless, still provides this information in print form because these devices can fail you just as electronic navigation systems can. The intent here is not to dissuade you from using calculators and computers. But you should also carry the ephemeris in (indestructible) book form.

In general, *Reed's Almanacs* present data that changes over time; this *Companion* contains information that is unchanging. However, to enable you to accomplish all the calculations in celestial navigation using a single volume, *Reed's* makes an exception to this rule by including the unchanging trigonometric tables in its *Nautical Almanac*, along with an explanation of their use.

If you're a beginner in celestial navigation, don't be deterred by a fear that the concept is complicated, or the calculations need be arduous, or the knowledge you need to identify stars is imposing. Rather, be encouraged that you can readily grasp the concept (starting with your reading of the next section), that the calculations require only simple arithmetic (or the quick and easy use of a calculator or computer), and that you can use star charts or other star-finding aids to avoid memorizing the locations of stars.

With an expenditure of effort (primarily to get comfortable using a sextant) and of relatively little money (most of it for a good sextant), you can join the dwindling ranks of mariners who can find their way across oceans by observing the stars, moon, planets, and sun. Your reward for your effort will be enhanced peace of mind offshore and satisfaction in practicing an ancient art.

## THE CONCEPT

When a heavenly body is directly over your head (at your zenith) you are, of course, at the point on earth directly underneath it — or, more precisely, at the point where a line between the body and the center of the earth intersects the earth's surface. A body at your zenith — your highest point in the sky — is 90° in angular distance from your horizon. That is, its altitude is 90°.

If the body is lower in the sky — altitude less than 90° — then you're some distance away from the point directly under that body — the point called the body's ground position (GP). The higher the body's altitude, the closer you are to its GP; the lower its altitude, the farther away you are. Any altitude measurement you get (other than 90°) places you on a circle of position centered on a GP with a radius related to altitude. Bodies high in the sky yield circles with short radii; those lower yield large circles.

**Advanced Nav.**

Consider the case of the North Star (Polaris), for example. (See fig. 1) The GP of Polaris is approximately at the North Pole. If you measured its altitude as 90°, you'd know you were right underneath it, or at the North Pole. If you observed Polaris on the horizon (zero altitude), you'd be on the equator; that is, on the circle with the largest possible radius, derived from the smallest possible altitude. Note the pattern here: When Polaris's altitude is 90°, your latitude is 90° N; when its altitude is 0°, you're at latitude 0°. With these relationships in mind, you'll need no prompting to conclude that you'd be at latitude 45° N if you measured the altitude of Polaris as 45°.

Because the GP of Polaris is at the North Pole, the circles of position (LOPs) you get from measuring its altitude are parallels of latitude. (See fig. 2.) That's convenient because the LOPs, being latitudes, are easy to plot. But you get latitude only from observing Polaris, or any other body when it's directly north or south of you — like the sun is at noon. To locate yourself in longitude you need at least one more LOP based on observing a body that's not directly north or south of you. That's where all the other stars, the planets, the moon, and the sun (at times other than noon) come in. You

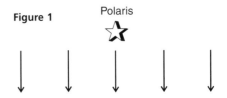

**Figure 1**

Polaris

Rays parallel because Polaris's distance relative to earth's diameter is virtually infinite.

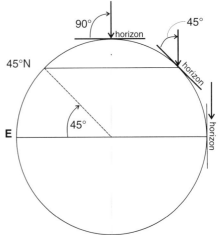

must observe one or more of them when they're somewhat east or west of you. And this is where the matter gets more complicated — but only slightly so.

Heavenly bodies appear to move across the sky as the earth rotates under them. Their GPs on earth follow this movement. Actually, they appear to rotate around Polaris, whose GP stays very close to the North Pole at all times. To get the GP of all these other bodies, you need to consult an almanac. And because the bodies are moving, you must enter the almanac with the time you observed the bodies. (The practice of celestial navigation was limited for centuries to determinations of latitude only because sufficiently accurate time measurements were not available at sea.)

There's another aspect to the complications involved in determining longitude. Because the circles of position derived from bodies east or west of you are not parallels of latitude, you must deal with a plotting prob-

**Figure 2**

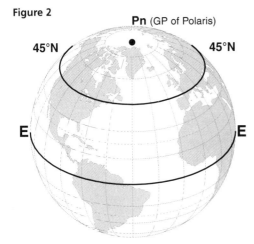

Pn (GP of Polaris)

45°N            45°N

E                    E

**Figure 3**

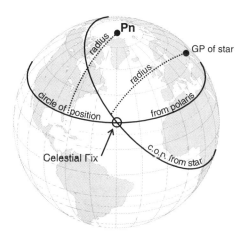

er than you expected, you'd know you were closer to the GP than you assumed. If lower, then you'd be farther away.

If your assumed position (AP) is anywhere near your actual position, then the distance between them can easily be plotted on a chart. So, you pick an AP near where your DR track puts you, calculate its direction and distance to the star's GP and the altitude corresponding to this calculated distance, and then observe the altitude to determine how far you are from the AP. You plot the AP on your chart and draw the LOP some distance from the AP — usually a few miles — either toward or away from the GP. (See fig. 4). You go through all of this to obviate the drawing of arcs with radii many hundreds of miles long.

lem. That problem is evident in the case of a body located, say, northeast of you at an altitude of 45°. (See fig. 3.) In this case, the distance between you and the body's GP would be 2,700 miles (45 x 60 miles in a degree). That is, the radius of the circle of position centered on the GP would be 2,700 miles. If you tried to plot this LOP directly on a chart, swinging an arc in your direction 2,700 miles from the GP, the chart's scale would have to be so small as to make your curved pencil line many miles wide. And, you'd have to use a chart projection that didn't distort the long radius. These plotting considerations are absent in the case of circles that are latitudes because of the way Mercator projections are constructed and marked.

To get around this plotting problem, you employ an ingenious technique cooked up by a Frenchman many generations ago, for which you should be unqualifiedly grateful, were it not for the fact that it gets you into the trigonometry part of the process. (Don't be dismayed; it just involves one more easily understood step.)

You set up a little experiment, making an assumption about where you are, and then testing that assumption. If you assumed you were 2,700 miles from a star's GP, for example, you'd know that its altitude should be 45°. If, when you measured its altitude, you found that it's not 45°, then you'd know that your assumption was wrong. If the observed altitude were high-

Trigonometry enters the process at the point that you calculate the distance and direction of your AP to the GP. That distance and angle are part of the so-called navigational triangle. The points and angles of this triangle are expressed in a composite of corresponding celestial and terrestrial terms. All heavenly bodies are assumed to be on a celestial sphere centered at the earth's center — a reasonable assumption because distances to all of them, though differing, can be considered as infinite. All angular measurements on the celestial sphere correspond to those on the earth's surface because the spheres share the same center. The names of these angles, however, are different. Latitude on the earth's surface is called declination on the celestial sphere. Longitude corresponds to hour angle which, unlike longitude, is measured only west from the Greenwich celestial meridian through 360°.

In figure 5 on page 215, the points of the navigational triangle are your assumed position (AP), the ground position of the body (GP), and the nearest pole (Pn). You locate the GP by finding its declination and hour angle from the almanac. (One side of the triangle, then, is Pn - GP, or 90° minus declination.) You know the latitude and longitude of your AP. So, you know another side of the triangle, Pn - AP (90° minus latitude). The angle between these sides is formed by the relationship between your AP's longitude and the body's hour angle.

213

This is called the local hour angle.

Surely you remember from your schooling in math that you can find the third side of a triangle and the angles it forms when you know two sides and their included angle. Well, now's the time to dust off and put that knowledge to good use. By plugging into a table, calculator, or computer the two known sides of the navigational triangle and the angle at Pn, you can get the side AP-GP, which is the distance you want to calculate, and the angle at your AP, which is the direction to the GP.

## The Celestial LOP

The length of the AP-GP side of the triangle (i.e., how far you are from the body's GP) is a function of the body's altitude, as stated earlier. More precisely, the side AP-GP is equal to 90° minus the altitude. This is called the zenith distance because it describes an arc on the celestial sphere between your zenith and the body. To plot an LOP, you compare the zenith distance you calculate from solving the triangle with the zenith distance you get from actually observing the body's altitude. This comparison tells you how many miles nearer to or farther from the body you are than you assumed (one minute of arc equals one nautical mile).

For example, if you calculate the zenith distance to be 40° and 5 minutes and observe it to be 40° and 10 minutes, you know that you're five miles farther from the GP than you assumed. You'd plot the results of this comparison as shown in figure 4. Because the radius of the circle of position is large, you can draw the small section at your position as a straight line at a right angle to the GP's direction.

That's all there is to getting a celestial LOP.

**Figure 4**

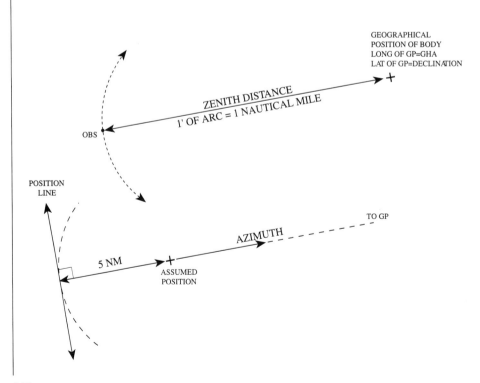

POSITION OF BODY
LONG OF GP=GHA
LAT OF GP=DECLINATION

ZENITH DISTANCE
1' OF ARC = 1 NAUTICAL MILE

OBS

POSITION LINE

TO GP

AZIMUTH

5 NM

ASSUMED POSITION

**Figure 5**

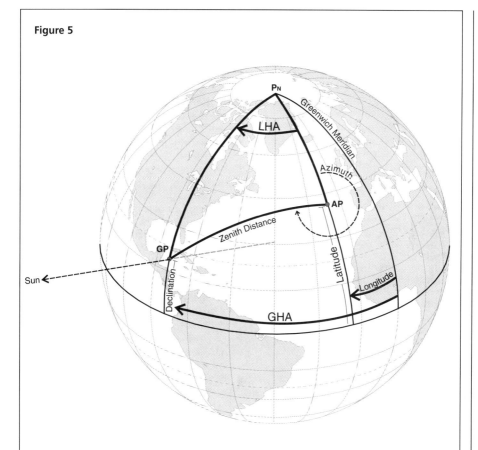

## The Celestial Triangle Illustrated

The navigator is on a passage from Bermuda to Europe. His sun sight gives him his zenith distance in angular form (often labeled **Ho**) from the **G**eographical **P**osition of the sun, which he can determine exactly by taking the exact time and date of his sight to the ephemeris (also known as the Nautical Almanac) and looking up the sun's **Dec**lination and **G**reenwich **H**our **A**ngle.

To make use of this information, the navigator then solves the celestial triangle with any of several means of sight reduction. He estimates an **A**ssumed **P**osition close to his real position so that he can derive two sides and one angle of the triangle. 90°– assumed latitude = one side. 90°– **Dec**. sun = second side. GHA sun – assumed longitude = the angle **LHA**. Sight reduction yields Hc (90° – the Zenith Distance ), which is compared to Ho (90° – measured Zenith Distance). The resulting intercept is plotted using the AP and the Azimuth of the sun (also derived from the sight reduction). The final result is a line of position (see fig. 4).

Note that from the sun's GP we can deduce that the season is either late spring or early summer and that this sight was taken in the late afternoon.

Advanced Nav.

## TIME

As stated earlier, the determination of all celestial LOPs, other than latitudes, depends on time. The earth's rotation makes all bodies appear to move. (Even Polaris moves a little.) If you watched them from the equator, their movement would translate into a rate of 900 miles per hour, 15 miles per minute, 1/4-mile per second. Although the distance covered in these time intervals lessens with increases in latitude, you can still see from these figures that small errors in timekeeping can cause substantial errors.

Happily, watches have gotten a lot better lately with the introduction of quartz technology, and costs of accurate watches have declined. Further, you can measure time accurately using a watch with an error — even a large error — if you know what the error is. And, you can know your watch's error more easily if its rate of error is constant; that is, if its gain or loss is consistent over time. Finally, you can get supremely accurate radio time signals on broadcasts available worldwide on frequencies of 2.5, 5, 10, 15, and 20 megahertz.

After reading the next several pararaphs, you'll be tempted, when asked the simple question, "What time is it?", to respond, "Compared to what?" The reason for being circumspect in your answer is that several different points of reference are used when expressing time. Time related to the Greenwich meridian is Greenwich time; time related to the central meridian of your time zone is zone time; and time related to the meridian at your location is local time.

To complicate things further, the sun, which serves as a focal point in timekeeping, is not consistent in its apparent movement. You can blame the inconsistency on factors related to the earth's orbit and rotation. Time based on the sun you actually see is called apparent time. To overcome the irregularities of apparent time, the time mavens have created a fictitious sun that moves with perfect regularity at the average rate of the real sun. The time based on this average movement is called mean time.

In celestial navigation, you use a mix of these kinds of time for differing purposes. You enter the almanacs with Greenwich Mean Time, for example, converting from your zone time by adding or subtracting a number of hours that varies with the difference in longitude between your zone and the Greenwich zone. For another example, when you observe the sun at noon to find your latitude, you do so at local apparent noon, the time the real sun crosses your meridian. To calculate this time in advance of the meridian crossing, you must convert from (mean) zone time. You do this by taking into account the difference in longitude between your meridian and your zone's central meridian, and also the difference on that day between mean and apparent time — a difference that's called the equation of time.

The essential relationship between time and longitude is nowhere more evident than in the almanac's arc-to-time conversion table (included on page 236). This table is based on the mean sun's movement across meridians at a rate of 360° per day, or 15° per hour. You use the table to convert back and forth between time and longitude. In it you find, without doing the arithmetic, that an arc of, say, 25° is equivalent to one hour and 40 minutes.

# WORLD MAP OF TIME ZONES

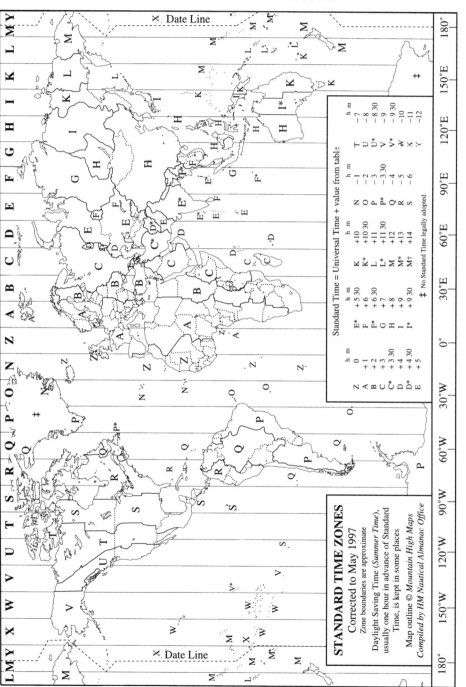

**STANDARD TIME ZONES**
Corrected to May 1997
Zone boundaries are approximate
Daylight Saving Time (*Summer Time*),
usually one hour in advance of Standard
Time, is kept in some places
Map outline © *Mountain High Maps*
*Compiled by HM Nautical Almanac Office*

Standard Time = Universal Time + value from table

| | h m | | h m |
|---|---|---|---|
| Z | 0 | E* | + 5 30 |
| A | + 1 | F | + 6 |
| B | + 2 | F* | + 6 30 |
| C | + 3 | G | + 7 |
| C* | + 3 30 | H | + 8 |
| D | + 4 | I | + 9 |
| D* | + 4 30 | I* | + 9 30 |
| E | + 5 | | |

| | h m | | h m |
|---|---|---|---|
| K | +10 | N | − 1 |
| K* | +10 30 | O | − 2 |
| L | +11 | P | − 3 |
| L* | +11 30 | P* | − 3 30 |
| M | +12 | Q | − 4 |
| M* | +13 | R | − 5 |
| M† | +14 | S | − 6 |

| | h m |
|---|---|
| T | − 7 |
| U | − 8 |
| U* | − 8 30 |
| V | − 9 |
| V* | − 9 30 |
| W | −10 |
| X | −11 |
| Y | −12 |

† No Standard Time legally adopted

‡ No Standard Time legally adopted

217

## GLOSSARY OF TERMS

The celestial sphere illustrated on the facing page has no defined outline in reality. For practical purposes, though, you can assume that it's a hollow sphere, of very large radius, with the earth at its center and all heavenly bodies located on its surface.

Because the earth's radius is relatively small, the observer's eye can be assumed to be at the center of the earth. Positions on the earth's surface, as well as parallels of latitude and meridians of longitude, can be projected from the center outward onto the celestial sphere.

**Altitude.** The angular height of an object above the visible horizon, measured on a vertical circle perpendicular to the horizon by a sextant.

**Amplitude.** The bearing of a heavenly body when rising or setting, measured from the east or west points of the observer's horizon.

**Apogee.** The position in the orbit of the Moon which is farthest from Earth. Opposite to perigee.

**Aphelion.** The farthest point in the orbit of Earth or another planet from the Sun, opposite to Perihelion.

**Apparent Time.** Time measured by the apparent Sun.

**Apparent Sun.** The actual visible Sun on which you can take observations.

**An Apparent Solar Day.** The interval between two consecutive transits of the apparent Sun over an observer's meridian.

**Apparent Noon.** The time when the apparent Sun is on the meridian of a place.

**Apparent Time.** Apparent solar time at any place is the measurement of the apparent Sun's angular distance from the antimeridian of that place.

**Arc.** A part of the circumference of any circle.

**Aries.** One of the constellations of the zodiac (see First Point of Aries).

**Ascension (Right).** See Right Ascension.

**Astronomical Day.** Composed of 24 mean solar hours, it begins at midnight on the civil day. It is reckoned from 0h. to 24h.

**Autumnal Equinox.** The time of the year when the Sun crosses the equator moving from north to south declinations.

**Azimuth.** The bearing of a heavenly body measured from the north or south points of the horizon.

**Azimuth Tables.** Tables that present the true bearing of a heavenly body for any latitude and time.

**Calendar Month.** The ordinary month in general use having 30, 31, or 28 (and in a leap year 29) days.

**Celestial Poles.** The North and South Poles of the earth projected from the earth's center onto the celestial sphere.

**Circumpolar Stars.** Stars that never set below the horizon at the place of observation.

**Civil Time** is composed of 24 mean solar hours divided into two equal portions. The first is marked "A.M.," from midnight to noon; the second is marked "P.M.", from noon to midnight. The civil year is 365 days (or 366 in a leap year).

**Conjunction.** Two celestial bodies in the same direction from Earth are in conjunction.

**Constellations.** The grouping of stars for identification purposes. The ancients gave these groups the names of fish, birds, or figures that they were thought to resemble.

**Culmination.** The time a heavenly body reaches its highest altitude. It culminates when it crosses the observer's meridian.

**Cycle.** The period of time between some celestial phenomenon and its repetition.

**Day.** See Apparent Time, Mean Day, and Sidereal Day.

**Declination.** The declination (dec.) of a body is its angular distance north or south of the celestial equator. Declination on the celestial sphere corresponds to latitude on Earth.

**Eclipse.** The period when one celestial body passes through the shadow of another.

**The Ecliptic.** The great circle on the celestial sphere on which the sun appears to move during its annual migration. Its plane is inclined 23° 27' to the plane of the celestial equator, an angle called the obliquity of the ecliptic.

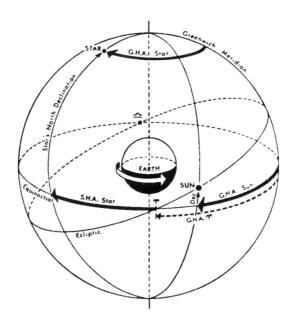

**Elevated Pole.** The celestial pole that is above the observer's horizon.

**Ephemeris (Ephemerides).** The special calendar showing the predicted timetable of the moving celestial bodies.

**Ephemeris Time (ET).** A conception of time for presentation of ephemerides of the Sun, moon, and planets.

**Equation of Time (Eq.T.).** The excess of mean solar time over apparent solar time. When apparent time is greater than mean time, the equation of time is a negative quantity and is prefixed with a minus sign.

**Equinoctial (or Celestial Equator).** The equinoctial is a great circle dividing the celestial sphere into two equal parts. It is in the same plane as Earth's equator.

**Equinox.** See Autumnal Equinox, also Vernal Equinox.

**First Point of Libra.** The autumnal equinoctial point, where the Sun's center crosses the equinoctial as it moves along the ecliptic and changes its declination from north to south each year. It is opposite to the First Point of Aries.

**First Point of Aries.** The point where the Sun's center crosses the celestial equator (equinoctial) when moving along the ecliptic and changing from south to north decli-

nation at the time of the vernal (or spring) equinox. See also Transit of Aries.

**Full Moon.** The Moon at the point that it's in "opposition" to the Sun, or on the Sun's antimeridian; that is, when it's on the meridian about midnight — 12 hours different from the Sun.

**Geographical Position.** The point on Earth's surface directly underneath a heavenly body. This point is defined by its declination (latitude) and its GHA (longitude).

**GHA** The coordinate in the heavens (measured 0° to 360° westward from the prime meridian) corresponding to longitude of the geographical position of the body.

**Gibbous Moon.** The phases of the Moon when the Moon's disc is more than half illuminated; that is, between first quarter and full moon and also between full moon and last quarter.

**Greenwich Mean Time (GMT).** The time at Greenwich by the mean sun and the standard to which all observations can be referred.

**Greenwich Hour Angle.** The angle at the Pole between the meridian at Greenwich and the meridian or hour circle through the body, measured westward from 0° to 360°.

**Greenwich Sidereal Time (GST).** The same as GHA Aries.

**Harvest Moon.** The full moon nearest the autumnal equinox.

**Hemisphere.** Half of a sphere. A plane (equator) passing through the center of a sphere (the earth) divides it into two equal parts — the northern and southern hemispheres.

**Horizontal Parallax (HP).** The difference in the angular measurement of the altitude of a body when viewed from the horizon and from Earth's center.

**Hour Angle.** The angle at the Pole between a reference meridian and the meridian through a body. Although it is an angular measurement, it often expresses time and so is called the hour angle.

**Hunter's Moon.** The full moon nearest October 21, not so pronounced as the harvest moon.

**Inferior Planet.** A planet whose orbit round the Sun is between Earth and the Sun. Only Mercury and Venus are inferior planets.

**Latitude (Terrestrial).** The angular distance of a place on Earth's surface north or south of the equator.

**Latitude (Celestial).** The angular distance of a celestial body north or south of the ecliptic.

**Leap Year.** The year consists of 365 1/4 days, but because the civil year consists of 365 days, the extra one-quarter day is added at the end of the fourth year (the leap year) as an extra day in February.

**Limb.** The edge (upper or lower) of the Sun or Moon's disc.

**Line, The.** The mariner's name for the equator. When a vessel moves from south to north latitude, or vice versa, she is said to "cross the line."

**Local Hour Angle (LHA).** The difference between the longitude of the geographical position of the body and the longitude of the observer. It's measured westward (0° to 360°) from the observer's meridian.

**Local Mean Time (LMT).** The mean time at any place on Earth's surface.

**Local Sidereal Time.** The LHA of the First Point of Aries at any instant reckoned (0-24 hours) westward from the meridian of a

place. It is also the angular distance of the meridian eastward from the First Point of Aries or the right ascension of the meridian (RAM).

**Longitude.** The angular distance between the Greenwich Meridian and the meridian passing through any place and measured east or west of Greenwich from 0° to 180°.

**Longitude of Time.** The difference between SMT and GMT. The difference of longitude between two places is the difference between the local mean times of the places.

**Lunar Distance.** The angular distance of the Moon from other heavenly bodies.

**Lunar.** Of the moon. (A lunar day is the time between two successive transits of the Moon over the same meridian.)

**Magnitude.** Relative brightness of a star or planet.

**Mean Time.** Time based on the mean solar day, which is the average of all the apparent solar days throughout many years. This mean sun is an imaginary celestial body that moves with a uniform speed equal to the average speed of the true Sun.

**Meridian.** An imaginary great circle extending between the North and South Poles.

**Meridian Altitude.** The altitude of a heavenly body when it's on the meridian.

**Meridian, Prime.** The meridian of Greenwich, England — longitude 0°.

**Moon's Age.** The number of days that have passed since the previous new moon.

**Nadir.** The point opposite the zenith; that is, the point of the heavens directly below the observer.

**New Moon.** The Moon is new when the Sun and Moon are on the same celestial longitude; that is, in conjunction. The term Is often incorrectly applied to the time when the Moon is first visible as a crescent in the west after sunset.

**Noon (Apparent).** The time when the center of the actual Sun is on the observer's meridian.

**Obliquity of the Ecliptic.** See Ecliptic.

**Occultation.** The point at which one heavenly body eclipses another.

**Opposition.** The point at which a heavenly body is 180° of longitude from another.

**Orbit.** The elliptical path of one heavenly body around another body.

**Parallax.** The apparent movement of an object when viewed from two different positions.

**Perigee.** The position in the Moon's orbit nearest Earth, opposite to apogee.

**Perihelion.** The point in the orbit of Earth or another planet when it is nearest to the Sun; opposite to aphelion.

**Phase.** The particular aspects of a heavenly body, as in phases of the Moon.

**Polar Distance.** The angular distance of a heavenly body from the nearer celestial pole.

**Prime Meridian.** See Meridian, Prime.

**Prime Vertical.** Vertical circle on the celestial sphere passing through east and west points of the horizon. A heavenly body is on the "prime vertical" when it bears east or west.

**Quadrature.** The point where the positions of the heavenly bodies differ by 90° of longitude. At first quarter and last quarter, the moon is in quadrature.

**Quarter, First and Last.** The phases of the Moon when the body is half illuminated; that is, when the Sun and Moon are 90° apart.

**Right Ascension (RA).** The angular distance eastward from the First Point of Aries to the point where the great circle through the Pole and the body cuts the equator. The number is always expressed in hours 0h. - 24h.

**Rising.** The ascent of a heavenly body above the horizon of the observer.

**Seasons.** The variation in climate and in the length of day and night due to the inclining of Earth's axis to the plane of its orbit.

**Semi-Diameter (SD).** Half the angular diameter of a heavenly body. The SD of the Sun and the Moon is roughly 16 minutes.

**Sidereal.** In relation to the stars.

**Sidereal Day.** The interval between two successive transits of the First Point of Aries over an observer's meridian. (See First Point of Aries.) Sidereal time is used by astronomers.

**Sidereal Hour Angle.** The angle at the Pole measured (from 0° to 360°) from the

meridian of Aries to the meridian of a star in a westerly direction.

**Signs of the Zodiac.** The twelve constellations through which the ecliptic runs. (See page 225).

**Signs of the planets.**

| | | |
|---|---|---|
| A The Sun | ⊕ The Earth. | L Saturn. |
| 2 The Moon. | F Mars. | N Uranus. |
| B Mercury. | K Jupiter. | + Nepturn. |
| C Venice. | | |

**Solstices.** The points at which the Sun is farthest from the celestial equator (i.e., declination 23.5° north or south).

**Superior Planets.** Planets whose orbits are outside that of Earth; that is, all planets except Mercury and Venus.

**Time.** See Apparent, Mean, Sidereal.

**Transit.** The passage of a heavenly body across an observer's meridian.

**Twilight.** The periods of the day when the Sun is slightly below the horizon. The observer doesn't experience complete darkness, which occurs when the Sun's center is 18° below the horizon. Civil twilight begins or ends when the sun is 6° below the horizon, at which time the sea horizon is clear and the brightest stars are visible — the most favorable time for stellar observations.

**Universal Time (UT).** Another name for Greenwich mean time.

**Vernal Equinox.** Also called the spring equinox, the point at which the Sun crosses the equinoctial from south to north (about March 21).

**Waxing** and **waning.** The Moon is waxing between new moon and full moon when its light increases and waning when its light decreases between full moon and new moon.

**Zenith.** The point on the celestial sphere directly above an observer; the opposite of nadir.

**Zenith Distance.** The angular distance of a body from an observer's zenith.

**Zodiac.** An imaginary belt of sky along the ecliptic, in which the Sun, Moon, and larger planets perform their revolutions. (See page 225)

**Advanced Nav.**

## THE FIXED STARS

Stars are called "fixed" because their position in relation to one another changes very little over long periods of time. All stars appear to move across the sky from east to west and cross your meridian about four minutes earlier each day. They don't move about the heavens at random as the Moon and the planets appear to do. The stars are at an immense distance from Earth and shine with their own light, unlike the Moon and planets, which shine with the reflected light of the Sun. The heavens abound in stars, but relatively few of them are bright stars that you can use for navigational purposes.

### Stellar Magnitudes

The magnitude of a star is a measure of its relative brilliance: A magnitude 1 star projects 100 times as much light as a magnitude 6 star; a magnitude 2 star is 100 times brighter than a magnitude 7 star, and so on. It follows, therefore, that a magnitude 0 star is 100 times brighter than a magnitude 5 star, and a star that is 100 times brighter than a star of magnitude 4 must have a magnitude of -1. Sirius, the brightest star in the heavens, has a magnitude of -1.6. Stars with magnitudes less than 1.0 are first magnitude stars (there are only 12). A sixth magnitude star is barely visible to the naked eye. The planets Venus and Jupiter have variable minus magnitudes of approximately -3.5 and -2.0, respectively. The Sun and the full moon have magnitudes of -26.7 and -12.5, respectively.

### Constellations

From ancient times, stars have been placed into groups called constellations and named according to their constellation. The brightest star in a constellation was prefixed with the Greek letter α (alpha), the second brightest star was prefixed ß (beta); and so on, in order of their brightness as, for example, α Andromedae and ß Andromedae. Proper names have also been given to the brightest of the fixed stars — especially in the northern hemisphere — as, for example, Alpheratz (α Andromedae); Mirach (ß Andromedae); Vega (Alpha Lyrae); Altair (Alpha Aquiliae); Canopus (Alpha Carinae); and Denebola (Beta Leionis).

To judge the angular distance between heavenly bodies, it's helpful to compare such distances with the known angular distance between specified stars or other reference points. The following angles can serve as a guide to estimating distances in the sky when using star charts.

| | |
|---|---|
| 360° | All round the horizon. |
| 180° | East to west along the horizon or through zenith. |
| 90° | Horizon to zenith. |
| 60° | Dubhe (Great Bear) to Caph (B Cassiopeiae). |
| 30° | Polaris to Caph (~ Cassiopeiae). |
| 23° | Vega to Deneb. |
| 20° | Betelguese to Rigel (Orion). |
| 5° | Merak to Dubhe (Pointers to the Plough). |
| 4° | Castorto Pollux. |

## How to Find the Principal Stars

You'll benefit from using a star map, atlas, or star-finding device like the Rude Starfinder, especially when you don't take star sights often. Many star maps and devices are graduated in right ascension, so in the table that follows the listing below the RA of each star is given, as well as its SHA. Generally, you use the brighter planets and stars, so the annual edition of *Reed's Almanac* has tabulated each month the position, in declination and GHA, of 60 principal stars. Each of these stars is numbered below in the same order used in the *Almanac*. The following notes will assist you in finding every one of these navigational stars. Pronunciations are also given for some of the stars; always accent the syllable marked. The descriptions that follow are best read while referring to the star charts on pages 227–229.

**(1) Alpheratz.** A line from the Pole Star through β Cassiopeiae (Caph) and produced the same distance beyond leads to Alpheratz (α Andromedae), which together with the stars Markab, Algenib, and Scheat form the Square of Pegasus, with Markab at the southwest corner. These are all bright stars and make an almost exact square that you can easily find.

**(2) Ankaa.** (α Phoenicis). A second magnitude star situated just east of a line from Achernar to Fomalhaut.

**(3) Schedar.** The brightest star in Cassiopeiae. This constellation is on the opposite side of the Pole Star to the Dipper and about the same distance away. It's in the shape of a "W" and is known as Cassiopeiae's Chair.

When the Great Bear (or Big Dipper) is on the meridian above the Pole, Cassiopeiae is on the meridian below the Pole, and the two constellations appear to revolve round the Pole Star at equal distances. A line drawn from Aldebaran through Algol intersects Schedar.

**(4) Diphda.** A star of second magnitude that lies by itself about halfway between the Square of Pegasus and Achernar.

**(5) Achernar.** (Ak'-er-nar). The brightest star in the constellation Eridanus in the Southern Hemisphere. It lies about 70° west of Canopus just off a line between Canopus and Fomalhaut.

**(6) POLARIS (or POLE STAR).** The North Star.

**(7) Hamal.** The brightest star in the constellation Aries. A line from Betelgeuse through Aldebaran leads to Hamal, which lies midway between Aldebaran and the Great Square of Pegasus.

**(8) Acamar.** A third magnitude star situated about 20° northeast of Achernar.

**(9) Menkar.** A second magnitude star that lies southwest of Aldebaran and forms the apex of a triangle (upside down) with Aldebaran and Hamal. A line from Sirius through Rigel about the same distance beyond points to Menkar (a Ceti).

**(10) Mirfak.** Lies north of Algol and on a line from Capella to Cassiopeiae.

**(11) Aldebaran** (Al-deb'-ar-an). This very bright red star lies to the north of Orion just a little off the line of the Belt and at the top of one of the arms of a V-shaped cluster of small stars — the Hyades. The Pleiades, a well-defined cluster of stars (The Seven Sisters) lie close to the Hyades and form a valuable skymark.

**(12) Rigel** (Ri'-jel). A bright star in the constellation Orion.

**(13) Capella** (Ca-pel'-la). A line drawn from the Pole Star away from the Great Bear, but perpendicular to the Pointers, leads to Capella. You'll readily recognize it as a bright yellow star. A line from Polaris to Rigel nearly intersects Capella, which is 45° from the Pole Star and 55° from Rigel.

You may also recognize it in a line from Menkar through the Pleiades about 30° northeast of that cluster of stars.

**(14) Bellatrix** (Bel'-la-trix). A bright star in the constellation Orion.

**(15) Elnath** (Nath). The second brightest star to Aldebaran in the constellation Taurus; it lies about halfway along a line between Orion's Belt and Capella.

**(16) Alnilam.** The middle star of the three bright stars in the center of Orion forming the Belt.

**(17) Betelgeuse** (Bet'-eljoox). In the constellation Orion, Betelgeuse has a reddish appearance rather like Aldebaran.

**(18) Canopus** (Can-o'-pus). a Carinae (formerly Argus). The second brightest star in the sky, but situated at 52° south declination. A line drawn from Bellatrix through the northern star in Orion's Belt passes to Canopus. It is almost due south from Sirius and a pale blue color.

**(19) Sirius** (Sir'-e-us). The Dog Star is magnificent in that it is the brightest star in the sky (surpassing in brilliance Mars and Saturn) and has a gorgeous pale blue color. The three stars in the Belt of Orion lead directly away from Aldebaran to Sirius, which lies southeast of Orion.

A fine heavenly curve is formed by Capella, Castor, Pollux, Procyon, and Sirius. See diagram of the constellation of Orion.

**(20) Adhara.** This is a first magnitude star that lies about 10° south of Sirius.

**(21) Castor and Pollux** (Kas'-ter and Pol'-lux). Known as the Twins, these two stars lie nearly halfway between the Dipper and Orion. A line from Rigel through the center star in Orion's Belt points to Castor. Pollux (the brighter star of the two) is found 4.5° to the south.

**(22) Procyon** (Pro'-se-on). A line drawn from Castor and Pollux to Sirius passes almost through Procyon, the little Dog Star.

**(23) Pollux.** See Castor and Pollux (#21).

**(24) Avior.** This first magnitude star lies far south (60° declination), about 30° southeast of Canopus and a little to the east of a line joining Canopus to Miaplacidus.

**(25) Suhail** (v Velorum). A second magnitude star south of Alphard and east-north-east of Canopus.

Advanced Nav.

**(26) Miaplacidus** β Carinae (formerly Argus). A far southerly first magnitude star, situated about halfway between Canopus and Acrux, but about 10° southwest of a line joining them.

**(27) Alphard.** This second magnitude star lies on a line drawn from the Great Bear Star Alioth through Regulus and about 20° beyond to the south-southwest. Its name means "the solitary one;" there is no other bright star near it.

**(28) Regulus** (Reg'-u-lus). A line from the Pole Star through the Pointers of the Dipper and continued about 45° leads close to Regulus. You can easily find this star because it's situated at the end of the "handle" of the "Sickle" (the shape of the constellation Leo) and is the brightest star in the group.

**(29) Dubhe.** The northern and brightest of the two pointers of the Great Bear.

**(30) Denebola** (De-neb'-o-la). The second brightest star in the constellation Leo. It lies about halfway along a line from Arcturus to Regulus.

**(31) Gienah** (γ Corvi). A second magnitude star situated southwest of Spica.

**(32) Acrux.** The brightest and most southerly star in the Southern Cross or Crux. Together with the bright stars, a and 13 Centauri, the Southern Cross, or Crux, forms the most remarkable constellation in the Southern Hemisphere. Unfortunately, it's not visible far north and only shows up over the horizon when you reach south latitudes in the 20s.

**(33) Gacrux** (γ Crucis) is nearly as bright as Mimosa (β Crux) and is situated at the top (north) of the Cross.

**(34) Mimosa** (γ Crucis). The second brightest star in the Crux; it lies at the eastern arm of the Cross.

**(35) Alioth.** One of the stars in the tail of the Great Bear.

**(36) Spica** (Spi'-ka). When the curve of three stars in the tail of the Great Bear is continued through Arcturus and about 30° beyond, it passes through Spica, a first magnitude star. Just southwest of Spica are four stars that look exactly like a Spanker sail — they're known as Spica's Spanker — whose gaff always points to Spica.

**(37) Alkaid** (Benetnasch). A first magni-

tude star situated at the extreme tail of the Great Bear.

**(38) Hadar** (β Centauri). The two Stars β and α Centauri lie close eastward of the Southern Cross and are called the Southern Cross Pointers. β Centauri is the nearer of the two to Crux.

**(39) Menkent** (θ Centauri). A second magnitude star situated about halfway between Spica and β Centauri and slightly east of a direct line.

**(40) Arcturus** (Ark-tu-rus). If you follow the Great Bear south away from the Pole Star for the same distance as the length of the Dipper itself, you'll see Arcturus (a yellow Star). There are three small stars just to the west of Arcturus that form a small triangle. Arcturus is the second brightest star in the Northern heavens.

**(41) Rigil Kent** (α Centauri). See No. 38. α Centauri is the nearest fixed star to the Earth.

**(42) Zuben'ubi** (α Librae). A second magnitude star situated on a line about halfway between Spica and Antares.

**(43) Kochab.** A second magnitude star in Ursa Minor.

**(44) Alphecca.** A second magnitude star in the constellation Corona Borealis, but the brightest in the heavenly jewel, the Northern Crown. A line drawn from Megrez through Alkaid (the last Star in the tail of the Great Bear) leads to Alphecca in the Northern Crown — an almost perfect semi-circular group of small stars. It lies a third of the distance from Arcturus to Vega about 20° east-northeast of Arcturus.

**(45) Antares** (An'-ta-rez). A line from Regulus through Spica the same distance beyond leads to Antares — a bright red star. It lies about 45° southwest of Altair.

**(46) Atria** (α Trianguli Australis). A first magnitude star and the brightest of the three stars lying at the southeast apex of the Southern Triangle, which lies southeast of Centaurus and about 45° due south of Antares.

**(47) Sabik** (π Ophuchi). A second magnitude star situated northeast of Antares about a quarter of the way toward Altair.

**(48) Shaula.** A first magnitude star lying 15° southeast of Antares, about a quarter of the way on a line drawn from Antares to Peacock (α Pavonis).

**(49) Rasalhague.** A second magnitude star lying about 25° west-northwest of Altair. It lies also on a line between Vega and Antares and forms a triangle with Altair and Vega.

**(50) Eltanin.** A second magnitude star lying about 10° north-northwest of Vega on a line from Altair through Vega.

**(51) Kaus Australis.** A second magnitude star lying with the many stars of the constellation of Sagittarius. It is difficult to identify and lies about 25° east-southeast of Antares, but east of a line from Antares to Peacock (No. 55).

**(52) Vega** (Ve'-ga). A line curving through Dubhe, Megrez, Alioth, and Mizar (see diagram of the Great Bear) and following to the west for about 35° leads close to Vega — the brightest and most beautiful star in the northern heavens with a fine pale blue color. You can also find Vega on a line from Arcturus through the Northern Crown Star (Alphecca) and extending about 40° beyond.

**(53) Nunki.** A second magnitude star lying among many others of the constellation Sagittarius about 35° due east of Antares.

**(54) Altair** (Al-tair'). Easily recognized as a bright star lying between two smaller stars that are close in line and point in the direction of Vega. A line from the Pole Star between Vega and Deneb and extended the same distance beyond leads to Altair.

**(55) Peacock.** This second magnitude star lies alone in 57° south declination about halfway between Achernar and Centauri on the same parallel of latitude (west from Achernar). It lies southeast of Antares, southwest of Fomalhaut, and about 65° due south of Altair.

**(56) Deneb** (Den'-eb). This first magnitude star lies east-northeast of Vega and is the brightest star in the constellation Cygnus (the Swan). A line drawn from Castor and Pollux through the Pole Star and extended the same distance beyond passes through Deneb, which is readily found at the top of a "Cross" of Stars (very similar to the Southern Cross). The constellation is usually known as the "Kite" for its shape. It lies about 25° east of Vega.

**(57) Enif** (ε Pegasi). A second magnitude star situated about halfway between Altair and Markab (Square of Pegasus).

**(58) Al Na'ir** (α Gruis). This second magnitude star lies west of β Gruis and is on a line about halfway between Fomalhaut and Peacock.

**(59) Fomalhaut** (Fom'-al-haut). A line drawn from Scheat through Markab (which forms one side of the Great Square of Pegasus) passes through Fomalhaut, which you can readily find because it has a small square of stars near it. Fomalhuat is situated about 45° south of Markab.

**(60) Markab.** Located in the southwest corner of the Square of Pegasus. A line from Altair northeast through the Dolphin, 50° from Altair will lead to Scheat. It lies about 45° to the east of Altair and about 45° north of Fomalhaut.

## SIGNS OF THE ZODIAC

The Zodiac is the belt or zone extending 8° on either side of the Ecliptic, which contains the apparent paths of the Sun, Moon and the principal planets. It is divided into twelve angular portions of 30° (equalling the circle of 360°), each portion containing one constellation or sign, termed collectively The Signs of the Zodiac.

The seasons associated with these signs are given right; however, owing to the precession of the equinoxes, the vernal equinox now actually occurs during Pisces instead of marking the First Point of Aries.

**Northern Signs**

| | | | | |
|---|---|---|---|---|
| Spring Signs | { | 1. a | Aries | 0° |
| | | 2. b | Taurus | 30° |
| | | 3. c | Gemini | 60° |
| Summer Signs | { | 4. d | Cancer | 90° |
| | | 5. e | Leo | 120° |
| | | 6. f | Virgo | 150° |

**Southern signs**

| | | | | |
|---|---|---|---|---|
| Autumn Signs | { | 1. g | Libra | 180° |
| | | 2. h | Scorpio | 210° |
| | | 3. i | Sagittarius | 240° |
| Winter Signs | { | 4. j | Capricornus | 270° |
| | | 5. k | Aquarius | 300° |
| | | 6. l | Pices | 330° |

Advanced Nav.

## ALPHABETICAL INDEX OF PRINCIPAL STARS

With their approximate places, 1998

| Proper Name | Bayer's Name (Constellation) | Mag | RA (h, m) | Dec (°) | SHA (°) | No |
|---|---|---|---|---|---|---|
| Acamar | θ Eridani | 3.1 | 2 58 | S 40 | 315 | 8 |
| Achernar | α Eridani | 0.6 | 1 38 | S 57 | 336 | 5 |
| Acrux | α Crucis | 1.1 | 12 27 | S 63 | 173 | 32 |
| Adhara | ε Canis Majoris | 1.6 | 6 59 | S 29 | 255 | 20 |
| Aldebaran | α Tauri | 1.1 | 4 36 | N 17 | 291 | 11 |
| Alioth | ε Ursae Majoris | 1.7 | 12 54 | N 56 | 167 | 35 |
| Alkaid | η Ursae Majoris | 1.9 | 13 47 | N 49 | 153 | 37 |
| Al Na'ir | α Gruis | 2.2 | 22 08 | S 47 | 28 | 58 |
| Alnilam | ε Orionis | 1.8 | 5 36 | S 1 | 276 | 16 |
| Alphard | α Hydrae | 2.2 | 9 28 | S 9 | 218 | 27 |
| Alphecca | α Coronae Borealis | 2.3 | 15 35 | N 27 | 126 | 44 |
| Alpheratz | α Andromedae | 2.2 | 0 08 | N 29 | 358 | 1 |
| Altair | α Aquilae | 0.9 | 19 51 | N 9 | 62 | 54 |
| Ankaa | α Phoenicis | 2.4 | 0 26 | S 42 | 353 | 2 |
| Antares | α Scorpii | 1.2 | 16 29 | S 26 | 113 | 45 |
| Arcturus | α Bootis | 0.2 | 14 16 | N 19 | 146 | 40 |
| Atria | α Triang Australis | 1.9 | 16 48 | S 69 | 108 | 46 |
| Avior | ε Carinae | 1.7 | 8 22 | S 60 | 234 | 24 |
| Bellatrix | γ Orionis | 1.7 | 5 25 | N 6 | 279 | 14 |
| Betelgeuse | α Orionis | 0.1–1.2 | 5 55 | N 7 | 271 | 17 |
| Canopus | α Carinae | −0.9 | 6 24 | S 53 | 264 | 18 |
| Capella | α Aurigae | 0.2 | 5 17 | N 46 | 281 | 13 |
| Castor | α Geminorum | 1.6 | 7 34 | N 32 | 246 | 21 |
| Deneb | α Cygni | 1.3 | 20 41 | N 45 | 50 | 56 |
| Denebola | β Leonis | 2.2 | 11 49 | N 15 | 183 | 30 |
| Diphda | β Ceti | 2.2 | 0 44 | S 18 | 349 | 4 |
| Dubhe | α Ursae Majoris | 2.0 | 11 04 | N 62 | 194 | 29 |
| Elnath | β Tauri | 1.8 | 5 26 | N 29 | 278 | 15 |
| Eltanin | γ Draconis | 2.4 | 17 56 | N 51 | 91 | 50 |
| Enif | ε Pegasi | 2.5 | 21 44 | N 10 | 34 | 57 |
| Fomalhaut | α Piscis Austrini | 1.3 | 22 58 | S 30 | 16 | 59 |
| Gacrux | γ Crucis | 1.6 | 12 31 | S 57 | 172 | 33 |
| Gienah | γ Corvi | 2.8 | 12 16 | S 18 | 176 | 31 |
| Hadar | β Centauri | 0.9 | 14 04 | S 60 | 149 | 38 |
| Hamal | α Arietis | 2.2 | 2 07 | N 23 | 328 | 7 |
| Kaus Australis | ε Sagittarii | 2.0 | 18 24 | S 34 | 84 | 51 |
| Kochab | β Ursae Minoris | 2.2 | 14 51 | N 74 | 137 | 43 |
| Markab | α Pegasi | 2.6 | 23 05 | N 15 | 14 | 60 |
| Menkar | α Ceti | 2.8 | 3 02 | N 4 | 314 | 9 |
| Menkent | θ Centauri | 2.3 | 14 07 | S 36 | 148 | 39 |
| Miaplacidus | β Carinae | 1.8 | 9 13 | S 70 | 222 | 26 |
| Mimosa | β Crucis | 1.5 | 12 48 | S 60 | 168 | 34 |
| Mirfak | α Persei | 1.9 | 3 24 | N 50 | 309 | 10 |
| Nunki | σ Sagittarii | 2.1 | 18 55 | S 26 | 76 | 53 |
| Peacock | α Pavonis | 2.1 | 20 26 | S 57 | 54 | 55 |
| POLARIS | α Ursae Minoris | 2.1 | 2 31 | N 89 | 323 | 6 |
| Pollux | β Geminorum | 1.2 | 7 45 | N 28 | 244 | 23 |
| Procyon | α Canis Minoris | 0.5 | 7 39 | N 5 | 245 | 22 |
| Rasalhague | α Ophiuchi | 2.1 | 17 35 | N 13 | 96 | 49 |
| Regulus | α Leonis | 1.3 | 10 08 | N 12 | 208 | 28 |
| Rigel | β Orionis | 0.3 | 5 14 | S 8 | 281 | 12 |
| Rigil Kent | α Centauri | 0.1 | 14 40 | S 61 | 140 | 41 |
| Sabik | η Ophiuchi | 2.6 | 17 10 | S 16 | 102 | 47 |
| Schedar | α Cassiopeiae | 2.5 | 0 40 | N 57 | 350 | 3 |
| Shaula | γ Scorpii | 1.7 | 17 33 | S 37 | 97 | 48 |
| Sirius | α Canis Majoris | −1.6 | 6 45 | S 17 | 259 | 19 |
| Spica | α Virginis | 1.2 | 13 25 | S 11 | 159 | 36 |
| Suhail | γ Velorum | 2.2 | 9 08 | S 43 | 223 | 25 |
| Vega | α Lyrae | 0.1 | 18 37 | N 39 | 81 | 52 |
| Zuben'ubi | α Librae | 2.9 | 14 51 | S 16 | 137 | 42 |

The last column refers to the number given to the star in this almanac. The star's exact position may be found according to this number on the monthly pages in *Reed's Nautical Almanac*.

## STAR CHART OF NORTHERN HEMISPHERE

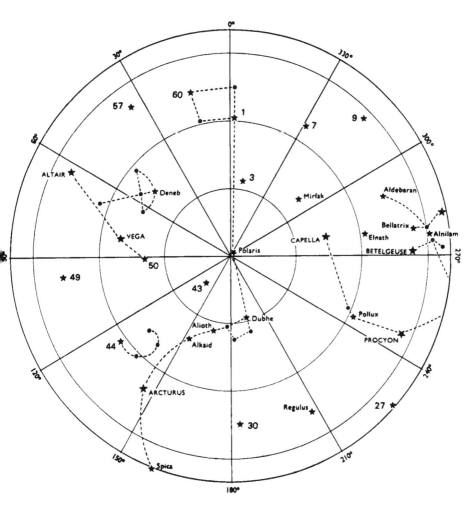

**\* Stars of the first magnitude**
**(capital letters)**

**● Stars of magnitude 2.0 to 1.0**
**(small letters)**

*Key to numbered stars*

| | | |
|---|---|---|
| 1. Alpheratz | 27. Alphard | 49. Rasalhague |
| 3. Schedar | 30. Denebola | 50. Eltanin |
| 7. Hamal | 43. Kochab | 57. Enif |
| 9. Menkar | 44. Alphecca | 60. Markab |

Advanced Nav.

## STAR CHART OF SOUTHERN HEMISPHERE

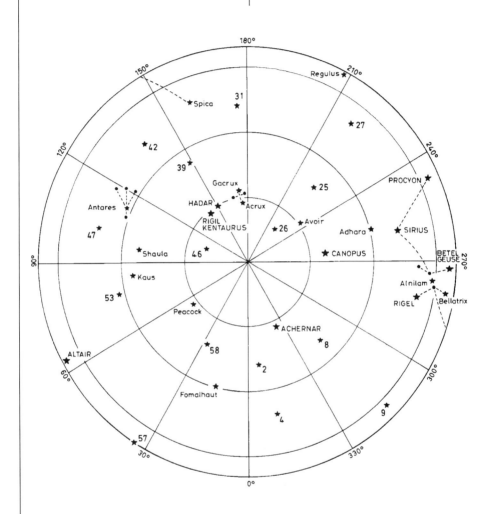

**\* Stars that are less bright than
mag. 2.0 but are listed and
numbered as Selected Stars**

**● Stars of lesser magnitude,
included to help identify
some constellations.**

*Key to numbered stars*

| | | |
|---|---|---|
| 2. Ankaa | 26. Miaplacidus | 46. Atria |
| 4. Diphda | 27. Alphard | 47. Sabik |
| 8. Acamar | 31. Gienah | 53. Nunki |
| 9. Menkar | 39. Menkent | 57. Enif |
| 25. Suhail | 42. Zuben'ubi | 58. Al Na'ir |

## AUXILIARY STAR CHARTS

### POLE-DIPPER-DUBHE-BENETNASCH-KOCHAB

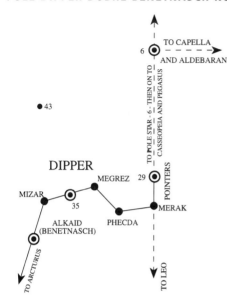

No. 6.   POLARIS.

No. 29. DUBHE.

No. 35. ALIOTH.

No. 43. KOCHAB.

No. 11. ALDERBARAN.

No. 13. CAPELLA.

Polaris — the Pole Star — familiar in the Northern Hemisphere, is always seen in the same part of the heavens, over the Pole of the Earth. It is the brightest star in the Little Bear (Ursa Minor). The position of Polaris in the Little Bear corresponds to the position of Alkaid (Benetnasch) 37 in the Great Bear. The Dipper or Great Bear (Ursa Major) is the easiest recognizable constellation in the northern heavens. A straight line through Merak and Dubhe — the Pointers — leads to Polaris.

### CAPELLA-POLLUX-SIRIUS-ORION-ALDE-BARAN

No. 11. ALDEBARAN.

No. 12. RIGEL.

No. 13. CAPELLA.

No. 14. BELLATRIX.

No. 17. BETELGEUSE.

No. 19. SIRIUS.

No. 21. CASTOR.

No. 22. PROCYON.

No. 23. POLLUX.

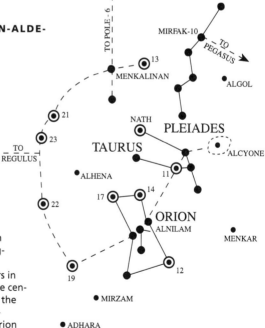

Orion is the finest constellation visible in the Northern Hemisphere, is easily recognized, and the many fine stars around it make it invaluable. The three bright stars in line form Orion's belt with Alnilam at the center and the sword hanging down below the belt. Four bright stars surround Orion — Betelgeuse, Bellatrix, Rigel and Saiph. Orion is near the meridian at midnight late in the year and therefore is only visible in northern latitudes in winter and early spring.

**Advanced Nav.**

## THE MOON'S PHASES

The time required for the Moon to make one orbit using the Sun as a reference point — that is, the interval between two successive new moons — is approximately 29.5 days and is called a synodical month, or a lunation. A sidereal month is the duration of one complete orbit with reference to a fixed star. Its interval from Perigee to Perigee or Apogee to Apogee is approximately 27 days.

A lunar day is the interval between two successive transits of the Moon over the same meridian. It averages about 24 hours and 50 minutes. The minutes in excess of 24 hours vary from 38 to 66 due to the irregular speed of the Moon along its orbit.

Because the Moon crosses the meridian later each day, there is always a day in each synodical month in which there is no meridian passage, another in which there is no moonrise, and another with no moonset. For example, if moonrise occurs at, say, 2330 on a Monday, the following moonrise may not occur until 0020 on Wednesday.

**Figure 1** (looking down onto the North Pole of the Earth) shows eight successive positions of the Moon as it orbits the Earth in a counterclockwise direction. It also shows how at all times one hemisphere of the Moon is illuminated by the Sun's rays while the opposite hemisphere is in total darkness. The eight positions are numbered commencing at the New Moon, Position 1.

**Figure 2** illustrates the appearance of the Moon's disc corresponding to each of the positions, numbered 1 to 8, in figure 1. This shows how the Moon looks to an observer in any latitude from which the Moon bears South at its meridian passage. If you are on the other side of the Moon, turn this diagram upside down.

**PHASES OF THE MOON**                               Referring to Figures 1 and 2

| Position No. | Moon's Phase | Age | Time of Mer. Pass (Approx) | Remarks |
|---|---|---|---|---|
| | | **Days** | **Hrs.** | |
| 1 | **New Moon** | 0 | 1200 | Sun and Moon "in conjunction." Moon not visible because only the dark hemisphere faces the Earth. |
| 2 | **Between New Moon and First Quarter** | 3-4 | 1500 | Visible as a crescent with its bow towards the West. Waxing. |
| 3 | **First Quarter** | 7 | 1800 | Moon 90° East of Sun (in East Quadrature). Visible as a half-disc with its bow towards the West. Waxing. |
| 4 | **Between First Quarter** | 11-12 | 2100 | Three quarters of the disc visible (called a Gibbous Moon), the more rounded side towards the West. Waxing. |
| 5 | **Full Moon** | 15 | 2400 | Moon on Sun's antimeridian, i.e., "in opposition." The whole of the illuminated hemishpere is visible. |
| 6 | **Between Full Moon and Last Quarter** | 18-19 | 0300 | Three quarters of the disc visible (called a Gibbous Moon), the more rounded side towards the East. Waning. |
| 7 | **Last Quarter** | 22 | 0600 | Moon 90° West of the Sun (in West Quadrature). Visible as a half-disc with its bow towards the East. Waning. |
| 8 | **Between Last Quarter and New Moon** | 25-26 | 0900 | Visible as a crescent with its bow towards the East. Waning. |

In low latitudes, moonrise and moonset occur a few minutes more than six hours before and after mer. pass., respectively. In high latitudes the times vary with changes in the Moon's declination.

**THE MOON'S PHASES**

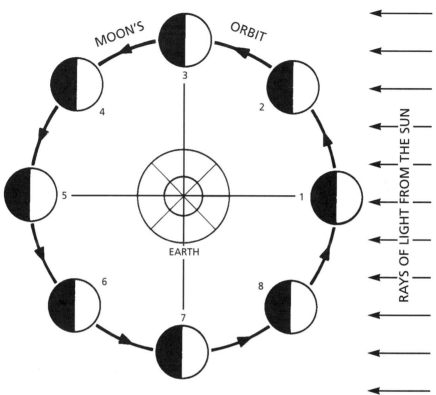

**Figure 1**
Successive positions (1 to 8) of the Moon along its orbit round the Earth.

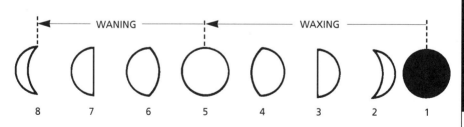

**Figure 2**
Phases of the Moon as viewed from the Earth's surface.

Advanced Nav.

## HOW TO RECOGNIZE THE PLANETS

The principal planets are Mercury, Venus, Earth, Mars, Jupiter, Saturn, Uranus, and Neptune.

Planets, including Earth, revolve round the Sun in orbits that vary with their differing distances from the Sun. They are all, however, situated in a belt of the celestial sphere about 8° on either side of the ecliptic called the Zodiac.

The planets, like Earth's satellite, the Moon, and the comets when visible, all receive their light from the Sun. Compared with Earth's orbit, the orbits of Mercury and Venus are closer to the Sun; they are called inferior planets. The other planets' orbits are outside Earth's orbit and are called superior planets.

Because their positions vary so much in comparison with the fixed stars, the planets are often called wandering stars. None of the visible planets ever twinkle like the stars. You may be able to distinguish them from stars by this characteristic.

Mercury is very close to the Sun and is seldom seen, so it's of little use to the navigator. Among the other planets, only Venus, Jupiter, Mars, and Saturn are visible to the naked eye and are navigationally important.

Venus is visible only for a short time after sunset and before sunrise because its orbit is between Earth and the Sun and it appears to cross and recross the Sun continually. The time of the meridian passage of Venus is constantly changing from about 9 a.m. to 3 p.m. Because Venus is so bright you can observe it during the daytime in clear weather when it's not too near the Sun, using a sextant equipped with a telescope. Many navigators get a splendid position during the day by observing Venus on the meridian and crossing its LOP with one from the Sun.

Venus has a bluish light and, with the exception of the Sun and Moon, is by far the brightest object in the heavens. Jupiter, although not as bright as Venus, is brighter than any fixed star. You can use it for a daytime fix with a powerful sextant telescope. Mars' distance from Earth varies; sometimes it's very bright and at other times very faint. Mars has a reddish color. Saturn is the least bright of the four planets and shines at the equivalent of a first magnitude star. It has a yellowish color.

The diameter of Jupiter is about three times that of Saturn and is quite apparent. Because their diameters vary, it's customary to observe the center of a planet to avoid any correction.

The notes on monthly planet pages in *Reed's Almanac* show whether the planet is a morning or evening planet, whether it's too close to the Sun for observation, and give its position in the heavens.

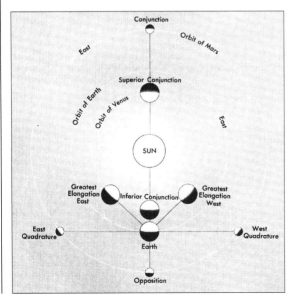

### Planet Mechanics

This diagram shows many of the terms for positions of the planets relative to earth. The ephemeris diary section of *Reed's Almanacs* makes use of these terms.

## AMPLITUDES

The bearing of the sun when rising or setting is known as its *amplitude*.

Amplitude is useful for calculating compass error because accurate time or sight reduction is not required. All that is required is to know the approximate latitude from the chart and the sun's approximate declination from this ephemeris.

With these values, the table on following pages will give you the true bearing of the sun at sunrise or sunset in any part of the world, up to latitude 66°. This bearing can be compared with your compass bearing at sunrise or sunset to deduce any deviation it might have.

**Notes:**
The "theoretical sunrise" is considered to take place at the moment when the sun's center is on the edge of the horizon to the eastward.

Due to refraction (i.e., the bending of rays of light when passing through the atmosphere), the sun appears higher than it actually is. It appears to rise before it is actually above the horizon, and it has actually set when you can still see a small portion of the limb. The rule of thumb is to take amplitude bearings, both at rising and setting, when the sun's lower limb is about half the sun's diameter above the horizon, as it is then that the center of the sun is actually on the horizon.

This table can also be used to find the true bearing at rising and setting of any celestial body other than the moon, within these declinations.

**Example:**
November 18th, on passage to Bermuda, DR 28°N, 64°30′ W, the sun rose bearing by compass 130°. The Variation from the chart was 14°W. Find the deviation.

In *Reed's Nautical Almanac* (or any other almanac) you will find that the sun's declination on this day is about S 19°. Going to the table on the next two pages with our declination and latitude, we get a bearing of 68°. The important note at the bottom of the table states:

**Name the Bearing the same as the Declination NORTH or SOUTH and EAST if rising, WEST if setting.**

Therefore, our answer is S 68°E — in other words, 68° east from 180°, or 112° on the compass rose. Now apply this to a typical compass table:

| | | | |
|---|---|---|---|
| + W | **T**rue | 112° | from table |
| – E | **V**ariation | 14°W | from chart |
| | **M**agnetic | 126° | |
| | **D**eviation | 4°W | deduce |
| | **C**ompass | 130° | actual reading |

You may also wish to draw the problem as shown below.

Note that this procedure will give you only the compass deviation for the heading that you are on when you took the bearing. To generate a deviation card, you can get separate bearings while steering the vessel on eight or more cardinal headings.

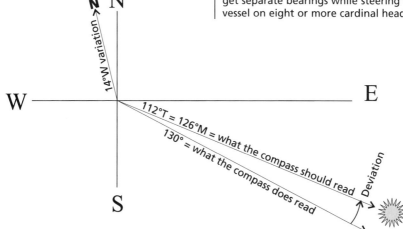

## SUN'S TRUE BEARING AT SUNRISE AND SUNSET

LATITUDES 0° to 66° DECLINATIONS 0° to 11°

| LAT | DECLINATION | | | | | | | | | | | |
|---|---|---|---|---|---|---|---|---|---|---|---|---|
|  | 0° | 1° | 2° | 3° | 4° | 5° | 6° | 7° | 8° | 9° | 10° | 11° |
| 0° to 5° | 90 | 89 | 88 | 87 | 86 | 85 | 84 | 83 | 82 | 81 | 80 | 79 |
| 6° | 90 | 89 | 88 | 87 | 86 | 85 | 84 | 83 | 82 | 81 | 79.9 | 78.9 |
| 7° | 90 | 89 | 88 | 87 | 86 | 85 | 84 | 83 | 81.9 | 80.9 | 79.9 | 78.9 |
| 8° | 90 | 89 | 88 | 87 | 86 | 85 | 84 | 82.9 | 81.9 | 80.9 | 79.9 | 78.9 |
| 9° | 90 | 89 | 88 | 87 | 86 | 85 | 83.9 | 82.9 | 81.9 | 80.9 | 79.8 | 78.9 |
| 10° | 90 | 89 | 88 | 87 | 86 | 84.9 | 83.9 | 82.9 | 81.9 | 80.9 | 79.8 | 78.8 |
| 11° | 90 | 89 | 88 | 87 | 86 | 84.9 | 83.9 | 82.9 | 81.9 | 80.8 | 79.8 | 78.8 |
| 12° | 90 | 89 | 88 | 87 | 85.9 | 84.9 | 83.9 | 82.9 | 81.8 | 80.8 | 79.8 | 78.8 |
| 13° | 90 | 89 | 88 | 86.9 | 85.9 | 84.9 | 83.8 | 82.8 | 81.8 | 80.8 | 79.7 | 78.7 |
| 14° | 90 | 89 | 88 | 86.9 | 85.9 | 84.8 | 83.8 | 82.8 | 81.8 | 80.7 | 79.7 | 78.7 |
| 15° | 90 | 89 | 88 | 86.9 | 85.9 | 84.8 | 83.8 | 82.8 | 81.7 | 80.7 | 79.6 | 78.6 |
| 16° | 90 | 89 | 87.9 | 86.9 | 85.8 | 84.8 | 83.8 | 82.7 | 81.7 | 80.6 | 79.6 | 78.6 |
| 17° | 90 | 89 | 87.9 | 86.9 | 85.8 | 84.8 | 83.7 | 82.7 | 81.6 | 80.6 | 79.5 | 78.5 |
| 18° | 90 | 89 | 87.9 | 86.9 | 85.8 | 84.8 | 83.7 | 82.6 | 81.6 | 80.5 | 79.5 | 78.4 |
| 19° | 90 | 89 | 87.9 | 86.8 | 85.8 | 84.7 | 83.7 | 82.6 | 81.5 | 80.5 | 79.4 | 78.4 |
| 20° | 90 | 88.9 | 87.9 | 86.8 | 85.8 | 84.7 | 83.6 | 82.6 | 81.5 | 80.4 | 79.4 | 78.3 |
| 21° | 90 | 88.9 | 87.9 | 86.8 | 85.7 | 84.7 | 83.6 | 82.5 | 81.4 | 80.4 | 79.3 | 78.2 |
| 22° | 90 | 88.9 | 87.9 | 86.8 | 85.7 | 84.6 | 83.5 | 82.5 | 81.4 | 80.3 | 79.2 | 78.1 |
| 23° | 90 | 88.9 | 87.9 | 86.7 | 85.7 | 84.6 | 83.5 | 82.4 | 81.3 | 80.2 | 79.1 | 78.0 |
| 24° | 90 | 88.9 | 87.8 | 86.7 | 85.6 | 84.5 | 83.4 | 82.3 | 81.2 | 80.1 | 79.0 | 78.0 |
| 25° | 90 | 88.9 | 87.8 | 86.7 | 85.6 | 84.5 | 83.4 | 82.3 | 81.2 | 80.1 | 79.0 | 77.9 |
| 26° | 90 | 88.9 | 87.8 | 86.7 | 85.6 | 84.4 | 83.3 | 82.2 | 81.1 | 80.0 | 78.9 | 77.8 |
| 27° | 90 | 88.9 | 87.8 | 86.6 | 85.5 | 84.4 | 83.3 | 82.1 | 81.0 | 79.9 | 78.8 | 77.6 |
| 28° | 90 | 88.9 | 87.8 | 86.6 | 85.5 | 84.4 | 83.2 | 82.1 | 80.9 | 79.8 | 78.7 | 77.5 |
| 29° | 90 | 88.9 | 87.8 | 86.6 | 85.5 | 84.3 | 83.1 | 82.0 | 80.9 | 79.7 | 78.6 | 77.4 |
| 30° | 90 | 88.9 | 87.7 | 86.5 | 85.4 | 84.2 | 83.1 | 81.9 | 80.8 | 79.6 | 78.5 | 77.3 |
| 31° | 90 | 88.9 | 87.7 | 86.5 | 85.4 | 84.2 | 83.0 | 81.8 | 80.7 | 79.5 | 78.3 | 77.1 |
| 32° | 90 | 88.9 | 87.7 | 86.5 | 85.3 | 84.1 | 82.9 | 81.7 | 80.6 | 79.4 | 78.2 | 77.0 |
| 33° | 90 | 88.8 | 87.7 | 86.4 | 85.3 | 84.0 | 82.8 | 81.7 | 80.5 | 79.3 | 78.0 | 76.9 |
| 34° | 90 | 88.8 | 87.6 | 86.4 | 85.2 | 84.0 | 82.7 | 81.5 | 80.3 | 79.1 | 77.9 | 76.7 |
| 35° | 90 | 88.8 | 87.5 | 86.3 | 85.1 | 83.9 | 82.7 | 81.4 | 80.2 | 79.0 | 77.8 | 76.5 |
| 36° | 90 | 88.8 | 87.5 | 86.3 | 85.0 | 83.8 | 82.6 | 81.3 | 80.1 | 78.8 | 77.6 | 76.3 |
| 37° | 90 | 88.7 | 87.5 | 86.2 | 85.0 | 83.7 | 82.5 | 81.2 | 80.0 | 78.7 | 77.4 | 76.2 |
| 38° | 90 | 88.7 | 87.5 | 86.2 | 84.9 | 83.6 | 82.4 | 81.1 | 79.8 | 78.5 | 77.3 | 76.0 |
| 39° | 90 | 88.7 | 87.4 | 86.1 | 84.8 | 83.6 | 82.3 | 81.0 | 79.7 | 78.4 | 77.1 | 75.8 |
| 40° | 90 | 88.7 | 87.4 | 86.1 | 84.8 | 83.5 | 82.1 | 80.8 | 79.5 | 78.2 | 76.9 | 75.6 |
| 41° | 90 | 88.7 | 87.3 | 86.0 | 84.7 | 83.4 | 82.0 | 80.7 | 79.4 | 78.0 | 76.7 | 75.3 |
| 42° | 90 | 88.6 | 87.3 | 86.0 | 84.6 | 83.3 | 81.9 | 80.6 | 79.2 | 77.8 | 76.5 | 75.1 |
| 43° | 90 | 88.6 | 87.3 | 85.9 | 84.5 | 83.1 | 81.8 | 80.4 | 79.0 | 77.6 | 76.4 | 74.9 |
| 44° | 90 | 88.6 | 87.2 | 85.8 | 84.4 | 83.0 | 81.6 | 80.2 | 78.8 | 77.4 | 76.0 | 74.6 |
| 45° | 90 | 88.6 | 87.2 | 85.7 | 84.3 | 82.9 | 81.5 | 80.1 | 78.6 | 77.2 | 75.8 | 74.3 |
| 46° | 90 | 88.6 | 87.1 | 85.7 | 84.2 | 82.8 | 81.3 | 79.9 | 78.4 | 77.0 | 75.5 | 74.0 |
| 47° | 90 | 88.5 | 87.1 | 85.6 | 84.1 | 82.6 | 81.2 | 79.7 | 78.2 | 76.7 | 75.2 | 73.7 |
| 48° | 90 | 88.5 | 87.0 | 85.5 | 84.0 | 82.5 | 81.0 | 79.5 | 78.0 | 76.5 | 75.0 | 73.4 |
| 49° | 90 | 88.5 | 86.9 | 85.4 | 83.9 | 82.4 | 80.8 | 79.3 | 77.7 | 76.2 | 74.6 | 73.1 |
| 50° | 90 | 88.4 | 86.9 | 85.3 | 83.8 | 82.2 | 80.7 | 79.1 | 77.5 | 75.9 | 74.3 | 72.7 |
| 51° | 90 | 88.4 | 86.8 | 85.2 | 83.6 | 82.0 | 80.4 | 78.8 | 77.2 | 75.6 | 74.0 | 72.3 |
| 52° | 90 | 88.4 | 86.7 | 85.1 | 83.5 | 81.9 | 80.2 | 78.6 | 76.9 | 75.3 | 73.6 | 71.9 |
| 53° | 90 | 88.3 | 86.7 | 85.0 | 83.3 | 81.7 | 80.0 | 78.3 | 76.6 | 74.9 | 73.2 | 71.5 |
| 54° | 90 | 88.3 | 86.6 | 84.9 | 83.2 | 81.5 | 79.7 | 78.0 | 76.3 | 74.6 | 72.8 | 71.0 |
| 55° | 90 | 88.2 | 86.5 | 84.8 | 83.0 | 81.3 | 79.5 | 77.7 | 75.9 | 74.2 | 72.4 | 70.6 |
| 56° | 90 | 88.2 | 86.4 | 84.6 | 82.8 | 81.0 | 79.2 | 77.4 | 75.6 | 73.7 | 71.9 | 70.0 |
| 57° | 90 | 88.2 | 86.3 | 84.5 | 82.6 | 80.8 | 78.9 | 77.1 | 75.2 | 73.3 | 71.4 | 69.5 |
| 58° | 90 | 88.1 | 86.2 | 84.3 | 82.4 | 80.5 | 78.6 | 76.7 | 74.8 | 72.8 | 70.9 | 68.9 |
| 59° | 90 | 88.0 | 86.1 | 84.2 | 82.2 | 80.2 | 78.3 | 76.3 | 74.3 | 72.3 | 70.3 | 68.2 |
| 60° | 90 | 88.0 | 86.0 | 84.0 | 82.0 | 80.0 | 77.9 | 75.9 | 73.8 | 71.8 | 69.7 | 67.6 |
| 61° | 90 | 87.9 | 85.9 | 83.8 | 81.7 | 79.6 | 77.5 | 75.4 | 73.3 | 71.2 | 69.0 | 66.8 |
| 62° | 90 | 87.9 | 85.7 | 83.6 | 81.4 | 79.3 | 77.1 | 74.9 | 72.7 | 70.5 | 68.3 | 66.0 |
| 63° | 90 | 87.8 | 85.6 | 83.4 | 81.2 | 78.9 | 76.7 | 74.4 | 72.1 | 69.8 | 67.5 | 65.1 |
| 64° | 90 | 87.7 | 85.4 | 83.1 | 80.8 | 78.5 | 76.2 | 73.9 | 71.5 | 69.1 | 66.7 | 64.2 |
| 65° | 90 | 87.6 | 85.3 | 82.9 | 80.5 | 78.1 | 75.7 | 73.2 | 70.8 | 68.3 | 65.7 | 63.2 |
| 66° | 90 | 87.5 | 85.1 | 82.6 | 80.1 | 77.6 | 75.1 | 72.6 | 70.0 | 67.4 | 64.7 | 62.0 |

**Name the Bearing the same as the Declination NORTH or SOUTH
and EAST if rising, WEST if setting.**

For example of how to use this table, see previous page.

## SUN'S TRUE BEARING AT SUNRISE AND SUNSET

LATITUDES 0° to 66°   DECLINATIONS 12° to 23°

| LAT. | DECLINATION | | | | | | | | | | | |
|---|---|---|---|---|---|---|---|---|---|---|---|---|
| | 12° | 13° | 14° | 15° | 16° | 17° | 18° | 19° | 20° | 21° | 22° | 23° |
| | ° | ° | ° | ° | ° | ° | ° | ° | ° | ° | ° | ° |
| 0° to 5° | 77.9 | 76.9 | 75.9 | 74.9 | 73.9 | 72.9 | 71.9 | 70.9 | 69.9 | 68.8 | 67.9 | 66.9 |
| 6° | 77.9 | 76.9 | 75.9 | 74.9 | 73.9 | 72.9 | 71.9 | 70.9 | 69.9 | 68.8 | 67.9 | 66.9 |
| 7° | 77.9 | 76.9 | 75.9 | 74.9 | 73.9 | 72.9 | 71.9 | 70.8 | 69.8 | 68.8 | 67.8 | 66.8 |
| 8° | 77.9 | 76.9 | 75.9 | 74.8 | 73.8 | 72.8 | 71.8 | 70.8 | 69.8 | 68.8 | 67.8 | 66.8 |
| 9° | 77.8 | 76.8 | 75.8 | 74.8 | 73.8 | 72.8 | 71.8 | 70.7 | 69.7 | 68.7 | 67.7 | 66.7 |
| 10° | 77.8 | 76.8 | 75.8 | 74.8 | 73.7 | 72.7 | 71.7 | 70.7 | 69.7 | 68.7 | 67.6 | 66.6 |
| 11° | 77.8 | 76.8 | 75.7 | 74.7 | 73.7 | 72.7 | 71.6 | 70.6 | 69.6 | 68.6 | 67.6 | 66.5 |
| 12° | 77.7 | 76.7 | 75.7 | 74.6 | 73.6 | 72.6 | 71.6 | 70.6 | 69.5 | 68.5 | 67.5 | 66.4 |
| 13° | 77.7 | 76.6 | 75.6 | 74.6 | 73.6 | 72.5 | 71.5 | 70.5 | 69.4 | 68.4 | 67.4 | 66.4 |
| 14° | 77.6 | 76.6 | 75.6 | 74.5 | 73.5 | 72.5 | 71.4 | 70.4 | 69.4 | 68.3 | 67.3 | 66.2 |
| 15° | 77.6 | 76.5 | 75.5 | 74.4 | 73.4 | 72.4 | 71.3 | 70.3 | 69.3 | 68.2 | 67.2 | 66.1 |
| 16° | 77.5 | 76.5 | 75.4 | 74.4 | 73.3 | 72.3 | 71.2 | 70.2 | 69.1 | 68.1 | 67.1 | 66.0 |
| 17° | 77.4 | 76.4 | 75.3 | 74.3 | 73.3 | 72.2 | 71.1 | 70.1 | 69.0 | 68.0 | 66.9 | 65.9 |
| 18° | 77.4 | 76.3 | 75.3 | 74.2 | 73.2 | 72.1 | 71.0 | 70.0 | 68.9 | 67.9 | 66.8 | 65.7 |
| 19° | 77.4 | 76.2 | 75.2 | 74.1 | 73.0 | 72.0 | 70.9 | 69.9 | 68.8 | 67.7 | 66.7 | 65.6 |
| 20° | 77.2 | 76.1 | 75.1 | 74.0 | 72.9 | 71.9 | 70.8 | 69.7 | 68.6 | 67.6 | 66.5 | 65.4 |
| 21° | 77.1 | 76.0 | 75.0 | 73.9 | 72.8 | 71.7 | 70.7 | 69.6 | 68.5 | 67.4 | 66.3 | 65.2 |
| 22° | 77.0 | 76.0 | 74.9 | 73.8 | 72.7 | 71.6 | 70.5 | 69.4 | 68.3 | 67.3 | 66.2 | 65.1 |
| 23° | 76.9 | 75.9 | 74.8 | 73.7 | 72.6 | 71.5 | 70.4 | 69.3 | 68.2 | 67.1 | 66.0 | 64.9 |
| 24° | 76.8 | 75.7 | 74.6 | 73.5 | 72.5 | 71.3 | 70.2 | 69.1 | 68.0 | 66.9 | 65.8 | 64.7 |
| 25° | 76.7 | 75.6 | 74.5 | 73.4 | 72.3 | 71.2 | 70.1 | 68.9 | 67.8 | 66.7 | 65.6 | 64.5 |
| 26° | 76.6 | 75.5 | 74.4 | 73.3 | 72.1 | 71.0 | 69.9 | 68.8 | 67.6 | 66.5 | 65.4 | 64.2 |
| 27° | 76.5 | 75.4 | 74.3 | 73.1 | 72.0 | 70.8 | 69.7 | 68.6 | 67.4 | 66.3 | 65.1 | 64.0 |
| 28° | 76.4 | 75.2 | 74.1 | 73.0 | 71.8 | 70.7 | 69.5 | 68.4 | 67.2 | 66.1 | 64.9 | 63.8 |
| 29° | 76.2 | 75.1 | 73.9 | 72.8 | 71.6 | 70.5 | 69.3 | 68.2 | 67.0 | 65.8 | 64.6 | 63.5 |
| 30° | 76.1 | 75.0 | 73.8 | 72.6 | 71.4 | 70.3 | 69.1 | 67.9 | 66.7 | 65.5 | 64.4 | 63.2 |
| 31° | 76.0 | 74.8 | 73.6 | 72.4 | 71.2 | 70.0 | 68.9 | 67.6 | 66.5 | 65.3 | 64.1 | 62.9 |
| 32° | 75.8 | 74.6 | 73.4 | 72.2 | 71.0 | 69.8 | 68.6 | 67.4 | 66.2 | 65.0 | 63.8 | 62.6 |
| 33° | 75.7 | 74.4 | 73.2 | 72.0 | 70.8 | 69.6 | 68.4 | 67.1 | 65.9 | 64.7 | 63.5 | 62.2 |
| 34° | 75.5 | 74.2 | 73.0 | 71.8 | 70.6 | 69.3 | 68.1 | 66.9 | 65.6 | 64.4 | 63.1 | 61.9 |
| 35° | 75.3 | 74.1 | 72.8 | 71.6 | 70.3 | 69.1 | 67.8 | 66.6 | 65.3 | 64.0 | 62.8 | 61.5 |
| 36° | 75.1 | 73.8 | 72.6 | 71.3 | 70.1 | 68.8 | 67.5 | 66.3 | 65.0 | 63.7 | 62.4 | 61.1 |
| 37° | 74.9 | 73.6 | 72.4 | 71.1 | 69.8 | 68.5 | 67.2 | 65.9 | 64.6 | 63.3 | 62.0 | 60.7 |
| 38° | 74.7 | 73.4 | 72.1 | 70.8 | 69.5 | 68.2 | 66.9 | 65.6 | 64.3 | 62.9 | 61.6 | 60.3 |
| 39° | 74.5 | 73.2 | 71.9 | 70.5 | 69.2 | 67.9 | 66.6 | 65.2 | 63.9 | 62.5 | 61.2 | 59.8 |
| 40° | 74.2 | 72.9 | 71.6 | 70.2 | 68.9 | 67.6 | 66.2 | 64.8 | 63.5 | 62.1 | 60.7 | 59.3 |
| 41° | 74.0 | 72.7 | 71.3 | 70.0 | 68.6 | 67.2 | 65.8 | 64.4 | 63.0 | 61.6 | 60.2 | 58.8 |
| 42° | 73.7 | 72.4 | 71.0 | 69.6 | 68.2 | 66.8 | 65.4 | 64.0 | 62.6 | 61.2 | 59.7 | 58.3 |
| 43° | 73.5 | 72.1 | 70.7 | 69.3 | 67.9 | 66.4 | 65.0 | 63.6 | 62.1 | 60.7 | 59.2 | 57.7 |
| 44° | 73.2 | 71.8 | 70.3 | 68.9 | 67.5 | 66.0 | 64.6 | 63.1 | 61.6 | 60.1 | 58.6 | 57.1 |
| 45° | 72.9 | 71.4 | 70.0 | 68.5 | 67.0 | 65.6 | 64.1 | 62.6 | 61.1 | 59.5 | 58.0 | 56.4 |
| 46° | 72.6 | 71.1 | 69.6 | 68.1 | 66.6 | 65.1 | 63.6 | 62.1 | 60.5 | 58.9 | 57.4 | 55.8 |
| 47° | 72.2 | 70.7 | 69.2 | 67.7 | 66.2 | 64.6 | 63.0 | 61.5 | 59.9 | 58.3 | 56.7 | 55.0 |
| 48° | 71.9 | 70.3 | 68.8 | 67.2 | 65.7 | 64.1 | 62.5 | 60.9 | 59.3 | 57.6 | 55.9 | 54.3 |
| 49° | 71.5 | 69.9 | 68.4 | 66.8 | 65.1 | 63.5 | 61.9 | 60.2 | 58.6 | 56.9 | 55.2 | 53.4 |
| 50° | 71.1 | 69.5 | 67.9 | 66.2 | 64.6 | 63.0 | 61.3 | 59.6 | 57.8 | 56.1 | 54.3 | 52.6 |
| 51° | 70.7 | 69.0 | 67.4 | 65.7 | 64.0 | 62.3 | 60.6 | 58.8 | 57.1 | 55.3 | 53.5 | 51.6 |
| 52° | 70.3 | 68.6 | 66.9 | 65.1 | 63.4 | 61.6 | 59.9 | 58.1 | 56.2 | 54.4 | 52.5 | 50.6 |
| 53° | 69.8 | 68.0 | 66.3 | 64.5 | 62.7 | 60.9 | 59.1 | 57.2 | 55.4 | 53.4 | 51.5 | 49.5 |
| 54° | 69.3 | 67.5 | 65.7 | 63.9 | 62.0 | 60.2 | 58.3 | 56.4 | 54.4 | 52.4 | 50.4 | 48.3 |
| 55° | 68.7 | 67.9 | 65.0 | 63.2 | 61.3 | 59.3 | 57.4 | 55.4 | 53.4 | 51.3 | 49.2 | 47.1 |
| 56° | 68.2 | 66.3 | 64.4 | 62.4 | 60.5 | 58.5 | 56.4 | 54.4 | 52.3 | 50.1 | 47.9 | 45.7 |
| 57° | 67.6 | 65.6 | 63.6 | 61.6 | 59.6 | 57.5 | 55.4 | 53.3 | 51.1 | 48.8 | 46.5 | 44.2 |
| 58° | 66.9 | 64.9 | 62.8 | 60.8 | 58.6 | 56.5 | 54.3 | 52.1 | 49.8 | 47.4 | 45.0 | 42.5 |
| 59° | 66.2 | 64.1 | 62.0 | 59.8 | 57.6 | 55.4 | 53.1 | 50.8 | 48.4 | 45.9 | 43.3 | 40.6 |
| 60° | 65.4 | 63.3 | 61.1 | 58.8 | 56.5 | 54.2 | 51.8 | 49.4 | 46.8 | 44.2 | 41.5 | 38.6 |
| 61° | 64.6 | 62.3 | 60.1 | 57.7 | 55.3 | 52.9 | 50.4 | 47.8 | 45.1 | 42.3 | 39.4 | 36.3 |
| 62° | 63.7 | 61.4 | 59.0 | 56.5 | 54.0 | 51.5 | 48.8 | 46.1 | 43.2 | 40.2 | 37.1 | 33.7 |
| 63° | 62.7 | 60.3 | 57.8 | 55.2 | 52.6 | 49.9 | 47.1 | 44.2 | 41.1 | 37.9 | 34.4 | 30.6 |
| 64° | 61.7 | 59.1 | 56.5 | 53.8 | 51.0 | 48.2 | 45.2 | 42.0 | 38.7 | 35.2 | 31.3 | 27.0 |
| 65° | 60.5 | 57.8 | 55.1 | 52.2 | 49.3 | 46.2 | 43.0 | 39.6 | 36.0 | 32.0 | 27.6 | 22.4 |
| 66° | 59.2 | 56.4 | 53.5 | 50.5 | 47.3 | 44.0 | 40.5 | 36.8 | 32.8 | 28.2 | 22.9 | 16.1 |

**Name the Bearing the same as the Declination NORTH or SOUTH**
**and EAST if rising. WEST if setting.**

Advanced Nav.

## ARC-TO-TIME CONVERSION TABLE

| Arc ° | Time h m | Arc ° | Time h m | Arc ° | Time h m | Arc ° | Time h m | Arc ° | Time h m | Arc ° | Time h m | Arc ' | Time m s | Arc '' | Time s |
|---|---|---|---|---|---|---|---|---|---|---|---|---|---|---|---|
| 0 | 0 00 | 60 | 4 00 | 120 | 8 00 | 180 | 12 00 | 240 | 16 00 | 300 | 20 00 | 0 | 0 00 | 0=0.0 | 0.00 |
| 1 | 0 04 | 61 | 4 04 | 121 | 8 04 | 181 | 12 04 | 241 | 16 04 | 301 | 20 04 | 1 | 0 04 | 1 | 0.07 |
| 2 | 0 08 | 62 | 4 08 | 122 | 8 08 | 182 | 12 08 | 242 | 16 08 | 302 | 20 08 | 2 | 0 08 | 2 | 0.13 |
| 3 | 0 12 | 63 | 4 12 | 123 | 8 12 | 183 | 12 12 | 243 | 16 12 | 303 | 20 12 | 3 | 0 12 | 3 | 0.20 |
| 4 | 0 16 | 64 | 4 16 | 124 | 8 16 | 184 | 12 16 | 244 | 16 16 | 304 | 20 16 | 4 | 0 16 | 4 | 0.27 |
| 5 | 0 20 | 65 | 4 20 | 125 | 8 20 | 185 | 12 20 | 245 | 16 20 | 305 | 20 20 | 5 | 0 20 | 5 | 0.33 |
| 6 | 0 24 | 66 | 4 24 | 126 | 8 24 | 186 | 12 24 | 246 | 16 24 | 306 | 20 24 | 6 | 0 24 | 6=0.1 | 0.40 |
| 7 | 0 28 | 67 | 4 28 | 127 | 8 28 | 187 | 12 28 | 247 | 16 28 | 307 | 20 28 | 7 | 0 28 | 7 | 0.47 |
| 8 | 0 32 | 68 | 4 32 | 128 | 8 32 | 188 | 12 32 | 248 | 16 32 | 308 | 20 32 | 8 | 0 32 | 8 | 0.53 |
| 9 | 0 36 | 69 | 4 36 | 129 | 8 36 | 189 | 12 36 | 249 | 16 36 | 309 | 20 36 | 9 | 0 36 | 9 | 0.60 |
| 10 | 0 40 | 70 | 4 40 | 130 | 8 40 | 190 | 12 40 | 250 | 16 40 | 310 | 20 40 | 10 | 0 40 | 10 | 0.67 |
| 11 | 0 44 | 71 | 4 44 | 131 | 8 44 | 191 | 12 44 | 251 | 16 44 | 311 | 20 44 | 11 | 0 44 | 11 | 0.73 |
| 12 | 0 48 | 72 | 4 48 | 132 | 8 48 | 192 | 12 48 | 252 | 16 48 | 312 | 20 48 | 12 | 0 48 | 12=0.2 | 0.80 |
| 13 | 0 52 | 73 | 4 52 | 133 | 8 52 | 193 | 12 52 | 253 | 16 52 | 313 | 20 52 | 13 | 0 52 | 13 | 0.87 |
| 14 | 0 56 | 74 | 4 56 | 134 | 8 56 | 194 | 12 56 | 254 | 16 56 | 314 | 20 56 | 14 | 0 56 | 14 | 0.93 |
| 15 | 1 00 | 75 | 5 00 | 135 | 9 00 | 195 | 13 00 | 255 | 17 00 | 315 | 21 00 | 15 | 1 00 | 15 | 1.00 |
| 16 | 1 04 | 76 | 5 04 | 136 | 9 04 | 196 | 13 04 | 256 | 17 04 | 316 | 21 04 | 16 | 1 04 | 16 | 1.07 |
| 17 | 1 08 | 77 | 5 08 | 137 | 9 08 | 197 | 13 08 | 257 | 17 08 | 317 | 21 08 | 17 | 1 08 | 17 | 1.13 |
| 18 | 1 12 | 78 | 5 12 | 138 | 9 12 | 198 | 13 12 | 258 | 17 12 | 318 | 21 12 | 18 | 1 12 | 18=0.3 | 1.20 |
| 19 | 1 16 | 79 | 5 16 | 139 | 9 16 | 199 | 13 16 | 259 | 17 16 | 319 | 21 16 | 19 | 1 16 | 19 | 1.27 |
| 20 | 1 20 | 80 | 5 20 | 140 | 9 20 | 200 | 13 20 | 260 | 17 20 | 320 | 21 20 | 20 | 1 20 | 20 | 1.33 |
| 21 | 1 24 | 81 | 5 24 | 141 | 9 24 | 201 | 13 24 | 261 | 17 24 | 321 | 21 24 | 21 | 1 24 | 21 | 1.40 |
| 22 | 1 28 | 82 | 5 28 | 142 | 9 28 | 202 | 13 28 | 262 | 17 28 | 322 | 21 28 | 22 | 1 28 | 22 | 1.47 |
| 23 | 1 32 | 83 | 5 32 | 143 | 9 32 | 203 | 13 32 | 263 | 17 32 | 323 | 21 32 | 23 | 1 32 | 23 | 1.53 |
| 24 | 1 36 | 84 | 5 36 | 144 | 9 36 | 204 | 13 36 | 264 | 17 36 | 324 | 21 36 | 24 | 1 36 | 24=0.4 | 1.60 |
| 25 | 1 40 | 85 | 5 40 | 145 | 9 40 | 205 | 13 40 | 265 | 17 40 | 325 | 21 40 | 25 | 1 40 | 25 | 1.67 |
| 26 | 1 44 | 86 | 5 44 | 146 | 9 44 | 206 | 13 44 | 266 | 17 44 | 326 | 21 44 | 26 | 1 44 | 26 | 1.73 |
| 27 | 1 48 | 87 | 5 48 | 147 | 9 48 | 207 | 13 48 | 267 | 17 48 | 327 | 21 48 | 27 | 1 48 | 27 | 1.80 |
| 28 | 1 52 | 88 | 5 52 | 148 | 9 52 | 208 | 13 52 | 268 | 17 52 | 328 | 21 52 | 28 | 1 52 | 28 | 1.87 |
| 29 | 1 56 | 89 | 5 56 | 149 | 9 56 | 209 | 13 56 | 269 | 17 56 | 329 | 21 56 | 29 | 1 56 | 29 | 1.93 |
| 30 | 2 00 | 90 | 6 00 | 150 | 10 00 | 210 | 14 00 | 270 | 18 00 | 330 | 22 00 | 30 | 2 00 | 30=0.5 | 2.00 |
| 31 | 2 04 | 91 | 6 04 | 151 | 10 04 | 211 | 14 04 | 271 | 18 04 | 331 | 22 04 | 31 | 2 04 | 31 | 2.07 |
| 32 | 2 08 | 92 | 6 08 | 152 | 10 08 | 212 | 14 08 | 272 | 18 08 | 332 | 22 08 | 32 | 2 08 | 32 | 2.13 |
| 33 | 2 12 | 93 | 6 12 | 153 | 10 12 | 213 | 14 12 | 273 | 18 12 | 333 | 22 12 | 33 | 2 12 | 33 | 2.20 |
| 34 | 2 16 | 94 | 6 16 | 154 | 10 16 | 214 | 14 16 | 274 | 18 16 | 334 | 22 16 | 34 | 2 16 | 34 | 2.27 |
| 35 | 2 20 | 95 | 6 20 | 155 | 10 20 | 215 | 14 20 | 275 | 18 20 | 335 | 22 20 | 35 | 2 20 | 35 | 2.33 |
| 36 | 2 24 | 96 | 6 24 | 156 | 10 24 | 216 | 14 24 | 276 | 18 24 | 336 | 22 24 | 36 | 2 24 | 36=0.6 | 2.40 |
| 37 | 2 28 | 97 | 6 28 | 157 | 10 28 | 217 | 14 28 | 277 | 18 28 | 337 | 22 28 | 37 | 2 28 | 37 | 2.47 |
| 38 | 2 32 | 98 | 6 32 | 158 | 10 32 | 218 | 14 32 | 278 | 18 32 | 338 | 22 32 | 38 | 2 32 | 38 | 2.53 |
| 39 | 2 36 | 99 | 6 36 | 159 | 10 36 | 219 | 14 36 | 279 | 18 36 | 339 | 22 36 | 39 | 2 36 | 39 | 2.60 |
| 40 | 2 40 | 100 | 6 40 | 160 | 10 40 | 220 | 14 40 | 280 | 18 40 | 340 | 22 40 | 40 | 2 40 | 40 | 2.67 |
| 41 | 2 44 | 101 | 6 44 | 161 | 10 44 | 221 | 14 44 | 281 | 18 44 | 341 | 22 44 | 41 | 2 44 | 41 | 2.73 |
| 42 | 2 48 | 102 | 6 48 | 162 | 10 48 | 222 | 14 48 | 282 | 18 48 | 342 | 22 48 | 42 | 2 48 | 42=0.7 | 2.80 |
| 43 | 2 52 | 103 | 6 52 | 163 | 10 52 | 223 | 14 52 | 283 | 18 52 | 343 | 22 52 | 43 | 2 52 | 43 | 2.87 |
| 44 | 2 56 | 104 | 6 56 | 164 | 10 56 | 224 | 14 56 | 284 | 18 56 | 344 | 22 56 | 44 | 2 56 | 44 | 2.93 |
| 45 | 3 00 | 105 | 7 00 | 165 | 11 00 | 225 | 15 00 | 285 | 19 00 | 345 | 23 00 | 45 | 3 00 | 45 | 3.00 |
| 46 | 3 04 | 106 | 7 04 | 166 | 11 04 | 226 | 15 04 | 286 | 19 04 | 346 | 23 04 | 46 | 3 04 | 46 | 3.07 |
| 47 | 3 08 | 107 | 7 08 | 167 | 11 08 | 227 | 15 08 | 287 | 19 08 | 347 | 23 08 | 47 | 3 08 | 47 | 3.13 |
| 48 | 3 12 | 108 | 7 12 | 168 | 11 12 | 228 | 15 12 | 288 | 19 12 | 348 | 23 12 | 48 | 3 12 | 48=0.8 | 3.20 |
| 49 | 3 16 | 109 | 7 16 | 169 | 11 16 | 229 | 15 16 | 289 | 19 16 | 349 | 23 16 | 49 | 3 16 | 49 | 3.27 |
| 50 | 3 20 | 110 | 7 20 | 170 | 11 20 | 230 | 15 20 | 290 | 19 20 | 350 | 23 20 | 50 | 3 20 | 50 | 3.33 |
| 51 | 3 24 | 111 | 7 24 | 171 | 11 24 | 231 | 15 24 | 291 | 19 24 | 351 | 23 24 | 51 | 3 24 | 51 | 3.40 |
| 52 | 3 28 | 112 | 7 28 | 172 | 11 28 | 232 | 15 28 | 292 | 19 28 | 352 | 23 28 | 52 | 3 28 | 52 | 3.47 |
| 53 | 3 32 | 113 | 7 32 | 173 | 11 32 | 233 | 15 32 | 293 | 19 32 | 353 | 23 32 | 53 | 3 32 | 53 | 3.53 |
| 54 | 3 36 | 114 | 7 36 | 174 | 11 36 | 234 | 15 36 | 294 | 19 36 | 354 | 23 36 | 54 | 3 36 | 54=0.9 | 3.60 |
| 55 | 3 40 | 115 | 7 40 | 175 | 11 40 | 235 | 15 40 | 295 | 19 40 | 355 | 23 40 | 55 | 3 40 | 55 | 3.67 |
| 56 | 3 44 | 116 | 7 44 | 176 | 11 44 | 236 | 15 44 | 296 | 19 44 | 356 | 23 44 | 56 | 3 44 | 56 | 3.73 |
| 57 | 3 48 | 117 | 7 48 | 177 | 11 48 | 237 | 15 48 | 297 | 19 48 | 357 | 23 48 | 57 | 3 48 | 57 | 3.80 |
| 58 | 3 52 | 118 | 7 52 | 178 | 11 52 | 238 | 15 52 | 298 | 19 52 | 358 | 23 52 | 58 | 3 52 | 58 | 3.87 |
| 59 | 3 56 | 119 | 7 56 | 179 | 11 56 | 239 | 15 56 | 299 | 19 56 | 359 | 23 56 | 59 | 3 56 | 59 | 3.93 |
| 60 | 4 00 | 120 | 8 00 | 180 | 12 00 | 240 | 16 00 | 300 | 20 00 | 360 | 24 00 | 60 | 4 00 | 60=1.0 | 4.00 |

## RADIOBEACON HALF-CONVERGENCY CORRECTION TABLE

| Mean Lat | Longitude Difference between Radio Station and Ship | | | | | | | | | | | | |
|---|---|---|---|---|---|---|---|---|---|---|---|---|---|
| | 2° | 4° | 6° | 8° | 10° | 12° | 14° | 16° | 18° | 20° | 22° | 24° | 26° |
| | 0.1 | 0.1 | 0.2 | 0.2 | 0.3 | 0.3 | 0.4 | 0.4 | 0.5 | 0.5 | 0.6 | 0.6 | 0.7 |
| 3 | 0.1 | 0.2 | 0.3 | 0.4 | 0.5 | 0.6 | 0.7 | 0.8 | 0.9 | 1.0 | 1.1 | 1.2 | 1.3 |
| 6 | 0.2 | 0.3 | 0.5 | 0.6 | 0.9 | 0.9 | 1.1 | 1.2 | 1.4 | 1.5 | 1.7 | 1.8 | 2.0 |
| 9 | 0.2 | 0.4 | 0.6 | 0.8 | 1.1 | 1.2 | 1.5 | 1.6 | 1.9 | 2.0 | 2.3 | 2.5 | 2.7 |
| 12 | 0.3 | 0.5 | 0.8 | 1.0 | 1.3 | 1.6 | 1.9 | 2.0 | 2.3 | 2.5 | 2.8 | 3.1 | 3.3 |
| 15 | 0.3 | 0.6 | 1.0 | 1.2 | 1.6 | 1.9 | 2.2 | 2.4 | 2.8 | 3.0 | 3.4 | 3.7 | 4.0 |
| 18 | 0.3 | 0.7 | 1.1 | 1.4 | 1.9 | 2.2 | 2.5 | 2.8 | 3.2 | 3.5 | 3.9 | 4.3 | 4.6 |
| 21 | 0.4 | 0.8 | 1.2 | 1.6 | 2.1 | 2.5 | 2.9 | 3.2 | 3.6 | 4.0 | 4.4 | 4.8 | 5.2 |
| 24 | 0.4 | 0.9 | 1.3 | 1.8 | 2.3 | 2.8 | 3.2 | 3.6 | 4.0 | 4.5 | 5.0 | 5.4 | 5.9 |
| 27 | 0.5 | 1.0 | 1.4 | 2.0 | 2.5 | 3.0 | 3.5 | 4.0 | 4.5 | 5.0 | 5.5 | 6.0 | 6.5 |
| 30 | 0.5 | 1.1 | 1.5 | 2.2 | 2.7 | 3.3 | 3.8 | 4.4 | 4.9 | 5.4 | 6.0 | 6.5 | 7.1 |
| 33 | 0.6 | 1.2 | 1.7 | 2.4 | 2.9 | 3.5 | 4.1 | 4.7 | 5.3 | 5.9 | 6.5 | 7.0 | 7.6 |
| 36 | 0.6 | 1.3 | 1.8 | 2.6 | 3.1 | 3.8 | 4.4 | 5.0 | 5.6 | 6.3 | 7.0 | 7.5 | 8.1 |
| 39 | 0.7 | 1.4 | 1.9 | 2.8 | 3.3 | 4.0 | 4.7 | 5.3 | 6.0 | 6.7 | 7.5 | 8.0 | 8.7 |
| 42 | 0.7 | 1.5 | 2.0 | 2.9 | 3.5 | 4.2 | 5.0 | 5.6 | 6.3 | 7.1 | 7.9 | 8.5 | 9.2 |
| 45 | 0.7 | 1.5 | 2.1 | 3.0 | 3.7 | 4.5 | 5.3 | 5.9 | 6.7 | 7.4 | 8.2 | 8.9 | 9.6 |
| 48 | 0.8 | 1.6 | 2.3 | 3.2 | 3.9 | 4.7 | 5.5 | 6.2 | 7.0 | 7.8 | 8.5 | 9.3 | 10.0 |
| 51 | 0.8 | 1.6 | 2.4 | 3.4 | 4.1 | 4.9 | 5.7 | 6.5 | 7.3 | 8.1 | 8.9 | 9.7 | 10.5 |
| 54 | 0.8 | 1.7 | 2.5 | 3.5 | 4.3 | 5.1 | 5.9 | 6.8 | 7.6 | 8.4 | 9.2 | 10.0 | 10.9 |
| 57 | 0.9 | 1.8 | 2.6 | 3.6 | 4.4 | 5.2 | 6.1 | 7.0 | 7.9 | 8.7 | 9.5 | 10.3 | 11.2 |

If two places on the chart are joined, first by a great circle and then by a straight line, the latter makes an angle with the great circle at each end. Each of these two angles may, for all practical purposes, be regarded as being equal to the **Half-Convergency.**

**It is important to remember that the straight line bearing on the Mercator chart always lies on the equatorial side of the great circle bearing.**

D/F bearings are all great circle bearings and must, therefore, be corrected for Half Convergency before they can be plotted on a Mercator chart.

**Half-Convergency Example:** A vessel in Lat. 15°20'N, Long. 50°20'W, obtains a Radio D/F bearing from a station in Lat. 53°40'N., Long 5°10'W. True bearing signalled as 070°.

Enter the above table with the mean latitude (53°40' + 50°20' = 104°00' ÷ 2) = 52°00', and the Diff. Long. (15°20'– 5°10') = 10°10'W., and by inspection the approximate correction is found to be 4°. By the rule above this must be applied toward the equator so 070° + 4° = 074°, which is the correct mercatorial bearing to plot.

### OMEGA STATIONS

| Ident Letter | Location | Lat. | Long. |
|---|---|---|---|
| A | Norway | 66°25'N | 13°09'E |
| B | Liberia | 6°18'N | 10°40'W |
| C | Hawaii | 21°24'N | 157°50'W |
| D | N. Dakota | 46°22'N | 98°20'W |
| E | La Réunion | 20°58'S | 55°17'E |
| F | Argentina | 43°03'S | 65°11'W |
| G | Australia | 38°29'S | 146°56'E |
| H | Japan | 34°37'N | 129°27E |

**Advanced Nav.**

237

## LORAN-C RATE TABLES

| PAIR | LOCATION (MASTER STATION LISTED FIRST) | |
|------|------|------|
| **GULF OF ALASKA, U.S.A.** | | |
| 7960-X | TOK JUNCTION, AK | NARROW CAPE, AK |
| 7960-Y | TOK JUNCTION, AK | SHOAL COVE, AK |
| 7960-Z | TOK JUNCTION, AK | PT. CLARENCE, AK |
| **WEST COAST, CANADA** | | |
| 5990-X | WILLIAMS LAKE, BC | SHOAL COVE, REVILLAGIGEDO I., AK |
| 5990-Y | WILLIAMS LAKE, BC | GEORGE, WA |
| 5990-Z | WILLIAMS LAKE, BC | PORT HARDY, VANCOUVER I., CANADA |
| **CENTRAL PACIFIC** | **THIS CHAIN HAS BEEN DISCONTINUED** | |
| **WEST COAST U.S.A.** | | |
| 9940-W | FALLON, NV | GEORGE, WA |
| 9940-X | FALLON, NV | MIDDLETOWN, CA |
| 9940-Y | FALLON, NV | SEARCHLIGHT, NV |
| **EAST COAST, CANADA** | | |
| 5930-X | CARIBOU, ME | NANTUCKET, MA |
| 5930-Y | CARIBOU, ME | CAPE RACE, NEWFOUNDLAND |
| 5930-Z | CARIBOU, ME | FOX HARBOR, NEWFOUNDLAND |
| **NORTHEAST, U.S.A.** | | |
| 9960-W | SENECA, NY | CARIBOU, ME |
| 9960-X | SENECA, NY | NANTUCKET, MA |
| 9960-Y | SENECA, NY | CAROLINA BEACH, NC |
| 9960-Z | SENECA, NY | DANA, IN |
| **SOUTHEAST, U.S.A.** | | |
| 7980-W | MALONE, FL | GRANGEVILLE, LA |
| 7980-X | MALONE, FL | RAYMONDVILLE, TX |
| 7980-Y | MALONE, FL | JUPITER, FL |
| 7980-Z | MALONE, FL | CAROLINA BEACH, NC |
| **GREAT LAKES, U.S.A.** | | |
| 8970-W | DANA, IN | MALONE,FL |
| 8970-X | DANA, IN | SENECA, NY |
| 8970-Y | DANA, IN | BAUDETTE, MN |

# EMERGENCY NAVIGATION

*We wish to credit David Burch with much of the inspiration for this chapter. His book,* Emergency Navigation, *published by International Marine, is the definitive work on the subject and we recommend it highly.*

Navigation is both an art and science. Nowhere is the blend more evident than in the techniques used to navigate when you've lost all or most of the gear you normally rely on. Deprived of this equipment, you must turn to the centuries-old techniques of the Polynesians and Phoenicians, whose navigation was thought to be more magic than science. When you borrow these techniques, you appreciate more fully the knowledge and skills of navigators who long ago preceded you.

Learning to make do with limited and crude equipment enhances your understanding of the basic concepts behind sophisticated new systems. You are forced to go through some of the same thought processes that experts program into those "black boxes." And, you're forced to rely on your senses as you more acutely hear, smell, feel, and look for clues about your position.

In short, familiarity with the tools of emergency navigation makes you a better navigator in any circumstance. Beyond that, practicing their use is fun — that is, when you're not coping with stressful emergency conditions.

This chapter describes a selected and limited number of techniques you can use far from shore when your normal instruments and systems fail. To conserve space, the techniques included here are only a sampling of the full array of possibilities. They don't include methods that are available when land is in sight or when you're proceeding along a coast in fog. The techniques described here are confined largely to the use of heavenly bodies for steering and finding your position. For example, this chapter does not describe how to use cloud and wave patterns.

You should be prepared to use all available emergency navigation methods when faced with total system failure. You may wish to consult other treatments of the subject like *Emergency Navigation*, which presents a more elaborate discussion of the material presented here and includes the full array of additional techniques.

## BASICS

### Using What You Have

Your offshore emergency kit should include a number of items that can help you find your way to port: a hiker's compass, a plastic sextant, pencils, waterproof paper, a waterproof quartz watch, and *Reed's Nautical Almanac*. You'd also be smart to carry a stick or two (each a couple of feet long), some string, a small weight, a flat pan that holds water, and — especially useful instruments — your arms and fingers. The crude devices that you can jury rig with these items, when combined with your eyes, ears, nose, and skin, can get you home.

### Dead Reckoning

A good first rule of emergency navigation is to know where you are when the emergency arises. Don't fail to keep close track of your position, even in midocean, on the presumption that you can always easily get an update. When all else fails, you can usually proceed for quite some distance with reasonable confidence based on careful dead reckoning. But your projected DR positions are only as good as their starting point. So don't be cavalier about your navigation on the grounds that no dangers are nearby. In an emergency, you're in much better shape if you have a good DR starting point.

### Estimating Speed

A good DR track also depends on carefully estimating speed through the water, and you can do so without a knotmeter by timing the movement of any floating object as it passes alongside your boat. Simply drop something off the bow of your boat and note the time it takes to reach the stern. Then apply a little math. Suppose it takes four seconds for the floating object to travel from the bow to the stern on your 40-foot boat. Multiply the object's speed, expressed in feet per second, (in this case, 10) by .6 to get your boat speed in knots — 6 knots, in this example.

This method's accuracy improves when the floating object passes over a longer distance. On a short boat, you can lengthen the object's travel time by tying it to one end of a light line with a measured length of, say, 100 feet. (Lacking a ruler or tape measure, estimate the line's length by extending your arms — if you're of average size, the distance between your fingertips is about a fathom.)

Tie the line to your stern, toss the tethered object overboard, and carefully time how long it takes for the line to stretch out to its full length (the point at which you start dragging the object along).

The term "knot" derives from a variant of this technique in which you tie knots at measured intervals along the line and note how long it takes for a certain number of knots to go by. Choose convenient intervals to simplify the math. If you place a knot every 10 feet, then the number of intervals (and fractions) that go by in six seconds is your speed in knots.

When estimating speed in this way without a watch, you'll have to fall back on the old trick of counting cadence — as in "one thousand and" equals one second. A good way to practice your rhythm before you need it is to use your favorite cadence to time the intervals of flashing lights.

## Estimating Leeway

When you're under sail and heading to weather, you need to take leeway into account in estimating the direction of your DR projection. When you're close-hauled, leeway can vary between 5° and 25° depending on wind strength, sea state, and your boat's performance characteristics. It falls off a lot when you fall off a little and ease the sheets.

You don't have to guess at leeway — you can measure it. You can do so crudely by looking astern and observing the angle that your wake forms with an imaginary extension of your centerline. You can be more precise by tying a light line to some point above your centerline amidships, trailing it freely astern, and measuring the angle it forms with your centerline. (See illustration.)

## Current

The problem with DR positions, of course, is that they don't take account of current. When you're in areas with significant amounts of current you must estimate and project its cumulative effect.

Pilot charts outline prevailing ocean cur-

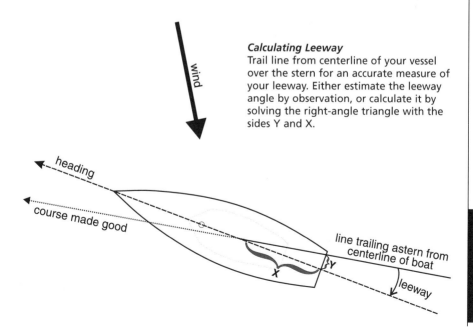

*Calculating Leeway*
Trail line from centerline of your vessel over the stern for an accurate measure of your leeway. Either estimate the leeway angle by observation, or calculate it by solving the right-angle triangle with the sides Y and X.

rents monthly. Ocean current strength and direction are often predictable because they follow the prevailing wind patterns: clockwise circulation around the perimeter of ocean basins in the Northern Hemisphere, and counterclockwise in the Southern Hemisphere.

Although the speed of ocean currents might average half a knot worldwide, it can be as high as three or four knots in some areas like the Gulf Stream between Florida and the Bahamas. In such areas, you can observe changes in water temperature and color and in wave characteristics to determine when you're in the Stream.

When you're very near shore you need to take account of currents induced by tides and local winds. In areas such as bays and other open basins with regular features you can sometimes relate tidal current strengths and directions (ebb and flood) to the times of rise and fall of the tide. Along straight coastal stretches tides induce a rotating current pattern with emphasis on movement along the shore rather than perpendicular to it. Because the flow direction reverses with tidal changes, these alongshore currents have little net effect over a day's coastwise travel.

In gauging the effect of local winds on current, you can use the rough rule that current speeds are about three percent of the speed of winds that blow for a half day or longer. In open Northern Hemisphere waters, the current's direction is about 30° to the right of the wind direction. So, for example, when a strong (20-30 knots) northwest wind blows (toward the southeast) for an extended period, you may have a wind-driven current heading in a southerly direction at a speed of maybe half a knot or more. (The foregoing estimates are deliberately imprecise because the rule is very general.)

### Dead Reckoning Errors

When you're forced to rely on dead reckoning for an extended period, you should be acutely aware that errors are cumulative. For example, if you could be reasonably confident, after taking all possible errors into account, that you were within 20 miles of your estimated position at the end of a day's run, you'd have to conjure with the possibility of being as much as 100

miles off after five days if the same factors continued to prevail. To keep this perspective, it helps to think of the range of possible errors in percentage terms. If your average daily run in the above example is 100 miles, then your error rate would be 20 percent. At that rate, your actual position might be up to 100 miles from your projected position after going an estimated 500 miles.

You're well advised to be thoughtful and realistic in placing outer limits on your error. In dead reckoning, isolate the elements that can contribute to error and don't underestimate their magnitude. When you're operating without reliable instruments, your speed estimates, measurements of direction, and knowledge of current can be quite crude. It's best to assign separate percentages to your course and speed errors and then combine them into a single rate. Mathematicians insist that the way to combine them is not to add them together, nor to use only the larger value. The right way (you guessed it) is more complicated.

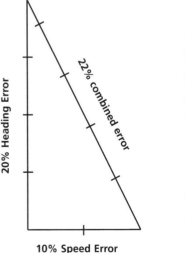

**10% Speed Error**

*Estimating Combined Errors*
This example shows how an estimated heading error of 20% and a speed error of 10% would combine to a total 22% error.

Adapted from *Emergency Navigation* by David Burch.

The math you use in combining errors can best be conveyed graphically. Draw a right triangle to scale, with the length of one side equal to the rate of speed error and the other to course error. The combined error is then equal to the length of the hypotenuse. (See illustration left.) So, for example, if you believe that your speed error could be as much as 10 percent and your course error 20 percent, your combined error (the hypotenuse) would be 22 percent. Note that the combined number is in between the larger single error (20) and the sum of the two (30). Also, imagine a triangle with sides of very unequal lengths. In it, the length of the hypotenuse is nearly identical to the length of the longer side. You can see, then, that the combined error is nearly the same as the larger error when the size of one error dominates.

This extended discussion of errors is included here because successful emergency navigation (indeed, all navigation) can hinge on taking errors fully into account. When you can't be sure where you are, it's important to know where you surely are not.

## STEERING WITHOUT A COMPASS

When steering by heavenly bodies you should keep in mind the pattern of their motions as the earth rotates under them. In the northern hemisphere, stars appear to rotate counterclockwise through the night around Polaris, the North Star. Stars that are close to Polaris do not rise or set; the others rise in the east and set in the west (as does the sun, of course). You can become familiar with this pattern while standing night watches and noting how it changes with changes in the seasons and in latitude. It helps to understand the directional orientation of the whole pattern, even though you may use only one body at a time to steer by.

Directions to bodies in the sky are easier to measure when they're near the horizon than when they're at high altitudes. Yet, bodies near the horizon are less bright than higher ones because their light passes through more atmosphere. On the other hand, the very brightness of the sun compels you to take to accuracy-reducing precautions to protect your eyes.

## STEERING BY THE STARS

At the risk of detracting from the importance of using the entire star pattern, this discussion focuses on three parts of the pattern: The North Star, the constellation Orion, and overhead stars. (The preceding chapter on celestial navigation provides important background for this section.)

### The North Star

Polaris is not located exactly at the north celestial pole, but it's so close that you can use it for steering purposes without making any corrections. It's a convenient directional reference point because it's virtually motionless during the night and through the seasons. It's easier to use when you're at lower latitudes because it doesn't appear high in the sky from such latitudes.

Polaris doesn't stand out when you're looking for it because it isn't a first magnitude star. To find it, locate the two pointer stars at the Big Dipper's cup end. Extend a line from these stars to a distance five times the distance between the pointers — and there's Polaris. You can use the angles subtended by your fingers at the ends of your fully extended arms to measure these and other angular distances.

When clouds cover the Big Dipper you can find Polaris by using the constellation Cassiopeia, which is on the opposite side of Polaris from the Big Dipper. (See the illustration on the next page for the relationship of Polaris to the Big Dipper and Cassiopeia.)

Because Polaris can be so important to your directional orientation, you may want to use it even when it's obscured by clouds. You can locate the cloud-covered Polaris by using the Big Dipper when it's still visible. To do this, you'll need a stick, string, and small weight. (See illustration on page 245.) Mark the stick with five segments, each equal in length to the distance between the Big Dipper's two pointer stars when you hold the stick up to them at arm's length. When you align the stick with the pointers, as shown in the figure, its end marks the location of Polaris behind the cloud cover. The weighted string tied to the stick's end brings the direction of Polaris down vertically to your horizon. Bringing the direction down is a particularly useful thing to do when Polaris, or any

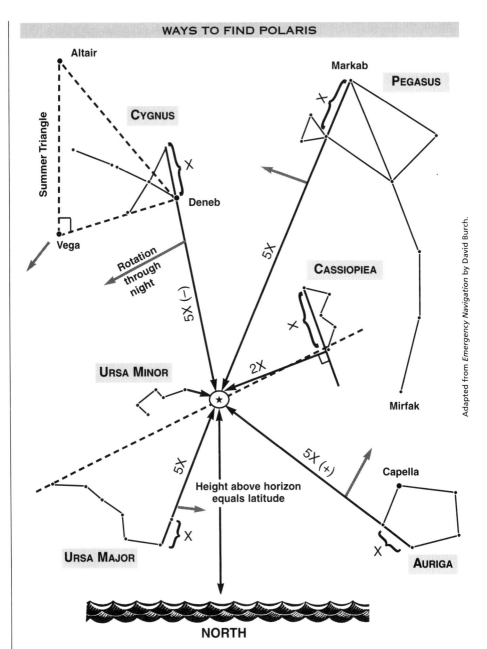

**WAYS TO FIND POLARIS**

Altair

Markab

**PEGASUS**

**CYGNUS**

Summer Triangle

X

Deneb

Vega

Rotation through night

5X (−)

5X

**CASSIOPIEA**

X

**URSA MINOR**

2X

Mirfak

5X (+)

Capella

5X

Height above horizon equals latitude

**URSA MAJOR**

X

X

**AURIGA**

*Adapted from Emergency Navigation by David Burch.*

**NORTH**

Many navigators are familiar with the technique of finding Polaris by using the two "pointer stars" on the outer edge of the Big Dipper (Ursa Major) to first establish the distance "X," and then point to Polaris five "X" lengths from the dipper. This illustration shows that relationship as well as five other constellations that point in some manner to Polaris. Note that the "X" distances vary from constellation to constellation, and in the cases of Auriga and Cygnus, the 5X distance is modified slightly.

## FINDING POLARIS BEHIND CLOUDS

other body, is high in the sky. You might want to use this jury-rigged device for this purpose even when a body is visible.

### Orion

Mintaka is the leading star in Orion's belt; the other two stars in the belt follow it as the constellation appears to move across the sky from east to west. Mintaka circles westward right above the equator and, because of this, its direction is exactly east when rising and west when setting.

Unless you're located on the equator, Mintaka doesn't remain directly east of you after rising and isn't directly west before setting. That is, it doesn't move in a plane vertical to your horizon. The angle its path makes with your horizon depends on your latitude. When you're closer to the equator, the path is more vertical; when you're farther away from the equator, the path is inclined more toward your horizon.

You can use even a rough knowledge of your latitude to describe the path of Mintaka's ascent and descent. And, in doing so, you can estimate how far from east or west Mintaka is at times after rising

and before setting and use it for steering over a several-hour period. One approach is to visualize Mintaka's path by tracing it back to the horizon after rising, or forward to the horizon before setting. To do this, hold a stick (again) up to Mintaka and incline it to the horizon at an angle equal to 90° minus your latitude. (See illustration on next page.) You use that formula because the angle varies inversely with latitude, as explained above. East or west is located where the inclined stick meets your horizon.

In midlatitudes or higher, you can use this method only up to about three hours after Mintaka rises or before before it sets because its path curves markedly when its direction departs substantially from east or west, as shown in the illustration.

### Overhead Stars

Any star passing directly overhead (through your zenith) is moving west as it does so. You can tell directions, then, by closely watching the movement of a star passing overhead. A weighted string suspended from a stick (again) can provide you with the needed point of reference.

Adapted from *Emergency Navigation* by David Burch.

**Emergency Nav.**

## USING ORION'S BELT TO FIND EAST

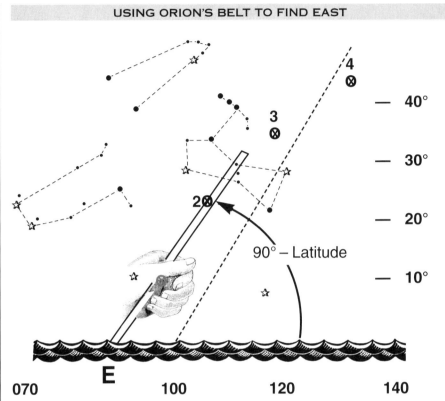

— 40°

3
⊗

— 30°

4
⊗

— 20°

90° – Latitude

— 10°

Adapted from *Emergency Navigation* by David Burch.

E

070          100          120          140

This illustration shows east being determined when you are approximately 35° north and Mintaka, the leading star of Orion's Belt, has risen about 2½ hours. The stick is held at 55° (90° – 35°). The ⊗'s mark the hourly progression of Mintaka rising. Best results are obtained up to three hours after rising. The dotted line shows how a sighting at 3½ hours yields a bearing almost 10° in error.

Sight up along the string to the tip of the stick held above your head. The tip indicates your zenith. With patience and practice, you can track a star's direction as it moves through your zenith.

A star that passes directly overhead won't stay on an east-west path throughout the night, though, unless you're looking at it from the equator. Only stars with zero declination, like Mintaka, rise at 090° and set at 270°. And those stars pass directly over your head only if you're at latitude 0°.

Stars that pass overhead have declinations equal to your latitude, so you can estimate an overhead star's declination when you have only a rough idea of your latitude. And, a star's declination is one

determinant of how far north or south of the east-west line it rises and sets. If you're in the Northern Hemisphere you know that a star passing directly overhead is heading for a point on the horizon that's north of west.

Here's a rule you can use to estimate the direction of an overhead star long after it has passed overhead — it's called the half-latitude rule. When the star descends to an altitude that equals your latitude, it is displaced from west by one-half your latitude. Therefore, when you're at latitude 30° north, for example, an overhead star is 15° north of west when its altitude is 30°. A way of gauging when the star's altitude equals your latitude is to compare its height with that of Polaris, whose altitude always equals your latitude.

When you're anywhere in the tropics, it's easier to get direction from overhead stars because they appear, from those latitudes, to rise and set north or south of the east-west line by an amount equal to your latitude. For example, an overhead star rises and sets 15° to the north of east-west when your latitude is 15° N. (This convenient relationship in the tropics may be one of the reasons the ancient Polynesians could make successful long distance passages.)

## STEERING BY THE SUN

Now — you're probably thinking — this is the easy part. Everyone knows how to tell direction from the sun. It rises in the east and sets in the west. Sorry, but it's not quite that simple. Steering by the sun can be as challenging as steering by the stars, or more so.

The sky is filled with stars — but there's only one sun. With a partial cloud cover, you'll likely be able to see some useful stars, but you may not be able to see the sun at all.

The best way to use the stars is to get directional orientation from the entire pattern they form in the sky. The sun, by itself, forms no pattern. Further, the sun's intense brightness prevents you from focusing on it for even an instant without risking eye damage. Finally, the sun doesn't usually rise at 090° or set at 270°.

### Sunrise/Sunset Observations

In the fall and winter, when the sun's declination is south, it rises and sets south of east-west. In the middle of this period, at the time of the winter solstice (around December 21), the sun's displacement from east-west on rising and setting (called its amplitude) is greatest. The pattern is the same in spring and summer, in reverse. Then the amplitude is north and reaches its maximum amount around June 21, at the summer solstice.

The sun's amplitude also varies with your latitude. It's greater at higher latitudes. You can derive, mathematically or graphically, the precise direction of sunrise and sunset from your latitude and the sun's declination; or you can use Amplitude Tables such as those at the end of Chapter 4,

*Advanced Navigation.* You can also make a fairly close estimate of these directions in an easy way by using the stars just before sunrise or just after sunset.

One way to relate the direction of sunrise to star directions is to steer directly toward Polaris just before morning twilight, maintain that course until sunrise (using the wave pattern as a reference), and then note (on a jury-rigged compass card) the relative bearing of the sun when it rises. You don't have to go so far as to alter course to the north when using this approach. You can relate the direction of sunrise to whatever star or star pattern you're steering by in the pre-dawn hours, if you feel they're providing a reasonably accurate guide. And, you can relate the direction of sunset to the placement of evening stars in the same way. You don't have to go through this process every day because the sun's amplitude changes only very slowly — if you don't change latitudes rapidly.

### Morning and Afternoon Observations

Unless you happen to be on the equator on March 21 or September 21 (when the sun's declination is zero), the sun won't ascend vertically after rising or descend vertically before setting. It usually changes direction significantly in the several hours after it rises and before it sets.

To use the sun with some accuracy while steering during those hours, you can track its changing direction in the same way you track the movement of your friend Mintaka in Orion's belt. (See previous page.) In this case, hold the stick up to the sun and incline it at an angle to the horizon equal to 90° minus your latitude to find the point of sunrise or sunset. This technique doesn't work as well with the sun as it does with Mintaka because the sun's declination changes with the seasons; Mintaka's always stays at zero. The inaccuracies resulting from not adjusting for the sun's changing declination are kept to a tolerable level, though, when your latitude and the sun's declination are not very far apart. This method won't be accurate enough, for example, when you're sailing at high north latitudes in the winter when the sun's declination is south — a situation you'd want to avoid more for reasons of frigid weather than for this inaccuracy.

## Midday Sun Observations

The sun is always directly north or south of you when it crosses your meridian at midday. The time it crosses your meridian is halfway between sunrise and sunset. (That's not necessarily, nor usually, when your watch reads 1200.) You can time the rise and set and divide the interval between these times by two to determine how long after sunrise the meridian crossing will occur. It's important to take the sun's sizable diameter into account when timing its rise and set. Always use the top or bottom edge against the horizon. If atmospheric conditions make it difficult to time the rise or set accurately, you can still find the time of meridian crossing by noting the time the sun is, say, 30° high after rising and before setting. As long as the altitudes are the same, you can use the same arithmetic as above to make the calculations. (Measuring altitude without a sextant is covered later.)

The nice thing about using the sun's direction at midday is that the timing is completely independent of your latitude and the sun's declination. Every day of the year, wherever in the world you are, the sun is either north or south of you halfway between its rising and setting. Because the sun is at its highest point in the sky when it crosses your meridian, you can theoretically tell from its height when it's directly north or south, without using a watch. However, that's not a practical possibility without using a sextant because the sun's height changes very slowly near the top of the arc that it describes across the sky each day.Without a very accurate altitude measurement, you can't pinpoint when it's at its highest point.

When you're able to time the meridian crossing, though, you may not need to confine your use of the sun for middle-of-the-day directions to the single midday point. When your latitude is far enough from the sun's declination so the sun gets no higher than about 45° at its highest point, you can get reliable directions from it within several hours before and after it bears directly north or south. Reasonably accurate measurements of the sun's direction are possible before and after noon based on a 15° per hour rate of movement. So with the sun bearing 180° at meridian crossing, it bears 165° one hour earlier and 195° one hour after the crossing.

## FINDING YOUR LATITUDE

### Latitude by the Sun at Noon

When you're using the sun at midday to get directions, you'll be tempted to use it also to determine your latitude in the manner described in the preceding chapter on celestial navigation. The sun's height varies with your latitude. So, when you know the sun's declination (gradually changing with the seasons) and measure its altitude, you can determine your latitude. And indeed, such determinations are part of the standard celestial navigation routine when you have a functioning sextant to measure altitudes accurately and an almanac to give you the sun's declination. Without a sextant, though, it's difficult to get a useful altitude of the sun because it's so bright and usually very high in the sky at noon.

With crude altitude-measuring devices you can usually get better accuracy observing the heights of lower bodies. The tolerances for measuring altitudes are much closer than for measuring directions. A 2° error in steering is often acceptable, but the same error in an altitude measurement places you 120 nautical miles from your actual position. You'd have to steer a long time with a 2° error before it would displace you by that distance. You see, then, that the requirements when you're measuring altitude are more exacting than when measuring directions.

### Timing the Day

Rather than measure altitude at noon, you can make better use of the sun by measuring the length of day to get your latitude. At most times of the year changes in latitude significantly affect the day's length — and the change is more pronounced around the times of the summer and winter solstices than at the spring and fall equinoxes, when the length of day and night is equal at all latitudes. Except for a few weeks near the equinoxes, you can find your latitude with useful accuracy by timing the interval between sunrise and sunset and using sunrise-sunset tables in *Reed's Nautical Almanacs* that relate the times of those events to latitude.

In this method, you need to make a correction to your timing of the day's length when you head west or east for any substantial distance during a day. When traveling west, you lengthen the time of daylight; you shorten it when traveling east. The amount of lengthening or shortening can be large enough (at the rate of four minutes for each degree of longitude change) to require a correction to your measurement of the day's length.

## Using Polaris to Find Latitude

As in finding direction, the idea of using the North Star to find latitude is simple: its altitude equals your latitude — approximately. The relationship between altitude and latitude is approximate because Polaris isn't exactly over the North Pole — it's off by about 4/5 of a degree. That small amount doesn't matter when you're using Polaris for direction, but it can place you off by as much as 48 nautical miles when you're using it to find your latitude. When you're measuring altitude with a crude device, with high potential for error, there's no point in compounding the error

by failing to adjust for Polaris's imperfect location.

You can make the adjustment without referring to an almanac by noting the orientation of Polaris to the two constellations that embrace it — the Big Dipper on one side and Cassiopeia on the other. (See illustration below.) The north celestial pole and Polaris are on a line that joins the trailing star of Cassiopeia and the end of the Big Dipper's handle. The Pole is 4/5 of a degree from Polaris on the Big Dipper side of the line. When the line is horizontal (hold up a stick up — again — to see its orientation), the altitudes of Polaris and the Pole are the same, so you don't have to make a correction. When the line is vertical, make a 4/5° (48') correction. When the line is inclined at an angle somewhere between horizontal and vertical you can figure out the intermediate value of the correction graphically by making a scale diagram of the geometric relationship between the North Pole and the star.

## FINDING THE CORRECTION TO THE ALTITUDE OF POLARIS

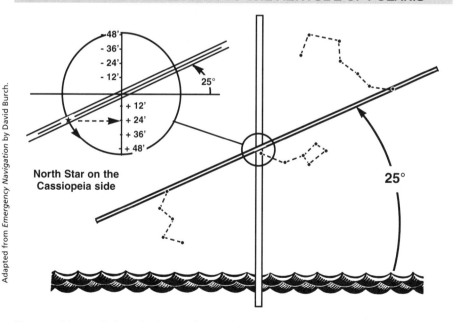

**North Star on the Cassiopeia side**

**25°**

Illustrated is a technique for interpolating the error in Polaris observations. Polaris is actually 48', or 4/5ths of a degree, away from the celestial north pole toward the trailing star in Cassiopeia. See text for further explanation of this diagram.

## Using Overhead Stars to Find Latitude

While you're examining the movement of a star passing through your zenith to get direction (as explained earlier), you can also use the star to get your latitude because its declination equals your latitude. If it were otherwise, the star wouldn't pass directly over your head. All you need to do is find a star of known declination that passes through your zenith. Simple idea, isn't it? Yes — although putting it to practical use can be difficult.

Because bright, easily recognized stars rarely pass exactly through your zenith, you usually have to measure the distance of a very high (and less bright) star from your zenith when it passes very close to that position. That measurement is not easy. One way to do it is to retrieve your weighted string tied to the end of your trusty stick and, positioned on your back at some comfortable place on deck, sight up the string to locate your zenith — at the top of the stick. Then, measure how far north or south of that point the star passes. That measurement tells you how far north or south your latitude is from the star's declination. (A technique for measuring such angular distances is covered later.)

## FINDING LONGITUDE

You can see from the foregoing that there are ways to determine latitude that don't rely on time and a watch, and that you can steer by methods that are independent of time. But you can't find longitude without knowing the time. As explained in the preceding chapter, time and longitude go hand in hand because the earth's daily rotation makes heavenly bodies appear to move along a westward path over a parallel of latitude. The rate of movement is 15° per hour. To orient yourself in longitude using these moving bodies, you need to know where they are at a point in time.

We keep time in relation to the sun's movement, and so, too, you can use the sun to determine your longitude. Without an accurate altitude-measuring instrument it's the easiest body to use because you can readily observe when it rises and sets.

The starting point in this process is to find Greenwich Mean Time (GMT) because *Reed's Nautical Almanac* (and others) gives the times of sunrise and sunset in GMT. To find GMT, first convert your watch time to zone time by adding or subtracting any known watch error. Then, convert your zone time to GMT by adding or subtracting the whole number of hours that your zone time differs from Greenwich time.

The sunrise-sunset table in *Reed's* tells you the time the sun rises and sets when you're on the Greenwich meridian for every day of the year. Because those times are affected by latitude, *Reed's Nautical Almanac* also provides a table that enables you to adjust the tabulated times to your latitude. Compare the times you get from the *Almanac* with the GMT of your observation of the sun's rise or set. Base your observation on the time the sun's top edge (upper limb) meets the horizon. The difference between the tabulated and observed times is equivalent to the difference between your longitude and Greenwich's longitude. A time difference of one hour is equivalent to 15°; one minute of time equals 15 minutes of longitude; four seconds of time equals one minute of longitude; and so on.

As an example, let's say your sailing off the east coast of the U.S. and observe the time of sunrise on your watch to be 05:59:50 (10 seconds before 0600). Taking into account the date of your last check of your watch's error and the daily rate of its error, you know that your watch was 10 seconds slow at the time of observation. So, convert your watch time to zone time by adding 10 seconds (bringing the time of observation up to 06:00:00). Convert the Eastern Standard Time that you're keeping to GMT by adding five hours — making the GMT of your observation of sunrise 11:00:00.

From *Reed's Almanac* you learn that the sunrise at the Greenwich meridian, when adjusted for your latitude, was 05:50:00. The difference in time (11:00:99 minus 05:00:00) is five hours and 10 minutes. You convert that into a longitude difference of 77.5° using the 15° per hour rate. Because the sun rose later at your meridian than at the Greenwich meridian, you know you're west of Greenwich — at longitude 77.5° W.

## JURY-RIGGED INSTRUMENTS

You know that you can turn the simplest materials into measuring devices. Fingers at the end of outstretched arms can give you a rough idea of angular distances along the horizon and in the sky. A stick, string, and small weight can serve multiple uses. It's possible, though, to go a step beyond these crude devices and fashion slightly more elaborate instruments from simple materials.

### Sextant Substitutes

When measuring angular distances you can improve on your fingers and arms by using a string and stick — this time, a flat stick like a ruler. Fasten one end of the string to the stick with a bridle so you can keep the stick perpendicular to the string. (See illustration on next page.) You'll be holding the string's other end in your mouth, so you might want to make a stop knot at its end to hold the end between your clenched teeth. The length of the string should correspond to the length of your extended arm (so you can comfortably stretch the string out to its full length).

Next, place marks along the stick at intervals that correspond to known angular distances. To do this, you'll need to remember the spacing between a few pairs of stars. The distance between the Big Dipper's pointer stars, for example, is 5.4°. Between each of the stars in Orion's belt it's 1.4°. Hold your makeshift instrument up to these pairs of stars, mark the intervals on the stick, and extend these markings along the stick's full length. You've just made a clever device that can provide you with useful angular distances up to 15° to 20°.

To measure larger angles, you can fashion a still more elaborate instrument using a tube, board, string, and small weight. Assemble them as illustrated on page 253, marking off the scale on the arc in graduations that relate to the length of its radius, as shown. When you sight along the tube, tilting it up to the heavenly body, the intersection of the weighted string and the arc indicate the body's altitude because you've calibrated the zero point on the arc to the horizon.

### A Homemade Compass

Did you ever make a magnetic compass in a long-ago science class in school? If not, it's about time you did. With it, you can augment the directional orientation you get from heavenly bodies.

You'll need to gather an iron-free container of water, a piece of iron that resembles a pin (perhaps a nail or paper clip), and some iron-free, buoyant materials on which the iron piece can float. When you float the pin-like object in still water so it can swing freely, it will orient itself along the north-south magnetic axis. By referring to other directional signs, you ought to be able to determine which end is pointing north. The slim piece of iron assumes the desired orientation with startling speed if you first rub it against a larger piece of magnetized material.

Have fun with these homemade instruments and with the techniques described in this chapter that accompany their use. Getting familiar with them will make you a better navigator and give you more peace of mind when you're offshore.

## DESIGN AND USE OF AN ANGLE STICK

Castor

4.5°

Pollux **E**

**D**

10°

1.4°

9°

6.7° 4.4° 5.5°

10.2°

5.4°

4.5° 7.9°

**F**

Figures A and C show this simple instrument in use. The design (B) consists of a ruler-size board or stick attached to a fixed length of string. The knot in the string goes in the user's mouth, and establishes a constant distance from eye to stick. The yoke keeps the measuring stick at a constant angle to the user. The measuring stick can be calibrated using known angular distances between stars. We've illustrated useful dimensions in the constellations Orion (D), Gemini (E), and Ursa Major (F). This device is very similar to one called a Kamal, used to navigate dhows around the Middle East in ancient times.

## DESIGN AND USE OF A PLUMB-BOB SEXTANT

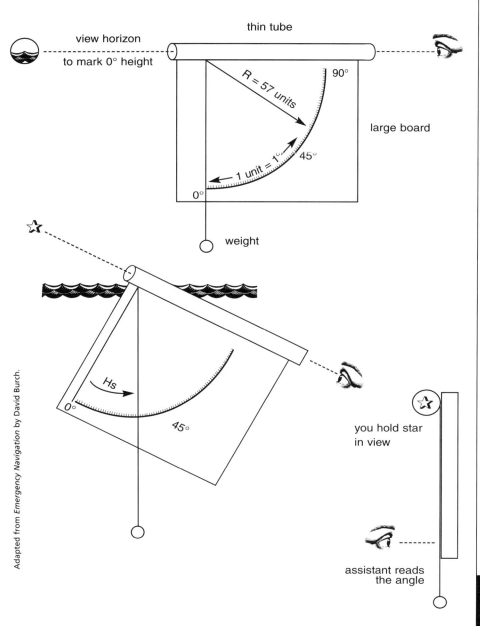

This is a challenging device to build. The trick is to scribe the 90° arc with a string or rule and then divide that distance into 57 parts to establish a 1° unit, and finally accurately mark those units along the arc. Using the instrument also requires care and patience because, of course, the plump-bob will swing around with the motion of your vessel. Unlike normal sextants, a visible horizon is not required.

Emergency Nav.

# COMMUNICATIONS

# RADIO

Effective, dependable communications are essential to safe boating and can do much to make it more pleasurable. It is not necessary to become an electronics expert to use radios well, but an understanding of the fundamentals can be a great help.

Communications for vessels include the following: radiotelephones —marine band, amateur (ham), citizens band — cellular telephones, satellites, and visual signaling. Each of these will be considered in turn.

## RADIO PRINCIPLES

To send information by radio there must be a transmitter that first generates electrical energy at radio frequencies and then modulates with the information to be sent and amplified to a higher power level. The final step is the radiation of the energy into space as a radio wave by an antenna.

On the other end, there is first a receiving antenna to pick up the radio wave, amplification, demodulation, further amplification, and dispersal as audio frequency energy by a speaker or earphones, or use of the received information in the form of data or graphics.

### Propagation

From a transmitting antenna, radio waves are normally radiated out in all horizontal directions. There are directional antennae, but these are not used in marine communications, except for satellites (discussed later). In the vertical plane, radio energy is radiated out both horizontally and in several lobes upward at various angles. The horizontal radiation is termed "ground waves;" the above-horizontal energy is in the form of "sky waves."

Ground waves reach out to the horizon and to distances beyond the horizon that vary with their radio frequency. In general, the lower the frequency the more they bend over the horizon and the farther they can be received. What happens to the energy radiated upward again depends on the frequency, the time of day, the season of the year, and the state of the 11-year sunspot cycle — it's a bit complicated! The

sky waves may be reflected back to earth by one of several layers of ionization in the ionosphere, or they may penetrate the layer or layers and continue outward in space. These layers form and dissipate at various times of the day, in different seasons, and changing sunspot conditions.

### The Radio Frequency Spectrum

The frequency of radio waves is measured in hertz (Hz)— cycles per second — the same as audio waves and electrical power. For radio, however, the numbers are so large that the units are kilohertz (kHz), megahertz (MHz), and gigahertz (GHz), for respective values of a thousand, a million, and a billion times a hertz.

The radio frequency spectrum is divided into bands from Extremely Low Frequency (ELF), below 3 kHz, up to Super High Frequency (SHF), 3 GHz to 30 GHz.

The radio bands of greatest interest to the typical small-craft skipper are first the VHF (30-300 MHz), and secondarily the MF (300 kHz–3 MHz) and HF (3-30 MHz) bands. Almost all communications needs will normally be met in these two areas of the radio spectrum. Lower frequencies may be used for navigation and higher frequencies for navigation and communication satellites.

### Modulation

For information such as voice, music, or data to be transmitted by radio, the basic carrier wave must be modulated. The band most used for marine communications, VHF, uses frequency modulation (FM). The carrier wave is steady in power level but is varied in frequency around that center frequency. The audio frequencies that are being transmitted determine the rate at which the radio frequency varies. The extent to which it varies, or deviates, determines the loudness level of the received audio information.

In the lower frequency MF and HF bands, the information is communicated by amplitude modulation (AM). With this method, the frequency does not vary; speech or other information is communicated by changing the strength of the transmitted signal. Originally, AM signals had half of their power in a central carrier, with the other half divided equally between two sidebands, on either side — *double-sideband* transmission. This type of modulation works, but it wastes three-quarters of the transmitter power. Advancing technology developed *single-sideband* radio, a system of modulation in which the carrier and one sideband were eliminated in the transmitter without diminishing the effectiveness of the communications. Although the system is still AM, it's referred to by the initials SSB.

Technically, either the upper or lower sideband can be used. The upper sideband is always used for marine communications. On amateur radio bands, the lower sideband is used on frequencies lower than 10 MHz and the upper sideband on higher frequencies.

## Modes of Operation

An understanding of the two different modes of radio operation used in marine communications is essential for the proper use of radio channels. On the VHF band, most communications are in the *simplex* mode, where only one station can transmit at a time. The other can only listen and await its turn to transmit. You cannot interrupt the person speaking as you can in an ordinary telephone call on shore — a mode called *duplex* communications. The same frequency is used by both, or all, stations for both transmitting and receiving.

When a vessel engages in ship-to-shore contacts with a marine operator, the mode is termed *half-duplex*. It is still not possible for the listener to interrupt the speaker, but the vessel transmits on one frequency and receives on another — the transmitting frequency of the shore telephone station. Note that ship-to-shore communications with marinas, bridges, and the like are simplex communications; only with marine operators is half-duplex used.

## Equipment

VHF radio consists of a transceiver, which contains both the transmitter and receiver (usually called a "radio" or "set"), plus an antenna. Equipment for SSB communications on MF and HF is a bit more complicated by the need for an antenna tuner and a ground connection.

### Transceivers

Marine radio sets for use on VHF are very user friendly with only three basic controls. One control selects the frequency for transmitting and receiving, using simple channel numbers rather than six-digit MHz values. Another sets the audio volume level for the received signal (it has no effect on how loud your signal will be at the other station), and a third sets the squelch level, which silences the normal background noise when no signal is being received. Other controls that may be found on transceivers let you quickly shift to the calling channel and scan a variety of channels. Other special features vary from set to set.

VHF sets can be mounted in a bracket, set into a bulkhead panel, or handheld. The mountable sets generally have the maximum allowable power of 25 watts, with a required low-power setting of one watt; Handheld radios have five or so watts and a low-power setting. The FCC requires that every VHF set be capable of operating on Channels 16 and 6 and a working channel, but in reality all sets, even the small handhelds, can tune to all channels; thus, this requirement is not really pertinent. See below for a discussion of the various channels.

Handheld VHF radios are useful on small craft because they can easily be removed when not in use, thus protecting them from the weather or theft. You can put them in waterproof bags and carry in a dinghy to keep in touch with the "mother ship." Adapters are available so that these units can be attached to a regular whip antenna, replacing the small flexible antenna mounted directly on the set. Handhelds use internal batteries and the maximum power is limited to about five watts, but with the larger antenna they can reach almost the same range as mounted sets.

FCC regulations prohibit the use of handhelds on shore or the use of regular marine channels for onboard communications.

Transceivers for SSB communications are larger than those for VHF, but are still small enough for easy mounting on boats of a size that would be interested in MF-HF radios.

Mounted transceivers are powered from the vessel's normal 12-volt DC sources. Often, handhelds can be connected through an adapter to the 12-volt system for operation or for recharging the set's internal battery.

257

All radio equipment that radiates a signal must be "Type Approved" by the FCC. This presents no problem when purchasing new or used sets because Type Approval is required before equipment may be offered for sale.

### Antennae

External antennae for VHF radios come in three different sizes. VHF waves are not reflected from the ionosphere, so communications are limited to the visible horizon plus a small percentage of additional range. Range can be increased by "squeezing down" the radiated energy that would normally go upward at an angle closer to the horizon down toward the surface of the water, increasing the power in a useful direction. Antennae are rated by the extent to which this is done, expressed in *decibels* (dB) of gain. Common types are 3 dB, 6 dB, and 8 or 9 dB; the higher gain antennae are longer. Handheld sets have an attached flexible rubber-covered antenna whose length is measured in inches — not very efficient, but quite convenient.

Antennae for MF-HF sets using single-sideband are physically much larger than those for VHF, but still not as large electrically as they should be. Vertical whip antennae are 18 to 23 feet or more in length and still must have an antenna tuner box to make up for a lack of physical length to properly match the transceiver. For sailboats, it is possible to insert insulators near the top and bottom ends of a backstay and use the electrically isolated portion as the antenna.

A further essential element of a SSB installation is a good ground connection (not needed with a VHF set).

## MARINE RADIO COMMUNICATIONS

Maritime radio operations are regulated by the Federal Communications Commission (FCC). The Rules and Regulations are contained in Part 80 of Title 47 of the Code of Federal Regulations (47CFR80), which can be found in larger libraries or on-line at:

*http://fatty.law.cornell.edu/uscode/47/.*

The marine airwaves are really semiregulated or self-regulated because the FCC has limited monitoring facilities. Citations for violations are few. The Coast Guard will occasionally tell stations misusing Channel 16 to move to another channel, but otherwise, proper use of the marine frequencies is largely a matter of knowledge and self-discipline.

### Station Licenses

Basically, FCC licenses are required for all equipment that radiates signals — transceivers, radar, EPIRBs, satcom, and the like — but not receivers and electronic navigation equipment. You submit an application for a ship station license (the term used by the FCC even for small craft) to the FCC on Form 506. Detailed instructions are included on the form; read them carefully to avoid having your application rejected and returned to you. You should check all boxes for types of equipment and frequencies that you have now *and might have in the future*; this will lessen the need to apply for a modification of the license if you add such equipment. A station to be licensed for MF/HF SSB use must first be licensed for VHF, but both can be included in a single application. The application and applicable fee (see below) should be mailed to:

*Federal Communications Commission*
*Marine Ship Service*
*P.O. Box 358275*
*Pittsburgh, PA 15251-5275*

A ship station license is valid for five years and can be renewed; use Form 506B and send the applicable fees. If there is a change of name or address of the licensee, or a change of the boat's name, the license need not be modified, but the FCC must be notified by letter (or Form 405A) to P.O. Box 1040, Gettysburg, PA 17325-1040. No notification is required for a simple change of equipment. *A license is not transferable* and cannot be used by a new owner if the boat is sold; nor can it be used by the licensee on a different boat even with the same equipment.

### Exemption

It should be noted, however, that non-commercial small craft operated wholly in U.S. waters with VHF equipment *are not required to have a marine radio license.* Radar and EPIRBs are also included in this waiver. If the craft uses SSB equipment, or goes into the waters of a foreign nation, or communicates with a station in another country, then there is a requirement for a station license. Merely cruising or fishing in international waters (beyond the 12-mile limit) does not require a license.

### Temporary License

So you can use your radio or other equipment immediately, you are instructed to keep a portion of Form 506; it serves as an interim license until you receive the permanent one. It provides for a temporary call sign, which should be used only until the permanent license and its call sign are received.

## Operator Licenses

A Restricted Radiotelephone Operator Permit is not required for operating a VHF marine radio in the circumstances described above where a station license is not needed. It is required for operating VHF equipment in foreign waters, or a SSB set in any waters. It is also required for operators on vessels that must comply with the Bridge-to-Bridge Radiotelephone Act (see Chapter 2, *Boating Regulations*) and on vessels over 65 feet in length on the Great Lakes. (There are higher grades of operator licenses, but a Restricted Permit is adequate.)

An applicant for a Restricted Radiotelephone Operator Permit must be a U.S. citizen or a foreign national authorized to work in the United States (there are some exceptions for special cases). There is no examination, but applicants must "certify" that they can hear and speak, keep a rough written log, and are familiar with the treaties, laws, and regulations governing marine radio use. Applicants must also certify that they need the Permit because of the type of vessel they work on or because of anticipated travel to a foreign country.

Application is made on Form 753. This, plus the applicable fee (see below), is mailed to:

*Federal Communications Commission*
*Restricted Permit*
*P.O. Box 358295*
*Pittsburgh, PA 15251-5295*

Detailed instructions are included on the form. Read them carefully to avoid having your application rejected and returned to you. A portion of Form 513 is retained as a temporary permit valid for 60 days.

A Restricted Radiotelephone Operator Permit is valid for the life of the holder.

## Application Forms and Fees

FCC forms are often packed with new radios, and marine electronic equipment dealers usually stock copies. If not available from these sources, obtain them by contacting the FCC at:

*Federal Communications Commission*
*Forms Distribution Center*
*2803 52nd Avenue*
*Hyattsville, MD 20781*
*Phone: 202-632-3676; Fax: 202-418-0177*
*Info line: 888-225-5322*
*www.fcc.gov/formpage.html*

Both station and operator licenses require a fee to accompany the application. The amount of these fees is subject to change (increase) annually; see any current edition of *Reed's Nautical Almanac* for the exact amount. Fees must be submitted in the form of check or money order; do not send cash.

Canada still requires station licenses and operator licenses for all radio use. For further information and applications, contact:

*Industry Canada*
*Radio Regulatory Branch*
*800 Slater Street*
*Ottawa, Ontario, KIA OC8*

The Canadian Coast Guard Pacific Region Marine Communications branch maintains an excellent Web page that includes the complete text of the Radio Operator's Study Guide:

*www.island.net/~comoxcg/main.htm*

## VHF Marine Service

VHF/FM marine radios operate in the frequency band of 156-163 MHz. Within this band are numerous channels spaced 25 kHz apart; numbered from 1 to 28, and 60 through 88. Each channel has a designated frequency, or pair of frequencies, but in everyday use only the channel number is used, with no reference to the megahertz value.

### FCC Definitions

The FCC Rules and Regulations contain a number of definitions that must be understood in order to properly interpret the channel allocations. (The definitions below have been condensed from the official text.)

A *commercial transport vessel* is one that is used primarily in commerce for transporting persons or goods to or from harbors, or within such port areas. Such a vessel may also be used in connection with the construction, maintenance, loading and unloading, moving, or salvage of other vessels, and related activities.

*Commercial communications* are those between stations on commercial transport vessels, or between shore stations and stations on commercial transport vessels. They must relate to the purposes for which the vessel is being used, including piloting, movement, and obtaining supplies and repairs.

*Noncommercial communications* are those between stations on other than commercial transport vessels, or between shore stations and stations on vessels other than commercial transport vessels; these communications must pertain to the needs of the vessel. Note that this "other than" category includes recreational (pleasure) craft, which are not recognized as a named category.

*Port operations communications* include communications in or near a port, in waterways, or at locks relating to the operational handling, movement, and safety of ships, and in an emergency to the safety of persons.

*Safety communications* covers the transmission and receipt of distress, alarm, urgent, or safety signals, and related messages which, if delayed, might adversely affect the safety of life or property.

### Channel Assignments

Specific uses are assigned to each channel, which are shown in the tabular listings at the end of this chapter. The most important ones are discussed in this section. Some channels that have an international assignment of a pair of frequencies for duplex operation are used in the United States for simplex communications; here only the lower of the two frequencies is used and an "A" is appended to the channel number. For example, 157.100 MHz is the lower of the two frequencies of international Channel 22; in the U.S. it is called 22A, or 22 Alpha, and is used as a simplex channel for communications between boats and the Coast Guard. VHF radios will have a switch or other means of changing between "Int." and "U.S." — in U.S. waters, be sure that this switch is set on "U.S."

Channel 16 is the most important channel — it is for distress and safety communications. It is also used for calling and reply, making the initial contact between two stations, except in areas where the Channel 9 is used for this purpose (see below). Using this channel for initial contacts between stations ensures that a maximum number of persons, on vessels and on shore, are listening on the frequency that carries distress calls. Channel 16 should *never* be used for routine conversations, no matter how brief.

Channel 6 is the main channel for inter-ship safety communications; it should not be used for any other purpose, nor by any station on shore.

Channel 13 is primarily the "Bridge-to-Bridge" channel, where "bridge" means the control station of a vessel. Many types of vessels are required to monitor this channel. It is used to coordinate vessel movements in meeting, crossing, and overtaking situations; in such cases, it can replace the otherwise required whistle signals of the International and Inland Navigation Rules. (Channel 67 is substituted in the lower Mississippi River.) In many areas, Channel 13 is also used to communicate with bridge and lock tenders.

Channel 9 is the primary channel for intership communications between commercial and noncommercial vessels. To relieve congestion on Channel 16, it is now being encouraged as a calling and reply channel for noncommercial craft. In some areas, Channel 9 is used for communicating with bridge tenders to relieve congestion on Channel 13.

Channel 22A, sometimes referred to as merely 22, is the normal working frequency for communications to Coast Guard stations and vessels; at times, the Coast Guard will request use of Channel 12 or other frequency.

Channel 70 is dedicated exclusively to establishing contact using Digital Selective Calling (DSC). The use of DSC has been slow to develop, but more and more equipment is either so equipped when purchased, or can be subsequently modified. DSC requires the use of a nine-digit "maritime mobile service identity" number; this can be requested on a ship station license application. Calls using DSC techniques can also be made on a working frequency if it is known that the other station listens to that frequency.

Note that *separate channels* are allocated for the use of commercial and noncommercial vessels. There are an adequate number of channels for each type of vessel, *if the traffic load is spread across all available channels* — all too often communications are concentrated on one or two channels; Channel 68 is frequently overused for boat-

to-boat communications. Each type of vessel, commercial or noncommercial, should use *only* a properly assigned channel. The only channel common to both commercial and noncommercial vessels in all areas is Channel 9 (there is also 79A and 80A on the Great Lakes, and 72 in the Puget Sound area).

Ship-to-shore communications to marine operators — called "public correspondence" communications by the FCC — have their own channels, one or more in each geographic area. These are duplex channels, with the vessel transmitting on one frequency and the shore station on a different frequency. Thus, boats cannot use unassigned public correspondence channels to talk among themselves.

Ship-to-shore communications to marinas, yacht clubs, and similar places — termed by the FCC as "private coast stations" — take place on simplex channels that have been authorized for that purpose, such as 9 or 68.

The National Weather Service has continuous broadcasts of current conditions and forecasts that are of considerable interest and value to those on the water. With very few exceptions, these transmissions are on channels Wx-1, Wx-2, or Wx-3, all of which are on all marine VHF transceivers (as well as other unused weather channels).

## MF-HF Single-Sideband Marine Service

Communications between vessels on VHF channels is normally limited to about 15-20 miles, sometimes less. The determining factor is not transmitter power, but antenna height at each end of the link. For this reason, sailboats and shore stations can reach farther than powerboats. To communicate

### SSB CHANNELS

These simplex single-sideband radiotelephone frequencies are provided for worldwide common use by ships of all categories, for communications with coast stations or other ships. These frequencies are shared and are not available for the exclusive use of any station.

**Note:** All duplex and simplex frequencies are upper sideband (USB), with assigned frequency 1.4 kHz above the listed carrier frequency.

### HF Simplex Channels

| | | | |
|---|---|---|---|
| 4146 | 6224 | 8294 | 12,353 |
| 4149 | 6227 | 8297 | 12,356 |
| | 6230 | | 12,359 |
| | | | 12,362 |
| | | | 12,365 |
| | | | |
| 16,528 | 18,825 | 22,159 | 25,100 |
| 16,531 | 18,828 | 22,162 | 25,103 |
| 16,534 | 18,831 | 22,165 | 25,106 |
| 16,537 | 18,834 | 22,168 | 25,109 |
| 16,540 | 18,837 | 22,171 | 25,112 |
| 16,543 | 18,840 | 22,174 | 25,115 |
| 16,546 | 18,843 | 22,177 | 25,118 |

### GMDSS Radiotelephone Channels

These simplex frequencies are designated under the Global Maritime Distress & Safety System for distress and safety communications and (except for 2182 kHz) are not normally guarded.

| | |
|---|---|
| 2182 kHz | 8291 kHz |
| 4125 | 12,290 |
| 6215 | 16,420 |

*This HF radiotelephone channel and frequency information was derived from Appendix 16 of the International Telecommunications Union (ITU) Radio Regulations.*

at greater distances, it is necessary to use medium- or high-frequency single-sideband equipment.

The MF-HF service operates in a number of bands at approximately 2, 4, 6, 8, 12, 16, 18, 22, and 25 MHz. Specific frequencies are designated in each of these bands for various types of communications. For brevity and convenience, many of these frequencies have been given channel numbers much like those used on VHF, except that these numbers have three or four digits, the first one or two of which relate to the frequency band concerned.

Frequencies are designated for specific types of communications — distress and safety, calling by voice or DSC, intership, public correspondence, narrow-band direct-printing, data, and facsimile. You can find information on specific frequencies for each type of communications in the applicable volume of *Reed's Nautical Almanac*, the operation manuals that accompany SSB radios, from marine electronics dealers, and, of course, in the FCC Rules and Regulations. Some important frequencies are discussed below.

### Distress Calling

In the MF band, the international radiotelephone distress, urgency, and safety frequency is 2180 kHz. This simplex frequency is also used for initial calls and replies (just like Channel 16 on VHF). The frequency 2191 kHz can be used for calling in areas where 2182 is heavily used.

When 2182 kHz does not have enough range, the frequencies 4125, 6215, 8291, 12290, and 16420 kHz can be used on a simplex basis for distress and safety communications. 4125 kHz may also be used for distress and safety communications between ship stations and aircraft.

Distress, urgency, and safety calls using DSC should use 2187.5, 4207.5, 6312.0, 8414.5, 12577.0, and 16804.5 kHz on a simplex basis.

### Working Frequencies

There are many working frequencies for MF and HF single-sideband communications using radiotelephony, and different frequencies for the other types of communications. There are also many pairs of duplex working channels for ship-to-coast public correspondence, designated by channel numbers, in the bands from 2 MHz to 22 MHz. In addition, there is a call and reply channel in each of the bands.

Each band also has simplex frequencies for intership or ship-to-coast communications, and a special set for use in the Mississippi River System. The frequency 2170 kHz is authorized for communications with the Coast Guard, and there are channels in the higher frequency bands as well.

## Operating Rules

The FCC Rules and Regulations — Code of Federal Regulations, Title 47, Part 80 — contains the legally required operation practices for marine radio communications. These cover the most basic situations, but they are not all-encompassing and must be supplemented by unofficial good operating procedures, to be discussed in the next subsection.

### Permissible Communications

First, transmissions must fit into one of the types of permissible communications defined previously in this chapter. *Marine radio is not CB!* Except for communications through marine operators into the public telephone system, personal and social conversations are not allowed. Ordinary contacts must relate to the needs of the vessel, such as navigational information, obtaining supplies and services, and the like. Marine radio channels are *not* the place to discuss the size of the fish you caught or where to meet for dinner.

### Calling and Working Channels

The basic system of marine communications is the use of separate *calling* and *working* channels. The objectives are to have the maximum number of stations listening on the calling channel in order to hear a distress call, yet have the minimum amount of transmissions on this channel so that it will be clear to hear a distress call. Upon establishing contact on a calling channel, stations must *immediately* shift to an appropriate working channel — no communications, no matter how brief, are permitted on the calling channel. This does not apply, however, to distress traffic.

On VHF, there are certain classes of ship stations (with minor exceptions) that must maintain a listening watch on Channel 16. Land-based stations must maintain a safety watch on Channel 16 unless excused by the FCC because there is a government (USCG) station covering the listening area.

Voluntarily equipped craft — those not required by any treaty, law, or regulation to maintain a listening watch — must listen on Channel 16 when the radio is turned on and is not being actively used for communication on another channel. Although recreational boats are encouraged to use Channel 9 for calling, this does not excuse them from the Channel 16 watch requirement. Essentially, all new radios have a *dual-watch* capability, and some have a *triple-watch* feature to enable listening on 16, 9, and a working channel. A voluntarily equipped vessel that maintains a DSC

## FREQUENCY SELECTION GUIDE

This chart is greatly simplified. The winter/summer cycle and sunspot activity will alter propagation. Generally, if you can hear traffic clearly you will be able to transmit successfully on the same channel or band. Always listen for other traffic before transmitting. After transmitting, wait several minutes for a response before trying again.

Listen to traffic lists and weather reports at various times. Use your radio log to record the best times and frequencies for communicating with these stations.

### Distance in Nautical Miles

| Local Time | 200-750 NM | 750-1500 NM | More Than 1500 NM |
| --- | --- | --- | --- |
| 0000 | 3-5 MHz | 6-9 MHz | 6-11 MHz |
| 0400 | 3-5 MHz | 4-7 MHz | 6-9 MHz |
| 0800 | 3-7 MHz | 6-11 MHz | 11-22MHz |
| 1200 | 4-7 MHz | 8-13 MHz | 13-22 MHz |
| 1600 | 4-7 MHz | 8-13 MHz | 13-22 MHz |
| 2000 | 3-7 MHz | 6-11 MHz | 11-22 MHz |

watch on Channel 70 is excused from a watch on Channel 16.

Each ship station operating on frequencies in the 1605-3500 kHz band must listen on 2182 for at least three minutes starting on the hour and 30 minutes past the hour.

For both compulsorily and voluntarily equipped vessels, calling may be done on an intership working channel if it is known that the other vessel is maintaining a simultaneous listening watch on both the calling channel and that working channel. Actually, this is a preferable procedure as it lessens transmissions on the calling and distress frequency.

Every radio channel is available for use on a shared basis. No individual station or group has any exclusive right. Stations must cooperate in the use of authorized frequencies in order to minimize interference and obtain the maximum use of the available channels.

### Distress Calls and Messages

Quite obviously, as safety is the primary reason for the marine communications system, *distress calls and traffic have absolute priority.*

Distress calls are identified with the word "MAYDAY," derived from the French for "Help me." Distress is defined as when a vessel is threatened with grave and imminent danger and requests immediate assistance — it is not to be used when you have run out of fuel, have a dead battery, are aground in good weather, or in other non-threatening situations. There is an established international format for a distress call and messages. The distress call precedes the distress message. It is spoken as follows:

*The distress signal MAYDAY spoken three times;*
*The words THIS IS;*
*The call sign, name, or other identification of the vessel in distress, spoken three times.*

The distress message is transmitted as follows:

*The distress signal MAYDAY;*
*The name of the vessel in distress;*
*Particulars of its position;*
*The nature of the distress;*
*The kind of assistance desired;*
*Any other information that might facili-*

*tate rescue, such as a description of the vessel and the number of persons on board.*

If the vessel is equipped with a device that will generate the radiotelephone alarm signal — two alternating tones of specified characteristics — this alarm should be transmitted for 30 to 60 seconds prior to the distress call.

In general, position should be given in terms of latitude and longitude coordinates, but can be given in terms of direction and distance from an identifiable geographic point.

It is extremely important that all portions of the distress call and message be spoken slowly and distinctly, clearly pronouncing each word. Having to repeat transmissions slows down the rescue operation.

If you transmit a distress message and receive no reply, send it again after a brief wait. If nothing is heard after several transmissions, try another channel, especially one on which you have communicated with or heard other stations recently.

You may be requested to transmit a "long count" — numbers from one to ten and back — or other signal for purposes of direction finding.

### If You Hear a Distress Call or Message

If you hear a Mayday call on Channel 16 or 2182 kHz, *do not immediately answer.* The call may have been heard directly by the Coast Guard, or other authorities, or by another vessel closer and better able than you to render assistance. Listen carefully, but do not transmit. However, after a few moments, if you do not hear anyone else better able to help, call the distressed vessel and let them know that their call has been heard. The official procedure is as follows:

*The distress signal MAYDAY;*
*The call sign, or other identification, of the vessel sending the distress message, spoken three times;*
*The words THIS IS;*
*The call sign, or other identification, of the station acknowledging receipt, spoken three times;*
*The word RECEIVED;*
*The word MAYDAY.*

Following this, you should give your position, your speed toward the distressed vessel, and your estimated time of arrival. You should also take immediate action to relay information about the situation to the Coast Guard and to any other vessels that might be in better positions to assist. The official procedure is as follows:

*The signal MAYDAY RELAY, spoken three times ;*
*The words THIS IS*
*The call sign, or other identification, of the transmitting station, spoken three times.*

If a radiotelephone alarm signal device is available, it should be activated for 30 to 60 seconds before transmitting the above.

## RADIO TELEPHONE ALPHABET

When sending any communication at sea in plain language, the following phonetic alphabet is used internationally:

| Letter | Word | Pronunciation |
|---|---|---|
| A | Alpha | AL FAH |
| B | Bravo | BRAH VOH |
| C | Charlie | CHAR LEE |
| D | Delta | DELL TAH |
| E | Echo | ECK OH |
| F | Foxtrot | FOKS TROT |
| G | Golf | GOLF |
| H | Hotel | HOH TELL |
| I | India | IN DEE AH |
| J | Juliett | JEW LEE ETT |
| K | Kilo | KEY LOH |
| L | Lima | LEE MAH |
| M | Mike | MIKE |
| N | November | NO VEM BER |
| O | Oscar | OSS CAH |
| P | Papa | PAH PAH |
| Q | Quebec | KEH BECK |
| R | Romeo | ROW ME OH |
| S | Sierra | SEE AIR RAH |
| T | Tango | TANG GO |
| U | Uniform | YOU NEE FORM |
| V | Victor | VIK TAH |
| W | Whiskey | WISS KEY |
| X | X-ray | ECKS RAY |
| Y | Yankee | YANG KEY |
| Z | Zulu | ZOO LOO |

Syllables to be emphasized are underlined.

### Control of Distress Traffic

The FCC Rules, following international procedures, state that the vessel in distress controls the distress traffic. In practice, if the Coast Guard is active in the rescue they will control the frequency.

The controlling station will normally announce a condition of *radio silence*, but whether or not such is formally established, a station having knowledge of the distress situation is forbidden to transmit on the frequency being used. Malicious or willful interference is subject to severe penalties. Radio silence is imposed by the controlling station announcing SEELONCE MAYDAY. If necessary, any other station may announce SEELONCE DISTRESS, but this should be done only with great care to avoid causing interference to important traffic on the frequency. The end of radio silence is announced by the transmission of the following:

*The distress signal MAYDAY;*
*The call "Hello all stations," spoken three times;*
*The words THIS IS;*
*The call sign, or other identification, of the station making the announcement, spoken three times;*
*The time of the announcement;*
*The name and call sign, or other identification, of the vessel that was in distress;*
*The words SEELONCE FINEE or PRU-DONCE.*

### Urgent Transmissions

In emergencies that do not warrant the transmission of a distress call and message, an *urgent* transmission can be sent. The urgency signal — PAN PAN, pronounced "pawn pawn" — indicates that the message that follows concerns the safety of a ship or aircraft, or other vehicle, or the safety of a person. This signal is spoken three times before the call. This can be an announcement of a situation and not necessarily a call for assistance. It is frequently used by the Coast Guard to advise all vessels to be on the lookout for an overdue craft or a person lost overboard.

### Safety Transmissions

The lowest level of priority transmissions is the *safety* message. It is preceded by the word "SECURITÉ," using the French pronunciation, "securitay." It is used preceding messages concerning the safety of navigation or important weather warnings.

Communications

## Station Identification

The FCC Rules require that transmissions be identified at the beginning of each *exchange* of transmissions with another station, not on each transmission individually. If the communications with another station extend more than 15 minutes (see *Time Limitations* below), station identification must be given every 15 minutes; if public correspondence is being exchanged with a shore station (marine operator), identification may be deferred until the end of the contact.

The regulations state that identification is made by "giving the call sign in English." A problem arises when a VHF station in domestic use has no license, and hence no call sign. It is suggested that the boat's name be used, or an unofficial call sign generated by adding "K" before the state registration number or "KUS" before the USCG documentation number.

Under normal communication conditions, it is not necessary to use phonetic equivalents for the letters of a call sign — doing so undesirably lengthens the transmission time. If phonetics are used, they should be from the standard international phonetic alphabet, listed on the previous page.

## Test Transmissions and "Radio Checks"

The FCC regulations set definite limitations on making test transmissions. The first and most basic restriction is that they must not interfere with communications in progress — *listen before you test*. The prescribed procedure is to announce "test," followed by station identification. If any station responds with "wait," any further transmission must be delayed for at least 30 seconds. Then "test" and identification can be repeated and, if no objection is heard, the test can continue. Test transmissions should consist of number counts or phrases that do not conflict with normal operating procedures. Test signals must not continue for more than 10 seconds and cannot be repeated until after one minute has elapsed.

The test described above is a one-way transmission to observe the operation of the equipment. "Radio checks" are requests for signal reports from another station. It is permissible to make such a call on Channel 16 or 2182 kHz, *but the rules require that there be a shift to a working*

channel for the actual exchange of information on signal readability and location. A simpler procedure is to listen on a working channel and call a station heard there for your signal report. The Coast Guard will participate in radio testing *only* when the calls are made by a representative of the FCC or a licensed technician doing installation or maintenance work. The calling for radio check is much overused; marine radio sets are highly reliable, and if one worked properly the last time it was used, it is extremely likely that it is still working satisfactorily.

## Time Limitations

Calls to a specific station must not continue for more than 30 seconds. If the called station does not reply, the call cannot be repeated until after an interval of two minutes. If three calls are so made, and no reply is received, calling cannot continue until 15 minutes have passed. If there is reason to believe that no harmful interference to other communications will be caused, this interval may be reduced to three minutes. These limitations do not apply to emergency communications involving safety.

Transmissions on Channel 16 and 2182 kHz must not exceed one minute, except for distress communications. All commercial communications must be limited to the minimum practicable transmission time. There is no regulatory limit on noncommercial communications, but common sense would indicate that they, too, be limited to the minimum practicable time. In ship-to-shore communications with private coast stations, a station on board a vessel must comply with instructions given by the shore station.

## Secrecy of Communications

Any person using the radio must observe the secrecy provisions of the Communications Act and International Radio Regulations. Basically, these state that no person may divulge to another person, except the addressee or his agent, any knowledge gained from receiving or intercepting radio transmissions not addressed to himself. Further, *no person may use such knowledge for his own benefit* — it's not legal for you to listen to other boats talking about where the fish are biting and then going there!

The secrecy laws do not apply to distress

communications or broadcasts for the general use of the public, but they *do apply* to all other transmissions and conversations heard on the air.

## General Operating Procedures

The FCC Rules and Regulations must, of course, be obeyed, but they do not cover all operating situations. There are other procedures that should be followed for the most efficient and effective communications. They are not legally required, but they do make good sense.

### Establishing Contact Between Boats

When you wish to contact another boat, the first thing you should do is listen on the calling channel *and* on the working channel that you will propose to the other craft. This will ensure that you don't interfere with another station on the calling channel, or with any emergency traffic on that frequency; it will also help to ensure that you will not encounter problems after you shift to a working channel.

Set your transceiver to a calling channel — 16, 9, or a prearranged working channel — and make your call to the other station as follows:

*The name of the other vessel; under normal conditions this should not need to be stated more than once, but if necessary, it can be given two or three times. It is not necessary to give the call sign of the other vessel, assuming that it has one and that you know it.*
*The words THIS IS.*
*The name of your boat and your call sign if you are in foreign waters. In U.S. waters, because so many craft do not now have call signs, it has become customary to omit yours if you do have one — this results in briefer transmissions, which is always desirable. If you know that the other boat is monitoring more than one channel, it is helpful to state the channel number that you are using so that the other operator will know on what channel to reply.*
*You can say the procedure word OVER, indicating the end of your transmission and your readiness to receive a reply, but it is normally not necessary on VHF with good reception conditions — it will be obvious when you stop talking.*

There is also a recommended procedure if you are on the receiving end of a call. On the same channel, respond as follows:

*The name of the boat that called, normally said only once. If you know the other operator well, or have recently been in communications with that boat, this portion of the reply can be omitted.*
*The words THIS IS.*
*The name of your boat, and your call sign if you are in foreign waters. In U.S. waters, because so many craft do not now have call signs, it has become customary to omit yours if you do have one — this results in briefer transmissions, which is always desirable.*
*The procedure word OVER. (This may be omitted under good conditions.)*

Normally, at this point the originating operator will propose a working channel; under good conditions, all that need be said is the number of the channel — for example, "69." Note that a single-digit channel can be referred to either with or without the leading zero — "9" or "09." The person who names the working channel must *not* shift to it until the other person has acknowledged the channel number, which can be done by merely stating that number. Much confusion can result if two people go to different working channels!

Alternatively, if the mariners have been in recent contact or habitually use a specific working channel, the person called may propose the working frequency, but should include his or her identification rather than make a more abbreviated transmission. The originating station accepts the proposed working channel, or objects and suggests another.

In either of these procedures, there must be clear agreement on the working channel to be used before a shift is made from the calling frequency.

### Calling a Private Coast Station

Establishing contact with a marina, yacht club, or similar business such as a towing service, follows essentially the same procedure as above. Here, however, abbreviated procedures are less likely to be used, with the exception of the omission of "over." The shore station will probably be the one to propose the working channel. Operators on board recreational boats should be wary of being told to shift to a commercial channel that is not authorized for their class of station — even though their sets are capable of operating on that channel.

267

## Calling a Public Correspondence Station

Although some marine operators do listen on Channel 16, they all listen on their working channel or channels. Transmissions on Channel 16 are lessened and time is saved if initial calls are made directly on the working channel. These frequencies are widely listed in cruising guides and other publications and can always be learned by calling a local boat or marina. When contact is established, give the operator the telephone number to be called and provide billing information as requested.

Marine operators holding traffic for vessels will call on Channel 16, but will normally direct the craft to reply on a specified working channel, with no transmission on 16.

## Bridge-to-Bridge Communications

In this era of modern radio communications, it was realized some years ago that navigational safety could be greatly enhanced by having direct voice contact between the persons controlling two ships that were approaching each other. Direct exchanges of information by voice about what each vessel intended to do are much better than the whistle signals of the Navigation Rules. In fact, the Rules allow vessels to substitute voice communications for whistle and light signals. Hence, the *Bridge-to-Bridge Communications* system was established and mandated by law and regulation for certain classes of vessels while in U.S. waters. These are:

All power-driven vessels 20 meters (65.6 feet) or more in length, while navigating. This includes commercial, noncommercial, and government-owned ships; U.S. and foreign flag.

All vessels of 100 gross tons or more while carrying one or more passengers, while navigating. Note that this includes sailing vessels of this size.

All towing vessels of 7.8 meters (26 feet) or more in length, while navigating. Presumably, such craft only become "towing vessels" when actually performing a tow.

All dredges and floating plants in or near a channel or fairway, while engaged in operations likely to restrict or affect the navigation of other vessels. An unmanned or intermittently manned floating plant

is not required to have a separate radiotelephone capability.

To meet the Bridge-to-Bridge requirements, a vessel must have a second radiotelephone installation for a continuous watch on Channel 13 (and *additionally* Channel 67 in the New Orleans and Lower Mississippi River area), in addition to the set used for the required watch on Channel 16 or VTS frequency. This radio must also be capable of operating on Channel 22A. A single "dual-watch" type of radio does *not* meet this requirement.

This radio must be monitored by the master or person in charge of the vessel, or by a person designated by the master or person in charge to direct the navigation of the vessel. The person on the Bridge-to-Bridge radio watch may perform other duties if they don't interfere with his or her ability to maintain that watch. This person must have a Restricted Radiotelephone Operator Permit or higher class of license.

Most small-craft navigators will not have to comply with the requirements of the Bridge-to-Bridge Act and its regulations, but they should be aware of the existence of the system. Skippers can make use of its capabilities when appropriate, such as when passing a tug and tow in a narrow waterway or getting around a dredge that is blocking the channel.

## Emergency Communications

2182 kHz is the international hailing and distress frequency in the medium-frequency band. It is monitored by most Coast Guard stations and all commercial vessels equipped for that frequency when underway.

Emergency medical advice may be obtained by contacting the Coast Guard on 2182 kHz or via one of the high-frequency channels listed below. The stations listed in the section on High Seas Radiotelephone Service (in the various editions of *Reed's Nautical Almanac*) will immediately transfer emergency calls to the nearest Coast Guard station. No charge is made for such calls when the vessel states it is an emergency involving the safety of life or property at sea.

The Coast Guard monitors the following frequencies as part of the CALL (Contact and Long Range Liaison) system. These frequencies are also used for voice weather broadcasts, navigation warnings, and medical communications. Allow at least one minute for a response before switching channels. The Coast Guard is monitoring many channels simultaneously and may not be able to respond immediately. (Not all frequencies are monitored twenty-four hours; see *Reed's Nautical Almanacs* for further information.)

| Channel | Transmit | Receive |
|---------|----------|---------|
| 424 | 4134 kHz | 4426 kHz |
| 601 | 6200 kHz | 6501 kHz |
| 816 | 8240 kHz | 8764 kHz |
| 1205 | 12242 kHz | 13089 kHz |
| 1625 | 16432 kHz | 17314 kHz |

## CONNECTIONS INTO THE PUBLIC TELEPHONE NETWORK

Three types of ship-to-shore radio services provide full connection coverage into the public telephone network for a wide range of needs: VHS Radiotelephone Service (VHF); Coastal Harbor Service (MF); and High Seas Radiotelephone Service (HF). Each is described fully on the following pages.

A network of marine radio stations along the nation's coastal waters and major inland waterways is maintained by common carriers. The marine operators or high seas operators at these stations are available to connect your calls at any time of the day or night. The radiotelephone equipment on board your vessel should be capable of radiating adequate power and equipped with appropriate radio channels for the radiotelephone service desired.

If you plan to use the public marine radiotelephone service regularly, it is important that you make arrangements with that service. These arrangements can be made at no charge and can expedite calling by saving the air time it would take to otherwise process your call. Users of the VHF and Coastal Harbor services are assigned Marine Identification Numbers (MINs), which can be obtained by contacting your local telephone company.

### VHF Ship-to-Shore Service

This system provides reliable operation and good transmission quality over distances of 20 to 50 miles via FM channels in the 156-162 MHz range. Since VHF provides essentially line-of-sight communications, antenna height and equipment quality aboard your vessel are basic to the distance of transmission. This service performs better than systems operating on the lower frequencies because there is less atmospheric noise at the higher VHF frequencies and there is virtually no ionospheric "skip," which could bring in interfering signals from hundreds or thousands of miles away. VHF must be used in preference to MF when the vessel is within range of a VHF shore station. For information on placing or receiving calls on VHF, see the Coastal Harbor Ship-to-Shore Service section below.

For additional information on VHF telephone coverage and service contact:

*Maritel Marine Communications System*
*452 Courthouse Road*
*Gulfport, MS 39507*
*1-888-627-4835*

### Coastal Harbor Ship-to-Shore Service

The operating range of this service is normally to distances up to 300 miles. Channels operating in the 2 MHz range are used along the East and West Coasts. Vessels may be registered for VHF and Coastal Harbor (MF) Radiotelephone Service by contacting the telephone company office serving the area in which your account is to be billed — normally a home or business location.

**Placing ship-to-shore calls (VHF or MF).** Monitor the desired coast station channel to determine that it is idle. If known, give the name of the coast station you are calling. When the marine operator answers, announce: "This is (ship's call sign) and my Marine Identification Number (or MIN) is (give number)." If you don't have a MIN, give the ship's name, call sign, and full billing information. Give the city and telephone number you wish to call. Proceed as directed. At the end of the conversation, repeat your ship's name and call sign and say "out."

**Placing shore-to-ship calls (MF or VHF).** To make a call to a vessel, contact the local telephone operator from any private or pay phone and ask for the marine operator. Give the operator the name of the ship you are calling, its call sign, and location if known. If the ship has a Selective Signaling Number, give this information, too. Then follow the operator's instructions.

Remember that the ship station generally operates using half-duplex (push-to-talk) techniques, so it is impossible for you to break in while the person on the vessel is talking.

**Receiving a call from shore.** A vessel's equipment must be operating and tuned to the appropriate channel before it can receive public coast station calls. Coast stations routinely make contact through VHF Channel 16 (156.8 MHz) unless the vessel is equipped with selective signaling which permits direct dialing on the coast station transmitting channel. When your vessel is called, announce: "This is (name of your vessel and call sign), over." Then proceed as instructed.

**Ship-to-ship calls via marine operator (VHF or MF).** Your marine operator can connect you with vessels that may be beyond your normal vessel-to-vessel transmitting range. To do so, contact the operator in the regular ship-to-shore fashion and give the name, call sign, location, and Selective Signaling Number (if known) of the vessel you are calling. On completion of the call, sign off by announcing your vessel's name and call sign.

## High Seas Ship-to-Shore Service

This service uses high frequencies (HF) to provide long-range radiotelephone communications with suitably equipped vessels throughout the world. Service is provided via public coast stations in the United States. These stations operate on various radio channels in the 4 through 23 MHz bands and are equipped for single-sideband operation. Propagation on the radio channels assigned to this service differs with the time of day, season, and vessel location. A good rule of thumb is to use the frequency on which you best hear the coast station; the frequency selection guide below can be helpful in determining where to listen.

Vessel operators contemplating use of this service may obtain information concerning choice of channels for given location, time, and season by calling or writing to the station operations manager. The addresses, telephone numbers, and operating frequencies for WOO, WOM, WAH, and WLO are listed in the various editions of *Reed's Nautical Almanac*. Radio equipment for high seas operation should be capable of employing various channels in 4 to 23 MHz bands. The following modes of transmission may be used:

A3A – Single-sideband, reduced carrier.
A3J – Single-sideband, suppressed carrier.

Normally, the higher radio frequency channels propagate over greater distances, so the most important factor is the band selected. For example, 4 MHz will only operate 100 miles (or a little more) at noon. When the sun nears the horizon, the range increases. At night, 4 MHz is excellent for over 800 miles. On the other hand, the 8 MHz band has a noontime range of about 600 miles, while at night the signal will travel several thousand miles. Higher frequency bands will often cover distances up to 10,000 miles.

**Placing ship-to-shore calls (HF).** First, select the channel for the coast station you wish to contact. Then LISTEN. Don't call until transmissions in progress have been completed. Before completing your call, the high seas traffic operator will ask for your name, the name and telephone number of the party you wish to reach, and the method of billing — paid, collect, marine credit card, or third number. Should you need time and charges information, advise the operator of this *before* your call is connected. After your call is completed, stand by until the technical operator releases the channel.

**Placing shore-to-ship calls (HF)**. To make a call to a vessel, contact the local telephone operator from any private or pay phone and ask for the high seas operator. Give the operator the name of the vessel you are calling, its call sign if you know it, and location if known. Then follow the operator's instructions. More specific information about the vessel — the channel generally monitored for receiving calls and the coast station through which calls are normally received — is often useful.

Remember that the ship station generally operates using half-duplex (push-to-talk) techniques, so it's impossible for you to break in while the person on the vessel is talking.

**Receiving shore-to-ship calls (HF).** You can receive an incoming call only when your receiver is turned on and tuned to the frequency of the coast station through which the call is being routed. When your vessel is called, answer the coast station on a working channel stating your vessel's name, call sign, and location. After contact has been established, the coast station operator will make any necessary adjustments to provide you with the best possible circuit for your telephone call.

**Traffic Lists.** All high seas stations continuously monitor vessels' transmitting channels. These stations periodically broadcast "traffic lists" — the names of the vessels for whom they are holding calls. Do not wait for a traffic list to be broadcast before making a call; demand calling is encouraged.

No calls are accepted on a channel just before it is scheduled to carry a traffic list or weather broadcast. However, when a call is in progress, the broadcast is omitted on the busy channel.

### AT&T High Seas Direct

AT&T High Seas Direct is a low-cost alternative to satellite communications and can be used to make phone calls anywhere in the world. The system works by combining computer-controlled equipment with existing maritime radiotelephone service and high frequency single-sideband technology.

AT&T High Seas Direct consists of an onboard handset with a built-in keypad and digital display. The handset plugs into a SSB radio and works with a coast station to process calls without having to contact

an operator. You dial directly to a phone number without an operator's assistance, using your five digit Personal Identification Number (PIN) and the area code and phone number of the party called. Although the high seas direct handset replaces the SSB microphone, the microphone should be kept onboard as an emergency backup.

Other features of high seas direct are a secure mode of communications by using the built-in scrambler and the ability to retrieve incoming calls and messages. The cost of using this service is less than calls made through a high-seas operator (currently around $1.29 per minute). Cost of high seas direct equipment (handset, handset cradle, and modem) is approximately $900.

Calls can be made in either an automatic or semi-automatic mode over designated high seas direct (HSD) frequencies. In the automatic mode, a frequency is selected by the unit's software. However, this may not always be the optimum frequency due to atmospherics and the nature of radio propagation. In that case, the user can manually select a designated high seas direct channel.

High seas direct can be used to make ship-to-ship calls as well as ship-to-shore. However, calls to 800 and 900 numbers are not possible.

For additional information on AT&T High Seas Direct contact:

*AT&T Maritime Services*
*650 Liberty Avenue*
*Union, NJ 07083*
*800-392-2067*

## CITIZENS BAND COMMUNICATIONS

The use of CB radios generally peaked more than a decade ago, although many of them are still around. From a safety viewpoint, CB sets are *not* a substitute for marine radios, but they still have a use — legally permissible communications of a social nature not allowed on marine channels.

A CB radio is inexpensive and easily installed, but it requires its own whip antenna. Finding a set that is specially constructed for use in a marine environment may be difficult, but a regular automotive set can be used if consideration is given to protecting it from rain and spray.

A station or operator license is not required for CB radio operation. There are, however, FCC regulations for the use of these sets. The equipment must be Type Accepted and cannot be modified; the use of high-power amplifiers is prohibited. A CB set cannot be used for any illegal activity or to transmit music or sound effects. The use of profane, obscene, or indecent language is forbidden, as is communication with stations in foreign countries, except Canada.

Call signs are not issued and identification is not required, although it is "encouraged." Unofficial call signs can be generated by adding "K" to the boat's state registration number, or adding "KUS" to the USCG documentation number.

Organizations sometimes create identification numbers for stations of their members. The use of a CB "handle" is permissible, but is not a substitute for more formal identification.

There are 23 basic CB channels, with an additional 17 on some sets — these are between 26.965 and 27.405 MHz. Reliable communications are limited to the horizon distance plus a small percentage more; occasionally there will be possibilities for contacts over much greater distances using sky waves. Channel 9 is reserved for "emergency communications involving the immediate safety of life or the immediate protection of property." The Coast Guard no longer listens on Channel 9, and monitoring by local authorities or groups provides only scattered coverage. *No vessel should depend on CB radio for obtaining assistance in an emergency.* Other than

Channel 9, there are no specific channel assignments. In many areas, though, groups of users have established specific uses for various purposes, such as fishing. If you are using CB communications, learn what coverage is available for Channel 9, and what groups are on other channels. There are no exclusive assignments for any channel to a individual user or group of users.

## AMATEUR (HAM) RADIO

Although there are many amateur ("ham") radio stations on boats, this is a communications service entirely separate and distinct from marine communications. It is probably most useful to boaters who cruise some distances from home waters. It cannot be used for business purposes, but it can be a means of keeping in touch with family and friends and for getting weather and port information for destinations yet ahead.

### Licenses

Operating an amateur radio station requires both a station license and an operator license. Station licenses, except for club stations, are all the same, but operator licenses are issued in various classes. To receive a license you must pass examinations on regulations, radio theory, and, with one exception, the Morse code. The exception is the "Codeless Technician" license, but that license is of little benefit to a cruising boater.

Licenses start at the Novice level, but again, this class is of limited benefit. A General Class license provides the minimum level of operating privileges for cruisers; Advanced and Extra Class licenses provide some additional privileges, but are not necessary. A General Class requires demonstrating the ability to receive and send Morse code at a speed of 13 words per minute. Reaching that speed takes practice, but it's definitely achievable. There is also an examination in FCC regulations and radio theory and practice. There are, however, excellent correspondence courses and study guides that contain the questions and answers. In many areas, ham radio clubs conduct classes or can assist in locating someone who will help a person prepare for the exam. A ham license is not easily obtained, but it is possible for just about anyone who is willing to study for it. More information can be obtained from the amateurs' organization, the American Radio Relay League at 225 Main Street, Newington, CT 06111-1494; or on the Web at *www.arrl.org*.

### Frequencies and Modes

Ham radio operates in bands of frequencies from 1.6 MHz up to 300 or more GHz. Within each band there are sub-bands for various types of modulation and classes of licensees. Subject to such restrictions, amateurs select their own transmitting frequencies. There are "nets" that habitually operate on a specific frequency at a given time, but no amateur "owns" any particular frequency. Power limits vary with the frequency band, but are generally much greater than for marine communications.

Many modes of operation are authorized. Morse code, also called CW, communications are still widely used, although less now than in decades past. Voice communications use FM on the VHF band and SSB on the lower frequencies. Double-sideband is still authorized but is seldom used. Other modes include radioteletype, fax, packet data transmissions between computers, and even two-way TV.

### Equipment

Transceivers for amateur radios look much like those for marine communications, but they are different in several respects.

Although many ham sets include marine frequencies, amateur radio transmitters are not Type Approved under Part 80 for use as ship stations, and cannot legally be used as such. (In a true emergency, anything can be used to obtain assistance.) As amateurs are deemed to be more technically qualified as a result of passing their license examinations, ham transmitters are less "idiot proof" than their marine equivalents. There are more controls and greater flexibility in tuning and adjusting, thus more opportunity for putting out a signal that might interfere with other stations. Conversely, though, many marine transceivers can be set for ham frequencies and legally, but less flexibly, used on them.

The receiver section of most ham HF transceivers can be tuned to any frequency within wide limits. This allows for its use with a modem to pick up weather facsimile

broadcasts to be fed to a personal computer and printer. Foreign news and music broadcasts can also be received.

Sets for the VHF ham bands can be either mounted or handheld. Like HF radios, they look similar to the equivalent marine transceivers. They have more controls, though, with greater flexibility of frequency selection and mode of operation.

Antennae for amateur stations on boats are essentially the same as for marine band communications, except that antenna tuners for HF transceivers are likely to be less automatic in operation.

### Operations

Most maritime ham radio operation is on HF bands at 3.5, 7, 10, 14, 18, and 21 MHz, with operation at 24 and 28 MHz when the sunspot cycle is favorable. There is some activity on the VHF bands, primarily 144 MHz, between members of local groups who often use *repeaters* to extend operating distances between stations. Operation is divided among established nets, regularly scheduled informal contacts between friends, and casual contacts. Refer to the current regional edition of *Reed's Nautical Almanac* for frequencies and times of nets. Although there is not formal or guaranteed safety capability, there is a long history of cases where ham radio has been the primary, or even sole, means of communications in emergencies at sea.

### CELLULAR TELEPHONES

There are actually two technologies to be considered here — the cellular telephone service and the personal communications service. The two are very similar and, in the public's eye, are the same. Here, we will lump them together as "cel phones." This means of communications has become vastly popular and the sets are seen everywhere.

On board a boat, a cel phone can be a valuable supplement to regular marine radio equipment, *but it is not a substitute*. It will enable you to dial telephone calls directly without having to go through a marine operator, and such calls will have greater privacy — persons on shore can place a call to you in the same manner as if you were on land. However, it is not a fully adequate means of sending a distress call

Communications

or other emergency message. In some areas, arrangements have been made for speed dialing the Coast Guard by entering "*CG" on the dialing pad, but before you depend on this means of communication, be sure that system is set up where you do your boating. A disadvantage of calling for help using a cel phone is that other boats in your vicinity, ones that might come to your assistance before the Coast Guard could reach you, will not hear you. Further, any craft responding to your call won't be able to home in on your signals, as they could if you were using VHF.

## The Cellular Telephone System

The cell phone system is an amalgamation of radio transmissions and the wired public telephone network. A large number of transmitter/receiver and antenna combinations are placed around an area, creating the "cells" of the system; these are interconnectd by the regular land line telephone network. A mobile unit automatically makes contact with the location best receiving its signals, and the contact is passed on to other cells as that unit moves along, again automatically, without the user being aware of the change. Each cell is connected into the landwire network, and calls are completed as if they had originated at a regular phone at home or the office. Although the direct range of a cell phone is very limited, the area over which it can be used is very extensive due to the large number of individual cells that are patched together by land lines.

### Equipment

The most widely used cel phone is the handheld unit, now often small and light enough to fold and put in your pocket.

A considerable number of special features for cel phones are available in various combinations:

*Programmable memories for emergency or frequently called numbers.*
*Selectable ringer or vibrator for incoming call alerting.*
*Automatic redial.*
*Indicator for battery and signal strengths.*
*Alphanumeric "scratchpad" for writing memos.*
*Call timer.*
*Capability for data transmission.*
*Dual NAM permitting use on two different cellular systems.*

On land, where there are cells all around, even the small power of a handheld — less than one watt — is enough to ensure adequate communications, particularly if it is used with an external antenna. On the water, where cells are probably much more distant, it is advisable to use a handheld with an external amplifier that will boost the power to the maximum allowable three watts. Alternatively, there are transportable, or "bag," models that have full power and their own larger battery to match; these can also be plugged into a boat's 12-volt DC electrical system. To increase range, a marine-type antenna, usually a 33-inch whip, should be used rather than a car-type antenna. Because cel phones operate at UHF frequencies — even higher than VHF — and have basically line-of-sight range, the antenna should be mounted as high as possible — a masthead location is not too high.

Other accessories available for cell phones include:

*Protective carrying cases.*
*External antennae for car rear windows or tops (magnetic mount).*
*Car 12-volt adapter/chargers for handhelds (usable on boats).*
*Power boosters for handhelds.*
*Extended life batteries.*
*Desktop chargers.*
*"Handsfree" kits.*

Because the technology is advancing so rapidly — analog sets are being replaced by digital equipment — a prospective purchaser of a cel phone should thoroughly investigate the various models and available services before making a purchase.

## E-MAIL USING HF CHANNELS

Using digital technology and a shipboard SSB connected through a modem to a laptop computer, e-mail can now be sent and received from vessels. Messages are sent and received using ASCII format, and binary files can be sent at up to 2400 bps.

E-mail systems can be tied into the U.S. Coast Guard's Automated Merchant Vessel Emergency and Rescue (AMVER) system, allowing your position to be tracked by the U.S. Coast Guard. Depending on the nature of service purchased, weather information and other navigational resources, such as Gulf Stream and ocean currents, charts can be received.

The cost for sending and receiving information is normally based on the amount of data sent, not minutes connected. To use e-mail at sea, an account must be set up with a participating company and their modem and software installed onboard.

Technical details and specifics on using a SSB radio for e-mail transmissions can be found in ICOM Marine's publication *Marine Single-Sideband Simplified* written by Gordon West. Contact:

*ICOM Marine Inc.*
*2380 116th Ave. NE*
*Bellevue, WA 98004-3036*
*Phone: 206-454-8155; Fax: 206-450-6057*

Several companies currently provide e-mail service:

*Mobile Marine Radio Inc.*
*7700 Rinla Avenue*
*Mobile, Alabama 36619-1199*
*Phone: 334-666-5110 or 800-343-1090*
*Fax: 334-660-9850; Telex: 782027 WLO UD*

*PinOak Digital*
*PO Box 360*
*Gladstone, NJ 07934-0360*
*Phone: 908-234-2020 or 800-PINOAK1*
*Fax: 908.234.9685; e-mail: info@pinoak.com*

*Globe Wireless*
*One Meyn Road*
*Half Moon Bay, CA 94019-2503*
*Phone: 415-726-6588 or 800-876-7234*
*Fax: 415-726-8604*

## WEATHER FACSIMILE BROADCASTS

Even though you may be beyond the reach of newspapers and television service, you don't have to do without accurate and up-to-date weather maps. Facsimile weather broadcasts are available on several HF channels; this service is often called *weatherfax*. See the regional editions of *Reed's Nautical Almanac* for frequencies and times of transmission from various shore stations.

Your vessel can have ether a self-contained facsimile printer that includes the radio receiver, a printer unit to attach to your regular HF communications transceiver, or a suitable modem attached to that transceiver and used with a personal computer and printer. The combined unit is easier to operate, but is more expensive.

A number of different charts are transmitted in sequence — surface analysis, prognosis for various times ahead, upper air at several levels, wave analysis, and more. Photos from weather satellites are also transmitted. Proper interpretation of the received images is required if they are to be of value, but this skill can be acquired and the results are far better than merely listening to audible broadcasts.(See Chapter 10, *Weather,* for an extensive discussion of weatherfax maps.)

## NAVTEX

NAVTEX is an international system of one-way broadcasts of offshore weather information, navigational warnings, ice warnings, Gulf Stream location, and distress messages.

All transmissions are on the same frequency, 518 kHz, with the individual stations transmitting in sequence on a normal four-hour schedule. The times of each broadcast are listed in the regional editions of *Reed's Nautical Almanac*.

A vessel has a small receiver that displays and prints out the information received. It can be programmed to receive every message, or only those of interest to the vessel on which it is installed. The receiver can be unattended, and messages will be stored for later review.

## SATELLITE COMMUNICATIONS

Access to a reliable, easy-to-use communications link can not only make any voyage safer and more enjoyable, but it allows one to operate a business office while at sea. Today, this is quite possible, as satellite communications systems, global and regional, are now available for vessels of all sizes. Satellite systems (Satcoms) designed for the marine environment have seen significant advances since their inception 20 years ago. They now provide voice, telex, fax, and data services to and from a vessel as easily as from a home or office telephone.

There are several maritime satcom standards for equipment and service that are available and in use for various classes of vessels. Systems for large vessels are available with up to six assigned channels; some models provide for operation of four simultaneous calls and data rates up to 64Kbit/s.

The smaller systems generally provide for one or two voice, a fax, and a data channel. Communications software is available to interconnect to Internet e-mail, as well as to transfer still video images taken on a digital camera.

## International Systems (Global Coverage)

**The International Maritime Satellite Organization** (INMARSAT), the global communications satellite consortium of member nations (now 81 countries), provides communications around the clock for vessels of all sizes voyaging in all oceans of the globe. These satellites, two for the Atlantic Ocean region, one for the Pacific Ocean region, and one for the Indian Ocean region, provide for complete global coverage with the exception of the far polar regions above about 76 degrees north and below 76 degrees south latitude.

The Inmarsat satellites are in geosynchronous orbit (GEO) over the equator; to anyone on earth, they appear as if they were standing still in space. Calls are set up and connected via the international switched telephony network using telephone/telex/data numbers established

for this purpose. This is similar in call setup to that used when making any public international terrestrial call. Each satellite providing coverage for an ocean region has a number assigned to it — the same as now exists for a country.

For example, to make a call to a vessel in the Atlantic from a telephone in the U.S., you would dial 011 (international call), 871 (Atlantic East Satellite), and the nine-digit Inmarsat telephone number assigned to the satcom. To call from the vessel to a shore number in the U.S. (Thomas Reed Publications, for example), you'd dial 001 (U.S. country code), 617 (Boston area code), 248-0084 #. The # symbol transmits the number string similar to the send key on a cellular phone.

**Inmarsat-A**, introduced in 1982, was the first satcom system. It's based on FM-modulated analog technology using very large antennae of a size and weight that makes them suitable only for large ships such as cruise liners, oil tankers, and large cargo vessels. Voice, fax, and data services are available for this system, including multiple channel operation and switched data up to 64Kbit/s. However, the Inmarsat-A system has been made more or less obsolete by

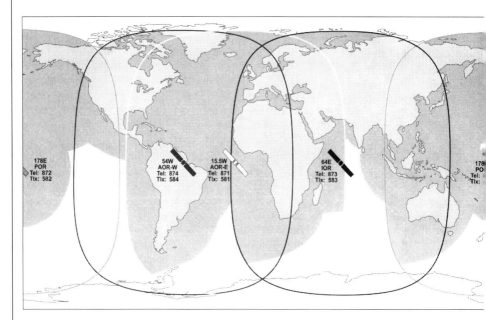

*INMARSAT A, B, C, D, E, & M coverage (shaded areas indicate spot beam coverage)*

the newer digital modulated systems. Although Inmarsat will continue to support the existing "A" systems as long as there is a requirement and demand, they will no longer approve new systems for manufacture.

**Inmarsat-B** is the digital successor to Inmarsat-A and conserves satellite bandwidth and power that results in additional capacity and lower charges for the second generation of Inmarsat satellites. The antennae size and weight stayed approximately the same, thereby making the system suitable for the same class of vessels as A, and for moving large data files for seismologic vessels and offshore oil platforms.

A range of specialized video services also became available at the 64 Kbit/s data rate using data compression techniques. It is possible to send high-quality photographs and compressed video to and from an onboard satcom. Ships can send and receive visual medical information during emergencies and disaster operations, and send and receive instant visual information on the repair of engines to an onshore agent who can then pinpoint the defect and quickly suggest methods of repair.

**Inmarsat-C** was developed as a low-cost satcom suitable for fitting on a vessel of any size, large or small. The system's size — it's slightly larger than a car radio with a small omnidirectional antenna — and weight made it especially suitable for

yachts and fishing vessels that were too small for the large Inmarsat-A or, as of late, B, installation. This system does not provide voice communications, but it does include a way to send text messages (fax/telex/e-mail) in a very short time. Inmarsat-B requires the user (at either end) to prepare the message/data on his or her end terminal (PC) and transmit it via the Inmarsat-C system. After a delay of a few minutes, the message may be viewed, printed, and/or stored. Any person familiar with electronic mail systems, including Internet e-mail, will readily understand how Inmarsat C functions to deliver and receive messages.

Shore-based service providers offer Internet e-mail connection and regularly updated weather reports, stock market information, medical information, and news. They also make possible a range of services such as data reporting, position reporting, and polling. Vessel operators can program their C satcom to transmit regular data reports, including GPS coordinates, on the condition of their vessel and other operational information to shore-based offices. Alternatively, shore-based managers and families of the boat operator can "poll," or interrogate, the vessel automatically or manually, receiving the same type of information.

Coupled with C's Enhanced Group Call (EGC) capabilities, vessels are able to automatically receive a category of messages

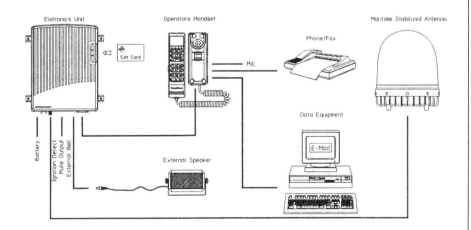

*Typical satcom setup*

known as SafetyNET. This service is directed to vessels in or approaching specific geographic regions such as an area around a storm warning, a hazard to navigation, or a ship in distress. The vessel only receives these safety at sea messages for the area the vessel is operating in. In addition, Inmarsat C's automatic distress calling feature, with fast and reliable alert calling to the Rescue Coordination Centers (RCC) in closest proximity to the vessel in distress, is unparalleled by any other marine communications system. For this reason, large-vessel operators who are required to meet the mandatory GMDSS requirements of the IMO (see Chapter 8, *Safety*) are installing Inmarsat-C in lieu of the larger and more expensive Inmarsat-A and B.

**Inmarsat-M** was introduced to complement the existing global services with a vessel satcom that would provided voice as well as fax and data, albeit at 2.4 Kbit/s for fax and data, versus 9.6 Kbit/s for Inmarsat-A and B. The marine M versions can be obtained with antennae one-third the weight and size of the A and B and at an equipment cost reduced by approximately half. This system is suitable for vessels approximately 70 feet and longer and is used on many large vessels complemented by an Inmarsat-C to meet their GMDSS requirement.

**Inmarsat Mini-M** is the latest and smallest marine system; it was introduced in late summer 1997. It provides the capability for voice, fax, and data service at 2.4Kbit/s at reduced service cost and is suitable for vessels as small as are practical for blue-water cruising. The smallest of these systems, the Mini-M has a fully stabilized five-pound tracking antenna (9.5" high and 8.5" in diameter); the below-decks equipment is the size of a notebook laptop PC. While this system can be used on vessels of any size, it fills the gap for vessels less than 70 foot nicely. This system was made possible with the launch of the Inmarsat third generation satellites in 1996-97, which have advanced, multiple-spot beam technology supplementing the traditional global beams. The spot beams concentrate the satellite's transmit signal energy to specific points of focus on the globe's surface, increasing signal strength and allowing for smaller antenna operation. Each of the four operational satellites provides overlapping spot beam coverage to 95 percent of

the world's continents and a significant part of the world's oceans. The illustration on the previous page depicts the Inmarsat global and spot beam coverage. It should be noted that less than complete coverage is available in midocean southern hemisphere, Atlantic, Indian, and Pacific Oceans for Mini-M. Vessels cruising in these latitudes should supplement their voice communications installation with Inmarsat-C.

To summarize, there have been three generations of Inmarsat satellites since Inmarsat was established in 1979. The first generation comprised a combination of satellites and packages on existing international satellites that were already in orbit when Inmarsat was formed. These were all analog FM-modulated systems and provided three ocean global beams for the Inmarsat network (now known as Inmarsat-A since the newer systems came on line).

In 1990, the second generation satellites, totally owned by Inmarsat, were launched. This second generation was still global beam only, but now could accommodate digital carriers which allowed the development of first Inmarsat-C, followed by M and then B, while still allowing capacity for the FM-modulated A service. Then, in 1996 and 1997, the third generation was launched which now has the high-powered spot beam technology onboard, as well capacity for digital and FM services on the global beams. This system now allows for the small Mini-M plus all of the earlier technologies/standards. With each generation more and more capacity has been added to accommodate the growing number of users in the maritime, land mobile, and aeronautical fields.

All standards — A, C, M, B, and Mini-M (listed in order of activation) — are in place and available. Inmarsat still supports A but the economics (double the cost for service) discourage its use and many large vessels are converting to B, M/C, or Mini-M/C. This is because of the 1999 GDMSS requirement by the IMO. Inmarsat A, B, and C qualify for GDMSS, but M and Mini-M do not.

**Low elliptical orbiting (LEO) satellite systems** will be introduced in 1998 and will offer small, handheld voice and messaging communicators with global coverage. The first of these, a handheld messaging communicator for use on the ORBCOMM Satellite Network, will be followed by the IRIDIUM voice plus data system. These devices may offer boaters very cost-effective offshore communications for safety and business. When they become commercially available, *Reed's Almanacs* will discuss them fully.

## Domestic Systems (Regional Coverage)

American Mobile Satellite Corporation (AMSC) is a U.S. public company with the principal shareholders being Hughes Communications, Singapore Telecom, and AT&T Wireless Services.

The AMSC satellite, like Inmarsat, is GEO over the equator and uses similar overlapping spot-beam technology focused on North and Central America, with a separate beam for coverage of Hawaii. The AMSC satellite system is backed up by a separate companion system, owned by TMI, Canada.

Launched in 1995, maritime coverage for the AMSC system is limited to the coastal regions of Central and North America from the northern borders of Colombia and Venezuela, covering the whole of the Caribbean, 200 miles off the West Coast, as far east as Bermuda, and ranging north to the Arctic Circle. A special spot beam is focused to provide 200-mile surrounding coverage for Hawaii (see illustration). AMSC service and equipment is similar to Inmarsat-M in size and capability (voice, fax

and data), with slightly higher data rates because of the more powerful spot beams. Until late 1996, the smallest marine stabilized antenna was 19 inches in diameter and weighed 30 pounds, making it suitable for vessels down to about 70 feet. In November 1996, a nonstabilized, broad-beam marine tracking antenna was introduced that was the size of a child's bicycle helmet and weighed in under three pounds, making it very suitable for vessels as small as 30 feet.

Similar regional satellite systems are in operation by OPTUS Communications, Sidney, for offshore coverage around Australia, and by Telécomunicaciónes de Mexico, using the same satcom equipment available to North and Central American users of the AMSC/TMI systems.

## Satcom Considerations for Small Vessels

Even with all of the advanced capabilities indicated above, satcom systems are easy to operate and don't require the protocols required for VHF, MF, and HF(SSB) radio. If you can operate a telephone, cellular phone, fax, or PC, you can operate any of the Inmarsat and AMSC Satcoms. Several Satcom models are available for each Inmarsat standard and for AMSC operation. Essentially, these consist of an above-the-deck stabilized auto tracking antenna

*American Mobile Satellite coverage*

(omnidirectional for C) encased in a small weatherproof dome. Below decks is the electronic and peripheral equipment such as a telephone, fax, and computer.

For global cruising, you should consider satcoms both for safety at sea and business communications. They should not be considered as a replacement for VHF, MHF, and HF (SSB) inter-ship and ship-to-shore hailing or navigation channel communications. Radio communications are not only required by regulation for this purpose, they are economically the most efficient when within range of other vessels and coastal facilities that are serviced by radio telephone. However, for consistent global communications and distress calling not affected by atmospherics and radio propagation effects, satcoms cannot be equaled by any other communications means.

Once you buy a satcom, you must register the equipment and obtain a satcom phone number. This process requires selecting an Inmarsat Service Provider or Authorized Accounting Authority and signing a service contract. This is similar to selecting a cellular service provider and arranging for service, but is somewhat more complicated because you must work with an international organization that requires strict IMO policy adherence. The service provider then submits the commissioning and registration forms to Inmarsat through the Inmarsat Routing Organization (RO) of the country of the vessel's registry. For example, if the vessel is registered in the U.S., the paperwork is submitted to the U.S. RO, Comsat. In Canada, paperwork is handled at Stratos Mobile Networks; in the U.K., it goes to British Telecom; in France, to French Telecom, etc.

Most routing organizations are also service providers, but you aren't obligated to use your nation's RO as your service provider. Inmarsat service providers represent a number of land stations that interconnect your call to the public-switched network. They compete internationally for your business and rates can vary as much as 25 percent. Service providers also have a host of value- added services such as prepaid and credit card arrangements and technical and medical assistance. Shopping for the best value makes sense.

Most satcoms are shipped with the neces-sary paperwork and instructions. If you are commencing a global voyage and purchasing Inmarsat equipment, don't wait until the last minute and expect to have the satcom installed and be on your way. When the paperwork is complete, in order, and the service agreement arranged, it can be as fast as a 12- to 24-hour turnaround time to become operational. However, if your paperwork is not in order, your service provider not arranged, and your vessel has foreign registry, it can take up to a week or more. Some vessel owners, for economic reasons, have their vessels registered (flagged) in countries different than in which they reside, which can add confusion to the commissioning process.

Generally, the dealer or distributor from whom you purchased the satcom will assist in the commissioning and registration process after purchase. Be careful, though, because some dealers are not fully versed in the commissioning requirements. Commissioning for an AMSC system is much simpler than for Inmarsat. However, there are more than one manufacturers of Satcom equipment for this system, and several distributors of both the satcoms and service. Because there are economic choices to be made in selecting equipment and a service provider, a specialized satcom consultant's advice may be helpful.

## Additional Satcom Information

Because the Inmarsat and AMSC equipment and service providers are many and varied, the following references will assist you in finding out more about equipment and service in your part of the world.

- For additional information or general Inmarsat system questions, contact Inmarsat Customer Relations at: 011-44-1-71-728-1777.

- For specific information on equipment manufacturers, dealers, service providers, and consultants listed by area of the world and country, consult the Inmarsat Internet home page:
  *www.inmarsat.org/inmarsat*
  In addition, you will find an excellent "Tool Box" section where you can download information on fax and data set-up for the Inmarsat satcoms, as well as obtain a handbook on SafetyNET and other system information.

- For additional information on the AMSC system and a list of distributors and dealers in service and equipment, contact AMSC SkyCell Customer Service, +1-703-758-6000, or on the internet at: *www skycell.com/services/marine.htm*
- U.S. Coast Guard information on SafetyNET can be found on the USCG Internet page: *www.navcen.uscg.mil/marcomms/gmdss /snet.htm*
- Free consultation to prospective satcom owners about selecting equipment and service providers, as well as help in completing the commissioning paperwork, can be obtained from Quest Telecom International, 1-207-664- 0122; e-mail: quest@hypernet.com; or the web: *www.hypernet.com/quest.html*

## EPIRBS

**Emergency Position Indicating Radio Beacons** (EPIRBs) are designed to alert rescue authorities in emergencies. EPIRBs are made in six different types:

Class A and B EPIRBs are the most common aboard cruising boats; they are the least expensive. These units transmit a simple characteristic signal on 121.5 and 243 MHz, similar to Emergency Locator Transmitters (ELTs) used on aircraft. Class A units are designed to float free from a sinking vessel and automatically activate. Class B units, which are less expensive, must be manually activated. Unfortunately, their detection range is limited due to several factors. They are intended to be received either by passing aircraft or by certain orbiting satellites. A passing aircraft must be listening on one of these frequencies and a satellite must be in line of sight of both the EPIRB and a ground terminal for detection to occur. These devices are subject to a high false alarm rate from satellites (over 99 percent). Consequently, confirmation will be required before search and rescue forces are dispatched. Caution: EPIRBs manufactured before October 1988 may have design or construction problems, or may not be detectable by satellite.

Class S EPIRBs are essentially Class B models that either float or are an integral part of a survival craft (lifeboats and liferafts).

Class C EPIRBs are now obsolete. They transmitted a distinctive signal on VHF Channels 16 and 15 and were intended for coastal waters. They were, however, relatively ineffective.

Category I and II EPIRBs transmit on both 406MHz and 121.5 MHz; the two categories correspond to Class AS and B. The 406 MHz signal is received by a satellite transponder. The information, which includes the vessel's identity, and may also include her position if the EPIRB is interfaced with a GPS or loran set, is immediately relayed to a ground station. It there is no ground station visible to the satellite, the information is stored and relayed as soon as one comes in view. The 121.5 MHz signal allows aircraft and rescue vessels to home in on the scene of distress.

A 406 MHz EPIRB does not require a FCC license, but as each has its own identification number — a 15-digit number built in by the manufacturer — it *must* be registered with NOAA so that the source of the signal can be identified. (Forms for registration are supplied with each EPIRB or may be obtained on the Internet.) Registration includes information on the vessel and its owner. If the boatowner's address or telephone number changes, the EPIRB must be re-registered; if the boat or EPIRB is sold, it must be re-registered by the new owner. Failure to register will greatly lessen the value of the EPIRB in an emergency — lives have been lost from failure to register.

The Coast Guard must certify Category I and II EPIRBs for sale in the U. S. Many commercial vessels are required to carry a Category I unit, including fishing boats.

**Testing EPIRBs.** The Coast Guard urges EPIRB owners to periodically examine them for watertightness, battery expiration date, and signal presence. FCC rules allow class A, B, and S EPIRBs to be turned on briefly (for three audio sweeps, or one second only) during the first five minutes of each hour. Signal presence can be detected by an FM radio tuned to 99·5 MHz or an AM radio tuned to any vacant frequency and located close to the EPIRB. Category I and II EPIRBs can be tested through their own self-test function.

The Coast Guard has up-to-date information on EPIRBs at:
*www.navcen.uscg.mil/marcomms/gmdss /EPIRB.HTM*

## SIGNAL FLAGS

**A full-color version of this illustration is on page 482.**
*(You may find this grayscale version useful for testing your knowledge of flag colors.)*

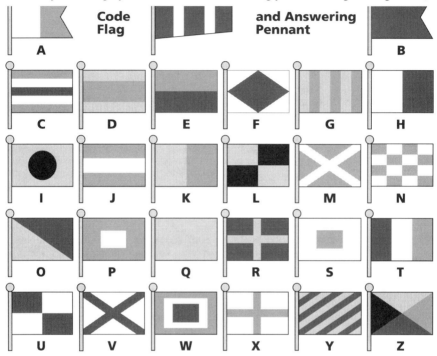

**Code Flag** and **Answering Pennant**

A  B
C  D  E  F  G  H
I  J  K  L  M  N
O  P  Q  R  S  T
U  V  W  X  Y  Z

### Numeral Pennants

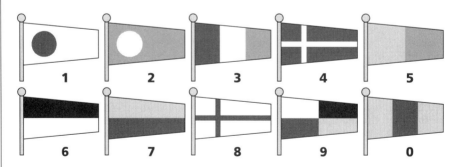

1  2  3  4  5
6  7  8  9  0

### Substitutes

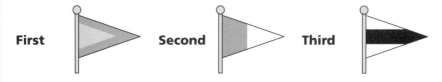

First    Second    Third

# SIGNALING BY FLAGS, LIGHTS, AND SOUND

Although almost all communications between vessels and from vessels to shore are accomplished by using radio, there are other methods that can, and sometimes are, used. Knowledge of signal communications can be very valuable if radio equipment is inoperative, or there is no common frequency between you and the station you wish to communicate with, or where there is a language difference. Vessels within sight or hearing of each other may communicate using code flags, flashing lights, or sound signals.

## THE INTERNATIONAL CODE OF SIGNALS

The International Code of Signals is published by the National Imagery and Mapping Agency as *Publication No. 102*. It is published in the nine most commonly used languages and it's well worthwhile to have a copy on board most small vessels.

Pub. 102 contains *signals* that can be sent by flag hoists, flashing light and sound, and other means. The International Morse code is used for flashing light and sound signals, as well as radiotelegraphy.

Signals basically consist of single letters and two-letter combinations; three-letter combinations, all starting with "M," are used solely for medical messages. Many signals can be expanded or made more specific with *complements*. These may express a variation in the meaning of the basic signal; questions and answers related to the meaning of the basic signal; or supplementary, specific, or more detailed meanings of the basic signal. Most complements consist of a single numeral, but there may be two, three, four, five, or six numerals when signaling such values as latitude and longitude, time, or date.

### Single-Letter Signals

Signals consisting solely of one letter are used for the most basic messages. Typical ones are listed below:

**A**  I have a diver down; keep well clear at slow speed.

**B**  I am taking in, or discharging, or carrying dangerous goods.

**D**  Keep clear of me — I am maneuvering with difficulty.

**H**  I have a pilot on board.

**K**  I wish to communicate with you.

**L**  You should stop your vessel instantly.

**O**  Man overboard.

**Q**  My vessel is healthy and I request free pratique.

**U**  You are running into danger.

**V**  I require assistance.

**W**  I require medical assistance.

**X**  Stop carrying out your intentions and watch for my signals.

**Y**  I am dragging my anchor.

There is also another set of single-letter signals that is used only with numerical complements to communicate azimuth or bearing, course, speed, latitude and longitude, or time and date.

Yet another set of single-letter signals, usually made by sound or radiotelephony, is used between icebreakers and assisted vessels.

### Two-Letter Signals

The General Signal Code consisting of signals of two letters, many with a single numerical complement, is used for many types of messages. Typical signals are:

**AC**  I am abandoning my vessel.

**AN**  I need a doctor.

**AQ**  I have injured/sick person (or number of persons indicated) to be taken off urgently.

**CB**  I require immediate assistance.

**CK**  Assistance is not (or is no longer) required by me (or vessel indicated).

**CP**  I am (or vessel indicated is) proceeding to your assistance.

**DV**  I am drifting.

**DX**  I am sinking (lat...long...if necessary).

**ED**  Your distress signals are understood.

**EL**  Repeat the distress position.

**FA**  Will you give me my position?

**FO**  I will keep close to you.

**GW** Man overboard. Please take action to pick him up (position to be indicated if necessary).

**IL** I can only proceed at slow speed.

**IT** I am on fire.

**JG** I am aground; I am in dangerous situation.

**JH** I am aground; I am not in danger.

**JW** I have sprung a leak.

**KJ** I am towing a submerged object.

**KM** I can take you (or vessel indicated) in tow.

**KQ** Prepare to be taken in tow.

**KT1** I am sending a towing hawser.

**LBI** Towing hawser is fast to chain cable.

**NC** I am in distress and require immediate assistance.

**NF** You are running into danger.

**NG** You are in a dangerous position.

**OQ** I am calibrating radio direction finder or adjusting compasses.

**PN** You should keep to leeward of me (or vessel indicated).

**PP** Keep well clear of me.

**QD** I am going ahead.

**QI** I am going astern.

**QQ** I require health clearance.

**RB** I am dragging my anchor.

**RU** Keep clear of me. I am maneuvering with difficulty.

**TP** Fishing gear has fouled my propeller.

**UY** I am carrying out exercises – keep clear of me.

**YG** You appear not to be complying with the traffic separation scheme.

**ZM** You should send (or speak) more slowly.

**ZS** My vessel is healthy and I request free pratique.

## FLAG HOIST SIGNALING

The most common use of the International Code of Signals is visual signaling using code flags. A set of flags consists of 26 flags for the letters of the alphabet, ten number pennants, three substitute pennants, and the answering pennant. (The U.S. Navy uses a fourth substitute and

calls them all "repeaters.") The substitutes are necessary because a set contains only one flag for each letter and some flag hoists require repetitions of one or more letters.

Five standard colors are used — red, white, blue, yellow, and black. Most of the flags are of two colors, selected and arranged for maximum contrast. Two flags are of a single color only, three use three colors, and one uses four colors.

Flag hoists are read from the top flag or pennant downward; if there is more than one hoist from a single spreader or yardarm, each hoist is read in turn from outermost inward. Full-color signal flags are illustrated on page 482. Additional details on flag hoist signaling can be found in Pub. 102.

## THE INTERNATIONAL MORSE CODE

Letters, numerals, and punctuation marks are signaled in the Morse code by combinations of dots and dashes. Letters have from one to four dots or dashes, numerals have five, and punctuation marks have six. The dots and dashes, and the spaces between them, are defined in terms of *units*. A dot is one unit in length and a dash is three units. The space between the dots and/or dashes within a character is one unit; the space between characters is three units; and the space between words is five units. The length of any unit is set by the method of signaling – much longer in sound or flashing light than radiotelegraphy.

The International Morse Code is shown on the next page.

Regardless of the method of signaling, you should not try to send at a speed greater than what you can do smoothly. You should also not send at a speed greater than that at which you can receive, lest you find yourself unable to keep up with the other operator.

### Flashing Light Signaling

Signaling by flashing light is carried out by using Morse Code. It is necessary to learn the dot-dash sequences and their meanings, and to practice sending and receiving, in order to be able to communicate with another vessel, up to several

## INTERNATIONAL MORSE CODE

| Letter | Character | Letter | Character |
|--------|-----------|--------|-----------|
| A | · — | N | — · |
| B | — · · · | O | — — — |
| C | — · — · | P | · — — · |
| D | — · · | Q | — — · — |
| E | · | R | · — · |
| F | · · — · | S | · · · |
| G | — — · | T | — |
| H | · · · · | U | · · — |
| I | · · | V | · · · — |
| J | · — — — | W | · — — |
| K | — · — | X | — · · — |
| L | · — · · | Y | — · — — |
| M | — — | Z | — — · · |

| Num'l | Character | Num'l | Character |
|-------|-----------|-------|-----------|
| 1 | · — — — — | 6 | — · · · · |
| 2 | · · — — — | 7 | — — · · · |
| 3 | · · · — — | 8 | — — — · · |
| 4 | · · · · — | 9 | — — — — · |
| 5 | · · · · · | 0 | — — — — — |

Ä (German) = AE (Danish) · — · —
Á or Å (Spanish or Scandinavian) · — — · —
Ch (German or Scandinavian) — — — —
É (French) · · — · ·
Ñ (Spanish) — — · — —
Ö (German) = Ø (Danish) — — — ·
Ü (German) · · — —

miles distant, either day or night. Proficiency at Morse Code is also required for most amateur (ham) radio licenses. Practice tapes and flash cards designed to improve your learning curve are available from several sources.

A signaling lamp (also known as an Aldis lamp) is needed for proper Morse Code signalling. It is portable and designed to operate on 12 volts. Few recreational boats carry these items today, so you may have to rely on your boat's searchlight, or even a flashlight. Lights are produced with the capability of sending a Mayday signal (SOS) automatically. These may be used to satisfy the Coast Guard distress signal requirement (see Chapter 2).

Signaling lamps must be pointed directly in the direction of the other vessel. Sights are attached to ensure you are pointing the light directly at the target. The usual range is several miles, both day and night. These lamps are very useful for rescue purposes, and even as an ordinary spotlight.

### Sound Signaling

Although signaling between vessels may be carried out by whistle using the Morse code for some of the signals from Pub. 102, this is a slow method and, unless in open waters, should never be resorted to. Confusion as to any sound signals given, or their misinterpretation, can have disastrous results. Sound signals are best left to those specified in the Navigation Rules.

## INTERNATIONAL DIVING FLAG

The International Code Flag A means:

**"I have a diver down; keep well clear at slow speed"**

In the United States, divers commonly show a red flag with a diagonal white stripe. The meaning of this flag is the same as International Code Flag A. The diving flag is frequently seen attached to a float, which in turn is attached to the diver by a tether. As the diver moves below the surface, the warning flag follows along. Unfortunately, this can give the diver a false sense of security – showing the diving flag does not relieve the diver of the responsibility of staying clear of channels and navigation aids. The dive flag should not be flown on a permanent basis, as is seen aboard some dive boats. The flag should only be used when divers are actually in the water.

With the increasing number of underwater swimmers and diving parties operating along the coasts and in the harbors, boaters are urged to keep well clear whenever they see the diving flag. Give any vessels flying this flag a very wide berth and proceed at slow speed. Keep in mind the possibility of floating tethers, lifelines, and other temporary obstructions in the vicinity of any divers. Divers near channels should have an observer stationed aboard the dive boat. Mariners are urged to contact the observer if in any doubt as to the location of dive operations.

Communications

## VHF MARINE CHANNELS AND THEIR USES

| Channel Number | Frequencies (MHz) Ship Transmit | Ship Receive | Channel Usage Intended Use |
|---|---|---|---|
| 01A | 156.050 | 156.050 | PORT OPERATIONS and COMMERCIAL only within the USCG designated Vessel Traffic Services (VTS) Area at New Orleans and lower Mississippi River. |
| 05A | 156.250 | 156.250 | PORT OPERATIONS only within the VTS radio protection areas of New Orleans and Houston. |
| 06 | 156.300 | 156.300 | INTERSHIP SAFETY. Required on all VHF-FM equipped vessels. For intership safety purposes, and search and rescue (SAR) communications with ships and aircraft of the U.S. Coast Guard. Must not be used for nonsafety communications. |
| 07A | 156.350 | 156.350 | COMMERCIAL (Intership and Ship-to-Coast). A working channel for commercial vessels to fulfill a wide scope of business and operational needs. |
| 08 | 156.400 | 156.400 | COMMERCIAL (Intership). Same as Channel 7A, except limited to intership communications. |
| 09 | 156.450 | 156.450 | COMMERCIAL and NONCOMMERCIAL. (Intership and Ship-to-Coast). Recommended as calling channel for noncommercial stations. Used for bridge tenders in some areas. |
| 10 | 156.500 | 156.500 | COMMERCIAL (Intership and Ship- to -Coast). Same as Channel 7A. |
| 11 | 156.550 | 156.550 | COMMERCIAL. Same as Channel 7A. VTS in designated areas. |
| 12 | 156.600 | 156.600 | PORT OPERATIONS. Restricted to the operational handling, movement, and safety of ships and, in emergency, to the safety of persons. VTS in designated areas. |
| 13 | 156.650 | 156.650 | NAVIGATIONAL (Ship's) Bridge-To-(Ship's) Bridge. This channel is available to all vessels and is required on large passenger and commercial vessels (including many tugs). Use is limited to navigational communications such as in meeting and passing situations. Abbreviated operating procedures (call signs omitted) and one watt maximum power (except in certain special instances) are used on this channel for both calling and working. For recreational vessels, this channel should be used for listening to determine the intentions of large vessels. This is also the primary channel used at locks and some bridges. |
| 14 | 156.700 | 156.700 | PORT OPERATIONS (Intership and Ship-to-Coast). Same as channel 12. Used for VTS in designated areas. |
| 15 | | 156.750 | ENVIRONMENTAL (Receive Only). A channel used to broadcast environmental information to ships such as weather, sea conditions, time signals for navigation, notices to mariners, etc. Most of this information is also broadcast on the weather (WX) channels. |

| 16 | 156.800 | 156.800 | DISTRESS, SAFETY, and CALLING (Intership and Ship-to-Coast). Required channel for all VHF-FM equipped vessels. Must be monitored at all times station is in operation (except when actually communicating on another channel). This channel is also monitored by the Coast Guard, public coast stations, and many limited coast stations. Calls to other vessels are normally initiated on this channel. Then, except in an emergency, you must switch to a working channel. |
| 17 | 156.850 | 156.850 | STATE CONTROL. Available to all vessels to communicate with ships and coast stations operated by state or local governments. Messages are restricted to regulation and control, or rendering assistance. Use of low power (one watt) setting is required by international treaty. |
| 18A | 156.900 | 156.900 | COMMERCIAL (Intership and Ship-to-Coast). Same as Channel 7A. |
| 19A | 156.950 | 156.950 | COMMERCIAL (Intership and Ship-to-Coast). Same as Channel 7a. |
| 20 | 157.000 | 161.600 | SHIP-to-COAST. |
| 20A | 157.000 | 157.000 | PORT OPERATIONS (Intership only). Available to all vessels. This is a traffic advisory channel for use by agencies directing the movement of vessels in or near ports, locks, or waterways. Messages are restricted to the operational handling, movement and safety of ships and, in emergency, to the safety of persons. |
| 21A | 157.050 | 157.050 | U.S. GOVERNMENT ONLY. |
| 22A | 157.100 | 157.100 | U.S. GOVERNMENT. Used as a working channel with USCG. |
| 23A | 157.150 | 157.150 | U.S. GOVERNMENT ONLY. |
| 24 | 157.200 | 161.800 | PUBLIC CORRESPONDENCE (Ship-to-Coast). Available to all vessels to communicate with public coast stations |
| 25 | 157.250 | 161.850 | PUBLIC CORRESPONDENCE (Ship-to-Coast). Same as Channel 24. |
| 26 | 157.300 | 161.900 | PUBLIC CORRESPONDENCE (Ship-to-Coast). Same as Channel 24. |
| 27 | 157.350 | 161.950 | PUBLIC CORRESPONDENCE (Ship-to-Coast). Same as Channel 24. |
| 28 | 157.400 | 162.000 | PUBLIC CORRESPONDENCE (Ship-to-Coast). Same as Channel 24. |
| 63A | 156.175 | 156.175 | Same as Channel 01A. |
| 65A | 156.275 | 156.275 | PORT OPERATIONS (Intership and Ship-to-Coast). Same as Channel 12. |
| 66A | 156.325 | 156.325 | PORT OPERATIONS (Intership and Ship-to-Coast). Same as Channel 12. |
| 67 | 156.375 | 156.375 | COMMERCIAL (Intership). Same as Channel 7A, except limited to intership communications. In the New Orleans VTS radio protection area, use is limited to NAVIGATIONAL bridge-to-bridge intership purposes. Available to NONCOMMERCIAL in Puget Sound area only. |

**Communications**

| 68 | 156.425 | 156.425 | NONCOMMERCIAL (Intership and Ship-to-Coast). A working channel for noncommercial vessels. May be used for obtaining supplies, scheduling repairs, berthing and accommodations, etc. from yacht clubs or marinas, and intership operational communications such as piloting or arranging for rendezvous with other vessels. Channel 68 is the most popular noncommercial channel and therefore is usually heavily congested. |
|---|---|---|---|
| 69 | 156.475 | 156.475 | NONCOMMERCIAL (Intership and Ship-to-Coast). Same as Channel 68. |
| 70 | 156.525 | 156.525 | DIGITAL SELECTIVE CALLING ONLY. |
| 71 | 156.575 | 156.575 | NONCOMMERCIAL (Intership and Ship-to-Coast). Same as Channel 68. |
| 72 | 156.625 | 156.625 | NONCOMMERCIAL (Intership). Same as Channel 68, except limited to intership communications; available for COMMERCIAL communications in Puget Sound area only |
| 73 | 156.675 | 156.675 | PORT OPERATIONS (Intership and Ship-to-Coast). Same as Channel 12. |
| 74 | 156.725 | 156.725 | PORT OPERATIONS (Intership and Ship-to-Coast). Same as Channel 12. |
| 77 | 156.875 | 156.875 | PORT OPERATIONS (Intership). Limited to intership communications to and from pilots concerning the docking of ships. Power limited to one watt. |
| 78A | 156.925 | 156.925 | NONCOMMERCIAL (Intership and Ship-to-Coast). Same as Channel 68. |
| 79A | 156.975 | 156.975 | COMMERCIAL (Intership and Ship-to-Coast). Same as Channel 7A. |
| 80A | 157.025 | 157.025 | COMMERCIAL (Intership and Ship-to-Coast). Same as Channel 7A. |
| 81A | 157.075 | 157.075 | U.S. GOVERNMENT ONLY. |
| 82A | 157.125 | 157.125 | U.S. GOVERNMENT ONLY. |
| 83A | 157.175 | 157.175 | U.S. GOVERNMENT ONLY. |
| 84 | 157.225 | 161.825 | PUBLIC CORRESPONDENCE (Ship-to-Coast). Same as Channel 24. |
| 85 | 157.275 | 161.875 | PUBLIC CORRESPONDENCE (Ship-to-Coast). Same as Channel 24. |
| 86 | 157.325 | 161.925 | PUBLIC CORRESPONDENCE (Ship-to-Coast). Same as Channel 24. |
| 87 | 157.375 | 161.975 | PUBLIC CORRESPONDENCE (Ship-to-Coast). Same as Channel 24. |
| 88 | 157.425 | 162.025 | PUBLIC CORRESPONDENCE. In the areas of the Puget Sound and Strait of Juan de Fuca and approaches, same as channel 24. |
| 88A | 157.425 | 157.425 | COMMERCIAL (Intership). Beyond 120 km from Puget Sound area, in the Great Lakes, and on the St. Lawrence Seaway, same as Channel 7A, except limited to intership use. Also available for communications between commercial fishing vessels and associated aircraft while engaged in commercial fishing. |

# SEAMANSHIP

7

Good seamanship is important to the proper operation of vessels of all types and sizes — from small dinghies to super-tankers. A skipper's study of the subject should never end.

## BOAT HANDLING — NORMAL CONDITIONS

A discussion of boat handling procedures for everyday conditions will not suffice for abnormal situations, which are usually more hazardous.

Powerboats can be divided into three general groups: single screw, twin screw, and directed thrust, which in turn can be divided as to the means of thrust — propeller or water jet. Be especially cautious if you are experienced with one type of boat but are asked to take the helm of another type.

For the most part, the discussion of single-screw powerboats below applies to sailing craft when auxiliary engines are in use. (A comment on the difference between powerboats and auxiliary powered sailboats is made at the end of this section.)

### Powerboats — Single Screw

The single-engine, single-propeller craft is the basic type of powerboat and there are many of these. An understanding of the fundamentals of boat handling should start here.

The forward-thrusting propeller may turn in either direction, referred to as right- or left-hand rotation. When viewed from astern, a right-hand propeller turns clockwise when propelling the boat ahead. There are probably more "right-handed" boats than "left-handed," but there are enough of the latter to warrant discussion here. Learn the basic principles and apply them to your craft, but also learn how the other type handles in case you are some-day handed the helm on such a boat. The right-handed craft will be considered in detail here; in general, the propeller reactions of a left-handed boat will be just the opposite.

A first consideration in boat handling is how it turns. A boat does not steer as a land vehicle does! A vessel of any size has a "turning point," about which it pivots when a change of direction is effected. Typically, this will be about one-third of the

way aft from the vessel's bow. As a result, when a turn is made in one direction, right or left, the bow turns that way, *but the stern swings out to the opposite side.* The location of the turning point may vary slightly, influenced by the hull's shape and draft, but it does exist, and recognition of this characteristic must be constantly in every skipper's mind.

*Going Ahead*

The stern of a boat with a single, right-hand propeller in forward gear tends to swing to starboard, giving a slight turn to port, even with the rudder centered. You can visualize this by thinking of the propeller as though it were rolling across the sea bottom. This torque effect, often referred to as "propeller walk," is slight if the propeller shaft is horizontal, but increases considerably if the shaft is angled downward, which is usually the case with inboard powerboats. (Consideration of why this happens, suction and discharge currents, unequal blade thrust, etc., is beyond the scope of the discussion here, but can be found in other reference texts.) The tendency to turn to port is usually easily handled by the helmsman, but if it becomes annoying, a small "trim tab" can be attached to the rudder and adjusted to neutralize the turning effect.

*In Reverse*

With the engine in reverse gear, the action is the opposite — the stern goes to port. Although the effect of propeller walk is no less when operating in reverse, it may seem more pronounced under some conditions. When using reverse gear to bring your vessel to a stop, make a tight turn, or leave a dock, the kick to port can be quite accentuated. These are conditions when the propeller may be spinning with substantial speed while you're making little or no way. At such times, your rudder has little or no ability to counter propeller walk. Remember, with a left-hand propeller, both of these actions will be just the opposite from that described above.

### Powerboats — Twin Screw

Craft with two engines and two propellers are commonly referred to as "twin-screw." This is not strictly true, though, because universally one propeller will be right-hand and the other left-hand (with the right-hand one on the starboard side, so that at the upper side both propellers are turning outward). The engines are usually identical, turning in the same direction; the reversal of one shaft's rotation is effected in the reduction gears. This has long been the situation for inboard-engine boats with conventional shafts and propellers.

Having two propellers rotating in opposite directions neutralizes the sideways tendency described above for single-screw vessels. Twin screws provide significant other boat handling advantages. Because each shaft is off to one side of the boat's centerline, each propeller exerts a turning force. This can be put to good use when maneuvering in close quarters — by putting one engine in forward gear and the other in reverse, you can make very sharp turns. By carefully manipulating the throttles, a twin-screw boat can normally be turned in place, with no forward or backward movement.

## Powerboats — Directed Thrust

This category includes propeller-driven craft with sterndrive units, frequently called "I-O" drives because they combine the features of inboard and outboard motors. Also included are craft with water-jet propulsion, mostly the ubiquitous personal watercraft (PWC), but now including large yachts. The common feature of all these vessels is the ability to turn their propulsive thrust from side to side for steering, without rudders. Craft of this type with a single propeller are still subject to the turning action described for a single-screw inboard boat with conventional shaft and propeller. However, counter-rotation is available when sterndrives and medium and larger size outboard engines are paired.

### Maneuvering

Here again we will consider first the single-screw powerboat (right-hand propeller) because it is the more difficult to maneuver.

#### Getting Underway

Ideally, there would be a gentle offshore breeze and you'd only need to cast off your lines, drift off a bit, and then go forward normally. Unfortunately, that's not the usual situation. If there is no such favorable wind (or current), or if the wind is pushing you into the pier or wharf, it's better to back away rather than go forward and bump your stern and quarter against the structure.

Because of the sideways swing of her stern — to port when reversing — the preferred way to dock is with the starboard side to. So positioned, the natural tendency is for the stern to swing away from the structure. If your "wrong side" is against the dock in an onshore breeze and you can't, therefore, use propeller walk to assist in kicking your stern away from the dock, you may have to use an after-bow springline (see next page) to angle out the stern enough to get away clearly. To do so, put the transmission in forward briefly. When you do, the line will prevent you from moving forward, the bow will be pulled into the dock, and the stern will angle out. Back out, get well clear, and then go ahead, at a slow speed until clear of other boats.

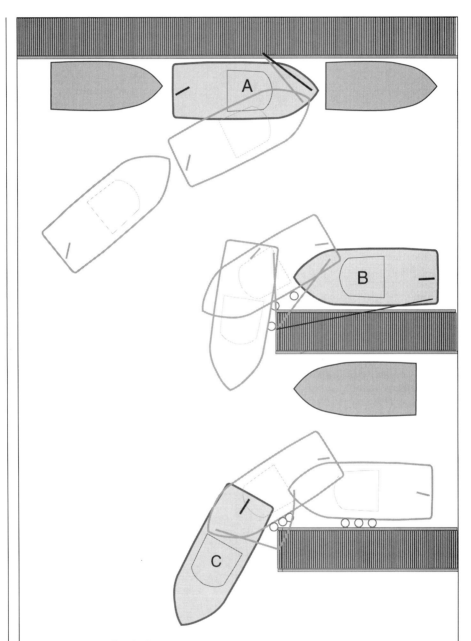

**Using springlines for docking**

Vessel A manages to dock in a tight space by coming in at a sharp angle, running an after-bow springline, and going ahead with hard right rudder. When departing, vessel A can use the same spring and left rudder to get its stern into the channel. Vessel B has used a forward-quarter spring and plenty of fenders to spring itself around the dock end and into its berth. Finally, vessel C uses a bow line which becomes an after-bow spring as they move forward, and aids their exit from a similar berth.

Twin-screw craft can use the turning effect of one engine ahead and one engine in reverse to turn the boat sufficiently so that backing out presents no problem. Such craft can dock either side to the pier or wharf as desired. Similarly, boats with directed-thrust can use their capability to turn sharply when backing away.

When leaving a mooring, boats of any type should be sure to back away so they don't get entangled with the mooring pennant; go ahead to either side of the buoy, but keep well clear.

### Underway

*The most important action while underway is to maintain a good lookout.* This is both common sense and one of the Navigation Rules on all waters. All too many collisions take place solely because no one on board was alert.

The next most important item is to remember that boats do not have brakes! You can't abruptly stop, or even slow down, a conventionally powered boat of substantial displacement. The reverse spin of the propeller you use to stop or slow takes effect only gradually — and in single-screw boats, it can induce a marked swing of the stern to one side.

Always keep in mind that a boat turns around a pivot point. When going forward, the effect of applying, say, a left rudder angle, is to swing the stern to starboard. When the pivot point is well forward of amidships (the normal case), the stern swings through a greater arc than the bow.

Every small-craft skipper should take systematic steps to become fully familiar with his or her own craft — learning how she reacts to currents, waves, and winds from all points; how she reacts to various throttle settings; as well as all the other handling characteristics. Take time to practice maneuvers in open areas. Practice docking your boat in an area that has plenty of open space, but imagine that other boats are alongside and set yourself a limited space into which you must dock your boat. Then practice getting out from a tight space, even if it is only imaginary. When you are asked to take the helm of a strange vessel, you may not be able to practice, so your best course of action is to take actions slowly and in small increments until you have the feel of that boat.

### Docking

Regardless of how many times you have done it before, or how favorable the conditions, the cardinal rule is "slow and easy." You should have just enough headway to have positive steering control — remember, you don't have any brakes. A steering failure or engine stall when reverse power is needed can result in great embarrassment, if not damage or injury.

Consider wind direction, and any current, too. You'll have the most control of your boat when heading into wind or current, or the stronger of the two if both are acting on you. Then, their effects work for you, not against you. If at all possible, avoid docking downwind or down-current. And never try to fend off with your hands, feet, or legs. Have fenders (not "bumpers") available for immediate use, but unless you're approaching a solid dock face, wharf, or lock side, don't put them out in advance — they could get hung up on a pile.

Before you approach a dock, think about which line you should first pass over to the dock. Consider what will happen if a dock attendant snubs the line while you're still moving forward. If the attendant has your bow line, your bow will be pulled abruptly into the dock. For this reason, many experienced skippers prefer to first pass over a line that is attached amidships. In any case, a good rule is to use the engine, not a line, to stop your boat.

If you're forced to dock downwind in a strong breeze you should, of course, consider using a sternline to guard against overshooting your mark. When you've stopped, you can use a bow line to help swing your stern into the dock.

If your bow gets caught by wind or current, your best bet is to use an after-bow springline. With that made fast to the shore, turn the wheel away from the shore and go ahead slowly on the engine (the shoreside engine if twin screw). This will hold your boat in to the structure even in a strong offshore breeze; this may be also all that you will need for brief stops.

When picking up a mooring, note how other craft are lying to their buoys and approach *slowly* on the same heading. Ideally, another crewmember will be on the bow with a boathook and can signal you how to steer when you can no longer see the buoy. If you should overrun the buoy, place the transmission in neutral to avoid fouling the pennant in the propeller and shaft. You'll likely drift clear from the push of the wind or current. If you can't use such a passive approach, then it's better to go forward and swing around for another pass. If possible, avoid going in reverse when the buoy is near your stern, because a reversed propeller is more likely to suck in the pennant (or any other line).

## Sailboats

The dynamics of sailing is another topic. Here, we will only consider the handling of sailing craft under power.

Basically, a sailboat not under sail is a powerboat — and it certainly is in the Navigation Rules. She is a single–screw craft, probably underpowered for her size and displacement, with a smaller and less effective propeller. It can be assumed that she will handle less efficiently than a powerboat of the same size; there are some sailboats that simply will not back in a straight line. Follow the guidance given above for single-screw powerboats, but move more slowly and cautiously.

### BOAT HANDLING — ADVERSE CONDITIONS

Because boating conditions are not always favorable, prudent skippers think ahead and prepare themselves and their craft for unfavorable conditions. The major adverse conditions are high wind and seas, and reduced visibility from fog or other causes.

## High Winds and Seas

High winds and high seas usually occur together, but occasionally there may be large swells from a distant storm in a location not experiencing strong winds. When high winds and seas do occur together, their combined effects should be judged in relation to the size of the craft involved and the experience of her skipper. Winds that are too strong for one boater might be perfect for another. The essential safety factor in handling your craft in strong winds and rough seas is your experience and your recognition of the risks you may face.

### Preparation

Being prepared for rough weather is a key element in riding it out with the least amount of stress and discomfort; it may even be the key to survival. The list below may not apply to all vessels, but it will provide a basis for tailoring one to your craft:

Close and secure tightly all windows, ports, and hatches.

Secure all loose items; stow smaller ones and lash down larger ones.

Get out the necessary number of PFDs; put them on *now*, before conditions get really bad.

Get out any emergency gear you might need — hand pumps, buckets, gear to shore-up windows and ports, sea anchor, EPIRB, etc.

Pump all bilges dry; repeat as necessary.

Bring your navigation plot up to date; recheck your position.

Consider possible changes of course to better weather the storm or to seek shelter.

Assign duties to each person; doing so will lessen confusion later when conditions worsen, and a person with something to do will worry less than one sitting idle.

### Head Seas

In almost all cases, heading directly into the waves, or nearly head on (or close-hauled under sail), will provide the safest and most comfortable conditions on board. A slow speed will also make things better — ease off on the throttle or shorten sail. If conditions worsen, reduce speed to the bare minimum to maintain steering control. Adjust your fore-and-aft trim to ensure that your boat will rise properly to meet the next wave after sliding down the back face of the preceding one.

### Running Before the Seas

Taking heavy seas from astern is risky and should be avoided if at all possible. If not, try to set your forward speed to allow the swells to pass under your boat as smoothly as possible. Take every precaution to prevent broaching; that is, being thrown sideways and out of control. Some hull shapes — for example, powerboats with broad sterns — are especially subject to broaching if the waves are allowed to get off the quarter. Other hull shapes, such as double-enders, will normally ride before the seas quite well. A drogue set out astern is very helpful, but must be carefully tended to prevent its line from becoming entangled in your rudders or propellers.

### Broadside to the Seas

This can be a very dangerous situation. The boat must ride up the face of a wave and down the backside, with a great tendency to roll. If you must head in a direction that would put you broadside to the waves, a good procedure is to "tack" either side of the track you must make good so you take the waves first on the bow at about a 45° angle and then on the stern at a 45° angle. Make each tack as long as possible to minimize the coming about. Slow down and try to pick a gap between the largest waves — they are not all the same size — to make your turn, and do it as quickly as possible so you're broadside for a minimum time.

### Extreme Conditions

In extreme conditions, skippers should consider removing all power — sail or engine — and trying to find a relatively comfortable, safe way to ride out the weather.

One option is lying a'hull; that is, allowing the vessel to simply sit and take it, perhaps deploying a sea anchor to hold the bow more into the wind and waves. Another option is "running under bare poles," or steering downwind with only the power of your vessel's windage — maybe even trailing tires, anchors, or whatever you can find to prevent your vessel from going down the faces of large waves so fast that you bury your bow into the wave ahead or broach.

Sailboats can use their sails to "heave to" in quite rough weather. The object is to maintain a steady course at the lowest possible speed and ensure that the vessel's motion is as comfortable as possible. The technique is simple:

Place the headsail in a backed position, either by hauling it to windward or — usually more easily — by changing tacks without shifting the headsail. Lash the tiller to leeward or set the wheel to windward. The amount of rudder angle you use will depend on your boat's sail plan and design, as well as on the conditions. So, too, you should adjust the trim of the mainsail.

If the boat falls off much, the main will power up, the vessel will gain speed, and the rudder will turn her up into the wind. If she heads up too far she will lose all way and the backed headsail will push her bow to leeward. The net effect of these forces working against each other is the vessel fore reaching slowly at maybe 60° off the wind, steadied by her sails, and steering herself.

With modern hulls of light displacement and narrow fin keels and transom hung rudders, it's especially important to achieve a favorable rudder angle and mainsail trim. The average cruising yacht should perform adequately once the owner has established the trim required. It is well worth your time trying out the maneuver initially in light winds to see how your vessel performs; then, practice again in heavier winds. "Heaving to" can be useful in even moderate weather to deal with a domestic crisis below decks or simply to enjoy a peaceful meal in the cockpit.

Two important points to remember: First, although the vessel may be moving very slowly through the water, its speed over the ground may be quite appreciable because of leeway; therefore, be sure that you have plenty of sea room. Second, maintain a good lookout at regular intervals. Remember, according to the Rules of the Road, you're an underway vessel even when you're hove to.

## Running Inlets

In some coastal regions, the junction of inland and ocean waters is a broad opening that can be traversed easily in all weather suitable for normal operations. Unfortunately, in other areas there is a restricted opening — an inlet — that can have strong river and/or tidal currents. Departing through such an inlet can be the most dangerous part of a day's outing on your boat — and returning from sea through the inlet can be even more hazardous. The restricted opening of an inlet, a strong current, running against a strong wind, and the generally shallower depths as compared with offshore, all combine to result in higher waves that can build to a crest and break — not good conditions for a small craft.

### Departing Through an Inlet

Going out through an inlet can be safer than coming in because you can better see the nature of the waves in the inlet, their size, and whether or not they are breaking. Exiting, you'll usually be heading into the waves and thus have better control of your boat. Further, if you don't like the conditions of the inlet, you have the option of turning back and trying again later.

Before you leave, consider the conditions you'll likely encounter if you plan to re-enter the same inlet. If you do decide to go out, remember that waves are usually more moderate in deeper water. So, make your run in those areas if you can. Most inlets are buoyed, and the Coast Guard attempts to keep up with changes in hydrography by relocating them, but buoys are not always where the best conditions are. Look over the situation and make your decisions based on the sea state you observe and the placement of the buoys. By far, the safest passage through an inlet is made by following a local boat, one that has done it before many times — but confirm by radio that the other skipper is indeed experienced at this inlet.

### Entering Through an Inlet

Although you won't encounter dangerous conditions at all inlets, and not all of the time at any particular inlet, there are many that have a well-deserved bad reputation. Shallow inlets can be particularly treacherous when a fast-moving ebb current is opposing a strong onshore wind and large ocean swells.

From offshore, it's difficult to assess the conditions and potential hazards at an inlet. You'll see only the backsides of the waves and be unable to determine their size and breaking characteristics. Also, you won't be able to accurately determine where the conditions are more favorable. This is the time to use your radio to get information from shore stations and/or craft on the inside. It's often a better idea, even in the face of rough weather offshore, to remain outside and await better conditions in an inlet — you will be safer riding the larger swells and waves in deep water than trying to get through the breaking surf of an inlet.

Because inlets are worse on ebbing tidal currents as the outward flow works against and under the incoming swells, the best conditions are generally at the time of slack or flood current — wait if you can.

If you must come through when conditions are difficult, take your time in deciding just how you are going to do it. Observe the waves — they generally run in "sets" with a fairly regular sequence of one or two large breakers followed by several smaller waves before the next large ones. Position your boat where you can move in to follow a larger wave, riding a smaller one. Prepare your craft: close all ports and hatches; secure all loose gear; brief everyone on board about what you are going to do and what you want them to do or not do; put on PFDs; and consider shifting weights toward the stern to reduce any tendency of the bow to dig in when riding down the forward slopes of waves.

When you feel that a large wave has passed, and the next one will be smaller, start your entrance. Watch the water ahead, *and behind*, your boat; control the speed of your boat, and try to match the speed of the waves. In a sailboat, if you can't match wave speed, try to go slowly enough so the waves pass you. Maintain directional control closely to avoid broaching.

## Reduced Visibility

Fog is the primary cause of reduced visibility, but haze, heavy rain, and snow all present problems for mariners, too. Running in these conditions presents two hazards — navigational errors and collisions. Preventing both of these begins with reducing your speed. The old saying, "Be able to stop in half the distance of visibility," doesn't appear in the Navigation Rules, but it is very good advice — even slower is better! A sailboat with an auxiliary engine, if under sail in fog, should have her engine available for immediate use, but you'll be better able to listen for fog signals and other helpful sounds if you leave the engine off until it's needed.

Fog signals must be sounded; the time interval specified in the Navigation Rules is the *minimum*. Vary your interval so that there is no possibility of your signals being in step with another vessel's, thereby preventing you from hearing them. Listening for another vessel's fog signals is just as important as sounding your own. If you have crew aboard, post a lookout well forward (and consider having another person aft if possible). The lookout should listen as well as look. Listen for other vessels, the sound of aids to navigation, breaking surf, and other helpful sounds. Lookouts are especially important if your helm station is inside. In the middle of a watch, switch bow and stern lookouts to provide some variety and increase alertness.

If your engines are noisy, periodically shift into idle, or even shut them down for a few minutes to listen for faint fog signals. The transmission of sound in foggy conditions is tricky; if you hear something, don't jump to a too-quick conclusion about its direction and distance — listen some more.

If several craft are traveling together, it is advisable that they stay close in a column formation, but one in which closely following vessels aren't directly behind the leader so they can easily steer clear if the lead vessel stops suddenly. If the fog is so thick that it is hazardous for them to be within sight of each other, each vessel should tow a floating object — an empty fuel container or a cushion works well — astern on a line of approximately 50 meters. Then, each vessel can keep its "station" in column by keeping that object in sight, rather than the craft ahead.

## Groundings

Despite vigilant efforts to stay off shoals, beaches, or rocks, groundings do happen. It is said that there are only two kinds of skippers — those who have run aground, and those who will run aground in the future. It is important that every captain be prepared for such an event — with knowledge and equipment.

### Immediate Actions

First, here is what you should *not* do when you run aground: Unless you are absolutely sure that it is a small shoal with deeper water ahead, *do not* apply power and try to push your way across — you will only put yourself harder aground. *Do not* immediately shift into reverse and increase engine power in an attempt to back off — you might suck up mud and bottom vegetation into the engine intake (watch for any signs of engine overheating), and you might further damage the propellers.

Instead, take time to assess the situation: Is any water coming into the hull? Where exactly are you? How did you get there? Where might deeper water lie? What is the state of the tide?

If you have a dinghy in the water, or can launch one, use it to take soundings all around your boat. If you are in a rocky area, it is especially important *not to attempt to refloat* the craft immediately. First, check for any hull damage — the rocks you are on might be the only things keeping your boat afloat! If the damage is considerable, set out an anchor or two to keep you in place for the time being. Even if you don't need any immediate assistance, you should radio the Coast Guard or other local authority. Advise them of your situation and your intended actions.

Let us assume that you are lucky and that the tide is rising (or will rise soon) and that the increased depths will be enough to float you free. Although you might get off sooner if another vessel pulled, letting the tide float you off is less stressful on your hull, if not on your crew. It may be necessary to set out an anchor in the direction of the wind and waves to prevent the rising tide from carrying you further up on the shoal.

If you are less lucky, and the tide is falling, quickly assess the situation and the possibility of refloating the boat before the tide goes down further. If this is not possible, determine how far it will go down. Will the hull need cushioning and supports as it lays over on its side? While you wait for the tide or assistance, you might want to use the opportunity to inspect and clean your hull's bottom. (An especially crafty skipper might even be able to convince others that that was why you went aground!)

### Getting Off

If you are only lightly stranded, you may be able to get off without assistance. First, determine where deeper water lies — this may or may not be the direction opposite to that from which you came. Then, try to reduce draft. In any type of craft, sail or power, you can empty water tanks if the supply isn't critical.

You might also place some heavy gear in a dinghy. On a sailboat, you can try reducing draft by taking a halyard out to one side, attaching it to an anchor or another boat, and pulling. Yet another maneuver is to put out an anchor in the direction in which you wish to move. If you have an anchor windlass or a sheet winch, use that to take in the line — this is called "kedging off." The anchor can be carried out by dinghy (with the line in the dinghy being paid out as it moves away from the vessel). If this isn't possible, the anchor can be supported on PFDs or buoyant cushions and floated out to where it is to be set — the longer the scope, the better.

If another craft is available to help you, run a line to that boat if it can pull in the desired direction. Be very careful that the other boat does not become stranded in the same shallow water; it may be necessary for the other boat to put out and tend an anchor to keep her clear. Be sure that both craft have deck fittings that can withstand the strain of the pull — typical recreational boats may not have such hardware.

If a pull is made, *keep all persons away from the line and beyond the ends of the line in both directions.* Various types of lines stretch to different degrees, but all stretch enough to act as slingshots if they break or if fittings pull out. Serious injury, or even death, are possible results of such failures.

Even if the other boat cannot pull to get you off, she may help by running back and forth and making as large a wake as possible. The waves formed in this wake may life your boat enough to get her off. (You should use this technique only where the bottom is soft enough to cushion your underbody.)

### ASSISTING ANOTHER VESSEL

There is an unwritten law of the sea that a mariner should offer assistance to anyone in need of help. The Federal Boating Safety Act of 1971 contains a "Good Samaritan" clause stating that anyone is protected who gratuitously and in good faith renders assistance at the scene of an accident or other boating casualty without the objection of any person being assisted. Such persons cannot be held liable for civil damages as a result of rendering assistance or for any act or omission in providing or arranging for salvage, towing, medical treatment, or other assistance where they act as ordinary, reasonably prudent persons would have acted under the same or similar circumstances.

#### Assistance In Groundings

If you are called upon to assist a boat that has run aground, you should agree to help — but not at the risk of endangering your own craft and crew. It's critical, of course, that the skipper of the assisting boat is absolutely certain of the depth of water — how closely can you approach, and from what direction? It may well be that the most practical assistance will be to call for help if the stranded craft has not already done so. Or, as mentioned above, perhaps the assisting boat can help by making a wake that will lift the grounded boat up enough so she can get off with her own engine power.

If a pull can be safely made, first consider the following factors: Is a line available of suitable diameter and length? (Don't worry about whose line is used; there is no issue of legal liability involved despite old sayings.) Are there deck fittings on *both* boats that can take the strain of a hard pull? (In some cases, a line can be fastened around the base of a mast, or even, theoretically, using a bridle around a cabin or the whole hull.) If these conditions are satisfactorily met, then the problem is getting the line across between the boats. This is probably most easily done from the assisting craft to the grounded boat. If the grounded boat can be approached closely enough, the simplest procedure is to toss the line over. Otherwise, a line may be taken over by dinghy or floated over with a PFD or buoyant cushion. The pull can be made by going either ahead or astern — usually determined by the location of suitable fittings on the assisting boat or the available depths of water. If you are doing the pulling by going ahead, *make sure that the point of attachment of the line is well forward of your stern* so that your maneuverability is not hampered.

If there is wind or current at a large angle to the direction of pull, the pulling vessel may want to put out an upwind anchor to keep from being swept sideways — both this anchor and the one put out by the stranded craft must be tended for the duration of the pull to ensure that they remain effective. A second anchor should be readily available in case the engine stalls during the pull.

## Towing

If you have pulled free a stranded vessel, she may have damaged her running gear and be unable to proceed under her own power. Or, you may encounter another boat that has engine failure or has run out of fuel. In either of these situations, you may be asked to tow the other craft to a safe harbor. You should do so if you won't be risking your vessel and those aboard. Remember — you might be the one needing a tow next time!

When towing another boat, some of the same considerations apply as discussed above in groundings. There must be suitable line and adequate deck fittings. The steady strain, when towing, will be less than when pulling off a grounded vessel, but if any seas are running there may be shock loads as the towline goes slack momentarily and then comes up tight. Both craft should have an anchor available for immediate use in the event the towline parts. Usually, a disabled boat can be most easily picked up by passing a line over from

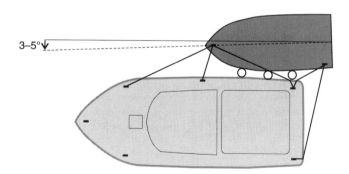

**Towing alongside, or "on the hip"**
This technique is useful for towing a vessel in close quarters. Canting the bow of the towboat inward 3–5° will help to balance steering.

the craft that is going to do the towing; again, don't worry about who furnishes the towline. If it isn't safe to get close enough to throw the line, it can be floated over, but take care that it doesn't get entangled in either boat's propeller or rudder. A polypropylene line (the kind used for waterskiing) floats and is good for this procedure; once it is across the gap between the boats it can be used to pull over the actual towing line.

If you have a choice, double-braid nylon is preferable for towing. Ordinary three-strand twisted nylon has too much stretch and, although polypropylene line floats, it lacks elasticity and strength.

### Towing Procedures

In open waters, the usual practice is to tow astern. Great care must be taken to attach the line to the towing craft well forward of the stern — her maneuverability will be severely hampered if done otherwise. Start slowly and take up the slack in the towline with care, and then continue the towing operation at a very moderate speed. If there are waves present, adjust the length of the towline so that the two craft are "in step," with both on a crest or in a trough at the same time — this will make for the smoothest pull with the minimum of jerks and sudden strains on the line.

It is important to maintain communications between the vessels concerned. (Handheld radios come in handy here.) Someone on the towing boat must be stationed aft and keep the towed boat under constant observation. That person should be able to cast the line off quickly or have some means of cutting the towline should an emergency require such action. The caution regarding not standing near or in line with the towline is just as applicable here as in pulling off a stranded boat.

When the boats get into more protected or more crowded waters, the towline should be shortened. It may be desirable to take the disabled craft alongside — "on the hip" is the term used by professional towing crews. The towing boat should place the disabled boat far enough forward so it can maintain effective steering. The towing boat, then, is on the hip of the boat being towed, which will provide the maximum maneuverability of the two-vessel combination. Before you reach your destination, consider how you are going to cast off the tow. Don't try to take the disabled boat all the way into the pier — just get it close enough for a line to thrown ashore, or have a smaller boat take over for the final few meters.

Remember, though, if your boat is not suitable, or you lack adequate crew to tow someone, just stand by until the Coast Guard, an assistance towing boat, or other suitable craft arrives on scene. Don't take on a task that you can't complete safely.

## DOCKING

Earlier in this chapter we considered how to get a boat alongside a pier or wharf safely and gracefully. Once alongside it must be kept in the desired position with lines to the shore. There are a number of docklines that can be used; each has a specific purpose. These lines may be of three-strand twisted nylon, but double-braid is easier on the hands. For docking, nylon works better than Dacron because it stretches more. It is essential that every craft has enough docklines and that they're long enough for the task.

### Lines

Bow and stern lines are used the most often. They run from the ends of a vessel to the shore, forward at the bow and aft at the stern, so that the distance between them is greater than the length of the vessel. If there are cleats on each side of the stern, it's usually best to run a sternline from the offshore side. These bow and sternlines may be all that are needed for making fast in good weather.

With just these lines, however, there will be some fore and aft movement of the boat with respect to the pier or wharf. When you want to reduce that movement (for example, when you want to keep fenders aligned against pilings), you can do so by using springlines, which are named by their location on the boat and the direction they run. An after-bow spring is attached at a side cleat well forward and runs aft to the shore. A forward-quarter spring is attached to a side cleat forward of the stern and runs forward to the shore. These are the preferred locations for attaching springlines to a boat, but variations may be necessary in the absence of cleats in the ideal locations. Cleats at the bow and stern may have to be used. There are also *forward-bow springs* and *after-quarter springs*, but these are used less often. A single springline is often very useful in coming into a berth or pivoting a boat to get out of a berth in tight quarters.

Springlines are often crossed as they run to the shore. Their length is determined by the change in level between the boat and the shore; they should be long enough to allow for tidal or other changes (as should other lines). Alternatively, the midpoint of a long line can be attached to an amidships cleat and the two ends run forward and aft to the shore.

There are also *breast* lines, which are relatively short lines that run directly from some part of the side of the vessel to the shore. Their primary use is for pulling in the boat for boarding and disembarking.

A point to remember about docklines is that the eye of the line should not be dropped over any lines already on the piling, unless it'll be the next line to be removed. The eye should be passed up through the eyes of lines already there and then dropped over the piling. This will facilitate removing any line without disturbing the others.

### Size and Length of Docklines

The size of docking lines will, of course, vary with the size of the craft. Lines for a 20-footer can be 3/8-inch in diameter; for a 30- to 40-footer, 1/2-inch lines are appropriate; and for a 40- to 50-foot craft, 5/8-inch lines are appropriate. Every boat except the very smallest should have at least four lines, two of which are as long or longer than the craft. Some boaters use docklines that are too large; the result is that they don't fit well on cleats and are harder to handle. When bad weather threatens, you may want to double your lines. In doing so, make sure that the lines are of equal length and will share the load — nothing is gained if one carries all the load until it breaks, and then the other is left to carry the load until it, in turn, breaks.

### Heaving a Line

Normally, as a boat approaches a pier or wharf, the docking lines are thrown, or *heaved*, across the gap. There is a right way, and several wrong ways, to do this. Docklines will carry some distance if heaved properly. If you are right-handed,

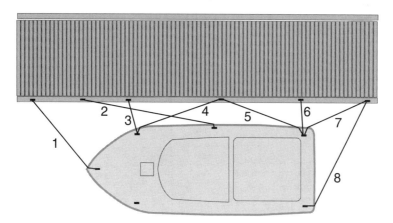

**Docklines illustrated:**

1. bow line
2. forward spring
3. forward (bow) breast
4. after-bow spring
5. forward-quarter spring
6. after-quarter breast
7. after-quarter spring
8. sternline

coil the line in your left hand, making the loops clockwise, and be sure that the coils are straight and smooth, with no reversed loops. Take about half of the loops in your right hand. Throw all of these loops in a smooth, forward-swinging motion. Let the loops in your left hand pay out freely — but make sure you don't lose the bitter end if it isn't secured to the boat! If you are left-handed, just reverse the above procedure.

Lines up to 5/8-inch or 3/4-inch diameter can be thrown as described above. If you must get a heavier line across, as might be needed for towing, first throw a lighter *messenger* line and use that to pull the heavier line across. If the distance is greater than normal, you can fasten a weight to the end of the messenger line to increase range and accuracy. Such a weight is often a fancy woven knot around a spherical weight, called a *monkey's fist*.

## ANCHORING

The ability to anchor securely is an essential part of seamanship. It may become necessary to anchor if you have engine or other problems where you have to call for assistance. Or, you may merely wish to anchor in a pleasant cove or harbor; "anchoring out" is often more pleasant than making fast at a crowded pier or wharf. In either case, the object is to secure the boat to the bottom in such a manner that it will not pull free in any anticipated weather conditions. The skipper must have both the proper equipment and the knowledge to use it correctly.

### Equipment

The gear needed for anchoring consists essentially of an anchor and rode, which may be either line or chain, with shackles to join the various segments. A tripline and float can be added. The combination of all the gear used for anchoring is often referred to as "ground tackle."

#### Anchors

There are many types of anchors, but here we only consider those most widely used. The *lightweight* type of anchor relies on its sizable surface area to dig into the bottom. One type of lightweight anchor, and perhaps the most widely used, is the

Danforth, which has two pivoting flukes that dig into the bottom. The Danforth can be made of either steel or high-strength aluminum. It holds well in mud or sand, but has a tendency to pull out of a bottom covered with weeds or grass because it often only lies on the top of such vegetation. It will hook into rocks or coral, but may be difficult to get free; it may also bend or break when so hooked. Many lightweight types of anchors will lie reasonably flat on deck and are easy to stow.

The *plow* anchor is very effective because it has sufficient weight to enable its fluke to dig into a variety of bottoms, but is awkward to stow on deck. It is popular with sailors and powerboaters whose craft have bow pulpits with rollers. There are a number of different manufacturers of plows, in addition to the original CQR model. The *Bruce* anchor is much like the plow, but has a fixed stock rather than one that pivots.

Minor types of anchors include the *Grapnel*, which has several (usually five) arms and flukes. The Grapnel has some application for anchoring, but it's most often used to drag along the bottom to recover lost chain or other gear. *Mushroom* anchors are used only for permanent moorings. Named for their shape, the large crown gradually sinks into a soft bottom and provides great holding power. Less often seen are anchors with stocks, such as a *kedge* anchor, whose name refers to its design, rather than how it is used. Anchors with stocks come in a variety of designs for different types of bottoms — relatively large flukes are used in sand; narrow, more pointed flukes are used to get down through grass and weeds.

The number and type of anchors for a particular craft should be largely determined by her size and intended cruising area. Any boat other than the very smallest should carry two anchors; three are even better.

#### The Anchor Rode

Connecting the anchor to the vessel is the *anchor rode*, which may be of either chain or line. Chain makes a good rode because its weight adds to the holding power of any anchor, but it is heavy and difficult to use. If the rode is comprised entirely of chain, it is almost always necessary to have an anchor windlass to raise it. Further, the weight of a sufficient length of chain may be a problem in the bow of a small craft, especially one with a sharp entry and limited buoyancy forward.

Line is favored by many for anchoring because its elasticity absorbs the shock load when anchoring in moderate to heavy swells. Three-stranded twisted nylon is preferred over double-braid line because it stretches more. If you use line for your rode, a length of chain several meters long should be inserted just above the anchor to counteract against any chafing on rocks or coral. The weight of this chain also keeps the lower end of the rode down against the bottom, thereby making the pull on the anchor more horizontal.

Do not make the mistake of using anchor line that's too large in diameter. Use a size that's adequate for strength, but not larger, because a larger size will stretch less and provide less of a cushioning effect on shock loads. *Shackles* are used to join the chain to the anchor and, if used, the line to the chain. The pin of every thimble should be secured against accidental unscrewing by using stainless steel wire or a plastic cable tie. Where line is to be made into an eye, use a *thimble*; it should be metal, except for the lightest rodes where a plastic thimble is acceptable.

### Triplines

A light line, called a tripline, is frequently attached to a ring or eye at the crown of the anchor — the opposite end at which the rode is attached. Polypropylene line, which floats, is most commonly used, and a small float is attached to the other end of the line. Basically, a tripline is intended to help pull an anchor out backwards if the flukes get caught in rocks, coral heads, or wreckage. Triplines have other handy uses — the float indicates where your anchor is located and might help you see if your anchor is holding or dragging (see below).

## Anchoring Procedures and Techniques

Even with the best of equipment, anchoring may not be secure and safe if you don't use the gear properly. Anchoring has often been called an art, but it is one that can be learned and improved upon with experience.

### Selecting an Anchorage

Except in an emergency, the first step in anchoring is deciding where to lower your anchor. You should take into account the prevailing winds, the bottom depth, the bottom composition, and the existence of other craft in the anchorage.

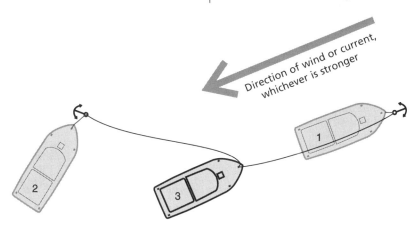

Direction of wind or current, whichever is stronger

**Setting two anchors:**
1) Set the first anchor upwind (or current); 2) Drop down current (wind) and set second anchor; 3) Adjust rodes to lay between anchors.

This is a particularly good technique in narrow waterways with strong reversing currents. To set two anchors in a blow, set them in a "V" toward the expected strongest wind.

Shelter from the wind is important because calmer water will put less strain on the ground tackle, as well as on the skipper's nerves. Be sure to consider any anticipated changes in wind direction and velocity. The composition of the bottom will affect the type of anchor you'll use, assuming that you have a choice. Ideally, the water should be deep enough so you won't have to worry about sitting on the bottom at low tide. However, deeper isn't always better. The deeper the water, the longer the rode must be, and so the greater your swinging circle will be. Anchoring in water that, at its lowest, will be two or three times the draft of your boat is a good practice if possible.

### Approaching the Anchorage

If there are other boats in the anchorage you have selected, look for a place where you will have adequate swinging room. Mentally estimate the swinging circles of the other boats — they'll be small if on moorings, larger if on anchors. Note how the other boats are lying to any wind and current. Reduce speed and enter the anchorage on the same heading as boats already anchored, slowing even more as you approach your chosen spot.

### Setting the Anchor

When you have reached just beyond where you want to anchor, check all headway and start a very slow backward movement — then, and only then, start lowering your anchor. Continue with slow sternway as you pay out the necessary length of rode. The proper length is determined by the desired *scope* — the ratio of the length of the rode in use to the distance to the bottom of the water. Note that this is not just the *depth* of the water — it is the value *plus* the height of the bow above the surface. The depth of the water used in calculating scope is the greatest depth that will occur while anchored; that is, the depth at high tide. For calm conditions, a scope of five is generally satisfactory when using a line rode; when using chain, a scope of three works well. For expected bad weather, increase these values to as much as ten and seven respectively.

It is helpful if the anchor line or chain is marked at regular intervals. When the proper length of rode has been let out, it should be removed from the anchor windlass (if one has been used) and the line

made fast to a Samson post, anchor bitts, or a cleat. Take several turns around the fitting, followed by one or two half-hitches to secure the bitter end. A chain rode is normally secured with a special fitting.

When the rode is fully extended, apply reverse power to make sure that the anchor is holding. If the water is clear enough, and the bottom has small features such as rocks or clumps of grass, you can simply watch them to see if your boat moves with respect to the bottom. If there are features on shore that can serve as a range, use them to determine if your boat is moving backward. But the simplest and surest way is to watch the float on your anchor's tripline. If, when you apply reverse power, the float bobs as usual, you are truly anchored. If you see the float moving through the water, then your anchor is moving, too.

Anchoring under sail is not as simple as doing so under power, but it can be done. Approach under reduced sail and follow the above procedures as best possible. Backing down is usually done by backwinding the mainsail.

The Navigation Rules, International and Inland, require that an anchored vessel hoist a black ball shape by day and show an all-round white light at night. The Inland Rules exempt a vessel less than seven meters in length from this requirement when not anchored in or near a channel or fairway, or near where other vessels normally navigate.

### Getting Underway

When you are ready to leave your anchorage, go forward slowly, taking in the anchor rode by windlass or by hand as it becomes slack. If all goes well, the anchor will break out of the bottom when the pull becomes nearly vertical and it can be hoisted to the surface; you may want to dip it up and down several times to wash off mud and grass.

If the anchor does not come free using normal procedures, position the bow of your craft directly above the anchor so the pull is vertical. Go forward slowly and see if this will not pull it free. If it seems to be firmly stuck, try turning your boat and pulling from different directions. If you have made a tripline a part of your ground tackle, pick up the float and pull the anchor out backward. There are also patented devices that can be rigged to an anchor and its rode to assist in its retrieval.

### Using Two Anchors

It is usually unnecessary, and sometimes undesirable, to use more than one anchor. If a second anchor is set to guard against dragging in a strong wind, it should be put out so that its rode forms an angle of roughly 45° with the first rode. This may be done if there is doubt about the holding power of the first anchor and the wind is expected to continue from the same general direction. If you use a second anchor to anticipate a reversal of tidal current, you should place it in a direction 180° from the first anchor. If squalls and thunderstorms are expected with widely shifting winds, having two anchors out can be dangerous. If the winds go "all the way around the clock," the two rodes can become entangled and either or both of the anchors can lose holding power and pull out — in some cases, one anchor is safer than two.

## ROPES AND LINES

Another essential part of seamanship is marlinespike seamanship — knowledge about rope, its use, and care. Rope is what you buy in bulk; when it's put to use aboard a boat or ship, it becomes line.

### Rope Basics

#### Types of Rope Construction

There are two main methods of rope construction: laid, or twisted, ropes (cable laid) — the traditional form of manufacture used when natural fiber ropes were in general use — and braided ropes. Braided ropes, now usually double braided with a braided cover over a braided core, have the great advantage of being far less liable to kink than a traditional laid rope. Some smaller single braided or eight-part braided rope is used for flag halyards, sail covers, and the like. Braided types of construction, of course, require special splicing techniques.

#### Types of Material Used in Ropes

In the "olden days," rope was made of natural fibers, mostly manila, but also hemp and others. They worked, but have now been superceded by manmade fibers with much better characteristics.

There are three main kinds of manmade fiber: nylon, polyester, and polypropylene. Nylon is the strongest of the three, followed by polyester and then polypropylene. Nylon, in addition to being very strong, is elastic and thus most suitable for dealing with shock loads (with anchors, for example), but is unsuitable for halyards where minimum stretch is essential.

Polyester has the useful combination of being strong and a low-stretch characteristic, thus making it suitable for most purposes on board. It is also available as pre-stretched, which is ideal for halyards, in both plaited and three–strand construction. (Dacron is a trademark of polyester rope.)

The main advantage of polypropylene is that it floats. Therefore, it's the most useful rope to use for dinghy painters and mooring pennants where a submerged rope could offer hazards to propellers.

Recent additions to manmade fibers are Spectra (brand name of Allied Chemicals) and Kevlar (brand name of DuPont). Both are very light with immensely strong filaments. In their present form, both new materials are mainly of interest to sailboat racers, where great strength and lightness are highly desirable, and cost and working life are of lesser importance than to the cruising sailor.

When using any of these new materials, you should read the manufacturers' recommendations regarding usage and care. For example, Kevlar is highly susceptible to chafing and bending and must be protected from sunlight. Spectra, on the other hand, is susceptible to long-term creep.

**Riding Turn on a Winch**

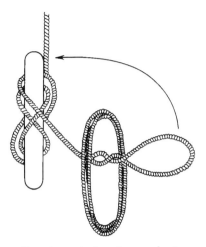

**Hanging a halyard on a cleat**

Manmade fiber ropes used on small craft are generally larger (stronger) than necessary to facilitate ease of handling. For example, the modern equivalent, in terms of strength, of the old 1½-inch circumference manila ropes would be far too small to handle comfortably today if used for sheets. The surface of the rope also has considerable bearing on its handling properties — ropes that are formed with a continuous filament (never possible with natural fibers) are immensely strong and very shiny in appearance. Rope that's formed of the staple or shorter filament has slightly lower strength than the continuous filament rope, but has a matte finish, which is obviously more desirable when the rope is frequently handled, as in the case of sheets.

### Handling and Care of Rope

Manmade fibers, as well as being much stronger than natural fibers, are very tolerant of those factors that reduced the working life of the latter. For example, synthetic lines can be stored while still damp and they won't rot (although you may see mildew on them). Physical damage must be guarded against (as with natural fibers); you should particularly bear in mind that rope under tension is easily damaged by chafe. Lines that are under tension but static (e.g., mooring lines) should be protected at any angular point or rough service by placing plastic tubing over the rope or parcelling it with canvas.

The effects of chafe from normal friction

surfaces such as sheaves, fairleads, and cleats is considerably reduced if the bearing surfaces are large. In the case of sheaves, the diameter should not be less than five times the diameter of the rope — and preferably more. The groove of a sheave should have such a radius that it supports one-third of the rope's circumference. Whenever possible, avoid making sharp "nips" in a rope. If, however, you have to lead a line through a sharp angle, the bearing surface of the lead should be smooth and at least that required of a sheave. Rope can be severely damaged if led through a thin shackle or eye bolt, particularly if the angle is sharp.

If possible, always avoid heavy shock loads. For example, when passing a towline between a stationary vessel and a moving one, never make both ends fast at once. The resulting jerk imposes a tremendous strain on the line which, if it does not damage it, may rip a cleat or bollard out. When one end has been made fast, the correct procedure at the other end is to make a figure-eight turn round the cleat or bitts, and allow the line to ease out smoothly as the load comes on. Then, check steadily and make fast as the vessel gathers way.

Riding turns on a winch (as illustrated on page 305), must be avoided. They are caused by a line wrongly led or tailed. Often they can only be undone by using another winch and a rolling hitch to take the strain off the line.

**Securing a coil**

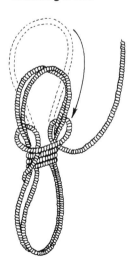

When coiling a line, always begin at the end that is made fast so that any twists or kinks can be chased along and run out at the far end. It is particularly important to ensure that load is never applied to a line when there is a kink in it; doing so will almost inevitably damage and weaken it. Rope that has been badly overloaded in any way may be identified by being unusually hard in parts. The hardness is caused by the heat that is produced by the overload friction that fuses some of the filaments together.

Unless lines are properly coiled, kinks will occur — with subsequent snags — when the line is run out. Nearly all laid ropes are right-handed and should be coiled clockwise to ensure smooth running out.

In practice, cleats on the masts of sailing yachts are seldom large enough to allow the fall of the halyard to be looped over the horn of the cleat without slipping off and becoming a confused tangle. When the halyard has been made up on the cleat and coiled, hold it close to the cleat, pull a short length through the coil, and twist and then loop it over the horn of the cleat, as shown in the upper left illustration.

Alternatively, a buntline hitch can be used. After coiling and looping, push the last loop through the center of the coil, capsize it over the top, and draw it tight, as shown on lower left. This is a very useful hitch to use when hanging up spare lines in a cockpit locker.

To make sure that your ropes wear evenly, it's a good idea to change them end for end occasionally.

The life of rope can be extended considerably by washing it in fresh water to get rid of salt crystal, grit, and dirt. Do your washing at the end of the season when laying up; the rope will remain soft and pliable during layup and will be nice and clean when the next sailing season begins. Use only soap powder — *not detergent* — to wash rope.

## Rope Specifications

This section on types of marine rope, breaking strains, and size selection is based on information provided by New England Ropes of New Bedford, Massachusetts. Special rope designs using proprietary fibers and construction are available only from New England Ropes. Other manufacturers may, or may not, have similar designs. In any case, this information is representative of the types of high-tech line available to today's boater.

*Specific Rope Types*

**3-Strand**. Traditional rope construction consisting of three equally sized strands twisted together to produce a very fine, durable rope. Standard designs are available in nylon, polyester, polypropylene, and specialized blends. Uses include hand and block lines, anchor and docklines, safety lines, and numerous other applications. Available in sizes up to one-inch diameter.

**Double Braids.** Exceptionally strong rope construction composed of a core braid contained within an outer braided jacket. Double braids are torque-free, have very good abrasion resistance, and offer excellent strength to weight ratios. Ropes are available in nylon, polyester, and combinations of fibers, including Kevlar and Spectra, that are designed to maximize the advantages inherent in different fiber classes. Uses include heavy marine applications, winch and stringing lines, recreational marine use, and numerous other applications. Available in sizes up to 10-inch circumference.

**12-Strand S-Braids.** Round single-braid rope construction designed to offer high strengths and ease of splicing. Single braids offer significant improvement in performance over twisted and eight-strand plaited ropes. Available in nylon, polyester, and a polyester/polypropylene blend. Uses include mooring and head lines, hand and block lines, and other general purpose applications. Available in sizes up to six-inch circumference.

**Parallel Core Rope.** Specialized construction consisting of a parallel fiber core wrapped with a double layer of polyester tape and covered with a braided jacket. Unlike other parallel core ropes, this rope is easily spliced using a technique similar to that used for double braids. The parallel core rope provides very high strength and exceptionally low elongation. It is designed for applications such as stringing lines where low stretch is a primary consideration. Available in sizes up to 1 1/8-inch diameter.

*Seamanship* (side tab)

**Multiline II.** A combination rope design in which each strand consists of a polypropylene core wrapped with 100 percent polyester cover yarns made of blended staple and filament fibers. Lighter and lower in strength then Dacron, but with similar stretch characteristics. Excellent UV resistance. Renders well around sheaves and winches.

**Nylon.** Highest strength and elongation. Ideal for uses requiring high energy absorption. Good UV resistance. Not affected by common alkalies or acids. Should not be exposed to strong mineral acids.

**Dacron.** DuPont's trade name for their polyester fiber. Much less elastic then nylon, with slightly lower strength. Not affected by common alkalies or acids. Excellent UV resistance. Very good wet or dry abrasion resistance. Renders well around capstans or winches.

**Polypropylene.** The lightest and lowest strength fiber used in commercial ropes; will float in water. Excellent resistance to most common chemicals, but highly susceptible to UV. Given its low melting point and high coefficient of friction over metal, it is recommended for noncritical use only.

**Nylon Double Braid.** Nylon cover/nylon core. Most elastic double-braid construction; has excellent energy absorbing characteristics. Good abrasion resistance wet or dry. Minimal strength loss due to UV. Affected by strong mineral acids. Ideal for uses where energy absorption is desired such as towing, mooring lines, slings, purse lines, and personnel safety lines.

**Polyester Double Braid.** Polyester cover/polyester core. Very low elongating construction — much less elastic than nylon. Excellent abrasion resistance wet or dry. Superior resistance to UV degradation. Excellent chemical resistance except to concentrated sulphuric acid and strong alkalies at elevated temperatures. Ideal for use where controlled elongation is required such as head lines, sailboat halyards, and sheets, bull ropes, and winch lines.

**Polyester/Nylon Double Braid.** Polyester cover/nylon core. Unique combination of fibers designed to provide a balanced rope construction of extremely high strength. Stronger than either nylon or polyester double braid, but offering elasticity similar to that of an all nylon rope. The polyester cover braid offers the same excellent abrasion and chemical resistance as found in the all-polyester rope. Ideal for uses requiring good energy absorption and very high strength such as mooring lines, winch lines, and commercial fishing lines.

**Spect-Set Double Braid.** Polyester cover/Spectra core. The strength member core design utilizes the exceptional performance properties of Spectra. High-tensile strength, very low stretch, and lightweight. The tough durable jacket provides excellent abrasion and chemical resistance. The core is provided with a special coating to reduce slipping between the cover and core. Ideal for winch lines, stringing lines, and replacement for steel cable.

**Nylon "S" Braid.** 100 percent nylon 12-strand single braid. Superior in strength and performance characteristics to three-strand and plaited rope constructions. The single-braid design will not rotate under load or hockle when a load is released. Stays firm and round under load. Easy to splice. Strips and renders well on winches and capstans. Designed to be used in place of three-strand and plaited ropes in all applications where improved performance is necessary, such as mooring lines, tow surge pennants, head lines, and other applications requiring high energy absorption.

**Polyester "S" Braid.** 100 percent polyester single braid. Highest strength S-braid available. Provides all the advantages associated with polyester in a torque-free, flexible construction that is ideally suited for use in marine applications. Uses include mooring lines, pilot lines, head and block lines, slings, and commercial fishing lines.

**Kevlar #100.** 100 percent braided Kevlar core and blended spun/filament polyester cover braid. This design is intended to derive maximum benefit from the ultra-high strength, low-stretch properties of Kevlar. Due to the susceptibility of Kevlar to abrade in bending situations, this construction is intended for use in situations such as standing rigging where the rope is not subjected to excessive bending loads.

**Sta-Set K-900.** Core braid consisting of a combination of Kevlar and Spectra fibers and a filament polyester cover. This design combines the best properties of the two strongest, lowest stretch fibers commercially available. Problems associated with the exclusive use of either of these fibers, such as the poor abrasion resistance of Kevlar or the creep and excessive slipperiness of Spectra, are virtually eliminated through the special blending of these two fibers in the core braid. As a result, this rope is ideally suited for both standing and running rigging applications, or any application requiring very high strength and low elongation.

## Tensile Strengths and Working Loads

The strengths listed in the adjacent tables are the approximate averages for new rope tested under ASTM (D-4268), or Cordage Institute test methods. The tensile strength is the load at which a new rope tested under laboratory conditions can be expected to break. However, to estimate the minimum tensile strength of a new rope,

reduce the approximate average by 15 percent. (Cordage Institute defines minimum tensile strength as two standard deviations below the average tensile strength of the rope.) Age, use, and the type of termination used, including knots, will lower tensile strength significantly.

The Cordage Institute specifies that the safe working load of a rope shall be determined by dividing the minimum tensile strength by the safety factor. Safety factors range from 5 to 12 for noncritical uses. The working load is a guideline for the use of a rope in good condition for noncritical applications and should be reduced where life, limb, or valuable property are involved, or for exceptional service such as shock, sustained loading, severe vibration, and the like.

## KNOTS, BENDS, AND HITCHES

The following simple bends and hitches are but a few of those used by professional mariners. They should, however, serve to meet most of the requirements of those operating small boats and yachts.

A **bend** is used to join the ends of two ropes.

A **hitch** secures a rope to another object.

*The Round Turn*

Although this is only the first movement in securing a line to a permanent fixture, there is much virtue in a round turn not always appreciated by small-boat owners. Always remember that a considerable weight can be held with relatively little effort by taking a round turn around a cleat or other secure object. A round turn should always be taken around an open-ended protrusion, such as a cleat, because then you won't have to let go of the rope. When coming alongside, a round turn or two will take the strain without the danger of jamming.

In an emergency, a quick turn around some strong object on board (and the rope then held away tight) will frequently prevent the bow or stern from swinging out into the tide at the wrong moment. Having stopped the craft's movement by the round turn, a judicious "slacking away" or "hauling in" using the samson post or cleat as a temporary "hold" is excellent seamanship. When the emergency is over, secure or remove the rope as desired.

**Round Turn and Two Half Hitches.** For securing a dinghy painter or the docklines of a small boat to a pile, mooring ring, and the like. It will never come adrift, but is easy to untie.

**Figure of Eight Knot.** To prevent the end of a small rope from accidentally running through a block or the deck lead for jib sheets, etc.

**Bowline.** The most commonly used loop knot. Will never capsize if properly formed. Used to make a loop in the end of a rope without splicing — made quickly and without hesitation when sending small mooring lines ashore.

**Sheet Bend.** Serves many purposes. Used for making a rope fast to the bight of another — i.e., bending the sheets to the sails — and securing the end of a small rope to that of a larger. If used to join ropes that are made of different materials, the ends should be seized back or the bend is likely to come adrift. (See also Double Sheet Bend.)

**Double Sheet Bend.** For securing a bosun's chair and for the same purposes as the sheet bend. The working end is tucked twice to give extra security.

**Clove Hitch.** A good hitch for securing a rope at intermediate points. It is not safe with a short end, but can be made secure with two half hitches around the standing part of the line. Difficult to untie after being subjected to heavy strain, especially when wet.

**Reef Knot.** Also called a "square knot"; has many uses. Excellent as a "binder" knot, joining the ends of small ropes — e.g., reef points when reefing and furl-  ing sail. Before leaving signal halyards or any "running ropes" not in use, always join the ends together in case wind blows them off the cleat and they become loose. CAUTION: Do not use this knot as a bend for tying two ropes together. If the ropes are of different size, or different materials, or one is stiffer than the other, the knot is very liable to capsize.

**Rolling Hitch.** A most practical knot much used at sea. After starting as a clove hitch, an additional hitch is made over the first between this and the standing part of the rope that effectively jams the hitch and prevents sideways pull. The simple form is finished off with a fur- ther hitch away 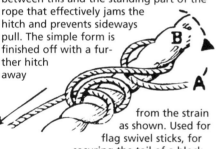 from the strain as shown. Used for flag swivel sticks, for securing the tail of a block to a larger rope, and for hanging off a rope on a stopper. It does not slip or "roll" under normal loading, but if subject- ed to heavy strain — as when stoppering off a mooring rope — the end (A), which does not carry the load, should be "backed and dogged," that is, backed against the hitch and twisted round the first rope (B) in long lays. The end is then held or stopped until the load can be transferred back to the larger rope.

**Carrick Bend.** For bending two hawsers or wire ropes together. Very secure and unlikely to jam. Each end tucks under/over four times.

**Timber Hitch.** Used for lifting a spar, timber, bale or plank. The turns should always be dogged with the lay of the rope. When used for towing a spar, or to keep a piece of timber pointing in one direction when being lifted, it should be used with a half hitch as illus- trated.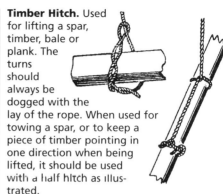

**Lighterman's Hitch.** Used by barge crews to make a towing eye in the end of a barge rope. The lighterman's hitch consists of a loop secured by a half hitch with two back tucks on the standing part. It will hold as well as any splice. Lobstermen use a sim- ilar technique, finishing a bowline in slip- pery poly line with a tuck or two.

**Sheepshank.** Used for shortening a rope temporarily. To make more secure, especial- ly if not subjected to a steady pull, the loops should be stopped to the standing part at points A and B.

*Knowing the most widely used knots — and knowing how to use them correctly — are unmistakable signs of a savvy mariner.*

## ROPE SPLICING

### Eye Splice

(1) Unlay the three strands at the end of the rope, enough to make at least three tucks —about one turn for each tuck — and form an eye by laying the opened strands on top of the standing part of the rope.

(2) Take the middle end (A) and tuck it, from right to left, underneath the nearest strand of the standing part.

(3) Pick up the left end (B) and tuck it — again from right to left — under the next strand to the left of the one under which (A) is tucked.

(4) Turn the whole splice over, then take the third end (C) and lead it over to the right of the third strand, so that the third tuck can, again, be made from right to left, as in step 3.

(5) There should now be one end coming out from under each strand on the standing part. If two ends come from under the same strand, the splice is wrong.

(6) Pull each end tight enough to make a tidy and snug fit. This completes the first round of tucks.

(7) For the second round, take each end over one strand and under the next towards the left. Pull each end tight.

(8) Repeat for the third round. Never use less than three rounds of tucks if the eye

is to bear any strain.

(9) If desired, for neatness, the splice can be tapered by adding additional rounds of tucks, first with halved strands and then by halving again before the final round.

### Short Splice

For joining two ropes of the same size together.

(1) Unlay the two ends to be joined—at least one turn for each round of tucks to be made.

(2) Marry these ends together, so that the strands of one rope lay alternately between the strands of the other.

(3) Hold firmly while making tucks. Tucks are made toward the left by passing each end, in turn, over one strand and under the next, in the same manner as described for the eye splice.

(4) If the line is to bear any strain, make at least three rounds of tucks each way.

### Long Splice

Seldom used, but very useful as a temporary measure; that is, until the rope can be replaced with a new one — for a line that is required to run through a block because the splice does not thicken it.

(1) Unlay the ends of two ropes to at least four times the distance required for a short splice.

(2) Marry the ends together as though about to begin a short splice.

**Eye Splice in
3 strand line**

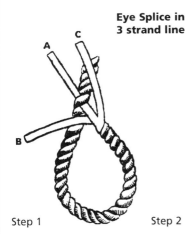

Step 1

Step 2

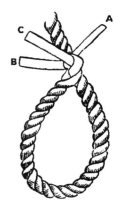

Step 3

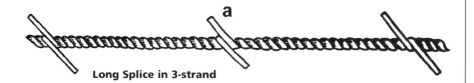

**Long Splice in 3-strand**

(3) Select two ends that cross one another from opposite sides, unlay one of them for some length, and lay into its place the opposite strand from the other rope until only a short piece is left. Cut off surplus from the end that is unlaid.

(4) Repeat with two more strands but work in the opposite direction.

(5) The third pair of strands (at 'a' in the illustration) are left in their original place, so that there are now three pairs of ends. Make an overhand knot with each pair so that the ends follow the lay of the rope and do not cross it.

(6) Pull very tight and then taper off by reducing the yarns in each strand.

## Back Splice

Where a line is not required to run through a block — when whippings are preferable — a back splice may be used to prevent the strands unlaying.

After unlaying the strands for the estimated distance, form a crown by interlacing the strands at the rope's end. Then tuck the strands "over one and under one" backward toward the standing part of the rope. This splice is only good with natural fiber ropes. With manmade fibers the rope ends can be fused together by heating.

## Eye Splice with Braided Rope

There are several ways to eye splice braided rope.

The illustration below shows how you can tuck an eye splice into double, four-part braid. The eye splice used is based upon the construction of the rope, which employs both "Z," or right-handed lay strands, and "S," or left-handed strands. After whipping or stopping at the point of splice, divide the various Z and S strands as shown and tuck in two pairs front and back of the work. Thereafter the paired

## Eye Splice in double four-part braid

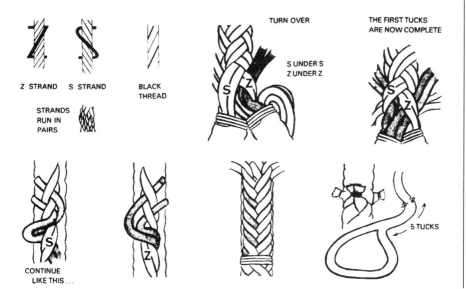

Z STRAND    S STRAND       BLACK THREAD

STRANDS RUN IN PAIRS

TURN OVER

S UNDER S
Z UNDER Z

THE FIRST TUCKS ARE NOW COMPLETE

CONTINUE LIKE THIS ...

5 TUCKS

313

strands are divided and tucked separately. Finish by seizing ends as illustrated on the previous page.

Another technique for eye splicing braided line is "sew & serve," illustrated below. It is important that stoppings, sewing, and finally serving are tight and neat, otherwise the eye splice resulting will be loose and weak. Pass the sail needle right through the rope each time and tug the stitch home tightly. Taper the unlaid rope yarns or it will be impossible to apply a serving to the decreasing diameter of the splice. Set up taut before attempting to serve. Use #16 waxed whipping polyester twine.

Note that the serving mallet shown in the illustration is not absolutely necessary, but is a great help toward getting a tight serve.

### Sew an Eye Splice in Braided Rope

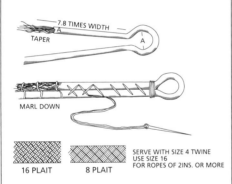

By Courtesy of Marlow

### Serving the Eye Splice

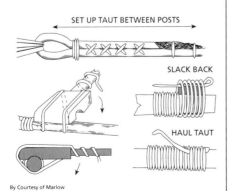

By Courtesy of Marlow

The third, and most commonly used, method of eyesplicing braided line is with a special fid that permits you to insert the end of the line back into the core of the braid. It works much like the braided bamboo Chinese finger puzzle that children play with. It is important to have the rope manufacturer's instructions and the right size fid to make one of these splices.

## ROPE WHIPPINGS

Whippings are extensively used with natural fiber ropes to secure the ends from unravelling, but with modern manmade fibers the ends of smaller ropes are usually fused together. There will always, however, be occasions when it is useful to be able to whip the end of a rope or seize an eye or thimble in the middle (e.g., double sheets).

### Common Whipping

1) Cut off a suitable length of twine and lay one end (D in fig.1 of the illustration) along the end of the rope.

2) Then take half a dozen or more tight turns around the rope and the twine, working toward the end of rope (down in the illustration) and against the lay. Pull each turn tight as it is made.

3) Now lay the other end of twine (BC in fig. 2) along the rope and over the turns already made.

4) With part A of the twine, continue to pass turns round over part B.

5) When the loop remaining at E becomes too small to pass over the rope's end, pull tight on C, which should pull the twine tightly under the whipping. Cut the ends off to finish (fig. 3).

An alternate method is to make the D in the illustration a loop with the twine end above the whipping. Then just wrap down with A until you have almost run out of twine, stick the A end through the loop, and pull it and the loop under the whipping with D end. In either case, these whippings will not stand up to much rough use.

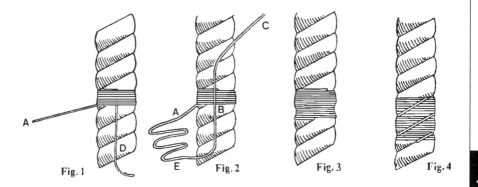

Fig. 1        Fig. 2        Fig. 3        Fig. 4

## Palm and Needle Whipping

This is more secure than the common whipping and is suitable for reef points, mooring lines, sheets, etc.

1) Thread a suitable length of twine through a sailmaker's needle.

2) Pass the needle under one strand and draw through most of the twine.

3) Take about a dozen or more turns of twine round the rope, working against the lay and pulling each turn tight as it is made.

4) Now stitch, by following round between each strand in turn with the needle, as in fig. 4, and thus tightly frapping the turns in between each strand.

## West Country Whipping

Useful when required to whip the bight of a line.

1) Place the middle of the twine against the rope, bring the two ends round in opposite directions, and make an over-hand knot.

2) Now bring the ends round (again, in the opposite direction) to the opposite side and make another overhand knot.

3) Continue overhand knotting the ends alternately on opposite sides of the rope.

4) Finish with a reef knot when sufficient turns have been made.

## ROPE STRENGTH & STRETCH TABLES

## Double Braid Ropes — 12 Strand S-Braids

| NOMINAL SIZE (inches) | | POLYESTER BRAID | | NYLON BRAID | | POLYESTER/NYLON | | SPECT-SET | | POLYESTER S-BRAID | | NYLON S-BRAID | | DA-PRO S-BRAID | |
|---|---|---|---|---|---|---|---|---|---|---|---|---|---|---|---|
| Dia. | Circ. | Weight Lbs./100 ft. | Average Tensile Strength | Weight Lbs./100 ft. | Average Tensile Strength | Weight Lbs./100 ft. | Average Tensile Strength | Weight Lbs./100 ft. | Average Tensile Strength | Weight Lbs./100 ft. | Average Tensile Strength | Weight Lbs./100 ft. | Average Tensile Strength | Weight Lbs./100 ft. | Average Tensile Strength |
| 3/16 | 9/16 | 1.1 | 1.2 | 0.9 | 1.2 | | | | | | | | | | |
| 1/4 | 3/4 | 2. | 2.3 | 1.6 | 2.2 | 1.9 | 2.5 | 2. | 4.6 | | | | | | |
| 5/16 | 1 | 3.1 | 3. | 2.5 | 3.4 | 3. | 3.9 | 3.2 | 7.4 | | | | | | |
| 3/8 | 1-1/8 | 4.4 | 4.4 | 3.4 | 4.7 | 4.3 | 5.6 | 4. | 9.5 | 4.2 | 5.3 | 3.7 | 5.2 | 3.2 | 4. |
| 7/16 | 1-1/4 | 6.1 | 6.6 | 4.9 | 6.6 | 5.8 | 7.5 | 5.2 | 12.5 | 5.7 | 7.1 | 5.1 | 7.1 | 4.3 | 5.4 |
| 1/2 | 1-1/2 | 8. | 8.5 | 6.3 | 8.5 | 7.6 | 10.5 | 7.5 | 16.9 | 7.4 | 9.3 | 6.6 | 9.2 | 5.6 | 7. |
| 9/16 | 1-3/4 | 10.1 | 11. | 8. | 11.7 | 9.6 | 12.5 | 9. | 21. | 9.3 | 11.6 | 8.4 | 11.8 | 7.2 | 9. |
| 5/8 | 2 | 12.6 | 14. | 11.7 | 13.5 | 11.9 | 15.5 | 11.1 | 27. | 11.5 | 14.4 | 10.4 | 14.6 | 9.3 | 11.6 |
| 3/4 | 2-1/4 | 17.5 | 22. | 14.3 | 19.4 | 17.1 | 23.2 | 15.7 | 37. | 16.6 | 20.8 | 15. | 17. | 12.6 | 15. |
| 7/8 | 2-3/4 | 23.7 | 29.9 | 19.4 | 26.3 | 23.3 | 30.3 | 19.9 | 51.5 | 22.6 | 24.3 | 19.3 | 23.2 | 17.5 | 19. |
| 1 | 3 | 33. | 38. | 25.4 | 34. | 30.4 | 40. | 26. | 63.5 | 30. | 32. | 23. | 28. | 24.5 | 26. |
| 1-1/8 | 3-1/2 | 42. | 46. | 35. | 46. | 38. | 50. | 35.3 | 77. | 38. | 41. | 31. | 37. | 33.9 | 34.5 |
| 1-1/4 | 3-3/4 | 49.8 | 55. | 40. | 52. | 45. | 58. | 40.6 | 85. | 44. | 47. | 36. | 43. | 38.9 | 39.2 |
| 1-5/16 | 4 | 57. | 61. | 45. | 58. | 57. | 73. | 46.3 | 98. | 50. | 54. | 41. | 49. | 44.3 | 44.3 |
| 1-1/2 | 4-1/2 | 68. | 72. | 58. | 74. | 68. | 87. | 58.5 | 115. | 63. | 63. | 52. | 62. | 56. | 55.4 |
| 1-5/8 | 5 | 85. | 89. | 71. | 90. | 80. | 101. | 72.3 | 145. | 78. | 77. | 64. | 77. | 69.1 | 67.9 |
| 1-3/4 | 5-1/2 | 101. | 104. | 89. | 110. | 97. | 121. | 87.4 | 168. | 94. | 92. | 77. | 92. | | |
| 2 | 6 | 123. | 124. | 102. | 126. | 115. | 143. | 104. | 192. | | | | | | |
| 2-1/8 | 6-1/2 | 144. | 145. | 119. | 145. | 134. | 168. | 122.1 | 222. | | | | | | |
| 2-1/4 | 7 | 168. | 166. | 138. | 166. | 157. | 194. | 141.6 | 258. | | | | | | |
| 2-1/2 | 7-1/2 | 196. | 190. | 159. | 189. | 180. | 222. | 162.5 | 285. | | | | | | |
| 2-5/8 | 8 | 216. | 212. | 181. | 213. | 203. | 248. | 184.9 | 318. | | | | | | |
| 2-3/4 | 8-1/2 | 246. | 234. | 204. | 237. | | | | | | | | | | |
| 3 | 9 | 293. | 278. | 228. | 261. | | | | | | | | | | |
| 3-1/4 | 10 | 344. | 326. | 282. | 319. | | | | | | | | | | |

Average tensile strength listed in thousands of pounds (1.5 = 1500)

# 3-Strand Ropes

| NOMINAL SIZE | NYLON | | DACRON | | MULTILINE II | | POLYPROPELENE | |
|---|---|---|---|---|---|---|---|---|
| Dia | Weight Lbs./100 ft. | Average Tensile Strength | Weight Lbs./100 ft. | Average Tensile Strength | Weight Lbs./100 ft. | Average Tensile Strength | Weight Lbs./100 ft. | Average Tensile Strength |
| 3/16* | 1.0 | 1,200 | 1.2 | 1,200 | ... | ... | 0.7 | 856 |
| 1/4* | 1.5 | 2,000 | 1.7 | 2,000 | ... | ... | 1.2 | 1,350 |
| 5/16* | 2.5 | 3,000 | 3.1 | 3,000 | 2.5 | 2,200 | 1.8 | 2,050 |
| 3/8* | 3.5 | 4,400 | 4.5 | 4,400 | 3.6 | 3,200 | 2.8 | 2,900 |
| 7/16* | 5.0 | 5,900 | 6.2 | 5,900 | 5.0 | 4,100 | 3.8 | 3,800 |
| 1/2* | 6.5 | 7,500 | 8.0 | 6,500 | 6.5 | 5,800 | 4.7 | 4,700 |
| 9/16* | 8.2 | 9,400 | 10.2 | 8,900 | ... | ... | 6.1 | 5,450 |
| 5/8* | 10.5 | 12,200 | 13.0 | 11,700 | 9.5 | 8,200 | 7.5 | 7,000 |
| 3/4* | 14.5 | 16,700 | 17.5 | 14,700 | 12.5 | 10,800 | 10.7 | 9,400 |
| 7/8* | 20.0 | 23,500 | 25.0 | 21,200 | 18.0 | 15,500 | 15.0 | 13,000 |
| 1* | 26.4 | 29,400 | 30.4 | 25,800 | 21.8 | 18,700 | 18.0 | 15,700 |

# Specialty Braided Ropes

| NOMINAL SIZE | NEREX | | PCR | | SPECTWELVE | | KEVLAR 100 | | STA-SET K900 | |
|---|---|---|---|---|---|---|---|---|---|---|
| (inches) Dia. | Weight Lbs./ 100 ft. | Average Tensile Strength | Weight Lbs./ 100 ft. | Average Tensile Strength | Weight Lbs./ 100 ft. | Average Tensile Strength | Weight Lbs./ 100 ft. | Average Tensile Strength | Weight Lbs./ 100 ft. | Average Tensile Strength |
| 3/16 | ...... | ...... | ...... | ...... | ...... | ...... | 1.4 | 2,300 | 1.3 | 2,200 |
| 1/4 | ...... | ...... | ...... | ...... | 1.4 | 6,200 | 2.2 | 3,600 | 1.9 | 3,600 |
| 5/16 | ...... | ...... | 3.4 | 4,400 | 2.2 | 9,900 | 3.1 | 5,000 | 2.8 | 5,800 |
| 3/8 | 4.7 | 6,300 | 4.4 | 5,500 | 3.2 | 14,400 | 4.7 | 8,300 | 4.2 | 8,700 |
| 7/16 | 6.4 | 9,000 | 5.9 | 7,400 | 4.3 | 18,500 | 6.5 | 11,000 | 5.3 | 12,200 |
| 1/2 | 8.9 | 11,900 | 7.9 | 9,600 | 5.8 | 26,500 | 8.7 | 15,500 | 7.2 | 15,800 |
| 9/16 | 10.5 | 15,100 | ...... | ...... | 7.1 | 32,000 | 10.9 | 19,600 | 9.5 | 20,100 |
| 5/8 | 13. | 17,900 | 12.3 | 15,000 | 8.8 | 40,000 | 13.6 | 22,000 | 12.0 | 24,500 |
| 3/4 | 18. | 23,500 | 17.7 | 21,600 | 12.7 | 52,000 | ...... | ...... | 17.0 | 35,000 |
| 7/8 | 25.5 | 33,100 | 24.1 | 30,700 | 17.2 | 69,500 | ...... | ...... | 22.5 | 48,000 |
| 1 | 33.3 | 43,300 | 32.0 | 38,400 | 23.3 | 88,000 | ...... | ...... | 31.0 | 60,000 |
| 1-1/8 | ...... | ...... | 39.5 | 49,000 | 29.5 | 108,000 | ...... | ...... | ...... | ...... |

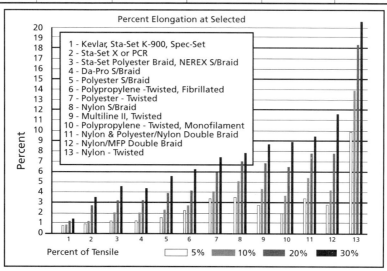

Percent Elongation at Selected

1 - Kevlar, Sta-Set K-900, Spec-Set
2 - Sta-Set X or PCR
3 - Sta-Set Polyester Braid, NEREX S/Braid
4 - Da-Pro S/Braid
5 - Polyester S/Braid
6 - Polypropylene -Twisted, Fibrillated
7 - Polyester - Twisted
8 - Nylon S/Braid
9 - Multiline II, Twisted
10 - Polypropylene - Twisted, Monofilament
11 - Nylon & Polyester/Nylon Double Braid
12 - Nylon/MFP Double Braid
13 - Nylon - Twisted

Percent of Tensile     5%    10%    20%    30%

## ROPE APPLICATIONS AND SIZING TABLES

Table courtesy of
New England Ropes
Pope's Island
New Bedford, MA 02740
508-999-2351

| | | 3-STRAND NYLON | 3-STRAND DACRON | 3-STRAND SPUN DACRON | DOUBLE BRAID NYLON | REGATTA BRAID | STA SET | STA SET X | STA SET X LITE | KEVLAR 65 | STA SET K-900 | SPECT SET | DACRON CORD |
|---|---|---|---|---|---|---|---|---|---|---|---|---|---|
| CHARACTERISTICS | DURABILITY/WEAR | | | | | | | | | | | | |
| | HANDLING | | | | | | | | | | | | |
| | SPLICEABILITY | | | | | | | | | | | | |
| | UV RESISTANCE | | | | | | | | | | | | |
| | STRETCH | VH | ML | ML | H | L | L | VL | VL | VVL | VVL | VVL | L |
| | STRENGTH | H | H | M | H | H | H | H | H | H | VH | VH | M |
| APPLICATIONS | ANCHOR LINE | | | | | | | | | | | | |
| | DOCKLINE | | | | | | | | | | | | |
| | TOWLINE | | | | | | | | | | | | |
| | HALYARDS | | | | | | | | | | | | |
| | SHEETS | | | | | | | | | | | | |
| | GUYS | | | | | | | | | | | | |
| | RUNNING BACKSTAYS | | | | | | | | | | | | |
| | CONTROL LINES | | | | | | | | | | | | |
| | TOPPING LIFT | | | | | | | | | | | | |
| | REEF LINES | | | | | | | | | | | | |
| | FURLING SYSTEM | | | | | | | | | | | | |
| | FLAG HALYARD | | | | | | | | | | | | |
| | LIFE PRESERVER LANYARDS | | | | | | | | | | | | |

**KEY**

H=HIGH   M=MEDIUM
L=LOW    V=VERY

EXCELLENT   VERY GOOD   GOOD   FAIR

### Dock and Anchor Line Chart

| Boat Length | Dock Lines | Anchor Line | Mooring Pendent |
|---|---|---|---|
| Up to 20' | 3/8 | 3/8 | 1/2 |
| 21–30' | 1/2 | 1/2 | 5/8 |
| 30–35' | 1/2 | 1/2 | 3/4 |
| 35–40' | 5/8 | 5/8 | 7/8 |
| 40–45' | 5/8 | 5/8 | 1 |

Consider these sizes as minimums for average size vessels of these lengths.

## SEAMANSHIP GLOSSARY

**ABAFT**            Aft of any particular point on the vessel; e.g., abaft the mast — behind the mast.
**Abeam**            At right angles to the fore and aft centerline.
**About**            To go about, to change tack by moving the bow through the wind.
**Aft**              Toward the stern of the vessel.
**Amidships**        Midway between stem and stern.
**Apparent wind**    The wind felt aboard the boat.
**Athwart**          From side to side.
**Avast**            To stop, to hold fast; e.g., avast heaving.
**Awash**            A vessel, wreck, or shoal so low that water constantly washes over.
**Aweigh**           Term to indicate that the anchor has broken out of the ground.

**BACK**             (a) Wind shifting counterclockwise; (b) To sheet a sail out to windward.
**Backstay**         Standing rigging from a masthead, leading aft to support the mast.
**Ballast**          Iron, lead, or other heavy weight placed in bottom of a ship to increase her stability.
**Bar**              A shoal in the approach to a harbor.
**Battens**          Thin pieces of wood or plastic set into the leech of the sail to preserve the shape.
**Beacon**           Aid to navigation, lighted or unlighted, radio or racon, set on the shore or rocks, or set into the bottom.
**Beam**             (a) Extreme width of a vessel; (b) Athwartships timber on which the deck is laid.
**Beam bearing**     Direction of objects when abeam; i.e., at right angles to the fore and aft line.
**Bearing**          Direction of an object.
**Bear away**        To put the helm up; i.e., steer further away from the wind or an object.
**Beating**          Sailing toward the direction of the wind by tacking.
**Becket**           Small rope circle; a simple eye.
**Belay**            To make a rope fast to a belaying pin or cleat.
**Bend**             Knot that connects two lines.
**Bight**            Any part of a rope between its ends; also a curve, a cove on a coastline, or in a channel.
**Binnacle**         The housing for the mariner's compass.
**Bitter end**       The last part of a cable left around the "bitts" when the rest is over-board.
**Bitts**            Pair of vertical wood or metal posts fixed on deck, to which ropes may be secured.
**Bluff**            (a) Steep shore; (b) Full-bowed vessel.
**Bobstay**          A stay for the bowsprit to prevent it lifting; from bowsprit end to stem at waterline.
**Bollard**          Heavy short post on a wharf or dock to secure ship's mooring lines.
**Bolt rope**        A strong rope sewn round the edge of sails to give strength and prevent tearing.
**Boom**             A spar for many purposes, such as to stretch out the foot of a fore-and-aft-sail.
**Boottop**          A band of paint at the waterline between "wind and water."
**Bower anchor**     Main anchor carried forward in a vessel.
**Bow**              Forward part of a vessel.
**Bowsprit**         Heavy spar from deck leading forward from stem head, to which head-sails are attached.
**Breast line**      Ropes leading at right angles to the centerline to a dock.
**Bridle**           A rope attached to both ends of a boat or object to lift it. Lifting tackle is attached to middle of the rope.

| | |
|---|---|
| **Bring up** | To stop, as to come to anchor. |
| **Broach** | When running, to accidentally turn and get broadside on to wind and sea. |
| **Bulkheads** | Partitions fore and aft or athwartships, forming separate compartments. |
| **Bulwarks** | A vessel's topsides that extend above the deck. |
| **Buoy** | A float with distinguishing name, shape, color or light. |
| **Burgee** | Pennant (pointed) shaped flag with design indicating the Yacht Club the vessel's owner belongs to. |
| **By the head** | Greater than normal draft forward. |
| **By the lee** | When running under sail, the wind blows over the same side as the mainsail. |
| **By the stern** | Greater than normal draft. |
| **CABLE** | (a) One-tenth nautical mile; (b) Anchor chain. |
| **Capstan** | A vertical cylindrical machine for veering or hoisting the anchor chain. |
| **Careen** | To heel a vessel over on one side by tackles to work on her bottom . |
| **Carry way** | To continue to move through the water. |
| **Carvel** | Edge-to-edge planking for a vessel's hull. |
| **Caulk** | To fill the side or deck seams with oakum or cotton to prevent leaking . |
| **Chainplates** | Metal strips fastened outside or inside the hull to take the rigging strain. |
| **Check** | To slowly stop a vessel's movement or to slowly ease a rope. |
| **Chine** | The fore and aft line of the hull where the bilge turns up toward the topsides of the hull. |
| **Claw off** | Working a vessel to windward off a lee shore. |
| **Cleat** | A two-pronged device for making ropes fast. |
| **Clew** | The corner of the sail where the leech meets the foot. |
| **Close-hauled** | Sailing close to the wind. |
| **Companion** | Ladder in a ship. |
| **Composite** | Construction using more than one material; e.g., a wooden boat with metal floors and frames. |
| **Con** | To give orders to the helmsman in narrow waters. |
| **Counter** | The overhanging portion of a stern. |
| **Course** | (a) The direction a vessel steers; (b) The squaresail set from a lower yard. |
| **Cradle** | The frame erected around and under a vessel to support her out of the water. |
| **Cringle** | Rope around a thimble, worked into a sail. |
| **Crown** | (a) Where the arms of an anchor meet the shank; (b) The knot where the strands of a rope are interlocked to start a backsplice. |
| **Crutch** | Fitting to support the boom when the sail is not raised. (also Gallows). |
| **DAVIT** | Crane for hoisting, lowering, and holding small boats in position on larger vessels. |
| **Dead reckoning** | The position found by calculation from course steered and speed through the water. |
| **Deadweight** | The carrying capacity of a vessel, measured by its displacement. |
| **Deckhead** | Underside of a deck; the roof of a ship's cabin. |
| **Deep** | Unmarked soundings of the lead line. |
| **Dolphin** | A structure built of a pile or collection of piles. |
| **Downhaul** | Line or tackle used to haul down sail or yard. |
| **Down helm** | Order to helmsman to put tiller away from the wind; up helm is toward the wind. |
| **Dowse** | (a) To extinguish a light; (b) To lower sail or spar quickly; (c) To spray with water. |
| **Draft** | The depth of water occupied by a vessel at any time. |
| **Drogue** | A sea anchor— a cone-shaped canvas bag to which the vessel lies in heavy weather to keep the bow pointing into the waves, or towed from the stern to slow the speed when running. |

| | |
|---|---|
| **EARRING** | Rope for bending sail or head cringle to a yard, or clew cringle to a boom. |
| **Ebb** | The period when the tide falls or flows from the land. |
| **Eddy** | Circular motion of the water unconnected with general water movement. |
| **Ensign** | The flag, usually carried at the stern, that denotes a vessel's nationality. |
| **Eye of the wind** | That point from which the wind is blowing toward the observer. |
| **FAIRLEAD** | A fitting for leading a rope around an obstruction to avoid friction. |
| **Fairway** | Shipping channel, normally the center of an approach channel. |
| **Fathom** | Nautical measurement of depth of six feet, or 1.83m. |
| **Fender** | Soft material usually formed in a cylindrical or spherical shape that prevents chafe between vessels, or vessel and pier. |
| **Fetch** | (a) To make. arrive at a desired point: (b) The distance from weather shore to ship. |
| **Fiddle** | Battens fitted to the edges of cabin tables or counters to prevent objects from sliding in rough weather. |
| **Flare** | The outward spread of a vessel's topsides; also a distress signal. |
| **Fix** | A position obtained by observing directions and distances to objects of known locations. |
| **Flashing** | Navigation light with duration of light less than dark, operating at regular intervals. |
| **Floor** | Athwartship structural member fastened to keel and lower ends of frames. |
| **Foot** | The lower edge of a sail. |
| **Fore and aft** | In line with the centerline — lengthways of the ship. |
| **Forward** | Toward the bow. |
| **Foul** | Opposite of clear, as "foul berth," "foul anchor,"or "foul bottom." |
| **Frap** | To bind ropes together or to bind a loose sail to prevent it flapping. |
| **Freeboard** | The distance from the waterline to the deck outboard edge. |
| **Freshen** | The wind "freshens" when it increases. |
| **Full and by** | Close-hauled, but with the sails continuously well filled. |
| **Furl** | Gathering in sail and securing it to its spar. |
| **GAFF** | The spar to which the head of a fore and aft sail is bent. |
| **Galley** | The kitchen of a vessel of any size. |
| **Gallows** | Frame of wood or metal for supporting the boom . |
| **Gimbals** | Two concentric rings to hold the compass or stove horizontal at all times. |
| **Go about** | To tack by putting the bow through the wind. |
| **Gooseneck** | A metal fitting that secures a boom to a mast — it allows the boom to swing and lift. |
| **Goose-winged** | When running with the aftersail out on the side opposite to the foresail. |
| **Ground** | (a) A ship touching bottom is said to ground; (b) Groundswell is long coastal swell. |
| **Gunter** | On a sliding gunter rig, the gaff is hoisted vertically, reducing the necessity for a tall mast. |
| **Gunwale** | The heavy top rail of a boat. |
| **Guy** | A rope or wire used to control a spar or derrick. |
| **HALYARDS** | Lines or tackles used to hoist sails or flags. |
| **Hanks** | Strong clip hooks that attach headsails to the mast stays. |
| **Harden up** | To bring the vessel closer to the wind. |
| **Hawse pipes** | Pipes leading down through the bow, through which the anchor cables are led. |
| **Hawser** | A heavy line used for mooring, kedging, towing, or as a temporary anchor line. |
| **Head** | Forward in a ship; headsails are those set forward of the foremast. |

| | |
|---|---|
| **Headboard** | A triangular board sewn into the top of a sail, to which the halyard is attached. |
| **Head sea** | Sea from ahead. (A beam sea is caused by wind blowing from abeam.) |
| **Heads** | Toilets in a ship. |
| **Heave the lead** | To take soundings with a lead line. |
| **Heave to** | A sailing vessel is hove to when a headsail is backed, thus reducing the way through the water. |
| **Heaving line** | Light line, knotted on one end to throw ashore when berthing, as a messenger for a larger mooring line. |
| **Heel** | A tilt from the upright; the foot of a mast. |
| **Helm** | The tiller or wheel. |
| **Hitch** | To make a rope fast to a spar or stay, but not to another rope. |
| **Holding ground** | The type of bottom for anchor; i.e., good or bad holding ground. |
| **Holiday** | An unpainted or unvarnished spot in a vessel. |
| **Hounds band** | A band around the mast with securing eyes for attaching the lower stays. |
| **Hull** | Structure of a vessel below deck level. |
| | |
| **INSHORE** | Toward the shore. |
| **Irons** | A vessel is "in irons" when caught head to wind and unable to fall off on either tack. |
| **Isophase** | Navigation light where duration of light and dark are equal. |
| | |
| **JACKSTAY** | A bar or rope on which anything travels; e.g., a rope leading along the deck, to which safety harnesses may be clipped. |
| **Jack staff** | Small staff in the bow, from which the jack is flown. |
| **Jib** | The triangular sail set as the forward headsail. |
| **Jibe** | To change tacks by swinging the stern through the wind, and/or to swing a fore and aft sail to swing from one side to the other. |
| **Jury** | A makeshift rig to replace a lost mast or rudder. |
| | |
| **KEDGE** | (a) A lightweight anchor; (b) To use that anchor to pull the vessel up to it. |
| **Keel** | The lowest part of the fore and aft backbone of a vessel. |
| **King spoke** | The spoke of the steering wheel which is upright when the rudder is amidships. |
| **Knot** | One nautical mile per hour. |
| | |
| **LACING** | The long line that secures the sail to a spar through eyelets. |
| **Lapstrake** | Planking when one edge overlaps the adjacent lower plank. |
| **Launch** | (a) To place a vessel into the water; (b) A small motor-tender. |
| **Lay** | To go; that is, lay aft or lay aloft, lay to (i.e., heave to), lay up, lay a course. The twisting of strands in a rope. |
| **Lazy** | An extra such as an extra lazy painter, i.e., a line not currently in use; a "lazy" sheet. |
| **Leech** | The after side of a fore-and-aft sail and the outer sides of a squaresail. |
| **Lead** | The lead weight at the end of the lead line used to find depth of water. |
| **Lee side** | The side away from the wind direction. |
| **Lee tide** | Tidal stream running with the wind. |
| **Leeward (loo'ard)** | Direction away from the wind. |
| **Leeway** | The sideways drift of a vessel from her course to leeward, due to wind pressure. |
| **Lifeline** | Line stretched fore and aft for crew to hold on to. |
| **Lift** | A rope or wire to support a spar; e.g., a topping lift. |
| **List** | Heel caused by having greater weight on one side. |
| **Log** | An instrument that records the distance run. |
| **Log book** | The record of events on board a ship, especially navigational. |
| **Loom** | (a) The reflection on the clouds of light from below; (b) An oar handle. |
| **Lubber line** | Line on the inside of a compass bowl indicating the ship's heading. |

| | |
|---|---|
| **Luff** | (a) To keep closer to the wind; (b) The forward edge of a sail. |
| **MAKE** | To attain; i.e., to "make harbor." To "make fast" is to secure. Tides that "make" increase. To "make sail" is to set sail. |
| **Marlinespike** | Pointed steel tool for opening strand of rope when splicing. |
| **Marry** | To fasten two ropes together end-to-end temporarily, so one can pull the other through a block. |
| **Masthead rig** | When the headstay is attached to the top of the mast. |
| **Messenger** | Line used to carry an object, such as another line. |
| **Midships** | Order to the helmsman to put the rudder fore and aft. |
| **Miss stays** | To stay up in the wind when tacking. |
| **Moor** | To moor is to lie with two anchors down. Vessels are said to moor to a dock when well made fast with several lines. |
| **NEAP TIDES** | Minimum range of tide, when the moon is in quadrature . |
| **Neaped** | A grounded ship is said to be "neaped" when the tide does not rise high enough to float her. |
| **OCCULTING** | Navigation light with duration of light more than dark. |
| **Offing** | Distance from land. |
| **Overhaul** | To pull slack into a tackle so there is no strain on any of its parts. |
| **PAY OUT** | To ease a chain or rope. |
| **Pintle** | A vertical pin on which the rudder is shipped. |
| **Pitching** | A ship's movement in a seaway that lifts and lowers the bow and stern. |
| **Pooped** | A vessel is said to have been "pooped" when a heavy sea comes inboard over the stern. |
| **Port** | The left side of a vessel looking forward. |
| **Port tack** | To sail with the wind on the port side. |
| **Porthole** | Watertight window in a vessel's side or superstructure for ventilation and light. |
| **RACON** | Beacon giving characteristic signal when triggered by a vessel's radar set. |
| **Rake** | The inclination of the mast in the fore and aft line from the vertical. |
| **Range** | A line formed when two objects are in line, one behind the other. |
| **Ratlines** | Horizontal ropes affixed to the shrouds as steps to facilitate climbing. |
| **Reach** | The courses of a sailing vessel between close-hauled and running. |
| **Reef** | To reduce sail area. |
| **Round turn** | A full turn around a bollard or post. |
| **Running rigging** | Rigging that is readily adjustable and generally used to control spars and sails. |
| **SAMSON POST** | Used to secure anchor or tow line. |
| **Scantlings** | The dimensions of a ship's timbers or other structural members. |
| **Sheer** | The rise of a ship's deck toward the bow or stern from amidships. |
| **Sheerstrake** | The upper line of plating or planking on the hull. |
| **Sheet** | Line or chain at lower corner of sail for regulating its trim. |
| **Shroud** | Standing rigging that supports a mast athwartships. |
| **Skeg** | A fixed vertical fin on the after side of which the rudder is attached. |
| **Slack water** | Stationary tidal stream. |
| **Slack in stays** | When a vessel is slow in coming about. |
| **Sole** | The floor of a cabin or cockpit. |
| **Sound** | To measure the depth of water by lead line or electronic means. |
| **Spring** | A mooring line that prevents a vessel moving fore and aft when tied up alongside a dock; e.g., an after spring is attached to the stern of the vessel and led to a bollard on the dock forward of the vessel to prevent it moving astern. |
| **Spring tides** | Tides when the moon is full or new, when the range of tide is greatest. |

| | |
|---|---|
| **Stand on** | To maintain course and speed. |
| **Standing rigging** | Stationary rigging that supports a spar. |
| **Starboard** | The right hand side of a ship facing forward. |
| **Starboard tack** | With the wind on the starboard side. |
| **Stem** | The forward part of a vessel's backbone, to which the planking at the fore end of the boat is affixed. |
| **Stern sheets** | The platform extending aft from the aftermost thwart. |
| **Sternpost** | The after portion of the backbone, to which the planking at the after end is affixed or, in the case of boats with transoms, the transom. |
| **Stiff** | Said of a vessel that is not easily heeled and returns quickly to the vertical, when heeling force is removed. |
| **Surge** | To allow a rope to slip on a power windlass while it is revolving; to allow a rope under tension to slip while on a cleat or bollard. |
| **TABERNACLE** | A structure on deck or cabintop to hold the foot of the mast when it doesn't run through the deck. It usually opens aft to allow the mast to be lowered. |
| **Tackle** | A purchase of ropes and blocks. |
| **Taffrail** | A rail around stern of vessel. |
| **Take up** | To tighten. |
| **Thwarts** | Planks placed across the boat to form seats. |
| **Tiller** | Lever for turning the rudder. |
| **Tide rode** | Said of an anchored vessel that is lying to the tide rather than the wind. |
| **Toggle** | A wooden pin with one end of a line seized to its middle to make fast to an eye. |
| **Transom** | The athwartships stern surface of a vessel; originally a board to which the after ends of the planking were secured. |
| **Traveller** | A metal bar parallel to the deck, running athwartships to allow a sail sheet to be led to either side. |
| **Trick** | A period at the wheel. |
| **Tumble-home** | A convex shape of a vessel's sides or stem. |
| **Turnbuckle** | A screw fitting for adjusting the tension of shrouds and stays. |
| **UNDER WAY** | When a vessel is not made fast. |
| **Up and down** | Vertical (said of the anchor rode). |
| **VANG** | (a) A guy for steadying a gaff; (b) Running rigging pulling a boom downward. |
| **Veer** | (a) To ease out a cable; (b) A clockwise shift of the wind. |
| **WARPING** | Moving a vessel by means of a hawser. |
| **Weather helm** | A boat has weather helm when it have a tendency to turn up into the wind. |
| **Weather side** | The side upon which the wind is blowing. |
| **Weather tide** | Where the tidal current is flowing against the wind. |
| **Wear ship** | (a) Changing tacks by turning a ship around before the wind; (b) Keeping the sails full (the opposite to coming about). |
| **Weigh** | To lift the anchor off the bottom. |
| **Wind rode** | Where an anchored vessel is lying to the wind rather than the tide. |
| **Windward** | Direction toward the wind. |
| **YARD** | A spar suspended from a mast to spread a sail. |
| **Yaw** | When the ship's head is swung from side to side by the action of the waves. |
| **Young flood** | The first movements in a flood tide. |

324

# SAFETY

8

# STAYING OUT OF TROUBLE

Safety at sea is not just a matter of carrying a packet of red flares or knowing how to make a radio call for assistance — it's an attitude.

You start with the knowledge that your craft is sound, well equipped, and suitable for the type of passage planned. You must have sufficient skills at navigation, seamanship, weather forecasting, and operating various boat systems to complete the voyage and cope with any situations that arise along the way. You must understand the capabilities of your crew (and yourself) and be able to manage them in all conditions. Finally, you must be able to analyze all these elements to make sound judgements in difficult situations.

Ultimately, almost every page of this book addresses safety on board a boat. The purpose of this particular chapter is to discuss a few safety subjects that don't fit neatly into other chapters, to describe some of the procedures that should be taken in an emergency, and to hypothesize on the repair of major systems.

## EQUIPMENT

The U.S. Coast Guard, and similar governmental organizations in other countries, have established minimum requirements for onboard safety and signaling equipment. If you are not already quite familiar with those regulations, please refer to them in Chapter 2, *Boating Regulations.*

It's obvious that a life jacket could save

your life; it's less obvious that a simple thing like a fuel filter, or the wrench to install it, could keep you and your vessel out of harm's way. It makes sense that every vessel should have its own customized equipment list. Checklists of maintenance tasks and gear to inspect before and during a voyage are also a good idea. Equipment that you *think* you have, but don't, is no help in an emergency — and having gear that doesn't work could be just as dangerous as not having it.

One item of equipment that sometimes doesn't get sufficient attention is clothing. Dressing right is good seamanship. As we edit this book, hearty men and women are racing across the Southern Ocean, their boats often averaging near 20 knots; these sailors are being exposed to gale force winds and deck-sweeping waves of freezing water. Modern boat design and technology make these speeds possible in relatively small boats, but the crews could not manage without having and using well-designed and well-made clothing.

Having clothes capable of keeping you comfortable during any conditions you might meet on a voyage increases your margin of safety. The windchill table at right shows the effects of wind and air temperature on exposed skin. The point at which the temperature and wind speed intersect on the graph indicates the windchill factor and the practical implications of the windchill factors are given below the graph. Note that "proper clothing" means protecting all skin areas from direct wind with sufficient thickness to prevent undue coldness. If clothing becomes wet or frost forms on it, it should be dried as soon as possible.

At the other end of the scale, excessive exposure to the sun can result in sunburn so severe that you can become incapacitated. Long-sleeve shirts and full-length pants that limit the amount of skin exposed to the sun's rays, combined with sun-blocking cream or lotion with a high SPF rating on all areas left exposed, are necessities when boating in hot and sunny conditions.

## FIRE PREVENTION

Small vessels normally use diesel or gasoline in their main engines, and kerosene, alcohol, or propane gas for cooking. Each fuel has its own hazards and virtues.

The flash point, i.e. the temperature at which a liquid gives off an inflammable gas, is much higher for diesel and kerosene than for gasoline or alcohol. Therefore, diesel and kerosene are safer under normal working conditions. All fuels, however, can become a fire risk if they come into contact with a very hot metal surface like an engine manifold or a hot stove burner, or if they are exposed to an electrical spark.

Fuel tanks, especially those for gasoline, should be placed away from the engine and exhaust pipe. The exhaust pipe should be well insulated and, if possible, fireproof thermal insulation should be placed between it and the fuel tanks. The best design minimizes long runs of hot pipe by using a water-cooled exhaust. Each tank must have a vent pipe to allow air to escape as the tank is filled and to flow back in as fuel is drawn out for consumption; the vent pipes must terminate on the outside of the hull near deck level. The fuel piping must be of the best quality and well secured, with no possibility of chafe. Rigid pipe tends to eventually crack due to vibration. If your fuel lines are flexible, inspect them frequently and replace them at regular intervals — before they leak! Armored flexible piping designed for marine use should be used.

Other than an actual spill of gasoline, the greatest fire danger on board is an accumulation of explosive vapors in the bilge. Both gasoline and propane vapors sink; you should make every effort to prevent their accumulation. A marine blower (spark proof) should be located in the engine compartment and fuel tank area — and

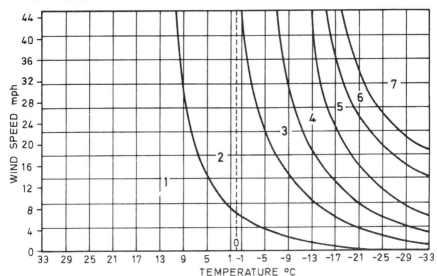

WINDCHILL GRAPH

1. Comfortable with normal precautions.
2. Can become uncomfortable on overcast days unless properly clothed.
3. Heavy outer clothing necessary even on clear days.
4. Heavy clothing is mandatory. Unprotected skin will freeze during prolonged period of exposure.
5. Multiple layers of clothing mandatory, especially protection for the face.
6. Proper face protection becomes mandatory. Do not venture on deck alone; exposure must be controlled by careful scheduling.
7. Survival conditions. Crew can become easily fatigued and mutual observation of fellow crewmembers is mandatory.

327

you should run it for at least four minutes before starting your engine. You can also install a vapor detector that will warn of dangerous accumulations. Last, don't forget your nose — use it after every fill up and before you start your engines.

Galley stove installations should be designed with safety in mind. Propane stoves should have automatic flame-failure devices on each burner that cut off the flow of gas if the fire is blown out for some reason. A solenoid switch can be installed directly at the propane tank; when the power is cut off, the flow of propane is cut off. The switch should be in a prominent location and have a light that indicates when it is turned on. The propane tanks should be stored in a vapor-tight locker that drains overboard, and spare tanks should also be stored on the outside of the boat. Be careful of deck-placed tanks — a gentle breeze can carry leaking gas vapors down the companionway.

If possible, the piping from the stove to the tanks should be one continuous run and all fittings should be sealed with gasdope or Teflon tape. Again, rigid pipe (copper) is prone to fracture after long periods of vibration. Many boaters prefer to have one long flexible pipe made up by a gas specialist. This is very heavy tubing that is extremely resistant to wear and not subject to vibration cracking. Of course, all piping must be well secured at frequent intervals.

Alcohol fuel remains popular in the U.S. because an alcohol fire can be extinguished with water. However, alcohol floats on water, so use plenty of water to extinguish a fire or you may just spread the flame. A spray bottle of water near the stove is handy both for galley grease fires and as an alcohol-fire extinguisher. When lighting an alcohol stove, never lean over the burners because flare-ups are common. When you're offshore, take even extra care when preheating alcohol or kerosene stoves — the lurching of your boat may send flaming liquid flying about the cabin and a very nasty burn is possible. A wick that clips onto the burner and allows the preheating liquid to be contained is a handy to keep aboard. These wicks are used to preheat pressurized kerosene lamps. Many experienced boaters use a small handheld torch to preheat the burners.

In summary:

1. Keep all compartments where explosive vapors can accumulate clear and well-ventilated.

2. Maintain all installations, both gas and liquid fuel, in a good condition — this means regular inspection. It also means inspecting electrical equipment that's installed where a spark could ignite an accumulation of gas.

3. Make sure your fire extinguishers are fully charged, inspected to date, and in locations where they can be readily reached when needed. See Chapter 2, *Boating Regulations,* for fire extinguisher requirements.

## Safe Fueling Procedures

Even with a properly designed and carefully maintained fuel system, there are hazards in the handling of gasoline and diesel fuel. Boats must be fueled carefully and in strict compliance with safe practices. (Diesel fuel is not explosive, although it is flammable; its more common hazard is pollution from a spill that results when a tank is over-filled.) Below are the correct procedures for safely fueling.

*Before Fueling*

1. If possible, fuel only during daylight. Do not fuel if an electrical storm is in the area.

2. Make sure that your craft is securely docked to the pier or wharf.

3. Stop engines, including the genset if one is on board. Turn off all electrical motors and other devices that might cause a spark. Open the master switch if the electrical system has one. Extinguish any galley fires.

4. Close all ports, windows, doors, hatches, etc., to prevent fumes from getting below decks.

5. Have all passengers and unneeded crew get off the boat and stand well clear.

6. Pass the word "No Smoking" on board and in the immediate vicinity.

7. Have a fire extinguisher readily available.

8. Determine the current fuel level and do not plan on taking on board an excessive amount.

9. For smaller boats, take portable tanks on shore and fill there.

### The Fueling Process

1. Keep the nozzle of the hose, or the spout of a can, in contact with the fill opening to prevent sparks from static electricity.

2. Do not drip or spill the fuel.

3. Do not overfill; take on board a bit less than the amount that would fill the tank completely — leave space for expansion. Do not fill a tank until it overflows.

### After Fueling

1. Close the fill opening immediately.

2. Wipe up any spills of gasoline; properly dispose of oily rags off the boat.

3. Open ports, windows, hatches, and doors; run the bilge exhaust blower for at least four minutes.

4. Check for any liquid fuel in the bilge or elsewhere inside the boat.

5. Use your nose — check for gas odors. If there are any, continue ventilation until it disappears. Over-ventilating never hurt anyone!

6. After the engines are started, cast off lines and get underway as quickly as possible. The greatest risk of explosion is in the first several minutes after leaving the fueling site — stay clear of piers and other boats for this time.

## WHAT IF'S?

Wise mariners engage in a lot of "what if?" thinking. What if that overweight crewmember falls overboard? What if a fuel tank springs a leak? What sort of emergencies can happen? What action will be necessary? Are the right spares and equipment carried on board? Have the crewmembers been properly trained?

Following are a few subjects that deserve your "what if" thinking — as well as your "What can I do to prevent the problem in the first place?" thinking.

### Man Overboard

This is one of the most difficult situations that can confront a skipper and one that often results in tragedy. When should crewmembers be required to use safety harnesses? Are there adequate attachment points on board and are the crew properly briefed on their locations?

In what situations can people go overboard? The only man overboard this editor has experienced during many days at sea was when a deckhand was knocked by a swinging pipe off an oilfield supply boat tied to an oil rig in calm conditions. His mandatory PFD saved his life. Among cruising people, it is said that more drownings occur when dinghying out to the parent vessel than when underway in her. Alcohol also contributes to many drownings and shipboard accidents. Life jackets should always be worn (especially by children) if there is the slightest danger. Many states now require life jackets on children under a specified age; if you go cruising out of your home waters, check the local regulations.

If someone does go overboard, how are you going to find him or her? Get back to them? Get them aboard? And, most important — what if the man overboard is you? (Turn to page 332 for a thorough discussion of man overboard procedures.)

### Collision at Sea

Although fortunately a rare occurrence, a collision still is a very real danger in high-density shipping areas. A sound knowledge of the Navigation Rules is necessary so you can quickly evaluate any close-quarters situation that may arise: Do you know for certain if you are in Inland or International Rules waters? Can you recall the sound signals for restricted visibility? Is your speed appropriate for current visibility conditions? Is your vessel on the correct course for crossing a shipping lane? (Remember Navigation Rule 10: "A vessel of less than 20m in length or a sailing vessel shall not impede the safe passage of a power-driven vessel following a traffic lane.") Even outside a traffic lane, a large vessel operating in confined waters (which may not appear to be confined waters to a small vessel) may be unable to take avoiding action — the responsibility for taking such action then lies squarely with the small vessel. It is important that such action be taken in good time and that it's obvious to all vessels involved in the close-quarters situation.

### Severe Weather

Why does rough weather become an emergency on one vessel and not on another? Have you closed all hatches and ports, firmly secured all deck gear, and prepared easy food for when conditions in the galley become difficult? If under sail, have you reefed down well ahead of any need for such action? Are you sure of your position on the chart and have you considered whether it would be wise to alter course for an alternative destination, bearing in mind the probable conditions to be expected on arrival?

Have you considered the alternatives to heaving to, such as running under bare pole or lying a'hull? Have you practiced heaving to in moderate conditions and assessed how your boat is likely to behave in more severe conditions? Will you have adequate sea room if the conditions get even worse than expected?

Are you and your crew taking care of yourselves — eating, sleeping, dressing right? A dry, warm, and well-fed crew can deal with trouble much more easily and capably than one that's wet, cold, and exhausted.

### Fire

Have you taken the normal precautions as described earlier in this section? Are you alert for other combustion sources like oily rags or cigarette smokers? Are your fire extinguishers accessible in any event? Fire at sea is perhaps the worst emergency that can occur in small craft because of the incredible speed with which it can spread and the lack of fire exits. A fire on land is bad enough; "burned to the waterline" is doubly so.

### Grounding

Have you thought about how you might extradite yourself from an accidental grounding? Would you be able to get out an anchor quickly? Could you reduce draft by moving weight or kedging from a mast top? Are you always aware of tidal height and current set when working around shallow areas? Do you know in which direction to turn if the water unexpectedly shallows?

### Power Failure

If your engine fails, will you be able to set an anchor quickly? Are you prepared to analyze and fix basic engine problems? Do you understand your fuel system and how to deal with contaminates in it? Do you know what to do if you get a rope wrapped in your propeller?

## FLOAT PLANS

The U.S. Coast Guard does not accept float plans from private boaters. However, many marinas and yacht clubs happy to do so. At the very least, prudent boaters will inform a friend or relative of their travel plans. Make sure they have a description of your vessel and other information that will make identification easier should the need arise. Be *very* sure to contact those concerned if you are unable make your destination or to return at the specified time. Printed on the opposite page is a sample float plan. Note also that several of the computer charting packages like ChartView by Nautical Software have options for printing a float plan, complete with a detailed route list.

## FLOAT PLAN

Complete this page before going boating and leave it with a reliable person who can be depended upon to notify the Coast Guard or other rescue organization should you not return as scheduled. Do not file this plan with the Coast Guard.

1. NAME OF PERSON REPORTING AND TELEPHONE NUMBER.

2. DESCRIPTION OF BOAT.  TYPE _____

    COLOR _____ TRIM _____ REGISTRATION NO. _____

    LENGTH _____ NAME _____ MAKE _____

    OTHER INFO. _____

3. PERSONS ABOARD

    NAME         AGE                ADDRESS & TELEPHONE NO.

4. DO ANY OF THE PERSONS ABOARD HAVE A MEDICAL PROBLEM?

    IF SO, WHAT? _____

5. ENGINE TYPE _____ H.P. _____

    NO. OF ENGINES _____ FUEL CAPACITY _____

6. SURVIVAL EQUIPMENT: (CHECK AS APPROPRIATE)

    PFDS    FLARES    MIRROR    SMOKE SIGNALS    FLASHLIGHT    FOOD

    PADDLES    WATER    OTHERS    ANCHOR    RAFT OR DINGHY    EPIRB

7. RADIO    YES / NO    TYPE _____

8. FROM _____ GOING TO _____

    EXPECT TO RETURN BY _____ (TIME) AND IN NO EVENT LATER THAN

9. ANY OTHER PERTINENT INFO. _____

10. AUTOMOBILE LICENSE _____

    TYPE _____ TRAILER LICENSE _____

    COLOR AND MAKE OF AUTO _____

    WHERE PARKED _____

11. IF NOT RETURNED BY (TIME) _____ _____

    CALL THE COAST GUARD, OR _____ (LOCAL AUTHORITY) _____

12. TELEPHONE NUMBERS _____

# WHEN TROUBLE STRIKES

Following are some notes about possible ways to cope with emergencies.

## MAN OVERBOARD

There are three main stages in a man overboard emergency. First, stop the vessel and return to the area of the accident; second, locate the victim and secure him or her alongside; and finally, recover the victim on board. All three stages must be carried out quickly and efficiently.

At the first instant you are aware of a man overboard, immediately throw over a lifering and/or any other handy floating objects that might help the victim to stay afloat, and that might help you locate the victim once you get the boat turned around. If you have a spare person on board, tell that person to do *nothing* but keep the victim in sight. If you have a running GPS or loran, mark your position (many units have a "MOB" button for this).

The next step is to get back to the victim and stop the vessel so that you can make the pick up. In a sailboat, this can be a complex maneuver. Different sailing manuals espouse different methods but, in truth, there is no single best method for all situations. The point of sail, the current sail configuration, and the crew available must all be factored into the most effective procedure to reverse your course without getting into more trouble.

Often, an effective way to turn around is the "reach-tack-reach," or "figure 8," method. As soon as possible, change your course to a reach and go *away* from the victim as far as necessary so that you can then tack and sail to a point downwind of him, followed by heading up and arriving at the victim with very little way on the vessel.

The quick-stop method is simple, rapid, and tailored to a weak and less-experienced crew. The procedure is to tack and leave the jib backed (adjusting the sheets if necessary) to enable the vessel to forereach back to the scene of the accident. After tacking, ensure that no ropes are over the side. When back near the site, start the auxiliary engine, furl the jib, and motor to where the person went overboard.

However you do it, it is usually not easy to get a sailboat stopped in a specific spot at sea, particularly in heavy weather, which is when a man overboard is most likely. Practice is invaluable: tie a fender to a bucket, throw it over without warning, and retrieve it.

Once you have precisely located the victim — often not easy to do if it has not been possible to maintain continuous visual contact — your next task is to secure him alongside. There are various pieces of equipment now available to assist the operation. One type consists of a pole with a stiff plastic loop on the end that can be dropped over the victim's head and shoulders. When suitably positioned, the loop can be tightened from the inboard end, thus enabling the victim to be firmly secured alongside. Another device consists of a lifering with a long floating line attached to the boat so that you can circle the victim and then pull him alongside.

The third and final stage of the operation, getting the person on board, can be the most difficult. A useful piece of equipment is a scrambling net, which consists of a strong net six feet by eight feet with four- or five-inch mesh. It's suspended from the stanchion bases and, apart from providing a comparatively easy method of scrambling aboard, it also enables a crewmember to stand in the net and assist the casualty aboard.

One occasionally hears that a transom-hung boarding ladder is useful in helping get overboard victims aboard, but nothing could be less useful if there is a heavy sea running. Although suitable as a swim ladder in calm conditions, in even moderate seas the transom will be rising and falling a matter of feet, and anyone in the water underneath such a ladder would be in a dangerous position. Recovery must be made amidships where the vessel's movement is at a minimum.

If the person in the water is unable to get back on board unaided, some form of mechanical aid is essential. Halyard winches, dinghy davits, and even anchor windlasses can be useful. Some vessels carry a block and tackle just for this purpose.

Whenever you are faced with a man overboard emergency, send out a Pan-Pan signal giving your vessel's name, position, and brief details of the emergency as follows: "Pan-Pan, (vessel name and call sign), (position), man overboard, request immediate assistance." It is far better to make a Pan-Pan call in good time and then cancel it if recovery is successful than to wait until it has proved impossible to recover the victim. If it is obvious that the crew stand no chance of getting the casualty aboard unaided, immediately send a MAYDAY call.

## FIRE

The following discussion of fire fighting is intended primarily for small vessels. An officer of a merchant ship is expected to have a good knowledge of fire drills, in general, and of particular precautions or methods of fire fighting required by a specific type of vessel or cargo. The skipper of a recreational boat or small commercial fishing craft should be similarly knowledgeable about potential dangers and the actions that should be taken.

**In case of fire:**

1. Alert all on board and tackle the fire, no matter how small, as a *major* incident. A fire can get out of hand with astonishing rapidity. Aim extinguishers at the base or center of the fire where they will probably have the greatest effect.

2. Instruct crewmembers to alter course or stop the craft (so that any wind is prevented from spreading the fire) and also to move the liferaft to a safe position and ensure that it is ready for launching. As rapidly as possible, without reducing the fire-fighting effort, get all hands into life jackets.

3. Close any hatches, ports, etc., to reduce the draft through the vessel.

4. If you can transmit by radio, inform the nearest ship or shore station of your predicament. It is better to later cancel an alarm than to be too late to send one.

5. Launch the dinghy or liferaft as soon as it is obvious that it will be required. If a dinghy, make sure that the survival kit (water, flares, etc.), is placed on board.

The above points may be dismissed as painfully obvious and indeed, they are, but they are intended to make the skippers of small vessels consider their equipment and their own general preparedness, as well as that of their crew, to deal with a danger on board. And remember — if you use water to fight a fire, start pumping the bilges without delay!

## ABANDONING SHIP

These notes apply to coastal waters in the Northern Hemisphere where one is unlikely to be adrift for more than five to seven days. The skippers of all small vessels should prepare a simple guide that explains the procedure for abandoning ship. The guide should include how to launch and use the the liferaft and the location of survival gear. Laminate the guide and display it permanently near the chart table/navigation area. In addition, you should have ready at all times a waterproof abandon ship box or bag, located near the liferaft or cabin entrance. The following is a list of suggested contents:

### Basic Survival Kit

- Container(s) of fresh water (with some air so they float), 2 quarts per person;
- Flares, smoke signals, dye markers, and signaling mirror;
- "Space" rescue blanket;
- Glucose sweets — 500 grams per person;
- Flashlight;
- Compass;
- Plastic bucket/bailer;
- 30 feet of line; and
- Emergency radio.

**If space and/or time allow:**

- Additional warm clothing, sleeping bags, sweaters, etc.;
- First-aid box;
- Ship's papers, money, passports (in waterproof packet);
- Chart(s);
- Sheath knife and other tools;
- Portable GPS or loran;
- Food — bread, chocolate, canned food, plus opener; and
- Your copy of *Reed's Nautical Almanac.*

**Two craft are better than one — if possible, take both liferaft and dinghy.**

## Procedure for Abandoning Ship

The decision to abandon ship is usually very difficult. In some instances, people have perished in their liferaft while their abandoned vessel managed to stay afloat; in others, people waited too long to successfully get clear of a foundering boat.

Once the decision is made, put on all available waterproof clothing, including gloves, headgear, and life jacket. Collect survival kit. Note present position. Send out MAYDAY message. Launch liferaft — attached to ship. Launch dinghy — attached to liferaft. Try to enter liferaft directly from the boat (if impossible, use minimal swimming effort to get on board).

Get a safe distance from the sinking vessel. Collect all flotsam — the most unlikely articles can be adapted for use under survival conditions. Keep warm — huddle bodies together. Remove all clothing from dead bodies and share between survivors. Keep dry — especially your feet. Stream sea anchor. Arrange lookout watches. Use flares only on skipper's orders — when there is a real chance of them being seen. Arrange for collecting rainwater. Ration water to maximum one-half quart per person per day, issued in small increments. Do not drink sea water or urine. If water is in short supply, eat only sweets from survival rations.

## EMERGENCY COMMUNICATIONS

When trouble strikes, there are many ways to communicate your distress and seek help. See the following sections in this book for detailed help:

- Chapter 6, *Communications,* for appropriate VHF or single-sideband radio channels and procedures for distress. Flag signals are at the end of Chapter 6.
- Chapter 1, *Navigation Rules,* for acceptable distress signals.
- Chapter 2, *Boating Regulations,* for more detail about distress signals (in Coast Guard requirements section).

A few additional thoughts:

- Flares are fast and effective — red for distress, white for collision avoidance.
- There are three levels of priority communications — distress, urgent, and safety, identified by MAYDAY, PAN-PAN, and SECURITE. Understand the differences.
- Panicked radio communications can confuse a rescue effort. Learn the proper procedures. Try to stay calm.

## ACT LIKE A CAPTAIN

At the beginning of this chapter, we said that safety is a matter of attitude. If you don't think so, consider the following:

A seamanship instructor we know teaches his students that being a good captain involves a certain amount of acting. He says that, particularly in emergency situations, the crew of a vessel look to their leader in an almost unconscious way to determine their own level of anxiety. If the captain projects a calm and confident attitude, the crew will be reassured — and since an anxious crew means poor judgement and performance, a captain should do all he or she can to keep the crew calm.

The idea here is not to lie to your crew, and certainly not to fake a fearless, macho manner — going down with the ship is a pretty dumb plan. The idea is that, by maintaining a calm, deliberate attitude in the face of a dire situation, you can help your crew remain effective and perhaps help save lives. If you need to fake that attitude to some degree, so be it.

# SEARCH AND RESCUE PROCEDURE

Around the coasts of the United States, Puerto Rico, and the U.S. Virgin Islands, the United States Coast Guard has the responsibility for coordinating search and rescue procedures (SAR) for vessels in distress.

Upon receiving distress calls, any coast radio station or public correspondence station will immediately contact the Coast Guard. The Coast Guard will normally request radio silence on the appropriate frequency for all vessels not involved in the emergency. They maintain a continuous watch on the emergency frequencies, which are VHF Channel 16 and 2182 kHz SSB. VHF Channel 70 will come into use as digital selective calling (DSC) equipment is installed at Coast Guard stations and on board USCG vessels.

If you hear a distress call, do *not* immediately transmit a response. First, listen carefully to determine if the Coast Guard has received the call and responded — or if another vessel is closer than you and better able to render assistance. Wait about two minutes — if the MAYDAY call is repeated and you don't hear anyone else responding, then call and attempt to establish communications with the distressed vessel. You should also try to call the Coast Guard and inform them of the situation.

If you can assist the stricken vessel without endangering your vessel and those on board, you should. The Federal Boat Safety Act of 1971 contains a "Good Samaritan" clause that states: "Any person . . . who gratuitously and in good faith renders assistance at the scene of a vessel collision, accident, or other casualty without objection of any person assisted, shall not be held liable for any act or omission in providing or arranging salvage, towage, medical treatment, or other assistance where the assisting person acts as an ordinary, reasonably prudent man would have acted under the same or similar circumstances."

If you hear a distress call that the Coast Guard cannot hear, you may have to act as an intermediate relay station. All vessels should immediately clear any channel upon which a distress call is being broadcast. If you hear the Coast Guard in communication with the disabled craft, continue to monitor the frequency, *but do not transmit* — your assistance may be needed later.

If the Coast Guard has been informed, they may call upon commercial assistance towing or salvage firms to come to the assistance of the disabled vessel if there is no immediate threat to the boat or its passengers. The Coast Guard does not maintain a list of approved commercial firms, nor do they inspect any firms to ensure their capabilities. In nonemergency situations, the Coast Guard will issue a "marine assistance radio broadcast." Commercial firms in the area may respond. It is up to the individual boater to negotiate terms and fees with the commercial firm.

Distress broadcasts transmitted by EPIRBs may be received by satellite or passing airplanes. All such transmissions are reported to the Coast Guard. If possible, the subject vessel will be contacted by other means. (See the section on EPIRBs in Chapter 6, *Communications*, for more information.)

It is essential that a distressed ship's position be given as precisely and accurately as possible if the original distress signal is made by radio — citing the latitude and longitude is the best. If the latitude and longitude can't be given, use the bearing (magnetic or true) and distance *from* a fixed object such as an inlet, lighthouse, or other aid to navigation. If time allows, include the type of ship or craft, the hull and trim colors (and, if applicable, the boat's sail configuration), along with brief details of lifesaving equipment aboard. The Coast Guard will want to know how many people are on board and if there are any injuries or other medical problems.

## RESCUE AT SEA BY HELICOPTER

Once a helicopter has become airborne from its base, how soon it locates the vessel and how effective it can be depends largely on the vessel itself.

A recreational boat in distress may not be expecting a helicopter rescue, particularly in view of the availability of rescue craft, but it is always advantageous to be prepared for this type of operation. A boat, particularly a small one, is not always easily identified from the air. The necessary precautions to ensure easy identification should form part of the seagoing equipment of a blue-water vessel. For example, sail numbers should be clearly marked, canvas dodgers should be boldly marked with the vessel's name and, if the dinghy is carried upside down on the deck, the vessel's name should be painted on its bottom.

Using a flare or smoke signal when the helicopter is sighted may materially speed up a rescue. Effective signals are the daylight, orange-colored smoke signal or a dye spread on the surface of the sea. Either of these is distinct from the air. Do not fire parachute flares while the helicopter is either directly overhead or close by.

Because of their operational limitations, helicopters should not be delayed at the scene of the rescue. If the vessel is large enough and free of significant masts, every effort should be made to provide a clear stretch of deck. A helicopter will approach the ship from astern and hover over the cleared area, heading into wind. For the helicopter pilot and crew to have as large an area of the ship as possible on which to operate, the ship should steam at a constant speed heading 30° to the right of the prevailing wind direction (so that the pilot of the helicopter, who sits in the right-hand seat, can best see the rescue operations). If this isn't possible, the ship should remain stationary, headed into the wind. If these conditions are met, the helicopter can lower onto and lift from the clear area the maximum length of the winch cable — about 200 feet. On no account should the trailing wire on the end of the basket or sling, when lowered to the vessel, be secured to any part of the vessel or allowed to become entangled. In all cases, an indication of wind direction is useful. Pennants and flags work for this purpose, as does smoke from the galley funnel, provided that there is not too much smoke.

The winch wire from a helicopter can carry a substantial charge of static electricity. The pilot will most likely dip the wire in the sea to release the charge before approaching your vessel.

Helicopter pilots are well practiced in rescuing survivors from either the sea or from a boat's deck. The victim, whether on deck or in the water, may be rescued by means of a sling or a basket. A crewmember may be lowered from the helicopter, together with the sling that is secured around the

victim's back and chest; both are then winched up into the helicopter.

If a victim on a deck is injured to the extent that using a harness around his or her back and chest would aggravate the injury or cause suffering, a crewmember from the helicopter is lowered onto the deck with a stretcher. The victim is placed in the stretcher, strapped in, and both stretcher and crewmember are winched up into the helicopter. If possible, the helicopter will be carrying a doctor who will be lowered to the deck to assist victims as necessary.

It is important to remember that a helicopter crew will not, under any circumstances, risk their winching cable becoming entangled with a small vessel's mast and rigging. Therefore, the crew on a sailboat must prepare to be picked up from the water at a safe distance from the craft. A liferaft or inflatable dinghy should be made ready and, on the approach of the helicopter, it should be streamed, complete with crew, on the end of at least a 100-foot line (longer is even better), firmly secured to the parent vessel — unless, of course, it's in danger of foundering.

The winch operator can then work in safety, well clear of the boat and her rigging. In the unfortunate event of their being no liferaft or inflatable dinghy, it will be necessary for the crew to get in the water when the helicopter has located them. Again, a long line (preferably polypropylene because it floats) should be streamed. The crew, with life jackets secured, can then drift to leeward attached to the line in a group. In the unlikely event that some members of the crew will have to remain in the water for an additional period, they will be able to return to the vessel by using the line.

On a small boat with no mast, the crew should remain on board unless otherwise instructed by the winch operator. Finally, remember that a helicopter cannot remain airborne indefinitely; watch for and carry out the winch operator's instructions exactly and immediately.

### High-Line Technique
In very bad weather, it may not be possible to lower the crewmember and harness directly onto the deck. In such a case, a rope extension of the winch line may be lowered to the vessel, which should be

taken in as the helicopter pays out her wire. Coil down the line on deck clear of snags, *but do not make it fast.* The helicopter will pay out the full scope of wire and descend, while the vessel's crew continue to take in the slack until the winch hook and sling are on board. The victim will then be secured in the harness and, when he or another member of the ship's crew signifies that he is ready, the helicopter will ascend and take in the wire. Pay out the extension rope, keeping enough weight on it to keep it taut, until the end is reached, then cast the end clear of the ship's side, unless further evacuation of crew is intended. Then, if possible, the end of the line should be retained on board to make recovery of the sling for the next person easier.

Rescue helicopters are fitted with marine VHF radios and may wish to communicate directly during transfer. Vessels with VHF should monitor Channel 16 (or other channel designated by the Coast Guard) and await instructions.

Remember: Keep clear of the main and tail rotors.

## AIRCRAFT SEARCHES AND SIGNALS

In general, night visual searches depend upon the ability of the survivors to indicate their positions by using pyrotechnics, lights, and fires. The searching aircraft can only hope to illuminate an accurately defined area, that is, on sighting red flares or flashing lights.

There are several patterns of searches, but the ones most likely to be used for missing craft or persons are the following:

**Expanding square search.** This procedure begins at a given point and expands in concentric squares. It is used to cover a limited area, usually when survivors are known to be in a relatively small area. To execute a square search, the aircraft flies in such a way as to make good the tracks shown in the diagram to the right.

**Track crawl search.** The procedure for this search is to fly along the known course from the last known position toward the intended destination and return on a parallel track at the sweep-width distance to one side of the original track. Then, the aircraft returns parallel to the original track on the other side, again at the sweep-width distance.

**Creeping line ahead search.** This procedure is used to search a rectangular area by a single aircraft. The aircraft proceeds to a corner of the search area and, flying at the allotted height, sweeps the area, maintaining parallel tracks. (See illustration next page.) The search area is usually long and narrow.

**Parallel track search.** This procedure is normally used when the search area is large and only the approximate location of the casualty is known. A uniform coverage is desired. The aircraft proceeds to a corner of the search area and, flying at the allotted height, sweeps the area maintaining parallel tracks. Successive tracks are flown parallel to each other until the area is covered. (See the illustration on the next page.)

### Aircraft Signals to Surface Assistance

To direct vessels that are in the vicinity of a vessel in distress to the assistance of the distressed vessel, aircraft may perform the following maneuvers in sequence:

1. Circle the surface assistance course at least once.

2. Cross the surface assistance course close ahead at low altitude while rocking the wings, opening and closing the throttle, or changing the propeller pitch.

3. Lead in the direction in which the surface assistance is to be directed.

When an aircraft is directing a surface vessel toward an aircraft or surface vessel

*Expanding square search*

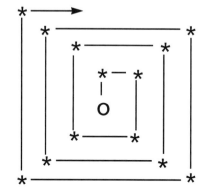

Safety

in distress and it wants to indicate that assistance of the surface vessel is no longer required, the aircraft crosses the surface vessel's wake close astern at low altitude while rocking the wings, opening and closing the throttle, or changing propeller pitch.

Repetition of any signal has the same meaning as when first used.

## GMDSS – A NEW ERA OF SAFETY AT SEA

The **Global Maritime Distress and Safety System** (GMDSS) is a new radio communication system for ships. It has already replaced the manual Morse code system on 500 kHz — the familiar "SOS"; it will ultimately replace voice radiotelephony on 2182 kHz and VHF Channel 16 with an automated ship-to-shore system using satellites and digital technology.

A set of safety regulations is in force, specifying the equipment ships must carry for disaster communications. The regulations form part of the GMDSS that has been formulated by the International Maritime Organization (IMO). These regulations apply to all ships carrying 12 or more passengers and to cargo vessels of 300 or more gross tons when such vessels are traveling on international voyages or in the open sea — these are termed "compul-

sory" ships. The regulations are being implemented incrementally; ships have until February 1999 to comply fully with the rules.

The GMDSS requirements do not apply to recreational or fishing vessels, small-passenger vessels operating domestically, or to vessels on the Great Lakes. However, GMDSS will eventually supplant the existing voice radio distress calling system and change watchkeeping on GMDSS ships. Thus, it may well be desirable for noncompulsory vessels to install digital selective calling (DSC) radios.

**What is GMDSS?** GMDSS takes advantage of the major technical advances in modern radio and satellite communications. The basic concept of GMDSS is that, in an emergency at sea, not only ships in the vicinity of the emergency, but also search and rescue authorities on shore should be alerted instantly so a rescue operation may be launched without delay.

To achieve this, GMDSS mandates the use of automated communications equipment for rapid and reliable links with shore. In addition, GMDSS provides for the dissemination of maritime safety information warnings. Every ship will be able, irrespective of the area in which it operates, to perform the communications that are essential for the safety of not only the ship itself, but of other ships operating in the same area.

*Creeping line ahead search*

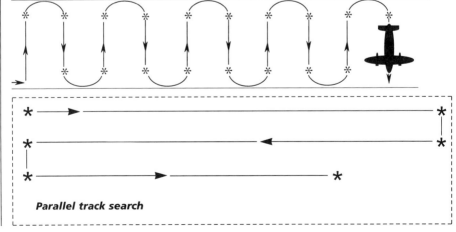

*Parallel track search*

IMO has specified nine principal communications functions that need to be performed by all ships and the equipment that would meet these requirements, depending on the zones in which they operate. These functions are: ship-to-shore, shore-to-ship, ship-to-ship distress alerting; search and rescue coordination communications; on-scene communications; transmitting and receiving position signals and maritime safety information; general radio communications; and bridge-to-bridge communications.

The communications equipment that must be carried by compulsory ships to perform these functions is determined by the area in which the vessel operates rather than its tonnage. GMDSS divides the seas into four different operating zones:

**Sea Area A1:** An area usually within 20 to 30 miles from land, within the range of shore-based VHF radio having digital selective calling (DSC) capability.

**Sea Area A2:** An area excluding A1, but within the range of shore-based MF radio (about 100 miles from shore) having DSC capability.

**Sea Area A3:** An area excluding A1 and A2, but within the range of services provided by the Inmarsat geostationary satellite system, which covers the whole globe, except small areas of navigable water in the polar regions.

**Sea Area A4:** All other areas outside areas A1, A2, and A3.

Most of the world's sea areas are in Sea Area 3 — Inmarsat service covers the globe between 70 degrees north to 79 degrees south latitude. The U.S. Coast Guard's DSC shore system will most likely cover Sea Area 2 by 1999. VHF facilities to establish Sea Area 1 along the U.S. coastline will not be fully in place until after the year 2000.

GMDSS requires that distress alerts reach a Rescue Coordination Center (RCC) uncorrupted and without delay; the alerts should pinpoint the tragedy at sea, provide the identity of the ship in distress, the nature of the emergency, and other relevant information. Initiation of an alert should be automatic or by the push of a button.

**Components.** The GMDSS consists of many separate systems; some are discussed below.

**The COSPAS-SARSAT System.** This is an international satellite-based search and rescue system established by the United States, Russia, Canada, and France. It can locate emergency transmissions on the frequencies used by Class A and B, and

GMDSS  Global Maritime Distress and Safety System

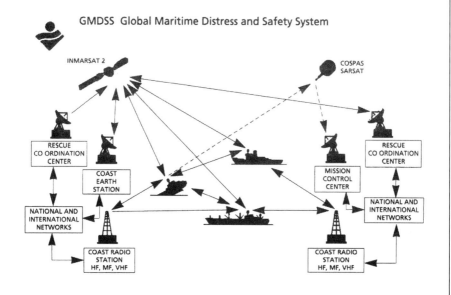

Category I and II Epirbs. The U.S. Coast Guard operates local-user terminals designed to receive EPIRB distress calls forwarded from COSPAS-SARSAT satellites. See Chapter 6 for description of the various types of EPIRBs.

**NAVTEX.** This is an international automated system for distributing maritime navigational warnings, weather forecasts and warnings, search and rescue notices, and similar information to ships. A small, low-cost and self-contained "smart" printing radio receiver installed near the helm of a ship or boat checks each incoming message to see if it has been received during an earlier transmission, or if it is of a category of no interest to that vessel. If it is a new and wanted message, it is printed on a roll of adding-machine paper; if not, it is ignored. No person need be present during a broadcast to receive vital information. See the applicable *Reed's Nautical Almanac* volume for stations and schedules.

**Satellites.** Satellite systems operated by the *International Mobile Satellite Organization (Inmarsat)* are important elements of the GMDSS. Inmarsat A and B (an updated version of A) provide ship-to-shore, ship-to-ship, and shore-to-ship tele-phone, telex, and high-speed data services, including a distress priority telephone and telex service to and from rescue coordination centers. Inmarsat C provides ship-to-shore, shore-to-ship, and ship-to-ship store-and-forward data and telex messaging, the capability for sending preformatted distress messages to an RCC, and the *SafetyNET* service — a service that works similarly to NAVTEX in areas outside of NAVTEX coverage.

**High Frequency.** The GMDSS includes HF radiotelephone and radiotelex (narrow-band direct printing) equipment, with calls initiated by digital selective calling (DSC). Worldwide broadcasts of maritime safety information are also made on HF narrow-band direct printing channels.

**Search and Rescue Radar Transponders (SARTs)** The GMDSS installation on ships includes one or more SARTs — devices that are used to locate distressed vessels or their survival craft by creating a series of dots on a rescue ship's 3cm radar display. The detection range between these devices and ships, depending upon the height of the ship's radar antenna and the height of the SART, is normally less than 10 miles.

# EMERGENCY REPAIRS

Mariners going offshore should be prepared to handle the breakdown of major systems. The discussions that follow are limited. You may not find techniques here that apply to your particular vessel, but you may be inspired to think through a repair solution that will work on your boat.

## JURY STEERING

The simplest form of emergency steering, which used to be standard issue in ships' lifeboats, was an oar. It could be put into a crutch, oarlock, or notch at the stern and used in the manner of the Viking ships. If your boat is small enough, an oar might work for you. If not, it's worth spending some time — before an emergency occurs — thinking about how you would install a jury steering system.

The first to do when the rudder or tiller breaks is stop the boat (turn off the engines and/or lower the sails) and investigate the cause. If the rudder is thrashing around you must take immediate steps to control it or it is likely to damage its gudgeons and pintles. Some boaters drill a hole through the outer lower end of the rudder blade, through which a line can be led to each side of the gunwale. This can serve as a brake on the rudder or as an emergency steering system.

If there is no hole in the rudder, one method of restraining it is to put a rope over the stern, secured on each side of the stern, and haul it tight against the rudder blade. If figure-of-eight knots are put into the rope, the blade will not be able to slip beyond the nearest knots. An alternative is to put lines on each side of a large shackle, from which the pin has been removed, and haul the shackle in tight over the aft end of the rudder blade. This method can be used as a rudimentary steering system, provided the shackle can be held in place, by easing on one line as the other is taken up to alter the rudder angle.

In a dire situation, you can even use a yachtsman's or fisherman's anchor to restrain the rudder. Put one line on one arm, another on the cable ring, and lower the anchor down the rudder so the blade is caught between the shank and arm.

If the tiller has broken, you can make an emergency one by lashing any suitable piece of wood or metal to the rudder head. When the boat has wheel steering, the usual cause of failure is one of the tiller lines. You should carry a spare wire that's already spliced to fit the system, but if one isn't aboard, you'll have to make a replacement or fit an emergency tiller.

With hydraulic steering systems, the usual cause of failure is a leak in the hydraulic pipelines. If the leak can be repaired and sufficient hydraulic fluid, or an acceptable temporary substitute, is on board, you're back in business. If insufficient spare fluid is available, a manual back-up steering system should be installed. All hydraulic steering systems should have stop valves in the pipelines and a method of isolating the wheel from the hydraulic rams so if the failure is due to some other cause, the wheel can be disconnected and an emergency tiller used atop the rudder post.

The most difficult repair is when the rudder stock breaks, because any jury steering system is going to have to be rigged directly to the rudder blade — and that means using one of the methods described earlier to control the angle of the blade.

When the entire rudder is lost, it is unlikely that the modern fin keel and skeg sailboat can be steered by balancing the sails (which was occasionally possible with the older, long keel designs, or with two-masted boats). However, it may be possible to control direction by setting the jib and hanking a small jib or storm sail to the backstay. The jib will provide power and hold the bow off the wind. By trimming the sheet on the small sail, the boat will tend to come into the wind; by easing the sheet, the boat will fall off. If the boat is fitted with a self-steering gear that has an auxiliary rudder, this might just work, but it would be unwise to put too much strain on it. You should reduce sail to keep the speed down.

The most obvious jury rudder is made by using a spinnaker pole or a similar spar over the stern like a steering oar. The inner end of the pole should be lashed to the backstay, which then acts as a pivot. Two lines should be led from the outer end of the pole, one to each side of the stern, where they pass through a block and then into the cockpit. Experimentation will show whether these lines need to be led to winches or whether they can be pulled and eased manually. If the pole is long enough, it may be possible to lash it to the backstay at a point on its length that allows the inner end of the pole to be operated like a crude tiller, with the fulcrum being at the backstay. However, this is hard work and the lines should be rigged for backup. The pole on its own will steer the boat as it is moved from side to side, but it will be much more effective if a plank, such as a bunk board, is bolted or lashed to it.

When the stern of the boat is narrow and the angle of the lines from the spinnaker pole back to the stern is acute, the tension required to pull the pole from side to side is considerable. It can be lessened by widening the angle. The easiest way to do this is to lash another spinnaker pole square across the stern of the boat, with blocks at each end, and lead the tiller lines through these blocks instead of the ones on the boat's gunwale.

## JURY RIGS

Being dismasted is a serious misfortune for a sailing boat. Dismasting tends to occur in heavy weather, usually because of the failure of some part of the rigging. In the quest for aerodynamic efficiency, some modern racing boats are rigged too lightly and, although modern materials are very strong, they are not indestructible.

One result of a dismasting in a monohull is that the boat's action will be much quicker because of the loss of the inertia aloft. Therefore, the repair work is made all the more difficult. If you are not far offshore, it's best to make for port under power once you have sorted out the mess. If, however, you are dismasted when you are in midocean and beyond the reach of outside help, you must improvise some kind of jury, or temporary, rig. Even if you have large fuel tanks, restoring some sail area will steady the motion of the boat and provide a modicum of sailpower.

## Jury Masts

If the boat is a ketch, yawl, or schooner, and the mainmast breaks, it may be possible to move the other mast into its position. Of course, in a ketch or yawl it may not be necessary to replace a broken mizzenmast because the boat may sail perfectly well under the sails on the mainmast alone.

In the event that the only mast has broken and been lost, a jury mast will have to be set up from what remains on board, such as the main boom, spinnaker poles, or bowsprit. If a stump of the mast remains, a spar, previously dressed with its shrouds, stays, and halyards, can be lashed upright to this stump.

A reasonable mast can be made by using two spars as sheer legs and setting up fore and backstays, but such a rig is only suited to a square sail, and another spar will be needed as a yard of sorts.

When a mast breaks, your first job is to clear the wreckage and recover as much usable rigging and bits of the mast as possible — these pieces may come in handy for making a jury rig. If part or all of the mast has gone overboard, it will be attached to the boat by shrouds and stays, so check that it is not endangering the hull of the boat.

Your next move depends upon the sea state. In anything worse than a small chop, it will be difficult or impossible to haul the mast on board, but the wreckage cannot be left lying alongside because it will likely knock a hole in the hull. If conditions permit, try to recover the sails intact and release all the rigging, but leave a sturdy line attached to a part of the mast or rigging, and then let go. A wooden mast will float clear of the boat; an aluminum one will sink. Either way, the goal is to keep the mast well clear of the boat but still attached so that it can be re-covered and used as part of the jury rig when the sea conditions improve.

Where the sea conditions are bad, and it is therefore dangerous to try and keep the mast attached, all the wreckage will have to be let go completely, and other items that remain on board must be used to make up the jury rig.

When conditions allow, haul the mast in alongside. Start by putting fenders over the side between the mast and the hull and lash the mast to the boat to reduce the relative movement between them. Next, remove the rigging by disconnecting it from the mast and then from the deck by undoing the turnbuckles and coiling it down. Doing so reduces the weight hanging over the side, lessens the load to be heaved on board, and eliminates clutter on the deck (thereby making your work there easier.)

Unless it is light, hauling the mast on board is not an easy task, and so should be tackled methodically. Move the mast fore and aft until its center of gravity is level with the midships section of the boat. Pass straps from the deck, down round the mast, back onto the deck again, and attach tackles to the upper end of the straps to form a simple sling.

If no suitable tackles are available, take a line from the upper part of the strap to a snatch block on deck in line with the strap's position and back to a winch. Alternatively, instead of using a strap, run a line from the winch through a snatch block and then down over the mast and up from beneath the mast to be secured to some strong point on deck.

On a large boat, you can use more than two straps, but on a boat of, say, 30 feet in length, two should be sufficient. The straps should be placed between six and 10 feet on either side of midships, depending on how the hull curves. If the hull is fairly straight, the straps may be farther apart.

Having rigged the tackles, start to take up the weight. If the mast refuses to come up the side easily, the job can be made easier by fitting a temporary ramp, angled down from the deck into the water, up which the mast can slide. Spinnaker poles or the main boom will do for the ramp. Each should be dropped over the side between the hull and the mast and then its top end hauled inboard. This will have the effect of moving the mast upward and away from the hull. The ramps should be fitted with fore and aft guys so that they cannot slip. Once the ramps are in place, hauling the mast on board with the slings should be a lot easier. Once the mast is aboard, lash it to the deck and start to assess what materials are available to set up your jury rig.

**Mast intact.** If the mast is deck-stepped and has gone over the side only because of rigging failure, it will probably still be intact. First, repair or replace the broken rigging. Even if the only material available is line, use it to set up temporary rigging replacements and make all as tight as possible. The rig is unlikely to be as strong as the original rigging, but it will provide some support, and if reduced sail is subsequently set, it should take the strain.

**Mast broken.** If the mast has broken, you have to decide which part of it to use for the jury rig. Normally, it makes sense to use the longest remaining section because more sail could be set. Sometimes, though, it's better to use a shorter section because it will be easier to set up — for example, when the top part of the mast is available with halyard sheaves and tangs intact for the rigging.

When a lower section of the mast is to be used and the break is just above a spreader, the spreader level will make a convenient point for the attachment of the fore and backstays. These can either be fastened directly to the mast just above the spreader, or tied off to a strap placed around the mast above the spreaders. Either way, the spreaders will prevent the new stays from slipping downward.

When the mast has broken close to the deck, leaving a stump, it is usually best to leave the stump and lash the jury mast to it. When stepping the mast, make a secure lashing to hold the foot of the jury mast to the bottom of the stump at deck level; once the mast is upright, lash it to the stump. The best way to lash is to take at least a dozen tight turns around the two pieces of the spar and finish by frapping the lashing between the two spars and tying it off. If there is space, put more than one such lashing around the spar.

**Stepping the mast.** There are two methods for re-stepping the mast. One is to push the mast forward with its head projecting out over the bow and its heel lashed to hold it at the mast step. Set up two spinnaker poles, or a spinnaker pole and main boom, as sheer legs over the deck, aft of the mast step, and hang a block from the apex of the sheer legs. To avoid damaging the deck, place pieces of wood beneath the heels of the spinnaker poles. Next, put lashings around the bottom of the poles and take them to secure points fore and aft so that the heels cannot slide. Lead a line from the masthead, or a point on the mast that would be the same height as the top of the sheer legs block when the mast is upright, through the block on the sheer legs, and down to a winch on deck. Attach the shrouds and the forestay to their rigging screws and then winch up the mast. The moment it is upright, secure the backstays and then dismantle the sheer legs.

The other method, which almost certainly has to be used if the mast is intact because it will be too long to extend safely over the bow, is to lay the mast on deck with its head over the stern. Rig sheer legs again, just forward of the mast step, and follow the same procedure. This time, however, it's the forestay that will have to be attached once the mast is upright.

In both systems, all the standing rigging, halyards, running backstays and so on, should be secured to the mast before it is stepped.

**Topmast broken.** When the upper part of the mast breaks off, leaving a substantial length of the mast still standing, the remaining length can be used to set sail. First, remove the wreckage. If the broken piece of the mast has not already fallen, lower it as gently as possible to the deck.

If there are no halyards left below the break, you will have to devise some way of getting aloft to rig temporary stays and halyards. Where there are two lower shrouds, the simplest system is to make ratlines. When the mast has only a single lower shroud, make a ladder by tying off lines between the mast and this shroud. This task may not be easy because the boat will become jerky without the extra weight.

Once it is possible to climb to the top of the broken mast, either put a jury mast knot around the top to attach stays, shrouds, and halyard blocks or, when the break is close above a spreader, attach these to the mast on a strap around the mast just above the spreader.

### Sprit and Gunter Jury Rigs

A very handy jury rig can be set up once a mast is stepped, using either the sprit or

gunter rigs. The sprit rig is practical when the lower part of the mainsail is intact. Any suitable spar can be lashed roughly in the position of the main boom gooseneck so that it can rotate a little. Its outer end is then lashed to a suitable point on the leech of the mainsail. The mainsail should be sewn along its new head and, if necessary, a rope should be sewn along this seam to provide extra strength.

The gunter rig is slightly more difficult to set up, but will work when the upper part of the mainsail survives and there is more length of mainsail than the mast remaining or the jury mast. The gunter rig is simple to handle and allows a higher sail to be set when the jury mast is short and it is not possible to put parrels on the upper part of the sail because they could not be hoisted above the spreaders.

### Jury Sails

If you are lucky, enough of the mast will remain to allow the mainsail, suitably reefed, to be set. However, if the mainsail is so badly torn that it cannot be repaired, some other sail will have to be set as a mainsail.

On a ketch, this could be the mizzen. On any boat, a jib or staysail can be used and set loose footed, with the clew taken out to the end of the main boom. Where possible, the sail should have its luff secured to the mast, be this its usual luff or its leech if the sail happens to fit better back to front. If the mast track remains, it is a simple job to sew sail slides onto the jury sail. If the track is unusable, it will be necessary to make up short lines to go around the mast; however, this will only work if there are no obstructions, such as spreaders, in the way.

Where it is not possible to make up any form of fore and aft sail, a square sail or a lateen sail may be the only answer. In both cases, a spar will be necessary. It is advisable to rig up a halyard for this yard and secure the halyard directly to the pivot point of the yard, or onto slings, so that both the sail and the yard can be lowered easily to the deck when necessary.

If none of the sails left on board will fit as a mainsail, it may be necessary to adapt them for the new rig. No one likes to cut up a perfectly good sail, but there may be no alternative.

## HULL LEAKS

Discovering a significant quantity of water in the bilges or, worse still, rising above the floorboards in the cabin, leads to one reaction — panic. Unfortunately, that's a less than desirable emotion to contend with when quick and careful thought and action are required.

### Finding the Source

While it may seem a good idea to devote all your energy to bailing, that's usually not a good idea. Other than switching on any nonautomatic bilge pumps and putting spare crew in charge of manual pumps and buckets, your first priority must be to find the source of the water — not always an easy job.

If the water is originating from a hole upwards of one inch (25 mm) square below the waterline, you have only a short time to locate the leak and stem it before the boat sinks or becomes unstable and capsizes.

Is the water fresh or salt? If fresh and you are boating in salt water, a potable water supply tank or line has developed a leak (turn off the electric potable water pump if fitted), or rainwater has been entering into a compartment in the boat, unnoticed over a period of time. In either case, there is no immediate danger. If you are sailing in fresh water, though, keep on checking.

Almost all cruising boats have a number of holes below the waterline: through-hull fittings, seacocks, instrument transducers, shaft logs, rudder shafts, keel bolts, anode studs, and prop shaft bracket fittings are some of the most common. Unless you are certain that you have collided with something that has damaged your hull, begin your investigation at these below-waterline areas.

Systematically check around all seacocks and close all nonessential ones until the leak has been found. Fractured hoses can be difficult to detect. On a boat that is significantly heeled over, sea toilet piping and submersible bilge pump through-hull fittings below the heeled waterline could be the source.

If the propeller shaft has been partially or completely pulled out of the boat, ensure the integrity of the rudder and shaft bracket mountings.

Check the cooling water circuit and exhaust on any working engines — the cooling pump is capable of pumping a large quantity of water straight into the bilge via any fractured lines. On powerboats fitted with outdrives, don't forget to look at the transom area in the engine compartment for failure of the rubber bellows sealing the drive.

If the boat has been taking heavy spray or green water, openings above the waterline such as anchor fittings, hatches, portholes, windows, through-deck chainplates, and blocked cockpit drains may be suspect.

If no immediate cause is found, hull damage is a possibility, and all internal parts of the hull so far uninspected should be examined as quickly as possible. If furnishings, fixed floors, or interior moldings conspire to hide some areas, look farther down toward the keel, where possible, to see if water is flooding from that direction.

### Taking Action

Most small-craft bilge pump systems are unable to stem the flow of a major leak unaided. Once a leak is located, you want to immediately reduce the volume of the leak to a level that the pumps can manage. The easiest method of stopping water from flowing through a broken below-waterline fitting, seacock, hose, or shaft that is completely missing, is to drive a round, tapered softwood plug into the hole. Packs of these plugs in assorted sizes are available at most major boating stores. To be most effective, suitable-sized plugs should be secured near all through-hull fittings, with spares carried in a handy locker well above the bilges. Remember that water pressure will try to force these temporary plugs out, so they need to be tended until secured in some way.

Instrument transducers often come with a spare solid plug to fill the hole while the transducer is being cleaned; these, too, should be kept in an easily found and accessible place in case of emergencies — preferably adjacent to the fitting.

If the hole is uneven, wrapping a rag around a plug may fill the gaps. Forcing cloth alone into place may also reduce the flow to manageable levels.

It may seem obvious, but even if it is going to take a relatively short time to locate a suitable material for a plug, try to constrict the flow with your hand if possible. A 2-inch (50 mm) hole 30 inches (0.75 m) below the waterline will let in around 40 gallons (180 L) every minute.

If the propeller shaft has become detached but is still inside the shaft log, the best solution is to push it back in place if at all possible. Hold it in place with a spare hose clamp until you can make a better, more permanent repair.

If there's damage to the hull you can rig a collision mat, which is a cloth (canopy, sail, or even a deflated inflatable without floorboards) that can be tied over the hole from the outside with ropes secured to the corners. Water pressure holds the mat against the hull, thereby substantially reducing the flow. Patented devices that work like umbrellas — they're pushed through the hole from the inside and open on the outside.

If you don't have a collision mat or the time to rig such a device, press bunk cushions against the damaged area from the inside to reduce the flow. Cushions can also be used to reduce water pouring in through shattered windows or failed hatches and portholes.

Aboard a sailboat, changing tack may reduce the pressure on any damage. On a fast powerboat, the hole may be in a region where, if the boat stays on the plane, the leak is stopped or reduced. A change of course or speed on all craft will also help if the leak is above the waterline. Again, by initially stemming the leak in any way possible, you gain time to solve the problem.

On both powerboats and auxiliary-powered sailing craft, the engine raw-water pump can serve well as an emergency bilge pump with considerable capacity. Stop the engine, close the seacock, and disconnect the hose. Put the end of the hose down into the bilge as far as it will reach and restart the engine. The water will be taken from the bilge ahead of the raw-water strainer; this is important, as there may be trash and small objects in the bilge water. Monitor this action closely to ensure that there is enough water for engine cooling — you don't want to risk damaging the impeller or overheating the engine. Using your engine's raw-water pump for this purpose is something you can plan for in advance by placing a T-fitting in the line between the seacock and the raw-water strainer. From this fitting, run a short length of hose into the bilge with a valve adjacent to the fitting. When you need the engine for emergency pumping, close the seacock and open the valve in the line leading to the bilge. If the water inflow to the bilge is less than the pump's capacity, the seacock can be partially opened to allow an adequate amount of water to reach the engine.

# EMERGENCY MEDICINE

**9**

*This chapter was entirely written by Dr. Paul Gill. We think that you will find it very informative, and surprisingly amusing. For a more thorough treatment of the subject, get Dr. Gill's* Onboard Medical Handbook, *published by International Marine.*

## LIFE-THREATENING EMERGENCIES

### The ABCs

No doubt you would know exactly what to do if your vessel hit a submerged ledge, fire broke out in the galley, or a crewmember fell overboard. You would react coolly and calmly with a well-rehearsed series of responses directed at evaluating and correcting the problem. Any onboard medical emergency should elicit the same efficient, rational response. You can evaluate and stabilize any seriously ill or injured person by tending to the ABCs:

**Airway:** If the victim is unconscious, open his airway using the jaw-thrust technique: put your fingers under each side of his jaw and lift up and forward *without tilting his head back*.

**Breathing:** Check to see if he is breathing by listening to his mouth and chest and observing his chest and abdomen. If his chest and abdomen are moving but you don't hear breath sounds, check the airway again. If you still don't hear breath sounds, give him two quick mouth-to-mouth breaths and go on to "Circulation."

**Circulation:** Control obvious bleeding (see

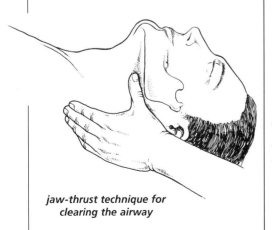

*jaw-thrust technique for clearing the airway*

below under *Shock*). Check for a pulse by putting your index and middle fingers over his windpipe and sliding them down alongside the neck muscle. If you don't feel one, start cardiopulmonary resuscitation (CPR).

### CPR

If you haven't taken a Basic Life Support course, you should contact your local hospital and sign up for one. Here is a brief review of CPR, which you can also think of in terms of ABC:

1. *Airway.* Shake the victim and shout her name. If she doesn't respond, place her on her back on a flat, stable surface, and open her airway using the jaw-thrust technique (see illustration). Put your fingers under each side of her jaw and lift it up and forward without tilting her head back. (Assume she has a neck injury until proven otherwise.)

2. *Breathing.* Kneel alongside the victim, and check to see if she is breathing by watching for movement of her chest and abdomen and listening for breath sounds with your ear against her chest. If she is not breathing, perform mouth-to-mouth breathing: pinch her nostrils, take a deep breath, seal your lips around her mouth, and giving her two full breaths.

3. *Circulation.* Check for pulses and, if absent, do chest compressions as follows.

   a. Place the heel of one hand on the lower half of the breast bone, and place your other hand over the first.

   b. Keeping your shoulders over her chest and your elbows locked, compress the chest at a rate of 60 per minute, stopping every 15 compressions to open the airway and give two breaths. The breastbone should be depressed 1.5 to 2 inches with each compression.

### Choking

If you are sitting in the galley eating breakfast one morning and your mate suddenly turns blue and grabs his throat, it's not your cooking. He's choking on a piece of food and will die of asphyxiation if you don't perform the Heimlich maneuver on him.

If he is talking or coughing and spluttering, *leave him alone*! His airway is only *partially* blocked. Encourage him to cough out

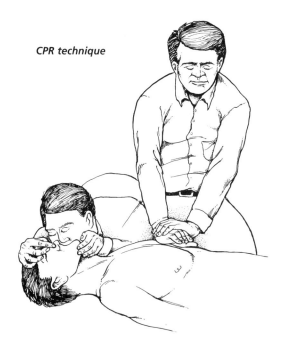

*CPR technique*

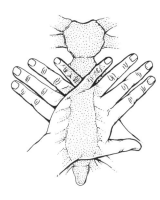

*proper hand position for chest compressions*

the food, but don't slap him on the back or perform the Heimlich maneuver.

If his face turns blue and he starts making a high-pitched, screechy noise, the obstruction is nearly complete. If he can't talk and clutches his throat with his hands, the obstruction is complete. In either case, it's time for you to perform the Heimlich maneuver — a series of abdominal thrusts that elevate the diaphragm and produce an artificial cough that expels the foreign object. Here are the American Heart Association's recommendations for treating the choking victim.

1. *The victim is standing or sitting, and conscious.* Stand behind her and wrap your arms around her waist. Make a fist with one hand and place the thumb side of the fist against her abdomen, just above the navel. Grab your fist with your other hand and press it into her abdomen with a quick, upward thrust (see illustration next page). Continue the thrusts until the airway is cleared or she loses consciousness. If she does lose consciousness, perform a finger sweep: open her mouth by grasping the tongue and lower jaw and lifting up. Then, insert the index finger of your other hand alongside the cheek to the base of the tongue. Hook the finger

behind the object and remove it from the mouth. (Be careful not to push the object deeper into the throat!) Then, give a series of mouth-to-mouth breaths. If you can't ventilate the lungs, perform six to ten abdominal thrusts; repeat the finger sweep and the mouth-to-mouth ventilations. Repeat the sequence of Heimlich maneuver, finger sweep, and mouth-to-mouth breathing until the airway is cleared.

2. *The victim is lying on the ground unconscious.* Place him in a supine position, and kneel astride his thighs. Place the heel of one hand against his abdomen just above the navel, and put the other hand over the first. Press into the abdomen with a quick upward thrust. Repeat the Heimlich maneuver, finger sweep, ventilation sequence as necessary.

3. *The victim is very obese or pregnant, and conscious.* Stand behind her, and wrap your arms around her chest. Place the thumb side of your fist on the middle of the breastbone, grab your fist with the other hand, and perform a series of backward thrusts until the airway is cleared or she loses consciousness.

4. *The victim is very obese or pregnant, and unconscious.* Place the victim on her back,

349

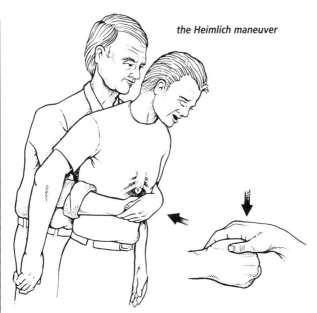

*the Heimlich maneuver*

lower ribs. Fractures of the xiphoid or ribs can lacerate the liver, spleen or lungs. And position the victim with his head lower than his trunk so that he won't regurgitate and aspirate his stomach contents.

## Shock

Shock is the failure of vital bodily functions that follows collapse of the circulation. It can be caused by severe bleeding (*hemorrhagic shock*), severe fluid loss from extensive burns or protracted vomiting and diarrhea (*hypovolemic shock*), heart failure (*cardiogenic shock*), severe allergic reactions (*anaphylactic shock*), or overwhelming infection (*septic shock*).

kneel alongside her, and place the heel of your hand on the lower half of the breastbone. Place the other hand over the first, and perform a series of thrusts. As above, repeat Heimlich maneuvers, finger sweeps, and ventilations until the airway is cleared.

5. *The choking victim is an infant.* If you are sure that the child is choking on an object, and not suffering from a severe cold, position the child head down so that he is straddling your forearm, and deliver four brisk blows between the shoulder blades with the heel of your hand. Then turn the infant face-up, position him on your thigh with his head down, and perform four chest thrusts, as described above.

6. *You are alone and choking.* Perform the Heimlich maneuver on yourself. Make a fist with one hand, and place the thumb side on the abdomen just above the navel. Grab the fist with the other hand, and press inward and upward in a quick, sharp, thrusting motion. If this doesn't work, press your abdomen across any firm surface, such as the steering wheel, air vent, or outboard motor.

**WARNING:** When doing abdominal or chest thrusts, be careful not to place your fist too near the xiphoid (a small bony projection at the bottom of the breastbone) or on the

Every cell in your body requires a steady supply of oxygen and nutrients from the blood and must be able to discharge carbon dioxide and other wastes into the blood. If shock persists for more than an hour, cellular metabolism fails and shock becomes irreversible and death inevitable.

Here's what happens if a great white shark bites off your leg. Pressure sensors in the large arteries in your chest and neck detect a drop in blood pressure and relay this information to the *vasomotor area* of the brain, the body's damage-control center. The vasomotor area then stimulates the sympathetic nervous system, a special network of nerves supplying the heart and blood vessels, to stabilize the circulation. If you are young, you could lose two to four pints of blood (25 to 30 percent of your blood volume) and show no outward sign of shock other than a rapid pulse and cool, moist skin. But, if you lost even a little more blood, you would go into irreversible shock.

*Recognizing Shock*

Assuming your shipmates heard your cries for help and hauled you back into the boat, here is what they would see, depending on the stage of shock you were in.

*Mild shock*: If you had lost less than two pints of blood, you would be alert, but cold, thirsty, weak, and lightheaded when you sat up. Your blood pressure would be normal, but you would have a rapid pulse (110 to 120 beats a minute) and your would be skin pale, cool, and damp.

*Moderate shock:* You have lost two to five pints of blood. You are thirsty and short of breath, and unable to help himself. Your speech is slurred, your skin is cold and clammy, your pulse is very rapid and thready, and your urine output meager (less than 30 milliliters per hour).

*Severe shock*: You have lost half or more of your blood volume (five pints plus) and the circulation to your heart and brain is poor. Your eyes are dull and glazed, your pupils dilated, your breathing shallow and rapid. You become restless and agitated, and then lethargic and comatose.

### Treating Shock

1. First, tend to the ABCs (see above).
2. Strip off the victim's clothing and examine him from head to toe, looking for serious injuries. Treat any head, neck, eye, chest, or abdominal injuries as described below, and splint any obvious fractures or dislocations (see below). Control bleeding by applying firm pressure directly over the wound with a bulky dressing or a clean towel or articles of clothing for several minutes. Then apply a sterile *compression dressing* (a bulky dressing consisting of ABD pads and several 4" x 4" dressing pads). If the wound continues to bleed, pack it with sterile gauze and cover it with a compression dressing.
3. After you have done everything possible to stabilize the victim's injuries, place him on his back with his legs bent at the hips, his knees straight, his feet elevated 12 inches, and his head down (the shock position). This position combats shock by promoting the return of venous blood to the heart.
4. Cover him with blankets and offer him warm fluids by mouth if he is alert. If you are medically trained, start two large-bore (16-gauge) peripheral intravenous lines and infuse lactated Ringer's solution or normal saline at a wide-open rate until the vital signs stabilize.
5. If it is cold and wet topside, carry the victim down into the cabin and check his vital signs, including his pulse and breathing rate and pattern, every few minutes.
6. Use the radio to call for help.

### Tourniquets

Tourniquets can be life-saving, but they can also damage muscles, nerves, and blood vessels. *Don't apply a tourniquet unless you are willing to write off the limb to save the victim.*

To make a tourniquet, fold a triangular bandage or a long strip of cloth into a band two inches wide. Place the tourniquet just above the wound; circle the limb with it twice and tie the ends in a square knot. Then, make a Spanish windlass by placing a six-inch piece of wood over the knot and tying it in place with a square knot. Rotate the windlass until the bleeding stops; then tie it in place with the free ends of the tourniquet. Keep the tourniquet exposed and don't release it unless advised to do so by physician or by emergency medical personnel.

## Near-Drowning

*"Ask them why they never learned to swim and they will probably retort with, 'Why learn?' Being able to swim is all right if you're fishing in some pond ashore; but out on the fishing banks—where would a man swim to?"*

–James B. Connolly, *The Book of the Gloucester Fishermen*

Drowning is suffocation by submersion in water. Near-drowning is survival for at least 24 hours after submersion. You can't breathe in oxygen and blow off carbon dioxide when you are underwater unless you have gills or a scuba tank. Consequently, the concentration of oxygen in the blood and tissues plummets (*hypoxemia*) and carbon dioxide levels rise (*hypercarbia*). The brain cannot operate without a steady flow of oxygen; hypercabia causes narcosis, so you pass out after a few minutes. High levels of carbon dioxide lead to a surplus of acids in the blood and tissues, which disrupts cellular metabolism in every organ.

### Treatment

In the old days, the drowning victim was often placed face down on a trotting horse or placed on or inside a barrel that was rolled back and forth in an effort to ventilate the lungs. Other strategies included warming the victim by lighting a fire near him, burying him in warm sand, putting him in a warm bath, or putting him to bed with a couple of volunteers; removing aspirated

Emergency Medicine

351

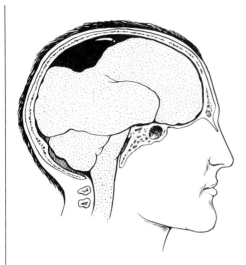

*subdural hematoma*

water by tickling his throat with a feather to induce vomiting; stimulating him by rectal and oral fumigation with tobacco smoke, or by squirting mixtures of oil, salt, and water into his mouth; and using a bellows to restore breathing or mouth-to-mouth breathing. Here is the modern approach.

1. Remove the victim from the water as quickly as possible, taking care to splint her neck if there are grounds to suspect a neck injury, (e.g., a dive into shallow water, a surfing accident).

2. If she is not breathing, use the jaw-thrust technique (see illustration on page 348) to open her airway, clear any debris from her mouth and throat, and start mouth-to-mouth ventilation while still in the water. If she has no pulse, start chest compressions as soon as you can position her on a firm surface.

3. Most submersion victims aspirate very small amounts of water, so don't waste time doing drainage procedures.

4. Re-warm her if she is hypothermic.

5. Continue CPR (see above) until you revive the victim or emergency medical personnel take over. If you're in a remote area, continue CPR until the victim has warmed to ambient temperature.

## HEAD AND NECK INJURIES

*"Groping blindly for the peak downhaul, I received a sharp blow in the face, then my neck was encircled in a vice-like grip and I soared aloft, caught in a bight of the downhaul whipped about by the flailing gaff. I knew no more until I hit the deck with a jarring shock..."*

Captain Richard England, *Schoonerman*

### Head Injuries

Serious head injuries were common in the days of commercial sail, when a sailor had to dodge falling marlinespikes, blocks, and tar pots, and bully captains and bucko mates enforced discipline with ample servings of handspike hash and belaying pin soup. Today you're more likely to get beaned by a jibing boom or smash your noggin on the cabin sole after tumbling down a wet companionway.

Here is how you should approach anyone with a head injury.

1. Check the ABCs (*A*irway, *B*reathing, and Circulation, see above).

2. Do a quick head-to-toe exam. *CAUTION!* Keep the neck rigidly immobilized (see below under *Neck Injuries*) until you are sure it isn't injured!

3. Evaluate the victim's mental status by checking the following:

   a. *Eye opening.* Does she open her eyes spontaneously, on command, or only in response to pain?

   b. *Verbal response.* Can you understand her speech? Does she make sense or is she confused and disoriented?

   c. *Motor response.* Does she obey simple commands (e.g., "squeeze my fingers")? If not, does she withdraw when you pinch or squeeze her arms?

   d. *Pupillary responses.* Are her pupils round and symmetrical? Do they constrict when you shine a light into her eyes?

If she wakes up after a short while and acts a little groggy, but her speech and movements are normal, she has probably suffered a *concussion*, which is a transient disruption of brain function. She may have short-term memory loss, headache, and irritability for a few days, but she'll be fine. If she remains unconscious, or wakes up for a short period and then lapses into a coma, she probably has an *epidural* or a *subdural hematoma* (bleeding between the brain and the skull — see illustration left). These hematomas are usually fatal if not treated quickly. Radio for emergency medical evacuation.

4. Look for skull fractures. A bruise behind the ear ("battle sign"), "raccoon eyes," bleeding from the ears, and drainage of clear fluid from the nose or ears are all signs of a *basilar skull fracture* (fracture of the base of the skull). If she has a scalp laceration, explore the wound gently with gloved hands. Is there a skull defect? Is the brain exposed? If there is no obvious open brain injury, run your finger over the surface of the skull. A depression denotes a *depressed skull fracture.* A skull fracture *per se* is not life threatening, but it may be complicated by underlying brain injury or intracranial bleeding and mandates immediate evacuation to a hospital. Don't try to clean an open skull fracture and *never pull a penetrating object out of the skull.* Simply apply a sterile dressing and keep the victim warm while awaiting evacuation.

### Neck Injuries

If your shipmate tumbles down an open hatch, or falls out of a bosun's chair and hits the deck head-first, assume that he has a neck injury. If he has an unstable spinal injury, any movement could cause irreparable spinal cord damage. Before you move him, do the following.

1. Ask him if his neck or back hurts. If he says no, and can move his head comfortably in all directions, serious neck injury is improbable.

2. Run your fingers down his spinal column from the base of his skull to his tailbone checking for tenderness.

3. If it hurts him to move his head or his spine is tender, have someone support his head while you wrap a rolled-up bath towel snugly around his neck and secure it with safety pins or adhesive tape (see illustration below). Then, without moving his neck, *gently* move him onto a long board or a pair of lashed oars and secure him to the board or lashed oars with rope or tape. Apply a fender or hardcover book to each side of his head and secure them with one or two long strips of tape running from one side of the board, across his forehead, and under the other side of the board. Now you can safely move him to the cabin.

If he has neck or back pain radiating down the arms or legs, numbness or tingling in the hands or feet, complete or partial loss of feeling in the arms or legs, weakness or paralysis of the arms or legs, a sustained erection, or inability to urinate, suspect a *spinal cord injury.* Arrange for evacuation.

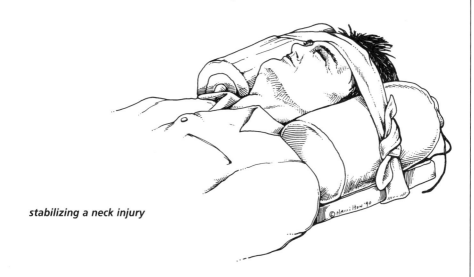

*stabilizing a neck injury*

## CHEST INJURIES

The chest operates like a bellows to pull air into your lungs with each breath. When the diaphragm (the muscle that separates the chest and abdominal cavities) contracts, it pulls down on the lower part of your chest cavity. This expands the chest and creates a relative vacuum that draws air through the respiratory tree and into the lungs. When the diaphragm relaxes, the chest cavity contracts, and the lungs recoil and deflate.

Here is how to evaluate a chest injury:

1. *Look.* Make sure her airway is clear and that she is breathing. Measure her respiratory rate (normal = 12 to 20 breaths per minute) and note her breathing pattern. Check her color. Her skin should be slightly pinkish; if her lips, ears, and fingertips are blue, she is in shock or respiratory failure. Are her neck veins bulging? Is her trachea (windpipe) in the midline, or deviated to one side? These are signs of *tension pneumothorax* (see below). Look for lacerations, puncture wounds, or asymmetrical movement of the chest.

2. *Feel.* Run your hands over the entire chest cage, front and back. Check for tenderness, abnormal movement, or crepitus (a grating sensation). Tenderness and crepitus suggest rib fracture. A bubbly feeling under the skin is caused by air that has escaped from a punctured lung.

3. *Percuss.* Tap on the chest with the ends of your long and index fingers. You should hear a slightly hollow sound from the collarbones to about the sixth rib in the front, and from the shoulder blades to about the tenth ribs in the back.

4. *Listen.* Put your ear to the victim's chest and listen while the victim takes a few deep breaths. If the upper airway is obstructed, you will hear loud, harsh breath sounds. Blood or fluid in the airways will produce a rattling sound. If you hear no breath sounds on one side, and that side also has a hollow sound when you tap on it, the victim probably has a *pneumothorax*. If the chest sounds dull when you tap on it, she probably has a *hemothorax* (see below).

### Blunt Chest Injuries

*Rib Fractures*
If you land chest-first on a winch, vent,

cleat, or bitt, you are going to bruise or crack one or more ribs. It's hard to distinguish between these injuries. They both cause terrific pain that worsens with deep breathing and trunk movement. If there is tenderness and crepitus over the injured area, and the pain is aggravated when you press on his breastbone when he is supine, you can be sure that he has at least one fractured rib. **Treatment:** Stabilize the fracture(s) by wrapping a six-inch elastic bandage around the chest at the level of the injured rib. Ice packs and analgesics help, too.

**WARNING:** Fractures of the lower ribs are sometimes associated with liver or spleen injuries. Examine the abdomen carefully and keep a close eye on your patient's vital signs and skin color. If he has abdominal pain or tenderness, or signs of shock, get on the radio and request immediate evacuation.

*Separated Cartilage*
The ribs are connected to the breastbone by bars of cartilage. A hard fall onto the front of the chest can disrupt the rib-cartilage junction, producing a separated cartilage. The victim will complain of a snapping sensation on deep breathing and exquisite pain a few inches below the nipple. **Treatment:** The same as for fractured ribs.

*Flail Chest*
Two or more fractures in each of three or more consecutive ribs produces a "flail chest," i.e., an unstable segment of the chest cage. The flail segment moves paradoxically with each breath; i.e., it sinks in when the rest of the chest is expanding with inspiration, and pushes out when the chest is contracting with expiration. This impedes the normal flow of air into and out of the lungs and the underlying lung is usually bruised. The victim may complain only of pain for a day or two, but then he'll develop progressively worsening shortness of breath and respiratory failure. **Treatment:** Get the victim to a hospital as quickly as possible.

*Pneumothorax (Collapsed Lung)*
When a fractured rib punctures a lung, air will flow out of the lung and into the chest cavity until the pressure in the chest cavity causes the lung to collapse. The signs and symptoms of pneumothorax include pain, shortness of breath, decreased breath sounds on the affected side, and a hollow sound when you tap over the affected side of the chest. **Treatment:** A small pneumoth-

orax may resolve spontaneously after a few days, but generally the victim needs to have a tube inserted into his chest to drain air from the chest cavity and reinflate the lung. Sit him up and make him as comfortable as possible while awaiting evacuation.

### Tension Pneumothorax

Sometimes a rib creates a one-way valve (flutter valve) when it punctures the surface of the lung, so that air flows only one way: out of the lung and into the chest cavity. This causes a *tension pneumothorax*. The chest cavity fills up with air under tension and pushes the heart, great vessels, and trachea over to the opposite side of the chest, compressing the uninjured lung. Kinks in the great veins prevent the return of venous blood to the heart, and the circulation collapses. The victim turns blue, her neck veins bulge, and she becomes extremely agitated and short of breath. She will die if her chest isn't decompressed immediately.

**Treatment:** Clean the skin with antiseptic solution and insert the largest sterile needle you have into the space between the second and third ribs just lateral to the nipple. Guide the needle over the top of the third rib and then straight into the chest until you hear a gush of air as the needle enters the chest cavity. The victim will improve dramatically after this lifesaving procedure. Leave the needle in place and arrange for emergency evacuation to a hospital.

### Hemothorax

Bleeding from fractured ribs can cause an accumulation of blood in the chest cavity, or *hemothorax*. A small hemothorax isn't a life-threatening injury, but a large one is. The victim will be anxious, in pain, pale, sweaty, and short of breath. His pulse will be rapid and his blood pressure low. His chest will sound dull when you percuss the injured side and breath sounds will be decreased on the injured side. **Treatment:** Make the victim as comfortable as possible while you arrange for evacuation to a hospital.

## Penetrating Chest Injuries

These were common injuries in Lord Nelson's navy when sailors were always getting poked with boarding pikes and cutlasses. One especially dangerous form of the

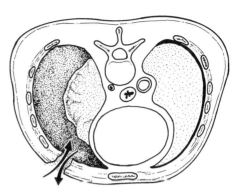

*sucking chest wound*

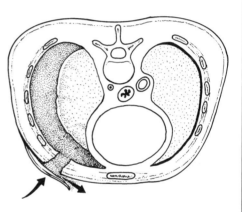

penetrating chest injury is the *sucking chest wound* (see illustration). This can result from a spear-gun injury, a fall onto the pointed end of a boathook or some other sharp object, or a swordfish attack. If the diameter of the wound approaches the diameter of the windpipe, air will be sucked through the wound into the chest cavity each time the victim takes a breath, and the lung will collapse. Little air will flow through the windpipe, and she will die if the problem isn't corrected fast.

**Treatment:** Cover the wound with a sterile dressing or any clean towel or cloth. Once the victim is stabilized, apply a sterile, petrolatum gauze dressing to the wound, and cover it with a sterile 4" x 4" gauze pad. Tape the pad on three sides only so that air can escape but not enter through the wound. Then radio for medical assistance.

355

### Abdominal Injuries

If a rogue wave slams you belly-down onto a vent or sampson post, you could lacerate or rupture your spleen or liver. Such injuries can be fatal if not diagnosed and treated in a timely fashion. But they can be hard to diagnosis. Anyone who sustains a hard blow to the upper abdomen or lower ribs should be observed carefully. Keep a weather eye out for early signs of shock: lightheadedness and weakness when the victim sits up; thirst; cool, damp skin; and rapid (110 to 120 beats per minute) pulse. Look for bruises, discoloration, or swelling on his chest and abdomen. Is his belly soft or rigid? Press your fingertips under his rib cage. Is there a tender area on either his right (liver) or left (spleen)? Now press over the rest of the abdomen. Local areas of tenderness and rigidity may be due to a bruise of the abdominal wall, but diffuse rigidity and tenderness, coupled with signs of early shock, suggest injury to an abdominal organ.

**Treatment:** Place the victim in the shock position (see above under "Shock"), cover him with blankets, and offer him fluids by mouth. If you can, start an intravenous line with a large-bore (16- or 18-gauge) catheter and infuse Ringer's lactate as rapidly as possible. Arrange for emergency evacuation as soon as possible.

### Kidney Injuries

Although well-protected by the abdominal organs in front and the lower ribs and thick spinal muscles in back, the kidneys are susceptible to injury from a hard fall or a whack in the back or flank by a flying boom or spinnaker pole. Pain in the back or the flank coupled with pink-tinged or grossly bloody urine (hematuria) are the usual symptoms. If the kidney is simply contused, the hematuria will stop after a few hours. If the victim feels weak and continues to pass pink or bloody urine, she may have lacerated or ruptured a kidney. **Treatment:** Same as for abdominal injuries (see above).

Cuts, burns, and splinters are as common as spray in the face for a mariner. You should be as familiar with their treatment as you are with your knots, bends, and hitches.

### Open Wounds

Open wounds are breaks in the skin. They range in seriousness from abrasions to amputations. Here is a systematic approach to treating them.

1. *Control the bleeding.* Apply firm pressure directly to the wound with a sterile dressing pad or a clean towel or rag. After a few minutes, the ends of the cut vessels constrict and a clot forms and plugs the hole in the vessel. Tourniquets are rarely necessary and are fraught with hazard (see above under "Shock").

2. *Inspect the wound.* After you have controlled the bleeding, inspect the wound. Determine its depth and check for damage to bones, tendons, ligaments, and blood vessels. If the wound is on a limb, check the pulses below the wound (see "A Systematic Approach to Skeletal Injuries" below) and test sensation below the wound and movement of hands and fingers or feet and toes.

3. *Clean the wound.* First, use a pair of tweezers to pick out any foreign matter you see in the wound. Next, use a bulb syringe to thoroughly irrigate the wound with irrigating solution (add an ounce of 10% povidone-iodine solution to two or three quarts of water). Then, gently wipe dirt out of the wound with a sterile gauze pad.

4. *Close the wound.* Any wound that is at high risk of infection, such as a fish bite or sting, is best left open. No matter how meticulous you are in cleansing the wound, it's impossible to remove every contaminant. Bacteria thrive on the blood and debris that accumulate in the depths of wounds, and closing a deep, dirty gash is a recipe for infection. It's better to leave such wounds open so that they can drain. But every wound has to be treated on its merits; the decision to close or not to close depends on its location and its depth, how dirty it is, and whether there are associated bone, joint, tendon or nerve injuries. When in doubt, leave the

wound open. Every wound will heal eventually, no matter what you do.

### Abrasions

When you scrape the skin over a bony prominence such as your knee or elbow, you get an abrasion. The superficial layer of skin is sheared off and dirt is often ground into the wound. **Treatment:** Cleanse the abrasion with an antiseptic solution, then cover it with a transparent dressing (Bioclusive or Tegaderm). Cover large abrasions with a multilayered bandage and change the dressing daily until a firm scab forms.

### Lacerations

A laceration is a wound made by tearing. Lacerations produced by a knife or by a nail or a screw protruding from a plank generally cause linear lacerations with regular wound edges. Blunt trauma, such as results from striking your knee against the chart table in the dark or dropping an anchor on your foot, causes jagged, stellate lacerations.

*Facial lacerations* can almost always be closed with tape skin closures. First, apply tincture of benzoin to the skin on either side of the wound to make the tapes adhere better, and spread antibiotic ointment on the wound. Then bring the wound edges together by applying a tape first to one wound edge, and then the other. Make sure that there are no gaps in the wound and that the edges are even.

In Canada and Europe, cyanoacrylate glue (Super Glue, Krazy Glue) is commonly used to close small, tension-free facial lacerations. Our FDA hasn't yet approved this use of cyanoacrylates, but here is the technique if you want to try it: Hold the wound edges together and squeeze enough glue onto the wound to cover the wound edges with a thin film. (Don't let the glue penetrate into the wound.) Then, maintain pressure on the wound until the glue dries (30 to 40 seconds). The glue is waterproof, so a dressing is unnecessary.

*Scalp lacerations* can easily be closed with surgical staples. Inspect and clean the wound in the usual manner, then press the wound edges together and staple them in place. Start in the middle of the laceration, and use the "divide and conquer" method until the wound edges are well-approximated. You can also close the wound by tying clumps of hair across it until the bleeding

stops. (Hair doesn't hold knots well, so use surgeons' knots — square knots with an extra throw.) Then apply a turban bandage using a roll of 4-inch roll gauze.

*Trunk and limb lacerations* should be closed with surgical staples or tape closures as appropriate, coated with antibiotic ointment, and covered with a multilayer sterile dressing. The first layer should be a nonabsorbent sterile dressing, such as Vaseline gauze (Adaptic). The next layer should consist of sterile gauze pads, followed by an ABD or Surgipad if the laceration is large. The dressings can be then be taped down or wrapped with roll gauze. Small lacerations can be closed with cyanoacrylate glue (see Facial Lacerations above). The glue may need to be reapplied periodically if the laceration is on a dynamic area, such as the elbow or back of the hand.

### Avulsions

An avulsion is what you get when you slice off a piece of skin (a fingertip, for example) with a knife. In a partial-thickness avulsion, only the top layers of the skin are lost; in a full-thickness avulsion all of the skin and some of the underlying fatty layer is lost.

An avulsion can't be closed, but it should be cleansed and covered with a sterile dressing. Skin will grow in from the sides and heal it as long as bone isn't exposed. If it is, or the avulsion is larger than a half-dollar, the avulsion may require skin grafting.

Avulsed skin that remains attached on one side is called a *flap*. Clean and dress a flap the way you would any other avulsion.

### Amputations

These are by no means rare injuries on shipboard. On large vessels, parting lines can whip through a man's legs like a hot knife through butter, and fingers and toes can easily be lopped off when caught in a bight in an anchor rode or a halyard. Bleeding from an amputated limb can lead to shock and death if not quickly controlled. If you can't control the bleeding with firm compression on the stump, you'll have to apply a tourniquet (see above under "Shock"). Amputated fingers can often be saved if they are surgically re-attached within six hours. First, cleanse the stump and apply a bulky dressing. Then, wash the severed finger, wrap it in sterile gauze, put it in a container inside an ice chest, and head for the nearest hospital. (*CAUTION!* Don't put the part directly on ice — the surgeon won't be able to re-attach it if it is frostbitten.) If you are offshore, contact the Coast Guard and request transport to a medical facility with replantation capabilities. If you are more than 10 or 12 hours from land, and helicopter transport isn't available, treat the stump like any other open wound.

### Puncture Wounds

Never ignore a puncture wound, no matter how trivial it may appear. Assume that the offending nail, splinter, or fish spine has driven bacteria and dirt deep into the tissues. It may even have punctured a blood vessel, nerve, tendon, or joint. Cleanse the wound thoroughly with antiseptic solution, and then cover it with antibiotic ointment and a bandage strip. If you haven't had a tetanus booster in 10 years, make sure you get one within 72 hours. (See section on "Venomous Marine Animals" for treatment of puncture wounds produced by the spines of venomous fish.)

### How To Remove a Fishhook

The string technique

1. Loop a 12-inch length of string around the curve of the hook, and wrap the ends around your index finger (see illustration).

2. Push down on the eye and shank of the hook with your free hand to disengage the barb.

3. Align the string with the shank's long axis. Then gently tug on the free ends of the string until it comes out through the entrance wound.

The Push and Snip Technique

1. If the barb is protruding through the skin, snip it off and back the hook out (see illustration).

2. If the barb isn't protruding, wash the skin around the wound with antiseptic solution, then numb it with an ice cube. Grasp the shank of the hook with a pair of needle-nose pliers and push the point of the hook through the skin.

3. Snip off or flatten the barb, then back the hook out.

### Splinters

Removing embedded splinters can be tougher than getting a ship out of a bottle. First, make sure you have good lighting. Press gently on the skin around the entrance wound to determine the orientation of the

splinter. Then, put your finger against the deep end of the splinter and push it toward the entrance wound. Grasp the exposed portion of the splinter with your tweezers and pull it out. Then clean and dress the wound. If you can't get it out, leave it alone. Soon it will fester and be expelled by the tissues.

**TWO WAYS TO EXTRACT A FISHHOOK**

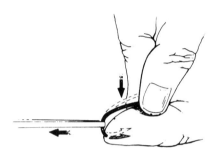

*the string technique*

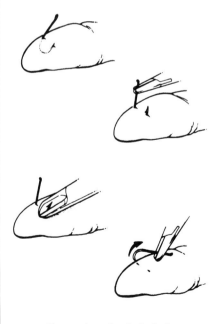

*the push and snip technique*

### Wet-to-Dry Dressings

Wet-to-dry dressings are a simple way to treat dirty wounds. Cover the wound with wet, sterile, gauze pads, and change them twice a day after they dry out. Wet-to-dries control infection by removing pus and necrotic debris.

## Contusions

Contusions are crush injuries to the skin and underlying fat and muscle that become swollen, painful, and discolored. A severe contusion of the thigh or buttocks can be complicated by a *hematoma*, a collection of blood within the muscle. Blunt trauma to the tip of a finger can cause a *subungual hematoma* (hematoma under the nail). **Treatment:** Rice is the key: *R*est, *I*ce, Compression, and *E*levation. Apply an ACE bandage to the contused limb from the base of the fingers or toes to above the contusion. Keep the limb elevated for 24 to 72 hours, apply ice wrapped in a towel for 15 minutes every two hours, and rest it as much as possible. Subungual hematomas hurt like the devil. Here's how to drain them:

1. Straighten one end of a paper clip.

2. Heat the tip of the clip over a flame. When it is red hot, press it through the discolored area of the nail until blood pours out of the hole you have made.

3. Apply a bandage strip after the bleeding stops.

## Strains

A strain ("pulled muscle" ) is an injury to the musculo-tendinous unit caused by over-stretching of the muscle or a sudden increase in the tension within the unit. When you overload a muscle, something has to give. Either the muscle itself tears, the tendon tears away from the muscle, or the tendon ruptures or tears away from its bony origin or insertion. A *Grade I strain* is simply the tightening you feel in a muscle while you're straining to lift a heavy object.

If you feel a tightening and then a pop, but can still move the injured part, you may have sustained a *Grade II strain*. Up to 50 percent of the muscle fibers are torn, and you can see and feel a defect in the muscle. If you feel a snap and hear a loud pop and can't contract the muscle, you likely have a *Grade III strain, i.e., a* complete rupture of the musculo-tendinous unit. **Treatment:** RICE (see above under "Contusions") will mini-

mize the bleeding, swelling, muscle spasm, and disability. First, splint the injured part and then put a soft pad over the injured muscle and secure it with an Ace bandage. Keep the limb elevated above heart level over the next 24 to 72 hours and apply ice for 15 minutes every two hours. After 48 hours, start soaking the injured part in a warm water bath. Gentle range-of-motion exercises help prevent shortening and weakening of the healing muscles. Grade I and most Grade II strains heal in a few days, more severe injuries require several weeks. A Grade III injury should be treated by a physician as soon as possible.

## Sprains

*Ligaments* are the thick, tough bands that stabilize the joints. When you slip on a slick deck and turn your ankle, the ligaments that support the ankle will tear either partially (mild or moderate sprain, Grade I or II) or completely (Grade III). The ankle becomes swollen, painful, and discolored. You may not be able to bear weight on it, and it may feel unstable. **Treatment:** RICE (see above under "Contusions") and splinting are the keys. Apply an ACE bandage or a splint to a sprained knee or ankle, and rest a sprained shoulder or elbow in a sling. Splint sprained wrists or hands in a "cock-up" splint by putting a balled-up pair of socks in the palm and splinting the wrist and hand to a long wooden or plastic slat. Sprained fingers should be buddy taped to the adjoining finger. Remove the splint or elastic bandage in 48 hours and start warm soaks and gentle range-of-motion exercises. Be patient — sprains take weeks to months to fully heal.

## Burns

Burns come in all varieties on shipboard — thermal, chemical, electrical, friction. The first step in treating a burn is to determine its depth, extent, and severity.

1. *Depth. First-degree burns* involve the *epidermis* (outer layer of the skin) only. The burned skin is painful and red. *Second-degree burns* extend to the outer portion of the dermis (deep layer of the skin). The burned skin is red or white, and blistered in areas. These are painful injuries. *Third-degree burns* destroy the epidermis and dermis and may extend to the fat, muscle, and bone. The skin is charred, or waxy and white; blood vessels can be seen

through translucent areas. The nerve endings are destroyed so these burns are painless. First- and second-degree burns are *partial-thickness* burns; third degree burns are *full-thickness* burns.

2. *Extent.* Estimate the extent of the burn using the "rule of nines" (see illustration).

3. *Severity. Minor burns* involve less than 15 percent body surface area (BSA). *Moderate burns* involve 15 to 25 percent BSA. *Major burns* are burns involving more than 25 percent BSA or serious burns of hands, feet, or genitals; burns with associated injury (e.g., fractures or head injury), or burns in patients with serious preexisting medical problems (e.g., heart disease or diabetes).

*Treatment*
*Minor and Moderate Burns.* First, wash the burn with mild soap and water. Use a cotton ball to gently remove dirt and debris, and scissors and tweezers to remove loose tissue. Then apply a 1/16-inch layer of silver sulfadiazine (Silvadene) cream (antibiotic ointment on facial burns), and cover the burn with an occlusive gauze dressing or Spenco 2nd Skin. Bandage fingers and toes individually, and leave burns of the face, neck, and genitals uncovered. Remove the dressing once or twice daily, wash the burn with mild soap, and reapply the burn ointment and dressing. Partial-thickness burns heal within seven to 10 days. A tetanus booster is recommended if more than five years has elapsed since the previous one.

*Major Burns.* Follow this sequence:

1. Remove the victim from the fire and strip off any burning or smoldering clothing.

2. Tend to the ABCs (see beginning of chapter).

3. Check for other injuries.

4. Replace fluid losses. Massive loss of plasma from extensive burns can rapidly lead to shock. If you can, start an intravenous (IV) line and administer Ringer's lactate solution according to this formula: 2-4 cc/kg body weight/% BSA burn Give one-half the amount in the first eight hours, and one-half in the next 16 hours. If you can't start an IV, and the victim is conscious, have her drink half a glass of

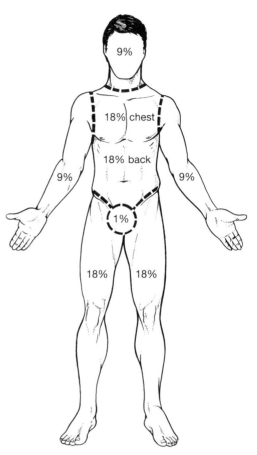

*rule of nines*

fluid (one-quarter glass for a child) every 15 minutes.

5. Radio for help.

6. Give pain medicine (by IV, preferably).

7. Wash the burns as described above. Cover extensive burns with clean sheets.

8. Keep the victim supine (prone if the burns are on the back) and warm while awaiting evacuation.

*Electrical Burns*
There is usually more than meets the eye in an electrical burn. You'll find an entrance and exit wound; what you won't see are the various degrees of thermal injury to the tissues traversed by the current, in proportion to their electrical resistance. Bone, muscles,

blood vessels, and nerves usually are most seriously injured. **Treatment:** First, remove the victim from the electrical source and administer CPR if necessary. Treat external burns as outlined above, and give the victim plenty by mouth or intravenously. Radio for medical assistance.

### Chemical Burns

Acids and alkali can cause deceptively deep burns. **Treatment:** Wash the exposed area with liberal amounts of water. Alkali can produce deep, destructive ocular burns, so irrigate the eyes *continuously* until the victim reaches a hospital if there has been eye exposure.

### Friction Burns

Every sailor has had a rope burn. They can range in severity from a mild abrasion to a deep burn. Treat friction burns the same as other thermal burns.

## Sunburn

Sunburn is an intense inflammatory response to ultraviolet radiation of wavelength 290 to 320 nm (ultraviolet B, or UVB). Your vulnerability to UVB is mostly a function of how much melanin you have in your epidermis. The more melanin you have, the darker you tan on exposure to sunlight and the less susceptible you are to sunburn. Your risk of sunburn is also determined by the time of day, time of year, atmospheric and surface conditions, and latitude.

Redness, itching, and exquisite pain start two to eight hours after sun exposure and peak in 24 to 36 hours. The skin may swell, blister, and slough. The redness fades over a period of one to four days, and the outermost layer of skin thickens and peels.

### Prevention

1. Stay out of the sun between 10 A.M. and 3 P.M., when UVR intensity is greatest.

2. Wear protective clothing: a visored hat, tight-weave, dyed, long-sleeve shirts, and long pants. Dry, tight-weave clothing blocks most UVR, but wet white clothing transmits nearly all UVR.

3. Use sunscreens liberally.

### Treatment

1. Take a cold shower or a dip in cool water.

2. Apply cold compresses, using a 50:50 solution of milk and ice water or Burow's solution.

3. Apply lotions such as Noxema or Cetaphil with 0.25% menthol.

4. Apply aloe vera gel.

## FRACTURES AND DISLOCATIONS

*"...the captain made a leap for the weather shrouds to get firm grip and not be washed away...but the sea and the ship's tremendous roll to leeward spun him over end for end— pitched him a somersault, still clinging to the lines. His head struck the steel bar at the foot of the shrouds...and cleft it open about a foot. A kneecap was knocked adrift, and he had other injuries. There he was, a dreadful sight, flung on his beam ends, blood gushing from his wounded head...a collarbone broken, unable to stand because of the leg injury, loss of breath, and a bellyful of sea water...Captain Miethe allowed himself to be helped to the little hospital down below.*

*Here he took command. The collarbone was no problem. The mate knew how to strap his shoulder up so that would mend.*

*As for the broken head, it was only skin and such: there was no fracture of that hard headpiece."*

Captain Alan Villiers, *War With Cape Horn*

I don't advocate belaying pin orthopedics. The safest approach to any fracture or dislocation on shipboard is to splint the injury until it can be tended by a physician. As long as bone ends are not protruding through the skin, and there is no sign of compromised circulation or nerve damage, definitive treatment can be delayed for a few hours. However, if you're in the Tasman Sea when your shipmate trips over the spinnaker pole and sustains a fracture-dislocation of the ankle, and his foot turns numb and pale, you will *have* to reduce the ankle in order to save his foot.

### An Orderly Approach to Skeletal Injuries

1. *Check the CMS.* CMS = Circulation, Motor function, and Sensation. Numbness, weakness, or diminished circulation in the extremity distal to (beyond) the fracture or dislocation means that displaced bone or fracture fragments are stretching or pressing on vessels or nerves. The victim may lose his hand or foot if you don't rec-

ognize and correct the problem. Here's how to check the CMS.

a. Circulation. Check the pulse at the wrist (just above the thumb side of the hand) or at the ankle (behind the inner knob), as appropriate. Then check the warmth and color of the fingers and toes. If they are cool compared to the uninjured side, and blue or pale instead of pink, the circulation is impaired.

b. Motion. Ask the victim to move the joints below the injury.

c. Sensation. Check for pain sensation by gently pinching the skin below the injury.

2. *Distinguish between bony injury and sprains or bruises.* Decide whether the injury is a fracture or dislocation or just a contusion or sprain. This is simple when the limb is grossly deformed or bone is protruding through the skin. If it isn't deformed, ask the victim to move the extremity. If he can move it through a normal range of motion, it's probably not fractured, and definitely isn't dislocated. Next, gently press on the bone, starting a few inches from the injured area. If it is fractured, it will be quite tender, and you'll feel *crepitus*, a grinding sensation caused by the bone ends rubbing together.

3. *Inspect the skin.* If bone is visible through an open wound, the victim has an *open fracture*. Open fractures are very serious injuries. They are usually contaminated with bacteria, and may be complicated by wound infection or osteomyelitis (bone infection).

## How to Reduce a Fracture

If the injured limb is not deformed, splint it in the position in which you find it. If it *is* deformed, the fracture is *displaced* and needs to be reduced to bring the fragments back into proper alignment. Reduction of a displaced fracture will relieve stretching and pressure on nerves and blood vessels near the fracture; reduce bleeding from the bone ends; prevent a closed fracture from becoming an open fracture; relieve pain; and enable you to splint the fracture.

### Open Fractures

Open fractures must be treated immediately. First, cover the wound with 4" x 4" gauze pads soaked in antiseptic solution and clean the skin around the wound with antiseptic solution. Then, reduce the fracture by pulling on the limb until the deformity is corrected. Cover the wound with a bulky dressing and immobilize the limb in a splint. Give cefadroxil, one gram immediately, and 500 mg every 12 hours, and arrange for evacuation.

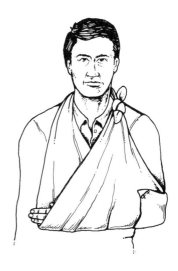

*sling construction*

## Splints

You can use a ready-made splint or you can improvise with an oar, gaff, fishing rod, magazine, charts, or any of a number of other shipboard items. Always keep these principles in mind when applying a splint:

- The splint should immobilize the joints above and below the fracture.

- Apply longitudinal traction to a fractured limb before applying a splint and splint dislocated limbs in the position in which you find them.

- The splint should be well padded, especially over bony prominences.

- The splint should provide some compression over the fracture site but should never impair the circulation.

## Common Upper Extremity Fractures

### Collar Bone (Clavicle)

You will note swelling, tenderness, and deformity over the clavicle. **Treatment:** Keep the arm in a sling (see illustration) until the victim can move the arm comfortably (seven to 10 days).

### Elbow

Fractures of the elbow are usually obvious. **Treatment:** Put the arm in a sling.

### Forearm

Either or both forearm bones (ulna and radius) may fracture following a direct blow to the area. **Treatment:** If the forearm is deformed and CMS is impaired, grasp the hand and pull gently but steadily on the limb until it looks straight and you can feel a strong pulse at the wrist. Then splint it and put the arm in a sling with the elbow flexed to 90 degrees.

### Wrist

If the injured wrist resembles an upside-down fork, it's fractured. But the absence of deformity doesn't mean that it's not fractured. **Treatment:** Immobilize the wrist in a *cock-up splint.* Have the victim hold a balled-up pair of socks in the palm of his hand and place his wrist and hand on a firm, 10-inch-long splint. Then wrap a three-inch elastic bandage around the hand from the knuckles to the upper forearm and put the arm in a sling. If the fingers are cold and blue, you may be dealing with a fracture-dislocation. Grasp the victim's hand as though you were going to shake hands and

pull straight out until the deformity is corrected. Then apply a cock-up splint.

### Finger Fracture

Fingers consist of three long bones, the *proximal* (closest to the hand), *middle,* and *distal phalanges.* They are frequently fractured on shipboard. **Treatment:** Reduce fractures of the proximal or middle phalanges by pulling on the finger until it looks straight. Then buddy tape the finger to the adjoining finger and encourage your patient to use the finger as normally as possible while the fracture heals.

### Fractures of the Spine

Falling out of a bosun's chair never hurt anyone, but those hard landings on the deck have caused more than a few *compression fractures* of the vertebrae and *fracture-dislocations* of the spine. The latter is usually associated with signs of spinal cord injury, i.e., weakness and loss of feeling below the chest or waist. **Treatment:** First, do a simple neurologic exam to rule out spinal cord injury. Have the victim raise his arms over his head against resistance and check his grip strength. Then have him flex his hips and knees and ask him to wiggle his toes. Check sensation by lightly poking both sides of his chest, his arms and hands, and his legs and feet with a pin. If you find no weakness or numbness, carefully log-roll him onto his side and thump over his spine from neck to tailbone. Localized tenderness suggests a fracture. Keep him immobilized until you can get him to a hospital.

### Pelvis, Hip, and Thigh

When the femur (thigh bone) is fractured, the thigh is swollen, deformed, and very painful, and the victim won't be able to move the injured leg. **Treatment:** Grasp the victim's foot and apply steady traction to the leg while an assistant applies counter-traction to the pelvis. When the thigh is straight, strap an oar, paddle, or spar from armpit to beyond the foot, and a shorter splint to the inner thigh from the groin to the foot (see illustration on page 364). Then put some padding under the knees to keep them slightly flexed. If you can't find a splint, strap the victim's legs together.

Hip fractures cause hip or groin pain. Pound the bottom of the victim's heel with your fist. If this produces pain in the groin, he probably has a hip fracture. Pain on movement of the leg and shortening and

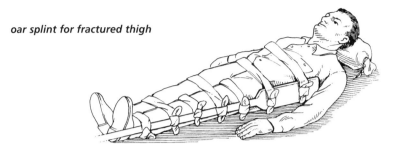

*oar splint for fractured thigh*

outward rotation of the leg are also signs of hip fracture. **Treatment:** Splint the leg as you would a fractured femur.

Pelvic fractures are rarely obvious. Put one hand over each iliac crest (the large bones on each side at waist level) and press toward the belly button. If this produces pain in the groin, or if there is tenderness to direct pressure over the iliac crests, groin, or pubic area, and if walking is impossible or difficult, the victim likely has a fractured pelvis. **Treatment:** Place some padding between her thighs and under her knees, then bandage her knees and ankles together.

Fractures of the pelvis, hip, and femur bleed internally, and are often associated with severe soft tissue injuries and shock. These people need to be transferred to a hospital.

### Kneecap

A contused kneecap will cause swelling and pain, but if you feel crepitus when you press down on the kneecap, it's probably fractured. **Treatment:** If there is no deformity, apply a cylindrical splint from groin to ankle and allow the victim to walk. If the kneecap is deformed, and the victim cannot straighten his knee, it may need to be surgically repaired. Apply a compression dressing (several layers of gauze and ABD pads secured with Kling gauze or an elastic bandage) and head for a hospital.

### Lower Leg

If you get thrown across the deck and slammed into the scuppers by a Southern Ocean greybeard, you may fracture your tibia (leg bone). Fractures of the upper tibia usually involve the knee joint, which may swell to the size of a mooring buoy. Frac-

tures of the shaft of the tibia are often angulated (bent out of alignment) and open, and the fibula (the smaller bone lateral to the tibia) is usually fractured also. **Treatment:** Pull on the ankle until the leg appears straight, then splint it. If bone is protruding from a wound, cleanse the wound with antiseptic solution and apply a sterile dressing before you reduce and splint the fracture.

### Ankle

If you find tenderness and crepitus when you press on the bony knobs on both sides of the ankles, you are probably dealing with a fracture and not a sprain. If the foot is discolored and bent at a weird angle, the ankle is fractured and dislocated. **Treatment:** Apply padding to the ankle and then secure a SAM splint to the bottom of the foot and up the back of the leg to the knee with an ACE bandage. If you don't have a SAM splint, place a pillow under the ankle and tape it across the front. If the ankle is dislocated, grasp the foot with the heel in your right hand and place your left hand over the top of the foot. Then pull out on the foot until the ankle snaps back into place. The victim will feel better immediately, and normal color will return to the foot as the circulation improves.

### Foot

If you fall off the bridge deck and land flat on your feet, you may fracture your heel or the metatarsals (long bones) of your feet. If your back hurts, you may have a compression fractures of the spine also. **Treatment:** Apply a large, soft dressing and ACE bandage to the heel and keep it elevated and iced. Wear wooden clogs or stiff-soled boots until metatarsal and big toe fractures heal.

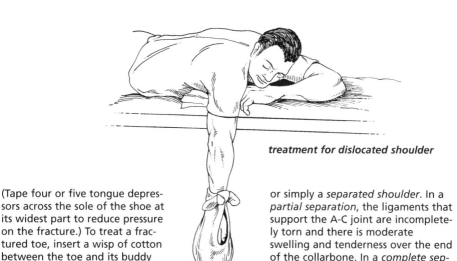

*treatment for dislocated shoulder*

(Tape four or five tongue depressors across the sole of the shoe at its widest part to reduce pressure on the fracture.) To treat a fractured toe, insert a wisp of cotton between the toe and its buddy and tape the two toes together.

## Dislocations

A dislocated joint is an orthopedic emergency. Blood vessels, nerves, muscles, and ligaments are stretched whenever a bone pops out of joint; the sooner the joint is reduced, the better.

### Shoulder

The shoulder can be levered out of joint by a backward force against an elevated arm, such as when you reach up to try to catch a jibing boom. The shoulder has a "squared off" appearance, the arm is held out from the body, and the victim can't place his hand on his uninjured shoulder. **Treatment:** 1. Have the victim lie face-down on the cabin top with the injured arm hanging down and attach 10 to 15 pounds of weight to his wrist with strips of cloth or gauze (see illustration above). The shoulder should slip back in joint within fifteen minutes. 2. Position the victim as above and sit or kneel next to him. Pull steadily on his upper arm until you feel the shoulder pop back into joint. After you have reduced the shoulder, place the arm in a sling and swathe for three weeks.

### Separated shoulder

If you trip over some uncoiled line and land on your shoulder, you may disrupt the acromio-clavicular (*A-C*) joint that joins the end of the collarbone and the shoulder blade (scapula). This is called an *A-C sprain,*

or simply a *separated shoulder*. In a *partial separation*, the ligaments that support the A-C joint are incompletely torn and there is moderate swelling and tenderness over the end of the collarbone. In a *complete separation*, the ligaments are completely torn and the end of the collarbone appears to ride high because it is no longer connected to the scapula. **Treatment:** Immobilize the shoulder in a sling until the pain and swelling subside.

### Elbow

A hard fall on an outstretched hand may drive the forearm bones backward out of the elbow joint. The elbow will be deformed; if you feel crepitus, it may be fractured *and* dislocated. **Treatment:** If the CMS is good, simply apply ice and put the arm in a sling. However, if you cannot feel a pulse at the wrist and the hand is turning blue, you must reduce the elbow in order to save the arm. Stand in front of the victim and apply steady longitudinal traction on the forearm while an assistant exerts countertraction on the upper arm. After the elbow is reduced, apply a compression dressing to the elbow and immobilize the arm in a sling for two weeks.

### Finger

Pull straight out on the digit with one hand and push against the base of the dislocated bone with the thumb of your other hand until the finger is reduced. Then buddy tape it to its partner for 10 days.

### Kneecap

Slowly straighten the knee while pushing inward on the kneecap. Once it's reduced, apply a long splint with the knee fully extended.

## HYPOTHERMIA AND COLD-WATER IMMERSION

*"The breaking seas made so much noise that I don't know just when in the night he died. I know he stopped moaning, and when daylight came I called to him to shake himself together, that day was coming after the long night. He made no answer, so thinking he must be asleep I called him again. I got no answer, and so I went to the bow to shake him up.*

*"He was dead—frozen stiff."*

James Brendan Connolly, *The Book of the Gloucester Fishermen*

Hypothermia is a drop in body temperature to below 95°. Unlike snakes and fish, humans and other mammals must maintain a nearly constant body temperature to survive. To do this, the body must balance heat production and heat losses. Body heat is lost through radiation, convection, and evaporation, and is generated by body metabolism. When the core temperature starts to drop, the body responds to the cold challenge by constricting blood vessels in the skin and muscles (creating a cold outer shell that insulates a warm internal core); shivering (which increases heat production up to 500 percent); inhibiting sweating (which limits evaporative heat losses); increasing its blood pressure, heart rate, and respiratory rate; and increasing the basal metabolic rate by increasing muscle tone throughout the body.

*Heat-Escape-Lessening-Posture*

## The Signs and Symptoms of Hypothermia

***Mild Hypothermia (temperature 90° to 95°)***
The victim is shivering, his speech is slurred, he moves slowly, and his skin is cool.

He may be confused and apathetic, and have difficulty handling sheets and lines, or holding navigational instruments.

***Severe Hypothermia (temperature below 90°)***
The victim is dejected and his skin is cold, blue, and mottled. He stops shivering and may hallucinate and act inappropriately, taking off his clothes or jumping in the water. His breathing and heartbeat slow. He becomes profoundly weak, his muscles become rigid, and he stops moving.

## Immersion Hypothermia

The good news about cold-water immersion is that you survive longer than you might think. That's also the bad news. Floating in ice water is not unalloyed pleasure. But as cold as you might feel on the outside, your core won't start to cool for at least 15 minutes, even in ice water. Once it does, however, your core temperature will plummet. After an hour and fifteen minutes, it will drop 86 degrees; at that point, you will likely lose consciousness and drown, or die of an irregular heartbeat. The average person can survive for 2.5 hours in 50° water, and for up to 12 hours in 68° water.

***Cold-Water Survival Techniques***
You lose body heat about 50 percent faster when you exercise in the water, so trying to swim for shore is rarely a wise move. But you may consider it if you are wearing a PFD and are within a half mile of shore. Generally, your best bet is to get as much of your body out of the water as possible by climbing up on the hull of your boat, if it is still afloat, or flotsam. You may feel colder out of the water, but you will cool much more slowly than you would in the water. If you can't get out of the water, limit skin exposure to the water by assuming the HELP (Heat-Escape-Lessening-Posture) position (see illustration). If you are with a group of people, huddle together and maximize upper body contact. And remember: a

powerful will to live is of supreme importance in cold-water immersion.

## Rescue and First Aid

A victim of mild hypothermia needs only some dry clothing, a blanket, and a hot, non-alcoholic drink. He'll recover quickly.

If the victim has been in cold water for more than 20 minutes, is lightly dressed, and has been swimming or treading water, treat her for profound hypothermia. Be very gentle with her. Her heart is cold and irritable, and rough handling can precipitate ventricular fibrillation, a lethal heart arrhythmia. If you allow her to move under her own power, or try to rewarm her, she may suffer from "afterdrop" (a sudden drop in core temperature when cold blood surges back to the heart from cold muscles). Carefully move her into the cabin, remove her wet clothing, gently dry her, and cover her with blankets. Then, apply hot packs to her neck, armpits, trunk, and groin, or have two people get undressed from the waist up, get into bed with her, and maintain close chest-to-chest contact. If you can start an intravenous line, infuse warmed (104°) intravenous fluids (Normal Saline or Ringer's Lactate solution). If she is alert, offer her a hot, nonalcoholic drink and something to eat while awaiting evacuation.

## VENOMOUS MARINE ANIMALS

Over the eons sea creatures have evolved a daunting array of cruelly efficient ways to defend themselves. He who enters Neptune's realm risks being injured or killed by fish that are armed with spines, fangs, sharp snouts, and venomous fins and tentacles.

### Stingrays

*"While exploring Chesapeake Bay, Captain John Smith hopped out of a boat barefoot onto a stingray, which had the temerity to stick its dart into his leg. It was a foolish act on the part of the fish, for Smith was no common man. Instead of trying to get clear of it, Smith held it to the bottom with his foot, drew his hanger, hacked the fish to pieces and ate several collops raw."*

Horace Beck, *Folklore and the Sea*

Stingrays range in size from several inches to 12 feet. They have flattened, diamond-shaped bodies with wing-like pectoral fins (see illustration) and long, whiplike tails equipped with one to four venomous stings, each one to 17 inches long. The sting has two rows of backward-pointing barbs and two grooves on its undersurface containing venom glands. Its sheath also contains venom glands and is coated with venom and mucus. After a stingray burrows into a sandy or muddy bottom in search of food, with

*Stingray with close-up of barb*

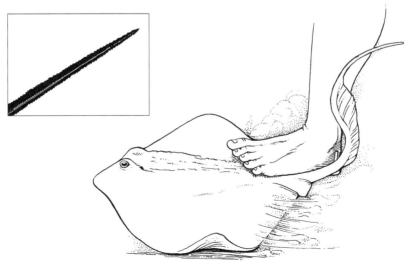

only its eyes, breathing hole, and tail showing, it's all but invisible. If you happen to step on it, its tail will reflexively snap up and bury the spine in your skin, causing a deep puncture wound or laceration. The sheath ruptures, and venom is released from the venom glands and driven deep into the wound, along with mucus and bacteria. The sheath and spine may remain in the wound as well.

**Symptoms:** Excruciating pain spreads throughout the limb, peaks in one hour, and then slowly subsides over the following six to 48 hours. The wound may bleed profusely. It will turn blue and then red, and swell as the venom destroys fat and muscle. Dizziness, fainting, weakness, nausea, and anxiety are common symptoms, but the victim may also experience vomiting, diarrhea, sweating, twitching of the muscles in the injured limb, pain in the groin or armpit, muscle cramps, headache, irregular heartbeat, and (rarely) paralysis, seizures, and death.

**Treatment:** Wash the wound thoroughly with salt water and remove as much debris as possible. Then immerse the limb in water as hot as you can stand for 30 to 90 minutes, or until the pain is relieved. (Heat inactivates the venom and relieves pain). While it is soaking, re-examine the wound and remove any remaining debris. Pack the wound open with sterile gauze and cover it with a sterile dressing. Reduce the risk of infection by taking TMP-SMX, one double-strength tablet every 12 hours, or ciprofloxacin, 500 mg every 12 hours, for two days.

## Scorpionfish

These are the most dangerous venomous fish in the sea. They hide in nooks and crannies on the sea bottom and blend into the background. Their dorsal, anal, and pelvic fins are tipped with 18 venomous, stingray-like spines that they can bury deep into the flesh of an unsuspecting swimmer or diver.

Scorpionfish, which include members of the Zebrafish, Scorpionfish, and Stonefish genera, are abundant in the waters off the Florida Keys, southern California, and Hawaii, and in the Gulf of Mexico.

**Symptoms:** Scorpionfish stings cause memorable pain that peaks in 60 to 90 minutes and wanes over a period of 6 to 12 hours. The wound swells and turns blue while the surrounding area becomes red and warm. Eventually, blisters form and the area around the wound becomes numb. The flesh may become infected, die, and slough off after a few days. Additional symptoms may include nausea, vomiting, weakness, headache, sweating, loss of consciousness, restlessness, delirium, shortness of breath, tremors, convulsions, paralysis, heart failure, ventricular fibrillation, and death.

**Treatment:** Scorpionfish envenomations are treated exactly like stingray injuries. An antivenin is available for stonefish envenomations from the Commonwealth Serum Laboratories in Melbourne, Australia. **Prevention:** It's hard to avoid accidental contact with an invisible fish, but try.

## Sponges

Sponges are animals, believe it or not. They don't bite, but they can give you an unpleasant rash, called "sponge diver's disease." The Hawaiian or West Indian *fire sponge* is a yellow-vermilion-orange sponge found in the waters off Hawaii and the Florida Keys. The *red moss sponge* is native to northeastern U.S. waters.

**Symptoms:** Contact with one of these sponges can cause a poison-ivy-like rash, swollen joints, malaise, nausea, fever, chills, muscle cramps, and dizziness. Spicules of silica or calcium carbonate that puncture the skin produce a burning rash.

**Treatment:** Wash the affected skin thoroughly with soap and water and remove spicules with adhesive tape. Apply dilute (5%) vinegar or 40% to 70% isopropyl alcohol compresses for 10 to 30 minutes four times a day, then cover the affected area with moisturizing cream or 1% hydrocortisone ointment. Use diphenhydramine to control itching. If a severe, blistering, rash develops, take prednisone every morning according to the following schedule: 80 mg days 1 through 3; 60 mg days 4 through 7; 40 mg days 8 through 10; 20 mg days 11 and 12; and 10 mg days 13 and 14.

## Coelenterates

Coelenterates (hydroids, jellyfish, sea anemones, and corals) are spineless, radially symmetrical animals with special stinging cells (*nematocysts*) lining their tentacles or mouths. Nematocysts consist of cysts filled with venomous fluid and a coiled thread.

When triggered, the thread fires out of the cyst like a tiny harpoon and strikes with sufficient force to penetrate skin and inject venom. Millions of nematocysts line the tentacles of jellyfish and Portugese men-of-war.

## Hydroids

Contact with the *feather hydroid* causes only mild skin irritation and itching. If you touch *fire coral* (which is not a true coral) you will suffer immediate burning pain, followed 30 minutes to several hours later by an itchy, red, bumpy rash or hives.

The *Portugese man-of-war* cruises tropical waters throughout the Atlantic and Pacific Oceans (see illustration). It has an iridescent purple sail and a 5- to 16-inch bladder filled with carbon monoxide and nitrogen monoxide which floats on the surface. Hanging down from the sail are a number of long (up to 100 feet), clear, nematocyst-studded tentacles. When an unsuspecting fish or human bumps into one of these nearly invisible tentacles, the impact triggers the release of hundreds of thousands of nematocysts.

**Symptoms:** Getting stung by a Portugese man-of-war can only be compared to being flogged with a cat-o'-nine-tails. First you will feel intense, burning pain locally or throughout your body. Then painful, itchy cross-hatching lines of red bumps and welts appear wherever nematocysts contacted your skin. These tentacle tracks may blister, bleed, ulcerate, become hyperpigmented, and leave permanent scars. You may have nausea and vomiting, weakness, anxiety, sweating, vertigo, runny eyes and nose, shortness of breath, headache, muscle spasms, kidney failure, a sense of impending doom, shock, and (rarely) death.

## Jellyfish

Numerous species of jellyfish populate Atlantic, Caribbean, and Pacific coastal waters. They look like Portugese men-of-war, but instead of having a sail that floats on the surface, jellyfish have a bell that floats below the surface, from which hang up to twelve hundred tentacles. The bells range from an inch to more than six feet across, and the tentacles may be over 120 feet long. Jellyfish venom is among the most potent toxins in nature. *Chironex fleckeri*, the feared box-jellyfish of northern Australian and western Indo-Pacific waters, can kill a human in 30 seconds. The stings of other jellyfish generally cause severe, burning pain and scattered bumps, wheals, or cross-hatched lines of welts on the skin. Severe envenomations may cause muscle spasms, vomiting, dizziness, confusion, chest pain, headache, shock and, not surprisingly, nightmares.

## Sea Anemones and Stony Coral

*Sea anemones* are flower-like coelenterates that grow on coral reefs and in shallow tidal pools. Their sting is mild, but they cause a rash that can become ulcerated and infected.

Ancient mariners believed that *stony corals* could ward off lightning, whirlwind, shipwreck, and fire. I'd rather be caught in a

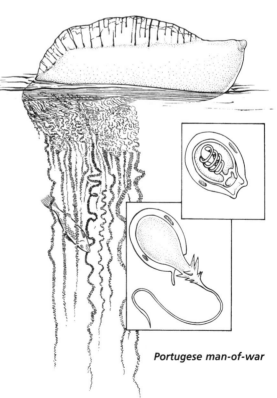

*Portugese man-of-war*

whirlwind than be flayed with the pointed horns and razor-sharp edges of this creature's calcareous outer skeleton. The cuts and abrasions cause burning pain, and itchy, red wheals that fade after an hour or two. This is called "coral poisoning." The wounds may blister, or become infected, ulcerate and slough, and take up to six weeks to heal.

*Treatment* of coelenterate envenomations:

1. Remove tentacles, using gloved hands or instruments.

2. Rinse the skin thoroughly with salt water. (*WARNING:* Fresh water and rubbing trigger nematocysts.)

3. Soak exposed skin in a 5% vinegar solution or 40% to 70 % isopropyl alcohol for 30 minutes (or until the stinging stops) to deactivate nematocysts. Add a few pinches of meat tenderizer to the vinegar or alcohol if you have any. Cover sea nettle stings with a baking soda slurry for 10 minutes and then scrape it off.

4. Remove residual nematocysts by applying shaving cream to the area and scraping the skin with a razor. Or make a paste with mud, baking soda, flour, or talc and scrape it off with a sharpened shell or knife.

5. Gently dry the skin and apply 1% hydrocortisone ointment.

6. Immobilize the injured part and keep it elevated above heart level.

## Echinoderms

### Crown of Thorns Starfish

This large starfish inhabits the Indo-Pacific area and the eastern Pacific from the Galapagos to the Gulf of California. Its surface is covered with sharp, venom-tipped spines that inflict painful wounds that bleed and swell. Multiple stings produce nausea, vomiting, swollen lymph nodes, numbness, and paralysis.

**Treatment:** Immerse the wound in hot water until the pain subsides, then irrigate it and remove debris.

### Sea Urchins

Sea urchins are nautical porcupines. They are covered with long, sharp, brittle spines that break off after puncturing the hide of a snorkeler or diver. Some of the spines carry venom, and small pincers scattered among the spines grab onto prey and continue to bite and inject venom as long as the victim moves. The spines penetrate deeply and cause wicked, burning pain, redness, swelling, and bleeding. Multiple spine punctures may cause nausea, numbness, weakness, abdominal pain, paralysis, difficulty breathing, fainting, muscle and joint pains, and (rarely) shock and death. One or two months after the original injury, a *granuloma* (a round, fleshy mass) may appear.

**Treatment:** Immerse the wound in hot water for 30 to 60 minutes to relieve pain, and carefully remove embedded spines. Spines can cause deep infections and granulomas, and those that puncture joints, nerves, or tendons will require surgical attention. (The body will resorb a thin spine in a few weeks; you can leave an inaccessible thin spine alone if it is not in or near a joint, nerve, or blood vessel.) Cleanse the wound thoroughly with antiseptic solution and, if the wound is deep, take TMP-SMX or ciprofloxacin twice daily for two days to ward off infection.

### Sea Cucumbers

These bottom-dwellers are found in deep and shallow waters world-wide. They can cause mild skin irritation or eye inflammation if the eyes are exposed to the toxin.

**Treatment:** Wash the exposed skin with 5% vinegar solution or isopropyl alcohol. Eye injuries should be evaluated by an ophthalmologist as soon as possible.

## GASTROINTESTINAL PROBLEMS

### Abdominal Pain

Diagnosing the cause of abdominal pain always reminds me of Winston Churchill's description of Russia as "a riddle wrapped in a mystery inside an enigma." Fortunately, as the ship's doctor, you don't have to make a precise diagnosis. Your job is simply to decide whether the patient is well enough to remain on board, or so sick that he needs to be transported to a hospital posthaste. While evaluating your patient, keep these potential causes of abdominal pain in mind.

### Problems Inside the Abdomen:

1. *Blockage of hollow organs.* The intestine, the gallbladder and its duct, and the ureters can, and frequently do, become blocked. When they do, the result is colicky pain and (usually) nausea and vomiting.

2. *Peritoneal inflammation.* The peritoneum is the thin membrane that lines the abdominal cavity. When blood, urine, digestive juices, or bacteria spill onto the peritoneum from a diseased or injured abdominal organ, it becomes inflamed. Appendicitis and cholecystitis often lead to peritoneal inflammation.

3. *Vascular problems.* A tear in the aorta in the chest (aortic dissection) or a leaking abdominal aortic aneurysm (stretching and weakening of the wall of the aorta) can cause terrific abdominal pain. A blood clot in the major artery to the intestines (mesenteric thrombosis) will cause pain and shock as the bowel dies.

### Problems Outside the Abdomen

1. *Chest problems.* Pneumonia, pneumothorax (collapsed lung), pulmonary embolus, esophageal spasm, and heart attack can all cause pain in the abdomen.

2. *Abdominal wall strain or injury.*

3. *Pelvic problems.* Ectopic pregnancies, ovarian cysts, and pelvic infections can be perceived as abdominal pain.

4. *Metabolic Problems.* Uncontrolled diabetes, spider and scorpion bites, and heavy-metal poisoning can cause abdominal pain.

After you have examined your patient, see if his illness falls into one of the following symptom groups:

1. *Abdominal pain only.* Pain is the only symptom early in the course of appendicitis, large bowel obstruction, kidney stone, and gall bladder attack.

2. *Central abdominal pain.* Simple intestinal colic, early appendicitis, early small bowel obstruction, pancreatitis, early mesenteric thrombosis, and heart attack.

3. *Severe central abdominal pain and shock.* Pancreatitis, mesenteric thrombosis, heart attack, ruptured aortic aneurysm, ruptured spleen, or ruptured ectopic pregnancy.

4. *Pain, vomiting, and distension (no rigidity).* Intestinal obstruction.

5. *Abdominal pain, constipation, distension.* Large bowel obstruction.

6. *Severe abdominal pain, collapse, and rigidity.* Perforation of the stomach or duodenum by a peptic ulcer; rarely, perforation of the gall bladder or appendix.

7. *Right upper quadrant pain and rigidity.* Gall bladder attack.

8. *Right lower quadrant pain and rigidity.* Appendicitis, kidney infection, ovarian cyst, or tubal pregnancy or infection.

9. *Left lower quadrant pain and rigidity.* Diverticulitis, kidney infection, ovarian cyst, or tubal pregnancy or infection.

### Some Common Causes of Abdominal Pain

#### Appendicitis

The appendix is a wormlike thing that hangs down from the colon. Infection of the appendix is called appendicitis. If an appendectomy is not performed within 24 to 48 hours or so, the appendix becomes gangrenous and ruptures, leading to peritonitis, a dangerous condition. The signs and symptoms of appendicitis, in their usual order of onset, include pain (upper or mid-abdominal first), then moving to the right lower quadrant; nausea, vomiting, and loss of appetite; tenderness in the right lower quadrant; rigidity of the abdominal muscles over the appendix; distension in the right lower quadrant; fever (low grade); and constipation. There is but one treatment for appendicitis: surgery.

#### Gallbladder Attack

*Gallstone (biliary) colic* begins with agonizing pain in the upper mid-abdomen or right upper quadrant when a gallstone plugs the cystic duct. The pain radiates to the right shoulder blade, and the patient usually vomits and breaks into a cold sweat. The attack usually subsides after the gallbladder expels the stone in one to four hours. In *acute cholecystitis* the gallbladder can't rid itself of the stone and becomes inflamed and infected. The right upper quadrant pain is aggravated by breathing, coughing, or pressure over the area. There will be a low-grade fever, slight elevation of the pulse, and nausea. There is no effective treatment for gallbladder colic outside of a hospital. Acute cholecystitis is a surgical emergency.

### Intestinal Obstruction

An intestinal obstruction is blockage of the normal movement of food and liquids through the intestinal tract. *Small bowel obstruction* is usually caused by scar tissue from previous abdominal surgery or by bowel becoming trapped in a hernia. *Large bowel obstruction* can be caused by hard stool in the rectum, by tumors, diverticulitis, or by twisting of a segment of the colon (volvulus).

Intestinal obstructions are bad news. When the intestine becomes blocked, the bowel distends with fluid and gas and loses

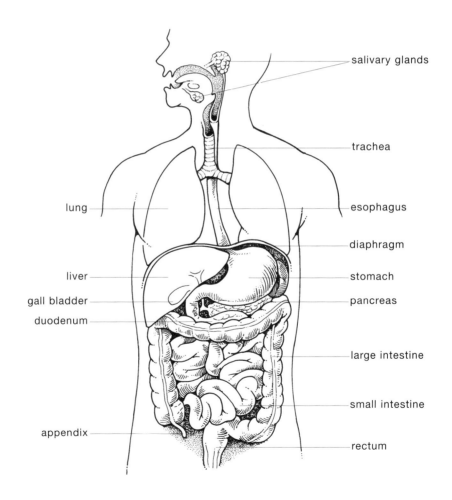

salivary glands

trachea

lung

esophagus

diaphragm

liver

stomach

gall bladder

pancreas

duodenum

large intestine

small intestine

appendix

rectum

*digestive system*

its ability to absorb water and nutrients. The patient starts to vomit and becomes severely dehydrated. He will die if the obstruction is not relieved.

Signs and symptoms include severe, cramping, midline abdominal pain; nausea and vomiting; abdominal distention; and abdominal rigidity and tenderness and shock if the obstruction is not relieved within several hours. The patient needs to be hospitalized.

### Intestinal Hernia

An intestinal hernia is the protrusion of bowel through an abnormal opening, usually in the groin. A *reducible hernia* is a lump in the groin or abdomen that the patient is able to push back into the abdominal cavity. If the hernia becomes acutely *incarcerated*, it will be painful and tender, and he won't be able to reduce it. If the blood supply to the incarcerated bowel is compromised, the hernia is said to be *strangulated*. The patient will exhibit all the signs and symptoms of bowel obstruction. **Treatment:** First, place the patient head down in a supine position and apply a warm compress over the hernia for a few minutes. Then gently try to push it back into the abdominal cavity. If you can't reduce it, or if it is tender, head for a hospital.

### Hemorrhoids

A hemorrhoid is a varicose vein in the anus. An *internal hemorrhoid* may cause bright red blood on the stool or toilet paper; if it prolapses (passes out of the anal canal), however, it may become infected or thrombosed, become very painful, and bleed profusely after defecation. *When* an *external hemorrhoid* becomes thrombosed it will turn blue and become firm and tender. **Treatment:** Warm sitz baths three times a day are the mainstay of treatment. If the thrombosed hemorrhoid has been there for more than 48 hours and is not tense or tender, warm sitz baths and a laxative may do the trick. If the thrombosis has been present for less than 48 hours, and is very painful, surgery may be indicated to give immediate relief. If your patient is incapacitated, he may beg you to excise the clot. Here's how you do it: Have him assume the prone position, then anesthetize the skin over the hemorrhoid with an ice cube. Then use a No. 10 scalpel to make an elliptical incision

in the skin over the hemorrhoid and remove the clot with a forceps. Tuck the corner of a small piece of gauze in the wound to control bleeding, and then apply a pressure dressing over it. Remove the dressing and gauze when the patient takes his first sitz bath eight to 12 hours later. If bleeding, pain, or uncontrollable itching become a problem, head for a hospital.

### Gastroenteritis

Gastroenteritis is the inflammation of the stomach and intestines, usually secondary to viral or bacterial infection. It causes vomiting and diarrhea which often lead to dehyration. **Treatment:** Mild dehydration can be corrected by drinking fruit juices, diluted ginger ale or cola drinks, or a sports drink. If you've had protracted diarrhea and feel lightheaded or dizzy, you need a solution with a higher electrolyte content. You can make up a good oral electrolyte solution by adding 1 tsp. of salt and 8 tsp. of sugar to a liter of water. Drink 8 oz. of the solution, plus as much plain water as you can, every 60 minutes. It's safe to eat staples such as rice, bananas, cereals, lentils, and potatoes, but avoid fats, dairy products, caffeine, and alcohol. You'll know you're rehydrated when you start passing large amounts of clear urine. Loperamide (Imodium) helps to control diarrhea, and promethazine (Phenergan) suppositories put the lid on vomiting. If you have a fever and blood in the stool, you need medical attention.

## GYNECOLOGIC PROBLEMS

Keep the following points in mind when a woman of child-bearing age complains of abdominal pain or vaginal bleeding:

1. A woman whose menstrual periods are usually regular is probably pregnant if more than four weeks have elapsed since her last menstrual period (LMP).

2. Abnormal vaginal bleeding is a complication of pregnancy until proven otherwise. A missed or late period followed by pelvic pain or abnormal vaginal bleeding should also be assumed to be a complication of pregnancy.

3. Any woman with lower abdominal pain or vaginal bleeding may have an ectopic pregnancy.

Emergency Medicine

## Early Pregnancy Complications

*Ectopic Pregnancy*
When a fertilized egg implants in the ovary, the fallopian tube, or some other extra-uterine site, an ectopic pregnancy results. If undetected, an ectopic pregnancy will eventually rupture, and bleeding will lead to shock and death. Women with a history of prior ectopic pregnancy, pelvic surgery, pelvic inflammatory disease, tubal ligation, therapeutic abortion, or use of an intrauterine device are at higher risk of ectopic pregnancy. Ectopic pregnancies typically announce their presence, after one or two missed periods, with crampy pain on one side of the pelvis, followed often by mild vaginal bleeding. After the tube ruptures, the pain will spread across the entire lower abdomen. On examining the patient, you may or may not detect abdominal rigidity and tenderness. **Treatment:** If you detect signs of shock, follow the instructions on pages 350 and arrange immediate evacuation to a hospital.

*Spontaneous Abortion (Miscarriage)*
Genetic defects, uterine abnormalities, or hormonal imbalances may lead to a miscarriage, usually prior to the eighth or ninth week of pregnancy. The initial symptom is mild, intermittent, or continuous vaginal spotting leading to heavy bleeding with passage of clots and tissue. Midline, cramping pain generally starts after the bleeding (unlike ectopic pregnancy, where pain precedes bleeding). In *threatened abortion*, there is minimal bleeding, while in *incomplete abortion* the bleeding is heavy until the fetus and placenta are expelled from the uterus. The abdomen remains soft and non-tender. **Treatment:** Instruct the woman with a threatened abortion to remain at bed rest and to abstain from sexual intercourse until she sees her obstetrician. She should use pads rather than tampons. An *incomplete abortion* may cause continuous vaginal bleeding until the uterus is emptied by dilation and curettage (D&C).

## Pelvic Pain in the Nonpregnant Woman

*Mittelschmerz*
Mittelschmerz (from the German, "middle pain") is pain associated with ovulation. It's a mild to moderately-severe, one-sided pain that comes in the middle of the menstrual cycle and lasts less than 24 hours. **Treatment:** Aspirin, ibuprofen, or naproxen are all effective.

*Ovarian Cyst*
A ruptured ovarian cyst causes many of the signs and symptoms of ectopic pregnancy or spontaneous abortion. Any woman in this condition needs immediate medical attention.

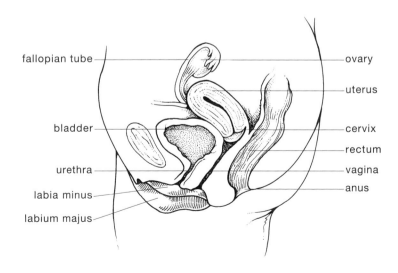

fallopian tube

ovary

uterus

bladder

cervix

rectum

urethra

vagina

anus

labia minus

labium majus

## CHILDBIRTH AT SEA

*"Death and taxes and childbirth! There's never any convenient time for any of them."*

Margaret Mitchell, *Gone With the Wind*

*figure 1*

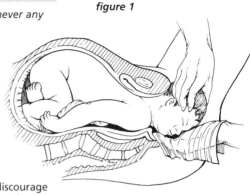

When a woman in labor tells you she wants to push the baby out, check to see if her cervix has dilated. Place her on her back with her heels drawn up to her buttocks and her knees apart. Then, using lubricant and, ideally, sterile gloves, place two fingers into the vagina and feel the baby's head. If you can feel a rim of tissue around it, the cervix is not fully dilated and you should discourage mother from pushing. If you can sweep your fingers all around his head and not feel any tissue, the cervix is fully dilated and mother is ready to deliver! If her perineum is bulging, or the baby's scalp is visible, delivery is imminent. Follow these steps:

1. Have mother empty her bladder. Then place her on her back, tilted slightly to one side, on a clean sheet. Elevate her buttocks on a couple of pillows, then spread her legs far apart with her heels near her buttocks.

*figure 2*

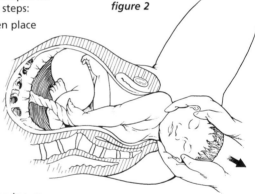

2. At the start of each contraction, ask mother to take a deep breath and hold it while she bears down. She can rest between contractions. If she expels feces, clean the perineum with mild soap and water.

3. As the head moves down during each contraction, gently stretch the perineum. When the baby's eyebrows emerge, place one hand on the baby's head and drape your other hand with a clean cloth. Ask mother to pant or breathe through her nose while you use your draped hand to gently lift the chin as the head emerges (fig. 1).

*figure 3*

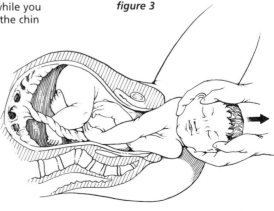

4. Check baby's neck to see if it is encircled by the umbilical cord. If it is, try to slip it over his head. If it is too tight, place two clamps on the cord, cut between them, and remove it. (If you don't have clamps, tightly tie two lengths of string around the cord before cutting it.)

5. Wipe baby's face and aspirate his mouth and nose with a bulb syringe to clear his airway. (Use your finger to clear the airway if you don't have a bulb syringe.)

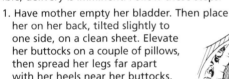

6. As mother pushes, place a hand on either side of the baby's head and push *down* gently until the anterior shoulder comes out (fig. 2). Then, pull *up* until the other shoulder is delivered. Now slide one hand down over baby's back and support his head as the rest of his body emerges (fig. 3).

7. Suction his airway again, and stimulate him to breathe by rubbing him vigorously with a towel. After he starts to breathe, wrap him in a warm blanket and place him on mother's abdomen to keep him warm.

8. Double clamp the umbilical cord near the baby's abdomen, then cut it with sterile scissors or knife.

9. Check mother's perineum for lacerations, and apply pressure with gauze bandages to any areas of active bleeding.

10. Check to see if the placenta has separated. If it has, the umbilical cord will be longer and there will be a gush of blood. Have mother push the placenta out while you pull gently on the umbilical cord.

11. Massage mother's uterus until it contracts and becomes firm and bleeding stops.

To reduce the risk of post-delivery infection, give mother cefadroxil, 500 mg every 12 hours for two days.

## URINARY PROBLEMS

### Kidney Stones

Only a man who has passed a kidney stone can truly say he understands the suffering a woman endures during childbirth. When the urine becomes supersaturated with calcium, oxalate, uric acid, or other minerals, crystals form that can grow and coalesce into stones. Stones can result from excessive excretion of insoluble minerals, a deficiency of natural inhibitors of stone formation, or urinary tract infection with certain types of bacteria. Dehydration increases the risk of stone formation in people with a predisposition to kidney stones.

**Signs and Symptoms:** When a stone starts to move the ureter toward the bladder, it causes excruciating pain in the abdomen or flank, nausea and vomiting, and a powerful urge to urinate. The patient will pace restlessly back and forth, holding one hand on his flank, and sweat profusely. As the stone progresses down the ureter, the pain will move into the testicle (groin or vulva in a woman). The urine may be pink-tinged.

**Treatment:** The good news about kidney stones is that 90 percent of them pass spontaneously. The bad news is that they can take an hour or longer to do so. Kidney stone colic requires industrial strength pain medication. If you can, start an intravenous line and infuse Ringer's lactate at 125 cc/hour, and give your patient Nubain, 10 mg IV. Give additional 5 mg injections of Nubain as necessary to control pain. (Nubain can be given intramuscularly in the same doses if you don't have intravenous access.) If you don't have Nubain, give him one or two oxycodone with acetaminophen (Tylox) tablets, or the strongest oral narcotic analgesic in your medicine chest. A Phenergan suppository will help to control nausea. When he passes the stone, his pain will suddenly disappear. If he does not pass it within a few hours, bring him to the nearest medical facility.

### Urinary Tract Infections

Urine is a great growth medium for bacteria and they don't have far to travel up a woman's short (1.6 inch) urethra to set up housekeeping. The average male urethra, by comparison, is eight inches long. Consequently, men have far less urinary tract infections than do women. Bladder bacteria populations grow exponentially after a woman has sexual intercourse, and "honeymoon cystitis" commonly follows an episode of intense sexual activity.

**Signs and Symptoms:** Painful urination, frequent urination, and lower abdominal pain are the usual signs of urinary tract infection. Pain in the flank or back can be caused by simple cystitis (bladder infection), but when that symptom is accompanied by fever, nausea, and malaise, the patient probably has acute pyelonephritis (kidney infection). If she has a vaginal discharge, her symptoms may be caused by a vaginal or pelvic infection.

**Treatment:** An otherwise healthy woman whose symptoms are of brief duration can be treated with 2 TMP-SMX double-strength tablets (Bactrim DS) as a single dose. A woman who has a history of urinary tract infections, diabetes, prolonged symptoms, or signs of pyelonephritis, and any man with a urinary tract infection, should be given TMP-SMX, 1 double-strength tablet twice daily for 10 days, cefadroxil (Duricef), 1 or 2 tablets twice daily for 10 days, amoxicillin, 500 mg 3 times daily for 10 days, or ciprofloxacin (Cipro), 250 to 500 mg every 12 hours for 10 days. High fever, vomiting, and persistent flank pain are all grounds for hospital admission.

### Urinary Retention

Urinary retention is the inability to fully empty the bladder. In men, it may be caused by phimosis or paraphimosis (see below),

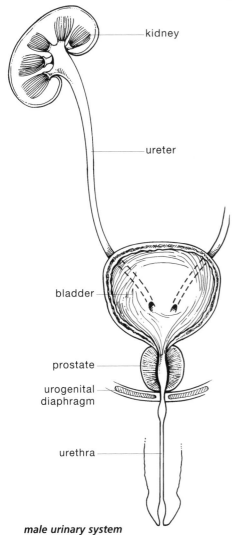

kidney

ureter

bladder

prostate

urogenital diaphragm

urethra

*male urinary system*

urethral stricture (narrowing of the urethra secondary to venereal infection), or an enlarged prostate gland. In women it can be caused by stretching and weakening of the bladder by chronic, infrequent voiding. In men or woman, it may be secondary to multiple sclerosis or diabetes, or a side effect of various medications, including antihistamines, Sudafed, and other "cold remedies," antispasmodics, amphetamines, and some of the older antidepressants.

**Signs and Symptoms:** The patient will be restless and complain of having a full bladder, despite frequent efforts to void. Her bladder will be distended, firm, and tender.

**Treatment:** The sound of running water is a powerful stimulus to the act of urination. Create this sound with a deck bucket or bilge pump, and allow a few minutes for the stimulus to work its way through the reflex arc from ears to brain to bladder. If this technique fails, you will have to catheterize the patient (if you have been trained to do so and have a catheter) or bring him to a hospital. Back pressure from a full bladder can damage the kidneys.

### MALE GENITAL PROBLEMS

As you can see from looking at the illustration on the next page, the male reproductive system is a rather complicated affair. All manner of things can go wrong with it, including the following:

### Balanoposthitis

Balanoposthitis is inflammation of the head of the penis (the glans) and the foreskin. When you retract the foreskin, you'll find the glans and inner surface of the foreskin to be tender, foul smelling, reddened, and covered with purulent material.

**Treatment:** Cleanse the area three or four times a day with mild soap and water and dry it thoroughly. Apply an antifungal cream, such as nystatin or clotrimazole, morning and night. If it appears as though the area is infected, take cefadroxil, 500 mg twice a day for one week. Chronic infection may be an early sign of diabetes mellitus.

Emergency Medicine

## Phimosis

Phimosis is the inability to retract the foreskin, usually due to infection, poor hygiene, or scarring. If the urethral opening becomes blocked, urination becomes impossible.

**Treatment:** Dilate the opening in the foreskin with a hemostat so that the patient can pass urine. Circumcision may be required later.

## Paraphimosis

Paraphimosis is the inability to pull a swollen, retracted foreskin back over the glans. This is a serious problem because the constricting band of foreskin can act like a tourniquet, blocking flow of venous blood out of the penis and arterial blood into the penis. If untreated, the penis can become gangrenous, mummify, and fall off.

**Treatment:** Try to compress the swollen foreskin and pull it back into its normal position. If you can't reduce it, you'd better lay a course for the nearest hospital.

## Fractured Penis

Trauma during sexual activity can cause a tear in the membrane that envelopes the erectile tissue. The patient will hear a "cracking" sound, and his penis will be swollen, tender, and discolored.

**Treatment:** If you are within reasonable distance of a hospital, have the patient hold an ice bag over the injured part while you take him there. If you are in a remote part of the world, keep him at bed rest with ice packs for 24 to 48 hours, then switch to moist heat and pressure dressings. Ten percent of patients will have permanent penile deformity and impaired sexual performance.

## Testicular Torsion

Normally, the lining of the testicle is attached to the back wall of the scrotum. A testicle that is not so attached is liable to twist and kink the spermatic cord and the testicular artery and vein. This can happen during strenuous physical activity, or it may happen during sleep. **Signs and Symptoms:** The patient will complain of sudden, severe pain in the lower abdomen, the groin, or the testicle, and he may have nausea and vomiting. The testicle and the scrotum on the involved side are swollen, tender, and firm. You may be able to see that the testicle lies high and horizontally in the scrotum.

**Treatment:** The twisted testicle will die if its blood supply isn't restored quickly. Arrange for immediate transport to a hospital.

## Epididymitis

Epididymitis is infection (usually bacterial) of the epididymis, the cordlike structure at the back of the testicle which stores sperm. **Signs and Symptoms:** The patient will complain of the gradual onset of pain in the

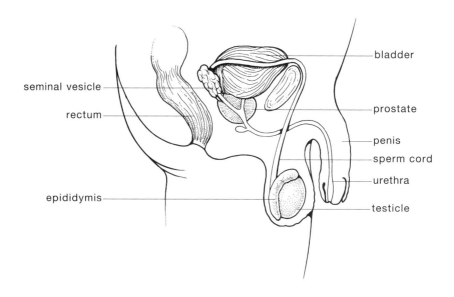

seminal vesicle  
rectum  
epididymis  
bladder  
prostate  
penis  
sperm cord  
urethra  
testicle

lower abdomen, groin, and testicle, and he may have frequent, painful urination as well. There will be local tenderness over the back of the testicle at first, but later you will only be able to feel a large, tender scrotal mass. It may be impossible to distinguish epididymitis from testicular torsion at this point.

**Treatment:** Bed rest with scrotal elevation in an athletic supporter, ice, and ibuprofen, 600 mg 4 times a day for 24 to 48 hours is standard treatment for epididymitis. In men under 40 years of age, the infection is likely to be due to gonorrhea or chlamydia, both of which are sexually transmitted diseases. They should receive tetracycline, 500 mg 4 times a day for 10 days, as well as amoxicillin, 3 grams as a single dose. Men over 40 should be treated with TMP-SMX, 1 double-strength tablet every 12 hours for 10 days. If there is any possibility that the patient has testicular torsion, bring him to the hospital.

## HEART ATTACK

A heart attack is an inconvenient thing no matter when or where it strikes. If you or one of your ship's company are visited with one while navigating the Magellan Strait or the Gulf Stream during hurricane season, it can be downright unpleasant. You'll need to recognize it for what it is and do what you can to stabilize the patient before arranging medical evacuation.

Heart attack, angina pectoris, and sudden death are the three most common manifestations of *coronary artery disease*. When the coronary arteries that supply blood to the myocardium (heart muscle) are blocked by cholesterol deposits, *myocardial ischemia* (insufficient blood flow) may result. The blood supply, which may be adequate at rest, cannot supply the myocardium with the extra oxygen-rich blood it needs when it has to work harder, as during physical exertion. Myocardial ischemia may cause *angina pectoris* or *acute myocardial infarction* ("heart attack").

Angina is a feeling of heaviness, squeezing, or pressure under the sternum lasting for 5 or 10 minutes. It may radiate to the neck, shoulders, or arms, and is usually brought on by exertion or emotional upset, and subsides with rest or nitroglycerin.

Acute myocardial infarction happens when a blood clot or spasm of a coronary artery causes prolonged ischemia and the myocardium infarcts (dies). Most heart attacks occur when the patient is at rest, and in the morning.

The victim may complain of a severe, crushing or squeezing pain under the sternum or all across the chest and upper abdomen that radiates down the arms or into the throat, neck, back, or jaw. He may describe it as the most excruciating pain he has ever experienced (one patient told me it felt like his testicles were on his chest and an elephant were standing on them), or he may try to tell you that it is just a bad case of indigestion.

It may feel like a severe angina attack, but it doesn't subside with rest or after taking nitroglycerin. Nausea, vomiting, shortness of breath, and cold sweats are prominent symptoms. His skin may be cold and clammy, his face ashen, and his lips and nail beds blue. His pulse may be rapid and irregular, and he may have a sense of impending doom. On the other hand, up to 20 percent of myocardial infarctions are painless. An older person may complain only of sudden shortness of breath, weakness, palpitations, or confusion.

### Treatment

Help your patient into a berth and place several pillows under his back so that he is in a semi-sitting position. Open the scuttles to let fresh air into the cabin, and loosen any restrictive clothing. If you have nitroglycerin tablets, put one under his tongue. Give an additional tablet every five minutes until he gets relief, up to a total of three tablets in 15 minutes. If the nitroglycerin relieves the pain, he probably had an angina attack. If not, assume that he is having a heart attack. Give him one aspirin tablet and reassure him and make him comfortable while you arrange for evacuation to the nearest hospital.

## THE SHIP'S MEDICINE CHEST

Whether you are a weekend cruiser or a circumnavigator, you should have a medical kit on board. Stock it with the items listed below that are appropriate to the specific needs of your crew, the medical skills of the best-trained individual on board, and the anticipated length of your voyage. Store the kit in a readily accessible place on your boat in a large tackle box so that you can easily transfer the kit into a survival craft if you need to abandon ship. And replace used items and dated medications after each cruise.

### Wound Care Materials

bar soap

antiseptic solution, two 4-oz bottles

latex surgical gloves, sterile and unsterile, various sizes

1% silver sulfadiazine cream (Silvadene), 400-gram jar

bulb irrigating syringe, 60 cc

2 20-cc syringes with 20-gauge needles

Vaseline gauze packing, 1/2" x 50 yds

antibiotic ointment, two 1-oz tubes (Neosporin, Bacitracin)

15 Adaptic dressings, 3" x 3"

24 sterile dressing pads, 4" x 4"

10 Kerlix or Kling roll bandages, 4" x 5 yds

8 Surgipads, 8" x 10", or ABD pads, 8" x 8"

2 rolls waterproof adhesive tape, 1" x 5 yds

8 Bioclusive or Tegaderm transparent dressings, 2" x 3" or 3" x 3"

Spenco 2nd Skin

surgical staples (Precise Five-Shot, 3M)

50 bandage strips (Band-Aids), 1" x 3"

20 skin-closure strips, 1/4" x 3"

20 skin-closure strips, 1/2" x 3"

compound benzoin tincture, 2 oz

4 sterile eye pads

Q-tip cotton swabs

silver nitrate sticks

(Store dressings and bandages in plastic bags or a watertight plastic container.)

*Bar soap:* Use to clean abrasions and superficial cuts and burns.

*Antiseptic solution:* Chlorhexidine (Hibiclens), Povidone-iodine (Betadine), and benzalkonium chloride are powerful germicides that should be used to clean open wounds.

*Silver sulfadiazine cream* is a topical antimicrobial used on burns to prevent infection.

*Bulb irrigating syringe:* can be used to irrigate wounds or to flush foreign matter from the eyes.

*Syringes and needles* are for irrigating wounds.

*Antibiotic ointment:* Dab a little on abrasions and cuts before applying a dressing. It's good for facial burns, too.

*Adaptic pads:* These nonadherent pads can be applied directly to a wound and won't stick.

*Sterile dressing pads:* Use them to clean or dress wounds. Their wicking action absorbs blood and fluids.

*Kling and Kerlix bandages:* These stretchy gauze rolls are terrific for securing splints, or as the final layer in a bulky wound dressing.

*Surgipads/ABDs* are ideal for applying pressure to bleeding wounds and as burn coverings.

*Bioclusive or Tegaderm dressings* are transparent dressings that keep out water and dirt, but not air. You can apply them to small cuts, abrasions, and blisters.

*Spenco 2nd Skin* is a hydrogel that makes a soothing dressing for open blisters and burns.

*Skin closure strips:* Take your pick from Steri-Strips (3M), Butterflies (Johnson & Johnson), Coverstrip Closures (Biersdorf), or Curi-Strips (Kendall). These easy-to-apply paper strips can be used to close most small lacerations. They'll stick better if you apply *tincture of benzoin* to the wound edges first.

*Silver nitrate sticks* are used to cauterize nose bleeds.

## Medications

100 analgesic tablets (aspirin, acetaminophen, or ibuprofen)

60 dimenhydrinate (Dramamine) tablets,
50-mg tablets, or

20 meclizine tablets, 25-mg tablets

*12 Transderm Scop patches

30 diphenhydramine (Benadryl) tabs, 25-
mg tablets

30 Imodium (loperamide) tablets

*10 Promethazine (Phenergan) 25-mg rec-
tal suppositories

*30 Tylox (oxycodone with acetaminophen)
tablets

*Nalbuphine (Nubain) 10 mg/cc, 10-cc
multi-use vial

60 melatonin 3-mg tablets

*100 penicillin VK 250-mg tablets

*100 trimethoprim-sulfamethoxazole
[TMP-SMX] (Bactrim DS) 800/160-mg
tablets

*100 tetracycline 500-mg tablets

*20 cefadroxil (Duricef) 500-mg tablets

Maalox or Mylanta, 20 oz

Caladryl lotion, 8 oz

12 Domeboro tablets

500 Vitamin C 500-mg tablets

lotrimin (clotrimazole) cream 1%, 30 g

hydrocortisone 1% cream, 60 g

hydrocortisone 1% ointment, 60 g

*fluocinonide (Lidex) 0.05% cream, 30 g

*30 prednisone 20-mg tablets

Cavit, 7-gram tube

Desitin ointment

5 one-liter bags of Ringer's lactate intravenous solution

intravenous tubing; intravenous catheters,
16 and 18 gauge, 5 of each

isopropyl alcohol, 40 to 70% solution

milk of magnesia

Eucerin with PABA

*30 Nitrostat (nitrogylcerine) 0.3 mg sub-
lingual tablets

aloe vera gel, 1 bottle

*2 EpiPen Autoinjectors

*Otic Domeboro

personal medications

*Prescription medicines. Show this list to
your physician. She can tailor it to your particular medical needs.

*Dramamine, meclizine* and *Transderm Scop*
patches are seasickness remedies.

*Diphenhydramine* (Benadryl) is an antihista-
mine used to treat allergic reactions, itching,
nausea, and insomnia.

*Imodium* tablets control diarrhea.

*Promethazine* suppositories control vomiting
and seasickness.

*Tylox* is a potent narcotic analgesic. Take
one or two tablets every 4 to 6 hours for
severe pain.

*Nalbuphine* is a potent narcotic analgesic.
Inject 10 mg into the shoulder muscle (del-
toid) every 3 to 6 hours for severe pain.

*Melatonin* is nature's sleeping pill.

*Trimethoprim-sulfamethoxazole, tetracycline,
cefadroxil, and penicillin vk* are antibiotics.

*Caladryl* dries and takes the itch out of poison ivy rashes. *Domeboro* tablets can be
used to make Burow's solution, an astrin-
gent, drying solution for poison ivy rash.

*Vitamin C* tablets will prevent scurvy, a
potential problem for castaways.

*Lotrimin cream* kills athlete's foot, jock itch,
and vaginal fungi.

*Hydrocortisone* is a steroid anti-inflammatory agent used to treat itchy, inflamed rashes.
Use hydrocortisone cream for weepy rashes,
and hydrocortisone ointment for dry rashes.

*Fluocinonide cream* is a potent steroid anti-
inflammatory preparation used to control
severe rashes. *WARNING*: Fluocinonide can
cause skin atrophy when applied to the face
or between the fingers or toes. Use a hydrocortisone preparation in these areas.

*Prednisone* is a powerful anti-inflammatory
steroid.

*Cavit* is a dental paste for emergency dental
repairs.

*Desitin ointment* contains zinc oxide. It is an
excellent physical sunblock and it helps to
heal skin fissures, cracks and ulcers.

*Isopropyl alcohol* can be used to treat jellyfish stings.

*Milk of magnesia* is an old standby for constipation.

*Eucerin with PABA* is a great moisturizing
lotion for dry skin and salt sores.

*Aloe vera gel* is an antibacterial agent and
emollient that is excellent for burns, abrasions, cuts, and dermatitis.

An *Epipen Autoinjector* is essential if you or any of your shipmates has a history of severe insect sting reactions.

*Otic Domeboro* is a 2% acetic acid solution in Burow's solution used to treat swimmer's ear.

## Miscellaneous

4 rubberized (ACE) bandages, 3" and 6"

4 instant cold packs

cravats

30 large safety pins

12 tongue blades

tweezers

hemostats, 2 straight and 2 curved

No. 3 stainless steel scalpel handle

Nos. 10, 11, and 20 scalpel blades, 3 of each

scissors

single-edge razor

pliers

moleskin

thermometer

pen light

magnifying glass

SAM splint

air splint

aluminum splint

enema kit

splinter forceps

blood pressure cuff

stethoscope

water-purification tablets (Potable Aqua, Globuline, Halazone)

Foley catheters, 14- and 16-Fr with 30-cc balloon, one of each

surgical lubricant

2 nasal tampons

2 pregnancy test kits

A compendium of your medical history (including family and personal history, operations, immunizations, allergies, list of prescription medications, a copy of your latest EKG, and name and phone numbers of physicians)

A copy of this book or, better, *The Onboard Medical Handbook*

*Rubberized bandages* are indispensable for wrapping sprains, securing splints to fractured limbs, and applying compression dressings to bruised muscles and large wounds.

A *cravat* is a triangular muslin bandage that you can use to make a sling or turban bandage, or to secure splints to fractured limbs.

*Safety pins* can be used as fishhooks, to hold your glasses together if you lose a screw, keep the airway open in an unconscious person, close gaping wounds, drain blisters and abscesses, remove splinters, and secure bandages, splints and slings.

*Tongue blades* are ideal for applying ointment to abrasions, rashes or burns, and make good temporary splints for fractured or dislocated fingers.

*Needle-nosed pliers* are handy for removing fishhooks.

*Moleskin* can be applied over blisters.

The *SAM splint* is a versatile, light, padded, malleable splint for fractured limbs.

*Air splints* are comfortable and easy to apply.

An *enema kit* may be one of your most treasured items on a long offshore cruise.

*WARNING*: Readers with chronic medical problems or a history of drug allergy, as well as all pregnant or breast-feeding women, should consult their physicians before taking any of the medications recommended in this book.

# WEATHER

## GENERAL WEATHER STRATEGIES

Meteorology is the scientific study of the atmosphere, embracing both weather (conditions at specific points or areas at a specific time) and climate (annual average or long-term conditions in the overall atmosphere). Marine meteorology is the study of atmospheric conditions over coastal and ocean areas.

Meteorology is divided into two main disciplines: analysis (observation) and prognosis (forecasting). Forecasts are based on the data collected during analysis.

**Analysis.** You can collect present-time meteorological data directly by observing local weather conditions. Sometimes you can use these observations for short-term local forecasts. You should also use, whenever available, the complex analytical data collected by the National Weather Service (NWS) and other government agencies from sophisticated sources, including automated offshore weather buoys and earth-orbiting satellites. This far-reaching data is used for both local forecasts and synoptic (large area) forecasts.

**Forecasts.** Forecasts cover specific geographic areas and project conditions to specified times in the future. Short-term marine forecasts cover a six- to 24-hour period and do not provide an adequate basis for long-term plans.

Long-term forecasts cover from 24 hours to 10 days and occasionally longer. Forecast accuracy decreases with time, so if you were given the choice of relying on one 48-hour forecast or two successive 24-hour forecasts, the two 24-hour prognoses would probably be the better choice.

The NWS uses multiple variables, nonlinear equations, and large amounts of data to produce a forecast. Even these sophisticated analyses and computer models can estimate only the likelihood of future conditions; they can't predict with certainty. The farther out in time a computer model extrapolates, the larger the uncertainty. You should use long-term forecasts beyond 72 hours to indicate the general trend of weather patterns rather than specific conditions in your location. You can identify the sources of weather forecasts in the "Resources" section of this chapter, which begins on page 413.

## Inshore/Offshore

The weather information you use depends on whether a substantial portion of your voyage will be coastal (within 25 miles of land) or offshore (more than 25 miles from land). This distinction is important because weather occurring where land and water meet can be quite different from open-ocean weather, even when both locations are under the influence of the same general weather pattern. These weather variations occur because land and water adsorb and radiate heat at different rates. Heat exchange plays a very important role in the formation of weather conditions. Marine weather forecasts often specify whether they're for coastal or offshore waters. Be careful to use the right one.

Keep in mind that even the best coastal forecasts can't include the effects of local terrain — for instance, a cliff-lined shore or a narrow current-filled river mouth — that can have powerful influences over local conditions. Use your local observations to augment a coastal forecast.

### Phases of a Voyage

When planning your weather strategy, it is helpful to divide your trip into three phases: pre-departure, en route, and pre-arrival.

**Pre-departure.** During the pre-departure phase, the key decisions are whether and when to leave port. For a daytrip, this decision is based in large part on current local conditions such as wind and seas at a harbor entrance, wind strength and direction relative to the coast, and tides and currents. You can use this data to gauge your ability to gain sea room and to maneuver safely. When you're heading out for another area, you should also consider reported conditions and local forecasts for areas you expect to reach a few hours to a day later.

Prior to departure on a voyage of more than a day's duration, you should also obtain 24-, 48-, 72-, and 96-hour projections and review various sources of weather information including broadcasts, surface and upper-air weather charts and, if possible, satellite images. (A discussion of the various types of weather charts follows later in this chapter.) Remember that weather is likely to be more dynamic during the change of seasons. Conditions can evolve and intensify more rapidly in fall and spring. To determine a good "weather window" for departure, you should always try to time your departure based on the most recent forecasts.

**En route.** While en route on a prolonged voyage, your weather strategy shifts to finding the most efficient and comfortable track for your vessel. It's important to think about "the big picture" and to obtain synoptic analyses and forecasts. You need to study weather patterns that are hundreds and even thousands, of miles away to determine what type of wind and seas they will bring and whether you can plot a course to avoid rough conditions.

**Pre-arrival.** When your destination is a day or two away, your focus should again be on coastal and local conditions — this time, to determine the safest way to make port at a desirable time. Consider not only coastal weather, but also how winds, waves, and tides will interact with coastal geography at your destination. Consider the probable sea state in areas of shoaling (at the Continental Shelf or near shore) and possible wind anomalies caused by prominent land masses. Consider also the possibility of fog when there is a significant temperature difference between the air and water.

## Weather Routing

To make the most of the abundant weather information (analysis and prognosis) available today, some commercial mariners and offshore yacht racers and cruisers hire professional shore-based weather routers. A router analyzes government and private weather data using various computer models. Then, you are given a package that typically contains weather prognoses for a week or more, including surface and upper-air weather charts, ocean current analysis (if appropriate), custom wind and sea state forecasts, and a suggested route based on your vessel's performance profile. Depending on the path and duration of your voyage, the router may also provide updates while you are at sea and propose alterations to the suggested route. A list of professional routers appears in the "Resources" section.

You can also do your own routing onboard. To approach the sophistication of professionals, you need a single-sideband radio or a satellite communication system to receive raw weather data, as well as an onboard computer and software that processes weather data, wind strength, barometric pressure, and your vessel's performance characteristics. The software then suggests a route that will allow your vessel to cover the distance between selected points in the shortest possible time.

## WEATHER SYSTEMS

Air near the earth's surface tends to move from areas of high pressure to areas of low pressure. The winds (and waves) that affect mariners are attributable mainly to that movement. In the absence of powerful local factors, a large difference in pressure between the highs and lows (a steep gradient) produces strong winds; a small difference (usually indicated by steady or slowly changing atmospheric pressure in your area) produces weak winds.

Pressure differentials are usually created in the first instance by the uneven heating of air. When air over a warm surface is heated, it expands and becomes lighter. It rises and the pressure over this warm area decreases. The process over a cold surface is reversed. There, the cooled air near the surface becomes heavier, contracts, and sinks. At higher levels, air moves horizontally to fill the space vacated by the sinking air. This adds to the total air mass over the cold region and increases the atmospheric pressure there.

Through this process heat is redistributed between warmer and colder regions. If this were a simpler world, a single circulating cell would be operating in each hemisphere. Rising warm air from the low pressure equatorial belt would flow at high altitudes toward the poles, where it would be cooled and sink to the surface in the high pressure polar regions and then flow south near the surface back toward the equatorial low.

In the real world, the process is much more complicated, mainly because the earth is spinning. The spin creates the Coriolis force, which induces the wind to curve to the right in the Northern Hemisphere and to the left in the Southern Hemisphere. The warm, polar-bound air from equatorial regions cools enough in comparison to surrounding air that it tends

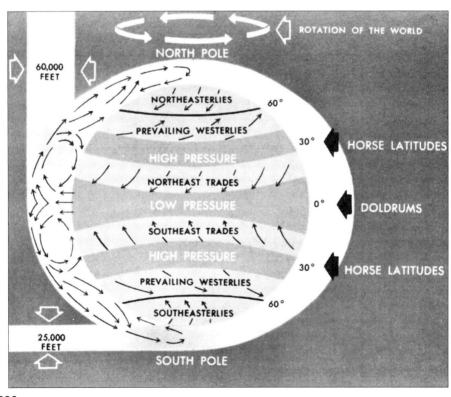

to sink when it reaches the vicinity of about 25 to 35 degrees of latitude, where the pressure is semi-permanently high. Likewise, the cold, equator-bound air from polar regions warms enough by the time it reaches the vicinity of 50 to 60 degrees of latitude that it tends to rise, creating a semi-permanent belt of low pressure there. So, in fact, there are three circulating cells in operation in each hemisphere, with separate prevailing wind patterns in each. At the surface, winds flowing from the east (the trade winds) prevail in the low latitude cell, while in the midlatitude cell, westerlies prevail. This entire pattern tends to shift north and south with seasonal changes.

To complicate things further, this prevailing pressure and wind pattern is subject to interruption, especially in the temperate, midlatitude region. A variety of factors there contributes to the frequent formation of transient high and low pressure systems that generally sweep eastward through the region. Because of the Coriolis force, winds tend to swirl clockwise around high-pressure centers and counterclockwise around lows in the Northern Hemisphere. This temperate region is also a common meeting place of warm air masses formed in lower latitudes and cold air masses formed in higher latitudes. The weather within each type of air mass has distinctly different characteristics. Fronts form at the boundary between differing air masses — cold fronts where the cold air mass is advancing on the warm mass, and warm fronts where the relatively warm air is advancing. Differing types of weather typically form along these frontal boundaries.

## Air Mass Weather

Air masses often cover large areas of the earth's surface with huge domes of air having fairly homogeneous temperature and humidity. They derive their character from the region where they're formed: Those formed over polar land regions tend to be cold and dry, for example; those over tropical water are likely to be warm and moist.

When air masses migrate away from their source region — which they often do — the weather associated with them is determined not only by their moisture and heat content, but also by the contrast in tem-

perature between the air and the surface they're passing over. In fact, the designation of an air mass as cold or warm is taken from the air's temperature in relation to surface temperature.

An air mass that's colder than the surface below is called a cold air mass. The air rises as it's heated by the warmer surface, and the rising (convective) currents bring instability to the area that can translate into vertically developed cumulus cloud formations and gusty wind at the surface. This instability is often accentuated during afternoon hours of maximum surface warmth and is diminished during relatively cold nights and early mornings.

In contrast, stability often characterizes the air in a warm air mass, in which the surface is colder than the air. The surface cools the air just above it, and vertical currents are not likely to form. When the air contains a high amount of moisture, low stratus-type clouds with horizontal development are likely to form, possibly accompanied by rain. As in cold-air masses, the daily heating and cooling of land beneath a warm air mass can affect its weather, as well. Because water heats and cools more slowly than land, the impact of daily temperature oscillations is less pronounced over offshore waters.

## Prevailing Weather Systems

Two semipermanent surface features control North Atlantic weather—the Icelandic Low and the widespread subtropical high known as the Bermuda or Azores High. The Icelandic Low is a region of low average atmospheric pressure (997 Mb) that is centered near Iceland for most of the year. Its pressure is lowest in winter when its center lies to the southwest of Iceland and its circulation is large enough to embrace the coast of northwestern Europe.

In summer, the Icelandic Low is relatively weak and its pressure is higher — around 1009 Mb. Then the Azores/Bermuda High strengthens and spreads. The center of this subtropical high remains to the south or southwest of the Azores throughout the year, but its average central pressure is somewhat higher in July (1025 Mb) than in January (1020 Mb). The pressure on its north side also rises in summer when the Icelandic Low is weak.

Weather

During spring (April and May), a ridge of high pressure often builds and extends northeast from the Azores in response to seasonal heating of the Northern Hemisphere. This process causes the prevailing west wind to gradually shift more to the southwest. From June to August the high pressure pattern is fairly constant. In late September and October, the subtropical high migrates farther south in the North Atlantic as heat is lost from the Northern Hemisphere, and this shift allows low-pressure systems to intrude more frequently.

The dominant weather feature along North America's West Coast is another subtropical high — the North Pacific High. In summer, it is centered north and east of Hawaii and its position is an important factor when choosing a route to the Hawaiian Islands. Its mean central pressure reaches a maximum of about 1026 Mb in July. The high promotes a general clockwise weather rotation in the North Pacific, bringing northwest winds along the U.S. coast from Puget Sound to Mexico. In the fall, the high moves southeast and shrinks in size, while the Aleutian Low strengthens and deepens over the Gulf of Alaska and the Bering Sea.

## Weather Along Fronts

The cold fronts formed at the leading edge of an advancing cold air mass can bring some dramatic, but usually quickly

## Weather Map Symbols

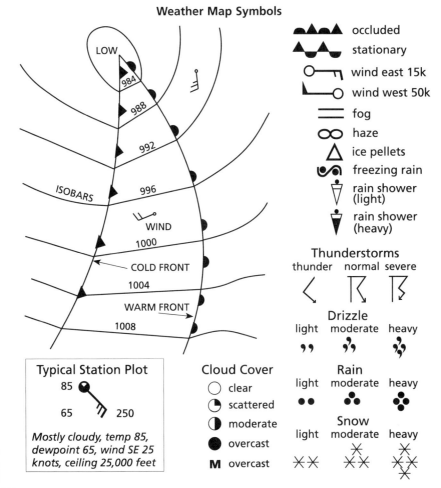

passing, conditions. The pressure is higher on the cold-air side of the front because the air there is more dense and heavy. The steeply sloped wedge of heavier cold air undercuts the warm air and lifts it up. If the rising warm air is stable, the result can be moderate vertical cloud formation and steady precipitation. If the lifted warm air is unstable, though, squalls and thunderstorms can punctuate the precipitation along the front. Squall lines can also form some 50 to 300 miles ahead of a fast-moving cold front. Conditions after a cold front passes also vary with stability — the stability of the cold air. When the advancing cold air is stable, clear skies are likely to follow the front's passage. When it's unstable, numerous clouds and scattered showers are possible.

The weather along warm fronts behaves in a different way. The advancing warm air rides up over the retreating cold air, but climbs up a slope that is much more gradual than the cold front wedge. The cloud and precipitation pattern can spread out ahead of the front for over 500 miles, in contrast to the relatively narrow band of special weather along cold fronts.

### Recognizing Cold Fronts

A cold front introduces a high-pressure area and its associated cooler, drier air. During the passage of a cold front, the barometric pressure can fall dramatically, creating a "V" pattern on the readout of a recording barograph (a barometer that includes a stylus that marks a paper-covered drum). Once the front has passed, the pressure will often rise rapidly.

In the Northern Hemisphere, the wind will shift clockwise around the compass, from east-southeast to south-southwest, before a cold front. Strong, gusty north-northwest winds will often follow behind the front.

The clouds accompanying a cold front are cumulus in nature and, although some may ride 50 to 100 miles ahead, most are found close to the actual front. The cloud pattern is not as regular as with a warm front. The time interval between the clouds' first appearance and the passage of the front are usually shorter (measured in hours rather than days) than with a warm front. Small cumulus clouds often appear just after the passage of a cold front due to

instability in the atmosphere, as mentioned above.

The temperature will remain fairly constant before a cold front arrives but will often fall rapidly behind the front, sometimes at rates of 5° to 10° F per hour.

The dew point will hold steady or rise slightly as a cold front approaches. Then it will likely fall quickly, sometimes even faster than the temperature, as cold, dry air moves in behind the front.

Showers at the cold front usually occur only in close proximity to the front. During winter in midlatitudes, precipitation may change from rain to snow and then snow flurries behind a cold front.

### Recognizing Warm Fronts

A warm front introduces a low-pressure area with its warmer, and usually moister, air. The barometric pressure will usually drop at the approach of a warm front, and then level off once the front has passed. When a warm front precedes a deep depression (an area of particularly low pressure indicating a severe storm), the pressure may fall as rapidly as 3 Mb per hour.

In the Northern Hemisphere, the wind will shift from east-northeast, to east-southeast, and to south-southwest as a warm front approaches and passes.

Clouds appear in the following order before a warm front: cirrus, cirrostratus, altostratus, nimbostratus, and stratus. These clouds will usually break up and may even clear out as the warm air moves in with its greater capacity to hold moisture. The temperature will rise, often dramatically, with the approach of a warm front, then level off after it passes.

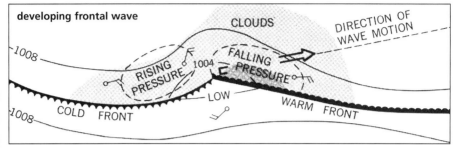

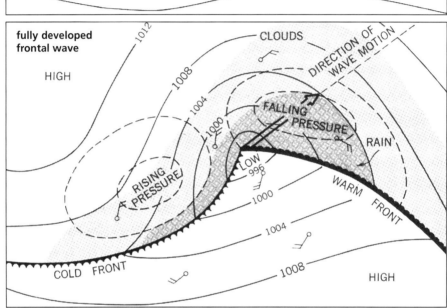

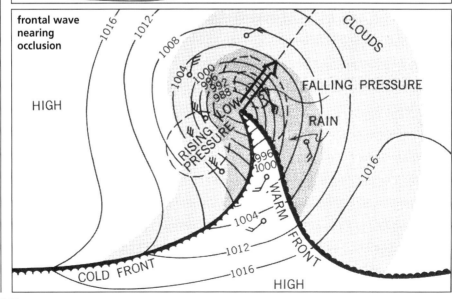

As a warm front approaches, the dew point will rise and the separation between the temperature and dew point will diminish. At the passage of the warm front, humidity will reach nearly 100 percent near the surface.

Precipitation usually precedes the passage of a warm front and is produced by middle and low clouds: altostratus, nimbostratus, and stratus. Precipitation is normally widespread and heavy. During winter in midlatitudes, precipitation starts as snow and often changes to sleet, freezing rain, and finally rain. The precipitation usually ends with the warm front passage.

## Stationary Front

Sometimes, weather systems stall and a front will stop moving forward or will oscillate back and forth. A stalled front is called a stationary front. Near a stationary front, the weather is often gray and dull with precipitation. Rain and snow may persist for days and changes in barometric pressure, wind, cloud, temperature, and dew point are usually slight. There will be little change until new developments in the upper-level airflow get the weather system moving again.

## Occluded Front

An occluded front forms where a faster moving cold front overtakes and combines with a warm front. The barometric pressure normally falls with the approach of an occlusion and rises with its passage. However, pressure may become steady for periods depending on whether the associated low-pressure system is deepening.

If you are in the Northern Hemisphere and located west of the occlusion, the wind will back from east-southeast, to east-northeast, and finally to north-northwest. If you are east of the occlusion, it will veer from east-southeast, to south-southeast, to south-southwest, and finally to west-southwest or west-northwest.

You'll usually find precipitation on both sides of an occluded front. The clouds associated with an occlusion are mixed and "pocket thunderstorms" may occur.

In midnorthern latitudes in winter, rain is likely if you are located east of the center of the low-pressure area associated with the occlusion. If you are west of the center, snow is likely.

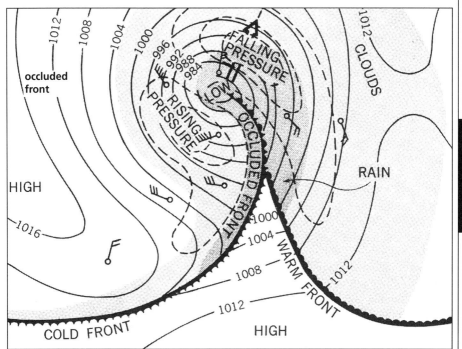

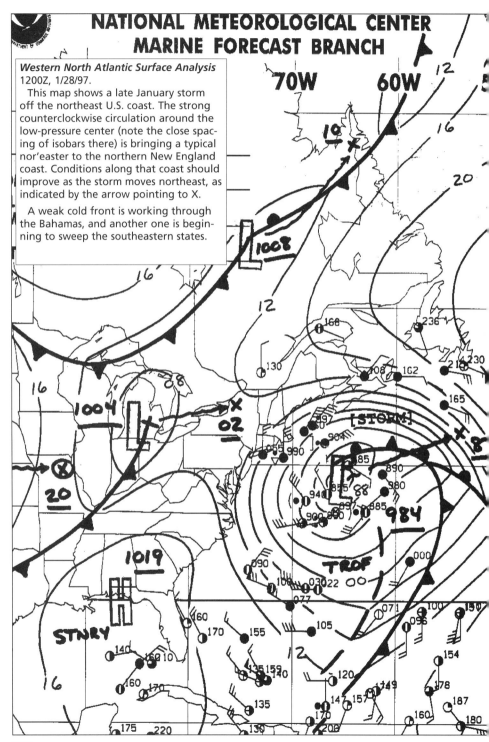

# NATIONAL METEOROLOGICAL CENTER
# MARINE FORECAST BRANCH

**Western North Atlantic Surface Analysis**
1200Z, 1/28/97.
  This map shows a late January storm off the northeast U.S. coast. The strong counterclockwise circulation around the low-pressure center (note the close spacing of isobars there) is bringing a typical nor'easter to the northern New England coast. Conditions along that coast should improve as the storm moves northeast, as indicated by the arrow pointing to X.

  A weak cold front is working through the Bahamas, and another one is beginning to sweep the southeastern states.

## WEATHER CHARTS

The following discussion focuses on four types of charts issued by the National Weather Service (NWS): surface, upper air, streamline, and sea state. Within each type are analysis (current conditions) and forecast (future conditions) charts. The NWS also issues imagery from geostationary and polar-orbiting weather satellites. Before and during an ocean voyage, you should study a variety of types of charts and satellite images. The more pieces of the weather puzzle you have, the more accurate your interpretation can be.

Mariners can obtain NWS charts in a number of ways (see "Resources," page 413). Some use a dedicated weather facsimile receiver; others use a computer and modem connected to a telephone landline, to a single-sideband receiver, or to satellite communications. In addition, private weather forecasters often prepare their own charts and transmit them to their clients via fax or e-mail.

### Surface Charts

A surface analysis chart is like a weather snapshot showing weather features at a specified time. A prognosis (forecast) chart projects into the future — some project 12 or 24 hours ahead and others at lengthening intervals up to five days. This discussion of surface charts focuses on surface analysis charts.

Every six hours at 0000Zulu (Greenwich Mean Time) 0600Z, 1200Z, and 1800Z, the National Weather Service Marine Forecast Branch produces synoptic (large-area) surface analysis charts for the Atlantic, Pacific, and the Gulf of Mexico. The surface analysis charts are usually available within 3.5 hours of the "valid" time. These surface charts are based on information from satellites, weather buoys, weather balloons, ship reports, and observations from aircraft and individuals.

**Surface Analysis Format.** Surface analysis charts cover a very large area so that mariners can use them to plot the locations and tracks of many weather systems, and to show the systems' locations relative to land.

Each ocean basin is shown on a Mercator projection with latitude and longitude

marked in 10-degree increments. Each surface chart is issued in two parts overlapping by ten degrees of longitude: 165 to 175 degrees west in the Pacific and 40 to 50 degrees west in the Atlantic. (The Gulf of Mexico is included in the western Atlantic chart.) Polar charts are produced on polar stereographic projections.

**Information Provided on Surface Analysis Charts.** Like the picture in the Chinese proverb that is worth more than ten thousand words, a surface analysis chart provides a wealth of information. (See sample chart.) Fronts are indicated by lines studded with solid black symbols as shown in the diagram on page 388.

The centers of low-pressure systems are marked with an L and a notation of the central barometric pressure. The centers of high-pressure systems are marked with an H and a notation of the central barometric pressure. Arrows projecting from the lows and highs ending in an X show the systems' projected tracks and both the predicted locations and pressure in 24 hours.

A low-pressure area is labeled "rapidly intensifying" if the low's central pressure drops 24 Mb or more in a 12- or 24-hour period. If a low-pressure system is forecast to become a gale (Force 8, 34 - 40 knots) or storm (Force 10, 48 - 55 knots), it is labeled "developing gale" or "developing storm." Pronounced thunderstorm activity is shown with comments on coverage and intensity.

Due to the uncertain movement of tropical weather systems, including hurricanes, forecast positions for these systems are often not shown on long-range forecast charts, but are only shown on 24-hour charts.

On surface analysis charts, atmospheric pressure is indicated by isobars (lines connecting points with equal barometric pressure). Isobars are drawn at intervals of 4 Mb of pressure. Outside the tropics, winds blow parallel to isobar lines, turning slightly inward around low-pressure systems (approximately 20 degrees—more at surface levels; less at higher levels) and outward around high-pressure systems. Wind speed is related to the spacing of the isobars. The closer the isobars, the greater the pressure gradient over a given distance and the stronger the winds.

Weather

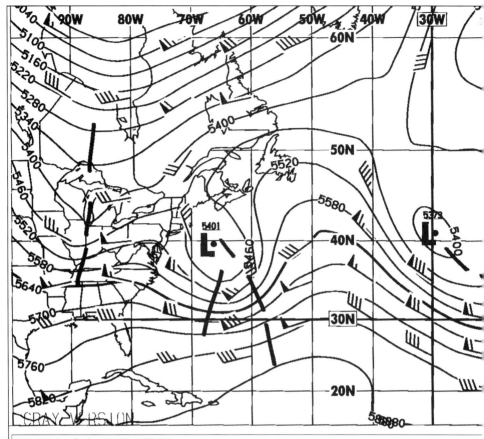

**500 MB Analysis** 1200Z, 1/29/98
Here is the high seas forecast that you could get by radio, navtex, or e-mail for this same period:

N ATLANTIC N OF 3N TO 31N W OF 35W INCLUDING CARIBBEAN SEA AND GULF OF MEXICO

WARNINGS...1200 UTC JAN 29...N OF 29N BETWEEN 75W AND 56W, WIND 30 TO 40 KT, SEAS 14 TO 20 FT. BY 1200 UTC JAN 31...WIND BELOW GALE FORCE.

SYNOPSIS AND FORECAST: 1200 UTC JAN 29...ATLC COLD FRONT 31N56W 20N66W. FORECAST 0000 UTC JAN 30...COLD FRONT 31N43W 23N59W.

1200 UTC JAN 29...EXCEPT AS NOTED IN WARNINGS SECTION...N OF 24N W OF COLD FRONT TO 78W, WIND W TO NW 20 TO 30 KT, SEAS 9 TO 16 FT. N OF 24N WITHIN 600 NM E OF COLD FRONT, WIND S TO SW 20 TO 30 KT, SEAS 8 TO 14 FT. BY 0000 UTC JAN 30...N OF 24N W OF COLD FRONT TO 70W, WIND W TO NW 20 TO 30 KT, SEAS 10 TO 18 FT. N OF 24N WITHIN 480 NM E OF COLD FRONT, WINDS S TO SW 20 TO 30 KT, SEAS 8 TO 14 FT. FORECAST 0000 UTC JAN 31...N OF 29N WITHIN 480 NM W OF COLD FRONT, WINDS NW TO W 20 TO 30 KT AND SEAS 10 TO 18 FT IN NW SWELL. N OF 25N WITHIN 420 NM E OF COLD FRONT WINDS SW TO S 20 TO 25 KT AND SEAS 8 TO 12 FT IN NW SWELL. ATLC 1200 UTC JAN 29...S OF 18N, WINDS E TO NE 20 KT AND SEAS 9 FT IN E SWELL. FORECAST 0000 UTC JAN 31...S OF 15N, WINDS E TO NE 20 KT, SEAS TO 9 FT. REMAINDER ATLC WINDS LESS THAN 20 KT AND SEAS LESS THAN 8 FT THROUGH 0000 UTC JAN 31. 1200 UTC JAN 29...CARIBBEAN COLD FRONT 20N70W 14N80W. FORECAST 0000 UTC JAN 31...COLD FRONT DISSIPATED. 1200 UTC JAN 29...W OF COLD FRONT, WINDS N 20 KT AND SEAS 8 FT. FORECAST 0000 UTC JAN 31...WINDS LESS THAN 20 KT AND SEAS LESS THAN 8 FT. REMAINDER CARIBBEAN WINDS LESS THAN 20 KT AND SEAS LESS THAN 8 FT THROUGH 0000 UTC JAN 31. GULF OF MEXICO WINDS LESS THAN 20 KT SEAS LESS THAN 8 FT THROUGH 0000 UTC JAN 31.

Data about surface winds as reported by buoys and ships is also included; wind direction is indicated on an eight-point compass rose along with notations about wind speed and cloud cover.

## 500 Mb Charts

Upper-air jet stream winds act as steering currents for surface weather and influence the formation of lows, highs, troughs, ridges, and fronts. When doing your own weather interpretation, you should compare surface analysis charts with upper-air charts to predict what forces will probably drive the surface weather for the next few days or longer.

The NWS issues many upper-air charts, each one identified by a specified atmospheric pressure. Mariners get the most useful information from the 500 Mb chart, which depicts the height above sea level where the atmospheric pressure equals 500 Mb. (Normal sea level pressure is 1013 Mb.) Five hundred Mb occurs at an altitude of approximately 18,000 feet, halfway up the earth's atmosphere and at the lowest level of jet stream activity. (See sample chart.)

The solid lines on 500 Mb (and other upper-air) charts connect points of equal elevation for a specified atmospheric pressure. Upper air wind speeds of 30 knots and greater are shown using directional "barbs" with "feathers" indicating five- and 10-knot increments. Wind speeds above 50 knots are noted with a solid triangular flag.

On a 500 Mb chart, the lines indicate elevations where the pressure is 500 Mb. These lines are called height contours and are similar to contour lines on surface topographical maps. (Recall that the lines on surface charts, in contrast, indicate varying pressures at the same — surface — elevation.) On an upper-air chart, the lines are drawn at intervals of 60 meters of altitude and are often labeled in decameters. For example, a line labeled 564 on a 500 Mb chart indicates a pressure of 500 Mb at a point 5,640 meters above sea level. Generally, the colder the air mass, the lower the altitude at which the pressure is at the specified amount. The elevations at 500 Mb are higher at the equator and lower at the poles.

The jet stream flows generally from west to east, but can meander north and south. Meridional flow refers to north-south motion that forms waves, or undulations, in the stream. Meridional flow mixes cold air from mid and high latitudes with warm air from lower latitudes and is a harbinger of unsettled and possibly stormy weather.

Zonal flow refers to a west-to-east motion (in both hemispheres) that has very little of the undulating, wavy motion found in meridional flow. In zonal flow there is not much mixing of cold and warm air and, generally, stable settled weather accompanies it.

**Troughs and Ridges.** When you examine a 500 Mb chart, first you should determine if the height contour lines reflect meridional or zonal flow, because the flow pattern is an excellent indicator of surface weather. In meridional flow, you should first look for the troughs (U-shaped dips in the Northern Hemisphere) and ridges (humps in the form of inverted U's). Second, you should compare these patterns to a surface analysis chart. Surface low-pressure systems often form near troughs, and surface high-pressure systems near ridges.

In midlatitudes, surface lows often form downstream (to the east) of jet stream troughs because the troughs induce an upward motion to the air. Surface highs are associated with upper-air ridges where the air is subsiding. (In the Southern Hemisphere these shapes are reversed.) Troughs that are sufficiently developed to induce the development of surface low-pressure systems are drawn on 500 Mb charts with a bold dashed line along their axis. Troughs and ridges at the 500 Mb level change slowly, often taking days, weeks, and occasionally months to change their flow pattern. This is why they are so useful in making surface weather forecasts.

If a low forms at the surface beneath an upper-level trough, the low system will usually move in the direction of the upper airflow, but at a forward speed of one-third to one-half the speed of the upper-air winds. Normally, surface wind speeds within the low will be half of the 500 Mb wind speed. For instance, if the wind speed in a trough is 60 knots at the 500 Mb level, the winds in the surface low will be in the 30-knot range.

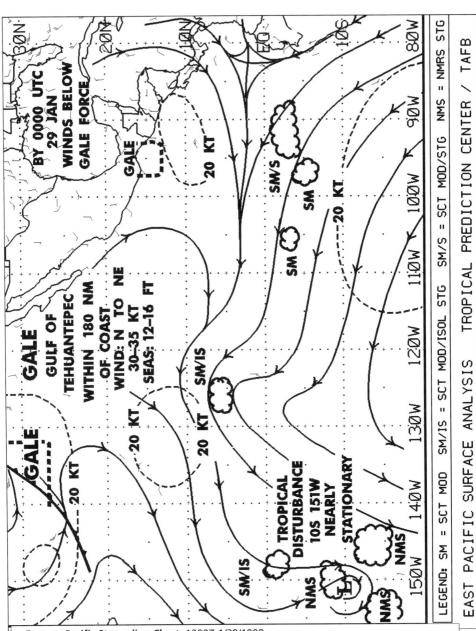

**Eastern Pacific Streamline Chart**, 1200Z 1/29/1998

Regions of significant thunderstorm or rain activity are enclosed with scalloped lines, resembling a hand-drawn cloud and are labeled according to coverage and intensity, as follows:

**ISOLD**: isolated showers and rain      **SCT**: scattered showers and rain

**MOD**: moderate intensity      **STG**: strong intensity

On a 500 Mb chart, the 564 line (delineating 5,640 meters) often receives special attention because it tends to mark the southern border (Northern Hemisphere) of Beaufort Force 7 (28- to 33-knot) surface winds in winter and Beaufort Force 6 (22- to 27-knot) surface winds in summer. This contour is drawn thicker and darker than other contours on the chart.

If jet stream winds in the area of a 500 Mb trough exceed 110 knots, there's a strong possibility of a rapidly intensifying low at the surface. Conditions that promote such development occur when a trough has pronounced north-south development that produces a healthy mix of warm and cold air; when there are large temperature differences within the atmosphere — especially in the spring and fall — and when an upper-level trough is located over a warm ocean current.

The amplitude (north-south height) and breadth (west-east) of troughs and ridges on a 500 Mb chart indicate the characteristics of the surface highs and lows beneath them. Generally, the greater the amplitude, the stronger the surface system because large amplitudes indicate that more cold dry air is mixing with warm moist air. Strong Northern Hemisphere upper-level ridges with extensive north-south development (high amplitude) are called "Omega blocks" because their shape on a chart resembles the Greek letter. Omega blocks will often divert or stall approaching low-pressure systems allowing high pressure to predominate.

The NWS generates 500 Mb analysis charts for the Atlantic and Pacific twice daily at 0000Z and 1200Z. Forty-eight-hour 500 Mb prognoses are also issued at those times. A 96-hour 500 Mb prognosis is issued once a day at 0000Z. Twelve-, 60-, and 120-hour 500 Mb forecasts may be issued when the normal 48- or 96-hour forecasts are not available.

Be aware that forecast data on surface charts is a blending or consensus derived from the forecast models of several national and international weather agencies and from forecasters' personal experience. Upper-air charts are computer generated and released without alteration. Because they are generated differently, these two types of charts may not coincide exactly in their analyses or prognoses.

## Streamline Charts

In midlatitudes, winds are usually caused by the differences in pressure between eastward-moving highs and lows. Below these latitudes in the tropics you're not likely, in most seasons, to find a succession of such moving highs and lows. Variations in pressure are normally slight. Consistent winds in this region are attributed more to the semipermanent subtropical high to the north, around which air flows in a large circular clockwise pattern — eastward flowing south of the high.

In mid and high latitudes, winds swirling around highs and lows blow parallel to isobar lines — or nearly so. Since tropical regions generally do not have well-formed high and low patterns, isobar lines are not useful indicators of tropical wind flow. Therefore, meteorologists use streamlines to show wind patterns in tropic areas. Streamlines are solid, bold, curved lines plotted parallel to surface airflow. Arrows indicate the wind direction. (See sample streamline chart.)

Wind information on a streamline analysis chart is obtained from ships' reports and from boundary layer analysis derived from satellite information. Boundary layer winds are winds within 2,000 feet of the earth's surface. This derived data is used for areas from which there is sparse information from ships.

Streamline analysis charts for the Pacific and Atlantic Oceans are issued twice daily (1200Z and 1800Z) by the National Weather Services Tropical Prediction Center, located at the National Hurricane Center in Miami, Florida. They cover the regions near the equator in the Atlantic and Pacific known as the Intertropical Convergence Zone (ITCZ). Streamline forecast charts provide prognoses — the expected movement of surface synoptic (large-scale) windflow patterns.

Streamline charts use the symbols (right) to indicate the stages of development of adverse conditions that originate in the tropics.

 = tropical disturbance

 = tropical depression

= tropical storm

 = hurricane

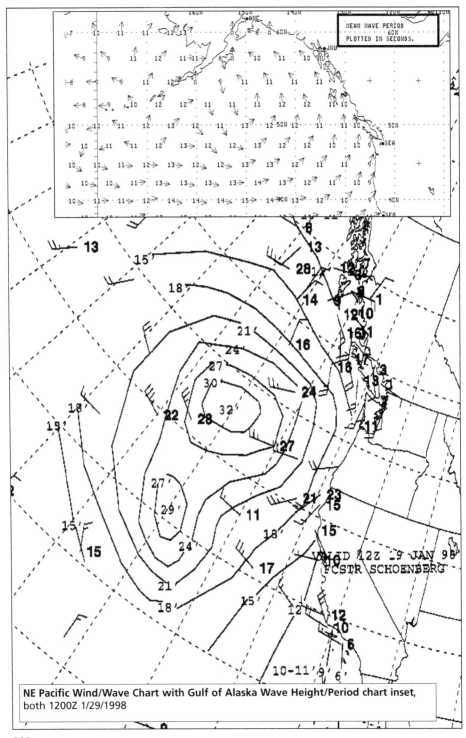

**NE Pacific Wind/Wave Chart with Gulf of Alaska Wave Height/Period chart inset,** both 1200Z 1/29/1998

On a tropical streamline analysis chart, tropical storms and hurricanes are noted with their name and latest advisory position. Hurricanes are designated using a six-digit code that provides general information about the system. For example, the code 160905 placed adjacent to a hurricane indicates that the system became developed and consistent on the 16th day of the month, it is the ninth tropical storm of the season, and it has been under analysis for five days.

## Sea-State Charts

The charts described above give you analyses and prognoses for the atmosphere. Sea-state analysis and prognosis charts give you conditions on the sea surface and provide valuable information about wave height and direction. (See sample sea-state analysis chart.) Sea-state analyses based on actual ship's reports are issued once a day by the Marine Prediction Center (MPC). Contour lines indicate wave height in feet or one-meter increments; arrows can be used to show the primary direction of the swells. In addition, maximum and minimum combined wind, wave, and swell heights are noted by the abbreviations MAX and MIN next to the average wave height amounts. Analysts derive the combined wave height by adding approximately one-third the height of the wind wave to the height of the swell. During the winter, the edge of the ice is depicted by a bold, jagged line.

In addition to the daily analyses, the MPC issues 48-hour sea state prognoses each day at 0000Z and 1200Z. These prognoses are based on ships' reporting and the short-range significant wave height forecast from the U.S. Navy and the National Center for Environmental Prediction. These prognosis charts use the same contour lines and symbols as the analysis charts.

If you use sea-state charts in conjunction with surface charts and 500 Mb upper-level charts, you will have a complete picture. A version of each of these three charts is issued at 0000Z and 1200Z. Using them together will help you locate and possibly avoid the worst weather and the largest seas.

## SINGLE OBSERVER FORECASTING

When you don't have access to professional analyses and forecasts, you can use the six basic indicators —-barometric pressure, wind direction/strength, cloud characteristics, temperature, humidity, and sea and wave characteristics — to make short-term marine forecasts for your location with some success. You can also use your local observations to augment coastal forecasts and identify micro phenomenon.

## Weather Instruments

Your observation of clouds and sea state is visual. The basic instruments for observing the other indicators are a barometer, a windvane/anemometer, a thermometer, and a hygrometer. You should always obtain information from several of these instruments and you should never depend on single observations or readings. Multiple readings over time show the amount and rate of change, which are more accurate indicators of weather trends than a single reading. Changes in barometric readings are especially important. A prudent navigator will enter barometric readings, wind direction and strength, cloud characteristics, temperature, sea state, and possibly humidity into the log at regular intervals.

**Barometer.** A barometer measures atmospheric pressure. A mercury barometer consists of a tube containing mercury in a vacuum. The level of the mercury rises and falls as the atmospheric pressure increases and decreases. The height of this column of mercury is measured in inches or millibars (see barometric conversion table).

Most modern barometers are aneroid models. ("Aneroid" means "not using fluid."). An aneroid barometer contains no mercury; its indicator is moved directly by atmospheric pressure. The works of this type of barometer consist of a bellows made of thin corrugated metal in a "box," from which almost all the air has been removed. The pressure exerted by the atmosphere on the outside of the box is magnified by a series of levers that activate a pointer on a dial. The readout is expressed in inches or millibars, just as in the case of a mercury barometer.

You don't need to correct an aneroid barometer for temperature or gravity, but you should correct it for height above sea level when you're using it on a body of fresh water that's not at sea level. Otherwise, to determine if your barometer's reading is correct, compare it to known sea-level pressure. (Local weather forecasts give sea level barometric pressure.) If your barometer's reading does not match, adjust the indicator by turning a screw on the back of the instrument case using a thin-ended screwdriver.

**Windvane/anemometer.** The typical anemometer consists of an impeller formed by a set of "cups" that scoop up the wind and rotate at a rate that corresponds to wind speed. The RPMs are translated electronically into wind velocity that can be read in a vessel's cockpit or navigation station. An anemometer and windvane on a moving vessel measure relative, not true, wind speed and direction. When using their readings in weather analysis, then, you should convert readings to true wind speed and direction.

**Thermometer.** The liquid in common liquid-in-glass thermometers (normally mercury) expands when heated and contracts when cooled to a greater extent than the glass that contains it. You sight the expansion and contraction on the Fahrenheit or Celsius scale. (See the table on page 530 to convert between Fahrenheit and Celsius.) Bimetal thermometers indicate the differing thermal expansion rates of two thin strips of dissimilar metals welded together. The feel of hot or cold air on your skin is not a reliable measure of temperature or its change because humidity and wind speed affect that feel and distort your sense of temperature.

**Hygrometer.** A hygrometer measures the water content of air using two thermometers—one containing a dry bulb and the other a wet bulb. As water evaporates from the surface of the wet bulb, heat is extracted and that thermometer reads less than the dry-bulb thermometer. The difference in readings indicates the humidity, or dampness, of the air. When the air contains a relatively high amount of water, the temperature difference between the wet and dry bulb thermometers is slight because little or no evaporation is occurring at the wet bulb.

When an air mass is saturated (100 percent humidity), a drop in temperature will cause the water vapor in the atmosphere to condense, forming rain, snow, or fog. The point at which the temperature is cool enough so that condensation begins is called the dew point. Using the dew point table (see page 417), you can find what decrease in temperature for a given humidity level will cause rain, snow or fog.

### Some Forecasting Rules of Thumb

**Fair Weather.** When the barometer is steady or rising at a steady rate, and very high cirrostratus clouds (mares' tails) or cumulus clouds are present, you can expect fair weather to continue for awhile. (See later section on clouds.)

**Rain.** Signs of approaching rain include a slowly falling barometer (about 0.14 Mb/hour), dark clouds with hard, defined outlines, or distant white, watery-looking clouds that increase, followed by an overcast murky vapor.

**Wind.** Strong winds and perhaps rain are

indicated if the barometer is falling or rising rapidly (1.0 Mb or greater). Hard, more sharply defined, edges on dark black clouds signal strong wind.

**Change in Wind Direction.** High upper clouds moving in a different direction from the lower clouds or from the surface wind signal a change in wind direction. These upper clouds can indicate the new direction of the surface wind.

## Atmospheric Pressure

Trends in atmospheric pressure can indicate the strength and stability of a weather system and can warn of approaching systems. If the sea level barometric pressure is above 1020 Mb and is steady or rising, fair weather is likely to last for another 24 hours. During unsettled weather, if there is a rapid rise in barometric pressure to 1030 Mb or higher, you can expect conditions to improve.

A falling barometer and a consistent, continual change in wind direction and strength usually indicate the approach of a low-pressure system that may still be six to 12 hours away from your area. A rapid barometric fall often indicates a strong weather system; a slow fall, a milder system. However, a slow fall to below 990 Mb often indicates a strong low-pressure system that has stalled or is moving slowly.

A rising barometer often indicates the onset of fair weather as a high-pressure system replaces a low-pressure system. In midlatitudes, a rapid rise in barometric pressure can indicate that the weather systems are moving rapidly, or that the pressure differential between two systems is large, or both. Although fair weather is imminent, upper-air instability can cause strong gusty winds for a day or so as the high-pressure center approaches. It's wise to remember that some of the strongest winds and seas associated with gales can come behind a cold front and appear after the barometer has begun to rise.

In northern midlatitudes, if the sky clears after the passage of a cold front and the wind veers to northwest, six to 12 hours of clear and cool weather should follow. During this time, you should keep a close watch on the barometer and wind. If the barometer begins to fall again, if the wind backs toward southwest, and if upper

## Weather Rhymes

These rhymes summarize rather neatly, and in an easily remembered form, a number of rules for the amateur weather forecaster. Although there is a considerable degree of truth in them, these rhymes are not infallible and you should use them with caution.

### The Barometer

Long foretold, long last,
Short notice, soon past,
Quick rise after low,
Sure sign of stronger blow.

When the glass falls low,
Prepare for a blow;
When it slowly rises high,
Lofty canvas you may fly.

At sea with low and falling glass
Soundly sleeps a careless ass,
Only when it's high and rising
Truly rests a careful wise one.

### Wind and Weather

A red sky at night is a sailor's delight,
A red sky in the morning is a sailorman's
    warning.

The evening red and morning gray
Are sure signs of a fine day,
But the evening gray and the morning
    red,
Makes the sailor shake his head.

Mackerel sky and mares' tails,
Make lofty ships carry low sails.

When the wind shifts against the sun,
Trust it not, for back it will run.

When rain comes before the wind,
Halyards, sheets and braces mind,
But when wind comes before rain
Soon you may make sail again.

If clouds are gathering thick and fast,
Keep sharp look out for sail and mast,
But if they slowly onward crawl,
Shoot your lines, nets and trawl.

clouds increase, then you can expect renewed inclement weather within six to 12 hours.

Low-pressure systems may approach from almost any direction, but in midlatitudes they usually approach from the west, following paths determined by the flow of upper-level winds called jet streams. In the Northern Hemisphere at these latitudes, an observer south of an approaching low will experience increasing and clocking winds—that is, winds that change direction in a clockwise direction. An observer north of a low's center will feel increasing and backing (shifting counterclockwise) winds. An observer in the path of a west-to-east-moving low will experience increasing winds from a steady easterly direction.

Apart from the large changes in barometric pressure due to the movement of weather systems, there is also a small diurnal (twice daily) pressure variation of not more than 0.5 Mb throughout the world. It's at its maximum at 1000 and 2200 local time and at its minimum at 0400 and 1600. Although this daily variation is often masked by larger changes in pressure, it's worth remembering when you are interpreting barometric trends.

## Wind

Because wind is the single most important weather element to mariners, a review of some fundamentals is presented here.

Wind is the movement of air over the earth's surface caused by differences in atmospheric pressure. These pressure differences are the result of variations in temperature and moisture between air masses. The difference in the atmospheric pressure over a specific distance is known as pressure gradient. The steeper the gradient, the stronger the wind. Air also moves vertically in the atmosphere, influencing the formation of high and low pressure systems as well as thunderstorms, waterspouts, and other local weather features.

Winds that blow from approximately the same direction throughout most of the year in the tropics are called "trade winds"; winds whose directions change with the sun's changing declination are termed "seasonal winds." The well-known monsoon of the Indian Ocean and the China Sea is an example of a seasonal wind.

You can estimate the speed of surface winds using the Beaufort Wind Scale (see table on page 418) that relates sea state to wind speed. A calm sea indicates winds of less than one knot, and 12 (the highest number) indicates winds of hurricane strength (63-plus knots). (See table on page 531 for conversion from knots to miles per hour and vice versa.)

**Effect of the Earth's Rotation.** Air moving over the earth's surface is deflected to the right in the Northern Hemisphere and to the left in the Southern Hemisphere due to the earth's rotation. This phenomenon is known as the Coriolis effect. Absent the Coriolis effect, winds would flow directly from high- to low-pressure centers. Because of the deflection caused by the Coriolis effect, winds circulate clockwise around areas of high pressure and counterclockwise around lows in the Northern Hemisphere. The reverse is true for the Southern Hemisphere. In addition, close to the earth, friction caused by surface topography affects wind direction. Surface winds angle somewhat more toward and away from pressure centers than do winds at 3,000 feet and higher.

A rule of thumb states that if an observer in the Northern Hemisphere faces into the

wind, low barometric pressure will lie to his or her right and high pressure to his or her left.

**Jet Streams.** In middle and high latitudes, upper-level winds called jet streams circle the globe from west to east at approximately 18,000 feet and higher. Not slowed by surface friction, these undulating ribbons of air often move at speeds in excess of 200 knots, although 50 to 150 knots is more normal.

Jet stream winds are caused by (1) the atmosphere's constantly seeking equilibrium by transferring hot air from equatorial regions to polar regions and (2) the deflection of airflow caused by the earth's rotation.

The strength and path of jet streams is important to surface mariners because jet streams act as steering currents for surface weather.

## Clouds

Clouds are gatherings of minute water drops, ice crystals, or both, held in suspension in the atmosphere. There are three primary forms:

- The heap cloud, cumulus, formed from strong vertical air motion (convection).
- The layer cloud, stratus, formed from more gradual horizontal and vertical ascent of air.
- The streak cloud, cirrus, composed of ice crystals.

The three cloud forms are subdivided into ten important modifications or principal cloud types based on cloud base height:

*High Clouds (10,000 – 60,000 ft)*
    Cirrus (Ci)
    Cirrostratus (Cs)
    Cirrocumulus (Cc)

*Middle Clouds (6,500 – 25,000 ft)*
    Altostratus (As)
    Altocumulus (Ac)

*Low Clouds (up to 6,500 ft)*
    Stratus (St)
    Stratocumulus (Sc)
    Nimbostratus (Ns)

*Variable – low to high*
    Cumulus (Cu)
    Cumulonimbus (Cb)

Following are some cloud descriptions and there are cloud photographs beginning on page 421.

**Cirrus clouds** are detached and have a delicate, fibrous, often silky appearance. They are usually white in color, not shaded. Cirrus clouds that look like separate brush strokes are popularly called "mares' tails."

**Cirrocumulus clouds** form small white flakes or very small globular masses without shadows. They are arranged in groups or lines with their configuration often resembling ripples or wave-created ridges of sand on the seashore.

**Cirrostratus clouds** create a transparent, whitish veil of fibrous or smooth appearance that totally or partially cover the sky and usually produce halo phenomena.

**Altocumulus clouds** are composed of fairly small elements, with or without shading. These clouds form laminae or rather flattened globular masses that appear in a layer or in patches.

**Altostratus clouds** form a striated or fibrous veil, more or less gray or bluish in color. They form a uniform layer covering all or part of the sky.

**Nimbostratus clouds** form a low, amorphous, and rainy layer. The color is dark gray and nearly uniform.

**Stratocumulus clouds** form globular masses or rolls that appear in a layer or patches. The smallest of the regularly arranged elements are fairly large; they are soft and gray with darker parts.

**Stratus clouds** form a low, gray layer with tops and bases at uniform heights. They're like fog that is not resting on the ground.

**Cumulus clouds** are thick with vertical development. Their upper surfaces are dome shaped and exhibit protuberances, while the base is nearly horizontal.

**Cumulonimbus clouds** are composed of heavy masses with great vertical development. The summits rise in the form of mountains or towers, and the upper parts have a fibrous texture and often spread out in the shape of an anvil.

The extent of cloud cover is sometimes expressed on a scale of zero to eight. These numbers represent eighths of sky covered and are called *oktas*. Zero represents a sky that is free of clouds; eight represents an entirely overcast sky with no patches of blue visible.

**Weather**

**Interpreting Clouds.** Of all cloud types, you should pay particular attention to cirrus and cirrostratus. These clouds can be your "early warning system," the first precursors of an advancing warm front associated with a low-pressure system that may still be hundreds of miles away.

Extended and well-defined cirrus contrails indicate very cold upper-level air. High cirrus clouds whose movement across the sky can be detected without reference to a stationary object indicate 100-knot or greater, jet stream winds. Winds of this speed can bring mixing of air and rapid changes within the atmosphere. If fine cirrus clouds increase and thicken into a sheet and form a halo around the sun or moon, then there is a high probability that inclement weather will follow within 12 to 24 hours. This prognosis is more reliable if the barometer is falling steadily and the wind changes direction and freshens.

Small- or medium-sized cumulus clouds form when air is lifted in response to heating from the surface land or water below it and indicate fair weather. Towering cumulus are formed in response to pronounced surface heating and an abundance of rising hot air. They can produce showers and squalls. In summer, ragged and vertically developed cumulonimbus clouds with very high tops often indicate thunderstorms.

There is not much change in sea-surface temperature between day and night; therefore, large active cumulus clouds can form over the ocean whenever the sea surface is warm enough to lift the air above it. In contrast, cumulus clouds often form over land during the day when the surface is heated significantly and then dissipate at night when the land cools.

## Temperature and Humidity

Although not particularly useful alone, when used in conjunction with other weather indicators, variations in temperature and humidity may provide you with some clues to forthcoming changes in weather. A heavy dew or frost shows that the sky was clear during the night, but this alone does not necessarily indicate that good weather will continue throughout the day. Haze probably indicates the presence of a temperature inversion (the air is colder at the surface than aloft) and is probably caused by sinking air around the perimeter of a high-pressure area. This often occurs during dry summer weather and indicates fair weather attending the high pressure.

**Sea Surface Temperature.** Because the sea surface is in direct contact with the overlying air mass, sea temperature is particularly important in meteorology. Water temperature changes more slowly than air, so water temperature can be used as a short-term "constant." The difference between sea and air temperatures can be a useful guide in identifying air masses. Polar air is colder than the sea; tropical air is warmer.

When the air temperature is rising and the sea is calm, the surface water temperature may be several degrees warmer than water a few feet deep. When the air temperature is falling and/or there are waves or tidal currents, the water temperature will be uniform from the surface downward. Waves and currents mix the water, and as the surface water cools, it becomes denser and sinks, which aids the mixing.

If you don't have a through-hull temperature sensor, you must draw a water sample to determine the surface water temperature. Draw water in a nonconductive canvas or rubber bucket from overside (not through your ship's plumbing). Read the temperature as soon as you've drawn the water and be sure your thermometer is fully immersed. Most thermometers will give accurate readings within 30 seconds of drawing the water.

**Identifying Currents with a Thermometer.** You can use sea temperature as a useful guide to identifying warm and cold currents. You'll often see a long line of foam at the meeting of two currents, one of which is colder and sinking below the other. Generally, you will find a difference in the water temperature on either side of the line.

You can identify the boundary of the Gulf Stream using a thermometer. The boundary at the north and west side of the Stream, known as the "north wall," is an area of noticeable temperature change. Waters east and south of the wall are warm; waters west and north are cold. The difference is most apparent near Cape Hatteras, but you can observe it anywhere along the Stream from the Straits of Florida to the Grand Banks. In addition to its main flow, the Gulf Stream often spins off huge warm- and cold-water eddies that a navigator can play to advantage. Although satellite imagery is probably the best way to locate these eddies, local sea-surface temperature readings will confirm whether you have found the eddy you are seeking.

**Fog.** Fog forms at sea when the water temperature is equal to or below the dew point temperature of the air at sea level. If the air near the sea surface contains a high concentration of salt particles (which attract moisture and encourage condensation), fog may form even before the air is cooled to its dew point. Fog often forms when a tidal flow or an ocean current brings colder water to the surface. This colder water may cool the surface air to its dew point.

There are a number of rules of thumb regarding the formation and dissipation of fog. A change in wind direction or speed may cause fog to thin or thicken. If the daytime sky above a fog bank is clear, fog is more likely to dissipate than if the sky is cloudy. Wisps at the edges and top of shallow fog often indicate clearing. A good indication of shallow fog is your ability to can see the masthead of a nearby vessel. Generally, on the open sea, fog clears with the arrival of a cold front or with an increase in the water temperature.

## Waves and Sea State

It's useful to distinguish between wind waves and swells. The former are generated by local winds; swells can be generated by gale or storm winds hundreds or thousands of miles away, or by moderate winds somewhat closer at hand. Swells are long, regular seas usually traveling in the same direction. A wave period (time between crests) of at least 10 seconds, or a wave length of at least 500 feet in open ocean, indicates that the wind that produced the swell must have been at least gale force (see Beaufort Wind Scale table and sea state photographs). Swells of lesser size can still have originated in a strong storm, but may have decayed in traveling a long distance from their place of origin. Swells travel outward (away) from the weather system that creates them. You can use the direction from which swells are coming as a rough indicator of the location of a tropical depression or midlatitude low-pressure system relative to your vessel.

A change in wind direction of more than 30 degrees can produce a new wave train. That is, the waves will begin to travel in a different direction. This can create confused seas where the new and old wave trains intersect. Often you will experience confused seas when two or more strong weather systems are close to each other or during the passage of a weather front.

## HURRICANES

Most hurricanes, known as cyclones or typhoons in the western Pacific and Indian Oceans, originate in the tropical oceans of the world. They are severe low-pressure areas with clearly defined circulation and sustained winds of over 63 knots. Barometric pressure at a hurricane's center can be so low that the sea surface will rise several feet. This rise in sea surface can combine with a piling up of wind-driven water to produce coastal storm surges of 20 feet or more. In 1988 the central pressure of Hurricane Gilbert dropped to 888 Mb (average sea-level pressure is 1013 Mb), setting a record low.

Hurricanes are among the world's most powerful weather systems and can produce winds over 200 knots. It is difficult to comprehend the power and strength of a mature hurricane. If converted to electricity, an average hurricane could meet the power demands of the United States for six months! A Class 5 hurricane can dominate

**Weather**

more than one million cubic miles of the earth's atmosphere and, in the open ocean, can create waves well over 50 feet high. If a small vessel directly encounters a fully developed hurricane, chances of survival are low.

The National Weather Service has designated June 1 through November 30 as North Atlantic hurricane season, with the greatest hurricane frequency and severity during August, September, and October. However, hurricanes often occur during other months of the hurricane season, and mariners should monitor tropical weather forecasts throughout the period.

The National Hurricane Center in Miami, Florida, tracks hurricanes in the North Atlantic and the Pacific east of 180°. The Central Pacific Hurricane Warning Center covers the eastern and central Pacific west of 140° W to the International Date Line (180°). Pacific waters west of the date line are covered by the Typhoon Warning Center.

## Formation

Most hurricanes are born when the atmosphere becomes burdened with heat at the equator and the earth's normal thermal circulation system fails to move this heat to polar regions at a rate sufficient to keep the earth's atmosphere in balance. Hurricanes are Mother Nature's overload protection and, as such, expedite movement of heat. Hurricanes are so efficient at extracting heat from the surface that the water temperature in a hurricane's wake usually has been reduced by several degrees.

A hurricane of tropical origin needs several ingredients to form: (1) a westerly moving tropical weather system, called a wave or trough; (2) a seawater temperature of 80°F or greater; and, (3) during the early stages of development, moderate-speed, low- and upper-level winds that change very little in speed and direction with changes in height — that is, winds with low sheer.

The first stage in the development of this type of hurricane is a tropical wave. A tropical wave is a trough at low latitudes. Unlike midlatitude depressions, which form from the top down, starting with upper-level troughs, tropical hurricanes develop from the bottom up, starting with lower-level troughs. A trough can grow over warm ocean water. When the surface water temperature is 80°F or higher, the moisture-laden air immediately above it begins to rise rapidly. As warm, moist air rises, it cools, causing the moisture to condense and release heat. This released heat warms the surrounding air so that it continues to rise. Supported by a steady influx of moist warm surface air, the system grows vertically.

When high-level winds draw off, or exhaust, this rising air, the atmospheric pressure at the surface drops, strengthening the wave. If these processes continue, and if the pressure continues to drop, the Coriolis effect, even though it's weak at low latitudes, will eventually induce a spin into the system, particularly as the system moves toward midlatitudes. When the system develops a clear circulation with sustained surface winds of 25 to 33 knots, it is classified as a tropical depression (low-pressure area). When further strengthening occurs and sustained surface winds exceed 34 knots, the system is designated a tropical storm and is assigned a name. When sustained winds exceed 63 knots, the storm becomes a hurricane. Fortunately, only a fraction of tropical waves become hurricanes each season.

At the same time it grows vertically, a tropical trough or wave moves westward at speeds averaging 10 to 20 knots. During peak season in the North Atlantic, tropical waves are often seen crossing the ocean in succession from east to west separated by four to eight degrees of longitude.

If you are in the Caribbean during hurricane season, pay careful attention to the wind direction. Any slow and steady change from the normal easterly direction could indicate the approach of a trough or wave. As a tropical wave approaches, you will see the wind back from east to northeast and north. As the trough passes, the wind will continue to back slowly until it reaches a southeasterly direction.

Using infrared sensors, weather satellites continually measure seawater temperature and send the data back to earth stations. If the sea surface temperature reaches 80°F early in the hurricane season, meteorologists at the National Hurricane Center become justifiably concerned, because this could indicate a very active season.

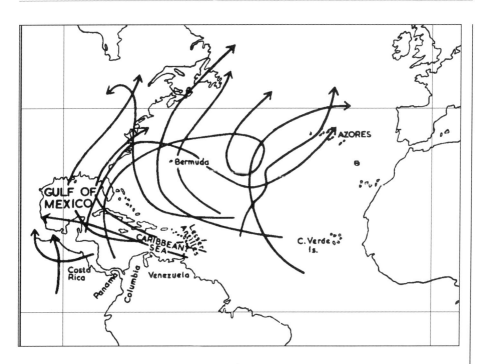

Hurricanes generally cover a smaller area than do extra-tropical depressions at mid-latitudes. They range in diameter from less than 100 to more than 500 miles. Centers, or "eyes," range from four to 25 miles across. The center is an area of very low atmospheric pressure and winds spiral inward, counterclockwise around it in the Northern Hemisphere. Spiral bands of intense rain, thunderstorms, and water-spouts/tornadoes emanate from the center and are most prevalent at the eye wall. Winds at the outer edge of a fully formed hurricane are light to moderate and gusty. They increase toward the center to very high sustained winds with even stronger gusts. Air movement within the eye itself is usually fitful and sometimes nearly calm. However, seas in the eye are heavy and confused because the winds surrounding the eye are shifting and violent. After the eye passes, hurricane-force winds will resume blowing, this time from the opposite direction.

### Hurricane Areas and Tracks

In the North Atlantic, most hurricanes form between the Cape Verde Islands near Africa and the Windward Islands of the Caribbean, over the western Caribbean, and over the Gulf of Mexico. (See chart of hurricane tracks.)

While some North Atlantic hurricanes, especially those that form southeast of Bermuda, may move northward in the beginning, the majority initially move west or northwest. Then they often follow a track forming a large right-hand (clockwise) curve. Some hurricanes pass to the east or north of the larger islands of the Caribbean, gradually turning to the northeast and east. Others pass over (or to the south of) the larger Caribbean islands and enter the Gulf of Mexico where they curve to the north or northeast.

A significant number of North Atlantic hurricanes, however, remain in low latitudes and do not curve appreciably northward. Erratic tracks incorporating complete loops, hairpin turns, and other irregularities sometimes occur. In the North Atlantic, movement of hurricanes to the southeast is rare, and when it does occur, it is only for a short duration.

The majority of hurricanes that move from the Atlantic into the Caribbean in August and September follow a west-northwesterly course in low latitudes, often reaching the U. S. East Coast before curving north and northeast. In late September and in October and November, hurricanes are likely to move to the north and east, passing through the Yucatan Channel or over Cuba, Florida, or the Bahamas. In October and November, movement of hurricanes is often toward the north into the open Atlantic.

Some severe North Atlantic depressions that don't originate in the tropics develop sustained hurricane-strength winds and are accorded hurricane status. Like other mid-latitude depressions, they are formed differently than tropical hurricanes, but they can have equally devastating effects.

The average forward speed of North Atlantic hurricanes is 10 to 13 knots. However, this varies considerably according to the location of the storm, its development, and the surrounding meteorological conditions. The highest rates of forward motion usually occur when a hurricane is moving north or northeast in midlatitudes.

Hurricanes that form in the tropics at the eastern edge of the North Pacific Ocean tend to follow a westerly path that misses the North American continent. However, some do curve north and then northeast and threaten the Baja peninsula and other parts of Mexico's west coast.

## Signs of Approach

One of the earliest signs of a hurricane's approach is the appearance of high cirrus clouds. They will converge toward a point on the horizon that indicates the direction from which the hurricane is approaching. You will see snow-white "mares' tails" when the hurricane center is 300 to 400 miles away.

Other early warning signs are long, heavy swells that can originate a considerable distance away and reach you two or three days in advance of the storm's arrival. This swell comes from the general direction of the hurricane.

During the "early warning" stage, there is usually a slight rise in barometric pressure, followed by continuously falling pressure.

As the hurricane center nears, the barometric pressure falls rapidly. The wind increases in speed and comes in heavy squalls. Changes in wind direction accelerate. When a center is close, rain is usually continuous, accompanied by furious gusts

of wind. The air is thick with rain and spume. Visibility is low; you can barely see even nearby objects.

As the hurricane's center recedes from you, barometric pressure rises and winds begin to subside. Seas also subside, but the wind decreases sooner. A fully risen sea can often take days to subside.

**Distance from the Center.** You can estimate roughly how far you are from the center of a hurricane using barometric pressure and wind velocity. If the barometric pressure falls slowly and wind speed increases gradually, then the center is distant. When the barometer falls rapidly and the wind increases rapidly, the center is near. This is confirmed if the winds blow from the same direction as the increasing waves.

**Bearing of the Center.** When you face into the wind, the center of a Northern Hemisphere hurricane will be approximately 115° to your right. In general, if you are facing into the wind, the wind will back to your left if the hurricane center is moving toward your left. If the wind veers to your right, the center is moving toward your right. If you are in the path of the center, the wind will remain from the same direction.

## Hurricane Avoidance

When plotting a hurricane, it is helpful to draw an imaginary line through the storm's center in the direction that the storm is moving. This line, often called the storm track or axis, divides the storm into two halves or semicircles. (See diagram.) In the Northern Hemisphere, the right half is called the "dangerous semicircle" because that is the area of the strongest winds. The left half is called the "navigable semicircle" because the wind strengths tend to be lower. As a rule, you should always navigate to increase your distance from the center of a hurricane, taking into account the storm's track and forward speed. And if you have a choice, avoid the right, or "dangerous," semicircle.

**Detection and Avoidance.** Prior to the availability of satellite imagery and to the use of sophisticated aircraft reconnaissance and computer-based numerical modeling, there was often little warning of an approaching hurricane. Frequently, mariners only realized a hurricane was imminent when the barometric pressure began to drop radically, a large swell appeared, and clouds covered the sky. Sometimes these events occurred just a day before a hurricane passed over an area, particularly if a hurricane was not very large in diameter.

For years, strategies for dealing with hurricanes were based on the assumption that a vessel might actually encounter a hurricane at sea. Using vectors, a navigator would plot the course that would provide the widest berth possible under the circumstances. Today with satellites, aircraft, and computer-forecasting models, navigators have a much better chance of avoiding hurricanes altogether.

### Tracking Tropical Weather Systems

Weather satellites use visible and infrared sensors to track tropical waves by locating their dense and vertically developed cumulus and cumulonimbus clouds. These clouds can have individual diameters of one to 50 miles and cloud clusters may have diameters from 50 to 500 miles. These cloud cells and clusters often do not form a consistent or continuous pattern because they are a product of uneven heating of the earth's equatorial regions, which is due to seasonal, geographic, and climatological variations. With uneven cloud formation, tropical weather can fluctuate rapidly. The transition from calm to squalls, and showers to clear skies, often occurs quickly and with little advanced warning.

In the tropics, cumulus and cumulonimbus clouds tend to align themselves with the axis of a low-pressure trough. The National Hurricane Center uses satellite imagery to produce a Tropical Surface Analysis (TSA) chart, which is a streamline chart. A TSA chart shows clouds and wind

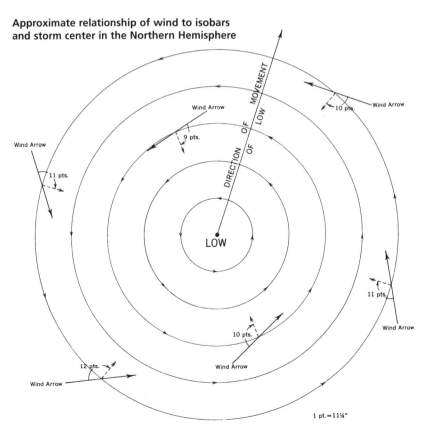

**Approximate relationship of wind to isobars and storm center in the Northern Hemisphere**

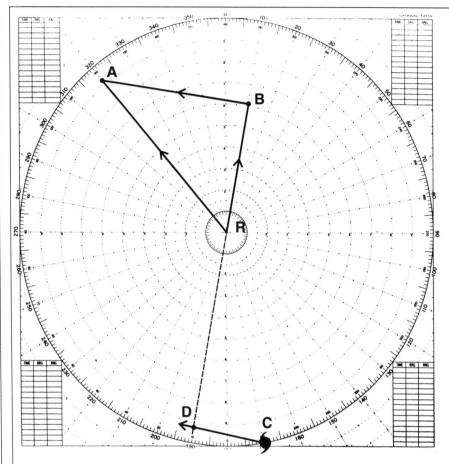

**Determining a course to avoid a hurricane (or storm) center**

**Example:** A tropical cyclone is estimated to be moving in direction 320° at 19 knots. Its center bears 170°, at an estimated distance of 200 miles from your vessel, whose maximum speed is 12 knots.

**Solution:**

Plot with your vessel remaining at the center as in radar plotting, page 200.

Plot the position of the storm center C (scale 20:1).

Plot the storm's speed vector, RA, using 2:1 scale for simplicity.

From A draw a line tangent to the 12 knot speed circle (labeled 6 at 2:1 scale).

From the center of the drawing, draw a perpendicular to this tangent line, locating point B.

The line RB is the required speed vector for the vessel. Its direction, 011°, is the required course. The path of the storm relative to your vessel will be along a line from C in the direction BA, if both maintain course and speed. The point of nearest approach will be at D, the foot of a perpendicular from your heading. RD equals 187 miles. The storm will move 72 miles, CD, to that point at a relative speed of about 15 knots, BA. Therefore, the point of nearest approach will be in about 4 hours 50 minutes.

resulting from horizontal convergence and ascending air. During hurricane season, streamline analysis is an important tool in detecting and tracking tropical waves that can be the breeders of full-fledged hurricanes. (For more information, see the "Streamline Charts" section above and the sample tropical streamline chart.)

The "Resources" section at the end of this chapter lists many sources of tropical advisories and forecasts, including weather charts, radio broadcasts, and web sites.

## CURRENTS

There are more than 50 notable ocean currents moving water over the earth's surface. (Forty-one of them are shown and/or listed on the map page 416 and the table page 427.) Major ocean currents can flow at rates of two knots or greater and persist over long periods (months, years, or longer). The major causes of ocean currents are prevailing winds and variations in the temperature and salt content of the seawater. We often think of these currents as streams or rivers, flowing with consistent direction and speed. In reality, ocean currents move at varying speeds and in varying directions. Some actually reverse direction in response to seasonal and climatic influences. Day-to-day observations of ocean currents often show speeds and direction that depart markedly from yearly averages. These variations are most frequently caused by changes in wind strength and direction. In addition, phenomena such as volcanic eruptions, El Niño events, and sunspots all affect global heat distribution and, ultimately, the movement of ocean currents.

Major ocean currents should not be confused with the many local coastal and inshore currents that are affected by tides, seasonal wind patterns, temperature differentials, coastal configuration, and land-water runoff. Coastal currents can affect the departure and arrival phases of your voyage. Detailed information about these currents can be found in coast pilots, local tide and current tables (see Chapter 11, *Tides and Currents,* and *Reed's Nautical Almanacs*).

### Some Facts About Major Ocean Currents

• Major ocean currents are located between the equator and 50 degrees north and south latitude.

• These currents turn clockwise in the Northern Hemisphere and counterclockwise in the Southern Hemisphere.

• In the Northern Hemisphere, currents on the western side of ocean basins are stronger than those on the eastern side.

• Currents are categorized as either warm or cold in comparison with the water outside their flow.

• Eddies of warm water associated with major currents normally circulate clockwise in the Northern Hemisphere; cold eddies circulate counterclockwise. The reverse applies in the Southern Hemisphere.

• Northern Indian Ocean currents reverse direction during monsoon season.

### Effects of Currents on Vessels

When planning a passage, you should consider the potential effect of any major ocean current you will encounter. A current can advance a vessel far along its intended track or can put it seriously off course. In this age of electronic charting and GPS navigation, plotting or compensating for a current is much easier than it was just a few years ago.

Consider ocean currents in relationship to anticipated weather. Wind that blows contrary to a current can produce abnormally high seas. A northerly wind against the Gulf Stream — that powerful ocean current that flows north-northeasterly off the U.S. East Coast for part of its route — can produce seas 50 percent higher than if the wind were not opposing the current.

When large waves occur in the Gulf Stream, the National Weather Service broadcasts a "north wall" bulletin. (North wall refers to the north or west edge of the Stream.) The north wall bulletin consists of a schematic chart of the Gulf Stream. Hatch marks indicate areas where seas are predicted to reach 14 feet in 30 knots of wind.

Ocean currents can have a strong effect on the weather. Fog and low-pressure systems may form when there is a significant difference in temperature between a

Weather

prevailing air mass and the air immediately above a current. Fog forms off the U.S. New England coast when the warm, moist air from the Gulf Stream region meets the much colder water north of the Stream. The California Current brings cold water from the Gulf of Alaska to the U.S. West Coast. Since there is no continental shelf to keep it offshore, the current passes close to the warm California coast. Cooling and fog result.

Low-pressure systems often form or intensify off the North Carolina coast when the warm air over the nearby Gulf Stream meets the cooler air over the land.

## Information About Currents

As you plan a voyage, a good source of information about major ocean currents—those that flow at a reasonably consistent pace and direction—is the *Atlas of Pilot Charts,* published jointly by the U.S. Department of Commerce and the Department of Defense (available through the U.S. Government Printing Office and local nautical chart agents). The atlas contains charts of the world's oceans on which green arrows show the prevailing direction and average speed of major currents. The atlas lists the location and temperature of the 10 ocean currents that have the most effect on a vessel, particularly a slow-moving one. Another useful planning tool is the computerized version of the *Atlas of Pilot Charts.* (See "Resources," page 413.)

Real-time or near-time plots of ocean currents are produced using infrared (IR) satellite imagery that displays surface water temperature using a false color palette. You can obtain these images with an onboard weather satellite receiving system, or from internet sources like the Rosenstiel School of Marine Science, *www.rsmas.miami.edu/images+pics.html*

Rosenstiel's home page displays IR images of major currents obtained from polar-orbiting satellites. Many of these images show resolutions down to one kilometer (.54 nautical mile). However, this is not real-time data; the images are delayed approximately three days. Another option is to obtain a current analysis derived from satellite imagery prepared by a professional and sent to you via fax or e-mail. (See "Resources.")

Real-time satellite imagery is potentially more useful for a vessel underway. However, satellite sensors cannot "see" through clouds, so real-time data can only be obtained on clear days.

## The Gulf Stream

The Gulf Stream rushes up the U.S. East Coast and then curves northeast toward northern Europe as part of the major clockwise rotary current around the edge of the North Atlantic ocean basin. The current on the west side of the North Atlantic is more developed and stronger than the current on the east side of the Atlantic.

Just as mountain streams tumble and turn, the Gulf Stream twists, splits, rejoins, and spins off eddies. Eddies of cold water form on the south or east sides of the main flow, and eddies of warm water form on the north and west sides. These eddies are often long-lasting; some are more than 100 miles across and have a rotational speed of two to four knots. Satellite imagery is particularly useful tool for identifying the location and size of eddies.

Eddies are caused by instabilities in the main current flow. Once they form, however, they can become very stable. Warm Gulf Stream eddies have lasted up to six months to one year; some cold eddies have lasted up to two years. A navigator should know the location and speed of Gulf Stream eddies in order to calculate set and drift, determine sea state, and plan an advantageous route.

## RESOURCES

### Books

The three regional editions of *Reed's Nautical Almanacs* — West Coast, East Coast, and Caribbean — contain detailed information on many weather prediction sources. Another good book is *Selected World Wide Marine Weather Broadcasts* published by the National Oceanographic and Atmospheric Administration (NOAA), U.S. Government Pub. # 003-017-00540-2

### Voice Broadcasts

**VHF.** NOAA operates 400 VHF transmitters in the United States, each with a range of 40 miles. These transmitters broadcast continuously, providing recorded analyses and forecasts (projected from six to 24 hours) for coastal waters. Seven frequencies from 162.400 to 162.550 Mhz allow for overlapping coverage. These forecasts are updated every few hours, more frequently if necessary, and intentionally are kept brief (about four to six minutes). Long-term weather features are not normally included, although significant features outside the forecast area such as hurricanes often will be highlighted. You can obtain information about VHF broadcasts from *Reed's Nautical Almanacs* or from:

*NOAA*
*National Weather Service*
*Warning and Forecast Branch*
*1325 East-West Highway*
*Silver Spring, MD 20910*
*www.nws.noaa.gov*

**Single Sideband.** The U.S. Coast Guard broadcasts complete offshore weather forecasts on SSB. These cover waters beyond 25 miles offshore. Forecasts usually last 20-25 minutes and provide more detail than VHF coastal reports. These forecasts are delivered by a droning synthesized voice known as "Perfect Paul." A very useful tool for getting the most out of these forecasts is a plastic weather area map used with dry markers.

Several of the SSB High Seas Radiotelephone Services, such as AT&T Maritime Services, also provide weather forecasts.

All the above forecasts are **not** broadcast continuously, so you need a broadcast schedule. You can find them in the books listed above or at the USCG navigation web site: *www.navcen.uscg.mil*

**Weather Nets.** Amateur or "Ham" radio can provide valuable weather information. There are a number of marine-oriented "Nets" providing weather information to all listeners — good examples are the Waterway Net and Herb Hilgenberg.

The Waterway Net begins each day at 0745 EST or EDT as applicable on 7268kHz, lower sideband. It primarily includes boats along the U.S. Atlantic and Gulf Coasts and the Caribbean area, but may also include boats on the Great Lakes and making Bermuda and trans-Atlantic passages. Weather reports are given for Atlantic and Gulf Coasts and the Southwest North Atlantic Ocean.

Herb Hilgenberg is an amateur weather forecaster who operates a very popular SSB weather net for offshore sailors. For many years Herb was based in Bermuda, but he now broadcasts from Ontario, Canada. Herb's station is VAX-498 and he begins his broadcasts at 4 p.m. Eastern Daylight Time (2000 UTC) daily on 12.359MHz upper sideband. Herb moves in a geographic pattern around the Atlantic, receiving weather condition reports from vessels and dispensing individual forecasts to them. If you have a ship's license to transmit, you may join the net; but listen first to learn Herb's protocol. Before your voyage, you may wish to contact Herb by fax at 905-681-7114.

*Reed's Nautical Almanacs* contain up-to-date information on these and other Ham Nets (and welcomes further information for publication).

If you are interested in becoming a licensed Ham operator, Radio Shack reportedly offers good introductory materials.

### Text Broadcasts

**Navtex.** NAVTEX is an internationally coordinated method of broadcasting distress, urgent, and safety messages and weather forecasts and warnings using small, low-cost printing receivers designed to be installed in the pilothouse of a vessel. A series of coast stations transmit NAVTEX radio teletype safety messages on medium frequency 518 kHz during preset time slots. Routine messages are normally broadcast four to six times daily. Urgent messages are broadcast on receipt, provided that an adjacent station is not transmitting. The

413

coverage of NAVTEX is reasonably continuous out to 200 nautical miles from the transmitting station. Interference from or receipt of stations farther away occasionally occurs at night. In the U.S., the Coast Guard is the responsible agency for NAVTEX operation.

To receive these broadcasts of notices and marine weather, mariners need a special NAVTEX receiver. Mariners who do not have NAVTEX receivers but have SITOR radio equipment can also receive these broadcasts by operating it in the FEC mode and tuning to 518 kHz. There are techniques to receive NAVTEX with a SSB or shortwave radio and a computer.

## Weather Charts

**Via facsimile receiver.** Contrary to rumors circulating over the last few years, neither the U.S. Coast Guard nor the U.S. Navy have plans to discontinue weather facsimile broadcasts in the near future. Despite budget constraints, the U.S. Coast Guard plans to continue its radiofacsimile broadcasts to meet both the needs of its cutters and public safety needs. The U.S. Navy has delayed suspending its broadcasts of marine weather information until at least 1998 because of delays in installing equipment in its ships. Navy radio weather facsimile broadcasts will cease once Navy ships have been fitted with new satellite equipment.

Broadcast schedules are listed in *Reed's*.

**Via the internet.** Using a laptop computer and modem, you can download weather charts for the Atlantic, Gulf of Mexico, and Pacific upon request. Your modem can be connected to a land (or cellular) telephone line if you're in port or to a single sideband radio or satellite communications if you are at sea.

The weather charts you receive via the Internet are broadcast within 3.5 hours of valid time. They are the same ones you receive on a weatherfax with the advantage that you don't have to wait for a broadcast. And there is no cost beyond your normal telephone charges. The central Web addresses for charts are:

*www.nws.noaa.gov*
*www.ncep.noaa.gov/MPC/*

The weather charts you will download are in a graphic file format called TIF. There are many flavors of this format, and NWS uses a somewhat exotic one that is highly compressed but also is incompatible with some graphics programs. If you have trouble viewing the files, first try every graphics program you have, then seek another graphic viewer or file conversion program.

**Via e-mail.** The Marine Prediction Center (MPC) of the National Centers for Environmental Prediction (which is also part of NOAA) will send text forecasts and weather charts to your e-mail address. There is more information about this service at the MPC Web site listed in the last section.

For information about receiving e-mail via SSB or satellite, see page 276 in Chapter 6, "Communications."

## Satellite Images

While the weather fax services mentioned above include some satellite images, it is now possible to receive weather imagery directly from the satellites. The companies listed below all have software/hardware products that make this possible. Some of these tools can also be used for receiving weather information via SSB/computer.

*OCENS*
*3257 16th Avenue W, Suite 6*
*Seattle, WA 98119*
*800-746-1462; 206-301-9137*
*www.ocens.com; freeberg@ocens.com*

*Software Systems Consulting*
*Products Group*
*615 S. El Camino Real*
*San Clemente, CA 92672*
*714-498-5784*
*www.ssccorp.com*

*SFWX, Inc.*
*POB 3370*
*Allentown, PA 18106 U.S.A.*
*610-395-4441*
*www.sfwx.com/softworks/*

## Weather Routing

You can hire a professional router to provide weather analyses/forecasts and charts from private and government sources. Routers not only interpret the weather, but also project the most efficient track for a vessel based on weather and the vessel's characteristics. Here is a partial list of weather routers:

Locus Weather / Ken McKinley
PO Box 804, 21 Elm St.
Camden, ME 04843-0804
207-236-3935; locuswx@midcoast.com

Commanders' Weather Corporation
154 Broad St., Suite 1517
Nashua, NH 03062
603-882-6789
104477,3462@compuserve.com
http://commandersweather.com/default.html

Bob Rice's Weather Window
39-4 North Main Street
Wolfeboro, NH 03894
603-569-4700

Ocean Strategies / Michael Carr
PO Box 24
Portland, ME 04108
207-766-4430
104643.1112@compuserve.com

Ocean Routes
680 West Maude Ave., Suite 3
Sunnyvale, CA 94086-3518
408-245-3600

Jenifer Clark – Gulf Stream Analysis
5902 Federal Ct.
Upper Marlboro, MD 20772
301-574-2871

## Currents

Two good publications for the study of ocean currents are the *Atlas of Pilot Charts* published by the U.S. National Imagery and Mapping Agency (NIMA) and *Ocean Passages for the World* published by the British Admiralty (Pub. #136). A computerized version of the Pilot Charts is sold as the "Visual Passage Planner":

Digital Wave
P.O. Box 326
Ft. Monmouth, NJ 07703

There is a sample section of a Pilot Chart on page 129. In the electronic charting section on page 201 is information on two companies whose software both predicts tidal currents and displays these currents on electronic charts.

---

### World Wide Web Note

All the Web sites listed in this book are also listed in the "Nautical Links" page of *Reed's* own Web site:

### www.treed.com

---

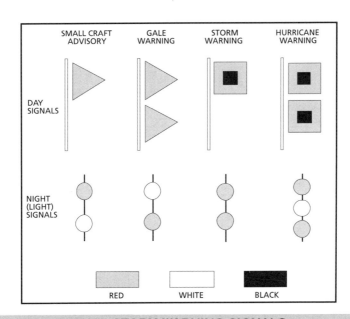

**VISUAL STORM WARNING SIGNALS**

These were formerly displayed by the Coast Guard at many locations. They are no longer maintained by the Coast Guard, but may be seen at yacht clubs, marinas, or flown by the coast Guard Auxiliary.

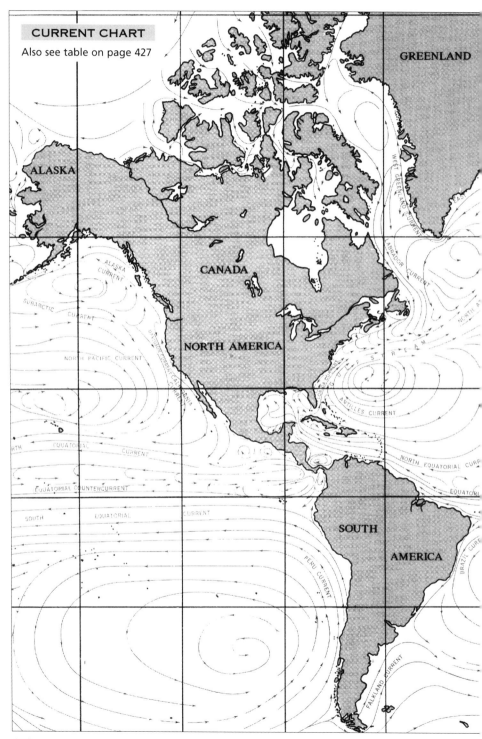

**CURRENT CHART**
Also see table on page 427

GREENLAND

ALASKA

CANADA

NORTH AMERICA

SOUTH

AMERICA

WEST GREENLAND CURRENT

EAST

LABRADOR CURRENT

NORTH A

ALASKA CURRENT

SUBARCTIC CURRENT

NORTH PACIFIC CURRENT

CALIFORNIA CURRENT

G U L F S T R E A M

ANTILLES CURRENT

NORTH EQUATORIAL CURRENT

RTH EQUATORIAL CURRENT

EQUATORIAL COUNTERCURRENT

SOUTH EQUATORIAL CURRENT

EQUATORI

PERU CURRENT

BRAZIL CURRE

FALKLAND CURRENT

## DEW POINT (°C) TABLE

| Dry Bulb °C | 0° | 0.2° | 0.4° | 0.6° | 0.8° | 1.0° | 2.0° | 2.5° | 3.0° | 3.5° | 4.0° | 4.5° | 5.0° | 5.5° | 6.0° | 6.5° | 7.0° | 7.5° | Dry Bulb °C |
|---|---|---|---|---|---|---|---|---|---|---|---|---|---|---|---|---|---|---|---|
| 40 | 40 | 40 | 40 | 39 | 39 | 39 | 38 | 37 | 36 | 36 | 35 | 34 | 34 | 33 | 32 | 32 | 31 | 30 | 40 |
| 39 | 39 | 39 | 39 | 38 | 38 | 38 | 37 | 36 | 35 | 35 | 34 | 33 | 33 | 32 | 31 | 31 | 30 | 29 | 39 |
| 38 | 38 | 38 | 38 | 37 | 37 | 37 | 35 | 35 | 34 | 34 | 33 | 32 | 32 | 31 | 30 | 29 | 29 | 28 | 38 |
| 37 | 37 | 37 | 37 | 36 | 36 | 36 | 34 | 34 | 33 | 32 | 32 | 31 | 30 | 30 | 29 | 28 | 28 | 27 | 37 |
| 36 | 36 | 36 | 35 | 35 | 35 | 35 | 33 | 33 | 32 | 31 | 31 | 30 | 29 | 29 | 28 | 27 | 26 | 26 | 36 |
| 35 | 35 | 35 | 34 | 34 | 34 | 34 | 32 | 32 | 31 | 30 | 30 | 29 | 28 | 28 | 27 | 26 | 25 | 24 | 35 |
| 34 | 34 | 34 | 33 | 33 | 33 | 33 | 31 | 31 | 30 | 29 | 29 | 28 | 27 | 26 | 26 | 25 | 24 | 23 | 34 |
| 33 | 33 | 33 | 32 | 32 | 32 | 32 | 30 | 30 | 29 | 28 | 28 | 27 | 26 | 25 | 25 | 24 | 23 | 22 | 33 |
| 32 | 32 | 32 | 31 | 31 | 31 | 31 | 29 | 29 | 28 | 27 | 26 | 26 | 25 | 24 | 23 | 23 | 22 | 21 | 32 |
| 31 | 31 | 31 | 30 | 30 | 30 | 30 | 28 | 28 | 27 | 26 | 25 | 25 | 24 | 23 | 22 | 21 | 21 | 20 | 31 |
| 30 | 30 | 30 | 29 | 29 | 29 | 29 | 27 | 27 | 26 | 25 | 24 | 24 | 23 | 22 | 21 | 20 | 19 | 18 | 30 |
| 29 | 29 | 29 | 28 | 28 | 28 | 28 | 26 | 25 | 25 | 24 | 23 | 22 | 22 | 21 | 20 | 19 | 18 | 17 | 29 |
| 28 | 28 | 28 | 27 | 27 | 27 | 27 | 25 | 24 | 24 | 23 | 22 | 21 | 20 | 20 | 19 | 18 | 17 | 16 | 28 |
| 27 | 27 | 27 | 26 | 26 | 26 | 26 | 24 | 23 | 23 | 22 | 21 | 20 | 19 | 18 | 18 | 17 | 16 | 15 | 27 |
| 26 | 26 | 26 | 25 | 25 | 25 | 25 | 23 | 22 | 22 | 21 | 20 | 19 | 18 | 17 | 16 | 15 | 14 | 13 | 26 |
| 25 | 25 | 25 | 24 | 24 | 24 | 24 | 22 | 21 | 20 | 20 | 19 | 18 | 17 | 16 | 15 | 14 | 13 | 12 | 25 |
| 24 | 24 | 24 | 23 | 23 | 23 | 23 | 21 | 20 | 19 | 19 | 18 | 17 | 16 | 15 | 14 | 13 | 12 | 11 | 24 |
| 23 | 23 | 23 | 22 | 22 | 22 | 21 | 20 | 19 | 18 | 17 | 17 | 16 | 15 | 14 | 13 | 12 | 10 | 9 | 23 |
| 22 | 22 | 22 | 21 | 21 | 21 | 20 | 19 | 18 | 17 | 16 | 15 | 14 | 13 | 12 | 11 | 10 | 9 | 8 | 22 |
| 21 | 21 | 21 | 20 | 20 | 20 | 19 | 18 | 17 | 16 | 15 | 14 | 13 | 12 | 11 | 10 | 9 | 8 | 6 | 21 |
| 20 | 20 | 20 | 19 | 19 | 19 | 18 | 17 | 16 | 15 | 14 | 13 | 12 | 11 | 10 | 9 | 7 | 6 | 5 | 20 |
| 19 | 19 | 19 | 18 | 18 | 18 | 17 | 16 | 15 | 14 | 13 | 12 | 11 | 10 | 9 | 7 | 6 | 4 | 3 | 19 |
| 18 | 18 | 18 | 17 | 17 | 17 | 16 | 15 | 14 | 13 | 12 | 11 | 10 | 8 | 7 | 6 | 4 | 3 | 1 | 18 |
| 17 | 17 | 17 | 16 | 16 | 16 | 15 | 14 | 13 | 12 | 11 | 9 | 8 | 7 | 6 | 4 | 3 | 1 | -0 | 17 |
| 16 | 16 | 16 | 15 | 15 | 15 | 14 | 12 | 11 | 10 | 9 | 8 | 7 | 6 | 4 | 3 | 1 | 0 | -2 | 16 |
| 15 | 15 | 15 | 14 | 14 | 14 | 13 | 11 | 10 | 9 | 8 | 7 | 6 | 4 | 3 | 1 | 0 | -2 | -5 | 15 |
| 14 | 14 | 14 | 13 | 13 | 13 | 12 | 10 | 9 | 8 | 7 | 6 | 4 | 3 | 1 | 0 | -2 | -4 | -7 | 14 |
| 13 | 13 | 13 | 12 | 12 | 11 | 11 | 9 | 8 | 7 | 6 | 4 | 3 | 1 | 0 | -2 | -4 | -7 | -9 | 13 |
| 12 | 12 | 12 | 11 | 11 | 10 | 10 | 8 | 7 | 6 | 4 | 3 | 1 | 0 | -2 | -4 | -6 | -9 | -12 | 12 |
| 11 | 11 | 11 | 10 | 10 | 9 | 9 | 7 | 6 | 4 | 3 | 1 | 0 | -2 | -4 | -6 | -9 | -12 | -15 | 11 |
| 10 | 10 | 10 | 9 | 9 | 8 | 8 | 6 | 4 | 3 | 2 | 0 | -2 | -3 | -6 | -8 | -11 | -15 | -19 | 10 |
| 9 | 9 | 9 | 8 | 8 | 7 | 7 | 4 | 3 | 2 | 0 | -1 | -3 | -5 | -8 | -10 | -14 | -18 |  | 9 |
| 8 | 8 | 8 | 7 | 7 | 6 | 6 | 3 | 2 | 0 | -1 | -3 | -5 | -7 | -10 | -13 | -17 |  |  | 8 |
| 7 | 7 | 7 | 6 | 6 | 5 | 5 | 2 | 1 | -1 | -3 | -4 | -7 | -9 | -12 | -16 |  |  |  | 7 |
| 6 | 6 | 6 | 5 | 5 | 4 | 4 | 1 | -0 | -2 | -4 | -6 | -9 | -11 | -15 |  |  |  |  | 6 |
| 5 | 5 | 5 | 4 | 4 | 3 | 2 | 0 | -2 | -4 | -6 | -8 | -10 | -14 | -15 |  |  |  |  | 5 |
| 4 | 4 | 4 | 3 | 2 | 2 | 1 | -1 | -3 | -5 | -7 | -10 | -11 | -14 | -18 |  |  |  |  | 4 |
| 3 | 3 | 3 | 2 | 1 | 1 | 0 | -3 | -5 | -7 | -8 | -11 | -14 | -17 |  |  |  |  |  | 3 |
| 2 | 2 | 2 | 1 | 0 | 0 | -1 | -4 | -5 | -8 | -10 | -13 | -16 |  |  |  |  |  |  | 2 |
| 1 | 1 | 1 | 0 | -1 | -1 | -2 | -5 | -7 | -9 | -12 | -15 | -10 |  |  |  |  |  |  | 1 |
| 0 | 0 | -1 | -1 | -2 | -2 | -3 | -7 | -9 | -11 | -14 | -18 |  |  |  |  |  |  |  | 0 |

In this table, lines are are ruled to draw attention to the fact that, above the line evaporation is going on from a water surface, while below the line it is going on from ice surface. Owing to this, interpolation must not be made between figures on different sides of the lines.

### Use of Dew Point Table:

Determine the difference in observed dry- and wet-bulb temperatures and enter the table in the column (depression of west bulb) with a heading closest to that difference. Go down that column until you reach a value in line with the observed dry-bulb temperature shown in the left and right margins. That value is the temperature at which condensation will occur.

Weather

## BEAUFORT WIND SCALE

| Beaufort Number | Mean Velocity Knots | Descriptive Term | Deep Sea Criterion | Probable Height of Waves in feet |
|---|---|---|---|---|
| 0 | Less than 1 | Calm | Sea like a mirror. | |
| 1 | 1-3 | Light | Ripples with the appearance of scales are formed but without foam crests. | .25 |
| 2 | 4-6 | Light breeze | Small wavelets, still short but more pronounced. Crests have a glassy appearance. | .5-1 |
| 3 | 7-10 | Gentle breeze | Large wavelets. Crests begin to break. Foam of glassy appearance. Perhaps scattered white horses. | 2-3 |
| 4 | 11-16 | Mod. breeze | Small waves, becoming longer; fairly frequent horses. | 3.5-5 |
| 5 | 17-21 | Fresh breeze | Moderate waves, taking a more pronounced long form; many white horses are formed. (Chance of some spray.) | 6-8.5 |
| 6 | 22-27 | Strong breeze | Large waves begin to form; the white foam crests are more extensive everywhere. (Probably some spray.) | 9.5-13 |
| 7 | 28-33 | Near gale | Sea heaps up and white foam from breaking waves begins to be blown in streaks along the direction of the wind. | 13.5-19 |
| 8 | 34-40 | Gale | Moderately high waves of greater length; edges of crests begin to break into spindrift. The foam is blown in well-marked streaks along the direction of the wind. | 18-25 |
| 9 | 41-47 | Strong gale | High waves. Dense streaks of foam along the direction of the wind. Crests of waves begin to topple, tumble and roll over. Spray may affect visibility. | 23-32 |
| 10 | 48-55 | Storm | Very high waves with long overhanging crests. The resulting foam in great patches is blown in dense white streaks along the direction of the wind. On the whole, the surface of the sea takes a white appearance. The tumbling of the sea becomes heavy and shock-like. Visibility affected. | 29-41 |
| 11 | 56-63 | Violent storm | Exceptionally high waves. (Small and medium-sized ships might for a time be lost to view behind the waves.) The sea is completely covered with long white patches of foam lying along the direction of the wind. Everywhere the edges of the waves crests are blown into froth. Visibility affected. | 37-52 |
| 12 | 63+ | Hurricane | The air is filled with foam and spray. Sea completely white with driving spray; visibility very seriously affected. | 45+ |

**Notes:**
1. It must be realized that it will be difficult at night to estimate wind force by the sea criterion.
2. The log effect between increase of wind and increase of sea should be borne in mind.
3. Fetch, depth, swell, heavy rain and tide effects should be considered when estimating the wind force from the appearance of the sea.

* This table is intended only as a guide to show roughly what may be expected in the open sea, remote from land. In enclosed waters, or when near land with an off-shore wind, wave heights will be smaller, and the waves steeper. **WARNING:** for a given wind force, sea conditions can be more dangerous near land than in the open sea. In many tidal waters, wave heights are liable to increase considerably in a matter of minutes.

**FORCE 0-4 — wind speed 0-16 knots; waves 0-5 feet (NOT SHOWN)**

**FORCE 5 (FRESH BREEZE) — wind speed 17-21 knots; waves 6-8 feet**
Moderate waves taking a more pronounced long form; many white horses; some spray.

**FORCE 6 (STRONG BREEZE) — wind speed 22-27 knots; waves 9-13 feet**
Large waves begin to form; white foam crests everywhere; spray.

Weather

**FORCE 7 (NEAR GALE) — wind speed 28-33 knots; waves 13–19 feet**
Sea heaps up; white foam from breaking waves begins to streak along wind direction.

**FORCE 8 (GALE) — wind speed 34-40 knots; waves 18–25 feet**
Edges of crests begin to break into spindrift; foam streaks well defined.

**FORCE 9 (STRONG GALE) — wind speed 41-47 knots; waves 23–32 feet**
Crests begin to topple, tumble and roll over. Spray may affect visibility on even large boats.

**FORCE 10 (STORM) — wind speed 48-55 knots; waves 29–41 feet**
Long overhanging crests; foam in great patches; sea surface takes a white appearance.

**FORCE 11 (VIOLENT STORM) — wind speed 56-63 knots; waves 37–52 feet**
Sea is completely covered with foam patches; wave crests blown into froth everywhere.

**FORCE 12 (hurricane) — wind speed 56-63 knots; waves huge**
The air is filled with foam and spray; sea completely white with driving spray.

**CIRRUS (Ci) (Mares's Tails), high clouds**
Cirrus increasing and thickening is a sign of unsettled weather.

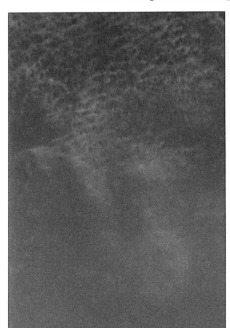

**CIRROCUMULUS (Cc) (Mackerel Sky), high clouds**
When these move rapidly and become Cirrostratus, unsettled weather is approaching.

Weather

**CIRROSTRATUS (Cs), high clouds**
A halo, as shown, is a sign of deteriorating weather approaching.

**ALTOCUMULUS (Ac), middle clouds**
Altocumulus in lines with castellated tops, as right, indicate thundery conditions.

**ALTOSTRATUS (As), middle clouds**
Can become a continuous layer of gray cloud from which rain will soon fall, Nimbostratus.

**CUMULONIMBUS (Cb), low to middle clouds**
Thunderstorm clouds, often accompanied by sudden squalls and rapidly changing winds.

Weather

**CUMULUS (Cu), low clouds**
Small Cumulus usually means fine weather; upward extension means trouble.

**STRATOCUMULUS (Sc), low clouds**
More frequent in the colder months; STRATUS (St) (not illustrated), featureless low cloud.

## CURRENTS OF THE WORLD

On page 416 is a simplified current chart for North and South America. On the following two pages are listed many of the world's ocean currents, with their average rate of drift and temperature/source remarks. For more complete information consult the appropriate *Pilot Charts* from the Defense Mapping Agency and Ocean Passages For The World (Pub. 136, British Admiralty).

| No. | Name | Average Drift miles per day | Remarks |
|-----|------|------------------------------|---------|
| 1 | N. Equatorial | 10-40 | Neutral temperature |
| 2 | Bahama | 10-50 | Neutral temperature |
| 3 | Caribbean counter current | | Neutral temperature |
| 4 | Gulf Stream | 10-70 | Warm at northern limit |
| 5 | N. Atlantic drift | 10-25 | Warm-considerable modifying effect on climate of Western Europe and the U.K. |
| 6 | Norwegian | | Warm |
| 7 | Irminger | 9 (average) | Neutral |
| 8 | E. and W. Greenland | 6-12 | Neutral – source of N. Atlantic icebergs |
| 9 | Labrador | 5-20 | Cold – source of fog and icebergs on the Grand Banks. |
| 10 | Canary | 10-35 | Cold – associated with upwelling |
| 11 | Azores | 11 (average) | Neutral |
| 12 | Portuguese | 10 (average) | Cold to neutral |
| 13 | Counter Equatorial | 10-30 | Neutral |
| 14 | S. Equatorial | 10-45 | Neutral |
| 15 | Guinea | 10-60 | Neutral |
| 16 | Brazil | 10-35 | Warm |
| 17 | Falkland | 10-40 | Cold |
| 18 | Brazil Inshore | 15 (average) | Cold. An extension of the Falkland current, may reach as far north as Rio de Janeiro in May to July |
| 19 | Southern Ocean Drift | 0-30 | Neutral – carries S. Atlantic icebergs, common to S. Atlantic, S. Pacific and S. Indian Ocean |
| 20 | Benguela | 10-50 | Cold. Associated with upwelling |
| 21 | Western Australian | 14 (average) | Inshore current sets south from March to August |
| 22 | Equatorial | | Similar to Atlantic |
| 23 | Counter Equatorial | | Similar to Atlantic |
| 24 | Mozambique | 0-30 | Neutral |
| 25 | East African coast | | Neutral. Average daily drift: November to January 16 miles; February to March 48 miles; May to September 48 miles. From July to September the daily drift may reach 170 miles to the south of Socotra |
| 26 | Agulhas | 10-40 | Warm. A counter current is found close inshore. |

**Note the change in direction with the change of the monsoon in the Red Sea, Arabian Sea, Bay of Bengal, and the China Sea.**

## CURRENTS OF THE PACIFIC OCEAN

| No. | Name | Average Drift miles per day | Remarks |
|---|---|---|---|
| 27 | N. Equatorial | 0-40 | Similar to the Atlantic |
| 28 | Counter Equatorial | 0-40 | Similar to the Atlantic |
| 29 | S. Equatorial | 0-40 | Similar to the Atlantic |
| 30 | Kuro Shio | 10-50 | Warm. The "Gulf Stream" of the Pacific |
| 31 | Oya Shio | 15-30 | Cold |
| 32 | Tsushima | | Warm |
| 33 | Liman | | Cold |
| 34 | Kamchatka | 5-10 | Neutral |
| 35 | N. Pacific drift | 10-20 | Warm |
| 36 | Aleutian | 3-7 | Neutral |
| 37 | Alaskan | 6 (average) | Neutral |
| 38 | Californian | 10-30 | Upwelling occurs off the coast of California. Between November and December and Davidson current sets northward close inshore. |
| 39 | East Australian | 0-25 | Warm |
| 40 | Peru | 0-30 | Cold. Upwelling along the coast. |
| 41 | Holy Child | Variable | Warm. Flows from January to March but is rather irregular |

# TIDES AND CURRENTS

# THEORY OF TIDES AND TIDAL CURRENTS

*If the Moon only passes over once per day, why do we have two usually equal tides where I live in the northeast U.S.? Why are they sometimes less equal? Why do some areas to the south sometimes experience a single tide cycle per day?*

*This section — originally published by the National Ocean Service — improved my understanding immensely.*

*Editor*

The word *tides* is a generic term used to define the alternating rise and fall in sea level with respect to the land, produced by the gravitational attraction of the moon and sun. To a much smaller extent, tides also occur in large lakes, in the atmosphere, and within the solid crust of the earth, acted upon by these same gravitational forces of the moon and sun. Additional nonastronomical factors such as configuration of the coastline, local depth of the water, ocean-floor topography, and other hydrographic and meteorological influences may play important roles in altering the range, the interval between high and low water, and times of arrival of the tides.

The most familiar evidence of the tides along our seashores is the observed recurrence of high and low water — usually, but not always, twice daily. The term *tide* correctly refers only to such a relatively short period, astronomically induced vertical change in the height of the sea surface (exclusive of wind-actuated waves and swell). The expression *tidal current* relates to accompanying periodic horizontal movements of the ocean water, both near the coast and offshore (but as distinct from the continuous stream-flow type of *ocean current*).

Knowledge of the times, heights, and extent of inflow and outflow of tidal waters is of importance in a wide range of practical applications such as the following: navigation through intracoastal waterways and within estuaries, bays, and harbors; work on harbor engineering projects such as the construction of bridges, docks, breakwaters and deep-water channels; the

establishment of standard chart datums for hydrography and for demarcating the seaward extension of shoreline property boundaries; the determination of a base line or "legal coastline" for fixing offshore territorial limits, both on the sea surface and on the submerged lands of the Continental Shelf; provision of information necessary for underwater demolition activities and other military engineering uses; and the furnishing of data indispensable to fishing, boating, surfing, and a considerable variety of related water sports activities.

## ASTRONOMICAL TIDE-PRODUCING FORCES

### General Considerations

At the surface of the earth, the earth's force of gravitational attraction acts in a direction inward toward its center-of-mass, and thus holds the ocean waters confined to this surface. However, the gravitational forces of the moon and sun also act externally upon the earth's ocean waters. These external forces are exerted as tide-producing, or so-called "tractive," forces. Their effects are superimposed upon the earth's gravitational force and act to draw the ocean waters to positions on the earth's surface directly beneath these respective celestial bodies (i.e., toward the "sublunar" and "subsolar" points).

High tides are produced in the ocean waters by the "heaping" action resulting from the horizontal flow of water toward two regions on the earth representing the positions of maximum attraction of the combined lunar and solar gravitational forces. Low tides are created by a compensating maximum withdrawal of water from regions around the earth midway between these two tidal humps. The alternation of high and low tides is caused by the daily (diurnal) rotation of the solid body of the earth with respect to these two tidal humps and two tidal depressions. The changing arrival times of any two successive high or low tides at any one location are the result of numerous factors to be discussed later.

## Origin of the Tide-Raising Forces

To all outward appearances, the moon revolves around the earth but, in actuality, the moon and the earth revolve together around their common center-of-mass, or gravity. The two astronomical bodies are held together by gravitational attraction, but are simultaneously kept apart by an equal and opposite centrifugal force produced by their individual revolutions around the center-of-mass of the earth-moon system. This balance of forces in orbital revolution applies to the centers-of-mass of the individual bodies only. At the earth's surface, an imbalance between these two forces results in the fact that there exists, on the hemisphere of the earth turned toward the moon, a net (or differential) tide-producing force that acts in the direction of the moon's gravitational attraction, or toward the center of the moon. On the side of the earth directly opposite the moon, the net tide-producing force is in the direction of the greater centrifugal force, or away from the moon.

Similar differential forces exist as the result of the revolution of the center-of-mass of the earth around the center-of-mass of the earth-sun system.

## Detailed Explanation of the Differential Tide-Producing Forces

The tide-raising forces at the earth's surface thus result from a combination of basic forces: (1) the force of gravitation exerted by the moon (and sun) upon the earth; and (2) centrifugal forces produced by the revolutions of the earth and moon (and earth and sun) around their common centers-of-gravity (mass). The effects of those forces acting in the earth-moon system will here be discussed, with the recognition that a similar force complex exists in the earth-sun system.

With respect to this center-of-mass of the earth-moon system (known as the barycenter), the above two forces always remain in balance (i.e., equal and opposite). Consequently, the moon revolves in a closed orbit around the earth without either escaping from, or falling into, the earth — and the earth likewise does not collide with the moon. However, at local points on, above, or within the earth, these two forces are not in equilibrium, and oceanic, atmospheric, and earth tides are the result.

The center of revolution of this motion of the earth and moon around their common center-of-mass lies at a point approximately 1,068 miles beneath the earth's surface, on

**FIG. 1 — The Monthly Revolution of the Earth and Moon around the Barycenter of the Earth-Moon System**

This revolution is responsible for a centrifugal force component ($F_C$) necessary to the production of the tides.

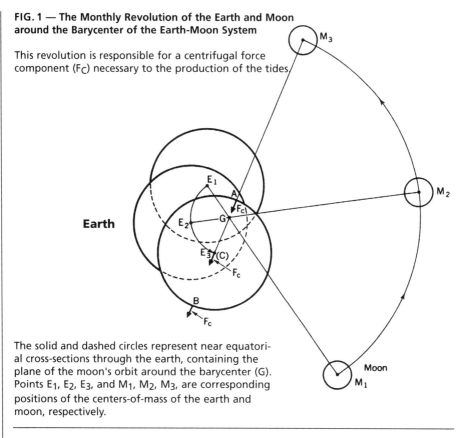

The solid and dashed circles represent near equatorial cross-sections through the earth, containing the plane of the moon's orbit around the barycenter (G). Points $E_1$, $E_2$, $E_3$, and $M_1$, $M_2$, $M_3$, are corresponding positions of the centers-of-mass of the earth and moon, respectively.

the side toward the moon, and along a line connecting the individual centers-of-mass of the earth and moon (see G, fig. 1). The center-of-mass of the earth describes an orbit ($E_1$, $E_2$, $E_3$) around the center-of-mass of the earth-moon system (G), just as the center-of-mass of the moon describes its own monthly orbit ($M_1$, $M_2$, $M_3$) around this same point.

**1. The Effect of Centrifugal Force.** It is this little-known aspect of the moon's orbital motion that is responsible for one of the two force components creating the tides. As the earth and moon whirl around this common center-of-mass, the centrifugal force produced is always directed away from the center of revolution in the same manner that an object whirled on a string around one's head exerts a tug upon the restraining hand. All points in or on the surface of the earth acting as a coherent body acquire this component of centrifugal

force, just as all points on an object whirled around the head tend to fly outward under the action of centrifugal force. And, since the center-of-mass of the earth is always on the opposite side of this common center of revolution from the position of the moon, the centrifugal force produced at any point in or on the earth will always be directed away from the moon. This fact is indicated by the common direction of the arrows (representing the centrifugal force F) at points A, C, and B in figure 1, and the thin arrows at these same points in figure 2.

It is important to note that the centrifugal force produced by the daily rotation of the earth *on its axis* must be completely disregarded in tidal theory. This element plays no part in the establishment of the differential tide-producing forces.

While space does not permit here, it may be graphically demonstrated that, for such

**FIG. 2 — The Combination of Forces of Lunar Origin Producing the Tides**
A north-south cross-section through the earth's center in the plane of the moon's hour angle; the dashed ellipse represents a profile through the spheroid composing the tidal force envelope; the solid ellipse shows the requiting effect on the earth's waters. (A similar complex of forces exists in the earth-sun system.)

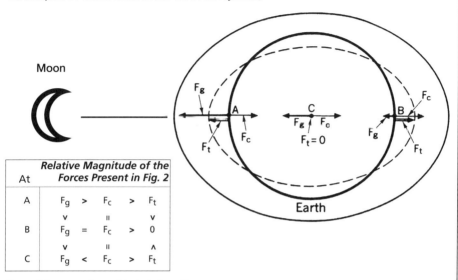

| At | Relative Magnitude of the Forces Present in Fig. 2 | | |
|----|------|------|------|
| A | $F_g$ > | $F_c$ > | $F_t$ |
|   | v | II | v |
| B | $F_g$ = | $F_c$ > | 0 |
|   | v | II | ∧ |
| C | $F_g$ < | $F_c$ > | $F_t$ |

Type of force and graphical designation

$F_c$ = Thin arrow = Centrifugal force due to earth's revolution around the barycenter
$F_g$ = Heavy arrow = Gravitational force due to the moon
$F_t$ = Double-shafted arrow = Resultant tide-raising force due to the moon

a case of revolution without accompanying rotation as above enumerated, any point on the earth will describe a circle around the earth's center-of-mass which will have the same radius as the radius of revolution of the center-of-mass of the earth around the barycenter. Thus, in figure 1, the magnitude of the centrifugal force produced by the revolution of the earth and moon around their common center-of-mass (G) is the same at point A or B or at any other point on or beneath the earth's surface. Any of these values is also equal to the centrifugal force produced at the earth's center-of-mass (C) by its revolution around the barycenter. This fact is indicated in figure 2 by the equal lengths of the thin arrows (representing the centrifugal force Fc) at points A, C, and B, respectively.

**2. The Effect of Gravitational Force.** While the effect of this centrifugal force is constant for all positions on the earth, the effect of an external gravitational force produced by another astronomical body may be different at different positions on the earth because the magnitude of the gravitational force exerted varies with the distance of the attracting body. According to Newton's Universal Law of Gravity, gravitational force decreases as the second power of the distance from the attracting body. As a special case, the *tide-raising* force varies inversely as the third power of the distance of the center-of-mass of the attracting body from the surface of the earth. Thus, in the theory of tides, a variable influence is introduced based upon the different distances of various positions on the earth's surface from the moon's center-of-mass. The relative gravitational attraction (F) exerted by the moon at various positions on the earth is indicated in figure 2 by arrows heavier than those representing the centrifugal force components.

433

## FIG. 3 — The Phase Inequality; Spring and Neap Tides

The gravitational attractions (and resultant tidal force envelopes) produced by the moon and sun reinforce each other at times of new and full moon to increase the range of the tides and counteract each other at first and third quarters to reduce the tidal range.

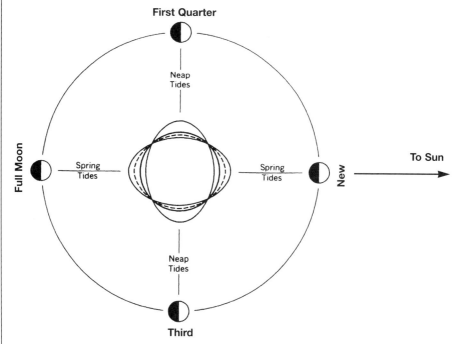

Looking down on the North Pole of the earth's figure (central solid circle). The two solid ellipses represent the tidal force envelopes produced by the moon in the positions of syzygy (new or full moon) and quadrature (first or third quarter), respectively; the dashed ellipse shows the smaller tidal force envelope produced by the sun.

### 3. The Net or Differential Tide-Raising Forces: Direct and Opposite Tides.

It has been emphasized above that the centrifugal force under consideration results from the revolution of the center-of-mass of the earth around the center-of-mass of the earth-moon system, and that this centrifugal force is the same anywhere on the earth. Since the individual centers-of-mass of the earth and moon remain in equilibrium at constant distances from the barycenter, the centrifugal force acting upon the center of the earth (C) as the result of their common revolutions must be equal and opposite to the gravitational force exerted by the moon on the center of the earth. This fact is indicated at point C in figure 2 by the thin and heavy arrows of equal length,

pointing in opposite directions. The net result of this circumstance is that the tide-producing force (Ft) at the earth's center is zero.

At point A in figure 2, approximately 4,000 miles nearer to the moon than is point C, the force produced by the moon's gravitational pull is considerably larger than the gravitational force at C due to the moon (the earth's own gravity is, of course, zero at point C). The smaller lunar gravitational force at C just balances the centrifugal force at C. Since the centrifugal force at A is equal to that at C, the greater gravitational force at A must also be larger than the centrifugal force there. The net tide-producing force at A obtained by taking the difference between the gravitational and centrifugal forces is in favor of the gravitational component — or outward toward the moon. The tide-raising force at point A is indicated in figure 2 by the double-shafted arrow extending vertically from the earth's surface toward the moon. The resulting tide produced on the side of the earth toward the moon is known as the *direct tide.*

At point B, on the opposite side of the earth from the moon and about 4,000 miles farther away from the moon than is point C, the moon's gravitational force is considerably less than at C. At point C, the centrifugal force is in balance with a gravitational force which is greater than at B. The centrifugal force at B is the same as that at C. Since gravitational force is less at B than at C, it follows that the centrifugal force exerted at B must be greater than the gravitational force exerted by the moon at B. The resultant tide-producing force at this point is, therefore, directed away from the earth's center and opposite to the position of the moon. This force is indicated by the double-shafted arrow at point B. The tide produced in this location halfway around the earth from the sublunar point, coincidentally with the direct tide, is known as the *opposite tide.*

**4. The Tractive Force.** It is significant that the influence of the moon's gravitational attraction superimposes its effects upon, but does not overcome, the effects of the earth's own gravity. Earth-gravity, although always present, plays no direct part in the tide-producing action. The tide-raising force exerted at a point on the earth's surface by the moon at its average distance from the earth (238,855 miles) is only about one 9-millionth part of the force of earth-gravity exerted toward its center (3,963 miles from the surface). The tide-raising force of the moon is, therefore, entirely insufficient to "lift" the waters of the earth physically against this far greater pull of the earth's gravity. Instead, the tides are produced by that component of the tide-raising force of the moon that acts to draw the waters of the earth horizontally over its surface toward the sublunar and antipodal points. Since the horizontal component is not opposed in any way to gravity and can, therefore, act to draw particles of water freely over the earth's surface, it

becomes the effective force in generating tides.

At any point on the earth's surface, the tidal force produced by the moon's gravitational attraction may be separated or "resolved" into two components of force: the one in the vertical, or perpendicular, to the earth's surface, and the other horizontal, or tangent, to the earth's surface. This second component, known as the *tractive* ("drawing") component of force is the actual mechanism for producing the tides. The force is zero at points on the earth's surface directly beneath and on the opposite side of the earth from the moon (since in these positions, the lunar gravitational force is exerted in the vertical — i.e., opposed to, and in the direction of, earth gravity, respectively). Any water accumulated in these locations by tractive flow from other points on the earth's surface tends to remain in a stable configuration, or tidal "bulge."

Thus, there exists an active tendency for water to be drawn from other points on the earth's surface toward the sublunar point (A, in fig. 2) and its antipodal point (B. in fig. 2), and to be heaped at these points in two tidal bulges. Within a band around the earth at all points 90° from the sublunar point, the horizontal or tractive force of the moon's gravitation is also zero, since the entire tide-producing force is directed vertically inward. There is, therefore, a tendency for the formation of a stable depression here. The words "tend to" and "tendency for" employed in several usages above in connection with tide-producing forces are deliberately chosen since, as will be seen below, the actual representation of the tidal forces at work is that of an idealized "force envelope," within which the rise and fall of the tides is influenced by many factors.

**5. The Tidal Force Envelope.** If the ocean waters were completely to respond to the directions and magnitudes of these tractive forces at various points on the surface of the earth, a mathematical figure would be formed having the shape of a prolate spheroid. The longest (major) axis of the spheroid extends toward and directly away from the moon, and the shortest (minor) axis is centered along, and at right angles to, the major axis. The two tidal humps and two tidal depressions are represented

### FIG. 4 — The Lunar Parallax and Solar Parallax Inequalities

Both the moon and the earth revolve in elliptical orbits and the distances from their centers of attraction vary. Increased gravitational influences and tide-raising forces are produced when the moon is at position of perigee, its closest approach to the earth (once each month) or the earth is at perihelion, its closest approach to the sun (once each year). This diagram also shows the possible coincidence of perigee with perihelion to produce tides of augmented range.

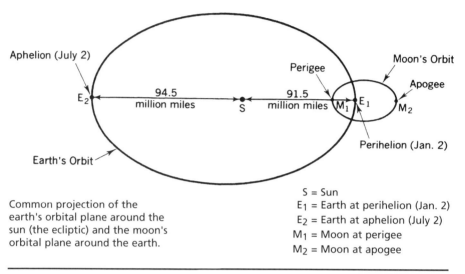

Common projection of the earth's orbital plane around the sun (the ecliptic) and the moon's orbital plane around the earth.

S = Sun
$E_1$ = Earth at perihelion (Jan. 2)
$E_2$ = Earth at aphelion (July 2)
$M_1$ = Moon at perigee
$M_2$ = Moon at apogee

in this force envelope by the directions of the major axis and rotated minor axis of the spheroid, respectively. From a purely theoretical point of view, the daily rotation of the solid earth with respect to these two tidal humps and two depressions may be conceived to be the cause of the tides.

As the earth rotates once in each 24 hours, one would ideally expect to find a high tide followed by a low tide at the same place six hours later; then a second high tide after 12 hours, a second low tide 18 hours later, and finally a return to high water at the expiration of 24 hours. Such would nearly be the case if a smooth, continent-free earth were covered to a uniform depth with water, if the tidal force envelope of the moon alone were being considered, if the positions of the moon and sun were fixed and invariable in distance and relative orientation with respect to the earth, and if there were no other accelerating or retarding influences affecting the motions of the waters of the earth. Such, in actuality, is far from the situation that exists.

First, the tidal force envelope produced by the moon's gravitational attraction is accompanied by a tidal force envelope of considerably smaller amplitude produced by the sun. The tidal force exerted by the sun is a composite of the sun's gravitational attraction and a centrifugal force component created by the revolution of the earth's center-of-mass around the center-of-mass of the earth-sun system, in an exactly analogous manner to the earth-moon relationship. The position of this force envelope shifts with the relative orbital position of the earth in respect to the sun. Because of the great difference between the average distances of the moon (238,855 miles) and sun (92,900,000 miles) from the earth, the tide-raising force of the moon is approximately 2½ times that of the sun.

Second, there exists a wide range of astronomical variables in the production of the tides caused by the changing distances of the moon from the earth, the earth from the sun, the angle which the moon in its orbit makes with the earth's equator, the superposition of the sun's tidal envelope of forces upon that caused by the

**FIG. 5 — The Moon's Declination Effect (Change in Angle with Respect to the Equator) and the Diurnal Inequality; Semidiurnal, Mixed, and Diurnal Tides**

A north-south cross section through the earth's center; the ellipse represents a meridian section through the tidal force envelope produced by the moon.

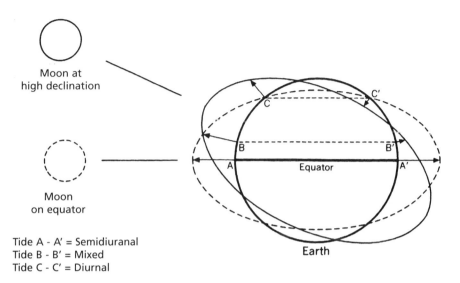

Moon at high declination

Moon on equator

Tide A - A' = Semidiuranal
Tide B - B' = Mixed
Tide C - C' = Diurnal

Equator

Earth

---

moon, the variable phase relationships of the moon, etc. Some of the principal types of tides resulting from these purely astronomical influences are described below.

### Variations in the Range of the Tides: Tidal Inequalities

As is shown in figure 6, the difference in height, in feet, between consecutive high and low tides occurring at a given place is known as the *range*. The range of the tides at any one location is subject to many variable factors. Those influences of astronomical origin will first be described.

**1. Lunar Phase Effects: Spring and Neap Tides.** It has been noted above that the gravitational forces of both the moon and sun act upon the waters of the earth. It is also obvious that, because of the moon's changing position with respect to the earth and sun (fig. 3) during its monthly cycle of phases (29.53 days), the gravitational attraction of moon and sun may variously act along a common line or at changing angles relative to each other.

When the moon is at new phase and full phase (both positions are called *syzygy*), the gravitational attractions of the moon and sun act to reinforce each other. Since the resultant or combined tidal force is also increased, the observed high tides are higher and low tides are lower than average. This means that the tidal range is greater at all locations that display a consecutive high and low water. Such greater-than-average tides resulting at the syzygy positions of the moon are known as *spring tides* — a term that merely implies a "welling up" of the water and bears no relationship to the season of the year.

At first- and third-quarter phases (quadrature) of the moon, the gravitational attractions of the moon and sun upon the waters of the earth are exerted at right angles to each other. Each force tends in part to counteract the other. In the tidal force envelope representing these combined forces, both the maximum and minimum force values are reduced. High tides are lower and low tides are higher than average. Such tides of diminished range

Tides & Currents

## FIG. 6 — Principal Types of Tides

Showing the moon's declinational effect in production of semidiurnal, mixed, and diurnal tides.

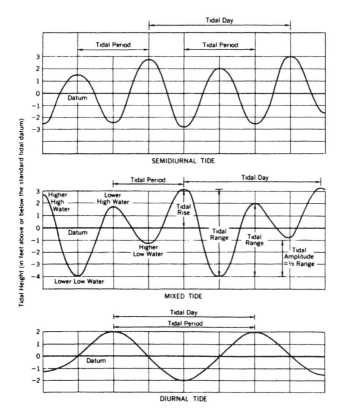

SEMIDIURNAL TIDE

MIXED TIDE

DIURNAL TIDE

are called *neap tides,* from a Greek word meaning "scanty."

**2. Parallax Effects (Moon and Sun).** Because the moon follows an elliptical path (fig. 4), the distance between the earth and moon will vary throughout the month by about 31,000 miles. The moon's gravitational attraction for the earth's waters will change in inverse proportion to the third power of the distance between earth and moon, in accordance with previously mentioned variation of Newton's Law of Gravitation. Once each month, when the moon is closest to the earth (perigee), the tide-generating forces will be higher than usual, thus producing above-average ranges in the tides. Approximately two weeks later, when the moon (at apogee) is farthest from the earth, the lunar tide-raising force will be

smaller, and the tidal ranges will be less than average. Similarly, in the sun-earth system, when the earth is closest to the sun (perihelion), about January 2 of each year, the tidal ranges will be enhanced, and when the earth is farthest from the sun (aphelion), around July 2, the tidal ranges will be reduced.

When perigee, perihelion, and either the new or full moon occur at approximately the same time, considerably increased tidal ranges result. When apogee, aphelion, and the first- or third-quarter moon coincide at approximately the same time, considerably reduced tidal ranges will normally occur.

**3. Lunar Declination Effects: The Diurnal Inequality.** The plane of the moon's orbit is inclined only about 5° to the plane of the earth's orbit (the ecliptic) and thus the moon in its monthly revolution around the earth remains very close to the ecliptic. The ecliptic is inclined 23 1/2° to the earth's equator, north and south of which the sun moves once each half year to produce the seasons. Similarly, the moon, in making a revolution around the earth once each month, passes from a position of maximum angular distance north of the equator to a position of maximum angular distance south of the equator during each half month. (Angular distance perpendicularly north or south of the celestial equator is termed *declination*.) Twice each month, the moon crosses the equator. In figure 5, this condition is shown by the dashed position of the moon. The corresponding tidal force envelope due to the moon is depicted, in profile, by the dashed ellipse.

Since the points A and A' lie along the major axis of this ellipse, the height of the high tide represented at A is the same as that which occurs as this point rotates to position A' some 12 hours later. When the moon is over the equator — or at certain other force-equalizing declinations — the two high tides and two low tides on a given day are similar in height at any location. Successive high tides and low tides are then also nearly equally spaced in time, and occur uniformly twice daily. (See top diagram in fig. 6.) This is known as the semidiurnal type of tides.

However, with the changing angular distance of the moon above or below the equator (represented by the position of the small solid circle in fig. 5), the tidal force envelope produced by the moon is canted, and differences between the heights of two daily tides of the same phase begin to occur. Variations in the heights of the tides resulting from the changes in the declination angle of the moon and in the corresponding lines of gravitational force action give rise to a phenomenon known as the *diurnal inequality.*

In figure 5, point B is beneath a bulge in the tidal envelope. One-half day later, at point B', it is again beneath the bulge, but the height of the tide is obviously not as great as at B. This situation gives rise to a twice-daily tide displaying unequal heights in successive high or low waters, or in both pairs of tides. This type of tide, exhibiting a strong diurnal inequality, is known as a mixed tide. (See the middle diagram in fig. 6.)

Finally, as depicted in figure 5, the point C is seen to lie beneath a portion of the tidal force envelope. One-half day later, however, as this point rotates to position C', it is seen to lie above the force envelope. At this location, therefore, the tidal forces present produce only one high water and one low water each day. The resultant diurnal type of tide is shown in the bottom diagram of figure 6.

## FACTORS INFLUENCING LOCAL HEIGHTS AND TIMES OF THE TIDES

It is noteworthy in figure 6 that any one cycle of the tides is characterized by a definite time regularity as well as the recurrence of the cyclical pattern. However, continuing observations at coastal stations will reveal — in addition to the previously explained variations in the heights of successive tides of the same phase — noticeable differences in their successive times of occurrence. The aspects of regularity in the tidal curves are introduced by the harmonic motions of the earth and moon. The variations noted both in the observed heights of the tides and in their times of occurrence are the result of many factors, some of which have been discussed in the preceding section. Other influences will now be considered.

The earth rotates on its axis (from one meridian transit of the "mean" sun until the next) in 24 hours. But as the earth rotates beneath the envelope of tidal forces produced by the moon, another astronomical factor causes the time between two successive upper transits of the moon across the local meridian of the place (a period known as the lunar or tidal day) to exceed the 24 hours of the earth's rotation period — the mean solar day.

The moon revolves in its orbit around the earth with an angular velocity of approximately 12.2° per day, in the same direction in which the earth is rotating on its axis with an angular velocity of 360° per day. In each day, therefore, a point on the rotating earth must complete a rotation of 360° plus 12.2°, or 372.2°, to "catch up" with the moon. Since 15° is equal to one hour of time, this extra amount of rotation equal to 12.2° each day would require an extra

439

period of time equal to 12.2°/15° x 60m/hr., or 48.8 minutes — if the moon revolved in a circular orbit and its speed of revolution did not vary. *On the average* it requires about 50 minutes longer each day for a sublunar point on the rotating earth to regain this position directly along the major axis of the moon's tidal force envelope, where the tide-raising influence is a maximum. In consequence, the recurrence of a tide of the same phase and similar rise (see middle diagram of fig. 6) would take place at an interval of 24 hours 50 minutes after the preceding occurrence, if this single astronomical factor known as *lunar retardation* were considered. This period of 24 hours 50 minutes has been established as the *tidal day.*

A second astronomical factor influencing the time of arrival of tides of a given phase at any location results from the interaction between the tidal force envelopes of the moon and sun. Between new moon and first-quarter phase, and between full moon and third-quarter phase, this phenomenon can cause a displacement of force components and an acceleration in tidal arrival times (known as *priming of the tides*), resulting in the occurrence of high tides before the moon reaches the local meridian of the place. Between first-quarter phase and full moon, and between third-quarter phase and new moon, an opposite displacement of force components and a delaying action (known as *lagging of the tides*) can occur, as the result of which the arrival of high tides may take place several hours after the moon has reached the meridian.

These are the two principal astronomical causes for variation in the times of arrival of the tides. In addition to these astronomically induced variations, the tides are subject to other accelerating and retarding influences of hydraulic, hydrodynamic, hydrographic, and topographic origin — and may further be modified by meteorological conditions.

The first factor of consequence in this regard arises from the fact that the crests and troughs of the large-scale gravity-type traveling wave system comprising the tides strive to sweep continuously around the earth, following the position of the moon (and sun).

In the open ocean, the actual *rise* (see middle diagram, fig. 6) of the tidally induced wave crest is only one to a few feet. It is only when the tidal crests and troughs move into shallow water, against landmasses, and into confining channels, that noticeable variations in the height of sea level can be detected.

Possessing the physical properties of a fluid, the ocean waters follow all of the hydraulic laws of fluids. This means that, since the ocean waters possess a definite, although small-internal, viscosity this property prevents their absolutely free flow and somewhat retards the overall movement of the tides.

Secondly, the ocean waters follow the principles of traveling waves in a fluid. As the depth of the water shallows, the speed of forward movement of a traveling wave is retarded, as deduced from dynamic considerations. In shoaling situations, therefore, the advance of tidal waters is slowed.

Thirdly, a relatively small amount of friction exists between the water and the ocean floor over which it moves — again, slightly slowing the movement of the tides, particularly as they move inshore. Further internal friction (or viscosity) exists between tidally induced currents and contiguous currents in the ocean — especially where they are flowing in opposite directions.

The presence of landmasses imposes a barrier to progress of the tidal waters. Where continents interpose, tidal movements are confined to separate, nearly closed oceanic basins and the sweep of the tides around the world is not continuous.

Topography on the ocean floor can also provide a restraint to the forward movement of tidal waters — or may create sources of local-basin response to the tides. Restrictions to the advance of tidal waters imposed both by shoaling depths and the sidewalls of the channel as these waters enter confined bays, estuaries, and harbors can further considerably alter the speed of their onshore passage.

In such partially confined bodies of water, so-called "resonance effects" between the free period of oscillation of the traveling, tidally induced wave and that of the confining basin may cause a surging rise of the water. Basically, this phenomenon is similar to the action of water when "sloshed" over the sides of a washbasin by repeatedly tilting the basin and matching the wave crests reflected from opposite sides of the basin.

All of the above, and other less important influences, can combine to create a considerable variety in the observed range and phase sequence of the tides — as well as variations in the times of their arrival at any location.

Of a more local and sporadic nature, important meteorological contributions to the tides known as "storm surges," caused by a continuous strong flow of winds either onshore or offshore, may superimpose their effects upon those of tidal action to cause either heightened or diminished tides, respectively. High-pressure atmospheric systems may also depress the tides, and deep low-pressure systems may cause them to increase in height.

## PREDICTION OF THE TIDES

In the preceding discussions of the tide-generating forces, the theoretical equilibrium tide produced, and factors causing variations, it has been emphasized that the tides actually observed differ appreciably from the idealized, equilibrium tide. Nevertheless, because the tides are produced essentially by astronomical forces of harmonic nature, a definite relationship exists between the tide-generating forces and the observed tides, and a factor of predictability is possible.

Because of the numerous uncertain and, in some cases, completely unknown factors of local control mentioned above, it is not feasible to predict tides purely from a knowledge of the positions and movements of the moon and sun obtained from astronomical tables. A partially empirical approach based upon actual observations of tides in many areas over an extended period of time is necessary. To achieve maximum accuracy in prediction, a series of tidal observations at any one location ranging over at least a full 18.6-year tidal cycle is required. Within this period, all significant astronomical modifications of tides will occur.

Responsibility for computing and tabulating — for any day in the year — the times, heights, and ranges of the tides — as well as the movement of tidal currents — in various parts of the world is vested in appropriate governmental agencies that devote both theoretical and practical effort to this task. The resulting predictions are based in large part upon actual observations of tidal heights made throughout a network of selected observing stations. The factors used to predict a particular station, both local and astronomical. are called its "harmonic constituents."

The U.S. National Ocean Service (NOS), a component of the National Oceanic and Atmospheric Administration of the U.S. Department of Commerce, maintains for this purpose a continuous control network of approximately 140 tide gauges that are located along the coasts and within the major embayments of the United States, its possessions, and United Nations Trust Territories under its jurisdiction. Temporary secondary stations are also occupied to increase the effective coverage of the control network. Tidal data are recorded on chart rolls and punched tape, and are translated onto magnetic tape for electronic computer processing, tabular printout, and analysis.

Predictions of the times and heights of high and low water are prepared by the National Ocean Survey for a large number of stations in the United States and its possessions as well as in foreign countries and United Nations Trust Territories.

The National Ocean Survey published six volumes of *Tide and Current Tables* each year. Now, NOS makes these predictions available to numerous private publishers like *Reed's* for printing and distribution. NOS also shares their harmonic constituents with software publishers who produce programs that can do the complex mathematics of predicting primary stations as well as the simple math of calculating secondary stations.

# TIDE AND CURRENT MISCELLANY

This *Companion* can not present regular tide or current prediction tables because it is not an annual publication. Here's what you will find in the rest of this chapter:

- Notes on important tide prediction terms, with general descriptions of typical U.S. tide phenomenon.
- A glossary of tide and current terms.
- Several ways to determine the height of the tide at any time between known high and low heights.
- A table for calculating current speed at any time when you know the times of slack and maximum ebb or flood.
- A section on wind-driven currents with data collected on both Atlantic and Pacific coasts, and a discourse on how to plot the combination of wind-driven and tidal currents.
- Tables on offshore rotary tidal currents along the U.S. Atlantic Coast.
- Tables on offshore tidal currents along some sections of the U.S. Pacific Coast.
- Finally, a list of U.S. tidal reference stations with their datum below mean sea level.

Note that some of this material is also published in *Reed's Almanacs*, but may not be in future editions.

## TIDE NOTES

*Reed's Nautical Almanacs* contain complete sets of tides for their respective regions, using data collected and maintained by the U. S. National Ocean Service (NOS), the Canadian Hydrographic Service (CHS), and the United Kingdom Hydrographic Service.

Each set of tables consists of daily predictions for a number of reference ("primary") stations; that is, locations that are particularly important to mariners, or whose tide pattern represents a large area. Following the reference tables are the secondary tables, with which you can calculate the tides at thousands of locations by referencing difference factors to the primary tables. Each *Almanac* also contains thorough instructions on how to use the tables.

Following are some notes about the particulars of tide tables:

**Typical tide curves:** The variations in the tide from day-to-day and from place-to-place are illustrated on the following pages by tide curves for representative ports along the Atlantic and Pacific coasts of the United States.

All three tide-curve types occur on the East Coast. In most locations, the tides follow a classic *semidiurnal* curve — two tides each day of similar height. In some southeastern waters, the tidal curve tends to be *mixed* — the height difference between one high and low is significantly less than the difference between the tidal day's other high and low or, during part of the tidal month there is only one high and low per tidal day. In the Gulf of Mexico, there are several locations that are *diurnal* — only one high and low per tidal day.

Illustrated on the opposite page are the tide curves for representative ports along the U.S. Atlantic Coast. Note how these curves correlate with the synopsis above. Further note that, at places with mixed or diurnal tides, it is particularly important to calculate the height as well as the time of the tides. In such locations, the tide cycle is closely related to the declination of the moon and its distance from earth. (Information about the moon's declination and distance can be found in the monthly pages of the *Ephemeris* chapter in each edition of *Reed's Nautical Almanac*.)

All three tide-curve types also occur on the West Coast. In many locations, there are semidiurnal tide curves, but throughout much of the area, the tidal curve is mixed. In Mexico, there are a few locations that are *diurnal*.

An illustration on the next page shows the tide curves for representative ports along the U.S. Pacific Coast. Note that one of the chief characteristics of the tide in this region is diurnal inequality; that is, the difference in heights of successive high or low waters. The largest inequality is in the low waters, although at Seattle there is also considerable difference between the two high waters on certain days. The

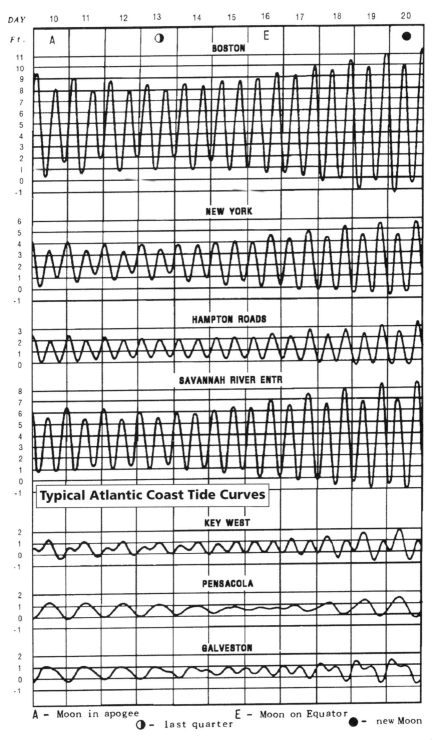

Typical Atlantic Coast Tide Curves

A - Moon in apogee          E - Moon on Equator
      ☽ - last quarter                        ● - new Moon

Tides & Currents

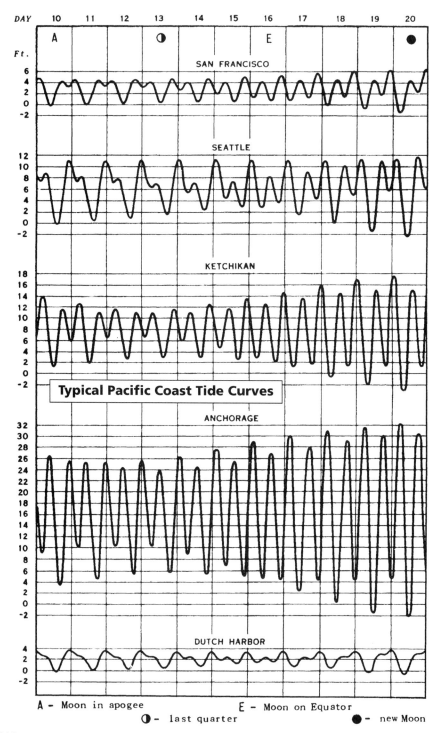

Typical Pacific Coast Tide Curves

A - Moon in apogee     E - Moon on Equator
◑ - last quarter          ● - new Moon

importance of this inequality at Seattle is demonstrated by the curve that shows that, at times, the two high waters of a day differ by more than four feet and the two low waters differ by more than eight feet.

At Ketchikan and Anchorage the inequality is less pronounced because of the large range of tide. There, the principal variations in the tide follow the changes in the moon's phase and distance. The tide at Anchorage is one of the largest in the world. At Unalaska and Dutch Harbor the tide is semidiurnal around the times the moon is on the equator, but becomes diurnal around the times of maximum north or south declination of the moon. (Information about the moon's declination and distance can be found in the monthly pages of the *Ephemeris* chapter in each edition of *Reed's Nautical Almanacs*.)

**Datum:** Tidal datums are very much like chart datums; they define the height of water that the chart or table maker has chosen as "0." There are a remarkable number of datum names and definitions in use throughout the world. Theoretically, the tide datum should not concern the mariner because it should be matched with the chart datum in use for that location. For instance, if you are using a tide table marked "U.S. Datum," zero feet represents Mean Lower Low Water (MLLW) — the average of the lower of the two low waters of each day. NOAA charts use the same datum. Therefore, you may simply apply the tide heights in the table to the charted depths; at the time of a six-foot tide over a charted eight-foot bottom, there should be 14 feet of water.

Canada uses Lowest Normal Tides (LNT) for its tide tables and charts, which are significantly different from the datum used in the United States. LNT is usually synonymous with Lower Low Water, Large Tides (LLWLT) — the average of the lowest low waters, one from each year of 19 years of predictions (the tide epoch). You may apply Canadian tide predictions directly to Canadian charts, but not to NOAA or NIMA charts. With the large tide ranges in Nova Scotia and New Brunswick, there are significant differences between LNT and MLLW. Consult the datum table on your chart to calculate the value you should subtract from Canadian height predictions to adjust them to your chart datum.

Tide tables for foreign locations marked *Chart Datum* are less definitive. NOS says on the subject: "For foreign coasts, a datum approximating to mean low water springs (MLWS), Indian spring low water, or the lowest possible low water is generally used." The tide datums are supposed to match the local charts for these waters, but often there are redundant charts originating in several different countries and they may use different chart datums. For maximum accuracy, you should check the datum used on your chart and then scan the low-tide heights in the table you are using to approximate its datum. Tide tables (like U.S.) with numerous tides less than zero feet per month use a MLLW-type datum. Tables with almost no minus tides per month use a datum like MLWS; and tables with no minus tides probably use Lowest Astronomical Tide (LAT) or LLWLT. The Bermuda and Bahamas tide tables appear to use the LAT datum favored by the British.

**Variation in sea level:** Changes in winds and barometric conditions cause variations in sea level from day-to-day. Generally, with onshore winds or a low barometer, the heights of both high and low waters will be higher than predicted; with offshore winds or a high barometer they will be lower. There are also seasonal variations in sea level, but these variations have been included in the predictions for each station. At ocean stations, the seasonal variation in sea level is usually less than half a foot. At stations on tidal rivers, the average seasonal variation in river level due to freshets and droughts may be considerably more than a foot. The predictions for these stations include an allowance for this seasonal variation, representing average freshet and drought conditions. Unusual freshets or droughts, however, will cause the tides to be higher or lower, respectively, than predicted.

**Number of tides:** At locations with semidiurnal or mixed tide curves, there are usually two high and two low waters daily. Tides follow the moon more closely than they do the sun, and the lunar (tidal) day is about 50 minutes longer than the solar day. This causes the tide to occur later each day, and a tide that has occurred near the end of one calendar day will be followed by a corresponding tide that may skip the next day and occur in the early morning of the third day. Thus, on certain days of each month, only a single high or a single low water occurs.

**Relation of tide to current:** In using tide prediction tables, bear in mind that they give the times and heights of high and low waters and *not* the times of turning of the current or slack water. For stations on outer coasts there is usually a small difference between the time of high or low water and the beginning of ebb or flood current, but for places in narrow channels, landlocked harbors, or on tidal rivers, the time of slack water may differ by several hours from the time of high- or low-water stand. The relation of the times of high and low water to the turning of the current depends upon a number of factors, so no simple or general rule can be given. (See the *Currents* chapter in *Reed's Nautical Almanacs* for more information.)

**Annual Inequality:** Seasonal variation in the water level or current, more or less periodic, due chiefly to meteorological causes.

**Apogean Tides or Tidal Currents:** Tides of decreased range, or currents of decreased speed, occurring monthly as the result of the moon being in apogee (farthest from the Earth).

**Automatic Tide Gauge:** An instrument that automatically registers the rise and fall of the tide. In some instruments, the registration is accomplished by recording the heights at regular intervals in digital format; in others, it's done by a continuous graph in which the height, versus corresponding time of the tide, is recorded.

**Benchmark (BM):** A fixed physical object or marks used as reference for a vertical datum. A tidal benchmark is one near a tide station to which the tide staff and

### A diagram of tidal datums and ranges (USA)

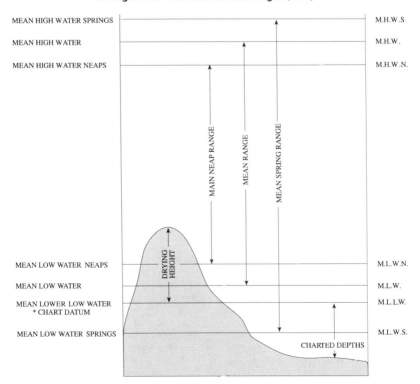

| | |
|---|---|
| MEAN HIGH WATER SPRINGS | M.H.W.S |
| MEAN HIGH WATER | M.H.W. |
| MEAN HIGH WATER NEAPS | M.H.W.N. |

MAIN NEAP RANGE  
MEAN RANGE  
MEAN SPRING RANGE

DRYING HEIGHT

| | |
|---|---|
| MEAN LOW WATER NEAPS | M.L.W.N. |
| MEAN LOW WATER | M.L.W. |
| MEAN LOWER LOW WATER * CHART DATUM | M.L.L.W. |
| MEAN LOW WATER SPRINGS | M.L.W.S. |

CHARTED DEPTHS

tidal datums are referred. A *Geodetic benchmark* identifies a surveyed point in the National Geodetic Vertical Network.

**Chart Datum:** The tidal datum to which soundings on a chart are referred. It is usually taken to correspond to low-water elevation of the tide, and its depression below mean sea level is represented by the symbol $Z_0$.

**Current:** Generally, a horizontal movement of water. Currents may be classified as *tidal* and *nontidal*. Tidal currents are caused by gravitational interactions between the sun, moon, and earth, and are a part of the same general movement of the sea that is manifested in the vertical rise and fall, called *tide*. Nontidal currents include the permanent currents in the general circulatory systems of the sea as well as temporary currents arising from more pronounced meteorological variability.

**Current Difference:** Difference between the time of slack water (or minimum current) or strength of current in any locality, and the time of the corresponding phase of the tidal current at a reference station, for which predictions are given in the *Tidal Current Tables.*

**Current Ellipse:** A graphic representation of a rotary current in which the velocity of the current at different hours of the tidal cycle is represented by radius vectors and vectorial angles. A line joining the extremities of the radius vectors will form a curve roughly approximating an ellipse. The cycle is completed in one-half tidal day or in a whole tidal day, according to whether the tidal current is semidiurnal or diurnal. A mixed current will give a curve of two unequal loops each tidal day.

**Current Meter:** An instrument for measuring the speed and direction, or just the speed, of a current.

**Datum (vertical):** For marine applications, a base elevation used as a reference from which to reckon heights or depths. It is called a *tidal datum* when defined by a certain phase of the tide. Tidal datums are local datums and should not be extended into areas that have differing topographic features without substantiating measurements. So they may be recovered when needed, such datums are referenced to fixed points known as *benchmarks*.

**Daylight Saving Time:** A time used during the summer in some localities in which clocks are advanced one hour from the usual standard time.

**Diurnal:** Having a period or cycle of approximately one tidal day. Thus, a tide is said to be diurnal when only one high water and one low water occur during a tidal day; a tidal current is said to be diurnal when there is a single flood and single ebb period in the tidal day. A rotary current is diurnal if it changes its directions through all points of the compass once each tidal day.

**Diurnal Inequality:** The difference in height of the two high waters or of the two low waters of each day. Also, the difference in speed between the two flood tidal currents or the two ebb tidal currents of each day. The difference changes with the declination of the moon and, to a lesser extent, with the declination of the sun. Generally, the inequality tends to increase with an increasing declination, either north or south, and to diminish as the moon approaches the Equator. *Mean diurnal high water inequality (DHQ)* is one-half the average difference between the two high waters of each day observed over a specific 19-year Metonic cycle (the National Tidal Datum Epoch). It is obtained by subtracting the mean of all high waters from the mean of the higher high waters. *Mean diurnal low water inequality (DLQ)* is one-half the average difference between the two low waters of each day observed over a specific 19-year Metonic cycle (the National Tidal Datum Epoch). It is obtained by subtracting the mean of the lower low waters from the mean of all low waters. *Tropic high water inequality (HWQ)* is the average difference between the two high waters of the day at the times of the tropic tides. *Tropic low water inequality (LWQ)* is the average difference between the two low waters of the day at the times of the tropic tides. Mean and tropic inequalities as defined above are applicable only when the tide is either semidiurnal or mixed. Diurnal inequality is sometimes called declinational inequality.

**Double Ebb:** An ebb tidal current where, after ebb begins, the speed increases to a maximum called *first ebb*. It then decreases, reaching a minimum ebb near the middle of the ebb period (at some places it may actually run in a flood direction for a short period). It then again ebbs to a maximum speed called *second ebb,* after which it decreases to slack water.

**Double Flood:** A flood tidal current where, after flood begins, the speed increases to a maximum called *first flood.* It then decreases, reaching a minimum flood near the middle of the flood period (at some places it may actually run in an ebb direction for a short period). It then again floods to a maximum speed called *second flood,* after which it decreases to slack water.

**Double Tide:** A double-headed tide; that is, a high water consisting of two maxima of nearly the same height, separated by a relatively small depression, or a low water consisting of two minima separated by a relatively small elevation. Sometimes called an *agger.*

**Duration of Flood and Duration of Ebb:** Duration of flood is the interval of time in which a tidal current is flooding; the duration of ebb is the interval in which it is ebbing. Together they cover, on an average, a period of 12.42 hours for a semidiurnal tidal current ,or a period of 24.84 hours for a diurnal current. In a normal semidiurnal tidal current, the duration of flood and duration of ebb will each be approximately equal to 6.21 hours, but the times may be modified greatly by the presence of a nontidal flow. In a river, the duration of ebb is usually longer than the duration of flood because of the freshwater discharge, especially during the spring when snow and ice melt are the predominant influences.

**Duration of Rise and Duration of Fall:** Duration of rise is the interval from low water to high water; duration of fall is the interval from high water to low water. Together they cover, on an average, a period of 12.42 hours for a semidiurnal tide, or a period of 24.84 hours for a diurnal tide. In a normal semidiurnal tide, the duration of rise and duration of fall will each be approximately equal to 6.21 hours, but in shallow waters and in rivers there is a tendency for a decrease in the duration of rise and a corresponding increase in the duration of fall.

**Ebb Current:** The movement of a tidal current away from shore or down a tidal river or estuary. In the mixed type of reversing tidal current, the terms "greater ebb" and "lesser ebb" are applied respectively to the ebb tidal currents of greater and lesser speed of each day. The terms "maximum ebb" and "minimum ebb" are applied to the maximum and minimum speeds of a current running continuously ebb, the speed alternately increasing and decreasing without coming to a slack or reversing. The expression "maximum ebb" is also applicable to any ebb current at the time of greatest speed.

**Equatorial Tidal Currents:** Tidal currents occurring semimonthly as a result of the moon being over the equator. At these times, the tendency of the Moon to produce a diurnal inequality in the tidal current is at a minimum.

**Equatorial Tides:** Tides occurring semimonthly as the result of the Moon being over the equator. At these times, the tendency of the Moon to produce a diurnal inequality in the tide is at a minimum.

**Flood Current:** The movement of a tidal current toward the shore or up a tidal river or estuary. In the mixed type of reversing current, the terms "greater flood" and "lesser flood" are applied respectively to the flood currents of greater and lesser speed of each day. The terms "maximum flood" and "minimum flood" are applied to the maximum and minimum speeds of a flood current, the speed of which alternately increases and decreases without coming to a slack or reversing. The expression "maximum flood" is also applicable to any flood current at the time of greatest speed.

**Great Diurnal Range (Gt):** The difference in height between mean higher high water and mean lower low water. The expression may also be used in its contracted form, diurnal range.

**Gulf Coast Low Water Datum:** A chart datum. Specifically, the tidal datum formerly designated for the coastal waters of the Gulf Coast of the United States. It was defined as mean lower low water when the type of tide was mixed, and mean low water when the type of tide was diurnal.

**Half-Tide Level:** See mean tide level.

**Harmonic Analysis:** The mathematical process by which the observed tide or tidal current at any place is separated into basic harmonic constituents.

**Harmonic Constants:** The amplitudes and epochs of the harmonic constituents of the tide or tidal current at any place.

**Harmonic Constituent:** One of the harmonic elements in a mathematical expression for the tide-producing force and in corresponding formulas for the tide or tidal current. Each constituent represents a periodic change or variation in the relative positions of the earth, moon, and sun. A single constituent is usually written in the form y=A cos(at+α), in which y is a function of time as expressed by the symbol t and is reckoned from a specific origin. The coefficient A is called the amplitude of the constituent and is a measure of its relative importance. The angle (at+α) changes uniformly and its value at any time is called the phase of the constituent. The speed of the constituent is the rate of change in its phase and is represented by the symbol "a" in the formula. The quantity α is the phase of the constituent at the initial instant from which the time is reckoned. The period of the constituent is the time required for the phase to change through 360° and is the cycle of the astronomical condition represented by the constituent.

**High Water (HW):** The maximum height reached by a rising tide. The height may be due solely to the periodic tidal forces, or it may have superimposed upon it the effects of prevailing meteorological conditions. Use of the synonymous term, high tide, is discouraged.

**Higher High Water (HHW):** The higher of the two high waters of any tidal day.

**Higher Low Water (HLW):** The higher of the two low waters of any tidal day.

**Hydraulic Current:** A current in a channel caused by a difference in the surface level at the two ends. Such a current may be expected in a strait connecting two bodies of water in which the tides differ in time or range. The current in New York City's East River, which connects Long Island Sound and New York Harbor, is an example.

**Knot:** A speed unit of one international nautical mile (1,852.0 meters or 6,076.11549 international feet) per hour.

**Low Water (LW):** The minimum height reached by a falling tide. The height may be due solely to the periodic tidal forces, or it may have superimposed upon it the effects of meteorological conditions. Use of the synonymous term, low tide, is discouraged.

**Lower High Water (LHW):** The lower of the two high waters of any tidal day.

**Lower Low Water (LLW):** The lower of the two low waters of any tidal day.

**Lunar Day:** The time of the rotation of the earth with respect to the moon, or the interval between two successive upper transits of the moon over the meridian of a place. The mean lunar day is approximately 24.84 solar hours long, or 1.035 times as long as the mean solar day.

**Lunar Interval:** The difference in time between the transit of them moon over the meridian of Greenwich and over a local meridian. The average value of this interval expressed in hours is 0.069 L, in which L is the local longitude in degrees, positive for west longitude and negative for east longitude. The lunar interval equals the difference between the local and Greenwich interval of a tide or current phase.

**Lunicurrent Interval:** The interval between the Moon's transit (upper or lower) over the local or Greenwich meridian and a specified phase of the tidal current following the transit.

*Examples:* Strength of flood interval and strength of ebb interval, which may be abbreviated to flood interval and ebb interval, respectively. The interval is described as local or Greenwich according to whether the reference is to the moon's transit over the local or Greenwich meridian. When not otherwise specified, the reference is assumed to be local.

**Lunitidal Interval:** The interval between the moon's transit (upper or lower) over the local or Greenwich meridian and the following high or low water. The average of all high-water intervals for all phases of the Moon is known as *mean high-water lunitidal interval* and is abbreviated to *high-water interval (HWI).* Similarly, the *mean low-water lunitidal interval* is abbreviated to *low-water interval (LWI).* The interval is described as local or Greenwich according to whether the reference is to the transit over the local or Greenwich meridian. When not otherwise specified, the reference is assumed to be local.

**Mean High Water (MHW):** A tidal datum. The arithmetic mean of the high-water heights observed over a specific 19-year Metonic cycle (the National Tidal Datum Epoch). For stations with shorter series, simultaneous observational comparisons are made with a primary control tide station to derive the equivalent of a 19-year value.

**Mean Higher High Water (MHHW):** A tidal datum. The arithmetic mean of the higher high-water heights of a mixed tide observed over a specific 19-year Metonic cycle (the National Tidal Datum Epoch). Only the higher high water of each pair of high waters, or the only high water of a tidal day is included in the mean.

**Mean Higher High Water Line (MHHWL):** The intersection of the land with the water surface at the elevation of mean higher high water.

**Mean Low Water (MLW):** A tidal datum. The arithmetic mean of the low-water heights observed over a specific 19-year Metonic cycle (the National Tidal Datum Epoch). For stations with shorter series, simultaneous observational comparisons are made with a primary control tide station in order to derive the equivalent of a 19-year value.

**Mean Low-Water Springs (MLWS):** A tidal datum. Frequently abbreviated "spring low water." The arithmetic mean of the low-water heights occurring at the time of the spring tides observed over a specific 19-year Metonic cycle (the National Tidal Datum Epoch).

**Mean Lower Low Water (MLLW):** A tidal datum. The arithmetic mean of the lower low-water heights of a mixed tide observed over a specific 19-year Metonic cycle (the National Tidal Datum Epoch). Only the lower low water of each pair of low waters, or the only low water of a tidal day, is included in the mean.

**Mean Range of Tide (Mn):** The difference in height between mean high water and mean low water.

**Mean River Level:** A tidal datum. The average height of the surface of a tidal river at any point for all stages of the tide observed over a 19-year Metonic cycle (the National Tidal Datum Epoch), usually determined from hourly height readings. In rivers subject to occasional freshets, the river level may undergo wide variations, and for practical purposes certain months of the year may be excluded in the determination of tidal datums. For charting purposes, tidal datums for rivers are usually based on observations during selected periods when the river is at or near low-water stage.

**Mean Sea Level (MSL):** A tidal datum. The arithmetic mean of hourly water elevations observed over a specific l9-year Metonic cycle (the National Tidal Datum Epoch). Shorter series are specified in the name; for example, monthly mean sea level and yearly mean sea level.

**Mean Tide Level (MTL):** Also called half-tide level. A tidal datum midway between mean high water and mean low water.

**Mixed Tide:** Type of tide with a large inequality in the high- and/or low-water heights, with two high waters and two low waters usually occurring each tidal day. Strictly speaking, all tides are mixed, but the name is usually applied to the tides intermediate to those predominantly semidiurnal and those predominantly diurnal.

**Neap Tides or Tidal Currents:** Tides of decreased range or tidal currents of decreased speed occurring semimonthly as the result of the Moon being in quadrature. The neap range (Np) of the tide is the average semidiurnal range occurring at the time of neap tides and is most conveniently computed from the harmonic constants. It is smaller than the mean range where the type of tide is either semidiurnal or mixed and is of no practical significance where the type of tide is diurnal. The average height of the high waters of the neap tides is called *neap high water* or *mean high water neaps (MHWN)* and the average height of the corresponding low waters is called *neap low water* or *mean low water neaps (MLWN)*.

**Perigean Tides or Tidal Currents:** Tides of increased range or tidal currents of increased speed occurring monthly as the result of the Moon being in perigee or nearest the earth. The perigean range (Pn) of tide is the average semidiurnal range occurring at the time of perigean tides and is most conveniently computed from the harmonic constants. It is larger than the mean range where the type of tide is either semidiurnal or mixed, and is of no practical significance where the type of tide is diurnal.

**Range of Tide:** The difference in height between consecutive high and low waters, the mean range is the difference in height between mean high water and mean low water. Where the type of tide is diurnal, the mean range is the same as the diurnal range. For other ranges, see great diurnal, spring, neap, perigean, apogean, and tropic tides.

**Reference Station:** A tide or current station for which independent daily predictions are given in the *Tide Tables* and *Tidal Current Tables,* and from which corresponding predictions are obtained for subordinate stations by means of differences and ratios.

**Reversing Current:** A tidal current that flows alternately in approximately opposite directions with a slack water at each reversal of direction. Currents of this type usually occur in rivers and straits where the direction of flow is more or less restricted to certain channels. When the movement is toward the shore or up a stream, the current is said to be flooding; when in the opposite direction, it is said to be ebbing. The combined flood and ebb movement, including the slack water, covers on an average 12.42 hours for the semidiurnal current. If unaffected by a nontidal flow, the flood and ebb movements each last about six hours, but when combined with such a flow, the durations of flood and ebb may be quite unequal. During the flow in each direction, the speed of the current varies from zero at the time of slack water to a maximum about midway between the slacks.

**Rotary Current:** A tidal current that flows continually with the direction of flow changing through all points of the compass during the tidal period. Rotary currents are usually found offshore where the direction of flow is not restricted by any barriers. The tendency for the rotation in direction has its origin in the Coriolis force and, unless modified by local conditions, the change is clockwise in the northern hemisphere and counterclockwise in the southern. The speed of the current usually varies throughout the tidal cycle, passing through the two maxima in approximately opposite directions and the two minima with the direction of the current at approximately 90° from the direction at time of maximum speed.

**Semidiurnal:** Having a period or cycle of approximately one-half of a tidal day. The predominating type of tide throughout the world is semidiurnal, with two high waters and two low waters each tidal day. The tidal current is said to be semidiurnal when there are two flood and two ebb periods each day.

**Set (of current):** The direction toward which the current flows.

**Slack Water:** The state of a tidal current when its speed is near zero, especially the moment when a reversing current changes direction and its speed is zero. The term is also applied to the entire period of low speed near the time of turning of the current when it is too weak to be of any practical importance in navigation. The relation of the time of slack water to the tidal phases varies in different localities. For standing tidal waves, slack water occurs near the times of high and low water; for progressive tidal waves, slack water occurs midway between high and low water.

**Spring Tides or Tidal Currents:** Tides of increased range or tidal currents of increased speed occurring semimonthly as the result of the Moon being new or full. The spring range (Sg) of tide is the average semidiurnal range occurring at the time of spring tides and is most conveniently computed from the harmonic constants. It is larger than the mean range where the type of tide is either semidiurnal or mixed, and is of no practical significance where the type of tide is diurnal. The mean of the high waters of the spring tide is called spring high water or mean high water springs (MHWS), and the average height of the corresponding low waters is called spring low water or mean low water springs (MLWS).

**Stand of Tide:** Sometimes called a platform tide. An interval at high or low water when there is no sensible change in the height of the tide. The water level is stationary at high and low water for only an instant, but the change in level near these times is so slow that it is not usually perceptible. In general, the duration of the apparent stand will depend upon the range of tide, being longer for a small range than for a large range, but where there is a tendency for a double tide the stand may last for several hours, even with a large range of tide.

**Standard Time:** A kind of time based upon the transit of the sun over a certain specified meridian, called the time meridian, and adopted for use over a considerable area. With a few exceptions, standard time is based upon some meridian that differs by a multiple of 15° from the meridian of Greenwich.

**Strength of Current:** Phase of tidal current in which the speed is a maximum; also the speed at this time. Beginning with slack before flood in the period of a reversing tidal current (or minimum before flood in a rotary current), the speed gradually increases to flood strength and then diminishes to slack before ebb (or minimum before ebb in a rotary current), after which the current turns in direction, the speed increases to ebb strength, and then diminishes to slack before flood completing the cycle. If it is assumed that the speed throughout the cycle varies as the ordinates of a cosine curve, it can be shown that the average speed for an entire flood or ebb period is equal to $2/\pi$ or 0.6366 of the speed of the corresponding strength of current.

**Subordinate Current Station:** (1) A current station from which a relatively short series of observations is reduced by comparison with simultaneous observations from a control current station. (2) A station listed in the *Tidal Current Tables,* for which predictions are to be obtained by means of differences and ratios applied to the full predictions at a reference station.

**Subordinate Tide Station:** (1) A tide station, from which a relatively short series of observations is reduced by comparison with simultaneous observations from a tide station with a relatively long series of observations. (2) A station listed in the *Tide Tables,* for which predictions are to be obtained by means of differences and ratios applied to the full predictions at a reference station.

**Tidal Current Tables:** Tables that give daily predictions of the times and speeds of the tidal currents. These predictions are usually supplemented by current differences and constants, through which additional predictions can be obtained for numerous other places.

**Tidal Difference:** Difference in time or height of a high or low water at a subordinate station and at a reference station, for which predictions are given in the *Tide Tables.* The difference, when applied according to sign to the prediction at the reference station, gives the corresponding time or height for the subordinate station.

**Tide:** The periodic rise and fall of the water resulting from gravitational interactions between the Sun, Moon, and Earth. The vertical component of the particulate motion of a tidal wave. Although the accompanying horizontal movement of the water is part of the same phenomenon, it is preferable to designate the motion as tidal current.

**Tide Tables:** Tables that give daily predictions of the times and heights of high and low waters. These predictions are usually supplemented by tidal differences and constants, through which additional predictions can be obtained for numerous other places.

**Time Meridian:** A meridian used as a reference for time.

**Tropic Currents:** Tidal currents occurring semimonthly when the effect of the Moon's maximum declination is greatest. At these times, the tendency of the Moon to produce a diurnal inequality in the current is at a maximum.

**Tropic Ranges:** The great tropic range (Gc), or tropic range, is the difference in height between tropic higher high water and tropic lower low water. The small tropic range (Sc) is the difference in height between tropic lower high water and tropic higher low water. The mean tropic range (Mc) is the mean between the great tropic range and the small tropic range. The small tropic range and the mean tropic range are applicable only when the type of tide is semidiurnal or mixed. Tropic ranges are most conveniently computed from the harmonic constants.

**Tropic Tides:** Tides occurring semimonthly when the effect of the Moon's maximum declination is greatest. At these times there is a tendency for an increase in the diurnal range. The tidal datums pertaining to the tropic tides are designated as tropic higher high water (TcHHW), tropic lower high water (TcLHW), tropic higher low water (TcHLW), and tropic lower low water (TcLLW) .

**Type of Tide:** A classification based on characteristic forms of a tide curve. Qualitatively, when the two high waters and two low waters of each tidal day are approximately equal in height, the tide is said to be semidiurnal; when there is a relatively large diurnal inequality in the high or low waters or both, it is said to be mixed; and when there is only one high water and one low water in each tidal day, it is said to be diurnal.

**Vanishing Tide:** In a mixed tide with very large diurnal inequality, the lower high water (or higher low water) frequently becomes indistinct (or vanishes) at time of extreme declinations. During these periods the diurnal tide has such overriding dominance that the semidiurnal tide, although still present, cannot be readily seen on the tide curve.

## HEIGHT OF TIDE AT ANY TIME

There are several methods to estimate the height of tide for a given time between predicted highs and lows. On these pages, we present the Rule of Twelfths, NOS's Table 3, and a graphic solution.

**Caution:** All of the methods presented here are based on the assumption that the rise and fall conform to simple cosine curves. The heights obtained will be approximate. The roughness of approximation will vary as the tide curve differs from a cosine curve. Semidiurnal tide curves tend to be closer to cosine curves than mixed or especially diurnal curves.

## THE RULE OF TWELFTHS
**A tide rises or falls** (approximately)

| | | |
|---|---|---|
| $^1/_{12}$ | of its range during the | **1st hour** |
| $^2/_{12}$ | of its range during the | **2nd hour** |
| $^3/_{12}$ | of its range during the | **3rd hour** |
| $^3/_{12}$ | of its range during the | **4th hour** |
| $^2/_{12}$ | of its range during the | **5th hour** |
| $^1/_{12}$ | of its range during the | **6th hour** |

This is very much an approximation, but it does give you a sense of how the tides accelerate and decelerate, and it gives you some tools with which to approximate intermediate heights.

For example, if the tide will rise 10 feet during its six-hour cycle, the law of twelfths suggests that after two hours it will have risen 2.5 feet:

$$(^1/_{12} + ^2/_{12}) = ^3/_{12} = ^1/_4 \times 10 = 2.5$$

If a tide will fall seven feet in its six-hour cycle, after four hours it will have fallen 5.25 feet:

$$^9/_{12} = ^3/_4 \times 7 = 5.25$$

## NOS TABLE

The National Ocean Service printed this table in their *Tide Prediction* books. First, read the footnote to the table on the next page. If you are confused — and you aren't alone! — you may wish to follow this example:

We'll find the height of tide at 0755 on a day when the predicted tides before and after 0755 are given as follows:

     morning low:   0522, 0.1 feet.
     morning high: 1114, 4.2 feet.

Therefore, the duration of rise is $11^h 14^m - 5^h 22^m = 5^h 52^m$. The time from the nearest high or low water is then $7^h 55^m - 5^h 22^m = 2^h 33^m$ (from low). The range of tide is given as $4.2 - 0.1 = 4.1$ feet.

We then enter the left-hand boldfaced column of the table and find the value nearest our value for the duration of rise and fall ($5^h 52^m$) — in

this case, $6^h 00^m$. Following across that row, we look for the tabular time that is closest to $2^h 33^m$, the time from the nearest tide — in this case, $2^h 36^m$. Staying in the $2^h 36^m$ column, we move into the bottom section of the table ("Correction to height") and look left to the left-hand boldfaced column to find the tabular value that is closest to our range of tide value (4.1 feet) — in this case, 4.0 feet. Matching the $2^h 36^m$ column and the 4.0 row, we arrive at a correction of 1.6 feet. Because the nearest tide was low, we add the correction to the low:

0.1 + 1.6 = 1.7-foot tide height at 0755.

## GRAPHIC METHOD

You can graph a typical tide using the *one-quarter, one-tenth rule*:

Plot the high- and low-water points in the order of their occurrence, measuring time horizontally and height vertically. Draw a light straight line connecting the points. Divide this line into four equal parts. At the quarter point adjacent to high water, draw a vertical line above the point; at the quarter point adjacent to low water, draw a vertical line below the point. Make the length of these lines equal to one-tenth of the range between the high and low waters used. Finally, draw a smooth curve through the points of high and low waters and the intermediate points, making the curve well rounded near high and low waters. This curve will approximate the tide curve, and heights for any time of the day may be scaled from it.

An example of the graphic method is illustrated below. Using the same predicted tides as in the above example, the approximate height at $7^h 00^m$ is 1 foot.

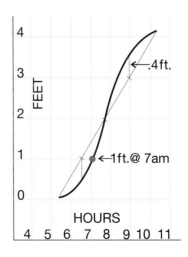

# HEIGHT OF TIDE AT ANY TIME

## Time from the nearest high water or low water

| Duration of Rise or Fall h.m. | h.m. | h.m. | h.m. | h.m. | h.m. | h.m. | h.m. | h.m. | h.m. | h.m. | h.m. | h.m. | h.m. | h.m. | h.m. |
|---|---|---|---|---|---|---|---|---|---|---|---|---|---|---|---|
| 4 00 | 0 08 | 0 16 | 0 24 | 0 32 | 0 40 | 0 48 | 0 56 | 1 04 | 1 12 | 1 20 | 1 28 | 1 36 | 1 44 | 1 52 | 2 00 |
| 4 20 | 0 09 | 0 17 | 0 26 | 0 35 | 0 43 | 0 52 | 1 01 | 1 09 | 1 18 | 1 27 | 1 35 | 1 44 | 1 53 | 2 01 | 2 10 |
| 4 40 | 0 09 | 0 19 | 0 28 | 0 37 | 0 47 | 0 56 | 1 05 | 1 15 | 1 24 | 1 33 | 1 43 | 1 52 | 2 01 | 2 11 | 2 20 |
| 5 00 | 0 10 | 0 20 | 0 30 | 0 40 | 050 | 1 00 | 1 10 | 1 20 | 1 30 | 1 40 | 1 50 | 2 00 | 2 10 | 2 20 | 2 30 |
| 5 20 | 0 11 | 0 21 | 0 32 | 0 43 | 0 53 | 1 04 | 1 15 | 1 25 | 1 36 | 1 47 | 1 57 | 2 08 | 2 19 | 2 29 | 2 40 |
| 5 40 | 0 11 | 0 23 | 0 34 | 0 45 | 0 57 | 1 08 | 1 19 | 1 31 | 1 42 | 1 53 | 2 05 | 2 16 | 2 27 | 2 39 | 2 50 |
| 6 00 | 0 12 | 0 24 | 0 36 | 0 48 | 1 00 | 1 12 | 1 24 | 1 36 | 1 48 | 2 00 | 2 12 | 2 24 | 2 36 | 2 48 | 3 00 |
| 6 20 | 0 13 | 0 25 | 0 38 | 0 51 | 1 03 | 1 16 | 1 29 | 1 41 | 1 54 | 2 07 | 2 19 | 2 32 | 2 45 | 2 57 | 3 10 |
| 6 40 | 0 13 | 0 27 | 0 40 | 0 53 | 1 07 | 1 20 | 1 33 | 1 47 | 2 00 | 2 13 | 2 27 | 2 40 | 2 53 | 3 07 | 3 20 |
| 7 00 | 0 14 | 0 28 | 0 42 | 0 56 | 1 10 | 1 24 | 1 38 | 1 52 | 2 06 | 2 20 | 2 34 | 2 48 | 3 02 | 3 16 | 3 30 |
| 7 20 | 0 15 | 0 29 | 0 44 | 0 59 | 1 13 | 1 28 | 1 43 | 1 57 | 2 12 | 2 27 | 2 41 | 2 56 | 3 11 | 3 25 | 3 40 |
| 7 40 | 0 15 | 0 31 | 0 46 | 1 01 | 1 17 | 1 32 | 1 47 | 2 03 | 2 18 | 2 33 | 2 49 | 3 04 | 3 19 | 3 35 | 3 50 |
| 8 00 | 0 16 | 0 32 | 0 48 | 1 04 | 1 20 | 1 36 | 1 52 | 2 08 | 2 24 | 2 40 | 2 56 | 3 12 | 3 28 | 3 44 | 4 00 |
| 8 20 | 0 17 | 0 33 | 0 50 | 1 07 | 1 23 | 1 40 | 1 57 | 2 13 | 2 30 | 2 47 | 3 03 | 3 20 | 3 37 | 3 53 | 4 10 |
| 8 40 | 0 17 | 0 35 | 0 52 | 1 09 | 1 27 | 1 44 | 2 01 | 2 19 | 2 36 | 2 53 | 3 11 | 3 28 | 3 45 | 4 03 | 4 20 |
| 9 00 | 0 18 | 0 36 | 0 54 | 1 12 | 1 30 | 1 48 | 2 06 | 2 24 | 2 42 | 3 00 | 3 18 | 3 36 | 3 54 | 4 12 | 4 30 |
| 9 20 | 0 19 | 0 37 | 0 56 | 1 15 | 1 33 | 1 52 | 2 11 | 2 29 | 2 48 | 3 07 | 3 25 | 3 44 | 4 03 | 4 21 | 4 40 |
| 9 40 | 0 19 | 0 39 | 0 58 | 1 17 | 1 37 | 1 56 | 2 15 | 2 35 | 2 54 | 3 13 | 3 33 | 3 52 | 4 11 | 4 31 | 4 50 |
| 10 00 | 0 20 | 0 40 | 1 00 | 1 20 | 1 40 | 2 00 | 2 20 | 2 40 | 3 00 | 3 20 | 3 40 | 4 00 | 4 20 | 4 40 | 5 00 |
| 10 20 | 0 21 | 0 41 | 1 02 | 1 23 | 1 43 | 2 04 | 2 25 | 2 245 | 3 06 | 3 27 | 3 47 | 4 08 | 4 29 | 4 49 | 5 10 |
| 10 40 | 0 21 | 0 43 | 1 04 | 1 25 | 1 47 | 2 08 | 2 29 | 2 51 | 3 12 | 3 33 | 3 55 | 4 16 | 4 37 | 4 59 | 5 20 |

## Correction to height

| Range of Tide Ft. | Ft. | Ft. | Ft. | Ft. | Ft. | Ft. | Ft. | Ft. | Ft. | Ft. | Ft. | Ft. | Ft. | Ft. | Ft. |
|---|---|---|---|---|---|---|---|---|---|---|---|---|---|---|---|
| 0.5 | 0.0 | 0.0 | 0.0 | 0.0 | 0.0 | 0.0 | 0.1 | 0.1 | 0.1 | 0.1 | 0.1 | 0.2 | 0.2 | 0.2 | 0.2 |
| 1.0 | 0.0 | 0.0 | 0.0 | 0.0 | 0.1 | 0.1 | 0.1 | 0.2 | 0.2 | 0.2 | 0.3 | 0.3 | 0.4 | 0.4 | 0.5 |
| 1.5 | 0.0 | 0.0 | 0.0 | 0.1 | 0.1 | 0.1 | 0.2 | 0.2 | 0.3 | 0.4 | 0.4 | 0.5 | 0.6 | 0.7 | 0.8 |
| 2.0 | 0.0 | 0.0 | 0.0 | 0.1 | 0.1 | 0.2 | 0.3 | 0.3 | 0.4 | 0.5 | 0.6 | 0.7 | 0.8 | 0.9 | 1.0 |
| 2.5 | 0.0 | 0.0 | 0.1 | 0.1 | 0.2 | 0.2 | 0.3 | 0.4 | 0.5 | 0.6 | 0.7 | 0.9 | 1.0 | 1.1 | 1.2 |
| 3.0 | 0.0 | 0.0 | 0.1 | 0.1 | 0.2 | 0.3 | 0.4 | 0.5 | 0.6 | 0.8 | 0.9 | 1.0 | 1.2 | 1.3 | 1.5 |
| 3.5 | 0.0 | 0.0 | 0.1 | 0.2 | 0.2 | 0.3 | 0.4 | 0.6 | 0.7 | 0.9 | 1.0 | 1.2 | 1.4 | 1.6 | 1.8 |
| 4.0 | 0.0 | 0.0 | 0.1 | 0.2 | 0.3 | 0.4 | 0.5 | 0.7 | 0.8 | 1.0 | 1.2 | 1.4 | 1.6 | 1.8 | 2.0 |
| 4.5 | 0.0 | 0.0 | 0.1 | 0.2 | 0.3 | 0.4 | 0.6 | 0.7 | 0.9 | 1.1 | 1.3 | 1.6 | 1.8 | 2.0 | 2.2 |
| 5.0 | 0.0 | 0.1 | 0.1 | 0.2 | 0.3 | 0.5 | 0.6 | 0.8 | 1.0 | 1.2 | 1.5 | 1.7 | 2.0 | 2.2 | 2.5 |
| 5.5 | 0.0 | 0.1 | 0.1 | 0.2 | 0.4 | 0.5 | 0.7 | 0.9 | 1.1 | 1.4 | 1.6 | 1.9 | 2.2 | 2.5 | 2.8 |
| 6.0 | 0.0 | 0.1 | 0.1 | 0.3 | 0.4 | 0.6 | 0.8 | 1.0 | 1.2 | 1.5 | 1.8 | 2.1 | 2.4 | 2.7 | 3.0 |
| 6.5 | 0.0 | 0.1 | 0.2 | 0.3 | 0.4 | 0.6 | 0.8 | 1.1 | 1.4 | 1.6 | 1.9 | 2.2 | 2.6 | 2.9 | 3.2 |
| 7.0 | 0.0 | 0.1 | 0.2 | 0.3 | 0.5 | 0.7 | 0.9 | 1.2 | 1.4 | 1.8 | 2.1 | 2.4 | 2.8 | 3.1 | 3.5 |
| 7.5 | 0.0 | 0.1 | 0.2 | 0.3 | 0.5 | 0.7 | 1.0 | 1.2 | 1.5 | 1.9 | 2.2 | 2.6 | 3.0 | 3.4 | 3.8 |
| 8.0 | 0.0 | 0.1 | 0.2 | 0.3 | 0.5 | 0.8 | 1.0 | 1.3 | 1.6 | 2.0 | 2.4 | 2.8 | 3.2 | 3.6 | 4.0 |
| 8.5 | 0.0 | 0.1 | 0.2 | 0.4 | 0.6 | 0.8 | 1.1 | 1.4 | 1.8 | 2.1 | 2.5 | 2.9 | 3.4 | 3.8 | 4.2 |
| 9.0 | 0.0 | 0.1 | 0.2 | 0.4 | 0.6 | 0.9 | 1.2 | 1.5 | 1.9 | 2.2 | 2.7 | 3.1 | 3.6 | 4.0 | 4.5 |
| 9.5 | 0.0 | 0.1 | 0.2 | 0.4 | 0.6 | 0.9 | 1.2 | 1.6 | 2.0 | 2.4 | 2.8 | 3.3 | 3.8 | 4.3 | 4.8 |
| 10.0 | 0.0 | 0.1 | 0.2 | 0.4 | 0.7 | 1.0 | 1.3 | 1.7 | 2.1 | 2.5 | 3.0 | 3.5 | 4.0 | 4.5 | 5.0 |
| 10.5 | 0.0 | 0.1 | 0.3 | 0.5 | 0.7 | 1.0 | 1.3 | 1.7 | 2.2 | 2.6 | 3.1 | 3.6 | 4.2 | 4.7 | 5.2 |
| 11.0 | 0.0 | 0.1 | 0.3 | 0.5 | 0.7 | 1.1 | 1.4 | 1.8 | 2.3 | 2.8 | 3.3 | 3.8 | 4.4 | 4.9 | 5.5 |
| 11.5 | 0.0 | 0.1 | 0.3 | 0.5 | 0.8 | 1.1 | 1.5 | 1.9 | 2.4 | 2.9 | 3.4 | 4.0 | 4.6 | 5.1 | 5.8 |
| 12.0 | 0.0 | 0.1 | 0.3 | 0.5 | 0.8 | 1.1 | 1.5 | 2.0 | 2.5 | 3.0 | 3.6 | 4.1 | 4.8 | 5.4 | 6.0 |
| 12.5 | 0.0 | 0.1 | 0.3 | 0.5 | 0.8 | 1.2 | 1.6 | 2.1 | 2.6 | 3.1 | 3.7 | 4.3 | 5.0 | 5.6 | 6.2 |
| 13.0 | 0.0 | 0.1 | 0.3 | 0.6 | 0.9 | 1.2 | 1.7 | 2.2 | 2.7 | 3.2 | 3.9 | 4.5 | 5.1 | 5.8 | 6.5 |
| 13.5 | 0.0 | 0.1 | 0.3 | 0.6 | 0.9 | 1.3 | 1.7 | 2.2 | 2.8 | 3.4 | 4.0 | 4.7 | 5.3 | 6.0 | 6.8 |
| 14.0 | 0.0 | 0.2 | 0.3 | 0.6 | 0.9 | 1.3 | 1.8 | 2.3 | 2.9 | 3.5 | 4.2 | 4.8 | 5.5 | 6.3 | 7.0 |
| 14.5 | 0.0 | 0.2 | 0.4 | 0.6 | 1.0 | 1.4 | 1.9 | 2.4 | 3.0 | 3.6 | 4.3 | 5.0 | 5.7 | 6.5 | 7.2 |
| 15.0 | 0.0 | 0.2 | 0.4 | 0.6 | 1.0 | 1.4 | 1.9 | 2.5 | 3.1 | 3.8 | 4.4 | 5.2 | 5.9 | 6.7 | 7.5 |
| 15.5 | 0.0 | 0.2 | 0.4 | 0.7 | 1.0 | 1.5 | 2.0 | 2.6 | 3.2 | 3.9 | 4.6 | 5.4 | 6.1 | 6.9 | 7.8 |
| 16.0 | 0.0 | 0.2 | 0.4 | 0.7 | 1.1 | 1.5 | 2.1 | 2.6 | 3.3 | 4.0 | 4.7 | 5.5 | 6.3 | 7.2 | 8.0 |
| 16.5 | 0.0 | 0.2 | 0.4 | 0.7 | 1.1 | 1.6 | 2.1 | 2.7 | 3.4 | 4.1 | 4.9 | 5.7 | 6.5 | 7.4 | 8.2 |
| 17.0 | 0.0 | 0.2 | 0.4 | 0.7 | 1.1 | 1.6 | 2.2 | 2.8 | 3.5 | 4.2 | 5.0 | 5.9 | 6.7 | 7.6 | 8.5 |
| 17.5 | 0.0 | 0.2 | 0.4 | 0.8 | 1.2 | 1.7 | 2.2 | 2.9 | 3.6 | 4.4 | 5.2 | 6.0 | 6.9 | 7.8 | 8.8 |
| 18.0 | 0.0 | 0.2 | 0.4 | 0.8 | 1.2 | 1.7 | 2.3 | 3.0 | 3.7 | 4.5 | 5.3 | 6.2 | 7.1 | 8.1 | 9.0 |
| 18.5 | 0.1 | 0.2 | 0.5 | 0.8 | 1.2 | 1.8 | 2.4 | 3.1 | 3.8 | 4.6 | 5.5 | 6.4 | 7.3 | 8.3 | 9.2 |
| 19.0 | 0.1 | 0.2 | 0.5 | 0.8 | 1.3 | 1.8 | 2.4 | 3.1 | 3.9 | 4.8 | 5.6 | 6.6 | 7.5 | 8.5 | 9.5 |
| 19.5 | 0.1 | 0.2 | 0.5 | 0.8 | 1.3 | 1.9 | 2.5 | 3.2 | 4.0 | 4.9 | 5.8 | 6.7 | 7.7 | 8.7 | 9.8 |
| 20.0 | 0.1 | 0.2 | 0.5 | 0.9 | 1.3 | 1.9 | 2.6 | 3.3 | 4.1 | 5.0 | 5.9 | 6.9 | 7.9 | 9.0 | 10.0 |

Before using this table, get the times and heights of the two tide events that your desired time of height falls between. Calculate the duration of time and the range of heights between the two events, and the time difference between your desired time and the nearest high or low.

Enter the table with the Duration of Rise or Fall boldfaced in the upper left column that is closest to your calculation. Scan that row to find the Time from Nearest High or Low closest to your difference. Use that column to enter the bottom section of the table. Find the row whose bold-faced value Range of Tide is closest to yours, and get your correction value where the row and column cross.

**When the nearest tide is high water, subtract the correction and vice versa.**

Tides & Currents

## SPEED OF CURRENT AT ANY TIME

Although the predictions in *Reed's* give only the slack and maximum currents, you can obtain the approximate speed of the current at any intermediate time by using the "Speed of Current at Any Time" table on the opposite page. Directions for using the table are given below it. Before using the table, you must first obtain the predictions for the day in question .

The examples below follow the numbered steps in the directions.

*Example 1:* Find the speed of the current in The Race at 6:00 on a day when the predictions that immediately precede and follow 6:00 are as follows:

1.  *Slack Water*     *Maximum (Flood)*
    Time            Time     Speed
    4:18            7:36     3.2 knots

    Directions under the table indicate that table A is to be used for this station.

2.  Interval between slack and maximum flood is 7:36 – 4:18 = 3h 18m. Column heading nearest to 3h 18m is 3h 20m.

3.  Interval between slack and time desired is 6:00 – 4:18 = 1h 42m. Line labeled 1h 40m is nearest to 1h 42m.

4.  Factor in column 3h 20m and on line 1h 40m is 0.7. The maximum flood

speed of 3.2 knots, multiplied by 0.7, gives a flood speed of 2.24 knots at 6:00 (or 2.2 knots since one decimal is sufficient).

*Example 2:* Find the speed of the current in the Harlem River at Broadway Bridge at 16:30 on a day when the predictions (obtained using the tide difference ratio) that immediately precede and follow 16:30 are as follows:

1.  *Maximum (Ebb)*     *Slack Water*
    Time         Speed     Time
    13:49        2.5 knots     17:25

    Directions under the table indicate that table B is to be used, since this station is referred to Hell Gate.

2.  Interval between slack and maximum ebb is 17:25 – 13:49 = 3h 36m. Hence, use column headed 3h 40m.

3.  Interval between slack and time desired is 17:25 – 16:30 = 0h 55m. Hence, use line labeled 1h 00m.

4.  Factor in column 3h 40m and on line 1h 00m is 0.5. The above ebb speed of 2.5 knots multiplied by 0.5 gives an ebb speed of 1.2 knots for the desired time.

When the interval between slack and maximum current is greater than 5h 40m, enter the table with one-half the interval between slack and maximum current and one-half the interval between slack and the desired time, and use the factor thus found.

## SPEED OF CURRENT AT ANY TIME
### TABLE A

**Interval between slack and maximum current**

| Interval between slack and desired time | h.m. 1 20 | h.m. 1 40 | h.m. 2 00 | h.m. 2 20 | h.m. 2 40 | h.m. 3 00 | h.m. 3 20 | h.m. 3 40 | h.m. 4 00 | h.m. 4 20 | h.m. 4 40 | h.m. 5 00 | h.m. 5 20 | h.m. 5 40 |
|---|---|---|---|---|---|---|---|---|---|---|---|---|---|---|
| h. m. | f. | f. | f. | f. | f. | f. | f. | f. | f. | f. | f. | f. | f. | f. |
| 0 20 | 0.4 | 0.3 | 0.3 | 0.2 | 0.2 | 0.2 | 0.2 | 0.1 | 0.1 | 0.1 | 0.1 | 0.1 | 0.1 | 0.1 |
| 0 40 | 0.7 | 0.6 | 0.5 | 0.4 | 0.4 | 0.3 | 0.3 | 0.3 | 0.3 | 0.2 | 0.2 | 0.2 | 0.2 | 0.2 |
| 1 00 | 0.9 | 0.8 | 0.7 | 0.6 | 0.6 | 0.5 | 0.5 | 0.4 | 0.4 | 0.4 | 0.3 | 0.3 | 0.3 | 0.3 |
| 1 20 | 1.0 | 1.0 | 0.9 | 0.8 | 0.7 | 0.6 | 0.6 | 0.5 | 0.5 | 0.5 | 0.4 | 0.4 | 0.4 | 0.4 |
| 1 40 | --- | 1.0 | 1.0 | 0.9 | 0.8 | 0.8 | 0.7 | 0.7 | 0.6 | 0.6 | 0.5 | 0.5 | 0.5 | 0.4 |
| 2 00 | --- | --- | 1.0 | 1.0 | 0.9 | 0.9 | 0.8 | 0.8 | 0.7 | 0.7 | 0.6 | 0.6 | 0.6 | 0.5 |
| 2 20 | --- | --- | --- | 1.0 | 1.0 | 0.9 | 0.9 | 0.8 | 0.8 | 0.7 | 0.7 | 0.7 | 0.6 | 0.6 |
| 2 40 | --- | --- | --- | --- | 1.0 | 1.0 | 1.0 | 0.9 | 0.9 | 0.8 | 0.8 | 0.7 | 0.7 | 0.7 |
| 3 00 | --- | --- | --- | --- | --- | 1.0 | 1.0 | 1.0 | 0.9 | 0.9 | 0.8 | 0.8 | 0.8 | 0.7 |
| 3 20 | --- | --- | --- | --- | --- | --- | 1.0 | 1.0 | 1.0 | 0.9 | 0.9 | 0.9 | 0.8 | 0.8 |
| 3 40 | --- | --- | --- | --- | --- | --- | --- | 1.0 | 1.0 | 1.0 | 0.9 | 0.9 | 0.9 | 0.9 |
| 4 00 | --- | --- | --- | --- | --- | --- | --- | --- | 1.0 | 1.0 | 1.0 | 1.0 | 0.9 | 0.9 |
| 4 20 | --- | --- | --- | --- | --- | --- | --- | --- | --- | 1.0 | 1.0 | 1.0 | 1.0 | 0.9 |
| 4 40 | --- | --- | --- | --- | --- | --- | --- | --- | --- | --- | 1.0 | 1.0 | 1.0 | 1.0 |
| 5 00 | --- | --- | --- | --- | --- | --- | --- | --- | --- | --- | --- | 1.0 | 1.0 | 1.0 |
| 5 20 | --- | --- | --- | --- | --- | --- | --- | --- | --- | --- | --- | --- | 1.0 | 1.0 |
| 5 40 | --- | --- | --- | --- | --- | --- | --- | --- | --- | --- | --- | --- | --- | 1.0 |

### TABLE B

**Interval between slack and maximum current**

| Interval between slack and desired time | h.m. 1 20 | h.m. 1 40 | h.m. 2 00 | h.m. 2 20 | h.m. 2 40 | h.m. 3 00 | h.m. 3 20 | h.m. 3 40 | h.m. 4 00 | h.m. 4 20 | h.m. 4 40 | h.m. 5 00 | h.m. 5 20 | h.m. 5 40 |
|---|---|---|---|---|---|---|---|---|---|---|---|---|---|---|
| h. m. | f. | f. | f. | f. | f. | f. | f. | f. | f. | f. | f. | f. | f. | f. |
| 0 20 | 0.5 | 0.4 | 0.4 | 0.3 | 0.3 | 0.3 | 0.3 | 0.3 | 0.2 | 0.2 | 0.2 | 0.2 | 0.2 | 0.2 |
| 0 40 | 0.8 | 0.7 | 0.6 | 0.5 | 0.5 | 0.5 | 0.4 | 0.4 | 0.4 | 0.4 | 0.3 | 0.3 | 0.3 | 0.3 |
| 1 00 | 0.9 | 0.8 | 0.8 | 0.7 | 0.7 | 0.6 | 0.6 | 0.5 | 0.5 | 0.5 | 0.4 | 0.4 | 0.4 | 0.4 |
| 1 20 | 1.0 | 1.0 | 0.9 | 0.8 | 0.8 | .07 | 0.7 | 0.6 | 0.6 | 0.6 | 0.5 | 0.5 | 0.5 | 0.5 |
| 1 40 | --- | 1.0 | 1.0 | 0.9 | 0.9 | 0.8 | 0.8 | 0.7 | 0.7 | 0.7 | 0.6 | 0.6 | 0.6 | 0.6 |
| 2 00 | --- | --- | 1.0 | 1.0 | 0.9 | 0.9 | 0.9 | 0.8 | 0.8 | 0.7 | 0.7 | 0.7 | 0.7 | 0.6 |
| 2 20 | --- | --- | --- | 1.0 | 1.0 | 1.0 | 0.9 | 0.9 | 0.8 | 0.8 | 0.8 | 0.7 | 0.7 | 0.7 |
| 2 40 | --- | --- | --- | --- | 1.0 | 1.0 | 1.0 | 0.9 | 0.9 | 0.9 | 0.8 | 0.8 | 0.8 | 0.7 |
| 3 00 | --- | --- | --- | --- | --- | 1.0 | 1.0 | 1.0 | 0.9 | 0.9 | 0.9 | 0.8 | 0.8 | 0.8 |
| 3 20 | --- | --- | --- | --- | --- | --- | 1.0 | 1.0 | 1.0 | 1.0 | 0.9 | 0.9 | 0.9 | 0.9 |
| 3 40 | --- | --- | --- | --- | --- | --- | --- | 1.0 | 1.0 | 1.0 | 1.0 | 0.9 | 0.9 | 0.9 |
| 4 00 | --- | --- | --- | --- | --- | --- | --- | --- | 1.0 | 1.0 | 1.0 | 1.0 | 0.9 | 0.9 |
| 4 20 | --- | --- | --- | --- | --- | --- | --- | --- | --- | 1.0 | 1.0 | 1.0 | 1.0 | 0.9 |
| 4 40 | --- | --- | --- | --- | --- | --- | --- | --- | --- | --- | 1.0 | 1.0 | 1.0 | 1.0 |
| 5 00 | --- | --- | --- | --- | --- | --- | --- | --- | --- | --- | --- | 1.0 | 1.0 | 1.0 |
| 5 20 | --- | --- | --- | --- | --- | --- | --- | --- | --- | --- | --- | --- | 1.0 | 1.0 |
| 5 40 | --- | --- | --- | --- | --- | --- | --- | --- | --- | --- | --- | --- | --- | 1.0 |

Use table A for all places except those listed below for Table B.
Use Table B for Cape Cod Canal, Hell Gate, C and D Canal, Deception Pass, Seymour Narrows, Isanotski Strait and all stations referenced to these tables.
1. From predictions find the time of slack water and the time and speed of maximum current (flood or ebb), one of which is immediately before and the other after the time for which the speed is desired.
2. Find the interval of time between the above slack and maximum current, and enter the top of Table A or B with the interval which most nearly agrees with this value.
3. Find the interval of time between the above slack and the time desired, and enter the side of Table A or B with the interval which most nearly agrees with this value.
4. Find, in the table, the factor corresponding to the above two intervals, and multiply the maximum speed by this factor. The result will be the approximate speed at the time desired.

Tides & Currents

## WIND-DRIVEN CURRENTS ATLANTIC & PACIFIC

A wind continuing for some time will produce a current, the speed of which depends on the speed of the wind. Unless the current is deflected by some other cause, the deflective force of the Earth's rotation will cause it to set to the right of the direction of the wind in the northern hemisphere, and to the left in the southern hemisphere.

The current produced at offshore locations by local winds of various strengths and directions has been investigated from observations made at lightships (all of which have since been removed). The averages obtained are given below and may prove helpful in estimating the probable current that may result from various winds at the locations listed, and elsewhere.

**Caution:** There were, of course, many departures from these averages of speed and direction, because the wind-driven current often depends not only on the length of time the wind blows, but also on factors other than the local wind at the time and place of the current. Mariners must not, therefore, assume that the given wind will always produce the indicated current.

It should be remembered, too, that the current that a vessel experiences at any time is the result of the combined actions of the tidal current, the wind-driven current, and any other currents such as the Gulf Stream or currents due to river discharge.

**Speed:** The following table shows the average speed of the current due to winds of various strengths.

**Direction:** The position of the shoreline with respect to the station influences considerably the direction of the currents due to certain winds. The table on pages 461 and 462 show for each station the average number of degrees by which the wind-driven current is deflected to the right or left of the wind. Thus, at the former location of the San Francisco Lightship, the table indicates that, with a north wind, the wind-driven current flows on the average 061° west of south; with an east wind it flows 023° north of west.

## The Combination of Currents

When using the current tables to determine the speed and direction of the current at any time, it is frequently necessary to combine the tidal current with the wind-driven current. The following methods indicate how the outcome of two or more currents may be easily determined.

**Currents in the same direction:** When two or more currents set in the same direction, it's a simple matter to combine them. The speed of the resultant current will equal the sum of all the currents and will set in the same direction.

For example, a vessel is near the Nantucket Shoals station at a time when the tidal current is setting 120° with a speed of 0.6 knot; at the same time, a wind of 40 miles per hour is blowing from the west. What current will the vessel be sub-

| Wind speed (miles per hour) | 10 | 20 | 30 | 40 | 50 |
|---|---|---|---|---|---|
| Average current speed (knots) due to wind at following lightship stations:* | | | | | |
| Boston and Barnegat | 0.1 | 0.1 | 0.2 | 0.3 | 0.3 |
| Diamond Shoal and Cape Lookout Shoals | 0.5 | 0.6 | 0.7 | 0.8 | 1.0 |
| All other locations on the Atlantic Coast | 0.2 | 0.3 | 0.4 | 0.5 | 0.6 |

| Wind speed (miles per hour) | 10 | 20 | 30 | 40 | 50 |
|---|---|---|---|---|---|
| Average current speed (knots) due to wind at following lightship stations:* | | | | | |
| San Francisco | 0.3 | 0.3 | 0.5 | 0.6 | 0.7 |
| Blunts Reef | 0.2 | 0.3 | 0.4 | 0.7 | 0.8 |
| Columbia River | 0.4 | 0.5 | 0.6 | 0.8 | 0.8 |
| Umatilla Reef | 0.2 | 0.6 | 0.9 | 1.0 | 0.9 |
| Swiftsure Bank | 0.5 | 0.5 | 0.5 | 0.7 | 0.8 |

* All of these lightships have since been removed.

ject to at that time? Since a wind of 40 miles per hour from the west will give rise to a current setting 120° with a speed of 0.5 knot, the combined tidal and wind-driven currents will set in the same direction (120°) with a speed of 0.6 +0.5 = 1.1 knots.

**Currents in opposite directions:** Combining currents that set in opposite directions is also a simple matter. The speed of the resultant current is the difference between the opposite setting currents; the direction of the resultant current is the same as that of the greater current.

As an example, let's determine the speed of the current at the Nantucket Shoals station when the tidal current is setting 205° with a speed of 0.8 knot, and when a wind of 40 miles per hour is blowing from the south. The current produced by a wind of 40 miles per hour from the south would set 025° with a speed of 0.5 knot. The tidal and wind-driven currents, therefore, set in opposite directions, the tidal current being the stronger. Hence the resultant current will set in the direction of the tidal current (205°) with a speed of 0.8 – 0.5 = 0.3 knot.

**Currents in different directions:** Combining two or more currents that set neither in the same nor in the opposite direction, although not as simple as the previous cases, is nevertheless not difficult. The best method is graphic. Taking the combination of two currents as the simplest case, draw a line from a given point (origin), whose direction is the direction of one of the currents to be combined and whose length represents the speed of that current to some suitable scale. From the end of this line, draw another line (to the same scale), whose direction and length represents the other of the currents to be combined. Finally, draw a line joining the origin with the end of the second line to give the direction and speed of the resultant current.

As an example, let's take Nantucket Shoals station at a time when the tidal current is 0.7 knot, setting 355°, and a wind of 50 miles per hour is blowing from the west-southwest. The wind-driven current, according to the table, would be about 0.6 knot setting 085°.

Using a scale of two inches to the knot, draw from point A in the diagram above,

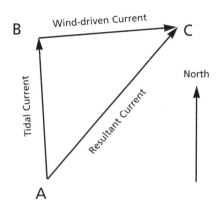

**Combination of tidal current and wind-driven current**

the line AB 1.4 inches in length directed 355° to represent the tidal current. From B, then draw the line BC 1.2 inches in length directed 085° to represent the wind current. The line AC represents the resultant current. When measured, it's found to be about 1.8 inches in length, directed 035° with a speed of 0.9 knot.

The combination of three or more currents is made in the same way as above. The third current to be combined is drawn from point C and the resultant current is given by joining the origin A with the end of the last line. A parallel rule and compass rose are convenient for drawing the lines; a protractor or polar coordinate paper may also be used. The paper form known as a maneuvering board (illustrated on pages 200 and 410) is very useful for this project.

# WIND-DRIVEN CURRENTS — ATLANTIC COAST

Average deviation of current to right of wind direction

[A minus sign (—) indicates that the current sets to the left of the wind]

| Wind from... Old Lightship Stations | Lat. ° ' | Long. ° ' | N | NNE | NE | ENE | E | ESE | SE | SSE | S | SSW | SW | WSW | W | WNW | NW | NNW |
|---|---|---|---|---|---|---|---|---|---|---|---|---|---|---|---|---|---|---|
| Portland | 43 32 | 70 06 | 24 | 14 | 9 | 8 | -2 | -14 | 0 | 26 | 15 | 18 | 18 | 24 | 15 | 34 | 13 | 18 |
| Boston | 42 20 | 70 45 | - | -1 | - | 21 | - | 32 | - | 29 | - | 20 | - | 2 | - | 19 | - | 15 |
| Pollock Rip Slue | 41 37 | 69 54 | 6 | 5 | 48 | -38 | 30 | -53 | -24 | -75 | -25 | 167 | 70 | 59 | 36 | 53 | 20 | 19 |
| Nantucket Shoals | 40 37 | 69 37 | 44 | 46 | 28 | 24 | 9 | 16 | 12 | 3 | 25 | 0 | 6 | 18 | 30 | 39 | 41 | 48 |
| Hen and Chickens | 41 27 | 71 01 | 16 | 14 | -7 | -1 | -14 | 3 | -39 | -36 | 25 | 55 | 35 | 30 | 20 | 16 | 16 | 8 |
| Brenton Reef | 41 26 | 71 23 | 34 | 25 | 22 | 19 | 25 | 1 | -7 | 8 | 27 | 48 | 23 | 41 | 41 | 31 | 21 | 24 |
| Fire Island | 40 27 | 73 11 | 35 | 23 | 15 | 8 | 2 | -17 | 31 | 55 | 40 | 41 | 31 | 14 | -2 | 0 | 25 | 37 |
| Ambrose Channel | 40 27 | 73 49 | 36 | 40 | 21 | 11 | 18 | 72 | 27 | 112 | 82 | 70 | 63 | 46 | 37 | 22 | 23 | 21 |
| Scotland | 40 27 | 73 55 | 16 | -12 | -26 | -36 | -61 | -36 | -92 | -150 | 90 | 33 | 77 | 44 | 15 | 30 | 27 | 13 |
| Barnegat | 39 46 | 73 56 | 6 | 5 | -13 | -9 | -16 | -7 | 33 | 54 | 55 | 30 | 14 | 8 | 0 | -5 | 21 | 29 |
| Northeast End | 38 58 | 74 30 | 30 | 14 | -3 | -11 | -20 | -31 | -42 | -28 | 37 | 44 | 25 | 18 | 7 | 16 | 25 | 18 |
| Overfalls | 38 48 | 75 01 | 28 | -6 | -1 | 2 | -40 | -56 | -78 | -22 | 68 | 28 | 55 | 54 | 32 | 31 | 32 | 45 |
| Winter-Quarter Shoal | 37 55 | 74 56 | 18 | -1 | -5 | -21 | -27 | -35 | -19 | 31 | 23 | 20 | 4 | 14 | 9 | 8 | 28 | 27 |
| Chesapeake | 36 59 | 75 42 | 18 | -2 | -4 | 5 | -6 | 23 | 73 | 71 | 57 | 38 | 27 | 26 | 22 | 18 | 15 | 22 |
| Diamond Shoal | 35 05 | 75 20 | 11 | 3 | -3 | 36 | 65 | 88 | 74 | 52 | 40 | 22 | 7 | -10 | -13 | -17 | -25 | -4 |
| Cape Lookout Shoals | 34 18 | 76 24 | 30 | 24 | 2 | 2 | -29 | - | 21 | 80 | 54 | 31 | 32 | 21 | 2 | 18 | 5 | -5 |
| Frying Pan Shoals | 33 34 | 77 49 | 34 | 34 | 18 | 6 | 2 | 9 | 48 | 55 | 48 | 38 | 26 | 14 | -7 | -12 | -27 | -6 |
| Savannah | 31 57 | 80 40 | 12 | 12 | -9 | -18 | -23 | -46 | 17 | 50 | 43 | 17 | 7 | -8 | -10 | 7 | 15 | 33 |
| Brunswick | 31 00 | 81 10 | 17 | -2 | -10 | -28 | -18 | -21 | 37 | 29 | 23 | 2 | 6 | -21 | -21 | -26 | 16 | 18 |
| St. Johns | 30 23 | 81 18 | 3 | -12 | -27 | -47 | -84 | 30 | 35 | 26 | 26 | 27 | 1 | 16 | -8 | -17 | 6 | 8 |

## WIND-DRIVEN CURRENTS

### AVERAGE DEVIATION OF CURRENT TO RIGHT OR LEFT OF WIND DIRECTION

### Pacific Coast

| Light Station* | San Francisco | | Blunts Reef | | Columbia River | | Umatilla Reef | | Swiftsure Bank | |
| --- | --- | --- | --- | --- | --- | --- | --- | --- | --- | --- |
| | Left | Right | Left | Right | Left | Right | Left | Right | Left | Right |
| Wind from: É | * | * | * | * | * | * | * | * | * | * |
| N.................. | --- | 061 | --- | 020 | --- | 035 | --- | 044 | --- | 100 |
| NNE.............. | --- | 027 | --- | 006 | --- | 027 | --- | 018 | --- | 054 |
| NE................ | --- | 030 | --- | 010 | --- | 009 | --- | 034 | --- | 048 |
| ENE.............. | --- | 031 | --- | 032 | --- | 029 | --- | 048 | --- | 033 |
| E .................. | --- | 023 | --- | 028 | --- | 017 | --- | 052 | --- | 027 |
| ESE .............. | --- | 029 | --- | 007 | --- | 002 | --- | 038 | --- | 018 |
| SE ................ | --- | 021 | 011 | --- | 008 | --- | --- | 025 | --- | 009 |
| SSE............... | --- | 005 | --- | 013 | 007 | --- | --- | 006 | --- | 001 |
| S .................. | 020 | --- | --- | 001 | 019 | --- | 006 | --- | 015 | --- |
| SSW ............. | 030 | --- | 011 | --- | 044 | --- | 013 | --- | 021 | --- |
| SW ............... | 049 | --- | 018 | --- | 074 | --- | 032 | --- | 068 | --- |
| WSW ........... | 040 | --- | 028 | --- | 121 | --- | 052 | --- | 088 | --- |
| W.................. | 051 | --- | 060 | 000 | 000 | 145 | 077 | --- | 090 | --- |
| WNW ........... | --- | 033 | --- | 002 | --- | 105 | 006 | --- | --- | 082 |
| NW ............... | --- | 016 | --- | 031 | --- | 078 | --- | 037 | --- | 130 |
| NNW ............ | --- | 017 | --- | 043 | --- | 053 | --- | 025 | --- | 111 |

\* All of these lightships have since been removed.

## ROTARY TIDE CURRENTS, OFFSHORE ATLANTIC

Offshore and in some of the wider indentations of the coast, the tidal current is quite different from that found in more protected bays and rivers. In these inside waters the tidal current is a reversing current. That is, it sets in one direction for a period of about six hours, after which it ceases to flow momentarily, and then sets in the opposite direction during the following six hours. Offshore, the current is not confined to a definite channel, so it changes its direction continually and never comes to a slack; therefore, in a tidal cycle of about 12.5 hours, it will have set in all directions of the compass. This type of current is therefore called a *rotary current*.

A characteristic feature of the rotary current is the absence of slack water. Although the current generally varies from hour to hour, this variation from greatest current to least current and back again to greatest does not give rise to a period of slack water. When the speed of the rotary tidal current is least, it is known as the *minimum current;* when it is greatest, it is known as the *maximum current*. The minimum and maximum speeds of the rotary current are thus related to each other in the same way as slack and strength of current — a minimum speed of the current following a maximum speed by an interval of about three hours and being followed in turn by another maximum after a further interval of three hours.

The tables on the next few pages list, for several offshore stations, the direction and average speed of the rotary tidal current for each hour of the tidal cycle referred to daily predictions for a reference station in *Reed's Nautical Almanac* (or in most other complete current tables).

The speeds given in these tables are average. The Moon at new, full, or perigee tends to increase the speeds 15 to 20 percent above average. When perigee occurs at or near the time of new or full Moon, the speeds will be 30 to 40 percent above average. Quadrature and apogee tend to decrease the speeds below average by 15 to 20 percent. When apogee occurs at or near quadrature, they will be 30 to 40 percent below average. The speeds will be about average when apogee occurs at or near the time of new or full Moon and also when perigee occurs at or near quadrature.

Note that the dates and times of the new, quarter, and full moon, apogee, and perigee can be found in the monthly moon tables in Chapter E, "Nautical Ephemeris," of *Reed's Nautical Almanacs;* the moon phases are also shown in the prediction tables for primary reference stations in Chapter C, "Currents."

The direction of the current is given in degrees, true, reading clockwise from 0° at north, and is the direction toward which the water is flowing.

The speeds and directions are for the tidal current only and do not include the effect of winds. When a wind is blowing, a wind-driven current will be set up that will be in addition to the tidal current. The actual current will be a combination of the wind-driven current and tidal current. (See "Wind-Driven Currents" and "The Combination of Current" in the previous section.)

As an example, in the following table the current at Nantucket Shoals is given for each hour after maximum flood at Pollock Rip Channel. Suppose you want to find the direction and speed of the current at Nantucket Shoals at 3:15 p.m. (15:15) Eastern Standard Time (EST) on a day when maximum flood at Pollock Rip Channel is predicted to occur at 13:20 EST. The desired time is therefore about two hours after maximum flood at Pollock Rip Channel, and from the following table the tidal current at Nantucket Shoals at this time is setting 15° true with an average speed of 0.8 knot. If this day is near the time of new Moon and about halfway between apogee and perigee, then the distance effect of the Moon will be nil and the phase effect alone will operate to increase the speed by about 15 percent, to 0.9 knot. If a wind has been blowing, determine the direction and speed of the wind-driven current as described in "Wind-Driven Currents" earlier in this chapter and combine it with the tidal current as explained in the section, "The Combination of Currents."

**Caution:** Speeds from 1.5 to 3 knots have been observed at most of the stations in this table. Near Diamond Shoal Light a speed of four knots has been recorded.

## ROTARY TIDAL CURRENTS

| | Georges Bank Lat. 41°50′N, Long. 66°37′W | | | Georges Bank Lat. 41°54′N, Long. 67°08′W | | | Georges Bank Lat. 41°48′N, Long. 67°34′W | |
|---|---|---|---|---|---|---|---|---|
| Time | Direction (true) Degrees | Velocity Knots | Time | Direction (true) Degrees | Velocity Knots | Time | Direction (true) Degrees | Velocity Knots |
| 0 | 285 | 0.9 | 0 | 298 | 1.1 | 0 | 325 | 1.5 |
| 1 | 304 | 1.1 | 1 | 325 | 1.4 | 1 | 332 | 2.1 |
| 2 | 324 | 1.2 | 2 | 344 | 1.5 | 2 | 342 | 2.0 |
| 3 | 341 | 1.1 | 3 | 0 | 1.2 | 3 | 358 | 1.3 |
| 4 | 10 | 1.0 | 4 | 33 | 0.7 | 4 | 35 | 0.7 |
| 5 | 43 | 0.9 | 5 | 82 | 0.8 | 5 | 99 | 0.8 |
| 6 | 89 | 1.0 | 6 | 118 | 1.1 | 6 | 126 | 1.3 |
| 7 | 127 | 1.3 | 7 | 138 | 1.5 | 7 | 150 | 2.0 |
| 8 | 147 | 1.6 | 8 | 153 | 1.2 | 8 | 159 | 1.9 |
| 9 | 172 | 1.4 | 9 | 178 | 1.1 | 9 | 169 | 1.7 |
| 10 | 197 | 0.9 | 10 | 208 | 0.9 | 10 | 197 | 1.2 |
| 11 | 232 | 0.8 | 11 | 236 | 0.8 | 11 | 275 | 0.9 |

| | Georges Bank Lat. 41°42′N, Long. 67°37′W | | | Georges Bank Lat. 41°41′N, Long. 67°49′W | | | Georges Bank Lat. 41°30′N, Long. 68°07′W | |
|---|---|---|---|---|---|---|---|---|
| Time | Direction (true) Degrees | Velocity Knots | Time | Direction (true) Degrees | Velocity Knots | Time | Direction (true) Degrees | Velocity Knots |
| 0 | 316 | 1.1 | 0 | 318 | 1.6 | 0 | 312 | 1.5 |
| 1 | 341 | 1.3 | 1 | 320 | 1.8 | 1 | 338 | 1.7 |
| 2 | 356 | 1.0 | 2 | 325 | 1.4 | 2 | 346 | 1.5 |
| 3 | 16 | 0.8 | 3 | 330 | 0.8 | 3 | 14 | 1.1 |
| 4 | 43 | 0.6 | 4 | 67 | 0.3 | 4 | 59 | 0.9 |
| 5 | 92 | 0.8 | 5 | 111 | 0.9 | 5 | 99 | 0.9 |
| 6 | 122 | 1.0 | 6 | 117 | 1.5 | 6 | 123 | 1.3 |
| 7 | 146 | 1.1 | 7 | 126 | 1.7 | 7 | 144 | 1.7 |
| 8 | 170 | 1.1 | 8 | 144 | 1.7 | 8 | 160 | 1.6 |
| 9 | 195 | 1.0 | 9 | 160 | 1.1 | 9 | 187 | 1.3 |
| 10 | 215 | 1.0 | 10 | 242 | 0.8 | 10 | 244 | 1.0 |
| 11 | 272 | 0.9 | 11 | 292 | 1.2 | 11 | 274 | 1.1 |

| | Georges Bank Lat. 41°29′N, Long. 67°04′W | | | Georges Bank Lat. 41°14′N, Long. 67°38′W | | | Georges Bank Lat. 41°13′N, Long. 68°20′W | |
|---|---|---|---|---|---|---|---|---|
| Time | Direction (true) Degrees | Velocity Knots | Time | Direction (true) Degrees | Velocity Knots | Time | Direction (true) Degrees | Velocity Knots |
| 0 | 277 | 1.0 | 0 | 305 | 1.4 | 0 | 319 | 1.5 |
| 1 | 302 | 1.2 | 1 | 332 | 1.6 | 1 | 332 | 2.0 |
| 2 | 329 | 1.4 | 2 | 355 | 1.6 | 2 | 345 | 1.4 |
| 3 | 348 | 1.3 | 3 | 15 | 1.4 | 3 | 9 | 0.8 |
| 4 | 15 | 1.2 | 4 | 38 | 1.1 | 4 | 42 | 0.6 |
| 5 | 48 | 1.1 | 5 | 77 | 0.9 | 5 | 80 | 0.7 |
| 6 | 85 | 1.2 | 6 | 112 | 1.2 | 6 | 118 | 1.0 |
| 7 | 122 | 1.4 | 7 | 141 | 1.6 | 7 | 138 | 1.3 |
| 8 | 145 | 1.5 | 8 | 162 | 1.6 | 8 | 154 | 1.4 |
| 9 | 166 | 1.3 | 9 | 187 | 1.5 | 9 | 169 | 1.5 |
| 10 | 194 | 1.2 | 10 | 214 | 1.4 | 10 | 188 | 1.3 |
| 11 | 223 | 1.1 | 11 | 252 | 1.2 | 11 | 236 | 0.9 |

| | Georges Bank Lat. 40°48′N, Long. 67°40′W | | | Georges Bank Lat. 40°49′N, Long. 68°34′W | | | Great South Channel, Georges Bank Lat. 40°31′N, Long. 68°47′W | |
|---|---|---|---|---|---|---|---|---|
| Time | Direction (true) Degrees | Velocity Knots | Time | Direction (true) Degrees | Velocity Knots | Time | Direction (true) Degrees | Velocity Knots |
| 0 | 304 | 0.9 | 0 | 301 | 1.2 | 0 | 320 | 0.7 |
| 1 | 340 | 0.9 | 1 | 326 | 1.5 | 1 | 331 | 0.9 |
| 2 | 353 | 0.8 | 2 | 345 | 1.4 | 2 | 342 | 1.1 |
| 3 | 29 | 0.6 | 3 | 8 | 1.1 | 3 | 3 | 1.0 |
| 4 | 56 | 0.6 | 4 | 36 | 0.8 | 4 | 23 | 0.8 |
| 5 | 83 | 0.6 | 5 | 69 | 0.8 | 5 | 63 | 0.4 |
| 6 | 107 | 0.9 | 6 | 106 | 1.0 | 6 | 129 | 0.7 |
| 7 | 140 | 1.0 | 7 | 139 | 1.4 | 7 | 140 | 0.9 |
| 8 | 156 | 1.0 | 8 | 153 | 1.5 | 8 | 164 | 1.0 |
| 9 | 175 | 0.9 | 9 | 175 | 1.4 | 9 | 179 | 1.0 |
| 10 | 202 | 0.8 | 10 | 201 | 1.1 | 10 | 190 | 0.8 |
| 11 | 245 | 0.8 | 11 | 237 | 0.9 | 11 | 221 | 0.6 |

**ALL STATIONS this page are referenced: Hours after maximum flood at Pollock Rip Channel**

Tides & Currents

463

## ROTARY TIDAL CURRENTS

| Nantucket Shoals Lat. 40°37′N, Long. 69°37′W | | | Great South Channel, Georges Bank Lat. 41°10′N, Long. 68°56′W | | | Davis Bank, Nantucket Shoals 15 miles SE of Nantucket I. Lat. 41°07′N, Long. 69°41′W | | |
|---|---|---|---|---|---|---|---|---|
| Time | Direction (true) Degrees | Velocity Knots | Time | Direction (true) Degrees | Velocity Knots | Time | Direction (true) Degrees | Velocity Knots |
| 0 | 323 | 0.6 | 0 | 318 | 0.5 | 0 | 15 | 1.5 |
| 1 | 355 | 0.7 | 1 | 349 | 0.7 | 1 | 28 | 2.1 |
| 2 | 15 | 0.8 | 2 | 352 | 1.1 | 2 | 33 | 2.4 |
| 3 | 38 | 0.8 | 3 | 356 | 1.0 | 3 | 35 | 2.1 |
| 4 | 55 | 0.8 | 4 | 359 | 0.7 | 4 | 37 | 1.1 |
| 5 | 85 | 0.7 | 5 | 18 | 0.4 | 5 | 128 | 0.4 |
| 6 | 125 | 0.6 | 6 | 106 | 0.4 | 6 | 197 | 1.2 |
| 7 | 162 | 0.7 | 7 | 157 | 0.7 | 7 | 204 | 1.9 |
| 8 | 192 | 0.8 | 8 | 165 | 1.0 | 8 | 205 | 2.2 |
| 9 | 212 | 0.8 | 9 | 173 | 1.0 | 9 | 206 | 2.2 |
| 10 | 232 | 0.8 | 10 | 180 | 0.8 | 10 | 213 | 1.6 |
| 11 | 257 | 0.7 | 11 | 204 | 0.6 | 11 | 307 | 0.7 |

| Davis Bank, Nantucket Shoals (west) 15 miles SE of Nantucket I. Lat. 41°03′N, Long. 69°47′W | | | Davis Bank, Nantucket Shoals (mid) 17.5 miles SE of Nantucket I. Lat. 41°02′N, Long. 69°43′W | | | Davis Bank, Nantucket Shoals (east) 18.5 miles SE of Nantucket I. Lat. 41°02′N, Long. 69°41′W | | |
|---|---|---|---|---|---|---|---|---|
| Time | Direction (true) Degrees | Velocity Knots | Time | Direction (true) Degrees | Velocity Knots | Time | Direction (true) Degrees | Velocity Knots |
| 0 | 346 | 0.9 | 0 | 23 | 0.8 | 0 | 30 | 0.6 |
| 1 | 28 | 1.2 | 1 | 27 | 1.5 | 1 | 36 | 1.3 |
| 2 | 47 | 1.3 | 2 | 28 | 1.9 | 2 | 38 | 1.5 |
| 3 | 73 | 1.1 | 3 | 29 | 1.8 | 3 | 50 | 1.4 |
| 4 | 103 | 0.8 | 4 | 46 | 1.1 | 4 | 80 | 1.1 |
| 5 | 132 | 0.9 | 5 | 115 | 0.4 | 5 | 105 | 0.8 |
| 6 | 182 | 0.8 | 6 | 191 | 1.2 | 6 | 178 | 0.6 |
| 7 | 215 | 1.2 | 7 | 202 | 1.9 | 7 | 230 | 1.3 |
| 8 | 240 | 1.1 | 8 | 215 | 1.7 | 8 | 235 | 1.7 |
| 9 | 251 | 0.9 | 9 | 225 | 1.5 | 9 | 238 | 1.4 |
| 10 | 267 | 0.7 | 10 | 233 | 0.9 | 10 | 241 | 1.0 |
| 11 | 302 | 0.7 | 11 | 270 | 0.2 | 11 | 265 | 0.3 |

| Nantucket Island, 28 miles east of Lat. 41°20′N, Long. 69°21′W | | | Monomoy Point, 23 miles east of Lat. 41°35′N, Long. 69°30′W | | | Nauset Beach Light, 5 miles NE of Lat. 41°56′N, Long. 69°54′W | | |
|---|---|---|---|---|---|---|---|---|
| Time | Direction (true) Degrees | Velocity Knots | Time | Direction (true) Degrees | Velocity Knots | Time | Direction (true) Degrees | Velocity Knots |
| 0 | 19 | 0.9 | 0 | 320 | 0.7 | 0 | 315 | 0.5 |
| 1 | 7 | 1.3 | 1 | 324 | 1.0 | 1 | 327 | 0.6 |
| 2 | 359 | 1.4 | 2 | 326 | 0.9 | 2 | 340 | 0.5 |
| 3 | 351 | 1.1 | 3 | 330 | 0.7 | 3 | 357 | 0.2 |
| 4 | 334 | 0.5 | 4 | 334 | 0.3 | 4 | 16 | 0.1 |
| 5 | 221 | 0.3 | 5 | 144 | 0.1 | 5 | 124 | 0.2 |
| 6 | 198 | 0.8 | 6 | 145 | 0.5 | 6 | 132 | 0.4 |
| 7 | 185 | 1.1 | 7 | 146 | 0.8 | 7 | 135 | 0.6 |
| 8 | 184 | 1.1 | 8 | 147 | 0.9 | 8 | 139 | 0.6 |
| 9 | 184 | 0.9 | 9 | 148 | 0.8 | 9 | 145 | 0.4 |
| 10 | 183 | 0.7 | 10 | 150 | 0.4 | 10 | 269 | 0.2 |
| 11 | 60 | 0.1 | 11 | 230 | 0.1 | 11 | 297 | 0.2 |

| Great Round Shoal Channel ent, Nantucket Sound ent Lat. 41°26′N, Long. 69°44′W | | | Great Round Shoal Channel Buoy 9, 0.3 ,miles NE of Lat. 41°24′N, Long. 69°55′W | | | Great Round Shoal Channel, 4 miles NE of Great Pt., Nantucket Sound Lat. 41°26′N, Long. 69°59′W | | |
|---|---|---|---|---|---|---|---|---|
| Time | Direction (true) Degrees | Velocity Knots | Time | Direction (true) Degrees | Velocity Knots | Time | Direction (true) Degrees | Velocity Knots |
| 0 | 32 | 1.6 | 0 | 47 | 1.0 | 0 | 80 | 0.8 |
| 1 | 45 | 1.4 | 1 | 60 | 1.3 | 1 | 88 | 1.1 |
| 2 | 68 | 1.3 | 2 | 70 | 1.3 | 2 | 96 | 1.3 |
| 3 | 95 | 1.1 | 3 | 91 | 0.8 | 3 | 104 | 1.0 |
| 4 | 140 | 0.8 | 4 | 153 | 0.5 | 4 | 129 | 0.5 |
| 5 | 192 | 1.2 | 5 | 211 | 0.7 | 5 | 213 | 0.5 |
| 6 | 210 | 1.5 | 6 | 234 | 0.9 | 6 | 267 | 1.1 |
| 7 | 220 | 1.5 | 7 | 247 | 1.3 | 7 | 275 | 1.4 |
| 8 | 235 | 1.2 | 8 | 252 | 1.1 | 8 | 280 | 1.2 |
| 9 | 264 | 0.9 | 9 | 260 | 0.9 | 9 | 284 | 0.7 |
| 10 | 303 | 0.8 | 10 | 305 | 0.3 | 10 | 328 | 0.2 |
| 11 | 350 | 1.2 | 11 | 35 | 0.4 | 11 | 42 | 0.4 |

*ALL STATIONS THIS PAGE are referenced: Hours after maximum flood at Pollock Rip Channel*

## ROTARY TIDAL CURRENTS

### Cuttyhunk I., 3.25 miles SW of Lat. 41°23′N, Long. 71°00′W

| Hours after maximum flood at Pollock Rip Channel | Direction (true) Degrees | Velocity Knots |
|---|---|---|
| 0 | 356 | 0.4 |
| 1 | 15 | 0.3 |
| 2 | 80 | 0.2 |
| 3 | 123 | 0.3 |
| 4 | 146 | 0.5 |
| 5 | 158 | 0.5 |
| 6 | 173 | 0.4 |
| 7 | 208 | 0.3 |
| 8 | 267 | 0.2 |
| 9 | 306 | 0.3 |
| 10 | 322 | 0.3 |
| 11 | 335 | 0.4 |

### Gooseberry Neck, 2 miles SSE of Buzzards Bay entrance Lat. 41°27′N, Long. 71°01′W

| Hours after maximum flood at Pollock Rip Channel | Direction (true) Degrees | Velocity Knots |
|---|---|---|
| 0 | 52 | 0.6 |
| 1 | 65 | 0.4 |
| 2 | 108 | 0.2 |
| 3 | 168 | 0.3 |
| 4 | 210 | 0.4 |
| 5 | 223 | 0.5 |
| 6 | 232 | 0.5 |
| 7 | 249 | 0.3 |
| 8 | 274 | 0.2 |
| 9 | 321 | 0.2 |
| 10 | 16 | 0.3 |
| 11 | 38 | 0.5 |

### Browns Ledge, Massachusetts Lat. 41°20′N, Long. 71°06′W

| Hours after maximum flood at Pollock Rip Channel | Direction (true) Degrees | Velocity Knots |
|---|---|---|
| 0 | 330 | 0.3 |
| 1 | 12 | 0.3 |
| 2 | 28 | 0.3 |
| 3 | 104 | 0.4 |
| 4 | 118 | 0.4 |
| 5 | 123 | 0.4 |
| 6 | 168 | 0.3 |
| 7 | 205 | 0.2 |
| 8 | 201 | 0.3 |
| 9 | 270 | 0.3 |
| 10 | 282 | 0.4 |
| 11 | 318 | 0.5 |

### Point Judith, Harbor of Refuge, Block Island Sound (west entrance) Lat. 41°22′N, Long. 71°31′W

| Hours after maximum flood at The Race | Direction (true) Degrees | Velocity Knots |
|---|---|---|
| 0 | 197 | 0.2 |
| 1 | 160 | 0.2 |
| 2 | 151 | 0.4 |
| 3 | 159 | 0.5 |
| 4 | 146 | 0.5 |
| 5 | 124 | 0.5 |
| 6 | 109 | 0.4 |
| 7 | 104 | 0.2 |
| 8 | 90 | 0.1 |
| 9 | 30 | 0.1 |
| 10 | 336 | 0.1 |
| 11 | 209 | 0.1 |

### Point Judith, 4.5 miles SW of Block Island Sound Lat. 41°18′N, Long. 71°33′W

| Hours after maximum flood at The Race | Direction (true) Degrees | Velocity Knots |
|---|---|---|
| 0 | 264 | 0.6 |
| 1 | 270 | 0.6 |
| 2 | 270 | 0.5 |
| 3 | 280 | 0.2 |
| 4 | 62 | 0.2 |
| 5 | 70 | 0.6 |
| 6 | 78 | 0.7 |
| 7 | 95 | 0.5 |
| 8 | 105 | 0.3 |
| 9 | 120 | 0.1 |
| 10 | 286 | 0.1 |
| 11 | 277 | 0.3 |

### Grace Point, 2 miles NW of Block Island Sound Lat. 41°12′N, Long. 71°38′W

| Hours after maximum flood at The Race | Direction (true) Degrees | Velocity Knots |
|---|---|---|
| 0 | 304 | 0.2 |
| 1 | 2 | 0.2 |
| 2 | 28 | 0.4 |
| 3 | 28 | 0.6 |
| 4 | 37 | 0.7 |
| 5 | 71 | 0.6 |
| 6 | 86 | 0.6 |
| 7 | 126 | 0.4 |
| 8 | 137 | 0.2 |
| 9 | 213 | 0.1 |
| 10 | 256 | 0.1 |
| 11 | 267 | 0.1 |

### Little Gull I., 3.7 miles ESE of Block Island Sound Lat. 41°11′N, Long. 72°02′W

| Hours after maximum flood at The Race | Direction (true) Degrees | Velocity Knots |
|---|---|---|
| 0 | 271 | 0.8 |
| 1 | 284 | 0.5 |
| 2 | 320 | 0.2 |
| 3 | 68 | 0.2 |
| 4 | 77 | 0.7 |
| 5 | 95 | 1.1 |
| 6 | 118 | 1.6 |
| 7 | 128 | 1.2 |
| 8 | 150 | 0.6 |
| 9 | 171 | 0.2 |
| 10 | 221 | 0.4 |
| 11 | 228 | 0.7 |

### Sandy Hook Approach Lighted Horn Buoy 2A, 0.2 mile W of Lat. 40°27′N, Long. 73°55′W

| Hours after maximum flood at The Narrows, N.Y. Harbor | Direction (true) Degrees | Velocity Knots |
|---|---|---|
| 0 | 313 | 0.4 |
| 1 | 325 | 0.3 |
| 2 | 356 | 0.2 |
| 3 | 55 | 0.2 |
| 4 | 94 | 0.3 |
| 5 | 118 | 0.4 |
| 6 | 136 | 0.6 |
| 7 | 147 | 0.5 |
| 8 | 177 | 0.2 |
| 9 | 256 | 0.2 |
| 10 | 290 | 0.3 |
| 11 | 298 | 0.4 |

### Fenwick Shoal Lighted Whistle Buoy 2, off Delaware coast Lat. 38°25′N, Long. 74°46′W

| Hours after maximum flood at Delaware Bay Entrance | Direction (true) Degrees | Velocity Knots |
|---|---|---|
| 0 | 342 | 0.2 |
| 1 | 349 | 0.2 |
| 2 | 357 | 0.1 |
| 3 | 43 | 0.1 |
| 4 | 110 | 0.1 |
| 5 | 135 | 0.2 |
| 6 | 150 | 0.3 |
| 7 | 165 | 0.3 |
| 8 | 185 | 0.2 |
| 9 | 226 | 0.1 |
| 10 | 282 | 0.1 |
| 11 | 318 | 0.2 |

### *Frying Pan Shoals, off Cape Fear Lat. 33°34′N, Long. 77°49′W

| Hours after maximum flood at Charleston | Direction (true) Degrees | Velocity Knots |
|---|---|---|
| 0 | 335 | 0.3 |
| 1 | 10 | 0.2 |
| 2 | 50 | 0.2 |
| 3 | 90 | 0.3 |
| 4 | 110 | 0.3 |
| 5 | 128 | 0.3 |
| 6 | 150 | 0.3 |
| 7 | 188 | 0.2 |
| 8 | 235 | 0.2 |
| 9 | 268 | 0.3 |
| 10 | 290 | 0.3 |
| 11 | 305 | 0.3 |

### Cape Romain, 5 miles SE of Lat. 32°57′N, Long. 79°17′W

| Hours after maximum flood at Charleston | Direction (true) Degrees | Velocity Knots |
|---|---|---|
| 0 | 6 | 0.2 |
| 1 | 38 | 0.2 |
| 2 | 55 | 0.3 |
| 3 | 67 | 0.3 |
| 4 | 93 | 0.3 |
| 5 | 114 | 0.3 |
| 6 | 167 | 0.2 |
| 7 | 212 | 0.2 |
| 8 | 242 | 0.3 |
| 9 | 244 | 0.4 |
| 10 | 262 | 0.3 |
| 11 | 292 | 0.3 |

### Cape Romain, 6.9 miles SW of Lat. 32°54′N, Long. 79°26′W

| Hours after maximum flood at Charleston | Direction (true) Degrees | Velocity Knots |
|---|---|---|
| 0 | 317 | 0.3 |
| 1 | 350 | 0.2 |
| 2 | 19 | 0.2 |
| 3 | 71 | 0.3 |
| 4 | 115 | 0.3 |
| 5 | 111 | 0.3 |
| 6 | 132 | 0.2 |
| 7 | 160 | 0.2 |
| 8 | 216 | 0.2 |
| 9 | 251 | 0.2 |
| 10 | 266 | 0.3 |
| 11 | 303 | 0.3 |

*Current during June-August usually sets eastward, average velocity ½ knots.*

Tides & Currents

## ROTARY TIDAL CURRENTS

**Capers Inlet, 1.9 miles east of**
**Lat. 32°50'N, Long. 79°40'W**

| Time | Direction (true) Degrees | Velocity Knots |
|---|---|---|
| 0 | 12 | 0.1 |
| 1 | 58 | 0.1 |
| 2 | 52 | 0.2 |
| 3 | 53 | 0.2 |
| 4 | 67 | 0.1 |
| 5 | 98 | 0.1 |
| 6 | 129 | 0.1 |
| 7 | 214 | 0.1 |
| 8 | 222 | 0.2 |
| 9 | 254 | 0.2 |
| 10 | 246 | 0.1 |
| 11 | 247 | 0.1 |

**Capers Inlet, 3.6 miles SE of**
**Lat. 32°49'N, Long. 79°38'W**

| Time | Direction (true) Degrees | Velocity Knots |
|---|---|---|
| 0 | 302 | 0.2 |
| 1 | 357 | 0.1 |
| 2 | 34 | 0.1 |
| 3 | 17 | 0.2 |
| 4 | 89 | 0.2 |
| 5 | 94 | 0.2 |
| 6 | 112 | 0.2 |
| 7 | 116 | 0.2 |
| 8 | 189 | 0.1 |
| 9 | 249 | 0.2 |
| 10 | 268 | 0.2 |
| 11 | 282 | 0.2 |

**Charleston Entrance,**
**37 miles east of**
**Lat. 32°42'N, Long. 79°06'W**

| Time | Direction (true) Degrees | Velocity Knots |
|---|---|---|
| 0 | 328 | 0.3 |
| 1 | 350 | 0.3 |
| 2 | 20 | 0.2 |
| 3 | 65 | 0.2 |
| 4 | 95 | 0.3 |
| 5 | 118 | 0.3 |
| 6 | 140 | 0.3 |
| 7 | 163 | 0.3 |
| 8 | 195 | 0.2 |
| 9 | 235 | 0.2 |
| 10 | 268 | 0.2 |
| 11 | 295 | 0.3 |

**Charleston Lighted Whistle Buoy**
**2C off Charleston Harbor entrance**
**Lat. 32°41'N, Long. 79°43'W**

| Time | Direction (true) Degrees | Velocity Knots |
|---|---|---|
| 0 | 300 | 0.2 |
| 1 | 332 | 0.2 |
| 2 | 17 | 0.1 |
| 3 | 55 | 0.2 |
| 4 | 77 | 0.3 |
| 5 | 93 | 0.3 |
| 6 | 117 | 0.3 |
| 7 | 153 | 0.2 |
| 8 | 207 | 0.2 |
| 9 | 242 | 0.2 |
| 10 | 260 | 0.3 |
| 11 | 275 | 0.3 |

**Folly Island, 2 miles east of**
**Lat. 32°39'N, Long. 79°52'W**

| Time | Direction (true) Degrees | Velocity Knots |
|---|---|---|
| 0 | 346 | 0.1 |
| 1 | 24 | 0.2 |
| 2 | 58 | 0.3 |
| 3 | 76 | 0.3 |
| 4 | 102 | 0.3 |
| 5 | 121 | 0.2 |
| 6 | 164 | 0.1 |
| 7 | 222 | 0.2 |
| 8 | 256 | 0.2 |
| 9 | 256 | 0.3 |
| 10 | 271 | 0.3 |
| 11 | 290 | 0.2 |

**Folly Island, 3.5 miles east of**
**Lat. 32°38'N, Long. 79°50'W**

| Time | Direction (true) Degrees | Velocity Knots |
|---|---|---|
| 0 | 322 | 0.1 |
| 1 | 47 | 0.2 |
| 2 | 69 | 0.2 |
| 3 | 86 | 0.2 |
| 4 | 96 | 0.2 |
| 5 | 115 | 0.2 |
| 6 | 148 | 0.1 |
| 7 | 215 | 0.1 |
| 8 | 256 | 0.2 |
| 9 | 260 | 0.2 |
| 10 | 265 | 0.2 |
| 11 | 285 | 0.1 |

**Martins Industry, 5 miles east**
**of, off Port Royal Sound**
**Lat. 32°06'N, Long. 80°28'W**

| Time | Direction (true) Degrees | Velocity Knots |
|---|---|---|
| 0 | 282 | 0.4 |
| 1 | 293 | 0.3 |
| 2 | 330 | 0.1 |
| 3 | 30 | 0.1 |
| 4 | 75 | 0.3 |
| 5 | 92 | 0.4 |
| 6 | 102 | 0.5 |
| 7 | 110 | 0.4 |
| 8 | 140 | 0.2 |
| 9 | 200 | 0.2 |
| 10 | 250 | 0.3 |
| 11 | 271 | 0.4 |

**Savannah Light, 1.2 miles SE of**
**Lat. 31°57'N, Long. 80°40'W**

| | Time | Direction (true) Degrees | Velocity Knots |
|---|---|---|---|
| | 0 | 296 | 0.3 |
| *Hours after maximum flood* | 1 | 308 | 0.2 |
| *at Savannah River Entrance* | 2 | 326 | 0.1 |
| | 3 | 45 | 0.1 |
| | 4 | 90 | 0.2 |
| | 5 | 107 | 0.3 |
| | 6 | 114 | 0.3 |
| | 7 | 123 | 0.3 |
| | 8 | 145 | 0.2 |
| | 9 | 213 | 0.1 |
| | 10 | 267 | 0.2 |
| | 11 | 283 | 0.3 |

*ALL STATIONS this page are referenced: Hours after maximum flood at Charleston*
*EXCEPT Savannah Light*

## Miscellaneous Atlantic Offshore Tidal Currents

Tidal currents at the following stations were also analyzed. They are not rotary currents, and their habits are not referenced to any daily predictions.

*Fire Island Inlet, N. Y., 22 mile south of:*
Tidal current is weak, averaging about 0.1 knot at strength.

*Fire Island Lighted Whistle Buoy 2 Fl:*
Tidal current is weak, averaging about 0.2 knot at strength.

*Ambrose Light, New York Harbor entrance.*
Tidal current is weak, averaging about 0.2 knot at strength.

*Cape May, N.J., 72 miles east of:*
Tidal current is weak, averaging about 0.1 knot at strength.

*Five-Fathom Bank Northeast Lighted Whistle Buoy 2FB:*
Tidal current is weak, averaging about 0.2 knot at strength.

*Winter-Quarter Shoal Lighted Whistle Buoy 6WQS, 9.2 miles SE of, off Assateague I:*
Tidal current is weak, averaging less than 0.1 knot.

*Cape Charles, 70 miles east of:*
Tidal current is weak, averaging about 0.2 knot at strength.

*Chesapeake Light, 4.4 miles NE of, off Chesapeake Bay entrance, Va:*
Tidal current is weak and variable.

*Cape Lookout Shoals Lighted Whistle Buoy 14:*
Tidal current is weak, averaging about 0.2 knot at strength.
Current during June-August usually sets eastward, averaging speed 0.5 knot.

*Ocracoke Inlet, 3.5 miles SSE of:*
Tidal current is weak, averaging about 0.1 knot at strength.

*Diamond Shoal Light, 3.9 miles SSW of:*
Tidal current is weak, averaging less than 0.1 knot at strength.
Current during June-August usually sets northeastward, average speed 0.75 knot.

*Frying Pan Shoals Light, 14.3 miles NW of:*
Tidal current is weak, averaging about 0.2 knot at strength.
Current during June-August usually sets eastward, average speed 0.5 knot.

*St. Johns Point, 5 miles east of, Fla:*
Tidal current is weak and averaging about 0.2 knot at strength.

*Fowey Rocks Light, 1.5 miles SW of:*
Tidal current is weak and variable.

This section deals with tidal currents found offshore from five to 20 miles from the coast. The data were based upon observations made through the cooperation of the U.S. Coast Guard at a number of lightship stations along the Pacific coast from San Francisco to Swiftsure Bank, off the coast of Washington.

**Rotary current:** Offshore, away from the immediate influences of the coast, the tidal current is quite different from the current found in inland tidal waters. Instead of setting in one direction for a period of six hours and in the opposite direction during the following period of six hours, the tidal current offshore changes its direction continually, so that in a period of about 12.5 hours it will have set in all directions of the compass. This type of current is therefore called a rotary current.

**Minimum current:** A characteristic feature of the rotary current is the absence of slack water. Although the current generally varies from hour to hour, this variation from greatest current to least current and back again to greatest current does not give rise to a period of slack water. When the speed of the rotary tidal current is least, it is known as the *minimum current;* when it is greatest it is known as the *maximum current.* The minimum and maximum speeds of the rotary current are thus related to each other in the same way as slack and strength of current, a minimum speed of the current following a maximum speed by an interval of about three hours and being followed in turn by another maximum after a further interval of three hours.

**Changes In tidal current:** The speeds of the tidal current given here are average speeds. Near the times when the Moon is full or new, the speeds of the tidal current will be about 20 percent, or one-fifth greater than the average. Near the times of the Moon's first and third quarters, the speeds will be smaller than the average by one-fifth.

**Effect of wind:** You should carefully note that, when wind is blowing, the current that a vessel will encounter is the resultant of the tidal and wind currents. Only the tidal currents together with the greatest

observed speed of the current at each light vessel are given here. Mariners are cautioned to combine with the tidal current the current brought about by any wind that may be blowing. Wind currents are given elsewhere in this chapter under the heading, "Wind-driven Currents."

**Direction and speed of current:** The direction of the current is true — not magnetic, and is the direction toward which the current is setting. The wind, when given, is in the direction from which it is blowing. The speed of the current is given in knots or nautical miles per hour.

**Reference to tides:** The tidal currents on the Pacific coast, like the tides, exhibit the feature known as diurnal inequality; that is, the two floods and two ebbs of a day are unequal. In the case of the tides, the higher of the two high waters of a day is known as *higher high water,* while the lower of the two is known as *lower high water.* For the two low waters of a day there are likewise distinctive names, the lower one being known as *lower low water,* while the higher one is known as *higher low water.* In certain instances it is convenient to refer the currents to the tides, and where this is done the following symbols are used to designate the different tides: HH for higher high water; LH for lower high water; LL for lower low water; and HL for higher low water.

*Point Lobos, 8.7 miles WSW of (former location of San Francisco Lightship), Calif:* The tidal current here is rotary, turning clockwise, as shown in figure 1, in which the average currents have been referred to each hour of the tides at San Francisco (Golden Gate). The diurnal inequality here is so great that the current is very largely diurnal; that is, during the greater part of the month the current changes direction at the rate of about 15° per hour, giving but one strength of flood and one strength of ebb in a day.

The speed of the tidal current here is generally small, as shown in the table below right, which represents the average conditions of figure 1.

In the column headed "Time," in the table opposite, the minus (—) sign before the hours indicates that the time referred to is before the particular tide; the plus (+) sign indicates that the time is after the tide. Thus, HH–3 in the table opposite and

**Figure 1**

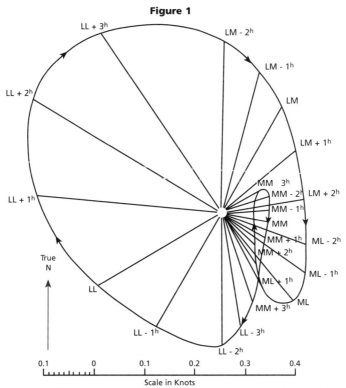

**Point Lobos Tidal Current Curve, former location of San Francisco Lightship**
**Referred to predicted time of the tide at San Francisco (Golden Gate), Calif.**

in figure 1 means three hours before higher high water, and LL+1 means one hour after lower low water.

The current observations at this location indicated a permanent current in a northwesterly direction of about 0.1 knot, which was especially noticeable during the winter months. This permanent current, therefore, increases the speed of the tidal currents that set in the northwesterly direction and decreases the speed of the tidal currents setting in the southeasterly direction.

| Point Lobos, 8.7 miles WSW (average of fig. 1) | | | | | |
|---|---|---|---|---|---|
| Time | Speed | Direction | Time | Speed | Direction |
| Tide Hrs | Knot | True | Tide Hrs | Knot | True |
| HH–3 | 0.1 | 060° | LL–3 | 0.2 | 170° |
| HH–2 | 0.1 | 070° | LL–2 | 0.3 | 180° |
| HH–1 | 0.1 | 085° | LL–1 | 0.3 | 210° |
| HH | 0.1 | 100° | LL | 0.3 | 240° |
| HH+1 | 0.1 | 120° | LL+1 | 0.3 | 275° |
| HH+2 | 0.1 | 145° | LL+2 | 0.4 | 300° |
| HH+3 | 0.2 | 160° | LL+3 | 0.4 | 325° |
| LH–2 | 0.3 | 000° | HL–2 | 0.2 | 110° |
| LH–1 | 0.3 | 015° | HL–1 | 0.2 | 125° |
| LH | 0.2 | 030° | HL | 0.2 | 140° |
| LH+1 | 0.2 | 050° | HL+1 | 0.2 | 150° |
| LH+2 | 0.2 | 080° | HL+2 | 0.1 | 130° |

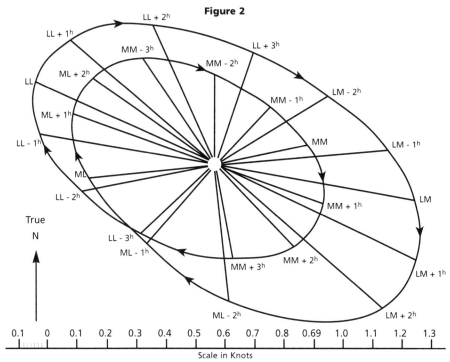

**Figure 2**

0.1  0  0.1  0.2  0.3  0.4  0.5  0.6  0.7  0.8  0.69  1.0  1.1  1.2  1.3

Scale in Knots

**Tidal Current Curve, Swiftsure Bank. Referred to predicted time of tide at Astoria, Oreg.**

When there is considerable runoff from San Francisco Bay, the combined tidal and nontidal current at the former lightship location generally attain a speed of 1.5 knots in a northwesterly direction. The greatest observed speed was 2.9 knots.

**Cape Mendocino Light,** 4.6 miles west of (former location of Blunts Reef Lightship), Calif: The tidal current here is rotary, but quite weak — it averages less than 0.1 knot. At strength of flood the current sets north, and at strength of ebb it sets south. Because the tidal current is weak, it's generally masked by wind currents or other nontidal currents. The observations indicated the existence of a nontidal current setting southwesterly with an average speed of 0.2 knot from March to November and northwesterly with a like average speed from November to March. The greatest observed speed was three knots.

**Columbia River Approach Lighted Horn Buoy R"C"** (former location of the Columbia River Lightship), coast of Oregon:

The tidal current here is rotary, turning clockwise, but rather weak. The speed of the current at strength is about 0.3 knots setting 020° on the flood and 200° on the ebb.

The current from the Columbia River completely masks the flood current. Observations show that there is a nontidal current at the buoy location with an average speed of 0.4 knot setting 235° from February to October and 295° from October to February. When there is considerable runoff from the river, the combined tidal and nontidal current at the buoy frequently attains a speed of two knots or more in a southwesterly direction: The greatest observed speed here is 3.5 knots.

**Cape Alava,** 4.4 miles west of (former location of Umatilla Reef Lightship), Wash: The tidal current here is only slightly rotary. Strength of flood comes about one-fourth hour after the strength of flood in the entrance to the Strait of Juan be Fuca, setting 345° with a speed of 0.3 knot.

| Swiftsure Bank (see fig. 2) | | | | | |
|---|---|---|---|---|---|
| Time | Speed | Direction | Time | Speed | Direction |
| Tide Hrs | Knot | True | Tide Hrs | Knot | True |
| HH–3 | 0.5 | 325° | LL–3 | 0.4 | 230° |
| HH–2 | 0.4 | 000° | LL–2 | 0.6 | 260° |
| HH–1 | 0.3 | 045° | LL–1 | 0.7 | 280° |
| HH | 0.4 | 080° | LL | 0.8 | 295° |
| HH+1 | 0.5 | 110° | LL+1 | 0.8 | 310° |
| HH+2 | 0.4 | 135° | LL+2 | 0.6 | 335° |
| HH+3 | 0.4 | 170° | LL+3 | 0.4 | 020° |
| LH–2 | 0.5 | 060° | HL–2 | 0.5 | 175° |
| LH–1 | 0.7 | 085° | HL–1 | 0.4 | 225° |
| LH | 0.8 | 100° | HL | 0.5 | 265° |
| LH+1 | 0.9 | 115° | HI +1 | 0.6 | 290° |
| LH+2 | 0.8 | 130° | HL+2 | 0.6 | 305° |

Strength of ebb comes about one-fourth hour after the strength of ebb in the strait and sets 165° with a speed of 0.3 knot.

The tidal current here is generally masked by nontidal currents brought about by winds or other causes. Observations indicated the existence of a nontidal current, setting about 350° with a speed of 0.7 knot from November to April, with the greatest speed during the month of December when it averaged about one knot. From April to November the nontidal current was variable, averaging 0.4 knot, generally in a southeasterly direction. With strong southeasterly winds the combined tidal and nontidal current attains a speed of two to three knots in a northerly direction. The greatest observed speed was 3.3 knots.

*Swiftsure Bank (Latitude 48°32′N.; Longitude 125°00′W.):* The tidal current is distinctly rotary, turning clockwise twice each day (see figure 2), in which the average currents have been referred to every hour of the tides at Astoria, Oregon. Because there is considerable difference between the speeds of the two revolutions that the tidal currents make each day, there are two distinct values for the flood and ebb currents, corresponding to the diurnal inequality of the tides.

The speed of the tidal currents here is generally small — less than one knot — as shown in the table top right, which represents the average conditions of figure 2.

In the first column of the table opposite, the letters under "Time" refer to the dif-ferent tides of the day. HH stands for higher high water; LH for lower high water; LL for lower low water; and HL for higher low water. The corresponding letters on figure 2 have a similar meaning. The minus (—) sign before the hours indicates that the time referred to is earlier than the particular tide; the plus (+) sign indicates that the time is after the tide. Thus, HH—3 means three hours before higher high water, and LL+1 means one hour after lower low water at Astoria, Oregon.

Note that the speeds and directions of the current given in the table refer only to the tidal current. Observations indicate the existence of a permanent current setting 315° with an average speed of 0.5 knot. This makes the northwesterly currents considerably stronger than the southeasterly. A southeasterly current of as much as 1.5 knots does not occur except with strong westerly or northwesterly winds, but northwesterly currents of two knots or more occur frequently. The greatest observed speed at Swiftsure Bank is three knots.

*Maui Island, Hawaii (Latitude 20° 46′ N; Longitude 155° 58′ W).* Observations indicate the existence of a permanent current setting north with an average speed of 0.7 knot. Combined with the tidal current, the northward current may have an average speed varying from slack to 1.4 knots. The greatest observed speed off Maui island was 2.7 knots.

Tides & Currents

471

## LIST OF U.S. TIDAL REFERENCE STATIONS

| Name of station | Datum below mean sea level | Name of station | Datum below mean sea level |
|---|---|---|---|
| **ATLANTIC COAST** | | | |
| Albany, New York | *2.5 | Newport, Rhode Island | 1.8 |
| Amuay, Venezuela | 0.6 | New York, New York | 2.6 |
| Baltimore, Maryland | 0.8 | Padre Island, Texas | 0.9 |
| Boston, Massachusetts | 5.2 | Pensacola, Florida | 0.6 |
| Breakwater Harbor, Delaware | 2.3 | Philadelphia, Pennsylvania | *3.5 |
| Bridgeport, Connecticut | 3.6 | Pictou, Nova Scotia | 3.9 |
| Charleston, South Carolina | 3.0 | Port Isabel, Texas | 0.8 |
| Cristobal, Panama | 0.5 | Portland, Maine | 4.9 |
| Dauphin Island, Alabama | 0.6 | Punta Gorda, Venezuela | 3.3 |
| Eastport, Maine | 9.7 | Reedy Point, Delaware | 3.0 |
| Fernandina Beach, Florida | 3.4 | St. John, New Brunswick | 14.5 |
| Galveston, Texas | 0.8 | St. Marks River Entrance, Florida | 1.9 |
| Grand Isle, Louisiana | 0.5 | St. Petersburg, Florida | 1.2 |
| Halifax, Nova Scotia | 4.3 | Sandy Hook, New Jersey | 2.6 |
| Hampton Roads, Virginia | 1.4 | San Juan, Puerto Rico | 0.8 |
| Isla Zapara, Venezuela | 2.7 | Santos, Brazil | 2.5 |
| Key West, Florida | 0.9 | Savannah, Georgia | 4.4 |
| Mayport, Florida | 2.5 | Savannah River Entrance, Georgia | 3.8 |
| Miami Harbor Entrance, Florida | 1.4 | Tampico Harbor, Mexico | 0.8 |
| Mobile, Alabama | 0.8 | Vaca Key, Florida | 0.5 |
| Montauk Pt., New York | 1.4 | Washington, D.C. | *1.6 |
| Nantucket, Massachusetts | 1.8 | Willets Point, New York | 3.9 |
| New London, Connecticut | 1.6 | Wilmington, North Carolina | *2.3 |
| **PACIFIC COAST** | | | |
| Aberdeen, Washington | 5.6 | Nushagak Bay, Alaska | 10.3 |
| Anchorage, Alaska | 16.0 | Port Chicago, California | 2.6 |
| Astoria, Oregon | *4.4 | Port Townsend, Washington | 5.0 |
| Cherry Point, Washington | 5.3 | Prudhoe Bay, Alaska | 4.5 |
| Cordova, Alaska | 6.7 | St. Michael, Alaska | 2.0 |
| Crescent City, California | 3.8 | Salina Cruz, Mexico | 1.9 |
| Guayaquil, Ecuador | *6.3 | San Diego, California | 2.9 |
| Guaymas, Mexico | 1.5 | San Francisco, California | 3.1 |
| Honolulu, Hawaii | 0.8 | Seattle, Washington | 6.6 |
| Humboldt Bay, California | 3.7 | Seldovia, Alaska | 9.5 |
| Juneau, Alaska | 8.5 | Sitka, Alaska | 5.2 |
| Ketchikan, Alaska | 8.0 | Sweeper Cove, Alaska | 2.1 |
| Kodiak, Alaska | 4.3 | Unalaska, Alaska | 2.2 |
| Los Angeles, California | 2.8 | Valdez, Alaska | 6.4 |
| Massacre Bay, Alaska | 1.9 | Vancouver, British Columbia | 10.0 |
| Nikishka, Alaska | 11.2 | Victoria, British Columbia | 6.1 |

Each datum figure above represents the difference in elevation between the local mean sea (or river) level and the reference level from which the predicted heights in NOS tide tables were calculated. Note that *Reed's* uses local predictions (and datums) in Canada and other countries outside the U.S. See the *Almanacs* for specifics about foreign datums.

Local mean sea level datum should not be confused with the National Geodetic Vertical Datum which is the datum of the geodetic level net of the United States. Relationships between geodetic and local tidal datums are published in connection with the tidal bench mark data of the National Ocean Service.     * Datum below mean river level.

# FLAGS

## UNITED STATES FLAG

The United States flag is also the United States ensign for use aboard boats of all sizes (this is the same flag as flown ashore). The flag should normally be flown from a staff at the stern of both powerboats and sailboats. Some power vessels have a mast with a gaff, which is the proper location for the flag. Gaff-rigged sailboats may also fly the flag from the aftermost gaff on the boat. Sailboats without a gaff sometimes fly the flag from the leech of the aftermost sail, about one-third of the way from the top. Of course, doing so means that the flag is doused when the sail comes down. In that case, it is proper to fly the flag from the stern staff while not underway. Some sailboats fly the flag from a backstay in the same manner as a stern staff. You can also fly the flag one-third of the distance from the top of the mast as you would a flag attached to the sail.

Some boats fly a special yacht ensign showing a circle of 13 stars on a blue field with a fouled anchor in the center. This flag is proper within the United States, but should not be flown in foreign waters.

The appropriate size for the U.S. flag is a matter of personal taste and practical considerations. You may want to fly a flag 72 inches long on July 4, but you may not want to do so on a regular basis. Most flags come in several standard sizes; the horizontal measure is the critical one. As a starting point, we offer the following suggested sizes:

| BOAT LENGTH IN FEET | LENGTH OF FLAG (horizontal) |
|---|---|
| 18 and under | 18 inches |
| 19 to 24 | 24 inches |
| 25 to 30 | 30 inches |
| 30 to 36 | 36 inches |
| 36 to 48 | 48 inches |
| 48 to 60 | 60 inches |

Keep in mind that there are no regulations within the United States requiring any particular size flag or, for that matter, any flag at all — except the Q flag when entering from a foreign port.

Generally, the U.S. flag is only flown from sunrise to sunset. In some harbors, yacht clubs fire a cannon at local sunset indicating the proper time to furl your flag. At sea, you only have to fly the national flag when encountering other vessels. Although it is proper to fly an illuminated flag at night, few small vessels do so.

Flying the U.S. flag upside down is understood as a sign of distress, although it is not an official signal.

## WORLD FLAGS

Anguilla

Antigua and Barbuda

Argentina

Aruba

Australia

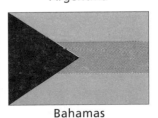
Bahamas

Barbados

Belgium

Belize

Bermuda

Brazil

British Virgin Islands

Canada

Cayman Islands

Columbia

Costa Rica

Cuba

Denmark

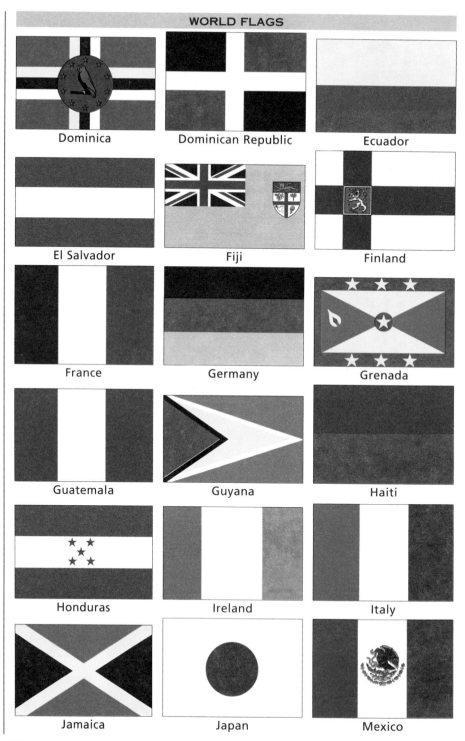

## WORLD FLAGS

Dominica

Dominican Republic

Ecuador

El Salvador

Fiji

Finland

France

Germany

Grenada

Guatemala

Guyana

Haiti

Honduras

Ireland

Italy

Jamaica

Japan

Mexico

**WORLD FLAGS**

Montserrat

Netherlands

Netherlands Antilles

New Zealand

Nicaragua

Panama

Portugal

Spain

St Kitts & Nevis

St Lucia

St Vincent & Grenadines

Sweden

Switzerland

Trinidad & Tobago

Turks & Caicos Islands

United Kingdom

United States of America

Venezuela

## CANADIAN PROVINCES & MISCELLANEOUS

| | | |
|---|---|---|
| Alberta | British Columbia | Manitoba |
| New Brunswick | Newfoundland | Northwest Territories |
| Nova Scotia | Ontario | Prince Edward Island |
| Quebec | Saskatchewan | Yukon |
| British Ensign | NATO | O.A.S |
| Olympic | Union Jack | United Nations |

## U.S. STATE FLAGS

| Alabama | Alaska | Arizona |
| Arkansas | California | Colorado |
| Connecticut | Delaware | District of Columbia |
| Florida | Georgia | Hawaii |
| Idaho | Illinois | Indiana |
| Iowa | Kansas | Kentucky |

Flags

## U.S. STATE FLAGS

Louisiana

Maine

Maryland

Massachusetts

Michigan

Minnesota

Mississippi

Missouri

Montana

Nebraska

Nevada

New Hampshire

New Jersey

New Mexico

New York

North Carolina

North Dakota

Ohio

## U.S. STATE FLAGS

Oklahoma

Oregon

Pennsylvania

Rhode Island

South Carolina

South Dakota

Tennessee

Texas

Utah

Vermont

Virginia

Washington

West Virginia

Wisconson

Wyoming

American Samoa

Puerto Rico

U.S. Virgin Islands

Flags

## INTERNATIONAL SIGNAL FLAGS

Code Flag and Answering Pennant

A · B · C · D · E · F · G · H · I · J · K · L · M · N · O · P · Q · R · S · T · U · V · W · X · Y · Z

**Numeral Pennants**

1 · 2 · 3 · 4 · 5 · 6 · 7 · 8 · 9 · 0

**Substitutes**

First · Second · Third

## COURTESY FLAGS

It is proper practice to fly a courtesy flag when sailing in a foreign country (the U.S. flag should still be displayed in its proper place). Generally, it's a good idea to obtain a selection of courtesy flags before leaving the U.S. because they are often hard to find in foreign ports. Although many countries have separate flags for use ashore and afloat, few will object if you fly their national flag as a courtesy flag. However, some countries do require that you fly the proper flag while in their waters.

A courtesy flag will generally be a small version of the national flag, measuring no more than 18 or 24 inches on the horizontal. It should be flown from the starboard spreader on sailboats, from the starboard side of a tower on sportfishing boats, or from an appropriate antenna or pole on the starboard side of a motor vessel. On two-masted boats the flag should fly from the forward mast's starboard spreader. A courtesy flag should always fly above other flags in the same location. When first entering a country, it is proper to fly only the yellow Q flag ("I request clearance"), but many boaters fly both the courtesy flag and the Q flag. Again, though, always fly the courtesy flag at the top of the hoist.

## STATE FLAGS

Within the United States it is common to fly the state flag appropriate to your home port. Some boaters fly the state flag as a courtesy flag for the state they are traveling through. State flags are flown in the same manner as courtesy ensigns on most boats. State flags may also be flown from the masthead or on a bow staff. They should not be flown on a stern staff.

## QUARANTINE FLAG

When entering a foreign port or when returning to the United States from a foreign port, the solid yellow Q flag should be flown from the starboard spreader or the appropriate location on the starboard side of a motor vessel. This flag is the International Code Flag for the letter Q. It means, "My vessel is healthy, I request free pratique." In practical terms it alerts the proper authorities that your vessel is requesting customs and immigration clearance into the country. It is often necessary to contact the authorities directly on the VHF radio in addition to hoisting the Q flag. In fact, many times you'll have to go ashore to call the authorities or visit their offices. Do not assume that your Q flag will get an immediate response from the busy officials.

## YACHT CLUB BURGEES

It is common for members of yacht clubs to fly their club's burgee, which is often a triangular pennant (swallowtail pennants are also used). Aboard sailboats, the proper place to fly a burgee is at the highest masthead. On many modern sailboats, though, the masthead is often cluttered with sensitive instruments, lights, and antennae. As a result, club burgees are often flown from the starboard spreader. If that location is used, the burgee should not fly above the courtesy ensign when in a foreign port. The position below the port spreader is inferior to the position below the starboard spreader. If you must fly so many flags that you need both port and starboard flag hoists, you must decide which flags should be most honored.

Rigging a masthead burgee requires that the flag be attached to a short staff. Attach one end of the halyard near the bottom of the staff and the other end anywhere from six inches to several feet (depending on the length of your staff) higher up. Then haul the staff up until the upper line dead-ends at the block. Pull the lower line taught to keep the staff vertical. The staff should be tall enough for the burgee to clear all of the masthead clutter.

On powerboats a burgee is usually flown from a bow staff. Powerboats with a mast may also fly a burgee from the masthead. If a gaff is present, that is the location of honor and is reserved for the U.S. flag.

## COAST GUARD ENSIGN

The United States Coast Guard has its own flag consisting of 16 red-and-white vertical stripes with the Coast Guard crossed anchors seal on them; a white field in the upper-left corner has a "flying eagle" symbol with a shield in the center. The flag is flown day and night by Coast Guard vessels.

Coast Guard Auxiliary vessels participating in official Coast Guard operations may fly an ensign showing the familiar red diagonal stripe on a white background with the crossed anchors seal of the auxiliary in the center. This flag is usually flown from a bow staff or a masthead position.

## U.S. CUSTOMS ENSIGN

The Customs Service has their own ensign that they fly from their vessels. It is similar to the Coast Guard ensign but features a larger eagle surrounded by an arc of stars. There are also 16 vertical red-and-white stripes, but there is no seal on this area.

## DRESSING SHIP

It is traditional for boats to "dress ship" when celebrating national holidays or special occasions. The International Signal Flags are stretched from bow to masthead and down to the stern. On multimasted vessels they should pass over the masts before descending to the deck. There are several different theories on designing a harmonious pattern for this display. We offer one suggested order as a starting point for your creativity:

Starting from the stern - E, Q, 3, G, 8, Z, 4, W, 6, P, 1, Code, T, Y, B, X, First Repeater, H, Third Repeater, D, F, Second Repeater, U, A, O, M, R, 2, J, 0 (zero), N, 9, K, 7, V, 5, L, C, S.

A tradition among cruisers is to dress ship with the courtesy flags from the ports visited on a long cruise. This is a fun way to enter your home port after a voyage.

# Boat & Ship Recognition

**13**

The following pages are intended only as a simple guide and to stimulate interest in the subject of ship and boat recognition. They illustrate some of the wide range of vessels you may expect to encounter at sea.

## TALL SHIPS

**Full-Rigged Ship.**  Sailing vessel with square sails on three or more masts. The few that remain today are used as training vessels.

**Barque.**  Three- to five-masted sailing ship, all of them square-rigged except the after-mast, which is fore-and-aft rigged.

**Brig**.  Two-masted sailing vessel developed from the brigantine and differing from it mainly by being square-rigged on both masts.

**Brigantine**.  Two-masted sailing ship, square-rigged on the foremast and fore-and-aft rigged on the mainmast.

**Barquentine.**  Sailing ship with three to five masts, all of them fore-and-aft rigged except the foremast, which is  square-rigged.

**Topsail Schooner.**  Two or more masted vessel, fore-and-aft rigged. The aftermast is taller than the foremast, which is set with one or more square topsails.

## SMALL BOATS

**Cape Cod Catboat.**  Single-masted fore-and-aft rigged sailing vessel with single gaff mainsail. The mast is stepped near the bow and the boom may overhang the stern. Many have been built as centerboarders, with transom-hung "barn-door rudders." Most are under 30 feet in length.

**Schooner.**  Usually double-masted fore-and-aft rigged sailing vessel with gaff sails abaft the masts. This example has a Marconi sail on the aft mast and a topsail set above the gaff main. Coastal trading schooners were built with up to five masts.

**Masthead Cutter.**  Single-masted fore-and-aft rigged sailing vessel with running bowsprit, mainsail, and two or more head-sails.

**Sloop.**  Single-masted fore-and-aft rigged sailing boat with single headsail set from the forestay.

**Gaff Cutter.**  Single-masted fore-and-aft rigged sailing craft with two headsails. A gaff yard supports the top edge of an additional topsail.

**Yawl.**  Two-masted fore-and aft rigged sailing vessel similar to the ketch but with a smaller mizzenmast abaft the rudder.

**Ketch.**  Two-masted fore-and-aft rigged sailing ship with mizzenmast situated aft of the main mast but forward of the rudder.

**Staysail Schooner.**  Two-masted fore-and-aft rigged sailing vessel, with mainsail and staysail set between the masts.

## WARSHIPS

**Frigate.**  Primarily intended for fast escort duties, the frigate is armed with a mixed array of guns, missiles, and torpedoes. It can be difficult to distinguish from the destroyer.

**Destroyer.**  A medium-sized fast warship with an armament of guns, torpedoes, guided missiles, and depth charges, noted for its high maneuverability. Also used as an escort vessel to provide powerful support in many actions.

**Landing Craft**.  Designed to carry a large number of troops and their vehicles during combined services landing operations. Carries only small arms for defense purposes.

**Fleet Service Vessel.**  An important role is played by these naval support vessels, which carry oil, fuel, ammunition, spare parts, and many other essential supplies. They are equipped with handling gear and most have a helipad situated aft.

**Mine Countermeasure Vessels**.  The mine-hunter, fitted with sonar equipment, searches for and classifies mines on the seabed, from a distance. The minesweeper is equipped with wires, magnetic cables, or acoustic gear to remove and destroy mines from the surface or seabed.

**Aircraft Carrier.**  Easily recognized by its enormous size. Used as a mobile air base at sea, the flat deck extends the length and width of the vessel and serves as a landing strip. Service speed is in excess of 30 knots.

## TALL SHIPS ILLUSTRATED

Full-Rigged Ship

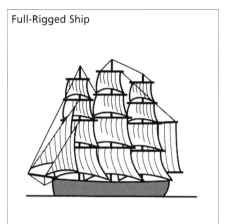

Three-Masted Barque

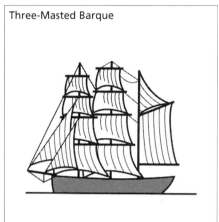

Brig

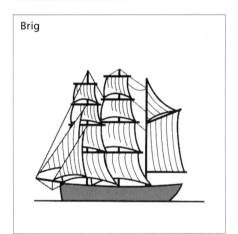

Brigantine

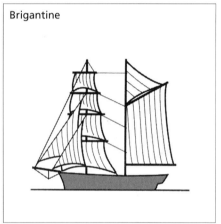

Barquentine

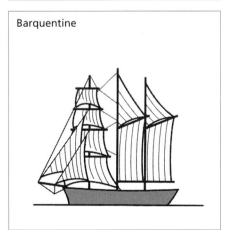

Topsail Schooner

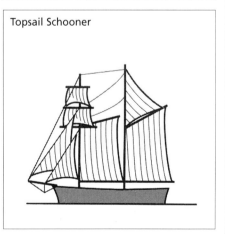

Boats & Ships

# SMALL BOATS ILLUSTRATED

Cape Cod Catboat
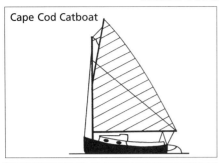

Schooner
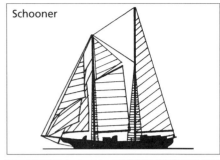

Masthead Cutter
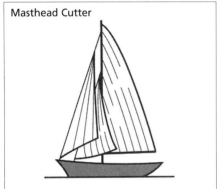

Sloop
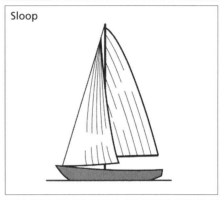

Gaff Cutter
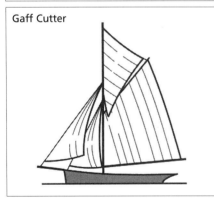

Yawl

Ketch
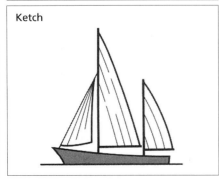

Staysail Schooner
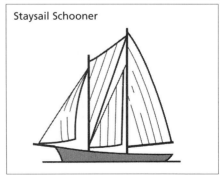

## WARSHIPS ILLUSTRATED

Frigate

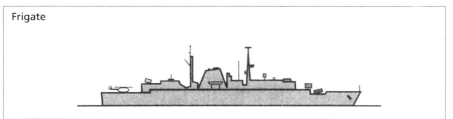

Destroyer

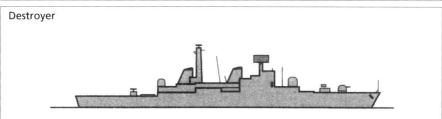

Landing Craft

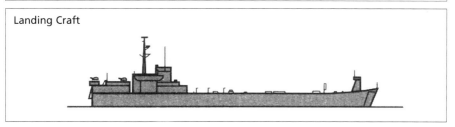

Fleet Service Vessel

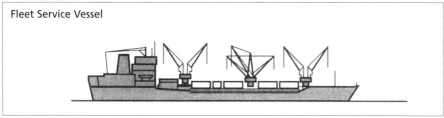

Minesweeper

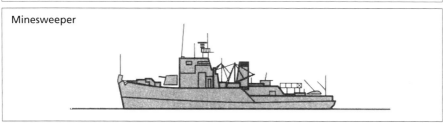

Aircraft Carrier

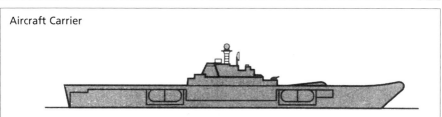

Boats & Ships

## MERCHANT SHIPS

***Passenger Liner.*** Mainly used today as a cruise liner, this type of vessel cannot be confused with any other form of sea transport. Its elegant lines and high superstructure present an individual profile. Capable of speeds in excess of 20 knots.

***Car Ferry.*** Passenger-car ferries are a familiar sight. They are designed so that the motorist can drive on and drive off the unobstructed vehicle decks without delay. Today, they are of considerable size and can attain high speeds.

***General Cargo Vessel.*** Designed to transport different types of cargo, their handling gear is an important feature. Cranes and derricks are carried on deck and facilitate the loading or discharging of cargo from the holds.

***Container Ship.*** The function of this vessel is to package cargo in large, standardized containers to facilitate shipping and handling, thereby leading to much quicker turn-arounds. Dry cargo is mainly shipped, but specialized units can handle liquid or refrigerated cargoes. Because these are very costly vessels, many are owned by a consortium of companies, some multinational.

***OBO Carrier.*** The oil/bulk/ore ship is different from a normal bulk carrier because of its wide range of deck fittings, vents, piping, and the steel hatch covers that encompass most of the width of the deck. The hull is subdivided, so the holds containing cargo such as grain or ore are flanked by oil tanks.

## WORK BOATS

***Chesapeake Bay Boat.*** This versatile vessel is seen throughout the Chesapeake Bay, either dredging for oysters or pulling crab-pots. Many were built of wood at local boatyards. They often have dry exhausts that may be heard at a good distance.

***Lobster Boat.*** This is a distinctly New England-style of workboat, although some are produced in yacht versions. The pots are usually hauled over the starboard side by a hydraulic winch. They may be carrying stacks of lobster pots on the stern.

***Shrimp Boat or Trawler.*** When underway, these vessels usually have the outriggers in the spread position for stability or to handle the nets. A large net is dragged astern with the aid of trawl doors that keep the mouth of the net open. The catch is hauled in over the stern.

***Multipurpose Tug.*** This high-performance vessel is suitable for a wide range of activities, including berthing, anchor handling, fire fighting, salvage, dive support, and hose flushing.

***Supply and Support Vessel.*** Used for servicing oil and gas rig installations and designed to cope with the adverse wind, weather and sea conditions often encountered, these vessels can carry a diverse range of cargoes, e.g. fuel oil, fresh water, ballast water, mud, brine, and cement.

***Fire-fighting Tug.*** Instantly recognizable by the two fire monitors positioned on a platform above the superstructure. Powerful pumps supply the monitors with either foam or water.

***Fish Factory Ship.*** This ship carries equipment for processing its catch on board including a complete freezing plant, which means that the vessel can remain at sea for much longer periods. Every process is carried out — the fish are cleaned, gutted, filleted, and so on, before finally being frozen and stored until return to port.

## MERCHANT SHIPS ILLUSTRATED

Passenger Liner

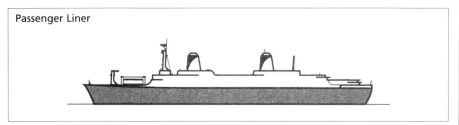

Car Ferry

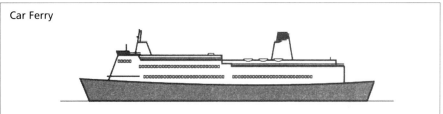

General Cargo Liner

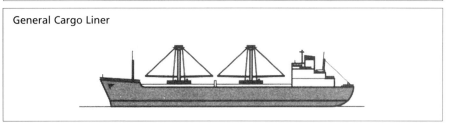

Container Ship

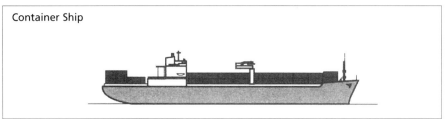

OBO Carrier

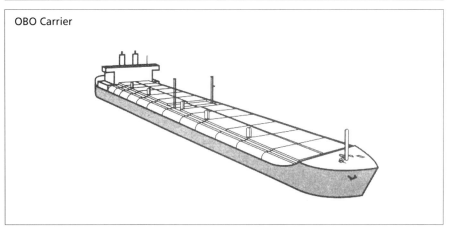

Boats & Ships

## WORK BOATS ILLUSTRATED

Chesapeake Bay Boat

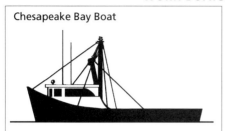

Lobster Boat

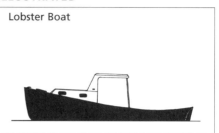

Shrimp Boat or Trawler

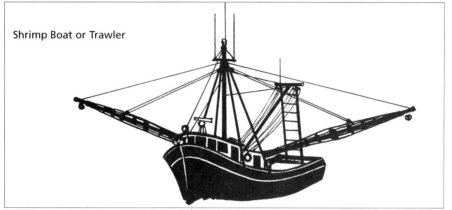

Multipurpose Tug

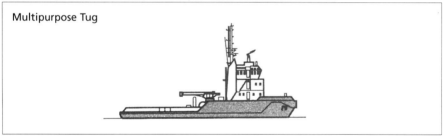

Factory/Freezer Ship

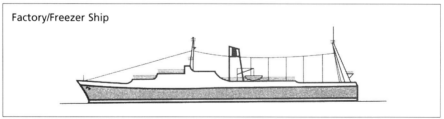

Offshore Supply Vessel

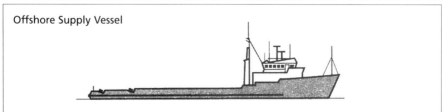

# DISTANCE TABLES

14

# ATLANTIC COAST —
## Montreal, Canada, to Panama Canal Zone
(Nautical Miles)

Figure at intersection of columns opposite ports in question is the nautical mileage between the two. Example: New York, N. Y., is 1399 nautical miles from San Juan, P. R.

**Port list (coordinates as printed):**

- PANAMA CANAL, (Pacific End) 8°53.0'N., 79°31.0'W
- Panama Canal (Atlantic Ent) 9°23.5'N., 79°55.3'W
- YUCATAN CHANNEL 21°50.0'N., 85°03.0'W
- San Juan, P. R. 18°27.8'N., 66°06.7'W
- Corpus Christi, Tex 27°48.8', 97°24.0'W
- Galveston, Tex 29°19.0'N. 94°47.0'W
- Port Arthur, Tex 29°49.5'N. 93°57.6'W
- NEW ORLEANS, La (via SW pass) 29°57.0'N. 90°03.7'W
- Mobile, Ala 30°42.5'N. 88°02.5'W
- Pensacola, Fla 30°24'N. 87°13.0'W
- Tampa, Fla 27°56.5'N. 82°26.7'W
- STRAITS OF FLORIDA 24°25.0'N. 83°00.0'W
- Key West, Fla 24°33.7'N. 81°48.5'W
- Jacksonville, Fla 30°19.2'N. 81°39.0'W
- Savannah, Ga 32°05.0'N. 81°05.7'W
- Charleston, S.C. 32°47.2'N. 79°55.52'W
- Wilmington, N.C. 34°14.0'N. 77°57.0'W
- DIAMOND SHOALS 35°08.0'N. 75°15.0'W
- Norfolk, Va 36°50.9'N. 75°17.9'W
- CHESAPEAKE BAY ENT 36°56.3'N. 75°58.6'W
- Baltimore, Md 39°16.0'N. 76°34.5'W
- Philadelphia, Pa 39°56.8'N. 75°08.3'W
- NEW YORK, N.Y. 40°42.0'N. 74°01.0'W
- NANTUCKET SHOALS 40°30.0'N. 69°25.0'W
- Boston, Mass 42°22.0'N. 71°03.0'W
- Portland, Maine 43°39.4'N. 70°14.7'W
- Gut of Canso (Lock) 45°45.0'N. 61°25.0'W
- Cabot Strait 47°07.0'N. 60°17.0'W
- MONTREAL, CANADA (St. Lambert Lock)

**Distance table (triangular). Columns, left to right: Montreal, Cabot Strait, Gut of Canso, Portland, Boston, Nantucket Shoals, New York, Philadelphia, Baltimore, Chesapeake Bay Ent, Norfolk, Diamond Shoals, Wilmington, Charleston, Savannah, Jacksonville, Key West, Straits of Florida, Tampa, Pensacola, Mobile, New Orleans, Port Arthur, Galveston, Corpus Christi, San Juan, Yucatan, Panama (Atl).**

| From \ To | Mon | Cab | Gut | Por | Bos | Nan | NY | Phi | Bal | Che | Nor | Dia | Wil | Cha | Sav | Jac | KW | Str | Tam | Pen | Mob | NO | PA | Gal | CC | SJ | Yuc | PanAtl |
|---|---|---|---|---|---|---|---|---|---|---|---|---|---|---|---|---|---|---|---|---|---|---|---|---|---|---|---|---|
| Cabot Strait | 681 | | | | | | | | | | | | | | | | | | | | | | | | | | | |
| Gut of Canso | 717 | 120 | | | | | | | | | | | | | | | | | | | | | | | | | | |
| Portland | 1276 | 595 | 484 | | | | | | | | | | | | | | | | | | | | | | | | | |
| Boston | 1318 | 637 | 526 | 100 | | | | | | | | | | | | | | | | | | | | | | | | |
| Nantucket Shoals | 1311 | 630 | 519 | 203 | 163 | | | | | | | | | | | | | | | | | | | | | | | |
| New York | 1534 | 853 | 742 | 426 | 386 | 223 | | | | | | | | | | | | | | | | | | | | | | |
| Philadelphia | 1682 | 1001 | 890 | 575 | 535 | 372 | 240 | | | | | | | | | | | | | | | | | | | | | |
| Baltimore | 1838 | 1157 | 1046 | 734 | 694 | 531 | 417 | 203 | | | | | | | | | | | | | | | | | | | | |
| Chesapeake Bay Ent | 1689 | 1008 | 896 | 584 | 544 | 361 | 267 | 163 | 150 | | | | | | | | | | | | | | | | | | | |
| Norfolk | 1716 | 1035 | 923 | 611 | 571 | 408 | 294 | 242 | 173 | 27 | | | | | | | | | | | | | | | | | | |
| Diamond Shoals | 1729 | 1048 | 936 | 628 | 588 | 425 | 345 | 322 | 269 | 117 | 144 | | | | | | | | | | | | | | | | | |
| Wilmington | 1948 | 1267 | 1155 | 847 | 807 | 644 | 564 | 541 | 486 | 366 | 402 | 145 | | | | | | | | | | | | | | | | |
| Charleston | 2014 | 1333 | 1221 | 913 | 873 | 710 | 630 | 607 | 552 | 429 | 476 | 197 | 102 | | | | | | | | | | | | | | | |
| Savannah | 2088 | 1407 | 1295 | 987 | 947 | 784 | 704 | 681 | 626 | 503 | 560 | 285 | 227 | 145 | | | | | | | | | | | | | | |
| Jacksonville | 2172 | 1491 | 1379 | 1071 | 1031 | 868 | 788 | 765 | 710 | 587 | 560 | 315 | 197 | 102 | 89 | | | | | | | | | | | | | |
| Key West | 2479 | 1798 | 1690 | 1387 | 1347 | 1184 | 1109 | 1086 | 1031 | 908 | 881 | 764 | 667 | 572 | 543 | 462 | | | | | | | | | | | | |
| Straits of Florida | 2540 | 1859 | 1751 | 1448 | 1408 | 1245 | 1170 | 1147 | 1092 | 969 | 942 | 825 | 728 | 633 | 504 | 437 | 73 | | | | | | | | | | | |
| Tampa | 2772 | 2091 | 1983 | 1680 | 1640 | 1477 | 1402 | 1379 | 1324 | 1201 | 1174 | 1057 | 960 | 865 | 755 | 540 | 347 | 232 | | | | | | | | | | |
| Pensacola | 2977 | 2296 | 2188 | 1885 | 1845 | 1682 | 1607 | 1584 | 1529 | 1406 | 1379 | 1262 | 1165 | 1070 | 960 | 703 | 510 | 437 | 305 | | | | | | | | | |
| Mobile | 3011 | 2330 | 2222 | 1919 | 1879 | 1716 | 1641 | 1618 | 1563 | 1440 | 1413 | 1296 | 1199 | 1104 | 994 | 773 | 544 | 471 | 389 | 89 | | | | | | | | |
| New Orleans | 3080 | 2399 | 2291 | 1988 | 1948 | 1785 | 1710 | 1687 | 1632 | 1509 | 1482 | 1365 | 1268 | 1173 | 1063 | 810 | 613 | 540 | 502 | 207 | 89 | | | | | | | |
| Port Arthur | 3240 | 2559 | 2451 | 2148 | 2108 | 1945 | 1870 | 1847 | 1792 | 1669 | 1642 | 1525 | 1428 | 1333 | 1223 | 1001 | 775 | 702 | 618 | 496 | 441 | 251 | | | | | | |
| Galveston | 3242 | 2561 | 2450 | 2150 | 2110 | 1947 | 1872 | 1849 | 1794 | 1671 | 1644 | 1527 | 1430 | 1335 | 1225 | 1001 | 780 | 709 | 605 | 504 | 446 | 249 | 89 | | | | | |
| Corpus Christi | 3347 | 2666 | 2558 | 2255 | 2215 | 2052 | 1977 | 1954 | 1899 | 1776 | 1749 | 1632 | 1535 | 1440 | 1330 | 1121 | 885 | 810 | 699 | 605 | 555 | 269 | 207 | 89 | | | | |
| San Juan | 2445 | 1764 | 1669 | 1531 | 1486 | 1334 | 1399 | 1375 | 1395 | 1225 | 1252 | 1114 | 1153 | 1138 | 1156 | 1121 | 966 | 880 | 1249 | 1448 | 1448 | 1557 | 1717 | 1719 | 1824 | | | |
| Yucatan Channel | 2730 | 2049 | 1937 | 1629 | 1589 | 1426 | 1346 | 1323 | 1268 | 1145 | 1118 | 1001 | 904 | 809 | 699 | 533 | 192 | 251 | 404 | 562 | 587 | 491 | 496 | 509 | 533 | 769 | | |
| Panama Canal (Atlantic Ent) | 3203 | 2522 | 2419 | 2373 | 2143 | 2103 | 1940 | 1926 | 1909 | 1858 | 1735 | 1591 | 1563 | 1517 | 1513 | 1467 | 1060 | 1001 | 1213 | 1342 | 1371 | 1396 | 1487 | 1493 | 1549 | 990 | 809 | |
| Panama Canal (Pacific End) | 3249 | 2568 | 2522 | 2419 | 2189 | 2149 | 1986 | 1972 | 1955 | 1904 | 1781 | 1637 | 1609 | 1563 | 1513 | 1559 | 1106 | 1047 | 1259 | 1380 | 1417 | 1442 | 1533 | 1539 | 1595 | 1036 | 855 | 46 |

* Quebec. Canada SUBTRACT 139 MILES

All tabular distances are by outside routes which can be used by the deepest draft vessel that the listed ports can accommodate. Lighter-draft vessels can save considerable mileage by transiting Canso Lock (Canada), the Cape Cod Canal (Massachusetts), and the Chesapeake and Delaware Canal (Delaware-Maryland); see the detailed tables. Gulf of Mexico distances are through the Shipping Safety Fairways.

# GULF OF MAINE — CALAIS, ME, TO CAPE COD, MA
(Nautical Miles)

Figure at intersection of columns opposite ports in question is the nautical mileage between the two. Example: Portland, Maine, is 100 nautical miles from Boston, Mass.

Ports along the diagonal (with positions):

- NANTUCKET SHOALS 40°30.0'N, 69°25.0'W
- Provincetown, Mass. 42°02.5'N, 70°10.0'W
- CAPE COD CANAL E ENT 41°46.8'N, 70°29.0'W
- Plymouth, Mass. 41°57.6'N, 70°39.8'W
- Scituate, Mass. 42°11.9'N, 70°43.5'W
- Boston, Mass. 42°22.0'N, 71°03.0'W
- Lynn, Mass. 42°27.3'N, 70°56.6'W
- Marblehead, Mass. 42°30.1'N, 70°50.7'W
- Salem, Mass. 42°31.3'N, 70°52.5'W
- Gloucester, Mass. 42°36.6'N, 70°39.6'W
- Rockport, Mass. 42°40.0'N, 70°36.5'W
- Newburyport, Mass. 42°48.6'N, 70°52.4'W
- Portsmouth, N.H. 43°04.6'N, 70°44.5'W
- York Harbor, Maine 43°07.9'N, 70°38.6'W
- Portland, Maine 43°39.4'N, 70°14.7'W
- Augusta, Maine 44°18.9'N, 69°46.4'W
- Bath, Maine 43°54.5'N, 69°48.7'W
- Wiscasset, Maine 43°59.5'N, 69°40.1'W
- Boothbay Harbor, Maine 43°51.0'N, 69°37.6'W
- Bangor, Maine 44°27.0'N, 68°54.0'W
- Bucksport, Maine 44°34.3'N, 68°48.0'W
- Searsport, Maine 44°27.0'N, 68°54.0'W
- Rockland, Maine 44°06.0'N, 69°05.5'W
- Stonington, Maine 44°09.2'N, 68°39.8'W
- Buck Harbour 44°20.3'N, 68°44.2'W
- Bar Harbor, Maine 44°23.5'N, 68°12.0'W
- Jonesport, Maine 44°31.9'N, 67°37.0'W
- Machiasport, Maine 44°41.9'N, 67°23.6'W
- Lubec, Maine 44°51.7'N, 66°59.0'W
- Eastport, Maine 44°54.3'N, 66°59.0'W
- Calais, Maine 45°11.4'N, 67°16.7'W

Distances read for each port (from that port to the ports lying toward Nantucket Shoals; the last figure in each row is the distance to Nantucket Shoals):

| From port | Distances (nautical miles) |
|---|---|
| Provincetown | 132 |
| Cape Cod Canal E Ent | 22, 144 |
| Plymouth | 20, 26, 144 |
| Scituate | 20, 29, 29, 143 |
| Boston | 21, 40, 52, 163 |
| Lynn | 13, 22, 40, 48, 159 |
| Marblehead | 14, 19, 22, 39, 48, 156 |
| Salem | 5, 18, 27, 45, 53, 159 |
| Gloucester | 12, 11, 22, 26, 43, 52, 155 |
| Rockport | 17, 24, 23, 37, 37, 50, 49, 157 |
| Newburyport | 16, 31, 38, 47, 51, 64, 72, 171 |
| Portsmouth | 22, 27, 40, 46, 56, 58, 73, 180 |
| York Harbor | 11, 25, 29, 42, 49, 58, 63, 75, 182 |
| Portland | 43, 56, 67, 79, 87, 86, 95, 97, 112, 203 |
| Augusta | 66, 94, 104, 116, 125, 132, 131, 141, 146, 142, 240 |
| Bath | 27, 40, 67, 72, 88, 94, 105, 109, 114, 119, 115, 213 |
| Wiscasset | 30, 57, 78, 89, 98, 105, 110, 118, 120, 115, 217 |
| Boothbay Harbor | 21, 23, 50, 36, 64, 74, 86, 95, 102, 110, 112, 115, 207 |
| Bangor | 87, 106, 131, 115, 126, 135, 145, 151, 162, 170, 176, 186, 191, 169, 267 |
| Bucksport | 17, 70, 89, 86, 86, 104, 126, 135, 143, 153, 160, 169, 174, 169, 250 |
| Searsport | 13, 30, 61, 80, 78, 90, 118, 126, 137, 145, 152, 161, 166, 161, 242 |
| Rockland | 23, 33, 50, 59, 71, 99, 107, 118, 126, 133, 142, 147, 142, 223 |
| Stonington | 20, 24, 47, 62, 81, 109, 119, 132, 133, 145, 153, 158, 155, 226 |
| Buck Harbour | 16, 22, 30, 68, 94, 123, 131, 138, 149, 157, 162, 165, 237 |
| Bar Harbor | 39, 53, 77, 94, 105, 130, 132, 154, 163, 169, 179, 184, 177, 243 |
| Jonesport | 34, 62, 70, 89, 96, 115, 124, 149, 167, 178, 189, 198, 203, 206, 257 |
| Machiasport | 20, 52, 80, 100, 107, 115, 144, 162, 184, 203, 217, 221, 224, 209, 271 |
| Lubec | 20, 40, 72, 91, 98, 126, 118, 133, 150, 161, 172, 196, 208, 215, 244, 233, 286 |
| Eastport | 3, 35, 42, 83, 102, 109, 130, 126, 142, 153, 162, 173, 183, 208, 200, 216, 221, 225, 242, 244, 297 |
| Calais | 24, 26, 61, 66, 98, 118, 125, 145, 152, 159, 176, 187, 214, 198, 222, 230, 241, 236, 245, 252, 261, 265, 259, 268, 270, 258, 312 |

Portland Lighted Horn Buoy P (LNB) (43°31.6'N, 70°05.5'W) to Portland 11.3 miles
Boston Lighted Horn Buoy B (LNB) (42°22.7'N, 70°47.0'W)

port to Provincetown; the distance via Matinicus Rock and Cape Ann is 235 miles. Distances from Eastport to Machiasport and other ports farther southward are via deep Head Harbor Passage, which is 8 miles farther than via shallow Lubec Channel.

Each distance is by shortest route that safe navigation permits between the two ports concerned. Vessels standing along the coast must make their own adjustments for non-direct routes. For example, the table shows a distance of 214 miles by direct route from Machias-

Distances

## COASTWISE — CAPE COD, MA, TO NEW YORK, NY
### (Nautical Miles)

Figure at intersection of columns opposite ports in question is the nautical mileage between the two. Example: New Bedford, Mass., is 74 nautical miles from New London, Conn.

Port labels with coordinates (listed top-right to bottom-left along the diagonal of the table):

|  |  |
|---|---|
| Port Newark, N. J. | 40°41.8'N, 74°09.0'W |
| Elizabethport, N. J. | 40°38.8'N, 74°11.2'W |
| Perth Amboy, N.Y. | 40°30.3'N, 74°15.7'W |
| NEW YORK (BATTERY), N. Y. | 40°42.0', 74°01.0'W |
| MONTAUK POINT, N. Y. | 40°42.0'N, 74°01.0'W |
| Port Jefferson, N. Y. | 40°57.0'N, 73°04.5'W |
| Greenport, N. Y. | 41°06.0'N, 72°21.5'W |
| Sag Harbor, N. Y. | 41°00.2'N, 72°17.7'W |
| Montauk, N. Y. | 41°02.8'N, 71°57.5'W |
| Stamford, Conn. | 41°01.8'N, 73°32.3'W |
| South Norwalk, Conn. | 41°05.7'N, 73°24.7'W |
| Bridgeport, Conn. | 41°10.3'N, 73°10.8'W |
| Stratford, Conn. | 41°11.3'N, 73°07.3'W |
| New Haven, Conn. | 41°17.4'N, 72°54.5'W |
| Hartford, Conn. | 41°45.0'N, 72°39.0'W |
| New London, Conn. | 41°21.4'N, 72°05.6'W |
| Stonington, Conn. | 41°19.9'N, 71°54.6'W |
| Great Salt Pond, R. I. | 41°11.1'N, 71°34.9'W |
| Providence, R. I. | 41°48.5'N, 71°24.0'W |
| Fall River Mass. | 41°42.4'N, 71°09.8'W |
| Newport, R. I. | 41°29.8'N, 71°19.8'W |
| New Bedford, Mass. | 41°38.1'N, 70°55.1'W |
| Woods Hole, Mass. | 41°31.4'N, 70°40.4'W |
| Vineyard Haven, Mass. | 41°27.3'N, 70°35.8'W |
| Nantucket, Mass. | 41°17.2'N, 70°05.7'W |
| NANTUCKET SHOALS | 40°30.0'N, 70°25.0'W |
| CAPE COD CANAL E ENT. | 41°46.8'N, 70°29.0'W |

Ambrose Light (40°27.5'N, 73°49.9'W.) to New York (The Battery). 20.7 miles

## Inside-Route — South Side of Long Island

### GREENPORT, N.Y., TO EAST ROCKAWAY INLET, N.Y.
(Nautical Miles)

Figure at intersection of columns opposite ports in question is the nautical mileage between the two. Example: Freeport is 61 nautical miles from Shinnecock Canal North End

The following are the ports listed in the triangular distance table, with their coordinates, followed by the stack of distance figures shown beneath each in the chart (nautical miles):

| Port | Coordinates | Distance figures (as charted) |
|---|---|---|
| Manasquan Inlet, N.J. | 40°06.1'N, 74°01.9'W | 40 |
| NEW YORK (The Battery) | 40°42.0'N, 74°01.0'W | 13, 27 |
| Rockaway Point | 40°32.4'N, 73°56.5'W | 9, 22, 31 |
| East Rockaway Inlet | 40°34.9'N, 73°45.4'W | 5, 14, 27, 36 |
| Long Beach | 40°35.7'N, 73°39.4'W | 6, 11, 20, 33, 42 |
| Freeport | 40°37.6'N, 73°34.9'W | 4, 5, 10, 19, 32, 41 |
| Jones Inlet | 40°34.4'N, 73°30.8'W | 4, 4, 8, 13, 22, 35, 44 |
| Jones Beach | 40°36.2'N, 73°30.8'W | 7, 11, 12, 15, 20, 29, 42, 51 |
| Amityville | 40°39.6'N, 73°24.8'W | 6, 13, 17, 18, 21, 26, 35, 48, 57 |
| Babylon | 40°41.2'N, 73°18.9'W | 8, 12, 16, 20, 21, 24, 29, 38, 51, 60 |
| Fire Island Inlet | 40°37.8'N, 73°18.6'W | 9, 5, 10, 17, 21, 21, 24, 29, 38, 51, 60 |
| Bay Shore | 40°42.8'N, 73°14.2'W | 13, 18, 17, 22, 28, 32, 36, 41, 50, 63, 72 |
| Patchogue | 40°45.5'N, 73°01.2'W | 6, 16, 21, 19, 24, 31, 35, 38, 44, 53, 66, 75 |
| Bellport | 40°45.1'N, 72°56.0'W | 11, 17, 27, 32, 30, 35, 42, 46, 49, 54, 63, 76, 85 |
| Moriches Inlet | 40°45.8'N, 72°45.3'W | 7, 15, 21, 30, 35, 34, 39, 45, 49, 53, 67, 80, 89 |
| Westhampton Beach | 40°48.2'N, 72°38.4'W | 9, 15, 23, 29, 39, 44, 42, 47, 54, 58, 61, 66, 75, 88, 97 |
| Shinnecock Inlet | 40°50.3'N, 72°28.6'W | 5, 12, 18, 26, 32, 41, 46, 45, 50, 56, 60, 64, 69, 78, 91, 100 |
| Shinnecock Canal, N. End | 40°53.9'N, 72°30.3'W | 8, 13, 20, 26, 34, 40, 49, 54, 53, 58, 64, 68, 69, 72, 77, 86, 99, 108 |
| Riverside | 40°55.0'N, 72°39.4'W | 22, 17, 22, 29, 35, 43, 49, 58, 63, 62, 67, 73, 77, 78, 81, 86, 86, 95, 108, 117 |
| Sag Harbor | 41°00.2'N, 72°71.7'W | 11, 21, 16, 21, 28, 34, 42, 48, 57, 62, 61, 66, 72, 76, 77, 80, 85, 85, 94, 107, 116 |
| Greenport | 41°06.0'N, 72°21.5'W | (base of chart) |

Ambrose Light (40°27.5'N, 73°49.9'W) to New York (The Battery), 20.7 miles

**Distances**

## HUDSON RIVER — NEW YORK, NY, TO TROY LOCK, NY
(Nautical Miles)

Figure at intersection of columns opposite ports in question is the nautical mileage between the two. Example: Poughkeepsie, N. Y., is 60 nautical miles from Albany, N. Y.

Ports (with positions):

- Troy Lock 41°45.1'N, 73°41.1'W
- Watervliet 42°43.7'N, 73°41.9'W
- Troy 42°43.7'N, 73°41.8'W
- Rensselaer 42°37.9'N, 73°45.1'W
- Albany 42°37.9'N, 73°45.3'W
- Coeymans 42°28.5'N, 73°47.4'W
- Coxsackie 42°21.0'N, 73°47.6'W
- Athens 42°15.7'N, 73°48.5'W
- Hudson 42°15.3'N, 73°48.1'W
- Catskill 42°13.0'N, 73°52.1'W
- Saugerties 42°04.4'N, 73°56.7'W
- Kingston 41°55.1'N, 73°59.0'W
- Hyde Park 41°47.3'N, 73°56.9'W
- Poughkeepsie 41°42.3'N, 73°56.5'W
- Newburgh 41°30.1'N, 74°00.3'W
- West Point 41°23.1'N, 73°57.3'W
- Peekskill 41°17.3'N, 73°56.0'W
- Haverstraw 41°11.8'N, 73°57.5'W
- Ossining 41°09.6'N, 73°52.3'W
- Nyack 41°05.4'N, 73°54.9'W
- Tarrytown 41°04.7'N, 73°52.2'W
- Yonkers 40°56.1'N, 73°54.3'W
- NEW YORK (The Battery) 40°42.0'N, 74°01.0'W

## COASTWISE — NEW YORK, NY, TO CHESAPEAKE BAY ENTRANCE, VA
(Nautical Miles)

Figure at intersection of columns opposite ports in question is the nautical mileage between the two.
Example: New York, N. Y., is 240 nautical miles from Philadelphia, Pa..

**Ports (with coordinates):**

- CHESAPEAKE BAY ENT. — 36°56.3′, 75°58.6′W
- Chincoteague, Va. — 37°56.3′, 75°22.8′W
- Ocean City, Md. — 38°19.b′, 75°05.6′W
- Indian River Inlet, Del. — 38°36.5′, 75°03.6′W
- Trenton, N. J. — 40°11.4′, 74°45.4′W
- U.S. Steel Basin, Pa. — 40°08.2′, 74°45.3′W
- Philadelphia, Pa. — 39°56.8′, 75°08.3′W
- Chester, Pa. — 39°50.0′, 75°22.0′W
- Marcus Hook, Pa. — 39°48.2′, 75°25.2′W
- Wilmington, Del. — 39°43.2′, 75°31.5′W
- CHES. & DEL. CANAL E. ENT. — 39°33.8′N, 75°32.8′W
- Harbor of Refuge, Del. — 38°49.0′N, 75°05.2′W
- DELAWARE BAY ENTRANCE — 38°50.5′N, 75°03.3′W
- Cape May Harbor, N. J. — 38°57.1′N, 74°52.6′W
- Atlantic City, N. Y — 39°22.6′N, 74°24.9′W
- Barnegat Inlet — 39°46.0′N, 69°25.0′W
- Manasquan Inlet, N. J. — 40°06.1′N, 74°01.9′W
- NEW YORK, N. Y. — 40°42.0′N, 74°01.0′W
- MONTAUK POINT, N. Y. — 41°01.7′N, 71°47.3′W
- NANTUCKET SHOALS — 40°30.0′N, 69°25.0′W

**Distance matrix (nautical miles):**

| From \ To | Ches. Bay Ent. | Chincoteague | Ocean City | Indian River | Trenton | U.S. Steel Basin | Philadelphia | Chester | Marcus Hook | Wilmington | Canal E. Ent. | Harbor of Refuge | Delaware Bay Ent. | Cape May | Atlantic City | Barnegat | Manasquan | New York | Montauk |
|---|---|---|---|---|---|---|---|---|---|---|---|---|---|---|---|---|---|---|---|
| Chincoteague | 69 | | | | | | | | | | | | | | | | | | |
| Ocean City | 100 | 41 | | | | | | | | | | | | | | | | | |
| Indian River Inlet | 118 | | 20 | | | | | | | | | | | | | | | | |
| Trenton | 270 | 187 | 147 | 129 | | | | | | | | | | | | | | | |
| U.S. Steel Basin | 265 | 182 | 142 | 124 | 5 | | | | | | | | | | | | | | |
| Philadelphia | 242 | 159 | 119 | 101 | 28 | 23 | | | | | | | | | | | | | |
| Chester | 227 | 144 | 104 | 86 | 43 | 38 | 15 | | | | | | | | | | | | |
| Marcus Hook | 224 | 140 | 101 | 83 | 46 | 41 | 18 | 3 | | | | | | | | | | | |
| Wilmington | 218 | 134 | 95 | 77 | 54 | 49 | 26 | | 8 | | | | | | | | | | |
| Canal E. Ent. | 206 | 83 | | 66 | 64 | 59 | 36 | 21 | 17 | 11 | | | | | | | | | |
| Harbor of Refuge | 155 | 71 | 31 | 14 | | 111 | 88 | 73 | 69 | 63 | 52 | | | | | | | | |
| Delaware Bay Entrance | 155 | 72 | 32 | 15 | | 110 | 87 | 72 | 68 | 62 | 51 | 2 | | | | | | | |
| Cape May Harbor | 141 | 80 | 40 | 24 | | | 126 | 103 | 88 | 84 | 78 | 17 | 16 | | | | | | |
| Atlantic City | 171 | 113 | 73 | 57 | | 159 | 136 | 121 | 117 | 111 | 100 | 49 | 50 | 37 | | | | | |
| Barnegat Inlet | 201 | 141 | 101 | 86 | | | 188 | 165 | 150 | 146 | 140 | 79 | 78 | 65 | 32 | | | | |
| Manasquan Inlet | 219 | 262 | 212 | 121 | 105 | 207 | 184 | 169 | 165 | 159 | 148 | 98 | 97 | 85 | 52 | 22 | | | |
| NEW YORK | 267 | 327 | 268 | 201 | 161 | 263 | 240 | 224 | 221 | 215 | 204 | 153 | 153 | 128 | 94 | 63 | 40 | | |
| MONTAUK POINT | 322 | 227 | 209 | 145 | 322 | 299 | 283 | 280 | 274 | 263 | 204 | 212 | 212 | 192 | 159 | 131 | 117 | 122 | |
| NANTUCKET SHOALS | 381 | 400 | 295 | 285 | | 395 | 372 | 356 | 353 | 347 | 336 | 285 | 285 | 271 | 242 | 221 | 212 | 223 | 113 |

---

Ambrose Light (40°27.5′N, 73°49.9′W) to New York (The Battery), 20.7 miles.
Five Fathom Bank Lighted Horn Buoy F (38°47.3′N, 74°34.6′W) to Philadelphia, 111 miles.
Delaware Lighted Horn Buoy D (38°27.3′N, 74°41.8′W) to Philadelphia, 116 miles.
Chesapeake Light (36°54.3′N, 75°42.8′W) to Norfolk, 42 miles; Baltimore, 165 miles.

**Distances**

## INTRACOASTAL WATERWAY — MANASQUAN INLET, NJ TO CAPE MAY CANAL, NJ

(Nautical Miles)

Figure at intersection of columns opposite ports in question is the nautical mileage between the two. Example: Atlantic City N. J., is 13 nautical miles from Ocean City, N. J.

| NEW YORK, N. Y. (The Battery)* 40°42.0'N, 74°01.0'W. | Shark river Inlet* 40°11.2'N, 74°00.5'W. | Manasquan Inlet* 40°06.1'N, 74°01.9'W. | Bay Head 40°03.8'N, 74°03.1'W. | Mantoloking 40°02.2'N, 74°03.4'W. | Toms River (Town) 39°56.9'N, 74°11.8'W. | Seaside Park 39°55.3'N, 74°05.0'W. | Forked River (town) 39°50.1'N, 74°11.7'W. | Barnegat Inlet 39°46.0'N, 74°06.3'W. | Beach Haven 39°34.0'N, 74°14.8'W. | Atlantic City 39°22.6'N, 74°24.9'W. | Mays Landing 39°26.9'N, 74°43.4'W. | Ocean City 39°17.3'N, 74°34.4'W. | Sea Isle City 39°09.4'N, 74°42.0'W. | Avalon 39°06.6'N, 74°44.0'W. | Stone Harbor 39°03.4'N, 74°46.0'W. | Wildwood 39°00.5'N, 74°49.8'W. | Cape May Harbor 38°57.1'N, 74°52.6'W. | Cape May Canal W. Ent. 38°58.0'N, 74°54.0'W. | CHES. & DEL. CANAL E. ENT. 39°33.8'N, 75°32.8'W. |
|---|---|---|---|---|---|---|---|---|---|---|---|---|---|---|---|---|---|---|---|
| 34 | | | | | | | | | | | | | | | | | | | |
| 40 | 6 | | | | | | | | | | | | | | | | | | |
| 44 | 9 | 4 | | | | | | | | | | | | | | | | | |
| 46 | 11 | 6 | 2 | | | | | | | | | | | | | | | | |
| 58 | 23 | 18 | 14 | 12 | | | | | | | | | | | | | | | |
| 54 | 20 | 14 | 10 | 9 | 7 | | | | | | | | | | | | | | |
| 63 | 29 | 23 | 19 | 17 | 15 | 10 | | | | | | | | | | | | | |
| 66 | 32 | 26 | 22 | 20 | 18 | 13 | 8 | | | | | | | | | | | | |
| 79 | 45 | 39 | 35 | 33 | 31 | 26 | 21 | 20 | | | | | | | | | | | |
| 97 | 62 | 57 | 53 | 51 | 49 | 44 | 39 | 38 | 18 | | | | | | | | | | |
| 124 | 90 | 84 | 80 | 79 | 77 | 71 | 66 | 65 | 45 | 30 | | | | | | | | | |
| 108 | 74 | 68 | 64 | 63 | 60 | 55 | 50 | 49 | 29 | 13 | 18 | | | | | | | | |
| 119 | 85 | 79 | 76 | 74 | 72 | 66 | 61 | 60 | 40 | 25 | 29 | 11 | | | | | | | |
| 123 | 89 | 83 | 79 | 77 | 75 | 70 | 65 | 64 | 44 | 28 | 33 | 15 | 4 | | | | | | |
| 128 | 94 | 88 | 85 | 83 | 81 | 75 | 70 | 69 | 49 | 34 | 38 | 20 | 9 | 5 | | | | | |
| 133 | 99 | 93 | 89 | 88 | 86 | 80 | 75 | 74 | 54 | 39 | 43 | 25 | 14 | 10 | 5 | | | | |
| 138 | 103 | 98 | 94 | 92 | 90 | 85 | 80 | 79 | 59 | 43 | 47 | 30 | 18 | 15 | 9 | 5 | | | |
| 142 | 108 | 102 | 98 | 96 | 94 | 89 | 84 | 83 | 63 | 47 | 52 | 34 | 23 | 19 | 14 | 9 | 4 | | |
| 190 | 156 | 150 | 146 | 144 | 142 | 137 | 132 | 131 | 111 | 95 | 100 | 82 | 71 | 67 | 62 | 57 | 52 | 48 | |

* Outside distances between New York and Manesquan Inlet.

## DELAWARE BAY AND RIVER
(Nautical Miles)

Figure at intersection of columns opposite ports in question is the nautical mileage between the two. Example: Salem, N. J., is 41 nautical miles from Philadelphia, Pa.

Places (with positions):

- Trenton, N. J. — 40°11.4'N, 74°45.4'W
- Bordentown, N. J. — 40°09.1'N, 74°43.0'W
- U.S. Steel Basin, Pa — 40°08.2'N, 74°45.3'W
- Burlington, N. J. — 40°04.9'N, 74°51.8'W
- Philadelphia, Pa. — 39°56.8'N, 75°08.3'W
- Schuylkill River Mouth, PA — 39°52.8'N, 75°11.9'W
- Chester, Pa. — 39°50.0'N, 75°22.0'W
- Bridgeport, N. J. — 39°48.0'N, 75°21.3'W
- Marcus Hook, Pa. — 39°48.2'N, 75°25.2'W
- Wilmington, Del. — 39°43.2'N, 75°31.5'W
- New Castle, Del. — 39°39.4'N, 75°33.6'W
- CHES. & DEL. CANAL E. ENT. — 39°33.8', 75°32.8'W
- Salem, N. J. — 39°34.6'N, 75°28.7'W
- Smyrna River Mouth, Del — 39°22.2'N, 75°30.2'W
- Bridgeton, N. J. — 39°25.5'N, 75°14.2'W
- Mauricetown, N. J. — 39°17.1'N, 74°59.5'W
- St. Jones River Mouth, Del. — 39°04.0'N, 75°22.5'W
- Cape May Canal W. Ent., N. J. — 38°58.0'N, 74°58.0'W
- Roosevelt Inlet, Del. — 38°47.7'N, 75°09.4'W
- DELAWARE BAY ENT. — 38°50.0'N, 75°03.3'W

Distance table (triangular):

| From \ | Tre | Bor | USS | Bur | Phi | Sch | Che | Brp | MHk | Wil | NCa | C&D | Sal | Smy | Bri | Mau | StJ | CMy | Roo |
|---|---|---|---|---|---|---|---|---|---|---|---|---|---|---|---|---|---|---|---|
| Bordentown | 4 | | | | | | | | | | | | | | | | | | |
| U.S. Steel Basin | 2 | 5 | | | | | | | | | | | | | | | | | |
| Burlington | 7 | 9 | 12 | | | | | | | | | | | | | | | | |
| Philadelphia | 16 | 23 | 25 | 28 | | | | | | | | | | | | | | | |
| Schuylkill River Mouth | 7 | 23 | 29 | 31 | 34 | | | | | | | | | | | | | | |
| Chester | 9 | 15 | 31 | 38 | 40 | 43 | | | | | | | | | | | | | |
| Bridgeport | 6 | 14 | 22 | 37 | 44 | 46 | 49 | | | | | | | | | | | | |
| Marcus Hook | 4 | 3 | 12 | 18 | 34 | 41 | 43 | 46 | | | | | | | | | | | |
| Wilmington | 8 | 11 | 11 | 19 | 26 | 42 | 49 | 51 | 54 | | | | | | | | | | |
| New Castle | 5 | 12 | 15 | 15 | 23 | 30 | 46 | 53 | 55 | 58 | | | | | | | | | |
| CHES. & DEL. CANAL E. ENT. | 7 | 11 | 17 | 17 | 21 | 21 | 29 | 36 | 52 | 59 | 61 | 64 | | | | | | | |
| Salem | 5 | 12 | 16 | 22 | 26 | 26 | 34 | 41 | 57 | 64 | 66 | 69 | | | | | | | |
| Smyrna River Mouth | 16 | 13 | 20 | 24 | 30 | 34 | 34 | 42 | 49 | 65 | 72 | 74 | 77 | | | | | | |
| Bridgeton | 25 | 39 | 36 | 43 | 47 | 53 | 57 | 57 | 65 | 72 | 88 | 95 | 97 | 100 | | | | | |
| Mauricetown | 51 | 39 | 54 | 51 | 58 | 62 | 68 | 72 | 72 | 80 | 87 | 103 | 110 | 112 | 115 | | | | |
| St. Jones River Mouth | 30 | 35 | 21 | 36 | 34 | 40 | 45 | 51 | 55 | 55 | 63 | 69 | 85 | 92 | 94 | 97 | | | |
| Cape May Canal W. Ent. | 21 | 26 | 47 | 36 | 51 | 48 | 55 | 59 | 65 | 69 | 69 | 77 | 84 | 100 | 107 | 109 | 112 | | |
| Roosevelt Inlet | 14 | 20 | 37 | 52 | 40 | 55 | 52 | 59 | 69 | 73 | 73 | 81 | 88 | 104 | 111 | 113 | 116 | | |
| DELAWARE BAY ENT. | 6 | 9 | 20 | 33 | 51 | 39 | 54 | 51 | 58 | 62 | 68 | 72 | 72 | 80 | 87 | 103 | 110 | 112 | 115 |

Distances

## CHESAPEAKE BAY
(Nautical Miles)

Figure at intersection of columns opposite ports in question is the nautical mileage between the two. Example: Washington, D. C., is 155 nautical miles from Annapolis, Md.

Ports (with coordinates):

- CHESAPEAKE BAY ENT. — 36°56.3'N, 76°58.6'W
- Norfolk, Va. — 36°50.9'N, 76°17.9'W
- Richmond, Va. — 37°31.4'N, 77°25.2'W
- Petersburg, Va. — 37°14.1'N, 77°24.0'W
- Hopewell, Va. — 37°19.0'N, 77°16.4'W
- Suffolk, Va. — 36°44.3'N, 76°35.0'W
- Newport News, Va. — 36°58.0'N, 76°26.0'W
- West Point, Va. — 37°31.6'N, 76°48.1'W
- Yorktown, Va. — 37°14.4'N, 76°30.5'W
- Cape Charles Va. — 37°15.9'N, 76°01.4'W
- Fredericksburg, Va. — 38°17.8'N, 77°27.2'W
- Crisfield, Md. — 37°58.9'N, 75°51.9'W
- Washington, D. C. — 38°52.4'N, 77°01.4'W
- Potomac River Mouth — 37°57.7'N, 76°16.7'W
- Salisbury, Md. — 38°21.9'N, 75°36.3'W
- Solomons, Md. — 38°19.2'N, 76°27.4'W
- Cambridge, Md. — 38°34.4'N, 76°04.3'W
- St. Michaels, Md. — 38°47.2'N, 76°13.2'W
- Annapolis, Md. — 38°59.0'N, 76°28.6'W
- Chestertown, Md. — 39°12.4'N, 76°03.8'W
- Baltimore, Md. — 39°16.0'N, 76°34.5'W
- Havre de Grace, Md. — 39°32.7'N, 76°05.0'W
- Chesapeake City, Md. — 39°31.8'N, 75°48.9'W
- CHES. & DEL CANAL E. ENT. — 39°33.8'N, 75°32.8'W

Triangular mileage table (distances by row, reading left to right):

- Norfolk: 27
- Richmond: 90, 101
- Petersburg: 28, 80, 92
- Hopewell: 10, 19, 70, 82
- Suffolk: 79, 89, 98, 29, 42
- Newport News: 21, 58, 68, 77, 12, 24
- West Point: 63, 78, 122, 123, 140, 66, 56
- Yorktown: 22, 55, 55, 114, 101, 132, 58, 34
- Cape Charles: 28, 50, 29, 48, 88, 97, 106, 32, 21
- Fredericksburg: 122, 132, 154, 143, 161, 201, 211, 220, 146, 136
- Crisfield: 129, 51, 64, 86, 86, 74, 92, 132, 142, 151, 77, 67
- Washington, D.C.: 121, 221, 146, 164, 186, 182, 185, 240, 233, 259, 185, 163
- Potomac River Mouth: 96, 27, 125, 50, 68, 90, 89, 89, 144, 137, 163, 89, 67
- Salisbury: 49, 141, 165, 87, 100, 122, 110, 128, 168, 178, 187, 113, 103
- Solomons: 51, 27, 118, 42, 150, 76, 87, 109, 97, 115, 155, 165, 174, 100, 92
- Cambridge: 39, 81, 58, 149, 72, 182, 107, 117, 140, 129, 147, 187, 197, 206, 132, 123
- St. Michaels: 36, 48, 89, 65, 156, 80, 190, 116, 126, 149, 138, 156, 196, 206, 215, 141, 132
- Annapolis: 25, 39, 45, 86, 64, 155, 77, 186, 112, 130, 152, 136, 152, 194, 204, 213, 140, 129
- Chestertown: 40, 59, 72, 78, 119, 96, 187, 110, 219, 146, 156, 178, 167, 185, 225, 235, 244, 170, 162
- Baltimore: 45, 66, 60, 84, 107, 98, 206, 132, 155, 174, 172, 170, 172, 228, 222, 247, 173, 150
- Havre de Grace: 41, 61, 45, 62, 78, 84, 124, 101, 115, 224, 163, 185, 190, 230, 240, 249, 175, 166
- Chesapeake City: 20, 49, 65, 52, 70, 85, 90, 130, 109, 121, 230, 179, 201, 196, 252, 271, 196, 174
- CHES. & DEL CANAL E. ENT: 13, 33, 62, 78, 65, 83, 98, 103, 143, 122, 134, 243, 169, 192, 214, 207, 209, 265, 259, 284, 209, 187

## POTOMAC RIVER
(Nautical Miles)

Figure at intersection of columns opposite ports in question is the nautical mileage between the two. Example: Colonial Beach, Va., is 63 nautical miles from Washington, D. C.

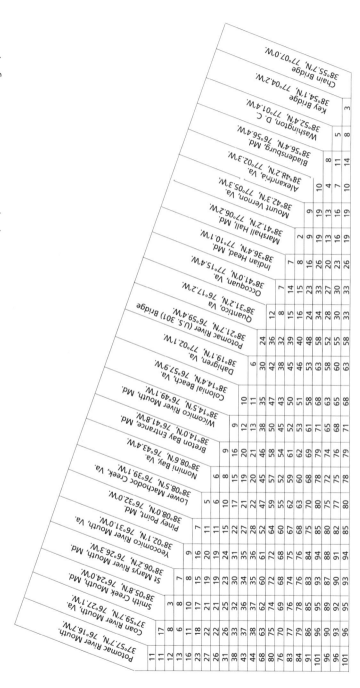

**Distances**

503

# COASTWISE — NORFOLK, VA, TO KEY WEST, FL
(Nautical Miles)

Figure at intersection of columns opposite ports in question is the nautical mileage between the two. Example: Norfolk, Va., is 503 nautical miles from Savannah, Ga.

**Ports and positions (as listed on the chart headers):**

- STRAITS OF FLORIDA — 24°24.0'N, 83°00.0'W
- Key West, Fla. — 24°33.7'N, 81°48.5'W
- Miami, Fla. — 25°47.0'N, 80°11.0'W
- Port Everglades, Fla. — 26°05.6'N, 80°07.0'W
- Port of Palm Beach, Fla. — 26°46.1'N, 80°03.0'W
- Stuart, Fla. — 27°12.2'N, 80°15.6'W
- Fort Pierce, Fla. — 27°27.1'N, 60°19.3'W
- Cape Canaveral, Fla — 28°24.6'N, 80°36.5'W
- St. Augustine, Fla. — 29°53.6'N, 81°18.5'W
- Jacksonville, Fla. — 30°19.2'N, 81°39.0'W
- Fernandina Beach, Fla. — 30°40.3'N, 81°28.0'W
- Brunswick, Ga — 31°08.0'N, 81°29.7'W
- Savannah, Ga. — 32°06.0'N, 81°05.7'W
- Port Royal, S. C. — 32°22.3'N, 80°41.6'W
- Charleston, S. C. — 32°47.2'N, 79°55.2'W
- Georgetown, S. C. — 33°21.4'N, 79°16.9'W
- Wilmington, N. C. — 34°14.0'N, 77°57.0'W
- Southport, N. C. — 33°54.8'N, 78°01.0'W
- Morehead City, N. C. — 34°42.8'N, 76°41.8'W
- DIAMOND SHOALS — 35°08.0'N, 75°15.0'W
- Norfolk, Va. — 46°50.9'N, 76°17.9'W
- CHESAPEAKE BAY ENTRANCE — 36°56.3'N, 75°58.6'W

**Distance table (nautical miles). Each row lists distances from the named port to the ports above it; the left-most value is the distance to the nearest adjacent port, the right-most value is the distance to the Straits of Florida.**

| From \ To | Straits | Key West | Miami | Pt Everglades | Palm Beach | Stuart | Ft Pierce | Cape Canaveral | St. Augustine | Jacksonville | Fernandina | Brunswick | Savannah | Port Royal | Charleston | Georgetown | Wilmington | Southport | Morehead | Diamond | Norfolk |
|---|---|---|---|---|---|---|---|---|---|---|---|---|---|---|---|---|---|---|---|---|---|
| Key West | 73 | | | | | | | | | | | | | | | | | | | | |
| Miami | 211 | 151 | | | | | | | | | | | | | | | | | | | |
| Port Everglades | 226 | 165 | 27 | | | | | | | | | | | | | | | | | | |
| Port of Palm Beach | 267 | 207 | 68 | 46 | | | | | | | | | | | | | | | | | |
| Stuart | 300 | 239 | 101 | 78 | 36 | | | | | | | | | | | | | | | | |
| Fort Pierce | 316 | 255 | 117 | 94 | 52 | 32 | | | | | | | | | | | | | | | |
| Cape Canaveral | 374 | 313 | 175 | 152 | 110 | 91 | 69 | | | | | | | | | | | | | | |
| St. Augustine | 475 | 414 | 276 | 253 | 211 | 192 | 167 | 120 | | | | | | | | | | | | | |
| Jacksonville | 523 | 462 | 324 | 301 | 259 | 240 | 214 | 167 | 56 | | | | | | | | | | | | |
| Fernandina Beach | 526 | 465 | 327 | 304 | 262 | 242 | 216 | 169 | 61 | 53 | | | | | | | | | | | |
| Brunswick | 549 | 488 | 350 | 327 | 285 | 268 | 242 | 195 | 90 | 82 | 50 | | | | | | | | | | |
| Savannah | 604 | 543 | 405 | 382 | 340 | 324 | 298 | 251 | 152 | 145 | 115 | 104 | | | | | | | | | |
| Port Royal | 605 | 544 | 406 | 383 | 341 | 324 | 298 | 251 | 157 | | 120 | 110 | 51 | | | | | | | | |
| Charleston | 633 | 572 | 434 | 407 | 369 | 353 | 329 | 283 | 199 | 197 | 166 | 156 | 102 | 90 | | | | | | | |
| Georgetown | 671 | 610 | 472 | | | | | 324 | 247 | 247 | 216 | 210 | 154 | 141 | 79 | | | | | | |
| Wilmington | 728 | 667 | 529 | 506 | 476 | | | 388 | 315 | 286 | 281 | 227 | 212 | 151 | 108 | | | | | | |
| Southport | 772 | 707 | 646 | 529 | 506 | 464 | 423 | 407 | 367 | 296 | 294 | 265 | 260 | 206 | 191 | 130 | 21 | | | | |
| Morehead City | | 764 | 711 | 646 | 573 | 561 | 550 | 509 | 476 | 438 | 377 | 379 | 352 | 346 | 295 | 284 | 220 | 87 | | | |
| Diamond Shoals | 825 | 764 | 626 | 603 | 561 | 549 | 530 | 495 | 440 | 443 | 416 | 410 | 359 | 348 | 285 | 248 | 219 | 198 | 105 | | |
| Norfolk | 969 | 908 | 770 | 747 | 705 | 693 | 674 | 639 | 584 | 587 | 560 | 554 | 503 | 492 | 429 | 392 | 363 | 342 | 249 | 144 | |
| Chesapeake Bay Entrance | 942 | 881 | 743 | 720 | 678 | 666 | 647 | 612 | 557 | 560 | 533 | 527 | 476 | 465 | 402 | 365 | 336 | 315 | 222 | 117 | 27 |

Chesapeake Light (36°54.3'N, 75°42.8'W) to Norfolk 42 miles; Baltimore, 165 miles.
Cape Fear River Entrance Lighted Buoy 2CF (33°49.5'N, 78°03.7'W) to Wilmington, 28 miles.
Charleston Entrance Lighted Whistle Buoy C (32°39.6'N, 79°40.9'W) to Charleston, 14.7 miles.
Savanah Light (31°57.0'N, 80°41.0'W) to Savannah, 25 miles.
St Johns River Entrance Buoy STJ (30°23.6'N, 81°19.1'W) to Jacksonville, 23 miles.
Key West Entrance Lighted Whistle Buoy KW (24°27.7'N, 8148.1'W) to Key West, 6.3 miles.

Each distance is by shortest route that safe navigation permits between the two ports concerned. The navigator must make his own adjustments for non-direct routes selected to run with or avoid the Gulf Stream. For example, the table shows a distance of 561 miles by direct route from Diamond Shoals to Port of Palm Beach; distances via adjusted routes are: Outer route 572 miles; Gulf Stream route 593 miles; Inner route, 628 miles.

# INSIDE ROUTE — NORFOLK, VA, TO FERNANDINA BEACH, FL

(Nautical and Statute Miles)

Figure at intersection of columns opposite ports in question is the nautical/statute mileage between the two. Example: Morehead City, N. C., is 445 nautical miles (512 statute miles) from Fernandina Beach, Fla.

Statute Miles

Nautical Miles

| Port | Norfolk | Elizabeth City | Hertford | Columbia | Edenton | Plymouth | Manteo | Belhaven | Washington | Ocracoke | Oriental | New Bern | Beaufort, N. C. | Morehead City | Swansboro | Jacksonville | Wrightsville | Wilmington | Southport | Little River | Bucksport | Georgetown | McClellanville | Charleston | Beaufort, S. C. | Savannah | Thunderbolt | Brunswick | Fernandina Beach |
|---|---|---|---|---|---|---|---|---|---|---|---|---|---|---|---|---|---|---|---|---|---|---|---|---|---|---|---|---|---|
| Norfolk, Va. 36°50.9'N, 76°17.9'W | | *89 | 102 | 102 | 113 | 121 | 92 | 138 | 180 | 151 | 184 | 207 | 204 | 205 | 230 | 266 | 283 | 314 | 308 | 344 | 377 | 405 | 430 | 467 | 536 | 585 | 583 | 685 | 717 |
| Elizabeth City, N. C. 36°18.1'N, 76°13.0'W | *77 | | 45 | 45 | 55 | 64 | 45 | 91 | 131 | 105 | 136 | 160 | 154 | 157 | 182 | 217 | 235 | 266 | 260 | 296 | 329 | 358 | 382 | 419 | 488 | 536 | 535 | 636 | 669 |
| Hertford, N. C. 36°11.6'N, 76°28.0'W | 89 | 39 | | 30 | 40 | 48 | 53 | 91 | 132 | 112 | 137 | 160 | 158 | 158 | 184 | 219 | 236 | 267 | 261 | 298 | 330 | 358 | 383 | 421 | 489 | 537 | 536 | 638 | 670 |
| Columbia, N. C. 35°55.0'N, 76°15.4'W | 89 | 39 | 26 | | 29 | 38 | 52 | 90 | 131 | 110 | 136 | 159 | 157 | 157 | 182 | 217 | 235 | 266 | 260 | 296 | 329 | 357 | 382 | 419 | 488 | 536 | 535 | 636 | 669 |
| Edenton, N. C. 36°03.3'N, 76°36.6'W | 98 | 48 | 35 | 25 | | 16 | 62 | 100 | 142 | 120 | 145 | 168 | 166 | 167 | 191 | 227 | 245 | 276 | 270 | 306 | 338 | 366 | 391 | 429 | 497 | 547 | 545 | 647 | 678 |
| Plymouth, N. C. 35°51.8'N, 76°45.6'W | 105 | 56 | 42 | 33 | 14 | | 70 | 109 | 150 | 130 | 154 | 178 | 175 | 175 | 201 | 237 | 254 | 285 | 280 | 315 | 349 | 376 | 402 | 438 | 508 | 556 | 555 | 656 | 688 |
| Manteo, N. C 35°54.6'N, 75°40.2'W | 80 | 39 | 46 | 45 | 54 | 61 | | 81 | 121 | 70 | 105 | 127 | 127 | 127 | 152 | 186 | 205 | 236 | 231 | 267 | 299 | 326 | 352 | 388 | 457 | 506 | 505 | 606 | 639 |
| Belhaven, N. C. 35°32.1'N, 76°37.4'W | 120 | 79 | 79 | 78 | 87 | 95 | 70 | | 45 | 49 | 49 | 72 | 70 | 70 | 96 | 131 | 150 | 181 | 175 | 211 | 243 | 270 | 296 | 334 | 402 | 451 | 450 | 551 | 582 |
| Washington, N. C. 35°32.6'N, 77°03.7'W | 156 | 114 | 115 | 114 | 123 | 130 | 105 | 39 | | 69 | 64 | 87 | 85 | 85 | 110 | 146 | 163 | 194 | 189 | 224 | 258 | 285 | 311 | 348 | 417 | 465 | 464 | 565 | 597 |
| Ocracoke, N. C. 35°06.8'N, 75°59.1'W | 131 | 91 | 97 | 96 | 104 | 113 | 61 | 43 | 60 | | 47 | 71 | 68 | 68 | 93 | 129 | 147 | 178 | 173 | 208 | 241 | 268 | 293 | 331 | 399 | 449 | 448 | 549 | 580 |
| Oriental, N. C. 35°01.5'N, 76°41.8'W | 160 | 118 | 119 | 118 | 126 | 134 | 91 | 43 | 56 | 41 | | 26 | 25 | 25 | 51 | 86 | 105 | 136 | 130 | 166 | 198 | 226 | 251 | 289 | 357 | 406 | 405 | 506 | 537 |
| New Bern, N. C. 35°06.1'N, 77°02.1'W | 180 | 139 | 139 | 138 | 146 | 155 | 110 | 63 | 76 | 62 | 23 | | 44 | 44 | 69 | 105 | 123 | 154 | 148 | 184 | 216 | 245 | 270 | 307 | 376 | 425 | 423 | 525 | 557 |
| Beaufort, N. C. 34°43.1'N, 76°40.2'W | 177 | 134 | 137 | 136 | 144 | 152 | 110 | 61 | 74 | 59 | 22 | 38 | | 3 | 28 | 63 | 81 | 112 | 107 | 143 | 175 | 203 | 229 | 266 | 334 | 383 | 382 | 483 | 514 |
| Morehead City, N. C. 34°42.8'N, 76°41.8'W | 178 | 136 | 137 | 136 | 145 | 152 | 110 | 61 | 74 | 59 | 22 | 38 | 3 | | 25 | 61 | 79 | 110 | 105 | 140 | 173 | 200 | 226 | 264 | 331 | 381 | 380 | 481 | 512 |
| Swansboro, N. C. 34°41.0'N, 77°07.3'W | 200 | 158 | 160 | 158 | 166 | 175 | 132 | 83 | 96 | 81 | 44 | 60 | 24 | 22 | | 36 | 53 | 64 | 79 | 115 | 147 | 175 | 200 | 238 | 306 | 356 | 353 | 456 | 487 |
| Jacksonville, N. C. 34°44.7'N, 77°26.3'W | 231 | 189 | 190 | 189 | 197 | 206 | 162 | 114 | 127 | 112 | 75 | 91 | 55 | 53 | 31 | | 55 | 86 | 81 | 116 | 148 | 177 | 203 | 239 | 308 | 357 | 356 | 457 | 489 |
| Wrightsville, N. C. 34°13.1'N, 77°48.8'W | 246 | 204 | 205 | 204 | 213 | 221 | 178 | 130 | 142 | 128 | 91 | 107 | 70 | 69 | 46 | 48 | | 31 | 25 | 61 | 94 | 122 | 147 | 184 | 253 | 302 | 300 | 402 | 434 |
| Wilmington, N. C. 34°14.0'N, 77°57.0'W | 273 | 231 | 232 | 231 | 240 | 248 | 205 | 157 | 169 | 155 | 118 | 134 | 97 | 96 | 73 | 75 | 27 | | 24 | 60 | 93 | 121 | 146 | 183 | 252 | 300 | 299 | 402 | 433 |
| Southport, N. C. 33°54.8'N, 78°01.0'W | 268 | 226 | 227 | 226 | 235 | 243 | 201 | 152 | 164 | 150 | 113 | 129 | 93 | 91 | 69 | 70 | 22 | 21 | | 36 | 69 | 97 | 122 | 159 | 228 | 276 | 275 | 376 | 409 |
| Little River, S. C. 33°52.2'N, 78°36.6'W | 299 | 257 | 259 | 257 | 266 | 274 | 232 | 183 | 195 | 181 | 144 | 160 | 124 | 122 | 100 | 101 | 53 | 52 | 31 | | 32 | 61 | 86 | 123 | 192 | 241 | 239 | 341 | 373 |
| Bucksport, S. C. 33°39.0'N, 79°05.6'W | 328 | 286 | 287 | 286 | 294 | 303 | 260 | 211 | 224 | 209 | 172 | 188 | 152 | 150 | 128 | 129 | 82 | 81 | 60 | 28 | | 28 | 53 | 91 | 159 | 208 | 206 | 308 | 339 |
| Georgetown, S. C. 33°21.4'N, 79°16.9'W | 352 | 311 | 311 | 310 | 318 | 327 | 283 | 235 | 248 | 233 | 196 | 213 | 177 | 174 | 152 | 154 | 106 | 105 | 84 | 53 | 24 | | 28 | 64 | 133 | 183 | 181 | 283 | 314 |
| McClellanville, S. C. 33°04.7'N, 79°27.6'W | 374 | 332 | 333 | 332 | 340 | 349 | 306 | 257 | 270 | 255 | 218 | 235 | 199 | 196 | 174 | 176 | 128 | 127 | 106 | 75 | 46 | 24 | | 37 | 106 | 155 | 153 | 255 | 287 |
| Charleston, S. C. 32°47.2'N, 79°55.2'W | 406 | 364 | 366 | 364 | 373 | 381 | 337 | 290 | 302 | 288 | 251 | 267 | 231 | 229 | 207 | 208 | 160 | 159 | 138 | 107 | 79 | 56 | 32 | | 69 | 120 | 119 | 220 | 251 |
| Beaufort, S. C. 32°25.6'N, 80°40.2'W | 466 | 424 | 425 | 424 | 432 | 441 | 397 | 349 | 362 | 347 | 310 | 327 | 290 | 288 | 266 | 268 | 220 | 219 | 198 | 167 | 138 | 116 | 92 | 60 | | 49 | 47 | 150 | 181 |
| Savannah, Ga. 32°05.0'N, 81°05.7'W | 508 | 466 | 467 | 466 | 475 | 483 | 440 | 392 | 404 | 390 | 353 | 369 | 333 | 331 | 309 | 310 | 262 | 261 | 240 | 209 | 181 | 159 | 135 | 104 | 43 | | 16 | 117 | 150 |
| Thunderbolt, Ga. 32°01.5'N, 81°02.8'W | 507 | 465 | 466 | 465 | 474 | 482 | 439 | 391 | 403 | 389 | 352 | 368 | 332 | 330 | 307 | 309 | 261 | 260 | 239 | 208 | 179 | 157 | 133 | 103 | 41 | 14 | | 101 | 133 |
| Brunswick, Ga. 31°08.0'N, 81°29.7'W | 595 | 553 | 554 | 553 | 562 | 570 | 527 | 479 | 491 | 477 | 440 | 456 | 420 | 418 | 396 | 397 | 349 | 349 | 327 | 296 | 268 | 246 | 222 | 191 | 130 | 102 | 88 | | 40 |
| Fernandina Beach, Fla. 30°40.3'N, 81°28.0'W | 623 | 581 | 582 | 581 | 589 | 598 | 555 | 506 | 519 | 504 | 467 | 484 | 447 | 445 | 423 | 425 | 377 | 376 | 355 | 324 | 295 | 273 | 249 | 218 | 157 | 130 | 116 | 35 | |

* 51 Statute miles via Dismal Swamp Canal * 44 nautical via Dismal Swamp Canal

Distances

# INSIDE-ROUTE — FERNANDINA BEACH, FL, TO KEY WEST, FL

(Nautical and Statute Miles)

Figure at intersection of columns opposite ports in question is the nautical/statute mileage between the two.
Example: St. Augustine, Fl., is 271 nautical miles (312 statute miles) from Miami, Fla.

Statute miles

| | Fernandina Beach | Jacksonville | St Augustine | Marineland | Daytona Beach | New Smyrna Beach | Titusville | Cocoa | Eau Gallie | Melbourne | Vero Beach | Fort Pierce | Salerno | Stuart | Port Mayaca | Clewiston | Moore Haven | Fort Myers | Jupiter | Port of Palm Beach | Fort Lauderdale | Port Everglades | Miami | Tavernier | Matecumbe Harbor | Marathon | Flamingo | Key West |
|---|---|---|---|---|---|---|---|---|---|---|---|---|---|---|---|---|---|---|---|---|---|---|---|---|---|---|---|---|
| Norfolk, Va. 36°50.9'N., 76°17.9'W | 717 | 758 | 778 | 796 | 831 | 846 | 879 | 898 | 915 | 918 | 952 | 966 | 990 | 995 | 1026 | 1053 | 1066 | 1122 | 1005 | 1018 | 1064 | 1067 | 1090 | 1150 | 1170 | 1203 | 1208 | 1244 |
| Fernandina Beach, Fla. 30°40.3'N., 81°28.0'W | | 41 | 60 | 79 | 114 | 130 | 162 | 181 | 198 | 201 | 235 | 249 | 273 | 278 | 310 | 336 | 349 | 406 | 289 | 302 | 348 | 350 | 373 | 435 | 453 | 486 | 491 | 527 |
| Jacksonville, Fla. 30°19.2'N., 81°39.0'W | | | 56 | 75 | 109 | 124 | 158 | 176 | 193 | 197 | 230 | 244 | 268 | 274 | 305 | 331 | 344 | 402 | 284 | 297 | 344 | 345 | 368 | 430 | 449 | 481 | 486 | 522 |
| St Augustine, Fla. 29°53.6'N., 81°18.5'W | | | | 18 | 53 | 68 | 101 | 120 | 137 | 140 | 174 | 188 | 212 | 217 | 248 | 275 | 288 | 344 | 227 | 241 | 287 | 289 | 312 | 373 | 392 | 425 | 430 | 466 |
| Marineland, Fla. 29°40.1'N., 81°13.0'W | | | | | 35 | 51 | 83 | 102 | 119 | 122 | 157 | 170 | 194 | 199 | 230 | 257 | 270 | 327 | 209 | 222 | 269 | 270 | 293 | 356 | 374 | 407 | 412 | 448 |
| Daytona Beach, Fla. 29°12.6'N., 81°00.7'W | | | | | | 16 | 48 | 67 | 84 | 87 | 121 | 135 | 159 | 165 | 196 | 222 | 235 | 292 | 175 | 188 | 235 | 236 | 259 | 321 | 339 | 372 | 377 | 413 |
| New Smyrna Beach, Fla 29°01.7'N., 81°55.1'W | | | | | | | 32 | 52 | 68 | 72 | 106 | 120 | 144 | 150 | 181 | 207 | 220 | 276 | 159 | 173 | 219 | 220 | 243 | 305 | 323 | 356 | 362 | 397 |
| Titusville, Fla. 28°37.3'N., 80°47.9'W | | | | | | | | 20 | 36 | 39 | 74 | 87 | 112 | 116 | 147 | 174 | 188 | 244 | 127 | 139 | 186 | 188 | 211 | 273 | 291 | 323 | 329 | 365 |
| Cocoa, Fla. 28°21.3'N., 80°43.1'W | | | | | | | | | 16 | 21 | 54 | 68 | 92 | 98 | 129 | 155 | 168 | 224 | 107 | 121 | 167 | 168 | 191 | 253 | 273 | 304 | 311 | 346 |
| Eau Gallie, Fla. 28°07.9'N., 80°37.1'WEau | | | | | | | | | | 3 | 38 | 52 | 76 | 81 | 112 | 138 | 152 | 208 | 91 | 104 | 151 | 152 | 175 | 237 | 257 | 288 | 293 | 329 |
| Melbourne, Fla. 28°05.0'N., 80°35.5'W | | | | | | | | | | | 34 | 47 | 71 | 77 | 108 | 135 | 148 | 205 | 87 | 100 | 147 | 148 | 171 | 234 | 252 | 284 | 290 | 326 |
| Vero Beach, Fla. 27°39.0'N., 80°22.4'W | | | | | | | | | | | | 14 | 38 | 44 | 75 | 101 | 114 | 170 | 53 | 67 | 113 | 114 | 137 | 199 | 219 | 250 | 257 | 292 |
| Fort Pierce, Fla. 27°27.5'N., 80°19.3'W | | | | | | | | | | | | | 24 | 30 | 61 | 87 | 100 | 157 | 39 | 53 | 99 | 100 | 123 | 185 | 205 | 236 | 243 | 278 |
| Salerno, Fla. 27°08.8'N., 80°11.6'W | | | | | | | | | | | | | | 9 | 40 | 67 | 81 | 137 | 20 | 32 | 79 | 80 | 104 | 166 | 185 | 216 | 222 | 258 |
| Stuart, Fla. 27°12.2'N., 80°15.6'W | | | | | | | | | | | | | | | 31 | 58 | 70 | 128 | 25 | 38 | 85 | 86 | 109 | 171 | 190 | 222 | 228 | 264 |
| Port Mayaca, Fla. 26°59.1'N., 80°36.8'W | | | | | | | | | | | | | | | | 26 | 40 | 96 | 56 | 69 | 116 | 117 | 141 | 203 | 221 | 253 | 259 | 295 |
| Clewiston, Fla 26°45.6'N., 80°55.2'W | | | | | | | | | | | | | | | | | 13 | 70 | 83 | 96 | 143 | 144 | 167 | 229 | 247 | 280 | 285 | 321 |
| Moore Haven, Fla. 26°50.0'N., 81°05.3'W | | | | | | | | | | | | | | | | | | 56 | 96 | 108 | 155 | 156 | 180 | 242 | 261 | 292 | 298 | 334 |
| Fort Myers, Fla. 26°38.9'N., 81°52.3'W | | | | | | | | | | | | | | | | | | | 152 | 166 | 212 | 213 | 236 | 298 | 318 | 349 | 356 | 390 |
| Jupiter, Fla. 26°56.8'N., 80°05.4'W | | | | | | | | | | | | | | | | | | | | 14 | 60 | 61 | 84 | 146 | 166 | 197 | 204 | 239 |
| Port of Palm Beach, Fla. 26°46.1'N., 80°03.0'W | | | | | | | | | | | | | | | | | | | | | 47 | 48 | 71 | 133 | 152 | 184 | 190 | 226 |
| Fort Lauderdale, Fla. 26°06.8'N., 80°07.2'W | | | | | | | | | | | | | | | | | | | | | | 1 | 24 | 86 | 106 | 137 | 144 | 178 |
| Port Everglades, Fla. 26°05.6'N., 80°07.0'W | | | | | | | | | | | | | | | | | | | | | | | 23 | 85 | 105 | 136 | 142 | 177 |
| Miami, Fla. 25°47.0'N., 80°11.0'W | | | | | | | | | | | | | | | | | | | | | | | | 62 | 82 | 113 | 120 | 154 |
| Tavernier, Fla. 25°00.7'N., 80°31.3'W | | | | | | | | | | | | | | | | | | | | | | | | | 22 | 54 | 60 | 96 |
| Matecumbe Harbor, Fla. 24°51.1'N., 80°44.5'W | | | | | | | | | | | | | | | | | | | | | | | | | | 33 | 40 | 75 |
| Marathon, Fla 24°42.2'N., 81°06.7'W | | | | | | | | | | | | | | | | | | | | | | | | | | | 39 | 48 |
| Flamingo, Fla. 25°08.5'N., 80°55.4'W | | | | | | | | | | | | | | | | | | | | | | | | | | | | 84 |

Nautical Miles

| | Norfolk | Fernandina Beach | Jacksonville | St Augustine | Marineland | Daytona Beach | New Smyrna Beach | Titusville | Cocoa | Eau Gallie | Melbourne | Vero Beach | Fort Pierce | Salerno | Stuart | Port Mayaca | Clewiston | Moore Haven | Fort Myers | Jupiter | Port of Palm Beach | Fort Lauderdale | Port Everglades | Miami | Tavernier | Matecumbe Harbor | Marathon | Flamingo |
|---|---|---|---|---|---|---|---|---|---|---|---|---|---|---|---|---|---|---|---|---|---|---|---|---|---|---|---|---|
| Fernandina Beach | 623 | | | | | | | | | | | | | | | | | | | | | | | | | | | |
| Jacksonville | 659 | 36 | | | | | | | | | | | | | | | | | | | | | | | | | | |
| St Augustine | 676 | 53 | 49 | | | | | | | | | | | | | | | | | | | | | | | | | |
| Marineland | 692 | 69 | 65 | 16 | | | | | | | | | | | | | | | | | | | | | | | | |
| Daytona Beach | 722 | 99 | 95 | 46 | 30 | | | | | | | | | | | | | | | | | | | | | | | |
| New Smyrna Beach | 735 | 113 | 108 | 59 | 44 | 14 | | | | | | | | | | | | | | | | | | | | | | |
| Titusville | 764 | 141 | 137 | 88 | 72 | 42 | 28 | | | | | | | | | | | | | | | | | | | | | |
| Cocoa | 780 | 157 | 153 | 104 | 89 | 58 | 45 | 17 | | | | | | | | | | | | | | | | | | | | |
| Eau Gallie | 795 | 172 | 168 | 119 | 103 | 73 | 59 | 31 | 14 | | | | | | | | | | | | | | | | | | | |
| Melbourne | 798 | 175 | 171 | 122 | 106 | 76 | 63 | 34 | 18 | 3 | | | | | | | | | | | | | | | | | | |
| Vero Beach | 827 | 204 | 200 | 151 | 136 | 105 | 92 | 64 | 47 | 33 | 29 | | | | | | | | | | | | | | | | | |
| Fort Pierce | 839 | 216 | 212 | 163 | 148 | 117 | 104 | 76 | 59 | 45 | 41 | 12 | | | | | | | | | | | | | | | | |
| Salerno | 860 | 237 | 233 | 184 | 169 | 138 | 125 | 97 | 80 | 66 | 62 | 33 | 21 | | | | | | | | | | | | | | | |
| Stuart | 865 | 242 | 238 | 189 | 173 | 143 | 130 | 101 | 85 | 70 | 67 | 38 | 26 | 8 | | | | | | | | | | | | | | |
| Port Mayaca | 892 | 269 | 265 | 216 | 200 | 170 | 157 | 128 | 112 | 97 | 94 | 65 | 53 | 35 | 27 | | | | | | | | | | | | | |
| Clewiston | 915 | 292 | 288 | 239 | 223 | 193 | 180 | 151 | 135 | 120 | 117 | 88 | 76 | 58 | 50 | 23 | | | | | | | | | | | | |
| Moore Haven | 926 | 303 | 299 | 250 | 235 | 204 | 191 | 163 | 146 | 132 | 128 | 99 | 87 | 70 | 61 | 34 | 11 | | | | | | | | | | | |
| Fort Myers | 975 | 353 | 349 | 299 | 284 | 254 | 240 | 212 | 195 | 181 | 178 | 148 | 136 | 119 | 111 | 83 | 61 | 49 | | | | | | | | | | |
| Jupiter | 873 | 251 | 247 | 197 | 182 | 152 | 138 | 110 | 93 | 79 | 76 | 46 | 34 | 17 | 22 | 49 | 72 | 83 | 132 | | | | | | | | | |
| Port of Palm Beach | 885 | 262 | 258 | 209 | 193 | 163 | 150 | 121 | 105 | 90 | 87 | 58 | 46 | 28 | 33 | 60 | 83 | 94 | 144 | 12 | | | | | | | | |
| Fort Lauderdale | 925 | 303 | 299 | 249 | 234 | 204 | 190 | 162 | 145 | 131 | 128 | 98 | 86 | 69 | 74 | 101 | 124 | 135 | 184 | 52 | 41 | | | | | | | |
| Port Everglades | 927 | 304 | 300 | 251 | 235 | 205 | 191 | 163 | 146 | 132 | 129 | 99 | 87 | 70 | 75 | 102 | 125 | 136 | 185 | 53 | 42 | 1 | | | | | | |
| Miami | 947 | 324 | 320 | 271 | 255 | 225 | 211 | 183 | 166 | 152 | 149 | 119 | 107 | 90 | 95 | 122 | 145 | 156 | 205 | 73 | 62 | 21 | 20 | | | | | |
| Tavernier | 999 | 378 | 374 | 324 | 309 | 279 | 265 | 237 | 220 | 206 | 203 | 173 | 161 | 144 | 149 | 176 | 199 | 210 | 259 | 127 | 116 | 75 | 74 | 54 | | | | |
| Matecumbe Harbor | 1017 | 394 | 390 | 341 | 325 | 295 | 282 | 253 | 237 | 223 | 219 | 190 | 178 | 161 | 165 | 192 | 215 | 227 | 276 | 144 | 132 | 92 | 91 | 71 | 19 | | | |
| Marathon | 1045 | 422 | 418 | 369 | 353 | 323 | 309 | 281 | 264 | 250 | 247 | 217 | 205 | 188 | 193 | 220 | 243 | 254 | 303 | 171 | 160 | 119 | 118 | 98 | 47 | 29 | | |
| Flamingo | 1050 | 427 | 423 | 374 | 358 | 328 | 315 | 286 | 270 | 255 | 252 | 223 | 211 | 193 | 198 | 225 | 248 | 259 | 309 | 177 | 165 | 125 | 123 | 104 | 52 | 35 | 34 | |
| Key West, Fla. 24°33.7'N., 81°48.5'W | 1080 | 458 | 454 | 405 | 389 | 359 | 345 | 317 | 301 | 286 | 283 | 254 | 242 | 224 | 229 | 256 | 279 | 290 | 339 | 207 | 196 | 155 | 154 | 134 | 83 | 65 | 42 | 73 |

## ST. JOHNS RIVER, FL
(Nautical Miles)

Figure at intersection of columns opposite ports in question is the nautical mileage between the two. Example: Weleka, Fla., is 66 nautical miles from Jacksonville, Fla.

**Ports (with coordinates):**

1. Lake Harney — 28°46.8'N, 81°03.2'W
2. Sanford — 28°49.1'N, 81°16.2'W
3. Astor-Volusia — 29°10.0'N, 81°31.4'W
4. Georgetown — 29°23.1'N, 81°38.3'W
5. Leesburg, Oklawaha River
6. Moss Bluff Lock, Oklawaha River
7. Silver Springs, Oklawaha River
8. Welaka — 29°28.8'N, 81°40.5'W
9. Crescent City — 29°25.8'N, 81°30.3'W
10. Palatka — 29°38.6'N, 81°37.6'W
11. Doctors Lake Inlet — 30°08.9'N, 81°41.2'W
12. Jacksonville — 30°19.2'N, 81°39.9'W
13. Broward River mouth — 30°24.6'N, 81°35.7'W
14. Intracoastal Waterway Route — 30°23.1'N, 81°27.7'W
15. Mayport — 30°23.7'N, 81°25.9'W
16. St Johns River mouth — 30°24.0'N, 81°23.8'W

| | 1 | 2 | 3 | 4 | 5 | 6 | 7 | 8 | 9 | 10 | 11 | 12 | 13 | 14 | 15 |
|---|---|---|---|---|---|---|---|---|---|---|---|---|---|---|---|
| 2 Sanford | 18 | | | | | | | | | | | | | | |
| 3 Astor-Volusia | 52 | 34 | | | | | | | | | | | | | |
| 4 Georgetown | 66 | 49 | 14 | | | | | | | | | | | | |
| 5 Leesburg | 148 | 131 | 96 | 82 | | | | | | | | | | | |
| 6 Moss Bluff Lock | 131 | 113 | 79 | 65 | 17 | | | | | | | | | | |
| 7 Silver Springs | 123 | 105 | 71 | 56 | 31 | 14 | | | | | | | | | |
| 8 Welaka | 75 | 57 | 23 | 8 | 75 | 58 | 50 | | | | | | | | |
| 9 Crescent City | 101 | 83 | 49 | 35 | 102 | 85 | 76 | 26 | | | | | | | |
| 10 Palatka | 93 | 75 | 41 | 26 | 94 | 76 | 68 | 18 | 20 | | | | | | |
| 11 Doctors Lake Inlet | 129 | 111 | 77 | 62 | 129 | 112 | 104 | 54 | 56 | 36 | | | | | |
| 12 Jacksonville | 141 | 123 | 89 | 75 | 142 | 125 | 116 | 66 | 69 | 48 | 12 | | | | |
| 13 Broward River mouth | 149 | 131 | 97 | 83 | 150 | 133 | 124 | 74 | 77 | 56 | 20 | 8 | | | |
| 14 Intracoastal Waterway Route | 157 | 139 | 105 | 91 | 158 | 141 | 132 | 82 | 85 | 64 | 28 | 16 | 8 | | |
| 15 Mayport | 159 | 141 | 107 | 93 | 160 | 143 | 134 | 84 | 87 | 66 | 30 | 18 | 10 | 2 | |
| 16 St Johns River mouth | 161 | 143 | 109 | 95 | 162 | 145 | 136 | 86 | 89 | 68 | 32 | 20 | 12 | 4 | 2 |

**Distances**

# GULF OF MEXICO —
## KEY WEST, FL, TO PORT BROWNSVILLE, TX
### (Nautical Miles)

Figure at intersection of columns opposite ports in question is the nautical mileage between the two. Example: Tampa, Fla., is 810 nautical miles from Corpus Christi, Tex.

**Ports (with positions), listed along the diagonal of the table:**

- Port Brownsville, Tex. 25°57.1'N, 97°24.0'W
- Port Isabel, Tex. 26°03.6'N, 97°12.8'W
- Corpus Christi, Tex. 27°48.8'N, 97°24.0'W
- La Quinta, Tex. 27°52.6'N, 97°15.1'W
- Point Comfort, Tex. (Lavaca Bay) 28°38.7'N, 96°33.3'W
- Freeport, Tex. 28°56.3'N, 95°20.4'W
- Houston, Tex. 29°45.0'N, 95°17.3'W
- Texas City, Tex. 29°22.7'N, 94°53.2'W
- Galveston, Tex. 29°19.0'N, 94°47.0'W
- Beaumont, Tex. 30°04.7'N, 94°05.2'W
- Orange, Tex. 30°05.3'N, 93°43.0'W
- Port Arthur, Tex. 29°49.5'N, 93°57.6'W
- Lake Charles, La. 30°13.1'N, 93°15.5'W
- Morgan City, La. 29°41.5'N, 91°12.9'W
- NEW ORLEANS, LA (SW Pass)* 29°57.0'N, 90°13.7'W
- New Orleans, La (South Pass)* 29°57.0'N, 90°03.7'W
- New Orleans, La (Gulf Outlet)* 29°57.0'N, 90°03.7'W
- Gulfport, Miss. 30°21.5'N, 89°05.5'W
- Pascagoula, Miss. 30°21.9'N, 88°33.8'W
- Mobile, Ala. 30°42.5'N, 88°00.5'W
- Pensacola, Fla. 30°24.0'N, 87°13.0'W
- Panama City, Fla. 30°08.2'N, 85°37.6'W
- Port St. Joe, Fla. 29°49.1'N, 85°18.8'W
- Tampa, Fla. 27°56.5'N, 82°26.7'W
- Port Tampa, Fla. 27°51.1'N, 82°33.3'W
- St. Petersburg, Fla. 27°46.0'N, 82°37.0'W
- Port Boca Grande, Fla. 26°43.2'N, 82°15.3'W
- Key West, Fla. 24°33.7'N, 81°48.5'W
- STRAITS OF FLORIDA 24°25.0'N, 83°00.0'W
- YUCATAN CHANNEL 21°50.0'N, 85°00.0'W

**Triangular distance matrix** (each row is a port; values read left-to-right from the adjacent listed port toward Port Brownsville):

| Port (row) | Distances (nautical miles) |
|---|---|
| Port Isabel | 13 |
| Corpus Christi | 15 · 142 |
| La Quinta | 112 · 137 · 154 |
| Point Comfort | 119 · 117 · 204 · 215 |
| Freeport | 127 · 154 · 160 · 247 · 258 |
| Houston | 52 · 84 · 89 · 170 · 206 · 212 |
| Texas City | 9 · 47 · 89 · 158 · 201 · 207 · 337 |
| Galveston | 27 · 116 · 120 · 152 · 230 · 270 · 275 · 309 |
| Beaumont | 22 · 26 · 111 · 115 · 154 · 234 · 266 · 271 · 376 |
| Orange | 83 · 94 · 105 · 132 · 148 · 208 · 244 · 249 · 358 · 369 |
| Port Arthur | 182 · 190 · 212 · 216 · 235 · 240 · 273 · 278 · 354 · 362 · 347 |
| Lake Charles | 278 · 454 · 460 · 466 · 441 · 451 · 489 · 508 · 545 · 550 · 569 · 580 |
| Morgan City | 298 · 472 · 493 · 492 · 465 · 470 · 508 · 508 · 545 · 550 · 574 · 599 |
| New Orleans (SW Pass)* | 304 · 479 · 488 · 486 · 446 · 476 · 513 · 514 · 564 · 564 · 588 · 604 |
| New Orleans (South Pass)* | 304 · 484 · 491 · 497 · 476 · 501 · 518 · 519 · 570 · 575 · 585 · 609 |
| New Orleans (Gulf Outlet)* | 330 · 506 · 515 · 519 · 498 · 514 · 538 · 539 · 594 · 580 · 605 · 618 |
| Gulfport | 171 · 236 · 253 · 269 · 288 · 308 · 333 · 385 · 397 |
| Pascagoula | 238 · 216 · 250 |
| Mobile | 271 · 269 · 278 |
| Pensacola | 149 · 170 · 188 · 206 · 213 · 222 · 274 · 288 · 295 |
| Panama City | 52 · 98 · 75 · 117 · 236 · 253 · 288 · 333 |
| Port St. Joe | 89 · 94 · 193 · 206 · 213 · 235 |
| Tampa | 42 · 154 · 139 · 200 |
| Port Tampa | 252 · 265 · 347 · 389 · 392 |
| St. Petersburg | 18 · 248 · 261 · 343 · 386 · 409 · 452 · 457 · 472 |
| Port Boca Grande | 8 · 18 · 240 · 252 · 334 · 377 · 401 · 444 · 459 · 467 · 488 · 498 |
| Key West | 100 · 109 · 113 · 294 · 281 · 372 · 413 · 414 · 436 · 474 · 512 · 564 · 717 · 704 · 707 · 690 · 695 · 714 · 752 · 747 · 816 · 806 · 811 · 816 · 814 · 880 · 855 · 866 |
| Straits of Florida | 73 · 150 · 219 · 228 · 232 · 369 · 381 · 437 · 471 · 469 · 492 · 513 · 524 · 540 · 581 · 715 · 700 · 722 · 726 · 702 · 707 · 746 · 743 · 797 · 802 · 807 · 782 · 793 |
| Yucatan Channel | 192 · 251 · 332 · 389 · 399 · 404 · 495 · 506 · 533 · 562 · 554 · 576 · 575 · 579 · 587 · 602 · 705 · 691 · 713 · 717 · 696 · 702 · 707 · 740 · 717 · 761 · 763 · 769 · 718 · 729 |

Sabine Pass buoy 32 (29°36.9'N, 93°48.3'W) to Port Arthur, 16.6 miles.
Galveston Bay entrance buoy GA (29°08.7'N, 94°25.8'W) to Galveston, 23 miles; Texas City, 28 miles; houston, 67 miles.
Aransas Pass entrance buoy AP (27°47.6'N, 96°57.4'W) to Corpus Christi, 25 miles.
Brazos Santiago entrance buoy BS (26°03.9'N, 97°06.6'W) to Port Brownsville, 17.5 miles.

All tabular distances are via STRAITS OF FLORIDA, (24°25.0'N, 83°00.0'W), and through the Shipping Safety Fairways. For distances from Key West to west Florida ports via Rebecca Shoal Channel. (24°24.4'N, 82°42.0'W). SUBTRACT 24 miles from Port Boca Grande distance. 17 miles from Tampa Bay distances, 9 miles from Port St. Joe and Panama City distances, and 5 miles from Pensacola distance

*Baton Rouge, La. (30°27.0'N, 91°11.7'W) ADD 115 miles.

Entrance lighted whistle buoy (24°27.7'N, 81°48.1'W) to Key West. 6.3 miles.
Entrance buoy T (27°35.3'N, 83°00.7'W) to Tampa. 43 miles.
Entrance buoy 1 (30°16.3'N, 87°17.5'W) to Pensacola. 11.5 miles.
Entrance buoy M (30°08.1'N, 88°03.9'W) to Mobile, 35 miles.
Mississippi River-Gulf Outlet approach buoy NO. (29°26.4'N, 88°56.9'W) to New Orleans. 73 miles.
South Pass entrance buoy 2 (28°58.7'N, 89°06.5'W) to New Orleans, 96 miles.
Southwest Pass entrance buoy SW (28°52.7'N, 89°25.9'W) to New Orleans, 102 miles.
Calcasieu Channel buoy 2B (29°27.3'N, 91°13.4'W) to Lake Charles, 50 miles.

## COASTWISE & INSIDE-ROUTE — KEY WEST, FL, TO APALACHICOLA, FL
### (Nautical Miles)

Figure at intersection of columns opposite ports in question is the nautical mileage between the two.
Example: Flamingo is 225 nautical miles from Clearwater.

**Port coordinates**

- Apalachicola, Fla. 29°43.5'N, 84°58.8'W
- Carrabelle. 29°51.0'N, 84°40.0'W
- St. Marks. 30°09.2'N, 84°12.2'W
- Cedar Key. 29°08.0'N, 83°01.9'W
- Tarpon Springs. 28°09.4'N, 82°45.8'W
- Clearwater. 27°58.5'N, 82°49.6'W
- Tampa. 27°56.5'N, 82°26.7'W
- St. Petersburg. 27°46.0'N, 82°37.0'W
- Bradenton. 27°30.0'N, 82°34.4'W
- Sarasota. 27°20.0'N, 82°32.9'W
- Venice. 27°06.7'N, 82°27.8'W
- Port Boca Grande. 26°43.2'N, 82°15.3'W
- Fort Myers. 26°38.9'N, 81°52.2'W
- Naples. 26°08.0'N, 81°47.6'W
- Everglades. 25°52.0'N, 81°23.1'W
- Cape Sable. 25°09.0'N, 81°11.0'W
- Flamingo. 24°08.5'N, 80°55.4'W
- Matecumbe Harbor. 24°51.1'N, 80°44.5'W
- Marathon. 24°42.2'N, 81°06.7'W
- Key West, Fla. 24°33.7'N, 81°48.5'W

| From \ To | Apalachicola | Carrabelle | St. Marks | Cedar Key | Tarpon Springs | Clearwater | Tampa | St. Petersburg | Bradenton | Sarasota | Venice | Port Boca Grande | Fort Myers | Naples | Everglades | Cape Sable | Flamingo | Matecumbe Harbor | Marathon |
|---|---|---|---|---|---|---|---|---|---|---|---|---|---|---|---|---|---|---|---|
| Carrabelle | 25 | | | | | | | | | | | | | | | | | | |
| St. Marks | 69 | 52 | | | | | | | | | | | | | | | | | |
| Cedar Key | 118 | 101 | 91 | | | | | | | | | | | | | | | | |
| Tarpon Springs | 164 | 147 | 145 | 68 | | | | | | | | | | | | | | | |
| Clearwater | 174 | 157 | 155 | 79 | 18 | | | | | | | | | | | | | | |
| Tampa | 218 | 202 | 200 | 123 | 63 | 47 | | | | | | | | | | | | | |
| St. Petersburg | 202 | 186 | 164 | 107 | 47 | 31 | 18 | | | | | | | | | | | | |
| Bradenton | 209 | 193 | 191 | 114 | 54 | 36 | 22 | | | | | | | | | | | | |
| Sarasota | 221 | 204 | 202 | 125 | 65 | 49 | 33 | 25 | | | | | | | | | | | |
| Venice | 234 | 218 | 216 | 139 | 79 | 63 | 61 | 47 | 39 | 15 | | | | | | | | | |
| Port Boca Grande | 262 | 245 | 244 | 167 | 107 | 91 | 89 | 75 | 67 | 43 | 28 | | | | | | | | |
| Fort Myers | 297 | 280 | 278 | 202 | 142 | 124 | 110 | 102 | 96 | 78 | 63 | 35 | | | | | | | |
| Naples | 316 | 299 | 297 | 221 | 160 | 145 | 143 | 129 | 120 | 116 | 88 | 82 | 54 | | | | | | |
| Everglades | 350 | 334 | 332 | 255 | 195 | 179 | 177 | 163 | 155 | 131 | 88 | 79 | | 38 | | | | | |
| Cape Sable | 379 | 362 | 360 | 284 | 223 | 208 | 205 | 192 | 183 | 159 | 145 | 117 | 107 | 71 | 49 | | | | |
| Flamingo | 396 | 379 | 377 | 301 | 240 | 225 | 222 | 209 | 200 | 176 | 162 | 134 | 124 | 88 | 66 | 17 | | | |
| Matecumbe Harbor | 411 | 394 | 392 | 316 | 255 | 240 | 237 | 224 | 215 | 191 | 177 | 149 | 139 | 103 | 81 | 32 | 35 | | |
| Marathon | 408 | 391 | 389 | 313 | 253 | 237 | 235 | 221 | 213 | 189 | 174 | 146 | 136 | 100 | 80 | 31 | 37 | 29 | |
| Key West, Fla. | 406 | 389 | 387 | 310 | 250 | 234 | 232 | 218 | 210 | 186 | 172 | 144 | 134 | 98 | 88 | 57 | 70 | 65 | 42 |

St. George Sound. Distances from Everglades northward are inside via Big Marco River and Gordon Pass.

Routes used in table: Hawk Channel between Marathon and Key West; Northwest Channel (Key West) and outside to places between Cape Sable and San Carlos Bay; thence inside to Anclote Keys; and thence outside to

**Distances**

509

Statute Miles

# INTRACOASTAL WATERWAY — APALACHICOLA, FL, TO PORT BROWNSVILLE, TX
### (Nautical and Statute Miles)

Figure at intersection of columns opposite ports in question is the nautical/Statute mileage between the two.

Example: Mobile, Ala., is 398 nautical miles (458 statute miles from Beaumont, Tex.

Port locations and coordinates (diagonal labels, top-right to bottom-left):

- Port Brownsville, Tex. 25°57.1'N, 97°24.0'W
- Port Isabel, Tex. 26°03.6'N, 97°12.8'W
- Port Mansfield, Tex. 26°33.4'N, 97°25.6'W
- Corpus Christi, Tex. 27°48.8'N, 97°24.0'W
- La Quinta, Tex. 27°52.6'N, 97°15.7'W
- Aransas Pass, Tex. 27°53.9'N, 97°08.0'W
- Rockport, Tex. 28°01.1'N, 97°02.9'W
- Port O'Connor, Tex. 28°26.5'N, 96°24.4'W
- Freeport, Tex. 28°56.3'N, 95°20.4'W
- Texas City, Tex. 29°22.7'N, 94°53.2'W
- Houston, Tex. 29°45.0'N, 95°17.4'W
- Galveston, Tex. 29°18.5'N, 94°48.1'W
- Port Arthur, Tex. 29°49.5'N, 93°57.6'W
- Beaumont, Tex. 30°04.6'N, 94°05.2'W
- Orange, Tex. 30°04.0'N, 93°43.3'W
- Lake Charles, La. 30°13.1'N, 93°15.5'W
- Morgan City, La. 29°41.3'N, 91°12.7'W
- Houma, La. 29°35.9'N, 90°42.6'W
- NEW ORLEANS, LA. 29°57.0'N, 90°03.7'W
- Gulfport, Miss. 30°21.4'N, 89°05.6'W
- Biloxi, Miss. 30°23.5'N, 88°52.0'W
- Pascagoula, Miss. 30°21.9'N, 88°33.8'W
- Mobile, Ala. 30°41.5'N, 88°02.2'W
- Pensacola, Fla. 30°24.0'N, 87°13.0'W
- Fort Walton Beach, Fla. 30°24.0'N, 86°36.7'W
- Panama City, Fla. 30°08.2'N, 85°37.6'W
- Port St. Joe, Fla. 29°49.1'N, 85°18.8'W
- Apalachicola, Fla. 29°43.5'N, 84°58.8'W

Nautical Miles

# PUERTO RICO AND VIRGIN ISLANDS
(Nautical Miles)

Figure at intersection of columns opposite ports in question is the nautical mileage between the two. Example: San Juan, Puerto Rico, is 80 nautical miles from Charlotte Amalie, St. Thomas.

**Ports (with coordinates):**

1. Krause Lagoon, St. Croix, V. I. — 17°42.5'N, 64°46.3'W
2. Frederiksted, St. Croix, V. I. — 17°42.9'N, 64°53.4'W
3. Christiansted, St. Croix, V. I. — 17°45.0'N, 64°42.0'W
4. Road Town, Tortola, B. V. I. — 18°25.3'N, 64°37.1'W
5. Cruz Bay, St. John, V. I. — 18°20.0'N, 64°47.8'W
6. Charlotte Amalie, St. Thomas, V. I. — 18°20.0'N, 64°55.5'W
7. Isabel Segunda, Vieques — 18°09.2'N, 65°26.7'W
8. Ensenada Honda, Culebra — 18°18.0'N, 65°17.0'W
9. Puerto Arecibo, P. R. — 18°28.9'N, 66°42.1'W
10. Bahía de Aguadilla, P. R. — 18°26.0'N, 67°09.6'W
11. Mayagüez, P. R. — 18°13.2'N, 67°09.7'W
12. Bahía de Guánica, P. R. — 17°57.5'N, 66°54.5'W
13. Bahía de Guayanilla, P. R. — 17°59.5'N, 66°46.4'W
14. Bahía de Tallaboa, P. R. — 17°58.9'N, 66°44.6'W
15. Ponce, P. R. — 17°58.2'N, 66°37.3'W
16. Bahía de Jobos, P. R. — 17°57.0'N, 66°13.3'W
17. Humacao, P. R. — 18°09.9'N, 65°44.6'W
18. Ensenada Honda, P. R. — 18°13.8'N, 65°37.4'W
19. Fajardo, P. R. — 18°20.2'N, 65°37.8'W
20. San Juan, P. R. — 18°27.6'N, 66°06.6'W

**Distance table (triangular).** For each origin port, distances are listed in the order shown in the table, reading from the nearest adjacent port toward Krause Lagoon (the right-most column).

|  |  |
|------|-----------|
| Frederiksted | 18 |
| Christiansted | 19, 35 |
| Road Town | 42, 46, 62 |
| Cruz Bay | 15, 37, 39, 55 |
| Charlotte Amalie | 11, 24, 38, 38, 54 |
| Isabel Segunda | 33, 40, 55, 54, 46, 62 |
| Ensenada Honda (Culebra) | 15, 24, 31, 47, 48, 42, 59 |
| Puerto Arecibo | 92, 87, 112, 115, 126, 135, 128, 144 |
| Bahía de Aguadilla | 40, 123, 118, 144, 146, 157, 166, 159, 176 |
| Mayagüez | 23, 58, 136, 161, 164, 175, 184, 171, 182 |
| Bahía de Guánica | 60, 70, 105, 109, 96, 126, 132, 147, 135, 122, 133 |
| Bahía de Guayanilla | 15, 67, 77, 112, 86, 117, 122, 137, 125, 112, 123 |
| Bahía de Tallaboa | 5, 16, 67, 76, 112, 85, 116, 121, 136, 124, 111, 122 |
| Ponce | 13, 14, 22, 74, 83, 118, 93, 79, 110, 116, 131, 119, 106, 117 |
| Bahía de Jobos | 31, 36, 37, 47, 96, 105, 140, 92, 76, 62, 93, 99, 113, 101, 89, 101 |
| Humacao | 48, 65, 71, 72, 82, 131, 123, 92, 31, 17, 50, 57, 71, 68, 58, 70 |
| Ensenada Honda (P. R.) | 11, 56, 74, 79, 80, 90, 115, 84, 12, 44, 65, 69, 72 |
| Fajardo | 14, 21, 65, 83, 88, 89, 99, 121, 103, 72, 25, 18, 46, 66, 68, 77 |
| San Juan | 40, 52, 59, 103, 152*, 145*, 145*, 138*, 92, 74, 43, 59, 55, 80, 82, 94, 103, 96, 112 |

\* Via Mona Passage

Limetree Bay, St. Croix, V. I. 1 mi. E of Krause Lagoon

Distances

## DISTANCES FROM PANAMA

**PANAMA, PANAMA**
(8°53'00N 79°31'00W) to:

**Junction Points:**

Bishop Rock, England (via Mona Passage), 4,388

Cape of Good Hope, Republic of South Africa, 6,466

Fastnet, Republic of Ireland (via Mona Passage), 4,247

Grand Banks South, 2,555

Honshu, Japan, 7,614

Ile d'Ouessant, France (via Mona Passage, 4,374

Montreal, Canada, 3,204

Punta Arenas, Chile, 3,932

Singapore (via San Bernardino Strait), 10,505

Strait of Gibraltar (via Anegada Channel), 4,351

Torres Strait, Australia (via Raine Island entrance), 8,451

Tsugaru Kaikyo, Japan, 8,004

Wilson Promontory, Australia (via Cook Strait), 7,842

Wilson Promontory, Australia (via Foveaux Strait), 7,770

Yucatan Channel, 855

**Ports**

Abraham Bay, Bahamas, 922

Acajutla, El Salvador, 833

Acapulco, Mexico, 1,426

Almirante, Panama, 198

Amapala, Honduras, 745

Amuay, Venezuela, 678

Angra dos Reis, Brazil, 4,527

Antilla, Cuba, 887

Antofagasta, Chile, 2,140

Apia, Samoa, 5,710

Apra, Guam, 7,988

Arica, Chile, 1,921

Auckland, New Zealand, 6,516

Avarua, Cook Islands, 5,092

Bahia de Samana, Dominican Republic, 1,015

Bahia Blanca, Argentina, 5,776

Bahia de las Calderas, Dominican Republic, 810

Baie Taio-Hae, Marquesas, 3, 826

Bahia Cayo Moa, Cuba, 853

Baltimore, Maryland, U.S.A. (via Windward Passage and Crooked Island Passage), 1,944

Barahona, Dominican Republic, 796

Barbers Point, Hawaii, U.S.A. 4,694

Barcelona, Venezuela, 1,014

Belize, Belize, 859

Bikini, Marshalls, 4,915

Boca de Tanamo, Cuba, 869

Bocas del Toro, Panama, 187

Bordeaux, France (via Mona Passage), 4,641

Boston, Massachusetts, U.S.A. (via Crooked Island Passage), 2,200

Bridgeport, Connecticut, U.S.A., 2,118

Bridgetown, Barbados, 1,280

Brisbane, Australia, 7,687

Brunswick, Georgia, U.S.A., 1, 581

Buenaventure, Colombia, 352

Cabedelo, Brazil, 3,149

Caibarien, Cuba, 1,138

Caldera, Chile, 2,302

Caleta Olivia, Argentina, 6,204

Callao, Peru, 1,350

Campeche, Mexico, 1,210

Cap Haitien, Haiti, 860

Cape Town, Republic of South Africa, 6,508

Carmen, Mexico, 1,289

Cartagena, Colombia, 324

Casilda, Cuba, 792

Catia la Mar, Venezuela, 873

Champerico, Guatemala, 954

Charleston, South Carolina, U.S.A., 1,607

Charlotte Amalie, Virgin Islands, 1,072

Charlottetown, Canada, 2,578

Chimbote, Peru, 1,158

Christmas Island, Line Islands, 4,751

Cienfuegos, Cuba, 815

Coatzacoalcos, Mexico, 1,420

Colon, Panama, 44

Comodoro Rivadavia, Argentina, 6,185

Coquimbo, Chile, 2,448

Corinto, Nicaragua, 683

Covenas, Columbia, 308

Dagu, China (via Osumi Kaikyo), 9,002

Dagu, China (via Tsugaru Kaikyo), 8,786

Dakar, Senegal, 3,738

Dalian, China (via Osumi Kaikyo), 8,843

Dalian, China (via Tsugaru Kaikyo), 8,627

Dutch Harbor, Alaska, U.S.A., 5,246

Easter Island, Pacific, 2,785

Enderbury Island, Phoenix Islands, 5,599

Eniwetak, Marshall Islands, 7,086

Ensenada, Mexico, 2,791

Esmeraldas, Ecuador, 472

Fanning Island, 4,805

Fort de France, Martinique, 1,202

Fort Liberte, Haiti, 881

Funafuti Island, Tuvalu, 6,217

Galveston, Texas, U.S.A., 1,536

Georgetown, Guyana, 1,558

Golfito, Costa Rica, 334

Conaives, Haiti, 805

Guantanamo, Cuba, 732

Guayaquil, Ecuador, 824

Guaymas, Mexico, 2,370

Guira, Venezuela, 1,200

Gulfport, Mississippi, U.S.A. (northbound), 1,431

Hakodate, Japan, 7,417
Halifax, Canada, 2,338
Hamilton, Bermuda, 1,702
Hilo, Hawaii, U.S.A., 4,527
Ho Chi Minh, Vietnam, 10,017
Hobart, Tasmania, 7,630
Hong Kong, B.C.C., 7,195
Honolulu, Hawaii, U.S.A., 4,685
Iloilo, Philippines, 9,235
Incheon, Republic of South Korea, 8,474
Iquique, Chile, 1,987
Isabel Segunda, Isla de Vieques, 1,060
Jacksonville, Florida, U.S.A., 1,559
Jaluit, Marshall Islands, 6,666
Jarvis Island, 1,173
Johnston Island, 5,359
Kahului, Hawaii, U.S.A., 4,605
Kaneohe Bay, Hawaii, U.S.A., 4,868
Kaunakakai, Hawaii, U.S.A., 4,633
Key West, Florida, U.S.A., 1,108
Kingston, Jamaica, 594
Kobe, Japan, 7,964
Kodiak, Alaska, U.S.A., 4,907
La Ceiba, Honduras, 709
La Guaira, Venezuela, 884
La Libertad, Ecuador, 674
La Libertad, El Salvador, 806
La Palma, Panama, 104
La Romana, Dominican Republic, 889
La Union, El Salvador, 748
Les Cayes, Haiti, 688
Levuka, Fiji Islands, 6,288
Limon, Costa Rica, 234
Los Angeles, California, U.S.A., 2,913
Lota, Chile, 2,825
Lucea, Jamaica, 579
Makassar, Sulawesi (via Selat Sagewin and Selat Salajar), 9,855
Malakal, Palau Islands, 8,674
Manila, Philippines (via Balintang Channel), 9,347
Manila, Philippines (via San Bernardino Strait), 9,370
Manzanillo, Cuba, 732
Mar del Plata, Argentina, 5,543
Maracaibo, Venezuela, 737
Matagorda Bay, Texas, U.S.A., 1,558
Matarani, Peru, 1,790
Mazatlan, Mexico, 2,006
Melbourne, Australia (via Foveaux Strait), 7,928
Midway Island, 5,707
Miller Anchorage, Bahamas, 1,115
Montecristi, Dominican Republic, 881
Monterey, California, U.S.A., 3,165
Montevideo, Uruguary, 5,379
Nagasaki, Japan (east of Honshu), 8,200
Nagasaki, Japan (west of Honshu), 8,299

Naknek, Alaska, U.S.A., 5,604
Nassau, Bahamas (via Windward Passage), 1,210
New Amsterdam, Guyana, 1,581
New Haven, Connecticut, U.S.A., 2,106
New Orleans, Louisiana, U.S.A. (northbound via South Pass), 1,444
New York, New York, U.S.A. (via Windward Passage and Crooked Island Passage), 2,018
Newcastle, Australia, 7,654
Nicaro, Cuba, 881
Nikolayevsk, Soviet Union, (south of Aleutian Islands), 7,293
Nikolayevsk, Soviet Union (via Unimak Passage), 7,296
Nome, Alaska, U.S.A., 5,834
Norfolk, Virginia, U.S.A. (via Windward Passage and Crooked Island Passage), 1,822
Noumea, New Caledonia, 6,982
Nukualofa, Tonga Islands, 5,953
Ocean Island, 6,724
Omura, Japan, 7,766
Oranjestad, Aruba, 661
Osaka, Japan, 7,969
Paamiut (Frederikshaab), Greenland, 3,558
Pago Pago, American Samoa, 5,656
Papeete, French Polynesia, 4,493
Paramaribo, Suriname, 1,691
Paranagua, Brazel, 4,607
Pearl Harbor, Hawaii, U.S.A., 4,692
Pedregal, Panama, 308
Petropavlovsk, Soviet Union, 6,492
Philadeplhia, Pennsylvania, U.S.A. (via Windward Passage and Crooked Island Passage), 1,989
Pisco, Peru, 1,458
Pointe a Pitre, Guadeloupe, 1,211
Ponape, Caroline Islands, 7,321
Ponce, Puerto Rico, 976
Port au Prince, Haiti, 817
Port Antonio, Jamaica, 625
Port Castries, St. Lucia, 1,203
Port Hueneme, California, U.S.A., 2,958
Port Limon, Costa Rica, 218
Port Neward, New Jersey, U.S.A., 2,021
Port Pirie, Australia, 8,467
Port of Spain, Trinidad, 1,202
Portland, Maine, U.S.A. (via Crooked Island Passage), 2,241
Portland, Oregon, U.S.A., 3,869
Porto Alegre, Brazil, 5,148
Prince Rupert, Canada, 4,303
Progreso, Mexico, 1,069
Puerto de Hierro, Venezuela, 1,192
Puerto la Cruz, Venezuela, 1,016
Puerto Armuelles, Panama, 306
Puerto Barrios, Guatemala, 823
Puerto Bolivar, 774

Distances

Puerto Cabello, Venezuela, 845
Puerto Cabezas, Nicaragua, 390
Puerto Cortez, Honduras, 776
Puerto Descado, Argentina, 6,222
Puerto Madryn, Argentina, 6,012
Puerto Manati, Cuba, 959
Puerto Montt, Chile, 3,177
Puerto Padre, Cuba, 948
Puerto Sandino, Nicaragua, 649
Puerto Sucre, Venezuela, 1,035
Puerto Vita, Cuba, 915
Punta Cardon, Venezuela, 674
Puntarenas, Costa Rica, 471
Quepos, Costa Rica, 415
Qingdao, China, 8,575
Rabaul, Papua New Guinea, 7,807
Raoul Island, Kermadec Islands, 6,125
Rio Gallegos, Argentina, 6,455
Rio Haina, Dominican Republic, 845
Roosevelt Roads, Puerto Rico, 1,054
Rotoava, Iles Tuamotu, 4,256
Salaverry, Peru, 1,109
Salina Cruz, Mexico, 1,170
Salvador, Brazil, 3,741
San Antonio, Chile, 2,644
San Diego, California, U.S.A., 2,843
San Felix, Venezuela, 1,535
San Francisco, California, U.S.A., 3,245
San Jose, Guatemala, 886
San Juan del Sur, Nicaragua, 590
San Juan, Peru, 1,590
San Juan, Puerto Rico, 1,036
San Lorenzo, Honduras, 762
Santa Barbara, California, U.S.A., 2,980
Santa Cruz del Sur, Cuba, 731
Santa Maria, Cuba, 814
Santa Rosalia, Mexico, 2,390
Santiago de Cuba, Cuba, 726
Santo Domingo, Dominican Republic, 846
Santos, Brazil, 4,609
Savannah, Georgia, U.S.A. (via Windward Passage and Crooked Island Passage), 1,606
Seattle, Washington, U.S.A., 4,020
Seward, Alaska, U.S.A., 4,916
Shanghai, China (via Osumi Kaikyo), 8,648
Shanghai, China (via Tsugaru Kaikyo), 8,566

Shimonoseki, Japan (east of Honshu), 8,153
Shimonoseki, Japan (west of Honshu), 8,081
Sitka, Alaska, U.S.A., 4,524
Skagway, Alaska, U.S.A., 4,739
St. Georges, Grenada, 1,161
St. John, Canada, 2,361
St. John's, Canada, 2,742
St. Marc, Haiti, 796
Suva, Fiji Islands, 6,325
Swan Island, Honduras, 605
Sweeper Cove, Alaska, U.S.A., 5,586
Sydney, Australia, 7,674
Talara, Peru, 826
Talcahuano, Chile, 2,805
Taltal, Chile, 2,225
Tampico, Mexico, 1,528
Tela, Honduras, 749
Tocopilla, Chile, 2,068
Truk, Caroline Islands, 7,685
Turbo, Colombia, 311
Turiamo, Venezuela, 858
Tuxpan, Mexico, 1,498
Unalakleet, Alaska, U.S.A., 5,967
Valparaiso, Chile, 2,616
Vancouver, Canada, 4,032
Veracruz, Mexico, 1,463
Victoria, Canada, 3,962
Vladivostok, Soviet Union, (north of Aleutian Islands, and La Perouse Strait), 7,757
Vladivostok, Soviet Union, (south of Aleutian Islands, and La Perouse Strait), 7,739
Vladivostok, Soviet Union, (via Tsugaru Kaikyo), 7,833
Wake Island, 6,673
Washington, D.C., U.S.A., 1,957
Wellington, New Zealand, 6,505
Whittier, Alaska, U.S.A., 4,958
Willemstad, Curacao, 742
Wilmington, North Carolina, U.S.A., 1,656
Weonsan, Democratic People's Republic of Korea, 8,038
Wotho, Marshall Islands, 4,882
Xiamen, China (via Osumi Kaikyo), 8,943
Xiamen, China (via Tsugaru kaikyo), 8,959
Yokohama, Japan, 7,682
Zamboanga, Philippines, 943

## PACIFIC OCEAN —
## PANAMA TO ALASKA TO HAWAII
(Nautical Miles)

Figure at intersection of columns opposite ports in question is the nautical mileage between the two. Example: San Francisco, Calif., is 2,091 nautical miles from Honolulu, Hawaii.

**Ports (with positions):**

- Midway Island, 28° 13.0'N, 177° 22.0'W.
- Port Allen, Hawaii, 21° 54.1'N, 159° 35.6'W.
- Nawiliwili, Hawaii, 21° 57.4'N, 159° 21.5'W.
- Pearl Harbor, Hawaii, 21° 20.0'N, 157° 58.3'W.
- Honolulu, Hawaii, 21° 18.5'N, 157° 52.3'W.
- Kahului, Hawaii, 20° 54.0'N, 156° 28.2'W.
- Kawaihae, Hawaii, 20° 02.3'N, 155° 49.9'W.
- Hilo, Hawaii, 19° 44.1'N, 155° 03.5'W.
- Kuliuk Bay, Alaska, 57° 51.6'N, 176° 37.6'W.
- UNIMAK PASS, ALASKA, 54° 20.0'N, 164° 45.0'W.
- Kodiak, Alaska, 57° 47.1'N, 152° 25.1'W.
- Anchorage, Alaska, 61° 14.2'N, 149° 53.3'W.
- Seward, Alaska, 60° 06.0'N, 149° 26.0'W.
- Port Valdez, Alaska, 61° 06.0'N, 146° 24.0'W.
- CAPE SPENCER, ALASKA, 58° 10.0'N, 136° 38.3'W.
- Sitka, Alaska, 57° 03.1'N, 135° 20.5'W.
- Ketchikan, Alaska, 55° 20.5'N, 131° 38.7'W.
- Seattle, Wash., 47° 36.2'N, 122° 20.3'W.
- SWIFTSURE BANK, WASH., 48° 31.0'N, 125° 00.0'W.
- CAPE FLATTERY, WASH., 48° 26.0'N, 124° 47.0'W.
- Portland, Oreg., 45° 33.0'N, 122° 41.7'W.
- Astoria, Oreg., 46° 11.7'N, 123° 50.0'W.
- San Francisco, Calif., 37° 48.5'N, 122° 24.0'W.
- Los Angeles, Calif., 33° 45.0'N, 118° 16.2'W.
- Long Beach, Calif., 32° 46.2'N, 118° 13.3'W.
- San Diego, Calif., 32° 43.0'N, 117° 10.5'W.
- PANAMA CANAL (Pac. Ent.), 8° 53.0'N, 79° 31.0'W.

**Distance matrix** (each row lists distances from the named port to ports listed above it, reading left-to-right toward Midway Island):

| From \ To → | … | … | Midway |
|---|---|---|---|
| Port Allen | | | 1042 |
| Nawiliwili | Port Allen 21 | | 1069 |
| Pearl Harbor | Nawiliwili 92 | Port Allen 96 | 1146 |
| Honolulu | Pearl Harbor 9 | Nawiliwili 102 · Port Allen 106 | 1150 |
| Kahului | Honolulu 89 · Pearl Harbor 94 | Nawiliwili 181 · Port Allen 193 | 1232 |
| Kawaihae | Kahului 85 · Honolulu 140 · Pearl Harbor 145 | Nawiliwili 230 · Port Allen 240 | 1278 |
| Hilo | Kawaihae 83 · Kahului 121 · Honolulu 196 · Pearl Harbor 201 | Nawiliwili 287 · Port Allen 297 | 1338 |
| Kuliuk Bay | Hilo 2198 · Kawaihae 2164 · Kahului 2099 · Honolulu 2061 · Pearl Harbor 2057 · Nawiliwili 1989 · Port Allen 1990 | | 1460 |
| Unimak Pass | Kuliuk Bay 463 · Hilo 2126 · Kawaihae 2296 · Kahului 2110 · Honolulu 2044 · Pearl Harbor 2028 · Nawiliwili 2024 · Port Allen 2057 | | 1680 |
| Kodiak | Unimak Pass 505 · Kuliuk Bay 968 · Hilo 2289 · Kawaihae 2542 · Kahului 2535 · Honolulu 2479 · Pearl Harbor 2477 · Nawiliwili 2230 · Port Allen 2289 | | 1990 |
| Anchorage | Kodiak 242 · Unimak Pass 688 · Kuliuk Bay 1151 · … | | 1972 |
| Seward | Anchorage 274 · Kodiak 175 · Unimak Pass 652 · Kuliuk Bay 1115 · … | | 1963 |
| Port Valdez | Seward 144 · Anchorage 385 · Kodiak 280 · Unimak Pass 761 · Kuliuk Bay 1224 · … | | 2184 |
| Cape Spencer | Port Valdez 400 · Seward 422 · Anchorage 641 · Kodiak 505 · Unimak Pass 987 · Kuliuk Bay 1450 · … | | 2203 |
| Sitka | Cape Spencer 85 · Port Valdez 479 · Seward 494 · Anchorage 708 · Kodiak 505 · Unimak Pass 564 · Kuliuk Bay 1027 · … | | 2305 |
| Ketchikan | Sitka 224 · Cape Spencer 307 · … | | 2088 |
| Seattle | Ketchikan 659 · Sitka 815 · Cape Spencer 976 · … 1234 · 1234 … | | 2250 |
| Swiftsure Bank | Seattle 134 · … | | 2570 |
| Cape Flattery | Swiftsure Bank 10 · Seattle 124 · … | | 2818 |
| Portland | Cape Flattery 238 · … | | — |
| Astoria | Portland 85 · Cape Flattery 153 · … | | 2694 |
| San Francisco | Astoria 567 · Portland 652 · Cape Flattery 683 · Swiftsure Bank 807 · … | | 2809 |
| Los Angeles | San Francisco 371 · Astoria 904 · Portland 989 · Cape Flattery 1020 · Swiftsure Bank 1144 · … | | 2724 |
| Long Beach | Los Angeles 3 · San Francisco 374 · Astoria 908 · Portland 992 · Cape Flattery 1024 · Swiftsure Bank 1148 · … | | 2792 |
| San Diego | Long Beach 94 · Los Angeles 95 · San Francisco 455 · Astoria 989 · Portland 1074 · Cape Flattery 1104 · Swiftsure Bank 1228 · Seattle 1575 · Ketchikan 1723 · Sitka 1787 · … | | 3031 |
| Panama Canal | San Diego 2867 · Long Beach 2939 · Los Angeles 2939 · San Francisco 3270 · Astoria 3803 · Portland 3888 · Cape Flattery 3920 · Swiftsure Bank — · Seattle 4044 · Ketchikan 4387 · Sitka 4538 · Cape Spencer 4603 · Port Valdez 4984 · Seward 4940 · Anchorage 5117 · Kodiak 4924 · Unimak Pass 5228 · Kuliuk Bay 5604 · Hilo 4527 · Kawaihae 4594 · Kahului 4609 · Honolulu 4685 · Pearl Harbor 4690 · Nawiliwili 4767 · Port Allen 4777 | | 5707 |

Distances

515

# HAWAII
(Nautical Miles)

Figure at intersection of columns opposite ports in question is the nautical mileage between the two.
Example: Hilo is 196 nautical miles from Honolulu.

**Ports (with positions):**

- Palmyra Island — 5° 52.5′N., 162° 08.0′W.
- Johnston Island — 16° 44.6′N., 169° 31.2′W.
- Midway Island — 28° 13.0′N., 177° 22.0′W.
- Nonopapa, Niihau — 21° 52.0′N., 160° 14.1′W.
- Hanalei, Kauai — 22° 12.9′N., 159° 30.1′W.
- Waimea, Kauai — 21° 57.4′N., 159° 40.4′W.
- Port Allen, Kauai — 21° 54.1′N., 159° 35.6′W.
- Nawiliwili, Kauai — 21° 57.4′N., 159° 21.5′W.
- Ahukini, Kauai — 21° 59.7′N., 159° 20.1′W.
- Pearl Harbor, Oahu — 21° 20.0′N., 157° 58.3′W.
- Honolulu, Oahu — 21° 18.5′N., 157° 52.3′W.
- Kalaupapa, Molokai — 21° 11.7′N., 156° 59.3′W.
- Haleolono, Molokai — 21° 05.2′N., 157° 15.2′W.
- Kaunakakai, Molokai — 21° 05.1′N., 157° 02.0′W.
- Kamalo, Molokai — 21° 02.9′N., 156° 52.7′W.
- Kaumalapau, Lanai — 20° 47.4′N., 156° 59.7′W.
- Kahului, Maui — 20° 54.0′N., 156° 28.2′W.
- Lahaina (Mala), Maui — 20° 53.5′N., 156° 41.5′W.
- Hana, Maui — 20° 45.6′N., 155° 59.1′W.
- Mahukona, Hawaii — 20° 11.2′N., 155° 54.2′W.
- Kawaihae, Hawaii — 20° 02.3′N., 155° 49.9′W.
- Kailua, Hawaii — 19° 38.6′N., 156° 00.0′W.
- Napoopoo, Hawaii — 19° 28.6′N., 155° 55.3′W.
- Hilo, Hawaii — 19° 44.1′N., 155° 03.5′W.

| To \ From | Hilo | Napoopoo | Kailua | Kawaihae | Mahukona | Hana | Lahaina | Kahului | Kaumalapau | Kamalo | Kaunakakai | Haleolono | Kalaupapa | Honolulu | Pearl Harbor | Ahukini | Nawiliwili | Port Allen | Waimea | Hanalei | Nonopapa | Midway | Johnston |
|---|---|---|---|---|---|---|---|---|---|---|---|---|---|---|---|---|---|---|---|---|---|---|---|
| Napoopoo | 120 | | | | | | | | | | | | | | | | | | | | | | |
| Kailua | 109 | 11 | | | | | | | | | | | | | | | | | | | | | |
| Kawaihae | 83 | 45 | 34 | | | | | | | | | | | | | | | | | | | | |
| Mahukona | 72 | 50 | 39 | 12 | | | | | | | | | | | | | | | | | | | |
| Hana | 85 | 84 | 73 | 48 | 36 | | | | | | | | | | | | | | | | | | |
| Lahaina (Mala) | 125 | 99 | 88 | 72 | 74 | 57 | | | | | | | | | | | | | | | | | |
| Kahului | 121 | 120 | 91 | 85 | 76 | 37 | 27 | | | | | | | | | | | | | | | | |
| Kaumalapau | 136 | 101 | 110 | 82 | 77 | 72 | 25 | 50 | | | | | | | | | | | | | | | |
| Kamalo | 137 | 112 | 102 | 86 | 95 | 59 | 15 | 30 | 25 | | | | | | | | | | | | | | |
| Kaunakakai | 145 | 120 | 109 | 93 | 102 | 80 | 23 | 39 | 21 | 12 | | | | | | | | | | | | | |
| Haleolono | 155 | 124 | 114 | 103 | 123 | 70 | 39 | 50 | 24 | 22 | 13 | | | | | | | | | | | | |
| Kalaupapa | 154 | 138 | 127 | 110 | 128 | 119 | 73 | 41 | 54 | 37 | 45 | 33 | | | | | | | | | | | |
| Honolulu | 196 | 157 | 147 | 140 | 133 | 124 | 78 | 89 | 60 | 61 | 52 | 40 | 53 | | | | | | | | | | |
| Pearl Harbor | 201 | 162 | 152 | 145 | 138 | 131 | 86 | 94 | 65 | 66 | 57 | 45 | 58 | 9 | | | | | | | | | |
| Ahukini | 287 | 245 | 236 | 230 | 223 | 210 | 165 | 181 | 151 | 153 | 144 | 132 | 143 | 96 | 92 | | | | | | | | |
| Nawiliwili | 287 | 244 | 235 | 230 | 223 | 210 | 165 | 181 | 151 | 153 | 144 | 132 | 144 | 96 | 92 | 5 | | | | | | | |
| Port Allen | 297 | 254 | 245 | 240 | 233 | 220 | 177 | 193 | 161 | 163 | 154 | 142 | 156 | 106 | 102 | 23 | 21 | | | | | | |
| Waimea | 303 | 260 | 251 | 246 | 246 | 226 | 199 | 194 | 172 | 173 | 160 | 148 | 162 | 112 | 108 | 29 | 27 | 8 | | | | | |
| Hanalei | 308 | 266 | 257 | 251 | 252 | 232 | 182 | 232 | 199 | 203 | 164 | 152 | 159 | 116 | 112 | 29 | 32 | 42 | 35 | | | | |
| Nonopapa | 332 | 287 | 278 | 277 | 262 | 262 | | | | | 193 | 181 | 194 | 147 | 143 | 65 | 63 | 45 | 40 | 52 | | | |
| Midway | 1338 | 1278 | 1232 | | | | | | | | | | | 1150 | 1146 | 1069 | | 1042 | | | | | |
| Johnston | 905 | 811 | 796 | | | | | | | | | | | 725 | 722 | 668 | | 656 | | | | 825 | |
| Palmyra | 959 | 928 | 1010 | | | | | | | | | | | 959 | 960 | 986 | | 979 | | | | 1606 | 785 |

# COASTWISE — SAN DIEGO, CA, TO CAPE FLATTERY, WA
### (Nautical Miles)

Figure at intersection of columns opposite ports in question is the nautical mileage between the two.

Example: San Francisco. Calif., is 652 nautical miles from Portland, Oreg.

**Ports (with coordinates):**

- San Diego, Calif. — 32° 43.0'N., 117° 10.5'W.
- Newport Beach, Calif. — 33° 37.1'N., 117° 55.5'W.
- Long Beach, Calif. — 32° 46.2'N., 118° 13.3'W.
- Los Angeles, Calif. — 33° 45.0'N., 118° 16.2'W.
- Port Hueneme, Calif. — 34° 09.0'N., 119° 12.4'W.
- Santa Barbara, Calif. — 34° 24.5'N., 119° 41.1'W.
- Port San Luis, Calif. — 35° 10.4'N., 120° 44.8'W.
- Monterey, Calif. — 36° 36.5'N., 121° 53.0'W.
- San Francisco, Calif. — 37° 48.5'N., 122° 24.0'W.
- Oakland, Calif. — 37° 48.5'N., 122° 19.5'W.
- Stockton, Calif. — 37° 57.2'N., 121° 18.8'W.
- Sacramento, Calif. — 38° 33.8'N., 121° 33.0'W.
- Eureka, Calif. — 40° 47.8'N., 124° 11.2'W.
- Crescent City, Calif. — 41° 44.5'N., 124° 11.4'W.
- Coos Bay, Oreg. — 43° 22.4'N., 124° 12.5'W.
- Gardiner, Oreg. — 43° 43.9'N., 124° 06.8'W.
- Florence, Oreg. — 43° 58.0'N., 124° 06.3'W.
- Newport, Oreg. — 44° 37.8'N., 124° 03.1'W.
- Depoe Bay, Oreg. — 44° 48.6'N., 124° 03.6'W.
- Garibaldi, Oreg. — 45° 33.3'N., 123° 55.1'W.
- Astoria, Oreg. — 46° 11.7'N., 123° 50.0'W.
- Longview, Wash. — 46° 06.3'N., 122° 57.7'W.
- Vancouver, Wash. — 45° 37.6'N., 122° 41.3'W.
- Portland, Oreg. — 45° 33.0'N., 122° 41.7'W.
- South Bend, Wash. — 46° 40.1'N., 123° 47.5'W.
- Aberdeen, Wash. — 46° 58.4'N., 123° 48.5'W.
- CAPE FLATTERY, WASH. — 48° 26.0'N., 124° 47.0'W.

**Distance matrix** (each row lists, in the order printed, the distances from that port to the ports listed above it in the table — the leftmost figure being to the nearest listed northern port and the rightmost figure being to Cape Flattery):

| Port | Distances (nautical miles) |
|---|---|
| Aberdeen | 117 |
| South Bend | 53, 131 |
| Portland | 13, 143, 238 |
| Vancouver | 45, 80, 156, 234 |
| Longview | 34, 85, 108, 159, 198 |
| Astoria | 58, 103, 138, 155, 186, 153 |
| Garibaldi | 16, 63, 115, 160, 196, 200, 179 |
| Depoe Bay | 50, 101, 146, 182, 198, 238, 258, 222 |
| Newport | 43, 54, 153, 198, 234, 258, 262, 209, 235 |
| Florence | 36, 69, 78, 127, 178, 223, 258, 281, 232, 273 |
| Gardiner | 42, 59, 92, 101, 201, 246, 281, 285, 327, 244, 298 |
| Coos Bay | 125, 140, 156, 188, 199, 245, 296, 341, 377, 383, 327, 321 |
| Crescent City | 64, 180, 195, 212, 244, 254, 301, 352, 397, 432, 436, 383, 395, 411 |
| Eureka | 307, 354, 467, 482, 486, 471, 496, 502, 534, 544, 591, 642, 687, 468 |
| Sacramento | 75, 303, 354, 467, 482, 496, 531, 541, 588, 639, 684, 719, 722, 727, 758 |
| Stockton | 78, 235, 287, 399, 414, 430, 463, 473, 520, 570, 615, 651, 719, 723, 670, 755 |
| Oakland | 3, 75, 232, 283, 396, 411, 427, 459, 469, 516, 567, 612, 647, 652, 598, 610, 686 |
| San Francisco | 78, 235, 287, 399, 414, 430, 463, 473, 520, 570, 615, 651, 655, 601, 613, 683 |
| Monterey | 96, 167, 171, 294, 346, 459, 474, 490, 522, 532, 579, 630, 675, 710, 714, 661, 673, 746 |
| Port San Luis | 121, 208, 276, 280, 403, 455, 567, 582, 599, 631, 641, 687, 739, 783, 819, 823, 769, 781, 854 |
| Santa Barbara | 91, 205, 287, 290, 358, 383, 485, 537, 649, 664, 681, 713, 723, 770, 821, 866, 901, 905, 852, 864, 937 |
| Port Hueneme | 29, 116, 228, 287, 358, 362, 485, 510, 561, 674, 689, 706, 737, 748, 794, 845, 890, 925, 930, 876, 888, 961 |
| Los Angeles | 62, 90, 175, 266, 371, 374, 445, 449, 569, 620, 736, 751, 768, 800, 810, 857, 904, 949, 985, 992, 935, 947, 1020 |
| Long Beach | 3, 66, 94, 179, 290, 374, 377, 446, 449, 572, 620, 733, 748, 764, 797, 810, 857, 906, 953, 988, 992, 939, 951, 1024 |
| Newport Beach | 25, 27, 81, 108, 193, 304, 389, 392, 460, 464, 587, 638, 751, 766, 782, 815, 825, 871, 906, 967, 1003, 1007, 953, 965, 1038 |
| San Diego | 78, 94, 95, 147, 174, 259, 370, 455, 458, 526, 530, 653, 704, 817, 832, 848, 881, 891, 937, 969, 1034, 1070, 1074, 1019, 1031, 1104 |

Entrance buoy SD (32° 37.3'N., 117° 14.7'W.) to San Diego, 8.3 miles.
Entrance buoy LB (32° 42.1'N., 118° 11.0'W.) to Long Beach, 4.9 miles.
Entrance buoy LA (33° 42.0'N., 118° 14.5'W.) to Los Angeles, 3.8 miles.
Entrance buoy SF (37° 45.9'N., 122° 41.5'W.) to San Francisco, 15 miles; Oakland 18.5 miles; Stockton 87 miles; Sacramento 91 miles.
Humboldt Bay entrance buoy HB (40° 46.4'N., 124° 16.2'W.) to Eureka, 5.5 miles.

Entrance buoy K (43° 22.2'N., 124° 23.0'W.) to Coos Bay (city), 13.3 miles.
Yaquina Bay entrance buoy CR (46° 11.1'N., 124° 11.0'W.) to Astoria, 17.8 miles; Longview 64 miles; Vancouver 98 miles; Portland 103 miles.
Willapa Bay entrance buoy W (46° 42.6'N., 124° 10.8'W.) to South Bend, 19 miles.
Grays Harbor entrance buoy GH (46° 51.9'N., 124° 14.3'W.) to Aberdeen, 21 miles.

**Distances**

## SAN FRANCISCO BAY AREA
### (Nautical Miles)

Figure at intersection of columns opposite ports in question is the nautical mileage between the two.
Example: Sacramento, California is 74 nautical miles from Napa, California.

Sacramento River

Chico Landing, 39° 42.6'N, 121° 56.6'W — 42
Colusa, 39° 13.0'N, 122° 00.0'W — 47, 89
Knights Landing, 38° 48.1'N, 121° 43.1'W — 29, 77, 119
Sacramento, 38° 33.8'N, 121° 33.0'W — 27, 56, 104, 146

San Joaquin R

Rio Vista, 38° 09.3'N, 121° 41.3'W — 100, 127, 204, 246
Hills Ferry, 37° 20.4'N, 120° 58.5'W — 74, 48, 75, 84, 132, 174
Stockton, 37° 57.2'N, 121° 18.8'W — 31, 103, 17, 44, 73, 121, 163

Suisun Bay

Antioch, 38° 01.1'N, 121° 48.7'W — 3, 35, 107, 14, 40, 69, 117, 159
Pittsburg, 38° 02.1'N, 121° 52.6'W — 14, 17, 48, 120, 26, 52, 81, 129, 171

San Pablo Bay

Benicia, 38° 02.4'N, 122° 08.2'W — 22, 36, 39, 70, 142, 48, 74, 103, 151, 193
Napa, 38° 17.7'N, 122° 16.9'W — 15, 8, 21, 24, 55, 127, 33, 59, 88, 136, 178
Vallejo, 38° 05.3'N, 122° 15.3'W — 28, 33, 46, 50, 81, 153, 58, 85, 114, 162, 204
Petaluma, 38° 14.1'N, 122° 38.2'W — 27, 17, 32, 35, 38, 69, 141, 47, 73, 102, 150, 192

San Francisco Bay

San Rafael, 37° 58.1'N, 122° 30.7'W — 11, 31, 21, 36, 25, 39, 42, 73, 145, 51, 77, 106, 154, 196
Sausalito, 37° 51.6'N, 122° 28.6'W — 7, 9, 29, 19, 34, 24, 37, 40, 71, 143, 49, 75, 104, 152, 194
Richmond, 37° 54.6'N, 122° 21.7'W — 14, 8, 16, 36, 26, 40, 30, 43, 47, 78, 149, 55, 81, 110, 158, 200
Oakland, 37° 48.2'N, 122° 19.5'W — 22, 32, 27, 35, 54, 44, 58, 49, 62, 65, 96, 168, 73, 100, 129, 171, 219
Redwood City, 37° 30.8'N, 122° 12.5'W — 16, 7, 17, 11, 19, 39, 29, 43, 33, 46, 50, 81, 153, 58, 84, 113, 161, 203
Hunters Point, 37° 43.1'N, 122° 21.5'W — 6, 22, 3, 11, 5, 13, 33, 23, 37, 27, 40, 44, 75, 147, 52, 78, 107, 155, 197
San Francisco, 37° 48.5'N, 122° 24.0'W

Statute Miles

## COLUMBIA RIVER SYSTEM

Figure at intersection of columns opposite ports in question is the nautical/statute mileage between the two.
Example: Astoria, Oreg., is 85 nautical miles (98 statute miles) from Portland, Oreg.

Diagonal port reference points (with coordinates):

- Columbia River Mouth, 46° 14.8'N, 124° 05.5'W
- Ilwaco, Wash., 46° 18.3'N, 124° 02.2'W
- Warrenton, Oreg., 46° 10.1'N, 123° 55.0'W
- Astoria, Oreg., 46° 11.7'N, 123° 50.0'W
- Longview, Wash., 46° 06.3'N, 123° 50.0'W
- St. Helens, Oreg., 45° 51.7'N, 122° 57.7'W
- Vancouver, Wash., 45° 37.6'N, 122° 41.3'W
- Bonneville Lock & Dam, 45° 38.3'N, 121° 56.8'W
- Hood River (town) Oreg., 45° 43.0'N, 121° 30.0'W
- The Dalles Lock & Dam, 45° 36.9'N, 121° 08.3'W
- John Day Lock & Dam, 45° 42.9'N, 120° 41.5'W
- Arlington, Oreg., 45° 43.6'N, 120° 12.2'W
- Umatilla, Oreg., 45° 55.4'N, 119° 20.5'W
- McNary Lock & Dam, 45° 56.4'N, 119° 17.9'W
- Port of Walla Walla, Wash., 46° 00.0'N, 118° 55.3'W
- Pasco, Wash., 46° 13.2'N, 119° 05.9'W
- Richland, Wash., 46° 16.5'N, 119° 16.1'W
- Portland, Oreg., 45° 33.0'N, 122° 41.7'W
- Oregon City, Oreg., 45° 21.5'N, 122° 36.5'W
- Salem, Oreg., 44° 56.2'N, 123° 03.1'W
- Albany, Oreg., 44° 38.3'N, 123° 06.2'W
- Corvallis, Oreg., 44° 34.0'N, 123° 15.3'W
- Harrisburg, Oreg., 44° 16.0'N, 123° 10.2'W
- Ice Harbor Dam, Wash., 46° 15.1'N, 118° 52.7'W
- Central Ferry, Wash., 46° 37.6'N, 117° 46.6'W
- Lewiston, Idaho, 46° 25.1'N, 116° 59.9'W
- Johnson Bar landing, Idaho

River segment labels: Columbia River · Willamette River · Snake River

Distances

Nautical Miles

## STRAIT OF JUAN DE FUCA AND STRAIT OF GEORGIA

(Nautical miles)

Figure at intersection of columns opposite ports in question is the nautical mileage between the two. Example: Port Angeles, Wash., is 69 nautical miles from Seattle, Wash.

| | CAPE FLATTERY, WASH. 48°26.0'N, 124°47.0'W | SWIFTSURE BANK, WASH. 48°31.0'N, 125°00.0'W | Neah Bay, Wash. 48°22.4'N, 124°36.5'W | Port Angeles, Wash. 48°25.0'N, 123°26.4'W | Victoria, Canada 48°25.0'N, 123°23.5'W | Port Townsend, Wash. 48°06.8'N, 122°45.2'W | Port Ludlow, Wash. 47°55.3'N, 122°41.0'W | Port Gamble, Wash. 47°51.3'N, 122°34.7'W | Everett, Wash. 47°59.3'N, 122°13.2'W | Point Wells, Wash. 47°47.1'N, 122°23.7'W | Seattle, Wash. 47°36.2'N, 122°20.3'W | Eagle Harbor, Wash. 47°37.2'N, 122°30.7'W | Bremerton, Wash 47°33.5'N, 122°38.0'W | Tacoma, Wash. 47°16.0'N, 122°26.0'W | Olympia, Wash. 47°03.1'N, 122°54.3'W | Roche Harbor, Wash. 48°36.6'N, 123°09.1'W | Friday Harbor, Wash. 48°32.2'N, 123°00.9'W | Anacortes, Wash. 48°31.4'N, 122°36.7'W | Bellingham, Wash. 48°45.1'N, 122°29.0'W | Blaine, Wash. 48°59.5'N, 122°45.9'W | Nanaimo, Canada. 49°10.1'N, 123°56.0'W | New Westminster, Canada. 49°12.0'N, 122°54.5'W |
|---|---|---|---|---|---|---|---|---|---|---|---|---|---|---|---|---|---|---|---|---|---|---|
| SWIFTSURE BANK, WASH. | 10 | | | | | | | | | | | | | | | | | | | | | |
| Neah Bay, Wash. | 10 | 20 | | | | | | | | | | | | | | | | | | | | |
| Port Angeles, Wash. | 61 | 71 | 54 | | | | | | | | | | | | | | | | | | | |
| Victoria, Canada | 62 | 71 | 55 | 19 | | | | | | | | | | | | | | | | | | |
| Port Townsend, Wash. | 86 | 96 | 79 | 32 | 34 | | | | | | | | | | | | | | | | | |
| Port Ludlow, Wash. | 100 | 110 | 93 | 46 | 48 | 16 | | | | | | | | | | | | | | | | |
| Port Gamble, Wash. | 104 | 114 | 97 | 50 | 53 | 21 | 10 | | | | | | | | | | | | | | | |
| Everett, Wash. | 117 | 127 | 110 | 63 | 66 | 34 | 26 | 28 | | | | | | | | | | | | | | |
| Point Wells, Wash. | 111 | 121 | 103 | 56 | 59 | 27 | 19 | 21 | 16 | | | | | | | | | | | | | |
| Seattle, Wash. | 124 | 134 | 116 | 69 | 72 | 40 | 32 | 34 | 30 | 14 | | | | | | | | | | | | |
| Eagle Harbor, Wash. | 123 | 133 | 115 | 68 | 71 | 40 | 32 | 34 | 29 | 14 | 8 | | | | | | | | | | | |
| Bremerton, Wash | 131 | 141 | 124 | 77 | 80 | 48 | 40 | 42 | 38 | 23 | 14 | 13 | | | | | | | | | | |
| Tacoma, Wash. | 143 | 153 | 136 | 89 | 91 | 59 | 52 | 53 | 49 | 34 | 25 | 25 | 29 | | | | | | | | | |
| Olympia, Wash. | 168 | 178 | 160 | 113 | 115 | 84 | 75 | 78 | 73 | 59 | 50 | 50 | 50 | 34 | | | | | | | | |
| Roche Harbor, Wash. | 83 | 92 | 76 | 36 | 25 | 41 | 54 | 58 | 71 | 64 | 77 | 76 | 85 | 96 | 121 | | | | | | | |
| Friday Harbor, Wash. | 87 | 96 | 80 | 37 | 30 | 30 | 44 | 48 | 62 | 54 | 67 | 67 | 76 | 86 | 112 | 12 | | | | | | |
| Anacortes, Wash. | 93 | 102 | 86 | 42 | 36 | 30 | 43 | 47 | 49 | 54 | 66 | 66 | 74 | 86 | 110 | 27 | 18 | | | | | |
| Bellingham, Wash. | 108 | 117 | 101 | 54 | 50 | 43 | 57 | 61 | 63 | 68 | 80 | 80 | 88 | 100 | 124 | 37 | 28 | 17 | | | | |
| Blaine, Wash. | 112 | 121 | 105 | 65 | 55 | 59 | 72 | 76 | 80 | 83 | 95 | 95 | 104 | 115 | 139 | 35 | 37 | 36 | 38 | | | |
| Nanaimo, Canada. | 145 | 154 | 138 | 99 | 89 | 97 | 111 | 115 | 118 | 121 | 134 | 134 | 142 | 154 | 177 | 66 | 69 | 76 | 75 | 55 | | |
| New Westminster, Canada. | 139 | 148 | 132 | 93 | 82 | 91 | 105 | 109 | 114 | 116 | 128 | 128 | 137 | 148 | 171 | 60 | 60 | 70 | 71 | 48 | 48 | |
| Vancouver, Canada. 49°17.4'N, 123°06.6'W | 141 | 150 | 133 | 95 | 83 | 92 | 106 | 110 | 115 | 117 | 129 | 129 | 138 | 149 | 173 | 62 | 62 | 71 | 72 | 48 | 36 | 41 |

## INSIDE PASSAGE — SEATTLE, WA TO CAPE SPENCER, AK
(Nautical Miles)

Figure at intersection of columns opposite ports in question is the nautical mileage between the two.
Example: Ketchikan, Alaska is 220 nautical miles from Juneau, Alaska.

**Ports (with coordinates):**

- CAPE SPENCER, ALASKA. 58°10.0'N., 136°38.3'W.
- Gustavus, Alaska. 58°23.3'N., 135°43.6'W.
- Skagway, Alaska. 59°26.8'N., 135°19.3'W.
- Haines, Alaska. 59°13.8'N., 135°26.1'W.
- Juneau, Alaska. 58°17.9'N., 134°24.7'W.
- Pelican, Alaska. 57°57.6'N., 136°13.8'W.
- Sitka, Alaska. 57°03.1'N., 135°20.5'W.
- Petersburg, Alaska. 56°48.9'N., 132°57.8'W.
- Port Alexander, Alaska. 56°14.8'N., 134°28.8'W.
- CAPE DECISION, ALASKA. 55°59.4'N., 134°08.1'W.
- Wrangell, Alaska. 56°28.2'N., 132°23.2'W.
- Craig, Alaska. 55°28.7'N., 133°09.2'W.
- Ketchikan, Alaska. 55°20.5'N., 131°38.7'W.
- Metlakatla, Alaska. 55°07.8'N., 131°34.2'W.
- Cape Chacon, Alaska. 54°40.6'N., 131°59.7'W.
- Hyder, Alaska. 55°54.2'N., 130°00.6'W.
- DIXON ENTRANCE, ALASKA. 54°28.0'N., 132°52.0'W.
- Victoria, Canada. 48°25.0'N., 123°28.5'W.
- Seattle, Wash. 47°36.2'N., 122°20.3'W.

**Triangular distance table** (each row lists distances from the named port to the ports that precede it in the list above, rightmost value = to Cape Spencer):

| From \ distances (nearest listed port → … → Cape Spencer) |
| --- |
| Gustavus: 32 |
| Skagway: 106  136 |
| Haines: 14  96  124 |
| Juneau: 88  100  82  110 |
| Pelican: 123  136  148  45  18 |
| Sitka: 79  162  176  187  136  85 |
| Petersburg: 159  108  179  191  166  136  195 |
| Port Alexander: 24  100  82  186  186  198  147  173 |
| Cape Decision: 76  95  206  206  157  204  215  208  193 |
| Wrangell: 75  99  40  170  248  148  219  231  164  235 |
| Craig: 111  49  73  113  144  206  253  264  213  242 |
| Ketchikan: 121  89  129  153  112  224  220  291  303  321 |
| Metlakatla: 16  109  104  143  167  126  238  235  305  317  307 |
| Cape Chacon: 32  76  123  125  149  146  220  254  325  337  318 |
| Hyder: 136  148  212  234  273  293  256  368  364  435  447  451 |
| Dixon Entrance: 169  34  66  77  157  126  150  221  332  288  359  371  319 |
| Victoria: 612  638  588  608  608  664  697  737  761  719  832  937  827  898  910  886  924 |
| Seattle: 72  664  690  640  660  659  716  749  788  812  771  883  989  879  950  962  938  976 |

# GULF OF ALASKA
## (Nautical Miles)

Figure at intersection of columns opposite ports in question is the nautical mileage between the two.
Example: Anchorage is 385 nautical miles from Port Valdez.

**Port positions:**

- False Pass: 54° 51.4'N, 163° 24.0'W
- UNIMAK PASS: 54° 20.0'N, 164° 45.0'W
- Unga: 55° 10.6'N, 160° 29.8'W
- Chignik: 56° 17.8'N, 158° 24.0'W
- Uyak: 57° 38.6'N, 154° 00.0'W
- Kodiak: 57° 47.1'N, 152° 25.1'W
- Anchorage: 61° 14.2'N, 149° 53.3'W
- Homer: 59° 36.0'N, 151° 24.0'W
- Seldovia: 59° 26.5'N, 151° 43.0'W
- Seward: 60° 06.0'N, 149° 26.0'W
- Latouche: 60° 03.3'N, 147° 54.1'W
- Whittier: 60° 46.8'N, 148° 39.6'W
- Port Valdez: 61° 06.0'N, 146° 24.0'W
- Cordova: 60° 33.4'N, 145° 45.3'W
- Yakutat: 59° 32.9'N, 139° 43.9'W
- CAPE SPENCER, ALASKA: 58° 10.0'N, 136° 38.3'W
- Sitka, Alaska: 57° 03.1'N, 135° 20.5'W
- CAPE DECISION, ALASKA: 55° 59.4'N, 134° 08.1'W
- DIXON ENTRANCE, ALAS.: 54° 28.0'N, 132° 52.0'W
- SWIFTSURE BANK: 48° 31.0'N, 125° 00.0'W

| | False Pass | Unimak Pass | Unga | Chignik | Uyak | Kodiak | Anchorage | Homer | Seldovia | Seward | Latouche | Whittier | Port Valdez | Cordova | Yakutat | Cape Spencer | Sitka | Cape Decision | Dixon Entrance |
|---|---|---|---|---|---|---|---|---|---|---|---|---|---|---|---|---|---|---|---|
| Unimak Pass | 86 | | | | | | | | | | | | | | | | | | |
| Unga | 187 | 135 | | | | | | | | | | | | | | | | | |
| Chignik | 289 | 236 | 122 | | | | | | | | | | | | | | | | |
| Uyak | 440 | 388 | 273 | 180 | | | | | | | | | | | | | | | |
| Kodiak | 505 | 453 | 338 | 245 | 80 | | | | | | | | | | | | | | |
| Anchorage | 688 | 636 | 521 | 428 | 264 | 242 | | | | | | | | | | | | | |
| Homer | 573 | 521 | 406 | 313 | 149 | 126 | 143 | | | | | | | | | | | | |
| Seldovia | 562 | 510 | 395 | 302 | 138 | 115 | 139 | 16 | | | | | | | | | | | |
| Seward | 652 | 600 | 485 | 392 | 228 | 175 | 274 | 158 | 147 | | | | | | | | | | |
| Latouche | 678 | 626 | 511 | 418 | 254 | 201 | 300 | 183 | 172 | 61 | | | | | | | | | |
| Whittier | 742 | 698 | 574 | 481 | 317 | 261 | 367 | 249 | 239 | 125 | 64 | | | | | | | | |
| Port Valdez | 761 | 709 | 595 | 501 | 337 | 280 | 385 | 267 | 257 | 144 | 83 | 96 | | | | | | | |
| Cordova | 763 | 711 | 597 | 503 | 339 | 282 | 387 | 270 | 260 | 146 | 85 | 96 | 78 | | | | | | |
| Yakutat | | 897 | 844 | 730 | 636 | 414 | 538 | 422 | 411 | 312 | 286 | 298 | 285 | 278 | | | | | |
| Cape Spencer | 987 | 926 | 811 | 717 | 505 | 641 | 591 | 525 | 467 | 422 | 395 | 413 | 400 | 393 | 141 | | | | |
| Sitka | 1027 | 980 | 865 | 772 | 564 | 708 | 647 | 636 | 580 | 494 | 467 | 492 | 479 | 472 | 231 | 85 | | | |
| Cape Decision | 1064 | 1016 | 892 | 811 | 613 | 763 | 729 | 718 | 636 | 553 | 525 | 542 | 529 | 522 | 295 | 162 | 95 | | |
| Dixon Entrance | 1120 | 1084 | 953 | 874 | 689 | 762 | 687 | 845 | 729 | 642 | 617 | 647 | 634 | 627 | 402 | 259 | 192 | 106 | |
| Swiftsure Bank | 1510 | 1473 | 1394 | 1301 | 1200 | 1124 | 1294 | 1178 | 1167 | 1100 | 1076 | 1113 | 1100 | 1093 | 869 | 739 | 681 | 588 | 500 |

## BERING SEA AND ARCTIC OCEAN
(Nautical Miles)

Figure at intersection of columns opposite ports in question is the nautical mileage between the two. Example: Port Moller is 618 nautical miles from Nome.

**Ports (with positions):**

- Alaska-Canada Boundary, 69°43.0'N, 141°00.0'W
- Barter Island, 70°09.0'N, 143°40.0'W
- Barrow, 71°18.0'N, 156°48.0'W
- Wainwright, 70°40.0'N, 160°00.0'W
- Point Lay, 69°48.0'N, 163°08.0'W
- Point Hope, 68°21.0'N, 167°18.0'W
- Deering, 66°06.0'N, 162°44.0'W
- CAPE PRINCE OF WALES, 65°37.6'N, 168°31.5'W
- Port Clarence, 65°17.1'N, 166°24.5'W
- Savoonga, 63°43.0'N, 170°27.0'W
- Nome, 64°29.0'N, 165°26.0'W
- Golovnin Bay, 64°22.3'N, 163°06.7'W
- Unalakleet, 63°53.0'N, 160°50.0'W
- St. Michael, 63°32.4'N, 161°54.8'W
- Apoorn Pass, 63°02.6'N, 163°22.3'W
- Hooper Bay, 61°29.0'N, 166°04.0'W
- Bethel, 60°49.0'N, 161°47.0'W
- Platinum, 59°01.5'N, 161°52.0'W
- Dillingham, 59°02.0'N, 158°29.0'W
- Naknek, 58°41.5'N, 157°16.0'W
- Meshik, 56°56.5'N, 158°49.0'W
- Port Moller, 55°59.0'N, 160°36.5'W
- St. Paul Island, 57°07.9'N, 170°17.9'W
- Massacre Bay, 52°48.9'N, 173°15.6'W
- Alcan Harbor, 52°44.0'N, 174°04.5'W
- Kiska, 51°58.3'N, 177°34.5'W
- Constantine Harbor, 51°24.0'N, 179°18.1'W
- Kuluk Bay, 51°51.6'N, 176°37.6'W
- Dutch Harbor, 53°52.7'N, 166°31.8'W
- UNIMAK PASS, 54°20.0'N, 164°45.0'W

**Distance table (triangular, selected readings):**

| Port | Distances to preceding ports |
|---|---|
| Barter Island | 62 |
| Barrow | 274, 337 |
| Wainwright | 77, 350, 412 |
| Point Lay | 86, 161, 434, 496 |
| Point Hope | 130, 211, 286, 560, 621 |
| Deering | 172, 302, 383, 458, 732, 794 |
| Cape Prince of Wales | 198, 166, 296, 377, 452, 725, 787, 846 |
| Port Clarence | 57, 255, 223, 354, 435, 510, 783, 850, 912 |
| Savoonga | 151, 323, 291, 312, 279, 291, 490, 566, 577, 901 |
| Nome | 139, 119, 114, 312, 279, 291, 490, 566, 577, 839, 850, 912 |
| Golovnin Bay | 62, 126, 254, 244, 238, 219, 417, 436, 515, 596, 672, 690, 963 |
| Unalakleet | 66, 230, 225, 228, 222, 420, 385, 534, 599, 674, 690, 945, 899, 961 |
| St. Michael | 35, 59, 110, 229, 209, 270, 388, 436, 518, 599, 722, 947, 963, 1007, 1025 |
| Apoorn Pass | 53, 88, 116, 276, 222, 685, 566, 647, 995, 945, 1010, 1007, 1058 |
| Hooper Bay | 259, 260, 286, 235, 200, 229, 420, 534, 515, 674, 722, 995, 1010, 1058 |
| Bethel | 454, 679, 680, 706, 655, 620, 624, 690, 883, 850, 980, 1061, 1137, 1472 |
| Platinum | 120, 565, 566, 592, 541, 507, 510, 576, 769, 866, 948, 1023, 1137, 1296, 1358 |
| Dillingham | 208, 322, 493, 718, 719, 744, 693, 659, 662, 728, 921, 889, 1019, 1100, 1175, 1448, 1513 |
| Naknek | 72, 202, 315, 486, 711, 712, 738, 693, 653, 656, 723, 915, 883, 1012, 1094, 1169, 1442, 1507 |
| Meshik | 118, 130, 179, 293, 459, 684, 685, 712, 660, 625, 628, 695, 887, 855, 985, 1066, 1141, 1414, 1477 |
| Port Moller | 88, 198, 207, 196, 310, 444, 676, 678, 703, 652, 618, 621, 689, 880, 848, 978, 1059, 1134, 1407, 1469 |
| St. Paul Island | 335, 381, 437, 207, 302, 415, 528, 529, 555, 470, 468, 529, 727, 695, 825, 906, 962, 1255, 1317 |
| Massacre Bay | 632, 934, 991, 1056, 1062, 1034, 921, 893, 830, 854, 1037, 1040, 1066, 1015, 970, 975, 1031, 1229, 1197, 1327, 1408, 1483, 1756, 1819 |
| Alcan Harbor | 33, 604, 920, 978, 1029, 1036, 1062, 893, 817, 931, 1007, 1015, 1018, 1044, 990, 945, 1008, 1206, 1174, 1304, 1385, 1460, 1733, 1795 |
| Kiska | 157, 526, 809, 912, 919, 951, 817, 789, 903, 897, 981, 984, 1009, 958, 919, 914, 975, 1173, 1141, 1271, 1352, 1427, 1700, 1762 |
| Constantine Harbor | 79, 185, 501, 769, 832, 871, 789, 903, 775, 776, 982, 985, 1011, 960, 920, 915, 976, 1174, 1142, 1272, 1353, 1428, 1701, 1763 |
| Kuluk Bay | 175, 235, 368, 396, 249, 287, 627, 694, 785, 662, 776, 903, 931, 981, 985, 835, 830, 891, 896, 1089, 1057, 1187, 1268, 1343, 1616, 1678 |
| Dutch Harbor | 407, 558, 616, 749, 777, 239, 256, 325, 432, 343, 464, 485, 721, 724, 750, 699, 659, 654, 720, 715, 913, 881, 1011, 1092, 1167, 1440, 1503 |
| UNIMAK PASS | 75, 463, 614, 672, 805, 833, 254, 208, 277, 384, 307, 421, 472, 708, 711, 737, 686, 646, 642, 708, 702, 900, 868, 998, 1079, 1155, 1428, 1490 |

**Distances**

# CONVERSIONS

**15**

## NAUTICAL MILES, STATUTE MILES, AND KILOMETERS

| NM | Km | SM | Km | NM | SM | SM | Km | NM |
|---|---|---|---|---|---|---|---|---|
| 1 | 1.852 | 1.15078 | 1 | 0.53996 | 0.62137 | 1 | 1.60934 | 0.86898 |
| 2 | 3.70 | 2.30 | 2 | 1.08 | 1.24 | 2 | 3.22 | 1.74 |
| 3 | 5.56 | 3.45 | 3 | 1.62 | 1.86 | 3 | 4.83 | 2.61 |
| 4 | 7.41 | 4.60 | 4 | 2.16 | 2.49 | 4 | 6.44 | 3.48 |
| 5 | 9.26 | 5.75 | 5 | 2.70 | 3.11 | 5 | 8.05 | 4.34 |
| 6 | 11.11 | 6.90 | 6 | 3.24 | 3.73 | 6 | 9.66 | 5.21 |
| 7 | 12.96 | 8.06 | 7 | 3.78 | 4.35 | 7 | 11.27 | 6.08 |
| 8 | 14.82 | 9.21 | 8 | 4.32 | 4.97 | 8 | 12.87 | 6.95 |
| 9 | 16.67 | 10.36 | 9 | 4.86 | 5.59 | 9 | 14.48 | 7.82 |
| 10 | 18.52 | 11.51 | 10 | 5.40 | 6.21 | 10 | 16.09 | 8.69 |
| 11 | 20.37 | 12.66 | 11 | 5.94 | 6.84 | 11 | 17.70 | 9.56 |
| 12 | 22.22 | 13.81 | 12 | 6.48 | 7.46 | 12 | 19.31 | 10.43 |
| 13 | 24.08 | 14.96 | 13 | 7.02 | 8.08 | 13 | 20.92 | 11.30 |
| 14 | 25.93 | 16.11 | 14 | 7.56 | 8.70 | 14 | 22.53 | 12.17 |
| 15 | 27.78 | 17.26 | 15 | 8.10 | 9.32 | 15 | 23.14 | 13.03 |
| 16 | 29.63 | 18.41 | 16 | 8.64 | 9.94 | 16 | 25.75 | 13.90 |
| 17 | 31.48 | 19.56 | 17 | 9.18 | 10.56 | 17 | 27.36 | 14.77 |
| 18 | 33.34 | 20.71 | 18 | 9.72 | 11.18 | 18 | 28.97 | 15.64 |
| 19 | 35.19 | 21.86 | 19 | 10.26 | 11.81 | 19 | 30.58 | 16.51 |
| 20 | 37.04 | 23.02 | 20 | 10.80 | 12.43 | 20 | 32.19 | 17.38 |
| 21 | 38.89 | 24.17 | 21 | 11.34 | 13.05 | 21 | 33.80 | 18.25 |
| 22 | 40.74 | 25.32 | 22 | 11.88 | 13.67 | 22 | 35.41 | 19.12 |
| 23 | 42.60 | 26.47 | 23 | 12.42 | 14.29 | 23 | 37.01 | 19.99 |
| 24 | 44.45 | 27.62 | 24 | 12.96 | 14.91 | 24 | 38.62 | 20.86 |
| 25 | 46.30 | 28.77 | 25 | 13.50 | 15.53 | 25 | 40.23 | 21.72 |
| 26 | 48.15 | 29.92 | 26 | 14.04 | 16.16 | 26 | 41.84 | 22.59 |
| 27 | 50.00 | 31.07 | 27 | 14.58 | 16.78 | 27 | 43.45 | 23.46 |
| 28 | 51.86 | 32.22 | 28 | 15.12 | 17.40 | 28 | 45.06 | 24.33 |
| 29 | 53.71 | 33.37 | 29 | 15.66 | 18.02 | 29 | 46.67 | 25.20 |
| 30 | 55.56 | 34.52 | 30 | 16.20 | 18.64 | 30 | 48.28 | 26.07 |
| 31 | 57.41 | 35.67 | 31 | 16.74 | 19.26 | 31 | 49.89 | 26.94 |
| 32 | 59.26 | 36.82 | 32 | 17.28 | 19.88 | 32 | 51.50 | 27.81 |
| 33 | 61.12 | 37.98 | 33 | 17.82 | 20.51 | 33 | 53.11 | 28.68 |
| 34 | 62.97 | 39.13 | 34 | 18.36 | 21.13 | 34 | 54.72 | 29.55 |
| 35 | 64.82 | 40.28 | 35 | 18.90 | 21.75 | 35 | 56.33 | 30.41 |
| 36 | 66.67 | 41.43 | 36 | 19.44 | 22.37 | 36 | 57.94 | 31.28 |
| 37 | 68.52 | 42.58 | 37 | 19.98 | 22.99 | 37 | 59.55 | 32.15 |
| 38 | 70.38 | 43.73 | 38 | 20.52 | 23.61 | 38 | 61.15 | 33.02 |
| 39 | 72.23 | 44.88 | 39 | 21.06 | 24.23 | 39 | 62.76 | 33.89 |
| 40 | 74.08 | 46.03 | 40 | 21.60 | 24.85 | 40 | 64.37 | 34.76 |
| 45 | 83.34 | 51.79 | 45 | 24.30 | 27.96 | 45 | 72.42 | 39.10 |
| 50 | 92.60 | 57.54 | 50 | 27.00 | 31.07 | 50 | 80.47 | 43.45 |
| 55 | 101.86 | 63.29 | 55 | 29.70 | 34.18 | 55 | 88.51 | 47.79 |
| 60 | 111.12 | 69.05 | 60 | 32.40 | 37.28 | 60 | 96.56 | 52.14 |
| 65 | 120.38 | 74.80 | 65 | 35.10 | 40.39 | 65 | 104.61 | 56.48 |
| 70 | 129.64 | 80.55 | 70 | 37.80 | 43.50 | 70 | 112.65 | 60.83 |
| 75 | 138.90 | 86.31 | 75 | 40.50 | 46.60 | 75 | 120.70 | 65.17 |
| 80 | 148.16 | 92.06 | 80 | 43.20 | 49.71 | 80 | 128.75 | 69.52 |
| 85 | 157.42 | 97.82 | 85 | 45.90 | 52.82 | 85 | 136.79 | 73.86 |
| 90 | 166.68 | 103.57 | 90 | 48.60 | 55.92 | 90 | 144.84 | 78.21 |
| 95 | 175.94 | 109.32 | 95 | 51.30 | 59.03 | 95 | 152.89 | 82.55 |
| 100 | 185.20 | 115.08 | 100 | 54.00 | 62.14 | 100 | 160.93 | 86.90 |

## FEET TO METERS / METERS TO FEET

| Feet | Meters | Feet | Meters | Meters | Feet | Meters | Feet |
|------|--------|------|--------|--------|-------|--------|--------|
| 1 | 0.30 | 26 | 7.92 | 1 | 3.28 | 26 | 85.30 |
| 2 | 0.61 | 27 | 8.23 | 2 | 6.56 | 27 | 88.58 |
| 3 | 0.91 | 28 | 8.53 | 3 | 9.84 | 28 | 91.86 |
| 4 | 1.22 | 29 | 8.84 | 4 | 13.12 | 29 | 95.14 |
| 5 | 1.52 | 30 | 9.14 | 5 | 16.40 | 30 | 98.43 |
| 6 | 1.83 | 31 | 9.45 | 6 | 19.69 | 31 | 101.71 |
| 7 | 2.13 | 32 | 9.75 | 7 | 22.97 | 32 | 104.99 |
| 8 | 2.44 | 33 | 10.06 | 8 | 26.25 | 33 | 108.27 |
| 9 | 2.74 | 34 | 10.36 | 9 | 29.53 | 34 | 111.55 |
| 10 | 3.05 | 35 | 10.67 | 10 | 32.81 | 35 | 114.83 |
| 11 | 3.35 | 36 | 10.97 | 11 | 36.09 | 36 | 118.11 |
| 12 | 3.66 | 37 | 11.28 | 12 | 39.37 | 37 | 121.39 |
| 13 | 3.96 | 38 | 11.58 | 13 | 42.65 | 38 | 124.67 |
| 14 | 4.27 | 39 | 11.89 | 14 | 45.93 | 39 | 127.95 |
| 15 | 4.57 | 40 | 12.19 | 15 | 49.21 | 40 | 131.23 |
| 16 | 4.88 | 41 | 12.50 | 16 | 52.49 | 41 | 134.51 |
| 17 | 5.18 | 42 | 12.80 | 17 | 55.77 | 42 | 137.80 |
| 18 | 5.49 | 43 | 13.11 | 18 | 59.06 | 43 | 141.08 |
| 19 | 5.79 | 44 | 13.41 | 19 | 62.34 | 44 | 144.36 |
| 20 | 6.10 | 45 | 13.72 | 20 | 65.62 | 45 | 147.64 |
| 21 | 6.40 | 46 | 14.02 | 21 | 68.90 | 46 | 150.92 |
| 22 | 6.71 | 47 | 14.33 | 22 | 72.18 | 47 | 154.20 |
| 23 | 7.01 | 48 | 14.63 | 23 | 75.46 | 48 | 157.48 |
| 24 | 7.32 | 49 | 14.94 | 24 | 78.74 | 49 | 160.76 |
| 25 | 7.62 | 50 | 15.24 | 25 | 82.02 | 50 | 164.04 |

## FATHOMS TO METERS / METERS TO FATHOMS

| Fathoms | Meters | Fathoms | Meters | Metres | Fathoms | Meters | Fathoms |
|---------|--------|---------|--------|--------|---------|--------|---------|
| 1 | 1.83 | 26 | 47.55 | 1 | 0.547 | 26 | 14.217 |
| 2 | 3.66 | 27 | 49.38 | 2 | 1.094 | 27 | 14.764 |
| 3 | 5.49 | 28 | 51.21 | 3 | 1.640 | 28 | 15.311 |
| 4 | 7.32 | 29 | 53.04 | 4 | 2.187 | 29 | 15.857 |
| 5 | 9.14 | 30 | 54.86 | 5 | 2.734 | 30 | 16.404 |
| 6 | 10.97 | 31 | 56.69 | 6 | 3.281 | 31 | 16.951 |
| 7 | 12.80 | 32 | 58.52 | 7 | 3.828 | 32 | 17.498 |
| 8 | 14.63 | 33 | 60.35 | 8 | 4.374 | 33 | 18.045 |
| 9 | 16.46 | 34 | 62.18 | 9 | 4.921 | 34 | 18.591 |
| 10 | 18.29 | 35 | 64.00 | 10 | 5.468 | 35 | 19.138 |
| 11 | 20.12 | 36 | 65.84 | 11 | 6.015 | 36 | 19.685 |
| 12 | 21.95 | 37 | 67.67 | 12 | 6.562 | 37 | 20.232 |
| 13 | 23.77 | 38 | 69.49 | 13 | 7.108 | 38 | 20.779 |
| 14 | 25.60 | 39 | 71.32 | 14 | 7.655 | 39 | 21.325 |
| 15 | 27.43 | 40 | 73.15 | 15 | 8.202 | 40 | 21.872 |
| 16 | 29.26 | 41 | 74.98 | 16 | 8.749 | 41 | 22.419 |
| 17 | 31.09 | 42 | 76.81 | 17 | 9.296 | 42 | 22.966 |
| 18 | 32.92 | 43 | 78.64 | 18 | 9.842 | 43 | 23.513 |
| 19 | 34.75 | 44 | 80.47 | 19 | 10.389 | 44 | 24.059 |
| 20 | 36.58 | 45 | 82.30 | 20 | 10.936 | 45 | 24.606 |
| 21 | 38.40 | 46 | 84.12 | 21 | 11.483 | 46 | 25.153 |
| 22 | 40.23 | 47 | 85.95 | 22 | 12.030 | 47 | 25.700 |
| 23 | 42.06 | 48 | 87.78 | 23 | 12.577 | 48 | 26.247 |
| 24 | 43.89 | 49 | 89.61 | 24 | 13.123 | 49 | 26.793 |
| 25 | 45.72 | 50 | 91.44 | 25 | 13.670 | 50 | 27.340 |

Conversions

## Inches to Millimeters     Millimeters to inches

| Inches | mm | Inches | mm | mm | Inches | mm | Inches |
|---|---|---|---|---|---|---|---|
| 1 | 25.40 | 15 | 381.00 | 1 | 0.0394 | 15 | 0.5906 |
| 2 | 50.80 | 20 | 508.00 | 2 | 0.0787 | 20 | 0.7874 |
| 3 | 76.20 | 25 | 635.00 | 3 | 0.1181 | 25 | 0.9843 |
| 4 | 101.60 | 30 | 762.00 | 4 | 0.1575 | 30 | 1.1811 |
| 5 | 127.00 | 35 | 889.00 | 5 | 0.1969 | 35 | 1.3780 |
| 10 | 254.00 | 40 | 1016.00 | 10 | 0.3937 | 40 | 1.5748 |

10 MILLIMETERS = 1 CENTIMETER. 100 CENTIMETERS (1000 MM) = 1 METER = 39.37 INCHES (3.3 FEET)

## Inches to Meters     Meters to Inches

| Inches | Meters | Inches | Meters | Meters | Inches | Meters | Inches |
|---|---|---|---|---|---|---|---|
| 1 | 0.0254 | 7 | 0.1778 | 0.1 | 3.937 | 0.7 | 27.559 |
| 2 | 0.0508 | 8 | 0.2032 | 0.2 | 7.874 | 0.8 | 31.496 |
| 3 | 0.0762 | 9 | 0.2286 | 0.3 | 11.811 | 0.9 | 35.433 |
| 4 | 0.1016 | 10 | 0.2540 | 0.4 | 15.748 | 1.0 | 39.370 |
| 5 | 0.1270 | 11 | 0.2794 | 0.5 | 19.685 | 1.1 | 43.307 |
| 6 | 0.1524 | 12 | 0.3048 | 0.6 | 23.622 | 1.2 | 47.244 |

TO CONVERT METERS TO CENTIMETERS, MOVE DECIMAL POINT TWO PLACES TO THE RIGHT

## Yards to Meters     Meters to Yards

| Yards | Meters | Yards | Meters | Meters | Yards | Meters | Yards |
|---|---|---|---|---|---|---|---|
| 1 | 0.91440 | 6 | 5.48640 | 1 | 1.09361 | 6 | 6.56168 |
| 2 | 1.82880 | 7 | 6.40080 | 2 | 2.18723 | 7 | 7.65529 |
| 3 | 2.74320 | 8 | 7.31520 | 3 | 3.28084 | 8 | 8.74891 |
| 4 | 3.65760 | 9 | 8.22960 | 4 | 4.37445 | 9 | 9.84252 |
| 5 | 4.57200 | 10 | 9.14400 | 5 | 5.46807 | 10 | 10.93614 |

MOVE DECIMAL POINT FOR HIGHER VALUES – e.g. 6,000 METERS = 6,561.68 YARDS

## Pounds to Kilograms     Kilograms to Pounds

| lb | kg | lb | kg | kg | lb | kg | lb |
|---|---|---|---|---|---|---|---|
| 1 | 0.454 | 6 | 2.722 | 1 | 2.205 | 6 | 13.228 |
| 2 | 0.907 | 7 | 3.175 | 2 | 4.409 | 7 | 15.432 |
| 3 | 1.361 | 8 | 3.629 | 3 | 6.614 | 8 | 17.637 |
| 4 | 1.814 | 9 | 4.082 | 4 | 8.818 | 9 | 19.842 |
| 5 | 2.268 | 10 | 4.536 | 5 | 11.023 | 10 | 22.046 |

## Gallons to Liters     Liters to Gallons

| Gallons | Liters | Gallons | Liters | Liters | Gallons | Liters | Gallons |
|---|---|---|---|---|---|---|---|
| 1 | 3·79 | 10 | 37·86 | 1 | 0.26 | 60 | 15.66 |
| 2 | 7·57 | 20 | 75·71 | 2 | 0.53 | 90 | 23.77 |
| 3 | 11·36 | 30 | 113·57 | 5 | 1.32 | 120 | 39.62 |
| 4 | 15·14 | 40 | 151·42 | 10 | 2.64 | 150 | 39.62 |
| 5 | 18·93 | 50 | 189·28 | 20 | 5.28 | 180 | 47.54 |

## Pints to Liters     Liters to Pints

| Pints | Liters | Pints | Liters | Liters | Pints | Liters | Pints |
|---|---|---|---|---|---|---|---|
| 1 | 0·47 | 6 | 2·84 | 1 | 2.11 | 6 | 12.68 |
| 2 | 0·95 | 7 | 3·31 | 2 | 4.23 | 7 | 14.79 |
| 3 | 1·42 | 8 | 3·79 | 5 | 6.34 | 8 | 16.91 |
| 4 | 1·89 | 9 | 4·26 | 10 | 8.45 | 9 | 19.02 |
| 5 | 2·37 | 10 | 4·73 | 20 | 10.57 | 10 | 21.13 |

## LENGTH, AREA, & VOLUME CONVERSIONS

**Length**

| | |
|---|---|
| 1 fathom | = 6 feet |
| 1 shackle | = 15 fathoms |
| 1 cable | = 608 ft (approx 100 fathoms) |
| 10 cables | = 1 international nautical mile |
| 1 international nautical mile | = 6,076.12 ft |
| | = 1.15 statute miles |
| | = 1,852 m |
| 1 statute mile | = 5280 ft |
| | = 1760 yd |
| | = 0.87 sea miles |
| kilometer (km) | = 1093.61yd |
| meter (m) | = 39.37in |
| centimeter (cm) | = 0.3937in |
| millimeter (mm) | = 0.03937in |

**Area**

| | |
|---|---|
| sq meter (m$^2$) | = 1.196yd$^2$ |
| sq centimeter (cm$^2$) | = 0.1550in$^2$ |
| sq millimeter (mm$^2$) | = 0.00155in$^2$ |

**Volume**

| | |
|---|---|
| cubic meter (m) | = 264 gallons |
| | = 1000 liters |
| | = 1.308yd$^3$ |
| | = 2.11 pints |
| centiliter (cl) | = 0.34 fl oz |
| milliliter (ml) | = 0.034 fl oz |
| 1 liter | = 30.272 ounces |
| 1 Imperial gallon | = 4.546 liters |
| 1 Imperial gallon | = 12 U.S. gallons |
| 1 U.S. gallon | = 0.83 Imperial gallons |

For **wind speed, temperature, and barometer** conversions, see following pages.

## SOLID & LIQUID WEIGHT MEASURES

**Weight**

1 long ton (British) = 2240lb = 1.12 short tons = 1.016 metric ton
1 short ton (USA and Canada) = 20 centals of 100lb each = 2000lb = 0.893 long tons = 0.907 metric tons
1 metric ton = 2,204.6lb = 1.1023 short tons = 0.9842 long tons = 1000kg
1 kilogram (kg)   = 2.2046lb
1 gram (g)        = 0.0353oz

**Nautical**

1 long ton (displacement) = 35cu ft salt water or 36 cu ft fresh water
1 ton (register) = 100 cu ft
1 ton (measurement) = 40 cu ft

**Fresh Water**

1 cu ft = 7·47 gallons and weighs 62·5 lbs
1 gallon =  3·79 liters and weighs 8·33 lbs
10 British gallons = approx. 12 American gallons
1000 liters =  1cu m
1 liter weighs approx 1kg

**Salt Water**

1 cu ft weighs 64 lb = 31·25 cu ft weighs 1 ton (U.S.)

## TEMPERATURE CONVERSIONS

| C° | F° | C° | F° | C° | F° | C° | F° | C° | F° |
|----|------|----|-------|----|-------|----|-------|----|-------|
| 00 | 32.0 | | | | | | | | |
| 01 | 33.8 | 21 | 69.8 | 41 | 105.8 | 61 | 141.8 | 81 | 177.8 |
| 02 | 35.6 | 22 | 71.6 | 42 | 107.6 | 62 | 143.6 | 82 | 179.6 |
| 03 | 37.4 | 23 | 73.4 | 43 | 109.4 | 63 | 145.4 | 83 | 181.4 |
| 04 | 39.2 | 24 | 75.2 | 44 | 111.2 | 64 | 147.2 | 84 | 183.2 |
| 05 | 41.0 | 25 | 77.0 | 45 | 113.0 | 65 | 149.0 | 85 | 185.0 |
| 06 | 42.8 | 26 | 78.8 | 46 | 114.8 | 66 | 150.8 | 86 | 186.8 |
| 07 | 44.6 | 27 | 80.6 | 47 | 116.6 | 67 | 152.6 | 87 | 188.6 |
| 08 | 46.4 | 28 | 82.4 | 48 | 118.4 | 68 | 154.4 | 88 | 190.4 |
| 09 | 48.2 | 29 | 84.2 | 49 | 120.2 | 69 | 156.2 | 89 | 192.2 |
| 10 | 50.0 | 30 | 86.0 | 50 | 122.0 | 70 | 158.0 | 90 | 194.0 |
| 11 | 51.8 | 31 | 87.8 | 51 | 123.8 | 71 | 159.8 | 91 | 195.8 |
| 12 | 53.6 | 32 | 89.6 | 52 | 125.6 | 72 | 161.6 | 92 | 197.6 |
| 13 | 55.4 | 33 | 91.4 | 53 | 127.4 | 73 | 163.4 | 93 | 199.4 |
| 14 | 57.2 | 34 | 93.2 | 54 | 129.2 | 74 | 165.2 | 94 | 201.2 |
| 15 | 59.0 | 35 | 95.0 | 55 | 131.0 | 75 | 167.0 | 95 | 203.0 |
| 16 | 60.8 | 36 | 96.8 | 56 | 132.8 | 76 | 168.8 | 96 | 204.8 |
| 17 | 62.6 | 37 | 98.6 | 57 | 134.6 | 77 | 170.6 | 97 | 206.6 |
| 18 | 64.4 | 38 | 100.4 | 58 | 136.4 | 78 | 172.4 | 98 | 208.4 |
| 19 | 66.2 | 39 | 102.2 | 59 | 138.2 | 79 | 174.0 | 99 | 210.2 |
| 20 | 68.0 | 40 | 104.0 | 60 | 140.0 | 80 | 176.0 | 100 | 212.0 |

## CONVERTING BAROMETER READINGS – INCHES TO MILLIBARS

| In. | Mill. | In. | Mill. | In. | Mill. | In. | Mill. |
|-------|-------|-------|-------|-------|--------|-------|--------|
| 27.00 | 914.3 | | | | | | |
| 27.05 | 916.0 | 28.05 | 949.9 | 29.05 | 983.8 | 30.05 | 1017.7 |
| 27.10 | 917.7 | 28.10 | 951.6 | 29.10 | 985.5 | 30.10 | 1019.4 |
| 27.15 | 919.4 | 28.15 | 953.2 | 29.15 | 987.2 | 30.15 | 1021.0 |
| 27.20 | 921.1 | 28.20 | 954.9 | 29.20 | 988.9 | 30.20 | 1022.7 |
| 27.25 | 922.8 | 28.25 | 956.6 | 29.25 | 990.6 | 30.25 | 1024.4 |
| 27.30 | 924.5 | 28.30 | 958.3 | 29.30 | 922.3 | 30.30 | 1026.1 |
| 27.35 | 926.2 | 28.35 | 960.0 | 29.35 | 944.0 | 30.35 | 1027.8 |
| 27.40 | 927.8 | 28.40 | 961.7 | 29.40 | 995.6 | 30.40 | 1029.5 |
| 27.45 | 929.5 | 28.45 | 963.4 | 29.45 | 997.3 | 30.45 | 1031.2 |
| 27.5 | 931.2 | 28.50 | 965.1 | 29.50 | 999.0 | 30.50 | 1032.9 |
| 27.55 | 932.9 | 28.55 | 966.8 | 29.55 | 1000.7 | 30.55 | 1034.6 |
| 27.60 | 934.6 | 28.60 | 968.5 | 29.60 | 1002.4 | 30.60 | 1036.3 |
| 27.65 | 936.3 | 28.65 | 970.2 | 29.65 | 1004.1 | 30.65 | 1038.0 |
| 27.70 | 938.0 | 28.70 | 971.9 | 29.70 | 1005.8 | 30.70 | 1039.7 |
| 27.75 | 939.7 | 28.75 | 973.6 | 29.75 | 1007.5 | 30.75 | 1041.4 |
| 27.80 | 941.4 | 28.80 | 975.3 | 29.80 | 1009.2 | 30.80 | 1043.1 |
| 27.85 | 943.1 | 28.85 | 977.0 | 29.85 | 1010.9 | 30.85 | 1044.8 |
| 27.90 | 944.8 | 28.90 | 978.6 | 29.90 | 1012.6 | 30.90 | 1046.4 |
| 27.95 | 946.5 | 28.95 | 980.3 | 29.95 | 1014.3 | 30.95 | 1048.1 |
| 28.00 | 948.2 | 29.00 | 982.1 | 30.00 | 1016.0 | 31.00 | 1049.8 |

### BAROMETER INDICATIONS

Certain fundamental principles may be helpful to remember concerning weather:

a **Low Pressure** shows unstable and changing conditions.
b **High Pressure** shows stable and continuing good conditions.
c **Steady Rise** shows good weather approaching.
d **Steady Fall** shows bad weather approaching.
e **Rapid Rise** shows better weather may not last.
f **Rapid Fall** shows stormy weather approaching rapidly.

## WIND VELOCITY CONVERSION TABLE

| Knots | Miles per hour | Knots | Miles per hour | Knots | Miles per hour | Knots | Miles per hour |
|---|---|---|---|---|---|---|---|
| 1 | 1.15 | 26 | 29.92 | 51 | 58.69 | 76 | 87.46 |
| 2 | 2.30 | 27 | 31.07 | 52 | 59.84 | 77 | 88.61 |
| 3 | 3.45 | 28 | 32.22 | 53 | 60.99 | 78 | 89.76 |
| 4 | 4.60 | 29 | 33.37 | 54 | 62.14 | 79 | 90.91 |
| 5 | 5.75 | 30 | 34.52 | 55 | 63.29 | 80 | 92.06 |
| 6 | 6.90 | 31 | 35.67 | 56 | 64.44 | 81 | 93.21 |
| 7 | 8.05 | 32 | 36.82 | 57 | 65.59 | 82 | 94.36 |
| 8 | 9.21 | 33 | 37.98 | 58 | 66.74 | 83 | 95.51 |
| 9 | 10.36 | 34 | 39.13 | 59 | 67.89 | 84 | 96.67 |
| 10 | 11.51 | 35 | 40.28 | 60 | 69.05 | 85 | 97.82 |
| 11 | 12.66 | 36 | 41.43 | 61 | 70.20 | 86 | 98.97 |
| 12 | 13.81 | 37 | 42.58 | 62 | 71.35 | 87 | 100.12 |
| 13 | 14.96 | 38 | 43.73 | 63 | 72.50 | 88 | 101.27 |
| 14 | 16.11 | 39 | 44.88 | 64 | 73.65 | 89 | 102.42 |
| 15 | 17.26 | 40 | 46.03 | 65 | 74.80 | 90 | 103.57 |
| 16 | 18.41 | 41 | 47.18 | 66 | 75.95 | 91 | 104.72 |
| 17 | 19.56 | 42 | 48.33 | 67 | 77.10 | 92 | 105.87 |
| 18 | 20.71 | 43 | 49.48 | 68 | 78.25 | 93 | 107.02 |
| 19 | 21.86 | 44 | 50.63 | 69 | 79.40 | 94 | 108.17 |
| 20 | 23.02 | 45 | 51.78 | 70 | 80.55 | 95 | 109.32 |
| 21 | 24.17 | 46 | 52.94 | 71 | 81.70 | 96 | 110.47 |
| 22 | 25.32 | 47 | 54.09 | 72 | 82.86 | 97 | 111.62 |
| 23 | 26.47 | 48 | 55.24 | 73 | 84.01 | 98 | 112.78 |
| 24 | 27.62 | 49 | 56.39 | 74 | 85.16 | 99 | 113.93 |
| 25 | 28.77 | 50 | 57.54 | 75 | 86.31 | 100 | 115.08 |

## FREQUENCY IN KILOHERTZ TO WAVELENGTH IN METERS
### for High-Frequency Broadcasting Bands

| 75 Meter Band | | 49 Meter Band | | 41 Meter Band | | 31 Meter Band | | 25 Meter Band | |
|---|---|---|---|---|---|---|---|---|---|
| kHz | Meters | kHz | Meters | kHz | Meters | kHz | Meters | kHz | Meters |
| 3900 | 76.92 | 5950 | 50.42 | 7100 | 42.25 | 9500 | 31.58 | 11700 | 25.64 |
| 3905 | 76.82 | 5955 | 50.38 | 7105 | 42.22 | 9505 | 31.56 | 11705 | 25.63 |
| 3910 | 76.73 | 5960 | 50.34 | 7110 | 42.19 | 9510 | 31.55 | 11710 | 25.62 |
| 3915 | 76.63 | 5965 | 50.29 | 7115 | 42.16 | 9515 | 31.53 | 11715 | 25.61 |
| 3920 | 76.53 | 5970 | 50.25 | 7120 | 42.13 | 9520 | 31.51 | 11720 | 25.60 |
| 3925 | 76.43 | 5975 | 50.21 | 7125 | 42.11 | 9525 | 31.50 | 11725 | 25.59 |
| 3930 | 76.34 | 5980 | 50.17 | 7130 | 42.08 | 9530 | 31.48 | 11730 | 25.58 |
| 3935 | 76.24 | 5985 | 50.13 | 7135 | 42.05 | 9535 | 31.46 | 11735 | 25.56 |
| 3940 | 76.14 | 5990 | 50.08 | 7140 | 42.02 | 9540 | 31.45 | 11740 | 25.55 |
| 3945 | 76.05 | 5995 | 50.04 | 7145 | 41.99 | 9545 | 31.43 | 11745 | 25.54 |
| 3950 | 75.95 | 6000 | 50.00 | 7150 | 41.96 | 9550 | 31.41 | 11750 | 25.53 |
| 3955 | 75.85 | 6005 | 49.96 | 7155 | 41.93 | 9555 | 31.40 | 11755 | 25.52 |
| 3960 | 75.76 | 6010 | 49.92 | 7160 | 41.90 | 9560 | 31.38 | 11760 | 25.51 |
| 3965 | 75.66 | 6015 | 49.88 | 7165 | 41.87 | 9565 | 31.36 | 11765 | 25.50 |
| 3970 | 75.57 | 6020 | 49.83 | 7170 | 41.84 | 9570 | 31.35 | 11770 | 25.49 |
| 3975 | 75.47 | 6025 | 49.79 | 7175 | 41.81 | 9575 | 31.33 | 11775 | 25.48 |
| 3980 | 75.38 | 6030 | 49.75 | 7180 | 41.78 | 9580 | 31.32 | 11780 | 25.47 |
| 3985 | 75.28 | 6035 | 49.71 | 7185 | 41.75 | 9585 | 31.30 | 11785 | 25.46 |
| 3990 | 75.19 | 6040 | 49.67 | 7190 | 41.72 | 9590 | 31.28 | 11790 | 25.45 |
| 3995 | 75.09 | 6045 | 49.63 | 7195 | 41.70 | 9595 | 31.27 | 11795 | 25.43 |
| 4000 | 75.00 | 6050 | 49.59 | 7200 | 41.67 | 9600 | 31.25 | 11800 | 25.42 |
| | | 6055 | 49.55 | 7205 | 41.64 | 9605 | 31.23 | 11805 | 25.41 |
| | | 6060 | 49.50 | 7210 | 41.61 | 9610 | 31.22 | 11810 | 25.40 |
| | | 6065 | 49.46 | 7215 | 41.58 | 9615 | 31.20 | 11815 | 25.39 |
| | | 6070 | 49.42 | 7220 | 41.55 | 9620 | 31.19 | 11820 | 25.38 |
| | | 6075 | 49.38 | 7225 | 41.52 | 9625 | 31.17 | 11825 | 25.37 |
| | | 6080 | 49.34 | 7230 | 41.49 | 9630 | 31.15 | 11830 | 25.36 |
| | | 6085 | 49.30 | 7235 | 41.47 | 9635 | 31.14 | 11835 | 25.35 |
| | | 6090 | 49.26 | 7240 | 41.44 | 9640 | 31.12 | 11840 | 25.34 |
| | | 6095 | 49.22 | 7245 | 41.41 | 9645 | 31.10 | 11845 | 25.33 |
| | | 6100 | 49.18 | 7250 | 41.38 | 9650 | 31.09 | 11850 | 25.32 |
| | | 6105 | 49.14 | 7255 | 41.35 | 9655 | 31.07 | 11855 | 25.31 |
| | | 6110 | 49.10 | 7260 | 41.32 | 9660 | 31.06 | 11860 | 25.30 |
| | | 6115 | 49.06 | 7265 | 41.29 | 9665 | 31.04 | 11865 | 25.28 |
| | | 6120 | 49.02 | 7270 | 41.27 | 9670 | 31.02 | 11870 | 25.27 |
| | | 6125 | 48.98 | 7275 | 41.24 | 9675 | 31.01 | 11875 | 25.26 |
| | | 6130 | 48.94 | 7280 | 41.21 | 9680 | 30.99 | 11880 | 25.25 |
| | | 6135 | 48.90 | 7285 | 41.18 | 9685 | 30.98 | 11885 | 25.24 |
| | | 6140 | 48.86 | 7290 | 41.15 | 9690 | 30.96 | 11890 | 25.23 |
| | | 6145 | 48.82 | 7295 | 41.12 | 9695 | 30.94 | 11895 | 25.22 |
| | | 6150 | 48.78 | 7300 | 41.10 | 9700 | 30.93 | 11900 | 25.21 |
| | | 6155 | 48.74 | | | 9705 | 30.91 | 11905 | 25.20 |
| | | 6160 | 48.70 | | | 9710 | 30.90 | 11910 | 25.19 |
| | | 6165 | 48.66 | | | 9715 | 30.88 | 11915 | 25.18 |
| | | 6170 | 48.62 | | | 9720 | 30.86 | 11920 | 25.17 |
| | | 6175 | 48.58 | | | 9725 | 30.85 | 11925 | 25.16 |
| | | 6180 | 48.54 | | | 9730 | 30.83 | 11930 | 25.15 |
| | | 6185 | 48.50 | | | 9735 | 30.82 | 11935 | 25.14 |
| | | 6190 | 48.47 | | | 9740 | 30.80 | 11940 | 25.13 |
| | | 6195 | 48.43 | | | 9745 | 30.79 | 11945 | 25.12 |
| | | 6200 | 48.39 | | | 9750 | 30.77 | 11950 | 25.10 |
| | | | | | | 9755 | 30.75 | 11955 | 25.09 |
| | | | | | | 9760 | 30.74 | 11960 | 25.08 |
| | | | | | | 9765 | 30.72 | 11965 | 25.07 |
| | | | | | | 9770 | 30.71 | 11970 | 25.06 |
| | | | | | | 9775 | 30.69 | 11975 | 25.05 |

## FREQUENCY IN KILOHERTZ TO WAVELENGTH IN METERS
### for High-Frequency Broadcasting Bands

| 19 Meter Band | | 16 Meter Band | | 13 Meter Band | | 11 Meter Band | |
|---|---|---|---|---|---|---|---|
| kHz | Meters | kHz | Meters | kHz | Meters | kHz | Meters |
| 15100 | 19.87 | 17700 | 16.95 | 21450 | 13.99 | 25600 | 11.72 |
| 15105 | 19.86 | 17705 | 16.94 | 21455 | 13.98 | 25610 | 11.71 |
| 15110 | 19.85 | 17710 | 16.94 | 21460 | 13.98 | 25620 | 11.71 |
| 15115 | 19.85 | 17715 | 16.93 | 21465 | 13.98 | 25630 | 11.71 |
| 15120 | 19.84 | 17720 | 16.93 | 21470 | 13.97 | 25640 | 11.70 |
| 15125 | 19.83 | 17725 | 16.93 | 21475 | 13.97 | 25650 | 11.70 |
| 15130 | 19.83 | 17730 | 16.92 | 21480 | 13.97 | 25660 | 11.69 |
| 15135 | 19.82 | 17735 | 16.92 | 21485 | 13.96 | 25670 | 11.69 |
| 15140 | 19.82 | 17740 | 16.91 | 21490 | 13.96 | 25680 | 11.68 |
| 15145 | 19.81 | 17745 | 16.91 | 21495 | 13.96 | 25690 | 11.68 |
| 15150 | 19.80 | 17750 | 16.90 | 21500 | 13.95 | 25700 | 11.67 |
| 15155 | 19.80 | 17755 | 16.90 | 21505 | 13.95 | 25710 | 11.67 |
| 15160 | 19.79 | 17760 | 16.89 | 21510 | 13.95 | 25720 | 11.66 |
| 15165 | 19.78 | 17765 | 16.89 | 21515 | 13.94 | 25730 | 11.66 |
| 15170 | 19.78 | 17770 | 16.88 | 21520 | 13.94 | 25740 | 11.66 |
| 15175 | 19.77 | 17775 | 16.88 | 21525 | 13.94 | 25750 | 11.65 |
| 15180 | 19.76 | 17780 | 16.87 | 21530 | 13.93 | 25760 | 11.65 |
| 15185 | 19.76 | 17785 | 16.87 | 21535 | 13.93 | 25770 | 11.64 |
| 15190 | 19.75 | 17790 | 16.86 | 21540 | 13.93 | 25780 | 11.64 |
| 15195 | 19.74 | 17795 | 16.86 | 21545 | 13.92 | 25790 | 11.63 |
| 15200 | 19.74 | 17800 | 16.85 | 21550 | 13.92 | 25800 | 11.63 |
| 15205 | 19.73 | 17805 | 16.85 | 21555 | 13.92 | 25810 | 11.62 |
| 15210 | 19.72 | 17810 | 16.84 | 21560 | 13.91 | 25820 | 11.62 |
| 15215 | 19.72 | 17815 | 16.84 | 21565 | 13.91 | 25830 | 11.61 |
| 15220 | 19.71 | 17820 | 16.84 | 21570 | 13.91 | 25840 | 11.61 |
| 15225 | 19.70 | 17825 | 16.83 | 21575 | 13.90 | 25850 | 11.61 |
| 15230 | 19.70 | 17830 | 16.83 | 21580 | 13.90 | 25860 | 11.60 |
| 15235 | 19.69 | 17835 | 16.82 | 21585 | 13.90 | 25870 | 11.60 |
| 15240 | 19.69 | 17840 | 16.82 | 21590 | 13.90 | 25880 | 11.59 |
| 15245 | 19.68 | 17845 | 16.81 | 21595 | 13.89 | 25890 | 11.59 |
| 15250 | 19.67 | 17850 | 16.81 | 21600 | 13.89 | 25900 | 11.58 |
| 15255 | 19.67 | 17855 | 16.80 | 21605 | 13.89 | 25910 | 11.58 |
| 15260 | 19.66 | 17860 | 16.80 | 21610 | 13.88 | 25920 | 11.57 |
| 15265 | 19.65 | 17865 | 16.79 | 21615 | 13.88 | 25930 | 11.57 |
| 15270 | 19.65 | 17870 | 16.79 | 21620 | 13.88 | 25940 | 11.57 |
| 15275 | 19.64 | 17875 | 16.78 | 21625 | 13.87 | 25950 | 11.56 |
| 15280 | 19.63 | 17880 | 16.78 | 21630 | 13.87 | 25960 | 11.56 |
| 15285 | 19.63 | 17885 | 16.77 | 21635 | 13.87 | 25970 | 11.55 |
| 15290 | 19.62 | 17890 | 16.77 | 21640 | 13.86 | 25980 | 11.55 |
| 15295 | 19.61 | 17895 | 16.76 | 21645 | 13.86 | 25990 | 11.54 |
| 15300 | 19.61 | 17900 | 16.76 | 21650 | 13.86 | 26000 | 11.54 |
| 15305 | 19.60 | | | 21655 | 13.85 | 26010 | 11.53 |
| 15310 | 19.60 | | | 21660 | 13.85 | 26020 | 11.53 |
| 15315 | 19.59 | | | 21665 | 13.85 | 26030 | 11.53 |
| 15320 | 19.58 | | | 21670 | 13.84 | 26040 | 11.52 |
| 15325 | 19.58 | | | 21675 | 13.84 | 26050 | 11.52 |
| 15330 | 19.57 | | | 21680 | 13.84 | 26060 | 11.51 |
| 15335 | 19.56 | | | 21685 | 13.83 | 26070 | 11.51 |
| 15340 | 19.56 | | | 21690 | 13.83 | 26080 | 11.50 |
| 15345 | 19.55 | | | 21695 | 13.83 | 26090 | 11.50 |
| 15350 | 19.54 | | | 21700 | 13.82 | 26100 | 11.49 |
| 15355 | 19.54 | | | 21705 | 13.82 | | |
| 15360 | 19.53 | | | 21710 | 13.82 | | |
| 15365 | 19.52 | | | 21715 | 13.82 | | |
| 15370 | 19.52 | | | 21720 | 13.81 | | |
| 15375 | 19.51 | | | 21725 | 13.81 | | |
| 15380 | 19.51 | | | 21730 | 13.81 | | |
| 15385 | 19.50 | | | 21735 | 13.80 | | |
| 15390 | 19.49 | | | 21740 | 13.80 | | |
| 15395 | 19.49 | | | 21745 | 13.80 | | |
| 15400 | 19.48 | | | 21750 | 13.79 | | |
| 15405 | 19.47 | | | | | | |
| 15410 | 19.47 | | | | | | |
| 15415 | 19.46 | | | | | | |
| 15420 | 19.46 | | | | | | |
| 15425 | 19.45 | | | | | | |
| 15430 | 19.44 | | | | | | |
| 15435 | 19.44 | | | | | | |
| 15440 | 19.43 | | | | | | |
| 15445 | 19.42 | | | | | | |
| 15450 | 19.42 | | | | | | |

## FAHRENHEIT-CENTIGRADE SCALE

| °F | 32 | 40 | 50 | 60 | 70 | 75 | 85 | 95 | 105 | 140 | 175 | 212 |
|----|----|----|----|----|----|----|----|----|-----|-----|-----|-----|
| °C | 0 | 5 | 10 | 15 | 20 | 25 | 30 | 35 | 40 | 60 | 80 | 100 |

## MPH-KM/H SCALE

| mph | 20 | 30 | 40 | 50 | 60 | 70 | 80 | 90 | 100 |
|-----|----|----|----|----|----|----|----|----|-----|
| km/h | 32 | 48 | 64 | 80 | 96 | 112 | 128 | 144 | 160 |

## TIRE PRESSURES

| lb/sq in | 20 | 22 | 24 | 26 | 28 | 30 | 32 | 34 |
|----------|----|----|----|----|----|----|----|----|
| kg/sq cm 1 | 41 | 1.55 | 1.69 | 1.83 | 1.97 | 2.11 | 2.25 | 2.39 |

## CLOTHING SIZES

**Men's Suits and Coats**

| | | | | | | | |
|-----|----|----|----|----|----|----|----|
| British | 36 | 38 | 40 | 42 | 44 | 46 | 48 |
| American | 36 | 38 | 40 | 42 | 44 | 46 | 48 |
| Continental | 46 | 48 | 50 | 52 | 54 | 56 | 58 |

**Men's Shirts**

| | | | | | | | |
|-----|----|----|----|----|----|----|----|
| British | 14 | 14½ | 15 | 15½ | 16 | 16½ | 17 |
| American | 14 | 14½ | 15 | 15½ | 16 | 16½ | 17 |
| Continental | 36 | 37 | 38 | 39/40 | 41 | 42 | 43 |

**Men's Shoes**

| | | | | | | | |
|-----|----|----|----|----|----|----|----|
| British | 7 | 8 | 9 | 10 | 11 | 12 | 13 |
| American | 7½ | 8½ | 9½ | 10½ | 11½ | 12½ | 13½ |
| Continental | 40½ | 42 | 43 | 44½ | 45½ | 47 | 48 |

**Men's Socks**

| | | | | | | |
|-----|----|----|----|----|----|----|
| British | 9½ | 10 | 10½ | 11 | 11½ | 12 |
| American | 9½ | 10 | 10½ | 11 | 11½ | 12 |
| Continental | 39 | 40 | 41 | 42 | 43 | 44 |

**Women's Dresses and Suits**

| | | | | | | |
|-----|----|----|----|----|----|----|
| British | 8 | 10 | 12 | 14 | 16 | 18 |
| American | - | 8 | 10 | 12 | 14 | 16 |
| Continental | - | 38 | 40 | 42 | 44 | 46 |

**Women's Shoes**

| | | | | | | | |
|-----|----|----|----|----|----|----|----|
| British | 4 | 4½ | 5 | 5½ | 6 | 7 | 8 |
| American | 5½ | 6 | 6½ | 7 | 7½ | 8 | 8½ |
| Continental | 37 | 37½ | 38 | 39 | 39½ | 40½ | 42 |

# Multilanguage Lexicon

**16**

## LEXICON TOPIC TRANSLATIONS

| ENGLISH | FRENCH | SPANISH | GERMAN |
|---|---|---|---|
| Prohibitions | Interdictions | Prohibiciones | Verbote |
| Types of vessel | Types de bateaux | Tipos de barco | Schiffstypen |
| Parts of vessel | Parties du bateau | Partes del barco | Schiffsteile |
| Masts & spars | Mâts | Mástiles y palos | Masten |
| Rigging | Gréement | Aparejo | Tauwerk |
| Sails | Voilure | Velas | Segel |
| Below deck | Cabine | Alcázar | Unterdeck |
| Navigation equipment | Equipement de navigation | Equipo de navegación | Navigations-ausrüstung |
| Engines | Moteurs | Motores | Motoren |
| Engine accessories | Accessoires moteur | Accesorios de motor | Motor-zubehör |
| Electrics | Electricité | Electricidad | Elektrik |
| Fuel and oil | Combustibles | Gasolina | Kraftstoffe |
| Metals | Métaux | Metales | Metalle |
| Lights | Lumières | Luz | Beleuchtung |
| Ship's papers | Papiers du bateau | Papeles del barco | Schiffspapiere |
| Tools | Outils | Herramientas | Werkzeuge |
| Chandlery | Fournitures maritimes | Pertrechos | Schiffsausrüstung |
| Food | Nourriture | Comida | Nahrungsmittel |
| Shops and places ashore | Boutiques et endroits à terre | Tiendas y sitios en tierra | Geschäfte und Orte an Land |
| In harbor | Au port | En el puerto | Im Hafen |
| First Aid | Premiers secours | Primer socorro | Erste Hilfe |

## PROHIBITIONS

| | | | |
|---|---|---|---|
| Prohibited area | Zone interdite | Zona prohibida | Gebiet mit Zutrittsverbot |
| Anchoring prohibited | Défense de mouiller | Fondeo prohibido | Ankern verboten |
| Mooring prohibited | Accostage interdit | Amarre prohibido | Anlegen verboten |

## TYPES OF VESSELS
### Private

| | | | |
|---|---|---|---|
| Sloop | Sloop | Balandra | Schaluppe |
| Cutter | Cotre | Cúter | Kutter |
| Ketch | Ketch | Queche | Ketsch |
| Yawl | Yawl | Yola | Jolle |
| Schooner | Goélette | Goleta | Schoner |
| Motorsailer | Voilier mixte | Motovelero | Motorsegler |
| Dinghy | Youyou, prame | Balandro | Dinghi, Beiboot |
| Launch | Chaloupe | Lancha | Barke |
| Motorboat | Bateau à moteur | Motora, bote a motor | Motorboot |
| Lifeboat | Bateau, Canot de sauvetage | Bote salvadidas | Rettungsboot |

| ENGLISH | FRENCH | SPANISH | GERMAN |
|---|---|---|---|
| | | **Commercial** | |
| Trawler | Chalutier | Pesquero | Schleppfischer |
| Tanker | Bateau-citerne | Petrolero | Tanker |
| Merchantman | Navire marchand | Buque mercante | Handelsschiff |
| Ferry | Transbordeur, bac | Transbordador | Fähre |
| Tug | Remorqueur | Remolcador | Schlepper |

## PARTS OF VESSEL

| ENGLISH | FRENCH | SPANISH | GERMAN |
|---|---|---|---|
| Stem | Étrave | Roda | Vordersteven |
| Stern | Poupe | Popa | Heck |
| Forecastle (fo'c's'le) | Gaillard d'avant | Castillo de proa | Vordeck |
| Forepeak | Pic avant | Pique de proa | Vorpiek |
| Cabin | Cabine | Camarote | Kabine |
| Chain locker | Puits à chaines | Caja de cadenas | Kettenkasten |
| Head | Toilette | Retrete | WC |
| Galley | Cuisine | Cocina | Kombüse |
| Chartroom | Salle des cartes | Cámara de derrota | Navigationsraum |
| Bunk | Couchette | Litera | Koje |
| Pipe cot | Cadre | Catre | Rohrkoje |
| Engine room | Chambre des machines | Cámara de máquinas | Motorraum |
| Locker | Coffre | Taquilla | Kasten |
| Bulkhead | Cloison | Mamparo | Schott |
| Hatch | Écoutille | Escotilla | Luke |
| Cockpit | Cockpit | Cabina | Cockpit |
| Sail locker | Soute à voiles | Pañol de velas | Segelkasten |
| Freshwater tank | Réservoir d'eau douce | Tanque de agua potable | Trinkwassertank |
| Rudder | Gouvernail | Timón | Ruder |
| Propeller | Hélice | Hélice | Schraube |
| Bilges | Cale | Sentina | Bilge |
| Keel | Quille | Quilla | Kiel |
| Gunwale (also gunnel) | Plat-bord | Borda, regala | Dollbaum |
| Rubbing strake | Bourrelet de défense | Verduguillo | Scheuerleiste |
| Tiller | Barre | Caña | Ruderpinne |
| Stanchion | Etançon, montant | Candelero | Pfosten |
| Bilgepump | Pompe de cale | Bombas de achique de sentina | Bilgenpumpe |
| Pulpit | Balcon avant | Púlpito de proa | Bugkanzel |
| Pushpit | Balcon arrière | Púlpito de popa | Heckkanzel |

## MASTS AND SPARS

| ENGLISH | FRENCH | SPANISH | GERMAN |
|---|---|---|---|
| Mast | Mât | Palo | Mast |
| Foremast | Mât de misaine | Palo trinquete | Fockmast |
| Mizzenmast | Mât d'artimon | Palo mesana | Kreuzmast |
| Boom | Bôme | Botavara | Baum |
| Bowsprit | Beaupré | Bauprés | Bugspriet |
| Bumpkin | Bout-dehors | Pescante de amura | Butluv |
| Spinnaker boom | Tangon de spi | Tangón de espí | Spinnakerbaum |
| Gaff | Corne | Pico cangrejo | Gaffel |
| Spreaders | Barres de flèche | Crucetas | Rahe |
| Jumper strut | Guignol | Contrete | Knickstange |

Lexicon

537

| ENGLISH | FRENCH | SPANISH | GERMAN |
|---------|--------|---------|--------|
| Truck | Pomme | Tope, galleta | Flaggenknopf |
| Slide | Coulisseau | Corredera | Rutsche |
| Roller reefing | Bôme à rouleau | Rizo de catalina | Drehreff |
| Worm gear | Vis sans fin | Husillo | Schneckentrieb |
| Solid | Massif | Macizo | Massiv |
| Hollow | Creux | Hueco | Hohl |
| Derrick | Grue | Pluma de carga | Ladebaum |

## RIGGING
### Standing

| | | | |
|---|---|---|---|
| Forestay | Étai avant, étai de trinquette | Estay de proa | Stagfock |
| Aft stay | Étai arrière | Estay de popa | Achternstag |
| Shrouds | Haubans | Obenques | Wanttaue |
| Stay | Étai | Estay | Stag |
| Bobstay | Sous-barbe | Barbiquejo | Wasserstag |
| Backstay | Galhauban | Brandal | Pardune |
| Guy | Retenue | Retenida, cabo de retenida viento | Spannseil, Topreep |

### Running

| | | | |
|---|---|---|---|
| Halyard | Drisse | Driza | Fall |
| Foresail halyard | Drisse de misaine | Driza de trinquetilla | Focksegelfall |
| Throat halyard | Attache de drisse | Driza de boca | Klaufall |
| Peak halyard | Drisse de pic | Driza de pico | Piekfall |
| Burgee halyard | Drisse de guidon | Driza de grímpola | Doppelstanderfall |
| Topping lift | Balancine | Amantillo | Hanger |
| Main sheet | Écoute de grand voile | Escota mayor | Großschot |
| Foresail sheet | Écoute de misaine | Escota de trinquetilla | Focksegelschot |
| Boom vang | Hale-bas de bôme | Trapa | Gaffelgeer |
| Rope | Cordage | Soga | Tau |
| Single block | Poule simple | Motón de una cajera | Einscheibiger Block |
| Double block | Poulie double | Motón de dos cajeras | Zweischeibiger Block |
| Sheave | Réa | Roldana | Seilscheibe |
| Shackle | Manille | Grillete | Schäkel |
| Pin | Goupille | Perno, cabilla | Bolzen |
| "D" shackle | Manille droite | Grillete en D | Augenschäkel |
| Snapshackle | Manille rapide | Grillete de escape | Schnappschäkel |

## SAILS

| | | | |
|---|---|---|---|
| Mainsail | Grand voile | Vela mayor | Großsegel |
| Foresail | Voile de misaine | Vela trinquete | Focksegel |
| Jib | Foc | Foque | Fock |
| Storm jib | Tourmentin | Foque de capa | Sturmfock |
| Trysail | Voile de sénau | Vela de cangrejo | Gaffelsegel |
| Genoa | Génois | Foque génova | Genua |
| Spinnaker | Spinnaker | Espínaquer, espí, foque balón | Spinnaker |
| Topsail | Flèche | Gavia | Topsegel |
| Mizzen sail | Artimon | Mesana | Kreuzsegel |
| Lugsail | Boile de fortune | Vela al tercio | Luggersegel |

| ENGLISH | FRENCH | SPANISH | GERMAN |
|---|---|---|---|

## Parts of Sails

| ENGLISH | FRENCH | SPANISH | GERMAN |
|---|---|---|---|
| Head | Point de drisse | Puño de driza | Topp |
| Tack | Point d'amure | Puño de amura | Halse |
| Clew | Point d'écoute | Puño de escota | Schothorn |
| Luff | Guindant | Gratil | Vorliek |
| Leech | Chute | Apagapenol | Achterliek |
| Foot | Bordure | Pujamen | Unterliek |
| Roach | Rond, échancrure | Alunamiento | Gillung |
| Peak | Pic | Pico | Piek |
| Throat | Gorge | Puño de driza | Klaue |
| Batten pocket | Étui, gaine de latte | Bolsa de tablillas y listones | Segelschalstück |
| Batten | Latte | Enjaretado | Schalstück |
| Cringle | Anneau, patte de bouline | Garrucho de cabo | Lägel |
| Seam | Couture | Costura | Naht |
| Sailbag | Sac à voile | Saco de vela | Segelsack |

## BELOW DECK

| ENGLISH | FRENCH | SPANISH | GERMAN |
|---|---|---|---|
| Toilet | Toilette | Retretes | WC |
| Toilet paper | Papier hygiénique | Papel higiénico | Toilettenpapier |
| Towel | Serviette | Toalla | Handtuch |
| Soap | Savon | Jabón | Seife |
| Cabin | Cabine | Camarote | Kabine, Kajüte |
| Mattress | Matelas | Colchón | Matratze |
| Sleeping bag | Sac de couchage | Saco de dormir | Schlafsack |
| Sheet | Drap | Sábana | Leintuch |
| Blanket | Couverture | Manta | Decke |
| Galley | Cuisine | Cocina | Kombüse |
| Cook stove | Cuisinière | Fogón | Herd |
| Frying pan | Poêle à frire | Sartén | Bratpfanne |
| Saucepan | Casserole | Cacerola | Kochtopf |
| Kettle | Bouilloire | Caldero | Kessel |
| Tea pot | Théière | Tetera | Teekanne |
| Coffee pot | Cafetière | Cafetera | Kaffeekanne |
| Knives | Couteaux | Cuchillos | Messer |
| Forks | Fourchettes | Tenedores | Gabeln |
| Spoons | Cuillères | Cucharas | Löffel |
| Can opener | Ouvre-boîtes | Abrelatas | Dosenöffner |
| Corkscrew | Tire-bouchon | Sacacorchos | Korkenzieher |
| Matches | Allumettes | Fósforos, cerillas | Zündhölzer |
| Dishwashing liquid | Liquide à vaisselle | Detergente | Geschirrspülmittel |

**Lexicon**

## NAVIGATION EQUIPMENT

| ENGLISH | FRENCH | SPANISH | GERMAN |
|---|---|---|---|
| Chart table | Table à cartes | Planero | Kartentafel |
| Chart | Carte marine | Carta náutica | Seekarte |
| Parallel ruler | Règle parallèle | Regla de paralelas | Parallellineal |
| Protractor | Rapporteur | Transportador | Winkelmesser |
| Pencil | Crayon | Lápiz | Bleistift |
| Eraser | Gomme | Goma | Radiergummi |
| Dividers | Pointes sèches | Compás de puntas | Stechzirkel |
| Binoculars | Jumelles | Gemelos | Fernglas |
| Compass | Compas | Compás | Kompaß |

| ENGLISH | FRENCH | SPANISH | GERMAN |
|---|---|---|---|
| Handbearing compass | Compas de relèvement | Alidada | Handpeilkompaß |
| Depthsounder | Echosondeur | Sondador acústico | Echolot |
| Radio receiver | Poste récepteur | Receptor de radio | Funkempfänger |
| Radio direction finder | Récepteur goniométrique | Radiogoniómetro | Peilfunkstation |
| Patent log | Loch enregistreur | Corredera de patente | Patentlog |
| Sextant | Sextant | Sextante | Sextant |

## ENGINES

| | | | |
|---|---|---|---|
| Gas engine | Moteur à essence | Motor de gasolina | Benzinmotor |
| Diesel engine | Moteur diesel | Motor diesel | Dieselmotor |
| Two-stroke | À deux temps | Dos tiempos | Zweitakt |
| Four-stroke | À quatre temps | Cuatro tiempos | Viertakt |
| Exhaust pipe | Tuyau d'échappement | Tubo de escape | Auspuff |
| Gearbox | Boîte de vitesses | Caja de engranajes | Getriebe |
| Gear lever | Levier de vitesses | Palanca de cambio | Schalthebel |
| Throttle | Accélérateur | Estrangulador | Drosselklappe |
| Clutch | Embrayage | Embrague | Kupplung |
| Stern tube | Tube d'étambot, arbre | Bocina | Stevenrohr |
| Fuel pump | Pompe à combustible | Bomba de alimentación | Kraftstoffpumpe |
| Carburetor | Carburateur | Carburador | Vergaser |
| Fuel tank | Réservoir de combustible | Tanque de combustible | Kraftstofftank |

## ENGINE ACCESSORIES

| | | | |
|---|---|---|---|
| Cylinder head | Culasse | Culata | Zylinderkopf |
| Jointing compound | Pâte à joint | Junta de culata | Dichtungsmaterial |
| Nut | Ecrou | Tuerca | Mutter |
| Bolt | Boulon | Perno | Bolzen |
| Washer | Rondelle | Arandela | Unterlegscheibe |
| Split pin | Coupille fendue | Pasador abierto | Splint |
| Asbestos tape | Ruban d'amiante | Cinta de amianto | Asbestband |
| Copper pipe | Tuyau de cuivre | Tubo de cobre | Kupferrohr |
| Plastic pipe | Tuyau de plastique | Tubo de plástico | Kunststoffrohr |

## ELECTRICS

| | | | |
|---|---|---|---|
| Voltage | Tension | Voltaje | Spannung |
| Amp | Ampères | Amperio | Ampère |
| Spark plug | Bougie | Bujía | Zündkerze |
| Dynamo | Dynamo | Dínamo | Dynamo |
| Magneto | Magnéto | Magneto | Magnet |
| Dynamo belt | Courroie de dynamo | Correa de dínamo | Dynamoriemen |
| Battery | Accumulateur | Batería | Batterie |
| Contact breaker | Interrupteur | Disyuntor | Unterbrecher |
| Fuse box | Boîte à fusibles | Caja de fusibles | Sicherungskasten |
| Switch | Commutateur | Interruptor | Schalter |
| Bulb | Ampoule | Bombilla | Glühbirne |
| Copper wire | Fil de cuivre | Cable de cobre | Kupferdraht |
| Distilled water | Eau distillée | Agua destilada | Destilliertes Wasser |
| Solder | Soudure | Soldadura | Löten |
| Flux | Flux | Flux | Flußmittel |
| Insulating tape | Ruban isolant | Cinta aislante | Isolierband |

| ENGLISH | FRENCH | SPANISH | GERMAN |
|---|---|---|---|
| | | **FUEL AND OIL** | |
| Gasoline | Essence | Gasolina | Benzin |
| Kerosene | Pétrole lampant | Petróleo | Kerosin |
| Diesel oil | Gas-oil | Gasoil | Dieselöl |
| Alcohol | Alcool à brûler | Alcohol desnaturalizado | Alkohol |
| Lubricating oil | Huile | Aceite de lubricación | Schmieröl |
| Two-stroke oil | Huile deux temps | Aceite de motor 2 tiempos | Zweitaktöl |
| Penetrating oil | Huile pénétrante, dégrippante | Aceite penetrante | Rostlösendes Öl |
| Grease | Graisse | Grasa | Fett |
| | | **METALS** | |
| Galvanized iron | Fer galvanisé | Hierro galvanizado | Verzinktes Eisen |
| Stainless steel | Acier inoxydable | Acero inoxidable | Rostfreier Stahl |
| Iron | Fer | Hierro | Eisen |
| Steel | Acier | Acero | Stahl |
| Copper | Cuivre | Cobre | Kupfer |
| Brass | Laiton | Latón | Messing |
| Aluminum | Aluminium | Aluminio | Aluminium |
| Bronze | Bronze | Bronce | Bronze |
| | | **LIGHTS** | |
| Navigation lights | Feux de bord | Luces de navegación | Navigationslichter |
| Masthead light | Feu de tête de mât | Luz del tope de proa | Topplicht |
| Spreader light | Feu de barre de flèche | Luz de verga | Rahenlicht |
| Port light | Feu de babord | Luz de babor | Backbordlicht |
| Starboard light | Feu de tribord | Luz de estribor | Steuerbordlicht |
| Stern light | Feu arrière | Luz de alcance | Hecklicht |
| Cabin lamp | Lampe de cabine | Lámpara de camarote | Kabinenbeleuchtung |
| Lamp glass | Verre de lampe | Tubo de lámpara | Lampenzylinder |
| Wick | Mèche | Mecha (para engrase) | Docht |
| | | **SHIP'S PAPERS** | |
| Certificate of Registry | Acte de francisation | Patente de navegación | Schiffszertifikat |
| Pratique | Libre-pratique | Plática | Verkehrserlaubnis |
| Ship's log | Livre de bord | Diario de navegación | Logbuch |
| Insurance certificate | Certificat d'assurance | Póliza de seguro | Versicherungsschein |
| Passport | Passeport | Pasaporte | Reisepaß |
| Customs clearance | Dédouanement | Despacho de aduana | Zollabfertigung |
| | | **TOOLS** | |
| Hammer | Marteau | Martillo | Hammer |
| Wood chisel | Ciseau à bois | Formón | Holzmeißel |
| Cold chisel | Ciseau à froid | Cortafrío | Kaltmeißel |
| Screwdriver | Tournevis | Destornillador | Schraubenzieher |
| Wrench (spanner) | Clé | Llave para tuercas | Spannschlüssel |
| Adjustable wrench | Clé anglaise | Llave ajustable | Verstellbarer Spannschlüssel |
| Saw | Scie | Sierra | Säge |
| Hacksaw | Scie à métaux | Sierra para metal | Bügelsäge |

Lexicon

541

| ENGLISH | FRENCH | SPANISH | GERMAN |
|---|---|---|---|
| Hand drill | Chignolle à main | Taladro de mano | Handbohrer |
| File | Lime | Lima | Feile |
| Wire cutters | Pinces coupantes | Cortador de alambre | Drahtschneider |
| Pliers | Pinces | Alicates | Zange |
| Wrench | Tourne-à-gauche | Llave de boca | Schraubenschlüssel |

## CHANDLERY

| | | | |
|---|---|---|---|
| Burgee | Guidon | Grímpola | Doppelstander |
| Ensign | Pavillon | Pabellón | Nationalflagge |
| Courtesy flag | Fanion de courtoisie | Pabellón extranjero | Gastflagge |
| Q flag | Pavillon Q | Bandera Q | Q-Flagge |
| Signal flag | Pavillon de signalis. (alphabetique) | Bandera de señales | Signalflagge |
| Anchor | Ancre | Ancla | Anker |
| Anchor chain | Chaîne d'ancre | Cadena de ancla | Ankerkette |
| Rope | Cordage | Soga | Tau |
| Hawser | Haussière | Estacha, amarra | Trosse |
| Synthetic rope | Cordage synthétique | Cuerda sintética | Synthetisches Tau |
| Nylon rope | Cordage de nylon | Cuerda de nylon | Nylontau |
| Dacron | Cordage de Tergal | Cuerda de terylene | Dacron-Tau |
| Hemp rope | Cordage de chanvre | Cuerda de cáñamo | Hanftau |
| Fender | Défense | Defensa | Fender |
| Lifebuoy | Bouée de sauvetage | Guindola | Rettungsboje |
| Cleat | Taquet | Cornamusa | Belegklampe |
| Winch | Winch | Cigüeña de cordelería | Deckwinde |
| Boathook | Gaffe | Bichero | Bootshaken |
| Oar | Aviron | Remo | Ruder, Riemen |
| Fairlead | Chaumard | Guía | Verholklampe |
| Eye bolt | Piton à oeil | Cáncamo | Augbolzen |
| Paint | Peinture | Pintura | Farbe |
| Varnish | Vernis | Barniz | Lack |
| Sandpaper | Papier de verre | Papel de lija | Schleifpapier |
| Foghorn | Corne de brume | Bocina de niebla | Nebelhorn |

## FOOD

| | | | |
|---|---|---|---|
| Cheese | Fromage | Queso | Käse |
| Butter | Beurre | Mantequilla | Butter |
| Bread | Pain | Pan | Brot |
| Milk | Lait | Leche | Milch |
| Jam | Confiture | Compota | Konfitüre |
| Marmalade | Confiture d'oranges | Mermelada | Marmelade |
| Mustard | Moutarde | Mostaza | Senf |
| Salt | Sel | Sal | Salz |
| Pepper | Poivre | Pimienta | Pfeffer |
| Vinegar | Vinaigre | Vinagre | Essig |
| Meat | Viande | Carne | Fleisch |
| Fish | Poisson | Pescado | Fisch |
| Fruit | Fruits | Frutas | Früchte |
| Vegetables | Légumes | Legumbres | Gemüse |
| Sausages | Saucisses | Embutidos | Wurst |
| Ham | Jambon | Jamón | Schinken |
| Beef | Boeuf | Carne de vaca | Rind |
| Pork | Porc | Carne de cerdo | Schwein |
| Lamb | Mouton | Carne de cordero | Lamm |
| Bacon | Lard fumé | Tocino | Speck |

| ENGLISH | FRENCH | SPANISH | GERMAN |
|---|---|---|---|
| Eggs | Oeufs | Huevos | Eier |
| Fresh water | Eau douce | Agua dulce | Süßwasser |

## SHOPS AND PLACES ASHORE

| ENGLISH | FRENCH | SPANISH | GERMAN |
|---|---|---|---|
| Grocer | Épicier | Tendero de comestibles | Lebensmittelgeschäft |
| Greengrocer | Marchand de légumes | Verdulero | Gemüsehändler |
| Butcher | Boucher | Carnicero | Metzgerei |
| Baker | Boulanger | Panadero | Bäckerei |
| Hardware store | Quincaillerie | Ferretero | Eisenwarengeschäft |
| Supermarket | Supermarché | Supermercado | Supermarkt |
| Market | Marché | Mercado | Markt |
| Yacht chandler | Fournisseur de marine | Almacén de efectos navales | Jachtausrüster |
| Sailmaker | Voilier | Velería | Segelhersteller |
| Garage | Garage | Garaje | Garage |
| Train station | Gare | Estación | Bahnhof |
| Bus | Autobus | Autobús | Bus |
| Post Office | Poste | Correos | Postamt |
| Bank | Banque | Banco | Bank |
| Pharmacist | Pharmacien | Farmacéutico | Apotheke |
| Hospital | Hôpital | Hospital | Krankenhaus |
| Doctor | Médecin | Médico | Arzt |
| Dentist | Dentiste | Dentista | Zahnarzt |

## IN HARBOR

| ENGLISH | FRENCH | SPANISH | GERMAN |
|---|---|---|---|
| Harbor | Bassin | Puerto | Hafen |
| Yacht harbor | Bassin pour yachts | Puerto de yates | Jachthafen |
| Fishing harbor | Port de pêche | Puerto pesquero | Fischerhafen |
| Harbormaster | Capitaine de port | Capitán de puerto | Hafenkapitän |
| Harbormaster's office | Bureau de Capitaine de port | Comandancia del puerto | Büro des Hafenkapitäns |
| Immigration officer | Agent du service de l'immigration | Oficial de inmigración | Einwanderungsbeamter |
| Customs office | Bureau de douane | Aduana | Zollbüro |
| Prohibited area | Zone interdite | Zona prohibida | Gebiet mit Zutrittsverbot |
| Anchoring prohibited | Défense de mouiller | Fondeo prohibido | Ankern verboten |
| Mooring prohibited | Accostage interdit | Amarre prohibido | Anlegen verboten |
| Lock | Écluse | Esclusa | Schleuse |
| Canal | Canal | Canal | Kanal |
| Mooring place | Point d'accostage | Amarradero | Anlegeplatz |
| Movable bridge | Pont mobile | Puente móvil | Bewegliche Brücke |
| Swing bridge | Pont tournant | Puente giratorio | Drehbrücke |
| Lifting bridge | Pont basculant | Puente levadizo | Zugbrücke |
| Ferry | Bac | Transbordador | Fähre |
| Harbor steps | Escalier du quai | Escala real | Hafenstufen |

## FIRST AID

| ENGLISH | FRENCH | SPANISH | GERMAN |
|---|---|---|---|
| Bandage | Bandage | Venda | Verband |
| Gauze (also lint) | Pansement | Gasa, hilacha | Verbandsmull |
| Adhesive bandage | Pansement adhésif | Esparadrapo | Klebepflaster |
| Scissors | Ciseaux | Tijeras | Schere |
| Safety pin | Épingle de sûreté | Imperdible | Sicherheitsnadel |
| Tweezers | Pince à épiler | Pinzas | Pinzette |

**Lexicon**

| ENGLISH | FRENCH | SPANISH | GERMAN |
|---|---|---|---|
| Thermometer | Thermomètre | Termómetro | Thermometer |
| Disinfectant | Désinfectant | Desinfectante | Desinfektionsmittel |
| Aspirin tablets | Aspirine | Pastillas de aspirina | Aspirin |
| Laxative | Laxatif | Laxante | Laxativ |
| Indigestion tablets | Pillules contre l'indigestion | Pastillas laxantes | Verdauungstabletten |
| Antiseptic cream | Onguent antiseptique | Pomada antiséptica | Antiseptische Salbe |
| Anti-seasickness pills | Remède contre le mal de mer | Píldoras contra el mareo | Pillen gegen Seekrankheit |
| Calamine lotion | Lotion à la calamine | Loción de calamina | Calamina-Lotion |
| Wound dressing | Pansement stérile | Vendajes para heridas | Wundverband |
| Stomach upset | Mal de coeur | Dolor de estómago | Magenverstimmung |

## CHART TERMS

### Light Characteristics

| | | | |
|---|---|---|---|
| F. | Fixe | f. | F. (Festfeuer) |
| Oc. | Occ. | Oc. | U.F. (Unterbrochenes Feuer) |
| Iso | Iso | Iso./Isof. | Iso. (Isophase) |
| Fl. | É | D. | B. (Blinkfeuer) |
| Q | Scint | Ct. | Ff. (Funkelfeuer) |
| IQ | Scint. dis. | Gp. Ct. | U.Ff. (Unterbrochenes Funkelfeuer) |
| Al. | Alt. | Alt. | Wf. (Wechselfeuer) |
| Oc.(..) | ... Occ. | Gp. Oc. Gr. Oc. | G.U.F. (Gruppen/ Unterbr.Feuer) |
| Fl.(..) | ... É | Gp. D. | G.B. (Gruppen/ Blinkfeuer) |
| Mo | Mo | Mo | Mo. (Morsecode) |
| FFI | Fixe É | F.D. | F. & B. (Festes und Blinkfeuer) |
| FFI.(..) | Fixe .. É | F. Gp. D./Gp. DyF. | F & B.G. (Festfeuer mit Blinkgruppen) |

### Compass Points

| | | | |
|---|---|---|---|
| North (N) South (S) | Nord (N) Sud (S) | Norte (N) Sur (S) | Norden (N) Süden (S) |
| East (E) West (W) | Est (E) Ouest (O) | Este, Leste (E) Oeste (W) | Osten (O) Westen (W) |
| Northeast (NE) | Nordé (NE) | Nordeste (NE) | Nordosten (NO) |
| North-Northeast (NNE) | Nord-Nordé (NNE) | Nornordeste (NNE) | Nordnordosten (NNO) |
| North by East | Nord quart Nordé | Norte cuarta al este (N4NE) | Nordnordosten |

### Colors

| | | | |
|---|---|---|---|
| Black | Noir (n) | Negro (n) | Schwarz |
| Red | Rouge (r) | Rojo (r) | Rot |
| Green | Vert (v) | Verde (v) | Grün |
| Yellow | Jaune (j) | Amarillo (am) | Gelb |
| White | Blanc (b) | Blanco (b) | Weiß |
| Orange | Orange (org) | Naranjo | Orange |
| Blue | Bleu (bl) | Azul (az) | Blau |
| Brown | Brun | Pardo (p) | Braun |
| Violet | Violet (vio) | Violeta | Violett |

| ENGLISH | FRENCH | SPANISH | GERMAN |
|---|---|---|---|
| **Radio and Aural Aids** | | | |
| Radiobeacon | Radiophare | Radiofaro | Funkbaken |
| Diaphone | Diaphone | Diáfono | Sirene |
| Horn | Nautophone | Nautófono | Schiffshorn |
| Siren | Sirène | Sirena | Sirene |
| Reed | Trompette | Bocina | Zungenhorn |
| Explosive | Explosif | Explosivo | Knallsignal |
| Bell | Cloche | Campana | Glocke |
| Gong | Gong | Gong | Gong |
| Whistle | Sifflet | Silbato | Pfeife |
| **Structure or Float** | | | |
| Dolphin | Duc d'Albe | Delfín, cetáceo | Dückdalbe |
| Light | Feu | Luz | Licht |
| Lighthouse | Phare | Faro | Leuchtturm |
| Light vessel | Bateau-feu | Faro flotante | Leuchtschiff |
| Light float | Feu flottant | Luz flotante | Leuchttonne |
| Beacon | Balise | Baliza | Bake |
| Column | Colonne | Columna | Säule |
| Dwelling | Maison | Casa | Wohnung |
| Framework Tower | Pylone | Armazón | Fachwerk-Turm |
| House | Bâtiment | Casa | Haus |
| Hut | Cabane | Choza, cabaña | Hütte |
| Mast | Mât | Mástil | Masten |
| Post | Poteau | Poste | Pfosten |
| Tower | Tour | Torre | Turm |
| Mooring buoy | Bouée de corps-mort | Boya de amarre muerto | Ankerboje |
| Buoy | Bouée | Boya | Tonne, Boje |
| **Type of Marking** | | | |
| Band | Bande | Bandas horizontales | Waagrecht gestreift |
| Stripe | Raie | Rayas verticales | Senkrecht gestreift |
| Checkered | à damier | A cuadros | Karo |
| Top mark | Voyant | Marea de tope | Toppzeichen |
| **Shape** | | | |
| Round | Circulaire | Redondo | Rund |
| Conical | Conique | Cónico | Kegelförmig |
| Diamond | Losange | Rombo | Raute |
| Square | Carré | Cuadrangular | Quadratisch |
| Triangle | Triangle | Triángulo | Dreieck |
| **Description** | | | |
| Destroyed | Détruit | Destruido | Zerstört |
| Occasional | Feu occasionnel | Ocasional | Gelegentlich |
| Temporary | Temporaire | Temporal | Vorübergehend |
| Extinguished | Eteint | Apagado | Gelöscht |
| **Tide** | | | |
| High water | Pleine mer | Pleamar | Hochwasser |
| Low water | Basse mer | Bajamar | Niedrigwasser |
| Flood | Marée montante | Marea entrante | Flut |
| Ebb | Marée descendante | Marea vaciante | Ebbe |
| Stand | Etale | Margen | Stauwasser |
| Range | Amplitude | Repunte | Gezeitenhub |
| Spring tide | Vive eau | Marea viva | Springflut |
| Neap tide | Morte eau | Aguas muertas | Nippflut |

**Lexicon**

| ENGLISH | FRENCH | SPANISH | GERMAN |
|---|---|---|---|
| Sea level | Niveau | Nivel | Wasserstand |
| Mean | Moyen | Media | Mitttel |
| Current | Courant | Corriente | Strömung |

## Chart Dangers

| | | | |
|---|---|---|---|
| Sunken rock | Roche submergée | Roca siempre cubierta | Blinde Klippe |
| Wreck | Epave | Naufragio (Nauf) | Wrack |
| Shoal | Haut fond (Ht. Fd.) | Bajo (Bo) | Untiefe |
| Obstruction | Obstruction (Obs.) | Obstrucción (Obston.) | Hindernis |
| | | | |
| Overfalls | Remous et clapotis | Escarceos, hileros | Überbrechende Seen |
| Dries | Assèche | Que vela en bajamar | Trockenwatt |
| Isolated Danger | Danger isolé | Peligro aislado | Isolierte Gefahr |

## Weather

| | | | |
|---|---|---|---|
| Weather forecast | Prévisions météo | Previsión meteorológica | Weersvoorspelling |
| Gale | Coup de vent | Duro | Sturm |
| Squall | Grain | Turbonada | Sturmbö |
| Fog | Brouillard | Niebla | Nebel |
| Mist | Brume légère ou mouillée | Neblina | Dunst |

## Dimensions

| | | | |
|---|---|---|---|
| Height | Tirant d'air | Altura | Höhe |
| Width | Largeur, de large | Ancho, anchura | Breite |
| Depth | Profondeur | Fondo, profundidad | Tiefe |
| Draft | Tirant d'eau | Calado | Tiefgang |

# TABLE OF USEFUL TABLES AND ILLUSTRATIONS

# INDEX

Index

Index

Index

# NOTES

## NOTES

NOTES

## NOTES